The
COMPLETE WORKS
of
FRANÇOIS
RABELAIS

A CENTENNIAL BOOK

One hundred books
published between 1990 and 1995
bear this special imprint of
the University of California Press.
We have chosen each Centennial Book
as an example of the Press's finest
publishing and bookmaking traditions
as we celebrate the beginning of
our second century.

UNIVERSITY OF CALIFORNIA PRESS

Founded in 1893

The
COMPLETE WORKS
of
FRANÇOIS
RABELAIS

Translated from the French by
DONALD M. FRAME

With a Foreword by
RAYMOND C. LA CHARITÉ

UNIVERSITY OF CALIFORNIA PRESS
Berkeley   Los Angeles   Oxford

A WAKE FOREST STUDIUM BOOK

WFS

Pro Humanitate

The Publisher wishes to acknowledge with gratitude the support given to this book by Joan Palevsky.

University of California Press
Berkeley and Los Angeles, California

University of California Press
Oxford, England

Library of Congress Cataloging-in-Publication Data

Rabelais, François, 1490-1553
[Works. English. 1991]
The complete works of François Rabelais / translated from the French by Donald M. Frame ; with a foreword by Raymond C. La Charité.
p. cm.
Includes bibliographical references.
ISBN 0-520-06400-3 (alk. paper)
1. Rabelais, François, ca. 1490–1553?—Translations into English.
I. Frame, Donald Murdoch, 1911–   . II. Title.
PQ1685.EF73   1991
843'.3—dc20   91-26198
                                                       CIP

Printed in the United States of America

1 2 3 4 5 6 7 8 9

The paper used in this publication meets the minimum requirements of American National Standard for Information Sciences—Permanence of Paper for Printed Library Materials, ANSI Z39.48-1984 ∞

Contents

BOOK 1
The Very Horrific Life of the Great Gargantua, Father of Pantagruel

CONTENTS

BOOK 2
Pantagruel, King of the Dipsodes, Restored to His Natural State with His Frightful Deeds and Exploits

BOOK 3

The Third Book of the Heroic Deeds and Sayings
of the Good Pantagruel

BOOK 4

The Fourth Book of the Heroic Deeds and Sayings of the Good Pantagruel

BOOK 5

The Fifth and Last Book of the Heroic Deeds and Sayings of the Good Pantagruel

6

Miscellaneous Writings

Abbreviations

(Other than those used in standard bibliographical works)

AN: (Maistre) Alcofribas Nasier.

BD: Brief Declaration.

BHR: *Bibliothèque d'Humanisme et Renaissance* (Geneva: Droz, 1941 to the present, 1 volume [3 issues] yearly).

EC: *Oeuvres de Rabelais,* édition critique, edited by Abel Lefranc et al., 6 volumes (Paris: Champion and Geneva: Droz, 1912–1955).

ER: *Etudes Rabelaisiennes,* 23 volumes (Geneva: Droz, 1956 to the present). Appears at irregular intervals: some monographs, some volumes of articles collected and introduced by one single editor; almost all historical in approach.

FC: Francesco Colonna (d. 1527), author of a popular fantasy romance much drawn on by R and by author of Book 5, the *Hypnerotomachia polyphili* (1492) or *Strife of Love in a Dream,* as translated by R. D. in 1592, an edition often reprinted.

FFM: *French Forum Monographs* (Lexington, Ky.: French Forum Publishers), continuing at irregular intervals, 74 volumes to date. Includes some collections of articles.

FFP: French Forum Publishers, as noted above.

FR: François Rabelais: *Ouvrage publié pour le quatrième centenaire de sa mort, 1553–1953* (Geneva: Droz and Lille: Giard, 1953). Twenty-three articles, mostly historical in approach by some leading scholars in the field.

FRS: *François Rabelais: A Study,* by Donald M. Frame (New York: Harcourt Brace Jovanovich, 1977).

G: *Rabelais: Oeuvres complètes,* edited by Pierre Jourda (Paris: Garnier, 1962), 2 volumes. A good scholarly reader's edition, for Book 5 follows a composite of texts: chapters 1–16 of *The Ringing Island,* then chapters 16–47 of the 1564 edition.

G and P: *Gargantua and Pantagruel*, here usually meaning all five books; to refer to Books 1 and 2 we use numerals.

GC: *Great Chronicles of Gargantua*.

HP: *Hypnerotomachia polyphili*, the book of Colonna listed above under his name.

LCLGLSM: Gérard Defaux's book *Le curieux, le glorieux, et la sagesse du monde*, FFM 34 (1982).

LI: *Rabelais: Oeuvres complètes*, Edition L'Intégrale, text and modern French version in columns side by side on each page, edited by Guy Demerson (Paris: Seuil, 1973). Despite the regrettably necessary two-column pages, the best scholarly reader's edition now available, and our guide and edition of reference for this translation.

NP: New Prologue to Book 4.

OC: Dedicatory Epistle to Cardinal Odet de Chastillon, Book 4.

OP: Old Prologue to Book 4.

P: Prologue.

PL: *Rabelais: Oeuvres complètes*, edited by Jacques Boulenger and Lucien Scheler (Paris: Gallimard [Pléiade ed.], 1955). A good scholarly reader's edition and the most convenient.

QL: *Le Quart Livre* (1552 definitive version), édition critique par Robert Marichal (1947; rpt. Geneva: Droz, 1967).

QL 1548: Robert Marichal, editor, "Facsimilé du Quart Livre de 1548," in *ER* 19 (1971) 151–174.

R: Rabelais.

RIB: *Rabelais's Incomparable Book: Essays on His Art*, edited by Raymond C. La Charité, FFM 62 (1986), 247 pp. Fourteen essays by fourteen contributors including the editor; uneven quality.

RR: *Romanic Review*, 1910 to present, quarterly, continuing, one volume per year.

Screech: M. A. Screech: *Rabelais* (London; Duckworth and Ithaca, Cornell University Press, 1979, 494 pp.).

TL: *Le Tiers Livre*, édition critique, commentée par M. A. Screech (Geneva: Droz, 1964).

Foreword

Donald M. Frame, born December 14, 1911, is no more. He died March 8, 1991, after a long, debilitating, and often painful series of medical problems. Unable to see the English translation of his beloved Rabelais through its final stages, he had hoped nonetheless to see it in print. Only the force of his will kept him going these past two years, and against all odds. In the end it was no match for the accumulation of strokes, infirmities, and afflictions that assailed him.

Don (my close personal relationship of almost 30 years makes it difficult for me to refer to him as Frame) first thought of translating Rabelais some forty years ago, and he often talked about the need for an accurate and idiomatic modern American English translation. From time to time, he would try various passages on me, and I remember fondly the many times he sent me into paroxysms of laughter with his gutsy and brilliant renditions of proper names. However, his first love, Montaigne, kept him occupied the entire course of his career. His biography, interpretation, and English translation of Montaigne—not to mention his study of Rabelais and his translations of Molière and Voltaire—brought him recognition as a world-class scholar, and he was unable to devote his energies to the extraordinarily difficult task of translating Rabelais until his retirement.

Upon retirement, Don's exclusive project was the "englishing" of Rabelais, and not just that of the four authentic books. He wanted all of Rabelais, including minor works and correspondence, whether in French or Latin, available in English. He was thoroughly familiar with the work of his predecessors (Sir Thomas Urquhart, W. F. Smith, Samuel Putnam, Jacques Leclercq, and J. M. Cohen) and could cite chapter and verse on what he considered to be good, bad, or suspect about their renditions. He preferred Urquhart (at times truly an English Rabelais) and Putnam (the best blend of accuracy and American English), but he always felt that the proper mixture of faithfulness to the original, based on a sure knowledge of sixteenth-century French, inventiveness, and liveliness of language had yet to be achieved. I once wrote of Don that "only a kindred soul—and a brilliant and sensitive interpreter—could have rendered the *Essais* in English as though it were Montaigne's original medium of expression," and this is in fact what he hoped to bring about with his translation of Rabelais.

As with all his previous work, he also wanted to reach the broadest possible audience—the student, the scholar, the nonspecialist—and to provide everyone with a judicious, meticulous, and honest interpretation, at once helpful and commanding assent. To that end he worked tirelessly; countless hours were spent chasing down obscure references and deciphering undecipherable creations and thorny passages. He put to use his vast knowledge of antiquity and his familiarity with scholarship on Rabelais in order to fashion a reliable guide. He left no stone unturned, queried friends and colleagues, and consulted his predecessors at every turn. He wanted his feel for Rabelais to be accompanied by scholarly solidity. I am convinced that readers will generally find *The Complete Works of François Rabelais* to be faithful, sensitive, scholarly, frequently brilliant, and the best contemporary English translation available.

Had circumstances and his health allowed it, Don would have made the entire work, from its inception to final execution, as perfect as anything so arduous can ever be. The reader should know that he spent better than ten years at his task, that he was beset by medical problems early on during this period, and that he last looked at any of it late in 1989. While it is true that he finished the entire project, it would be an understatement to say that he provided the University of California Press with a pristine, clean, and polished manuscript.

Over time, Don sent the Press more than 2,000 pages of typescript, many of them barely legible. I used to joke that he had undoubtedly bought the very first typewriter ever made and that it had come with only one ribbon. His typewritten pages were legendary. But, in the aggregate, this was a minor problem. Because of the duration of the project, his advancing age, his failing health, and his diminishing powers, a number of inconsistencies, inaccuracies, and omissions began to appear in his text as he labored, through several versions, to make corrections, emendations, and additions. When responding to various queries put to him, it was never clear which of the many versions he was looking at so that many editorial decisions had to be made on the basis of inference.

Early on, Don was asked to set aside many of his longer notes. In order to retain them in some fashion, he began an extensive Glossary, but not all of the note material was included, and page references were often to the typescript (and not infrequently to earlier versions) rather than to Rabelais's books and chapters, the system adopted throughout *The Complete Works of François Rabelais*. Moreover, the Glossary was not complete, but Don was satisfied that it would do.

A major problem was that the original manuscript did not link the remaining notes to the text, for the most part. In the course of preparing various versions of the typescript, Don dropped corresponding note numbers in the text, wrote new notes or rewrote earlier ones without inserting appropriate numbers in the text, and at times note numbers in the text referred to earlier versions of the translation and notes. Some notes were left unfinished, ellipsis points indicating that he would return to the matter when he had been able to clear it up.

As for the translation itself, the manuscript contained omissions and eyeskips—words, lines, paragraphs, and an occasional page—as well as repetitions, especially when multi-columned matter was involved. This probably came about because of the retyping of various versions of the work.

Every effort has been made to restore and to redo the work as Don had originally done it and intended it to be. I became associated with this endeavor last year, but by far the hardest part of it all was done by Susan Gallick, Don's copyeditor for the University of California Press. Without her patient and painstaking attention to every aspect of the project, I doubt very much that it would yet be ready for press.

In addition to his wife Kathleen, who was always available and helpful no matter the query, Marianne S. Meijer deserves special mention for her assistance and friendship to Donald Frame.

Raymond C. La Charité

Translator's Note

Although five English versions of Rabelais have been published, four of them within the last hundred years, all have serious weaknesses, and only one is readily available (the others barely if at all); we trust that there is room for this, the sixth, in all. I have believed this for some forty years; and when in 1950 I reviewed a book (by J. C. Powys, *Rabelais* [London: Bodley Head, 1948]) on R that included a partial translation, I undertook to show its qualities by comparing it with existing complete versions through a sampling of passages (*RR* 42 [1950] 287–290) in an assessment that I still maintain.

I found Sir Thomas Urquhart (London: Moring, 1653), as did Powys, savory and picturesque but too much Urquhart and at times too little R; too often the reader must guess whom he is reading, author or translator. I have borrowed some succulent phrases (especially oaths and insults) gratefully but been wary of the sense in the Urquhart. W. F. Smith (1899; 2d ed. Cambridge: Cambridge Univ. Press, 1934) writing at the turn of the century, was an excellent scholar; but he shuns R's obscenities and lacks his raciness. Powys labels him "too stately, courtly, and refined." I have used Smith for his erudition on Gargantua's games (1.22). That of Samuel Putnam (1929; rpt. New York: the Viking Press, 1946), arguably the best we have, is readily available in the Viking Portable selections, fully available (if still in print) only in a huge edition few can afford. Powys found it dangerously anachronistic; I find it so rarely. The version of Jacques Leclercq (1936), which Powys had not seen, is brilliant but rather independent of R; Leclercq encumbers R's text with his own notes, and often, like Urquhart, leaves the reader uncertain whom he is reading. J. M. Cohen's translation (Penguin, 1955) has come since Powys's book; of it more shortly.

In 1950, disappointed in all extant versions, I ventured my notion of the perfect translator of R: that he or she "should combine the imagination, daring, and gusto of the brilliant creator with the humility and solid learning of the true scholar."[1] (I now fear that any such paragon would be too busy with his or her own creative work to devote the required time and attention to translating anyone, even R; but one may hope.) My aim in this version, as always, is fidelity (which is not always literalness): to put into standard American English what I think R would (or at least might) have written if he were using that English today.

The one English translation now available, Cohen's in Penguin (1955), although in the main sound, is marred by his ignorance of sixteenth-century French: in the Prologue to Book 1, he renders "combien que" (although) by "seeing that" (the exact opposite); and some of his renderings of R's proper names are shaky ("Wordspinner" for Trouillogan, for example). For much of R's text, however, the everyday part, his resourceful experience as a translator makes him our best guide. My debts to earlier translators are considerable. Except for Smith and Putnam, however, not one offers enough annotation and any but the minimal texts; for each book, one prologue and the story text; thus for Book 4, no Old Prologue or Brief Declaration; and in Cohen, no Dedicatory Epistle. For inclusion our model has been the French scholarly readers' editions (PL, G, and LI); and where these disagree (order in PL, much in G), LI, the latest and best.

Because R needs ample annotation, which threatens to swamp the text, to restrict the length and number of notes we offer a Selected Glossary, explained there at the start; notes are marked in the text by superscript numerals.

My debts for help in this task are so many that they must be bare and brief: to the translators just listed; to the scholars so listed in the Introduction, for many facts and insights; to the completed EC volumes; to the scholarly texts of individual books (1–4), especially for their Indexes. Two grants have freed my time for this enterprise: from the National Humanities Center for 1982–1983; and a two-year Fellowship for Translation (1984–1986) from the NEA; my gratitude is great.

Thanks to the many colleagues and friends in the field (not listed separately here to save space) for steady, constant moral support and recommendations whenever asked. My many medical problems in these last few years have increased my debt of loving gratitude to my wife Kathleen, who has added cares for these to her other commitments and kept me free for this work at all times, besides furthering it by photocopying, mailing, and myriad other jobs now beyond my powers.

If I thought it was appropriate for a translation to bear a dedication, I would ask her leave to dedicate this one to her.

Donald M. Frame
Alexandria, VA, USA

Introduction

François Rabelais

The latest Webster's Collegiate Dictionary defines R as "French humorist and satirist" and Rabelaisian as "marked by gross robust humor"; my 1975 Columbia Encyclopedia calls him "one of the great comic geniuses in world literature" and expatiating thus on his book: R's novel is "one of the world's masterpieces, as gigantic in scope as the physical size of its heroes," adding that "under its broad humor, often ribald," lie "learned discussions of education, politics, and philosophy," while the entire book radiates R's zest for living.

I cite these summaries not as straw men but as bases to modify and build on (for R defies summary) as needed; adding my sense that most fairly literate and educated opinion today (formed from parts of Books 1–2 alone) holds roughly this view of R: "An ancient French author, monk or doctor or both or some such thing (remind me to look it up) who late in life wrote a funny, very dirty book about giants."[1] This composite needs one major addition and a few modifications: that for Books 1–2, R, who loves to mystify, creates a narrator and purported author, Master Alcofribas Nasier, Abstractor of Quintessence (AN), the sophist scamp who introduces both books, serves as R's "comic mask," doubles at will as a character in the tale, and shares with R both the combined letters of both his names and many of R's loves and detestations.[2]

First, I would modify or change their terms humor, humorist, and novel. The self-mocking touch of true humor appears only in Prologues 1–2 in AN's spoofing of his own "utterly veracious" punditry; elsewhere all R's comic barbs aim outward. Second, I would reserve the term novel for a half century after R's dates of composition (1532–1552), for the richer texture and characterization of a Don Quixote, and use for R's book his own term "merry new chronicles" or simply comic story or tale. Tale suggests the fiction that of course this is; but story, by its ambiguity, serves R's book better. Here we use both terms interchangeably to mean R's entire narrative or at times the happenings it relates. Third, is this book really about giants? We take that as a given; yet in only one-third (13 of 34 chapters) of Book 2, one-fourth (14 chapters of 58, all these in the first two-thirds of the book) of Book 1, and nowhere later (in 3–5) do they appear as giants. And even as giants, their sizes vary hugely (from about 100 feet to over 1,000 miles) with each episode.[3] With such part-time giants of such variable dimensions, what shall we say of their physical size except the obvious: this depends on what R finds best suited to his purposes for each giant episode!

Later, Cervantes in *Don Quixote* offers clues to his play with fact and fiction; and still later in *Jacques the Fatalist* Diderot enjoys being even more explicit. R, loving to mystify, after a few hints, leaves the enigma to his readers to solve if they can.

Without forgetting our modifications, we note here two salient peculiarities of R's story: he wrote Book 2 before he wrote Book 1; and Book 5 is probably in the main unauthentic (see the introductory note to 5), even though Book 4 has no conclusion. Book 5 is the best of these we have; it may be not far from what before his death he may have planned, and it may be in large part by R. We offer it here for the sake of maximal completeness.

LIFE

Whereas our knowledge of R's book is sketchy, ours of many basic facts of his life recalls Fastilent's costume: "nothing in front and nothing in back, and sleeves to match" (4.49). Born (either in 1483 or around 1494) in or near old Chinon, on the Vienne near the Loire, perhaps in the nearby family farmhouse La Devinière, he was the fourth child and third son of Antoine Rabelais, an eminent Chinon lawyer. We know nothing of his childhood or schooling (La Baumette?) or just when or why (by 1510–1511, and for study and a living?) he entered, as a novice, the strict religious order of the Observantine Franciscans. Our first glimpse of him is as priest and monk, in Le Puy Saint-Martin, an Observantine monastery in Fontenay-le-Comte (now Vendée, then Poitou), a busy town west of Poitiers and northeast of La Rochelle; versed in the law and rapidly learning Greek from his fellow priest Pierre Amy (or Lamy, d. 1525), and with him welcomed among the Hellenist jurists hosted by André

Tiraqueau (1480–1558), such as future Master of Requests Amaury Bouchard and rhétoriqueur Jean Boucher (see below, 6.2–6.4, 6.6).

Late in 1520, prodded by Amy, R had ventured to write to the greatest Hellenist of his day, Guillaume Budé (1468–1540; see below, 6.1), also adviser to King Francis I and eminent public servant, who had encouraged Amy. Having no reply, and again under Amy's prodding, on March 4, 1521 R again wrote Budé a long Latin letter with much Greek (even a concluding quatrain) as credential: our first sure date for R, sure glimpse of him, and sample of his prose. His crushing sense of Budé's eminence and of his own nullity makes this tediously apologetic, though understandably so; but it shows him at home in Greek, fluent in Latin, committed to the "New Learning" based on languages and stressing Greek, and shows the hostility of religious and other vested interests to this threat to their authority. A reminder of this came soon (1523?), when Sorbonne pressure impelled R's and Amy's superiors to take away their Greek books long enough to lead both men to look around elsewhere. Amy left the monastery and the order and found more tolerant environs for the two remaining years of his life.[4]

R was more fortunate. His first strong patron-protector, Bishop Geoffroy d'Estissac of Maillezais (Vendée), transferred him about ten miles under his own wing and roof in his Benedictine monastery of Saint-Pierre de Maillezais and priory of Ligugé, R's happy home (we think) until he went to Paris some time in 1527–1530 for serious solid medical studies sponsored (and subsidized?) by d'Estissac.

There he fathered two illegitimate children (as a priest, he could not marry), François and Junie, legitimized by Pope Paul III in 1535. He next moved to the medical faculty of Montpellier, France's finest, matriculating September 30, 1530, then receiving a Bachelor's degree November 1; this speed (for a two-year course) is presumably explained by his Paris studies earlier. For seven years this faculty was his home. On January 6, 1532 he joined colleagues to play in the zany old farce, *The Man Who Married a Dumb Wife;* he had lectured in spring 1531 on works of Hippocrates and Galen;[5] and his course notes and text were published in 1532 in Lyon by the erudite Sebastian Gryphius.

On that November 1 he became (for just over two years) a doctor in the big old Hôtel-Dieu. Probably just before then, spurred (AN tells us) by the huge sale of the anonymous *Great Chronicles* (GC) of Gargantua, he published the first book he wrote of his tale, *Pantagruel,* purportedly as a sort of sequel about the giant son of that folk hero. Its phenomenal instant success led to lame imitations by others but first to his own *Pantagrueline Prognostications,* all alike (the one for 1533 is item 6.8 below), published by late 1532, then two years later (1534?) to *Gargantua* (Book 1), a second version of the tale.

In 1534 R enjoyed his first stay in Rome, as physician to the ailing Bishop of Paris, Jean du Bellay (1492–1560), from February 1 to March, busy mainly on a topography of ancient Rome that he gave up when a good one came out, by one Marliani, which R dedicated to Du Bellay (6.10 below) and published August 31, 1534, in Lyon. Winter 1534–1535 was bad for Reformist sympathizers, blamed for twin provocations (October 17–18 and January 13), the famous Affair of the Placards and its virtual repetition, the conspicuous posting all over France, even on the king's chamber door, of violent attacks on the papacy and the mass, leading the king, previously sympathetic to Reform, to see it as disturbing sedition. The ensuing furor probably explains R's sudden apparent flight in February, without notice, from his post and from Lyon. By spring, however, the furor had calmed; on May 21 Du Bellay was named a cardinal, and on July 15 left for Rome, his physician R[6] with him or soon after, for his most productive stay, which won him from Pope Paul III absolution for his "apostasy" in quitting monastic residence without full authorization; a welcome back, if he liked, among the Benedictines; and full permission to go on practicing medicine as before; and from Cardinal du Bellay a place in his Benedictine abbey of Saint-Maur-les-Fossés, being installed February 11, 1536. When it was secularized soon after, this made R a secular priest, an ideal situation.

His next two years were rather peaceful, with his two degrees at Montpellier and 1537–1538 course there on Hippocrates's *Prognostics.* Of his years 1538–1540 we suspect a summer 1539 in Montpellier, and we know of the birth and early death of a third illegitimate, his son Théodule. R spent most of 1540–1542 serving the remarkable, dedicated French governor of Turin, Jean du Bellay's elder brother Guillaume, seigneur de Langey (1491–1543), equally cultivated and tolerant, his kin in convictions as in blood, brilliant diplomat, commander, and administrator, R's greatest hero out of all the greats he served. R was with him regularly in Turin, and on his few brief trips back to France (we think as both physician and secretary); and Langey left him a bequest (later erased by debts and legal fees) in his will, dated November 10, 1542. Soon after, feeling near death, Langey left for home, dying on the way but on French soil, on January 9, 1543. His death was in R's view a national disaster, which, uniquely, he relates with full attendant detail (4.27), as one of his many mourning friends. R helped escort the body to Le Mans, and returned there March 5 for the burial.

Another heavy blow soon followed (May 30), the death of another protector friend, Geoffroy d'Estissac; and then came two bad years, with R's first formal censure by the Sorbonne in 1543 for the Paris Parlement, a fierce surprise attack from the wildly eccentric but respected Royal Professor Guillaume Postel (1510–1581), prototype of R's "Maniacal Pistols" of 4.32, who charged that all Evangelicals were really crypto-Mohammedans—yet another weapon for R's enemies.

Another censorable listing came on August 19, 1544, and that September an agreement between king and emperor to reduce their mutual hostilities and thus free each other for suppressing heresy; this of course made persecution worse over western Europe. Worst of all, on January 8, 1545 Jean du Bellay's secretary Jean Bribart was burned at the stake. When on July 1, the Paris Parlement contrived a new form of preemptive censorship, R's prospects for later publication looked bad; but on September 19, 1545, King Francis granted him a six-year royal privilege for any book of his then or to come; and it must have been about then that Queen Margaret of Navarre gave her consent for his dizain dedicating Book 3 to her "abstracted spirit, rapt in ecstasy" (3.FM).

So sometime before Easter in 1546 R published Book 3 in the enemy's bailiwick, Paris (Christian Wechel), also for the first time under his own name and profession with no comic mask—a most audacious act. Around February, however, he left France for friendlier Imperial Metz (where the Du Bellays had agents and influence), which employed him (as doctor or counselor?); and he stayed there over a year. But his personal security was not financial; and on February 6, 1547, he sent Du Bellay an anguished appeal for money enough to live.

When Henry II succeeded his father on April 1, 1547, he showed tolerance for a time, and on July 27 sent his trusted Du Bellay to Rome to watch over French interests. On his way there with him as a doctor, R left for publication in Lyon with François Juste the sketchy 1548 version of Book 4. Our only relic of this his longest stay in Rome, the unrewarding Shadow Battle, sheds no light on either the author or the man. Returning from Rome (in latter 1549?), R spent part of summer 1550 at Saint-Maur with his convalescent cardinal; and Chastillon, on a visit to Du Bellay, confirmed to R his assurance of protection and support, later first helped prepare(?), then witnessed R's best royal privilege ever, from Henry II, for ten years, for any or all works of his, past or future. R was given in January 1551 two nonresident curacies, one just south of Paris, and Saint-Christophe-du-Jambet (Sarthe). On January 28, 1552, again in Paris (Michel Fezandat) and under his own name, appeared R's completed definitive Book 4, the last we know he wrote. A report that he was in prison that October was false. On January 9, 1553, for reasons unknown (ill health?), he resigned both curacies. He died later that year (April 9?) and was buried in Paris, Rue des Jardins, in the church cemetery of Saint-Paul Parish.

The Book

The first book R wrote, *Pantagruel,* no kin to the GC, opens with a long imaginary genealogy (chap. 1) from just after Cain and Abel down via Gargantua to Pantagruel, and offers a lively narrator and purported author, and thus a comic mask for R and an opening for comic ambiguity. Many journeymen had labored in this giant vein and produced dozens of crude yarns such as GC for their undemanding public. So had two Italians of real talent, Luigi Pulci in his verse mock epic *Morgante Maggiore* (1482) about a giant who served under Charlemagne, and Tofilo Folengo (*Merlin Coccai,* 1492–1554), with his verse *Opus macaronicum* or *Baldus,*[7] whose hero has as followers the blundering Giant Fracassus and the resourceful rascal Cingar, a model for R's Panurge; R drew on both but mainly the latter. However, R was the first real genius to illustrate this field. In both his first two books, as we noted, AN adds complexity and ambiguity; R draws on Lucian for the use and the spoofing of the tall tale; and by also using both satire and comedy based on words, ideas, and issues of the time, he rounds out a work of real literature, while enriching his story are his wide readings in the ancients and in his master Erasmus.

His book generally builds on the traditional framework: genealogy of the hero, birth and infancy, childhood, youth and education; then in manhood a victorious war against a wicked aggressor. Here genealogy, birth, infancy, and childhood lead in chapter 5 to a tour of provincial universities ending near Paris. Then for half the whole book (chaps. 6–22) R explores a few byways (student Latinizer in 6), erudition run amok in the Saint-Victor Library in 7, learning and the ideal education in 8, leading in 9 to the raffish polyglot Panurge, whom Pantagruel is to love all his life, and who shortly (after an interlude in chaps. 10–13 on the lunatic lawsuit between Lords Kissass and Sniffshit and Pantagruel's Solomonic verdict) takes center stage on his own for seventeen chapters, with his escape from the Turks (14), plans for the walls of Paris and the corollary tale of the lion, fox, and old woman (15), his ways in general (16), shameless ways to get money (from poorboxes, collection plates, and so on (17), his victory as Pantagruel's deputy over Thaumaste in the debate in signs (18–20), his vain propositions to the lady of Paris and nasty revenge when she turns him down (21–22). Then after the call to war (23), he solves the riddle of the ring (24), persuades Pantagruel to sit out the war while he takes charge, destroys the enemy Dipsodes by his ruses (25–26, 28), then helps give Pantagruel the courage to fight and destroy Werewolf's 300 giants (29)—alone—and later replaces Epistémon's head (regrettably cut off in battle but found cradled in his dead arms) on his shoulders and restores him to life to relate what hell is really like: topsy-turvy, the first now last and the last now first (30). Back home victorious, he and his prince dispose comically of the fallen aggressor Anarche (31); then R offers two Lucianesque episodes that send humans inside the giant: AN exploring inside his mouth (32) and the miners (33) sent to clean out his constipated bowels. A conclusion (34) then announces wonders to come (a few of which will) soon to delight the readers.

The second book R wrote, *Gargantua* (Book 1, 1534 or 1535), also generally follows the traditional plan but fills it out with less episode and more satire (as of Janotus in chaps. 18–20), and serious bits that seem straightforward (bad old education, 21–23, and good new, 23–24), monks and pilgrimages (40, 45) and war, especially the aggressive kind (25–51 in general, notably 25–33, 46–51); finally the account (52–57) of the utopian abbey of Thélème (Greek "will"), the antimonastery Gargantua built to suit Frère Jean's wishes in reward for his heroic prowess (far eclipsing his own) in the victorious war: its rationale, subsidization, and splendid construction (52–53); types excluded and types welcomed (54); facilities and attire (55–56); its one rule, "Do what you will," why and how it works, and the unanimism that results; and concluding the book, the Prophetic Enigma (58), probably in the main by court poet Mellin de Saint-Gelais,[8] Pantagruel's sad reading of it as predicting persecution ahead, then Frère Jean's, ingeniously comic, as a tennis game. And with this, on this note, the book ends.

Books 1 and 2, close in time, plot, and giant theme, are generally linked and compared, usually in favor of Book 1: freer from old models, more coherent, neater in aim and construction, richer in ideas known to be dear to R. However Book 2's ebullient spontaneity and untrammeled freedom, the patterns and unity all its own, have won it, especially of late, many able and articulate champions.[9]

As against R's usual interval of two to four years between books of his tale, eleven or twelve elapsed (1534 or 1535 to 1546) between publication of his second book written (1) and his third (3); we do not know just why, but both theories and reasons abound. I attribute much of it to the risky venture he was attempting after tiring of the unchallenging sure-fire success of his giant stories, this probably after long hesitation before deciding to try this erudite book with no more giants, physical action, regular story line, comic mask, or fictive narrator or purported author, but under his own name and profession, and publishing it in Paris, at the heart of enemy country, where many thirst to see him burn.

In his Prologue he clearly suggests his anxiety with a story used by Lucian (to express his uneasiness over mixing lowbrow comedy with high-flown dialogue),[10] of how Egyptian King Ptolemy, son of Lagus, after procuring two freakish creatures to entertain his people, was dismayed to see them received with abomination.[11] R's further discussion of his own venture recalls how he later thanks Chastillon (4.OC) for pulling him out of deep despondency from the unrelenting lies and slanders of his enemies and of his consequent decision to give up writing his book; for in the Prologue R first expresses his anxiety about his book's reception and his fear that it may be found "ridiculous and monstrous," before reassuring himself that all his readers possess a good measure of Pantagruelism, so that they will never take in bad part things they know issue from "a good, free, and honest heart," and will content themselves with good will even where power is weak. (To be sure, in the Prologue he then specifies which readers he welcomes and which not; whereas to Chastillon, understandably, he voices no such second thoughts or uncertainties.)

If my hunch is sound that his decision to make the try followed long hesitation, he may even be deriding this in Panurge's inability to make up his mind. But he must have wondered: Can I write a good book of this sort? And even if I can and do, will my readers like it, my topers, gouties, poxies, and others? Will they accept such a book from me? This and his anxiety about its reception called for careful deliberation, careful planning, and careful execution, all of which suggests at least one time-consuming false start. If we add to all this the new minor works and new editions of the G and P, especially the virtual expurgation in the new revision of 1542; R's times in Montpellier for advanced degrees and giving lectures; his trips to Rome and to Metz (probably not very productive for writing his story); and the two apparently bad years already noted, from mid-1543 to mid-1545, his delay in writing his story seems not so surprising.

Book 3 begins with Pantagruel's colonizing the unreformed Dipsodes of Book 2 with a law-abiding implant of his happily subject Utopians, then works its circuitous way to its main subject, Panurge's itch to marry, dread of cuckoldry if he does, and resulting inaction. First we meet the Panurge of Book 3 as Pantagruel rewards his wartime cunning with the castleship of Salmagundi[12] (chap. 2), which allows him to run through its revenue and pile up record debts in record time, then (2–4) display his glib sophistry by showing the virtues and advantages of debt, the horror of a world without it, the utopia where it prevails. Near the end of this, one term, the duty or debt (le debvoir) of marriage, dimly heralds what is to come; but first (5) Pantagruel asserts that he detests debt and debtors, quotes Plato and Saint Paul on what debts are licit, and turns down Panurge's plea, to be left a few to provide him company, with a sharp command to drop the subject.

We next (6) learn why Mosaic law gave newlywed men one year's exemption from military service (Panurge adds his own lustful theory), then (chap. 7) learn of Panurge's change to bizarre attire because a flea in his ear gives him an irresistible itch to marry. But his equal fear of cuckoldry leaves him helpless to decide, craving advice, thus ready for the thirteen consultations forming the body of the book. Naturally he starts with his wise prince and master Pantagruel, who tells him (9) to make up his mind and then act on it; but Panurge's squeeze between lust and dread leads to a comical exchange: Pantagruel keeps telling him to decide and act, while Panurge meets every such counsel with a querulous "but what if"; and each man's every rejoinder begins with the ending of the previous one, until Panurge accuses Pantagruel (3.10) of answering only with the "Ricochet song"; then for the nth time Pantagruel vainly urges him to decide and act, and this time tells him what a man must accept and do if he really wants to marry: one must "go into it at a venture, eyes blindfolded, bowing your head, kissing the ground, since once and for all you want to go into it. No other assurance about it could I possibly give you."

Pantagruel then suggests the first of the many authorities that Panurge may wish to consult, Virgilian lots,[13] which they explore in 12–14 and there set the unchanging pattern of these consultations: consultant's often enigmatic but unfavorable response; Pantagruel's echoing unfavorable clarification; and Panurge's highly implausible but ingeniously optimistic reading in rebuttal. Several consultants will agree with Pantagruel's "Decide, then act," and with the Thélémite "Do what you will," but of course always with the corollary "but accept the consequences": the beatific dying poet Raminagrobis (21), the benign sage theologian

Hippothadée (30, 35), and the ephectic philosopher Trouillogan (36). The final consultation, with the fool (jester) Triboullet (46), leads to Panurge's decision (47) to seek as ultimate consultant the divine Bottle, and thus to the voyage (Books 4–5) that makes up the rest of the tale. Preparations for the trip then bring on this book's final piece (49–52) on the magical virtues of the herb Pantagruelion, which include some of those of hemp, flax, at times asbestos. And with this barely related bit the book ends.

Book 4 tells the first part of the voyage announced late in 3. There are two versions (1548 and 1552), the former in effect a first installment on the completed, definitive Book 4 of 1552. Its eleven chapters interpolated, to form chapters 1–25 of the total of 67 in the 1552 edition. Each version has its own prologue, unrelated to the other; and with the 1552 text appear also a Dedicatory Epistle to Cardinal Odet de Chastillon (OC) and the Brief Declaration (hereafter BD) designed to clarify some of the book's difficult or obscure terms. Apart from the additions, the texts common to both versions are enough alike to obviate any need to offer both texts entire; notes suffice to show the variants; but the BD, the OC, and the two prologues are each unique; and although the BD may be inauthentic (see the first note for BD), we offer it here too for the sake of completeness.

The short Old Prologue (OP) explains the phrase "croquer pie" (to have a drink, literally "nibble magpie") as originating long ago in a horrific battle between two vast flocks, of the jays and the magpies, ending in the defeat and slaughter of the magpies, followed by one tame jay's practice of inviting any visitors to "croquer pie." From there, R turns to a fierce denunciation of his calumniators as lying "spitters in the basin" who have befouled his work and snatched it away from his patients, for whom it was written; and in conclusion an invitation (to these calumniators) to hang themselves, promptly, while he still has the tree and the rope that he will gladly provide, and gratis. (This blast will find a better place in 1552 in the OC as partial explanation of his heavy debt to the cardinal.)

The New Prologue (NP) of 1552, about twice as long as the old even without its burden of complaint, soon defines Pantagruelism, as "a certain gayety of spirit confected in disdain for fortuitous things," but centers in its moral of *médiocrité* (moderation in desire and aspiration, not unlike Christian humility), embodied in its honest hard-working hero Couillatris, a poor woodchopper, who on losing his indispensable hatchet howled so loud and long to get it back that Jupiter sent down Mercury to test his honesty by letting him choose his own out of a triad including with it one of gold and one of silver. Choosing his own, he is rewarded with a bonus of the other two that makes him rich for life: the moral and centerpiece of this rich prologue.

The book (4) tells of the early part of Panurge's questing voyage (with Pantagruel and the others) to hear the word of the divine Bottle. Its main focus is on the exotic places, customs, and characters encountered or described on the islands they visit or pass near: notably the Shysteroos of Procuration (12–16), whose living comes from the drubbings they receive for their services; the long-lived Macrobes (25–28) of the Macraeons' Island who explain the portents or the deaths of their hero neighbors; the antinatural monster Fastilent (29–32), anatomized in detail by Xenomanes, and whose spiritual heirs Pantagruel finds all around; his enemy victims the Chitterlings of the Wild Island, so fearful of him that they take Pantagruel for him and attack him by mistake, then are cut to pieces by Frère Jean's embattled cooks, and (the survivors) pardoned by Pantagruel; those mutual foes the downtrodden Popefigs (45–47, with the farmer, his shrewd wife, and the naive young devilkin) and the fat-cat Papimaniacs (48–54, glutted from all the French gold extracted by their infamous Decretals, revering anyone who has seen the pope), with their manic bishop, Grosbeak, drooling at thoughts of pope or Decretals but invoking torture and death for any who do not agree; Messere Gaster (Sir Belly), "First Master of Arts in the World" (57–62), inventor of all crafts that foster human life and civilization, but in turn exacting full obedience on the spot of all living creatures, even gods; lastly that true Antiparnassus, the Island of Thieves (Ganabin, 66–67), which, as they pass by, they salute with a cannon salvo, prompting Panurge's panic fear and the bowel movement whose product he hails triumphantly in conclusion as "Hibernian saffron!" For all its exoticism, both the book's most memorable episodes just display unedifying human conduct: Panurge's encounter (5–8) with the offensive sheep merchant Dindenault, whose arrogance richly earns the drowning (with all his sheep and shepherds) that his ingenious customer gets him to bring about; and the terrible tempest (17–24) that endangers every life and reveals Panurge's cowardly self-pity, Frère Jean's active courage, and Pantagruel's anguished Christian resignation to God's will when he has done all he can to save his party but thinks it is all in vain.

Two related quirks in both versions raise questions: does Book 4 have a distinguishable narrator or not? If so, is he one of the travelers or not? And, again if so, when? AN is never named in it, as he is in 2.32, or clearly absent, as from 3 on, but Panurge twice addresses him in person, in 4.18 as "Master Stargazer," and as "Sir Abstractor" in 4.20; and yet nowhere else in 4 does he seem clearly there on stage. Perhaps related are the inconsistencies in the forms (of verbs and pronouns) R uses to refer to the company: third person plural at first (they or them), implying his absence from the company, then first person (we or us) for the rest of 4 and nearly all 5, implying his presence in their midst. This change (for more on which see the introductory note to 4), hardly noticeable in 1552 at the start of chapter 5, in 1548 shows clear early but not initially in chapter 2; thus I think R made it early in his writing of the 1548 Book 4; and suspect he inserted those two addresses at that time but no others; and I doubt that matters much in any case, as the change in persons does.

Authentic or not, Book 5 in some ways follows 4: it takes the travelers to their goal, the Bottle and its word; its main subject too is exotic places, customs, and characters met or described. But except for the opening "Continuing on our way" (5.1), no real linkage is attempted, though 4.67 leaves party and readers still off Ganabin with Panurge and his fouled breeches: Pantagruel did tell him to clean up and change, but he may be still guarding his Hibernian saffron. Also, the Ringing Island part (chaps. 1–8) is no continuation but, just as it seems, the start of a new book.

Book 5 offers other problems beside doubtful authenticity: three different basic texts for chapters 1–16, two for the rest, and such basic differences among these as inclusion and numbering of chapters (where, as always, we follow the 1564 ed. and LI). Noteworthy episodes run from the humanoid birds of the Ringing Island (chaps. 1–8), through the Furred Cats of the Wicket and the Law, past Queen Quintessence of Entelechy (18–24) with her officers, their wondrous cures and idiot projects, and her chess pageant; past the lusty Semiquaver Friars (26–27), Satin Land and Lanternland (29–32), to the island of the Bottle, start of the long account (33–47) of the rest of the trip, overland walk, access, descent down the 108 tetradic steps to temple level; long fond descriptions of its wonders: intricate mathematical construction, sumptuous materials, elaborate workmanship; self-opening doors; fountain, lamps, and surrounding columns; and mosaic paving that depicts Bacchus's bloody conquest of India.

Chapter 42 tells how the fountain's magic water tasted like the wine each drinker imagined; 43, how Priestess Bacbuc of the Bottle dressed Panurge to get its word; 44, his presentation, then the long-awaited word, *Trinch*. When Panurge asks: "Is that all?" Bacbuc interprets the word in much the Thélémite sense, as follows: "you yourselves be the

interpreters of your own undertaking" not far from "Do what you will."
This seems a neat conclusion, perhaps too neat to suit R, who likes to
undercut his solemnities (as 4.28); so in 46 he offers the frenzied Bacchic
rhyming (instigated, curiously enough, by Pantagruel) of his two companions—Panurge eager, Bacchically vinous, above all lascivious; Frère
Jean reluctant, crude, irreverently obscene—that completes the responses
(45–46) to the word of the Bottle in parody that debases all the preceding
lofty talk. The final chapter (47) of the book belongs to Bacbuc, hostess to
the party and priestess of the Bottle, who extols her world below as both
richer (in hidden treasures) and nobler (in preferring giving to getting)
than ours above ground; supplies the party amply with food and drink;
equips them with a magic water that will provide favoring winds for their
long voyage home; and finally (5.47) bids them bon voyage and godspeed
and sends them on their way. When they reach their ships waiting safe in
port, the book and story end. Bacbuc has the last word, but the Dionysiac
rhyming also lingers in the mind.

We hope this long conclusion does not seem to imply that we accept
the book as authentic; for in the main we do not. And with that, at least
for now so much for Book 5.

To avoid clutter, we have bypassed R's miscellaneous writings up to
now. For clarity, we now group them roughly by genre, for genre and
date seem to be the main determinants. R's humanistic and Evangelical
views inform his letters to Budé and Erasmus (6.1 and 6.7 below) and
most of his epistles (6.2, 6.4–6, 6.10). Most of the prognostications and
almanacs offer a few dates (fairs and such) and comically obvious truisms,
while ridiculing man's claims for accurate prediction, which belongs
to God alone; the verse oddments seem negligible; and the jolly uproari-
ous letter to Hullot echoed much later by Flaubert, shows this vein in
this genre and R's familiar abomination of Lent. The derivative *Shadow
Battle* (6.21) sheds no light on R as author or otherwise; and of course the
Latin Sapphic Ode (6.22) is not by R but by his patient-patron Cardinal
Du Bellay.

Among all these, to me the most rewarding are R's missive letters,
6.12–6.14, of December–January–February 1535–1536, to Geoffroy
d'Estissac in Maillezais, giving specifics about R's successful petition to
the pope—procedures, problems, costs, and happy ending; and, more
generally, about his life on such a trip, thus a sense of his daily life anywhere; much about problems of communication by letter, especially
across national frontiers and when interception was a risk, before the days
of government postal services; and we learn how he solved them. Here

too we find in R an alert, informed reporter on the events that come into his ken but possibly not into his bishop's in Maillezais; comings, goings, and doings of the mighty of western Europe or their representative, which sharpens our sense of how power was wielded then; its influence by money; the secular weakness of the papacy; and the nearly dictatorial power of the Emperor over continental Europe excepting France. And such are the main features of these 22 miscellaneous works.

GENERAL

If the broadly comic style is the most Rabelaisian, still it is only one of his many, for he speaks with many voices. François Rigolot's *Les Langages de Rabelais,*[14] our best book in this area, distinguishes four of these; but since his divisions and subdivisions confuse me, here I use my own: (1) that of the presenter and storyteller AN; (2) the broadly comic, often ribald voice of both Panurge and Frère Jean; of the giants as small children and their interlocutors; also of many transitory characters, from Picrochole and his henchmen in 1 to Dindenault in 4 and many others passim; (3) the lofty humanistic (or, with Thomas Greene, angelic) voice of the mature giants and many transitory characters, from Ulrich Gallet at its extreme to the wise Hippothadée in 3.30 and 35, the good old Macrobe in 4.25–27, the guiding Lady Lantern in 5, and lastly in its final chapters Bacbuc; and (4) the ordinary normal voice of most of Pantagruel's friends: Carpalim, Epistémon (when not a pedant), Eudémon, Eusthenes, Gymnaste, and Ponocrates; often of the narrator AN; and of many minor transitory characters throughout the book.

R likes to juxtapose voices, especially those as contrasting as the angelic-humanistic and the ribald or broadly comic, as when Gargantua, while rejoicing in the birth of his fine giant son, laments his wife Badebec's untimely death in childbirth, first in earnest mourning, then in grotesque giant calculation, as he passes from "my darling, my love, my little cunt" to "to be sure, she had one a good three acres and two sesterees in size," or when among the Macraeons Pantagruel has finished telling his moving story of the death of Christ and stayed a moment in contemplation, as a token of his deep emotion R tells us: "we saw the tears flow down his cheeks, as big as ostrich eggs. God take me if by one single word I'm lying about it" (4.28). Similar comic cappings are that by Frère Jean in 1.58 of Pantagruel's reading of the Prophetic Enigma, and much later (5.46) that of the lofty descriptions of the temple and discourses of Bacbuc (5.37–45) by the tipsy Dionysiac rhymings of Panurge and Frère Jean. A striking aspect of these encounters is their urbanity as neither clashes nor confrontations: when the time comes each gives way to the other. Nor are they fully reconciled or resolved into a unison: Pantagruel never quite convinces Panurge, nor (Heaven help us) does Panurge convince Pantagruel. No, these and all opposites live their independent lives in a Pantagruelic symbiosis that is one of the charms and distinctions of R's book.

Notable throughout are three aspects related to style: R's lyrical obscenity, lexical intoxication, and love of orality. About his obscenity, Rigolot notes rightly that men of his day found straightforward talk about all bodily functions so natural that the term and even the concept of obscenity were hard to find; the now familiar decorum that banished many of them from polite converse was to come later. Clearly, however, R was indeed concerned—without disgust—with what Mikhail Bakhtin calls "the lower bodily stratum," and in the mode of the carnival, which he loved. Of the main types of obscenity, R's is rarely erotic, normally scatological; when he comes close to the erotic he tends to skirt it or turn it into the grotesquely comic, as in the example above from 2.3. He uses 36 terms for *copulate*,[15] many of his own invention; but none are titillating, all are animal, mechanical, or simply bizarre. But he enjoys talk of healthy elimination, liquid or solid, and his young Gargantua relates lyrically (and partly in verse) his finding ideal bliss in the perfect ass-wipe formed by a gosling's neck. One fine example shows R turning the near-erotic into the grotesquely comic. In the prologue to 3, after the tale of the dismal reception of Ptolemy's freaks, R thinks of his Pantagruelic readers and takes hope again, but adds that he wants none but these, no "mist-swallowers, . . . doriphagous giants, or other such monsters." "About the hood-brained pettifoggers," he then goes on, "the nit-picking sticklers for details, don't talk to me, I beseech you in the name and reverence of our four buttocks that engendered you and the life-giving kingpin that for that time coupled them." (The French is even more sonorously majestic.)[16] Samples of R's lexical intoxication are his elongated terms for lightly taken injuries (4.15), the longest two over 20 syllables long and over one line of text; but comparable others abound, for R is in love with words.

For over two millennia, from the Greek Semonides, then Roman laconism, down to the present via Pascal[17] in the 1650s economy has dominated the western esthetic; and most of us need it. We know that brevity, the soul of wit, is at the heart of good style.[18] If two words tell the story, better two than four, ten would be anathema. R turns this dogma on its head and seems to say: myriad lovely words are waiting to be used; use causes no wear, but renewal and proliferation; so if a writer has free choice, why stop at a meager two and leave all the rest idle? Great artists make their own rules, and R's is an esthetic of exuberance, cornucopian. Even so Lady Macbeth, happily for us, does not just say the blood she imagines on her hands will not wash off. No, says she, it "will rather / The multitudinous sea incarnadine, / Making the green one red."

R's love of orality shows in his wide use of dialogue and drama: he tells his story in dramatic scenes. Loving to talk himself, his characters share that love. And this penchant grows with each edition. Relating (2.4) what the infant Pantagruel, having lately eaten a cow and a bear, did when left alone chained in his cradle while his father gave a banquet, R first (1532) wrote: "Here is what he did. He tried . . . ". Next (1534) the rhetorical question: "What did he do? He tried . . . " And by 1542 it was dialogue of a sort: "What did he do? What he did, my good folk? Listen. He tried . . . " Orality, dialogue, drama are key aims and practices in all R.

Our frequent use of the terms humanism (humanist) and Evangelicalism calls for clarifying their meaning for R and his France. Webster's calls this humanism (in part) "the revival of classical letters . . . and emphasis on secular concerns characteristic of the Renaissance." I would note also its stress on languages (mainly Greek, also Hebrew) for giving access to the wellsprings of western thought and culture. Webster's defines "Evangelicalism" (*not* Evangelism) as "emphasizing salvation by faith in the atoning death of Jesus Christ through personal conversion, the authority of Scripture, and the importance of preaching as contrasted with ritual." Much like Protestantism but neither militant nor dogmatic, it sought Church Reform along these lines from within. Although the conservative Council of Trent (1545–1563), R's "national council of madmen" (Chesil: 4.18; 4.35; 4.64), was to seal its doom by flat rejection of any such thing, in R's time it was a viable creed, that of many leaders of thought and letters: the great Erasmus, queen Margaret of Navarre and her entourage, R himself, the poet Marot, humanist storyteller Bonaventure Des Périers (*Cymbalum Mundi*), and many others.

Both humanism and Evangelicalism aimed to go back beyond medieval clouds and error to the pure original texts, especially texts of the Gospel and the purity of primitive Christianity. Thus these trends were natural allies: most Evangelicals were humanists, and many humanists were Evangelicals or sympathizers. Main opponents were conservative powers (religious and other), led by the Sorbonne and its secular ally or arm the Parlement of Paris, who saw both trends as threats to their vested authority and interests. For most of his reign King Francis I, fond of arts and letters and hating the Sorbonne, leaned to the Evangelicals; but strong advisers on each side, and provocations, his late years especially were vacillating. R's commitment to both positions, clear in all his work in many ways, is most explicit in G and P (1.17; 1.20; 1.40; 1.45), but these are only some of many.

R's fortunes are little known: one general overview;[19] Marcel de Grève's careful studies of R's early reception in France, England, Holland (*L'Interprétation de Rabelais au XVIe siècle*); Marcel Tetel's on Italy (*Rabelais et l'Italie* [Florence: L.S. Olschki, 1969]); little else. His impact elsewhere long seems slight except for Johann Fischart's German adaptation in 1575, more of which later. French readers first saw just another giant yarn spinner; then a Lutheran, then Erasmian, then a source for the *Satire Ménippée;* after 1600 a source for freethinkers Gassendi, Viau, Patin, leading to Molière, La Fontaine and Mme de Sévigné.

Generally, however, neoclassical concision, Cartesian logic, and pious decorum frowned on R; and La Bruyère probably voiced the delight of few, the disgust of many, in calling R a monstrous mixture of delicacy and filth, the best and the worst.[20] Voltaire long held this mixed view, finding R a buffoon merry but tedious at times, philosophizing only in his cups, whereas Diderot, an admirer from early, shows a disciple's debt in *Jacques the Fatalist* around 1770. By then Voltaire, at war with infamy, by 1767 saw R's use of a hidden marrow as his mask, and him as an ally whose book was a bitter masked attack against privilege, the Church, and other bêtes noires of his.[21] And although this escapes Beaumarchais, one Ginuené wrote a manifesto on this book title, *Of Rabelais's Authority in the Present Revolution.* And clearly the Revolution adopted him, as it did many others.[22]

I believe it was this subversive playing the clown which formed the base for the unfathomable mocker of nineteenth-century French Romantics, placed at the top with Homer, Dante, Shakespeare by Hugo (for him a "priest of laughter"[23]) and Chateaubriand, for whom he was source and founder of all French letters. And Jules Michelet makes him a Panourgos, just about everything great in his time.[24] Flaubert sets him among the greatest for his serenity and power. He reads him constantly and says he never goes to sleep without having read a chapter of "the sacrosanct, immense, and superlatively beautiful Rabelais.[25] Amid such a chorus of raves, George Sand's blunt candor comes as a refreshing break. Enchanted by his great gifts, she still loathed his obscenity, once even planned to join another in preparing an expurgated edition, and says she often wanted to tell him: "Divine master, you are a dreadful pig!"[26] However, the dominant view of her century was the worshipful one of his Romantic enthusiasts.

Early English readers thought him a mere jester, but Urquhart's free but rich racy translation brought new keener readers and soon admirers, Swift's early (*Tale of a Tub*, 1704), especially *Gulliver's Travels* (1727) and much later Sterne in his letters and *Tristram Shandy* (1759–1767), whose work is an eloquent tribute. The nineteenth century brought English admirers from Romantics Coleridge, Southey, and Browning to Kingsley in midcentury and much later an enthusiast in Swinburne.[27] Yeats made one notation about R in his puzzling *A Vision*. Probably the commoner Victorian view of R, however, was the curious one of Walter Besant in his *French Humorists,* where he praises R to the skies for a host of virtues and a "great moral teacher," but charges him with destroying earnestness in France for years to come, and in a damning summation estimates "that no writer who ever lived has inflicted such lasting damage on his country."[28]

In our century R's readers have spread wide with translations into Italian, Spanish, Hungarian, Polish, Greek, Romanian, Russian, and Japanese. A Chinese postage stamp has claimed him as a Marxist. Russian, German, and American scholars, like French and English, contribute to our sense of R. He has so many French and Anglophone admirers that space allows only a minute sampling; in France Jules Renard, Anatole France, Pierre Louys, Barrès, Alain, Apollinaire, Tzara, Claudel, Gide, Giraudoux, Aymé, Céline, Butor, his adoring Barrault; English Catholics Belloc, Chesterton, D. B. Wyndham Lewis; Eliot and Auden; J. C. Powys. Aldous Huxley relished R's acceptance of even the muck of life: as he puts it, of this "improbable world where flowers spring from manure, and reverent Fathers of the Church mediate on the divine mysteries while seated on the privy."[29] But Orwell saw this in R as "coprophilia," a "preoccupation with the W. C.," unhealthy; and R himself "exceptionally perverse, morbid . . . a case for psycho-analysis."[30]

Few agreed. A most intriguing case is James Joyce. He wrote a friend in 1927 that he had never read R (as all assumed he had) but meant to, and had read a little in a book on his language.[31] In Joyce's works (*Notebooks for Finnegans Wake,* etc.) there are terms and allusions clearly from R; but their order almost proves that Sainéan is their source. If he had read R through with care, I strongly doubt he could have resisted taking more from such a kindred spirit. And he must at least have made a start; for in *Ulysses,* late in Molly Bloom's final soliloquy, she complains of "some of those books (Poldy) brings me the works of Master François somebody supposed to be a priest about a child born out of her ear because her bumgut fell out a nice word for any priest to write and her arse as if any fool wouldn't know what that meant. I hate that pretending of all things with that blackguards face on him anybody can see its not truth." Clearly, among Francophones and Anglophones R is still very much alive today.

R scholarship, unimpressive earlier, boomed early in this century, led by Abel Lefranc in the positivist mode then reigning, stressing facts and figures, rarely concerned with esthetics or critical assessment; but as critics such as Parer and Symons, later Eliot and the "New Criticism," exposed the inadequacies of that approach, a slow but powerful shift began in R studies. In 1910 a young Viennese scholar (Leo Spitzer) won a German doctorate with a study of word-formation (as in R) as a stylistic means or medium.[32] Of course the prevalent positivism went on undisturbed; but he was not, and in 1939, as an eminence in the field now transplanted in the United States at Johns Hopkins, he opened fire with an article, "The So-called Realism of R," deflating that strange claim, which even Lanson endorsed, and belaboring the worst excesses and lacks of the old school. This of course had more impact than his work in 1910; but it shed less light on R's esthetics than it seemed to promise; and the tide still flowed with the historical, which Febvre greatly enriched in the 1940s with his psychological and socio-economic insights. Spitzer showed his hand more clearly and sociably in *Linguistics and Literary History* in 1948, urging the uniting of the two and illustrating this with four long studies (40–50 pages each) of one great Spanish author and three French "Le prétendu réalisme de Rabelais," fashioning a coherent view of each one's corpus from close reading of a short sample—recalling Horace's "Exungue leonem" and the Flaubert-Maupassant "Petit fait significatif."[33] But all the method's brilliance could not conceal its subjectivity (is there such a claw or sample, and is this it?), nor did the four long monologues involve the reader.

A slightly younger German-born scholar of comparable experience, Erich Auerbach (1892–1957), by then at Yale, had solved this problem already in his luminous *Mimesis,*[34] a collection of twenty shorter pieces (27–28 pages each) on short literary passages quoted fully or in large part, in English translation but also (except for Homer) the original, the passages drawn from Homer's Greek, classical and medieval Latin, medieval French, R and Montaigne, and ten European writers in four modern vernaculars concluding with Virginia Woolf—a dazzling introduction to western literature by true *explication de texte* and close reading. Through forty years of kaleidoscopic change it has held its high place as a classic.

Spitzer, rejoining the fray in 1960 with "Rabelais et les rabelaisants," his harshest blast, barely notes one Auerbach article (but not this book) as he denounces the articles composing the 1953 *FR*, ancestor volume of the *ER* series, honoring the fourth centenary (of R's death).[35]

Another view and aspect of R emerged in 1968 and 1970 with the English and French translations of *Rabelais and His World* by the Russian Mikhail Bakhtin (composed in 1940), which ignores Pantagruelism and virtually all of Books 3–5 to show R as a populist in revolt, on behalf of the comic ribald carnival spirit that loves to turn things upside down, against the dominant neoclassical literary culture, nobiliary and bourgeois, and its decorum that suppresses as foul the "open body" and "lower bodily stratum."[36] While its esthetic concern is incidental, Bakhtin's book added one more voice against the Pantagruelic and the positivistic, usually bourgeois, senses of R; and in the 1960s and 1970s, mainly in the wake of Spitzer and Auerbach, the pendulum has swung far onto the esthetic side, with adepts of approaches stylistic, structuralist, post-structuralist, deconstructionist, and so on, joined in bashing historicism as they have vied for center stage.

Broader, less programmatic aims seem basic to Manuel de Diéguez's *Rabelais par lui-même* (1960) and Alfred Glauser's *Rabelais créateur* (1966) and to Floyd Gray as he followed his valuable article on the prologue to Book 1 (*EE* 56 [1965] 12–21) with his 1974 book *Rabelais et l'écriture*; while Barbara Bowen further explored ambiguity and paradox (in both R and Montaigne) in her 1972 *Age of Bluff*.[37]

In 1973 Gérard Defaux set a good example in *Pantagruel et les sophistes* when, after calling this the "Quarrel of Ancients and Moderns" of our time, he stated his own position and reminded us all that our studies require two basics—knowledge and understanding—based on solid fact and historical sense of time and place but leading to judgment and assessment.[38] Both are needed: the solid base for the crowning judgment, also that judgment and assessment to crown that base as our ultimate goal. Surely this alliance of forces and methods is what is needed now, and any further bashing is counterproductive.

In the years since then, Defaux has produced a valuable article on Alcofribas, "Rabelais et son masque comique," and another rich book, centered on Panurge and Ulysses.[39] Other scholars in quest of assessment based on sound understanding include two already noted, Barbara Bowen and François Rigolot, Terence Cave with his *Cornucopian Text*,[40]

Raymond C. La Charité with many books and articles since 1967, especially in praise of *Pantagruel,* and Edwin M. Duval.[41]

Especially encouraging is the large number of these aged still around fifty and so likely to have much still to offer. And proven R experts such as Thomas M. Greene who lately have been active mainly in other areas of the field may well return to R's Diogenic cask for another draft or so. We may not have among us a second J. J. Lowes to give us a *Road to Bacbuc* or *Road to Ganabin* to rival his classic *Road to Xanadu* of 1927, or another Erich Auerbach to offer what today might have to be an unmimetic *Mimesis,* or someone to bring to R studies what Richard A. Sayce brought to his work on Montaigne; such beacon lights are rare. But if constructive combining of forces supplant bashing, as now seems likely, right now, with so many fine scholars having probably many good years still ahead, for the rest of this millennium and beyond, the outlook for Rabelais studies seems bright.

LES
ŒUVRES
de Maître
F. RABELAIS

J. B. Scotin Sculp.

BOOK 1

The Very Horrific Life
of the Great

GARGANTUA

Father of

PANTAGRUEL

Composed of old by
MASTER ALCOFRIBAS
Abstractor of Quintessence

A Book Full of Pantagruelism

To The Readers

You friends and readers of this book, take heed:
Pray put all perturbation far behind,
And do not be offended as you read:
It holds no evil to corrupt the mind;
Though here perfection may be hard to find,
Unless in point of laughter and good cheer;
No other subject can my heart hold dear,
Seeing the grief that robs you of your rest:
Better a laugh to write of than a tear,
For it is laughter that becomes man best.

Author's Prologue

Most illustrious topers, and you, most precious poxies—for to you, not to others, my writings are dedicated—Alcibiades, in Plato's dialogue entitled *The Symposium*, praising his master Socrates, incontrovertibly the prince of philosophers, among other things says he is like the Sileni. Sileni were in olden times little boxes, such as we see nowadays in apothecaries' shops, painted on the outside with merry frivolous pictures, such as harpies, satyrs, bridled goslings, saddled ducks, flying goats, harnessed stags, and other such paintings imagined at will to set everyone laughing (such was Silenus, master of good old Bacchus); but inside they preserved fine drugs such as balm, amergris, amomum, musk, civet, precious stones, and other valuables.

Such he said was Socrates, because, seeing him from the outside and estimating him by his external appearance, you wouldn't have given a shred of onion peel for him, so ugly in body was he and ridiculous in bearing, pointed nose, glance like a bull's, face of a madman, simple in manners, rustic in clothing, poor in fortune, unlucky in women, inept for all offices of the commonwealth, always gibbering, always dissembling his divine learning, but, on opening the box, you would have found inside a heavenly drug beyond price: superhuman understanding, wondrous virtue, invincible courage, matchless sobriety, certain contentment, perfect assurance, incredible disesteem for everything on account of which humans so lie awake, run, labor, sail, and fight.

To what purpose, you may well ask, does this prelude and essay point? It's inasmuch as you, my good disciples, and a few other unoccupied madmen, reading the merry titles of certain books of our creating, such as *Gargantua, Pantagruel, Tosspint, On the dignity of codpieces, On peas with bacon cum commento*, etc., too easily judge that inside there is nothing treated but mockeries, tomfooleries, and merry falsehoods, seeing that the outward sign (that is the title) is commonly received without further inquiry as derision and jest. But it is not fitting to assess the works of humans so lightly, for you say yourselves that the robe does not make the monk, and a man may wear a Spanish cape who in courage has no relation to Spain. That is why you must open the book and carefully consider what is expounded in it. Then you will recognize that the drug contained inside is of quite other value than the box promised, that is to say that the matters here treated are not so foolish as the title above claimed.

And, even in case in the literal sense you find these matters rather jolly and corresponding to the name, you should not stop there, as the Sirens' song, but interpret in a higher sense what peradventure you thought was said casually. Did you ever pick a lock and swipe some bottles? Son of a bitch! Call back to memory the way you looked. Did you ever see a dog coming upon some marrow bone? That is, as Plato says, Book 2 of *The Republic*, the most philosophic animal in the world.[1] If seen one you have, you were able to note with what devotion he watches it, with what care he guards it, with what fervor he holds it, with what prudence he starts on it, with what affection he breaks it, with what diligence he sucks it. What leads him to do this? What is the hope of his endeavor? What good does he aspire to? Nothing more than a little marrow. True it is that this little is more delicious than the much of all the others, because marrow is the food elaborated to perfection by nature, as Galen says, *iij Fácu. natural.*, and *xj De usu parti.* [*On the natural faculties, Book 3*, and *On the parts of the body and their functions, Book 11*].

After this example it behooves you to be wise enough to sniff out and assess these exquisite books, to be light footed in pursuit and bold in the encounter; then by careful reading and frequent meditation, break the bone and suck out the substantific marrow—that is to say what I mean by these Pythagorean symbols, in the certain hope of being made more astute and brave by the said reading; for in this you will find quite a different taste and more abstruse doctrine, which will reveal to you some very lofty sacraments and horrific mysteries, concerning both our political state and our domestic life.

Do you believe in all good faith that Homer, writing the *Iliad* and *Odyssey*, ever thought of all the allegories with which he has been calked by Plutarch, Heraclides Ponticus, Eustathius, Cornutus, and what Poliziano stole from them?

If you believe it, you come nowhere near my opinion by either hand or foot, which affirms that these were as little thought of by Homer as were the sacraments of the Gospel by Ovid in his *Metamorphoses*, as a certain Friar Booby [Frère Lubin], a real bacon-snatcher, has tried to demonstrate, on the chance that he might meet up with folk as crazy as he, and, as the proverb says, a cover worthy of the pot.

If you don't believe that, on what grounds will you not do so with these merry new chronicles, although, while dictating them, I had no more thought of it than you, who peradventure were drinking as I was? For in the composition of this lordly book, I neither wasted nor ever employed any more or other time than that which was established for taking my bodily refection, that is to say eating and drinking. And indeed that is the right time for writing these lofty matters and this profound knowledge, as Homer well knew how to do, paragon of all philologists, and Ennius, father of the Latin poets, as Horace testifies, although one boor said that his songs smelled more of wine than of oil!

One no-good says as much of my books; but shit on him! The fragrance of wine, how much more appetizing, laughing, inviting, heavenly, and delicious it is than that of oil! And I shall glory as much in people's saying about me that I have spent more on wine than on oil as Demosthenes did when they said of him that he spent more on oil than on wine. To me it is due honor and glory to be called and reputed a good fellow and jolly companion, and in that name I am welcome in all good companies of Pantagruelists.

Demosthenes was reproached by one sourpuss claiming that his orations smelled like the cleanup rag of a filthy dirty oil-seller. Therefore interpret all my deeds and words in the most perfect sense; hold in reverence the cheese-shaped brain that is stuffing you with these fine idiocies, and, as best you can, always keep merry.

So now rejoice, my loves, and merrily read the rest, all for
the ease of your body and advantage of your
kidneys! But listen, you donkeypricks
(may boils and blains rack you!),
remember to drink to me
in return, and I'll
drink to you all
on the spot.

5

CHAPTER 1

*Of the genealogy
and antiquity of Gargantua.*

I refer you to the Pantagrueline chronicle to renew your knowledge of the genealogy and antiquity from which Gargantua came to us. In this you will hear at greater length how the giants were born into this world, and how from them, in a direct line, sprang Gargantua, father of Pantagruel; and you will not be angry if for the present I forbear, although the matter is such that the more it was recalled, the more your lordships would like it; for which you have the authority of Plato, in his *Philebus* and *Gorgias,* and of Flaccus, who says that some accounts, no doubt such as these, are all the more delightful the more they are repeated.

Would God that everyone knew his own genealogy as certainly, from Noah's Ark down to this day! I think that many today are emperors, kings, dukes, princes, and popes on earth, who are descended from relic-peddlers and firewood-haulers; just as, conversely, many are poorhouse beggars, wretched and suffering, who are descended from the blood and lineage of great kings and emperors, considering the prodigious transfer of reigns and empires: from the Assyrians to the Medes, from the Medes to the Persians, from the Persians to the Macedonians, from the Macedonians to the Romans, from the Romans to the Greeks, from the Greeks to the French.[1]

And, to give you knowledge of myself who am speaking, I think I am descended from some rich king or prince of the olden times; for you never saw a man who had more desire than I do to be a king and rich, so as to live luxuriously, do no work, not worry, and enrich my friends and all men of worth and learning. But in this I take comfort, that in the other world I shall in fact be greater than at present I would even dare to wish.

Do you comfort your unhappiness in such a thought, or a better one, and drink cool, if that can be done.

To return to our sheep,[2] I tell you that by a sovereign gift of the heavens there has been preserved for us the antiquity and genealogy of Gargantua, more complete than any other except that of the Messiah, which I do not speak of, for I have no right to, also the devils (that is, the calumniators and hypocrites) oppose it. And it was found by Jean Audeau in a field he owned near the Gualeau Arch, below the *Olive,* as you head for Narsay; in having its ditches cleaned, the diggers with their picks struck a great bronze tomb, immeasurably long, for they never found the end of it because it went too far into the mill-dams of the Vienne. Opening this in a certain place stamped on the outside with a goblet around which was written in Etruscan the letters HIC BIBITUR [HERE YOU DRINK], they found nine flagons in the order in which they put nine-pins in Gascony, of which the one in the middle covered a huge, stout, big, gray, pretty little moldy little book smelling more but not better than roses.

In this was the said genealogy found, written out at great length in chancery letters, not on paper, not on parchment, but on elm bark; these, however, so worn with age that you could hardly make out three in a row.

I, unworthy as I am, was summoned to it, and, with great reinforcement from spectacles, practicing the art by which one can read invisible letters, as Aristotle teaches,[3] I transcribed it, as you can see by Pantagruelizing, that is to say by drinking your fill and reading the horrific deeds of Pantagruel.

At the end of the book was a little treatise entitled *The Antidoted Frigglefraggles.* The rats and moths, or (lest I tell a lie) other harmful creatures had nibbled off the beginning; the rest I have inserted here below, out of reverence for antiquity.

CHAPTER 2

The antidoted Frigglefraggles,
found in an ancient monument.

ave?[1] ome the man who laid the Cimbrians low,
through the air, fearing the morning dew.
'his coming made the basins overflow,
As butter in his drawers and fell right through.
—hen grandmother was sprinkled with it too,
she cried aloud: "Please, mister, fish him out;
His beard is filthy from that loathsome stew;
Or bring a ladder if there's one about."

To lick his slipper, some folks used to say,
Helped more than the indulgences you buy;
But an affected blackguard passed that way,
Fresh from the hollow where the sunfish lie,
Who said: "Hands off, lords, honor God on high;
The eel is here, and in this hidden spot;
There you will find (if from close up you spy)
Deep down inside his amice's greatblot."

When time came for the chapter to be read,
Inside, a young calf's horns was all they found:
"I feel my miter's depths so cold," he said,
"My brain is freezing there and all around."
They warmed him with the scent of turnip-ground,
And he, contented, stayed home by the fire,
Once a new lime tree on a little mound
We made for shrewish people full of ire.

Their talk was all about Saint Patrick's Hole,
Gibraltar, many other holes as well:
If these as one deep scar could be made whole,
And put an end to every coughing spell.
Since it was thought discourteous, strange to tell,
To see them thus yawning in every breeze;
If haply well closed up, as in a spell,

They could be used as human guarantees.

This verdict left the raven plucked and bald,
By Hercules, of Libya well rid.
"What?" Minos said, "why am I too not called?
Except for me, everyone else is bid.
And then they'd have me keep my wish quite hid
To furnish them oysters and frogs galore!
Damme if ever I (which God forbid!)
Take mercy on their distaff-selling store."

To tame them then Q. B. came limping by;
Trim starlings got him through surrounding foes.
—Kin to great Cyclops of the one round eye,
The sifter slaughtered them. All, blow your nose!
Few buggerings then on this heath arose,
That were not balked in time upon the mill.
Run all, see that the warning bugle blows:
You never did have much, but now you will.

Soon after that, Jupiter's chosen bird [the eagle]
Resolved to wager on the weaker side,
But, seeing them so furiously stirred,
Fearing the empire ravaged from outside,
Preferred to steal fire from the heavens wide,
Out of the tree trunk where red herrings' sold,
Than to subject calm air, whate'er betide,
To sayings of the Massoretes of old.

All was agreed, each detail sharp and clear,
In spite of Ate with the heron's thigh,
Who sat there seeing old Penthesilea,
Thought to be selling cress for all to buy.
"Aside, vile collier's wife!" was then the cry,
"Is it for you to be here in our way?
You tore the Roman banner from on high,
That drew on the old parchment, so they say."

Except that Juno sought the evening dew,
With her great lord, beneath the rainbow's glow,
She'd have had such a hard time to go through,
That wear and tear on all her clothes would show.

It was agreed then that two eggs should go
To her from Hades' queen beneath the ground,
And in case ever she was fettered so,
Upon the hawthorn hill she should be bound.

After seven months (take away twenty-two),
He who destroyed Carthage in olden days
Sat down courteously between the two,
Asking for his bequest, with no delays,
Or that they share the lot in fairer ways,
Heeding the law as by a cobbler sewn,
Serving a little soup in many trays
To his workmen who made the deed his own.

The year will come, signed with a Turkish bow,
Five spindles, and three bottoms-of-the-pot,
When the back of a king too crude to show,
Under a hermit's robe shall be a sot.
Alas! For one pederast you will not,
I trust, let all this acreage go down;
Then stop! Let no one imitate this blot;
Go join the brother of the serpents brown.

This year just past, The One Who Is shall reign,
Together with His good old friends, at peace.
Nor crash nor smash shall dominate again;
Then all good will at last shall find surcease
For heaven-dwellers in its belfry peal'
Then the stud-stallions, idled by caprice,
Shall like a royal palfrey triumph feel.

And so this time of sleight-of-hand shall last,
Until such time as Mars is chained for fair.
Then comes one who all others has surpassed,
Delightful, handsome, nice beyond compare.
Lift up your hearts, and to this feast repair,
My subjects all, for one has passed away,
Whom no reward would lure back here from there,
So high will then be praised the olden day.

At last the man who was of wax shall stay
In the hinge by the hammer-wielder's side.

Petitioners no more "Sire, Sire" shall say
To a mountebank who holds the nightmare tied.
Hoy, give a man a cutlass stout and wide,
Soon the round-headed ringings would be clean,
And one might well with baling twine deride
The storehouse of abuses we have seen.

CHAPTER 3

*How Gargantua was carried
eleven months in his mother's belly.*

GRANDGOUSIER was a great joker in his time, loving to drink hearty as well as any man who was then in the world, and fond of eating salty. To this end, he ordinarily had on hand a good supply of Mainz and Bayonne hams, plenty of smoked ox tongues, an abundance of salted mullets, a provision of sausages (not those of Bologna, for he feared Lombard mouthfuls), but of Bigorre, of Longaulnay, of La Brenne, and of La Rouergue.

In his prime, he married Gargamelle, daughter of the king of the Parpaillons, a good looking wench, and these two together often played the two-backed beast, so that she became pregnant with a handsome son and carried him until the eleventh month.

For that long, indeed longer, can women bear a belly, especially when it is some masterpiece and a personage who in his time is to perform great feats, as Homer says that the child with which Neptune made the nymph big was born a full year afterward. For as A. Gellius says [Aulus Gellius, Book 3], that long time befitted the majesty of Neptune, so that in it the child should be formed to perfection. For a like reason, Jupiter made the night he lay with Alcmene last forty-eight hours, for in less time he could not have created Hercules, who cleansed the world of monsters and tyrants. My lords the old Pantagruelists conformed to what I say and declared not only possible but also legitimate, the child born to the wife in the eleventh month after her husband's death.

Hippocrates's book, *De alimento,* Pliny, *li. vij, cap. v* [Book 7, chapter 5],

Plautus, in Cistellaria [*The Casket*], Marcus Varro, in the satire named *The Testament,* alleging the authority of Aristotle on this matter, Censorinus's book, *De die natali* [*On the birthday*], Aristotle, *lib. vij, capi iij et iiij, De natura animalium* [in Book 7, chapters 3 and 4 *On the nature of animals*], Gellius, *lib. iij, cap xvj* [Book 3, chapter 16], Servius *in Egl.* [*On the Eclogues*] in explaining the line of Virgil—*Matri longa decem,* etc.—and a thousand other madmen, whose number has been increased by the lawmen, *ff. De suis et legit., l. intestato § fi.,* and in *Autent. De restitut. et ea quae parit in xj. mense* [*On their own and legitimates,* the Law on intestates, last paragraph]. Furthermore, their Robidilardic law has been besmeared with this Gallus, *ff. De lib. et posthu.,* and *l. septimo ff. De stat. homi.* and a few others whom for the present I dare not name. Thanks to such laws, widowed wives can freely play clinchcrupper all they like in their free time, two months after their husbands' death.

I ask you as a favor, my good fellow topers, if you find any of these who are worth opening your codpiece for, climb aboard and bring them to me. For if they are impregnated in their third month, their offspring will be heir to the deceased; and, once the pregnancy is known, they boldly push on further, and let 'er rip, since the paunch is full! Julia, daughter of Emperor Octavian, abandoned herself to her drum beaters only when she felt herself pregnant, even as the ship takes on its pilot only when it is first calked and loaded. And if anyone blames them for getting themselves rataconniculated thus during their pregnancy, considering that the animals never endure the masculating male upon their big bellies, they will answer that those are animals, but they are women, fully understanding the fair little rights of superfetation, as Popilia answered, as reported by Macrobius, *lib. ii Saturnal* [*Saturnalia Book 2*].

If the devil doesn't want them to conceive, someone will have to twist the spigot, and mouth closed.

CHAPTER 4

*How Gargamelle, while pregnant with Gargantua,
ate a great abundance of tripes.*

THE occasion and manner in which Gargamelle gave birth was this, and, if you don't believe it, your fundament is escaping you!

Her fundament was escaping her one day after dinner, the third day of February, for having eaten too many *gaudebillaux*. *Gaudebillaux* are fat tripes of *coiraux*. *Coiraux* are oxen fattened in the manger and *in prés guimaulx*. *Prés guimaulx* are those that grow grass twice a year. Of these they had killed three hundred and sixty-seven thousand and fourteen to be salted on Shrovetide, so that in the spring they should have beef in season in heaps, so as to have, at the beginning of the meals, a brief commemoration of salty things the better to get into the wine-drinking.

The tripes were copious, as you understand, and so delicious that everyone was licking his fingers for them. But the great four-person deviltry[1] lay in this, that they couldn't be kept long, for they would have rotted, which seemed indecent. So it was concluded that they should guzzle them without losing time. To do this they invited all the burghers of Sinay, Seuillé, La Roche Clermauld, and Vaugaudry, without omitting Le Coudray Montpensier, the Ford of Vède, and other neighbors, good drinkers all, good company, and good skittle players.[2]

That good man Grandgousier took very great pleasure in this and ordered to have everything served in ladlefuls. However, he told his wife to eat the last, seeing that she was nearing her time, and that all this tripery was not very recommendable food. "A person," said he, "is very eager to eat shit, who eats the sack thereof." Notwithstanding these remonstrances, she ate sixteen hogsheads, two bushels, and six pecks. O what lovely fecal matter must have been swelling up inside her!

After dinner, they went pell-mell to the Willow Grove, and there, on the sturdy grass, they danced to the sound of joyous flutes and sweet bagpipes, so gaily that it was heavenly fun to watch them sport.

CHAPTER 5

The palaver of the potted.

Then in the same place they started talking about dessert. Then flagons got going, hams trotting, goblets flying, glasses clinking:

"Draw!"

"Pass it here!"

"Turn it on!"

"Mix it!"

"Let me have it without water . . . That's it, my friend."

"Toss me off this glass gallantly."

"Come up with some claret for me, a weeping glass."

"A truce on thirst!"

"Ah, false fever, won't you go away?"

"My faith, gammer, I can't get tippling."

"You have a cold, my dear?"

"Yes indeed."

"Saint Quenet's belly! Let's talk about drinking."

"I drink only at my own times,[1] like the pope's mule."

"I drink only in my breviary, like a good Father Superior."[2]

"Which came first, thirst or drinking?"

"Thirst, for who would have drunk without thirst during our time of innocence?"

"Drink, for *privatio presupponit habitum* [privation presupposes habit]. I'm a cleric.

"Faecundi calices quem non fecere disertum?" [Whom did fertile cups not make eloquent?]

"We innocents drink only too much without thirst."

"Not I, a sinner, without thirst, and if not present, at least future, anticipating it, as you understand. I drink for the thirst to come. I drink eternally. For me it's an eternity of drinking, and drinking for eternity."

"Let's sing, let's sing, let's strike up a motet!"

"Where's my funnel?"

"What! I drink only by proxy [par procuration]!"

"Do you wet your whistle to get dry, or dry yourself to get wet?"

"I don't understand theory; of practice I do make some use."

"Hurry up!"

15

"I'm wetting, I'm drinking, all for fear of dying. Keep drinking, you'll never die."

"If I don't drink, I'm dry; then I'm dead. My soul will flee away into some frog pond. In dryness the soul can never dwell."

"You wine stewards, creators of new forms, from not drinking make me drinking!"

"Perennity of sprinkling through these parched and sinewy innards!"

"He drinks for nothing who gets no feeling from it."

"This stuff is going into my veins; the pissery won't get anything out of it."

"I'd gladly wash off the tripes of that calf I dressed this morning."

"I've ballasted my stomach well."

"If the paper of my bonds and bills drank as well as I do, my creditors would get their wine well enough when the time came to produce their titles."

"That hand is ruining your nose."

"O how many others will come in before this one goes out!"

"To drink at so shallow a ford is likely to break their breast straps."[3]

"This is what is called snaring flagons."

"What's the difference between a bottle and a flagon?"

"A big one, for a bottle is closed with a cork, a flagon with a prick."[4]

"That's a good one!"

"Our fathers drank well and emptied the pots."

"That's well shitten sungen. Let's drink!"[5]

"This one is going to wash the tripes. Won't you send anything to the river?"

"I drink no more than a sponge."[6]

"I drink like a Templar."

"And I *tanquam sponsus* [like a bridegroom]."

"And I *sicut terra sine aqua* [like a land without water]."

"What's a synonym for ham?"

"It's a compeller of drinks; it's a pulley. By means of a pulley you send the wine down into the cellar; by the ham into the stomach."

"Come on now, drink up now! There isn't a full load. "Respice personam: pone pro duos; bus non est in usu [Consider the person; put for two; bus is not in use]."[7]

"If I went up as well as I put it down, I'd long since have been up in the air."

"Thus did Jacques Coeur his millions gain."

"Thus do forests grow again."

"Thus did Bacchus conquer India."

"Thus philosophized Melinda."[8]

"A little rain beats down a big wind. Long drinking bouts break up the thunder."[9]

"But if my prick pissed such urine as that, would you really want to suck it?"

"Pass it here, page; I'll insinuate my nomination to you in my turn."

"Toss it off, Will! There's still another pot."

"I appear as appelant against thirst, even as against abuses. Page, draw up my appeal in due form."

"This snippet!"

"Once I used to drink it all; now I don't leave any."

"Let's not hurry and let's be sure and pile it all up."

"Here are tripes worth anteing for and *gaudebillaux* beyond compare from that dun ox with the black stripe. Oh, for heaven's sake, let's curry-comb it to the fullest."[10]

"Drink, or I'll . . ."

"No, no!"

"Sparrows won't eat unless you tap them on the tail; I drink only if you coax me."

"*Lagona edatera!*[11] There's not a rabbit burrow in all my body where this wine doesn't ferret out thirst."

"This one whips it out well."

"This one will banish it for me for good."

"Let's proclaim here, to the sound of flagons and bottles, that anyone who has lost his thirst need not look for it here: long clysters of drinking have driven it out of doors."

"Great God made the planets [planettes] and we make all the plates clean [platz netz]."

"I have the Word of God in my mouth: *Sitio*."[12]

"The stone called ἄβεστος [asbestos] is not more inextinguishable than my Paternity's thirst."[13]

"Appetite comes as you eat, Hangest of Le Mans used to say; thirst goes away as you drink."

"What's a remedy against thirst?"

"The opposite of the one against a dog's bite: keep running after the dog, he'll never bite you; keep drinking before thirst, it'll never happen to you."

"I've caught you napping; I'm waking you. Eternal wine steward [sommelier], keep us from napping [somme]. Argus had a hundred eyes to see with; a wine steward needs a hundred hands, like Briareus, to pour out indefatigably."

"Let's wet, hey-ho, it's no good being dry!"

"Some white! Pour it all, by the devil! Pour it all, fill 'er up; my tongue is peeling."

"Lans, trinque!"

"Here's to you, mate! Merrily, merrily!"

"So! So! So! That's really swilled, that is."

"O lachryma Christi!"[14]

"That's from La Devinière, it's pineau wine!"

"O what a nice white wine!"

"And, 'pon my soul, it's just a taffeta wine."[15]

"Ho, ho, it's one eared, well wrought, and of good wool."[16]

"Mate of mine, take heart!"

"For this game we'll not steal, for I've made a raise."[17]

"Ex hoc in hoc! [From this into that!]." There's no magic about it; each one of you saw it; I'm past master at it."

"Ahum! Ahum! I'm a mast paster."

"O those drinkers! O those thirsties!"

"Page my friend, fill it up here and crown the wine, please."

"In cardinal style!"

"Natura abhorret vacuum [Nature abhors a vacuum]."

"Would you say a fly had drunk of thus?"

"In Breton style!"

"Neat, neat, at this *piot!*"

"Swallow it, it's herb tea!"

CHAPTER 6

How Gargantua was born
in a very strange fashion.

Wᴴɪʟᴇ they were carrying on this small talk about drinking, Gargamelle began to feel bad in her lower body, at which Grandgousier got up off the grass and started comforting her honorably, thinking it was childbirth, and telling her that she was out to grass under the Willow Grove and that soon she would be making new feet; thus it behooved her to take new courage at the arrival of her baby, and although the pain was somewhat of an unpleasantness for her, that at all events it would be brief, and the joy that would soon follow would wipe away all this misery, so that she would have left only the memory of that.

"Have a sheep's courage," he kept saying, "dispatch this one, and soon let's make another."

"Hah!" said she, "it's easy for you to talk! All right, by God, I'll try my best, since you want me to. But would to God you had cut it off!"

"What?" said Grandgousier.

"Hah!" said she. "You really are a fine one! You know what I mean."

"My member?" said he. "By the nanny-goat's blood! If you see fit, bring me a knife!"

"Ah!" said she, "God forbid! God forgive me! I don't say that in earnest, and don't you do one thing more or less for what I said. But I'll have a tough time on my hands today, God help me, and all through your member, to make you feel good."

"Courage, courage!" said he. "Don't worry about a thing, and let the four front oxen do the job. I'm going off to have another drink. If you should have any trouble meanwhile, I'll stay nearby. If you whistle in your palm, I'll come to you."

A little while after this she began to sigh, lament, and cry out. Immediately there came up midwives in piles from all directions, and, feeling her from below, they found a few lumps of filthy matter with a rather bad taste, and they thought it was the child; but it was the fundament escaping her, from the loosening of the right intestine (which you call the bumgut) from having eaten too many tripes, as we have declared herein above.

Whereat a dirty old hag in the group who had a reputation as a great medic and had come here from Brizepaille near Saint-Genou sixty years before, made her a restringent so horrible that all her sphincters were contracted and tightened up to such a point that you could hardly have pried them open with your teeth; which is a mighty horrible thing to think; in the same way that the devil, writing down the yacketyyack of two old French wenches at Saint Martin's Mass, stretched the parchment just with his teeth.

By this mishap were loosened the cotyledons of the matrix, through which the infant sprang up into the vena cava; and, climbing up by the diaphragm up above the shoulders, where the said vein divides in two, took the route to the left, and came out through the left ear.

As soon as he was born he cried out, not "Wa, Wa!" like other babies, but at the top of his lungs: "A drink, a drink, a drink!" as if inviting everybody to drink, so well that he was heard in all the regions of Beusse and Bibarois.

I suspect that you do not firmly believe this strange nativity. If you don't believe it, I should worry! but a good man, a sensible man, believes what he's told and what he finds in books. Is it contrary to our law, our faith, contrary to reason, contrary to the Holy Scripture? For my part, I find nothing written in the Holy Bible that is against it. But if such had been the will of God, would you say He couldn't have done it? Hey, for mercy's sake, don't ever muddlefuddle your minds with these vain thoughts, for I tell you that to God nothing is impossible, and, if He wanted, from now on women would have their children that way through the ear.

Was not Bacchus engendered through Jupiter's thigh?

Wasn't Rocquetaillade born out of his mother's heel?

Wasn't Minerva born out of Jupiter's brain, by way of his ear?

Adonis out of the bark of a myrtle tree?

Castor and Pollux, out of the shell of an egg laid and hatched by Leda? But you would be much more amazed and astonished if I now expounded to you the whole chapter in Pliny in which he talks about strange and unnatural births; however, I am not as barefaced a liar as he was. Read Book 7 of his *Natural History,* chapter 3, and stop pounding on my understanding.

CHAPTER 7

How the name was given to Gargantua,
and how he inhaled the piot *wine.*

T HAT good man Grandgousier, as he was drinking and kidding with the
others, heard the horrible cry his son had uttered upon entering the
daylight of this world, when he roared and demanded "Drink! Drink!" At
which he said: "How big yours is!" (*supple*, your throat). Hearing which,
those present said that he therefore should really have the name
Gargantua, since such [Que grand tu as!] had been his father's first words
at his birth. To which he [Grandgousier] agreed, and his mother liked it
very well, on the example and intimation of the ancient Hebrews. And,
to appease him, they gave him enough to drink to burst his windpipe;
then he was carried over the baptismal font and baptized, as is the custom
of good Christians.

And there were assigned for him seventeen thousand nine hundred and
thirteen cows from Pontille and Bréhémont to give him his ordinary
milk. For it was impossible to find an adequate wet nurse in the whole
countryside, considering the great quantity of milk required to feed him,
although certain Scotist doctors have asserted that his mother nursed him
and that she could draw from her breasts fourteen hundred and two casks
and nine pipes of milk each time, which is not likely, and the proposition
was declared mammalogically scandalous, offensive to pious ears, and
smacking from afar of heresy.[1]

In that state he spent up to a year and ten months, at which point, on
the advice of the doctors, they began to carry him, and by Jean Denyau's
ingenuity a fine ox cart was made. In this they began to take him merrily
here and there; and it was good to see him, for he had a good mug and
almost eighteen chins; and he yelled only a very little; but he beshat
himself all the time, for he was wonderfully phlegmatic in the buttocks,
both by his natural disposition and by the accidental arrangement that had
come to him from inhaling too much September broth. And he inhaled
not a drop of it without cause, for if he happened to be feeling low,
angry, or sorry, if he stamped his feet, cried, or yelled, on bringing him a
drink they brought him back to himself; and promptly he stayed quiet
and happy.

One of his nurses told me, swearing her faith on it, that he was so accustomed to doing this, that at the mere sound of pints and flagons he went into ecstasy, as if he were tasting the joys of paradise. With the result that they, considering this heavenly disposition, to give him some fun in the morning, would make some glasses ring with a knife or some flagons with their stopper, or pintpots with their lids, at which sound he grew merry, hopped up and down, and himself rocked himself, nodding his head, playing tunes with his fingers, and giving the baritone with his tail.

CHAPTER 8

How they dressed Gargantua.

As he was at this age, his father ordered that clothes be made for him of his own colors, which were white and blue. Indeed, men went to work on it, and they were made, cut, and sewn in the fashion that was correct then. From the old charts in the Chamber of Accounts in Montsoreau, I find that he was dressed in the following way:

For his shirt were used nine hundred ells of Chasteleraud linen, and two hundred for the gussets, which were diamond shaped and put under the armpits; and it was not gathered; for the gathering of shirts was invented only since the seamstresses, when the point of their needle was broken, began functioning with the tail end.

For his doublet were taken up eight hundred and thirteen ells of white satin, and for the points fifteen hundred and nine and a half dogskins. Then people began to attach the hose to the doublet, and not the doublet to the hose; for that is something against nature, as Ockham fully declared in writing on the *Exponibles* of Master Haultechaussade [Highhosiery].[1]

For his hose were taken up eleven hundred and five and a third ells of white worsted. And they were slashed in the form of columns, chamfered and crenelated in back, so as not to heat up the kidneys. And within each slash there hung as much blue damask as was needed. And note that he had very handsome legs, well proportioned to the rest of his build.

For the codpiece were taken up sixteen and a quarter ells of this same cloth. And the form of it was like a flying buttress, most merrily fastened with two beautiful gold buckles, caught up by two enamel hooks, in each of which was set a big emerald the size of an orange. For—as Orpheus says, in his book *De lapidibus* [*On stones*], and Pliny, in his last book—it has the virtue of erecting and comforting the natural member.

The outlet of the codpiece was of a cane's length, slashed like the hose, with the beautiful blue damask floating as before. But if you saw the lovely gold embroidery and the attractive pleating with precious stones, garnished with fine diamonds, fine rubies, fine turquoises, fine emeralds, and great Persian pearls, you would have compared it to a lovely cornucopia, such as you see in the antique shops, and such as Rhea gave to the two nymphs Adrastea and Ida, wet nurses of Jupiter—always gallant, succulent, always verdant, always flourishing, always fructifying, full of humors, full of fruits, full of delights. I acknowledge God if it was not good to see it! But I will expound much more about it in the book I have done *On the dignity of codpieces.*[2] But I will tell you one thing, that if it was very long and very full, so was it well furnished inside and well victualed, and wholly unlike the hypocritical codpieces of a bunch of fops, which are full only of wind, to the great disadvantage of the feminine sex.

For his shoes were taken up four hundred and six ells of blue crimson velvet. And they were daintily slashed with parallel lines joined in uniform cylinders. For their soles were used eleven hundred brown cowhides, cut into codtail shape. For his coat were taken up eighteen hundred ells of blue velvet, dyed in the grain, bordered with fair vine shoots and embroidered in the middle with silver pintpots done in silver thread, intermixed with bands of gold and many pearls; denoting that he would be a good tosspint in his day. His belt was of three hundred and one-half ells of silk serge, half white and half blue (or I am badly mistaken).

His sword was not Valencian, nor his dagger Saragossan, for his father hated those potted hidalgos like devils; but he had a beautiful wooden sword and his dagger of boiled leather, gilded and painted to suit anyone.

His purse was made of an elephant's tool, which was given him by Herr Pracontal, procurator of Libya.

For his robe were taken up nine thousand six hundred ells less two-thirds of blue velvet as above, all tinseled with gold thread in a diagonal figure, from which in the right perspective there came a nameless color such as you see on the neck of a turtledove, which wondrously delighted the eyes of the spectators.

For his bonnet were taken up three hundred and two and a quarter ells of white velvet. And the shape of it was wide and round, to fit the head, for his father used to say that these bonnets Marrabaise [Spanish Jewish] style, made like a pie crust, would some day bring misfortune to their clean shaven wearers.

For his plume he wore a fine big blue feather, taken from a pelican from the country of Hyrcania, hanging very daintily over his right ear.

For his cap brooch he had, in a gold plate weighing sixty-eight marks [34 pounds], a suitable figure in enamel, in which was portrayed a human body having two heads, turned one toward the other, four arms, four feet, and two rumps, such as Plato in the *Symposium* said human nature was in its mystical beginning, and around it was written in Ionic lettering: ΑΓΑΠΗ ΟΥ ΖΗΤΕΙ ΤΑ ΕΑΥΤΗΣ "Love seeketh not her own," [1 Cor. 13.5].

To wear around his neck, he had a gold chain weighing twenty-five thousand and sixty-three gold marcs [12,531.5 pounds], made in the shape of great bayberries, between which were worked great green jaspers, engraved and cut into dragons surrounded by rays and sparks, as once King Necepsos wore; and it came down as far as the navel in his upper stomach, from which all his life he derived the emolument the Greek doctors know.

For his gloves were put to serve sixteen goblin skins, and three werewolf skins for the border of them; and they were made for him of such material by order of the Saint-Louand cabalists.

For his rings (which his father wanted him to wear to renew the old sign of nobility, he had, on the index finger of his left hand, a carbuncle as big as an ostrich egg, very daintily set in Egyptian gold. On the medical [middle] finger of the same hand he had a ring made of the four metals welded together in the most marvelous fashion that was ever seen, without the steel rubbing the gold or the silver crushing the copper; the whole thing was made by Captain Chappuys and Alcofribas, his good assistant. On the medical finger of his right hand he had a ring in spiral form, in which were set a perfect Balas-ruby, a pointed diamond, and a Physon emerald of inestimable value, for Hans Carvel, the great jeweler of the king of Melinda, assessed them at a value of sixty-nine million eight hundred and ninety-four thousand and eighteen long-woolled sheep; and such was the estimate of the Fuggers of Augsburg.

CHAPTER 9

Of the colors and livery of Gargantua.

GARGANTUA'S colors were white and blue, as you could have read above, and by these his father wanted people to understand that this was a celestial joy to him; for white to him meant joy, pleasure, delights, and rejoicing; and blue, celestial things.

I understand very well that as you read these words, you are laughing at the old toper and saying that white means faith and blue firmness. But without emotion, heat, or upset (for the times are dangerous), answer me, if you see fit. I shall use no other constraint toward you or others, whoever they may be; only I will tell you one word from the bottle.[1]

Who incites you? Who is stinging you? Who tells you that white means faith and blue firmness? A paltry book,[2] one which is sold by peddlers and book salesmen, with the title *The Blazon of Colors*. Who composed it? Whoever it was, he was prudent in this, that he did not put his name to it. For the rest, I don't know which I should marvel at first in him, his arrogance or his stupidity: his arrogance, which without reason, cause, or likelihood, dared to prescribe by his personal authority what things would be denoted by the colors, which is the practice of tyrants wanting their will to take the place of reason, not of the wise and learned who by reason satisfy the readers; his stupidity, which considered that, without other demonstrations and worthwhile arguments, people would regulate their devices by his doltish propositions.

Indeed (as the proverb says, there's always plenty of shit in a crapper's ass) he found some leftover imbeciles from the time of the high bonnets, who put faith in his writings and cut out their sayings according to these, harnessed their mules by them, dressed their pages, bordered their gloves, fringed their beds, painted their signs, composed songs, and (what is worse) perpetrated impostures and cowardly tricks secretly against modest matrons.[3]

In similar darkness are engulfed those court show-offs and name-changers who, wanting their mottoes to signify *espoir* [hope; then pronounced "espwère"], have depicted a sphere [sphère], birds' feathers [pennes] for pains [poines, then pronounced "pwènes"], *ancholie* for melancholy [mélancholie], the two-horned moon for "to live in growth" [*vivre en croissant,* meaning "to live in growing" or "in a crescent"], a broken

bench for bankruptcy [banc rompu pour bancque roupte], *non* and a
corslet for *non durhabit* [either "not a sturdy costume" or "it will not last"],
a bed without a canopy [*lict sans ciel,* with that *l* then silent] for a licentiate
[licencié], which are homonyms so stale, so uncouth and barbaric, that
someone should attach a foxtail to the collar of, and make a cow turd
mask for each and every one who would henceforth try to use them in
France, since the restoration of good letters.[4]

For the same reasons (if I am to call them reasons and not daydreams),
I would have a *penier* [*panier,* "basket"] painted to denote that I am being
made to suffer [pener]; and a mustard-pot [pot à moustarde] to show that
it *moult tarde* [is getting very late...for my heart] and a piss-pot, that's an
official [either an ecclesiastical judge or a chamber-pot]; and the depths of
my breeches, that's a *vaisseau de petz* [farts, homonym of *paix* "peace"];
and my codpiece is the *greffe des arrestz* [either "bulletin board for sentences, etc.," or "stem subject to hardening"]; an *estront de chien* [dog turd]
for the *tronc de céans* [inner sactuary] where lies the love of my lady.

Very differently did the Egyptian sages act once upon a time, when
they wrote with letters they called hieroglyphics, which no one understood who did not understand, and everyone understood who understood, the virtue, property, and nature of the things represented by these;
on which Orus Apollo has composed two books in Greek, and you have
a bit of it in the motto of My Lord the Admiral,[5] which Octavian
Augustus first wore.

But my little skiff will go no further between these unpleasant gulfs and
fords; I return to come ashore at the port from which I set out. I do
indeed hope to write about this more fully some day,[6] and demonstrate,
by both philosophical reasons and authorities accepted and approved from
all antiquity, what colors and how many there are in nature, and what
may be designated by each one—if God saves me the mold of my bonnet:
that is, my wine pot, as my grandmother used to say.

CHAPTER 10

Of what is signified by the colors white and blue.

So white signifies joy, solace, and blitheness and signifies it not wrongly but in good right and by just claim, which you can verify if, putting your prejudices behind you, you want to hear what I shall now explain to you. Aristotle says that assuming two things contrary in their species, like good and evil, virtue and vice, cold and hot, white and black, pleasure and pain, joy and sorrow, and so forth, if you couple them in such a way that one contrary of one species goes reasonably well with one contrary of another, it follows that the other contrary goes suitably with the other residue. Example: virtue and vice are contraries of one species; so are good and evil, if one of the contraries of the first species goes with one of the second—like virtue and good; for it is known that virtue is good—so will the two residues, which are evil and vice, for vice is bad. This rule of logic being considered, take these two opposites, joy and sadness, then these two, white and black, for they are physically contrary; and so thus it is that black means sorrow, and rightly white means joy.

And this significance is not instituted by human imposition but received by universal consent, which the philosophers call *jus gentium,* universal law valid in all countries. As you know well enough, all peoples, all nations (I except the Syracusans and a few Argives whose souls were askew), all languages, wanting to show their sadness externally, wear black clothes, and all mourning is done in black, which universal consent is not realized unless nature gives some argument and reason, which each and every man can understand immediately without being taught by anyone, which we call natural law.

By white, by the same natural deduction, everyone has understood joy, blitheness, solace, pleasure, and delectation.

In past time, the Thracians and Cretans marked the very fortunate and joyful dates with white stones, the sad and unfortunate with black.

Is not night sinister, sad, and melancholy? It is black and obscure by privation. Does not brightness rejoice all nature? It is whiter than anything there is. To prove which I could refer you to Lorenzo Valla's book against Bartolus; but the testimony of the Gospel will content you: in

Matthew 17 it is said that at the Transfiguration of Our Lord, His clothes were made "white as the light," by which luminous brightness He gave His three apostles to understand the idea and picture of the eternal joys. For by brightness are all humans delighted, as you have the remark of an old hag who had no teeth left in her head, but still said: "Light is good." And Tobit (chapter 5), when he had lost his sight and Raphael greeted him, replied: "What joy could I have, who do not see the light of heaven?" In such color the angels attested the joy of the whole universe at the Resurrection of the Savior (John 20) and at His Ascension (Acts 1). In like raiment Saint John the Evangelist (Revelation 4 and 7) saw the faithful dressed in the heavenly, beatified Jerusalem.

Read the old histories, Greek as well as Roman. You will find that the town of Alba (first model of Rome) was both built and named for the discovery of a white sow.[1]

You will find that if it was decreed that anyone, after gaining victory over the enemy, should enter Rome in a triumphant state, he entered in a chariot drawn by white horses; the same for one who entered in ovation;[2] for by no sign or color could they more certainly express joy at their coming than by whiteness.

You will find that Pericles, leader of the Athenians, wanted to have that part of his soldiers who by lot had drawn white beans, spend the whole day in joy, solace, and rest, while those of the other part fought.[3] I could expound to you a thousand other examples and instances in this connection, but this is not the place.

By means of this knowledge you can solve a problem that Alexander of Aphrodisias pronounced insoluble: why the lion, who by his mere cry and roar terrifies all animals, fears and reveres only a white rooster. For, as Proclus says, in his book *De sacrificio et magia* because the presence of the virtue of the sun, which is the organ and storehouse of all earthly and sidereal light, is more symbolized by, and related to, the white rooster as much for this color as for its specific property and order, than to the lion. He says further that devils have often been seen in leonine form, which in the presence of a white rooster have suddenly disappeared!

This is the reason why the Galli (that is the French, so called because they are naturally as white as milk which the Greeks called *gala*) are fond of wearing white plumes on their bonnets; for by nature they are joyous, candid, gracious, and well liked, and for their symbol they have the flower whiter than any other, that is, the lily.

If you ask how by the color white nature leads us to understand joy and cheer, I reply that the analogy and conformity is this. For—as white externally divides and disperses the sight, manifestly dissolving the visive spirits, according to Aristotle in his *Problems* and his *Perspectives* (and you see this by experience when you pass snow covered mountains, so that you complain that you cannot look at them well, as Xenophon says happened to his men, and as Galen explains fully in Book 10, *De usu partium*)—just so the heart is internally dispersed by surpassing joy and suffers manifest dissolution of the vital spirits[4] which can be so increased that the heart would remain despoiled of its sustenance and consequently life would be extinguished from this excess of joy, as Galen says in Book 12 of *Method* [*On practice*], Book 5 *De locis affectis* [*On the locations of illnesses*], and Book 2 *De symptomaton causis* [*On the causes of symptoms*], and as has been attested to happen in times past, by Marcus Tullius [Cicero], Book 1 of *Quaestio. Tuscul.* [*Tusculan disputations*], Verrius, Aristotle, Livy, after the batttle of Cannae, Pliny, Book 7, chapters 32 and 53, Aulus Gellius, Books 3 and 15, and others, to Diagoras of Rhodes, Chilon, Sophocles, Dionysius, tyrant of Sicily, Philippides, Philemon, Polycrata, Philistion, M. Juventus, and others who died of joy; and as Avicenna says (in *ij canone* and *lib. de viribus cordis)* of saffron, which so rejoices the heart that it robs it of life, if one takes it in excessive doses, by dissolution and excessive dilation. Here, see Alexander of Aphrodisias, Book 1 of the *Problems*, chapter 19, and for cause.[5]

But what's this? I'm getting further into this matter than I planned at the start. So here I'll take down my sails, putting off the rest to the book dealing with this, and I will say in a word that blue certainly signifies heaven and celestial things, by the same token as white signified joy and pleasure.

CHAPTER 11

Of the childhood of Gargantua.

Gargantua, from the age of three to five years, was brought up and taught in every appropriate branch of learning by his father's order, and spent that time like the little children of the region: to wit, drinking, eating, and sleeping; eating, sleeping, and drinking; eating, sleeping, and drinking; sleeping, drinking, and eating.

He was always wallowing in the mud, getting his nose dirty, messing up his face, wearing down his shoes at the heel, gaping after flies,[1] and running happily after butterflies, over whom his father held sway. He pissed on his shoes, shat in his shirt, blew his nose on his sleeves, sniveled in his soup, and made a mess everywhere, and drank out of his slipper, rubbed his stomach with a basket. He sharpened his teeth with a clog, washed his hands with soup, combed his hair with a goblet, sat between two saddles with his tail on the ground, covered himself with a wet sack, drank while he ate his dips, ate his *fouace* without bread, bit while laughing, laughed while biting, often spat in the basin, farted for fat, pissed against the sun, hid in the water for rain, struck while the iron was cold, had empty thoughts, gave himself airs and graces, flayed the fox, said the monkey's paternoster, returned to his sheep, turned the sows out to hay, beat the dog in front of the lion,[2] put the cart before the oxen, scratched himself where he did not itch, drew worms from his nose, bit off more than he could chew, ate his white bread first, shod grasshoppers, tickled himself to make himself laugh, ate heartily in the kitchen, offered the gods straw for wheat, had the Magnificat sung at matins and found it most appropriate, ate cabbage and shat leeks, could tell flies in milk, pulled the legs off flies, scraped paper smooth, besmeared the parchment, made his getaway on foot, pulled on the goatskin (of wine), counted without his host, beat the bushes without catching any litle birds, thought that clouds were brass skillets and bladders lanterns, took two grindings out of one bag, played the donkey to get some bran, made a mallet of his fist, caught cranes at the first leap, wanted to have coats of mail made link by link, always looked a gift horse in the mouth, jumped from rooster to donkey, put one ripe [grape] between two greens, made a ditch out of earth, kept the moon from the wolves, hoped to catch larks if the skies fell, made a virtue of necessity, made a dip to match his bread, cared as little about the shaven as the clipped, every morning flayed the fox. His father's little dogs ate out of his dish; he likewise would bite their ears, and they would scratch his nose; he would blow in their rump, and they would lick his jowls.

And you know what, lads? May barrel fever shake you! That little rascal was always feeling up his nurses, from top to bottom and from front to rear—giddap, burro—and already beginning to exercise his codpiece, which each and every day his nurses would adorn with lovely bouquets, fine ribbons, beautiful flowers, pretty tufts, and they spent their time bringing it back and forth between their hands like a cylinder of salve, then they laughed their heads off when it raised its ears, as if they liked the game.

One would call it my little spigot, another my ninepin, another my coral branch, another my stopper, my cork, my gimlet, my ramrod, my awl, my pendant, my *rude esbat roidde et bas* [near homonyms meaning "my sturdy sport stiff and low"], my erector, my little red sausage, my little rogue of a prick.

"It's mine," one would say.

"No, mine," would say another.

"And I," another would say, "shan't I get anything? My word, then, I'll cut it off."

"Huh, cut it off!" said another. "You'd hurt him, Madam; do you go cutting their things off children? He'd be Sir No'tail."

And, for him to play with like the children hereabouts, they made him a fine windmill with the sails of a windmill of Mirebalais.

CHAPTER 12

Of Gargantua's hobbyhorses.

THEN, so that he should be a good horseman all his life, they made him a fine big hobbyhorse, which he would make to prance, curvet, kick, and dance all together, walk, pace, trot, rack (go at a fast pace), gallop, amble, go the pace of a hobby, a hackney, a camel, or a wild ass, and had the color of his hair changed (as the monks do with Dalmatians according to the feast days), bay, sorrel, dappled grey, rat-dun, roan, cow, speckled, skewbald, piebald, white.

He himself made a horse for the hunt of a big post on wheels, another from a winepress beam, for everyday use, and from a great oak, a mule with a blanket for his chamber.

Besides these, we had ten or twelve for relays and seven for the post. And he put them all to bed right near him.

One day, the Lord of Breadinsack came to visit his father in great pomp and a fine retinue, on which day there had also come to him the Duke of Freelunch and the Count of Wetwind. 'Pon my word, the lodging was a little tight for so many people, and particularly the stables; so the chief steward and the furrier of the said Lord Breadinsack, to find out if there were empty stables anywhere else in the house, addressed Gargantua, a young lad, asking him secretly where the stables were for the big horses, thinking that children are prone to disclose everything.

Then he led them up the great steps of the château, passing through the second hall, into a great gallery by which they entered a great tower, and, as they climbed up by other steps, the furrier said to the chief steward:

"This child is playing a trick on us, for the stables are never at the top of the house."

"That's your misunderstanding," said the chief steward, "for I know places, at Lyon, at La Baumette, and elsewhere, where the stables were at the highest point of the house; so perhaps in back there's an exit to the upper level."

"But I'll ask for it more firmly."

Then he asked Gargantua: "My little dandy, where are you taking us?"

"To the stable," he replied, "of my big horses. We'll be right there, let's just go up these steps."

Then, passing them through another big room, he took them into his room, and said, closing the door:

"Here are the stables you're asking for; here's my gennet, my gelding, my courser, my hackney."

And, leading them to a great lever: "I give you," said he, "this Frieslander; I got him from Frankfurt, but he shall be yours; he's a good little horse, and a hard worker. With a goshawk tercel, a half dozen spaniels, and two greyhounds, you're king of the partridges and hares all this winter."

"By Saint John!" said they, "we sure have had it! At this point we've got the monk."

"I say you're wrong on that," said he, "he hasn't been here for three days."

Now guess which of the two they had more occasion for, to hide for shame, or to laugh for the fun.

At this point, as they were going down all confounded, he asked: "Would you like a whimwham?"

"What's that?" say they.

"That," he replied, "is five turds to make you a muzzle."

"For today," said the chief steward, "if we're roasted—never will we burn in the fire, for we're larded to a turn. O you little cutey, you've decked our horns with straw; I'll see you pope [pape] some day."

"So I mean to be," said he; "but then you'll be a butterfly [papillon], and this nice little popinjay [papeguay] will be a perfect hypocrite [papelard]."

"Well, well," said the furrier.

"But," said Gargantua, "guess how many stitches there are on my mother's blouse."

"Sixteen," said the furrier.

"You're not speaking Gospel," said Gargantua; "for there are a hundred in front [cent for sens davant] and a hundred behind [cent for sens derrière], and you miscounted them extremely badly."

"When?" said the furrier.

"When," said Gargantua, "they made a spigot of your nose to draw a hogshead of shit, and a funnel of your throat to put it into another vessel, for the bottoms were blown out."

" 'Odsbody!" said the chief steward, "we've found a smart talker. Mister prattler, God keep you from harm, you have such a fresh mouth!"

Coming down thus in great haste, under the stairway they dropped the big lever he had loaded them with; at which Gargantua said: "Devil take it, what bad horsemen you are! Your curtal fails you in case of need. If you had to go from here to Cahusac, which would you prefer, to ride horseback on a gosling, or to lead a sow on a leash?"

"I'd rather drink" said the furrier.

And so saying, they went into the downstairs hall where were the whole crew, and, telling this novel story, made everybody laugh like a pile of flies.

CHAPTER 13

*How Grandgousier recognized
the marvelous mind of Gargantua
by the invention of an ass-wipe.*

Toward the end of the fifth year, Grandgousier, returning from defeating the Canarrians, went to see his son Gargantua. There he was delighted, as such a father might be, seeing such a child of his, and, as he embraced him, he questioned him in various ways on little childish matters.

And he drank his fill with him and his nurses, of whom with great care he asked, among other things, whether they kept him white and clean. To this Gargantua made reply that he had so arranged it that in the whole kingdom there was no boy cleaner than he. "How's that?" said Grandgousier.

"I discovered," said Gargantua, "by long and painstaking experiments a way to wipe my ass, the most lordly, the most excellent, the most expedient that was ever seen."

"What's that?" said Grandgousier.

"As," said Gargantua, "I shall relate to you presently."

"I wiped myself with a lady's velvet mask, and found it good, for the softness of the silk part gave me a most pleasant feeling in my fundament; another time with one of their hoods, and it was just the same; another time with a neckerchief.

"Another time with ear-flaps of crimson satin, but the gilding of a batch of shitty spheres that were on it scratched my behind; may Saint Anthony's fire burn the bum-gut of the goldsmith who made them and the lady who wore them!

"That pain passed when I wiped myself with a page's bonnet, well plumed, Swiss fashion. Then, shitting behind a bush, I found a March-born cat; I wiped myself on him but his claws ulcerated my whole perineum.

"I cured myself of that by wiping myself with my mother's gloves, well perfumed with malzoin.[1]

"Then I wiped myself with sage, fennel, anise, marjoram, roses, gourd leaves, cabbages, beets, vine leaves, mallows, mullein (which is rump scarlet), lettuce, and spinach leaves—much good they did to my leg—with dog's mercury, persicaria, with nettles, with comfrey; but from it I got the Lombard bloody flux, of which I was cured by wiping myself with my codpiece.

"Then I wiped myself with the bed linen, the blanket, the curtains, a cushion, a rug, a green carpet, a rag, a napkin, a handkerchief, a dressing gown. In all I found more pleasure than do many people when they scrape them."

"All right," said Grandgousier, "which ass-wipe did you find the best?"

"I was just getting there," said Gargantua, "and soon you'll have the *tu autem*.[2] I wiped myself with hay, with straw, with rushes, with litter, with wool, with paper. But

> The ballocks always get a smear,
> When paper's used to wipe the rear."

"What!" said Grandgousier, "my little ballock, have you gotten stuck to the pot,[3] that you're rhyming already?"

"Yes indeed," said Gargantua, "my king, I'm rhyming that and much more, and in rhyming I often catch cold [en rimant...m'enrime]. Listen to what our privy says to the crappers:

> Shithard,
> Squirthard,
> Farthard,
> Turd spray,
> Your bum
> Has flung
> Some dung
> Our way.
> May you burn in Saint Anton's fire!
> Unless
> You dress
> Your mess,
> And wipe it clean ere you retire!

"Would you like some more of it?"

"Yes indeed," replied Grandgousier.

"Then," said Gargantua:

RONDEAU

While shitting th'other day I felt
The tax I'm owing to my tail;
Then did another scent prevail:
From tip to toe I foully smelt;
For this boon then I would have knelt:
To have a girl I could impale
      While shitting.

Soon in her pee-hole she'd have felt,
Crudely or not, my trusty nail;
This while her fingers formed a belt
To guard my bunghole and my tail,
      While shitting.

"Now tell me I don't know anything about it! Mother o' God [Par la mer Dé]! I didn't actually compose them, but, on hearing them recited by Grandma [dame grand] whom you see there, I've retained them in the game-pouch of my memory."

"Let's get back," said Grandgousier, "to our subject."

"Which one?" said Gargantua, "shitting?"

"No," said Grandgousier, "wiping your ass."

"But," said Gargantua, "will you pay for a puncheon of Breton wine if I make a monkey out of you on this subject?"

"Yes, indeed," said Grandgousier.

"There's no need," said Gargantua, "to wipe your ass unless there is filth; filth can't be there unless you shit; so shit you must before wiping your ass."

"Oh!" said Grandgousier, "what good sense you have, my little lad! In these next few days I'll make you a doctor in merry learning, by heaven! For you have more reason than years. So go on with your ass-wipative discourse, I pray you. And, by my beard! For one puncheon you shall have sixty casks, I mean of that good Breton wine, which does not grow in Brittany, but in that good Verron region."

"Afterward I wiped myself," said Gargantua, "with a kerchief, with a pillow, with a slipper, with a game-pouch, with a basket, but oh what an unpleasant ass-wipe! Then with a hat. And note that among hats, some are smooth, some shaggy, others velvety, others taffeta, others satin. The best of all is the hairy kind, for it gives a very good abstersion of the fecal matter.

"Then I wiped myself with a hen, with a rooster, with a chicken, with a calf's skin, with a pigeon, with a cormorant, with a lawyer's pouch, with a riding hood, with a coif, with a lure.

"But, to conclude, I say and maintain that there is no ass-wipe like a good downy gosling, provided you hold his head between your legs. And believe me on this, on my honor. For you feel in your asshole a mirific pleasure both from the softness of the said down and from the temperate warmth of the gosling, which is easily communicated to the bum-gut and other intestines, until it reaches the region of the heart and brain. And don't think that the beatitude of the heroes and demigods, who are around the Elysian Fields, lies in their asphodel or nectar, as these old women say. It lies, in my opinion, in that they wipe their asses with a gosling, and such is the opinion of Master John of Scotland."

CHAPTER 14

How Gargantua was instructed
by a sophist in Latin letters.

Having heard these remarks, that good fellow Grandgousier was transported with wonder, considering the lofty sense and marvelous understanding of his son Gargantua. And he said to his nurses:

"Philip, king of Macedon, recognized the good sense of his son Alexander from his adroitly managing a horse; for the said horse was so terrible and unruly that no one dared get on him, because he threw all his riders hard, breaking the neck of one, another's legs, another's brains, another's jaws. Considering which, in the hippodrome (which was the place where they walked the horses and did tricks on them), he noted that the horse's frenzy came only from the fright he took at his shadow. So climbing up on him, he had him run heading into the sun, so that the shadow fell behind, and by that means he made the horse gentle to his will. At which the father recognized the divine understanding there was in him, and had him very well tutored by Aristotle, who at the time was above all philosophers of Greece.

"But I tell you that in this sole talk I've had before you with my son Gargantua I recognize that his understanding partakes of some divinity, so keen, so subtle, profound, and serene do I find him; and he will attain the supreme summit of wisdom, if he is well taught. So I want to turn him over to some learned man to indoctrinate him according to his capacity, and I want to spare no effort or expense."

As a result, they assigned him to a great sophist named Master Thubal Holofernes, who taught him his alphabet so well that he could say it by heart backward; and he was at it five years and three months. Then he read him the *Donatus, Facetus, Theodolet,* and Alanus *in Parabolis,* and he was at it thirteen years six months and two weeks.

But note that meanwhile he was teaching him to write Gothic style,[1] and he wrote all his books, for the art of printing was not yet in use.

And he ordinarily carried around a great writing desk weighing more than seven thousand hundredweights, of which the pen case was as big and stout as the great pillars of Ainay,[2] and the inkwell hung from it on great iron chains that would bear a ton of merchandise.

Then he read him *De modis significandi,*[3] with the commentaries of Windbucker [Heurtebize], Rascal [Fasquin], Too-many-of-'em [Tropditeulx], Galahad, John-calf [Jean le Veau], No 'count [Billonio], Vaginatus [Brelinguandus],[4] and a pile of others; and he was at it over eighteen years and eleven months. And he knew it so well that on a test he could give it by heart, and he proved to his mother on his fingers that "De modis significandi non erat scientia [there was no science of the modes of signifying]." Then he read him the *Compostum,* on which he was fully sixteen years and two months, when his said tutor died; and it was in the year one thousand four hundred and twenty, from the pox that hit him.[5]

Afterward, he had another old wheezer named Jobelin Bridé, who read him Hugutio, Eberard's *Grecismus,* the *Doctrinal,* the *Parts of speech,* the *Quid est,* the *Supplementum,* Marmotretus, *De moribus in mensa servandis* [*On the etiquette for the dinner table*], Seneca, *De quatuor virtutibus cardinalibus* [*On the four cardinal virtues*], *Passavantus cum commento* [*Passavent with commentary*], and *Dormi secure* [*Sleep right*] for the feasts, and a few others of the same kidney. By reading which he became as wise as any man we ever baked.[6]

CHAPTER 15

How Gargantua was put under other teachers.

F ROM all this his father perceived that he was really studying very well and putting all his time into it; nevertheless, he was getting nothing out of it, and, what was worse, he was getting crazy, stupid, all dreamy and idiotic.

On complaining of this to Don Philip Des Marais, viceroy of Papeligosse,[1] he gathered that it would be better for him to learn nothing than such books under such teachers, for their learning was nothing but stupidity and their wisdom was nothing but trash, bastardizing the good and noble minds and corrupting all flower of youth.

"To prove that this is so," said he, "take one of these young men of the present day, who has studied just two years. In case he doesn't have better judgment, better command of words, better speech than your son, and better bearing and civility in society, consider me forever a bacon trimmer from La Brenne." Which Grandgousier liked very well, and ordered that it be done thus.

In the evening, at supper, the said Des Marais brought in a young page of his from Villegongys named Eudémon, so well combed, well dressed, well brushed, that he looked much more like a little cherub than a man. Then he said to Grandgousier: "Do you see this young lad? He's not yet twelve; let's see, if you think fit, what a difference there is between the learning of your daydreaming theologians[2] of the old days and the young folk of today."

Grandgousier was pleased with the test, and he ordered the young page to speak his piece. Then Eudémon, asking permission to do so of the said viceroy, his master, cap in hand, open face, red mouth, eyes steadfast, and his gaze fixed on Gargantua with youthful modesty, got to his feet and began to praise him and exalt him, first for his virtues and good behavior, secondly for his learning, thirdly for his nobility, fourthly for his bodily beauty, and, for the fifth part, gently exhorted him to revere his father in every observance, who was going to such lengths to have him well educated; finally he asked him to be willing to take him on as the least of his servants, for he asked for the present no other gift of the heavens than to be granted the favor of pleasing him by some agreable service. He set forth all this with such appropriate gestures, such distinct pronunciation, such an eloquent voice, and a speech so richly ornate and truly Latin, that he seemed more like a Gracchus, a Cicero, or an Emilius of bygone days than a youngster of this century.

On the contrary, Gargantua's whole reaction was that he started crying like a cow and hid his face in his bonnet, and it was not possible to draw a word out of him any more than a fart from a dead donkey. At which his father was so wrathful that he wanted and tried to kill Master Jobelin. But the said Des Marais kept him from it by a fine remonstrance he made him, so that his ire was moderated. Then he ordered him [Jobelin] to be paid his wages and to be set to tippling very sophistically; and that, that done, he be sent to all the devils.

"At least," he kept saying, "for this day he'll be hardly any expense to his host, if by chance he should die drunk as an Englishman."

With Master Jobelin gone out of the house, Grandgousier consulted with the said viceroy on what preceptor they might give him, and it was agreed between them that to that position should be appointed Ponocrates, preceptor to Eudémon, and that they should all three go to Paris together, to see what were the studies of young men in France at that time.

CHAPTER 16

How Gargantua was sent to Paris,
and of the enormous mare that bore him,
and how she killed the ox-flies of Beauce.

IN that same season, Fayolles,[1] fourth king of Numidia, sent from the land of Africa to Grandgousier a mare, the greatest and most enormous that was ever seen (you know well that Africa always brings something new), for she was as big as six elephants, and had feet divided into toes like Julius Caesar's horse, and hanging ears just like Languedoc nannygoats, and a little horn in her ass. For the rest, her coat was a burnt sorrel spotted with dapple-gray. But above all she had a horrible tail, for it was, give or take a little, as stout as the pillar of Saint Mars near Langeais,[2] and just as square, with locks no more nor less interwoven than ears of wheat. If you wonder at this, wonder even more at the tails of the Scythian rams, which weighed more than thirty pounds, and the Syrian sheep, to whose tail (if Thenaud is telling the truth) they have to attach a cart to carry it, it's so heavy. You don't have that kind, you flatland lechers.

And it was brought by sea, in three carracks and a brigantine, as far as the port of Olonne in the Talmont country. When Grandgousier saw it: "Here," said he, "is just what I need to take my son to Paris. Now then, all will go well. He will be a great cleric in the time to come. Were it not for my lords the beasts, we would all live like clerics."[3]

The next day, after drinking (you understand), Gargantua hit the road with his tutor Ponocrates, and with them Eudémon, the young page. And because it was fair weather and quite temperate, his father had tawny boots made for him; Babin calls them buskins.

Thus they went joyously on their long road, and always had a good time, until above Orléans. In the said area was a huge forest about thirty-five leagues long and seventeen or thereabouts wide [et de largeur dix et sept, ou environ]. It was so horribly fertile and abounding in ox-flies and hornets that it was a real den of brigands for the poor mares, donkeys, and horses. But Gargantua's mare honorably avenged all the outrages perpetrated against the animals of its kind, by a trick the insects did not in the least suspect. For as soon as they had entered the said forest and the hornets had gone on the attack, she unsheathed her tail, and, skirmishing, shoo-flied them so well that in so doing she knocked down the whole wood. Striking out in all directions, right and wrong, hither and yon, here and there, above, below, she knocked down woods as a reaper does grass, so that since then there have been neither woods nor hornets, but the whole region was reduced to open country.

Seeing which, Gargantua took great pleasure without otherwise boasting of it, and said to his men: "I think this is beautiful [Je trouve beau ce]," wherefore this region has since been called La Beauce. But their whole lunch was just yawning; in memory of which today the gentlemen from Beauce lunch by yawning,[4] and are very well off for it, and spit only the better for it.

Finally they arrived in Paris, in which place he refreshed himself for two or three days, living it up with his men, and inquiring what learned men were then in town and what kind of wine they were drinking.

CHAPTER 17

*How Gargantua paid his welcome to the Parisians
and how he took the great bells of
Notre Dame Church.*

A few days after they had refreshed themselves, he looked over the town and was seen by everybody in great astonishment, for the populace of Paris is so stupid, so silly, and so inept by nature that a juggler, an indulgence peddler, a mule with its cymbals, a fiddler in the middle of a crossroads, will draw more people than would a good Evangelical preacher.

And they followed him so annoyingly that he was constrained to take a rest upon the towers of Notre Dame. Being in that place and seeing so many people around him, he said clearly: "I think these louts want me to pay my welcome and my *proficiat*.[1] That makes sense. I'm going to give them their wine, but it will be only *par rys* [for a laugh; homonym of Paris].

Then, with a smile, he undid his fine codpiece and, brandishing his tool in the air, he bepissed them so ferociously that he thereby drowned two hundred and sixty thousand four hundred and eighteen of them, not counting the women and little children. A certain number avoided this piss-flood by speed of foot, and, when they were at the topmost point of the University, sweating, coughing, spitting, and out of breath, they began to curse and swear, some in anger, others *par rys*: "Carimary, carimara! Holy Ladylove,[2] we are bathed *par rys!*" Wherefore since then the city has been called Paris, which theretofore was called "Leucecia," as Strabo says, Book Four, that is to say in Greek "Whitey," for the white thighs of the ladies of the said place. And because at this new imposition of the name everyone present swore by all the saints of his parish, the Parisians, who are made up of all peoples and all types, are by nature both good swearers and good jurists and just a bit arrogant; therefore Joaninus de Barranco, in his book *De copiositate reverentiarum* [*On the abundance of scrapes and bows*], judges that they are called "Parrhésiens" in Greek, that is to say proud in their manner of speaking.

That done, he considered the great bells that were in the said towers and made them ring most harmoniously. As he did, the thought came to him that they would make a very fine jingles for the neck of his mare, which he wanted to send back to his father loaded with Brie cheeses and fresh herring. In fact, he took them to his lodging. Meanwhile, there came by a master mendicant of the Order of Saint Anthony, questing for hog meat, who, to make himself heard from far off and make the bacon tremble in the larder, tried to carry these off furtively, but honorably left them, not because they were too hot, but because they were somewhat too heavy to carry. He was not the one from Bourg, for he's too good a friend of mine.

The whole town was stirred to an uproar, as you know they are so prone to be that foreign nations are amazed at the patience of the kings of France, who do not check them otherwise than by good justice, considering the disadvantages that come out of it from day to day. Would God I knew the workshop in which these schisms and plots are fabricated, so as to place them in evidence for the brotherhood of my parish!

Believe me the place where the people assembled, all befooled and upset, was Nesle,[3] where then was, now no longer is, the oracle of Leucecia. There the case was set forth and the mishap of the bells announced. After thorough ergoing pro and contra, it was concluded in Baralipton that they would send the oldest and ablest member of the Faculty [of Theology] to remonstrate to him the horrible inconvenience of the loss of these bells; and, notwithstanding the remonstrances of some members of the University that this task befitted an orator better than a sophist, for this assignment was chosen our Master Janotus de Bragmardo.

CHAPTER 18

How Janotus de Bragmardo was sent
to recover the great bells from Gargantua.

M ASTER Janotus, hair cropped Caesarine fashion,[1] wrapped in his old-style liripipion [Sorbonne doctoral hood] and his stomach well fortified with quince pastries and holy water from the cellar,[2] betook himself to Gargantua's lodging, driving in front of him three red muzzled beadles, and dragging after him five or six Masters Inerts,[3] well befouled inside and out.

At their entry Ponocrates met them and was inwardly fearful at seeing them so strangely accoutered and supposed they were some sort of mummers out of their wits. Then he inquired of one of the said masters inerts of the band what was the purpose of this mummery. The answer was that they were asking to have the bells returned to them.

As soon as he heard this statement, Ponocrates ran to tell Gargantua the news, so that he should be ready with his response and deliberate on the spot on what was to be done. Gargantua, advised of the case, called aside Ponocrates his tutor, Philotomie his steward, Gymnaste his squire, and Eudémon, and conferred briefly with them on both what was to be done and to be said in reply. All agreed that they should be taken to the buttery and there made to drink like fish, and, so that this wheezer should not get vainglorious over his returning the bells at his request, while he was toping they should summon the city provost, the rector of the Faculty, the vicar of the church, to whom, before the sophist had stated his commission, they would deliver the bells. After that, with these people present, they would hear his fine harangue, which was done. And when the aforementioned had arrived, the sophist was brought into the main hall and began as follows, coughing:

CHAPTER 19

The harangue of Master Janotus de Bragmardo
to Gargantua to recover the bells.

"Ahem, ahem, ahem! *Mna dies,*[1] Sir, *et vobis,* Gentlemen [Good day... and to you]. It would only be fair that you should return our bells to us, for we need them badly. Ahem, ahem, harrumph! We had once turned down good money for them from the people of London in Cahors, so had we from those of Bordeaux in Brie,[2] who wanted to buy them for the substantific quality of the elementary disposition that is enthronificated, in the terresterity of their quidditative nature to extraneize the hot blasting mists and the whirlwinds from over our vines—not really ours, but close by here, for if we lose the *piot,* we lose everything, both sense and law.

"If you return them to us at my request, I'll get out of it six strings of sausages and a good pair of hose that will do my legs much good, unless they don't keep their promise. Ho! By God, *Domine* [Lord], a pair of hose is good, 'et vir sapiens non abhorrebit eam [and a man of sense will not be averse to it].' Ha ha! Not everyone who wants a pair of hose gets one, well I know that as regards myself! Think of it, *Domine:* I've been matagrobolizing this fine harangue for eighteen days: 'Reddite que sunt Cesaris Cesari, et que sunt Dei Deo' [Render unto Caesar the things that are Caesar's, and unto God the things that are God's, Luke 20.25]. There lies the hare [i.e., the gist of the problem].

"By my faith, *Domine,* if you want to sup in my rooms, 'Odsbody! 'charitatis nos faciemus bonum cherubin' [barbaric Latin for "nous ferons bonne chère (ubin)," which means "we'll have ourselves a time!"] 'Ego occidi unum porcum, et ego habet bon vino' [Again butchered Latin: "I've killed a hog, and I have good wine"]. But of good wine you can't make bad Latin. Come now, 'de parte Dei, date nobis clochas nostras [For the Lord's sake, give us our bells].' Look, on behalf of the Faculty I am giving you a *Sermones de Utino*[3] so that, *utinam,* you will give us our bells. 'Vultis etiam pardonos? Per Diem, vos habebitis et nihil poyabitis' [*Per Diem,* for *Per Deum,* "By God, you shall have pardons and not pay a cent"]. O, Sir, *Domine, clochidonnaminor nobis!* My word, *est bonum urbis* [for: *est bona urbs,* "it's a good city"]. Everybody uses them. If your mare enjoys having them, so does our Faculty, 'quae comparata est jumentis insipientibus et similis facta est eis, psalmo nescio quo' [which has been compared to silly mares and has become like them, in I don't know what Psalm]. I had noted it well in my notebook, 'et est unum bonum Achilles' [and it's a good Achilles, i.e., a clincher]. Ahem, ahem, harrumph!

"There now! I'm proving to you that you must give them to me. *Ego sic argumentor* [I adduce proof of this thus]:

" 'Omnis clocha clochabilis, in clocherio clochando, clochans clochativo clochare facit clochabiliter clochantes. Parisius habet clochas. Ergo gluc.'[4]

"Ha ha, ha ha, now that's talking! It's in *tertio prime,* in *Darii*[5] or else-where. 'Pon my soul, I've seen the time when I was a devil in argument, but now I don't do anything but prattle any more, and all I need from now on is good wine, good bed, back to the fire, belly to the table, and a plenty deep ladle. Hey, *Domine,* please, 'in nomine Patris et Filii et

Spiritus Sancti, amen,' give us back our bells, and God keep you from harm, and Our Lady of Health,[6] 'qui vivit et regnat per omnia secula seculorum, amen.' Ahem, ahem, hymphymph, harrumph ahem, hmphhmph!

" 'Verum enim vero, quando quidem, dubio procul, edepol, quoniam, ita certe, meus Deus fidus,'[7] a city without bells is like a blind man without a stick, a donkey without a crupper, and a cow without cymbals. Until you've given them back to us, we won't stop shouting after you like a blind man who has lost his stick, braying like a donkey without a crupper, and bellowing like a cow without cymbals.

"Some Latinizer or other, living near the Hôtel Dieu, once said, alleging the authority of one Taponnus—I'm wrong, it was Pontanus, a secular poet—that he wished they were made of feathers and the clapper was a fox's tail, because they engendered the chronic[8] in the tripes of his brain when he was composing his carminiform verses. But clunk, bingety-bang, bangety-bong, smack, thump, whack, he was declared a heretic; we make them as if out of wax. And further deponent saith not. 'Valete et plaudite. Calepinus recensui.' "[9]

CHAPTER 20

*How the sophist took home his cloth
and how he had a suit against the other masters.*

THE sophist had no sooner finished than Ponocrates and Eudémon broke out laughing so heartily that they nearly gave up their souls to God, no more nor less than Crassus, seeing a jackass eating thistles, and Philemon, seeing a donkey eating the figs that had been fixed for his dinner, died by dint of laughing. Together with them Master Janotus began to laugh, all three competing, so that tears came to their eyes through the violent concussion of the substance of the brain, at which were squeezed out these lachrymal humidities and made to flow through next to the optic nerves. Wherein by them was Democritus shown to be Heraclitizing and Heraclitus Democritizing.

When this laughter had completely subsided, Gargantua consulted with his men on what was to be done. On that Ponocrates advised that they have that fine orator drink again, and, seeing that he had given them more fun and made them laugh more than *Songecreux* [Daydreamer, a jester] would have done, that they give him the ten strings of sausages mentioned in the jolly harangue, with a pair of hose, three hundred logs of firewood, twenty-five hogsheads of wine, a bed with a triple layer of goose down, and a very capacious deep dish, things which he said were necessary for his old age.

The whole thing was done as they had planned, except that Gargantua, doubting that they would find hose right away suitable for his legs, also doubting in which style they would suit the said orator best—the martingale, which is with a drawbridge at the tail the better to crap, or mariner's style the better to relieve the kidneys, or Swiss style to keep the lower belly warm, or codtail style for fear of heating up the loins—had him delivered seven ells of black cloth, and three of white wool for the lining. The wood was carried by the porters; the Masters of Arts carried the sausages and dishes; Master Janotus insisted on carrying the cloth. One of the said Masters, named Master Jousse Bandouille, remonstrated to him that this was neither honorable nor befitting his position and that he should give it to one of them. "Ha!" said Janotus, "you donkey, you are not concluding *in modo et figura* [in proper form]. That's how much use the *Suppositions*[1] and the *Parva logicalia* are. *Panus pro quo supponit?* [To what, or whom does the cloth relate?]"

"*Confuse* [Confusedly]," said Bandouille, "*et distributive* [and distributively]; to each one his or its share."

"I'm not asking you, you donkey," said Janotus, "*quo modo supponit,* but *pro quo* [not in what way it relates, but to what]; that, you donkey, is *pro tibiis meis* [to my shins]. And therefore I shall carry it *egomet* [myself], *sicut suppositum portat adpositum* [as the substance bears the accident]."

Thus he carried it off furtively, as Pathelin did his cloth. The best part was when the wheezer, triumphantly, right in a plenary session held in the Mathurins, demanded his hose and his sausages; for they were peremptorily denied him, inasmuch as he had got them from Gargantua, according to the information reported on this. He remonstrated to them that that had been a free gift and out of his liberality, by which they were not in the least released from their promises. This notwithstanding, the reply to him was that he should be content with reason, and that he would not get one scrap more.

"Reason!" said Janotus, "we use none of that in here. Miserable traitors, you're good for nothing; the earth does not bear any people wickeder than you, I know full well. By God's spleen! I'll inform the king of the enormous abuses that are fabricated in here by your doing and by your own hands, and may I be a leper if he doesn't have you all burned alive as buggers, traitors, heretics, and seducers, enemies of God and of virtue!"

At these words, they brought complaints against him; he, for his part, had them summoned to appear. In sum, the lawsuit was retained by the court, and there it still is. The masters, for the time, made a vow never to wash again; Master Janot, with his adherents, made a vow not to blow their noses until the matter was settled by a definitive judgment.

By these vows they have remained down to the present both dirt caked and snotty, for the court has not yet closely scrutinized all the papers; the verdict will be handed down at the next Greek Calends, that is to say never, as you know they do more than is natural even against their own articles. For the articles of Paris chant that God alone can do infinite things. Nature makes nothing immortal, for she sets an end and period to all things produced by her; for *omnia orta cadunt* [all that is born dies], etc., but these mist-swallowers make the lawsuits pending before them infinite and immortal. By so doing, they have given rise to and verified the saying of Chilon the Lacedaemonian, consecrated at Delphi, that Misery is companion to Lawsuit and people pleading in them miserable, for sooner do they find an end to their life than to the right they claim.

CHAPTER 21

*Gargantua's mode of study according to
the teaching of his sophist tutors.*

WITH the first days spent thus and the bells put back in their place, the citizens of Paris, in gratitude for this consideration, offered to maintain and feed his mare for as long as he liked (which pleased Gargantua very much) and sent her to live in the forest of Bière [now Fontainebleau]. I think she is no longer there now.

That done, with all his sense he wanted to study at the discretion of Ponocrates; but he, for the start, ordered him to do as he was accustomed to, so he might understand by what means, over such a long time, his former tutors had made him so smug, stupid, and ignorant.

So he arranged his time in such a way that he ordinarily woke up between eight and nine o'clock, whether it was daylight or not;[1] thus had ordained his former tutors, citing what David says: "Vanum est vobis ante lucem surgere" ["It is pointless for you to get up before the light," Psalms 127.2]. Then he waggled his legs as he sat, bounced about and tumbled in the bed for some time the better to brighten up his animal spirits; and he dressed according to the season, but he was fond of wearing a great long robe of heavy frieze furred with foxskins; after that he combed his hair with Almain's comb, that was the four fingers and the thumb, for his tutors said that to comb one's hair, wash, and clean up any other way, was to waste time in this world.

Then he crapped, pissed, threw up, belched, yawned, farted, spat, coughed, sobbed, sneezed, blew his nose like an archdeacon, and ate breakfast to put down the bad air: fine fried tripes, beautiful carbonadoes, fair hams, fine game stews, and many early morning dips as snacks.

Ponocrates remonstrated to him that he should not eat so soon after getting out of bed without first taking some exercise. Gargantua replied:

"What? haven't I had enough exercise? I roled around in bed six or seven times before I got up. Isn't that enough? Pope Alexander did thus on the advice of his Jewish doctor, and he lived until he died in spite of the envious. My first masters got me accustomed to it, saying that breakfast gave one a good memory; therefore they had their first drink then. I find myself very well off for it and dine only the better for it; and Master Thubal (who was first in his year's *licence* in Paris) used to tell me that the whole advantage is not in running very fast but rather in leaving promptly; likewise the health of our humanity lies not in drinking it down in huge drafts like ducks but in drinking in the morning; *unde versus* [whence the verses]:

> Early to rise—a bad idea;
> Early to drink is better cheer."

After eating a hearty breakfast he went to church, and they carried for him a big heavy breviary in a case, weighing, both in grease and in clasps and parchment, give or take a little, eleven hundredweight six pounds. There, he heard twenty-six of thirty masses. Meanwhile the prayer reader came to his place, muffled like a hoopoe, having antidoted his breath very well with a lot of vineyard strup; with him he muttered all those litanies, and thumbed hidden rosaries so carefully that not one beat of them fell to the ground.

On leaving the church, they brought him on an ox-cart a heap of Saint-Claude rosaries, each as big as a hat form; and, walking through the cloisters, galleries, or garden, he said more of them than sixteen hermits.

Then he studied for some paltry half hour, his eyes resting on his book; but (as the comic poet says) his soul was in the kitchen.

So, pissing a full urinal's worth, he sat down to table, and, because he was naturally phlegmatic, he began his meal with a few dozen hams, smoked ox tongues, salt mullets, chitterlings, and other such precursors of wine.

Meanwhile four of his men threw into his mouth, one after the other, continuously, mustard by the pailful. Then he drank a horrific draft of white wine to relieve his kidneys. Afterward, he ate according to the season, food to suit his appetite, and he stopped eating when his belly was dilated.

For drinking he had no end nor rule, for he said that the bounds and limits of drinking were when, as the person drank, the cork in his slippers swelled upward a half a foot.

CHAPTER 22

Gargantua's games.

THEN, most lazily mumbling a snatch of grace, he washed his hands with fresh wine, cleaned his teeth with a pig's foot, and chatted joyfully with his men. Then, when the green cloth was laid out, they brought out plenty of cards, plenty of dice, and enough boards for checkers or chess. There he played:

Flush,	Primiera,
Grand slam,	Robber,
Trump,	Prick and spare not,
One hundred,	The spinet,

Poor Moll,
Pass ten,
Pair and sequence,
Beggar my neighbor,
The turned card,
Lansquenet,
Let him speak that hath it,
Marriage,
Opinion,
Sequences,
Tarots,
Gulls,
Snorer,
Honors,
Chess,
The men's morris,
Raffles,
Three dice,
Nick nock,
Queen's game,
Backgammon,
Fell down,
Needs must,
Mop and mow,
Shuffleboard,
Hopscotch,
Heads or tails,
Spillikins,
Hunt the slipper,
Coddling the hare,
Trudge-pig,
The horn,
The madge-owlet,
Pinpricks,

The fib,
Trente et un,
Three hundred,
Odd man out,
Take miss,
Cuckow,
Teetotum,
I have it,
Who does one thing does the other,
Cockall,
Losing Lodam,
Torture,
Gleek,
Morra,
Fox and geese,
Black and white,
Mumchance,
Tables,
Lurch,
Sbaraglino,
All tables,
Copsbody,
Draughts,
Primus, secundus,
Keys,
Odds or evens,
Huckle-bones,
Lawn billiards,
The moping owl,
Tug of war,
Magpies,
The Shrovetide ox,
Hinch pinch and laugh not,
Unshoeing the ass,

Sheep to market,
I sit down,
Buskins,
Chucker-out,
Hamstool,
Marseilles figs,
Bowman shot,
Tobogganing,
Selling oats,
Hide and seek,
Irons out of the fire,
Nine-stones,
The finding of the saint,
Pear tree,
The Breton jig,
The sow,
Cubes,
Quoits,
Fouquet,
The return course,
The dart,
Chaw-turd,
Short bowls,
Dogs' ears,
My desire,
Rush bundles,
Hodman blind,
Sweepstakes,
The pursuit,
In a row,
The humming-top,
The peg-top,
Scarred face,
Fast and loose,

Giddap, Neddy,
Gold-beard,
Draw the spit,
Gossip, lend me your sack,
Thrust out,
The fly,
Flay the fox,
Hold the pass,
Blow the coal,
Quick and dead judge,
The false clown,
The hunchback courtier,
Hinch-pinch,
Bumbasting,
Barlibreak,
Belly to belly,
Pushpin,
The ball is mine,
Nine-pins,
Flat bowl,
Pick-a-back to Rome,
Sly Jack,
Shuttlecock,
Smash crock,
Whirlygig,
Short staff,
Spur away,
The ferret,
Cob-nut,
The cherry pit,
The whip-top,
The hobgoblin,
Pushball,
Fatass,

The cock-horse,

The brown beetle,

Fair and gay goes Lent away,

Leap-frog,

Fart-in-throat,

The swing,

The small bowl,

Tic-tac-toe, my first go,

Nine hands,

The fallen bridges,

Bull's-eye,

Blindman's bluff,

Spy,

Cricket,

Cup and ball,

The trades,

Dot and go one,

Fillips,

The bolting cloth,

The greedy glutton,

Defendo,

Bascule,

The madge-owlet,[1]

The dead beast,

The dead pig,

The pigeon has flown,

Fagots,

Crossing,

Coin in the tail-pocket,

Hark forward,

Gunshot crack,

Out of school,

The feathered dart,

The bull's eye

Saint Cosma, I come to worship you,

I catch you napping,

The forked oak,

The Wolf's tail,

Billy boy, give me my lance,

The shock of wheat,

Baste the Bear,

Cross questions and crooked answers,

Harry-racket,

Bridled Nick,

Battledore and shuttlecock,

Bob-cherry,

Frogs and toads,

Pestle and mortar,

The queens,

Heads and points,

Wicked death,

Lady, I wash your cap,

Sowing oats,

Windmills,

Pirouetting,

Hind the plowman,

Butting rams,

Climb the ladder,

The salt rump,

Twos and threes,

Jump in the bush,

Hide and seek,

The buzzard's nest,

The fig,

Mustard-pounder,

The relapse,

Duck your head,

Crane-dance,

53

| Slash and cut, | Flirts on the nose, |
| Larks, | Flicks. |

After playing well, sifted, passed, and bolted the time, it was time to have a little drink—that was eleven gallons [peguadz] per man—and, right after banqueting, to stretch out and sleep two or three hours on a nice bench or a nice big bed, meanwhile to think no evil and speak no evil.

Ponocrates would point out to him that it was a bad regimen to drink that way after sleeping.

"That," Gargantua replied, "is the real life of the [holy] Fathers, for by nature I drink salty, and sleeping was worth that much ham."

Then he would start to study a bit, and Paternosters forward march! The better to expedite, and more by the book, he would climb on an old mule that had served nine kings. So, mouth mumbling and head nodding, he would go and see some rabbit caught in the nets.

Once back, he hied himself into the kitchen to see what roast was on the spit.

And he had a very good supper, on my conscience! and liked to invite a few neighborhood topers with whom, drinking their fill, they would tell tales old and new. Among others he had as domestics Lords du Fou, de Gourville, de Grignault, and de Marigny.

After supper there came into place the nice wooden Gospels, that is to say plenty of gameboards, or nice cards for flush. One-two-three, or "I'll take my chances" to make it short, or else went to see the wenches thereabout; then little banquets amid collations and after-collations, then he would sleep without a break until eight o'clock the next morning.

CHAPTER 23

How Gargantua was taught
by Ponocrates in such a regimen
that he did not waste an hour of the day.

WHEN Ponocrates learned of Gargantua's loose mode of life, he decided to teach him letters in a different way, but he put up with it for the first few days, knowing that nature does not endure sudden mutations without great violence.

So in order to begin his task better, he requested a learned doctor of that time named Master Theodore, to consider whether it was possible to put Gargantua back on a better track; and he purged him canonically with hellebore of Anticyra, and by that medicament scoured out all the alteration and perverse habit of his brain. By that means also Ponocrates had him forget everything he had learned under his former tutors, as Timotheus used to do with his pupils who had been taught under other musicians.

The better to do this, he introduced him into the companies of learned men who were there, in emulation of whom there grew in him the spirit and the desire to study in a very different way and make something of himself.

Afterward, he put him in such a regimen of study that he didn't waste any hour whatever of the day but used all his time in letters and honorable learning.

So Gargantua woke up about four o'clock in the morning. While they were rubbing him down,[1] there was read to him loud and clear some page of the Holy Scripture, with a delivery appropriate to the matter, and assigned to that was a young page, a native of Basché, named Anagnostes. According to the gist and argument of this lesson, he often gave himself up to revering, adoring, praying, and beseeching the good God, whose majesty and marvelous judgments the reading demonstrated.

Then he went to the private places to make an excretion of natural digestions. There his preceptor repeated what had been read, expounding to him the most obscure and difficult points.

As they were returning, they considered the state of the sky: whether it was such as they had noted it to be the evening before, and into what signs[2] was entering the sun, also the moon, for that day.

This done, he was dressed, combed, tidied up, accoutered and perfumed, during which time they repeated to him the lessons of the day before. He himself would say them by heart and found on them a few practical cases concerning the human estate, which they sometimes extended up to two or three hours, but ordinarily they stopped when he was fully dressed.

Then for three full hours he was read to.

That done, they went out, still discussing the subjects of the reading, and disported themselves in the Bracque, or the fields, and played ball, or tennis, or the triangular ball game, gallantly exercising their bodies as they had their souls.

Their entire play was solely in liberty, for they left off the game when they pleased, and ordinarily stopped when their bodies were sweating or they were in any other way tired. So when they were well dried and rubbed down, they changed their shirts, and, strolling gently, went to see whether the dinner was ready. Waiting there, they clearly and eloquently recited a few sayings from the lesson.

Meanwhile, Sir Appetite came, and at an opportune moment they sat down to table. At the beginning of the meal was read some amusing story of ancient exploits, until he had taken his wine.

Then (if it seemed good) they continued the reading or began to converse joyously together, speaking, for the first months, of the virtues, properties, effectiveness, and nature of everything they were served at table: of bread, water, salt, the meats, fish, fruits, herbs, roots, and the preparation thereof. Doing which he learned in a short time the passage pertinent to this in Pliny, Athenaeus, Dioscorides, Julius Pollux, Galen, Porphyry, Oppian, Polybius, Heliodorus, Aristotle, Aelian, and others.

These discussions held, often, to be more assured about them, they had the aforesaid books brought to table. And he retained in his memory so well and entirely the things said, that for that time there was no doctor who knew half as much about it as he did.

Afterward, they talked about the lessons read in the morning, and, completing their meal with some quince confection, he picked his teeth with a pick from a mastic tree, he washed his hands and eyes with fine fresh water, and they gave thanks to God with some nice canticles composed in praise of the divine munificence and benignity. That done, they brought cards, not to play, but to learn a thousand nice little tricks and novel inventions, which came out of arithmetic.

In that way he came to be very fond of this numerical knowledge, and every day, after dinner and supper, he spent time on it as entertainingly as he used to do on dice or cards. So much so that he learned of it both theory and practice, so well that Tunstal, the Englishman, who had written amply on it, confessed that really, in comparison with him, he understood nothing but High German.

And not only of this one, but also of all the other mathematical sciences, such as geometry, astronomy, and music;[3] or, while awaiting the natural concoction and digestion of his meal, they formed a thousand joyous geometric instruments and figures, and likewise they practiced the laws of astronomy. Afterward, they delighted themselves in singing musically in four or five parts, or on a set theme, to their throats' content. As regards musical instruments, he learned to play the lute, the spinet, the harp, the German flute and the one with nine holes, the viola, the sackbut.

This hour thus employed and digestion completed, he purged himself of natural excrements, then set himself to his principal study for three hours or more, both in the morning's reading and in pursuing the book undertaken, and also in drawing and forming well the ancient Roman letters.[4]

This done, they went out of their house, and with them a young gentleman from Touraine named Squire Gymnaste, who was showing him the arts of chivalry.

So, changing his clothes, he climbed on a courser, a cob, a gennet, an Arabian, a light horse, and he gave him a hundred laps, having him leap in the air, jump the ditch and the fence, turn short in a circle, both to the right and to the left.

There he did not break a lance—for it's the silliest thing to say: "I broke ten lances in a tourney or in a battle": a carpenter would do it as well—but it is praiseworthy glory with one lance to have broken ten of one's enemies. So with his steel-tipped lance, sturdy and stiff, he would break open a door, pierce a harness, uproot a tree, spit a ring, carry off an armed saddle, a halberd, a gauntlet. All this he did armed from tip to toe. As regards riding his horse to keep time with the trumpets, and making little clicking sounds to urge on his horse, no one could do them better than he. The horse jumper from Ferrara was just a monkey by comparison. He was singularly expert in jumping rapidly from one horse to another without touching the ground—and these horses were called *desultory* [Latin for "to jump from"; cf., French *destriers*]—and in mounting from either side, lance in fist, without stirrups, guiding his horse at will without a bridle, for such things are useful for military training.

Another day he would practice with the battle-ax, which he wielded so well, so vigorously recovered it from every thrust, so adroitly lowered it to strike out in a circle, that he was passed as a knight-at-arms in the field and in all trials. Then he brandished the pike, swung the two-handed sword, the hack sword, the Spanish rapier, the dagger, and the poniard, both armed and unarmed, with a buckler, with a cape, with a tiny round buckler. He hunted the stag, the roebuck, the bear, the fallow deer, the wild boar, the hare, the partridge, the pheasant, the bustard. He played with the big ball, and, with both foot and fist, sent it flying through the air. He wrestled, he ran, he jumped—not with a hop, not with the German leap; for, said Gymnaste, such jumps are useless and no good in war—but with one jump broke a window at the height of a lance.

He swam in deep water, right side up, on his back, sidestroke, using his whole body, just his feet, one hand in the air, and holding a book in it crossed the whole river Seine without wetting it, as Julius Caesar used to do. Then with one hand by main force he got into the boat; then threw himself back into the water, head first, sounding the depth, explored the hollows of the rocks, dived into the abysses and the gulfs. Then he turned the boat about, stirred it, took it swiftly, slowly, with the current, against it, held it fast in the sluice, guided it with one hand, with the other, laid about him with a great oar, hoisted the sail, climbed up the mast by the shrouds, ran along the rigging, adjusted the compass, took down the bowlines, handled the rudder.

Emerging from the water, he vigorously climbed up the mountainside and came down as readily; went up the trees like a cat, jumped from one to the other like a squirrel, and took down great branches like another Milo. With two well-steeled poniards and teated bodkins he climbed to the top of a house like a rat, and came down from top to bottom with such adroitness of limb that he was not in the least hurt by the fall.

He threw the dart, put the stone,[5] threw the javelin, the boar-spear, the halberd, drew the bow full out, bent over his chest the powerful siege crossbows, took aim with the harquebus by eye, set up the cannon, shot at the mark, at the popinjay, uphill, downhill, straight ahead, to one side, and to the rear like the Parthians.

They fastened a cable for him around some lofty tower, with one end on the ground; by this with both hands he climbed it, then came down so fast and surely that you could do no better on a level plain.

They suspended a great pole for him between two trees; he hung from this by his hands, and moved back and forth on it so fast without his feet touching, that you could not catch him, even running at full speed.

And to exercise his chest and lungs, he shouted like all the devils. I once heard him calling Eudémon all the way from the Saint-Victor Gate to Montmartre. Stentor at the battle of Troy never had such a voice. And to toughen his muscles, they had made him two great lead weights, each weighing eight thousand seven hundredweights, which he called *altères* [dumbbells]; and he picked these up off the ground in each hand, lifted them in the air over his head and held them thus, without budging, for three quarters of an hour or more, which took inimitable strength.

He played at barriers with the strongest, and when the tussle came, he kept his feet so sturdily that he would let the most venturesome see if they could budge him from his place, all this as Milo used to do, in imitation of whom he would also hold a pomegranate in his hand and give it to anyone who could take it away from him.

Having thus spent his time, and been rubbed down, cleaned up, and refreshed with a change of clothing, he went back at a gentle pace, and, as they passed by certain fields or other grassy places, they inspected the trees and plants, comparing them with the books of the ancients who had written about them, such as Theophrastus, Dioscorides, Marinus, Pliny, Nicander, Macer, and Galen; and they brought back whole handfuls to their lodgings, which were put in the care of a young page named Rhizotome, together with some little mattocks, pickaxes, grubbing forks, spades, pruning knives, and other instruments needed for good botanizing.

When they had arrived at the house, while supper was being prepared, they repeated certain passages of what had been read, and sat down at table.

Note here that the supper was copius and ample, for he took as much as he needed to sustain and nourish himself, which is the true diet prescribed by the art of good and sure medicine, although a pile of imbecile doctors, harassed in the workshop of the sophists, advise the contrary.

During this meal was continued the reading from dinner as long as seemed good; the rest was taken up with good conversation, all lettered and profitable.

After saying grace, they set themselves to singing musically, playing harmonious instruments, or those little tricks they do with cards, dice, or goblets, and stayed there, having a wonderful time and sometimes disporting until time for sleep; sometimes they would go and join in the companies of lettered folk, or of people who had seen foreign countries.

In full nighttime, before retiring, they would go into the most open space in their house to see the countenance of the sky, and they noted the comets, if there were any, and the figures, positions, oppositions, and conjunctions of the stars. Then with his tutor he briefly recapitulated, in the manner of the Pythagoreans, all he had read, seen, learned, done, and understood, in the course of the entire day.

So they prayed to God the Creator, worshiping Him and reaffirming their faith in Him, glorifying Him for His immense goodness, and giving Him thanks for all the time past, they commended themselves to His divine clemency for the whole future.

That done, they entered upon their rest.

CHAPTER 24

How Gargantua used his time
when the air was rainy.

If it happened that the air was rainy and intemperate, the entire time before dinner was spent as usual, except that he had a fine bright fire lit to correct the intemperateness of the air. But after dinner, instead of the exercises, they stayed in the house and, as a kind of recreation, played at baling hay, splitting and sawing wood, and threshing sheaves of wheat in the barn; then they studied the art of painting and sculpture, or called into use the ancient practice of the game of tables, as Leonicus has written about it and as our good friend Lascaris plays it. As they played, they rehearsed the passages of the ancient authors in which is taken or mentioned some metaphor on the said game.

Likewise, they either went to see how metals were drawn or how artillery was cast; or they went to watch the lapidaries, goldsmiths, and cutters of precious stones; or the alchemists and coin minters, or the makers of great tapestries, the weavers, the velvet makers, watchmakers, mirror makers, printers, organists, dyers, and other such kinds of workmen; and, always treating to wine, they learned and observed the skill and inventiveness of the trades.

They went to hear public readings, solemn acts, rehearsals, declamations, the pleading of the nice lawyers, the sermons of the Evangelical preachers.

He passed through the halls and places assigned for fencing, and there, against the masters, tried his hand with all weapons, and taught them by evidence that he knew as much about it as they, if not more.

Instead of botanizing, they visited the shops of the druggists, herb sellers, and apothecaries, and considered attentively the fruits, roots, leaves, gums, seeds, exotic unguents, also at the same time how they were adulterated.

He went to watch the jugglers, conjurers, and sellers of quack medicines, considered their moves, their tricks, their somersaults and spiels, especially those of Chauny[1] in Picardy, for by nature they are great prattlers and fine jokers in the matter of green monkeys.[2]

When they had returned after supper, they ate more soberly than on other days and foods more desiccative and attenuating, so that the intemperate humidity of the air, communicated to the body by necessary proximity, might by this means be corrected, and should not be harmful to them because they had not exercised as was their custom.

Thus was Gargantua governed, and he continued this procedure from day to day, profiting as you understand a young man may who has good sense, according to his age, in such practice thus continued, which, although at the beginning it seemed difficult, in its continuation was so sweet, mild, and delightful, that it was more like a king's pastime than a schoolboy's study.

However, Ponocrates, to give him a respite from this vehement contention of spirits, once a month selected a bright serene day, on which they moved out from town in the morning either to Gentilly, or Boulogne, or Montrouge, or the Charanton Bridge, or Vanves, or Saint-Cloud. And there they spent the whole day having the most fun they could think of, mocking, jesting, drinking their fill, playing, singing, dancing, rolling about in some lovely meadow, robbing sparrows' nests, catching quail, fishing for frogs or crayfish.

But even though the day was spent without books and readings, spent without profit it was not, for in the lovely meadow they recited some beautiful verses of Virgil's *Agriculture* [*Georgics*], of Hesiod, of Politian's *Rusticus,* quoted a few pleasing epigrams in Latin, then turned them into rondeaus and ballades in French.

As they feasted, they separated the water from diluted wine, as Cato teaches, in *De re rust* [*On agriculture*, chap. 111], and Pliny, with a goblet made of ivy; washed the wine in a basin full of water, then drew it off with a tube; ran the water from one glass into another; and built several little automatic machines, that is to say which moved by themselves.

CHAPTER 25

How there was aroused
between the fouaciers *of Lerné*
and the men of Gargantua's country
a great dispute
from which were built up great wars.

At that time, which was the vintage season, and the beginning of the autumn, the shepherds of the region were busy guarding the vines and keeping the starlings from eating the grapes.

At which time the *fouaciers* of Lerné were passing by the great highway, taking ten or twelve loads of *fouaces* to town.

The shepherds asked them courteously to let them have some for their money, at the market price. For note that grapes with fresh *fouace* are a heavenly food to eat for breakfast, especially the pinaux grapes, fig grapes, muscadines, verjuice grapes, the looseners for those who are constipated in the belly, for they make them go off the length of a boat spear, and often, thinking to fart, they beshit themselves, wherefore these are known as vintage tricksters.

Not in the least inclined to grant their request were the *fouaciers,* but what is worse, they badly insulted them, calling them[1] expendable, snaggle-teeth, carrot-top clowns, roisterers, shit-in-beds, drunks, sly knaves, ne'er-do-wells, guzzlers, potbellies, swaggerers, good-for-nothings, ruffians, paltry customers, sycophant varlets, slovenly louts, strutting coxcombs, jeering joltheads, jobbernol goosecaps, coddipol loggerheads, codshead loobies, ninnyhammer flycatchers, boobs, wiseacres, swellheads, teeth-rattlers, turd-herders, shitten shepherds, and other such defamatory epithets, adding that it was not for them to eat fine *fouaces,* but they should be content with coarse lumpy bread and rye-loaf.

To this outrage one of them named Frogier, personally a very honorable man and a notable young fellow, replied mildly:

"How long ago did you grow horns, that you've got so high-and-mighty? My word, you used to sell it to us, and now you refuse. That's not the way to treat good neighbors, and we don't treat you that way when you come here to buy our fine wheat from which you make your cakes and *fouaces.* Moreover, we would have thrown in some of our grapes into the bargain; but Holy Mother of God,[2] you might well repent of this and some day you'll have to deal with us. Then we'll do the same to you; and keep that in mind!"

Whereupon Marquet, chief standard-bearer of the confraternity of the *fouaciers,* said to him:

"Really, you're mighty cocky this morning; you ate too much millet last evening. Come here, come here, I'll give you some of my *fouace.*"

Then Frogier in all simplicity approached, pulling out of his baldric an eleven-denier piece, thinking that Marquet was going to bring out some of his *fouaces* for him; but he struck him across the legs with his whip so hard that the welts showed. Then he tried to get out of there in flight; but Frogier shouted "Help!" "Murder!" all he could, and also threw at him a stout cudgel that he carried under his arm, and hit him on the coronal [fronto-parietal] suture of the head, over the crototaphic [temporal] artery of the right side, in such a way that Marquet fell off his mare; he seemed more a dead man than alive.

Meanwhile the farmers, who were shelling walnuts nearby, came running up with their big staffs and banged on these *fouaciers* as on green rye. The other shepherds and shepherdesses, hearing Frogier's cry, came on with their slings and cudgels, and pursued them with hard-thrown stones so small that it seemed they were hail. Finally they caught up with them and took about four or five dozen of their *fouaces;* nevertheless, they paid for them at the customary price, and gave them also a hundred walnuts and three basketfuls of white grapes. Then the *fouaciers* helped Marquet, who was terribly wounded, to remount, and they went back to Lerné, without continuing on the road to Parilly, uttering strong and sturdy threats against the ox-herds, shepherds, and farmers of Seuillé and Sinays.

That done, both the shepherds and the shepherdesses made a great feast of these same *fouaces* and fine grapes, and had a hearty laugh together to the sound of the bagpipe, making fun of the high-and-mighty *fouaciers,* who had come to grief for not having crossed themselves with the right hand[3] that morning; and with great chenin[4] grapes they neatly dressed Frogier's legs, so that he soon healed.

CHAPTER 26

How the inhabitants of Lerné,
at the command of Picrochole, their king,
made an unexpected attack on Gargantua's shepherds.

THE *fouaciers,* back in Lerné, before eating or drinking, immediately betook themselves to the capitol [their capitol], and there, before their king, Picrochole, third of that name, set forth their complaint, showing their baskets broken, their caps mussed, their robes torn, their *fouaces* taken, and above all Marquet grievously wounded, saying that it had all been done by the shepherds and farmers of Grandgousier, near the great highway, beyond Seuillé.

He instantly flew into a frenzied rage, and, without asking himself what or how, he had the ban and the arrière-ban proclaimed throughout his country, summoning each and every man, on pain of the halter, to assemble under arms in the great square in front of the château, at the stroke of noon.

The better to support his endeavor, he sent to have the drum beaten around the town. He himself, while his dinner was being prepared, went to get his artillery placed, his ensign and standard unfurled, and to have loaded up plenty of munitions, both of arms and of victuals.

As he dined, he issued his assignments, and by his edict Lord Paltry [Trepelu] was put in charge of the vanguard, in which were numbered sixteen thousand and fourteen harquebusiers, thirty-five thousand and eleven mercenaries.

In charge of the artillery was Grand Master of the Horse Blowhard [Toucquedillon]; in this were numbered nine hundred and fourteen great bronze guns in the form of cannons, basilisks, serpentines, culverins, bombards, falcons, bases,[1] *spiroles,*[2] and other pieces. The rearguard was entrusted to Duke Scrapepenny [Raquedenare]; in the main body stayed the king and the princes of his kingdom.

Thus summarily accoutered, before setting out, they sent three hundred light horses, under the leadership of Captain Windswallower [Engoulevent], to reconnoiter the countryside, but, after searching diligently, they found all the surrounding country in peace and quiet, without any sort of gathering.

Learning this, Picrochole ordered each and every man to march under his own ensign in haste. Thereupon without order or measure they took to the fields one after the other, wasting and pillaging everything wherever they passed, without sparing poor man or rich, or place sacred or profane; they took away oxen, cows, bulls, calves, heifers, ewes, sheep, lambs, nannygoats, rams, hens, capons, chickens, goslings, ganders, geese, pigs, sows, piglets; knocking down walnuts, harvesting vines, carrying off the vinestocks, shaking down all the fruits from the trees. It was an incomparable disorder that they wrought, and they found no one to resist them; but each and every one threw himself at their mercy, beseeching them to be treated more humanely, considering that they had for all time been good and amiable neighbors, and against them they never commited any excess or outrage to be ill-used by them so suddenly, and saying that God would punish them for it shortly. To which remonstrances they made no other answer except that they would teach them to eat *fouace*.

CHAPTER 27

How a monk of Seuillé saved the abbey close
from being sacked by the enemy.

So much did they do and wreck, pillaging and thieving, that they arrived at Seuillé, and despoiled men and women alike, and took what they could; nothing was too hot or too heavy for them. Although the plague was there throughout most of the houses, they went in everywhere, plundered all that was inside, and never did one of them run any danger, which is a pretty marvelous thing; for the curates, vicars, preachers, physicians, surgeons, and apothecaries who went to examine, bind up, cure, preach to, and admonish the sick had all died of the infection, and these pillaging and murderous devils never got ill. How does that come about? Think about it, I beg you.

The town thus pillaged, they betook themselves to the abbey with horrible tumult but found it well locked and closed, wherefore the bulk of the army marched beyond it toward the Ford of Vède, except seven companies of foot and two hundred lances[1] that remained there and broke down the walls of the close so as to ruin the whole vintage.

The monks, poor devils, didn't know which one of their saints to offer their prayers to. At all events, they had *ad capitulum capitulantes* [the call to the chapter] rung. There it was decreed that they would form a beautiful procession with nice preachings, and litanies *contra hostium insidias* [against the snares of the enemy], and fine responces *pro pace* [for peace].

In the abbey at the time there was a claustral monk named Frère Jean des Entommeures [Friar John of the Hashes],[2] young, gallant, frisky, cheerful, very deft, bold, adventurous, resolute, tall, thin, with a wide open throat, well fixed for a nose, a great dispatcher of hours, a great unbridler of masses, a fine polisher-off of vigils, to sum it all up briefly a real monk if ever there was one since the monking world first monked in monkery; for the rest a cleric to the teeth in breviary matter.

This man, hearing the noise the enemies were making around the close of their vineyard, went out to see what they were doing, and, noting that they were harvesting their close, on which was based their drink for the whole year, he returns to the church choir, where the other monks were as stunned as bell-founders,[3] and, seeing them singing *Ini, nim, pe, ne, ne, ne, ne, ne, ne, tum, ne, num, num, ini, i, mi, i, mi, co, o, ne, no, o, o, ne, no, ne, no, no, no, rum, ne, num, num.*[4] "That," said he, "is well shitten sungen![5] Power of God, why don't you sing

> Baskets farewell, vintage is done?

"Devil take me if they aren't inside our close and cutting both vine stocks and grapes so well that, 'Odsbody! it'll be four years with nothing to glean in there. Saint James's belly! what will we poor devils drink meantime? Lord God, *da mihi potum* [give me drink]!"

Then said the claustral prior: "What is this drunkard going to do here? Take him away to prison for me. To disturb so the divine service [*service divin*]!"

"But," said the monk, "the wine service [*service du vin*], let's see to it that it is not disturbed; for you yourself, My Lord Prior, love to drink of the best. So does every good man; never does a noble man hate good wine: that's a monastic precept. But these responses you're singing, by God are not in season."

"Why are our hours short in harvest and vintage times, and long all winter? The late Friar Macé Pelosse, of happy memory, a real zealot (or devil take me) of our religion, told me, I remember, that the reason was so that in that season we should get the wine well pressed and made, and that in winter we should inhale it.

"Listen, gentlemen, you who love wine: 'Odsbody, now follow me! For boldly, may Saint Anthony burn me if those men are to taste the *piot* who didn't rescue the wine! God's belly, the goods of the Church! Ha, no, no, devil take it! Saint Thomas the Englishman was certainly willing to die for them; if I died at it, wouldn't I likewise be a saint? I'll never die at it, however, for I make that happen to the others."

So saying, he took off his great monk's habit and seized a staff of the cross, which was of the heart of the sorb apple tree, as long as a lance, round to fit the fist, and a little decorated with fleurs-de-lis, all almost obliterated. Thus he went forth in a fine cassock, put his frock scarfwise, and with his staff of the cross fell so lustily upon his enemies, who were gathering grapes without order, or ensign, or trumpet, or drum, amid the close—for the standard—and ensign-bearers had put down their standards and ensigns by the walls, the drummers had knocked in their drums on one side to fill them with grapes, the trumpeters were loaded down with bunches of grapes, everyone was in disarray—so he charged down upon them so hard, without a word of warning, that he bowled them over like pigs, striking out right and left, in the old fencing style.

For some, he beat their brains out, for others he broke arms and legs, for others he dislocated the vertebrae of the neck, for others demolished the kidneys, beat down the nose, blackened the eyes, split open the jaws, knocked teeth down their throat, shattered the shoulderblades, mortified the shins, blasted out the thighbones, crushed the forearms.

If anyone tried to hide among the thicker vine stocks, he battered his entire spine and dashed his loins like a dog.

If anyone tried to get away in flight, he made that one's head fly into pieces by rupturing the lambdoidal [occipitoparietal] suture.

If anyone climbed a tree, thinking to be in safety there, with his staff he impaled him by the fundament.

If some old acquaintance of his called out to him: "Ah, Frère Jean, my old friend, I give up!"

"Indeed you certainly must," he would say; "but also you shall give up your soul to all the devils."

And immediately he would blast him. And if anyone was so seized by rashness that he tried to resist him face to face, there he showed the strength of his muscles, for he pierced right through his chest through the interior mediastine and the heart. To others, hitting them under the hollow of the ribs, he wrought havoc on their stomach, and they promptly died. Others he struck so fiercely on the navel that he made their tripes come out. To others, passing between the ballocks, he pierced the bum-gut. Believe me, it was the most horrible sight you ever saw.

Some cried out: "Saint Barbe!"

Others: "Saint George!"

Others: "Sainte Nytouche [Saint Touch-me-not]!"

Others: "Our Lady of Cunault of Loreto! of Good Tidings! of La Lenou! of Rivière!"

Some made vows to Saint James.

Others to the Holy Shroud of Chambéry, but it burned up three months later, so completely that they couldn't save a single shred of it.

Others to Cadouin.

Others to Saint-Jean-d'Angely.

Others to Saint Eutropius of Saintes, to Saint-Mesmes of Chinon, to Saint Martin of Candes, to Saint Clouaud of Sinays, to the relics of Javerzay, and a thousand other little saints.

Some died without speaking, others spoke without dying. Some died speaking, others spoke dying.

Others cried aloud: "Confession! Confession! *Confiteor* [I confess] *Miserere* [Lord have mercy]! *In manus!* [Into Thy hands . . . I commit my spirit; according to St. Luke 23.46, the dying words of Christ on the Cross]."

So loud was the cry of the wounded that the prior of the abbey came out with all his monks, and they, when they perceived these poor folk tossed thus amid the vines and mortally wounded, confessed a few of them. But while the priests were busy confessing them, the little monklets ran up to where Frère Jean was and asked him how he wanted them to help him. To which he replied that they should slit the throats of those he had already wounded. So you know with what weapons? With fine whittles, which are little half-knives, with which the little children of our region shell walnuts.

Then, with his staff of the cross, he reached the breach the enemy had made. Some of the monklets had carried off the ensigns and standards to their rooms to make garters of them. But when those who had confessed tried to get through the breach, the monk knocked them senseless, saying:

"These are confessed and repentant, and have got pardons; they're going to Paradise, straight as a sickle,[6] and as the road to Faye."

Thus, by his prowess, were defeated all those of the army who had entered the close, up to the number of thirteen thousand six hundred and twenty-two, not counting the women and little children, that's always understood.

Never did Maugis the Hermit bear himself so valiantly with his pilgrim's staff against the Saracens, he of whom it is written in the exploits of the four sons of Aymon, as did the monk against the enemy with the staff of the cross.

CHAPTER 28

How Picrochole took by storm
La Roche Clermauld,
and the regret and difficulty that
Grandgousier felt
about undertaking war.

WHILE the Monk was skirmishing as we have said against those who had entered the close, Picrochole in great haste crossed the Ford of Vède with his men, and attacked La Roche Clermauld, at which place he was offered no resistance whatever, and, because it was already night, he decided to put up with his men in that town and cool the stinging of his wrath.

In the morning he stormed the bulwarks and château, and fortified it very well, and stocked it with the necessary munitions, thinking to make that his retreat if he attacked elsewhere, for the place was strong both by art and by nature because of its situation and site.

Now let's leave them there and return to our good Gargantua, who is in Paris, fully intent on the study of good letters and on athletic exercises, and good old Grandgousier, his father, who after supper is warming his balls by a fine big bright fire, and, while waiting for some chestnuts to roast, writing on the hearth with a stick burnt at one end with which you stir up the fire, and telling his wife and family fine tales of olden times.

One of the shepherds who was guarding the vineyards, named Pillot [diminutive of Pierre: Petey], came before him at that moment and told him in full of the excesses and pillage that Picrochole, king of Lerné, was perpetrating in his lands and domains, and how he had pillaged, devastated, and sacked the entire country, except for the close of Seuillé, which Frère Jean des Entommeures had saved, to his honor, and at present the said king was at La Roche Clermauld and was there fortifying himself, he and his men, with great urgency.

"Alas! Alas!" said Grandgousier, "what is this my good people? Am I dreaming, or is it true what they tell me? Is Picrochole, my good old friend from all time, wholly bound to me by race and alliance, coming and attacking me? What prompts him? What pricks him on? Who has given him such advice? Oh, oh, oh! My God, my Savior, help me, inspire me, advise me on what is to be done! I protest, I swear before Thee, so mayest Thou be favorable to me! If ever I did any displeasure or harm to him or his people, or pillage in his lands; but, quite on the contrary, I have helped him with men, money, favor, and counsel in every case where I could discern his advantage. So his having outraged me to such a point can be only through the Evil Spirit. Good God, Thou knowest my heart, for from Thee nothing can be hidden; if by chance he had gone mad, and, to restore his brain to him, Thou hadst sent him here, give me both the power and the knowledge to return him to good teaching by the yoke of Thy holy Will.

"Oh! oh! oh! my good people, my good friends and loyal servants, shall I be obliged to summon you to help me? Alas! my old age required henceforth nothing but repose, and all my life I have striven for nothing so much as peace; but I must, as I clearly see, burden my weary enfeebled shoulders with armor, and take into my trembling hand the mace to help and safeguard my poor subjects. Reason so wills it, for by their labor I am supported and by their sweat I am fed, I, my children, and my family. This notwithstanding, I shall not undertake war until I have tried all the arts of peace. On that I am resolved."

Thereupon he had his council summoned, and set forth the affair just as it was, and it was decided that they should send some prudent man to Picrochole to find out why he had so suddenly abandoned his repose and invaded lands to which he had no claim whatever; furthermore, they should send for Gargantua and his men, to support the country and defend it in its need. All this suited Grandgousier, and he ordered that it be done thus. So he immediately sent his lackey, Basque, to seek out Gargantua at top speed, and he wrote to him as follows:

CHAPTER 29

The tenor of the letter
that Grandgousier wrote to Gargantua.

"The fervor of your studies obliged me for a long time not to recall you from that philosophical repose, if my trust in our friends and former confederates had not now spoiled the security of my old age. But since such is this fated destiny that I should be troubled by those in whom I trusted most, I am forced to recall you to the aid of the people and property which are entrusted to you by natural law.

"For, even as arms are feeble outside if good counsel is not in the house, so is the endeavor and counsel vain which at the opportune time is not carried out and put into effect by valor.

"My intention is not to provoke, but to appease; not to attack, but to defend; not to conquer, but to protect my loyal subjects and hereditary lands, which Picrochole has invaded without cause or occasion, and from day to day pursues his mad enterprise with excesses intolerable to free men.

"I have made it my duty to moderate his tyrannical anger, offering him everything I thought might content him, and several times have sent an envoy in friendly manner to him to learn in what way, by whom, and how, he felt himself outraged; but from him I have had no reply but willful defiance and that in my lands he claimed simply to rule by right.

"From which I have recognized that eternal God has abandoned him to the rudder of his own free will and sense, which cannot but be wicked if it is not continually guided by divine Grace,[1] and, to confine him in his duty and bring him back to his senses by painful experience, has sent him here to me.

"Therefore, my well-beloved son, as soon as you can, when you have read this letter, come in haste to my aid, not so much to aid me (which nevertheless you should do by nature out of pity) as your people, whom by reason you should save and preserve. The exploit shall be accomplished with the least possible bloodshed and, if it is possible, by more expedient devices, stratagems, and ruses of war we shall save all the souls and send them back joyfully to their homes.

"Very dear son, the peace of Christ our Redeemer be with you.

"Give Ponocrates, Gymnaste, and Eudémon my greetings.

"The twentieth of September.[2]

Your father,
GRANDGOUSIER."

CHAPTER 30

How Ulrich Gallet was sent to Picrochole.

THIS letter dictated and signed, Grandgousier ordered Ulrich Gallet, his Master of Requests, a wise and discreet man whose valor and good counsel he had tested in varied and contentious affairs, to go to Picrochole and remonstrate to him what had been decreed by them.

At that very hour that good man Gallet left, and, having crossed the ford, he asked the miller about Picrochole's situation; who answered that his men had left him neither rooster nor hen, and that they had barricaded themselves in La Roche Clermauld, and that he advised him to go no further, for fear of the watch, for their frenzy was enormous. He readily believed this, and for that night put up at the miller's.

The next morning he betook himself with the trumpeter to the gate of the château, and asked the guards to have him speak to the king for his sake.

When these words were announced to the king, he in no way consented to have them open the gate to him, but he went up onto the bulwark and said to the ambassador:

"What's new? What do you want to say?"

Thereupon the ambassador spoke as follows:

CHAPTER 31

The speech made by Ulrich Gallet to Picrochole.

"No more just cause for grief can arise between men than if, from the source from which they expected favor and good will, they receive harm and damage. And not without cause (although without reason), many, having suffered such an accident, have considered this indignity to be less tolerable than their very life, and, in case they have been unable to correct it either by force or by other device, they themselves have robbed themselves of that light.

"Thus it is no wonder if King Grandgousier, my master, is by your frenzied and hostile arrival seized with great displeasure and perturbed in his understanding. A marvel it would be if he had not been moved by the incomparable excesses which have been perpetrated upon his lands and subjects by you and your men, from which has been omitted no example whatever of inhumanity, which is such a great grievance in itself, for the cordial affection with which he has always cherished his subjects, that it could not be more so to any mortal man. However, it is grievous to him beyond human estimation, inasmuch as those grievances and wrongs have been committed by you and your men, who from all memory and antiquity had, you and your forefathers, formed a friendship with him and all his ancestors, which until now you had together kept as inviolably sacred, guarded and maintained it, so well that not only he and his men, but the barbarian nations, Poitevins, Bretons, Manceaux, and those who live beyond the Canary Islands and Isabella, considered it as easy to demolish the firmament and to raise the abysses above the clouds as to sever your alliance, and they dreaded it so in their enterprises that they never dared provoke, irritate, or damage one for fear of the other.

"There is more. That sacred friendship so filled this clime that few people dwell today anywhere on the continent and the isles of the Ocean who have not ambitiously hoped to be received into it by pacts drawn up by you, esteeming your confederation as highly as their own lands and domains; so that in all memory there has not been a prince or a league so mad or so haughty as to have dared attack, I do not say just your lands, but those of your confederates; and if by headstrong counsel they have undertaken some new enterprise against them, once the name and title of your alliance was understood, they immediately left off their undertakings.

"Then what frenzy stirs you, breaking all alliance, treading underfoot all friendship, transgressing all right, to invade his lands as an enemy, without having in any way been harmed, or irritated or provoked by him or his men? Where is good faith? Where is law? Where is reason? Where is humanity? Where is the fear of God? Do you think that these outrages are hidden from the eternal spirits and from sovereign God, Who is the just recompenser of our enterprises? If you think so, you are wrong, for all things will come before His Judgment. Is it fated destinies or influences of the stars that will make an end of your peace and repose? Thus all things have their end and their period, and, when they have come to that highest point, they are thrown down in ruins, or they cannot remain long in such a state. That is the end of those who cannot moderate their fortunes and prosperities by reason and temperance.

"But, if it were thus fated that your happiness and repose were thus due now to come to an end, did it have to be by troubling my king, the man by whom you were established? If your house had to fall into ruin, was it necessary that in its ruin it should fall upon the hearth of the man who adorned it? The thing is so far outside the bounds of reason, so abhorrent to common sense, that it can hardly be conceived by human understanding, and until it is it will remain incredible among foreigners that the certain and attested effect gives them to understand that nothing is holy or sacred to those who have emancipated themselves from God and reason to follow their perverse affections.

"If some wrong had been done by us to your subjects and domains, if favor had been shown by us to those to whom you wish ill, if in your affairs we had not always succored you, if by us your name and honor had been wounded, or, to put it better, if the Calumniating Spirit, trying to lead you into evil, by fallacious appearances and delusory fantasies fixed it in your understanding, that we had done to you things unworthy of our ancient friendship, you should first have inquired into the truth, then admonished us of it; and we would have satisfied your heart's desire so that you would have had occasion to be content. But (O eternal God!) what is your undertaking? Would you wish, like a perfidious tyrant, thus to pillage and dissipate my master's kingdom? Have you found him so slothful and stupid that he would not, or so destitute of men, money, counsel, and military skill that he could not resist your unjust attacks?

"Leave these lands immediately, and tomorrow for the entire day be back in your lands, without committing any disorder or violence along the way; and pay a thousand gold besants for the damages you have done in these lands. You will hand over half of it tomorrow, the other half at the coming Ides of May next, leaving us meanwhile as hostage Dukes Turnmill [Tournemoule], Droopytail [Basdefesses], and Smallfry [Menuail], also Prince Bugscratcher [Gratelles], and Viscount Guzzler [Morpiaille]."

CHAPTER 32

*How Grandgousier, to buy peace,
had the* fouaces *returned.*

WITH this that good man Gallet was silent; but Picrochole makes no answer to his whole discourse except: "Come and get 'em, come and get 'em! They've got fine ballocks and soft ones,[1] they'll knead some *fouace* for you."

Then Gallet returns to Grandgousier, whom he found on his knees, head bare, bent over a little nook of his study, praying God to be willing to soften Picrochole's choler and bring him back to the path of reason, without going about it by force. When he saw the good man back, he asked him:

"Ha! my friend, what news do you bring me?"

"There is no order," said Gallet; "this man is completely out of his mind and abandoned by God."

"Yes, but," said Grandgousier, "my friend, what cause does he claim for this excess?"

"He exposed no cause to me," said Gallet, "except that he said to me in anger a few words about *fouaces*. I don't know whether some outrage may have been committed against his *fouaciers*."

"I want," said Grandgousier, "to understand him well before deciding anything about what is to be done."

Then he sent him to find out about his affair, and found it to be true that a few *fouaces* had been taken by force from Picrochole's men and that he said Marquet had first wounded Frogier in the legs with his whip. And it seemed to his whole council that he should defend himself with all his might. This notwithstanding, Gargantua said:

"Since all that's at stake is a few *fouaces,* I'll try to satisfy him, for I'm too reluctant to wage war."

So he inquired how many *fouaces* had been taken, and, learning it was four or five dozen, he ordered that five cartfuls be made that night, and that one of them be *fouaces* with fine butter, fine egg yokes, fine saffron, and fine spices, to be distributed to Marquet, and that for his hurt he would give him seven thousand and three philippuses [gold coins] to pay the barbers[2] who had bandaged him, and besides gave him the farm of La Pomardière in perpetuity, in freehold for him and his heirs. To conduct the whole thing and pass it through he sent Gallet, who along the road near the Willow Grove had great bunches of canes and reeds plucked, and had these decked around each of the carts and each of the carters; he himself held one in his hand, trying thereby to make it known that they were asking for nothing but peace and were coming to buy it.

Having come to the gate, they asked to speak to Picrochole on behalf of Grandgousier. Picrochole never would let them enter, and sent word to them that he was busy, but that they should say what they wanted to Captain Blowhard [Toucquedillon], who was setting up some artillery piece or other on the walls. Then that good man said to him:

"My Lord, to draw you out of this dispute and take away any excuse for not returning to our former alliance, we now return to you the *fouaces* over which there is the dispute. Our men took five dozen; they were very well paid for; we so love peace that we now return to you five cartfuls, of which this one shall be for Marquet, who is complaining the most. Besides, to make him wholly content, here are seven thousand and three philippuses that I deliver to him, and for the harm that he might claim, I give up to him the farm of La Pomardière, in perpetuity, in freehold for him and his heirs. See, there is the deed of conveyance. And for God's sake, let us henceforth live in peace, and you withdraw merrily into your lands, giving place here, where you have no right whatever, as you fully confess, and friends as before."

Blowhard told the whole story to Picrochole, and envenomed his heart the more, so he said to him:

"These clowns are really scared. By God, Grandgousier is shitting in his pants, the poor toper. It's not his thing to go to war, but rather to empty flagons. I think we should keep these *fouaces* and the money, and for the rest hasten to fortify ourselves here and pursue our fortunes. Do they think they're dealing with a gull, to feed us these *fouaces*? Here's how it is: the good treatment and the great familiarity you offered them have made you contemptible to them: pat a lout, and he'll bat you; bat a lout, and he'll pat you."³

"Sa, sa, sa," said Picrochole, "by Saint James, they'll catch it! Do as I have said."

"One thing," said Blowhard, "I want to warn you about. We're rather badly victualed here and meagerly provided with belly armor. If Grandgousier laid siege right now I'd go and have all my teeth yanked out except for leaving three, and as many to your men as to me: with these we'll still be only too quick to eat up our provisions."

"We," said Picrochole, "have only too much victuals. Are we here to eat or to give battle?"

"To give batle, yes indeed," said Blowhard, "but the dance comes from the paunch, and where hunger rules, strength is exiled."⁴

"All this chatter!" said Picrochole. "Seize what they brought."

At that they took money and *fouaces* and oxen and carts, and sent them [the men] back without saying a word, except that they should not come so near again for the cause that they would tell them tomorrow. So with nothing accomplished they returned to Grandgousier and told him the whole thing, adding that there was no hope of inducing them to peace unless by strong live war.

CHAPTER 33

How certain counselors of Picrochole,
by rash advice, placed him in the utmost peril.

WHEN the *fouaces* had been ransacked, there appeared before Picrochole the Duke of Smallfry [Menuail], Count Swashbuckler [Spadassin], and Captain Crapham [Merdaille], and they said to him:

"Sire, today we're making you the most fortunate, most knightly prince there has ever been since the death of Alexander of Macedon."

"Put your hats on," said Picrochole.¹

"Many thanks, Sire," said they, "we're only doing our humble duty. The plan is this:

"You will leave some captain in garrison with a small band of men, to guard the place, which seems pretty strong, both by nature and by the ramparts set up by your devising. Your army you will divide in two, as you understand only too well. One part will go and fall upon Grandgousier and his men. By it he will be easily defeated at the first attack. There you will recover heaps of money, for the lout has plenty of cash; lout, we say, because a noble prince never has a penny. To lay up treasure is a loutish act.

"The other part, meanwhile, will drive toward Aunis, Saintonge, Angoumois, and Gascony, likewise Périgord, Médoc, and the Landes. Without resistance they will take towns, châteaux, and fortresses. At Bayonne, at Saint-Jean-de-Luz, and Fontarabie, you will seize all the ships, and, skirting the coast toward Galicia and Portugal, you will pillage all the seaports as far as Lisbon, where you will get a fresh store of all the supplies needed by a conqueror. 'Odsbody, Spain will surrender, for they're nothing but clowns! You'll pass through the Strait of the Sibyl [of Seville, or Strait of Gibraltar], and there you will erect two columns more magnificent than those of Hercules in perpetual memory of your name, and that strait shall be called the Picrocholine Sea. When you've passed the Picrocholine Sea, here is Barbarossa surrendering as your slave."

"I," said Picrochole, "shall grant him mercy."

"Yes indeed," said they, "provided he has himself baptized. And you will attack the kingdoms of Tunis, Hippo, Algiers, Bona, Cyrene, and, boldly, all Barbary. Passing on beyond, you will hold in your hands Majorca, Minorca, Sardinia, Corsica, and other islands of the Ligurian and Balearic Sea. Skirting the coast on your left, you will dominate all Gallia Narbonensis [Narbonic Gaul, or Languedoc], Provence, and the Allobrogians, Genoa, Florence, Lucca, and farewell Rome! Poor Mister de Pope is already dying of fear."

"'I' faith," said Picrochole, "I'll never kiss his slipper."

"Italy taken, here are Naples, Calabria, Apulia, and Sicily all sacked, and Malta too. I'd just like to see those comical knights, formerly of Rhodes, resist you, to see what they're made of." [2]

"I'd like," said Picrochole, "to go to see Loreto."

"Not at all, not at all," said they; "that will be on the way back. From there we shall take Candia, Cyprus, Rhodes, and the Cyclades Islands, and fall back upon the Morea. We have it. By Saint Ninian, Lord protect Jerusalem, for the Sultan doesn't compare with you in power."

"Then I," said he, "will have the temple of Solomon rebuilt."

"Not yet," said they, "wait a bit. Don't ever be so hasty in your enterprises. Do you know what Octavian Augustus used to say? *Festina lente*

[Make haste slowly]. You had better first have Asia Minor, Caria, Lycia, Cilicia, Lydia, Phrygia, Mysia, Bithynia, Carrasia, Satalia, Samagria, Castamena, Luga, Sebasté, all as far as the Euphrates."

"Shall we," said Picrochole, "see Babylon and Mount Sinai?"

"There's no need to," said they, "at this time. Really, hasn't that been ranging enough, to have crossed the Caspian Sea and ridden over the two Armenias and the three Arabias?"[3]

"By my faith," said he, "we're ruined! Ah, poor souls!"

"What is it?" said they.

"What shall we have to drink in those deserts? For Julian Augustus and all his army died of thirst there, so they say."

"We," said they, "have already arranged for everything. In the Syrian Sea you have nine thousand and fourteen great ships loaded with the best wines in the world; they've arrived in Jaffa. There, there were twenty-two hundred thousand camels and sixteen hundred elephants, which you will have captured in a hunt near Sigeilmès, when you entered Libya, and furthermore you had the whole caravan to Mecca. Didn't they supply you with wine aplenty?"

"True," said he, "but we didn't have it cool to drink."

"By the virtue," said they, "not of any little fish! A hero, a conqueror, an aspirant and claimant to universal empire cannot always have his comforts. God be praised that you have come safe and sound, you and your men, all the way to the river Tigris!"

"But," said he, "meanwhile what is the part of our army doing that defeated that swilling clown Grandgousier?"

"They're not idling," said they; "we'll meet them shortly. They have taken for you Brittany, Normandy, Flanders, Hainault, Brabant, Artois, Holland, and Zeeland. They've crossed the Rhine over the bellies of the Swiss and the Lansquenets, and a part of them have conquered Luxembourg, Lorraine, Champagne, Savoy as far as Lyon, at which place they found your garrisons returning from the naval conquests in the Mediterranean Sea; and they reassembled in Bohemia, after sacking Swabia, Württemberg, Bavaria, Austria, Moravia, and Styrie; then together they fell fiercely upon Lübeck, Norway, Sweden, Dacia [Denmark], Gothia [southern Sweden], Greenland, the Easterlings, as far as the Glacial [Arctic] Sea. That done, they conquered the Orkney Islands and subjugated Scotland, England, and Ireland. From there, sailing through the Sandy Sea, and past the Sarmatians, they have vanquished and dominated Prussia, Poland, Lithuania, Russia, Wallachia, Transylvania, Hungary, Bulgaria, and Turkey, and they are in Constantinople."

"Let's go join them," said Picrochole, "as soon as possible, for I want to be emperor of Trebizond. Shan't we kill all those Turk and Moham-medan dogs?"

"What the devil," said they, "shall we do then? And you'll give their goods and lands to those who have served you honorably."

"Reason," said he, "wills it. That's equity. I give you Carmania, Syria, and all Palestine."

"Ah!" said they, "Sire, that's good of you. Many thanks. God prosper you always!"

Presently there was an old gentleman experienced in many hazards and a real campaigner, named Echephron [Greek "Sensible"], who, hearing these remarks, said:

"I'm much afraid that this whole undertaking will be like the farce about the milk jug, over which a shoemaker was dreaming himself rich; then, when the jug broke, he had nothing for dinner. What is your objective in all these fine conquests? What shall be the goal of so many travails and excursions?"

"It will be," said Picrochole, "that when we're back, we'll rest at our ease."

Then says Echephron: "And if by chance you don't come back, for the trip is long and perilous, isn't it better for us to rest now, without putting ourselves into all these dangers?"

"Oh," said Swashbuckler [Spadassin], "here's a fine dotard! Why, let's go hide in the chimney corner, and spend our time there with the ladies stringing pearls or spinning, like Sardanapalus. He who ventures nothing has neither horse nor mule, as Solomon said."

"He who ventures too much," said Echephron, "loses horse and mule," replied Malcon.[4]

"Enough!" said Picrochole; "let's go on. All I fear is those devilish legions of Grandgousier's. While we're in Mesopotamia, if he should fall upon our rear, what's the remedy?"

"A very good one," said Crapham [Merdaille]. "A nice little order that you will send the Muscovites will put in your camp in a moment four hundred and fifty thousand picked fighters. Oh! If you'll make me your lieutenant general in this, I renounce flesh, death, and blood! I'd kill a comb for a haberdasher![5] I'll strike, I'll catch. I'll kill, I'll abjure!"

"Onward, onward!" said Picrochole, "and let him who loves me follow me!"

CHAPTER 34

*How Gargantua left the city of Paris
to succor his country,
and how Gymnaste met the enemy.*

At this time, Gargantua, who had left Paris immediately on reading his
father's letter, riding on his great mare, had already passed the Pont de la
Nonnain [Nun's Bridge], he, Ponocrates, Gymnaste, and Eudémon, who
to follow him had all taken post horses. The rest of his retinue was
coming by regular day's journeys, bringing all his books and philosophic
apparatus.

When he arrived at Parilly, he was informed by Gouguet[1] how
Picrochole had fortified himself at La Roche Clermauld and had sent
Captain Tripet with a great army to attack the Wood of Vède and
Vaugaudry and that they had ravaged everything, down to the last hen, all
the way to the winepress at Billard, and that it was a strange thing and
difficult to believe the excesses they were committing all over the region.
So much so that he frightened him, and he didn't quite know what to say
or do. But Ponocrates advised him that they should betake themselves to
the Lord of Vauguyon, who for all time had been their friend and confed-
erate, and by him they would be better informed on all matters, which
they promptly did, and found him well decided to help them; and his
opinion was that he should send one of his men to reconnoiter the
country and find out what condition the enemy was in, so as to proceed
by a plan made according to the status of the moment. Gymnaste offered
to go; but it was decided that for a better plan he should take with him
someone who knew the ways and the wrong turns and the streams thereabouts.

So he and Prelingand [Sprightly], a squire of Vauguyon, set out, and
without fear scouted around in all directions. Meanwhile Gargantua took
a little rest and food with his men, and had his mare given a peck of oats,
that is, seventy-four hogsheads and three bushels. Gymnaste and his companion rode so far that they encountered the enemy scattered and in bad
order pillaging and robbing everything they could; and, from as far off as
they spied him, they came running up in a crowd and tried to rob him.
At that he shouted to them:

81

"Gentlemen, I'm a poor devil; I ask you to have mercy on me. I still have a crown or so left; we'll drink with it, for it's arum *potabile* [potable gold]; and this horse shall be sold to pay my welcome fee; that done, retain me as one of your own, for never did a man know better how to take, lard, roast, and dress—indeed, Pardy! dismember and season a hen—than I right here; and for my *proficiat* [initiation], I drink to all good companions."

Then he uncovered his leather canteen, and, without putting his nose into it, took a pretty decent drink. The ruffians kept looking at him, opening their jaws a whole foot with their tongues hanging out like greyhounds, waiting to drink afterward; but Tripet, the captain, at that point ran up to see what was up. To him Gymnaste offered his container, saying:

"Here, captain, be bold and have a drink. I've tried it, it's La Foye Monjault wine."

"What?" said Tripet, "is this rascal mocking us? Who are you?"

"I'm a poor devil," said Gymnaste.

"Ha!" said Tripet, "since you're a poor devil, it's right that you should pass on your way, for every poor devil passes without toll or duty; but it is not customary that poor devils should be so well mounted. Therefore, Sir Devil, get off so I can have the horse, and if he doesn't carry me well, you, Master Devil, shall carry me, for I very much like having a devil carry me off."

CHAPTER 35

*How Gymnaste killed Captain Tripet
and others of Picrochole's army.*

Hearing these words, some of them began to take fright and kept crossing themselves with might and main, thinking he was a devil in disguise. And one of them, named Good John, a captain of the Francs-Taupins, pulled out his prayerbook from his codpiece and shouted rather loud: "*Agios ho Theos* [Greek: "God is holy"]. If you are of God, speak up! if you are of the Other, then go away!" And he wasn't leaving, which several of the band heard, and left the company, while Gymnaste noted and considered it all.

Therefore he made as if to get off his horse, and when he was hanging on the side you mount on [the left], he nimbly did the stirrup-trick,[1] with his short sword at his side, and, having passed underneath his horse, flung himself into the air and stood with his feet on the saddle, his tail turned toward the horse's head. Then he said: "My case is going backward."

Then, in the position he was in, he made a leap on one foot, and, turning to the left, never failed to regain his former posture without varying in any way. At which said Tripet: "Ha! I won't do that one for the moment, and for cause."

"A turd!" said Gymnaste, "I missed; I'm going to undo that leap."

Then by great strength and agility he did the leap as before but turning to the right. That done, he put the thumb of his right hand on the pommel of his saddle and raised his whole body in the air, supporting his whole body on the muscle and sinew of the said thumb, and thus turned himself around three times. On the fourth, twisting his whole body backward without touching anything, he gathered himself up stiff and straight between his horse's ears, holding his whole body in the air on the thumb of his left hand, and in that posture he did the windmill flourish; then, striking with the flat of his right hand in the middle of the saddle, he gave himself such a fling that he alighted on the crupper, as the ladies do.

That done, quite at ease he passed his right leg over the saddle and put himself in position to ride on the crupper.

"But," said he, "I'd better get myself between the saddlebows."

So, leaning both thumbs on the crupper in front of him, he threw himself back in the air head over heels and landed in good shape between the saddlebows, and there he made over a hundred turns with his arms outstretched in a cross, and, so doing, he kept shouting in a loud voice: "I'm raging, devils, I'm raging, I'm raging! Hold me, devils, hold me, hold!"

While he was swinging around thus on this horse, the ruffians in great consternation were saying to one another: "Mother of God, he's a goblin or a devil in this disguise. 'Ab hoste maligno libera nos, Domine [From the wicked enemy deliver us, Lord].'" And they fled along the road, looking behind them like a dog making off with a goose wing.

Then Gymnaste, seeing his advantage, got off his horse, unsheathed his sword, and charged the haughtiest of them with mighty blows, and threw them down in great heaps, hurt, wounded, and slain, without meeting any resistance; they thinking that he was a famished devil, both for the marvelous stunts he had performed and for the things Tripet had said to him, calling him "poor devil"; except that Tripet treacherously tried to split his skull with a lansquenet's sword; but he was well protected, and of that blow felt only the weight; and promptly turning about, he made a feint thrust at the said Tripet, and while he was protecting himself above, with one blow he sliced him through the stomach, the colon, and half the liver; from which he fell to the ground, and, in falling, he gave up more than four potfuls of dips, and his soul mixed in amid the dips.

That done, Gymnaste draws back, mindful that cases of chance must never be carried to their last extreme, and that all good knights do well to treat their good fortune reverently, without pressing it or straining it; and, climbing on his horse, he gives him the spur, making straight toward Vauguyon, and Prelingand with him.

CHAPTER 36

*How Gargantua demolished
the château of the Ford of Vède,
and how they crossed the ford.*

WHEN he had come, he related the state he had found the enemy in, and told of the stratagem he had used, alone against their whole troop, affirming that they were nothing but ruffians, pillagers, and brigands, ignorant of all military discipline, and that they should set out boldly, for it would be very easy to knock them over like animals.

Whereupon Gargantua climbed on his great mare, accompanied as we have said before, and, finding on his way a great tall tree (which they commonly called Saint Martin's Tree because thus had grown a pilgrim's staff that Saint Martin had planted there), he said:

"Here's what I needed: this tree will serve me as a staff and a lance." And he easily yanked it out of the ground, stripped off the boughs, and trimmed it to suit his pleasure.

Meanwhile his mare had pissed to relieve her belly; and it was in such abundance that she made a flood for seven leagues around, while the piss-stream drained down in the Ford of Vède; and it swelled so against the current that the whole band of the enemy was drowned in great horror, except for some who had taken the road toward the hillsides on the left.

Gargantua, arrived at the Wood of Vède, was notified by Eudémon that inside the château there was some remnant of the enemy; and to find out about this matter Gargantua shouted as loud as he could:

"Are you there or aren't you? If you are there, be there no more; if you aren't there, I have nothing to say."

But a ruffian cannoneer who was at the machicolations fired a cannon shot at him and hit him fiercely on the right temple; however, for all that, he did him no more harm than if he had thrown a plum at him.

"What's that?" said Gargantua. "Are you throwing grape seeds at us now? The harvest will cost you dear," actually thinking the cannonball was a grapeseed.

Those who were inside the château busy with pillage [amuzez à la pille], hearing the noise, ran to the towers and fortresses, and fired at him over nine thousand and twenty-five falcons and harquebus shots, all aiming at his head, and they came so thick and fast that he exclaimed: "Friend Ponocrates, these flies around here are blinding me; give me some branch from those willows to drive them away," thinking that those artillery stones and lead cannonballs were gadflies. Ponocrates informed him that they were no other kind of flies than artillery shots they were firing from the castle. Then he banged his great tree against the castle, and with mighty blows he knocked down both towers and fortresses and dashed it all down to the ground. By this means were shattered and smashed to pieces all those who were therein.

Leaving there, they reached the mill bridge and found the ford covered with dead bodies in such a crowd that they had choked up the millstream, and these were the ones who had perished in the mare's urinary deluge. There they had to deliberate how they could cross in view of the obstacle of the corpses. But Gymnaste said:

"If the devils have crossed, I'll cross perfectly well."

"The devils," said Eudémon, "crossed to carry off damned souls."

"Saint Ninian!" said Ponocrates, "then by a necessary consequence he'll cross over."

"Right, right," said Gymnaste, "or else I'll remain on the way."

And, giving the spurs to his horse, he freely crossed over beyond without his horse ever taking fright at the dead bodies; for he had accustomed him (according to Aelian's teaching) not to fear dead souls or bodies — not by killing people, as Diomedes killed the Thracians, and Ulysses put his enemies' bodies in front of his horses' feet, as Homer tells us [*Iliad*

10.488-500]—but by putting a scarecrow amid his hay and having him ordinarily pass over it when he gave him his oats.

The three others followed him without fail, except Eudémon, whose horse plunged his right foot up to the knee in the paunch of a great fat oaf who was there on his back drowned and he couldn't pull it out; so he remained stuck until Gargantua with the end of his stick dug a hole in the rest of the oaf's tripes in the water, while the horse lifted his foot; and (what is a marvelous thing in hippiatry) the said horse was cured of a ring-bone he had on that foot by the touch of that fat ruffian's bowels.

CHAPTER 37

How Gargantua, in combing his hair,
made artillery shells fall out of it.

O̲ɴ leaving the bank of the Vède, a short time afterward they came to the château of Grandgousier, who was waiting for them most eagerly. On Gargantua's arrival, they feasted with might and main; never did you see people merrier, for the *Supplementum Supplementi Chronicorum* [*Supplement to the Supplement to the Chronicles*] says that Gargamelle died of joy there. For my part, I don't know a thing about it, and mighty little I care about her or anybody else.[1]

The truth was that Gargantua, changing his clothes and sprucing himself up with his comb (which was a hundred canes long, set with great whole elephants' tusks), with each stroke made to fall out more than seven artillery shells, which had remained amid his hair at the demolition of the Wood of Vède. Seeing which, his father Grandgousier thought they were lice, and said to him:

"Gracious, my good son, have you brought all the way here some Montaigu sparrowhawks? I didn't know you were in residence there."

To which Ponocrates replied: "My Lord, don't think that I put him into that louse-ridden school they call Montaigu. Better I had wanted to put him among the beggars of Saint-Innocent, in view of the enormous cruelty and villainy I have known there. For far better treated are the galleyslaves among the Moors and Tartars, the murderers in criminal prison, indeed even the dogs in your house, than are these poor wights in the said school; and if I were king of Paris, devil take me if I didn't set fire to it and burn up the principal and regents who permit this inhumanity to be practiced in front of their eyes!"

Then, lifting one of those artillery shells, he said: "These are artillery shells your son Gargantua received a while ago while passing before the Wood of Vède, by the treachery of your enemies. But they got such a reward for it that they all perished in the ruin of the château, like the Philistines by Samson's device, and those who were crushed by the tower of Siloam, of whom it is written in Luke 13. These men in my opinion we should pursue while luck is with us, for opportunity has all its hair on the forehead; when it has passed you by, you can no longer call it back; it is bald in the back of the head and never turns around."

"Indeed," said Grandgousier, "but it shall not be at this time, for I mean to regale you for this evening, and pray be most welcome."

That said, they prepared supper, and as extras were roasted: sixteen oxen, three heifers, thirty-two calves, sixty-three fat kids, ninety-five sheep, three hundred suckling pigs stewed in must, eleven score partridges, seven hundred woodcocks, four hundred capons from Loudun and Cornouaille,[2] six thousand chickens and as many pigeons, six hundred Guinea hens, fourteen hundred young hares, three hundred and three bustards, and seven hundred cockerels. Of venison they could not get any so promptly, except eleven wild boars sent by the Abbot of Turpenay,[3] and eighteen fallow deer given by the Lord de Grammont, as well as seven score pheasants sent by the Lord des Essars,[4] and a few dozen ringdoves, teal, bitterns, curlews, plovers, grouse, young lapwings, sheldrakes, black and white waterfowl, spoonbills, herons, young and grown coots, egrets, storks, *arbennes* [a land fowl], orange flamingoes (which are phenicopters), land-rails, turkeys, lots of buckwheat porridge, and a store of broths.

No mistake, there was no lack of victuals aplenty, and they were handsomely prepared by Dishlicker [Fripesaulce], Hodgepodge [Hoschepot], and Verjuicesacker [Pilleverjus], cooks to Grandgousier.

Johnny [Janot], Michael [Miquel], and Cleanglass [or Emptyglass; Verrenet] fixed the drinks very well.

CHAPTER 38

How Gargantua in a salad ate six pilgrims.

THE story requires us to relate what happened to six pilgrims coming from Saint-Sébastien, near Nantes, who, to get lodging that night, for fear of the enemy had hidden in the garden upon the pea-straw, between the cabbages and the lettuce.

Gargantua found himself a bit thirsty, and asked if someone could find him some lettuce to make a salad, and, hearing that there was some of the finest and biggest in the country, for the heads were as big as plum trees or walnut trees, decided to go there himself, and carried off in his hand what seemed good to him. With it he carried off the six pilgrims, who were so afraid that they dared neither speak nor cough.

So, as he was washing it in the fountain, the pilgrims were whispering to one another: "What's to be done? We're drowning here, amid the lettuce. Shall we speak? But if we speak, he'll kill us as spies."

And as they were deliberating thus, Gargantua put them with the lettuce on one of the dishes of the house, as big as the cask of Cisteaux,[1] and, with oil and vinegar and salt, was eating them as a pick-me-up before supper, and had already swallowed five of the pilgrims. The sixth was in the dish, hidden under a lettuce leaf, except for his staff, which showed above it. Seeing it, Grandgousier said to Gargantua:

"That's a snail's horn there; don't eat it."

"Why not?" said Gargantua. "They're all good all this month."

And, pulling out his staff, he picked up the pilgrim with it, and was eating him nicely; then he drank a horrific draft of *pineau,* and they waited for supper to be ready.

The pilgrims, eaten thus, pulled themselves as best they could out away from the grinders of his teeth, and thought they had been put in some deep dungeon in the prisons, and, when Gargantua drank the great draft, thought they would drown in his mouth, and the torrent nearly carried them off into the gulf of his stomach; however, jumping with the help of their staffs as the Michelots do, they got to safety in the shelter of his teeth. But by bad luck one of them, feeling the surroundings with his staff to find out if they were in safety, landed it roughly in the cavity of a hollow tooth and struck a nerve in the jawbone, by which he caused

Gargantua very sharp pain, and he started to cry out with the torment he endured.

So, to relieve himself of the pain, he had his toothpick brought, and, going out toward the young walnut tree, he dislodged milords the pilgrims. For he caught one by the legs, another by the shoulders, another by the knapsack, another by the pouch, another by the scarf; and the poor wretch who had hit him with the staff he hooked by the codpiece; however, this was a great piece of luck for him, for he pierced open for him a cancerous tumor that had been tormenting him since they had passed Ancenis.

So the dislodged pilgrims fled through the vineyard at a fine trot, and the pain subsided. At which time he was called to supper by Eudémon, for everything was ready.

"Then," said he, "I'm going to piss off my trouble."

Then he pissed so copiously that the urine cut the road for the pilgrims, and they were forced to cross the great drink. Passing from there by the edge of the wood, in the middle of the road, they all fell, except Fournillier, into a great trap made to catch wolves in the net, from which they escaped thanks to the resourcefulness of the said Fournillier, who snapped all the snares and ropes. Having got out of there, for the rest of that night they slept in a shack near le Couldray, and there were comforted for their misfortune by the kind words of their companion called Trudgealong [Lasdaller], who demonstrated to them that this adventure had been foretold by David in the Psalms [124]: "Cum exurgerent homines in nos, forte vivos deglutissent nos," when we were eaten in a salad with a grain of salt; "cum irasceretur furor eorum in nos forsitan aqua absorbuisset nos," when he drank a great draft; "torrentem pertransivit anima nostra," when we crossed the great drink; "forsitan pertransisset anima nostra aquam intolerabilem" of his urine, with which he cut our road. "Benedictus Dominus, qui non dedit nos in captionem dentibus eorum. Anima nostra, sicut passer erepta est de laqueo venantium," when we fell into the trap; "laqueus contritus est," by Fournillier, "et nos liberati sumus. Adjutorium nostrum, etc."[2]

CHAPTER 39

*How the monk was feasted by Gargantua,
and his fine talk at supper.*

WHEN Gargantua was at table and the first course of the morsels was wolfed down, Grandgousier began to relate the source and cause of the war between him and Picrochole, and he came to the point of narrating how Frère Jean des Entommeures had triumphed in the defense of the abbey close, and praised him above the exploits of Camillus, Scipio, Pompey, Caesar, and Themistocles.

Then Gargantua asked that he be sent for right away, so they might consult with him on what was to be done. By their will his majordomo went to fetch him, and brought him back merrily, with his staff of the cross, on Grandgousier's mule. When he had arrived, myriad caresses, myriad hugs, myriad good-days were given: "Hey there, Frère Jean, my great cousin, by the devil, I want an embrace, my friend! Give me a hug!"

"Here, my ballock I want to crush you with embraces!"

And Frère Jean kept chuckling. Never was a man so courteous and gracious.

"Here, now, here!" said Gargantua, "a stool near me, at this end."

"Suits me," said the monk, "since you wish it so. Pour, my child, pour; it will refresh my liver. Pass me some to gargle with."

"Deposita cappa [Robe off]," said Gymnaste; "let's take off that gown."

"Ho, pardy!" said the monk. "My gentleman, there's a chapter *in statutis Ordinis* [in my chapter's statutes] that would not like that."

"A turd," said Gymnaste, "for your chapter! That robe is breaking your shoulders; take it off."

"My friend," said the monk, "let me keep it, for, by God, I drink only the better for it; it makes my body all joyful. If I leave it off, milords the pages will make garters of it, as was done to me once at Coulaines. Furthermore, I'll have no appetite. But if in this costume I sit down to table, I'll drink, by God, both to you and to your horse, and merrily. God save the company from harm! I had supped; but for all that I shall not eat any less, for I have a stomach well paved, hollow as Saint Benedict's Boot, always open like an advocate's pouch. Of all fish except tench,[1] take a partridge's wing or a nun's thigh. Isn't it a merry way to die when you die with a stiff prick? Our prior is very fond of white capon meat."

"In that," said Gymnaste, "he's not like the foxes, for of the capons, hens, and chickens they snatch, they never eat the white."

"Because," said Gymnaste, "they have no cooks to cook them, and, if they're not competently cooked, they stay red, not white. The redness of meat is a sign that it's not cooked enough, except for lobsters and crayfish, which are cardinalized in cooking."

"Holy God's Day, as Bayard used to say," said the monk, "then the Hospitaler of our abbey has his head undercooked, for he has eyes as red as an alderwood bowl. This young hare's drumstick is good for the gouties. Speaking of trowels,[2] why is it that a lady's thighs are always cool?"

"That problem," said Gargantua, "is neither in Aristotle, nor in Alexander of Aphrodisias, nor in Plutarch."

"It's for three reasons," said the monk, "why a place is naturally cooled: *primo,* because water always runs all the way down; *secundo,* because it's a dark, obscure, and shadowy place, where the sun never shines; thirdly, because it is continually ventilated by winds from the northern breeze hole, the smock, and, besides, the codpiece. And merrily! Page, to our tippling! Smack, smack, smack! How good is God, Who gives us this good *piot!* I swear to the Almighty, if I'd lived in the time of Jesus Christ, I'd certainly have kept the Jews from taking Him at the Garden of Olivet [Gethsemane]! Also Devil take me if I would have failed to cut the hamstrings of Milords the Apostles, who fled like such cowards after supping well, and left their good Master in His need! I hate worse than poison a man who flees when it's time for knife-play.

"Hah, why am I not king of France for eighty or a hundred years? By God, I'd make curtal [short-tail] dogs of those runaways at Pavia! An ague strike them! Why didn't they die rather than leave their good prince in his plight? Isn't it better and more honorable to die battling valiantly than to flee despicably? . . . We'll have hardly any goslings to eat this year . . . Ha, my friend, give me some of that pork. The devil! There's no more must! *germinavit radix Jesse.*[3] I renounce my life, I'm dying of thirst. This wine is not all that bad. What wine were you drinking in Paris? Devil take me if I didn't keep a house there over six months open to all comers!

"Do you know Friar Claude des Hauts-Barrois? O what a good companion he is! But what's got into him? He's been doing nothing but study since I don't know when. For my part, I don't study. In our abbey we never study, for fear of the mumps. Our late abbot used to say that it's a monstrous thing to see a learned monk. By God, my friend, sir 'magis magnos clericos non sunt magis magnos sapientes [broken Latin: the most learned clerics are not the wisest].'... You never saw so many hares as there are this year. I haven't been able to get a goshawk or a tassell anywhere in the world. Monsieur de la Belonnière had promised me a lanner, but he wrote me not long ago that it had got short-winded. The partridges will eat our ears off[4] this year. I get no pleasure fowling with a tunnel-net, for I catch cold at it. If I don't run, if I don't raise a rumpus, I'm not at all comfortable. True it is that when I jump over the hedges and bushes, my robe leaves some of its hair behind. Go to the devil if a single hare escapes him. A lackey was taking him to My Lord de Maulévrier, and I robbed him. Am I doing wrong?"

"Frère Jean," said Gymnaste, "by all the devils, no!"

"So," said the monk, "here's to all those devils, while they last! Power of God! what would that limper[5] have done with it? 'Odsbody! He gets more pleasure when someone presents him with a pair of good oxen!"

"How's that?" said Ponocrates, "you're swearing, Frère Jean?"

"That's only," said the monk, "to adorn my speech. Those are colors of Ciceronian rhetoric."

CHAPTER 40

Why monks are shunned by everyone
and why some people have bigger noses
than others.

"By my faith as a Christian!" said Eudémon. "It sets me wondering, considering how nice this monk is, for he delights us all. And so how is it that monks are driven from all good companies, which call them spoil-sports, just as bees drive the drones from around their hives?"

> "Ignavum fucos pecus,"
> (dist Maro)
> "a praescepibus arcent."

> ["The drones, lazy cattle,"
> says Maro

"they drive from their stables."]
[Virgil *Georgics* 4.168]

To which Gargantua replied:

"There is nothing so true as that the robe and the cowl bring on themselves the opprobria, insults, and maledictions of the people, just as the wind called Caecias attracts the clouds.[1] The determining reason is that they eat the shit of the world, that is to say the sins, and as shit-eaters, they are cast back into their privies of a house. But if you understand why a monkey in a family is always mocked and harried, you will understand why monks are avoided by all, both old and young. A monkey does not guard the house, like a dog; he does not haul the plow, like an ox; he produces neither milk nor wool, like the sheep; he does not carry a burden, like the horse. What he does is to beshit and mess up everything, which is why from everyone he receives mockeries and beatings. Likewise, a monk (I mean one of these idle monks) does not toil like the peasant, does not guard the country like the warrior, does not cure the sick like the physician, does not preach or instruct people like the good Evangelicalist teaching doctor, does not transport the commodities and things necessary to the commonwealth like the merchant. That is why by everyone they are hooted at and loathed."

"True," said Grandgousier, "but they pray to God for us."

"Nothing less," replied Gargantua.[2] "True it is that they bother their entire neighborhood by dint of incessantly jangling their bells."

"True," said the monk, "a mass, a matins, and a vesper well rung are half said."

"They mutter a great plenty of legends and psalms not in the least understood by them; they recite plenty of paternosters interlarded with long *Ave Marias,* without thinking about them or understanding them; and that I call God-mock, not prayer. But God help them if they pray for us, and not for fear of losing their bread and thick dips. All real Christians, of all ranks, places, times, pray to God, and the Spirit prays and intercedes for them, and God takes them into His mercy. Now such is our good Frère Jean. Therefore everyone wants him in their company. He's no bigot; he's no ragamuffin; he's honorable, cheerful, determined, good company; he works; he toils; he defends the oppressed; he comforts the afflicted; he succors the wretched; he guards the abbey close."

"I do much more," said the monk, "for while dispatching our matins and anniversaries in the choir, I also make crossbow strings, I polish bolts and quarrels,[3] I make nets and pouches to catch rabbits. Never am I idle. But here now, some drink! Some drink here!

"Bring the fruit; it's chestnuts from Estroc Wood, with good new wine, there you are a composer of farts. You're not yet drunk in here. By God, I drink at all fords, like a Proctor's horse!"[4]

Gymnaste said to him: "Frère Jean, wipe off that drop that's hanging from your nose."

"Ha ha!" said the monk, "could I be in danger of drowning, seeing that I'm in the water up to my nose? No, no. *Quare?* [Why?] *Quia* [Because] it comes out of me all right, but none goes in, for it's well medicated with vine leaves. O my friend, if anyone had winter boots of such leather, he might boldly fish for oysters, for they would never let in water."

"Why," said Gargantua, "does Frère Jean have such a fine nose?"

"Because," said Grandgousier, "God so willed it, Who has made us in such form and for such an end as a potter makes his vessels."

"Because," said Ponocrates, "he was one of the first at the nose-fair. He took one of the biggest and finest."

"Giddap! [Trut avant]" said the monk. "According to true monastic philosophy, it's because my wet nurses had soft teats; in suckling her, my nose went in as into butter, and it rose and grew like dough in the kneading trough. Hard teats of wet nurses make children snubnosed. But merrily, merrily! 'Ad formam nasi cognoscitur ad te levavi [By the form of the nose is known, I raised unto Thee].'[5] I never eat sweetmeats. Page, to the tippling! Item, toasted snacks!"

CHAPTER 41

How the monk put Gargantua to sleep,
and of his hours and breviary.

WHEN supper was over, they consulted about the matter in hand, and
it was agreed that around midnight they should go out scouting to find
out what watch and ward the enemy was keeping; and meanwhile they
would rest a bit to be fresher. But Gargantua could not get to sleep by any
means whatever. So the monk said to him:

"I never sleep really comfortably except when I'm at the sermon or
when I'm praying to God. I beseech you, let's you and me begin the
seven psalms [of penitence: nos. 6, 32, 37, 51, 101, 129, 142] to see if you
won't soon be asleep."

The device suited Gargantua very well, and, beginning the first psalm
[6], on the point of the Beati quorum ["Blessed are those," in NEB 32.1:
"Happy the man whose..."], they both fell asleep. But the monk never
failed to wake up before midnight, he was so accustomed to the time of
claustral matins. Once he was awake, he waked all the others, singing at
the top of his lungs the song:

> O, Regnault, awake now, wake;
> O, Regnault, awake.

When they were all awake he said: "Gentlemen, they say matins begin
with coughing[1] and supper with drinking. Let's do the converse; let's
now begin our matins with drinking; and this evening, to start supper,
we'll see who can cough the best."

Then said Gargantua: "To drink so soon after sleeping is not living on
a medical regimen. We should first scour our stomach of superfluities and
excrements."

"That," said the monk, "is nicely medicated! May a hundred devils
jump on my body if there aren't more old drunkards than there are old
doctors! I've reached agreement with my appetite on such a pact that it
always goes to bed with me, and I see to it well during the day; also it gets
up with me. You can look after your castings[2] if you like, I'm going after
my tiring."

"What tiring do you mean?" said Gargantua.

"My breviary," said the monk; "for, just as the falconers, before feeding their birds, make them tire [*tyrer*, "tug and prey"] on some hen's foot to purge their brain of rheum and whet their appetite, so, taking my little breviary in the morning, I scour my lungs, and there I am ready to drink."

"After what use,"[3] said Gargantua, "do you say these fine hours?"

"After the use of Fécamp," said the monk, "with three Psalms and three lessons, or nothing at all for any who want none. I never subject myself to hours: hours are made for man, not man for hours. Therefore I do mine in stirrup style: I shorten or lengthen them when I see fit: 'brevis oratio penetrat celos, longa potatio evacuat cyphos [A short prayer penetrates the heavens, a long drinking-bout exhausts the cups].' Where is that written?"

" 'Pon my word," said Ponocrates, "I don't know, my little pillicock, but you're too much!"

"In that," said the monk, "I'm like you. But *venite apotemus.*"[4]

Then they prepared carbonadoes aplenty and fine prime dips, and the monk drank his fill. Some kept him company, the others forbore. Afterward every man began to arm and accouter himself, and they armed the monk against his will, for he wanted no other armor than his robe in front of his stomach and the staff of the cross in his fist. At all events, to please them he was armed cap-à-pie and mounted on a good Naples charger, and a stout short sword at his side, and with Gargantua, Ponocrates, Gymnaste, Eudémon, and twenty-five of the most venturesome of Grandgousier's household, all armed to advantage, lance in fist, mounted like Saint George, each with a harquebusier on his crupper.

CHAPTER 42

*How the monk encourages his companions
and how he hanged from a tree.*

Now the valiant champions are on their way to their adventure, fully determined to find out what encounter they must seek and what they must guard against when the day comes for the great horrible battle. And the monk encourages them, saying:

"Lads, have no fear or doubt, I'll lead you safely. God and Saint Benedict be with you! If I had the strength to match my courage, 'sdeath! I'd pluck them for you like a duck! I fear nothing except artillery. However, my staff of the cross shall play the devil. By God, any one of you who ducks, devil take me if I don't make a monk of him in my place and wrap him in my robe! It's good medicine for men's cowardice. Haven't you heard of Monsieur de Meurles's greyhound, who was no good in the field? He put a robe over his head. 'Odsbody! Not a hare or a fox got away from him; and what is more, he covered all the bitches in the area, he who before was impotent and *de frigidis et maleficiatis* [one of the frigid and bewitched]."

The monk, speaking these words in anger, passed under a walnut tree, heading toward the Willow Grove, and caught the visor of his helm in the stump of a big branch of the walnut tree. Nevertheless, he gave the spur fiercely to his horse, who was touchy under the spur, so that the horse bounded forward, and the monk, trying to unfasten his visor from the stump, lets go the bridle and hangs by his hand from the branches, while the horse slips out from under him. In this way the monk remained hanging from the walnut tree and shouting "Help!" "Murder!" also protesting about treachery.

Eudémon was the first to see him, and said, calling Gargantua:

"Sire, come and see Absalom hanged!" Gargantua, coming up, considered the countenance of the monk and the posture in which he was hanging, said to Eudémon:

"You've hit it wrong, comparing him to Absalom, for Absalom hanged himself by the hair; but the monk, clean shaven, hanged himself by the ears."

"Help me!" said the monk, "in the devil's name! Isn't this a fine time for chitchat? You remind me of the Decretalist preachers, who say that anyone who sees his neighbor in danger must, on pain of three-pronged excommunication, rather admonish him to make confession and put himself in a state of grace than help him.

"So when I see them fallen into a stream and about to be drowned, instead of going to fetch them and giving them a hand, I'll preach them a fine long sermon *de contemptu mundi et fuga seculi* [on contempt for the world and flight from the secular],¹ and, when they're stone dead, I'll go fish for them"

"Don't move, my cutey," said Gymnaste, "I'm coming to get you, for you're a nice little monachus:

> Monachus in claustro
> Non valet ova duo:
> Sed, quando est extra,
> Bene valet triginta.
>
> [A monk, cloistered from view,
> Is worth one egg, not two;
> But once outside the door,
> He's worth thirty or more.]

"I've seen more than five hundred hanged men, but I never saw one who had better grace in dangling, and if I could match it, I'd want to hang all my life."

"Will you," said the monk, "have preached enough soon? Help me, by God, since by the Other you won't. By the robe I wear, you'll repent of this *tempore et loco prelibatus* [in due time and place]."

Then Gymnaste got down off his horse, and, climbing up the walnut tree, with one hand he lifted the monk by the gussets, and with the other freed his visor from the stump of the branch, and thus let him fall to the ground, and himself after. When he was down, the monk rid himself of all his armor and threw one piece after another about the field, and, picking up his staff of the cross again, got back on his horse, which Eudémon had kept from running away.

Thus they joyously go their way, taking the road to the Willow Grove.

CHAPTER 43

How Picrochole's scouting party
was met by Gargantua,
and how the monk killed
Captain Tiravant [Forward March],
and then was taken prisoner
by the enemy.

Picrochole, on the report of those who had escaped the rout when Tripet was untriped, was seized with great anger, hearing that the devils had attacked his men, so he held his council all night, at which Hastycalf and Blowhard concluded that he could defeat all the devils in hell, if they came; at which Picrochole did not wholly believe nor did he mistrust it.

Therefore he sent sixteen hundred knights led by Count Tiravant to reconnoiter the country, all mounted on light horses, as a scouting party, all well sprinkled with holy water, and each having as his insignia a stole worn like a scarf, against all hazards, if they should meet the devils, so that by virtue of this Gringorian[1] water and of the stoles they should make them disappear and vanish. So they ran to the outskirts of La Vauguyon and La Maladerie but never found a soul to talk to; whereupon they went back to the upper road, and in the shepherd's hut near Le Couldray they found the pilgrims alive, whom, tied and manacled, they carried off as if they were spies, in spite of their exclamations, adjurations, and requests. When they had come down from there toward Seuillé, they were heard by Gargantua, who said to his men:

"Comrades, here is an encounter, and in number they are ten times more numerous than we. Shall we charge them?"

"What the devil else shall we do then?" said the monk. "Do you value men by their number, not by their valor and boldness?" Then he shouted: "Let's charge the devils, let's charge!"

Hearing which, the enemy thought they surely were real devils, so they began to flee with bridle down, except Tiravant who set his lance at the ready and with it struck the monk with full force in the middle of his chest; but, meeting the horrific frock, the lance was blunted at the point as if you were striking a little candle against an anvil. Then the monk with his staff of the cross hit him between the neck and collar on the acrimion

99

bone so hard that he stunned him and made him lose all sense and movement, and he fell at the horse's feet. And, seeing the stole that he was wearing like a scarf, he said to Gargantua:

"These are just priests; that's only the beginning of a monk. By Saint John, I'm a complete monk; I'll kill them for you like flies."

Then he ran after them at full gallop, so that he caught the last of them, and beat them down like rye, striking out at random.

Gymnaste immediately asked Gargantua whether they should pursue them, to which Gargantua said: "Not at all, not at all; for according to true military discipline one must never reduce his enemy to the point of despair; for such necessity multiplies his strength and increases his courage, which was almost downcast and failed; and there is no better way out to safety for stunned and exhausted men than to have no hope of safety. How many victories have been snatched from the hands of victors by the vanquished when they have not been content with reason but have tried to put all to the sword and destroy their enemy totally, without being willing to leave a single one to bear the news. Always open to your enemy all gates and roads, and rather make a bridge of silver to send them away."

"True," said Gymnaste, "but they have the monk."

"Do they have the monk?" said Gargantua, " 'Pon my honor it shall be to their hurt!"

"But so as to provide for all hazards, let's not pull back yet; let's wait here in silence, for I think I know enough about our enemies' resourcefulness. They are guided by chance, not by plan."

While they were waiting thus under the walnut trees, meanwhile the monk kept on in pursuit, charging everyone he met without having mercy on anyone, until he encountered a knight carrying on his crupper one of the pilgrims. And there, as he wanted to sack him, the pilgrim cried out: "Ha, Sir Prior, my friend, Sir Prior, save me, please!"

Hearing this call, the enemies turned about to the rear, and, seeing that it was only the monk that was causing this trouble, belabored him with blows as you load on an ass with wood. But of all this he felt nothing, especially when they struck his robe, such tough skin he had. Then they gave him two archers to guard him, and, turning around, saw no one opposing them; therefore they thought Gargantua had fled with his band. So then they ran toward the young walnut trees as vigorously as they could to meet them, and left there the monk alone with two archers on guard.

Gargantua heard the noise and the horses' neighing and said to his men:

"Comrades, I hear the sound of our enemies, and already I perceive some of them coming against us in a crowd. Let's close in tight together here and hold the road in good order. By that means we can receive them to their ruin and to our honor."

CHAPTER 44

How the monk got rid of his guards,
and how Picrochole's scouting party
was defeated.

THE monk, seeing them leave in disorder, conjectured that they were going to charge on Gargantua and his men, and was extremely unhappy that he couldn't help them. Then he noticed the bearing of his two archers on guard, who would gladly have run after the troop to pillage something there, and kept looking toward the valley into which they were going down. Moreover he was reasoning, saying:

"These people are very inexperienced in feats of arms, for they never asked for my word and did not take away my sword."

Immediately after, he drew his sword and struck the archer holding him on his right, cutting right through his jugular veins and the sphagitid arteries of his neck, with the uvula, as far as the two glands [the adenoids], and, drawing the blow back, opened up the spinal marrow between the second vertebra and the third; there the archer fell stone dead. And the monk, turning aside his horse to the left, ran upon the other, who, seeing his companion dead and the monk with the advantage over him, cried in a loud voice:

"Ah, Sir Prior, I surrender! Sir Prior, my good friend, Sir Prior!"

And the monk was likewise shouting: "Sir Posterior, my friend, Sir Posterior, you're going to get some on your posteriors!"

"Ah!" the archer kept saying, "Sir Prior, my sweetheart, Sir Prior, God make you abbot!"

"By the habit I wear," said the monk, "here I'm going to make you a cardinal. Do you ransom people in religious orders? You shall have a red hat today by my hand."

And the archer kept shouting: "Sir Prior, Sir Prior, Sir future abbot, Sir Cardinal, Sir Everything! Ha ha! Hey, hey, No, Sir Prior, my good Sir Prior. I give myself up to you!"

"And I give you up," said the monk, "to all the devils."

Then with one blow he cut off his head, slicing his scalp over the *os petrux* [stony bones, the lower part of the temporal bone], and taking off the two parietal bones and the parietal suture with a large part of the frontal bone, in doing which he cut through the two meninges and deeply opened up the two posterior ventricles of the brain; and the brain remained hanging over the shoulders by the skin of the pericranium to the rear, in the form of a doctoral cap, black on top, red on the inside. So he fell to the ground stone dead.

That done, the monk gives the spur to his horse and continues on the way the enemy was going, who had encountered Gargantua and his comrades on the highroad and were so diminished in number, because of the enormous slaughter Gargantua had done with his great three, Gymnaste, Ponocrates, Eudémon, and the others, that they were beginning to retreat in haste, all frightened and perturbed in sense and mind, as if they saw the very semblance and form of death before their eyes.

And—as you see a donkey, when he has a Junonic gadfly at his tail, or a fly that is stinging him, run hither and yon without road or path, casting his load on the ground, breaking his bridle and reins, without breathing at all or taking a rest, and you don't know what's driving him, for you see nothing touching him—so fled these men, robbed of their sense, without knowing the cause for fleeing; they were merely pursued by a panic terror that they had conceived in their souls.

When the monk saw that their whole thought was nothing but to take to their heels, he gets off his horse and climbs on a big rock that was on the road, and with his great sword kept striking on these fugitives with all his might, without holding back or sparing himself. So many did he kill and bring down that his sword broke into two pieces. At that the thought struck him that this was enough massacring and killing, and that the rest of them should escape to bear the news of this.

Therefore he seized in his fist an axe from those who lay there dead, and went back onto the rock, spending his time watching the enemy flee and tumble down among the dead bodies, except that he made them all leave their pikes, swords, lances, and harquebuses; and those who were carrying the bound pilgrims he would put on foot and deliver their horses to the said pilgrims, keeping them with him in the shelter of the hedge, also Blowhard [Toucquedillon], whom he held prisoner.

CHAPTER 45

*How the monk brought the pilgrims,
and the kind words that Grandgousier spoke
to them.*

THIS scouting party completed, Gargantua withdrew with his men, except the monk, and at daybreak they came to Grandgousier, who, in his bed, was praying to God for their safety and victory, and, seeing them safe and sound, embraced them with much love and asked for news of the monk. Gargantua answered him that no doubt their enemies had the monk. "Then," said Grandgousier, "they'll have an unhappy surprise," which had been quite true. Therefore the saying is still in use "to give someone the monk."

Thereupon he ordered a very good breakfast prepared to refresh them. With the whole thing prepared, they called Gargantua; but he was so depressed because the monk did not appear that he would neither eat nor drink.

All of a sudden the monk arrives, and, from the poultry-yard gate, he shouted: "Fresh wine, fresh wine, Gymnaste, my friend!"

Gymnaste went out and saw it was Frère Jean bringing five pilgrims and Blowhard prisoner. Whereat Gargantua went out to meet him, and they gave him the best welcome they could and brought him before Grandgousier, who questioned him about his whole adventure. The monk told him everything, both how they had taken him, how he had recovered the pilgrims and brought Captain Blowhard. Then they fell to banqueting merrily all together.

Meanwhile Grandgousier was questioning the pilgrims about what region they were from and where they were going. Trudgealong replied for all; "Lord, I am from Saint-Genou in Berry; this one is from Paluau; this one is from Onzay; this one is from Argy; this one is from Villebrenin. We're coming from Saint-Sébastien near Nantes, and are returning thence by little day's journeys."

"All right," said Grandgousier, "but what were you going to Saint-Sébastien to do?"

"We were going," said Trudgealong, "to offer our prayers against the plague."

"O, you poor folk," said Grandgousier, "do you think the plague comes from Saint-Sébastien?"

"Yes indeed," said Trudgealong, "and our preachers assert it."

"Really," said Grandgousier, "do the false prophets announce such abuses to you? Do they in this way so blaspheme God's just men and saints that they make them out like those devils who do nothing but harm among humans, as Homer writes [*Iliad* 1.9 ff.] that the plague was sent into the Greek host by Apollo, and as the poets invent a pile of Vedioves [*Vejoves* or Anti-Joves] and other maleficent divinities? Thus one hypocrite at Sinay was preaching that Saint Anthony set fire to legs, Saint Eutropius made people dropsical [hydropic], Saint Gildas made people mad, Saint Genou brought on the gout. But I made such an example of his punishment, although he called me a heretic, that from that time on not one hypocrite has dared to enter my lands; and I am amazed if your king lets them preach such scandal in his kingdom; for they are more to be punished than those who by magical art or other device would have spread the plague around the country. The plague kills only the body, but such impostors poison souls."

As he was saying these words, the monk came in, very purposeful, and asked them: "Where are you from, you poor wretches?"

"From Saint-Genou," said they.

"And," said the monk, "how is Abbé Tranchelion, that good toper? And the monks, what kind of life are they leading? 'Odsbody, they're corking your wives while you're out roaming as pilgrims [cependent que estes en romivage]!"

"Heh heh heh!" said Trudgealong, "I have no fear about mine, for anyone who sees her by day will never break his neck to go visit her by night."

"That's hitting the nail right on the thumb!" said the monk. She could be as ugly as Proserpina, by God, she'll get the tumble, seeing there are monks around, for a good workman puts all pieces of material to work indiscriminately. Even the shadow of an abbey steeple is fertile."

"It," said Gargantua, "is like the water of the Nile in Egypt if you believe Strabo; and Pliny, Book 7, chapter 3, opines that it comes from leaves, from clothes, and from bodies."

Then said Grandgousier: "Go your way, poor folk, in the name of God the Creator; may He be a perpetual guide to you, and henceforth don't be easy marks for these otiose and useless trips. Look after your families, each man work in his vocation, bring up your children, and live as the good Apostle Saint Paul teaches you to do. So doing, you will have the protection of God, the angels, and the saints with you, and there will be neither plague nor trouble that will do you harm!"

Then Gargantua took them to have their refection in the dining hall; but the pilgrims did nothing but sigh, and said to Gargantua: "O how happy is the country that has such a man as its lord! We are more edified and instructed by these words than by all the sermons ever preached to us in our town."

"That," said Gargantua, "is what Plato says, Book 5 of the *Republic* [473d]: that commonwealths would be happy when the kings would philosophize or the philosophers would reign."

Then he had their wallets filled with victuals and their bottles with wine, and to each one he gave a horse to relieve him the rest of the way, and a few crowns to live on.

CHAPTER 46

How Grandgousier humanely treated his prisoner Blowhard.

BLOWHARD was presented to Grandgousier and questioned by him on Picrochole's enterprise and affairs, what his aim was in this tumultuous disturbance. To which he replied that his aim was to conquer the whole country, if he could for the injury done to his *fouaciers*.

"That," said Grandgousier, "is undertaking too much; he who bites off too much cannot chew [qui trop embrasse peu estrainct]. It is no longer the time to conquer kingdoms thus with damage to our own Christian neighbor and brother. This imitation of the ancient Herculeses, Alexanders, Hannibals, Scipios, Caesars, and others like them is contrary to the Gospel's profession, by which we are commanded to guard, save, rule, and administer each man his own lands and countries, not hostilely to invade the others; and what the Saracens and barbarians once called exploits are now called brigandages and wicked deeds. He would have done better to restrain himself within his own house, governing it royally, than to come invading in mine, hostilely pillaging it; for by governing it he would have augmented it; and by pillaging me he shall be destroyed.

"Go your way in the name of God, follow good undertaking; remonstrate to your king the errors that you recognize, and never advise him having regard for your individual profit, for with the commonweal the individual is also lost. As for your ransom, I give it entirely to you and intend that your horse and arms be returned to you.

"Thus should we do between neighbors and old friends, seeing that this difference of ours is not properly war; as Plato, Book 5 of the *Republic* [470c], wanted it called not war but sedition when some Greeks moved against others, which, if by bad fortune it comes to pass, he orders that we use with all modesty. If war you call it, it is merely superficial; it does not enter the deep recess of our hearts, for no one is outraged in honor, and, all in all, it is only a question of repairing some mistake committed by our men, I mean both yours and ours, which, although you took cognizance of it, you should have let pass, for the people quarreling were more to be condemned than remembered, especially with me satisfying their grievances, as I offered to do. God will be just assessor of our conflict, Whom I beseech rather to remove me by death from this life and have my goods perish before my eyes, than that He be in any way offended."

These words completed, he called the monk, and in front of them all asked him: "Frère Jean, my good friend, are you, who took Captain Blowhard, here present?"

"Sire," said the monk, "he is of age and discretion; I would rather have you know this by his confession than by my word."

Then said Blowhard: "Lord, it is truly he who took me, and I give myself up freely as his prisoner."

"Did you," said Grandgousier, "put him to ransom?"

"No," said the monk. "That's no concern of mine."

"How much," said Grandgousier, "would you like for his capture?"

"Nothing, nothing," said the monk; "that's not my motive."

Then Grandgousier ordered that, in Blowhard's presence, there be counted out to the monk sixty-two thousand *saluts* for his capture, which was done while they prepared the collation for the said Blowhard, whom Grandgousier asked whether he wanted to stay with him or if he preferred to return to his king. Blowhard answered that he would take the course that he would advise him to.

"Then," said Grandgousier, "go back to your king, and God be with you." Then he gave him a handsome sword from Vienne, with its gold scabbard made with fine vine-leaf ornaments in worked gold and a gold collar weighing seven hundred and two thousand marcs [half-pounds], and ten thousand crowns, as an honorable present.

After these words, Blowhard climbed on his horse. Gargantua, for his security, gave him thirty men-at-arms and six score archers under Gymnaste's leadership to conduct him as far as the gates of La Roche Clermauld if necessary.

When he had left, the monk returned to Grandgousier the sixty-two thousand *saluts* he had received, saying: "Sire, it is not now that you should be making such gifts. Wait for the end of this war, for one never knows what matters may come up, and war waged without a good supply of money has only a short breath of vigor. Funds are the sinews of battle."

"Then" said Grandgousier, "at the end of it I'll content you with some honorable reward, you and all those who have served me well."

CHAPTER 47

How Grandgousier sent for his legions,
and how Blowhard killed Hastycalf,
then was killed by order of Picrochole.

IN these days, the people of Bessé, of the Marché Vieux [Old Market], the Bourg Saint-Jacques, Trainneau, Parilly, Rivière, Roches Saint-Paul, Vaubreton, Pautillé, le Bréhémont, Pont-de-Clam, Cravant, Grandmont, Les Bourdes, Chosé, Varennes, Bourgueil, the Isle-Bouchard, le Croullay, Narsay, Candé, Montsoreau, and other neighboring places, sent envoys to Grandgousier to tell him that they were informed of the wrongs that Picrochole was doing him, and, because of their old alliance, they offered him all their power, both in men and money and in other munitions of war.

The money from them all amounted, by the pacts they had with him, to six score and fourteen [134] millions and two crowns and a half of gold. The men were fiften thousand men-at-arms, thirty-two thousand light horses, eighty-nine thousand harquebusiers, a hundred and forty thousand mercenaries, eleven thousand two hundred cannons, double cannons, basilisks, and spiroles, of pioneers forty-seven thousand; the whole force victualed and paid up for six months and four days. This offer

Grandgousier neither refused nor accepted completely; but, thanking them greatly, he said he would wind up this war by such tactics that there would be no need to tie up so many honorable men.

Only he sent a man to bring, in order, the legions he ordinarily maintained in his places of La Devinière, Chavigny, Gravot, and Quinquenais, in number amounting to two thousand five hundred men-at-arms, sixty-six thousand foot soldiers, twenty-six thousand harquebusiers, two hundred large pieces of artillery, twenty-two thousand pioneers, six thousand light horses, all in companies, so well furnished with their paymasters, quartermasters, marshals, armorers, and other men necessary to provision for battle, so well trained in military art, so good at recognizing and following their ensigns, so prompt to hear and obey their captains, so ready to run, so adept in striking, so prudent in adventure, that they seemed more like a harmony of pipe organs and arrangement of clockwork than an army or militia.

Blowhard, on arriving, presented himself to Picrochole and told him what he had seen and done. In the end he advised, in strong words, that they reach agreement with Grandgousier, whom he had found to be the best man of honor in the world, adding that there was neither profit nor reason in thus molesting his neighbors, from whom they had never had any but good treatment, and, in regard to the main point, that they would never come out of this enterprise except to their great harm and misfortune, for the power of Picrochole was such that Grandgousier could easily destroy them. He had not finished these words when Hastycalf said very loudly:

"Very unfortunate is the prince who is served by such men, who are so easily corrupted as I find Blowhard to be; for I see that his heart is so changed that he would gladly have joined our enemies to fight against us and betray us, if they had been willing to keep him; but since valor is praised and esteemed by all, both friends and enemies, so is wickedness soon recognized and suspected, and, even supposing the enemy use this for their advantage, still they always hold traitors and the wicked in abomination."

At these words, Blowhard, impatient, drew his sword and with it ran Hastycalf through a little above the left nipple, from which he immediately died, and pulling his sword out of his body, he said roundly:

"So perish anyone who blames loyal servitors!"

Picrochole, immediately flew into a rage and, seeing the sword and scabbard thus stained, said: "Had this weapon been given you for you, in my presence, to kill feloniously my good friend Hastycalf?"

Then he ordered his archers to cut him to pieces, which was done on the spot so cruelly that the whole room was covered with blood; then he had Hastycalf's body honorably buried and Blowhard's thrown over the walls into the valley.

The news of these outrages spread throughout the army, whereat many began to murmur against Picrochole, so much that Clutchpuss [Grippeminault] said to him: "Lord, I don't know what will be the outcome of this undertaking. I see that your men are ill-assured in their hearts. They are considering that we are ill-provided with victuals and already reduced in number by two or three sorties. However, there is a great reinforcement of manpower coming to your enemy. If we are once besieged, I don't see how it can be but to our total ruin."

"Shit, shit!" said Picrochole. "You're like Melun eels, you scream before you're skinned. Just let 'em come!"

CHAPTER 48

How Gargantua attacked Picrochole
in La Roche Clermauld, and defeated
the said Picrochole's army.

GARGANTUA had entire charge of the army. His father stayed in his stronghold, and, encouraging them by kind words, he promised great gifts for those who should perform a few exploits. Then they reached the Ford of Vède, and, by boats and bridges lightly made, they crossed over in one move. Then, considering the site of the town, which was high and advantageous, he deliberated that night on what was to be done. But Gymnaste said to him:

"Lord, the nature and temperament of the French is such that they are good for nothing except at the first rush. Then they are worse than devils; but if they delay they are worse than women. My view is that at the present time, after your men have had a breather and a little food, you make the assault."

This advice was found good. So then he sets out the whole army right into the field, putting the reserves on the side of the rising ground. The monk took with him six companies of footsoldiers and two hundred men-at-arms, and with great dispatch crossed the marshes, and got just above Puy on the highway to Loudun.

Meanwhile the assault continued. Picrochole's men didn't know whether the better course was to come out and receive them or to guard the town without budging. But he sortied furiously with some band of men-at-arms of his house, and he was received and saluted with cannon shots that hailed down toward the slopes, whereupon the Gargantuists pulled back to the valley the better to give place to the artillery.

Those of the town defended the best they could, but their shots passed overhead and beyond without hitting anyone. Some of the band, saved from the artillery, proudly bore down on our men, but to little advantage, for they were all received between the ranks, and were thrown to the ground. Seeing this, they wanted to pull back; but meanwhile the monk had occupied the passage, wherefore they took to flight without order or discipline. Some wanted to give chase to them, but the monk held them back, fearing that in following the fugitives they would lose their ranks and that at that point those of the town would charge upon them. Then, waiting for a time and seeing no one appear against them, he sent Phrontiste to advise Gargantua to come forward to reach the hillside on the left, to block Picrochole's retreat by that gateway. Gargantua did this with all dispatch and sent there four legions of Sebaste's company; but they could not reach the top without meeting face to face Picrochole and those who had scattered with him. Then they charged hard upon them, but were greatly harmed, however, by those who were on the walls, with arrow and artillery shots. Seeing which, Gargantua went in great force to succor them, and his artillery began to beat on this section of the walls, so much that the whole strength of the town was pulled back there.

The monk, seeing this side, which he held besieged, stripped of men and guards, courageously headed toward the fort, and did so well that he got a foothold on it, and so did some of his men, thinking that those who come up during a conflict cause more fear and dread than those who fight them. At all events he caused no fright at all until all his men had reached the wall, except the two hundred men-at-arms that he left outside for any mischance.

Then he shouted horribly, and his men with him, and in all fierceness they ran together toward the east [read; west] gate, where the disarray was, and from the rear they overthrew all their force. The besieged, looking in all directions and seeing that the Gargantuists had won the town, surrendered to the monk at his mercy. The monk made them give up weapons and armor and all pull back and shut themselves in the churches, and seized all the staffs of the cross and assigned men to the doors to keep them from coming out; then, opening the east [read; west] gate, he went out to help Gargantua.

But Picrochole thought that help was coming to him from the town, and in arrogant rashness ventured out more than before, until Gargantua shouted: "Frère Jean, my friend, Frère Jean, welcome in good time."

Then Picrochole and his men, knowing that everything was desperate, took flight everywhere. Gargantua pursued them as far as Vaugaudry, killing and massacring, then sounded the retreat.

CHAPTER 49

How Picrochole in flight
was surprised by ill fortune,
and what Gargantua did after the battle.

Picrochole, thus in despair, fled toward L'Isle-Bouchard, and at the Rivière road his horse, which stumbled and fell, at which he was so indignant that with his sword he killed him in his choler. Then, finding no one to give him a new mount, he tried to take a donkey from the mill that was nearby; but the millers thumped him all over and stripped him of his clothes, and gave him a wretched peasant blouse to cover himself with.

Thus the poor choleric went his way; then, crossing the water at Port-Huault and relating his ill fortunes, he was informed by an old hag that his kingdom would be returned to him at the coming of the cocklicranes. Since then no one knows what has become of him. However, I was told that at present he is a poor porter in Lyon, choleric as before, and always inquiring of strangers about the coming of the cocklicranes, hoping certainly, according to the old woman's prophecy, to be restored to his kingdom at their coming.

After their retreat, Gargantua first called the muster-roll of his men and found that few of them had perished in battle, to wit a few footsoldiers of Captain Tolmère's band and Ponocrates, who had got a harquebus shot on his doublet. Then he had them given refreshment, each in his company, and ordered the paymasters to have the meal defrayed and paid for, and for no one to commit any outrage in the town, seeing that it was his, and that after their meal they should appear in the square in front of the château, and there they would be paid for six months, which was done. Then he had assembled before him in the said square all those who there remained of Picrochole's side, to whom, in the presence of all his princes and captains, he spoke as follows:

CHAPTER 50

The speech that Gargantua made to the vanquished.

"Our fathers, forefathers, and ancestors in all memory have been of this sense and nature, that for the battles accomplished by them they have been more prone to erect, as memorial signs of the triumphs and victories, trophies and monuments in the hearts of the vanquished by mercy, than on the lands they conquered, by architecture; for they rated higher the living memory of humans acquired by liberality than the mute inscriptions on arches, columns, and pyramids, subject to the calamities of the weather and to each and every man's envy. Well enough you may remember the mildness they used to the Bretons at the battle of Saint-Aubin du Cormier, and at the demolition of Parthenay. You have heard, and hearing admired, the good treatment they gave to the barbarians of Hispaniola, who had pillaged, depopulated, and sacked the maritime borders of Olonne and Talmondais.

"All this hemisphere has been filled with the praise and congratulations that you and your fathers offered when Alpharbal, king of Canarre, not sated with his good fortunes, furiously invaded the region of Aunis, practicing piracy in all the Armorican Islands and adjacent regions. He was captured and vanquished in a set naval battle by my father, whom God keep and protect. But what then? Whereas other kings and emperors, indeed those who have themselves called Catholics, would have treated him courteously, lodged him amiably with him in his palace, and with incredible kindliness sent him back with a safe-conduct, laden with gifts, laden with favors, laden with all the services of friendship. What came of it?

"He, back in his lands, assembled all the princes and estates of his kingdom, expounded to them the humanity he had found in us, and asked them to deliberate on this in such a way that the world would find it an example, as in us it had been of honorable graciousness, so in them it would be of gracious honorability. There it was decreed by unanimous consent that they would offer up entire their lands, domains, and kingdoms, to do with at our free will.

"Alpharbal in person immediately went back with nine thousand and thirty-eight great cargo ships, bringing not only the treasures of his house and kingly line but almost the whole country; for, as he was embarking to set sail to the northeast wind,[1] every man, in a crowd, threw into his ship gold, silver, rings, jewels, spices, drugs, and aromatic perfumes, popinjays, pelicans, monkeys, civet-cats, spotted weasels, porcupines. There was no son reputedly of a good mother who did not throw in whatever extraordinary thing he had.

"Once arrived, he wanted to kiss my said father's feet; the act was judged unworthy and was not tolerated, but he was embraced sociably. He offered his presents, which were not accepted, for not seeming equitable. He yielded, by the decree of the estate, his lands and kingdom, offering the transaction signed, sealed, and ratified by all those who should perform it; this was totally refused, and the contracts cast into the fire. The end was that my said father began to lament for pity and weep copiously, considering the free good will and simplicity of the Canarrians, and, by exquisite words and fitting sayings, he played down the good turn he had done them, saying he had done them no good that was worth even a button, and, if he had shown them any decency, he was bound to do so. But all the more did Alpharbal exaggerate it.

"What was the outcome? Whereas for his ransom, taken at its most extreme, we could have tyrannically demanded twenty times a hundred thousand crowns and retained as hostages his eldest children, they have made themselves perpetual tributaries, obliged themselves to give us each year two millions of refined gold at twenty-four carats. These are paid to us here the first year; in the second, by their free will, they paid of it twenty-three thousand crowns, the third twenty-six thousand, the fourth three million, and thus always increasing, by their good pleasure, we shall be constrained to forbid them to bring us anything more. That is the nature of gratuity, for a good turn freely done to the man of reason continually grows by noble thought and remembrance.

"Not wanting therefore to degenerate in any way from the hereditary kindliness of my parents, I now absolve and deliver you, and make you free and clear as before. Moreover, on leaving the gate you will be paid, each for three months, to let you retire to your homes and families; and conducting you to safety will be six hundred men-at-arms and eight thousand foot soldiers, under the command of my squire Alexander, so that you may not be injured by the peasants. God be with you!

"I regret with all my heart that Picrochole is not here, for I would have given him to understand that without my wish, without any hope of aggrandizing either my property or my name, this war was waged. But since he is lost, and no one knows where or how he has vanished, I want his kingdom to remain entire for his son, who, because he is too young in age (for he is not yet quite five years old), he will be governed and taught by the ancient princes and learned men of the kingdom. And, inasmuch as a kingdom thus left desolate would be easily ruined if someone did not check the covetousness of its administrators, I order and will that Ponocrates be superintendent over all his tutors, with the authority requisite for this, and assiduous with the child until he knows him to be fit and able to govern by himself.

"I consider that overly weak and lax facility in pardoning evildoers is an occasion for them thenceforth to do evil out of this pernicious confidence in mercy. I consider that Julius Caesar, an emperor so kindly that Cicero said of him that his fortune had nothing more sovereign about it but that he could, and his virtue nothing better about it but that he always would, save and pardon each and every one; he nevertheless, this notwithstanding, at certain points rigorously punished the authors of rebellion.

"Following these examples, I want you to deliver up to me before leaving:

"First, that fine Marquet, who was the source and first cause of this war by his vain arrogance; second his *fouacier* companions, who were negligent in correcting his headstrong madness on the spot; and finally all the councilors, captains, officers, and domestics of Picrochole, who must have incited, praised, or advised him to burst out of his limits in order thus to disturb us."

CHAPTER 51

*How the Gargantuist victors
were rewarded after the battle.*

Wₕₑₙ this speech had been made by Gargantua, the seditious men requested by him were delivered, except Spadassin, Merdaille, and Menuail, who had fled six hours before the battle, one as far as the Col d'Agnello, without a halt, one as far as the Val de Vire, one as far as Logrono,[1] without taking a look behind them or catching their breath on the road, and two *fouaciers,* who perished in the battle. No other harm did Gargantua do them but to order them to work the presses at his printing house, which he had just established.

Then he had those of them who had died there buried honorably in the Vallée des Noirettes and the Champ de Bruslevielle.[2] The wounded he had bandaged and treated in his great hospital. Afterward he gave thought to the damage done in the town and to its inhabitants, and had them reimbursed for all their losses on their declaration and oath, and had a strong castle built there, assigning to it men and watch to defend it better in future against sudden uprisings.

On leaving, he graciously thanked all the soldiers of his legions who had been present at this defeat, and sent them back to winter in their stations and garrisons, except certain of the decuman whom on that day he had seen to perform certain exploits, and the company captains, whom he brought with him to Grandgousier.

On seeing them coming, that good man was so joyful it would be impossible to describe it. So he offered them a feast, the most magnificent and most delicious since the time of King Ahasuerus. When they left the table, he distributed to each of them the whole ornamentation of his sideboard, with a weight of eighteen hundred thousand and fourteen gold besants in great antique vases, great pots, great basins, great cups, goblets, candelabra, bows, boats, flowerpots, comfit boxes, and other such plate, all in massive gold, besides the precious stones, enamel, and workmanship, which, in the estimation of all, exceeded their matter in value. Besides, he counted out from his coffers to each one twelve hundred thousand crowns in cash, and furthermore to each of them he gave in perpetuity (except if they died without heirs) his châteaux and neighboring lands, according as these were suited to them. To Ponocrates he gave La Roche Clermauld, to Gymnaste Le Couldray, to Eudémon Montpensier, Le Rivau to Tolmère, to Ithybole Montsoreau, to Acamas Candé, Varennes to Chronacte, Gravot to Sebaste, Quinquenais to Alexandre, Ligré to Sophrone, and thus with his other places.

CHAPTER 52

*How Gargantua built for the monk
the abbey of Thélème.*

THERE remained only the monk to provide for, and Gargantua wanted to make him abbot of Seuillé, but he refused it. He tried to give him the abbey of Bourgueil, or of Saint-Florent, whichever one would suit him better, or both if he liked the idea; but the monk gave him the decisive answer that he wanted no charge or government:

"For how," said he, "could I govern others, who cannot possibly govern myself?[1] If it seems to you that I have done, or might do in future, service pleasing to you, grant me this, to found an abbey of my own devising."

Gargantua liked this request and offered all his property of Thélème, next to the Loire River, two leagues from the great forest of Port-Huault [or of Chinon]; and he asked Gargantua to institute his religious order in the opposite way from all the others.

"Then first of all," said Gargantua, "there must never be walls built around it, for all other abbeys are proudly walled."

"Yes indeed," said the monk, "and not without cause; where wall [mur] is, front and rear, there is abundant murmur [mur-mur], envy, and mutual conspiracy."

Furthermore, seeing that in certain monasteries in this world, it is a practice that, if any woman enters (I mean of the decent modest ones), they scour the place where they passed; it was ordained that, if a monk or a nun entered there by chance, they would painstakingly scour all the places where they had passed. And because in the monasteries of this world everything is compassed, limited, and regulated by hours, it was decreed that there should never be any clock or sundial whatever, but all works would be dispensed according to the occasions and opportunities; for, Gargantua used to say, the greatest waste of time he knew of was to count the hours—what good comes of that? And the greatest folly in the world was to govern oneself by the ring of a bell and not at the dictation of good sense and understanding.

Item, because at that time no women were put into convents except those who were one-eyed, lame, hunchbacked, ugly, ill-made, mad, senseless, bewitched, and blemished, nor men [into monasteries] unless rheumatic, ill-born, dumb, and household pests.

"By the way," said the monk, "a woman who is neither fair nor good, what is she good for?"[2]

"To put into a convent," said Gargantua.

"True," said the monk, "and to make shirts."

It was ordained that none should be received there but the fair, well-formed and well-natured[3] women, and the handsome, well-formed and well-natured men.

Item, because in the convents of women men did not enter unless furtively and clandestinely, it was decreed that never would women be there unless men were there also, nor men there unless women were there too.

Item, because both men and women, once received into orders, after the year of probation, were forced and constrained to remain in them perpetually for all their life, it was decreed that both men and women received there should leave them when they saw fit, freely and wholly.

Item, because ordinarily the religious made three vows, to wit of chastity, poverty, and obedience, it was constituted that they could honorably be married, that each one should be rich and live at liberty.

As regards the lawful age, women were received there from age ten to age fifteen, men from age twelve to age eighteen.

CHAPTER 53

*How the abbey of the Thélémites
was built and endowed.*

For the building and furnishing of the abbey, Gargantua had delivered in cash twenty-seven thousand eight hundred and thirty-one long-woolled sheep; and for each year, until the whole thing was completed, he assigned from the receipts of La Dive sixteen hundred and sixty-nine thousand sun-crowns, and as many crowns of the Pleiades.[1] For its founding and maintenance he gave in perpetuity twenty-three hundred and sixty-nine thousand five hundred and fourteen rose nobles as a freehold endowment, exempt from all burdens and services, and payable each year at the abbey gate; and to this he gave them fine letters-patent.

The building was hexagonal in shape in such a way that at each angle was built a stout round tower, sixty paces in diameter, and they were all alike in width and appearance. The River Loire flowed on the northerly side. On its bank was situated one of the towers, named Artice [Arctic]; and heading toward the orient was another named Calaer [Greek *Kala* + *aer*, cf., English *Belair*]; the other then following, Anatole [Greek: western land, from *anatole* "sunrise," cf., *Anatolia*]; the one after that, Mesembrine [Greek: southern, or relating to noon]; the one after that Hesperia [Greek: western land, used of Italy]; the last, Cryere [Greek *Kryeros*, "icy"]. The whole was built in six stories, counting as one the cellars underground. The second was vaulted in the form of a basket handle; the rest had ceilings of Flanders plaster in the form of lamp bases, the roof covered with lead backing with figures of little manikins and animals well garnished and gilded, with the gutters that came out of the wall between windows painted in a diagonal figure in gold and azure down to the ground, where it ended in great eaves-gutters that led into the river below the lodging.

The said building was a hundred times more magnificent than is Bonnivet,[2] or Chambord, or Chantilly, for in it were nine thousand three hundred and thirty-two rooms, each one furnished with an inner chamber, study, garde-robe [either wardrobe, or, more probably, privy], chapelle [either kitchen or, more probably, chapel],[3] and opening into a great hall. Between each tower and the next, in the middle of the said building, was a winding staircase, inside the said building, whose steps were in part porphyry, in part Numidian stone [red marble], in part serpentine marble [green, with red and white spots], twenty-two feet long, three fingers thick, the arrangement in the number of ten between each landing. On each landing were two fine antique arches, by which the light was admitted, and by them one entered a cabinet made with lattice windows, of the width of said staircase. And it went up above the roof, and there ended in a pavilion. By this staircase you entered from each side into a great hall, and from the halls into the chambers.

From the Artice tower to the Cryere were the fine big libraries, in Greek, Latin, Hebrew, French, Tuscan, and Spanish, divided among different floors according to the languages. In the middle was a marvelous staircase, whose entryway was from outside the building symmetrically made six fathoms wide and accommodating six men-at-arms, who, with lance on thigh, could ride up together abreast all the way up on top of the entire building.

From the Anatole Tower to the Mesembrine were fine big galleries, painted all over with ancient exploits, histories, and descriptions of the earth. In the middle was a similar way up and a gate such as we told of on the river side. Over that gate was written, in antique letters, what follows:

CHAPTER 54

Inscription placed over the great gate of Thélème.

Hypocrites, bigots, do not enter here,
Blanched sepulchers, who ape the good and true,[1]
Idiot wrynecks, worse than Goths to fear,
Or Ostrogoths, who brought the monkeys near;
Imbecile sneaks, slippered impostors too,[2]
Furred bellybumpers, all, away with you!
Flouted and bloated, skilled in raising hell:
Go elsewhere your abusive wares to sell.

> Your wicked ways
> Would fill my days
> With evil strife;
> By your false life
> Would mar my lays
> Your wicked ways.

Here enter not, shysters athirst for fees,
Clerks, lawyers, who devour the common folk,
Bishops' officials, scribes and pharisees,
Doddering judges, binding at your ease
God-fearing people to a common yoke;
Your salary waits on the hangman's stroke.
Go there and bray; here no excessive loot
Should in your courts occasion any suit.

> No suits or jangles,
> No legal wrangles,
> Are here in play.
> We come for fun today.
> If law must have its say,
> You've bags full of tangles,
> Jingles and jangles.

Enter not, misers, userers, this hall,
Gluttons for money, piling up the stuff,
Gold-grabbers, quick to swallow mist and all,

Hunchbacked, flatnosed, your coffers full, you bawl
For more; a thousand marks is not enough,
Your stomachs never fill, for they're too tough;
Go on, scrawny-faced dastards, pile away:
I hope death strikes you down this very day.

> Their inhuman face
> Herein has no place;
> Let it take the air
> And get shaved elsewhere.
> Quickly then displace
> Their inhuman face.

Here enter not, you sottish mastiff curs,
You troublemakers, full of jealous spite,
And you, fomenters of seditious stirs,
Goblins and sprites, whom Dangier[3] ever spurs;
Latin or Greek, no wolf should cause such fright;
And poxies rotted with your noisome blight
Take hence your wolfish sores to feed at ease,
The crusted stigmas of a foul disease.

> Honor, praise, delight,
> Herein find their site,
> Always merrily,
> All well bodily,
> So we claim aright
> Honor, praise, delight.

Here enter, you, and very welcome be,
And doubly so, each goodly gentle knight,
This is the place where taxes all are free,
And incomes fit for living merrily.
Come thousands, from great lord to puny wight;
You shall be as my family in my sight,
Sprightly and jolly, cheery, always mellow,
Each one of us a very pleasant fellow.

> Companions clean,
> Witty, serene,
> Sans avarice;
> For civil bliss

These tools are keen,
Companions clean.

Here enter too, all you who preach and teach
The Gospel live and true, though many hound;
You'll find a refuge here beyond their reach
Against the hostile error you impeach,
Whose false style spreads its poison all around:
Enter, we'll found herein a faith profound,
And then confound, aloud or penned unheard,
The foemen who oppose the Holy Word.

The Word of grace
We'll not efface
From this God's shrine;
Let each entwine
In close embrace
The word of grace.

Here too, ladies of high degree,
With a free heart come and be happy here,
Flowers of beauty, faces heavenly,
Of upright bearing, gracious modesty,
This is the place where honor is most dear,
Gift of the high Lord whom we all revere,
Our patron, who established it for you,
And gave much gold to make it all come true.

Gold given by gift
Gives a golden shrift,
For the giver stored,
And makes rich reward
As a wise man's shift,
Gold given by gift.

CHAPTER 55

How the manor of the Thélémites ran.

In the middle of the inner court was a magnificent fountain of fine alabaster; above it, the three Graces with cornucopias, and they spouted water from their nipples, mouth, ears, eyes and other openings of the body.

The inside of the lodging on the said inner court was set on great pillars of chalcedony and porphyry, with fine antique arches, within which were fair galleries, long and ample, adorned with paintings and horns of stags, unicorns, rhinoceroses, hippopotamuses, elephants' tusks, and other sights to see.

The ladies' lodging comprised the part from the Artice tower as far as the Mesembrine Gate. In front of the said ladies' lodging, to provide them with entertainment, between the first two towers, on the outside, were the lists, the hippodrome, the theater, and the swimming pools, with the marvelous baths in three stages,[1] well furnished with all accommodations, and myrtle water aplenty.

Next to the river was the beautiful pleasure garden; in the middle of this, the fine labyrinth between the other two towers were the tennis courts and the court for the big ball. On the side of the Cryere was the orchard, full of all fruit trees, all ranged in quincuncial order. At the end was the great park, abounding in all kinds of game.

Between the third towers were the butts for the harquebus, the bow, and the crossbow; the offices, outside the Hesperia Tower, one storey high; the stables beyond the offices; the falconry in front of them, run by falconers most expert in the art, was supplied annually by the Candiots, Venetians, and Sarmatians with all sorts of specimen birds: eagles, gerfalcons, goshawks, great falcons, lanners, falcons, sparrowhawks, merlins, and others, so well trained that, leaving the château to play in the fields, they took everything they encountered. The kennel for the hounds was a little farther on, heading for the park.

All the rooms, public and private, and studies, were hung with tapestries of various sorts, according to the seasons of the year. All the pavement was covered with green cloth. The beds were all embroidered. In each back room was a mirror of crystal set in a frame of fine gold, garnished all around with pearls, and it was of such a size that it really could represent the whole person. At the exits of the public rooms of the ladies' lodgings were the perfumers and hairdressers, through whose hands the men passed when they went to visit the ladies. Each morning these furnished the ladies' chambers with rose water, orange-flower water, and myrtle water, and each lady with a precious casket breathing forth every kind of aromatic drugs.

CHAPTER 56

How the religious of Thélème, men and women, were dressed.

THE ladies, at the time of the first founding, dressed at their own pleasure and fancy. Later they reformed themselves of their own free will in the following fashion.

They wore scarlet or purple hose up above the knee, by just three fingers' breadth, and that border was adorned with fine embroidery and slashes. The garters were of the color of their bracelets, and covered the knee above and below. The shoes, pumps, and slippers were of crimson, red, or violet velvet, slashed like lobster wattles.

Over the smock they put on a lovely kirtle of some fine silk camblet. Over this they put the farthingale of taffeta, white, red, tawny, gray, etc., over it, the frock of silver taffeta made of embroidery of fine gold, and interlaced with needlework, or, as they saw fit and depending on how the weather looked, of satin, damask, or velvet: orange, tawny, green, ashen, blue, bright yellow, crimson, white, cloth of gold, cloth of silver, gold or silver purl, or embroidery, according to the feast days.

The gowns, according to the season, were of cloth of gold with silver fringe, of red satin covered with gold purl, of white, blue, black, or tawny taffeta, silk serge, silk camblet, velvet, silver broadcloth or cambrick, gold tissue, or purfled with gold in various portraits.

In summer, on some days, instead of gowns they wore flowing robes with the aforesaid adornments, or some Moorish style burnouses, of violet velvet with gold fringe over silver purl, or with a golden cord, studded the crossings with little Indian pearls. And always the handsome panache, according to the colors of the cuffs, and well garnished with gold spangles. In winter, gowns of taffeta of colors as above, fur trimmed with lynx, black weasel, Calabrian marten, sable, and other precious furs.

Their rosaries, rings, chain necklaces, carcanets, were of fine precious stones, carbuncles, rubies, Balas rubies, diamonds, sapphires, emeralds, turquoises, garnets, pearls and excellent margarites.

The headgear was according to the season: in winter, French style; in spring, Spanish style; in summer, Tuscan; except for Sundays, on which they wore French accouterments, because that is more honorable and smacks more of matronly modesty.

The men were dressed in their fashion: below, hose of worsted or serge cloth, scarlet, purple, white, or black; the breeches, of velvet in these colors or very nearly matching, embroidered and slashed as they designed; the doublet in cloth of gold or silver, in velvet, satin, damask, taffeta, in the same colors, slashed, embroidered, and decked out to their taste; their points, in silk of the same colors; the tags, of well-enameled gold; the coats and jerkins of cloth of gold, cloth of silver, or velvet purfled to taste; the gowns as precious as the ladies; the silk belts of the color of the doublets; each man with a handsome sword at his side, its handle gilt, its scabbard of velvet, decked with many gold rings and buttons; a white plume above, neatly divided by gold spangles at the end of which dangled lovely rubies, emeralds, etc.

But such sympathy was there between the men and the women that on each day they were dressed with similar adornment, and, so as not to fail in this, certain gentlemen were appointed to tell the men each morning what livery the ladies wanted to wear that day, for that was all at the ladies' decision.

In readying such neat clothes and rich adornments as these do not suppose that the men or the women wasted any time at all; for the wardrobe masters had each morning everything ready to put on, and the chamber ladies were so well trained, that in a moment they were accoutered from tip to toe. And to have these accouterments more readily available, around the Thélème wood was a great block of houses a half a league long, well lit and varied, where the goldsmiths lodged, the lapidaries, embroiderers, tailors, makers of gold thread, weavers of velvet, tapestry makers, and upholsterers; and there they each worked at his craft, and everything for the aforesaid men and women religious. These [craftsmen] were furnished with material and cloth by the hands of Lord Nausiclete, who for each year brought them seven shiploads from the islands of Perlas and the Cannnibals, laden with gold ingots, raw silk, pearls, and precious stones. If a few union pearls were getting too old and losing their natural whiteness, these [craftsmen] renewed them by their art by giving them to a few handsome roosters to eat, as they give castings [purges] to falcons.

CHAPTER 57

How the Thélémites were regulated
in their way of life.

All their life was laid out not by laws, statutes, or rules but according to their will and free choice. They got up out of bed when they saw fit, drank, ate, worked, slept when they came to feel like doing so; no one waked them, no one forced them either to drink or to eat or to do anything else whatever. Thus Gargantua had established it. In their rule was only this clause:

DO WHAT YOU WILL [FAY CE QUE VOULDRAS],[1]

because people who are free, well born, well bred, moving in honorable social circles, have by nature an instinct and goad which always impels them to virtuous deeds and holds them back from vice, which they called honor. These people, when by vile subjection and constraint they are oppressed and enslaved, turn aside this noble affection by which they freely tended toward virtue, to throw off and infringe this yoke of servitude: for we always undertake forbidden things and covet that which is denied us.

By this freedom they were moved to laudable emulation all to do what they saw a single one liked. If some man or woman said: "Let's drink," they all drank; if one said: "Let's go play in the fields," they all went. If it was to fly a bird or to hunt, the ladies, mounted on fine hackneys, with their proud palfrey, each carried on her daintily gauntleted fist either a sparrowhawk, or a lanner, or a merlin. The men carried the other kinds of hawks.

So nobly were they taught that there was none among them, man or woman, who could not read, write, sing, play harmonious instruments, speak five or six languages, and compose in these in both verse and prose.

Never were there seen such brave gentlemen, so noble and worthy, so dextrous and skilful both on foot and mounted, more brisk and lively, more nimble and quick, or better able to handle any kind of weapon than were there. Never were there seen ladies so fair, so dainty, less tiresome, more skilled with their hands, with the needle, for every honorable and free womanly act, as were there.

For this reason, when the time had come when anyone in this abbey, either at the parents' request or for other reasons, wanted to leave there, he took along one of these ladies, the one who had taken him for her devoted suitor, and they were married, and, if they had lived well at Thélème in devotion and friendship, they continued still better in marriage; moreover, they loved each other at the end of their days as on the first day of their wedding.

I do not want to forget to set down for you a riddle which was found in the foundations of the abbey on a great bronze plate. It was as follows:

CHAPTER 58

A prophetic riddle.

Poor mortal men, awaiting happiness,
Lift up your hearts and hear this my address:
If it is licit firmly to opine
That by the bodies which above us shine,
The human mind may of itself win through   5
Thus to announce the things that will come true,
Or if somehow by divine power one may
Have knowledge of the fate to come some day,
So as we judge by reason and good sense
The course and destiny of years long hence,   10
I make it known, for him who wants to hear,
That in this coming winter will appear,
Or sooner yet, right in this very space,
A kind of men, as if a certain race,
Weary of rest and fretful of delay,   15

Who frankly will proceed, in open day,
To suborn men in every walk of life
To disputation and to outright strife.
And he who listens and believes them true
20   (Whatever harm or damage they may do),
Will soon inflame to conflict past amends
Friends and close kinfolk against kin and friends;
The brazen will shamelessly conspire
And pit himself against his proper sire;
25   Even the great, sprung from a noble race,
From their own subjects shall rebellion face.
The duty then of honor and of awe
No longer shall enjoy the force of law,
For they will say that all in turn should go
30   Right to the top and then return below,
And on this point such mêlées shall ensue
Comings and goings, discord, much ado,
That in no history of marvels old
Was such a tale of troubles ever told
35   Then we shall see that many men of merit,
Pricked by the goad of hot and lusty spirit,
And over trustful in their thirst for strife,
Die in their flower after too short a life.
And no one then can leave this course behind,
40   Once he has set on it his heart and mind,
Until he fills, by violence and heat,
Heaven with noise and earth with marching feet.
Then just as much authority will rest
With faithless men as with the trusty best;
45   For all will follow the belief and mood
Of the untaught and stupid multitude,
Whose thickest dolt their chosen judge shall be.
O what a baneful deluge all shall see!
Deluge, I say indeed, and with good reason,
50   For this travail will not be out of season,
Nor Mother Earth delivered from her course,
Until she spurts waters with sudden force,
So that the soberest and least extreme,
Still fighting, shall be watered in this stream,
55   And rightly, for their part, wrapped in this fight,

Will not have pardoned, in its bitter spite,
Even dumb animals and harmless fowls,
Till it has used their muscles and their bowels,
Not with sacrifice to the gods in mind,
But for the common service of mankind   60
I leave you now to ponder in your soul
How best to order and arrange the whole,
And what repose, amid this fearful din,
The round machine[1] may hide its body in.
The happiest, who most of it possess,   65
To spoil and ruin it will forbear less,
And in more ways than one will labor still
To make it slave and prisoner to their will,
Till the poor thing sees all recourse evade her
Except to the Creator God Who made her;   70
And, for the worst of her sad accident,
The sun, before it seeks the occident,
Will let pitch darkness quite obscure the light,
More than would an eclipse or natural night,
Whence at one blow its freedom will be gone,   75
And Heaven's grace and light, which on it shone;
Or at least desolate will remain.
But she, before this ruin, loss, and pain,
Will long have shown, as token of her state,
A vast tremor, so violent and great,   80
That even Etna was not so harassed
When it upon a Titan's son was cast;[2]
And no less sharp and sudden was the quake
That poor Inarime[3] was felt to make
When huge Typhoeus, mad for all to see,   85
Flung down entire mountains into the sea
Thus all too soon it shall be disarranged,
Much for the worse, and then so often changed
That those who held it long will step aside,
Leave it to others to be occupied.   90
Then will be near the good and proper day
This exercise to end and put away;
For the great floods that all this talk inspire
Will lead each man to think he should retire;
And nonetheless, ere everyone depart,   95

A purpose will appear in every heart,
A giant flame whose bitter heat is bent
On finishing these floods and the event.

In fine, when all these incidents are past,
100   Then the elect shall be refreshed at last,
Filled with all goods and manna from the Lord,
And furthermore, by honorable reward
Enriched; finally, let the others go
Stripped and denuded. That is reason, so
105   That when this work is done in such a state,
Each man may have his own predestined fate.
Such was the pact. O how we should revere
Whoever to the end can persevere!

The reading of this document completed, Gargantua sighed deeply and
said to the company: "It is not just from today that people brought back
to the Evangelicalist belief are persecuted; but blessed is he who is not
scandalized and who will always aim at that mark that God, by His dear
Son, has set before us, without being distracted or led astray by his carnal
appetites."

The monk said: "What, in your understanding, do you think is designated by this riddle?"

"How's that?" said Gargantua. "The continuance and upholding of
divine truth."

"By Saint Goderan," said the monk, "such is not my explanation: the
style is that of Merlin the Prophet. Give it allegories and interpretations as
ponderous as you like, and speculate about it, you and everybody else,
just as you please. For my part, I think there is no other sense to it than
a description of the game of tennis[4] hidden under obscure words. The
suborners are the men who get up games, who are ordinarily friends; and
after two chases, the one who was in the service court goes out of it and
the other goes in. They believe the first person who says whether the ball
goes over or under the cord. The waters are the sweats; the racket strings
are made of lamb or goat guts; the round machine is the pelota or ball.
After the game, the players refresh themselves before a bright fire and
change their shirts, and gladly they feast, but most joyfully the winners.
And so good cheer!"

BOOK 2

PANTAGRUEL

King of the Dipsodes
Restored to His Natural State
with his
FRIGHTFUL DEEDS
and
EXPLOITS

Composed by the
LATE MASTER ALCOFRIBAS
Abstractor of Quintessence

Dizain by Master Hugues Salel[1]

To the Author of this Book

If writers who both teach and entertain
Are honored by their fellow men, I find
That your pursuit of praise shall not be vain.
The proof is that your understanding mind
Has in this book so cleverly combined
Pleasure and profit for the general weal,
That you, a new Democritus, I feel,
Make merry at the human enterprise.
So give us more; for praise both sure and real,
If not on earth, awaits you in the skies.

Prologue of the Author

Most illustrious and most valorous champions, who gladly devote your-selves to all things nice and honorable, not long ago you saw, read, and came to know the *Great and Inestimable Chronicles of the Enormous Giant Gargantua*,[2] and, as true faithful, you had the courtesy to believe them, and you have spent your time many times with the honorable older and younger ladies, telling them beautiful long stories from these when you ran out of things to say, which makes you most worthy of great praise and eternal remembrance.

And it would be my will that everyone should leave his own job, take no heed of his trade, and forget about his own affairs, to see to these entirely, without his mind being involved elsewhere, until he knew them by heart, so that if the art of printing ceased or in case all books perish, in the time to come they might be taught accurately to his children and pass them as if from hand to hand to his successors and survivors like some religious cabala;[3] for there is more fruit in it than may be supposed by a whole great bunch of swashbucklers all covered with crusts who under-stand much less about these little jollities than does even Raclet about the *Institutes*.[4]

I've known a good number of powerful high lords who, on their way to hunt big game or set birds flying after ducks, if it happened that the quarry was not found in its traces, or the falcon took to hovering as the prey got away in flight; they were very disappointed, as you can well understand; but their refuge and comfort, was to keep from catching cold and to recall the inestimable deeds of the said Gargantua.

There are others around the world (these are no silly tales) who, when in great pain from a toothache, after spending all their means on medicines with no profit, found no more expedient remedy than to wrap the said *Chronicles* between good hot cloths and apply them to the place where it hurt, sprinkling them with a little *poudre d'oribus* [powdered dung].

133

But what am I to say of the poor poxies and gouties? How many times we have seen them, at the moment when they were well greased and duly anointed, as their face shone like the lock-plate of a larder, and their teeth were chattering like organ or spinet keys when someone plays on them, and their throat was frothing like a wild boar's that the dogs have run down into the toils! What did they used to do then? Their whole consolation was only to hear some page of the said book read, and we have seen some who used to give themselves to a hundred pipes of old devils in case they had not felt some manifest relief in the reading of the said book when they were being held in limbo,[5] neither more nor less than women in labor when they were read the *Life of Saint Marguerite,* then? Find me a book, in whatever language, whatever faculty and area it may be, that has such virtues, properties, and prerogatives, and I'll pay for a pint of tripes. No, gentlemen, it is peerless, incomparable, and un-matched. I maintain this up to the stake *exclusive*[6] [but no further]. And as for those who would maintain the contrary, consider them abusers, prestinators,[7] and misleaders.

Quite true it is that certain occult properties may be found in certain topnotch books, in whose number is found *Fessepinte* [*Tosspint*], *Orlando Furioso, Robert le Diable, Fierabras, William the Fearless, Huon de Bordeaux, Montevieille* and *Matabrune*;[8] but they are not to be compared with the one we're talking about. People have unfailingly recognized by experience the great profit and great utility that came from the said *Gargantuan Chronicle*; for more of these have been sold by the printers in two months than there will be Bibles sold in nine years.

So I, your humble slave, wanting to augment your pastime further, offer you at present another book of the same caliber, were it not that it is a little more objective and trustworthy than the other one. For do not suppose (if you don't want to make a mistake knowingly) that I speak of it as the Jews used to speak about the Law. I was not born on such a planet, and it has never happened that I lied, or gave assurance of anything that was not truthful. I speak of this like a lusty pelican [onocrotale], or rather crapponotary [crotenotaire] of martyred suitors and crunchnotary [crocquenotaire][9] of amours: *Quod vidimus testamur* ["we testify to what we have seen," John 3.11]. This is about the horrible deeds and exploits of Pantagruel, whom I have served as a menial ever since I got through as a page until the present, when by his leave I have come to visit this cow country of mine and see if any relative of mine was still alive.

And so, to make an end of this prologue, even as I give myself to a thousand basketfuls of fine devils, body and soul, tripes and bowels, in case I lie by a single word in the whole story; so likewise, may Saint Anthony's Fire burn you, the falling sickness spin you, squinancy [péché de jeunesse] and the wolf in your stomach truss you,

> Erysipelas with piercing flare,
> As stinging thin as a cow's hair,
> With quicksilver to make it firm,
> Plunge up your bunghole till you squirm.

And, like Sodom and Gomorrah, may you fall into sulfur, fire, and the abyss, in case you do not firmly believe all I will relate to you in this present Chronicle!

CHAPTER 1

Of the origin and antiquity
of the great Pantagruel.

IT will not be a useless or idle thing, seeing that we are at leisure, to remind you of the first source and origin from which was born to us the good Pantagruel; for I see that all good historiographers have treated their Chronicles thus; not only the Arabs, barbarians, and Latins, but also the Greeks and Gentiles, who were everlasting drinkers.

So you should note that at the beginning of the world (a long time ago, more than forty times forty nights back, to reckon as the ancient Druids did),[1] soon after Abel was slain by his brother Cain, the earth, steeped in the blood of the just, for a certain year was very fertile in all fruits that are produced for us from her loins, and especially in great medlars—for three of them made up a bushel.

In that year the calends were found throughout the breviaries of the Greeks. The month of March was missing from Lent, and mid-August was May. In the month of October, it seems to me, or else in September (to make no mistake, for I want to be careful to avoid that), came the week so renowned in the annals, which is called the week of the three Thursdays; for there were three of them, because of the irregular bissextiles, when the sun swerved a little to the left, as *debitoribus*,[2] and the moon varied more than five fathoms in her course, and there was manifestly seen the trembling movement in the firmament known as Aplanes, so much so that the middle Pleiad, leaving its companions, declined toward the equinox, and the star called Spica left of Virgo, moving back toward the Balance; which are mighty frightening events, and matters so tough and difficult that the astrologers cannot get their teeth into them; and indeed they would have to have very long teeth to reach that far! You may count on this, that everyone gladly ate of the said medlars, for

they were fair to the eye and delicious to the taste; but even as Noah—
that holy man (to whom we are so obliged and beholden that for us he
planted the vine, whence we get that nectarean, delicious, precious, celestial, joyous, and deific liquor that we call *piot*)—was fooled when he
drank it, for he did not know its great virtue and power;[3] likewise, the
men and women of that time ate with great pleasure of that fine big fruit.

But very varied accidents befell them, for there came upon all a most
horrible swelling of the body, but not all in the same place. For some
swelled in the belly and their bellies grew a hump like a tun, of whom it
is written, *Ventrem omnipotentem* [Almighty Belly],[4] who were all good
folks and merry blades; and of this race were born Saint Paunchy and
Shrove Tuesday.[5]

Others swelled at the shoulders, and grew so hunchbacked that they
were called Montifers, as if to say Mountain-bearers. You will see some of
these around of different sexes and dignities, and of this race came Aesop,
whose fine deeds and words you have in writing. Others swelled in the
member that is called nature's plowman, so that theirs was wonderfully
long, big, stout, plump, verdant, and lusty in the good old style, so that
they used it as a belt, winding it five or six times around their body; and
if it happened to be at the ready with the wind astern, to see them you
would have said that they were men with their lances set to go jousting at
the quintain. And of these the race is lost, as the women say, for they
continually lament that

> There are no more big ones like that, etc.

You know the rest of the song.

Others grew so enormously in the matter of balls that three of them
quite filled a hogshead. From these are descended the ballocks of
Lorraine, which never dwell in a codpiece; they always come down to
the bottom of the breeches.

Others grew in the legs, and to see them you would have thought they
were cranes or flamingos, or else walking on stilts; and the little grammar-
school kids called them *iambus*.[6]

Others grew so much in their nose that it was like the flute of an
alembic, all mottled, all sparkling with pimples, sprouting, empurpled,
and all spangled, a mosaic, and embroidered with gules,[7] and such as you
have seen on Canon Panzoult and Piédeboys [Woodfoot], the doctor
from Angers, from which race there are few who loved herb tea, but all
were lovers of Septembral potion. Naso [Grand Nez] and Ovid[8] origi-
nated from those, and all those of whom it is said: "Lord only knows..."[9]

Others grew in the ears, which soon were so big that out of one of them they made up a doublet, breech, and long jacket, while with the other they covered themselves with a Spanish-style cape; and they say that in the Bourbonnais that descendance still lasts, whence the phrase "Bourbonnais ears."

Others grew in length of body. And of these came the giants, and of that line Pantagruel. And the first was Chalbroth,[10] who begat Sarabroth, who begat Faribroth, who begat Hurtaly, who was a great downer of dips and ruled at the time of the Flood; who begat Nimrod, who begat Atlas, who by his shoulders kept the heavens from falling; who begat Goliath, who begat Eryx, inventor of the goblet game; who begat Titus, who begat Orion, who begat Polyphemus, who begat Cacus, who begat Etion, who was the first man to get the pox, for not drinking cool in summer; as Bartachim attests; who begat Enceladus, who begat Ceus, who begat Typhoeus, who begat Aloeus, who begat Otus, who begat Aegeon, who begat Briareus, who had a hundred hands; who begat Porphyry, who begat Adamastor, who begat Antaeus, who begat Agatho, who begat Porus, whom Alexander the Great met in battle. Porus begat Aranthas, who begat Gabbara, who first invented drinking toasts; who begat Goliath of Secundilla, who begat Offot, who built himself a terribly fine nose by drinking out of a barrel; who begat Artachaeus, who begat Oromedon, who begat Gemmagog, who was the inventor of buckled shoes; who begat Sisyphus, who begat the Titans, of whom was born Hercules, who begat Enoc, a great expert at getting mites out of hands; who begat Fierabras, who was vanquished by Oliver, peer of France and comrade to Roland; who begat Morgante, who was the first man in the world to play at dice with his spectacles; who begat Fracassus, of whom Merlin Coccai has written;[11] of whom was born Ferragus,[12] who begat Flycatcher, who first invented smoking ox tongue by the fireplace; for theretofore people salted them as they do hams; who begat Bolivorax, who begat Longus, who begat Gayoffe, whose balls were of poplar and his prick of sorb apple wood; who begat Greedygut [Maschefain], who begat Ironburner [Bruslefer], who begat Windswallower [Engolevent], who begat Galahad, the inventor of flagons; who begat Millelingo [Mirelangault], who begat Galaffre, who begat Falourdin, who begat Roboaster, who begat Sortibrant of Coimbra, who begat Bruslant de Monmiré [Brushant de Mommière], who begat Bruyer, who was vanquished by Ogier the Dane, peer of France; who begat Maubrun [Mabrun], who begat Donkeyfucker [Foutasnon], who begat Hacquelebac, who begat Grainprick [Vitdegrain], who begat Grand

Gosier [Grandgousier], who begat Gargantua, who begat the noble Pantagruel, my master.

I quite understand that in reading this passage you are raising within yourselves a very reasonable doubt and asking how it can possibly be, since at the time of the Flood everyone perished except Noah and seven persons with him in the Ark, in whose number the said Hurtaly[13] was not included.

The question is no doubt well taken and quite apparent; but the answer will content you, or my wits are ill calked. And since I was not around at the time to tell you it any way I please, I'll cite you the authority of the Massoretes, good ballocky types and fine Hebraic bagpipers, who affirm that indeed Hurtaly was not in Noah's ark, indeed he couldn't have got in, for he was too big; but he was sitting on top astride it, one leg on one side, one leg on the other, like little children on hobbyhorses, and as the Great Bull of Bern, who was killed at Marignano,[14] was riding on his mount astride a great stone-throwing cannon, an animal with a fine amble, and no mistake. In this way he saved after God, the said ark from shipwreck; for he set it in motion with his legs, and with his foot he turned it wherever he wanted as they do with the rudder of a ship. The people inside sent him victuals aplenty through a chimney, in recognition of the good he was doing them; and sometimes they conferred together, as did Icaromenippus with Jupiter, according to Lucian's report.

Have you understood that well? Then drink a good snort without water. For, if you don't believe it, "nor do I," said she.[15]

CHAPTER 2

Of the nativity of the highly redoubtable Pantagruel.

Gargantua, at the age of four hundred four score and forty-four years, begat his son Pantagruel by his wife Badebec, daughter of the king of the Amaurots in Utopia, who died in childbirth; for he was so wonderfully big and heavy that he could not come into the light of day without choking his mother.

But to understand fully the cause and reason for his name, which was given him at his baptism, you must note that there was such a great drought that year in all the land of Africa that there passed thirty-six months three weeks four days thirteen hours and a little bit more without rain, with the heat of the sun so violent that the whole earth was parched. And even in the time of Elijah[1] it was no hotter than it was then, for there was no tree above ground that had either leaf or flower. The grasses had no verdure, the streams and springs were dried up; the poor fish deserted by their elements wandered screaming horribly about the land; the birds fell from the air for lack of dew; the wolves, foxes, stags, boars, deer, hares, rabbits, weasels, badgers, and other animals, were found dead all over the fields, their throats gaping. As regards men, it was most pitiful. You would have seen them with their tongues hanging out, like greyhounds that have run for six hours; many threw themselves into the wells; others climbed into a cow's belly to be in the shade, and Homer calls them Alibantes.[2]

The whole country was at anchor. It was a piteous thing to see the travail of humans to protect themselves from this horrific drought. For it was all anyone could do to save the holy water in the churches from being used up; but they so ordered it, on the advice of My Lords the Cardinals and the Holy Father, that no one dared take more than one helping. Even so, when anyone went into the church, you would have seen them by the score, poor parched wretches coming in behind the priest who was distributing it, their jaws gaping to have one tiny droplet, like the wicked rich man [of Luke 16.19–25], so that none of it should be lost. O how happy that year was the man who had a cool, well-stocked cellar!

The Philosopher relates, in dealing with the question why sea water is salty, that in the time when Phoebus gave over the driving of his lucific chariot to his son Phaethon, the said Phaethon, ill schooled in the art and not knowing how to follow the ecliptic line between the two tropics of the sun's orbit, strayed off his track and came so close to earth that he dried up all the countries lying underneath, burning a great part of the sky that the philosophers call the *Via lactea* and fiddlefaddlers call Saint James's Way, although the cockiest poets say that that area is where Juno's milk spilled when she suckled Hercules; then the earth was so heated that it burst into an enormous sweat, from which it sweated out the entire sea, which therefore is salty, as all sweat is salty, which you will say is true if you will taste your own—or else that of the poxies when they make them sweat—it's all one to me.

Almost the same thing happened in the said year; for one Friday, when all were busy with their devotions and were making a fine procession with lots of litanies and fine preachers, imploring Almighty God to cast a merciful eye on them in such great distress, great drops of water were visibly seen coming out of the ground, just as when a person sweats copiously. And the poor folk began to rejoice, as if it had been a thing very profitable for them; some even said that there was not one drop of moisture in the air from which any rain might fall, and the earth did not supply the default of that. Other learned men said it was rain from the Antipodes, such as Seneca tells about in the fourth book of his *Quaestiones naturales,* speaking of the origin and source of the River Nile. But they were wrong about it, for when the procession was over, when everyone wanted to gather up some of this dew and drink a whole jug of it, they found that it was nothing but brine, saltier and worse than sea water.

And because on that very day was born Pantagruel, his father pinned on him such a name; for *panta,* in Greek, amounts to saying "all" and *gruel* in Hagarene amounts to "thirsty"; meaning to signify that at the time of his nativity the earth was all thirsty, and seeing in a spirit of prophecy that one day he would be the dominator of the thirsties, which was demonstrated to him at that very moment by another more evident sign. For when his mother Badebec was bearing him, and the midwives were waiting to receive him, there issued first from his belly sixty-eight salt-vendors, each one tugging by the halter a mule all loaded with salt; after which came out nine dromedaries laden with hams and smoked ox tongues, seven camels loaded with baby eels; then twenty-five cartloads of leeks, garlic, onions, and chives, which really terrified the said midwives; but some of them said:

"Here are good provisions. You see, we were drinking only meagerly, not eagerly;[3] this is simply a good sign, these are goads to wine."

And as they were prattling with one another with such small talk, here comes Pantagruel, all hairy as a bear, and at this in a spirit of prophecy one of them said:

"He's born with all his hair on,[4] he'll do wonders; and if he lives, he'll be a grownup."

CHAPTER 3

How Gargantua mourned
for the death of his wife Badebec.

Wʜᴇɴ Pantagruel was born, who do you suppose was all stunned and perplexed? His father Gargantua. For, seeing on the one hand his wife Badebec dead, and on the other his son Pantagruel born so big and handsome, he didn't know what to say or do; and the uncertainty that troubled his understanding was whether he was to weep in mourning for his wife, or laugh aloud for joy over his son. On one side and the other he had sophistical arguments enough to choke him; for he shaped them very well *in modo et figura,*[1] but he could not resolve them; and in this way he remained stuck like a mouse in pitch[2] or a kite caught in a snare.

"Am I to weep?" he said. "Yes, and why? My good wife is dead, who was the most *this,* the most *that,* in all the world. Never will I see her again, never will I find another like her; it's an inestimable loss for me! O God what had I done to Thee to punish me so? Why didst Thou not send death to me first, before her? For to live without her is just languishing for me! Ah, Badebec, my darling, my love, my little cunt—to be sure, she had one a good three acres and two sesterees in size—my little tenderloin, my codpiece, my gym shoe, my slipper, never will I see you. Ah, poor Pantagruel, you have lost your good mother, your sweet nurse, your beloved lady! Ah, traitorous death, so hostile you are to me, so outrageous, to snatch from me her to whom by right immortality was due!"

And so saying, he wailed like a cow. But then suddenly, when Pantagruel came back to mind, he guffawed like a calf.

"Ho, my little son," he kept saying, "my ballock, my little imp, how pretty you are, and how grateful I am to God for giving me such a handsome son, so merry, so smiling, so pretty! Ho ho ho! How happy I am! Let's drink, ho, and put aside all melancholy! Bring some of the best, rinse the glasses, on with the tablecloth, put out those dogs, blow that fire up, send those poor on their way, but give them what they're asking! Take my gown, let me wear just my doublet, the better to regale the gossips!"

So saying, he heard the litany and *Mementos,*[3] of the priests bearing his wife to the earth, whereupon he left off his good talk and was suddenly transported elsewhere, saying:

"Lord God, must I again be sad? That grieves me; I'm no longer young, I'm getting old, the weather is dangerous, I may catch a fever and be all besotted. 'Pon my word as a gentleman,[4] it's better to weep less and drink more! My wife is dead. Well, in God's name (*da jurandi*)[5] I won't bring her back by my tears. She's fine, she's in paradise at least, if not better yet; she's praying to God for us, she no longer worries about our miseries and calamities; the same thing hangs over our heads, so God help the rest of us! I must be thinking of finding another.

"But here's what you do," he said to the midwives (Where are they? Good folks, I can't see you).[6] Go to the burial of her. I'll rock my baby son right here, for I feel quite parched, and might be in danger of falling ill; but first have a good stiff drink; for you'll feel the better for it, believe me on my honor."

Following these directions, they went to the burial and funeral, and poor Gargantua stayed home. And meanwhile he composed this epitaph, to be engraved in the manner that follows:

> She bore my child, and childbirth laid her low.
> Alas, fair Badebec, to come to this!
> In face as lean and fair as any crow,
> Spanish-thin body, belly round and Swiss.
> Pray God He take her to eternal bliss,
> Forgiving her if ever she did stray.
> Never did this her body go amiss;
> And died the year and day she passed away.

CHAPTER 4

Of Pantagruel's childhood.

I find in the ancient historiographers and poets that many people have been born into the world in very strange fashions, which would be too long to relate. Read Book 7 of Pliny, if you have the leisure. But you never heard of one as wonderful as Pantagruel's, for it was hard to believe how he grew in body and in strength in a short time, and Hercules was nothing, who, while in his cradle killed two snakes, for the said snakes were very small and frail; but Pantagruel, while still in his cradle, did some very frightful things.

I forbear from telling you how at each of his meals he imbibed the milk of four thousand six hundred cows, and how, to make him a saucepan to cook his pap in, all the braziers were busied from Saumur in Anjou, from Villedieu in Normandy, and from Bramont in Lorraine. And they gave him the said pap in a big bowl which at present is still at Bourges,[1] near the palace; but his teeth were already so tough and strong that with them he broke off a big piece of the said bowl, as very clearly appears.

On a certain day, toward morning, when they wanted to have him suck milk from one of his cows (for of nurses he never had any other sort, so the story goes), he got one of his arms free from the bonds that held him in the cradle, and up and takes the said cow under the hams and ate her two udders and half her belly, with the liver and kidneys, and would have eaten her all up, but that she was screaming horribly as if the wolves had her by the legs, at which scream people came up, and took the said cow away from Pantagruel; but they could not manage to help his keeping the shin just as he was holding it, and he was eating it nicely as you would a sausage; and when they tried to take away the bone, he promptly swallowed it as a cormorant would a little fish; and after that he started saying:

"Good! Good! Good!" for he still did not know how to speak very well; meaning to say that he had found it very good, and all he needed was more of the same. Seeing which, those who had him bound with big cables, such as are those they make at Tain for the salt trip to Lyon, or as are those of the great ship *Françoyse*[2] that is in the port of Le Havre de Grace in Normandy.

But once when a big bear that his father was bringing up escaped, and came to lick his face, for the nurse had not swabbed off his lips properly, he broke free of the said cables as easily as Samson from among the Philistines, and up and took Mister Bear and tore him in pieces like a chicken, and made himself a fine tidbit of him for that meal.

Wherefore Gargantua, fearing that he might hurt himself, had four stout iron chains made to bind him, and flying buttresses, well mounted, for his cradle. And of these chains you have one at La Rochelle, which they raise at night between the two great towers in the harbor; another is in Lyon, another in Anger, and the fourth was carried off by the devils to bind Lucifer, who was breaking loose at that time, because he was extraordinarily tormented by a colic for having eaten for his breakfast the soul of a sergeant in a fricassee. On this you may well believe what Nicolas de Lyra says about the passage in the *Psalter* [Psalms 136.20] where it is written *Et Og regem Basan* [And Og king of Basjan], that the said Og, while still little, was so strong and robust that he had to be bound into his cradle with iron chains [see de Lyra's commentary on Deuteronomy, and the text of Deuteronomy 3.3–4]. And thus he [Pantagruel] remained quiet and peaceful, for he could not break the said chains so easily, especially because he had no room in the cradle to give a shake with his arms.

But here is what happened the day of a great banquet his father Gargantua was giving for all the princes of his court. I really believe that all the court officers were so busy serving the feast that no one thought of poor Pantagruel, so he was left off in a corner. What did he do?

What did he do, my hearties? Listen.[3]

He tried to break the chains of the cradle with his arms; but he could not, for they were too strong. So he banged his feet so hard that he broke off the end of his cradle, which, however, was a great beam seven span square, and, once he had got his feet out, he slid down as best he could, so that his feet touched ground; and then with great power he hoisted himself upright, carrying the cradle bound thus on his back, like a tortoise climbing up against a wall; and to look at him it seemed he was a great five-hundred-ton carrick standing on end.

In that state he came into the hall where they were banqueting, and boldly, so that he quite frightened the people there; but inasmuch as he had his arms bound inside, he couldn't take anything to eat, and was bending down with great difficulty to lick up some little mouthful with his tongue. Seeing this, his father readily understood that he had been left without anything to eat, and ordered him to be unbound from the said chains, this with the advice of the princes and lords present; beside which, too, Gargantua's doctors said that if he were kept in the cradle that way, he would all his life be subject to kidney stones. When he was unchained, they had him sit down, and fed him very well; and he knocked this said cradle into over five hundred thousand pieces by hitting it in the middle with his fist out of spite, protesting that he would never go back there.

CHAPTER 5

*Of the deeds of the noble Pantagruel
in his youth.*

THUS Pantagruel went on growing from day to day and thrived visibly, at which his father rejoiced by natural affection, and had him made, since he was small, a crossbow to play at hunting little birds, which nowadays is called the great crossbow of Chantelle,[1] then sent him to school to learn and to spend his youth.

And thus he came to Poitiers to study, and profited well by it; in which place, seeing that the students were sometimes at loose ends and did not know how to spend the time, he had compassion on them, and one day took, from a huge mass of rock that they call Passelourdin, a big boulder about twelve fathoms square and fourteen span thick, and set it on four pillars in the middle of a field, very casually; so that the said students, when they didn't know what else to do, might spend their time climbing on the said boulder and feasting there with flagons, hams, and pasties galore, and scratching their names on it with a knife; and now it is called The Raised Stone [La Pierre Levée]. And in memory of this, today no one is entered as matriculated in the said University of Poitiers, unless he has drunk of the Caballine spring of Croustelles, gone to Passelourdin,[2] and climbed up onto the Raised Stone.

Subsequently, reading the fair chronicles of his ancestors, he found that of Geoffroy de Lusignan, known as Geoffroy Sabertooth, grandfather of the cousin-in-law of the elder sister of the aunt of the son-in-law of the uncle of his mother-in-law's daughter-in-law, was buried at Maillezais; so one day he took French leave to pay him a visit as a good man should. And, leaving Poitiers with some of his mates, they passed through Ligugé, visiting the noble Abbé Ardillon, through Lusignan, through Sansay, through Celles, through Colognes, through Fontenay-le-Comte, paying their respects to the learned Tiraqueau; and from there they reached Maillezais, where he visited the sepulcher of the said Geoffroy Sabertooth, which gave him a little scare, seeing how he is represented as a madman, drawing his great scimitar halfway out of its scabbard; and he kept asking the cause of this. The canons of the said place said there was no other cause than

Pictoribus atque Poetis,[3] etc.

that is to say that painters and poets have the freedom to portray whatever they wish at their pleasure. But he did not rest content with their reply, and said:

"He is not portrayed thus without cause; and I suspect that at his death someone did him some wrong, for which he is asking vengeance of his relatives. I will look into this more fully, and will do about it what reason demands."

Then he went back, but not to Poitiers; rather he wanted to visit the other universities of France, so, going via La Rochelle, he put to sea and came to Bordeaux, where he found not much going on except the dockers playing cards on the riverbank.

From there he came to Toulouse, where he learned right well to dance and to play with the two-handed sword, as is the way of the students at the said university; but he did not stay long when he saw that they had their teachers burned alive like red herrings, saying: "God forbid I should die that way, for I'm parched enough by nature without heating myself up any further."

Then he came to Montpellier, where he found very good Mireval wines and merry company;[4] and he thought of starting to study medicine; but he considered that doctors smelled like old devils of enemas. Therefore he determined to study law; but seeing that there were only three mangy law experts and one bald one at the said place, he left; and on the road he made the Pont du Gard and the Amphitheater at Nimes, in less than three hours, which nevertheless seem to be works more divine than human; and he came to Avignon, where he had been three days when he became enamored; for the women there love to play clinchcruppers, because it's papal territory.

Seeing which his tutor, Epistémon by name, took him out of there and away to Valence[5] in Dauphiné; but he saw that there was not much doing there and that the town roughnecks used to beat up the students, which made him angry; and one fine Sunday when everyone was dancing in public and one student tried to join in the dance, the roughnecks wouldn't let him. Seeing which, Pantagruel gave chase to them all right up to the edge of the Rhône, and tried to get them all drowned; but they took cover like moles in the ground, a good half league under the Rhône. The opening still shows there.[6]

Afterward he left, and in three steps and a hop came to Angers, where he was just fine, and would have stayed for some time had the plague not driven them out.

So he came to Bourges, where he studied quite a long time, and learned a lot in the law school; and sometimes he used to say that the law books seemed to him a beautiful golden gown that was bordered with shit. "For," he said, "there are no books in the world so beautiful, so ornate, so elegant, as are the texts of the *Pandects;* but their border, to wit, the gloss by Accursius, is so foul, unspeakable, and smelly, that it's nothing but sewage and sludge."

Leaving Bourges, he came to Orléans, and there found many loutish students who made a big fuss over him when he arrived; and in a short time with them he learned to play tennis so well that he was a master at it; for the students of the said place are great practitioners of that.

And sometimes they would take him to the Islands to enjoy the game of Push-it-in [poussavant]; and as regards beating his brains out in hard studying, he did none of that, for fear of weakening his eyesight, especially since one of his professors, a character, often said in his lectures that there is nothing so bad for the eyesight as eye disease. And one day when they gave a licentiate in law to one of the students he knew who had no more knowledge of it than he could carry, but to make up for it knew a lot about dancing and playing good tennis, Pantagruel composed the epitome and motto of the licentiates of the said university, saying:

> A tennis ball at your command,
> A tennis racket in your hand,
> A law to quote (misunderstood):
> You're fit for your licentiate's hood.[7]

CHAPTER 6

How Pantagruel met a Limousin[1]
who counterfeited the French language.

ONE day, I don't know when, Pantagruel was strolling with his companions after supper near the gate by which you go to Paris. There he met a very natty student coming along that road, and, after they had exchanged greetings, asked him:

"My friend, where are you coming from at this time of day?"

The student answered: "From the alme, inclyte, and celebrated academy that is vocitated Lutece."

"What does that mean?" asked Pantagruel of one of his men.

"It means," he said, "from Paris."

"So you come from Paris?" he said. "And how do you spend your time, you gentleman students, in the said Paris?"

Replied the student: "We transfretate the Sequana at the dilucule and crepuscule; we deambulate through the compita and quadrivia of the city; we despumate the Latial verbocination, and, like verisimilar amorabunds, we captate the benevolence of the omnijunctive, omniform, and omnigenous feminine sex. On certain diecules, we invisitate the lupanars, and, in venerean ecstasy, inculcate our vereters into the most recondite recesses of the pudenda of these most amiable meretricules;[2] then we cauponize, in the meritorius tabernae of the Fir Cone, the Castle, the Magdalen, and the Mule, lovely vervecine spatulae, performinate with petrosil; and if, by force of fortune, there is a rarity of pecunia in our marsupiae, and these are drained of ferruginous metal, for the scot we dimit our codices and oppignorated vestments, prestolating the tabellaries to come from the patristic penates and Lares."[3]

To which Pantagruel said: "What the devil language is this? By God, you're some sort of heretic."

"No, Signor," said the student; "for liberissimily, as soon as there illucesces some minutule sliver of daylight, I denigrate into one of these so well architectated minsters, and there, irrorating myself with fair lustral water, I mumble a snatch of some missic precation of our sacricules. And, submirmillating my horary precules, I elave and absterge my anima of its nocturnal inquinations. I revere the Olympicoles, I worshipfully venerate the supernal astripotent. I delectate and redame my proximates.

I serve the Decaligic prescripts, and, according to the faculty let of my vis, do not discede from them the width of an unguicule. Veriform indeed it is that, by reason that Mammon does not supergurgitate a drop into locules, I am just a bit rare and slow to supererogate eleemosynae to these egents, queritating their tipe hostiately."⁴

"Oh, turds, turds, turds," said Pantagruel, "what is this lunatic trying to say? I think he's concocting some devilish language here, and putting a spell on us like some enchanter."

To which one of his men said: "My Lord, beyond a doubt this fop is trying to counterfeit the language of the Parisians; but he does nothing but flay Latin, and thinks he's Pindarizing that way; and it really seems to him that he's some great orator in French, because he disdains the common way of speaking."

To which Pantagruel said: "Is that true?"

The student replied: "Signor Missayre, my genius is not nately apt for what this flagitious nebulon says, to excoriate the cuticle of our Gallic vernacule, but viceversically I fervidly operate, and by veles and rames applicate myself to locuplete it from the Latinicome redundance."⁵

"By God!" said Pantagruel, "I'll teach you to talk; but first answer me: Where are you from?"

To which the student said: "The primeval origin of my aves and ataves was indigenous to the Lemovic regions, where requiesces the corpus of the agiotate Saint Martial."⁶

"I quite understand," said Pantagruel; "you're a Limousin, that's the size of it, and here you want to counterfeit the Parisian. All right, come here now, let me give you a lick with the comb!"

Then he took him by the throat and said to him: "You flay Latin; by Saint John, I'll make you flay the fox, for I'm going to skin you alive."

Then the poor Limousin started saying: "Hey, lookee here, gempmun. Oh, Saint Marsault, hep me. O, O, lemme be, i' the name o' Goddsmighty, and doan' touch me no more."

To which Pantagruel said: "Now you're talking naturally."

And so he left him, for the poor Limousin was beshitting all his breeches, which were made codtail style and not full-bottom, at which Pantagruel said: "Saint Alipentin! What civet!⁷ Devil take the turnip-eater, he stinks so!"

And he left him. But this gave him such an aftershock for all his life, and he was so parched, that he often said that Pantagruel had him by the throat, and a few years later he died the Roland's death, this being done by divine justice, and demonstrating what the philosopher says, and Aulus

Gellius: that it befits us to talk according to the accepted language, and, as Octavian Augustus used to say [see Aulus Gellius 1.10], that we should avoid derelict words with the same diligence as ships' masters avoid rocks at sea.

CHAPTER 7

How Pantagruel came to Paris, and of the fair books of the Library of Saint-Victor.

AFTER Pantagruel had studied very well in Orléans [Aurelians], he determined to visit the great University of Paris. But before leaving, he was notified that there was a great enormous bell at Saint-Aignan in the said Orléans, in the ground for the last two hundred and fourteen years, for it was so big that by no contrivance whatever could they even get it out of the ground, although they had applied to it all the means set down by Vitruvius, *De architectura,* Albertus, *De re aedificatoria,* Euclid, Theon, Archimedes, and Hero, *De ingeniis;* for all this was no use at all. Wherefore, willingly bowing to the humble request of the citizens and inhabitants of the said city, he determined to carry it to the bell tower destined for that.

Indeed, he came to the place where it was and lifted it out of the ground with his little finger, as easily as you would a sparrowhawk's jingle. And before carrying it to the bell tower, Pantagruel undertook to play an aubade with it throughout the town, and have it rung in all the streets, while carrying it in his hand, which greatly delighted everyone; but one great misfortune resulted, for, from his carrying it thus and ringing it in all the streets, all the good Orléans wine turned and spoiled, which people noticed only the following night, for everyone felt so thirsty from having drunk of the turned wines that they did nothing but spit as white as Maltese cotton, and said: "We've got the Pantagruel, and our throats are salty."

This done, he came to Paris with his men. And at his entry everyone came out to see him—as you well know, the populace of Paris is stupid by nature: stupid, natural, sharp, and flat—and they looked at him in great consternation, and not without great fear that he might carry off the Law Courts somewhere else, into some land *a remotis* [far away], as his father had carried off the bells of Notre-Dame to fasten on his mare's neck.

And after he had stayed there a certain length of time and had studied extremely well in all the seven liberal arts, he was wont to say that it was a good town to live in but not to die in, for the gravediggers at Saint-Innocent's used to warm their tails with dead men's bones.[1] And he found the Library of Saint-Victor most magnificent, especially certain books he found in it, of which the repertory follows; and *primo*:[2]

Bigua salutis [The cart of salvation].

Bragueta juris [The codpiece of the law].

Pantofla decretorum [The slipper of the decrees].

Malogranatum vitiorum [The pomegranate of vices].

The Nest Egg of Theology.

Le Vistempenard des Prescheurs, composé par Turelupin [*The Feather Duster of the Preachers,* composed by Hooligan].

La Couillebarine des Preux [The Elephant Balls of the Worthies].

The Saltpeter of the Bishops.[3]

Marmotreus *De baboinis et cingis, cum commento d'Orbellis* [Marmosetus, *On baboons and monkeys, with comments by des Orbeaux*].[4]

Decree of the University of Paris concerning the gorgiasity of harlots.

The Apparition of Saint Gertrude to a Nun of Poissy in Labor.

Ars honeste pettandi in societate [*The art of farting decorously in society*], by Master Hardouin.

The Mustard-Pot of Penitence.

The Leggings, alias the Boots, of Patience.

Formicarium artium [The anthill of the College of the Arts].

De brodiorum usu et honestate chopinandi, per Silvestrem Prieratem, Jacospinum [*On the use of broths, and on respectable tippling,* by Silvester of Prierio, a Jacobite].

The Wittol in Court.

The Notaries' Sweet Spot.

The Marriage Packet.

The Crucible of Contemplation.

The Balderdash of Law.

The Goad to Wine.

The Spur of Cheese.

Decrotatorium scholarium [The scouring-brush of the students].

Tartaretus, *De modo cacandi* [Craparetus, *On the methodology of shitting*].

The Fanfares of Rome.

Bricot, *De differentiis soupparum* [*On the distinctions between dips*].

Le Culot de Discipline [The Bottom Line of Discipline].

The Gym Shoe of Humility.

Le Tripier de bon Pensement [*The Tripod of Worthy Thinking;* sounds like "The Tripe of Good Paunch-Filling"].

The Caldron of Magnanimity.

The Entangling Enticements of the Confessors.

The Curates' Flick on the Nose.

Reverendi Patris Fratris Lubini, Provincialis Bavardie, *De croquendis lardonibus libri tres* [Reverend Father Friar Gulligut Smellsmock, Provincial of Prattleborough, *On the nibbling of bacon snacks, three books*].

Pasquilli, Doctoris marmorei, *De capreolis cum chardoneta comedendis, tempore Papali ab Ecclesia interdicto* [Pasquin, the Marmoreal Doctor,[5] *On eating roe-deer with artichokes in Lenten time when it is forbidden by the Church*].

The Invention of the Holy Cross,[6] for six characters, played by the clerics of Sharpersville.

The Spectacles of the Roming [lit. Rome-bound; but also roaming] *Pilgrims.*

On the manner of making black puddings, by Mayr.

The Bagpipe of the Prelates.

Beda, *De optimitate triparum* [*On the optimity of tripes*].[7]

The Advocates' Lament over the Reform of Goodies [dragées].[8]

The Pettifoggery of the Attorneys.

On peas with bacon, with commentary [cum commento].

The Goodies of Indulgences.

The most Illustrious doctor of both branches of the law, Master Pilferus Scrapepenny, *On coping with the idiocies of the glosses of Accursius, a most lucidly unraveled treatise.*

The Stratagems of the Franc-Archer of Baignolet.[9]

Franc-Taupin, *On military matters, with illustrations,* by Weakknees [Tevoti].

On the practice and utility of skinning horses and mares, written by Our Master de Quebecu.

The Sauciness of the Husbandmen.

Our Master Rostocostokickintheass, *On serving mustard after the meal,* fourteen books, collected by Master Vaurillon.[10]

The Groom's Party of the Church Officers.

A most subtle question, whether a chimera, bombinating in the void, can devour second intentions, and it was debated for ten days at the Council of Constance.

The Insatiable Appetite of the Advocates.

The Jumblebotches [barbouilamenta] *of Scotus.*

The Batwing Headgear of the Cardinals.

On removing spurs, eleven decades, by Master Albericum de Rosata.

By the same, *On a military occupation of the hair, three books.*

The Entry of Antonio de Leiva into the Territory of Brazil.[11]

Marforio, a scholarship student with a baccalaureate in Rome, *On skinning and pulping the cardinals' mules.*[12]

Response by him *Against those who say that the pope's mule eats only at his hours.*

Prognostication that begins: "To Silvius Bullyballock," offered by Our Master Emptyhead [Silvi Triquebille . . . M.n. Songecruyson].

Nine novenas of Bishop Boudarin, *On the profits from emulgences,* with a papal privilege for three years, no more.

The Shittershatter [chiabrena] of the Maidens.

The Shaven Tail of the Widows.

The Capuchin [coqueluche] *of the Monks.*[13]

The Pray-Acting of the Celestine Fathers.

The Toll-Collection of Mendicancy.

The Tooth-Clatter of the Down-and-Outers.

The Rat-Trap of the Theologians.

The Mouthpiece of the Master of Arts.

The Single-Tonsured Scullions of Ockham.

Our Master Saucelicker, *On scrutinifications of the canonical hours, forty books.*

The Tumbletorium of the Confrairies, author unknown.

The Bottomless Pit of the Gluttonous Monks.

The Goatstink of the Spaniards, supercockcrowed by Brother Inigo.[14]

The Worming-Powder of the Sad Sacks.

The Poltroonery of Matters Italian, by Master Brûlefer.[15]

R. Lullius, *On the casual tomfooleries of princes.*

The Twatatorium of hypocrisy, author Jacob Hochstraten, hereticometrist.[16]

Hotballs [chaultcouillons], *On the guzzling-bouts of doctoral candidates and doctors,* eight highly lively books.

The Fart-Volleys of the Bullists, Copyists, Scriveners, Brief-Writers, Referencaries, and Daters, compiled by Regis.

Perpetual Almanac for Gouties and Poxies.

The way to sweep out glues [Maneries ramonandi fournellos], by Master Eccium.[17]

The String of the Merchants.

The Creature Comforts of Monastic Life.

The Gallimaufry of the Bigots.

The History of the Hobgoblins.

The Mendicancy of the Well-Paid Soldiers.

The Booby Traps of the Ecclesiastical Judges.

The Thatch of the Treasurer's Roofs.

The fun and games of the sophists [Badinatorium sophistarum].

Antipericatametanaparbeugedamphicribrationes merdicantium.[18]

The Symbolic Snail of the Rhymesters.

The Propelling Bellows of the Alchemists.

The Flimflam of the Questing Friars, Pickscraped Up, by Brother Serratis.

The Shackles of Life in Orders.

The Rackets of the Tumblers.

The Elbow-Rest of Old Age.

The Provender-Bag of Nobility.

Monkey's Paternoster.

The Handcuffs of Piety.

The Kettle of Ember Days.

The Judge's Cap of Political Life.

The Fly-Whisk of the Hermits.

The Capuchin of the Penitentiary Priests

The Backgammon of the Banging Friars.

Blockheadus, *On the life and decency of show-offs* [*De vita et honestate*].

Moral interpretations [*Moralisationes*] *of the Sorbonic lyripipion*, by Master Doltium.

The Knickknacks of the Travelers.

The Medications of the Potative Bishops.[19]

The Clangjanglings [*Tarraballationes*] *of the doctors of Cologne against Reuchlin.*[20]

The Ladies' Jingle-Bells.[21]

The Martingale[22] *of the Crappers.*

The Whirligigs of the Tennis-Scorers, by Friar Poopball [F. Pedebilletis].

The Clodhoppers of Stoutheartedness.

The Masquerades of the Sprites and Goblins.

Gerson, *On the removability of a pope by the Church.*[23]

The Broom of the Titled and the Graduates.

Johannes Dytebrodius,[24] *On the terribility of excommunications, a headless little book* [*libellus acephalos*].

The device for invoking devils and she-devils, by Master Guingolfus.[25]

The Hodgepodge of the Perpetual Beggars.

The Morris Dance of the Heretics.

The Crutches of Cajetan.

Babybib, the Cherubic Doctor,[26] *On the origin of the hairypaws and the rites of the wrynecks* [*De origine patepelutarum et torticollorum ritibus*], *seven books.*

Sixty-Nine Well-Thumbed Vintage Breviaries.

The Midnight Mass [*Godemarre*][27] *of the Five Orders of Mendicant Friars.*

The Lady Skinner of Rascals, extracted from the tawny boot incornifistibulated in the *Angelic Summa.*[28]

The Brooder Over Cases of Conscience.

The Pot-Belly of Presiding Judges.

The Donkeyprickery of the Abbots.

Sutoris [Couturier], *Against someone who called him a scoundrel, and that scoundrels are not condemned by the Church.*

The commode-pot of the medics [Cacatorium medicorum].

The Chimney-Sweep of Astrology.

Fields of enemas [Campi clysteriorum], by S. C.[29]

The Fart-Puller of the Apothecaries.

The Kissass of Surgery.

Justinian, *De cagotis tollendis* [*On the exaltation of hypocrites*].

The Antidotery of the soul [*Antidotarium animae*].

Merlin Coccai, *On the fatherland of the devils.*

Of which some are already in print, and the others are now being printed in that noble city of Tübingen.[30]

CHAPTER 8

*How Pantagruel, while in Paris,
received a letter from his father Gargantua,
and a copy of the same.*

PANTAGRUEL studied very well, as you understand well enough, and profited accordingly, for he had understanding enough for two, and a memory with a capacity of twelve skins and bottles of oil, and, as he was thus staying there, one day he received from his father a letter couched in the following manner:

"Very Dear Son,

"Among the gifts, graces, and prerogatives with which God Almighty the Sovereign Plasmator endowed and adorned human nature in its beginning, this one seems to me singular and excellent by which it can, in its mortal state, acquire a species of immortality, and, in the course of our transitory life, perpetuate its name and its seed, which is done by lineage sprung from us in lawful marriage. Whereby is to some extent restored to us what was taken from us by the sin of our first parents, who were told that because they had not been obedient to the command of God the Creator, they would die, and by death would be reduced to nothing that most magnificent plasmature in which man had been created.

"But, by this means of seminal propagation, there remains in the children what was lost in the parents, and in the grandchildren what perished in the children, and so on in succession until the hour of the final judgment, when Jesus Christ will have restored to God the Father His kingdom, peaceful, out of all danger and contamination of sin; for then will cease all generations and corruptions, and the elements will be through with their continual transmutations, seeing that peace, so greatly desired, will be consummate and perfected, and that all things will be reduced to their end and period.[1]

"So not without just and equitable cause I give thanks unto God, my Preserver, for having given me the power to see my hoary old age flower again in your youth; for when, by the pleasure of Him Who rules and orders all things, when my soul shall leave this human habitation, I shall not account myself to be totally dying, but passing from one place to another, considering that in you and through you I remain in my visible image in this world, living, seeing, and frequenting honorable people and my friends as I used to; which association of mine has been, thanks to the help and grace of God, not without sin, I confess (for we all sin, and continually beseech God to erase our sins), but without reproach.

"Wherefore, even as in you abides the image of my body, if the soul's behavior did not likewise shine out, you would not be judged the guardian and treasure-house of the immortality of our name, and the pleasure I would take in seeing this would be small, considering that the least part of me, which is the body, would remain, and the best, which is the soul (and by which our name remains held in benediction among men), would be degenerated and adulterated; which I do not say from any distrust I might have of your virtue, which has already been tested for me before now, but to encourage you the more strongly to profit, from well to better. And what I write you at present is not so much in order that you may live in this virtuous way, as that in living and having lived thus you may rejoice, and refresh yourself with as good a heart, for the future.

"You may well remember how, to perfect and consummate this undertaking, I have spared nothing, but have assisted you just as if I had no other treasure in this world but to see you once in my life absolute and perfect both in virtue, honor, and valor, and in every liberal and praiseworthy branch of learning, and to leave you so, after my death, as a mirror representing the person of myself your father, and if not as excellent and such in fact as I wish you to be, assuredly indeed such in desire.

"But even though my late father, of esteemed memory, Grandgousier, had devoted all his endeavor to having me profit in all politic perfection and learning, and my labor and application corresponded very well to his desire, indeed surpassed it, nonetheless, as you may well understand, the time was not so suitable or favorable for letters as it is at present, and I did not have the abundance of such tutors as you have had.

"The time was still dark, and smacking of the infelicity and calamity of the Goths,[2] who had brought all good literature to destruction; but, by God's goodness, in my day light and dignity has been restored to letters, and I see such improvement in these that at present I would hardly be accepted into the lowest class of little grammar-school boys, I who in my prime was reputed (not wrongly) the most learned man of the said century, which I do not say out of vain boastfulness—although I might honorably do so in writing you, as you have the authority of Marcus Tullius in his book *On old age*, and Plutarch's statement in the book entitled *How a man may praise himself without opprobrium*—but to instill in you the desire to aim still higher.

"Now all branches of learning are reestablished, languages restored: Greek, without which it is shameful for a man to call himself learned; Hebrew, Chaldean, Latin; truly elegant and correct printings are now customary, which were invented in my time by divine inspiration, as was, conversely, artillery by diabolical suggestion. The whole world is full of erudites, of very learned teachers, of very ample libraries; and, in my judgment, neither in Plato's time, nor Cicero's, nor Papinian's, were there such facilities for study as we see now; and henceforth no one must appear in public or in company if he is not well polished in Minerva's workshop.

"I see today's brigands, hangmen, adventurers, and grooms more learned than the scholars of my time. What am I to say next? Women and girls have aspired to his celestial laud and manna of good learning, with the result that at the age I am now, I have been constrained to learn Greek letters, which I had not despised like Cato but had not had time to master in my youth; and I am prone to take delight in reading Plutarch's *Moralia,* Plato's *Dialogues,* the *Monuments* of Pausanias, and the *Antiquities* of Athenaeus, as I await the hour when it shall please God my Creator to call me and bid me depart from this earth.

"Wherefore, my son, I exhort you to employ your youth to profit well in studies and virtues. You are in Paris, you have your tutor Epistémon: one of them by live spoken instructions, the other by laudable examples, can teach you.

"I intend and want you to learn languages perfectly: first Greek, as Quintilian will have it; secondly, Latin; then Hebrew for the Holy Writ, and likewise Chaldean and Arabic; and for you to form your style, as regards Greek, in imitation of Plato; as for Latin, of Cicero. Let there not be a history you do not have present in your memory, for which you will find help in the cosmography of those who have written about it.

"Of the liberal arts, geometry, arithmetic, and music, I gave you a little taste when you were still small, at age five or six; go after the rest, and know all the canons of astronomy, but leave aside divinatory astrology and Lully's art as abuses and vanities.

"Of civil law, I want you to know the fine texts by heart, and collate them philosophically. And as for the knowledge of nature's works, I want you to devote yourself to that with care: let there be no sea, stream, or spring, whose fish you do not know; all the birds of the air, all the trees, shrubs, and bushes of the forests, all the herbs of the earth, all the metal hidden in the bowels of the depths, the precious stones of the entire Orient and Southern Hemisphere: let nothing be unknown to you.

"Then carefully review the books of the Greek, Arabian, and Latin doctors, without disdaining the Talmudists and Cabalists, and, by frequent dissections,[3] get yourself a perfect knowledge of the other world, which is man.[4] And for certain hours of the day begin to get acquainted with the Holy Scriptures, first in Greek the New Testament and Acts of the Apostles, then the Old Testament in Hebrew. In sum, let me see you an abyss of knowledge; for now that you are growing up and becoming a man, you will have to come forth out of this tranquillity and repose of study, and knighthood and the use of arms to defend my house and succor our friends in all their affairs against the assaults of evildoers.

"And I want you shortly to test how much you have gained, which you cannot do better than by maintaining conclusions in every branch of knowledge, publicly, before all comers and against all comers,[5] and frequenting the literati who abound both in Paris and elsewhere.

"But because according to Solomon the wise, wisdom does not enter into an ill-disposed soul, and science without conscience[6] is but ruin of the soul—it behooves you to serve, love, and fear God, and in Him put all your thoughts and all your hope; and by faith formed of charity,[7] be adjoined to Him, in such wise that you will never be sundered from Him by sin. Hold suspect the abuses of the world; set not your heart on vanity, for this life is transitory, but the word of God abides eternally. Be helpful to all your neighbors, and love them as yourself. Revere your tutors. Shun the company of those you don't want to resemble; and as for the graces that God has granted you, these do not receive in vain. And when you know you have all the learning acquired yonder, return to me, so that I may see you and give you my blessing before I die.

"My son, the peace and grace of Our Lord be with you. *Amen.*

"From Utopia, this seventeenth day of the month of March,

Your father,
GARGANTUA."

This letter received and read, Pantagruel took fresh heart and was inflamed more than ever to profit; so that, to see him study and progress, you would have said that his mind among the books was like fire amid the heather, so tireless and enthusiastic it was.

CHAPTER 9

How Pantagruel found Panurge,
whom he loved all his life.

Oₙₑ day Pantagruel, strolling outside the city near the Abbaye Saint-Antoine, chatting and philosophizing with his men and a few students, met a man of handsome stature and elegant in every bodily feature, but pitiably wounded in various parts, and in such sorry condition that he seemed to have made his escape from the dogs, or rather he looked like an apple picker from the Perche country.

From as far off as Pantagruel saw him, he said to his companions:

"Do you see that man coming along the Charanton Bridge road? 'Pon my word, he is poor only in fortune, for from his physiognomy I assure you that Nature brought him forth from some rich and noble line, but the accidents that happen to the adventurous have reduced him to such penury and indigence."

And as soon as he was right up among them, he asked:

"My friend, I request you please to stay here a bit and answer the questions I ask, and you will not be sorry, for I am very eager to give you what help I can in the plight I see you in, for I have great pity for you. Therefore, my friend, tell me: Who are you? Where are you coming from? Where are you going? What are you seeking? And what is your name?"

The fellow answers him in the Germanic tongue:

"Juncker, Gott geb euch Glück unnd hail. Zuvor, lieber Juncker, ich las euch wissen, das da ir mich von fragt, ist ein arm unnd erbarmglich ding, unnd wer vil darvon zu sagen, welches euch verdruslich zu hoeren, unnd mir zu erzelen wer, vie vol, die Poeten unnd Orators vorzeiten haben gesagt in irem Sprüchen und Sentenzen, das die Gedechtnus des Ellends unnd Armuot vorlangs erlitten ist ain grosser Lust." [1]

To which Pantagruel replied: "My friend, I don't understand a thing of this gibberish; so, if you want to be understood, speak another language."

Then the fellow answered him: "Al barildim gotfano dech min brin alabo dordin falbroth ringuam albaras. Nin porth zadikim almucathim milko prin al elmim enthoth dal heben ensouim: kuthim al dum alkatim nim broth dechoth porth min michais im endoth, pruch dal maisoulum hol moth dansrilrim lupaldas im voldemoth. Nin hur diavosth mnarbotim dal gousch palfrapin duch im scoth pruch galeth dal Chinon, min foulchrich al conin butathen doth dal prim."[2]

"Do you make anything out of that?" said Pantagruel to the others.

To which Epistémon said: "I think it's a language of the Antipodes; the devil himself couldn't get his teeth into it."

Then said Pantagruel: "Mate, I don't know if the walls will understand you, but not one of us understands a word."

Then the fellow said: "Signor mio, voi vedete per exemplo che la cornamusa non suona mai, s'ela non a il ventre pino; cosi io parimente non vi saprei contare le mie fortune, se prima il tribulato ventre non a la solita refectione, al quale è adviso che le mani e li denti abbui perso il loro ordine naturale et del tuto annichillati."[3]

To which Epistémon retorted: "As much out of one as the other."

Then said Panurge: "Lard, ghest tholb be sua virtiuss be intelligence ass yi body schall biss be naturall relvtht, tholb suld of me pety have, for nature hass ulss egualy maide; bot fortune sum exaltit hess, an oyis deprevit. Non ye less viois mou virtius deprevit and virtiuss men discrivis, for, anen ye lad end, iss non gud."[4]

"Even less," responded Pantagruel.

Then said Panurge: "Jona andie, guaussa goussyetan behar da erremedio, beharde, versela ysser lan da. Anbates, otoyyes nausu, eyn essassu gourr ay proposian ordine den. Non yssena bayta facheria egabe, genherassy badia sadassu noura assia. Aran hondovan gualde eydassu nay dassuna. Estou oussyc eguinan soury hin er darstura eguy harm. Genicoa plasar vadu."[5]

"Are you there, Genicoa?" replied Epistémon.

At which Carpalim said: "Sain Ninian! you're a fucking Scotchman, or I miss my guess."

Then Panurge replied: "Prug frest strinst sorgdmand strochdt drhds pag brleland Gravot Chavigny Pomardière rusth pkalhdracg Devinière près Nays: Bouille kalmuch monach drupp delmeupplistrincq dlrnd dodelb up drent loch minc stzrinquald de vins ders cordelis hur jocststzampenards."[6]

At which Epistémon remarked: "Are you speaking Christian, my friend, or Pathelin language. No, that's Lanternese talk."

Then said Panurge: "Heere, ie en spreeke anders geen taele, dan kersten taele: my dunct nochtans, al en seg ie v niet een woordt, myuen noot v claert ghenonch wat ie beglere; gheest my unyt bermherticheyt yet waer un ie ghevoet mach zunch."[7]

To which Pantagruel retorted: "As much as that."

Then said Panurge: "Seignor, de tanto hablar yo soy cansado. Por que suplico a Vostra Reverentia que mire a los preceptos evangeliquos, para que ellos movant Vostra Reverentia a lo que es de conscientia; y si ellos non bastarent para mover Vostra Reverentia a piedad, supplico que mire a la piedad natural, la qual yo creo que le movra como es de razon, y con esto non digo mas."[8]

To which Pantagruel replied; "All right my friend, I have no doubt whatever that you can speak various languages well; but tell us what you want in some language we can understand."

Then said the fellow: "Myn Herre, endog, jeg med inghen tunge talede, lygesom boeen, ocg uskvvlig creatner! Myne Kleebon, och my ne legoms magerhed uudviser allygue klalig huvad tyng meg meest behoff girereb, som aer sandeligh mad och drycke: hwarfor forbarme teg omsyder offvermeg; och bef ael at gyffuc meg nogeth; aff huylket ieg kand styre myne groeendes maghe lygeruss son mand Cerbero en soppe forsetthr. Soa shal tue loeffve lenge och lycksaligth."[9]

"I think," said Eusthenes, "that the Goths spoke thus, and, if God so willed it, thus would we speak with our rump."

Then said the fellow: "Adoni, scolom lecha. Im ischar harob hal habdeca, bemeherah thithen li kikar lehem, chancathub: Laah al Adonai chonen ral."[10]

To which Epistémon replied: "Now I *have* fully understood: for this is Hebrew talk very eloquently pronounced."

Then said the fellow: "Despota ti nyn panagathe doiti sy mi uc artodotis? horas gar limo analis comenon eme athlios. Ce en to metaxy eme uc eleis udamos, zetis de par emu ha u chre, ce homos philologi pandes homologusi tote logus te ce rhemata peritta hyrparchin, opote pragma asto pasi delon esti. Entha gar anancei monon logi isin, hina pragmata (hon peri amphisbetumen) me phosphoros epiphenete."[11]

"What?" said Carpalim, Pantagruel's lackey. "That's Greek, I understood it. And how so? have you lived in Greece?"

Then said the fellow: "Agonou dont oussys vou denaguez algarou, nou den farou zamist vous mariston ulbrou, fousquez vou brol tam bredaguez moupreton den goul houst, daguez daguez nou croupys fost bardounnoflist nou grou. Agou paston tol nalprissys hourtou los echatonous, prou dhouquys brol panygou den bascrou noudous caguons goulfren goul oust troppassou."[12]

"It seems to me I understand," said Pantagruel: "for either this is the language of my country of Utopia, or else it sounds like it."

And as he meant to begin some remark, the fellow said: "Jam toties vos, per sacra, perque deos deasque omnis obtestatus sum, ut, si qua vos pietas

permovet, egestatem meam solaremini, nec hilum proficio clamans et
ejulans. Sinite, queso, sinite, viri impii,

Quo me fata vocant.

"Abire, nec ultra vanis vestris interpellationibus obtundatis, memores
veteris illius adagii, quo venter famelicus auriculis carere dicitur."[13]

"Really, my friend," said Pantagruel, "don't you know how to speak
French?"

"Indeed I do very well, My Lord," replied the fellow, "thank God. It's
my native mother tongue, for as a youngster I was born and brought up
in the garden of France, that is Touraine."

"Then," said Pantagruel, "tell us what is your name, and where you
come from; for 'pon my word, I've already taken such a great liking for
you that if you will grant me my will, you will never budge from my
company, and you and I will form a new pair in friendship such as was
that which existed between Aeneas and Achates."

"My Lord," said the fellow, "my real proper baptismal name is
Panurge, and at present I am coming from Turkey, where I was taken as
a prisoner when to my misfortune we went to Mytilene,[14] and I'd be glad
to tell you my adventures, which are more wonderful than those of
Ulysses; but since you wish to keep me with you—and I gladly accept the
offer, and protest that I will never leave you, were you to go to all the
devils—we shall have, at a more convenient time, ample leisure for me to
tell them; for at the present moment I have a very urgent need to feed:
sharpened teeth, empty stomach, dry throat, clamorous appetite, everything is set and ready. If you want to put me to work, it will be a pleasure
for you to watch me guzzle. For Heaven's sake, arrange it."

Then Pantagruel ordered them to take him to his lodging and bring
him victuals aplenty, which was done, and he ate very well that evening,
and went to bed right after, and slept until dinner time the next day, so
that it took him only three steps and a hop from bed to table.

CHAPTER 10

*How Pantagruel equitably judged
a marvelously difficult and obscure controversy,
so justly that his judgment
was pronounced most admirable.*

Pantagruel, fully mindful of his father's letter and admonitions, one day decided to test out his learning.

Accordingly, at all the city's crossroads he posted conclusions[1] in the number of nine thousand seven hundred and sixty-four, in all fields of learning, in these touching on all the gravest doubts there were in all these fields.

And first of all, on the Rue du Feurre, he maintained them against all the theologians, for a period of six weeks, from four o'clock in the morning until six in the evening, except for a two-hour interval for eating and refreshment.

And present at this were most of the lords of the Court, the masters of requests, presidents, councillors, treasury men, secretaries, advocates, and others, together with the sheriffs of the said city, besides the doctors and the professors of canon law. And note that most of these really took the bit in their teeth; but notwithstanding their ergos[2] and fallacies, he made monkeys of them all, and showed them all visibly that they were just calves in frocks.

Whereat everyone began sounding off and talking about his marvelous learning, even to the gammers, washerwomen, women brokers, women roast meat sellers, penknife sellers, and others, who, when he passed in the street, used to say: "He's the one!" At which he took pleasure, as did Demosthenes, prince of Greek orators, when a huddled old woman, pointing her finger at him, said: "That's the one!" [See Erasmus *Adages* 1.10.43].

Now in this very season there was a suit pending in court between two great lords, one of whom was Milord of Kissass, plaintiff, on the one hand, and Milord of Sniffshit, defendant, on the other, whose controversy was so lofty and difficult in point of law that the court of the Parlement could make out of it nothing but High German.

Wherefore, by command of the king, were assembled the four stoutest

167

and most learned men of all the Parlements of France, together with the Great Council, and all the principal professors of the universities, not only of France but also of England and Italy, like Jason, Philippus Decius, Petrus de Petronibus, and a pile of other old Rabanists. Thus assembled, for the space of forty-six weeks they had not been able to get their teeth into it or understand the case clearly to put it into law in any way whatever, at which they were so vexed that they were foully beshitting themselves for shame.

But one of them, named Du Douhet, the most learned, expert, and prudent of them all, one day when they were all philogrobilized in the brain, said to them:

"Gentlemen, we've been here a long time now already without doing anything but spend, and we can find neither bottom nor shore in this matter, and the more we study it the less we understand about it, which is a great shame to us and burden on our conscience; and in my opinion we shall come out of it only to our dishonor, for in our deliberations we do nothing but prattle. But here is what has occurred to me. You have certainly heard of that great personage named Master Pantagruel, who has been recognized to be learned beyond the capacity of the present day in the great disputations he has held publicly against all comers? My advice is that we call him and confer with him about this matter, for never will man get to the bottom of this if that man does not."

To which all these councillors and doctors willingly consented.

And so they sent for him immediately, and asked him to be good enough to canvas the case and scrutinize it thoroughly, and make his report to them on it as he should see fit to in real legal form; and they delivered into his hands the briefsacks and documents, which made up almost a load for four stout jackasses.

But Pantagruel said to them: "Gentlemen, are the two lords who have this lawsuit between them still alive?"

To which he was answered "yes."

"Then what the devil," said he, "is the use of all these tumblejumbles of papers and copies you're handing me? Isn't the best thing to hear their dispute by the spoken word rather than to read these babooneries, which are nothing but deceits, diabolical wiles of Cepola, and subversions of justice? For I am sure that you and all those through whose hands the lawsuit has passed have contrived whatever you could pro and contra, and, in case their controversy was patent and easy to judge, have obscured it by stupid and irrational reasons and inept opinions of Accursius, Baldus, Bartolus, De Castro, De Imola, Hippolytus, Panormitanus, Bertachin,

Alexander, Curtius and those other old curmudgeons who never understood the slightest law of the *Pandects,* and were nothing but fat blackheads, ignorant of everything necessary for the understanding of the laws.

"For, as is fully certain, they had no knowledge of any language either Greek or Latin, but only Gothic and barbarian; and nevertheless the laws are taken first of all from the Greeks, as you have Ulpian's testimony, *l. posteriori De orig. juris,* and all the laws are full of Greek words and sayings; and secondly, they are all drawn up in Latin, the most elegant and ornate there is in the whole Latin language, and I would not readily except from this either Sallust, or Varro, or Cicero, or Seneca, or Livy, or Quintilian. So how could those old dreamers have been able to understand the text of the laws, who never set eyes on a good book in the Latin language, as appears manifestly from their style, which is the style of a chimney sweep or a cook and bottlewasher, not of a jurisconsult?

"Furthermore, seeing that the laws are extracted from the milieu of moral and natural philosophy, how are these idiots to understand it who, by God, have studied less philosophy than my mule. In regard to humane letters and knowledge of antiquities and history, they were loaded with them like a toad with feathers, yet of these matters the laws are all full, and cannot be understood without them, as some day I will demonstrate to you more evidently in writing.

"Therefore, if you want me to take cognizance of this lawsuit, first of all have all these papers burned for me, and secondly have the two gentlemen come before me in person, and when I have heard them, I'll tell you my opinion on this, without the slightest feigning or dissimulation."

Which a few of them spoke against, since you know that in all companies there are more fools than wise men and the larger part always outnumbers the better one, as Livy says, speaking of the Carthaginians. But the said Du Douhet manfully upheld the contrary maintaining that Pantagruel had spoken well, that these registers, bills of inquest, replications, discreditings, supportings, and other such deviltries were nothing but subversions of justice and prolongation of suits, and that the devil would carry them all off if they did not proceed otherwise, according to Evangelical and philosophical equity.

In short, all the papers were burned, and the two gentlemen summoned in person. And then Pantagruel said to them:

"Are you the ones who have this vast disagreement between you?"

"Yes, Sir," said they.

"Which one of you is the plaintiff?"

"I am," said Lord Kissass.

"Now, my friend, tell me your business point by point and in truth; for 'Odsbody, if you lie about it in one single word, I'll take your head right off your shoulders and show you that in matters of justice and judgment one must speak nothing but the truth. Therefore take good care not to add or subtract anything in the account of your case. Speak on."

CHAPTER 11

How lords Kissass and Sniffshit
pleaded before Pantagruel without advocates.

So Kissass began in the following manner:
"My Lord, it is true that a gammer of my household was taking some eggs to sell in the market . . . "
"Do put your hat on,[1] Kissass," said Pantagruel.
"Many thanks, My Lord," said Kissass. "But to come to the point, there was passing between the two tropics six half-sous toward the zenith and a halfpenny, inasmuch as the Riffian Mountains that year had had a great sterility of boobytraps, resulting from a sedition of Fiddlefaddles [Ballivernes] arisen between the Gabblers [Barragouyns] and the Accursianists favoring the rebellion of the Swiss, who had assembled up to the number of a good angle to go handseling on the first hole in the year, when you give a sop to the oxen and the key to the charcoal to the maids for them to give the oats to the dogs.
"All night long, hand on the pot, they did nothing but dispatch papal bulls on foot, bulls on horseback, to hold back the boats, for the tailors wanted to make, out of the pilfered leftovers, a sackbut to cover the Ocean Sea, which for the time was pregnant with a potful of cabbage, in the opinion of the hay balers; but the doctors said that from its urine they recognized no evident sign, in the bustard's step, of eating axes with mustard, unless the Gentlemen of the Court gave a command in B-flat to the pox not to go gleaning after the silkworms, for the roughnecks already had a good start on dancing the estrindore[2] to a diapason, one foot in the fire and the head in the middle, as good old Ragot used to say.
"Ah, gentlemen, God moderates all things at His pleasure, and against

the adversities of fortune a carter broke his whip flicking noses. It was on the way back from La Bicoque,[3] when they gave Numbskullus de Cressponds [Antitus des Crossonniers] his Master's License in all doltishness; as the canon lawyers say: 'Beati lourdes, quoniam ipsi trebuchaverunt [Blessed are the dolts, for they have stumbled and fallen].' But what makes Lent so high, by Saint Fiacre of Brie, is nothing else but that

> Pentecost
> Never comes but at a cost;
> May, on we go again,
> Big wind yields to little rain.[4]

"Considering that the sergeant put the bull's eye so high at the butts that the court clerk did not therefore orbicularly lick his fingers feathered with goose plumes; and we manifestly see that everyone takes the rap for it, unless they look ocularly in perspective toward the fireplace, to the spot where hangs the sign of the wine with forty hoops, which are necessary for twenty stockings at five years' respite. At the very least, who would not rather loose the bird before slaps in the face than uncover him, for you often lose your memory when you put your hose on backward. So, God keep from harm Thibaut Mitaine!"[5]

Then said Pantagruel: "Easy now, my friend, easy, speak quietly, without anger. I understand the case, so go on."

"Now, Sir, said Kissass, "the said gammer, saying her *Gaude Marias* and *Audi Nos,*[6] could not protect herself against a backhand feint arising by virtue of the privileges of the University, except by warming herself at an angle with a basin, covering it with a seven of diamonds and giving it a flying stab as near the place as possible where they sell the old rags that the Flemish painters use when they want to put horseshoes on the grasshoppers right, and I very much marvel that the world does not lay eggs, since it's so nice to brood over them."

Here Lord Sniffshit tried to interrupt and say something, so Pantagruel said to him:

"Here, by Saint Anthony's belly, is it for you to speak without command? Here I am sweating and straining to understand the way your disagreement comes about, and you still come pestering me? Peace, in the devil's name, peace! You'll talk all you like when this man has finished. Go on," he said to Kissass, "and don't hurry."

"So," said Kissass, "seeing that the Pragmatic Sanction made no mention of it, the pope set everyone at liberty to fart at their ease, if the hose linings were not streaked, whatever poverty there might be in the world, provided one did not cross oneself with the scum of the earth, the rainbow, newly forged in Milan to hatch larks, consented that the gammer should burst the tail of the sciatic nerves on the complaint of the ballocky little fishes who then were necessary in order to understand the construction of old boots.

"Wherefore Johncalf, her cousin Gervais, stirred up by a piece of firewood, advised her not to place herself at that risk of seconding the wriggling steam without first dipping the paper in alum until *pille, nade, jocque, fore:*[7] for

Non de ponte vadit, qui cum sapientia cadit

[He does not walk from the bridge who falls in wisely],[8]

considering that the Gentlemen of the Treasury did not agree in totting up the lampreys, of which had been built the *Lunettes des Princes,*[9] newly printed in Antwerp.

"And there, Gentlemen, is what gives a bad report, and I believe the opposing party *in sacer verbo dotis:*[10] for, wishing to satisfy the king's pleasure, I had armed myself cap-à-pie with belly timber to go and see how my grape pickers had slashed their tall caps the better to play tumblemaid, and the weather was somewhat dangerous from the fair, so that several free-archers had been kept out of the parade, notwithstanding that the chimneys were high enough according to the proposition of friend Baudichon's windgalls and malanders.

"And by that means it was a great year for snailshells in the whole Artois region, which was no small improvement for my lords the firewood haulers, when they ate the shells without unsheathing and unbuttoned at the belly. And if I had my will everyone would have as fine a voice: people would play far better tennis for it, and those little tricks that people play to etymologize clogs would go down more easily into the Seine to serve forever at the Font aux Meusniers, as was once decreed by the king of Canarre, and the decision on it is still in the registry in here.

"Therefore, My Lord, I request that by your Lordship be stated and declared as is reasonable, with costs, damages, and interest."

Then said Pantagruel: "My friend, do you want to say anything more?"

Replied Kissass: "No, Sir, for I have told the whole *tu autem,* and have not altered a thing, on my honor."

"Then you," said Pantagruel, "My Lord Sniffshit, say what you want to, and be brief, but without leaving out anything that will serve the purpose."

CHAPTER 12

*How Lord Sniffshit
pleaded before Pantagruel.*

Then Milord of Sniffshit began as follows:

"My Lord and Gentlemen, if the iniquity of men were easily seen in categorical judgment, as flies can be recognized in milk,[1] the world, *quatre boeufs,*[2] would not be as rat-eaten as it is, and there would be many ears on earth that would have been gnawed away too laxly: for although everything the opposing party has said is of real down, quite true as to the letter and story of the *factum,* nevertheless, Gentlemen, hidden beneath the pot of roses are trickery and little entangling enticements.

"Must I endure that at the moment when I'm eating my lunch with my fellows, without speaking or thinking any harm, they come and vex and harass my brain, and play the antic, saying:

> He who drinks as he eats his dip,
> When he's dead, doesn't see one bit?[3]

"And, Holy Mother, how many great captains have we seen right on the battlefield, when they were giving out big chunks of the confraternity's holy bread so as to deliberate more handsomely, play the lute, sound off with the tail, and do little platform jumps! But now the world is all untracked from the corners of the bales of Leicester fleeces: one man becomes debauched, the other five, four, and two, and if the court does not impose some order, it will be as bad gleaning this year as it was, or else it will make goblets. If a poor person goes to the vats to get his muzzle lit up with cow-turds or to buy winter boots, and with sergeants passing, or else the men of the watch, receive the decoction of a clyster or the fecal matter of a chamber pot on the racket they make must one therefore pare down the testoons and fricassee the crown pieces? Are they wooden?

"Sometimes we think one thing but God does the other, and, when the sun is down, all animals are in the dark. I don't want to be believed on that unless I prove it decisively by people in broad daylight.

"In the year thirty-six, I had bought a German curtal, tall and short, of rather good wool and dyed in the grain, so the goldsmiths assured me, nevertheless the notary put some *cetera* on it. I'm not cleric enough to catch the moon in my teeth, but, at the butter pot where they were sealing the vulcanic instruments, the rumor was that the salt beef made you find the wine without a candle, even were it hidden at the bottom of a collier's sack and shod and bound with the headpiece and greave required for properly fricasseeing *rusterie,* that is, sheep's head. And it's just what they say in the proverb, that it is good to see black cows in burnt woods when you're enjoying your amours. I had Milords the clerics consulted about the matter; and for their conclusion they resolved in *frisesomorum*[4] that there is nothing like reaping in summer in a cellar well furnished with paper and ink, with pens and penknife from Lyon on the Rhône, taradiddle folderol [tarabin, tarabas]; for as soon as the suit of armor smells of garlic, rust eats out its liver, then all you do is peck back wrynecked, skirting after-dinner sleep. And that is what makes salt so dear.

"Gentlemen, do not believe that at the time when the said gammer snared the spoonbill with birdlime the better to endow the sergeant's witness, and when the innards for black pudding beat about the bush by way of the userer's purses, there was nothing better for guarding yourself from the cannibals than to take a bunch of onions, tied with three hundred turnips, and a little bit of calves' chawdron [a spicy sauce of chopped entrails], of the best alloy the alchemists have, and thoroughly smear and calcinate one's slippers fee fie fo fum, with a nice hayrack sauce, and hide in some little mole-hole, always saving the bacon snacks.

"And if the dice won't give you any throw but ambesace[5] and a chance for three at the big end, set the lady on the corner of the bed, feel her up hi diddle diddle, and drink bottoms up *depiscando grenoillibus* [unconcerned about the frogs], with fine buskined hose; that will be for the little molting goslings, who are having fun playing blow-out-the-candle, while waiting to beat the metal and heat the wax for the drinkers of good ale.

"Quite true it is that the four oxen in question had slightly short memories; at all events, since they knew the scale, they had no fear of any cormorant or Savoy duck, and the good folk of my region had good hopes for them, and said:

"These children will become great in algorism: this will be a rubric of the law for us. We cannot fail to catch the Wolf, setting our hedges on top of the windmill, of which the opposing party has spoken. But the great Devil himself became envious and set the Germans to the rear, who tippled like the devils: 'Herr, trink, trink!' Each scoring for two, for there is no likelihood that in Paris on the Petit Pont, hens on straw, and ever were they as cocky as swamp hoopers, unless they really sacrificed the pimples to the newly-forged ink with cursive or printed capital letters, it's all one to me, provided the book's headband does not breed worms there.

"And, putting the case that in the coupling of running dogs the lady jesters had sounded the catch before the notary had delivered his report by cabalistic art, it does not follow (saving better judgment by the Court) that six acres of meadow in full measure made three butts of fine ink without paying cash on the line, considering that at King Charles's [Charles VIII] funeral[6] they had the fleece in the open market for one two and one—I mean, on my oath, a wool fleece.

"And I ordinarily see in all good bagpipes that when they go piping to lure birds, by making three sweeps with a broom around a fireplace and insinuating their nomination, all they do is tense their loins and blow in her tail, if by chance it is too hot, and set 'em up in the other alley [quille luy bille],

> The letter seen and read, straightway
> The cows were back that very day.[7]

"And a similar decision was rendered on Saint Martin's Day in the year seventeen for the bad covering of Louzefougerouse,[8] to which may it please the court to give due consideration.

"I do not say indeed that one may not dispossess, in equity and with just cause, those who would drink of holy water, as they do with a weaver's trident, of which they make suppositories for those who won't hand over unless for good compensation.

" 'Tunc,' Gentlemen, 'quid juris pro minoribus? [Then what law for minors?].' For the common usage of the Salic Law is that the first firebug who steals the cow, who blows his nose in the middle of the chant without solfa-ing the cobbler's stitches, in Hail-Mary times must sublimate the penury of his member with moss gathered when you catch cold at midnight mass, to give the strappado to these Anjou wines that trip you up, neck to neck, Breton fashion.

"Concluding as above, with costs, damages, and interest."

After Lord Sniffshit had finished, Pantagruel said to Lord Kissass: "My friend, do you want to make any reply?"

To which Lord Kissass replied: "No, Sir, for I have spoken nothing but the truth about it, and in God's name let us have an end to our difference, for we are not here without great expense."

CHAPTER 13

How Pantagruel gave his decision
on the disagreement between the two lords.

THEN Pantagruel rises and assembles all the presidents, councillors, and doctors there present, and says to them: "Now then, gentlemen, you have heard, *vive vocis oraculo* [from the oracle in its living voice], the disagreement in question. What do you think about it?"

To which they replied: "We have indeed heard it, but we haven't understood devil a bit of the cause of it. Wherefore we beg you with one voice and implore you by your mercy to be willing to pronounce the sentence as you see it, and *ex nunc prout ex tunc* [from now just as from then], we find it agreeable and ratify it with our full consent."

"Well, Gentlemen," said Pantagruel, "since it is your wish, I shall do so; but I do not find the case as difficult as you do. Your paragraph *Cato,*[1] the law *Frater*, the law *Gallus*, the law *Quinque pedum*, the law *Vinum*, the law *Si dominus*, the law *Mater*, the law *Mulier bona*, the law *Si quis*, the law *Pomponius*, the law *Fundi*, the law *Emptor*, the law *Pretor*, the law *Venditor*, and so many others, are much more difficult, in my opinion."

And after that remark, he walked a turn or two around the hall, thinking very deeply, as one could judge, for he was groaning like a donkey that is saddled too tight, thinking that he must do right by each and every one, without differentiating or favoring anyone; then he went back to sit down and began to pronounce the decision as follows:

"Having seen, understood, and carefully assessed the disagreement between the Lords of Kissass and Sniffshit, the court says to them:

"That, considering the horripilation of the bat gallantly declining from the festival solstice to make passes at rifles that have been checkmated by the pawn by the evil vexations of the lucifuges which are around the latitude of Rome from an ape on horseback bending a crossbow backward, the plaintiff had just cause to calk the galleon that the gammer was inflating, one foot shod and the other bare, reimbursing him low and stiff in his conscience for as many knicknacks as there is hair on eighteen cows, and as many for the embroiderer.[2]

"Likewise he is declared innocent of the privileged case of the streaks of dried turd that he was thought to have incurred because he could not shit blithely, by the decision of a pair of gloves perfumed with fart-volleys fragrant of walnut tapers such as they use in his region of Mirebalais, releasing the bowline with the bronze bullets, from which the stable boys, like military commanders, made pies of his peas and beans interbasted by the lore with the sparrowhawk jingles made of Hungarian point which his brother-in-law carried as a memorial in a nearby basket, embroidered in gules with three chevrons weary of close scrutiny, at the angular blind from which they shoot at the vermiform popinjay with the fox-tail broom.

"But in that he charges the defendant that he was a cobbler, a cheese eater, and a man who tarred mummies, that this has not been found true on shaking it down, since the said defendant has disputed it well, and the court condemns him to pay three porringerfuls of cemented curds, prelorelitanted and codpieced as is the custom of the country, to the said defendant, payable at mid-August, in May; but the said defendant will be bound to furnish hay and tow for stopping up guttural caltrops, confustibulated with gobbets well scrutinized on the kneecap.

"And friends as before, without cost and with good reason."

This decision pronounced, the two parties departed, both content with the verdict, which was an almost incredible thing: for it had not come about since the great rains[3] and will not happen for thirteen jubilees that two parties, both contending in contradictory judgment, should be equally contented with a definitive verdict.

As for the councillors and other doctors who were present there, they remained swooning in ecstasy for a good three hours, and all ravished in admiration of the more than human wisdom of Pantagruel, which they had clearly recognized in the deciding of this judgment, so difficult and thorny, and they would have been there yet, except that people brought a lot of vinegar and rose water to restore to them their accustomed sense and understanding, for which God be everywhere praised.

CHAPTER 14

*How Panurge relates the way in which
he escaped from the hands of the Turks.*

PANTAGRUEL'S decision was immediately known and understood by everyone, and printed in large numbers, and entered in the court archives, so that people began to say:

"Solomon, who on a hunch restored the child to its mother, never demonstrated such a masterpiece of wisdom as the good Pantagruel has done. We are fortunate to have him in our country."

And indeed, they tried to make him master of requests and president in the Court; but he refused everything with gracious thanks:

"For," he said, "there is too much servitude in those offices, and those who exercise them can be saved only with great difficulty, in view of the corruption of men, and I think that, if the empty seats of the angels are not filled with a different kind of men, for thirty-seven jubilees we shall not have the Last Judgment, and Cusanus will be mistaken in his conjecture; and I inform you of this early. But if you have a few hogsheads of good wine, I would willingly accept a present of them."

Which they did willingly, and sent him the best in the city, and he drank pretty well; but poor Panurge drank of it valiantly, for he was as dry and emaciated as a red herring; so he went plodding along at it like a lean cat.

And someone admonished him, when he was half out of breath from a great tankard full of red wine, saying: "Easy, mate! You're drinking like a madman." "Devil take me," said he. "You're not talking to one of your little Paris sippers, who don't drink any more than a finch, and, like the sparrows, don't take their beakful unless you tap them on the tail. Oh, buddy, if I went up as well as I put it down [si je montasse aussi bien comme je avalle], I'd already be with Empedocles above the sphere of the moon! but I don't know what the devil this means: this wine is very good and truly delicious but the more I drink of it the thirstier I am. I think the shadow of My Lord Pantagruel engenders the thirsties, as the moon breeds catarrhs."

At which those present started laughing. Seeing which, Pantagruel said: "Panurge, what do you have to laugh about?"

"My Lord," said he, "I was telling them how very unhappy those devils the Turks are not to drink a drop of wine. If there were no other harm in Mahomet's *Alcoran,* still I would hardly place myself under his law."

"But now, tell me" said Pantagruel, "how you escaped from their hands?"

"By God, My Lord," said Panurge, "I won't lie about it in a single word.

"The blasted Turks had put me on a spit, all larded like a rabbit, for I was so emaciated that otherwise my flesh would have made very bad meat; and in that state they were having me roasted alive. Even as they were roasting me, I was commending myself to the Divine Grace, keeping in mind good Saint Lawrence, and I kept hoping in God that He would deliver me from that torment; which was done in a very strange way; for even as I was most heartily commending myself to God, crying: 'Lord God, help me! Lord God, save me! Lord God, take me out of this torment in which these treacherous dogs are holding me for maintaining Thy law!' the roaster fell asleep by the divine will, or that of some benign Mercury, who cleverly put to sleep Argus, who had a hundred eyes.

"When I saw that he was no longer turning me around and roasting me, I look at him and see that he's falling asleep. Then with my teeth I pick up an ember by the side where it isn't burned, and toss it in the lap of my roaster, and another I toss, the best I can, under a camp bed near the fireplace where lay my Mister Roaster's straw mattress.

"Immediately the fire caught in the straw, and from the straw to the bed, and from the bed to the ceiling, which was paneled with pine cut like lamp bottoms. But the good one was that the fire I had thrown into my villain roaster's lap burned his entire groin and was catching on his balls; but he himself stank so that he didn't smell it until daylight, and, jumping up like a stupid goat, he shouted out the window all he could: 'Dal baroth, dal baroth!' which amounts to saying 'Fire, fire!' and came straight for me to throw me all the way into the fire, and he had already cut the cords they had tied my hands with and was cutting the bonds on my feet.

"But the master of the house, hearing the cry of fire and already smelling the smoke from the street, where he was strolling with a few other pashas and mussafis,[1] ran up as hard as he could to give help and carry out his baggage.

"As soon as he arrives he pulls out the spit I was spitted on and killed my roaster stone dead; and he died from this for lack of proper direction or some other reason; for he ran the spit a little above the navel toward the right flank and pierced the third lobe of his liver, and the blow moving upward penetrated his diaphragm; and, running through his pericardium, the spit came out through the top of his shoulders between the spondyls [vertebrae] and the left shoulder-blade.

"True it is that on his drawing the spit out of my body I fell to the ground near the andirons, and the fall did me little harm, at all events not much, for the lard strips broke the shock.

"Then my pasha, seeing that the situation was desperate and his house was burned beyond reprieve and all his property lost, gave himself up to all the devils, calling Grilgoth, Astaroth, Rappallus, and Gribouillis, each nine times.[2] Seeing which, I felt more than a nickel's worth [pour plus de cinq solz] of fright, with this fear: Now the devils will come to carry off this lunatic; might they be just the people to carry me off too? I'm already half roasted. My lard strips will be the cause of my trouble, for these devils have a taste for lard strips, as you have the authority of the philosopher Iamblichus and Murmault in his Apologia *De bossutis et contrefactis pro magistros nostros* [*On hunchbacks and the deformed, for our masters*]. But I made the sign of the cross, shouting 'Agyos athanatos, ho Theos! [God is Holy and Immortal!].'[3] And no one came.

"Knowing this my rogue wished to pierce his heart with my spit, and to that purpose had set it against his breast, but it could not enter because it was not sharp enough even though he pressed with all his force.

"So I came up to him and said: 'Missaire Buggerino, now you're wasting your time, for you'll never kill yourself that way; yes, you will wound yourself with a good blow, and languish all your life in the hands of the barber-surgeons; but if you want, I'll kill you clean outright, so you won't feel anything; and take my word for it, for I've killed many others who have found themselves well off for it."

"Ah, my friend," he said, "please do! And for doing it I'll give you my purse. Here! Here it is! There are six hundred seraphs in it, and a few perfect diamonds and rubies."

"And where are they?" said Epistémon.

"By Saint John!" said Panurge, "they're a long way off if they're still going":

Mais où sont les neiges d'antan?

[But where are the snows of yesteryear]

"That was the greatest concern that was felt by the Parisian poet Villon."[4]

"Do finish," said Pantagruel, "I ask you, so we may know how you handled the pasha."

"On my word as a good man," said Panurge, "I'm not lying in one word. I bind him up with a miserable strip of linen that I find there, half burned, and tie him up saucily, hand and foot, with my cords, so thoroughly that he could not have resisted; then I thrust my spit through his throat and hanged him, attaching the spit to two big hooks that used to hold halberds; and I up and light a fine fire underneath, and was busy toasting my fine milord as you do red herrings in the fireplace. Then, taking his purse and a little javelin that was on the hooks, I run away at a fine gallop, and Lord knows how I smelled like a shoulder of mutton![5]

"When I had come down into the street, I found everybody there, having come up to the fire with lots of water to put it out, and seeing me half roasted, they naturally had pity on me and threw all their water on me and cooled me off joyously, which did me very much good; then they gave me something to eat, but I wasn't eating much, for they gave me only water to drink, in their way.

"No other harm did they do me, except for one ugly little Turk, hunchbacked in front, who kept furtively nibbling my lard strips; but I gave him such a hard knock on the fingers with my javelin that he didn't come back a second time; and one young Corinthian wench,[6] who had brought me a pot of East Indian Emblic plums conserved in their manner, and who was looking at my poor fly-bitten fellow here, how he had come out of the fire, for then he was reaching only down onto my knees. But note that that roasting completely cured me of a sciatica that I had been subject to for over seven years, on the side on whch my roaster let me burn when he went to sleep.

"Now while they were keeping busy with me, the fire was gaining, don't ask how, and catching more than two thousand houses, so that one of them noticed it and shouted out, saying: 'Mahomet's belly, the whole city is burning and we're wasting time here!' So everyone went off to his everyhome [Ainsi chascun s'en va à sa chascunière].[7]

"As for me, I make my way toward the gate. When I was on the little rise that is next to it, I turn around to the rear, like Lot's wife, and I saw the whole city burning, at which I was so happy I thought I'd beshit my breeches for joy; but God punished me proper for it."

"How so?" said Pantagruel.

"Even," said Panurge, "as I was watching that beautiful fire in high glee, snickering and saying: 'Ah, poor fleas, poor mice, you're going to have a bad winter, the fire is in your bed-straw!' out came more than six, indeed more than thirteen hundred and eleven dogs, large and small, all together out of the city, fleeing the fire. As soon as they came, they ran right at me, smelling the odor of my wretched half-roasted flesh, and they would have devoured me then and there if my good angel had not inspired me well, teaching me a very opportune remedy against tooth trouble."

"And for what reason," said Pantagruel, "were you afraid of tooth trouble? Weren't you cured of your colds?"

"Holy Palm Sunday! [Pasques de soles!]," replied Panurge, "is there any greater tooth trouble than when the dogs have you by the legs? But suddenly I thought of my lard strips and kept throwing them into the midst of them. Then the dogs went and fought among themselves with bared fangs to see which one would get the lard strip. By that device they left me, and also I left them, scrapping with one another. So I escaped lusty and merry, and long live roasting!"

CHAPTER 15

How Panurge teaches a very new way
of building the walls of Paris.

O NE day Pantagruel, to refresh himself from his studies, was strolling in the direction of the Saint-Marceau suburb [les faulxbours Sainct Marceau], wanting to see the Gobelin country seat. Panurge was with him, as always carrying under his gown a flagon and an odd piece of ham; for without that he never went out, saying it was his bodyguard. No other sword did he wear, and when Pantagruel wanted to give him one, he replied that it would heat up his spleen.

"True," said Epistémon, "but if someone attacked you, how would you defend yourself?"

"With strong gusts from a clean pair of heels," he replied, "provided that thrusts were forbidden."

On their way back, Panurge kept looking over the walls of Paris, and said to Pantagruel in derision: "Just look at these fine walls! O how strong they are, and in good shape to protect molting goslings! By my beard, they are appropriately bad for such a city as this, for a cow with one fart could knock down over six fathoms of them."

"O my friend," said Pantagruel, "are you well aware of what Agesilaus said when he was asked why the great city of Lacedaemon was never girded with walls? For, pointing to the inhabitants and citizens of the town, so very expert in military knowhow and so strong and well armed, 'here,' he said 'are the city walls,' meaning that there is no wall but of bone, and that cities and towns could have no safer and stronger wall than the valor of the citizens and inhabitants.

"Thus this city is so strong by the multitude of the warlike people who are in it that they do not worry about building other walls. Furthermore, if anyone wanted to wall it around like Strasbourg, Orléans, or Ferrara, it would be impossible, so excessive would be the costs and expenses."

"True," said Panurge, "but it still is a good thing to have some semblance of stone when you are invaded by your enemies, were it only to ask: 'Who's out there.'

"As regards the numerous costs you say are necessary if anyone wanted to wall it, if my lords of the city want to give me some good pot of wine, I'll teach them a very novel way in which they can build them at a very low cost."

"How?" said Pantagruel.

"Don't tell it to anyone," said Panurge, "if I teach you it."

"I see that women's whatchamacallits [les callibistrys] in this part of the country are cheaper than stones. Of these they should build the walls, arranging them in good architectural symmetry and putting the biggest in the front ranks, and then, building them up donkey-back style, arrange the mediums and the little ones, and then make fine intermingled assortment, in diamond points as in the great tower of Bourges, of all those stiffened weapons that dwell on claustral codpieces. What devil could break down such walls? There is no metal so resistant to blows. And then, if the culverins came and rubbed up against them, you would see (by God!) immediately distilled from them some of that blessed fruit of the pox, as fine as rain, dry in the devil's name. Moreover, lightning would never strike them; and why? They are all blessed or consecrated. I see only one drawback to this."

"Ho ho, ha ha ha!" said Pantagruel, "and what's that?"

"It's just that flies are extraordinarily fond of them, and would swarm around and leave their droppings there, and there would be the work spoiled. But here's how you'd remedy that: you'd have to brush the flies away thoroughly with nice foxtails, or big donkey pricks from Provence. And speaking of that, I want to tell you (on our way to supper) a good example noted by Frater Lubinus's book *De compotationibus mendicantium*.

"In the time when animals spoke (not three days ago), a poor lion, walking around in the Forest of Bièvre and saying his prayers, passed under a tree that a poor charcoal burner had climbed to cut some wood; seeing the lion, he threw his axe at him and gave him an enormous wound in the thigh. So the lion, limping, ran around and made such a racket through the forest that he met a carpenter, who willingly looked at his wound, cleaned it out as best he could and filled it with moss, telling him to keep brushing his wound off well so the flies could not leave their droppings in it, while waiting for him to go find some carpenter's herb.

"So the lion, all cured, was strolling through the forest, at a time when an everlasting old woman was cutting kindling and gathering firewood through the said forest; who, seeing the lion coming, fell over backward from fear in such wise that the wind blew her dress, petticoat, and smock way up over her shoulders. Seeing which, the lion ran up out of pity to see if she had done herself any harm, and, considering her what's-its-name, said: 'O poor woman, who has wounded you so?'

"As he said this, he noticed a fox, and called and said to him: 'Friend fox, this way, over here, we need you.'

"When the fox had come, he said to him: 'Buddy, my old friend, this gammer has been very grievously wounded between the legs, and there is manifest solution of continuity. Look how big the wound is: five and half span. It came from an axe; I suspect the wound is an old one. Anyway, so the flies don't come, brush it off good and hard, please both inside and out. You have a good long tail: shoo-fly my friend, shoo-fly, I beg you, and meanwhile I'm going to get some moss to put in there, for that's how we must succor and aid one another. Shoo-fly hard; that's it, my friend, shoo-fly well, for that wound needs to be brushed often; otherwise the person can't be comfortable, so shoo-fly well, my little friend, brush away. God has generously endowed you with a tail; yours is big and proportionately thick; brush hard and don't get bored with it. A good shoo-flier who is continuously shooing flies away with his brush never will be shoo-flied by flies. Shoo-fly, you old goat! shoo-fly, my little sprite! I won't be long.'

"Then he goes off to get a lot of moss, and when he was a little distance away he cried out, speaking to the fox: 'Keep right on shoo-flying well, buddy; shoo-fly, and don't ever get weary of shoo-flying well. I'll get you hired for wages to shoo-fly for Dom Pedro of Castile. Just keep shoo-flying, shoo-fly, and nothing more.'

"The poor fox was brushing away both near and far, inside and out; but the pestilent old woman was fizzling and farting and stinking like a hundred devils. The poor fox was very uncomfortable, for he didn't know which side to turn to get away from the perfume of the fizzles; and as he turned, he saw that in behind there was another opening, not as big as the one he was brushing, from which was coming this foul stinking wind.

"Finally the lion comes back, carrying over eighteen bales worth of moss, and began to put in the wound with a stick he brought along, and he had already put in fully sixteen and a half bales and was marveling: 'What the devil! This wound is deep: you could get in over two cartloads of moss.'

"But the fox advised him: 'O lion old buddy, my friend, please don't put all the moss in there; keep a little of it, for there's also under here another opening that stinks like five hundred devils. I'm poisoned with the smell of it, it stinks so.'

"So they should keep the flies off the walls and post hired shoo-fliers on them."

Then said Pantagruel: "How do you know the women's pudenda are so cheap? For in this town there are many good women, chaste and virgins."

"Et ubi prenus? [And where do you get that?]," said Panurge. "I'll tell you, not my opinion of it, but my real certainty and assurance. I'm not boasting about having filled four hundred and seventeen of them since I've been in this town—and that's only nine days—but this morning I ran across a good man who, in a sort of knapsack much like Aesop's, was carrying two little girls two or three years of age at most, one in front, the other behind. He asks me for alms, but I made reply that I had more ballocks than *deniers,* and after that I ask him 'Good man, are these two girls virgins?' 'Brother,' he said, 'I've been carrying them this way for two years, and as regards this one in front, whom I see continuously, in my opinion she's a virgin; however, I wouldn't want to stick my finger in the fire for it. As for the one I'm carrying behind, honestly I don't know a thing about it.'"

"Really," said Pantagruel, "you're good company; I want to dress you in my livery."

And he had him dressed gallantly in the manner of the time it was then, except that Panurge wanted the codpiece on his breeches to be three feet long and square, not round, which was done and it did one good to see it. And he often said that people had not yet recognized the advantage and utility there is in wearing a big codpiece; but time would teach them some day, even as in time all things have been invented.

"God preserve from harm" he used to say, "the fellow whose long codpiece has been worth a hundred and sixty thousand and nine crowns in one day! God preserve anyone who by his long codpiece has saved a whole city from dying of hunger! And, by God, I'll write a book *On the convenience of long codpieces* when I have more leisure."

Indeed, he composed a fine big book on it with illustrations, but it's not yet printed, as far as I know.

CHAPTER 16

Of the ways and dispositions of Panurge.

Panurge was of medium height, neither too tall nor too small, and he had a rather aquiline nose, shaped like a razor handle; and at that time he was of the age of thirty-five or thereabouts, fit for gilding like a lead dagger,[1] in his person a very likely fellow, except that he was somewhat of a lecher, and by nature subject to a malady that in those days was called

Faulte d'argent, c'est douleur non pareille.

[Lack of money, that is unmatched pain.]

However, he had thirty-three ways of finding some for his needs, of which the most usual and honorable was by way of theft furtively perpetrated: an evildoer, cheat, boozer, idler, robber, if any there was in Paris, and for the rest the nicest guy in the world;[2] and he was always contriving something against the sergeants and against the watch.

For he would collect three or four ruffians, and toward evening have them drink like Templars; after that he would take them below Sainte-Geneviève or near the Collège de Navarre, and, at the time when the watch was coming up that way which he could tell by putting his sword to the pavement, and his ear next to it—and when he heard his sword quivering, it was an infallible sign that the watch was near—at that moment then, he and his companions would take a dung cart and set it in motion, shoving it with might and main on its way down; and thus he threw all the watch onto the ground like pigs, and then they fled in the other direction; for in less than two days he knew all the streets, lanes, and crossways in Paris like his *Deus det* [God grant (us His peace)].[3]

Another time he would make, in some fine square where the said watch was to pass, a train of cannon powder, and, at the moment when it was passing, he would set fire to it, and then have his fun watching how graceful they were in flight, as they thought Saint Anthony's Fire had them by the legs.

And as for the poor masters of arts, he persecuted them above all others; when he encountered one of them in the street, he never failed to do him some harm: now putting a turn in their formal hoods, now attaching little fox-tails or rabbit ears behind, or some other trick.

One day, when the watch had been assigned to be on the Rue du Feurre, he made a mud-pie composed of lots of garlics, galbanum, asafoetilda, and castoreum, of good warm turds, and steeped it in ooze from pocky sores; and very early in the morning he greased and anointed the whole pavement with it, so that the devil himself could not have stood it. And all these fine folk were throwing up their guts in front of everybody, as if they had flayed the fox: and ten or twelve of them died of the plague, fourteen were lepers, eighteen were goutie, and over twenty-seven got the pox from it. But he didn't worry the least bit about it, and ordinarily carried a whip under his gown, with which unremittingly he whipped the pages he found taking wine to their masters, to keep them moving along.

In his jacket he had more than twenty-six little pouches and pockets, always full, one with a little lead die, and a little knife, sharp as a skinner's needle, with which he cut purses; another, with vinegar, which he threw into the eyes of anyone he met; another, with burdocks feathered with little gosling or capon plumes, which he threw onto the gowns and bonnets of worthy people; and often he made them fine horns of these, which they wore all over town, sometimes all their lives; and sometimes he put some on the women too, over their hoods, to the rear, shaped like

a man's member; in another, a heap of little paper cones all full of fleas
and lice, which he borrowed from the grave diggers at Saint-Innocent's,
and he threw them, with nice little reeds or pens you write with, onto
the collars of the snootiest ladies he found, and especially in church.

He never sat up above in the choir, but always stayed in the nave
among the women, both at mass and at vespers as well as at the sermon;
in another, provision aplenty of fish hooks and clasps, with which he
often coupled men and women together in companies where they were
crowded, and, when they tried to separate, they tore all their dresses; in
another, a tinder box equipped with a wick, matches, flint, and all other
gear needed for this purpose; in another, two or three burning mirrors,
with which he sometimes drove men and women crazy and put them out
of countenance in church; for he said there was nothing but an inversion
between "femme folle à la messe" and "femme molle à la fesse" ["a
woman wild in the mass" and "a woman mild in the ass"]; in another, he
had a store of needles and thread, with which he played a thousand
devilish little tricks.

Once, leaving the Law Court, in the Great Hall, when a Franciscan was
to say the Councillors' Mass, he helped him get dressed and robed; but in
dressing him, he sewed his alb onto his robe and shirt, and then withdrew
when the Gentlemen of the Court came and sat down to hear the said
mass. But when it came to the *Ite, Missa est,* and the poor friar tried to
take off his alb, he took off with it both robe and shirt, which were
thoroughly sewn together, and so he stripped to the shoulders, displaying
his thingumajig to all the world, and undoubtedly it was no small one.
And the friar kept on tugging; but he uncovered himself all the more,
until one of the Gentlemen of the Court said: "What's this, does this fine
friar want to have us give the offertory and kiss his ass? Saint Anthony's
Fire kiss him!"

From then on it was ordained that the poor fine friars should no longer
strip themselves in front of other people, but in their sacristy: especially
not in the presence of women, for that could be for them the occasion for
the sin of envy. And people asked why it was that friars had such long
tools. The said Panurge solved the problem very well, saying:

"What makes donkeys ears so big is the fact that their mothers didn't
put any little bonnet on their heads; as De Alliaco says in his *Suppositions.*[4]
For a similar reason, what makes the tools of the poor blessed fathers so
long is that they don't wear breeches with any bottom, and their poor
member stretches out at liberty unbridled, and thus goes dangling down
onto the knees, as do rosary beads on women. But the reason why it is

proportionately stout is that in that dangling the humors of the body go down into the said member; for according to the lawmen, agitation and continual motion is the cause of attraction."

Item, he had another pocket full of itching-powder, some of which he tossed down the backs of the women he saw to be the cockiest, and thus made them strip in front of everyone, others dance like a rooster on hot coals, or a drumstick on a drum, still others walk the streets;[5] and he ran after, and for those who stripped, he held his cape over their backs like a courteous and gracious man.

Item, in another he had a little oil flask full of old oil, and when he came across either a woman or a man who had a fine robe, he greased and befouled all the best-looking parts, on the pretext of touching them and saying: "This is good material, good satin, good taffeta, Madame; God grant you your noble heart's desire! You have a brand-new robe, my newfound friend; God keep you in it!"

So saying, he would put his hand on their collar. With that the nasty stain stayed there forever, so extraordinarily engraved on soul, body, and renown, that the devil himself couldn't have got it out; then in conclusion he would say to them: "My lady, take good care that you don't fall; for here is a big dirty hole in front of you."

In another, he had a pocketful of very subtly powdered euphorbium, and in it he put a handsome, finely worked handkerchief, which he had stolen from the fair courthouse laundress as he took a flea from under her breast, one which, however, he had put there; and when he found himself in the company of a few good ladies, he would work the conversation onto the subject of lingerie, and put his hand on their bosom, saying: "And is this work Flemish or from Hainault?" And then he would pull out his handkerchief and say: "Look, here, look at the workmanship on this: is it from Foutignan or Foutarabie?" And he would shake it very hard under their nose and start them sneezing for hours without respite. And meanwhile he would fart like a cart horse, and the women would laugh and say:

"What, you're farting, Panurge?"

"No, I'm not, Madame," he would say; "but I'm tuning in for counterpoint to the music you're making with your nose."

In another, a picklock, a screwhook, a skeleton key, and a few other iron tools, so that there was no door nor strongbox whose lock he could not pick.

In another, a whole pouchful of little goblets, with which he played very craftily: for he had fingers supple as Minerva, or Arachne, and at one time he had hawked quack medicine; and when he changed a testoon or some other coin, the changer would have had to be sharper than Maistre Mousche [Master Slick] for Panurge not to cause each time to vanish into thin air five or six big *blancs,* visibly, manifestly, without causing any wound or lesion whatever of which the changer would have felt so much as the breath.

CHAPTER 17

*How Panurge got pardons
and married off old women,
and of the lawsuits he had in Paris.*

ONE day I found Panurge rather a bit depressed and taciturn, and I fully suspected that he hadn't a *denier;* so I said to him:

"Panurge, you're sick, from what I see in your face, and I understand the trouble: you have a flux of the purse; but don't worry: I still have six *sous* and a half that never saw father or mother, which will not fail you any more than the pox in your need."

To which he answered me: "Oh, a turd for the money! I'll have only too much some day, for I have a philosopher's stone, which draws money to me out of purses as the magnet draws iron. But do you want to get pardons?"[1] said he.

"Well, by my word," I answer him, "I'm no great pardoner in this world; I don't know if I shall be in the other. But all right, let's go to it, in God's name, for a denier's worth, no more no less."

"But then," said he, "lend me a *denier,* at interest."

"Not at all, not at all," said I, "I give it to you with all my heart."

"*Grates vobis, Dominos,*"[2] said he.

So off we went, beginning at Saint-Gervais, and I got pardons only at the first box, for I'm content with little in these matters; then I was saying my little petitions and prayers to Saint Bridget; but we got them at every box, and always left money to each of the pardoners.

From there we betook ourselves to Notre-Dame, to Saint-Jean, to Saint-Antoine, and so with the other churches where there were pardons for sale. For my part, I wasn't getting any more, but him, at every box he would kiss the relics and give to each. To be brief: when we were back, he took me for a drink to the Cabaret du Chasteau and showed me ten or twelve of his pockets full of money. At which I made the sign of the Cross and said:

"Where did you get all that money in such a short time?"

To which he replied that he had taken it from the pardons plates: "For when I gave them my first denier," said he, "I put it in so supplely that it seemed it was a big half-sou. So with one hand I took twelve *deniers,* indeed a good twelve *liards* or double *liards* at the least and with the other, three or four *sous,* and thus through all the churches we've been to."

"True enough," said I, "but you're damning yourself like a snake, and you're a thief and committing sacrilege."

"Yes indeed," said he, "as it seems to you; but as for me, it doesn't seem so to me; for the pardoners give it to me when they tell me, as they offer me the relics to kiss. *Centuplum accipies* [Thou shalt receive a hundredfold; Mathew 19.29], that I should take a hundred deniers for one: for *accipies* is spoken after the manner of the Hebrews, who use the future instead of the imperative, as you have it in the law *Diliges Dominum* and *Dilige* ["Thou shalt love the Lord" and "Love"]. Thus when the pardoner says to me *Centuplum accipies,* he means *Centuplum accipe* [Receive a hundredfold]; and thus it is expounded by Rabbi Kimy and Rabbi Ben Ezra and all the Massoretes; and *ibi* Bartolus [there Bartolus, i.e., Bartolus agrees]. Furthermore, Pope Sixtus gave me fifteen hundred francs of income for curing him of a cankerous tumor, which was torturing him so that he was nearly lamed for his whole life. So, since he is not so [lame], I take my payment with my own hands from the said ecclesiastical treasure."

"Oh, my friend," said he, "if you only knew how I feathered my nest from the crusade, you'd be really flabbergasted. It was worth more than six thousand florins to me."

"And where have they gone?" said I, "for you haven't a halfpenny of them."

"Where they came from," said he; "they did nothing but change masters."

"But I used a good three thousand to marry off, not the young girls, for they find only too many husbands, but these great everlasting old women, who hadn't a tooth in their chops, considering this: These good women made very good use of their time in their youth, and played clinchcruppers with their tails until no one wanted any of it any more; and, by God, I'll get them pushed up one more time before they die! In that way, I would give one a hundred florins, another six score, another three hundred, according to how loathsome, detestable and abominable they really were; for the more horrible and execrable they were, the more I had to give them; otherwise the devil himself wouldn't have been willing to cork them. I would go right away to some big firewood-hauler and arrange the marriage myself; but before showing him the old women, I would show him the crown coins and say: 'Buddy, here's something for you if you want to tumblebumble for one good shot.' From that point on the poor dopes rumpchumped like old mules.

"So I would have them get good and ready by feasting, drinking of the best, and would give the crones spices aplenty to put them in rut and in heat. To conclude they would plug away like all good souls, except that for those who were horribly ugly and decrepit, I had them put a bag over their faces.

"However, I lost many of them [the coins] in lawsuit."

"And what lawsuits could you have?" said I. "You have neither house nor land."

"My friend," said he, "the ladies of this town had discovered, on the instigation of the devil in hell, a type of collar or neckpiece cut very high, which concealed their breasts so well that you couldn't put your hand on them from below any more, for the cleft in these garments they had put in the rear, and they were all closed up in front, at which the poor lovers, doleful and pensive, were unhappy. One fine Tuesday I presented to the Court a petition bringing suit against the said ladies, and, remonstrating the great losses I would suffer from this, protesting that, in the same way, I would have the codpiece of my breeches sewn on in back, if the Court did not impose order in this. To sum it up, the ladies formed a syndicate, displayed their fundaments, and appointed attorneys to defend their cause; but I prosecuted them so lustily that by a sentence of the Court it was decreed that these high neckpieces would no longer be worn, unless they were slit a little bit in front. But it cost me plenty.

"I had another suit, very filthy dirty, against Master Fify and his crew, so that they should no longer read clandestinely, by night, *The Puncheon Barrel* or the *Fourth Book of Sententiae,* but in bright broad daylight, and that in the schools of the Rue du Feurre, in front of all the other sophists; and here I was condemned to pay costs, because of some technicality in the sergeant's report.

"Another time I brought a complaint to the Court against the mules of the presidents and councillors and others, to the effect that when they were put out to champ their bits in the Court's backyard the councillors' wives should make them bibs, so that they should not mess up the pavement with their drool, and so that the Court page could comfortably play on it with dice or coxbody [reniguebieu],[3] without soiling their breeches at the knees. And on that I got a good decision; but it cost me a lot. So now count up how much the little banquets cost me that I give the Court page every day or so."

"And to what purpose?" said I.

"My friend," said he, "you have no pastime in this world. I have some, more than the king; if you wanted to join forces with me, we'd do the devil's own tricks."

"No, no," said I, "by Saint Adauras,[4] for some day you'll be hanged."

"And some day you," said he, "will be buried. Which is the more honorably done, in the air or the earth. Hey, you great ox! While these pages were banqueting, I'm tending their mules, and I cut the stirrup on the mounting side [the left], so that it holds by only a thread. When the fat puffed-out councillor, or someone else, has taken his start up to climb on, they all fall flat as pigs in front of everybody, and give us over a hundred francs worth of laughing matter. But I laugh even harder when, back home, they have Mister de Page beaten like green rye. That way I don't care what it cost me to banquet them."

To sum it all up, he had, as I've said above, sixty-three ways of getting money; but he also had two hundred and fourteen of spending it, besides the repairs right below the nose.

CHAPTER 18

How a great scholar from England
wanted to debate against Pantagruel,
and was vanquished by Panurge.

In these same days, a learned man named Thaumaste, hearing the fame and renown of the incomparable learning of Pantagruel, came from the land of England with this sole intention: to see Pantagruel and come to know him, and to test whether such was his learning as was the renown of it.

Indeed, once arrived in Paris, he betook himself toward the house of the said Pantagruel, who was staying at the Hôtel Saint-Denis,[1] and at that moment was strolling in the garden with Panurge, philosophizing in the manner of the Peripatetics. On first entering, he had quite a start from fear, seeing him so tall and stout; then he greeted him as is the fashion, courteously, saying to him:

"Quite true it is, says Plato, prince of philosophers, that if the face of learning and wisdom were corporeal and visible to the eyes of humans, it would excite everyone to admiration of it. For merely the report of this spread through the air, if it is received by the ears of the studious and the lovers of it who are known as philosophers, lets them neither rest nor sleep in peace; so much does it stimulate and inflame them to come running to the spot, and see the person in whom knowledge is said to have established her temple and to produce her oracles.

"As was manifestly demonstrated to us in the case of the Queen of Sheba, who came from the limits of the Orient and the Persian Sea, to see the order of the house of Solomon the wise, and to hear his wisdom;[2] in Anacharsis, who, from Scythia, went all the way to Athens to see Solon; in Pythagoras, who visited the Memphitic[3] soothsayers; in Plato, who visited the Magi of Egypt and Archytas of Tarentum; in Apollonius of Tyana, who went all the way to Mount Caucasus, passing through the Scythians, the Massagetae, and the Indians, navigated the great river Physon as far as the land of the Brahmins to see Hiarchus, and traveled in Babylonia, Chaldea, Media, Assyria, Parthia, Syria, Phoenicia, Arabia, Palestine, Alexandria, and as far as Ethiopia, to see the Gymnosophists.

"We have a similar example in Livy, to see and hear whom many studious people came to Rome from the farthest confines of France and Spain.

"I do not dare to count myself in the number and rank of such perfect people as these; but indeed I do want to be put down as a studious man and a lover not only of letters but also of men of letters.

"In fact, hearing the fame of your most inestimable learning, I have left country, kinfolk, and home, and betaken myself here, reckoning as nothing the length of the road, the tedium of the sea voyage, the unfamiliarity of the country, just to see you and confer with you about certain passages in philosophy, in geomancy, and in the Cabala, about which I have doubts and cannot satisfy my mind, which if you can resolve for me, I make myself from now on your slave, myself and all my posterity, for I have no other gift to offer in return that I consider adequate.

"I will put them down in writing, and tomorrow I'll make it known to all the learned men in town, so that we may debate publicly about these before them.

"But here is the way I mean for us to debate. I don't want to debate *pro* and *contra,* the way these stupid sophists do in this town and elsewhere. Likewise, I don't want to debate in the manner of the Academics by declamation, nor by numbers either, as Pythagoras used to do and as Pico della Mirandola tried to do in Rome; rather I want to debate by signs alone, without speaking; for the matters are so arduously difficult that human words would not suffice to explain them to my satisfaction.

"Therefore, may it please your Magnificence to be present there. It will be in the great hall of the Collège de Navarre, at seven o'clock in the morning."

These words completed, Pantagruel said to him honorably: "My lord, of the graces God has given me I would not want to deny anyone a share, in so far as lies within my power; for all good comes from Him, and His pleasure is that it be multiplied when we find ourselves among worthy people fit to receive this celestial manna of honorable learning, in whose number I already clearly perceive that you hold the first rank; because of which, I notify you that at any hour you will find me ready to grant each and every one of your requests, according to my poor powers, even though I should rather learn from you than you from me; but, as you have proclaimed, we shall confer together about your doubts, and shall seek the solution to them even to the depths of the inexhaustible well in which Heraclitus[4] used to say truth is hidden.

"And I greatly applaud the method of debate you have proposed to wit by signs, without speaking; for by doing that, you and I will understand each other, and we will keep away from those handclappings that those idiot sophists go in for when people debate, just when they are at the best point in the argument.

"So tomorrow I shall not fail to be at the time and place you have set me, but I ask that between us there be neither dispute nor tumult and that we seek neither honor nor men's applause, but truth alone."

To which Thaumaste replied; "My lord, God keep you in His grace; and I thank you that your high Magnificence is willing so much to condescend to my little worth. So farewell until tomorrow."

"Farewell," said Pantagruel.

Gentlemen who read this present writing, do not suppose that anyone was ever more elevated and transported in thought than that night were both Thaumaste and Pantagruel; for the said Thaumaste said to the concierge at the Hôtel de Cluny, where he was staying, that in all his life he had never found himself as thirsty as he was that night:

"I do believe," said he, "that Pantagruel has me by the throat. Order some drinks for us, please, and see to it that we have fresh water to gargle my throat."

On the other side, Pantagruel stretched his mind to its highest pitch, and kept doing nothing all night but brood over:

> Béda's book *De numeris et signis* [*On numbers and signs*];
>
> Plotinus's book *De inenarrabilibus* [*On unnarratables*];
>
> Proclus's book *De magia* [*On magic*];
>
> The books of Artemidorus *Per onirocriticon* [*On the meaning of dreams*];
>
> Of Anaxagoras *Peri Semion* [*On signs*];
>
> Of Ynarius *Peri Aphaton* [*On unutterables*];
>
> The books of Philistion;
>
> Hipponax *Peri Anacphoneton* [*On things unpronounced*];

and a pile of others, so much that Panurge said to him:

"My Lord, give up all these thoughts and go to bed; for I sense that you are so stimulated in mind that you would soon fall into some quotidian fever from this excess of thinking. But after first drinking twenty-five or thirty good drafts, go to bed and sleep your fill, for tomorrow I'll reply to Mister Englishman and debate with him, and in case I don't set him speechless [ad metan non loqui], speak ill of me."

"Yes," said Pantagruel; "but Panurge, my friend, he is wondrously learned; how will you be able to satisfy him?"

"Very well," replied Panurge. "I beg you, don't talk to me about it any more, and let me take care of it. Is there any man as learned as the devils are?"

"Truly, no," said Pantagruel, "without special divine grace."

"And nevertheless," said Panurge, "I've often argued with them and made monkeys of them and set them on their tails. Therefore rest assured about this high and mighty Englishman, that tomorrow I'll have him shitting vinegar in front of everybody."

So Panurge spent the night tossing the pot with the pages and gambling all the points of his breeches at *primus et secundus* and peck-point. And when the appointed time came, he brought his master Pantagruel to the place assigned, and, take my word for it, there was no one great or small in Paris who was not present there, with this thought:

"That devil Pantagruel, who convinced all those shifty sophist nincompoops, will get his comeuppance now, for that Englishman is one more Vauvert devil. We'll see who comes out on top."

With everyone thus assembled, Thaumaste was waiting for them, and when Pantagruel and Panurge came into the hall, all those students, young and older, started clapping their hands, as is their doltish custom. But Pantagruel shouted, as loud as the sound of a double cannon, saying:

"Peace, in the devil's name peace! by God, you wretches, if you bother me with your racket here, I'll cut off your heads, every one of you."

At which statement they all sat as startled as ducks, and did not even dare cough, even if they had eaten fifteen pounds of feathers, and all were so thirsty just from that voice alone that their tongues were hanging half a foot out of their chops, as if Pantagruel had salted their throats.

Then Panurge began to speak, saying to the Englishman: "Lord, have you come here to dispute contentiously about these propositions that you have set forth, or rather to learn and know the truth about them?"

To which Thaumaste replied: "Lord, nothing brings me here if not an honest desire to know what I have had doubts about all my life, and I have not found a book or a man who has satisfied me in solving the doubts that I have set forth. And as regards disputing in a contentious way, I do not want to do it; indeed it is too vile a thing, and I leave it to these scoundrelly sophists,[5] who in their disputations seek not truth, but contradiction and strife."

"Then" said Panurge, "if I, who am a little pupil of my master Lord Pantagruel, satisfy and content you in all and throughout, it would be an unworthy thing to bother my said master with this. Therefore it will be better for him to preside, judging our statements and contenting you further, if it seems to you that I have not satisfied your studious desire."

"Truly," said Thaumaste, "that is very well said. So begin."

Now note that Panurge had put on the end of his long codpiece a lovely lock of silk, red, white, green, and blue, and inside it had put a fine orange.

CHAPTER 19

How Panurge made a monkey
of the Englishman who argued by signs.

So with everyone present listening in proper silence, the Englishman raised both his hands separately high in the air, closing all his fingertips in the shape called hen's rump in Chinonais talk, and struck one with the other by the nails four times; then he opened them, and thus with the flat of one, struck the other with a sharp noise. One more time he joined them as above, struck twice, and, opening them, four times more; then replaced them, joined and extended one next to the other, seeming as if praying piously to God.

Panurge suddenly raised his right hand in the air, then put the thumb of it inside the nostril on that side, holding the four fingers extended and close together in a line parallel to the tip of his nose, closing his left eye all the way and winking the right with a deep lowering of the eyebrow and eyelid; then he raised his left hand high, squeezing together hard and extending the four fingers and raising the thumb, and he was holding it in a line directly corresponding to the position of the right, with a cubit and a half of distance between the two. That done, he lowered both hands in a similar gesture down against the ground; finally he held them at the middle, as if pointing straight at the Englishman's nose.

"And if Mercury . . . " said the Englishman.

There Panurge interrupts him to say: "Mummer, you spoke!"[1]

Then the Englishman made a sign like this. His left hand, wide open, he raised high in the air, then closed the fingers of it into a fist, and placed the extended thumb on the tip of his nose. Immediately afterward he raised his right hand wide open and lowered it wide open, linking the thumb to the place enclosed by the little finger of the left, and moved the four fingers of the right slowly through the air; then, conversely, he did with the right what he had done with the left, and with the left what he had done with the right.

Panurge, undismayed by this, hoisted into the air his supercolossal codpiece with his left hand, and with the right took out of it a white rib of beef and two pieces of wood of the same shape, one of black ebony, the other of flesh-pink Brazilwood, and placed them between the fingers of it in proper symmetry, and, clicking them together, made a sound such as the lepers do in Brittany with their castanets, only better resounding and more harmonious; and with his tongue, drawn back into his mouth, he hummed joyously, still looking at the Englishman.

The theologians, physicians, and surgeons thought that by this sign he was implying that the Englishman was a leper.

The councillors, jurists, and decretists thought that by doing this he meant to conclude that some sort of human felicity consisted in the leper's state, as Our Lord used to maintain once upon a time [Luke 16.24].

The Englishman was not frightened at this, and, raising both hands into the air, he held them in such a position that he squeezed the three main fingers into a fist and passed the thumbs between the index and middle fingers, and the little fingers remained at their full extension; thus he presented them toward Panurge, then coupled them in such a way that the right thumb touched the left and the left little finger touched the right.

At this Panurge, without saying a word, raised his hands and with them made a sign like this. With his left hand he joined the nail of the index finger to the thumbnail, making a sort of ring in the space in the middle, and on his right hand he squeezed all his fingers into a fist except the right index, which he pushed and pulled back and forth between the two aforementioned ones of the left hand. Then on his right hand he extended the index and middle fingers, separating them as much as he could and pointing them toward Thaumaste. Then he put the thumb of his left hand on the corner of his left eye, extending the whole hand like a bird's wing or a fish's fin, and moved it very daintily back and forth; and he did as much with his right on the corner of his right eye.

Thaumaste began to turn pale and tremble, and made him this sign. With his right hand he struck the middle finger on the palm muscle beneath the thumb, then made the right index finger into a ring like the left; but he did so from underneath, not from on top, as did Panurge. Then Panurge claps one hand against the other and blows in his palm. This done, he again puts the index finger of the right hand inside the ring of the left, pulling it back and forth several times. Then he struck out his chin, looking intently at Thaumaste.

The spectators, who understood nothing of these signs, understood clearly that in that way he was wordlessly asking Thaumaste:

"What do you mean by that?"

Sure enough, Thaumaste started sweating great drops, and certainly looked like a man transported in lofty contemplation. Then he bethought himself, and put all the fingernails of his left hand against those of the right, opening his fingers as if they had been semicircles, and raised his hands as high as he could in this sign.

At which Panurge promptly put the thumb of his right hand under his jawbone, and the little finger of it into the ring of the left, and in that position clicked his lower teeth very melodiously against the uppers.

Thaumaste, with a great effort, got up, but in getting up he let a great baker's fart, and he stank like all the devils in hell. The spectators started stopping up their noses, for he was beshitting himself in his perplexity. Then he raised his right hand, closing it in such a way that he brought all the ends of his fingers together, and he put his left hand flat open on his chest.

Whereat Panurge pulled out his long codpiece with its silken lock and extended it a cubit and a half, and held it in the air with his left hand, and with his right took his orange, threw it in the air several times, and on the eighth hid it in his right fist, very quietly holding it up; then he began to shake his fine codpiece, showing it to Thaumaste.

After that, Thaumaste began to puff out both cheeks like a bagpiper, and was breathing as if he were blowing up a pig's bladder.

Whereat Panurge put one finger of his left hand in his asshole, and with his mouth sucked in air as when we eat oysters in the shell or sip up our broth. That done, he opens his mouth a little, and struck on it with the flat of his right hand, thereby making a loud deep sound as if it came from the surface of the diaphragm by the trachean artery; and he did it sixteen times.

But Thaumaste was still puffing like a goose. Then Panurge placed the index of his right in his mouth, squeezing it very tight with the muscles of his mouth. Then he pulled it out, and in pulling it he made a big noise, as do little boys when they fire turnip pellets with a popgun; and he did it nine times.

Then Thaumaste cried out: "Aha! Gentlemen, the great secret. He put his hand in up to the elbow."

Then he pulled out a dagger he had, holding it point down.

Whereat Panurge took his long codpiece and kept shaking it as hard as he could against his thighs; then he put both hands, linked in the shape of a comb, on his head, sticking out his tongue as far as he could and rolling his eyes around in his head like a drying nannygoat.

"Ah, I understand!" said Thaumaste, "but then what?" and made this sign: he put the hilt of his dagger against his chest, and on the point put the flat of his hand, turning back his fingertips a little. Whereat Panurge lowered his head on the left side and put his middle finger on his right ear, raising his thumb aloft. Then he crossed both arms over his chest, coughed five times, and on the fifth tapped his right foot on the ground. Then he raised his left arm, and, squeezing all the fingers into a fist, held his thumb against his forehead, with his right hand striking his chest six times.

But Thaumaste, as if not content with this, put the thumb of his left on the tip of his nose, closing the rest of the said hand.

Then Panurge put his two forefingers in each side of his mouth, pulling it open all he could and showing all his teeth, and with his two thumbs he pulled his eyelids way down deep, making a pretty ugly grimace, so it seemed to the spectators.

CHAPTER 20

*How Thaumaste recounts the virtues
and knowledge of Panurge.*

THEREUPON Thaumaste got up, and, taking his bonnet off his head, softly thanked the said Panurge, then said to all the spectators:

"My lords, at this moment I may well say the words of the Gospel [Matthew 12.42; Luke 11.31]: 'Et ecce plus quam Salomon hic [And behold, here is a greater than Solomon].' You have here in your presence an incomparable treasure: that is My Lord Pantagruel, whose renown had attracted me from the farthest reach of England to confer with him about the insoluble problems of magic, alchemy, the cabala, geomancy, astrology, as well as of philosophy, which I had on my mind.

"But now I am indignant at renown, which seems to be envious of him for it reports only the thousandth part of what in fact there is.

"You have seen how this mere pupil has satisfied me and told me more about it than I was asking; moreover, he has opened to me and at the same time resolved other inestimable doubts. Wherein I can assure you that he has opened for me the true well and abyss of encyclopedic knowledge, indeed in such a way that I did not think these were jestings, and I'll have it printed so that everyone may learn from him as I have done;

whence you might judge what the master would have said, seeing that the pupil performed such an exploit; for 'Non est discipulus super magistrum' ['The pupil is not above his master,' Matthew 10.24]. In any case God be praised, and I thank you most humbly for the honor you have paid us at this event. May God reward you for it eternally."

Similar words of thanksgiving Pantagruel delivered to the entire audience, and leaving there, he took Thaumaste to dinner with him; and believe me, they drank with bellies unbuttoned (for in those days they closed their bellies with buttons, like today's collars)—until they didn't know whether they were coming or going. Holy Mother, how they pulled on the goatskin! and the flagons kept going round and they kept swigging:

"Draw one!"

"Gimme!"

"Page, wine!"

"Put it here, in the devil's name, put it here!"

There wasn't a one who didn't drink twenty-five or thirty hogsheads; and do you know how? "Sicut terra sine aqua" ["Like earth without water," Proverbs 30.16]; for it was hot, and moreover, they had raised a thirst.

As regards the exposition of the propositions set forth by Thaumaste, and the meaning of the signs they used in debating, I would expound them to you according to their relations to one another, but I have been told that Thaumaste made of them a great book, printed in London, in which he declares everything without omitting a thing. Therefore I forbear for the present.

CHAPTER 21

*How Panurge was smitten
by a great lady of Paris.*

P<small>ANURGE</small> began to get a reputation around the town of Paris for this disputation he maintained against the Englishman, and from then on he put his codpiece to good use, and had it decorated with Roman style embroidery. And people praised him publicly, and a song was written about him, which the little children would sing going to pick up mustard,[1] and he was welcome in all companies of ladies and gentlewomen, and thus he became cocky, so much that he tried to give her comeuppance[2] to one of the great ladies of the city. In fact, leaving out a pile of long prologues and protestations ordinarily made by those sad and contemplative Lent-lovers who don't touch flesh at all, he said to her one day:

"My lady, it would be most useful for the whole commonwealth, pleasurable for you, honorable to your line, and necessary for me, that you should be covered by my breed;[3] and take my word for it, for experience will demonstrate it to you."

The lady, at this remark, set him back more than a hundred leagues, saying: "You crazy wretch, have you any right to talk to me that way? Whom do you think you're talking to? Go away, never come near me again; for but for one little thing, I'd have your arms and legs cut off."

"Well, now," said he, "it would be all the same to me to have my arms and legs cut off, on condition that you and I should have a nice roll in the hay together, playing the stiff lowdown in-and-out game;[4] for (showing his long codpiece) here is Master Johnny Jumpup [Maistre Jean Jeudy], who will sound you an antic dance that you'll feel to the marrow of your bones. He's a lusty one, and so expert at finding out the little out-of-the-way spots and swellings in and around the crotch and in the rat-trap that after him there's no need for dusting."

To which the lady replied: "Be off, you wretch, be off. If you say one more word to me, I'll call my men and have you beaten to a pulp right here."

"Oh," said he, "you're not as bad as you say, or I'm much mistaken in your physiognomy; for sooner would the earth climb up to the heavens and the heavens descend into the abyss, and would the whole order of nature be perverted, than that in such a great beauty and elegance as yours there should be one drop of gall or malice. It is well said that hardly

> Has there ever been a belle
> Who was not unkind as well.
>
> [Veit-on jamais femme belle
> Qui aussi ne feust rebelle.]

But that is said about those common beauties. Yours is so excellent, so unique, so heavenly, that I believe nature set it in you as a paragon to give us to understand how much she can do when she wants to employ all her power and all her knowledge.

"All that is in you is nothing but honey, nothing but sugar, nothing but celestial manna.

"It is to you that Paris should have awarded the golden apple, not to Venus, or Juno, or Minerva; for never was there so much magnificence in Juno, so much wisdom in Minerva, so much elegance in Venus, as there is in you.

"O celestial gods and goddesses, how happy will be the man to whom you grant that boon to embrace this lady, to kiss her, and to rub his bacon with her. By God, that will be me, I see it clearly, for already she is madly in love with me; I know it and am predestined for it by the Fates. So, to save time, let's push-thrust-straddle!"[5]

And he tried to embrace her, but she made as if to go to the window to call the neighbors for help. Then Panurge soon left and said to her as he fled:

"My lady, wait for me here; I'll go fetch them myself, don't give yourself the trouble."

So off he went, without worrying very much about the refusal he had had, and had none the less fun for it.

The next day he was in the church at the time when she was going to mass. As she came in he gave her holy water, bowing deeply before her; afterward he knelt down beside her familiarly and said to her:

"My lady, know that I'm so in love with you that I can't piss or shit. I don't know what you think about it; if some harm came to me, how would things stand?"

"Go away," said she, "go away, it's no concern of mine; leave me alone here to pray to God."

"But," said he, "play inversions with *A creek rises for a handsome punt* [A Beaumont le Vicomte]."[6]

"I couldn't do that," said she.

"That," said he, "makes *A prick rises for a handsome cunt* [A beau con le vit monte]." And on that point, pray God to give me what your noble heart desires, and of your mercy give me these paternoster beads."

"Here you are," said she, "and don't pester me any more."

This said, she tried to pull out her paternoster beads, which were of lemonwood, with big gold markers for every ten. But Panurge promptly pulled out one of his knives and cut them off clean, and took them to the pawnshop, saying to her:

"Do you want my knife?"

"No, no," said she.

"But," said he, "apropos, it is quite at your command, body and gods, tripes and bowels."

Meanwhile the lady was not very happy about her paternosters, for that was one of her ways to keep in countenance in church, and she was thinking: "This fine prattler is some braggart, a man from a foreign country; I'll never get my paternoster beads back. What will my husband say to that? He'll get angry with me; but I'll tell him that a robber cut them off of me in church, and he'll believe it easily when he sees the bit of ribbon still at my belt."

After dinner Panurge went to see her, carrying in his sleeve a big purse full of law-court counters and tokens, and started saying to her:

"Which of us two loves the other more, you me or I you?"

To which she replied: "As far as I'm concerned, I don't hate you, for, as God commands, I love everyone."

"But apropos," said he, "aren't you in love with me?"

"I've already told you ever so many times," said she, "not to talk to me that way any more; if you say any more about it, I'll show you that I'm not the one for you to talk to in this dishonorable way. Get out of here, and give me back my paternosters so my husband won't ask me for them."

"How's that, madame?" said he, "your paternosters? No I won't, on my youth;[7] but I'm quite willing to give you some others.

"Will you like some better in nicely enameled gold in the shape of great spheres or nice love-knots, or else all massive like gold ingots? Or do you want them of ebony, or big hyacinths, great cut garnets, with markers of fine turquoise or of lovely marked topazes, fine sapphires, or beautiful rubies with great markers of twenty-four carat diamonds?

"No, no, that's too little. I know of a beautiful chaplet of fine emeralds, with markers of dappled ambergris, at the clasp a giant Persian pearl as big as an orange! It costs only twenty-five thousand ducats, and I want to make you a present of it, for I have enough ready cash for it."

And as he said this, he jingled his tokens together as if they were sun-crowns.

"Do you want a piece of bright crimson velvet dyed in scarlet, or a piece of embroidered or crimson-dyed satin? Do you want chains, gilded jewelry, headbands, rings? All you have to do is say yes. Up to fifty thousand ducats, that's nothing to me."

By virtue of these words he made her mouth water. But she said to him: "No, thank you; I want nothing from you."

"By God," said he, "Me, I want something from you, but it's something that won't cost you anything, and you'll have no less left. Look (showing his long codpiece), here is Master Peter Pecker [Maistre Jean Chouart] asking for a nest."

And next he tried to embrace her; but she started screaming, however not too loud. Then Panurge turned his mask around and said to her: "So you won't let me do my thing a bit any other way? Shit on you. You're not entitled to such a gift or such honor; rather, by God, I'll have you ridden by the dogs!"

And, that said, he ran away at a good pace, for fear of blows, of which by nature he was afraid.

CHAPTER 22

How Panurge played a trick on the Parisian lady
that was not at all to her advantage.

Now note that the next day was the great holiday of Corpus Christi, on which all the women dress up in their Sunday best, and for that day the said lady had put on a very beautiful gown of crimson satin, and a very precious white velvet petticoat. On the day before, Panurge searched high and low so hard that he found a bitch in heat,[1] which he tied with his belt and took into his room, and fed her very well on the said day and all night. In the morning he killed her and cut out of her what the Greek geomancers know, and cut it in pieces as fine as he could, and carried them off well concealed and went to where the lady was to go to follow the procession, as is the custom at the said festival; and when she came in, Panurge gave her holy water, greeting her very courteously, and a little while after she had said her personal prayers, he goes and joins her in her pew and gave her a rondeau in writing in the following form:[2]

RONDEAU

For this time when I dared to make my plea,
To you, fair one, I found you cold to me,
Driving me off with no hope of return,
In word or deed, by doubt or speech too free.
If you viewed my lament so hostilely,
Right to my face you could have said to me:
My friend, please take your leave; let us adjourn
    For this one time.

Harmless I speak my mind thus candidly,
When I remonstrate to you how in me
The spark your beauty lights must ever burn;
For nothing do I ask, but that in turn
You tumble blithely into bed with me
    For this one time.

And, just as she was opening the paper to see what it was, Panurge promptly strewed the drug he had over her in various places, and especially in the folds of her sleeves and of her gown, then said to her:

"My lady, poor lovers are not always at ease. As for me, I hope that the bad nights, the torments and troubles that the love of you keeps me in will serve for a deduction of so many pains in purgatory. At the very least pray God that he give me patience in my plight."

Panurge had no sooner finished these words when all the dogs that were in the church ran up to this lady, for the smell of the drug he had sprinkled over her. Great and small, stout and tiny, they all came, freeing up their members, and sniffing her and pissing all over her. It was the dirtiest mess in the world.

Panurge chased them off just for a bit, then took his leave of her, and withdrew into a chapel to watch the sport, for those nasty dogs pissed all over all her clothes, to the point where a big greyhound pissed on her head, the others in her sleeves, the others on her crupper; and the little ones pissed on her shoes, so that all the women around her had much to do to save her.

And Panurge kept right on laughing, and said to one of the lords of the city: "I think that lady is in heat, or else some greyhound has covered her recently."

And when he saw that all the dogs were busy growling over her as they do around a bitch in heat, he left there and went to fetch Pantagruel.

In all the streets where he found dogs, he gave them a kick and said: "Aren't you going to the wedding with your friends? Come on, come on, devil take you, come on!"

And on arrival at their lodging, he said to Pantagruel: "Master, I beg you, come and see all the dogs in the land gathered around a lady, the fairest in this town, and they want to ride her."

To which Pantagruel readily agreed, and saw the show, which he found very fine and novel.

But the good part was the procession, in which were to be seen over six hundred thousand and fourteen dogs around her, giving her a thousand annoyances; and everywhere she passed, newcomer dogs followed in her tracks, pissing along the roadway where her clothes had touched.

Everybody stopped at this spectacle, watching the antics of those dogs, who jumped up as high as her neck and ruined all those fine accouterments for her; to which she could find no remedy except to retire into her house, and dogs kept going after and she kept hiding, and chambermaids kept laughing.

When she had gone into her house and closed the door after her, all the dogs came running up from half a league around, and so sturdily bepissed the door of her house that they made a stream of their urines that ducks could have swum in, and it's that stream that now passes by Saint-Victor, in which Gobelin dyes his scarlet, for the specific virtue of these pisshounds, as was once preached publicly by our master d'Oribus.

So help you God, a mill could have milled with it; however, not as much as those of the Bazacle in Toulouse.

CHAPTER 23

How Pantagruel left Paris,
hearing news that the Dipsodes were invading
the land of the Amaurots,
and the reason why the leagues
are so short in France.

A short time after, Pantagruel heard that his father Gargantua had been translated to Fairyland by Morgan, as were Ogier and Arthur of old; likewise that on hearing the report of this translation, the Dipsodes had burst out of their boundaries and laid waste a large area of Utopia, and were holding besieged the great city of the Amaurots. So he left Paris without saying good-bye to anyone, for the matter was urgent, and came to Rouen.

Along the way, when Pantagruel saw that the leagues in France were much too short, compared to other countries, he asked Panurge the reason for this; and he told him a story that Marotus du Lac, monk, puts in the *Deeds of the Kings of Canarre,* saying that:

"In olden times, countries were not measured in leagues, miles, stadia, or parasangs, until King Pharamond divided them up, which was done in the following manner: he picked up in Paris a hundred handsome sprightly young blades, good and purposeful, and a hundred beautiful Picard wenches, had them well feasted and entertained, then summoned them and to each lad gave his wench, with expense money, ordering them to go to various places this way and that, and at every point where they corked their wenches they should put up a stone, and that could be one league.

"The lads set out joyously, and because they were fresh and rested, they friggle-fraggled at every little field, and that is why the leagues in France are so short.

"But when they had traveled a long way, and were already tired as poor devils, and there was no more oil in their lamp, they didn't tup as often, and were quite content (I mean of course the men) with one lousy little time a day. And that is what makes the leagues so long in Brittany, in Les Landes, in Germany and other more distant lands. Others propose other reasons; but that one seems the best to me."

To which Pantagruel readily agreed. Leaving Rouen, they arrived in Honfleur, where there put out to sea Pantagruel, Panurge, Epistémon, Eusthenes, and Carpalim. At which place, while waiting for a propitious wind and calking their ship, Pantagruel received from a lady of Paris (who he had been close to for a good length of time) a letter addressed at the top:

"To the best beloved of the fair, and the least faithful of the valiant, P. N. T. G. R. L."

CHAPTER 24

A letter that a messenger brought
to Pantagruel from a lady of Paris,
and the explanation of a phrase
inscribed in a gold ring.

WHEN Pantagruel had read the address, he was quite appalled, and asking the messenger the name of the woman who had sent it, he opened the letter, and found nothing written in it, but only a gold ring with a flat-cut diamond. Then he called Panurge and showed him the thing.

At which Panurge said to him that the sheet of paper was written on, but in such a subtle fashion that you couldn't see any writing.

And to find this out, he held it to the fire, to see if the writing was done with sal ammoniac slaked with water.[1]

Then he put it in water, to see if the letter was written with tithymal juice.

Then he held it in front of a candle, if it wasn't written with the juice of white onions.

Then he rubbed part of it with walnut oil, to see if it was not written with fig-tree lye.

Then he rubbed part of it with milk from a woman nursing her first-born daughter, to see if it was not written with toad's blood.

Then he rubbed a corner with the ashes of a swallow's nest, to see if it was written with the juice found in winter-cherries.

Then he rubbed another edge with ear wax, to see if it was written with crow's gall.

Then he dipped it in vinegar, to see if it was written with spurge juice.

Then he oiled it with bat grease, to see if it was written with whale sperm that is called ambergris.

Then he put it very gently in a basin of cold water and promptly pulled it out, to see if it was written with stone alum.

And, seeing that he couldn't make out anything, he called the messenger and asked him: "Mate, didn't the lady who sent you here give you a stick to carry?" thinking it was the trick that Aulus Gellius relates.

And the messenger answered him: "No, sir."

Then Panurge wanted to have the man's head shaved, to find out if the lady had someone write in strong ink on his shaven head what we wanted to send. But, seeing that his hair was very long, he left off, considering that in so short a time his hair wouldn't have grown so long.

Then he said to Pantagruel: "Master, by God's virtues, I don't know what to do or say about it. To find out whether there is anything written here, I have employed part of what is set down about it by Messere Francesco di Nianto, the Tuscan, who wrote on the way to read invisible letters, and what Zoroaster writes, *Peri grammato acriton* [*On ill-distinguishable letters*], and Calpurnius Bassus, *De literis illegibilibus* [*On unreadable letters*]; but I can't see a thing there, and I think there's nothing else but the ring. Now let's see it."

Then, looking at it, they found written inside in Hebrew:

LAMAH HAZABTHANI[2]

So they called Epistémon and asked him what they meant. To which he replied that they were Hebrew words signifying: "Why hast thou forsaken me?" Whereupon Panurge promptly replied:

"I understand the case. Do you see this diamond? It's a fake diamond. So this is the explanation of what the lady means;

Say, false lover,[3] why hast thou forsaken me?

Which explanation Pantagruel promptly understood, and he remembered how, on leaving, he had not said farewell to the lady; and it saddened him, and he would have been inclined to return to Paris to make his peace with her. But Epistémon brought back to his mind the parting of Aeneas from Dido, and the remark of Heraclides of Tarentum that when the ship is at anchor and there is an emergency, it is better to cut the rope than to lose time untying it, and that he should leave aside all other thoughts and get on to his native city, which was in danger.

Indeed, an hour later the wind arose known as north-northwest, to which they set full sails, and took to the open sea, and in a few days, passing by Porto Santo and Madera, they put in at the Canary Islands.

Leaving there, they passed by Cape Blanco, Senegal, Cape Verde, by Gambia, by Sagres, by Melli, by the Cape of Good Hope, and went ashore in the kingdom of Melinda.[4]

On leaving there, they set sail to the Transmontane [north] wind, passing by Meden, Uti, Udem, Gelasim, the islands of the Fairies, and near the kingdom of Achoria; finally they arrived at the port of Utopia, three leagues and a little more away from the city of the Amaurots.

When they were on land and a little bit refreshed, Pantagruel said: "Lads, the city is not far from here. Before we go any further, it would be well to deliberate about what is to be done, so as not to be like the Athenians, who never consulted unless after the fact. Are you resolved to live and die with me?"

"Yes, Lord," they all said, "rest assured of us as of your own fingers."

"Now, then," said he, "there is just one point that keeps me in suspense and doubtful: this is, that I don't know in what order and what number are the enemies who are holding the city besieged; for, if I knew that, I would go ahead with greater assurance. Therefore let's confer together on the way we can find it out."

To which they all said together:

"Let us go see, and you wait for us here; for, with all of today, we'll bring you back certain information."

"I," said Panurge, "undertake to enter into their camp through the midst of the guards and the watch, and feast with them and thrust [screw] at their expense, without being recognized by anyone; to inspect their artillery, and all the captains' tents, and strut past their troops, and never be found out. The devil himself could not outsmart me, for I'm of the lineage of Zopyrus."[5]

"I," said Epistémon, "know all the stratagems and exploits of the valiant captains and champions of times past, and all the ruses and tricks of military science. I'll go, and even if I should be discovered and found out, I will escape by making them believe whatever I please about me, for I am of the lineage of Sinon."[6]

"I," said Eusthenes, "will enter right through their trenches, in spite of the watch and all the guards, for I'll pass over their bellies and break their arms and legs, were they as strong as the devil, for I am of the lineage of Hercules."

"I," said Carpalim, "will get in there if the birds get in. For my body is so nimble that I will have leapt over their trenches and cut on through beyond their whole camp before they've noticed me, and I have no fear of either dart or arrow, or horse, however swift, even were it Persius's, Pegasus's, or Pacolet's, and I'll escape safe and sound ahead of them. I undertake to tread on the sheaves of wheat or the grass of the meadows without its bending under me, for I am of the lineage of Camilla the Amazon."

CHAPTER 25

How Panurge, Carpalim, Eusthenes, Epistémon,
Pantagruel's companions, very subtly
defeated six hundred and sixty knights.

As he was saying that, they caught sight of six hundred and sixty knights advantageously mounted on light steeds, who were running up to see what ship it was that had newly arrived in port, and were riding at top speed, to capture them if they could have.

Then said Pantagruel: "Lads, pull back into the ship. See, here are some of our enemies coming on the run; but I'll up and kill them here and now like animals, even were they ten times as many. Meanwhile pull back in, and enjoy the show."

Then Panurge replied: "No, My Lord, it's not right for you to do that; but instead you pull back into the ship, you and the others, for I'll undo them all alone; but we mustn't delay. You there, forward!"

At which the others said: "That's well said, My Lord, you pull back, and we'll help Panurge here, and you'll find out what we can do."

Thereupon Pantagruel said: "All right, I'm willing; but in case you should be the weaker, I'll not fail you."

Then Panurge pulled two great ropes out of the ship and attached them to the capstan on the main deck and put them on land and made of them two long hoops, the one reaching further, the other inside it, and said to Epistémon:

"Go on into the ship, and when I give you the signal, turn the capstan on the main deck hard and fast so as to pull in the two ropes to you."

Then he said to Eusthenes and Carpalim: "Lads, wait here, and present yourselves freely to the enemy and obey them, and make as if to surrender. But watch that you don't go inside the circle of those ropes; keep pulling back outside."

And promptly he went inside the ship, and took a load of straw and a barrel of gunpowder and spread them over the space enclosed by the ropes, and stood by with a firebrand.

Suddenly the horsemen arrived in full force, and the first ones charged up close to the ship, and because the bank was slippery, they fell, they and their horses, to the number of forty-four. Seeing which, the others approached, thinking they had met resistance on arrival. But Panurge said to them:

"Gentlemen, I think you hurt yourselves; pardon us, for it's not our doing, but the slipperiness of the sea water, which is always oily. We surrender to your good pleasure."

So also said his two companions and Epistémon, who was on the main deck.

Meanwhile Panurge was moving away, and, seeing that they were all within the loop of the ropes, and that his two companions had moved away from it, making room for all these knights, who were crowding up to see the ship and who was in it, suddenly shouted to Epistémon: "Pull! Pull!"

Then Epistémon started to pull on the capstan, and the two ropes became entangled among the horses and threw them all to the ground quite easily with the horsemen; but they, seeing this, tugged at their swords and tried to cut them, whereupon Panurge sets the fire to the train, and had them all burned there like damned souls. Men and horses, not a one escaped, except one who was mounted on a Turkish horse, who got away in flight; but when Carpalim noticed him, he ran after him so fast and nimbly that he caught him in less than a hundred paces, and, vaulting onto the crupper of his horse, clutched him from the rear and brought him to the ship.

This defeat completed, Pantagruel was very joyous, and showered wondrous praise on the ingenuity of his companions, and had them refresh themselves and joyfully feed well upon the bank and drink their fill until their bellies touched the ground, and their prisoner with them like one of the family, except that the poor devil was not sure that Pantagruel would not devour him whole, which he could have done, his throat was so wide, as easily as you would a little sugar candy, and he wouldn't have measured any higher in his mouth than a grain of millet in a donkey's gullet.

CHAPTER 26

How Pantagruel and his companions
were fed up with eating salt meat,
and how Carpalim went hunting
to get some venison.

AND so, as they were banqueting, Carpalim said: "Hey, by Saint Quenet's belly, shan't we ever eat venison? This salt meat completely parches me. I'm going to bring you a thigh of one of those horses we got burned; it will be well enough roasted."

Just as he was getting up to do this, he spied at the edge of the woods a fine big roebuck, which had come out of the heavy growth, in my opinion, when it saw Panurge's fire. Instantly he ran after it so hard that he seemed like a bolt shot from a crossbow, and caught it in an instant, and as he ran caught in his hands out of the air:

Four great bustards,
Seven bitterns,
Twenty-six gray partridges,
Thirty-two red ones,
Sixteen pheasants,
Nine woodcocks,
Nineteen herons,
Thirty-two ringdoves.

And with his feet he killed ten or twelve young hares and rabbits, some of each, who at the time were past pageship,

Eighteen coots, paired together,
Fifteen young wild boars,
Two badgers,
Three big foxes.

So, striking the roebuck across the head with his scimitar, he killed it, and, bringing it in, he collected his hares, coots, and young wild boars, and shouted out from as far away as he could be heard, saying:

"Panurge, my friend, vinegar! vinegar!"

Whereas good old Pantagruel thought he had a pain in the heart and ordered him to be brought vinegar. But Panurge quite understood that there was hare on the hook; indeed, he showed the noble Pantagruel how Carpalim was bearing a fine roebuck on his neck and had his whole belt studded with hares.

Promptly Epistémon made, in the name of the nine Muses, nine fine old-style wooden sputs; Eusthenes helped skin, and Panurge set two battle saddles with the armor of the knights in such an arrangement that they served as andirons, and made their prisoner the turnspit, and roasted their venison in the fire in which the knights burned.

And afterward, great feasting with vinegar aplenty. The devil to anyone who held back. It was a triumph just to see them guzzle.

Then said Pantagruel: "Would God each of you had two pairs or sparrowhawk's jingles on your chin and I had on mine the great chimes of Rennes, Poitiers, Tours, and Cambrai, to see the aubade we would give by the chomping of our chops."

"But," said Panurge, "we'd better think about our business a bit, and thereby we'll be able to give our enemies their comeuppance."

"That's good advice," said Pantagruel.

Therefore he asked the prisoner: "My friend, tell us the truth, and don't lie to us about anything, if you don't want to be skinned alive, for I'm the one who eats little children. Tell us in full the order, number, and strength of the army."

To which the prisoner replied: "My Lord, know for the truth that in the army are: three hundred giants, all armed with freestone, wondrous big, however not quite as big as you, except for one who is their leader and is named Werewolf, and he is wholly armed with Cyclopean anvils; a hundred and sixty-three thousand foot soldiers, all armed with goblin skins,[1] strong courageous men; eleven thousand four hundred men-at-arms; three thousand six hundred double cannons and countless siege artillery; ninety-four thousand pioneers; a hundred and fifty thousand whores, lovely as goddesses."

"That's for me," said Panurge . . .

"Some of whom are Amazons, others from Lyons, others from Paris, Touraine, Anjou, Poitou, and Normandy, Germany; of all lands and all tongues there are some."

"Yes," said Pantagruel, "but is the king there?"

"Yes, Sire," said the prisoner, "he is here in person, and we call him Anarche, king of the Dipsodes, which amounts to saying the Thirsties, for you never saw people so parched or drinking more readily, and his tent is under the guard of the giants."

"Good enough," said Pantagruel, "Up, lads, are you ready to come at it with me?"

To which Panurge answered: "God confound any man who deserts you! I've already figured how I'll kill them all dead as pigs for you, so not one will get his hamstring free of the devil; but I am a bit worried about one thing."

"And what's that?" said Pantagruel.

"It's how," said Panurge, "I'll be able to get the time to impale the whores who are there during this after-dinner time, so that not one will escape without my beating her drum in the usual manner."

"Ha, ha ha," said Pantagruel.

And Carpalim said: "To the devil of Biterne! By God, I'll stuff some of them!"

"And I," said Eusthenes, "how about me, who haven't got mine up since we moved out of Rouen, at least so that the needle climbed up to ten or eleven o'clock, and that even though mine is hard and strong as a hundred devils?"

"Indeed," said Panurge, "you shall have some of the plumpest and best rounded."

"How's this?" said Epistémon, "everyone's going to bestraddle and I'm to lead the donkey? Devil take whoever does any such thing. We'll use the rights of war: *Qui potest capere capiat* [Catch as catch can]."

"No, no," said Panurge, "but tie your donkey to a hook and straddle like the rest."

And good old Pantagruel laughed at everything, then said to them: "You're counting without your host. I'm much afraid that before night-fall, I'll see you in a state where you won't have much desire to get a hard on, and where you'll be ridden down with great blows of pike and lance."

"Enough," said Epistémon, "I'll give them to you ready to roast or boil, to fricassee or put in a pastry. They are not in such great number as Xerxes had, for he had three hundred thousand fighters, if you believe Herodotus and Trogus Pompeius, and nevertheless Themistocles undid them with a few. Don't worry, for Heaven's sake!"

"Shit, shit, shit," said Panurge. "My codpiece alone will dust off the men, and Saint Ballhole [Sainct Balletrou], who resides in it, will scour out all the women."

"Then up an' at 'em, lads," said Pantagruel; "let's get on the march."

CHAPTER 27

*How Pantagruel set up a trophy
in memory of their exploits,
and Panurge another in memory of the hares.
How Pantagruel of his farts engendered the
little men, and of his fizzles the little women,
and how Panurge broke a big stick
over two glasses.*

"Before we leave here," said Pantagruel, "in memory of the exploits you performed just now, I want to set up a trophy in this place."

So each and every one of them, in great delight and with little village songs, set up a great lance, on which they hung: one little saddle, one horse's headpiece, bosses, stirrup, leathers, spurs, a coat of mail, a suit of steel armor, a battle-axe, a broad-sword, a gauntlet, a mace, gussets, greaves, a gorget, and so for all the apparatus required for a triumphal arch or a trophy.

Then in eternal remembrance, Pantagruel wrote the victory inscription as follows:

> 'Twas here the valor was made manifest
> Of four stout heroes, resolute and bold,
> Who in good sense, if not in armor dressed,
> Like Scipios or Fabius of old,
> Six hundred sixty knights did seize and hold,
> And burned them up, as easily as straws.
> The lesson, kings and pawns, I now unfold.
> Wit conquers might; that's one of nature's laws.
>> To win the prize
>> Not in us lies.
>> Our Master still
>> High in the skies,
>> Hid from our eyes,
>> Moves to fulfill,
> Not for the great or strong, His holy will,
> But for his chosen, we must realize.

So wealth and honor shall his cup o'erfill
Whose prayer to God in faith and hope shall rise.

While Pantagruel was writing the aforesaid verses, Panurge set on a high stake the horns of the roebuck and the skin and right forefoot of it; then the ears of three young hares, the saddle of a rabbit, the jawbones of a hare, the wings of two bitterns, the feet of two ringdoves, a flagon of vinegar, a horn where they put the salt, their wooden spit, a larding stick, a miserable caldron all full of holes, a saucepan, an earthenware salt box, and a Beauvais goblet.

And in imitation of Pantagruel's verses and trophy, wrote what follows:

Here were the foes set on their ass to rest
Right merrily, by four good men and bold,
That we might feast Lord Bacchus with the best,
Meanwhile drinking like fish wine clear and cold,
Saddle and rump of hare, together rolled,
Soon were engulfed in feasters' hungry maws,
Followed by salt and vinegar, we're told,
And scorpions for corresponding cause.
  When summer fries,
  With burning skies,
  To drink our fill,
  For cool is wise,
  In any size,
  This fills the bill.
And eating hare can make you ill,
Sans vinegar to spice the prize.
Vinegar makes it what you will;
A lesson you must memorize.

Then said Pantagruel: "Come, lads, there's too much thinking about food; one hardly sees it happen that great banqueters perform fine feats of arms. There's no shade like that of banners, stream like that of (sweating) horses, and clattering like that of armor."

At this Epistémon started smiling and said: "There's no shade like that of a kitchen, no steam like that of pies, and clattering like that of cups."

To which Panurge responded: "There's no shade like that of bed curtains, no steam like that of tits, and clattering like that of ballocks."

Then, on getting up, he let a fart, gave a jump and a whistle, and shouted loud and joyously: "Long live Pantagruel!"

Seeing this, Pantagruel tried to do as much; but from the fart he let the earth trembled for nine leagues around, and from this and the befouled air he begat more than fifty-three thousand little men, deformed dwarfs, and with a fizzle he loosed he begat as many stooped little women, such as you see in many places, who never grow unless, like cows' tails, downward, or like Limousin turnips, in a circle.

"How's this?" said Panurge, "are your farts this fruitful? By the Lord, here are fine gym-shoe men, and fine fizzle women; we must get them to marry one another, and they'll engender horse flies."

Which Pantagruel did, and called them Pygmies, and set them to live in an island near there, where they have multiplied greatly since; but the cranes continually make war on them, from whom they defend themselves courageously, for those little bits of men, whom in Scotland they call currycomb handles, are apt to be choleric. The physical reason for this is that they have their heart near the shit.

At this same time Panurge took two glasses of the same size that were there, and filled them with all the water they could hold, and put one on one stool and the other on another, separating them by a distance of five feet; then took a javelin shaft about five and a half feet long and put it on top of the two glasses, so that the two ends of the shaft just touched the edges of the glasses. That done, he took a big stake, and said to Pantagruel and the others:

"Gentlemen, watch and see how easily we shall gain victory over our enemies, for, even as I shall break this shaft over the glasses without the glasses being in the least broken or cracked, indeed, what is more, without a single drop of water spilling out, just so we shall break the heads of our Dipsodes without one of us being wounded and without losing any of our property. But so you may not think there is any enchantment, look, he said to Eusthenes, hit it as hard as you wish in the middle with this stake."

Which Eusthenes did, and the shaft broke cleanly into two pieces without a drop of water spilling from the glasses.

Then he said: "I know lots of others; let's just go ahead with confidence."

CHAPTER 28

How Pantagruel won the victory
very strangely over the Dipsodes and giants.

AFTER all this talk, Pantagruel called their prisoner and sent him back, saying: "Go on away to your king and his camp, and tell him news of what you have seen, and to make up his mind to offer me a feast around noon tomorrow; for as soon as my galleys have arrived, which will be tomorrow morning at the latest, I'll prove to him by eighteen hundred thousand combatants and seven thousand giants, all bigger than I am as you see me, that he acted madly and against reason to up and attack my country this way."

Wherein Pantagruel pretended to have an army at sea. But the prisoner replied that he surrendered as his slave and was content never to return to his own people, but rather to fight with Pantagruel against them, and asked him, in God's name, to permit it.

To which Pantagruel would not consent, but ordered him to leave shortly and go as he had said, and gave him a box full of euphorbium and chameleon thistle grains stewed in brandy into a sort of compote, ordering him to take it to his king and tell him that if he could eat one ounce of it without a drink, he could resist him without fear.

Thereupon the prisoner, with clasped hands, implored him that at the time of his battle he should have pity on him. Thereupon Pantagruel said to him:

"After you've announced everything to your king, put all your hope in God, and He will not forsake you; for as for me, although I am strong, as you can see, and have an infinity of men in arms, nevertheless I hope not in my strength or my diligence, but all my trust is in God, my protector, Who never forsakes those who have put their hope and their thought in Him."

That done, the prisoner asked him to make a reasonable arrangement regarding his ransom. To which Pantagruel replied that his purpose was not to pillage or ransom human beings, but to enrich and reform them in complete liberty:

"Go your way," said he, "in the peace of the living God, and never follow bad company, lest ill befall you."

The prisoner gone, Pantagruel said to his men: "Lads, I gave this prisoner to understand that we have an army at sea, and withal that we would make an attack on them only tomorrow around noon, with the purpose that they, fearing the great arrival of men, should keep busy tonight setting things in order and putting up their ramparts; but meanwhile my intention is for us to charge upon them around the time of the first sleep."

Let us leave Pantagruel and his followers and talk of King Anarche and his army. When the prisoner had arrived, he betook himself before the king and told him how there had come a great giant, Pantagruel, who had undone and cruelly roasted the six hundred and fifty-nine knights, and he alone had escaped to bring the news; moreover, he had been charged by the said giant to tell him that he should prepare dinner for him the next day around noon, for he was planning to attack him at the said hour.

Then he gave him that box in which were the preserves. But the instant he had swallowed a spoonful, his throat was so badly burned, and his palate so ulcerated, that his tongue peeled, and, no matter what remedy they gave him, he could find no relief except to drink without letup; for as soon as he took the goblet from his mouth, his tongue would burn. Therefore all they did was pour wine down his throat with a funnel.

Seeing which, all his captains, pashas, and guards tasted the said drugs to see if they were so thirst-provoking; but the same thing happened to them as to their king. And they all plied the pot so well that the rumor went around the whole camp how the prisoner was back and the next day they were to sustain an attack, and that the king and captains, together with the guardsmen, were already preparing for this, and that by drinking the barrels dry. Therefore each and every man in the army began swilling, guzzling, and tippling to match. In short, they drank so well and so much that they fell asleep like pigs, without order, throughout the camp.

Now let's go back to good old Pantagruel and tell how he behaved in this affair.

Setting out from the location of the trophy, he took the mast of their ship in his hand like a pilgrim's staff, and put inside its scuttle two hundred and thirty-two puncheons of white Anjou wine, out of his stock brought from Rouen, and attached to his belt the ship, chockfull of salt, as easily as the lansquenets carry their little baskets, and thus set out on his way with his comrades. When he was near the enemy's camp, Panurge said to him:

"Lord, do you want to do something nice? Take this Anjou white wine out of the scuttle and let's have a real drink here Breton-fashion."

With which Pantagruel readily went along, and they drank up so clean that not one single drop remained of the two hundred and thirty-seven puncheons, except one leather bottle from Tours, which Panurge filled for himself, for he called it his *Vade mecum* [Go with me], and a few wretched dregs for vinegar.

When they had had good tugs at the jug, Panurge gave Pantagruel some devilish concoction of drugs to eat composed of *lithontripon* [a stonebreaker], *nephrocatharticon* [a kidney purge], quince preserves with cantharides, and other diuretics. That done, Pantagruel said to Carpalim:

"Go inside the town, climbing up the wall like a rat, as you well know how to do, and tell them that at this moment they are to make a sortie and charge upon the enemy as hard as they can; and, that once said, come down taking a lighted torch with you, wherewith you shall set on fire all the tents and pavilions in the camp. You are to shout as loud as you can with your great voice, and leave the said camp."

"Yes," said Carpalim, "but would it be a good thing for me to spike all their artillery?"

"No, no," said Pantagruel, "but set fire to their powder stores."

Obedient to this, Carpalim left immediately and did as had been decreed by Pantagruel, and all the combatants who were in the town made a sortie out of it. And, when he had set fire throughout the tents and pavilions, he passed lightly over them without their feeling any hint of it, so deeply were they snoring and sleeping. He came to the place where the artillery was and set fire to their munitions (but that was the danger). The fire caught so instantaneously that it almost burned poor Carpalim, and had it not been for his wondrous rapidity, he was fricasseed like a pig; but he got away so vigorously that a bolt shot from a crossbow does not fly faster.

When he was outside the trenches, he shouted so frightfully that it seemed that all the devils were unchained. At which sound the enemy awoke—but do you know in what shape?—as stupefied as at the first sound of Matins, which in the Luçon region they call ball-rub [frotte couille].

Meanwhile, Pantagruel started scattering the salt he had in his boat, and, because they were sleeping with their jaws open and gaping, he filled their entire throats with it, so much so that these poor devils were coughing like foxes and shouting:

"Ah Pantagruel, you're really heating up our embers!"

Suddenly Pantagruel got the urge to piss, because of the drugs that Panurge had given him, and he pissed in the middle of their camp, so well and copiously that he drowned them all; and there was a special flood for ten leagues around. And the story relates that if his father's big mare had been there and had pissed likewise, there would have been a greater flood than Deucalion's, for she never once pissed but that she made a stream greater than are the Rhône and the Danube.

Seeing which those who had come out of the town said: "They've all died cruelly, see the blood flow."

But they were wrong about it, thinking, of Pantagruel's urine, that it was the enemy's blood; for they saw it only by the firelight from the tents, and some slight bit of brightness from the moon.

The enemy, on waking up, seeing on the one hand the fire in their camp, and on the other the urinary deluge and flood, didn't know what to say or do. Some said it was the end of the world and the Last Judgment, which is to be consummated by fire; others, that the sea gods, Neptune, Proteus, Tritons, and others, were persecuting them, and that in fact it was salt sea water.

O, who can relate how Pantagruel bore himself against the three hundred giants? O my muse, my Calliope, my Thalia, inspire me at this moment, restore to me my spirits, here is the *pons asinorum* [ass's bridge] of logic, here is the pitfall, here is the difficulty of succeeding in expressing the horrible battle that was fought.

If I had my wish, might I now have a vial of the best wine ever drunk by those who will read this most veracious history!

CHAPTER 29

How Pantagruel defeated the three hundred giants armed with freestone and their captain Werewolf.

THE giants, seeing that their whole camp was drowned, carried off their king, Anarche, around their neck, the best they could, out of the fort, as did Aeneas with his father Anchises at the time of the burning of Troy [*Aeneid* 1.866 ff., 2.975 ff.]. And when Panurge caught sight of them, he said to Pantagruel:

"Lord see there the giants have come out: beat on them with your mast, gallantly, with the old-style swordplay, for now's the time when you must show yourself a man of mettle. And for our part we shall not fail you. And I'll boldly kill a lot of them for you. For why not? David certainly killed Goliath easily. And then that great lecher Eusthenes, who's as strong as four oxen, won't spare himself. Take courage, cut right through them slash and thrust."

Then said Pantagruel: "For courage, I have over fifty francs' worth. But what of it! Hercules never dared take on two against one."

"That," said Panurge, "is so much shit in my nose. Are you comparing yourself with Hercules? You, by God, have more strength in your teeth and more sense in your ass than Hercules ever had in his entire body and soul. A man is as good as he thinks he is."

As they were saying these words, here comes Werewolf with all his giants; and he, seeing Pantagruel all alone, was overcome by rashness and arrogance in his hope of slaying the poor guy. So he said to his companion giants:

"You lowland lechers, by Mahomet, if any one of you tries to fight against these two, I'll give him a cruel death! I want you to let me fight alone; meanwhile you'll have your fun watching us."

Then all the giants drew back with their king nearby, where the flagons were, and with them Panurge and his companions; he was making like someone with the pox, twisting his neck and wringing his hands; and in a hoarse voice he said: "I swear to God, mates, we're not at war. Give us something to eat, while our masters fight it out."

To which the king and his men consented, and had them banquet with them. Meanwhile Panurge was busy telling the Turpin stories[1] and *exempla* of Saint Nicholas; Mother Goose stories [le conte de la Ciguoingne].

So Werewolf came at Pantagruel with an all-steel mace weighing nine thousand seven hundred quintals [hundred-weights] and two quarterns, all of Chalybean steel, on the end of which were thirteen diamond points, the least of which was as big as the greatest bell of Notre-Dame de Paris; it may peradventure have been short of this by a nail's breadth, or, lest I misstate, by the back of one of those knives they call "ear-cutters" [couppe aureille], but for a bit, neither front nor back—and it was enchanted, so that it could never break, and whatever he touched it with immediately broke. So therefore, as he came near in all his great pride, Pantagruel, raising his eyes to heaven, with all his heart commended himself to God, making a vow as follows:

"Lord God, Who hast always been my Protector and Savior, Thou seest the distress I am now in. Nothing brings me here but natural zeal; as Thou hast vouchsafed to humans to guard and defend themselves, their wives, children, country, and family in a case where it would not be Thy affair, which is faith; for in such matters Thou wilt have no collaborator but that of Catholic confession and service of Thy Word, and Thou hast forbidden us all other arms and defenses, for Thou art the Almighty, Who, in Thine own affair and where Thy cause is involved, canst defend Thyself far more than can be supposed, Thou Who hast a thousand thousands of hundreds of millions of legions of angels, the least of whom can slay all humans and turn heaven and earth as he pleases, as clearly appeared long ago with Sennacherib's army [2 Kings 19.35]. So if Thou art pleased at this point to come to my aid, I vow to Thee that throughout all lands, both in this country of Utopia and others, where I have power and authority, I will have Thy Gospel preached pure, simple, and entire, so that the abuses of a bunch of hypocrites [papelars] and false prophets, who, by human institutions and depraved inventions, have envenomed the whole world, will be driven forth from around me."

Then was heard a voice from heaven, saying: *Hoc fac et vinces,* that is to say: "Thus do, and thou shalt conquer."[2]

Then, when Pantagruel saw that Werewolf was approaching with jaws wide open, came against him boldly and cried out all he could: "Death to you, villain! Death to you!" to give him a scare, as the Lacedaemonians taught men to do, by his horrible cry. Then from his boat that he was wearing at his belt he threw at him eighteen barrels and one *minot* of salt, with which he filled his throat and gullet, and his nose, and his eyes.

Irritated at this, Werewolf launched a blow with his mace against him, trying to knock out his brains. But Pantagruel was smart, with a fast eye and feet: thus he took a step back with his left foot; but he didn't manage well enough to keep the blow from falling on the boat, which shattered into four thousand and eighty-six pieces and spilled out the rest of the salt on the ground.

Seeing this, Pantagruel gallantly reached out his arms and, in line with the art of the battle-axe, smashed him full force with the big end of his mast above the nipple, and, drawing it back to the left, gave him a slash between the neck and shoulders; then, putting his right foot forward, poked him a violent thrust in the balls with the top point of his mast, at which the scuttle broke and poured out three or four puncheons of leftover wine. Wherefore Werewolf thought he had cut open his bladder, and that the wine was his urine coming out.

Not content with this, Pantagruel tried to hit him again with a glancing blow; but Werewolf, taking one step forward, raised his mace and tried to bring it down on Pantagruel with all his might; and indeed hit so hard with it that if God had not succored the good Pantagruel, he would have split him in two from the top of his head down to the depth of his spleen; but the blow went by on the right because of Pantagruel's swift agility, and his mace plunged into the ground more than seventy-three feet through a great mass of rock from which he struck out fire in a volume of over nine thousand and six tuns.

When Pantagruel saw that he was busied tugging at his mace, which was sticking fast in the earth amid the rock, he runs up on him and tries to beat in his head decisively; but by bad fortune his mast just touched Werewolf's mace, which (as we said before) was enchanted; and by that means his mast shattered three fingers' breadth from the handle, which left him more stunned than a bell founder,[3] and he cried out;

"Hey, Panurge, where are you?"

Hearing which, Panurge said to the king and the giants; "By God! they'll hurt themselves if someone doesn't separate them." But the giants were as cheerful as if they were wedding guests.

Then Carpalim tried to get up and help his master; but one giant said to him: "By Golfarim, nephew of Mahomet, if you budge from here, I'll put you down in the bottom of my hose, as we do with a suppository! Anyway, I'm constipated in my belly and can hardly *cagar* [shit], unless by dint of grinding my teeth."

Then Pantagruel, thus deprived of a stick, picked up the tip of his mast again, striking out at random right and left on the giant; but he was doing him no more harm than you would by snapping your finger on a blacksmith's anvil.

Meanwhile Werewolf kept tugging his mace out of the ground, and had it already out and was making ready to smite Pantagruel with it, who was quick in his moves and was sidestepping all his blows, until once seeing Werewolf threatening him, saying: "Villain, now I'm going to chop you into mincemeat; never again will you make poor folks thirsty!"

Pantagruel gave him such a hard kick in the belly that he threw him on his back with his legs in the air, and he up and dragged him around that way flay-ass further than a bowshot.

And Werewolf kept hollering, spitting up blood from his throat: "Mahom! Mahom! Mahom!"

At this cry the giants got up to help him. But Panurge told them: "Gentlemen, don't go there, if you'll listen to me; for our master is insane, striking out in all directions and not looking. You'd come out of it badly."

But the giants took no heed, seeing that Pantagruel had no stick.

When he saw them coming, Pantagruel took Werewolf by both feet and raised his body in the air like a pike; and with this armed with anvils, hit out among these freestone-armed giants, beat them down as a mason strikes off chips of stone, and no one made a stand before him whom he did not knock to the ground. Whereby, at the shattering of these stony suits of armor, such a horrible tumult was caused that there came back to my mind when the great Butter Tower that used to be at Saint-Etienne in Bourges, melted in the sun. Meanwhile Panurge, and with him Carpalim and Eusthenes, were slitting the throats of those who were struck to the ground.

You may rest assured that not one of them escaped; and Pantagruel, to see him, looked like a reaper who with his scythe (that was Werewolf) was cutting down the grasses in a meadow (those were the giants) but in this flailing Werewolf lost his head. That was when Pantagruel knocked down with it, one whose name was Gobblechitterling,[4] who was heavily armed [armé à hault appareil]; that was with freestone, one splinter of which cut all the way through Epistémon's throat; for otherwise the rest of them were lightly armed, that is to say with tufa for some, for others slate.

Finally, seeing that they were all dead, he threw Werewolf's body as hard as he could against the city, and it fell on the belly in the main square of the said city, and in its fall killed a burned tomcat, a soaked tabbycat, a field duck, and a bridled gosling.

CHAPTER 30

How Epistémon had his chop headed off,[1]
was cleverly cured by Panurge,
and how they got some news
of the devils and the damned.

THIS gigantic destruction completed, Pantagruel withdrew to the area of the flagons, and called Panurge and the others, who came back to him safe and sound, except Epistémon, who did not show up at all, at which Pantagruel was so woeful that he wanted to kill himself. But Panurge said to him:

"Come now, My Lord, wait a bit, and we'll look for him among the dead, and see the truth of the whole matter."

So then as they were looking, they found him stiff, stone dead, and his head between his arms, all bloody. Then Eusthenes exclaimed:

"Ah! wicked death, you have snatched from us the most perfect of men!"

At which cry Pantagruel stood up, in the greatest grief ever seen in the world, and said to Panurge:

"Ah, my friend, the omen of your two glasses and javelin shaft was only too deceiving!"

But Panurge said: "Don't shed one tear, lads, for he's still all warm, and I'll cure him for you as healthy as he ever was."

"So saying he took the head, and kept it warm in his codpiece, to keep it out of the wind. Eusthenes and Carpalim carried the body to the spot where they had feasted, not in the hope that he would ever get well, but so that Pantagruel should see it. However, Panurge kept comforting them, saying:

"If I don't make him well, I want to lose my head (which is a madman's wager)—leave off these tears and help me."

Thereupon he cleaned off the neck, and then the head, very nicely with good white wine, and sprinkled on it some quack dungpowder [pouldre de diamerdis] that he always carried in one of his pockets; after that he anointed them with I know not what ointment; and he fitted them together precisely, vein to vein, sinew to sinew, vertebra to vertebra, so that he should not be wrynecked (for such people he hated unto death). That done, he took fifteen or sixteen stitches around it with a needle, so that it should not fall off again, and then spread around it a little of an unguent that he called resuscitative.

Suddenly Epistémon began to breath, then to open his eyes, then yawn, then sneeze, then let a big household fart. At which Panurge said:

"Now he is certainly cured."

And he gave him a glass of strong crude white wine to drink, with a piece of sugared toast.

In this way Epistémon was cleverly cured, except that he was hoarse for over three weeks, and had a dry cough, which he never could remedy except by dint of drinking.

And then and there he began to speak, saying that he had seen the devils, and had had a familiar chat with Lucifer, and had a grand old time in hell and around the Elysian Fields, and he warranted, before us all, that the devils were good company.

As regards the damned, he said he was very sorry that Panurge had called him back to life so soon: "For," said he, "I was having a wonderful time seeing them."

"How so?" said Pantagruel.

"They don't treat them," said Epistémon, "as badly as you'd think; but their status is changed in an extraordinary way, for I saw Alexander the Great mending old breeches and earning his poor living that way.

Xerxes was hawking mustard,

Romulus was a salt vendor,

Numa, a nailsmith,

Tarquin a tacquin [penny-pincher],

Piso, a peasant,

Sulla, a ferryman,

Cyrus was a cowherd,

Themistocles a glazier,

Epaminondas, a maker of mirrors,

Brutus and Cassius, surveyors,

Demosthenes, a vine-dresser,

Cicero, a fire-kindler,

Fabius, a rosary-stringer,

Artaxerxes, a ropemaker,

Aeneas, a miller,

Achilles, a scurvy wretch,
Agamemnon, a pot-licker,
Ulysses, a reaper,
Nestor, an ironmonger,
Darius, a privy-cleaner,
Ancus Martius, a calker,
Camillus, an errand boy,
Marcellus, a bean sheller,
Drusus, a blowhard,
Scipio Africanus was hawking lye in a clog,
Hasdrubal was a lantern maker,[2]
Hannibal, a poulterer,
Priam was selling old rags,

Lancelot of the Lake was a skinner of dead horses. All the Knights of
the Round Table were poor day-laborers, tugging on the oar to cross the
rivers Cocytus, Phlegethon, Styx, Acheron, and Lethe when milords the
devils want to have some fun on the water, just like the boat-women of
Lyon and the gondoliers of Venice; but for each crossing they get nothing
but a flick on the nose, and, toward evening, some scrap of moldy bread.

Trajan was a frog fisher,
Antoninus, a lackey,
Commodus, a worker in jet,
Pertinax, a walnut sheller,
Lucullus, a roaster,
Justinian, a bauble maker,
Hector was a scullion,
Paris was a ragged wretch,
Achilles, a hay baler,[3]
Cambyses, a muleteer,
Artaxerxes, a pot scourer,
Nero was a fiddler, and Fierabras his valet; but he did Nero a thousand
    dirty tricks, and made him eat coarse bread and turned wine, while
    he ate and drank of the best.
Julius Caesar and Pompey worked at tarring ships,

Valentin and Orson stoked the stoves of hell and were mask scrapers,
Giglan and Gawain were poor swineherds,
Geoffroy Sabertooth was a match vendor,
Godfrey of Bouillon, a wood engraver,
Jason was a bell ringer,
Don Pietro of Castille, a relic peddler,
Morgante, a beer brewer,
Huon of Bordeaux was a barrel hooper,
Pyrrhus, a scullery knave,
Antiochus was a chimney sweep,
Romulus was a cobbler of gym shoes,
Octavian, a paper scraper,
Nerva was a stable boy,
Pope Julius, a hawker of little pot-pies, but he no longer wore his
    buggerish beard,
Jean de Paris was a boot greaser,
Arthur of Britain cleaned grease off caps,
Perceforest, a firewood hauler,
Pope Boniface the Eighth was a pot skimmer,
Pope Nicholas the Third was a papermaker,
Pope Alexander was a rat catcher,
Pope Sixtus, an anointer of poxies.

"How's that?" said Pantagruel, "are there poxies down there?"
"Yes indeed," said Epistémon, "I never saw so many. For, take my
word, those who haven't had the pox in this world have it in the other."
"By Gar," said Panurge, "then I'm quit of it; for I've been into it all the
way down the Hole of Gibraltar, and filled the Pillars of Hercules, and
brought down some of the ripest!"

Ogier the Dane was an armor furbisher,
King Tigranes was a roofer,
Galen Restored, a mole catcher,
The Four Sons of Aymon, tooth pullers,
Pope Calixtus was a cunt barber,
Pope Urban, a lard snatcher,

Melusine was a scullery maid,
Matabrune, a washerwoman,
Cleopatra, an onion peddler,
Helen, a placer of chambermaids,
Semiramis, a lice killer for vagabonds,
Dido was selling mushrooms,
Penthesilea peddled cress,
Lucrece was a nurse,
Hortensia, a flax spinner,
Livia, a scraper of verdigris.

In this way, those who had been great lords in this world earned their poor wretched slovenly living down there. On the contrary, the philosophers and those who had been indigent in this world, down yonder were great lords in their turn.

"I saw Diogenes strutting about in his finery, with a great purple robe and a scepter in his right hand, and he was driving Alexander the Great crazy whenever he hadn't mended his breeches well, and paying him with great whacks of his stick. I saw Epictetus dressed gallantly French style, under a lovely arbor, with ladies galore, making merry, dancing, in any case living it up, and near him sun-crowns aplenty. And above the trellis were written these words for his motto:

To hop, to skip, to dance and play,
To drink the good wine red and white,
And to do nothing else all day
But count your sun-crowns with delight.

"Then, when he saw me, he courteously invited me to dine with him, which I gladly did, and we toped theologically. Meanwhile Cyrus came by to ask him for a *denier*, in honor of Mercury, to buy a few onions for his supper. 'No, nothing doing,' said Epictetus, 'I don't give *deniers*. Here, you rascal, here's a crown piece; now be a good man.' Cyrus was very pleased to have come across such booty; but the other knavish kings who are down there, like Alexander, Dariua, and others, stole it at night.

"I saw Pathelin, treasurer for Rhadamanthus, bargaining for some little pot pies that Pope Julius was hawking, and he asked him

" 'How much a dozen?'

" 'Three half-sous,' said the pope.

" 'Huh,' said Pathelin, 'three cracks with the stave! Give me some, you rogue. Give me some, and go get some more.'

"The poor pope went away in tears. When he came before his pastrycook master, he told him someone had taken his pot pies; whereupon the pastry-cook gave him a whipping, so well that his skin wouldn't have been any use to make bagpipes.

"I saw Master Jean Lemaire impersonating the pope, and he had all those poor kings and popes of this world kiss his feet; and putting on the dog [faisant du grobis], he gave them his blessing, saying:

" 'Get your pardons, scoundrels, get them, they're cheap. I absolve you *de pain et de souppe* [of bread and dips],[4] and dispense you from every being good for anything.'

"And he called Caillette and Triboulet, and said: 'My Lord Cardinals, dispatch their bulls: to each one a bang on the loins with a pike.' Which was done immediately.

"I saw Master François Villon, who asked Xerxes: 'How much mustard is a *denrée* [a denier's worth]?'

" 'One denier,' said Xerxes. To which the said Villon said: 'A quartan fever to you, you rogue. A half-sous's measure is worth only a copper denier, and here you go overcharging us for victuals.'[5] Thereupon he pissed in his spill-pail, as do the mustard peddlers in Paris.

"I saw the Franc-Archer de Bagnolet, who was an inquisitor of heretics. He came upon Perceforest pissing against a wall on which was painted Saint Anthony's Fire.[6] He declared him a heretic, and would have had him burned alive had it not been for Morgante, who, for his initiation and other small fees, gave him nine barrels of beer."

Then said Pantagruel: "Save us all these fine stories for another time; only tell us how the userers are treated here."

"I saw them," said Epistémon, "all busy searching for rusty needles and old nails amid the gutters in the streets, as you see the beggars doing in this world; but a hundred-weight of this old iron junk is worth only a bit of bread; and at that the market for it is bad. So the poor wretches sometimes go more than three weeks without eating a piece or a crumb, and work day and night waiting for the coming fair; but this labor and misery they don't remember, so active and so accursed are they, provided that at the year's end they earn some miserable denier."

"Now," said Pantagruel, "let's have a bit of refreshment, and let's drink, lads, for the drinking is good all this month."

Then they unsheathed their flagons in piles, and had a great feast on the camp provisions; but poor King Anarche couldn't cheer up, at which Panurge said:

"What trade shall we pick out for Milord the King here, so he may already be expert in the craft when he's off yonder to all the devils?"

"Really," said Pantagruel, "that's a good idea of yours. So do what you please; I give him to you."

"Many thanks," said Panurge. "I can't say no to that present, and I like it from you."

CHAPTER 31

How Pantagruel entered the city of the Amaurots and how Panurge married off King Anarche and made him a hawker of green sauce.

AFTER that wondrous victory, Pantagruel sent Carpalim into the city of the Amaurots to tell and announce how King Anarche was captured and all their enemies defeated. This news heard, there came out before him all the inhabitants of the city, in good order, and in great triumphal pomp, with divine gladness, and led him into the city; and fine bonfires were lit for joy all over the city, and fair round tables, garnished with victuals aplenty, were set up around the streets. It was a renewal of the golden age of Saturn, such a good time was had by all.

But Pantagruel, to all the senate assembled, said: "Gentlemen, while the iron is hot one must strike; likewise, before we relax any further, I want us to go and take by storm the entire kingdom of the Dipsodes.

"Therefore let those who want to come with me be ready for tomorrow after a drink, for then I shall set out on the march. Not that I need more men to help me conquer it, for I might as well hold it already; but I see that this city is so full of inhabitants that they can't get around in the streets.

"So I'll take them as a colony into Dipsody, and give them the whole country, which is beautiful, healthy, and fruitful and pleasant above all the countries in the world, as many of you know who have gone there in other days. Let each and every one of you who wants to come there be ready as I have said."

This plan and deliberation was divulged through the city, and the next day, in the square in front of the palace, there were people in the number of eighteen hundred and fifty-six thousand and eleven, not counting the women and little children. Thus they began to march straight into Dipsody, in such good order that they looked like the children of Israel when they left Egypt [Exodus 14] to cross the Red Sea.

But before continuing this undertaking, I want to tell you how Panurge treated his prisoner Anarche. He remembered what Epistémon had told him, how the kings and the rich of this world were treated around the Elysian Fields, and how they then earned their living at vile and filthy jobs.

Therefore one day he dressed up his said king in a fine little linen doublet, all slashed like an Albanian's cap, and nice sailor's breeches, without shoes (for, he said, they would spoil his vision), and a little blue cap with one big capon's feather—I'm wrong, I think he had two—and a handsome blue and green belt, saying that this livery suited him well, seeing that he had been perverse.[1] In this state he brought him before Pantagruel and said to him:

"Do you recognize this clown?"

"No, indeed," said Pantagruel.

"It's Milord the pluperfect king;[2] I want to make a good man of him. These devils the kings are nothing but dumb calves; they know nothing and they're good for nothing, except to do harm to their poor subjects, and trouble the whole world by making war, for their wicked and detestable pleasure. I want to set him to a trade, and make him a hawker of green sauce. So now start shouting: 'Don't you need some green sauce?' "

And the poor devil shouted.

"That's too soft," said Panurge; and he took him by the ear and said: "Sing louder, in the key of G. So, you poor devil! You have a strong throat, you've never been so lucky as not to be king any more."

And Pantagruel enjoyed it all. For I make bold to say that he was the best nice little chap there ever was from here to the end of a stick. So Anarche was a good green-sauce hawker.

Two days later, Panurge married him off to an old whore, and himself gave the wedding feast with fine sheep's heads, good slices of roast pork with mustard, and other good roast meat with garlic—of which he sent five loads to Pantagruel, all of which he ate, he found them so appetizing;

and to drink, fine small wine and good sorb apple wine; and for them to dance to, he hired a blind man who sounded the tune on his fiddle.

After dinner, he brought them to the palace, and showed them to Pantagruel, and said to him, pointing to the bride:

"She's not likely to fart."

"Why not?" said Pantagruel.

"Because," said Panurge, "she's well split open."

"What's the point?" said Pantagruel.

"Don't you see," said Panurge, "that the chestnuts you roast by the fire, if they are whole, they fart like mad? and to keep them from farting, you split them open. And so this new bride is well split open at the bottom, so she won't fart."

Pantagruel gave them a little lodging next to the low street, and a stone mortar to beat their sauce on. And in that state they set up their little household, and he was as nice as a green-sauce hawker as ever was seen in Utopia; but I've been told since that his wife beats him like plaster, and the poor idiot doesn't dare defend himself, he's so stupid.

CHAPTER 32

How Pantagruel with his tongue
covered a whole army,
and what the author saw inside his mouth.

Now as Pantagruel with all his band entered upon the lands of the Dipsodes, everyone was delighted at this, and immediately surrendered to him, and, of their own free will, brought him the keys to all the cities he went to, except for the Almyrodes, who tried to hold out against him, and made reply to his heralds that they would not surrender unless for good reason.

"What," said Pantagruel, "do they ask for better ones than hand on pot and glass in fist? Come on, I want them put to the sack."

So then they all fell into marching order, as if intending to give the attack. But on the way, passing over a great open field, they were caught in a heavy rain shower. At which they began to shiver and huddle close to one another. Pantagruel seeing this, he had them told by the captains that it was nothing and that he could see well above the clouds that it would be only a little dew, but at all events that they should fall into ranks and he intended to cover them. Then they lined up in good order and well closed up, and Pantagruel put his tongue out only a half way, and with it covered them as a hen does her chickens.

Meanwhile I, who am telling you these stories so truly, had hidden myself under a burdock leaf, which was no less wide than the Bridge of Monstrible; but when I saw them thus well covered, I went over to them to take shelter, which I could not do, there were so many of them: as the saying goes, at the end of the ell the cloth runs out. So I climbed up above as best I could, and I walked a good two leagues on his tongue until I entered his mouth.

But, O ye gods and goddesses, what did I see there? Jupiter confound me with his three-forked thunder if I lie. I was walking along there as you do in Saint-Sophia in Constantinople and I saw great rock formations, like the mountains of the Danes, I think that were his teeth, and great plains, great forests, big strong cities no less large than Lyon or Poitiers. The first person I found was a chap who was planting cabbages. At which, in amazement, I asked him:

"My friend, what are you doing here?"

"I'm planting cabbages," said he.

"And how and what for?" said I.

"Ah, sir," said he, "not everyone can have balls as heavy as a mortar, and we can't all be rich. I earn my living that way, and I take them to sell in the market in the city that is behind here."

"Jesus," said I, "then there's a new world here?"

"To be sure," said he, "it's hardly new; but they do indeed say that outside of here there's a new earth where they have both sun and moon, and all sorts of fine carryings-on; but this one is older."

"All right, my friend," said I, "but what's the name of that city where you take your cabbages to sell?"

"It's name," said he, "is Aspharagos [Gullettown], and they are Christians, good people, and will give you a great time."

In short, I decided to go there. Now on my road I came upon a fellow setting snares for pigeons, and I asked him: "My friend, where do these pigeons come to you from?"

"Sire," said he, "they come from another world."

Then it occurred to me that when Pantagruel yawned, pigeons in whole flocks flew into his throat, thinking it was a dovecote.

Then I went into the city, and found it beautiful, quite strong and in nice air; but on the way in, the gatekeepers asked me for my health certificate, at which I was most astonished, and asked them:

"Gentlemen, is there danger of plague here?"

"Oh, my Lord!" said they, "people near here are dying so fast that the tumbrel keeps running through the streets."

"Dear God!" said I, "and where?"

At which he told me that it was at Larynx and Pharynx, which are two large cities such as Rouen and Nantes, rich and doing good business, and the cause of the plague was a foul stinking exhalation that had issued from the gulfs not long ago, from which over twenty-two hundred and sixty thousand and sixty persons have died in a week. Then I thought and calculated, and decided it was a stinking breath that had come from Pantagruel's stomach when he ate all that garlic sauce, as we have said above.

Leaving there, I passed between the rock formations, which were his teeth, and managed to climb up on one, and there found the loveliest places in all the world, fine big tennis courts, nice galleries, fair meadows, vines galore, and an infinity of country villas in the Italian style, amid fields full of delights, and there I stayed a good four months, and never had it so good as then and there.

Then I came down by the back teeth to get to the lips; but on my way was robbed by brigands while going through a big forest, which is near the region of the ears.

Then I found a little hamlet on the way down, I've forgotten its name, where I had an even better time than ever, and earned a little bit of money to live on. Do you know how? By sleeping; for they hire people by the day to sleep, and they earn five or six *sous* a day; but those who snore really hard earn a good seven *sous* and a half. And I was telling the senators how I had been robbed in the valley, and they told me that in all truth the people on the other side were evildoers and brigands by nature, from which I learned that just as we have the countries on this side and on the far side of the mountains [the Alps], so have they on this side and on the far side of the teeth; but it's much nicer on this side and the air is better.

At that point I began to think that it is very true what they say, that half the world doesn't know how the other half lives seeing that no one had yet written about that country, in which there are over twenty-five inhabited kingdoms, not counting the deserts and one great arm of the sea; but I have composed a book about it entitled *History of the Gorgias*,[1] for thus I have named them because they live in the throat [la gorge] of my master Pantagruel.

Finally I wanted to get back, and, passing through his beard, I threw myself down on his shoulders, and from there slid down to the ground and fell in front of him.

When he noticed me, he asked me: "Where are you coming from, Alcofribas?"

I answered him: "From your throat, sir."

"And how long have you been there?" said he.

"Since you set out," said I, "against the Almyrodes."

"That," said he, "is over six months ago. And what did you live on? What did you drink?"

I answered: "Lord, the same as you, and of the choicest morsels that passed down your throat I took my toll."

"All right," said he, "but where did you shit?"

"In your throat, my Lord," said I.

"Ha ha! you're a jolly good fellow," said he. "We have, with the help of God, conquered the whole country of the Dipsodes; I give you the castleship of Salmagundi."

"Many thanks, Sir," said I. "You do much more good for me than I have deserved of you."

CHAPTER 33

How Pantagruel was sick,
and the way in which he got well.

A short time after, the good Pantagruel fell ill and was so griped in the stomach that he could not eat; and because one trouble never comes alone, he got a case of hot piss that gave him more torment than you would think; but his doctors helped him, and very effectively, with lenitive and diuretic drugs aplenty, made him piss away his trouble.

His urine was so hot that since that time it has still not cooled, and you have some in France in various places, according as it took its flow, and they call it hot baths such as

At Cauterets,[1]

At Limoux,

At Dax,

At Balaruc,

At Neris,

At Bourgon-Lancy and elsewhere.

In Italy,

At Monte Grotto,

At Abano,

At Sancto Petro de Padua [San Pietro Montagnone, near Abano],

At Saint Helen [Santa Elena Battaglia, near Monte Grotto],

At Casa Nova,

At Sancto Bartholomeo, in the county of Bologna,

At La Porretta,

And a thousand other places.

And I am greatly astounded at a heap of crazy philosophers and doctors, who waste time arguing whence comes the heat of the said waters, or whether it is because of the borax or the sulfur, or the alum, or the saltpeter that is inside the mine; for they do nothing but prattle, and it would be more worth their while to go rub their ass with a thistle than waste their time that way arguing about something they don't know the origin of: for the solution is easy, and there's no need to inquire further: that these baths are hot because they came out through a hot piss of the good Pantagruel.

Now, to tell you how he was cured of his main trouble, I leave aside here how, for a light laxative, he took:

Four hundredweight of scammony from Colophon,

Six score and eighteen cartfulls of cassia,

Eleven thousand nine hundred pounds of rhubarb,

Not counting the other ingredients.

You must understand that, on the advice of the doctors, it was then decreed that they would remove what was giving him the trouble in his stomach. For this they made seventeen great copper globes, bigger than the one in Rome at Virgil's needle, so made that they could open them at the middle and close them with a spring.

Into one entered one of his men bearing a lantern, and a lighted torch, and thus Pantagruel swallowed it like a little pill.

Into five others there entered three peasants, each having a shovel hanging from his neck.

Into seven others entered seven firewood haulers each one having a basket around his neck, and thus they were swallowed like pills.

When they were inside the stomach [Quand furent en l'estomach], each one released his spring and they came out of their cabins, and first the man bearing the lantern, and thus they fell over half a league into a horrible gulf, more stinking putrid than Mephitis,[2] or the marsh of Camarina, or the foul lake Sorbonne, which Strabo writes about, and, had it not been that they had very well antidoted their heart, their stomach, and their wine-pot (which they call the noggin), they would have been suffocated and snuffed out by these abominable vapors. O what perfume, O what fundament, to befoul the dainty masks of lively young lasses!

Afterward, groping and smelling their way, they approached the fecal matter and the corrupted humors; finally they found a great heap of ordure. Then the pioneers beat on it to break it up, and the others, with their shovels, filled the baskets with it; and when all was well cleaned out, each one got back into his globe. That done, Pantagruel makes an effort to throw up, and there they came joyously out of their pills—it reminded me of when the Greeks came out of the Trojan horses—and by this means he was cured and restored to his earlier health.

And of those brass pills you have one at Orléans on the steeple of the Eglise de Sainte-Croix.

CHAPTER 34

*The conclusion of the present book,
and the author's excuse.*

Now, Gentlemen, you have heard a beginning of the horrific history of my lord and master Pantagruel. Here I shall make an end to this first book; my head aches a bit and I clearly sense that the registers of my brain are rather a bit muddled by this September broth.[1]

You shall have the rest of the story at these Frankfurt Fairs coming up soon, and there you shall see: how Panurge got married, and was cuckolded right from the first month of his marriage; and how Pantagruel found the philosopher's stone, and the way to find it and use it; and how he crossed the Caspian Mountains; how he sailed over the Atlantic Ocean, and defeated the cannibals, conquered the Perlas Islands; how he married the daughter of the king of India named Prester John; how he fought against the devils and set fire to five chambers of hell, and sacked the great black chamber, and cast Proserpina into the fire, and broke four of Lucifer's teeth and a horn on his ass; and how he visited the regions of the moon to see if in truth the moon was not whole, but women had three quarters of it in their head; and myriad other little jollities, all true. Those are fine carryings-on.

Good night to you, Gentlemen. *Pardonnante my,* and don't dwell so much on my faults as on your own.[2] If you say to me: "Master, it would seem to me that it was no great wisdom on your part to write us these idiocies and comical tomfooleries," I reply to you that you are not much wiser to waste your time in reading them.

At all events, if you read them as a merry pastime even as I wrote them to pass the time, you and I are more deserving of pardon than a big bunch of Sarabaites, bigots, snails, hypocrites, fakers, bellybumpers, monks in buskins, and other such sects of people, who have disguised themselves like masters to deceive people.

For, giving the common populace to understand that they are occupied only in contemplation and devotion, fasts and mortifying their sensuality, if not really to sustain and nourish the puny fragility of their human nature, on the contrary they live it up, God knows how well.

Et Curios simulant, sed bacchanalia vivunt.

[And ape a saintly style,
Carousing all the while.]
[Juvenal, *Satires* 2.3]

You can read it in big lettering and illumination on their red snouts and barrel-sized guts, except when they perfume themselves with sulfur.

As regards their study, it is entirely consecrated to the reading of the Pantagruelic books, not so much to pass the time joyously as to harm someone wickedly, to wit by articulating, monorticulating, torticulating, buttock-wagging, ballock-shaking, and diaboliculating that is to say calumniating. Doing which, they are like those village scavengers who dig up and spread around little children's shit, in the season, for all kinds of cherries, so as to find the pits and sell these to the druggists, who make pomander oil out of them.

These shun, abhor, and hate as much as I do, and you will be well off for it, upon my word, and, if you want to be good Pantagruelists (that is to say to live in peace, joy, and health, always having a good time), never trust people who look out through a hole.[3]

End of the Chronicles of Pantagruel, King of the Dipsodes,

Restored to Their Natural State, with His Rightful

Exploits, Composed by the Late Master

Alcofribas, Abstractor of

Quintessence.

BOOK 3

The Third Book
of the
HEROIC DEEDS AND
SAYINGS
of the Good

PANTAGRUEL

Composed by
MASTER FRANÇOIS
RABELAIS[1]
Doctor of Medicine

Revised and Corrected by the Author
On the Basis of Ancient Censure
The aforesaid author implores his kindly readers
to refrain from laughing until the seventy-eighth book.

François Rabelais

To the Spirit of the Queen of Navarre[1]

Abstracted spirit, rapt in ecstasy,
Who while you haunt the skies, your origin,
Have left your servant host as you roam free,
Your well-matched body—quick to discipline,
Heeding you, for this pilgrim's life we're in—
Sans sentiment, and to emotion slow;
Wouldn't you care for just a while to go
Out of the heavenly manor where you dwell,
To see in their third section here below
The joyous deeds of good Pantagruel?

Royal Privilege[1] (of 1545)

Francis,[2] by the grace of God, King of France:
to the Provost of Paris

Bailiff of Rouen, Seneschals of Lyon, Toulouse, Bordeaux, Dauphiné, Poitou, and all our other justices and officers and their lieutenants, and to each of them as shall pertain to him, greetings [salut].[3] On behalf of our dear and well-loved Master François Rabelais, Doctor of Medicine of our University of Montpellier, it has been set forth to us that, this petitioner having hitherto offered for printing several books, notably two volumes of the heroic deeds and sayings of Pantagruel, no less useful than delightful, the printers have corrupted and perverted these books in many places,[4] to the great displeasure and detriment of the said petitioner and disservice to the readers, wherefore he has abstained from publishing the sequel and remainder of the said heroic deeds and sayings;[5] however, he was importuned daily by the learned and studious folk of our kingdom and asked to put into use as well as into print the said sequel.

He has besought us to grant him a privilege so that no one may go about printing them or putting them up for sale except for those [copies] that he would have printed by booksellers, expressly, to whom he would give his true and correct copies, and this [privilege] for the period of ten consecutive years, beginning on the day and date of the printing of the said books.

Wherefore we, having considered these things, wishing good letters promoted throughout our kingdom for the utility and erudition of our subjects, have given the said petitioner leave, license, and permission to have printed and put on sale, by such booksellers as he shall see fit, his said subsequent works about the heroic deeds of Pantagruel, beginning with the third volume, with the right and power to correct and revise the first two heretofore composed by him, and to print them or have them printed anew, to put them on sale or have them put on sale anew; [meanwhile] issuing prohibitions and injunctions on our behalf, on great and certain penalties, confiscation of the said books printed and arbitrary fines, to all printers and others whom putting or having put on sale, the books mentioned above, without the will and consent of the said petitioner, within the term of six consecutive years, beginning on the day and date of the printing of the said books, on pain of confiscation of the [copies of] said books and of arbitrary fines. To do this we have given, and do give, each one of you as it pertains to him, full power, commission, and authority; we order and command all our justices, officers, and subjects, that by our present leave, privilege, and commission they cause, allow, and permit the said petitioner to enjoy and make use of this peaceably; [order you] to be obeyed in doing this, for thus it is our pleasure that it be done. Given at Paris, the nineteenth day of September, the year of our Lord one thousand five hundred and forty-five, and of our reign the xxxi [31st]. So signed: by the counsel: Delaunay. And sealed with a simple tongue [queue] of yellow wax.

Royal Privilege[1] (of 1550)

Henry,[2] by the grace of God, King of France, to the Provost of Paris, Bailiff of Rouen, Seneschals of Lyon, Toulouse, Bordeaux, Dauphiné, Poitou, and to all our other justices and officers, or their lieutenants, and to each one of them just as it shall pertain to him, greetings and affection. On behalf of our dear and well-loved Master François Rabelais, Doctor of Medicine, it has been set forth to us that, the said suppliant having heretofore given for printing several books—in Greek, Latin, French, and Tuscan, notably certain volumes about the heroic deeds and sayings of Pantagruel, no less useful than delectable: (that) the said printers had perverted, corrupted, and depraved in many places. That furthermore they had printed many other, scandalous books, in the name of the said suppliant, to his great displeasure, prejudice, and ignominy, [books] totally disavowed by him as false and supposititious; which, subject to our good pleasure and will, he wished to suppress. Furthermore, to revise and correct the others of his that were avowed, but depraved and disguised, as it is said, and to reprint them anew. Likewise [he wishes] to bring out and put on sale the sequel to his heroic deeds and sayings of Pantagruel. Humbly beseeching us thereupon to grant him the letter of ours that is necessary and suitable for this.

So it is for this reason that we, inclining freely to the petition and request of the said Master François Rabelais, petitioner, and wishing to treat him well and favorably in this matter. To him for these reasons and other good considerations impelling us to this, we have permitted, granted and authorized, and by our certain knowlege and royal power and authority, do permit, grant, and authorize, by these presents, that he may, and it be lawful for him to, by such printers as he shall determine, have printed, displayed, and put up for sale, each and all the said books and sequel to Pantagruel, composed and undertaken by him—both those that have already been printed and which for that purpose will by him be revised and corrected, and also those new ones that he proposes to bring out. Likewise (he may) suppress those that are falsely attributed to him.

And in order that he may have the means to meet the costs necessary to open the said printing: we have by these presents most expressly prohibited and forbidden, we do prohibit and forbid, all other booksellers and printers of this our kingdom and our other lands and seigniories, from going about printing or having printed, displayed, and put up for sale, any of the aforesaid books, old or new, during the time and term of ten ensuing consecutive years, beginning on the day and date of the printing of the said books, without the will and consent of the said petitioner [exposant]—and [this] on pain of confiscation of books found to have been printed to the detriment of this our present permission, and [on pain of] arbitrary fine.

So we will, and command each one of you, in your own regard and howsoever it shall pertain to you, that you maintain, keep, and observe our present leave, license, and permission, bans and prohibitions. And if any were to be found to have contravened them, proceed against them and institute proceedings against them on the aforesaid penalties and in other ways. And have the aforesaid suppliant enjoy and use, fully and peaceably, during the said time, beginning and all the rest as is stated above. Ceasing and causing to cease any troubles or hindrances to the contrary: for such is our pleasure. Notwithstanding any ordinances, restrictions, commands, or prohibitions whatsoever contrary to this. And because in various places you will have to proceed with these presents, we will that upon our official certification of these as exact copies [au vidimus d'icelles], under the royal seal, they be trusted just as is this present original.

Given at Saint-Germain-en-Laye on the sixth day of August, the year of Our Lord one thousand five hundred and fifty. And of our reign the fourth.

By the King, with the Cardinal [Odet] de Chastillon present.

Signed:
DU THIER

Prologue of the Author,

Master François Rabelais,
for the third book
of the heroic deeds and sayings
of the good Pantagruel.[1]

Good folk, most illustrious topers, and you, most precious poxies, did you ever see Diogenes, the Cynic philosopher? If you have seen him, you hadn't lost your sight, unless I've completely departed from my intelligence and logical sense. It's a fine thing to see the brightness of the wine and sun (crowns) [veoir la clairté du vin et escuz Soleil]. I call to witness the man born blind, so renowned in the most Holy Bible [Mark 10.51], who, having the choice to ask for all he wanted, by the command of Him Who is Almighty and Whose word is in a moment shown forth in deed, asked for nothing more than to see.

Item, you are not young, a quality competent for more than physically,[2] philosophizing in wine, not in vain [*vin* and *vain* are homonyms], and for being from now on in the Bacchic council, in order in assaying to assess [pour en lopinant opiner] the substance, color, odor, excellence, eminence, properties, faculty, virtues, effect, and dignity of the blessed and much-desired *piot* [vino].

If seen him you have not (as I am easily induced to believe), at least you have heard speak of him. For his name and renown throughout the air and the whole heaven has up to now remained memorable and famous enough, and then you're all sprung from Phrygian blood (or I'm mistaken), and, if you haven't as many gold crowns as Midas had, yet you do have a certain something of his about you that the Persians prized in their spies [otacustes] and which was most desired by the Emperor Antoninus, something for which later the Rohan serpentine got the nickname, Fine Ears.[3]

If you haven't heard of him I want to tell you now a story to make a start on the wine (so drink up) and the talk (so listen), informing you (so that you may not by simplicity be fooled like unbelievers) that in his time he was one rare and joyous philosopher in a thousand. If he had a few imperfections, so have you, so have we. Nothing, except God, is perfect. Yet the fact is that Alexander the Great, although he had Aristotle for his household tutor, held him in such high esteem that he wished, in case he were not Alexander, to be Diogenes of Sinope.

When Philip, king of Macedon, undertook to besiege and destroy Corinth, the Corinthians, alerted by their spies that he was coming against them in great array and with a big army, were all, not unreasonably, frightened, and were not negligent in each making it his business to resist his hostile approach and defend their city.

Some were bringing back from the fields and into the fortresses movables, cattle, grains, wines, fruits, necessary victuals, and munitions.

Others were repairing walls,
setting up bastions,
squaring off ravelins,
digging ditches,
cleaning out countermines,
setting up gabions in the defenses,
arranging high platforms,
emptying casemates,
putting new bars on roads upon the walls,
erecting high platforms for artillery,
rebuilding counterscarps,
cementing curtain walls,
setting up snipers' posts,
raising ramps to the parapets,
mortising barbicans,
reinforcing machicolations,
rebinding portcullises,
stationing sentinels,
sending out patrols.

Every man was on the watch, every man was carrying his basket. Some were polishing corslets, varnishing cuirasses, cleaning housings, frontstalls, habergeons, brigandines, helmets, beavers, metal skullcaps, double pikes, horsemen's headpieces, morions, coats of mail, jazerants, brassarts, tasses, gussets, gorgets, arm-plates and thigh-plates, jointed corslets, hauberks, targets, bucklers, greaves, foot-pieces, spurs.

Others were readying bows, slings, crossbows, pellets, catapults, fire-arrows, fireballs, fire-pots, fire-rings, grenades, stone-throwing ballistae, and scorpions, and other warlike machines made to repel and destroy siege towers.

They were sharpening boar spears, pikes, hooks, halberds, crooks, long-handled billhooks, lances, assagais, pitchforks, partisans, maces, battle-axes, darts, dartlets, javelins ancient and modern, hunting spears. They were whetting scimitars, cutlasses, back swords, tucks, hangers, broad old-style short-swords, poniards, knives, blades, three-edged daggers.

Everyone was exercising his poniard; everyone was scouring the rust off his hanger. No woman was there, however old and prudish, who did not get her harness furbished; for, as you know, the old-time Corinthian women were courageous in combat.

Diogenes, seeing them turning everything upside down with such fervor, and not being employed by the magistrates to do anything, for a few days contemplated their behavior without saying anything. Then, as if excited by martial spirit, he flung his cloak around him like a scarf, trussed up his robe like an apple picker, handed an old comrade of his his wallet, his books, and his writing tablets, took a fine esplanade out of the city toward Cranion, a hill and promontory near Corinth, rolled over to it the earthenware barrel that served him as a house against the assaults from the sky, and, exerting his arms in great vehemence of spirit, veered it,[4]

> twisted it, scrambled it, garbled it,
> churned it, turned it, overturned it,
> rustled it, hustled it, muscled it,
> bustled it, castled it, passeled it,
> hasseled it, wrassled it, dangled it,
> bangled it, wrangled it, poked it,
> stroked it, woke it, yoked it,
> provoked it, tumbled it, bumbled it,
> rumbled it, humbled it, preened it,
> cleaned it, liened it, careened it,
> bricked it, blocked it, blathered it,
> gathered it, spattered it, roused it,

raised it, bashed it, lanced it,
pried it, tried it, charmed it,
armed it, harmed it, tethered it,

feathered it, caparisoned it, brought it down below from atop, precipitated it off Cranion, then brought it back up from below to the top, as Sisyphus did with his stone; so much so that he barely missed knocking a hole in it.

Seeing this, one of his friends asked him what cause impelled him thus to torment his body, his spirit, and his barrel. To which the philosopher replied that being employed on no other business by the commonwealth, he harried his barrel this way amid this people so fervent and occupied, not alone to seem a slacker and an idler.

I likewise, although free from fear, am nonetheless not free from care,[5] seeing that I am held to be of no account worth putting to work, and considering that throughout this whole most noble kingdom of France, both on this side of the mountains and beyond them [deçà, delà les mons], today each and every man is earnestly exerting himself and working, partly on the fortification of his fatherland and defending it, partly on repelling the enemy and harming them, all this in such fair polity, such wonderful ordering, and to such evident advantage for the future (for henceforth shall France be superbly bordered [bournée], shall the French be secured in repose) that little restrains me from coming to the opinion of the good Heraclitus, that war was the father of all good things, and from believing that war in Latin is said to be beautiful [bellum, belle] not by antiphrasis, as have supposed certain patchers of old Latin iron,[6] because in war they saw no goodness and beauty, but absolutely and simply, for the reason that in war appears every kind of good and beauty, there is hidden every kind of evil and ugliness. As proof that this is so, the wise and peaceable King Solomon knew no better way to represent the ineffable perfection of the divine wisdom than by comparing it to the ordering of an army in camp.

So for not being enrolled and placed in the ranks of our men in the offensive part, since they have judged me to be too feeble and impotent, and in the other, which is defensive, not being employed at all, even if it were in carrying hods, burying sewage, binding, kindling, or breaking up clods,[7] it didn't matter to me, I thought it a more than moderate shame to be seen an idle spectator of so many valiant, eloquent, and knightly personages, who in the sight and spectacle of all Europe are playing this notable fable and tragic comedy,[8] not to put out my utmost effort myself, and not to accomplish by it that little, my all, that I had left. For scant glory seems to me to accrue to those who employ on it only their eyes, for the rest sparing their strength, concealing their gold crowns, hiding their silver, scratching their head with one finger, like disenchanted no-goods, gaping at flies like idiot moon-calves, flapping their ears like Arcadian donkeys at the musicians' song and by their faces signifying in silence that they consent to the prosopopoeia [performance].

This choice and option taken I thought I would perform no useless and importunate exercise if I agitated my Diogenic barrel, which alone has been left me from the shipwreck incurred in the past at the lighthouse by the Strait of Malencounter. By this dingledangling of my barrel, what do you think I will accomplish? By the virgin tucking up her skirts?[9] I don't know yet. Wait a minute while I sniff down a snifter from this bottle; it's my one real Helicon. It's my Caballine spring, my one and only enthusiasm. Here drinking I deliberate, I discourse, I resolve and conclude. After the epilogue,[10] I laugh, I write, I compose, I drink. Ennius drinking wrote, writing drank. Aeschylus (if you put any faith in Plutarch, in his *Symposiaca [Questiones naturales]* drank composing, drinking composed. Homer never wrote on an empty stomach. Cato never wrote except after drinking. This so that you may not say that I live like this without the example of those well praised and best prized. It's good and fresh enough, as you might say just at the start of the second degree;[11] God, the good God Sabaoth (that is to say, of the armies) be eternally praised for it. If you folks likewise drink one big swig or two little swigs under your cloak, I see no problem in that provided you praise God a bit for everything.

So since it is my lot or destiny (for not to every man is it granted to enter and inhabit Corinth [Horace *Epistles* 1.18.36]), my intention is to be so little idle and unprofitable, that I will set myself to serve the one and the other sort of folk. Among the diggers, pioneers, and rampart-builders, I will do what Neptune and Apollo did in Troy under Laomedon, what Renaud de Montauban did in his last days: I'll serve the masons, I'll put on to boil for the masons; and once the meal is over, to the sound of musical pipes I'll measure the musery of the musers [je . . . mesureray la musarderie des musars].[12] Thus did Amphion fund, build, and construct, by playing on his lyre, the great famous city of Thebes. For the combatants I'm again going to pierce my barrel, and from the draft, which by two preceding volumes (if by the printers' imposture they had not been perverted and jumbled) was well enough known to you, draw them, from the vintage of our afterdinner pastimes, a gallant third draft and

257

consecutively a merry fourth, of Pantagruelic sayings;[13] by me it will be licit to call them Diogenic. And since comrade I may not be, they shall have me as loyal steward of the feast,[14] within my small power offering refreshment for their return from alarms, and tireless, I say, in praise of their exploits and glorious feats of arms. I shall not fail them, by *lapathium acutum*[15] of God, if Mars[16] should not fail in Lent; but he'll be careful not to do that, the old lecher.

However, I remember reading that when Ptolemy, son of Lagus one day, among other spoils and booties of his conquests, offered the Egyptians, in the midst of the theater an all-black Bactrian camel and a slave motley colored in such a way that half of his body was black, the other white (not divided in latitude at the diaphragm as was that woman sacred to the Indian Venus who was noted by the Tyanian philosopher between the river Hydaspes and Mount Caucasus, but in the perpendicular dimension, things not yet seen in Egypt), he hoped by these novelties to augment the people's love for him. What comes of it? At the presentation of the camel all were frightened and indignant; at the sight of the motley-colored man some sneered, others abominated him as an infamous monster, created by an error of nature. In sum, the hope he had of pleasing the Egyptians, and by this means extending the affection they naturally bore him, slipped out of his hands. And he understood that they took more pleasure and delight in things beautiful, elegant, and perfect, than ridiculous and monstrous. After that he held both the slave and the camel in such scorn that soon after, through negligence and lack of proper treatment, they exchanged life for death.

This example makes me oscillate between hope and fear, afraid that in place of anticipated contentment I encounter what I abhor, my treasure proves to be lumps of coal, instead of Venus, I come up with Whiskers the dog,[17] instead of serving them I offend them, instead of pleasing them I displease, and my outcome be such as that of Euclion's Rooster, made so famous by Plautus in his *Pot* [*Aularia* 3.4] and by Ausonius in his *Gryphus* and elsewhere, who, for having discovered the treasure in his scratching, had his coat thrust.[18] Should that come to pass, ought it to get my goat? It has happened in the past; happen it still could. No it won't by Hercules! I recognize in them all a specific form and individual property that our ancestors called Pantagruelism, on condition of which they never take in bad part things they know issue from a good, free, and honest heart. I have seen them ordinarily take good will in payment and be content with that, even when weakness in power has been associated with it.

With that point expedited, I return to my barrel. Up and at this time, mates! Fill up your mugs, lads! If it doesn't seem good to you, leave it. I'm not one of those importunate fossilophers,[19] who by force, outrage, and violence, constrain the fellows and comrades to toss her down, which is worse. Every worthy toper, every worthy goutie, when thirsty, coming to this barrel of mine, is not to drink if he doesn't want to; if they want to, and the wine pleases the taste of the Excellency of their Excellencies [la seigneurie de leurs seigneuries], let them drink freely, frankly, boldly, without paying a thing, and not spare it. Such is my decree. And have no fear that the wine will run out, as it did at the wedding in Cana in Galilee [John 2.1–11]. As much as I draw from the spigot, I'll funnel in through the bung. Thus will the barrel remain inexhaustible. It has a living spring and a perpetual vein. Such was the golden bough sacred to the subterranean goddess, so celebrated by Virgil [*Aeneid* 6.63ff., 110–140, 174 ff]. It's a real cornucopia of joyfulness and jesting. If at some point it seems to you to be exhausted down to the lees, it will, however, not be dry. Good hope lies at the bottom, as in Pandora's bottle,[20] not despair, as in the jar of the Danaids.[21]

Mark well what I have said, and what manner of people I invite. For (that no one be misled), on the model of Lucilius, who protested that he wrote only for his Tarentines and Cosenzans, I have pierced it only for you, good people, topers of the first vintage and gouties in your own right. The doriphagous giants [les géans doriphages avalleurs de frimars],[22] mist-swallowers, have occupations[23] enough, and enough pouches on the hook for venison; let them see to that if they will. This is not their game here.

About the hood-brained pettifoggers, the nitpicking sticklers for details, don't talk to me, I beseech you in the name and reverence of the four buttocks that engendered you and the life-giving kingpin that for that time coupled them [Des cerveaulx à bourlet, grabeleurs de corrections, ne me parlez, je vous supplie on nom et révérence des quatre fesses qui vous engendrèrent, et de la vivificque cheville qui pour lors les coupploit.] As for the pious hypocrites, even less although they are all out-and-out poxies, equipped with unquenchable thirst and insatiable mastication. Why? Because they are not of good, but of evil, and of that evil from which we daily beseech God to be delivered, although they sometimes impersonate beggars. Never did an old monkey make a pretty face.

Behind me, curs! Out of here, impostors! Out of my sunlight, you devil's rabble! Are you high-tailing it here to screw up my wine and piss in my barrel? Look, here's the stick that Diogenes ordered in his will to be placed next to him after his death to clobber and drive away these coffin-haunting spooks and Cerberian curs. Out of here, you phonies! In the name of the devil, out! Are you still there? I give up my share of Papimania,[24] if I can just catch you. Grr. Grrr. Grrrrr! Avaunt, Avaunt! Will they ever go? May you never be able to crap except under the lash of stirrup leathers, never piss but with the strappado, never get hot pants except from a beating!

CHAPTER 1

How Pantagruel transported
a colony of Utopians into Dipsody.

PANTAGRUEL, having utterly conquered the country of Dipsody, transported into it a colony of Utopians in the number of 9876543210 men (not counting the women and little children), artisans in all trades and professionals in all liberal disciplines, so as to refresh, populate and adorn the said country, which was otherwise ill inhabited and for the most part a wilderness. And he transported them not so much for the excessive multitude of men and women who had multiplied like locusts in Utopia—you understand well enough, there is no more need to inform you of it further, that the Utopian men had genitals so fertile, and the Utopian women wombs so ample, gluttonous, tenacious, and architecturally well cellulated, that after every ninth month seven children at the very least, both males and females, were born of each marriage, in imitation of Judaic people in Egypt (if De Lyra is not delirious)—also not so much for the fertility of the soil, salubriousness of the climate, and advantages of the country of Dipsody, as in order to contain it in its duty and obedience by a new importation of his faithful ancient subjects, who in all memory of man had known, recognized, avowed, or served, no other lord than him.

And who, when they were born and came into the world with their mothers' milk also imbibed the sweetness and kindness of his rule, and in this were ever confected and reared, which offered certain hope that they would sooner give up this bodily life than that primal sole subjection naturally due to their prince, whithersoever they might be dispersed and transported. And not only such would they be and the children successively born of their blood, but also they would maintain in that fealty and obedience the nations newly annexed to his empire.

This indeed happened, and in no way was he frustrated in his planning.

For if the Utopians, before this transmigration, had been loyal and truly grateful, the Dipsodes, after associating with them for a few days, were even more so, by I know not what fervor natural in all humans at the beginning of all operations that are to their taste. Only they complained, calling on all the heavens and the moving intelligences, that they had not known sooner of the renown of the good Pantagruel.

So you will note here, topers, that the way to maintain and retain newly acquired countries is not (as certain tyrannical spirits[1] have opined, to their hurt and dishonor) by plundering, forcing, harassing, ruining the peoples and ruling them with iron rods, in short eating and devouring the peoples in the way for which Homer [*Iliad* 1.231] calls the wicked King Demovorous, that is to say, devourer of his people. In this connection I shall not cite you the old stories, but shall merely recall to your memory what your fathers have seen of this, and you yourselves, if you're not too young. Like a newborn child we must nurse them, cradle them, fondle them. Like a newly planted tree we must support them, secure them, defend them against all storms, damages and calamities. Like a person saved from a long potent illness and coming to convalescence, we must coddle them, spare them, restore them. So that they may inwardly conceive this opinion, that there is no king or prince in the world whom they would want less as an enemy, opt for more as a friend. Thus Osiris, the great king of the Egyptians, conquered the whole earth not so much by force of arms as by relieving harassment, teaching how to live well and in health, by comfortable laws, graciousness, and good deeds. Therefore he was surnamed by everyone the great god Evergetes (that is to say Benefactor) by order of Jupiter given to one Pamyla.

Hesiod, in his *Theogony*,[2] locates the good daemons (call them if you will angels or genii) as mediators between gods and men, superior to men, inferior to gods. And because through their hands riches and good things come to us from heaven, and they are continually beneficent to us, always preserving us from harm, he says they act the part of kings, since always to do good, never harm, is a peculiarly kingly way to act. Thus was Alexander of Macedon emperor of the universe. Thus was the whole continent possessed by Hercules, relieving humans of monsters, oppressions, exactions, and tyrannies, governing them with good treatment, maintaining them in equity and justice, in a benign government suiting the site of the countries instituting them, supplying what was lacking, pricing down what was plentiful, and pardoning the entire past with eternal oblivion of all preceding offense, as was the Amnesty of the Athenians, when by the prowess and steadfastness of a Thrasybulus the tyrants were driven out, later expounded in Rome by Cicero and renewed under Emperor Aurelian.[3]

These are the philters, snares, and lures of love, by which peacefully one retains what one had painfully conquered. And no more happily can a conqueror reign, be he king, prince, or philosopher, than by making Justice succeed Valor. His valor appeared in the victory and conquest, his justice will appear in that he will give laws by the will and kind affection of the people, and publish edicts, establish religions, do right to each and every man, as the noble poet Maro [Virgil *Georgics* 4.559-561] says of Octavian Augustus:

> Although the victor, yet he managed still
> To govern by the conquered people's will.[4]

That is why Homer, in his *Iliad* [1.375 and 3.236], calls good princes and great kings Κοσμήτορας λαῶν, that is to say adorners of peoples. Such was the consideration of Numa Pompilius, second king of the Romans, a just statesman and philosopher, when he ordained that to the god Terminus, on the day of his festival, which was called Terminalia, nothing was to be sacrificed that had died, teaching us that in peacetime it is fitting to guard and control the bounds, frontiers, in peace, friendliness, and geniality, without soiling our hands with blood and pillage. Anyone who acts otherwise will not only lose his gain but also will suffer this scandal and opprobrium, that he will be thought to have acquired it wickedly and wrongly, on the grounds that the gain perished in his hands. For ill-got things perish ill; and even though all his life he may have enjoyed it peaceably, if nonetheless the gain perishes in his heirs, the like scandal will lie upon the deceased; and his memory will be accursed as a wicked conqueror. For you say as a common proverb: "Of ill-got things the third heir shall have no joy."

Note also, you true-blue gouties, in this matter, how by this means Pantagruel made two angels out of one, an outcome opposite to Charlemagne's decision when he made two devils out of one when he transported the Saxons into Flanders and the Flemings into Saxony. For being unable to keep the Saxons annexed by him to his empire in subjection, but that would burst into rebellion if by chance he was drawn away into Spain or other far-off land, he transported them into a land of his naturally obedient, to wit Flanders; and the Hainaulters and Flemings, his natural subjects he transported into Saxony with no fear for their loyalty even though they were transmigrating into foreign lands. But it turned out that the Saxons continued in their original rebellion and obstinacy, and the Flemings in Saxony imbibed the ways and the contrariness of the Saxons.[5]

CHAPTER 2

How Panurge was made lord of Salmagundi in Dipsody and ate his wheat in the blade.

IN ordering the government of Dipsody, Pantagruel assigned to Panurge the castleship of Salmagundi in each year worth 6789106789 royals[1] in assured petty cash, not including the certain revenue from June bugs and snailshells, which year in year out amounted to between 2435768 and 2435769 long-woolled sheep. Sometimes it came to 123454321 seraphs[2] when it was a good year for snailshells and choice June bugs. But this was not every year. And so well and prudently did Milord the new Lord of the Manor govern himself that in less than a fortnight he had squandered the revenue, certain and uncertain, of his castleship for three years. He did not really squander[3] it, as you might say, on founding monasteries, erecting churches, building schools and hospitals, or tossing his bacon to the dogs; but he spent it on myriad joyous little banquets and feasts open to all comers, especially good companions, young girls, and cute wenches, felling woods, burning the big logs to sell the ashes, taking money in advance, buying dear, selling cheap, and eating his wheat in the blade.[4]

Pantagruel, notified of the matter, for all that was not in the least indignant, angry, or vexed inside. I've already told you, and yet again I tell you, that he was the best nice little big little fellow that ever buckled on a sword. All things he took in good part, all actions he interpreted for the good; never did he torment himself, never did he take offense; else he would have quite departed from out the deific manor of reason [aussi eust-il esté bien forissu du déificque manoir de raison], if otherwise he had let himself be affected; for all the goods that Heaven covers and earth holds in all its dimensions—height, depth, length, and width—do not deserve to stir our affections or trouble our senses and spirits.

Only he drew Panurge aside and gently pointed out to him that if he would live that way and not husband his resources differently, impossible it would be, or at least very difficult, to make him rich.

"Rich?" retorted Panurge. "Is that what you'd set your mind on? Had you made it your concern to make me rich in this world? Just put your mind to living joyously, in the name of God and the good man![5] May no other concern, no other care, be received into the sacrosanct domicile of your celestial brain. May the serenity thereof never be troubled by any clouds whatever of thought laced with pain and distress. With you living joyous, lusty, cheerful, I shall be only too rich. Everyone cries: 'Thrift, thrift!' but a man or two talks about thrift who knows not what it is. I'm the one whose advice they should take. And from me this time you shall take notice that what is imputed to me as vice has been imitation of the University and Parlement of Paris, places in which resides the true source and living archetype of pantheology and also for all justice. Heretic he who doubts it, and does not firmly believe it. At all events in one day they devour their bishop [Ilz toutesfoys en un jour mangent leur évesque] or the revenue of the bishopric (it's all one) for one entire year, indeed for two sometimes; that's on the day when he comes into it. And there's no way to be excused from this, if he would not be stoned on the spot.

"It has also been an exercise of the four cardinal virtues [A esté aussi acte des quatre vertus principales].

"Of prudence, in taking money in advance, for you never know who may bite or kick [car on ne sçayt qui mord ne qui rue]. Who knows if the world will last another three years? And even if it should last longer, is there any man so insane as to dare promise himself to live three years?

> Never had man the gods so much his way
> As to be sure to live another day.[6]

"Of commutative justice,[7] buying dear (I mean on credit), selling cheap (I mean for cash). What does Cato say in his *Husbandry* [*De re rustica* 2.55.7] on that subject? The paterfamilias, he says, must be a perpetual seller. By this method it is impossible for him not to become rich at last, if his provisions hold out.

"Distributive [justice],[8] giving food to good (I mean good) companions, whom Fortune had cast, like Ulysses, on the rocks of a good appetite with no supply of food, and the nice (I mean nice) young French wenches (I mean young; for, according to Hippocrates's saying, youth is intolerant of hunger, especially if it is vivacious, lively, fast-moving, curveting), which wenches willingly and heartily give pleasure to good men and are Platonic and Ciceronian to the point where they think they are born into the world not for themselves alone, but share their persons partly with their country, partly with their boyfriends [font part à leur patrie, part à leurs amis].

"Of strength, knocking down the big trees [en abastant les gros arbres], like a second Milo; wiping out the dark forests, lairs of wolves, wild boars, foxes, hideouts of brigands and murderers, burrows of assassins, workshops of counterfeiters, hideaways for heretics, and leveling them into bright open fields and fair heaths, playing the oboes[9] [haulx boys], and preparing the seats for Judgment Night.

"Of temperance, eating my wheat in the blade, living on salads and roots like a hermit, emancipating myself from sensory appetites, and thus saving up for the cripples and the afflicted. For by so doing I save on weeders, who make money; the reapers, who like to drink, and without water; the gleaners, who must have their cake; the threshers, who, on the authority of Virgil's Thestylis,[10] leave no garlic, onion, or shallot in the gardens; the millers, who are ordinarily robbers; and the bakers, who are hardly any better. Is that a petty saving? Besides the damage from the field mice, the residues in the granaries, and what is eaten by the weevils and mites?

"From wheat in the blade you make nice green sauce, simple to concoct and easy to digest, which refreshes your brain, cheers your animal spirits, rejoices your sight, opens up your appetite, delights your taste, fortifies your heart, tickles your tongue, brightens your color, strengthens your muscles, tempers your blood, revives your diaphragm, freshens your liver, unstops your spleen, relieves your kidneys, purges your bladder, lulls your loins, limbers up your vertebrae, empties your ureters, dilates your spermatic vessels, tightens up your cremasters, cleans out your bladder, fills up your genitals, straightens your foreskin, encrusts your gland, erects your member, gives you a good belly, makes you do things well: belch, fizzle, fart, shit, urinate, sneeze, sob, cough, spit, vomit, yawn, blow your nose, puff, inhale, breathe, snore, sweat, get your pecker up, and myriad other rare advantages."

"I quite understand," said Pantagruel, "you are inferring that dull-witted people could not spend so much in a short time. You are not the first to conceive that heresy. Nero maintained it and admired above all humans his uncle Gaius Caligula, who in a few days, by wondrous ingenuity, had spent all the patrimony and wealth that Tiberius had left him. But instead of keeping and observing the culinary and sumptuary laws of the

Romans, the *leges* Orchia, Fannia, Didia, Licinia, Cornelia, Lepidania, Antia, and those of the Corinthians, by which it was strictly forbidden to each and every one to spend more per year than his annual income allowed, you have performed Protervia, which among the Romans was a sacrifice like that of the Paschal lamb among the Jews: you were supposed to eat up everything edible, throw the rest into the fire, save nothing for the morrow. I can justly say of you what Cato said of Albidius, who, after eating up all he possessed by excessive expenditure, since all that was left was one house, he set fire to it, so as to say *consummatum est*,[11] even as later Saint Thomas Aquinas said when he had eaten up the whole lamprey. Let it pass [Cela non force].

CHAPTER 3

How Panurge praises debtors and creditors.

"But," asked Pantagruel, "when will you be out of debt?"

"At the Greek Calends," replied Panurge, "when everyone will be happy and you will be heir to yourself. God preserve me from being out of it. Then I would no longer find anyone who would lend me a penny. He who leaves no leaven in the evening will never make his dough rise in the morning. Do you always owe something to someone? By him will God be continually implored to give you a good, long, and happy life, fearing to lose his debt; always will he speak well of you in all companies, always will acquire for you new creditors, so that by means of them you may make payment, and with other men's earth fill his ditch.

"When once upon a time in Gaul, by the ordinance of the druids, serfs, servants, and attendants were all burned alive at the funerals and obsequies of their masters and lords, weren't they good and scared that their masters and lords would die, for they all had to die together? Didn't they continually pray to their great god Mercury, with Dis, the father with the ducats,[1] to keep them in health for a long time? Weren't they careful to treat and serve them well, for together they could live, at least, until death? Believe me, in even more fervent devotion your creditors will pray God that you live, will fear that you may die, the more so because they love the sleeve more than the arm,[2] the penny more than life; witness the userers of Landerousse not long ago, who hanged themselves when they saw the price of wheat and wines go down and good weather return."

As Pantagruel made no reply, Panurge went on:

"Honest to goodness [vray bot]! When I really think of it, you put me right back behind the eight-ball,[3] reproaching me for my debts and creditors! Why, in that sole quality I considered myself august, reverend, and redoubtable, in that, surpassing the opinion of all philosophers (who say nothing is made out of nothing), having nothing and no primal matter, I was a maker and creator.

"I had created what? All those lovely fine creditors. Creditors are (I maintain right up to the stake exclusively)[4] fine good creatures. Whoever lends nothing is an ugly evil creature, a creature of the great foul fiend of hell.

"And made what? Debts. O rare and antiquarian thing! Debts, I say, exceeding the number of syllables resulting from coupling all the consonants with all the vowels, a number once conceived and counted by the noble Xenocrates. If by the numerosity of creditors you estimate the perfection of debtors, you make no mistake in practical arithmetic.

"Will you believe how happy I am when every morning I see around me these creditors, so humble, so serviceable, and full of scrapes and bows? And when I note that when I show one of them a more open face and better greeting than to the others, the rascal thinks that he will get his quittance first, thinks he will have his day first, and supposes that my smile is ready money? It makes me think I'm still playing God in the Saumur passion play surrounded by His angels and cherubim. They are my candidates, my parasites, my glad-handers, my good-day-sayers, my perpetual speechmakers. And I truly thought it was in debts that consisted the heroic mountain of virtues described by Hesiod,[5] in which I was first in my class for my *licence*,[6] toward which all humans seem to tend and aspire (but few climb it, because the way up is difficult), since today I see everyone in a fervent desire and clamourous appetite to make new debts and creditors.

"However, not all are debtors who would be; not all make creditors who want to. And you want to oust me from this sable-smooth felicity? You ask me when you shall be out of debts?

"There's much worse than that; I give myself to Saint Babolin the good saint if all my life I've not considered debts to be a sort of connecting link between Heaven and earth, a unique interrelationship of the human race—I mean without which all humans would soon perish—

peradventure to be that great soul of the universe, which, according to the Academics, gives life to all things.

"As proof of this, in a serene state of mind imagine the idea and form of some world—take, if you see fit, the thirtieth of those imagined by the philosopher Metrodorus, or the seventy-eighth of Petron—in which there is not one debtor or creditor: a world without debts. There, among the stars, there will be no regular course whatever. All will be in disarray. Jupiter, not thinking himself a debtor to Saturn, will dispossess him of his sphere, and with his Homeric chain [*Iliad* 8.19–27; 15.19–22] will suspend all the intelligences, gods, heavens, daemons, heroes, devils, earth, sea, all elements. Saturn will join forces with Mars, and they will put this whole world into confusion. Mercury won't be willing to subject himself to the others, no longer will be their Camillus, as he was called in the Etruscan language; for he is not their debtor in anything. Venus will not be venerated. The moon will remain bloody and dark: on what ground will the sin impart his light to her? He was in no way bound to. The sun will not shine on their earth, the stars will exert no good influence there, for the earth was desisting from lending them nourishment by vapors and exhalations, by which (Heraclitus was wont to say, the Stoics to prove, Cicero to maintain) the stars were fed [maintenoit estre les estoilles alimentées].

"Among the elements there will be no sympathizing, alternation, or transmutation whatever, for the one will not repute himself obliged to the other; he hadn't lent him anything. Of earth will water not be made; fire will not warm the earth. The earth will produce nothing but monsters, Titans, Aloidae, and giants; rain will not rain there, nor light shine there, nor wind blow there, nor will there be summer or autumn there. Lucifer will loose his bonds and, issuing from the depths of hell with the Furies, the Pains, and horned devils, will try to dislodge from the heavens all the gods of both the greater and the lesser peoples.

"This nothing-lending world will be nothing but bitchery, a more unearthly wrangle than the election of the University Rector in Paris, a more confused deviltry than that of the Doué plays. Among humans one will not save the other; there'll be no use his shouting: 'Help! Fire! Man overboard! Murder!' No one will go and help. Why? He hadn't lent anything; no one owed him anything. No one feels anything to lose in his fire, in his shipwreck, in his ruin, in his death. And likewise he didn't lend anything. And likewise he wouldn't have lent anything afterward.

"In short, from this world will be banished Faith, Hope, Charity, for men are born to aid and succor men. In place of these will succeed

Mistrust, Contempt, Rancor, and the cohort of all evils, all curses, and all miseries. You will really think that there Pandora had poured out her bottle. Men to men will be wolves, werewolves, and goblins, as were Lycaon, Bellerophon, Nebuchadnezzar; brigands, assassins, poisoners, evildoers, evil-thinkers, evil-willers, and everyone bearing hatred against all, like Ishmael, like Metabus, like Timon of Athens, who for that reason was surnamed μισάγθρωπος [misanthropos]. So that an easier thing it would be in nature to nourish the fish in the air, feed the stags at the bottom of the ocean, than to endure this rascally scoundrelly rabble of a world, which lends nothing. My faith, I really hate them!

"And if on the model of this loathsome peevish world lending nothing you imagine the other, little world, which is man,[7] in him you'll find a terrible jinglejangle. The head will not want to lend the sight of its eyes to guide the feet and hands; the feet will not deign to carry the head. The hands will stop working for it. The heart will be annoyed at working so much for the members' pulse and will no longer lend to them. The lungs will no longer make it a loan of their bellows. The liver will not send it blood for its upkeep. The bladder won't want to be indebted to the kidney: the urine will be stopped. The brain, considering this unnatural carrying-on, will go off into a reverie and will give no feeling to the nerves, nor movement to the muscles. In sum, in this disrupted world, owing nothing, lending nothing, borrowing nothing, you will see an even more pernicious conspiracy than Aesop represented in his fable.[8] And it will perish beyond a doubt; not only will it perish, but it will perish soon, were it Aesculapius himself. And the body will promptly fall into putrefaction; the soul, all indignant, will take its flight to all the devils, after my money [l'âme toute indignée prendra course à tous les Diables, après mon argent]."[9]

CHAPTER 4

*Continuation of Panurge's speech
in praise of creditors and debtors.*

"O_N the contrary, imagine a different world in which everyone lends, everyone owes, all are debtors, all are lenders.

"O what harmony there will be among the regular movements of the heavens! I think I hear it as well as Plato ever did. What sympathy among the elements! O how Nature will delight in her works and productions! Ceres laden with wheat; Bacchus, with wines; Flora, with flowers; Pomona, with fruits; Juno in her serene air, herself serene, salubrious, pleasant. I'm lost in this contemplation. Among humans, peace, love, fondness, fidelity, repose, banquets, feasts, joy, blitheness, gold, silver, small change, chains, rings, merchandise will trot about from hand to hand. No lawsuit, no war, no dispute; no one there will be a userer, no one a sneak, no one stingy, no one a refuser.

"Honest to God, won't that be the age of gold, the reign of Saturn, the model of the Olympian regions in which all other virtues give way. Charity alone reigns, governs, dominates, triumphs? Everyone will be good, everyone will be beautiful, everyone will be just. O happy world! O people of that happy world! O thrice and four times blessed! It seems to me I'm there. I swear to you by honest-to-goodness [Je vous jure le bon Vraybis] that if this world, blessed world, thus lending to each and every one, refusing nothing, had a pope teeming with cardinals and associates of his sacred college, in a few years you would see there saints more clustered, more miracle working, with more readings, more prayers, more batons, and more tapers, than are all those of the nine bishoprics of Brittany,[1] excepting only Saint Ives.

"Consider how the noble Pathelin, wanting to deify, and by divine praises place all the way up in the third heaven Guillaume, Jousseaulme's father, said nothing more than

> Always did he heed
> Requests for loans for all in want or need.[2]

"O what a lovely statement! On that pattern imagine all our microcosm, *id est* little world, which is man, in all his members lending, borrowing, owing, that is to say in his natural state. For Nature created man only to lend and borrow. No greater is the harmony of the heavens than will be that of his polity. The intention of the Founder of this microcosm is to maintain in it the soul, which He has placed there as a guest, and life. Life consists in blood. Blood is the seat of the soul.[3] Therefore this microcosm labors at one sole task, to form blood continually. In this formation are all the members in their proper function; and their hierarchy is such that without stopping one borrows from the other, one to the other is debtor. The material and metal fit to be transmuted into blood is given by nature: bread and wine. In these two are comprised every kind of food, and from this it is called *companage* [victuals] in Langue d'Oc. To find, prepare, and concoct these [icelles . . . cuire], the hands work, the feet travel and carry this whole machine; the eyes guide everything; the appetite, in the orifice of the stomach, with the help of a little bitter melancholy, which is transmitted to it from the spleen, exhorts to take in food. The tongue makes trial of it; the teeth chew it; the stomach receives it, digests it, and chylifies it. The mesaraic veins suck out of it what is good and suitable, discarding the excrements, which by an expulsive property are voided outside by conduits made for that, then carry it to the liver; from that point on it transmutes it and makes blood of it.

"Then what joy do you suppose there is among these members [ces officiers], when they have seen this stream of gold [the blood], which is their one restorative? No greater is the joy of the alchemists when, after long labors, with great care and expense, they see the metal transmuted in their furnace.

"So then each member prepares itself and puts forth its powers to purify and refine this treasure. The kidneys, by the emulgent veins [the renal conduits], draw off from it the aquosity that you call urine, and by the ureters pass it down below. Way down it finds its own receptacle, that is the bladder, which at an opportune time voids it outside. The spleen draws off from it the earthy part and the lees, which you call melancholy [black bile]. The bile duct draws off from it the superfluous choler.[4] Then it is transported into another workshop to be better refined: that's the heart, which by its diastolic and systolic movements subtilizes it and inflames it, so that by the right ventricle it brings it to perfection and through the veins sends it to all the members. Each member draws it to itself and feeds on it at will: feet, hands, eyes, all of them; and then they are made into debtors, who before were lenders. By the left ventricle it makes it so subtle that it is called spiritual, and it sends it to all the members by its arterie, to warm up and ventilate the other blood from the veins. The lungs with their lobes and bellows never stop refreshing it. In gratitude for this boon the heart imparts the best of it to them by the pulmonary artery. In fine, it is so refined within the marvelous network that afterward are made from it the animal spirits, by means of which the soul imagines, discourses, resolves, deliberates, reasons, and remembers.

"Goshamighty [Vertus guoy]! I drown, I get lost, I go astray, when I enter the profound abyss of this world thus lending, thus owing. Believe me, a divine thing is lending, owing is a heroic virtue. Still that is not all. This lending, owing, borrowing world is so good that when this feeding is completed, it is already thinking about lending to those who are not yet born, and by lending perpetuating itself if it can and multiplying itself in images like itself; these are children. To this end each member cuts and clips off a portion of the most precious part of its nourishment and sends it back down below; there Nature has prepared opportune vessels and receptacles for it, by which, flowing down to the genitals through long roundabout windings, it receives adequate form and finds suitable places, in man just as in woman, to preserve and perpetuate the human race. The whole thing is done by loans and debts from one to another; therefore, it is called the duty or debt [le debvoir] of marriage.[5]

"A penalty is imposed by nature on the refuser, a sharp vexation among the members, and frenzy among the senses; to the lender a reward assigned, pleasure, blitheness, and voluptuousness."

CHAPTER 5

How Pantagruel detests debtors and creditors.

"I understand," said Pantagruel, "and you seem to me a good advocate and devoted to your cause. But preach and plead from now to Whitsunday, in the end you'll be dumbfounded at how you won't have persuaded me one bit, and by your fancy talk you'll never make me go into debt. 'Owe nothing,' says the Holy Apostle [Saint Paul: Romans 13.8], 'save love and mutual affection.'

"You're using on me here beautiful representations and descriptions, and I like them very much; but I tell you that, if you imagine a boastful blusterer [un affronteur efronté et importun emprunteur] and bothersome borrower coming anew into a town already informed of his ways, you'll find that at his entry the citizens will be in more fear and trepidation than if the plague had entered in such attire as the Tyanian philosopher[1] found it wearing at Ephesus. And I believe the Persians were not mistaken in considering that the second vice was lying, and the first was being in debt.[2] For debts and lies are ordinarily allied together.

"I don't mean to infer for all that never must we owe, never must we lend. There is no man so rich that he may not at some time owe. There is no one so poor that one may not at some time borrow from him. The occasion will be such as Plato stated it in his *Laws* [8.866b],[3] when he ordains that a man is not to let the neighbors draw water from his well until they had first dug and probed in their own meadows until they found that kind of earth they call *céramite* (that is potter's clay) and there had not come upon a spring or dripping of water. For this earth by its substance, which is greasy, strong, slippery, and dense, retains humidity, and does not easily allow runoff or evaporation.[4]

"Thus it is a great disgrace always, in every place, to borrow from each and every one, rather than to work and earn. Only then (in my judgment) should one lend, when the person, by working, has been unable to gain by his labor or when he has suddenly fallen into an unexpected loss of his goods.

"Therefore let's drop this subject, and from now on don't get involved with creditors; of the past I set you free."

"The least I should do, the most I can," said Panurge, "in this matter will be to thank you; and if the thanks are to be measured by the affection of the benefactors, that will be infinitely, eternally; for the love that by your grace you bear me is beyond the bounds of estimate, it transcends all weight, all number, all measure; it is infinite, eternal. But if you measure it by the caliber of the benefits and the contentment of the recipients, that will be rather laxly. The good things you do for me are much much more than belong to me, more than I have deserved of you, more than my merits warranted, I am forced to confess it but by no means as much as you think in this matter.

"That's not what bothers me, that's not what irks and gripes me. For from now on, being quit, what face am I going to wear? Believe me, I'll look bad for the first months, seeing that I'm neither trained nor accustomed to it. I'm very much afraid so.

"Besides, from now on not a fart will be born in all Salmagundi that won't get sent back to my nose. All the farting farters in the world say:

274

'That for the quit!' My life will soon end, I foresee it. And I'll die all pickled in farts. If some day as a restorative for farting for good women suffering acutely from windy colic the doctors are not satisfied with the ordinary medicament, the mummy of my lousy befarted body will be a remedy at hand for them. By taking the least little bit of it, they will fart more than they understand.

"That's why I would like to ask you to leave me some hundred-odd debts, as King Louis the Eleventh, on casting out of lawsuits Milles d'Illiers, bishop of Chartres, was importuned by him to leave him one or two to practice on. I would rather give them [my creditors] my snailshellery, and with it my Junebuggery, however, without drawing anything out of the principal."

"Let's drop this subject," said Pantagruel, "I've already told you that once."[5]

CHAPTER 6

Why newlyweds were exempt from going to war.

"B UT," asked Panurge, "in what law was it instituted and established that those who should plant a new vineyard, those who should build a new lodging, and newlyweds, would be exempt from going to war for the first year?"

"In the law of Moses," said Pantagruel.

"Why," asked Panurge, "the newlyweds? About the vine-planters, I'm too old to be concerned; I agree in the concern for the vintagers; and the fair new builders with dead stones are not inscribed in my book of life. I build only with live stones: that is men."

"In my judgment," replied Pantagruel, "it was so that for the first year they should enjoy their loves at their pleasure, keep busy in the produc-tion of lineage, and make provision of heirs. Thus, at the least, if in the second year they were killed in war, their name and coat of arms would remain in their children. Also so that their wives should be certainly known to be either barren or fertile (for the one-year trial seemed to them sufficient, considering the mature age at which they got married), in

275

order after their first husbands' deaths to be able to bestow them better in second marriages: the fertile on those who would wish to multiply in children; the barren on those who would not want any, and would take them for their virtues, learning, good graces, simply for domestic comfort and household maintenance."

"The preachers of Varennes," said Panurge, "detest second marriages as crazy and indecent."

"They're welcome," said Pantagruel, "to a nice juicy quartan fever."

"Yes indeed," said Panurge, "and so is Friar Sheathing-it [Enguainnant], who, preaching at Parillé, right in his sermon, inveighing against second marriages, swore up and down, and offered to give himself to the swiftest devil in hell in case he wouldn't rather deflower a hundred maidens than one widow.

"I think your reason is sound and well founded. But what would you say if this exemption were granted them for the reason that, in the course of this first year, they would have thumped their newly-won ladyloves so roundly (as is their rightful debt and duty), and so drained their spermatic vessels, that it left them all bedraggled, all unmanned, all enervated and drooping, so that when the day of battle came they would sooner take a dive like ducks than stand up with the fighters and valiant champions in the place where Enyo stirs the mêlée and the blows are handed out, and under the banner of Mars that would not strike one blow worthy of the name? For the great blows would have landed under the bed-curtains of his ladylove Venus.

"As proof that this is so, we still see nowadays, among other relics and mementos of antiquity, that in all good houses, after I know not how many days, they send these newlywed men to see their uncle, to get them away from their wives and meanwhile rest them up and revictual them, the better to combat on their return, although often they have neither uncle nor aunt; in the same manner as King Pétaud, after the battle of the Cornets [des Cornabons], did not fire us, strictly speaking, I mean me and Courcaillet [Quailpiper], but sent us to refresh ourselves in our houses. He's still looking for his. My grandfather's godmother used to say, when I was little, that

> Paternosters and praying
> Are fine for those whom they concern.
> A fifer going haying
> Can outdo two on their return.[1]

276

"What leads me to this opinion is that the vine-planters hardly used to eat grapes or drink wine of their labor during the first year; and the builders, for the first year, did not live in their new-made lodgings, on pain of dying there from failure in breathing out, as Galen learnedly noted in Book 2 *On difficulty in breathing*.[2]

"I didn't ask this without well-grounded grounds or without well-resounding reason [sans cause bien causée, ne sans raison bien résonnante]. No offense to you."

CHAPTER 7

How Panurge had a flea in his ear,
and left off wearing his magnificent codpiece.

On the morrow Panurge had his ear pierced Judaic style and fastened in it a little gold ring with silver thread inlay, in the bezel of which was set a flea. And the flea was black, so that you may have no doubt about anything (it's a fine thing to be well informed in every case), the expense for which, as reported to his *bureau,* each quarter amounted to hardly more than the marriage of one Hyrcanian tigress, as you might say 600,000 maravédis. At such excessive expenditure he grew angry when he was quit, and afterward fed it in the fashion of tyrants and attorneys: on the sweat and blood of his subjects.

He took four ells of *bureau;* dressed himself in it as a long gown with a single closure; left off wearing his breeches; and attached spectacles to his bonnet.[1]

In such state he presented himself to Pantagruel, who found the disguise strange, especially no longer seeing his lovely magnificent codpiece, in which, as in a holy anchor, he was wont to constitute his last refuge against all shipwrecks of adversity.

Since the good Pantagruel did not understand this mystery, he questioned him, asking what this new disguise meant.

"I have a flea in my ear," said Panurge; "I want to get married."

"I wish you well," said Pantagruel; "you've just made me very happy. To be sure, I wouldn't hold on to a red-hot iron as a bet on it. But this is not the attire of lovers, thus to have breeches at half-mast and let your shirt hang down over your unbreeched knees, with a long gown of brown frieze [*bureau*], which is an unusual color for full-length gowns among men of quality and virtue.

"If some adherents to heresies and individual sects have dressed in this in times past, although many have imputed it to trickery, imposture, and affectation of tyranny over the crude populace, I do not therefore want to blame them and in that to make a sinister judgment of them. Let every man be full of his own ideas,[2] especially in matters alien, extraneous, and indifferent, which are in themselves neither good nor bad, because they do not issue from our hearts and thoughts, which are the workshop producing all good and all evil: good, if good it is, with the disposition ruled by the pure spirit; bad, if by the evil spirit and the disposition is depraved. Only I don't like novelty and disdain for common usage."

"The color," replied Panurge, "is *aspre aux potz* [harsh on pots; homonym of *apropos*]. Apropos (that's my *bureau*),[3] I mean henceforth to run my affairs and check closely on them. Since now for once I'm quit, you've never seen a meaner man than I'll be, unless God helps me.

"See my spectacles here. To see me from a distance you'd rightly say it's Friar Jean Bourgeois. I think in this coming year I'll once more preach a crusade. God keep the ballocks from harm!

"Do you see this *bureau*? Believe me, in it consists some occult quality known to few people. I put it on only this morning, but already I'm wild, I'm unsheathing, I'm sizzling to be married and go to work like a brown devil upon my wife, with no fear of sticks or a beating. O what a great householder I'll be![4] After I die they'll have me burned on an honorific pyre, to get the ashes in memory and model of the perfect householder. 'Odsbody! On this bureau of mine my paymaster had better not play around with stretching the *esses*,[5] or my fists would go trotting all over him!

"Look me over, front and rear: this is the form of a toga, ancient attire of the Romans in time of peace. I took the pattern of it from Trajan's column in Rome, also from the triumphal arch of Septimius Severus. I'm tired of war, tired of buff coats and foot soldiers' cassocks. My shoulders are all worn down from wearing harness. Farewell arms, hail togas! At least for all this coming year, if I'm married, as you told me yesterday, by the law of Moses.

"As regards the breeches, my great-aunt Laurence used to tell me long ago that they were made for the codpiece. I believe it by the same inference as that mad wag Galen, Book 9 *Of the function of our members* [*De usu partium* 8.5] says the head is made for the eyes. For nature might have put our heads at our knees or our elbows; but, arranging the eyes to spy out afar, she set them in the head like a staff of the highest point of the body; as we see that lighthouses and high towers are erected above seaports so that the beacon may be seen from afar.

"And because I would like, for a certain length of time, a year at the least, to draw breath free from the military art, that is to say to marry, I'm no longer wearing a codpiece, or consequently breeches. For the codpiece is the first piece of the harness to arm the warrior. And I maintain up to the stake (exclusively, you understand) that the Turks are not properly armed, since wearing codpieces is expressly forbidden in their laws."

CHAPTER 8

*How the codpiece is the first piece
of harness among warriors.*

"Do you mean," said Pantagruel, "to maintain that the codpiece is the first piece of military harness? That's a very paradoxical and novel doctrine, for we say that with the spurs you begin to arm yourself."

"I do maintain it," replied Panurge, "and not wrongly do I maintain it.

"See how nature, wanting to perpetuate and continue to all successive ages the plants, trees, shrubs, herbs, and zoophytes once created by her without the species dying out, even though the individuals perish, carefully armed their germs and seeds, in which this perpetuity consists, and protected and covered them, by admirable ingenuity, with husks, sheaths, hulls, pits, tiny skins, shells, ears down, bark, prickly spines, which are for them like fair strong natural codpieces. Examples are manifest in peas, beans, string beans, walnuts, clingstone peaches, cotton, colocynths, wheats, poppies, lemons, chestnuts, generally all plants in which we clearly see that the germ and seed is more covered, protected, and armed than any other part of them. Not thus did nature provide for the perpetuation of the human race, but created man naked, tender, fragile, without either offensive or defensive arms, in a state of innocence and original golden age, as an animal, not a plant, as an animal, I say, born to peace not to war, an animal born to wondrous enjoyment of all fruits and vegetal plants, an animal born to peaceful domination over all beasts.

"When there came the multiplication of malice among humans that succeeded the iron age and Jupiter's reign, the earth began to produce nettles, thistles, thorns, and such other kinds of rebellion among vegetables against man; moreover, almost all the animals, by fated disposition, emancipated themselves from man and tacitly conspired together to serve him no more, obey him no longer in so far as they could resist, but harm him according to their capacity and power.

"Thereupon man, wanting to maintain his original enjoyment and continue his original domination, also being unable conveniently to do without the service of several animals, had the need to arm himself anew."

"By the Holy Mother of Goose!"[1] exclaimed Pantagruel, "since the last rains you've become a great fossilopher, or rather I mean philosopher."

"Consider," said Panurge, "how nature inspired him to arm himself, and what part of his body he first began to arm. By God's power, it was his balls,

> And Priapus, that good signor,
> When he had done, asked her no more.

"Thus testifies the Hebrew captain and philosopher Moses, affirming that he armed himself with a fine gallant codpiece, by most lovely invention made of fig leaves, which are natural and completely suitable in stiffness, indentations, embossing, polish, size, color, odor, virtues, and ability to cover and arm ballocks.

"Excepting only the horrific ballocks of Lorraine, which come down unbridled right to the bottom of the hose, shun the manor of the lofty codpiece, and are out of all order; witness Viardière, the noble Valentin,[2] whom I found one May Day in Nancy, so as to be more gorgeous, scouring his ballocks, which were stretched out on a table, like a Spanish-style cape.

"So henceforth we must not say, unless we want to; speak improperly, when we send the *franc-taupin* off to war:

> 'Stevie [Tevot], save the wine-pot,'

(that's the noggin): we must say:

'Stevie, save the milk-jug,'

that's the balls, by all the devils in hell! The head lost, perishes only the person; the balls lost, would perish all human nature.

"That's what impelled the gallant Cl. Galen, in Book 1 *On sperm* [*De spermate*], to conclude that it would be better (that is, less bad) to have no heart than to have no genitals. For there, as in a sacred repository, consists the preserving germ of the human line. And for less than a hundred francs I'd be ready to believe that those are the very stones of which Deucalion and Pyrrha restored the human race, abolished by the deluge fabled by the poets.[3]

"That's what led the valiant Justinian, in Book 4 *De cagotis tollendis*[4] [*On the elevation of hypocrites*], to locate the supreme good in shorts and codpieces [summum bonum in braguibus et braguetis].

"For this and other reasons, as Lord de Merville[5] was trying on a new harness one day to follow his king in war (for his ancient half-rusted one he could no longer use well, because for a number of years the skin of his belly had gone far away from his kidneys), his wife considered, in a thoughtful spirit, that he was taking little care of the common packet and staff of their marriage,[6] seeing that he was arming it only with chain mail, and came to the conclusion that he should arm it very well and gabion it with a stout jousting helmet that was hanging useless in his den. About her are written these verses in the third book of *The Shitter-Shatter of the Maidens*:[7]

> Seeing her husband armed from tip to toe,
> Save for the codpiece, heading for the fray,
> One woman said: "To keep you safe today,
> My love, protect the part I cherish so."
> Could any scoffer rate her counsel low?
> No, no, I say; because her greatest fear,
> Seeing it lively, was to let it go—
> That precious morsel that she held so dear.[8]

"So leave off your amazement at this novel attire of mine."

CHAPTER 9

How Panurge takes counsel of Pantagruel
to learn whether he should marry.

A s Pantagruel made no reply, Panurge went on and said with a deep sigh:

"My Lord, you have heard my plan, which is to marry, unless by bad fortune all the holes should be closed, shut, and locked; I beseech you by the love you have borne me for so long, tell me what you think about it."

"Since once," said Pantagruel, "you've cast the die and have thus decreed it and made a firm plan to do it, there's nothing more to say about it; all that remains is to put it into execution."

"True," said Panurge, "but I wouldn't want to execute it without your counsel and favorable advice."

"My advice is favorable," said Pantagruel, "and I counsel you to."

"But," said Panurge, "if you knew that my best course was to stay just as I am, without undertaking anything new, I'd rather not marry at all."

"Don't marry at all, then," replied Pantagruel.[1]

"All right," said Panurge, "but would you want me to stay all alone this way all my life without conjugal company? You know that it is written: *veh soli* [woe unto him who is alone]. A man alone never has such solace as you see among the married."

"Then get married, in God's name," replied Pantagruel.

"But," said Panurge, "what if my wife made me a cuckold, for you know it's a big year for them, that would be enough to drive me beyond the bounds of patience. I like cuckolds perfectly well, and they seem like fine people to me, and I enjoy their company, but for the life of me I wouldn't want to be one. That's a point that has too sharp a point."

"No point in it then, don't get married," responded Pantagruel; "for Seneca's dictum is true without any exception: whatever you've done to others, be sure that others will do to you."

"Do you say that," asked Panurge, "without exception?"

"Without exception he says that," replied Pantagruel.

"Oho!" said Panurge, "by the wee devil! He means either in this world or the other. All right, but since I can no more do without a wife than can a blind man without a stick (for the drill must get its exercise, other-

282

wise I couldn't live), isn't it better for me to take on with me some good worthy woman, rather than change from day to day with continual danger of a beating, or at the worst the pox? For no decent woman ever meant anything to me. (And no offense to their husbands.)"

"Then get married, in God's name!" replied Pantagruel.

"But," said Panurge, "if God so willed, and it came about that I married some worthy woman and she beat me, I'd be worse off than Job's tercel,[2] if I didn't go stark raving mad. For I've been told that these oh-so-virtuous women usually have a nasty temper; and so they have good vinegar in the house.[3] My temper would be even worse, and I'd beat her outlying parts [batteroys] with might and main: that is to say arms, legs, head, lungs, liver, and spleen; I would tear her clothes to shreds so badly in every way, that that great old Devil would lie in wait for her damned soul. From all this ruckus I'd like to be free for this year, and happy not to get into it at all."

"Then don't get married at all," said Pantagruel.

"All right," said Panurge, "but being in the state I'm in, quit and not married—mind you, I say quit at a bad time; for if I were very deep in debt, my creditors would be only too concerned about my Paternity—but quit and unmarried, I have no one to care as much about me and bear me such love as they tell me conjugal love is. And if by chance I fell ill, I would be treated only wrong way round. The sage [Ecclesiasticus 36.25–26] says: 'Where there is no wife (meaning wife and mother, in lawful marriage), a patient is in a sorry plight.' I've seen clear evidence of this in popes, legates, cardinals, bishops, abbots, priests, and monks. Now there you'll never get me."

"Get married then, in the name of God!" replied Pantagruel.

"But if," said Panurge, "while I might be ill and impotent for the duties [debvoir] of marriage, my wife, impatient of my languor, abandoned herself to others, and not only did not help me in my need but also made fun of my calamity and (worse yet, robbed me, as I have often seen happen, that would complete my pretty picture and drive me to go run about the streets in my doublet."

"Then don't go about getting married," replied Pantagruel.

"All right," said Panurge, "but in no other way would I ever have legitimate sons or daughters, in whom I would have hope of perpetuating my name and coat of arms; to whom I can leave my inheritances and acquisitions (I'll have some beauties one of these mornings, have no doubt of it, and furthermore I'll be a great payer-off of mortgages), with whom I can have fun when otherwise I'd be feeling low, as every day

I see your most benign and good-natured father do with you, and as all good people do in the privacy of their own home. For being quit, not being married, suppose by some mishap I were made wretched! . . . Instead of consoling me, it seems to me that over my trouble you're making merry!"

"Marry then, in the name of God!" replied Pantagruel.[4]

CHAPTER 10

How Pantagruel points out to Panurge
that advice about marriage is a difficult thing,
and of Homeric and Virgilian lots.

"Your advice," said Panurge, "subject to correction, is like the Ricochet song.[1] It's nothing but sarcasms, mockeries, and contrary repetitions. One group cancels out the other. I don't know which ones to rely on."

"Accordingly," replied Pantagruel, "in your propositions there are so many ifs and buts that I can't possibly base or resolve anything upon them. Aren't you certain of your will? The main point lies there: all the rest is fortuitous and dependent on the fated dispositions of heaven.

"We see a good number of people so happy in this encounter that in their marriage there seems to shine forth some idea and representation of the joys of paradise. Others are so unhappy in it that the devils who tempt the hermits around the deserts of the Thebaid and Montserrat[2] are not more so. You have to go into it at a venture, eyes blindfolded, bowing your head, kissing the ground, since once for all you want to go into it. No other assurance about it could I possibly give you.

"Now, here's something you might do if you see fit. Bring me the works of Virgil, and, opening them with your fingernail three times running, we'll explore, by the verses whose numbers we agree on, the future lot of your marriage. For, as by Homeric lots a man has often come upon his destiny.

"Witness Socrates in prison, who, hearing this bit of verse from Homer spoken of Achilles, in *Iliad* 9 [363]."

Ἤματι χεν τρίτατῳ Φθίην ἐρίβωλον ἱχοίμην.

I shall arrive without further delay,
At fertile Phthia, right on the third day.[3]

He foresaw that he would die on the third day thereafter, and assured Aeschines of it, as Plato writes in his *Crito* [44b], Cicero in Book 1 of *De divinatione,* and Diogenes Laertius.

"Witness Opilius Macrinus, to whom, wishing to know whether he would be emperor of Rome, there came by chance this saying from the *Iliad* 8 [102–103]

Ὦ γέρον, ἦ μάλα δή σε νέοι τείρουσι μαχηταί,
Σὴ δὲ βίη λέλυται, χαλεπὸν δέ σε γῆρας ὀπάζει ...

Old man, these tough young fighters are too strong,
And age won't let you hold on very long.

"Indeed he was already old, and, having held the empire for only one year and two months, by powerful young Heliogabalus he was dispossessed and slain.

"Witness Brutus, who, wanting to explore the fate of the battle of Pharsalia, in which he was killed, came upon this verse spoken by Patroclus in the *Iliad* 16 [849]:

Ἀλλά με μοῖρ᾽ ὀλοὴ χαὶ Λητοῦς ἔχτανεν υἱός.

By the cruel frown of Fate I was undone,
And by the rancor of Latona's son.

"That's Apollo, whose name served as the watchword on the day of that battle.

"Also by Virgilian lots in olden times were known and foreseen remarkable things and matters of great importance, indeed even to the winning of the Roman empire, as happened to Alexander Severus, who in this kind of lot came upon this written verse of the *Aeneid* 6 [851]:

Tu regere imperio populos, Romane, memento.

Remember, Roman, o'er the world to rule.

"Then after a number of allotted years was really and in fact made emperor of Rome.

"In the case of Hadrian, Roman emperor, who, being in doubt and anxiety to know what was Trajan's opinion of him and what feeling he had for him, took counsel by Virgilian lots and came upon this verse in the *Aeneid* 6 [808–810]:

> Quis procul ille autem, ramis insignis olivae
> Sacra ferens? Nosco crines insanaque menta
> Regis Romani . . .
>
> Bearing the olive branches, who is he?
> His hair and priestly gown show him to be
> The aged Roman king.

"Then was he adopted by Trajan, and succeeded him as emperor.

"In the case of Claudius the Second, highly praised emperor of Rome, on whom by lot fell this verse written in the *Aeneid* [1.265]:

> Tertia dum Latio regnantem viderit aestas
>
> While the third summer saw his Latian reign.

"In fact he ruled for only two years. To that very man, inquiring about his brother Quintilius, whom he wanted to bring into the government of the empire with him, there came this verse of the *Aeneid* 6 [869]:

> Ostendent terris hunc tantum fata
>
> Fate will but show this man unto the lands.

"This thing came to pass, for he was killed seventeen days after assuming the management of the empire; this same fate fell to Emperor Gordian the Younger.

"To Clodius Albinus, eager to hear his good fortune, came what is written in the *Aeneid* 6 [857]:

> Hic rem Romanam magno turbante tumultu
> Sistet eques, etc.

> This knight shall hold aloft the place of Rome
> While great disturbance dominates at home,
> Subduing Carthaginian and Gaul,
> And handing their revolts a heavy fall.

"To the Divine Claudius [II, Roman emperor A.D. 268–270], the emperor who preceded Aurelian, concerned about his posterity, came this verse from the *Aeneid* I [278]:

> His ego nec metas rerum, nec tempora pono

> For these no bounds are set, no deadlines drawn.

Accordingly he had a long genealogy of successors.

"In the case of Master Pierre Amy,[4] when he tried to learn whether he should escape the hobgoblins, and came upon this verse of the *Aeneid* 3 [44]:

> Heu! Fuge crudeles terras, fuge littus avarum.

> Woe! Flee this cruel land, this evil shore.

And then escaped from their hands safe and sound.

"A thousand others, whose adventures it would be too long-winded to relate, which happened according to the pronouncement of the verse come upon by lot.

"I do not want to imply, however, lest you be misled by it, that this lot is universally infallible."

CHAPTER 11

How Pantagruel points out
that fortune-telling by throwing dice is unlawful.

"This," said Panurge, "would be sooner done and dispatched with three fine dice."

"No," said Pantagruel, "that kind of divination is deceitful, illicit, and extremely scandalous. Don't ever trust it. That accursed *Book of Games of Chance*[1] was invented long ago by our enemy the infernal calumniator; near Boura in Achaea and in front of the statue of Bouraic Hercules he once used to lead, and at present in many places leads, many a simple soul to fall into his snares. You know how my father Gargantua in all his kingdoms has forbidden it, burned it with all its types and pictures, and completely banned, suppressed, and abolished it, as a very dangerous plague.

"What I've said about dice I likewise say to you about knucklebones; it's a comparably deceptive game of chance. And don't allege to me to the contrary the fortunate case of the knucklebones that Tiberius made in the fountain of Aponus at Geryon's oracle. Those cases are the bait with which the Calumniator draws simple souls to eternal perdition.

"To satisfy you all the same, I'm quite content that you should throw three dice on this table. From the number of points that come up we'll take the verses on the page you will have opened to. Do you have some dice there in your purse?"

"A game-pouch full," said Panurge. "That's the green amulet against the Devil,[2] as Merlin Coccai explains in the second book *Of the country of the devils*. The Devil would catch me unawares[3] if he came upon me with no dice."

The dice were brought out and cast, and fell showing five, six, and five points.

"That's sixteen," said Panurge. "Let's take the sixteenth verse on the page. I like the number, and I think we'll be well set. I'll hurl myself through all the devils in hell, like a bowling ball through a game of skittles or a cannonball through a battalion of foot soldiers. Let anyone who wants to beware of the devils, in case I don't bolt my future wife that many times on my wedding night."

"I have no doubt of it," said Pantagruel; "there was no need to take such a horrific oath on it. The first time will be a fault and count fifteen.[4] On getting off your perch you'll make it up; that way it'll make sixteen."

"And so," said Panurge, "that's how you understand it? Never was a slip up made by the valiant champion who does sentry duty for me in my lower belly. Have you ever found me in the confraternity or the defaulters? Never, never, to the very end never. I do it without fail, like a holy father. Just ask the players!"

These words finished, there were brought out the works of Virgil. Before opening them, Panurge said to Pantagruel:

"My heart is beating through my body like a mitaine.[5] Just touch my pulse a bit in this artery in the left arm. From its frequency and elevation you'd think I was being belabored at a thesis defense in the Sorbonne. You wouldn't advise, before going any further, that we invoke Hercules and the Tenite goddesses, who are said to preside over the Chamber of Lots?"[6]

"Neither the one nor the others," replied Pantagruel. "Just open it up with your fingernail."

CHAPTER 12

How Pantagruel explores by Virgilian lots
what sort of marriage Panurge's will be.

Panurge, opening the book, came upon this verse in the sixteenth line [Virgil, *Eclogues* 4.63]:

Nec Deus hunc mensa, Dea nec dignata cubili est.

No god bid her to table, no goddess to her couch.

"This one," said Pantagruel, "is not to your advantage. It signifies that your wife will be a slattern, consequently yourself a cuckold.

"The goddess you will not have favorable is Minerva, a greatly feared virgin, a powerful goddess, thunder-darting, enemy of cuckolds, of fops, adulterers, enemy of lascivious women, who do not keep faith promised to their husbands and who abandon themselves to other men. The god is Jupiter, hurling down thunder and lightning from the skies. And you will note in the doctrine of the ancient Etruscans that the *manubiae* (so they called the Vulcanian thundercasts) belong to her alone (an example of this was given in the burning of the ships of Ajax, son of Oileus) and to Jupiter her capital father.[1] To other Olympian gods it is not permitted to hurl lightning; therefore, they are not so dreaded by humans.

"I'll tell you more, and you're to take it as drawn from high mythology. When the giants undertook war against the gods, the gods at first made light of such enemies, and said there was not enough work here for their pages. But when they saw, by the work of the giants, Mount Pilion placed upon Mount Ossa and Mount Olympus already shaken loose to be set atop the two of them, they were all frightened. So Jupiter held a general council. There it was agreed by all the gods that they would valiantly prepare for defense. And because they had many times seen battles lost because of the women who were among the armies getting in the way, it was decreed that for the time they would banish out of the skies into Egypt and toward the confines of the Nile all that sluttery of goddesses disguised as weasels, martens, bats, shrew-mice, and other metamorphoses. Minerva was retained to hurl lightning with Jupiter, as goddess of letters and of war, of counsel and execution, goddess both armed, goddess dreaded in heaven, in the air, on sea, and on land."

" 'Od's belly!" said Panurge, "could I really be the Vulcan the poet speaks about?[2] No, I'm neither lame, nor a counterfeiter, nor a black-smith, as he was. Peradventure my wife will be as beautiful and attractive as his Venus, but not a trollop like her, nor I a cuckold like him. That lousy crookshank had himself declared a cuckold by a decision and in full view of all the gods. As for that, take it in reverse.

"This lot denotes that my wife will be virtuous, modest, and faithful, not a bit armed; bashful, neither brainless nor, like Pallas, taken out of a brain; and that handsome Jove will never be a rival to me, never will dip his bread into my dip, even if we should eat together at table.

"Consider his deeds and fine exploits. He was the sturdiest wencher and most infamous *cor* . . . —I mean *bordelier*[3]—that ever was, always lecherous as a wild boar; sure enough, he was nursed by a sow on Mount Dicte in Crete, if Agathocles the Babylonian is not lying; and more goatish than any goat; and so others say that he was suckled by Amnalthea, a nannygoat. By the powers of Acheron! for one day's stint he rammed out the third part of the world, beasts and men, rivers and mountains; that was Europe. Because of that ramming the followers of Ammon had him portrayed in the shape of a ram ramming, a horned ram.

"But I know how a man must protect himself from that horny character. Believe me, he won't find some stupid Amphitryon, some idiot Argus with his hundred eyeglasses, a coward Acrisius, a silly goosecap Lucus of Thebes, a dotard Agenor, a phlegmatic Asopus, a hairy-pawed Lycaon, a doltish Corytus of Tuscany, a stout-backed Atlas.

"He might transform himself a hundred and another hundred times into a swan, a bull, a satyr, into gold, into a cuckold, as he did when he deflowered his sister Juno, into an eagle, into a ram, into a pigeon, as he did when he was in love with the maiden Phthia, who lived in Aegium; into fire, into a snake, indeed into a flea, into Epicurean atoms, or magistronostrally [magistronostralement] into second intentions. I'll hook him with my crook. And do you know what I'll do to him? 'Odsbody [Corbieu]! what Saturn did to his father Heaven, Uranus (Seneca has predicted it of me and Lactantius confirmed it): what Rhea did to Atys. I'll up and cut his balls off right flush with his tail, not a hair's breadth less. For that reason he will never be pope, for he has no testicles [testiculos non habet]."

"Easy now, Sonny," said Pantagruel, "easy now! Open for the second time." Then he came upon this verse:

> Membra quatit, gelidusque coit formidine sanguis.

> He breaks his bones and shatters all his limbs;
> Which turns his blood to ice; his vision swims.

"It denotes," said Pantagruel, "that she will drub you, back and belly."

"Conversely," replied Panurge, "that prediction is about me and says that I will beat her like a tiger if she makes me angry. Martin Wagstaff will perform that function. If I have no stick, Devil devour me if I would not eat her alive and kicking, as Cambles, king of the Lydians, ate his."

"You," said Pantagruel, "are mighty courageous. Hercules would not fight you in this frenzy. But that's what they say, that one poor Joe [le Jan] is as good as two, and Hercules never dared fight alone against two."

"I'm a poor Joe?" said Panurge.

"Not at all, not at all," replied Pantagruel. "I was thinking of two kinds of backgammon."

On the third try he came upon this verse [*Aeneid* 2.782]:

Faemineo praedae et spoliorum ardebat amore.

She burned with eagerness, as women will,
To rob the baggage and to take her fill.

"It signifies," said Pantagruel, "that she will rob you. And I can see you in really good shape according to these three lots: you will be a cuckold, you will be beaten, you will be robbed."

"On the contrary," replied Panurge, "this verse signifies that she will love me with a perfect love. Never did the Satirist [Juvenal] lie about it when he said that a woman burning with supreme love sometimes takes pleasure in robbing her lover. Do you know of what? A glove, a clasp, some trifle, nothing of importance.

"Likewise these little fusses, these hassles, that sometimes arise between lovers, are like new fresheners and spurs of love. Just as we see, for example, cutlers sometimes hammer on their whetstones the better to sharpen iron blades. This is why I take these lots to my great advantage. Otherwise I appeal."

"Appeal," said Pantagruel, "one never can against judgments decided by lot and Fortune, as our ancient jurists attest, and Baldus says so, L. *ult.* C. *de leg.*

"The reason is because Fortune recognizes no superior to whom one may appeal from her and her judgments. And in this case the ward cannot be restored to his full rights, so he says clearly in L. *Ait praetor.* § *ult. ff. de minor.*"

CHAPTER 13

*How Pantagruel advises Panurge
to foresee by dreams
the fortune or misfortune of his marriage.*

"Now, since we don't agree with one another on the expounding of the Virgilian lots, let's try another art of divination."

"What one?" asked Panurge.

"A good one," replied Pantagruel, "ancient and authentic; that's by dreams; for by dreaming under the conditions prescribed by Hippocrates in his book Περι ἐνυπνίων [*On dreams*], Plato, Plotinus, Iamblichus, Synesius, Aristotle, Xenophon, Galen, Plutarch, Artemidorus Daldianus, Herophilus Q. Calaber, Theocritus, Pliny, Athenaeus, and others, could often foresee future things.

"There's no need to prove it to you at greater length. You understand it by vulgar example when you see how, with children nicely cleaned, well fed and suckled, the wet nurses go off and amuse themselves in freedom, as being for that time let off to do what they will for their presence around the cradle would seem useless. In that fashion our soul, when the body is asleep and digestion is completed in all parts, nothing more being necessary in it until awakening, amuses itself and again sees its native country, which is heaven.[1]

"From there it receives notable participation in its primal rights, origin, and in contemplation of that infinite intellectual sphere whose center is in every place and the circumference nowhere (that is God, according to the doctrine of Hermes Trismegistus), where nothing happens, nothing passes, nothing decays; it notes not only things past in our movements here below but also future things; and by its senses and organs exposing them to friends, it is called soothsaying and prophetic. True it is that it [the soul] does not report them in such purity as it has seen them in, being impeded by the imperfection and frailty of the bodily senses; as the moon, receiving light from the sun, does not communicate it as such—as lucid, as pure, as vivid and ardent, as it had received it. Therefore also needed for these somnial vaticinations is an interpreter who is adroit, wise, industrious, expert, rational, and an absolute oneirocritic and oneiropole;[2] thus they are called by the Greeks.

"That is why Heraclitus used to say that by dreams nothing was exposed to us, nothing was hidden from us, only we are given a signification and indication of things to come for our happiness or unhappiness, or for the happiness or unhappiness of others. The Holy Scriptures attest it, profane history makes it certain, exposing to us myriad cases that came out according to the dreams both of the person dreaming and of others.

"The Atlantides and those who live on the island of Thasos, one of the Cyclades, are deprived of this commodity (dreams), for in their countries no one ever dreamed. Also deprived were Cleon of Daulia, Thrasymedes, and in our time the learned Frenchman Villenovanus,[3] who never dreamed.

"So tomorrow, at the time when rosy-fingered Aurora [Dawn] drives away the shades of night, set yourself to dreaming deeply. Meanwhile strip yourself of all human passion: love, hatred, hope, and fear.

"For, as of old the great soothsayer Proteus, being disguised and transformed into fire, water, a tiger, a dragon, and other strange masks, did not predict things to come; to predict them he had to be restored into his own natural shape: indeed man cannot receive divinity and the art of vaticination unless when the part in him that is most divine (that is Nous and Mens) is quiet, tranquil, peaceful, not occupied or distracted by outside passions and emotions."

"I'm willing," said Panurge. "Must I have little or much for supper this evening? I do not ask without cause. For if I do not sup well and plentifully, I don't sleep worth a hoot; I do nothing but daydream, as empty of dreams as my belly then was."

"No supper at all," replied Pantagruel, "would be best, considering your well-fed condition and habit. Amphiarus, an ancient soothsayer, wanted those who received his oracles in dreams to eat nothing at all that day and not to drink wine for three days before. We shall not employ such an extreme and rigorous diet.

"To be sure, I do believe that a man full of food and surfeited has difficulty taking note of spiritual things; I am not, however, of the opinion of those who, after long and obstinate fasts, think they penetrate further into the contemplation of celestial things.

"You may remember well enough how my father Gargantua (whom in honor I name) often told us that the writings of these fasting hermits were as insipid, jejune, and sour-spittled as were their bodies when they composed them, and that it was hard for the spirits to remain good and serene when the body was in inanition, seeing that the philosophers and doctors affirm that the animal spirits arise, are born, and are active in the arterial blood, purified and refined to perfection with the marvelous network that lies beneath the ventricles of the brain; giving us the example of a philosopher who thinks he is in solitude and outside the mob, the better to comment, discourse, and compose, while nevertheless around him dogs bark, wolves howl, lions roar, horses neigh, elephants trumpet, serpents hiss, donkeys bray, grasshoppers chirp, turtledoves lament—that is to say, he had more disturbances around him than if he had been at the fair of Fontenay or Niort; for hunger was in the body; to remedy which the stomach barks, the eyesight dazzles, the veins suck out some of the very substance of the flesh-forming members, and draw back down below that wandering spirit, negligent of the treatment of its natural nursling and guest, which is the body; as if the bird on the fist wanted to take its flight into the air and should be instantly brought down by the leaches.

"And in that connection alleging to us the authority of Homer, father of all philosophy, who says [*Iliad* 18.20] that the Greeks put an end to their tears of mourning for Patroclus, Achilles's great friend, then, and no sooner when hunger spoke up and their bellies protested that they would furnish no more tears. For in bodies drained by long fasting there was no longer the wherewithal to weep and shed tears.

"Moderation is in every case praised, and there you shall hold to it. For supper you shall eat not beans, not hares or any other flesh, not octopus (which is called polyp), not cabbages or other foods that might trouble and obfuscate your animal spirit. For, as the mirror cannot present the simulacra of the things set before it and expose it if its polish is beclouded by breaths or by cloudy weather, so the spirit does not receive the forms of divination by dreams if the body is disquieted and troubled by the vapors and steams from the preceding foods, because of the sympathy between the two, which is indissoluble.

"You shall eat good Crustumenian and Bergamot pears, one apple of the shortshank pippin type, a few Tours plums, a few cherries from my orchard. And there will be no reason why you must fear that from this your dreams may come out doubtful, fallacious, or suspect, as some Peripatetics have declared them to be in the autumn season, which the ancient prophets and poets teach us mystically, saying that vain and fallacious dreams are hidden beneath the leaves fallen to the ground, because in autumn the leaves fall from the trees. For that natural fervor that abounds in new fruits and that by its ebullition evaporates in the animal parts (as we see that most do) has long since expired and been dissolved. And you shall drink nice water from my spring."

"The condition," said Panurge, "is a bit hard on me. I consent to it all the same, whatever the cost, protesting that tomorrow I'll have breakfast early, right after my dreamings. Moreover, I commend myself to the two gates of Homer [*Odyssey* 19.562–567], to Morpheus, to Icelon, to Phantasus and Phobetor. If they help me in case of need, I'll erect to them a joyous altar all made of fine down. If I were in Paeonia in the temple of Ino between Oetylus and Thalames, by her would my perplexity be resolved by dreaming with fair joyful dreams."[4]

Then he asked Pantagruel: "Wouldn't it be a good thing if I put a few laurel branches under my pillow?"

"There's no need," said Pantagruel. "That's a superstitious thing, and there's nothing but misconceptions in what is written about it by Serapion Ascalonites, Antiphon, Philochorus, Artemon, and Fulgentius Planciade. I would say as much to you about the left shoulder of the crocodile or of the chameleon, with all respect to old Democritus; as much about the stone of the Bactrians named Eumetrides; as much about the horn of Ammon: so the Ethiopians call a golden-colored precious stone in the shape of a ram's horn, as is the horn of Jupiter Ammon; saying that the dreams of those who wear it are as infallible as are divine oracles. Peradventure it's what Homer and Virgil [*Aeneid* 6.993] write about the two gates of dreams, to which you are commended. One is of ivory, through which enter confused, fallacious, and uncertain dreams, as through ivory; however thin it is, it is impossible ever to see anything: its density and opacity prevent the penetration of the visive spirits[5] and reception of the visible species. The other is of horn, by which enter the certain, true, and infallible dreams, just as through horn, by virtue of its shining gloss and diaphaneity, all species appear certainly and distinctly."

"You mean to infer," said Frère Jean,[6] "that the dreams of horned cuckolds, such as Panurge will be, with the help of God and of his wife, are always true and infallible?"

CHAPTER 14

Panurge's dream
and the interpretation thereof.

ABOUT seven o'clock the following morning, Panurge appeared before Pantagruel, there being in the room Epistémon, Frère Jean des Entommeures, Ponocrates, Eudémon, Carpalim, and others, to whom, on Panurge's arrival, Pantagruel said:

"Here comes our dreamer."[1]

"That remark," said Epistémon, "once cost a lot, and was sold very dear, to Jacob's children."

Thereupon said Panurge:

"I've certainly been to Billy's in the Land of Nod.[2] I dreamed ever so much and more, but I don't understand one bit of it. Except that in my dreams I had a young wife, sprightly, perfectly beautiful, who was treating and entertaining me sweetly like her little darling. Never was a man more delighted or more joyous. She was caressing me, tickling me, feeling me, smoothing my hair, kissing me, hugging me, and in sport making me two pretty little horns over my forehead. In the midst of our play I was remonstrating to her that she should put them above my eyes, the better for me to see what I'd like to but with them, so that Momus should not find in such a thing anything imperfect and worthy of correction, as he did in the placement of bovine horns.[3] The wanton, notwithstanding my remonstrance, kept fixing them even further forward on me. And in this she didn't hurt me a bit, which is a wonderful fact.

"A little later it seemed to me that I was transformed, I know not how, into a drum, and she into an owlet. At that point my sleep was interrupted, and I awoke all vexed, perplexed, and indignant. Now there you see a fine platterful of dreams, have a good feast on them, and explain it as you understand it. Let's go have breakfast, Carpalim."

"I understand," said Pantagruel, "if I have any judgment in the art of divination by dreams, that your wife will not actually, and to outward appearance, plant horns on your forehead, such as the satyrs wear, but that she will keep neither faith nor conjugal loyalty to you, but will abandon herself to others, and will make you a cuckold. That point is clearly exposed by Artemidorus, as I said.[4]

"Also you will not be metamorphosed into a drum, but you will be beaten by her like a drum at a wedding;[5] nor she into an owl; but she will rob you, as is the nature of the owl. And you see, your dreams are in conformity with the Virgilian lots: you will be a cuckold; you will be beaten; you will be robbed."

Thereupon Frère Jean broke out and exclaimed:

"He's telling by God the truth, you'll be a cuckold, my fine fellow, I assure you, you'll have beautiful horns. Heh, heh, heh, our own Master de Cornibus,[6] God preserve you! Give us a few words of preaching, and I'll pass the hat around the parish."

"The other way around," said Panurge, "my dream presages that in my marriage I'll have all goods in plenty together with the horn of abundance.

"You say they'll be satyr's horns. *Amen* [to that], *amen, fiat! fiatur! ad differentiam papae!*[7] Thus I'd eternally have my gimlet at the ready and indefatigable, as the satyrs have. A thing that all men desire, and few are granted it by the heavens. In consequence, a cuckold never, for the lack of that is the cause *sine qua non,* the sole cause of making husbands cuckolds.

"What makes vagabonds beg? It's because in their homes they haven't the wherewithal to fill their sacks. What makes the wolf come out of the woods? Lack of carnage. What makes wives into strumpets? You understand me well enough. I ask milords the clerics, milords the presidents of courts, counselors, attorneys, procurators,[8] and other commentators on the venerable rubric *De frigidis et maleficiatis* [*On the frigid and spellbound*].

"You (pardon me if I'm mistaken) seem to me evidently to err in interpreting horns as cuckoldry. Diana wears them on her head in the form of a fine crescent. Is she therefore a cuckold? How the devil could she be a cuckold, who was never married? For mercy's sake, speak correctly, for fear she may make you some horns on the model of those she made for Actaeon.[9]

"Good old Bacchus likewise wears horns. Pan, Jupiter Ammon, so many others. Are they cuckolds? Could Juno be a whore? For this would follow by the figure called *metalepsis.*[10] Just as calling a child, in the presence of his father and mother, *champis* or *avoistre,*[11] that amounts to saying civilly, tacitly, that the father is a cuckold and the mother a strumpet.

"Let's speak more nicely. The horns my wife was making me are horns of abundance and of plenty of all goods. I pledge my faith on it. Furthermore, I'll be joyful as a marriage drum, always sounding, always snoring, always buzzing and farting. Believe me, that's the luck of my good fortune. My wife will be dainty and pretty as a lovely little owlet. Anyone who doesn't believe it,

> Off to the gallows straight from hell,
> While we sing Noel, Noel.[12]

"I note," said Pantagruel, "the last point you have stated and compare it with the first. At the beginning you were all steeped in delight over your dream. At the end you awoke with a start, vexed, perplexed, and indignant . . . "

"True," said Panurge, "for I hadn't dined!"

"All will go into desolation, I foresee. Know for a fact that any sleep ending with a start and leaving the person vexed and indignant either means or presages, trouble.

"Means trouble, that is to say a cacoëthic [cacoethe], malignant, pestilent, occult disease, latent within the center of the body, which through sleep, which always reinforces the concoctive power (according to the theorems of medicine), would begin to declare itself and move toward the surface. At which sad movement would repose be shattered and the first sensitive element [13] admonished to have compassion on it and provide for it. As they put it in proverbs: rouse a hornet's nest, stir up Lake Camarine, wake a sleeping cat.

"Presages trouble, that is to say when, by the behavior of the soul in the matter of somnial divination, it gives us to understand that some misfortune is destined and prepared for it, which will shortly come to light in its effect.

"Example: in the dream and frightful awakening of Hecuba, in the dream of Eurydice, wife of Orpheus, of which Ennius says that they waked with a start and terrified. And so afterward Hecuba saw her husband Priam, her children, her country slaughtered and destroyed; Eurydice soon afterward died miserably.

"In Aeneas dreaming that he was talking to the defunct Hector, suddenly waking with a start. And so it was that very night that Troy was sacked and burned down. Another time, dreaming that he sees his family gods and Penates and waking in dread, he suffered on the following day a horrible tempest at sea.

"In Turnus, who, incited by a fantasy vision of the infernal Fury to begin war against Aeneas, waked with a start all indignant; then he was, after long tribulations, killed by this Aeneas. A thousand others.

"When I tell you stories about Aeneas, note that Fabius Pictor says that nothing was done or undertaken by him, nothing happened to him, which he had not known of beforehand and foreseen by divination through dreams.

"Reason is not lacking in these examples. For if sleep and repose is a special gift and benefit of the gods—as the philosophers maintain and the poet attests [*Aeneid* 2.268–269], saying:

> This was the time when sleep, at heaven's behest,
> Comes graciously to bring tired humans rest.

"Such a gift cannot be ended in vexation and indignation without foreboding great unhappiness. Otherwise would rest not be rest, a gift not a gift, coming not from the friendly gods but from the hostile devils, as in the common saying: ἐχθρῶν ἄδωρα δῶρα [a gift from enemies is no gift].[14]

"As if the paterfamilias, sitting at an opulent table with a good appetite at the start of his meal, is seen to jump to his feet in fright. Anyone not knowing the reason might be astonished. But you see! He had heard his manservants shout 'Fire!' His maidservants cry 'Stop thief!' His children cry 'Murder!' He had to run to the spot to remedy matters and restore order.

"Actually I remember that the cabalists and massoretes, interpreters of Holy Scripture, explaining in what way one could make out the truth by discernment about angelic apparitions (for sometimes Satan's angel transforms himself into an angel of light), say that the difference between the two is in that the benign, consoling angel, appearing to man, terrifies him at the beginning, consoles him in the end, leaves him happy and satisfied; the malign seducing angel delights him at the start, but in the end leaves him perturbed, vexed, and perplexed."

CHAPTER 15

*Panurge's excuse
and exposition of the monastic cabala
in the matter of salt beef.*

"Gᴏᴅ," said Panurge, "keep from harm him who sees well and hears not a sound![1] I see you very well, but I don't hear you one bit. And I don't know what you're saying. A famished belly has no ears. I'm bellowing by God in a wild frenzy of hunger. I've gone through too extraordinary an ordeal. It'll take a sharper man than Master Magic[2] to get me to do dreaming this year. No supper at all, by the Devil? A plague on it! Come on, Frère Jean, let's go have breakfast. When I've had a good big breakfast and my stomach is well victualed and foddered, then all right, if there were need and in case of necessity I'd get along without dinner. But to have no supper at all? Plague take it! That's a mistake. That's a scandal in nature.

"Nature made the day to exercise in, to work, and for each man to go about his business; and in order to do that more aptly, she supplies us with a candle, that's the bright joyful light of the sun. In the evening she begins to take it away and tells us tacitly: 'Lads, you're good folk. That's enough work. The night is coming: it is time to cease your labor and restore yourselves with good bread, good wine, good food, then amuse yourselves a bit, go to bed, and rest, so as to be fresh the next day and cheerfully ready for work as before.'

"Thus the falconers do. When they've fed their birds, they have them fly off their feed: they let them digest on the perch, which was very well understood by the good pope who first instituted fasts. He ordered men to fast until the hour of nones;[3] the rest of the day was set at liberty to feed. In the olden times, few men dined, except, you might say, the monks and canons (and indeed they have no other occupation: all days are feast days to them, and they diligently observe one claustral proverb: *de missa ad mensam*—from mass to table—and would not put off, even if waiting for the arrival of the abbot, plumping themselves down at table: there, while they guzzle, the monks wait for the abbot all he wants, but not otherwise, or for any other consideration), but everyone supped, except a few wool-gathering dreamers, which is why supper is called *coena,* that is to say common to all.

"You know this very well, Frère Jean. Come on, my friend, by all the devils, let's go! My stomach is baying with frantic hunger, like a dog. Let's toss it many dips in its gullet to appease it, after the example of the sibyl toward Cerberus. You love the dips served at prime; I prefer the greyhound's dips[4] with a piece of powdered beef, nine lessons' worth."

"I understand you," replied Frère Jean. "That metaphor is drawn from the claustral cooking pot. The powdered beef [le laboureur], that's the ox that labors or has labored; nine lessons' worth, that is to say cooked to perfection.

"For the good religious fathers, by a certain cabalistic institution of the ancients, not written, but passed down from hand to hand, in my time, on rising for matins, performed certain notable preambles before entering the church: they crapped in the crapperies, pissed in the pisseries, spat in the spitteries, coughed melodiously in the cougheries, daydreamed in the daydreameries, so as not to bring anything foul into the divine service. These things done, they piously betook themselves into the holy chapel [saincte chapelle]—thus in their lingo was named the claustral kitchen— and piously urged that the beef be put on the fire for the breakfast of the monks, brothers of Our Lord. They themselves often lit the fire beneath the cooking pot.

"Now it's true that, when matins had nine lessons, they got up earlier for a reason, and also increased in appetite and thirst by the baying at the parchment[5] more than when matins were hemmed over with one or three lessons only. Getting up earlier, by the aforesaid cabala, sooner was the beef on the fire; being there more, it remained more done; remaining more done, it was more tender, wore down the teeth less, delighted the palate, lay less heavy on the stomach, nourished the good monks more, which is the sole aim and primary intention of the founders, in contemplation of the fact that they hardly at all eat to live, they live to eat, and have only their life in this world. Let's go, Panurge!"

"At this point," said Panurge, "I've understood you, my velvety ballock, claustral and cabalic ballock. I'm concerned for the cabal itself as the capital. The principal, interest, and charges I forgo.[6] I content myself with the expenses, since you have given us such a learned rehearsal on the singular subject of the culinary and monastic cabala. Come on, Carpalim! Frère Jean, my baldrick,[7] let's go! Good day to you all, my good lords! I have dreamed enough to have a drink. Let's go!"

Panurge had not finished that remark when Epistémon cried aloud, saying:

"A very common and ordinary thing it is among humans to understand, foresee, recognize, and predict the misfortune of others. But how rare a thing it is to predict, foresee, and understand one's own misfortune! And how wisely Aesop pictured this in his *Fables*,[8] saying that every man is born into this world wearing a wallet about his neck, in the front pouch of which hang the misfortunes of others, always exposed to our sight and knowledge; in the rear pouch hang our own faults and misfortunes, and they are never seen or heard, except by those who enjoy the benevolent regard of the heavens."

CHAPTER 16

*How Pantagruel advises Panurge
to consult with a sibyl of Panzoust.*

A short time later, Pantagruel sent for Panurge and said to him:

"The inveterate love I have borne you for a long sequence of time incites me to think of your welfare and profit. Hear my idea; I've been told that at Panzoust, near Le Croulay, there is a very famous sibyl, who predicts all future things; take Epistémon for company, get yourself to her, and hear what she'll tell you."

"She may," said Epistémon, "peradventure be a Canidia, a Sagana, a pythoness and witch. What makes me think so is that this place has a bad name for abounding in witches even more than Thessaly ever did. I'll not go willingly. The thing is illicit and forbidden in the law of Moses."

"We're certainly not Jews," said Pantagruel, "and it's not an acknowledged or attested fact that she's a witch. Let's put off until your return the sifting and assessing of these matters.

"How do we know but that she's an eleventh sibyl, a second Cassandra? And even if she were not a sibyl and didn't deserve the name of sibyl, what risk do you run by consulting with her about your perplexity? Especially considering that she is thought to know more, to understand more, than is usual in her region or her sex. What harm is there in always finding out and always learning, even if it's from a sot, a pot, a dipper, a mitten, or a slipper?[1]

"Remember that Alexander the Great, having won the victory over

King Darius at Arbela, in the presence of his satraps, once refused an audience to a fellow, then repented of it in vain thousands and thousands of times [mille et mille foys]. He was in Persia, victorious, but so far from his hereditary kingdom of Macedonia that he was most distressed not to have been able to think up any way to get news of it, both because of the enormous distance between the two places and of great rivers blocking the way, the impediment of the deserts, and the barrier of the mountains. In this predicament and troubled quandary, which was no small matter (for someone could have occupied his country and kingdom and installed there a new king and a new colony long before he had warning of it to prevent it), there appeared before him a man from Sidon, an able and sensible merchant, but for the rest rather poor and unimpressive in appearance, who announced and affirmed to him that he had found a way and means by which his country could be notified in less than five days of his Indian victories, and he of the state of Macedonia and Egypt. He considered the promise so preposterous and impossible that he never would lend an ear to him or grant him an audience.

"What would it have cost him to hear and understand what the man had invented? What harm, what damage would he have incurred to find out what was the means, what was the way, that the man wanted to show him?

"Nature seems to me to have formed us not without cause with our ears open, setting on them no gate or closure whatever as she did with the eyes, tongue, and other openings in our bodies. I believe the cause is so that always, every night, we may be continually able to hear, and by hearing perpetually to learn; for that is the sense, above all others, most apt for learning. And perhaps that man was an angel, that is to say a messenger sent by God, as was Raphael to Tobias. He disdained him too promptly; he repented of it for too long afterward."

"You speak well," replied Epistémon, "but you'll never make me believe that it's a very advantageous thing to take counsel and advice from a woman, in such a region."

"I," said Panurge, "find myself very well off for women's advice, and especially old women's. On consulting them I always produce one or two extraordinary stools. My friend, they are real pointer dogs, real rubrics of the law books.[2] And those people speak quite properly who call them sage women ["sages femmes" or "midwives"]. My custom and my style is to call them *presage* women. Sage they are, for adroitly they know. But I call them *presage,* for they foresee divinely and foretell certainly things to come. Sometimes I call them not *maunettes* but *monettes,*[3] like the

Romans' Juno, for from them always come to us salutary and profitable admonitions. Inquire about it of Pythagoras, Socrates, Empedocles, and Our Master Ortuinus.[4]

"Likewise I praise to the high heavens the ancient institution of the Germans, who prized old women's advice at the value of the sanctuary standard and cordially revered it; by their counsels and replies they prospered as happily as they had wisely received them. Witness old Aurinia and that good mother Velleda in the time of Vespasian.

"Believe me, feminine old age is always abounding in zibeline[5] quality—I meant to say sibylline. Come on, with the help, come on, with the power, of God, come on! Good-bye, Frère Jean, I commend my codpiece to you."

"Very well," said Epistémon, "I'll follow you, protesting that if I have warning that she is using lots of enchantment in her replies, I'll leave you at the door, and you shall no longer be accompanied by me."

CHAPTER 17

*How Panurge speaks
to the sibyl of Panzoust.*

THEIR trip took three days. On the third, on a mountain crest, under a great ample chestnut tree, they were shown the soothsayer's abode. With no difficulty they entered the thatched cottage, ill-built, ill-furnished, all blackened from smoke.

"No matter!" said Epistémon, "Heraclitus, a great Scotist and darksome philosopher,[1] showed no astonishment on entering a similar house, explaining to his sectarians and disciples that the Gods resided there just as well as in palaces full of delights. And I think that such was the hut of the very famous Hecale, when she regaled young Theseus there; such also that of Hireus and Oenopion, in which Jupiter, Neptune, and Mercury did not disdain to enter, feed, and lodge, in which in a pisspot,[2] to pay their way, they forged Orion."

In a corner of the hearth they found the old woman.

"She," exclaimed Epistémon, "is a real sibyl and a faithful portrait represented true to life by Homer's τῇ χαμινοῖ [the old furnace-woman: *Odyssey* 18.27]."

The old woman was ill-favored, ill-dressed, ill-nourished, toothless, blear-eyed, hunchbacked, runny-nosed, languid; and she was making a green cabbage soup with a rind of bacon and some old broth from a soup bone.

"Mother of pearl!"[3] said Epistémon, "we've muffed it. We won't get any answer at all out of her, for we don't have the golden bough!"[4]

"I've provided for it," replied Panurge, "I have it here in my game-pouch in a golden ring in the company of some nice joyous carolus."

These words spoken, Panurge bowed deeply to her, presented her with six smoked ox tongues, a great butter-pot full of curds, a horn-shaped drinking glass furnished with drink, a ram's-ballock purse full of new-minted carolus, finally with a deep bow put on her ring finger a beautiful gold ring, in which was magnificently set a toadstone from Beusse.[5] Then in a few words he explained to her his motive in coming, courteously requesting her to tell him her advice and what good fortune his projected marriage would have.

The old woman remained in silence for some time, pensive and grinding her teeth, then sat down on the bottom of a cask, took in her hands three spindles, turned and twisted them between her fingers in various ways; then tested their points, kept the most pointed one in her hand, tossed aside the other two under a millet mortar. After that, she took her spools and turned them nine times. At the ninth turn, without touching them any longer, she considered the movement of the spools and waited until they came to full rest. Later I saw that she took off one of her clogs (we call them *sabotz*), raised her apron over her head as priests put up their amice when they want to sing mass, then with an old speckled cloth of many colors tied it under her throat. Thus decked out, she drew off a great draft from the drinking glass, took from the ram's ballock three carolus, put them in three nutshells and set them on the bottom of a feather-pot, gave three turns with a broom over the hearth, threw into the fire a half bundle of heath and a branch of dry laurel. She watched it burn in silence and saw that as it burned it made no sputtering or noise whatever. Thereupon she gave a frightful cry, muttering between her teeth a few barbarous words with a strange ending, in such a way that Panurge said to Epistémon:

"By the power of God, I'm trembling! I think I'm under a charm; she doesn't speak Christian. See how she seems to me four span taller than she was when she covered her head with her apron. What's the meaning of this movement of her chaps? What's the point of this shrugging of her shoulders? To what purpose does she quaver with her lips like a monkey dismembering crayfish? My ears are ringing; it seems to me I hear Proserpina crying out; soon the devils will come out on the spot. O what ugly beasts! Let's get out of here! Serpent of God, I'm dying of fear! I don't like devils one bit; they vex me and are most unpleasant. Let's get out of here! Farewell, Madame, many thanks for your help! I won't marry at all, no indeed! I give it up from now on just as before."

Thus he was starting to run out of the room; but the old woman got ahead of him, holding the spindle in her hand, and went out into a garden near her house. Here there was an old sycamore; she shook it three times, and on eight leaves that fell from it, summarily, with the spindle she wrote a few short verses. Then she tossed them to the wind and said to them:

"Go look for them if you want; find them if you can; the fated destiny of your marriage is written on them."

These words said, she withdrew into her lair, and on the doorstep trussed herself up, dress, petticoat, and smock, all the way to her armpits, and showed them her tail. Panurge saw it, and said to Epistémon:

" 'Odsbodikins, there's the sibyl's hole." [6]

Suddenly she barred the door after her, and was not seen thereafter. They chased after the leaves and collected them, but not without great effort, for the wind had strewn them among the bushes in the valley. And arranging them in order one after another, they found this statement in verse: [7]

Husk or shell
She'll undo;

Pregnant swell,
Not with you.

Suck a spell
Your sweet tip;

Flay you well,
Save a strip.

CHAPTER 18

*How Pantagruel and Panurge diversely interpret
the verses of the sibyl of Panzoust.*

WHEN the leaves were collected, Epistémon and Panurge returned to
Pantagruel's court, part joyous, part vexed. Joyous for the return; vexed
for the labor of the road, which they found rugged, stony, and poorly laid
out. About their trip they made a full report to Pantagruel about the
condition of the sibyl. Finally they presented him with the sycamore
leaves and showed him what was written in the little verses. Pantagruel,
having read the whole thing, said to Panurge with a sigh:

"You're really in good shape! The sibyl's prophecy exposes to you what
was already signified to us both by the Virgilian lots and by your own
dreams; that by your wife you will be dishonored, that she will make you
a cuckold, abandoning herself to others and becoming pregnant by someone else; that she will rob you of some good part, and that she will beat
you, flaying and bruising some member of your body."

"You understand as much," replied Panurge, "in the expounding of
these recent prophecies as does a sow in spices. Don't be offended if I say
so, for I'm feeling a little vexed. The opposite is the truth. Take good
heed of my words. The old woman says: Even as the bean is not seen if
it is not shucked, so my virtue and my perfection would never be brought
to renown if I were not married. How many times have I heard you say
that the magistracy and the office reveal the man and bring to light what
he had in his belly, that then is certainly known what kind of man the
person is and what he's good for when he's called to the handling of
affairs. Before then, when the man is in private, it is not known what
kind of man he is, any more than is known of a bean in the husk. So
much for the first point.

"Otherwise, would you want to maintain that the honor and good
renown of a decent man should depend on the tail of a whore?

"The second says that my wife will become pregnant (here understand
the prime felicity of marriage), but not with me.[1] 'Odsbody, I believe it!
It will be with a handsome tiny little child that she'll be pregnant. I'm
already full of love for him, and already I'm quite doting on him; he'll be
my little cutie. No vexation in the world, however great and violent, will
henceforth enter my mind that I'll not pass it off, just by seeing him, and

hearing him prate in his childish prattle. And blessed be the old woman! I'd like, honest to Gosh [Vraybis], to set up for her in Salmagundi some good source of revenue, not some annuity like giddy bachelors of arts, but a solid landed one like fine doctor professors. Otherwise, would you have my wife bear me within her loins, conceive me, deliver me, and have people say: 'Panurge is a second Bacchus, he's twice born, he's a rené [reborn], as was Hippolytus, as was Proteus, once of Thetis and secondly of the mother of the philosopher Apollonius, as were the two Palici, beside the river Simethos in Sicily. His wife was big with him. In him is renewed the ancient palintocia of the Megarians and the palingenesis of Democritus? Wrong! Don't ever speak to me about it.

"The third says that my wife will suck my sweet tip. I'm ready and waiting. You understand well enough that that's the single-ended stick that hangs between my legs. I swear and promise to you that I'll always keep it succulent and well victualed. She won't suck it on me in vain. In it eternally there'll be that little peck's worth, or better. You explain this bit allegorically and interpret it as robbery and theft. I praise the explanation, I like the allegory, but not in your sense. Perhaps the sincere affection you bear me draws you to the adverse and refractory side, as the clerics say that love is a marvelously fearful thing and that a good love is never without fear.

"But (according to my judgment) you understand within yourselves that theft, in this passage, as in many other ancient Latin writers, means the sweet fruit of amourettes, which Venus wills to be secretly and furtively plucked. Why, tell me in good faith? Because the little business, performed on the sly, between two closed doors, across the stairs, behind the tapestry, on a pile of loose kindling, is more pleasing to the Cyprian goddess (and that's where I stand, without prejudice to higher authority)[2] than performed in view of the sun, Cynic style, or under precious canopies, between golden curtains, at long intervals, to one's heart's content, using a crimson flyswatter, and chasing away the flies with a brush of Indian feathers, and the female picking her teeth with a little bit of straw that she had meanwhile plucked out from deep down in the straw mattress.

"Otherwise, would you want me to tell you that she will rob me by sucking, as the women of Cilicia (witness Dioscorides) draw in the grain from the oak?[3] Wrong. He who robs does not suck but snatches, nor swallows but wraps up, carries off, and plays 'Now you see it, now you don't.'

"The fourth says that my wife will flay it for me, but not all. O what a nice thing to say! You interpret it to mean beating and bruising. That's hitting the nail on the thumb, speaking of masons and trowels![4] I beseech you, raise your minds a little from earthly thought to the lofty contemplation of the wonders of nature, and here do you yourselves condemn yourselves for the mistakes you have committed in perversely expounding the prophetic statements of the divine sibyl.

"Putting, but not admitting or conceding the case that my wife, on the instigation of the enemy from hell, tried and undertook to do a bad turn, defame me, make me a cuckold up to my ass, rob me and outrage me, still she won't bring off her plan and undertaking. The reason that prompts me to say this is founded on this last point, and is extracted from the depth of monastic Pantheology. Friar Arthur Tailpusher[5] once told me it, and it was on a Monday morning, as we were together eating a bushel of minced veal pies, and at that it was raining, I remember; God give him good day!

"The women, at the beginning of the world or soon after, conspired together to flay the men alive completely, because the men wanted to lord it over them everywhere. And this decree was promised, confirmed, and sworn among them by the holy blood of the Goose.[6] But O the vain undertakings of women! O the great frailty of the female sex! They began to skin man, or flay him as Catullus puts it with the part they most delight in, that's the muscular, cavernous member, over six thousand years ago, and yet they still have got only to the head of it. Whereat, out of spite the Jews in circumcision cut and trim themselves, preferring to be called snipped and shorn marranos, rather than skinned by women, like the other nations. My wife, not degenerating from this enterprise, will flay it for me if it isn't so, I freely consent to this, but not all, I assure you, my good king."

"You," said Epistémon, "are not responding to the fact that the laurel branch, under our eyes, with her observing and exclaiming in a frightful frenzied voice, was burning without any noise or sputtering at all. You know that this is a sad augury and a vastly redoubtable sign, as is attested by Propertius, Tibullus, Porphyry the subtle philosoher, Eustathius on Homer's *Iliad*, and others."

"Really now," responded Panurge, "you're citing me some curious little calves! They were crazy as poets and dotards as philosophers, as full of sheer madness as was their philosophy."[7]

CHAPTER 19

*How Pantagruel praises
the counsel of mutes.*

PANTAGRUEL, these words finished, remained silent rather a long time and seemed greatly pensive. Then he said to Panurge:

"The malicious spirit is leading you astray, but listen. I've read that in times past the surest and most truthful oracles were not those given out in writing or proffered in words; many times mistakes were made even by those who were esteemed subtle and ingenious, both because of the uncertainties, ambiguities, and obscurities of the words and because of the brevity of the pronouncements; therefore was Apollo, god of vaticination, surnamed Λοξίας [Loxias]. Those that were expounded by gestures and signs were considered the most truthful and certain. Such was the opinion of Heraclitus. And thus did Jupiter vaticinate in Ammon; thus did Apollo prophesy among the Assyrians. For this reason they portrayed him with a long beard and dressed like an old person of sober sense, not naked, young, and beardless, as the Greeks did. Let's make use of this method; and do you, by signs without speaking, take counsel of some mute."

"I agree to that," replied Panurge.

"But," said Pantagruel, "the mute should properly be deaf from birth and consequently mute. For there is no mute more natural than one who has never heard."

"How do you mean that?" replied Panurge. "If it were true that no man ever spoke who had never heard speech, I would lead you to infer logically a very preposterous and paradoxical position. But let it go. So you don't believe what Herodotus writes [*History* 2.2] about the two children kept in a hut by the will of Psammetichus, king of the Egyptians, and brought up in perpetual silence, who after a certain particular time pronounced this word: *becus,* which in the Phrygian language means 'bread.' "

"Not a word of it," replied Pantagruel. "It's a misstatement to say that we have a natural language: languages exist by arbitrary institutions and conventions of peoples; words as the dialecticians say, signify not by nature but by our pleasure.[1] I do not make this statement to you without occasion. For Bartolo, *1. prima de verb. oblig.* [Bartolus, in the first law *Of words of obligation*], relates that in his time there was in Gubbio a certain Messer Nello de Gabrielis, who by accident had become deaf: this notwithstanding, he understood any Italian man, however cryptically he spoke, by the sight of his gestures and his lip movements. Moreover, I've read in an elegant learned author[2] that Tiridates, king of Armenia, visited Rome in Nero's time and was received in honorable pomp and ceremony, so as to maintain him in eternal friendship with the Roman senate and people, and there was not one memorable thing in the city that was not shown and exposed to him. On his departure the emperor made him great excessive gifts; besides, he gave him the option to choose whatever he liked best in Rome, with the sworn promise not to turn him down, whatever he asked for. He asked only for one farce-player whom he had seen at the theater, and, not understanding what he was saying, understood what he was expressing by signs and gesticulations; stating that under his dominion were peoples of various tongues, to answer and speak to whom he had to use several interpreters; this man alone would suffice for all. For in the matter of signifying by gestures, he was so excellent that he seemed to speak with his fingers.

"Therefore you must choose a mute deaf from birth, so that his gestures and signs may be naturally prophetic, not feigned, prettified, or affected. It still remains to be known whether you would want to take such advice from a man or a woman."

"I," said Panurge, "would gladly take it from a woman, were it not that I fear two things; one, that women, whatever things they see or represent to themselves in their minds, or think they imagine it's the entry of the sacred Ithyphalus; whatever gestures, signs, and appearances one may make in their sight and presence, they interpret and refer them to the moving act of bolting [elles les interprètent et réfèrent à l'acte mouvent de belutaige]. Therefore we would be misled, for the woman would think that all our signs were venereal. Remember what happened in Rome two hundred and sixty years after its founding: a young Roman gentleman, meeting on Mount Coelion a Latin lady named Verona, deaf and dumb from birth, asked her with Italian gestures, in ignorance of this deafness, what senators she had met on the way up. She, not understanding what he was saying, imagined it was what she had on her mind, and what a young man naturally asks of a woman. And so by signs (which in love-making are incomparably more alluring, effective, and valuable than words), she drew him aside into her house, made signs to him that she liked the game. Finally, without saying a word by mouth, they made a fine duet of tail-pushing.

"The other, that they would make no reply at all to our signs; they would promptly fall over backward, as really consenting to our unspoken requests. Or else, if they made us any signs responsive to our pro-poundings, these would be so wanton and ridiculous that we ourselves would think their thoughts were venereal. You know how, at Croquignoles, when the nun Sister Bigass [Soeur Fessue] was made preg-nant by the young lay friar Stickitinstiff [Dam Royddimet][3] and the preg-nancy known, she, summoned by the abbess in chapter meeting and accused of incest, excused herself, alleging that it had not been by her consent; it had been by violence and by the strength of Friar Stickitinstiff.

"When the abbess answered and said: 'Wicked girl, this was in the dormitory; why didn't you cry for help? We would have run to your assistance!' She answered that she dared not cry out in the dormitory because in the dormitory there was eternal silence. 'But,' said the abbess, 'you wretch, why didn't you signal to your roommates?' 'I kept signaling all I could with my tail,' replied Bigass, 'but no one came to help me.' 'But,' said the abbess, 'you bad girl, why didn't you come and tell me right away and bring a regular accusation against him? That's what I would have done if the same thing had happened to me, to demonstrate my innocence.' 'Because,' replied Bigass, 'fearful of remaining in sin and a state of damnation, for fear I might be beaten to it by sudden death, I made confession to him before I left the room, and he gave me as a penance not to reveal it to anyone. Too enormous a sin it would have been to reveal his confession, and too detestable in the sight of God and the angels. It might peradventure have been reason for fire from heaven to have burned down the whole abbey, and for us all to have fallen into the abyss with Dathan and Abiram.' "[4]

"You'll never," said Pantagruel, "make me laugh at that. I know well enough that all monkery is less afraid to transgress God's commandments than their provincial statutes. So take a man; Goatsnose [*Nazdecabre*, Langue d'Oc for *Nez-de-Chèvre*] seems to me suitable. He's deaf and dumb from birth."

CHAPTER 20

How Goatsnose replies
to Panurge in signs.

GOATSNOSE was summoned and arrived the next day. Panurge, on his arrival, gave him a fatted calf, half a hog, two puncheons of wine, a load of wheat, and thirty francs in small change; then he brought him before Pantagruel, and, in the presence of the gentlemen of the chamber, made him this sign: he yawned at some length, and, in yawning, outside his mouth, with the thumb of his right hand he traced the shape of the Greek letter called *Tau,* with frequent repetitions. Then he raised his eyes to heaven and rolled them around in his head like a nannygoat aborting, coughed as he did so, and deeply sighed. That done, he pointed to his lack of a codpiece, and then under his shirt took his poniard[1] full in his fist and clicked it melodiously between his thighs; then leaned over, bending his left knee, and remained holding both arms clasped one over the other on his chest.

Goatsnose kept looking at him curiously, then raised his left hand in the air and kept all the fingers thereof closed into a fist except the thumb and index finger, which he joined gently by the two nails.

"I understand," said Pantagruel, "what he means by this sign. It denotes marriage, and moreover the trentenary [thirty-year] number, according to the theory of the Pythagoreans. You will be married."

"Many thanks," said Panurge, turning toward Goatsnose, "my little chief steward, my galley-master, my gendarme, my police sergeant."

Then he raised the said left hand higher in the air, extending all five of the fingers thereof and stretching them as far apart from one another as he could.

"Here," said Pantagruel, "he insinuates to us more fully, by signifying the quinary number,[2] that you will be married, and not only engaged, wedded, and married, but besides, that you will live together and your life will go on as a feast. For Pythagoras used to call the quinary number a nuptial one, of wedding and consumated marriage, for this reason, that it is composed of the triad, which is the first odd and superfluous[3] number, and of the dyad, which is the first even number, as of male and female coupled together. Indeed in Rome, long ago, on the wedding day, they used to light five wax torches, and it was not legal to light any

314

more, even at the marriage of the richest, nor fewer, even at the marriage of the most indigent. Moreover, in times past, the pagans used to implore five gods, or one god for five benefits, upon those whom they were marrying: Jupiter the nuptial god, Juno as presiding over the feast, Venus the beautiful, Pitho the goddess of persuasion and fine talk, and Diana for help in the travail of childbirth."

"O," said Panurge, "that nice Goatsnose! I want to give him a farm near Cinais and a windmill in Mirebalais."

This done, the mute sneezed with remarkable violence and shaking of his entire body, turning aside to the left.

"By the power of the Lard above [vertus beuf de boys]!"[4] said Pantagruel, "what's that? That's not to your advantage. It signifies that your marriage will be unfelicitous and unhappy. That sneeze, according to Terpsion's doctrine, is the Socratic daemon, which, done on the right, means that boldly and with assurance one may go ahead with what one has planned: the start, progress, and outcome will be good and happy; done on the left, to the contrary."

"You," said Panurge, "are always taking things at their worst and raising troubles like another Davus. I don't believe a word of it. And I never heard of that old fogy Terpsion except as a deceiver."

"However," said Pantagruel, "Cicero says about it I forget[5] what in the second book of De divinatione [240, par. 84]."

Then he [Panurge] turns toward Goatsnose and makes him a sign like this: he rolled up his eyelids, twisted his jaws from right to left, stuck his tongue halfway out of his mouth. That done, he put his left hand, except for the middle finger, which he kept perpendicularly on his palm, and thus set it on the place for his codpiece; the right hand he kept closed into a fist, except for the thumb, which he turned straight backward under his right armpit, and then set it above the buttocks, on the place the Arabs call Al Katim. Immediately afterward he changed and held his right hand in the position of the left, and put it on the place for the codpiece; the left he held in the position of the right, and placed it on the Al Katim. This changing of hands he repeated nine times. On the ninth, he returned his eyelids to their natural position; did the same thing also with his jaws and his tongue; then he cast his squint-eyed glance upon Goatsnose, wiggling his lips as monkeys do when free to, and as rabbits do when eating oats in the sheaf.

Thereupon Goatsnose raised his right hand in the air wide open, put the thumb thereof up to the first joint between the third joints of the middle finger and the ring finger, squeezing rather hard around the thumb, and pulling back into his fist the remaining joints of these, and extending out straight the index and little fingers. His hand thus arranged he placed on Panurge's navel, continually moving the said thumb, and leaning his hand on the little and index fingers as on two legs. Thus with his hand he climbed successively over the belly, the stomach, the chest, and the neck of Panurge; then to the chin, and into his mouth put the aforesaid waggling thumb; then he rubbed his nose with it, and climbing on beyond up to the eyes, made as if to put them out with his thumb.

At that Panurge got mad and tried to pull away and shake off the mute. But Goatsnose went right on, with this waggling thumb touching now his eyes, now his forehead and the edges of his cap. Finally Panurge cried out and said:

"By God, Master Fool, you'll get a beating if you don't leave me alone! If you annoy me any more, you'll get a mask from the back of my hand over your whoring face!"

"He's deaf," said Frère Jean. "He can't hear a word you're saying, old ballock. Signal him with a hail of punches on the snout."

"What the devil," said Panurge, "does this Master Knowitall [Maistre Alliboron] think he's doing? He almost poached my eyes in butter sauce [poché les oeilz au beurre noir]. By God, *da jurandi* [excuse my swearing], I'll feast you with a banquet of nose-tweaks, alternating with double flicks."

Then he left, "blowing him the bird."[6] The mute, seeing Panurge on his way, got ahead of him forcibly and made this sign: he lowered his right arm toward the knee as far as he could extend it, closing all the fingers into a fist and putting his thumb between the middle and index fingers; then with his left hand he rubbed the inside of the elbow of the aforesaid right arm, and little by little, with this rubbing, raised that hand into the air to the elbow and above, suddenly brought it down as before, then at intervals raised it again, lowered it again, and displayed it to Panurge.

Panurge, angry at this, raised his fist to hit the mute; but in reverence for Pantagruel's presence he held back. Then said Pantagruel:

"If the signs vex you, how much more will the things signified vex you! Every truth harmonizes with every truth. The mute means and signifies that you will be married, a cuckold, beaten, and robbed."

"The marriage," said Panurge, "I concede; I deny the rest. And I beg you to do me the favor of believing that never had a man such good luck with women and horses as is predestined for me."

CHAPTER 21

How Panurge takes counsel
of an old French poet named Raminagrobis.[1]

"I never thought," said Pantagruel," I'd meet a man as obstinate in his preconceptions as I see you are. At all events, to clear up your doubt, my notion is that we should leave no stone unturned. Hear my idea. Swans, which are birds sacred to Apollo, when nearing their death, especially on the Meander, a river in Phrygia (I say this because Aelian and Alexander Myndius write of having seen several of them die elsewhere, but none sang as they were dying) sing; so that a swan's song is a certain presage of its coming death, and it does not die without first having sung [et ne meurt que praealablement n'ayt chanté]. Likewise poets, who are under Apollo's protection, when nearing their death, ordinarily become prophets and sing by Apollonian inspiration, vaticinating about future things.

"I have often heard, moreover, that every old man, decrepit and near his end, easily divines things to come. I remember that Aristophanes, in one of his comedies [*Knights* v.61] calls old people sibyls;

Ο δὲ γέρων σιδυλλιᾶ

[The old man acts as a sibyl.]

For as we, standing on the pier and seeing from afar the sailors and travelers in their ships on the open sea, watch them only in silence and earnestly pray for their happy landing; but when they approach the harbor, in both words and gestures we greet them and congratulate them on having arrived at a safe haven with us; so the angels, heroes, and good demons (according to the doctrine of the Platonists)[2] seeing humans close to death as to a very safe and salutary haven, a haven of repose and tranquillity outside of earthly troubles and cares, greet them, console them, talk with them, and already begin to pass on to them the art of divination.

"I will not allege to you the ancient examples of Isaac, Jacob, Patroclus to Hector, Hector to Achilles, Polymnestor to Agamemnon and Hecuba, the Rhodian celebrated by Posidonius, Calanus the Indian to Alexander the Great, Orodes to Mezentius, and others; I want only to recall to your memory the learned and valiant knight Guillaume du Bellay, formerly Lord of Langey, who died on Mount Tarare on the tenth of January, in the climacteric year of his life,[3] and by our count in Roman reckoning the year 1543. The three or four hours before his death, tranquil and serene in sense, he employed in vigorous words predicting for us what we have in part seen, in part are awaiting as coming; although for that time these prophecies seemed to us somewhat preposterous and strange, because at the time there appeared to us no sign heralding what he was predicting.

"We have here, near La Villaumère, a man who is both old and a poet: that is Raminagrobis, who in his second marriage wedded La Grande Guorre[4] [the pox?], whence was born the fair Basoche. I've heard that he's at death's door and in the final moments of his decease; get yourself into his presence and hear his song. It may be that from him you'll get what you're aiming for and that by him Apollo will resolve your doubt."

"I want to," replied Panurge. "Let's go there right away, Epistémon, for fear death may come to him first. Will you come, Frère Jean?"

"I will most gladly," replied Frère Jean, "for love of you, old ballock. For I do love you with all my heart and liver."

On the instant, they took to the road, and, reaching the poetic dwelling, found the old man in the death throes with joyful bearing, open face, and luminous glance.

Panurge, greeting him, put on his left hand, middle finger, as a pure gift, a gold ring, in the bezel of which was a fine big oriental sapphire; then, in imitation of Socrates, he offered him a white cock,[5] which, once set on his bed, head raised, in great delight shook his plumage, then sang loudly on a very high note.

This done, Panurge asked him courteously to tell and expose his judgment on the doubt about the projected marriage.

The good old man ordered pen, ink, and paper to be brought him. And this was promptly delivered to him. Thereupon he wrote what follows:[6]

> Take the lady, take her not;
> If you take her, good for you;
> But if taking her will not do,
> You will have picked the wiser lot.
> Go at an amble, go at a trot;
> Draw back, go right into the spot;
>   Take the lady, take her not . . .

Fast, eat twice what others got;
All that had been redone, undo;
All that had been undone, redo;
Wish her long life and death on the spot,
    Take the lady, take her not . . .

Then he handed this to them and said to them: "Go, my children, in the keeping of the great God in heaven, and bother me no more about this matter or any other there may be. I have today, which is the last day of May and of me [de May et de moy], driven out of my house with great fatigue and difficulty a bunch of ugly, filthy, pestilential creatures, black, piebald, tawny, white, ashen, speckled, which would not let me die in peace and comfort, and, by fraudulent prickings, harpyish snatchings, and waspish importunities, all forged in the smithy of I know not what insatiability, kept dragging me out of that sweet state of mind to which I was consenting, as I contemplated and saw, and already touched and tasted, the bliss and felicity that the good God has prepared for His faithful and elect in the other life and the state of immortality. Depart from their footsteps, don't be like them, disturb me no more, and leave me in silence, I beseech you!"

CHAPTER 22

How Panurge champions the order
of the mendicant friars.

As he came out of Raminagrobis's room, Panurge, as if quite terrified, said: "I do believe, by the power of God, that he's a heretic, or devil take me! He speaks ill of the good mendicant Franciscan and Jacobin friars, who are the two hemispheres of Christendom, by whose gyrognomic circumbilivagination,[1] as on two caelivagous filendopoles,[2] all the antonomatic matagrabolism[3] of the Roman Church, feeling itself pestiferated by any jabbering of error or of heresy, homocentrically gives a violent start. But what, by all the devils, have those poor devils the

Capuchins and Minims done to him? Aren't they battered enough, the poor devils? Aren't they smoke-begrimed and perfumed enough with misery and calamity, those poor sad sacks scraped up out of Ichthyophagia? 'Pon my word, Frère Jean, is he in condition to be saved? He's on his way, by God, damned as a serpent, to thirty thousand scuttlefuls of devils! To speak ill of those good valiant pillars of the Church! Do you call that poetic frenzy? I can't be content with that: he's sinning foully, he's blaspheming against religion. I'm extremely scandalized by it."

"I," said Frère Jean, "don't care a rap about it. They speak ill of everyone; if everyone speaks ill of them it's no skin off my nose. Let's see what he's written."

Panurge read the old man's writing attentively, then said to them: "He's not making sense, the poor boozer. I excuse him, however; I think he's near the end of his rope; let's go write his epitaph! From the answer he gives us, I'm as wise as we ever baked in the oven.[4] Listen here, Epistémon, old pot. Don't you find him mighty categorical in his answers? By God, he's a slick, choplogic, natural-born sophist. I'll bet he's a marrano-belly, how careful he is not to make any mistake in his words! He answers only in disjunctives;[5] he can't help speaking the truth, for it's enough for the truth of these that one part should be true. O what a sharp operator! By Santiago de Bressuire,[6] are there still some of that sort around?"

"Thus," responded Epistémon, "was the great prophet Tiresias wont to protest at the start of all his divinations, saying clearly to those who took counsel from him: 'What I say will either happen or not happen.[7] And that's the style of prudent prognosticators.'"

"All the same," said Panurge, "Juno put out both his eyes."[8]

"True," replied Epistémon "out of spite that he had given a better judgment than she had on the problem proposed by Jupiter."

"But," said Panurge, "what devil possesses this Master Raminagrobis who thus to no purpose, for no reason or occasion, speaks ill of the poor blessed Jacobin, Minor, and Minim fathers? I'm greatly scandalized by it, I swear, and I can't keep quiet about it. He has sinned grievously. His soul is going off to thirty thousand basketfuls of devils."

"I understand you," replied Epistémon, "and you yourself scandalize *me* greatly, perversely applying to the mendicant friars what the good poet was saying about the fleas, bedbugs, gnats, flies, mosquitoes, and other such creatures, which are some black, some tawny, some ashen, some tanned and swarthy, but all bothersome, tyrannical, and annoying, not only for the sick but also healthy and vigorous. Possibly he may have ascarids, lumbrics, and tapeworms inside his body. Peradventure he is suffering (as happens in Egypt in places beside the Red Sea as common and ordinary thing) in the arms and legs from some sting by the speckled Guinea worm that the Arabs call *meden*. You do ill by explaining his words otherwise, and you wrong the good poet by disparagement and the said friars by the imputation of such meanness. We must always interpret all things about our neighbor for the good."

"Start giving me lessons," said Panurge, "in spotting flies in milk!"[9] By God's power, he's a heretic. I mean a full-fledged heretic, a heretic as fit for burning as any little clock.[10] His soul is flying off to thirty thousand cartloads of devils. Do you know where to? 'Odsbody, my friend, right beneath Proserpina's toilet seat, inside the chamber pot where she delivers the fecal product of her enemas, on the left side of the great caldron, just three fathoms from Lucifer's claws on the way toward the black chamber of Demogorgon.[11] O the wretch!"

CHAPTER 23

*How Panurge makes a speech for
returning to Raminagrobis.*

"Let's go back," continued Panurge, "and admonish him about his salvation. Let's go in the name of God, let's go in the power of God. It will be a charitable work done by us: at least, if he loses his life, let him not damn his soul! We'll lead him into contrition for his sin, to ask pardon of the most blessed fathers, absent as well as present—and we'll put it in writing, so that after his death they won't declare him a heretic and damned, as the hobgoblins did with the provost's wife of Orléans— and give them satisfaction for the insult by ordering for the holy fathers throughout all the monasteries of this province plenty of handout snacks, plenty of masses, plenty of obits and anniversaries;[1] and that on the anniversary of his death they may forever get fivefold helpings, and that the great flagon, full of the best, may trot from row to row around their tables, both of the humming drones, the lay priests and guzzlers, and of the priests and clerics, both of the novices and of the professed. Thus will he be able to obtain God's pardon.

"Oh-oh! I'm going far off the track in what I'm saying! Devil take me if I'm going there! Power of God, the room is already full of devils! Already I hear them belaboring and beating the devil out of one another to see who'll gulp down the Raminagrobidic soul and be the first to carry it, hot off the spit [de broc en bouc] to Messer Lucifer. Shoo! Get out of there. I'm not going there; devil take me if I go. Who knows but that they might commit a *qui pro quo* [mistake in identity] and instead of Raminagrobis, snatch away poor old Panurge, now quit of his debts? They've often just missed doing so when I was saffron-tinted and in debt.

"Get out of there! I'm not going. I'm like to die, by God, from sheer frenzy of fear. To find yourself among famished devils! Among factious devils! Among devils at work! Get out of there! I'll bet that for the same fear, at his burial there won't be a Jacobin, a Franciscan, a Carmelite, a Capuchin, a Theatine, or a Minim friar. And no fools they! Besides, he left them nothing in his will. Devil take me if I go! If he's damned, too bad about him! Why did he keep speaking ill of the holy fathers? Why had he driven them out of his room at the moment when he most needed their help, their pious prayers, and their saintly admonitions? Why in his will didn't he leave them at least a few snacks, a little to gorge on, a little belly-lining, to these poor folk who have nothing in the world but their lives? If anyone wants to go, let him go! Devil take me if I go! If I went, the devil *would* take me. A pox on it! Get out of there!

"Frère Jean, do you want thirty thousand cartloads of devils to carry you off in a moment? Do three things; give me your purse, for the cross[2] stands against enchantments, and there could happen to you what happened to Jean Dodin, district tax collector of Le Couldray at the Ford of Vède,[3] when the soldiers broke the planks. This well-hung fellow, meeting on the bank Adam Couscoil,[4] an Observantine Franciscan from Mirebeau, promised him a frock on condition he would carry him pickaback across the water on his shoulders; for he was a powerful rascal. Friar Couscoil trusses himself up to his ballocks and loads him onto his back, like a nice little Saint Christopher, the said requester Dodin.

"Thus he was carrying him gaily, as Aeneas carried his father Anchises out of the burning of Troy [*Iliad* 2.948 ff.], singing a lovely *Ave maris stella*. When they reached the ford's deepest point, above the mill wheel, he asked him if he hadn't any money on him. Dodin answered that he had a whole pouchful, and that he shouldn't mistrust his promise of a new frock. 'How's that?' asked Friar Couscoil. 'You know very well that by a specific section of a rule of our order, we are strictly forbidden to carry money on us. You really are a wretch for making me sin on that point. Why didn't you leave your purse with the miller? No mistake, you're going to be punished for that right now. And if I ever get you in our chapter at Mirebeau, you'll get the *Miserere* right through to the *Vitulos!*'[5] Suddenly he unloads and tosses your Dodin right into the deep water head first.

"Heeding this example, Frère Jean, my sweet friend, so that the devils may carry you off in greater comfort for you, don't carry any cross on you. The danger in it is evident: if you have money bearing a cross, they'll throw you on some rocks, as eagles throw tortoises to break them, witness the peeled skull of the poet Aeschylus; and you would get hurt, my friend; I'd be very sorry about it.

"Or else they'll drop you into some sea, I don't know where, far away, as Icarus fell; and thereafter it would be called the Entommeric Sea.

"Secondly, be quit, for devils are very fond of the quit, I know that well as regards me. The lechers never stop ogling me and paying court to me, which they didn't used to do when I was saffron-tinted and indebted. The soul of a man in debt is all feverish and emaciated. It's not meat for devils.

"Thirdly, with your 'froc et domino de grobis,'[6] go back to Raminagrobis. In case thirty thousand boatloads of devils don't carry you off thus qualified, I'll pay for your drink and firewood.[7] And if, for your safety, you want to have company, don't come looking for me, no sir! I'm telling you. Get out of there, I'm not going there. Devil take me if I go!"

"I wouldn't be so very worried about them, peradventure," replied Frère Jean, "as you might think once I had my cutlass in my fist."

"You're absolutely right," said Panurge, "and you speak about it like a doctor subtle in lard.[8] In the time when I was studying at the Toledo School, the Reverend Father in the Devil Picatris, Rector of the Diabolological Faculty, used to tell us that devils naturally fear the gleam of swords as well as the light of the sun. Indeed, Hercules, going down into hell to all the devils, did not frighten them as much, having only his lion's skin and his club, as did Aeneas later [*Aeneid* 6.260 ff.], being covered with a glittering harness and equipped with his well-furbished and rust-free cutlass, with the help and counsel of the Cumean sibyl. That was perhaps the reason why Lord Gian Giacomo Trivulzio,[9] dying at Chartres, called for his sword and died with naked sword in hand, laying all about his bed like a valiant knight, and by this sword-play putting to flight all the devils who were lying in wait for him on his passage to death.

"When you ask the Massoretes and cabalists why devils never enter the earthly paradise, they give no other answer but that at the gate is a cherubim holding a flaming sword in his hand. For, to speak of true Toledan diabology, I confess that devils cannot really die of sword-strokes; but I maintain, according to the said diabolology, that they can undergo solution of continuity,[10] as if with your cutlass you cut across a flame of burning fire or a thick dark smoke. And they scream like devils at this feeling of dissolution, which is painful as the devil to them.

"When you see the clash of two armies, do you think, billyballock, that such a great horrible noise as you hear comes from human voices? from the crashing of harnesses? from the clatter of horse armor? from the bang-ing of maces? from the clanging of pikes? from the shattering of lances? from the screaming of the wounded? from the sound of drums and trum-pets? from the neighing of the horses? from the thunder of pistols and cannons? True, there is some of that, I must confess. But the great tur-moil and principal racket comes from the anguish and ululation of the devils, who, lying there pell-mell in wait for the poor souls of the wounded, unexpectedly receive sword-strokes and suffer dissolution of continuity of their airy and invisible substances: as if, to some lackey swiping bacon strips from the spit, Master Slobby (the cook)[11] gives a hard bang on the fingers with his stick; then they howl and cry like the devil, as Homer says of Mars, when he was wounded by Diomedes before Troy [*Iliad* 5.859–860], shouted in a louder voice and more horrific din than ten thousand men would make all together.

"But what I am getting to? We're talking about furbished harnesses and gleaming swords. That's not how it is with your cutlass. For from discontinuation of function and lack of exercise, it is, 'pon my word, rustier than the keyhole of an old powdering tub. Therefore do one of two things: either clean it up nice and neat from the rust, or, leaving it rusty as it is, be sure you don't go back into Raminagrobis's house. For my part I'm not going there. Devil take me if I go!"

CHAPTER 24

How Panurge takes counsel
of Epistémon.

Leaving La Villaumère and returning toward Pantagruel, on the way Panurge addressed Epistémon and said to him:

"Old friend and comrade, you see the perplexity of my mind. You know so many good remedies! could you help me out?"

Epistémon spoke up and pointed out to Panurge how the general conversation was all taken up with jokes about his disguise, and advised him to take a bit of hellebore, in order to purge the peccant humor in him, and to resume his ordinary dress.

"Epistémon, my pal," said Panurge, "I've taken a fancy to get married. But I'm afraid I'll be a cuckold and unfortunate in my marriage. Therefore I've made a vow to saint Francis the Younger, who is held in great devotion by all women at Plessis-lèz-Tours, for he is the first founder of the Good Men,[1] whom they naturally desire—a vow to wear spectacles on my bonnet, to wear no codpiece on my breeches, until I've had a clear solution to this perplexity of my mind."

"That," said Epistémon, "is truly a fine joyous vow. I'm amazed at you, that you don't come back to yourself and recall your senses from this wild distraction back to their natural tranquillity. When I hear you speak, you remind me of the vow of the long-haired Argives, who, having lost the battle against the Lacedaemonians in the dispute over Thyreae,[2] made a vow not to wear any hair on their heads until they had recovered their honor and their land, also of the vow of that comical Spaniard Michael d'Oris, who wore a piece of a greave on his leg [qui porta le trançon de grève en sa jambe].

"And I don't know which of the two would be more worthy and deserving to wear the fool's motley and hare's ears,[3] this glorious champion or Enguerrand de Monstrelet,[4] who tells such a long, detailed, and boring story about it, forgetting the art and manner of writing history, handed down by the philosopher of Samosata. For, as you read his long account, you think it must be the beginning and occasion of some mighty war or notable mutation of kingdoms; but when all is said and done, you laugh at the silly champion and the Englishman who defied him and at Enguerrand, their scrivener, who drivels worse than a mustard pot. The mockery is like that for Horace's mountain,[5] which kept loudly crying out and complaining, like a woman in the labor of childbirth. At her cries and lamentations all the neighborhood came running up in the expectation of seeing some wonderful and monstrous delivery; but finally all that was born of her was a little mouse [souriz]."

"I'm not ready to smile [*soubrys,* homonym of *souriz*] about that," said Panurge. "It's the lame mocking the halt [se mocque qui clocque]. So I'll do as my vow requires. Now it's been a long time that you and I have sworn faith and friendship together by Jupiter Philios; tell me what you think about it: should I marry or not?"

"Assuredly," said Epistémon, "it's a hazardous matter; I feel much too inadequate to resolve it. And if ever was true in the art of medicine the dictum of old Hippocrates of Lango [Cos]: 'Judgment is difficult,'[6] it is most true in this matter. True, I have in my imagination a few ideas by means of which we might have a determination of your perplexity; but they don't completely satisfy me. Certain Platonists say that anyone who can see his *Genius*[7] can understand their doctrine very well, and I don't advise you to trust it. There are many mistakes in it. I've seen it tried out in the case of a studious and curious gentleman in the land of Estangourre [East Anglia]. That's the first point.

"There's another. If we were still in the reign of the oracles of Jupiter in Ammon, Apollo in Lebadia, Delphi, Delos, Cyrrha, Patara, Tegyra, Praeneste, Lycia, Colophon; at the Castalian Spring, near Antioch in Syria; among the Branchidae, of Bacchus in Dodona; of Mercury, Phares near Patras; of Apis in Egypt; of Serapis in Canopus, Faunus in Maenalia and at Albunea near Tivoli; of Tiresias at Orchomenus; of Mopsus in Cilicia; of Orpheus in Lesbos; of Trophonius in Leucadia [read: *Lebadia*]; I would advise you (or peradventure I would not) to go there and hear what would be their judgment on your undertaking. But you know that they've all become muter than fish since the coming of that Savior King of ours, at which came to an end all oracles and all prophecies, just as when the bright sunlight comes, there disappear all sprites, lamias, lemurs, werewolves, hobgoblins, and spirits of darkness. Now, even if they were still in authority, I would not readily advise putting faith in their replies; too many people have been deceived by them.

"Furthermore, I remember that Agrippina reproached the fair Lollia with having questioned the oracle of Apollo Clarius to learn whether she would be married to the Emperor Claudius. For that reason she was first banished and later ignominiously put to death."[8]

"But," said Panurge, "let's do better yet. The Ogygian Islands are not far from the port of Saint-Malo; let's take a trip there after we've spoken to our king. In one of the four, the one looking out most toward the setting sun, they say, and I've read it in good ancient authors, that there live several diviners, soothsayers, and prophets; and that Saturn is there, bound with fine gold chains in a rock of gold, fed on ambrosia and divine nectar, which are brought to him daily from the heavens in abundance by I know not what kind of birds (perhaps they are the same ravens that in the deserts fed Saint Paul the first hermit),[9] and he predicts openly, to each and everyone who wants to hear his lot, his destiny and what is to happen to him. For the Fates spin nothing, Jupiter considers and plans nothing, that good old father Saturn does not know in his sleep. It would be a great shortening of our labor if we hear him a bit about this perplexity of mine."

"That," replied Epistémon, "is too evident an imposture and too fabulous a fable. I won't go."

CHAPTER 25

*How Panurge takes counsel
of Her Trippa.*

"SEE, however," went on Epistémon, "what you'll do around here before we go back to our king, if you'll be guided by me. Here, near L'Isle-Bouchard, lives Her Trippa: you know how by the arts of astrology, geomancy, chiromancy, metopomancy, and others of the same ilk, he predicts all things to come. Let's confer with him about your affair."

"About that," replied Panurge, "I don't know a thing. I do know this well: that one day when he was talking to the Great King about celestial, transcendent things, the court lackeys, along the steps, between the doors, were tumbling his wife, who was rather passable, to their hearts' content. And he, seeing all ethereal and terrestrial things without spectacles, discoursing about all events past and present, predicting the whole future, failed only to see his wife having a romp, and never got word of it. Very well! Let's go to him, since that's how you want it. One cannot possibly learn too much."

The next day they arrived at Her Trippa's dwelling. Panurge gave him a wolf-skin robe, a big well-gilded short-sword with a velvet sheath, and fifty lovely angels [angelotz]; then he conferred with him privately about his business.

The moment he arrived Her Trippa looked him in the face and said: "You have the metoscopy and physiognomy of a cuckold, I mean a notorious and defamed cuckold."

Then, studying Panurge's right hand all over, he said: "This disastrous line I see here above the Mons Jovis was never in any hand but a cuckold's."

Then with a stylus he hastily pricked a number of scattered points, joined them together by geomancy, and said: "No truer is truth itself than it is certain that you'll be a cuckold soon after you're married."

That done, he asked Panurge for the horoscope of his nativity. When Panurge had given it to him, he promptly drew in his houses of heaven[1] in all their parts, and, considering the site and aspects in their triplicities, he heaved a great sigh and said:

"I had already clearly predicted that you[2] would be a cuckold; in that you could not fail; here, furthermore, I have fresh assurance of it. And I affirm to you that you'll be a cuckold. Besides, you'll be beaten by your wife and by her you'll be robbed, for I find the seventh house[3] malign in all aspects and open to the battering of all signs bearing horns, such as Aries, Taurus, Capricorn, and others. In the fourth I find a falling off of Jove, together with a tetragonal aspect of Saturn associated with Mercury. You're going to be well peppered with the pox [bien poyvré], my fine fellow."

"I am, am I?" replied Panurge. "A nice quartan fever to you, you old fool! When the cuckolds all get together, you'll be the standard-bearer. But where did I get this worm here between my two fingers?"

As he said this, he pointed straight at Her Trippa his index and middle fingers in the form of two horns, and closed all the others into a fist. Then he said to Epistémon:

"Here you see a real-life Ollus[4] out of Martial, who devoted all his attention to observing and understanding other people's troubles and miseries; meanwhile, his wife was running *le brelant* [tenoit le brelant].[5] For his part, poorer than Irus,[6] and at the same time more cocky, arrogant, and insufferable that seventeen devils, in a word πτωχαλαζών [penniless braggart], as the ancients most appropriately called such scurvy rabble. Come on, let's leave this crazy fool right here, this candidate for a strait jacket, to rave his fill with his private devils. I wouldn't be very quick to believe that the devils would serve such a dolt. He doesn't know the first point of philosophy, which is 'know thyself,' and, preening himself on seeing a mote in someone else's eye, he doesn't see a great beam that blocks out both his own. He's just the kind of Polypragmon described by Plutarch. He's another Lamia[7]—who in strangers' houses, in public, had sharper eyes than a lynx, but in her own house was blinder than a mole; at home she saw nothing, for when she came back in from outside, she took out of her head her eyes, removable as a pair of eyeglasses, and hid them in a clog fastened behind the door of her house."

At these words, Her Trippa picked up a tamarisk branch.

"He's choosing well," said Epistémon, "Nicander calls it one for divination."

"Do you want," said Her Trippa as he went on, "to know the truth about it more amply by pyromancy,[8] aeromancy,[9] so justly celebrated by Aristophanes in his *Clouds*, by hydromancy, by lecanomancy, once so celebrated among the Assyrians and tried out by Hermolaus Barbarus? In a basin full of water I'll show your wife having a romp with two ruffians."

"When," said Panurge, "you stick your nose up my ass, don't forget to take off your glasses."

"By catoptromancy,"[10] said Her Trippa as he went on, "by means of which Divus Julianus, emperor of Rome, used to foresee what was to happen to him? You won't need any spectacles: you'll see her in a mirror getting plugged just as clearly as if I showed her to you in the temple of Minerva near Patras. By coscinomancy, once observed so religiously in the ceremonies of the Romans? Let's have a sieve and some tongs, and you'll see a devil of a sight. By alphitomancy, noted by Theocritus in his *Pharmaceutria,* and by aleuromancy, mixing wheat with flour? By astragalomancy. I have the plans all ready in here. By tyromancy. I have a Bréhémont cheese ready at hand. By gyromancy, I'll have you turn around and around in circles, and you'll fall to the left every time, I assure you. By sternomancy. My word, your chest is pretty ill-proportioned. By libanomancy. All you need is a little incense. By gastromancy? which in Ferrara was long used by the lady Jacoba Rhodigina,[11] an engastrimythe [ventriloquist]? By cephalomancy? which the Germans used to use, roasting an ass's head over burning coals. By ceromancy? there, by melted wax dropped into water, you'll see the faces of your wife and her drummer boys. By capnomancy? On burning coals we'll put some poppy and sesame seed: O what a gorgeous thing!

"By axinomancy? Just provide here an axe and a piece of jade, which we'll put on the embers; O how admirably Homer uses it on Penelope's suitors [*Odyssey* 21.420–423]! By onymancy? Let's have some oil and some wax. By tephramancy? You'll see ashes in the air showing your wife in a fine state. By botanomancy? I have some sage leaves here at hand. By sycomancy? O what a divine art! In fig leaves! By ichthyomancy,[12] once so celebrated and widely practiced by Tiresias and Polydamas, as certain as was done in Dina's pond in the wood sacred to Apollo in the land of the Lycians? By choeromancy?[13] Let's have plenty of hogs, and you shall have their bladders. By cleromancy? as they find the bean in the cake on the eve of Epiphany? By anthropomancy? which was used by Heliogabalus, emperor of Rome? It's a bit annoying, but you'll put up with it well enough, since you're a destined cuckold. By sibylline stichomancy? By onomatomancy? What's your name?"

"Crunchcrap [Maschemerde]," said Panurge.

"Or else by alectryomancy?[14] Here I'll draw a pretty boundary map, which, as you see and watch me, I'll divide into twenty-four equal parts; on each one I'll write a letter of the alphabet; on each letter I'll place a grain of wheat; then I'll turn loose a virgin cock to go over it: you'll see, I pledge you, that he'll eat the grains placed on the letters C. O. Q. U. S. E. R. A. [coqu sera: "cuckold he'll be"], as fatidically as when, under the Emperor Valens, when he was in perplexity to know the name of his successor, the soothsaying alectryomantic cock ate upon the letters Θ. E. O. Δ.[15]

"Do you[16] want to learn about it by the art of haruspicy? or by exispicy? by augury taken from the flight of birds, the song of birds of omen, the dance of ducks dropping grain on the ground?"

"By turdspicine [Par estronspicine]!"[17] retorted Panurge.

"Or else by necromancy? I'll suddenly bring back to life for you someone who died not long ago, as did Apollonius of Tyana for Achilles, as did the witch of Endor in the presence of Saul [1 Samuel 28.7–10], and this former dead man will tell us the total, no more nor less than at Erichtho's invocation a deceased man told Pompey the whole outcome of the battle of Pharsalia.[18] Or, if you're afraid of the dead, as all cuckolds naturally are, I'll just use sciomancy."

"Go to the devil," replied Panurge, "you crazy lunatic, and get yourself frigged by some Albanian:[19] then you'll have a pointed hat. Why the devil don't you advise me as well to hold an emerald, or a hyena stone,[20] under my tongue? or to lay in a stock of hoopoes' tongues and green frogs' hearts? or to eat of the heart and liver of some dragon so as to hear my destinies in the voice of swans and song of birds, as the Arabs used to do in the land of Mesopotamia?[21] Thirty devils take the horned cuckold, the marrano, sorcerer to the devil, enchanter to the Antichrist! Let's go back to our king. I'm sure he won't be pleased with us, if he once hears that we came here into the lair of this begowned devil. I repent of having come here, and would gladly give a hundred nobles and fourteen commoners[22] on condition that the man who used to blow in the bottom of my breeches would shortly shine up his mustaches for him with his spittle. Good Lord! How he smelled me up with vexation and deviltry, with enchantments and sorcery! May the devil run off with him! Say amen, and let's go drink. I won't have a really good time for two days, no, for four."

CHAPTER 26

How Panurge takes counsel
of Frère Jean des Entommeures.

Panurge was vexed by Her Trippa's remarks, and, after passing the hamlet of Huymes,[1] he addressed Frère Jean, stammering and scratching his left ear, and said to him:

"Cheer me up a bit, you old rascal. I'm feeling all matagrabolized[2] in my mind from that devil-ridden lunatic's remarks. Listen, my bonny ballock,

Brawny ballock,
Well-based ballock,
Leaded ballock,
Felted ballock,
Shrewd ballock,
Clay ballock,
Convoluted ballock,
Streamlined ballock,
Self-assured ballock,
Smoothed ballock,
Figured ballock,

331

Hammered ballock,
Sworn ballock,
Grain-filled ballock,
Frenzied ballock,
Whippersnapper ballock,
Hooded ballock,
Varnished ballock,
Brazil-wood ballock,
Organized ballock,
Long-range siege ballock,
Thrusting ballock,
Frantic ballock,
Piled-up ballock,
Stuffed ballock,
Polished ballock,
Poudrebif [a condiment] ballock,
Positive ballock,
Genitive ballock,
Gigantic ballock,
Oval ballock,
Claustral ballock,
Virile ballock,
Ballock of respect,
Ballock at leisure,
Massive ballock,
Manual ballock,
Absolute ballock,
Big-membered ballock,
Twin ballock,
Turquoise ballock,
Shining ballock,
Currying ballock,
Urgent ballock,
Inducing ballock,

Prompt ballock,
Fortunate ballock,
Well-fed-ox ballock,
Rich quality ballock,
Requested ballock,
Little-tail ballock,
Radish ballock,
Ursine [bear-like] ballock,
Ballock with a lineage,
Patronymic ballock,
Waspish ballock,
Algamala[3] [amalgam] ballock,
Robust ballock,
Ballock with an appetite,
Helpful ballock,
Redoubtable ballock,
Affable ballock,
Memorable ballock,
Palpable ballock,
Bardable[4] [fit to bear barbed armor] ballock,
Tragic ballock,
Transpontine ballock,
Digestive ballock,
Incarnative ballock,
Sigillative [sealing] ballock,
Stallioning ballock,
Made-over ballock,
Thundering ballock,
Hammering ballock,
Strident ballock,
Clashing ballock,
Dashing ballock,[5]
Lecherous ballock,
Lusty ballock,

Broaching ballock,
Miscarried ballock,
Hard-scrutinized ballock,
Bolting [belutant] ballock,
Renowned ballock,
Native-born ballock,
Milky ballock,
Calked ballock,
Restored ballock,
Gargoyle's ballock,
Steel-tipped ballock,
Antique ballock,
Well-born ballock,
Interlarded ballock,
Burgher's ballock,
Unwiped ballock,
Tarred ballock,
Appointed ballock,
Desired ballock,
Ebony ballock,
Boxwood ballock,
Latin ballock,
Grappling ballock,
Rash ballock,
Coveted ballock,
Encircled ballock,
Swollen ballock,
Pretty ballock,
Lusty ballock,
Gerundive ballock,
Active ballock,
Vital ballock,
Magisterial ballock,
Monkish ballock,

Subtle ballock,
Relay ballock,
Audacious ballock,
Lascivious ballock,
Gluttonous ballock,
Resolute ballock,
Big-headed ballock,
Courteous ballock,
Fecund ballock,
Whistling ballock,
Neat ballock,
Community ballock,
Brisk ballock,
Impetuous ballock,
Barking ballock,
Usual ballock,
Exquisite ballock,
Fey ballock,
Picardent [a good grape] ballock,
Guelph ballock,
Triage ballock,
Household ballock,
Trim ballock,
Diopter [alidade][6] ballock,
Algebraic ballock,
Gracious ballock,
Insuperable ballock,
Agreeable ballock,
Frightful ballock,
Profitable ballock,
Notable ballock,
Muscular ballock,
Subsidiary ballock,
Satiric ballock,

Repercussive ballock,
Convulsive ballock,
Restorative ballock,
Masculining ballock,
Donkeying ballock,
Fulminating ballock,
Sparkling ballock,
Ramming ballock,
Aromatizing ballock
Diaspermatizing [sperm-spreading] ballock,
Snoring ballock,
Thieving ballock,
Nodding ballock,
Drumming ballock,
Rumpling ballock,
Tumbling ballock,

harquebus-firing ballock, tail-pushing ballock, Frère Jean, my friend, I bear you very great reverence, and I was saving you as the best for the last: I beg you, tell me your opinion: should I marry or not?"

Frère Jean answered him in a blithe spirit, saying: "Get married, in the devil's name, get married, and carillon me double carillons of ballocks. I say, and I mean, as soon as you can do it. By this evening have the banns announced and get the bedstead ready for action. Power of God, until when do you want to hold back? Don't you know very well that the end of the world is coming near? Today we're two rods and half a fathom nearer to it than we were yesterday. The Antichrist is already born, so I've been told. True it is that he still does nothing but scratch his wet nurses and governesses, and he isn't yet displaying the treasures,[7] for he's still little. 'Crescite. Nos qui vivimus, multiplicamini'[8] [broken Latin: 'Increase. We the living, and multiply'] (so it is written in breviary matter), as long as a sack of wheat isn't worth three *patacz,* and a puncheon of wine only six blancs. Would you really want to be found with your ballocks full at the Last Judgment, 'dum venerit judicare [when He shall have come to judge]'?"

"You," said Panurge, "have a most limpid and serene mind, Frère Jean, my metropolitan ballock, and you speak pertinently. This is what Leander of Abydos in Asia was praying for as he was swimming across the sea of the Hellespont to visit his ladylove Hero of Sestos in Europe, to Neptune and all the gods of the sea:

> If you will help me get there safe and sound,
> Little I care if coming back I'm drowned.[9]

"He didn't want to die with his ballocks full. And I'm inclined to think that from now on, in all my Salmagundia, when they want to execute some malefactor in justice, a day or two beforehand they should have him plug away like a pelican,[10] so thoroughly that in all his spermatic vessels there remain not enough to fashion a Greek letter Y.[11] So precious a thing must not be witlessly lost! Peradventure he will engender a man. So he will die without regret, leaving man for man."

CHAPTER 27

*How Frère Jean
joyously advises Panurge.*

"By Saint Rigomé," said Frère Jean, "Panurge, my gentle friend, I'm not advising you to do anything I wouldn't do in your place. Only be careful and always keep well in mind to link up your scores and keep them going. If you ever let up, you're ruined, you poor guy, and there will happen to you what happens to wet nurses. If they stop giving milk to children, they lose their milk. If you don't continually exercise your tool, it will lose its milk and serve you only as a game-pouch. I give you fair warning, my friend. I've seen this experience in many who couldn't when they wanted to, for they hadn't done it when they could have. Thus by disuse are lost all privileges, so say the clerics. Therefore, son, keep all those low-born troglodyte common folk in a state of perpetually plowing the soil. See to it that they don't live like gentlemen, on their incomes, without doing a thing."

"Lord, no," replied Panurge, "Frère Jean, my left ballock, I'll believe you. You really go right to the point. Without exception or circumlocution you have plainly dissolved any fear that could have intimidated me. Thus may it be granted you by the heavens always to operate stiff and low! So now on your say-so I shall marry. There'll be no mistake. And then I'll always have beautiful chambermaids when you come to see me, and you shall be the protector of their Sorority.[1] So much for the first part of the sermon."

"Listen," said Frère Jean, "to the oracle of the bells of Varennes. What are they saying?"

"I hear them," replied Panurge. "Their sound, 'pon my thirst, is more fatidic than that of Jupiter's caldrons in Dodona. Listen:

> Get married, get married,
> Marry, marry.
> If you get married, married, married,
> Very well off you'll be, you'll be, you'll be
> Marry, marry.

"I assure you that I'll marry: all the elements invite me to. Let this word be to you as a wall of bronze.

"As for the second point, you seem to be somewhat doubtful, indeed mistrustful, of my Paternity, as having the stiff god of the gardens none too favorable. I beseech you to do me this favor: to believe that I have it at my command, docile, full of goodwill, attentive, obedient in all things and everywhere. I need only loose his leashes, I mean his point, show him his prey from close up, and tell him: 'Tallyho, pal!' And even if my future wife should be as gluttonous for venereal pleasure as ever was Messalina or the Marchioness of Winchester[2] in England, I beg you to believe that mine is even more copious for contentment.

"I am unaware of what Solomon says [Proverbs 30.15–16], and he spoke about it as a cleric and as one who knew. Since his time, Aristotle has declared that woman's nature is in itself insatiable; but I want it known that I have an indefatigable weapon of the same caliber. Don't hold up to me as models those fabulous wenchers Hercules, Proculus Caesar, and Mahomet, who boasts in the Koran that he has in his genitals the strength of sixty ship-calkers.[3] He lied, the lecher. Don't tell me about the Indian so celebrated by Theophrastus, Pliny, and Athenaeus, who, with the aid of a certain herb, used to do it seventy times and more in one day. I don't believe a word of it; the number is suppoditious. I beg you not to believe it. I beg you to believe (and you won't be believing anything that isn't true) that my nature, my sacred Ithyphallus,[4] Messer Thingumajig of Albinga [Messer Cotal d'Albingues], is the *prime del monde*.[5]

"Listen here, old ballock. Did you ever see the frock of the monk from Castres? When they set it down in some house, whether in the open or under cover, suddenly, by its horrific power, all the residents and inhabitants of the said place went into the rut, beasts and people, men and women, even to the rats and the cat. I swear to you that in my codpiece in other days I have known a certain even more extraordinary energy.

"I won't speak to you of any house or shack, any sermon or market; but at the passion play they were performing at Saint-Maixent,[6] when I came in onto the ground floor of the theater one day, I saw that by the virtue and occult property of this, suddenly everyone, actors as well as spectators, entered into such terrific temptation that there was no angel, human, devil, or she-devil who didn't want to plug away. The director-prompter [*le portecole* for *le protecole*] tossed away his copy; the actor playing Saint Michael came down by the stage heaven; the devils came out of hell and started carrying away all these poor little females; even Lucifer broke his chains. In short, seeing the disarray, I got out of that place, after the example of Cato the Censor, who, seeing that because of his presence the festival of Flora was in disorder, gave up being a spectator."[7]

CHAPTER 28

*How Frère Jean comforts Panurge
about his fear of cuckoldry.*

"I understand you," said Frère Jean, "but time subdues all things: there is no marble or porphyry that does not have its old age and decay. If you're not at that point right now, after a few years I'll hear you confessing that some people's balls are hanging down for lack of a game-pouch. Already I see the hair on your head graying. Your beard, by its shadings of gray, white, tan, and black, seems to me a world map. Look here: there is

Asia; here are Tigris and Euphrates. There's Africa; here are the Mountains of the Moon.[1] Do you see the marshes of the Nile? on the near side is Europe. Do you see Thélème? This sheer white tuft is the Hyperborean Mountains.[2] By my thirst, my friend, when the snows are in the mountains, I mean by that the head and chin, there's not much heat in the valleys of the codpiece!"

"A fine case of chilblains to you!" replied Panurge. "You don't understand your topics.[3] When the snow is on the mountains, the lightning, the thunderbolts, the leg ulcers, the pocky sores, the thunder, the storms, all the devils are in the valleys. Do you want to see this by experience? Go to Switzerland and consider Lake Wunderberlich, four leagues from Berne, on the way to Sion. You reproach me with my graying hair, and do not consider how it is in the nature of leeks, in which we see the head white and the tail green, straight, and vigorous.

"True it is that in myself I recognize a certain sign indicative of old age, I mean green old age; don't tell a soul: it shall remain a secret between the two of us. It is that I find wine better and more savory to my taste than I used to. I fear encountering bad wine. Note that that argues something of the setting sun and signifies that noon is past. But then what? Still a jolly good fellow, as much as ever or more so. I'm not afraid on that score, by the devil. That's not what bothers me. I'm afraid that by some long absence of our King Pantagruel, whom I must perforce accompany, yes, even were he to go to all the devils, my wife may make me a cuckold. That's the key word, for all those I've spoken to about it threaten me with it and affirm that it is thus predestined by the heavens."

"Not everyone," replied Frère Jean, "is a cuckold who wants to be. If you're a cuckold, *ergo* your wife will be beautiful, *ergo* you will be well treated by her, *ergo* you will have friends aplenty, *ergo* you will be saved. These are monastic topics. You'll be a better man for it, you old sinner. You never had it so good. You won't lose a thing by it. Your property will grow even more. If it is predestined thus, would you want to contravene it? Say, withered ballock,

Moldy ballock,
Oversodden ballock,
White-livered ballock,
Cold-benumbed ballock,
Downcast ballock,
Desiccated ballock,

Broken-down ballock,
Failing ballock,
Beshitten ballock,
Prostrate ballock,
Clogged ballock,
Skimmed ballock,
Suppressed ballock,
Balky ballock,
Ground ballock,
Dissolute ballock,
Ballock with a cold,
Drained ballock,
Disgraced ballock,
Drooping ballock,
Drip-drained ballock,
Burst ballock,
Stirred-up ballock,
Mitered ballock,
Bartered ballock,
Trumperied ballock,
Messed-up ballock,
Emptied ballock,
Chagrined ballock,
Unhafted ballock,
Putrified ballock,
Fizzly ballock,
Malandered[4] ballock,
Eunuch ballock,
Castrated ballock,
Emasculated ballock,
Befloured ballock,
Herniated ballock,
Gangrenous ballock,
Scabby pockmarked ballock,

Tattered ballock,
Subdued ballock,
Cocky ballock,
Paltry ballock,
Trepanned ballock,
Swarthy ballock,
Unmanned ballock,
Much-read ballock,
Ballock with St. Anthony's Fire,
Detriped [disemboweled] ballock,
Mildewed ballock,
Apoplectic ballock,
Overdiluted ballock,
Slashed ballock,
Cupped ballock,
Cropped ballock,
Chapped ballock,
Short-winded ballock,
Fusty ballock,
Beery ballock,
Fistulous ballock,
Languorous ballock,
Impotent ballock,
Hectic ballock,
Worn ballock,
Monkey ballock,
Matagrabolized ballock,
Macerated ballock,
Paralytic ballock,
Degraded ballock,
Benumbed ballack,
A bat's ballock,
Fart-volley ballock,
Sunburned ballock,

Torn ballock,
Stupefied ballock,
Numbstruck ballock,
Stinking ballock,
Appelant ballock,
Barred-in ballock,
Assassinated ballock,
Burglarized ballock,
Neglected ballock,
Matafain [stove-cooked black wheat cake] ballock,
Rubberneck ballock,
Customerless ballock,
Musty ballock,
Dangling ballock,
Appellant ballock,
Left ballock,
Deseeded ballock,
Incongruous ballock,
Mellow ballock,
Buggered ballock,
Beshitten ballock,
Pacified ballock,
Expressed ballock,
Paltry ballock,
Putative ballock,
Worm-eaten ballock,
Bowed-down ballock,
Wretched ballock,
Poorly-tempered ballock,
Corked ballock,
Diaphanous ballock,
Disgusted ballock,
Trifled-with ballock,
Ill-filled ballock,

Reproved ballock,
Pettifogged ballock,
Blistered ballock,
Besmeared ballock,
Wrinkled ballock,
Haggard ballock,
Blunted ballock,
Dejected ballock,
Furbished ballock,
Afflicted ballock,
Castrated ballock,
Mortified ballock,
Unhinged ballock,
Scurvy ballock,
Varicose ballock,
Wormy ballock,
Lame ballock,
Frigglefraggled ballock,
Decanted ballock,
Stubby ballock,
Fondled ballock,
Scorched ballock,
Raveled ballock,
Donkeypricked ballock,
Marinated ballock,
Extirpated ballock,
Constipated ballock,
Pocky ballock,
Slapped ballock,
Buffeted ballock,
Cupped ballock,
Cuffed ballock,
Scarfaced ballock,
Enfeebled ballock,

Stinking ballock,
Pushed ballock,
Chilly ballock,
Scrupulous ballock,
Cracked ballock,
Rancid ballock,
Diminutive ballock,
Grim ballock,
Wiseguy ballock,
Rusty ballock,
Vile ballock,
Antedated ballock,
One-armed ballock,
Confused ballock,
Churlish ballock,
Overwhelmed ballock,
Ballock aground,
Desolate ballock,
Decadent ballock,
Solecizing ballock,
Thin ballock,
Ulcerated ballock,
Patched ballock,
Numbstruck ballock,
Annihilated ballock,
Zero ballock,
Threadbare ballock,
Ballock sick with an ague,

"Ballock away to the devil, Panurge my friend, since it is so predestined for you; would you make the planets reverse their course? all the heavenly spheres go off track? propose error to the Moving Intelligences? blunt the spindles? slander the bobbins? reproach the reels? condemn the spools for spun thread? unwind the skeins of the Fates? A tough quartan fever to you, ballocker! You'd do worse than the Giants.[5]

"Come here, billicullion. Would you rather be jealous with no reason than a cuckold without knowing it?"

"I wouldn't like," said Panurge, "to be either one. But if I'm once informed of it, I'll get things straightened out, or the world will run out of sticks. Listen to what the bells are telling me, at this point when they're nearer:

> Marry not, marry not,
> Not, not, not, not,
> If you marry (marry not, marry not,
> Not, not, not, not),
> Sorry you'll be, you'll be, you'll be,
> Cuckold you'll be.

"Worthy power of God! I'm beginning to get annoyed. Now you people, you befrocked brains, don't you know any remedy for it? Has Nature so stripped humans that a married man cannot pass through this world without falling into the abysses and dangers of cuckoldry?"

"I mean to teach you," said Frère Jean, "an expedient by means of which your wife will never make you a cuckold without your knowledge and consent."

"I pray you to, velvety ballock," said Panurge, "So speak up, my friend."

"Take," said Frère Jean, "Hans Carvel's ring, the great lapidary of the king of Melinda.[6] Hans Carvel was a learned, expert, studious man, a worthy man, with good sense and good judgment, genial, charitable, giving alms, philosophical, moreover blithe, a good companion, and a joker if ever there was one; a wee bit paunchy, nodding his head, and rather awkward in person. In his old age he married the daughter of the bailiff Concordat,[7] young, pretty, frisky, gallant, attractive, much too gracious toward her neighbors and servants. Whence it came about that after a few weeks he became jealous as a tiger of her and suspicious that she was getting her tail drummed elsewhere. To obviate which he told her her fill of nice stories about the miseries brought on by adultery; often read her the legend of worthy women;[8] preached modesty to her; made up for her a book of praises of conjugal fidelity strongly detesting the wickedness of wanton wives; and gave her a beautiful necklace all covered with oriental sapphires. This notwithstanding, he saw her so ready and on good terms with his neighbors that his jealousy grew worse and worse.

"One night among others, in bed with her with such tormenting ideas in his mind, he dreamed that he was talking with the Devil and telling him his troubles. The Devil was comforting him and put a ring on his middle finger, saying:

" 'I give you this ring; as long as you have it on your finger, your wife will not be carnally known by anyone else without your knowledge and consent.'

" 'Many thanks indeed,' said Hans Carvel, 'Sir Devil. I'll deny Mahomet if anyone ever takes it off my finger.'

"The Devil disappeared. Hans Carvel, overjoyed, woke up and found that he had his finger in his wife's whatsitsname. I was forgetting to tell you that she was pulling back her tail, as if to say: 'Yes, no, that's not the thing to put there'; and then it seemed to Hans Carvel that someone was trying to rob him of his ring.

"Isn't that an infallible remedy? Follow this example, if you ask me, and you'll have your wife's ring continually on your finger."

Here ended the talk and the trip.

CHAPTER 29

How Pantagruel calls a meeting of
a theologian, a doctor, a jurist, and a philosopher
to help Panurge's perplexity.

ONCE back in the palace, they told Pantagruel the story of their trip and showed him the statement of Raminagrobis. Pantagruel, after reading and rereading it, said:

"I haven't yet seen a reply that I like better. He means, in sum, that in the undertaking of marriage each man must be the arbiter of his own thoughts and take counsel of himself. Such has always been my opinion, and I told you as much the first time you spoke to me about it. But you were tacitly making fun of this, I remember, and I recognize that *philautie*[1] and self-love is deceiving you. Let's do something different. Here's what: All that we are and we have consists in three things; the soul, the body, the property. For the conservation of each of the three respectively are destined nowadays three kinds of people: theologians for the soul, doctors for the body, jurists for the property. My idea is that on Sunday we have here for dinner a theologian, a doctor, and a jurist. Together with them we will confer about your perplexity."

"By Saint Picault,"[2] replied Panurge, "we won't get anywhere that way; I can see that clearly already. And just see how the world has gone to seed: we put our souls in trust to the theologians, who for the most part are heretics; our bodies to the doctors, who all loathe medications and never take medicine; and our property to the lawyers, who never go to law with one another."

"Spoken like a courtier," said Pantagruel. "But the first point I deny, seeing that the main, indeed the total and unique occupation of the good theologians is employed by deeds, by words, and by writings, in extirpating errors and heresies (that's how far they are from being stained with them), and in implanting deeply in human hearts the true living Catholic faith. The second I praise, seeing the good doctors set to rights the preventive and health-preserving part in their own regard so well that they have no need of the therapeutic and curative part by medications. The third I concede, seeing the good lawyers so involved in their pleadings and legal responses for others that they have no time or leisure to look out for their own.

"Therefore, next Sunday, let's have as theologian our Father Hippothadée;[3] as doctor, our master Rondibilis;[4] as jurist, our friend Bridoye;[5] and still I think we should go into the Pythagorean tetrad, and let's have as extra fourth our trusted liege the philosopher Trouillogan,[6] considering especially that the perfect philosopher, such as Trouillogan is, gives a positive answer on all doubts that are proposed. Carpalim, see to it that we have all four next Sunday for dinner."

"I think," said Epistémon, "that you couldn't have chosen better in the whole country. I say this not only as regards the perfections of each one in his field, which are beyond any hazards of judgment, but, moreover, in that Rondibilis is married, had not been; Hippothadée never was and is not; Bridoye has been and is not; Trouillogan is and has been. I'll relieve Carpalim of one task. I'll go and invite Bridoye (if that suits you), who is an old acquaintance of mine and whom I want to talk with for the good and advancement of a worthy learned son of his, who is studying at Toulouse under the direction of the very learned and virtuous Boyssonné."[7]

"Do," said Pantagruel, "as you see fit. And find out if I can do anything for the advancement of the son and for the dignity of Lord Boyssonné, whom I love and revere as one of the ablest men there is today in his field. I'll work on that most cordially."

CHAPTER 30

*How Hippothadée,[1] the theologian,
gives advice to Panurge
on the undertaking of marriage.*

On the following Sunday the dinner was no sooner ready than the guests appeared, except Bridoye, who was deputy-governor of Fonsbeton [lieutenant de Fonsbeton]. When they brought on the second service [the dessert], Panurge, with a deep bow, said:

"Gentlemen, all that's at issue is one word. Should I marry or not? If my doubt is not cleared up by you, I consider it insoluble, as are Alliaco's *Insolubilia*. For you are all selected, chosen, and singled out, each in his respective field, like fine peas on the sifter."

Father Hippothadée, after Pantagruel's invitation and the bows of all those present, replied with incredible modesty:

"My friend, you ask advice of us, but first you must advise yourself. Do you feel importunately in your body the prickings of the flesh?"

"Very strongly," replied Panurge, "no offense to you, Father."

"No offense taken," said Hippothadée, "for it is far better to marry than to burn in the fire of concupiscence."[2]

"That's the way to talk, that is," exclaimed Panurge, "gallantly, without circumbilivaginating[3] about the bush. Many thanks, Our Father, Sir! I'll marry and no mistake, and I invite you to my wedding. Cocksbody![4] We'll have quite a party. You shall have my colors to wear, and we'll have goose to eat, and my wife won't roast it! Also I'll ask you to lead off the first dance of the bridesmaids, if you'll be good enough to do me all that honor, in return for the same. There remains one little scruple to resolve. A little one, I say, less than nothing. Won't I be a cuckold?"

"No indeed, my friend," said Hippothadée, "if God please."

"Oh, Lord and His power help us!" exclaimed Panurge. "Where are you sending me back to, good folk? To the conditionals,[5] which in dialectic admit of all contradictions and impossibilities. If my transalpine mule could fly, my transalpine mule would have wings. If God please, I won't be a cuckold; I'll be a cuckold, if God please. Good Lord, if it were a condition I could obviate, I wouldn't despair at all. But you send me back to God's privy council, to the chamber of His petty pleasures. Where do you Frenchmen find the road to get there? Our, Father, Sir, I think the best thing for you will be not to come to my wedding. The noise and bustle of the wedding guests would shatter your whole head and brain.[6] You like repose, silence, and solitude. You won't be coming, I think. And then you dance rather poorly and would feel embarrassed to lead off the first dance. I'll send you some rissoles up to your room, also some wedding colors. You'll drink our health, if you please."

"My friend," said Hippothadée, "take my words in good part, I beg you. When I say to you: 'If God please,' am I doing wrong? Is it ill spoken? Is it a blasphemous or scandalous condition? Isn't it honoring the Lord, Creator, Protector, Preserver? Isn't it recognizing Him as our sole Giver of all good? Isn't it declaring that we all depend on his benignity, that without Him we are nothing, are worth nothing, can do nothing, if His holy grace is not infused over us? Isn't it setting a canonical exception to all our enterprises, and entrusting all that we propose to what shall be disposed by His holy will, in heaven as it is on earth? Isn't it truly sanctifying His blessed name? My friend, you will not be a cuckold, if God please. To find out what is His pleasure in this, there is no need to fall into despair, as over something abstruse, and to understand which you have to consult His privy council and travel into the chamber of His petty pleasures. The good God has done us this good, that He has revealed, announced, and openly described them, in the Holy Bible.

"There you will find that you will never be a cuckold, that is to say that your wife will never be a wanton, if you take her descended from good people, brought up in virtues and decency, having associated with and frequented only company of good moral conduct, loving and fearing God, loving to please God by faith and observation of His holy commandments, fearing to offend Him and lose His grace by lack of faith and transgression of His divine law, in which adultery is rigorously forbidden, and she is ordered to cleave solely to her husband, cherish him, serve him, love him totally after God.

"To reinforce this teaching, you, on your side, shall maintain her in conjugal affection, shall continue in uprightness, shall set her a good example, shall live continently, chastely, virtuously in your household, as you want her to live for her part; for even as that mirror is not called good and perfect that is most adorned with gilt and precious stones, but which truly represents the forms set before it, so that a wife is not to be most esteemed who might be rich, beautiful, elegant, born of noble race, but who tries the most to form herself in good grace with God and conform to her husband's ways. See how the moon takes no light either from Mercury, or Jupiter, or Mars, or any other planet or star that is in the sky; she receives it only from the sun, her husband, and receives from him no more than he gives her by his infusion and aspects. Thus shall you be to your wife as a model and exemplar of virtues and decency. And you shall continually implore God's grace for your protection."

"So you want me," said Panurge, pointing the ends of his mustaches, "to marry the capable wife described by Solomon [Proverbs 31.10]. She's dead, and no mistake. I've never seen her that I know of, God forgive me! Thanks anyway, Father. Here, eat a bit of marzipan: it will help you with your digestion; then you'll drink a cup of red and white hippocras:[7] it's good for your health and stomach. Let's move on."

CHAPTER 31

How Rondibilis, the doctor, advises Panurge.

PANURGE continued his remarks, saying: "The first words spoken by the man who was gelding the brown monks at Saussignac,[1] after gelding Friar Hotear,[2] were 'Bring on the rest [aux aultres]!' I say likewise: 'Bring on the rest!' Here now our Master Rondibilis, Sir, speed me along. Should I marry or not?"

"By the ambles of my mule!" replied Rondibilis, "I don't know what I should reply to this problem. You say you feel within yourself the sharp prickings of sensuality? I find in our Faculty of Medicine, and we have taken it from the conclusion of the ancient Platonists, that concupiscence is cured by five means: By wine."

"I believe it," said Frère Jean. "When I'm good and drunk, I ask for nothing but to sleep."

"I mean," said Rondibilis, "by wine taken intemperately. For from intemperance in wine there comes to the body a chilling of the blood, a slackening of the sinews, a dispersal of generative seed, a numbing of the senses, an impairment of the movements, which are all handicaps to the act of generation. Indeed, you see Bacchus, god of drunkards, portrayed beardless and in women's dress, as completely effeminate, and as a gelded eunuch. It is otherwise with wine taken temperately. The ancient proverb shows this, in which it is said that Venus catches cold without the company of Ceres and Bacchus. And it was the opinion of the ancients, according to the account of Diodorus Siculus, and especially of the Lampsacians, as Pausanias attests, that Messer Priapus was the son of Bacchus and Venus.

"Secondly, by certain drugs and plants, which make a man frigid, spellbound, and impotent for generation. Experience shows this in the Heraclean water lily [nymphaea heraclia], the amerine [agnus castus], willow, hempseed, honeysuckle [periclymenoa], tamarisk, Abraham's balm [vitex], mandrake, hemlock, the small orchid, the skin of a hippopotamus, and others, which inside human bodies, both by their elementary virtues and by their specific properties, either freeze and mortify the reproductive germs, or dissipate the spirits that were to lead them to the places destined by nature, or obstruct the passages and conduits by which they could be ejected. As, on the contrary, we have some that head up, excite, and empower man for the venereal act."

"I don't need them, thank God!" said Panurge. "How about you, Master? No offense, however. What I'm saying about this is not from any ill will I bear you."

"Thirdly," said Rondibilis, "by assiduous toil. For in this is brought about such great dissolution of the body that the blood, which is dispersed through it for the nourishment of each and every member, has no time, nor leisure, nor capacity to create this seminal exudation and superfluity of the third concoction.[3] Nature in special circumstances reserves it for herself, as being far more necessary for the preservation of her individual than for the multiplication of the human species and race. Thus Diana is called chaste, who constantly toils at the hunt. Thus once upon a time the camps were called chaste[4] in which athletes and soldiers continually worked.

"Thus Hippocrate writes, lib. *De aere, aqua et locis* [in his book *On air, water, and places*] of certain races in Scythia, who in his time were more impotent than eunuchs for venereal sport, because they were continually on horseback and at work. As, on the contrary, the philosophers say that Idleness is the mother of Lechery. When Ovid used to be asked why Aegisthus became an adulterer, he would answer nothing except that he was idle; and if anyone removed Idleness from the world, soon would perish Cupid's arts; his bow, his quiver, his arrows would be a useless burden to him; never would he strike anyone with them. For he is by no means such a good archer that he can hit cranes flying through the air and stags springing from the woods, as the Parthians certainly used to do, that is to say humans bustling about and working. He asks to have them quiet, sitting, lying down, and idle. In fact Theophrastus, when sometimes asked what sort of creature, what sort of thing he thought amours were, said that they were passions of idle minds. Diogenes likewise used to say that lechery was the occupation of people not otherwise occupied. Therefore Canachus the Sicyonian, a sculptor, wanting to make it understood that idleness, laziness, and listlessness were the determinants of bawdry, made his statue of Venus seated, not standing, as all his predecessors had done.

"Fourthly, by fervent study. For in it is produced an incredible dissolution of the spirits, to such a point that not enough remains to propel this generative exudation to the destined places and inflate the cavernous nerve, whose function is to project it out for the propagation of mankind. To prove that this is so, observe the posture of a man attentive to some study: you'll see in him all the arteries of the brain taut as the string of a crossbow to provide him deftly with sufficient spirits to fill the ventricles of the common sense,[5] of the imagination and apprehension, of reasoning and decision, of memory and recollection, and to run nimbly from one to the other by the conduits manifest in anatomy at the end of the wondrous network in which the arteries end, which took their origin from the left chamber of the heart and refined the vital spirits in long meanderings so as to make them animal.[6] So that in such a studious person you will see all the faculties suspended, all the external senses halted; in short you will judge him not to be living in himself, but to be abstracted out of himself by ecstasy, and you will say that Socrates was not misusing the term when he said that philosophy was nothing else but meditation on death.[7] Peradventure this is why Democritus blinded himself, considering less the loss of his sight than the diminution of his contemplations, which he felt to be interrupted by the wandering of his eyes.[8]

"Thus is said to be virgin Pallas, goddess of wisdom, tutor of studious folk; thus are the Muses virgins; thus the Graces remain in eternal chastity. And I remember reading that Cupid, when occasionally asked by his mother Venus why he did not attack the Muses, replied that he found them so beautiful, so pure, so decent, so modest and continually occupied—one in contemplation of the stars, another in computation of numbers, another in the measurement of geometrical bodies, another in rhetorical invention, another in poetic composition, another in the arrangement of music—that when he came near them, he would unstring his bow, close up his quiver, and put out his torch, for shame and for fear of harming them. Then he would take the bandage off his eyes so as to look them in the face more openly and hear their charming songs and poetic odes. In that he took the greatest pleasure in the world, so much so that often he felt himself quite ravished by their beauties and fine graces and went to sleep to their harmony. So far was he from wanting to attack them or distract them from their studies.

"Under this heading I include what Hippocrates writes in the aforementioned book, speaking of the Scythians, and in his book entitled *De genitura* [*On breeding*], saying that all humans are impotent for generation who have once had their parotid arteries cut (which are beside the ears), for the reason exposed above when I was speaking to you about the dissolution of the spirits and of the spiritual blood of which the arteries are the receptacles;[9] also because he maintains that a great part of the reproductive seed issues from the brain and the spinal column."

"Fifthly, by the venereal act."

"I was waiting for you there," said Panurge, "and take that one for my own. Let anyone who wants use the preceding ones."

"That," said Frère Jean, "is what Friar Scyllino, Prior of Saint-Victor near Marseille, calls maceration of the flesh. And I am of the opinion (so was the hermit of Sainte-Radégonde above Chinon) that the hermits of the Thebaid could not more aptly macerate their bodies, subdue that lecherous sensuality, put down the rebellion of the flesh, than by doing it twenty-five or thirty times a day."

"I see Panurge," said Rondibilis, "well proportioned in his members, well tempered in his humors, well constituted in his spirits, at a competent age, at an opportune time, of a steady will to be married: if he meets a woman of similar temperament, together they will engender children worthy of some transpontine[10] monarchy. The sooner the better, if he wants to see his children provided for."

"Our Master, Sir," said Panurge, "I shall be, have no doubt of it, and soon. During your learned speech this flea I have in my ear has tickled me more than it ever did. I'll count on you for the party. We'll have a good time and a half, I promise you. You'll bring your wife, if you please, with her lady neighbors, that's understood. So here we go, all fair and aboveboard!"

CHAPTER 32

How Rondibilis declares that cuckoldry
is naturally one of the attributes of marriage.

"THERE remains," went on Panurge, "one little point to clear up. In other days you have seen on the banner of Rome: S. P. Q. R., *Si Peu Que Rien.*[1] Won't I be a cuckold?"

"Haven of Mercy [Havre de Grâce]!" exclaimed Rondibilis, "What are you asking me? Whether you'll be a cuckold? My friend, I am married; you will be after all this. But write this dictum in your brain with an iron stylus, that any married man is in danger of being a cuckold. Cuckoldry is naturally one of the attributes of marriage. The shadow follows the body no more naturally than cuckoldry follows marriage. And when you hear said of anyone these three words: 'He is married,' if you say: 'Then he is, or has been, or will be, or may be a cuckold,' you will not be called an inexpert architect of natural consequences."

"By the belly and bowels of all the devils!" cried Panurge, "what are you telling me?"

"My friend," replied Rondibilis, "Hippocrates, going one day from Lango [Cos] to Polystylo [Thrace] to visit the philosopher Democritus, wrote a letter to his old friend Dionysius, in which he asked him, during his absence, to take his [Hippocrates'] wife to her parents, who were honorable people of good repute, not wanting her to stay in her house alone; nevertheless, asking him to watch over her carefully and take note of wherever she went with her mother and what people should visit her at her parents. 'Not,' he wrote, 'that I don't trust her virtue and modesty, which from times past has been made clear and known to me; but she is a woman, that's all.'

"My friend, the nature of women is represented for us by the moon both in other respects and in this one: that they hide, dissimulate, and constrain themselves in the sight and presence of their husbands. In the absence of these, they take their advantage, have themselves a good time, gad about, trot about, lay aside their hypocrisy, and declare themselves, even as the moon does not appear in heaven or on earth in conjunction with the sun, but only in opposition to it, when at her greatest distance from the sun, she shines forth in all her plenitude and appears full, especially at nighttime. Thus are all women women.

"When I say woman, I mean a sex so fragile, so variable, so mutable, so inconstant and imperfect, that Nature (speaking in all honor and reverence) seems to me to have strayed from that good sense by which she had created and formed all things, when she built woman.[2] And, having thought about it one hundred and five hundred times, I don't know what to conclude, unless that in creating woman she had regard more to man's social delectation and the perpetuation of the human species than to the perfection of individual femininity. Certainly Plato does not know in what category he should place them, that of reasonable animals or that of brute beasts.[3] For Nature has placed in their body, in a secret place inside, an animal, a member, which is not in men, in which are sometimes engendered certain salty humors, nitrous, boracic, acrid, biting, tearing, bitterly tickling, by whose pricking and painful titillation (for this member is all nerves and acutely sensitive), their entire body is shaken, all their senses transported, all desires internalized, all thoughts confused, so that if Nature had not sprinkled their foreheads with a little shame, you would see them, as if beside themselves, chasing the codpiece, more frightfully than ever did the Proetids,[4] the Mimallonids, or the Bacchic Thyades on the day of their Bachanals, because this terrible animal has connections with all the main parts of the body, as is evident in anatomy.

"I call it animal, following the doctrine of both the Academics and the Peripatetics. For if automotion is a certain indicator of an animate being, as Aristotle writes, and if all that by itself moves itself is called animal, then Plato rightly calls it animal, recognizing in it independent motions of suffocations, precipitation, corrugation, and indignation, indeed so violent that by them very often is ravished from woman every other sense and movement, as if it were a lipothymy, a swoon, epilepsy, apoplexy, and a real semblance of death. Furthermore, we see in this a manifest distinction of odors, and women, aware of it, avoid the stinking ones and follow the aromatic.

"I know that Cl. Galen tries to prove that these are not independent and self-impelled movements, but accidental, and that others of his sect labor to demonstrate that this is not in it a sensitive discrimination between odors, but a different capacity, proceeding from the diversity of the odoriferous substances. But if you examine carefully, and weigh in the balance of Critolaus, their statements and reasons, you will find that, both in this matter and in many others, they have spoken heedlessly and in the wish to correct their elders, more than in the quest for truth.

"Into this dispute I shall not enter further. Only I will say to you that no small praise is due to upright women, who have lived chastely and blamelessly, and have had the virtue to bring this frenzied animal to obedience, to reason. And I will conclude if I add this, that when this animal is satiated (if satiated it can be) by the food that Nature has prepared for it in man, all its individual motions have reached their goal, all its appetites are put to sleep, all its furies pacified. Therefore don't be astonished if we are in perpetual danger of being cuckolds, we who do not always have in abundance the wherewithal to pay it off and satisfy it to contentment."

"By the powers of others than little fishes!"[5] said Panurge, "don't you know any remedy for it in your art?"

"Indeed I do, my friend," replied Rondibilis, "and a very good one, which I use; and it is written down in a famous author, eighteen hundred years ago.[6] Listen."

"By the power of God," said Panurge, "you're a good man, and I love you all my blessed fill! Eat a bit of this quince pastry: quinces are suitable for closing the opening of the ventricle because of some happy stypticity that is in them, and they help in the first digestion. But what am I doing? I'm talking Latin in front of clerics! Wait until I give you a drink in this Nestorean[7] goblet. Will you have another draft of white hippocras? Don't be afraid of the quinsy, no indeed [Ne ayez paour de l'esquinance, non]. There's neither squinancy in it, nor ginger, nor amomum seed. There's nothing but lovely sifted cinnamon and nice refined sugar, with good white wine from the vintage of La Devinière, in the vineyard with the big sorb-apple tree above the crow-infested walnut tree [du grand Cormier, au dessus du Noyer groslier]."

CHAPTER 33

*How Rondibilis, the doctor,
gives a remedy for cuckoldry.*

"At the time," said Rondibilis, "when Jupiter established the estate of his Olympian household and the calendar of all his gods and goddesses, having set up for each and every one the day and season of his festival, assigned places for their oracles and pilgrimages, ordained their sacrifices . . ."

"Didn't he do," asked Panurge, "as did Tinteville,[1] Bishop of Auxerre? The noble pontiff loved good wine, as does every worthy man; therefore, he had especial care and concern for the vine-shoots, forefather of Bacchus. Now the fact is that for several years he saw the vine-shoots lamentably ruined by the frosts, drizzles, cold mists, hoar frosts, ice storms, chills, hailstorms, and calamities, that came on the feast days of Saints George, Mark, Vitalis,[2] Eutropius, and Philip, on Holy Cross Day, Ascension Day, and others, which come in the season when the sun passes under the sign of Taurus [April 22]. And he got this idea, that the aforementioned are saints that hail, freeze, and spoil the vine-shoots; therefore, he wanted to transfer their festivals to winter, between Christmas and Epiphany, allowing them, in all honor and reverence, to hail and freeze them all they wanted; the freeze then would be in no way harmful, but evidently profitable, to the vine-shoots; to put in their places the festivals of Saint Christopher, Saint John the Beheaded [the Baptist], Saint Magdalen, Saint Anne, Saint Dominic, Saint Lawrence, indeed to assign mid-August to May.[3] At which festivals, so far is anyone from being in danger from frost that there are no tradesmen so much in demand as sellers of cold drinks, arrangers of arbors, and coolers of wine."

"Jupiter," said Rondibilis, "forgot that poor devil Cuckoldry, who at that point was not present; he was in Paris pleading some lousy case for one of his tenants and vassals. I know not how many days afterward, Cuckoldry heard how he had been bilked, stopped his pleading, for a new concern not to be excluded from the estate, and appeared in person before the great Jupiter, alleging his earlier merits and the good and pleasing services he had done him in other days, and urgently requesting him not to leave him without feast day, without sacrifices, without honor. Jupiter kept making excuses, pointing out that all his benefices were distributed and that his estate was closed. However, he was so importuned by Messer Cuckoldry that at last he put him on the estate list and ordained for him on earth honor, sacrifices, and a festival.

"His festival was (because there was no empty and vacant spot in the whole calendar) in competition with the goddess Jealousy and on the same day; his dominion, over married men, especially those who should have beautiful wives; his sacrifices, suspicion, mistrust, surliness, lying in wait, investigation, and spying by husbands on their wives, with a rigorous recommendation to each and every man to revere and honor him, celebrate his festival twofold, and make him the aforementioned sacrifices, on pain and prescription that to those who would not honor him as is said, Messer Cuckoldry would not offer aid, or help, never would he take account of them, never would enter their houses, never would frequent their companies, whatever pleas they might make to him but would let them rot away eternally alone with their wives, without any rival, and would shun them forever as heretic and sacrilegious folk, as is the practice of the other gods toward those who do not honor them duly: of Bacchus toward vine growers, of Ceres toward farmers, of Pomona toward fruit growers, of Neptune toward sailors, of Vulcan toward blacksmiths, and so for the rest. Attached, as well, was an infallible promise that to those who (as they say) should stop work for this festival, cease all business, neglect their own affairs to spy on their wives, lock them up and mistreat them out of Jealousy, as the ordinance of his[4] sacrifices requires, he would be continually favorable, would love them, keep company with them, be in their houses day and night; never would they be destitute of his presence. I have spoken."

"Ha, ha, ha!" said Carpalim, laughing, "that's an even more natural remedy than Hans Carvel's ring. Devil take me if I don't think so! The nature of women is like that. Even as lightning does not shatter and burn any except hard, solid, resistant materials, it does not stop for soft, empty, and yielding things: it will burn the sword of steel without damaging the velvet scabbard; it will consume the bones in bodies without hurting the flesh that covers them; so women never sense the contentiousness, subtlety, and contrariness of their minds, unless toward what they know is prohibited and forbidden them."

"Indeed," said Hippothadée, "some of our doctors say that the first woman in the world, who the Hebrews call Eve, would hardly have entered into temptation to eat the fruit of all knowledge, if it had not been forbidden her. To prove that this is so, consider how the wily Tempter reminded her in his first words of the prohibition made against this, as if meaning to infer: 'It is forbidden you, so you must eat of it or you would not be woman.'"

CHAPTER 34

How women ordinarily covet forbidden things.

"At the time," said Carpalim, "when I was running a bawdy house in Orléans, I had no more valuable rhetorical trick or more persuasive argument for the young ladies to draw into my nets and lure them into the sport of amours than pointing out to them vividly, manifestly, how their husbands were jealous of them. I certainly hadn't invented this: it is written up, and we have laws, examples, reasons on the subject and daily experiences of it. Having this persuasion in their noggins, they will infallibly make their husbands cuckolds, by God (no swearing intended)! even if they had to do as did Semiramis, Pasiphae, Egesta, the women of Mendes Island in Egypt, whom Herodotus and Strabo hold up to our blame, and other such bitches."

"Really," said Ponocrates, "I've heard that Pope John XXII, when he passed one day through the abbey of Thrustitindeep [Coingnaufond], was asked by the abbess and some discreet nuns to grant them an indult by means of which they could confess to one another, under the seal of confession.

"'There is nothing' said the pope, 'that I won't gladly grant you. But I see one problem in it, which is that confession must be kept secret. You women would have a hard time concealing it.'

"'We'd do it very well,' said they, 'and better than the men do.'

"On that very same day the Holy Father left a box in their keeping, in which he had a little linnet put, asking them gently to lock it up in some safe secret place, promising them, on a pope's word, to grant them the terms of their request if they kept it secret, meanwhile strictly forbidding them to go and open it, on pain of ecclesiastical censure and eternal excommunication. No sooner was this prohibition made than their brains were sizzling with eagerness to see what was inside, and they could hardly wait for the pope to go out the door to get on with it. The Holy Father, having given them his blessing, retired to his quarters. He wasn't yet three steps from the abbey when the good ladies rushed in a crowd to open the forbidden box and see what was inside. The next day the pope visited them, with the intention (as it seemed to them) of dispatching them their indult. But before starting to talk, he gave orders to have his box brought him. It was brought him; but the little bird was no longer in it. Thereupon he remonstrated to them that it would be too hard a thing for them to keep confessions secret, seeing that only for so short a time they had kept secret the box so stringently entrusted to them."

"Our master, Sir, a most hearty welcome to you. It gave me great pleasure to hear you, and I praise God for everything. I hadn't ever seen you since back at Montpellier, when with our old friends Ant. Saporta, Guy Bouguier, Balthazar Noyer, Tolet, Jean Queutin, François Robinet, Jean Perdrier, and François Rabelais, you played in the moral comedy of *The Man Who Married a Dumb Wife.*"[1]

"I was there," said Epistémon. "The good husband wanted to have her speak. She did speak, by the skill of the doctor and the surgeon, who cut off a restricting cord under her tongue. With her speech recovered she talked and talked, so much that her husband went back to the doctor for a remedy to shut her up. The doctor replied that he had indeed in his craft remedies to make women talk, but none to shut them up; the only remedy for this interminable talking by his wife was deafness in the husband. The rascal became deaf, through I know not what spell they cast. His wife, seeing that he had become deaf, that she was talking in vain, he wasn't hearing her, went mad. Then, when the doctor asked for his fee, the husband replied that he really *was* deaf and couldn't hear his request. The doctor cast over his back some powder or other by virtue of which he went crazy. Thereupon the crazy husband and the mad wife joined forces together and beat up the doctor and surgeon so badly that they left them half dead. I've never laughed so hard as I did at that crazy farce."[2]

"Let's get back to our sheep," said Panurge. "Your Lords, translated from gibberish into French, mean that I should boldly marry and not worry about being a cuckold. That's really hitting the nail on the thumb! Our Master, Sir, I really think that on our wedding day you'll be busy elsewhere with patients and unable to show up. I'll excuse you.

> Stercus et urina medici sunt prandia prima.
> Ex aliis paleas, ex istis collige grana.
>
> [Urine and dung for doctors make fine meals,
> From one they gather straw, from the other grain.]

"You've got it wrong," said Rondibilis, "the second line goes like this:

Nobis sunt signa, vobis sunt prandia digna.

[Mere signs to us, to you they're worth dishes.]

"If my wife is ill, I'd want to check her urine, feel her pulse, and examine the condition of her lower belly and umbilical parts, before going any further, as Hippocrates orders us to do, *Aphorisms* Book 2, no. 35."

"No, no," said Panurge, "that's not the point. That's for us jurists, who have the rule *De ventre inspiciendo*.[3] I fix her a mighty enema. Don't abandon your more urgent business elsewhere. I'll send you some rissoles to your house, and you'll always be our friend."

Then he went up to him, and, without a word, slipped into his hand four rose nobles. Rondibilis took them all right, then said in alarm, as if indignant:

"Heh, heh, heh! Sir, you didn't need to. Many thanks all the same. From wicked people I never accept anything. From good people I never refuse. I'm always at your service."

"For pay," said Panurge.

"That's understood," said Rondibilis.

CHAPTER 35

How Trouillogan, the philosopher,
treats the difficulty of marriage.

WHEN these words were ended, Pantagruel said to Trouillogan, the philosopher:

"Our trusty liege, from hand to hand the torch has come to you [De main en main vous est la lampe baillée]. It's your turn now to respond. Should Panurge marry or not?"

"Both," replied Trouillogan.

"What are you telling me?" asked Panurge.

"What you've heard," replied Trouillogan.

"What have I heard?" asked Panurge.

"What I said," replied Trouillogan.

"Aha! Is that where we stand?" said Panurge. "I'll pass. So now then, should I marry or not?"

"Neither one," replied Trouillogan.

"Devil take me," said Panurge, "if I'm not losing my mind, and may he take me if I understand you! Wait a bit. I'll put my eyeglasses on this left ear, to hear you more clearly!"

At that moment, Pantagruel noticed near the door of the room Gargantua's little dog, whom he called Kyne, because that was the name of Tobias's dog.[1] So he said to the entire company:

"Our king is not far from here, let's rise."

These words were not finished when Gargantua entered the banquet hall. Everyone rose to make him a bow. Gargantua, having graciously greeted the company, said:

"My friends, you'll do me the pleasure, pray, not to leave your places or your talk. Bring me a chair to this end of the table. Give me something to let me drink to the company. Pray be most welcome. Now tell me, what were you talking about?"

Pantagruel answered that at the point when they brought on the dessert, Panurge had put forward a problematical matter, to wit, whether he should marry or not, and that Father Hippothadée and Master Rondibilis had delivered themselves of their answers; when he came in, his trusty liege Trouillogan was answering. And first, when Panurge asked him: "Should I marry or not?" he had answered: "Both at the same time"; the second time had said: "Neither one." Then Panurge complains about such incompatible and contradictory answers and protests that he doesn't understand a word of it.

"I understand it, I think," said Gargantua. "The answer is like what an ancient philosopher said when asked whether he had some woman whose name they gave him. 'I have her as my love,' said he, 'but she doesn't have my love. I possess her, I'm not possessed by her.' "[2]

"A similar answer," said Pantagruel, "was made by a servant girl from Sparta. She was asked whether she'd ever had business with a man. She answered: 'No, never, although men had sometimes had business with me.' "[3]

"So," said Rondibilis, "let's count ourselves as neuter in medicine, and in philosophy in the middle, by participation in both extremes and by dividing the time now in one extreme, now in the other."

"The Holy Apostle,"[4] said Hippothadée, "seems to me to have stated it more clearly when he said: 'Let those who are married be as if unmarried; let those who have a wife be as if they had no wife.' "

"I interpret," said Pantagruel, "having and not having a wife in this way: that having a wife is having her for such use as Nature created her for, which is for the aid, pleasure, and society of man; not having a wife is not getting slack by hanging about her, not contaminating for her sake that unique and supreme affection that man naturally owes to God, not giving up the duties he naturally owes to his country, the commonwealth, his friends, not disregarding his studies and business to be continually making up to his wife. Taking in this way having and not having a wife, I see no incompatibility or contradiction in the terms."

CHAPTER 36

Continuation of the replies of Trouillogan,
the ephectic [1] and Pyrrhonian philosopher.

"Your talk sounds good,"[2] replied Panurge. "But I believe I've gone down into the dark well in which Heraclitus used to say Truth is hidden. I can't see a thing, I can't hear a sound, I feel all my senses numbed, and I'm much afraid I'm under a spell. I'll talk in a different style. Our trusty liege, don't move. Don't pocket anything. Let's change the way we throw the dice, and let's talk without disjunctives.[3] These ill-joined phrases annoy you, from what I can see. Now then, in God's name, should I marry?"

TROUILLOGAN. It seems likely.

PANURGE. And if I don't marry?

TROU. I don't see any disadvantage in that.

PAN. You don't see any?

TROU. No, or my eyes deceive me.

PAN. I find more than five hundred.

TROU. Count them.

PAN. I mean roughly speaking, and using a certain number for an uncertain one, a definite for an indefinite: that is to say, many.

TROU. I'm listening.

PAN. I can't get along without a woman,[4] by all the devils!

TROU. Get those ugly beasts[5] out of here!

PAN. In God's name, so be it! For my Salmagundians say that to sleep alone or without a woman is a brutish life, and such Dido kept calling it in her lamentations.[6]

TROU. At your service.

PAN. 'Odsbodikins![7] I'm doing fine. Then shall I marry?

TROU. Peradventure.

PAN. Shall I be well off for it?

TROU. Depends how it turns out.

PAN. And if I strike it lucky, as I hope to do, shall I be happy?

TROU. Rather.

PAN. Let's turn this the other way around. And if I strike it unlucky?

TROU. My excuses for it.

PAN. But advise me, I beseech you: what should I do?

TROU. What you will.[8]

PAN. Pish tush.[9]

TROU. No invocations, please.

PAN. In God's name, so be it! I don't want a thing except what you'll advise me. What do you advise me about this?

TROU. Nothing.

PAN. Shall I marry?

TROU. I wasn't there.

PAN. Then I won't marry at all?

TROU. I can't do another thing about it.

PAN. If I'm not married, I'll never be a cuckold.

TROU. I was thinking about that.

PAN. Let's put the case that I'm married.

TROU. Where shall we put it?

PAN. I mean, take the case that married I am.

Trou. I'm otherwise engaged.

Pan. That's shit in my nose [merde en mon nez]! Good Lord, if I
only dared have a little swearing session under my gown, what a
relief that would be! All right, then, patience! So then, if I'm
married, I'll be a cuckold?

Trou. It would seem so.

Pan. If my wife is virtuous and chaste, I'll never be a cuckold?

Trou. You seem to me to speak correctly.

Pan. Listen.

Trou. All you want.

Pan. Will she be virtuous and chaste? Only this point remains.

Trou. I doubt it.

Pan. You've never seen her?

Trou. Not that I know of.

Pan. Then why do you doubt something you don't know about?

Trou. For cause.

Pan. And if you knew her?

Trou. Even more.

Pan. Page, my cutey, hold my cap for me here. I'm giving it to
you, except for my spectacles; go down into the courtyard and
swear a wee half hour for me. I'll swear for you whenever you
want. But who will make me a cuckold?

Trou. Someone.

Pan. By the ox-belly of wood,[10] I'll give you a good drubbing,
Mister Someone!

Trou. So you say.

Pan. May the devil, the one who has no whites in his eyes, take me
then, if I don't also lock my wife up Bergamask style[11] whenever
I go out of my seraglio.

Trou. Mend your talk.

Pan. That's doggone well shitten sungen[12] for all the speeches. Let's
come to some decision.

Trou. I'm not contradicting that.

Pan. Wait. Since from that area I can't draw any blood from you,
I'll try to bleed you from another vein. Are you married or not?

366

TROU. Neither one, and both at the same time.

PAN. God help us! I'm sweating, 'sdeath! with effort, and I feel my digestion interrupted. All my phrènes,[13] métaphrènes, and diaphragms are in suspense and tensed to incornifistibulate[14] what you're saying and answering into the game-pouch of my understanding.

TROU. That's not my problem.

PAN. Giddap![15] Our trusty liege, are you married?

TROU. So I think.

PAN. You had been another time?

TROU. It's possible.

PAN. Did you find yourself well off for it the first time?

TROU. It's not impossible.

PAN. This second time, how do you find yourself off for it?

TROU. As my fated lot will have it.

PAN. But then what? Speaking seriously, do you find yourself well off for it.

TROU. It's likely.

PAN. Here now, in the name of God, by Saint Christopher's burden, I might just as well try to draw a fart out of a dead donkey as an opinion out of you. Still, I'll get you this time. Our trusty liege, let's shame the devil in hell, let's confess the truth. Have you ever been a cuckold? I mean you who are right here, not you who are over yonder at the tennis court.

TROU. No, unless it is predestined.

PAN. By the flesh, I swear off! By the blood,[16] I quit! By the body, I give up! He gets away from me.

At these words, Gargantua rose and said: "Praise be to the good God in all things. As far as I can see, the world has grown pretty sharp since first I knew it. Is that where we stand? So then today the most learned and prudent philosophers have entered the think-tank and school of the Pyrrhonists,[17] aporrhetics, skeptics, and ephectics. Praise be to the good Lord! Truly from now on it will be possible to catch lions by the thick hair, horses by the mane, oxen by the horns, wild oxen by the muzzle, wolves by the tail, goats by the beard, birds by the feet; but never will such philosophers be caught by their words.[18] Good-bye, my good friends."

These words uttered, he withdrew from the company. Pantagruel and the others ranted to follow him but he wouldn't permit it.

When Gargantua had left the room, Pantagruel said to the guests: "Plato's Timaeus, at the beginning of the gathering, counted the guests; we, conversely, count them at the end. One, two, three: where is the fourth? Wasn't that our friend Bridoye?"

Epistémon replied that he had been to his house to invite him, but hadn't found him. A messenger from the Myrelinguais Parlement in Myrelingues had come to fetch him and set a date for him to appear in person before the members to state his reason for some decision he had made. Therefore he had left the day before, so as to present himself on the day assigned and not fall into default or contempt of court.

"I want," said Pantagruel, "to hear what this is all about. It's been over forty years that he's been a judge at Fonsbeton; during that time he has handed down more than four thousand definitive decisions. Two thousand three hundred and nine decisions handed down by him were appealed by the parties condemned to the sovereign court of the Myrelinguais Parlement in Myrelingues; all were ratified, approved, and confirmed by it, the appeals dismissed and annulled. So for him to be summoned now in person in his old age, him who through all past time has lived so righteously in his office, cannot be without some disaster. I want to be helpful to him with all my power, in equity. I know that today the wickedness of the world has grown so much worse that the best cause really needs support [. . . bon droict a bien besoing d'aide]. And I plan to go to work on that shortly, for fear of some surprise."

Then the tables were cleared and removed.[19] Pantagruel gave his guests precious and honorable gifts of rings, jewels, and plate of both gold and silver, and, after thanking them cordially, retired to his room.

CHAPTER 37

*How Pantagruel persuades Panurge
to take counsel of some fool.*[1]

As Pantagruel was retiring, from the gallery he noticed Panurge looking like a dreamer in a fog and wagging his head, and said to him:

"You look to me like a mouse ensnared in pitch:[2] the more it tries to get free of the pitch, the more it gets stuck. You likewise, straining to get yourself out of the nets of perplexity, remain stuck in them more than ever, and I know no remedy for it but one. Listen. I've often heard it as a popular proverb that a fool may well teach a wise man. Since you are not fully satisfied with the replies of the wise, take counsel of some fool; it may be that by so doing you will be satisfied and contented more to your taste. By the advice, counsel, and prediction of fools, you know how many princes, kings, and commonwealths have been preserved, how many battles won, how many perplexities solved.

"There's no need now to remind you of the examples. You will agree on this reason: for even as a man who keeps close watch on his private and domestic affairs, who is vigilant and attentive to the management of his household, whose mind is not wandering, who misses no chance whatever to acquire and amass property and riches, who shrewdly knows how to obviate the drawbacks of poverty, you call worldly wise, although he may be an idiot in the estimation of the celestial Intelligences; even so it is necessary, in order to be wise in their eyes, I mean sage and presage [sage et praesage] by divine aspiration and apt to receive the gift of divination, for a man to forget himself, empty his senses of all earthly affection, purge his spirit of all human solicitude, and look at everything with unconcern, which is popularly imputed to folly.

"In this manner was the great soothsayer Faunus, son of Picus, king of the Latins, called *Fatuel*[3] by the common herd.

"In this manner we see among traveling players, in the distribution of parts, that the character of the Fool and Jester is always played by the most competent and expert actor of their troupe.

"In this manner the mathematicians say there is the same horoscope at the birth of kings and of fools. And they give the example of Aeneas and Choroebus, who Euphorion says was a fool, who had the same date of origin.[4]

"I'll not be off the subject if I tell you what Jo. André says about a canon of a certain papal rescript addressed to the mayor and burghers of La Rochelle, and after him Panormitanus on this same canon, Barbatia on the *Pandects,* and recently Jason in his *Consilia,*[5] about Seigny Joan, noted Paris fool, great-grandfather of Caillette. This is the case:

"In Paris, in the roastshop section of the Petit Châtelet, in front of a roaster's stall, a porter was eating his bread in the steam from the roast and finding it, thus perfumed, very savory indeed. The roaster was letting him go ahead. Finally, when all the bread was guzzled, the roaster grabs the porter by the collar, and wanted him to pay him for the steam of his roast. The porter kept saying that he had in no way damaged his meat, taken nothing of his, was in no way his debtor. The steam in question was evaporating outside; one way or another it was being lost; never had it been heard that in Paris steam from a roast had been sold in the street. The roaster kept replying that he was not responsible for feeding porters with the steam from his roast, and swearing that in case he didn't pay him he would take away his load-hooks.

"The porter draws his cudgel and was setting himself ready in defense. The altercation was great. The rubberneck populace of Paris came running up to the dispute from all sides. There happened to be there at the right time Seigny Joan the fool, citizen of Paris. Having espied him, the roaster asked the porter: 'Do you want to let this noble Seigny Joan settle our dispute?' 'Yes, by the goose's blood,'[6] said the porter.

"Thereupon Seigny Joan, after hearing their dispute, ordered the porter to pull him out some silver coin from his baldrick. The porter put into his hand a Tournois philippus.[7] Seigny Joan took it and put it on his left shoulder as if checking whether it was of proper weight; then rang it on the palm of his left hand as if to hear whether it was good alloy; then put it on his right eyeball as if to see if it was well stamped. All this was done in great silence of the whole rubberneck populace, as the roaster waited confidently and the porter in despair. Finally he rang it on the counter several times. Then, in presidential majesty, holding his fool's bauble in his fist as if it were a scepter and putting on his cap of monkey marten[8] skins with its paper ears ridged like organ pipes, giving two or three good preliminary coughs, he announced in a loud voice:

" 'The Court informs you that the porter who ate his bread in the steam of the roast has civilly paid the roaster with the sound of his money. The said Court orders everyone to withdraw to his everyhome,[9] without costs, and for cause.'

"This decision of the Parisian fool seemed so equitable, and indeed admirable, to the aforesaid doctors, that they doubt whether, in case the matter had been decided by the Parlement of the said place, or by the Rota in Rome, or indeed by the Areopagites, it would have been more judicially decided by them. Therefore consider whether you want to take counsel of some fool."

CHAPTER 38

How Triboullet is blazoned [1]
by Pantagruel and Panurge.

" 'Pon my soul," replied Panurge, "I do want to! I think my bowels are loosening; a while ago they were tight and constipated. But even as we chose the fine cream of wisdom as counsel, so I would like someone to preside at our consultation who was a fool to a supreme degree."

"Triboullet," said Pantagruel, "seems to me competently a fool."

Panurge replied: "Properly and totally a fool."

PANTAGRUEL	PANURGE
Fatal fool,	Arrant[2] fool
Fool by nature,	B sharp and B flat fool
Celestial fool,	Landed fool,
Jovial fool,	Joyous and playful fool,
Mercurial fool,	Pretty, giddy fool,
Lunatic fool,	Fool with pompoms,
Erratic fool,	Pimply fool,
Eccentric fool,	Fool with bells,
Ethereal and Junonian fool,	Laughing and venereal fool
Arctic fool,	Bottom-of-the-barrel fool,
Heroic fool,	Best-of-the-vat fool,
Genial fool,	Fool of the first pressing,
Predestined fool,	Fool from rising time,

371

August fool,
Caesarian fool,
Imperial fool,
Royal fool,
Patriarchal fool,
Original fool,
Loyal fool,
Ducal fool,
Pennon fool,
Lordly fool,
Palatine fool,
Principal fool,
Pretorial fool,
Total fool,
Elected fool,
Curial fool,
Primipilar[4] fool,
Triumphant fool,
Vulgar fool,
Domestic fool,
Exemplary fool,
Rare, peregrine fool
Aulic fool,
Civil fool,
Popular fool,
Familiar fool,
Notable fool,
Favorite fool,
Latin fool,
Ordinary fool,
Dreaded fool,
Transcendent fool,
Sovereign fool,
Special fool,

Original fool,
Papal fool,
Consistorial fool,
Conclavist fool,
Bullist fool,
Synodal fool,
Episcopal fool,
Doctoral fool,
Monkish fool,
Fiscal fool,
Absurd fool,
Hooded fool,
Fool with simple tonsure,
Cotal[3] fool,
Graduate fool in folly,
Table-companion fool,
Fool first in his *licence,*
Train-bearing fool,
Fool in supererogation,
Collateral fool,
Fool *a latere,*[5] *altéré* [thirsty],
Silly fool,
Passing fool,
Brancher[6] fool,
Haggard fool,
Nice fool,
Mail-clad fool,
Pilfering fool,
Fool with tail regrown,
Starling-colored fool,
Doting fool,
Exquisite fool,
Puffed-up fool,
Supercockaloricky[7] fool,

Metaphysical fool,
Ecstatic fool,
Categorical fool,
Preachable fool,
Decuman[8] fool,
Officious fool,
Fool in perspective,
Algorismic fool,
Algebraic fool,
Cabaline fool,
Talmudic fool,
Algamala[9] fool,
Compendious fool,
Abbreviated fool,
Hyperbolic fool,
Antonomatic fool,
Allegorical fool,
Tropological[11] fool,
Pleonastic fool,
Capital fool,
Cerebral fool,
Cordial fool,
Intestine fool,
Hepatic[12] fool,
Splenetic fool,
Windy fool,
Legitimate fool,
Azimuthal fool,
Almicantarath[13] fool,
Proportioned fool,
Architrave fool,
Pedestal fool,
Paragon fool,
Celebrated fool,

Corollary fool,
Levantine fool,
Zibeline fool,
Crimson fool,
Fool dyed in the grain,
Bourgeois fool,
Feather-duster fool,
Masthead fool,
Modal fool
Second-intentional fool,
Niggardly fool,
Heteroclite fool,
Summist[10] fool,
Abbreviating fool,
Morris-dancing fool,
Well-bulled fool,
Mandatory fool,
Cowl-wearing fool,
Titular fool,
Covert fool,
Grim-visaged fool,
Well-tooled fool,
Ill-fettered fool,
Ballocky fool,
Crabbed fool,
Ventilated fool,
Culinary fool,
Fool of high growth,
Rack fool,
Wretched fool,
Catarrhal fool,
Braggart fool,
Twenty-four-carat fool,
Bizarre fool,

Cheerful and buxom fool,
Solemn fool,
Annual fool,
Festival fool,
Recreative fool,
Villatic fool,
Amusing fool,
Privileged fool,
Rustic fool,
Ordinary fool,
Fool at all hours,
Fool in diapason,
Resolute fool,
Hieroglyphic fool,
Authentic fool,
Fool of value,
Precious fool,
Fanatical fool,
Fantastic fool,
Lymphatic fool,
Panic fool,
Alembicated [distilled] fool,
Unirritating fool,

Egregious fool,
Foolishly a fool,
Fool with batons,
Fool with a bauble,
Fool from a good angle,
Fool with a wide swath,
Stumbling fool,
Superannuated fool,
Country-style fool,
Full-busted fool
Vainglorius fool,
Swaggering fool,
Slovenly fool,
Fool in his shorts,
Fool with a pattern [à patron],
Fool with a hood [à chapron],
Double fool,
Damascene fool,[14]
Variegated fool,
Azimina fool,
Baritone fool,
Flyspecked fool,
Harquebus-proof fool,

PANT. If there was good reason why long ago in Rome they called the Feast of Fools Quirinals, one might rightly institute in France the Triboulletinals.

PAN. If all fools wore a crupper, he would get his buttocks wellchafed, raw.

PANT. If he were the god Fatuel, whom we talked about, his father would be *Bonadies* [Good Day], his mother *Bonadea* [Good Goddess].

PAN. If all fools went at an amble, although he has a crookshank, he would pass them by a good fathom. Let's go in his direction without waiting. From him we'll get some fine solution; I'm expecting it.

"I want," said Pantagruel, "to attend Bridoye's judgment.[15] While I go to Myrelingues, which is beyond the River Loire, I'll send Carpalim to bring Triboullet here from Blois!"[16]

Then was Carpalim dispatched. Pantagruel, accompanied by his familiars, Panurge, Epistémon, Ponocrates, Frère Jean, Gymnaste, Rhizotome, and others, took the road for Myrelingues.

CHAPTER 39

How Pantagruel attends
the trial of Judge Bridoye,
who decided lawsuits by the chance of dice.

On the following day, at the appointed time, Pantagruel arrived in Myrelingues. The president, senators,[1] counselors asked him to come in with them and hear the decision on the causes and reasons that Bridoye would advance why he had rendered a certain verdict against Assessor Toucheronde,[2] which did not seem quite equitable to this centumviral[3] Court.

Pantagruel enters willingly and finds Bridoye sitting there in the middle of the *parquet*,[4] and, for all reasons and excuses, answering nothing but this, that he had grown old and hadn't as good eyesight as he used to, alleging many miseries and calamities that old age brings with it, which "not. per Archid. d. lxxxvj. c. tanta [are noted by the Archdeacon in *Distinctio*, section 86, chapter Tanta]."[5] Therefore he did not make out as distinctly as in the past the spots on the dice. So it might be that in the way in which Isaac, old and seeing poorly, took Jacob for Esau,[6] thus, in deciding the lawsuit in question, he had taken a four for a five, especially since he reported that he had then used his little dice. And that, by the intent of the law, natural imperfections are not to be imputed to crime, as is clear from "ff. de re milit. l. qui cum uno, ff. de reg. jur. l. fere ff. de edil. ed. per totum, ff. de term. mo., l. Divus Adrianus; resolu. per Lud. Ro. in l. si vero, ff. solu. matri." And if anyone did otherwise he would be accusing not man, but nature, as is evident "in l. maximum vitium. C. de lib. praeter."[7]

"What dice do you mean, my friend?" asked Trinquamelle, grand president of this Court.

"The dice," answered Bridoye, "of judgments, *alea judiciorum*,[8] of which it is written by 'Doct. 26. q. ij. c. Sors; l. nec emptio. ff. de contrah. empt. l. quod debetur. ff. de pecul. et ibi Barthol.'[9] And which dice you gentlemen ordinarily use in this sovereign Court of yours; so do all other judges in deciding lawsuits, according to what has been noted about it by D. Henri Ferrandat,[10] and 'no. gl. in c. fin. de sortil. et l. sed cum ambo., ff. de judi., ubi doct.' [where the learned doctors] note that chance is very good, honorable, useful, and necessary for the settlement of lawsuits and dissensions. Even more clearly this has been said by Bal., Bart. and Alex. 'C. communia de l. Si duo.' "

"And how," asked Trinquamelle, "do you proceed, my friend?"

"I shall reply briefly,"[11] answered Bridoye, "according to the teaching of the 'l. Ampliorem, par. in refutatoriis, C. de appella.' and what is said in 'Gl. l. j. ff. quod met. cau. Gaudent brevitate moderni.'[12] I do as you gentlemen do, as is the practice in judicature, to which our laws command us always to defer: 'ut no. extra. de consuet. c. ex literis, et ibi Innoc.' Having well seen, reviewed, read, reread, papered, and leafed through the complaints, summonings, appearances, commissions, inquests, preparatories, statements, allegations, depositions, replications, petitions, questionings, rebuttals, rejoinders, second replies, written testimonies, exceptions, anticipatories, evocations, referrals, referrals back, determinations, reasons for a stay, reasons for rejecting, reconciliations, reliefs, acknowledgments, acts, and other such goodies and spices from one part and the other, as a good judge must do, according to what has been noted about it by 'Spec.[13] de ordinario par. iij., et tit. de offi. om. ju. par. fi.' and 'de rescriptis praesenta., par. j.'

"I set at one end of the table in my study all the defendant's sacks and shot for him first, as you gentlemen do.[14] And this is 'not., l. Favorabiliores, ff. de reg. jur., et in c. cum sunt, eod. tit. lib. vj,' which says: 'Cum sunt partium jura obscura, reo favendum est potius quam actori.'

"That done, I set the plaintiff's sacks, as you gentlemen do, on the other end, *visum visu* [face to face]. For, 'opposita juxta se posita magis elucescunt [placed facing one another, opposites become clearer], ut not. in l. j., par. videamus, ff. de his qui sunt sui vel alie. jur. et in l. munerum j. mixta ff. de muner, et honor.' Likewise and at the same time, I shoot for him."

"But, my friend," asked Trinquamelle, "how do you recognize the obscurity of the claims of the litigating parties?"

"As you gentlemen do," answered Bridoye, "to wit, when there are many sacks on one side and on the other. And then I use my little dice, as you gentlemen do, pursuant to the law 'Semper in stipulationibus,[15] ff. de reg. jur.,' and the capital-letter law in verse, 'q. eod. tit.'

Semper in obscuris quod minimum est sequimur,

[In obscure cases we always take minimum action,]

adopted in canon law 'in c. in obscuris, eod. tit. lib. vj.'

"I have other, big dice, very handsome and harmonious, which I use, as you gentlemen do, when the matter is more liquid, that is to say when there are fewer sacks."

"That done," said Trinquamelle, "how do you pass sentence, my friend?"

"As you gentlemen do," replied Bridoye: "I pronounce sentence in favor of the one whose chance, by the lot of the judicial, tribunian, praetorial dice,[16] comes out first. Thus it is ordained by our laws 'ff. qui po. in pig., l. potior. leg. creditor., C. de consul., l. j. Et de reg. jur., in vj: Qui prior est tempore potior est jure.' "[17]

CHAPTER 40

How Bridoye explains the reasons
why he examined the lawsuits
that he decided by the chance of dice.

"Yes, my friend," asked Trinquamelle, "but since you make your decisions by chance and the casting of dice, why don't you try that chance the very day and hour when the parties in dispute appear before you, without any further delay? What use do you make of the writs and other documents contained in the sacks?"

"As you gentlemen do," replied Bridoye, "I use them for three things that are exquisite, requisite, and authentic.

"First, for form's sake, for lack of which there is no value in what one has done, as is very well proven by 'Spec. tit. de instr. edi. et tit. de rescrip. praesent.' Besides, you know only too well that often, in judicial proceedings, the formalities destroy the substantive materials. For, 'forma mutata, mutatur substantia. ff. ad exhib., l. Julianus; ff. ad leg. falcid., l. Si is qui quadringenta. Et extra., de deci., c. ad audientiam, et de celebra. miss. c. in quadam.'

"Secondly, like you gentlemen, I use them as a worthy and salutary exercise. The late Mr. Othoman Vadare, a great doctor, as you would say, 'C. de comit. et archi. lib. xij,' has told me many a time that the lack of bodily exercise is the sole cause of the paucity of health and shortness of life of you gentlemen and of all officers of the law, which had been noted very well before him by Bart. 'in l. j. C. de senten. quae pro eo quod.' Therefore are conceded to us, in turn, as to you gentlemen, 'quia accessorium naturam sequitur principalis, de reg. jur. lib. vj. et l. cum principalis, et l. nihil dolo., ff. eod. titu.; ff. de fidejusso., l. fidejussor. et extra de offic. de leg. c. j.,' certain games offering decent and recreative exercise, 'ff. de al. lus. et aleat., l. solent. et autent. ut omnes obediant, in princ. coll. vij, et ff. de praescript. verb. l. si gratuitam et l. j, C, de spect. lib. xj.' And such is the opinion of 'D. Thomae, in secunda secundae quaest. clxviij,' most appropriately cited by D. Alberic de Ros., who 'fuit magnus practicus' and a solemn doctor, as Barbatis attests 'in prin. consil.' The reason is set forth 'per gl. in proaemio. ff., par. ne autem tertii':

> Interpone tuis interdum gaudia curis.[1]
>
> [Take a few merry breaks between cares.]

"In fact, one day in the year 1489, having some monetary business in the chamber of the Lord Commissioners of the Treasury, and entering by pecuniary permission of the usher—as you gentlemen know, 'pecuniae obediunt omnia [all things obey money],' and Bald. has said so in 'l. Singularia, ff. si certum pet. et Salic. in l. recepticia, C. de constit. pecun. et Card. in Cle. j., de baptis.' I found them all playing 'Baste the Bear'[2] as a salubrious exercise, before or after a meal; it's all or one to me provided that 'Hic no [Here note]' that the game of 'Baste the Bear' is worthy, salubrious, ancient, and legal, 'a Musco inventore, de quo. C., de petit.

haered., l. si post motam.' And 'Muscarii, id est' people who play 'Baste the Bear' are excusable by law 'l. j., C., de excus. artif., lib. x.'

"And at that point the 'Bear' was Mr. Tielman Picquet,[3] I remember, and he was laughing at how the gentlemen of the said Court were ruining their bonnets by basting him on the shoulders; he was saying that this notwithstanding they were not excusable to their wives on their return home from the Court, by 'c. j., extra de praesump., et ibi gl.' Now, 'resolutorie loquendo [I make bold to say],' I would say, like you gentlemen, that in this palatine world[4] there is no exercise like this one or more aromatic than this: emptying sacks, leafing through papers, marking up booklets, filling baskets, examining lawsuits, 'ex Bart. et Jo. de Pra.[5] in l. falsa de condit. et demon. ff.'

"Thirdly, like you gentlemen, I consider that time ripens all things; by time all things come into evidence; time is the father of truth, 'gl. in l. j., C. de servit., Autent.,[6] de restit. et ea quae pa., et Spec. tit. de requis. cons.' That is why, like you gentlemen, I stay, delay, and put off the judgment, so that the suit, well ventilated, scrutinized, and batted around, may be borne more easily by the losing parties, as 'no. glo. ff. de excu. tut., l. Tria onera':

> Portatur leviter, quod portat quisque libenter.
>
> [Gladly is borne what each man gladly bears.]

In judging it when it is raw, green, and at the beginning, there would be the danger of the harm that doctors say occurs when they lance an abscess before it is ripe, when they purge some harmful humor from the human body before it is digested. For, as it is written in 'Autent., Haec constit. in Inno. const. prin.,' and repeated, 'gl. in c. Caeterum. extra, de jura. calum.':

> Quod medicamenta morbis exhibent, hoc jura negotiis.
>
> [What drugs do for diseases, laws for business do.]

Moreover, Nature teaches us to pluck and eat fruits when they are ripe, 'Instit. de re. di par. is ad quem, et ff. de acti. empt., l. Julianus,' to marry off girls when they are ripe, 'ff. de donat. int. vir. et uxo., l. cum hic status, par. si quis sponsa., et 27. q., j., c., Sicut' says 'gl.':

Jam matura thoris plenis adoleverat annis
Virginitas,[7]

[By now the maidenhood, fit for the marriage bed,
For years enough had ripened,]

to do nothing except in full maturity, 'xxiij. q. ij. par. ult.' and 'xxxiij.
d. c. ult.' "

CHAPTER 41

*How Bridoye tells the story
of the settler of lawsuits.*

"**I** remember on this subject," said Bridoye as he went on, "that at the
time when I was studying law at Poitiers under Blackstone's Commentaries,[1] there was a man at Smarve[2] by the name of Perrin Dendin, an
honorable man, a good plowman, singing well in the church choir, and
about the age of most of you gentlemen, who used to say that he had seen
that great fellow Lateran Council, with his broad red hat, and with him
his wife, the good lady Pragmatic Sanction, with her wide headband of
sky-blue satin and her great jet rosary.

"This worthy man used to settle more lawsuits than were decided in
the whole Hall of Justice in Poitiers, in the court of Montmorillon, in the
market-hall of Parthenay-le-Vieux, which made him venerated in the
entire neighborhood. From Chauvigny, Nouaillé, Croutelles, Esgne,
Ligugé, La Motte, Lusignan, Vivonne, Mezeaulx, Estables, and adjacent
places, all disputes, lawsuits, and controversies were adjusted by his solu-
tions as if by a sovereign judge, although judge he was not, but a worthy
man,[3] 'Arg. in l. sed si unius., ff. de jureju., et de verb. oblig., l.
continuus.' There was not a hog killed in the whole neighborhood of
which he didn't get some of the roast pork and blood puddings. And
almost every day he was a guest at a banquet, a wedding feast, a christen-
ing, a churching,[4] and in the tavern—to effect some reconciliation, you

understand, for never did he reconcile the parties but that he had them drink together, as a symbol of reconciliation, perfect accord, and joy renewed, 'ut no. per doct., ff. de peri. et comm. rei. vend. l. j.'

"He had a son named Tenot[5] Dendin, a great roister and gallant man, s'help me God, who likewise tried to mediate and reconcile litigants, as you know that

> Saepe solet similis filius esse patri,
> Et sequitur leviter filia matris iter,[6]
>
> [The son is wont to take after the sire,
> And daughters to their mothers' ways aspire,]

'ut ait gl., vj. q., j. c. Si quis; g. de cons., d. v. c. j. fi.; et est no. per doct., C. de impu. et aliis subst., l. ult. et l. legitimae, ff. de stat. hom., gl. in l. quod si nolit, ff. de edil. ed., l. quis, C. ad le. Jul. majest. Excipio filios a moniali susceptos ex monacho, per gl. in c. Impudicas, xxvij q.j.' And among his titles he assumed that of the Settler of Suits.

"In this business he was so active and vigilant—for 'vigilantibus jura subveniunt [the laws assist the vigilant], ex. l. pupillus, ff. quae in fraud. cred., et ibid. l. non. enim., et Instit. in proaemio,' that as soon as he sniffed out 'ut ff. si quad. pau. fec., l. Agaso, gl. in verbo olfecit i. nasum. ad culum posuit [that according to the *Pandects,* if a quadriped is said to have caused any misery, law Agaso, gloss at the words *he sniffed,* he stuck his nose in his ass],' and he heard that in the region any lawsuit or dispute was afoot, he butted in to try to reconcile the parties. It is written:

> Qui non laborat non manige ducat,[7]
>
> [He who does not work shall not eat],

and so says 'gl. ff. de dam. infect., l. quamvis,' and *currere* faster than a pace

> Vetulam compellit egestas,
>
> [Need makes the old hag run at a gallop,]

'gl., ff. de lib. agnos., l. Si quis pro qua facit; l. Si plures, C. de cond. incer.' But in such an operation he fared so poorly that never did he settle any controversy whatever, however small a one you might mention.

Instead of settling them, he irritated and embittered them even more. You know, gentlemen, that

> Sermo datur cunctis, animi sapientia paucis,
>
> [Speech is given to all, a wise mind to but few,]

'gl. ff. de alie. ju. mu. caus. fa., l. ij.' And the tavern-keepers of Smarve used to say that in his day they didn't sell as much settlement wine (so they called the good Liguge wine) in a year as they used to do in half an hour in his father's time.

"It happened that he complained about it to his father and was blaming, as the causes of his failure, the perversity of the men of his time, holding up against him the claim that if in the old days people had been that perverse, litigious, unruly, and irreconcilable, he [his father] would not have won the title of such an irreversible arbitrator as he had. In which Tenot was acting against equity, by which children are forbidden to reproach their own fathers, 'per gl. et Bar., l. iij par. si quis, ff. de condi. ob caus., et Autent., de nup., par. sed quod sancitum, coll. iiij.'

" 'You have,' replied Perrin, 'to go about it differently, my son Dendin. Now,'

> When *oportet* comes in play,
> Things just must be done that way,

'gl. C. de appell., l. eos etiam.' That's where the problem [le lièvre] lies. You never settle disagreements: Why? You take them at the beginning, when they are still green and raw. I settle them all: why? I take them near their end, quite ripe and digested. Thus says 'gl.':

> Dulcior est fructus post multa pericula ductus,
>
> [Sweeter is fruit through many perils grown,]

'l. non moriturus, C. de contrah. et comit. stip.' Don't you know that in the common proverb they say: Happy is the doctor called in on the waning of the illness. The illness was of itself nearing its final crisis, even without the doctor's coming in. My litigants likewise were winding down by themselves to the final goal of pleading, for their purses were empty; of themselves they were ceasing to prosecute and solicit: there was no more dough in the wallet to solicit and prosecute with:

Deficiente pecu, deficit omne, nia[8]

[If mo is lacking, all is lacking, ney.]

"Missing was only someone for a go-between and mediator, to save both parties from the pernicious shame of it being said: 'This one gave in first; he first spoke of settlement; he tired first; his case was not the stronger; he felt the saddle chafing him.' At that point, Dendin, I'm Johnny on the spot, like bacon in peas. That's my joy. That's my profit. That's my good fortune. And I tell you, my nice looking son Dendin, that by this method I could bring peace, or at least truces, between the Great King and the Venetians, between the emperor and the Swiss, between the English and the Scots, between the pope and the Ferrarese. Shall I go further? So help me God, between the Turk and the Sophy; between the Tartars and the Muscovites.

"Understand me clearly. I would take them at the point where both sides would be weary of making war, would have emptied their coffers, exhausted their subjects' purses, sold their domain, mortgaged their lands, consumed their victuals and munitions. Then, in the name of God or of His Mother, they are forcibly forced to catch their breath and moderate their felonies. That's the teaching in 'gl. xxxvii d. c. Si quando':

Odero si potero, si non, invitus amabo."[9]

[I will hate if I can, if not I'll grudging love.]

CHAPTER 42

*How lawsuits are born,
and how they come to perfection.*

"T<small>HAT</small> is why," said Bridoye as he went on, "like you gentlemen, I temporize, waiting for the ripeness of the lawsuit and its perfectedness in all its members: these are writs and sacks. 'Arg. in l. si major., C. commu. divi. et de cons., d. j, c. Solennitates, et ibi gl.'[1]

"A lawsuit when first born seems to me, as to you gentlemen, shapeless and imperfect. As a new-born bear has neither feet nor hands, skin, hair, nor head; he's just a piece of rough and shapeless flesh; the she-bear, by dint of licking,[2] brings this to perfection of the members 'ut no. doct., ff. ad leg. Aquil., l. ij. in fi.'

"So I see, like you gentlemen, lawsuits born at their beginnings shapeless and without members. They have only one or two documents, that's an ugly beast for the time. But when they are well packed, stacked, and sacked [entassez, enchâssez et ensachez], they may truly be said to have shape and limbs. For 'forma dat esse rei [form gives the thing being], l. si is qui, ff. ad leg. falci. in c. cum dilecta, extra de rescrip. Barbatia consil. 12, lib. 2,' and before him 'Bald in c. ulti. extra de consue., et l. Julianus, ff. ad exhib., et l. quaesitum. ff. de lega. iij.' The manner is such as is stated by 'gl. p. q. j. c. Paulus':

> Debile principium melior fortuna sequetur.
>
> [Better fortune will follow a weak start.]

"Like you gentlemen, similarly the sergeants, ushers, summoners, shysters, procurators, commissioners, advocates, investigators, notaries public, notaries, registrars, and lower-court judges, 'de quibus tit. est. lib. iij Cod.,' sucking very hard and continuously on the parties' purses, engender for their lawsuits head, feet, claws, beak, teeth, hands, veins, arteries, nerves, muscles, humors. These are the sacks, 'gl. de cons., d. iiij. c. accepisti.'

> Qualis vestis erit, talia corda gerit.
>
> [As is the jacket, such the heart he wears.]

Hic no. [Here note] that in this regard happier are the litigants than the ministers of justice, for

> Beatius est dare quam accipere,[3]
>
> [It is more blessed to give than to receive,]

'ff. comm., l. iij. et extra de celebra. Miss., c. cum Marthae, et 24. q. j. c. Odi. gl.'

> Affectum dantis pensat censura tonantis.
>
> [Thundering Jupiter weighs the giver's disposition.]

Thus they make the lawsuit perfected, gallant, well informed, as stated in *gl. can.*:

> Accipe, sume, cape sunt verba placentia papae,
>
> [Accept, receive, and take are words that please the pope,]

which Alber. de Ros. has stated more clearly *in verb. Roma.*:

> Roma manus rodit, quas rodere non valet, odit.
> Dantes custodit, non dantes spernit et odit.
>
> [Rome gnaws the hands, hates hands it cannot gnaw;
> Protects the giver, spurns and hates those who do not give.]

The reason why?

> Ad praesens ova, cras pullis sunt meliora,
>
> [Today's eggs rather than tomorrow's chicks,]

'ut est glo., in l. quum hi, ff. de transac.' The disadvantage of the converse is stated 'in gl. c. de allu., l. F.':

> Cum labor in damno est, crescit mortalis egestas.[4]
>
> [When work avails not, mortal poverty grows.]

"The true etymology of lawsuit [procès] is that in its pursuit [prochatz] it must have many sacks [prou sacs]. On this we have some heavenly quips:

> Litigando jura crescunt.
> Litigando jus acquiritur.
>
> [The laws grow by litigation.
> Justice is earned by litigation.]

" 'Item gl. in c. Illud, ext. de praesumpt., et C. de prob., l. instrumenta, non epistolis, l. non nudis,'

> Et cum non prosunt singula, multa juvant.[5]
>
> [And when lone efforts fail, multiple efforts help.]

"True," replied Trinquamelle. "But, my friend, how do you proceed in a criminal action, when the guilty party has been caught *flagrante crimine*?"

"Like you gentlemen," replied Bridoye, "I allow and command the plaintiff to get a good sound sleep before the case opens, then appear before me, bringing me a good judicial attestation of his sleep, according to the 'gl., 32. q. vij. c. Si quis cum,'

> Quandoque bonus dormitat Homerus.[6]
>
> [Sometimes good Homer nods.]

"This act engenders some other members; from that one is born another, even as link by link is made a coat of mail. Finally, by inquiry, I find the lawsuit well formed and perfected in its members. Thereupon I go back to my dice. And such furbishing is not done by me without reason and notable experience.

"I recall that in the camp at Stockholm[7] a Gascon named Gratianauld, a native of Saint-Sever, having lost all his money at gambling and being very vexed about it—as you know, 'pecunia est alter sanguis [money is another blood], ut ait Anto. de Butrio,[8] in c. accedens., ij, extra. ut lit. non contest.,' and Bald. 'in l. si tuis, C. de op. li. per no., et l. advocati, C. de advo div. jud.: Pecunia est vita hominis et optimus fidejussor in necessitatibus,' on leaving the game, in front of all his comrades, kept calling out loudly: 'By ox's head, laddies, may cask fever bat you down! Now that my twenty-four bits[9] are lost, I'd just as soon also hand out some knocks, bangs, and whacks. Is there any one of you who'd like to take me on and fight it out with me?[10] When no one answered his invitation, he passes on to the camp of the *Hondrespondres*[11] [the English], and kept repeating these same words, inviting them to fight with him. But these last-named kept saying: 'The Gascon sets himself up to fight with any one of us, but he's more inclined to steal: therefore, dear ladies, keep an eye on the baggage.' And none of their contingent offered to fight. Therefore the Gascon passes on to the camp of the French freebooters, saying the same thing as before and inviting them lustily to combat, with little Gascon gambols. But no one answered him. Then the Gascon, at the end of the camp, lay down near the tents of stout Christian, Chevalier de Crissé,[12] and went to sleep.

"At that point a freebooter, having likewise lost all his money, came out with his sword, determined to fight with the Gascon, inasmuch as he had lost like him [Juvenal, *Satires*, no. 13, v.134]

Ploratur lachrymis amissa pecunia veris,

[With real tears he laments the money lost,]

says 'glos. de paenitent. dist. 3, c. sunt plures.' Indeed, after looking for him all through the camp, finally he found him asleep. So then he said to him: 'Hey, on your feet! Sonnyboy of all the devils, get up; I've lost my money just as well as you have. Let's go have a good scrap together and bang each other around good and proper. Have a look, my tuck is no longer than your rapier.'

"The Gascon, still all dazed, answered him: 'By Saint Arnault's head,[13] who are you, to come waking me up? May tavern fever bat you down! Oh, by Saint-Sever, patron saint of Gascony, I was just having a good sleep when this here now no-good came around pestering me.' The freebooter kept inviting him again to fight; but the Gascon said to him: 'Hey, you poor guy, I'd skin you alive, now that I'm rested. Go get a bit of rest the way I did, then we'll fight.' Even as he had forgotten his loss, he had lost his urge to fight. In short, instead of fighting each other and possibly killing one another, they went off to have a drink together, each one on money loaned for his sword. Sleep had done this good deed, and pacified the ardent frenzy of these two worthy champions. Here apply the golden words of Giovanni Andrea[14] 'in c. ult. de sent. et re judic. libro sexto':

Sedendo et quiescendo fit anima prudens."

[Quiet and rest give prudence to the soul.]

CHAPTER 43

*How Pantagruel excuses Bridoye
about the verdicts
rendered by the chance of dice.*

WITH that Bridoye was silent. Trinquamelle ordered him to leave the courtroom, which was done. Then he said to Pantagruel:

"Reason will have it, most august Prince, not only by the obligation in which by infinite kindnesses you hold this Parlement and the whole Marquisate of Myrelingues, but also by the good sense, discerning judgment, and admirable learning that great God, Giver of all good things, has placed in you, we should offer you the decision in this matter of Bridoye, so novel, so strange and paradoxical, who in your presence, sight, and hearing, has confessed to making judgments by the chance of dice. So we beg you to be willing to pass judgment as it shall seem to you juridical and equitable."

To this Pantagruel replied: "Gentlemen, my estate lies not in professing to judge lawsuits, as you know. But since you are pleased to do me so much honor, instead of performing the function of judge, I'll assume that of petitioner.

"In Bridoye I recognize many qualities by which he would seem to me to merit pardon in the case in point. Firstly, old age; secondly, simplicity: in both of which you understand full well what ease our laws and statutes grant in pardon and excuse for a misdeed. Thirdly, I recognize another point, likewise drawn from our laws, in favor of Bridoye: it's that this one and only fault should be abolished, extinguished, and absorbed in the immense sea of so many equitable judgments that he has handed down in the past, and that in forty years and more no act of his has been found deserving of reprehension. As if, into the River Loire, I were to cast a drop of sea water: for that one and only drop, no one would call it salty.

"And it seems to me that in this there is something, I know not what, of God, Who has brought to pass and determined that in these judgments by chance all the preceding verdicts have been found good in this venerable and sovereign Court of yours—God Who, as you know, often wills to have His glory appear in the befuddlement of the wise, the humbling of the mighty, and the exaltation of the simple and humble.

"I'm willing to waive all these points. I will only beg you—not by that obligation that you profess toward my house, which I do not recognize, but the sincere affection that from all antiquity you have found in us, both on the near side and the far side of the Loire, for the maintenance of your estate and dignities—that for this one time you pardon and forgive him upon two conditions; first, that he satisfy or put a sufficient surety for the satisfaction of the party wronged by the injustice of the sentence in question: for the fulfillment of this article, I will provide sufficiently. And secondly, that for his subsidiary and in the weighty charge of administering justice, you would be pleased to give him someone younger, learned, prudent, expert and virtuous in counseling, on whose advice henceforth he will conduct his judicial proceedings.

"In case you should want to depose him completely from his office, I will ask you very earnestly to bestow him on me as a present and a pure gift. I'll find places and estates enough in my kingdoms to employ him and make use of him. For this I shall beseech the good God, Creator, Preserver, and Giver of all good things, to keep you forever in His holy Grace."

These words spoken, Pantagruel made a bow to the whole Court and left the courtroom. At the door he found Panurge, Epistémon, Frère Jean, and others. There they mounted their horses to go back to Gargantua.

Along the way Pantagruel was telling them point by point the story of the judgment of Bridoye. Frère Jean said that he had known Perrin Dendin at the time when he was staying at Fontenay-le-Comte under the noble Abbé Ardillon.[1] Gymnaste said he was in the tent of stout Christian, Chevalier de Crissé, when the Gascon answered the freebooter. Panurge was raising some difficulty over believing the good fortune of the judgments by chance, especially for such a long time. Epistémon said to Pantagruel:

"They tell us a parallel story about a provost of Montlhéry.[2] But what would you say about that good fortune with the dice continued over so many successive years? For one or two judgments given like that I wouldn't be astonished, especially in matters in themselves ambiguous, intricate, entangled, and obscure."

CHAPTER 44

How Epistémon[1] tells a strange story
of the perplexities of human judgment.

"As was[2] the controversy argued before Cneius Dolabella, proconsul in Asia. This is the case: A woman in Smyrna had by her first husband a child named A. B. C. When her husband died, after a certain time she remarried and, by her second husband, had a son named F. E. G. It happened (as you know, rare is the affection of stepfathers, fathers-in-law, and stepmothers toward the children of deceased first fathers and mothers) that this husband and his son secretly, treacherously, in ambush, killed A. B. C.

"The woman, learning of the treachery and wickedness, would not let the crime remain unpunished, and brought about the death of them both, avenging the death of her first son. She was apprehended by the law and brought before Cneius Dolabella. In his presence she confessed the deed, without any dissimulation; only she alleged that by right and by reason she had killed them. That was the state of the case.

"He found the affair so ambiguous that he didn't know to which side to lean. The woman's crime was great, who had killed her second husband and son. But the cause of the murder seemed to him so natural—and, as it were, founded in the law of nations, seeing that they had killed her first son, the two of them together, treacherously, in ambush, not having been outraged or injured by him, but only out of greed to possess the whole inheritance—that, for the decision, he sent to the Areopagites in Athens to learn what would be their advice and verdict on this.

"The Areopagites made reply that a hundred years later they should send them the contending parties in person to answer to certain questions that were not contained in the trial record. That was to say that the perplexity and obscurity of the matter seemed to them so great that they didn't know what to say or judge about it.

"If anyone had decided the case by the chance of dice, he would not have been wrong, come what might: if against the woman, she deserved punishment, seeing that she had taken into her hands the vengeance, which belonged to the law; if for the woman, she seemed to have had cause for atrocious grief.

"But, in Bridoye, the continuation over so many years astonishes me."

"I cannot," responded Pantagruel,[3] "answer your question categorically, I must confess. Conjecturally, I would attribute this good fortune to the benevolent aspect of the heavens and the favor of the Moving Intelligences. These—in consideration of the simplicity and sincere good intent of Judge Bridoye, who, mistrusting his knowledge and capacity, knowing the inconsistencies and contradictions of the laws, edicts, customs, and ordinances, knowing the wiles of the Infernal Calumniator (who often transforms himself into a messenger of light by his ministers, the perverse advocate, counselors, prosecuting attorneys, and other such officers, turns black into white, fancifully makes it seem to each party that it is in the right—as you know, there is no cause so bad but that it finds its advocate, without that there would never be a lawsuit in the world), should commend himself humbly to God the Just Judge, call celestial grace to his aid, and trust himself to the Sacrosanct Spirit for the hazard and perplexity of a definitive judgment, and by that chance should explore its decision and good pleasure, which we call a verdict—these Intelligences would move and turn the dice to make them fall in favor of the man who, armed with a just complaint, should request to have his rights maintained by justice; as the Talmudists say, there is no harm whatever contained in chance, and only by chance, in human anxiety and doubt, is the divine will manifested.

"I would not want to think or say, nor indeed do I believe, that the all too evident iniquity and corruption of those responsible for justice in this Myrelinguais Parlement in Myrelingues is so extraordinary that a lawsuit could not be decided worse by casting dice, come what might, than it is now, passing through their hands full of blood and perverse inclination. Considering especially that their entire rule-book in common law was given by one Tribonianus, an unbeliever, infidel, barbarian, so malicious, so perverse, so avaricious and wicked, that he used to sell laws, edicts, bills, constitutions, and ordinances for cash on the line to the highest bidder. And thus he cut their pieces for them by these little bits and scraps of the laws they have in use, suppressing and abolishing the rest, which worked for the total law, for fear that, if the total law remained and the books of the ancient jurists were seen in the exposition of the twelve tables[4] and edicts of the praetor, his wickedness would be clearly known to everyone.

"Therefore it would often be better (that is to say less harm would come of it) for the parties in dispute to walk over caltrops[5] than to entrust themselves for their rights to these men's responses and judgments, even as Cato in his day wished and advised that the law court should be paved with caltrops."

CHAPTER 45

*How Panurge takes counsel
of Triboullet.*

On the sixth day following, Pantagruel got back at the time when Triboullet had arrived by water from Blois. Panurge, on Triboullet's arrival, gave him a well-inflated pig's bladder, resounding because of the dried peas that were inside; also a well-gilded wooden sword; also a little game-pouch made of a tortoise shell; also a wicker-covered bottle full of Breton wine, and two dozen Blandureau apples.[1]

"How's that?" said Carpalim, "is he as crazy as a good round cabbage?"[2]

Triboullet girded on the sword and the game-pouch, took the bladder in his hand, ate part of the apples, drank all of the wine. Panurge kept looking at him curiously and said:

"I still have never seen a fool—and yet I've seen over ten thousand francs' worth—who didn't drink gladly and in long drafts."

Then he explained his business to him in elegant rhetorical terms. Before he had finished, Triboullet gave him a big punch with his fist between the two shoulders, gave him back the bottle into his hand, kept flicking his nose with the pig's bladder, and as his whole answer said to him, shaking his head very hard:

"By God, God, crazy fool, beware monk! Buzançais bagpipe!"[3]

These words uttered, he moved away from the company and kept playing with the bladder, delighting in the melodious rattling of the pea.

After that, it was not possible to drag any word whatever out of him. And when Panurge wanted to question him further, Triboullet drew his wooden sword and tried to strike him with it.

"Now we're really in great shape [Nous en sommes bien, vrayement]!" said Panurge. That's a fine solution. Good and crazy he is, there's no denying that; but crazier still is the man who brought him to me, and supremely crazy I, for communicating my thoughts to him."

"That," said Carpalim, "is aimed straight at my visor."

"Without getting worked up," said Pantagruel, "let's consider his gestures and his words. In these I observed notable mysteries, and I'm no longer as amazed as I used to be that the Turks revere such madmen as Musaphis and prophets. Did you consider how his head shook and wagged before he opened his mouth to speak? By the teaching of the ancient philosophers, by the ceremonies of the Magi, and the observations of the jurists, you may judge that this movement was prompted by the coming and inspiration of the prophetic spirit, which, entering abruptly into a weak and tiny substance (as you know, a big brain cannot be contained within a small head), shook it up in such a way as doctors say a tremor comes upon the members of the human body, partly from the weight and violent impetuosity of the burden borne, partly from the weak capacity of the organ bearing it.

"A manifest example is in those who, on an empty stomach, cannot carry a big goblet full of wine in their hand without their hands trembling. This the Pythian prophetess prefigured to us of old when, before responding with the oracle, she would shake her domestic laurel. Thus Lampridius says that the Emperor Heliogabalus, in order to be reputed a diviner, throughout many festivals of his great idol,[4] among his fanatical eunuchs used to shake his head publicly. Thus Plautus declares in his *Asinaria*[5] that Surias used to walk along shaking his head, as if frenzied and out of his senses, frightening everyone who encountered him. And elsewhere [*Trinummus* 5.2.45], explaining why Charmides used to shake his head, he says it was in ecstasy.

"Thus Catullus tells us, in Berecynthia and Atys [*Elegies* 63.23], of the place where the maenads, Bacchic women, priestesses of Bacchus, frenzied diviners, bearing boughs of ivy, used to shake their heads. In a similar case did the gelded Galli, priests of Cybele, in celebrating their festivals. Wherefore she is so named, according to the ancient theologians; for Κυβίσται means to turn, to twist, to shake one's head, and act like a wryneck.

"Thus Livy writes that in the Bacchanalia in Rome, men and women seemed to vaticinate, because of a certain shaking and agitation of the body that they affected. For the common voice of the philosophers and the opinion of the people was that the power of prophecy was never given by the heavens without frenzy and shaking of the trembling and shuddering body, not only when this was receiving it but also when it was manifesting and declaring it.

"In fact Julian, a notable jurist, when sometimes asked whether a slave should be considered sane who, in the company of fanatical and frenzied people, had conversed and peradventure prophesied, but without such shaking of the head, replied that he would be considered sane. Thus nowadays we see tutors and preceptors shake their pupils' heads, as you do a pot by the handles, by pinching and pulling their ears (which, according to the Egyptian sages, are the members consecrated to Memory), to restore their senses, then perchance far afield in strange thoughts and as it were made skittish by disorderly desires, to good philosophical learning, which Virgil [*Eclogues* 6.3–4] confesses about himself in his shaking by Apollo Cynthius."

CHAPTER 46

How Pantagruel and Panurge diversely interpret the words of Triboullet.

"H E says you're a fool?[1] And what kind of fool? A crazy fool, who in your old age wants to bind and enslave yourself in marriage. 'Beware monk!' 'Pon my honor, that by some monk you will be made a cuckold. I stake my honor on it, and nothing greater could I stake, even were I sole and peaceful ruler in Europe, Africa, and Asia.

"Note how much I rely on our morosophe,[2] Triboullet. The other oracles and replies have determined that you will peacefully be made a cuckold, but had not yet clearly expressed by whom your wife would be led into adultery and you cuckolded. This noble Triboullet tells that. And the cuckoldry will be notorious and extremely scandalous. Must your conjugal bed be defiled and contaminated by monkery?

"He says further that you will be the Buzançais bagpipe,[3] that is to say well horned, antlered, and cornute [bien corné, cornard et cornu]. And just as he, wanting to ask King Louis XII for the salt controllership at Buzançais for his brother, asked for a bagpipe, so you likewise, thinking to marry some good, honorable woman, will marry a woman empty of prudence, full of wind and arrogance, loud mouthed and unpleasant, like a bagpipe.

"Note further that with the bladder he kept flicking you on the nose, and gave you a punch on the backbone: that presages that you will be beaten, flicked on the nose, and robbed, as you had robbed the little children of Vaubreton of the pig's bladder."[4]

"On the contrary," replied Panurge. "Not that I mean to exempt myself shamelessly from the domain of folly. I'm its vassal and belong to it, I confess. Everyone is mad. In Lorraine, Fou is near Tou by sound discernment. Everything is mad. Solomon says that infinite is the number of fools.[5] From infinity nothing can be subtracted, to it nothing added, as Aristotle proves.[6] And a crazy fool would I be if, being a fool, a fool I did not think myself. That is what likewise makes the number of maniacs and madmen infinite. Avicenna says that infinite are the species of mania.

"But the rest of his words and gestures work for me. He says to my wife: 'Beware monk!' That's a sparrow[7] that she will cherish, like the one that Catullus's Lesbia had, who will go flying after flies and spend his time on that, as cheerily as ever did Domitian the flycatcher.

"He says further that she will be a village girl, and pleasant as a lovely bagpipe from Saulieu or Buzançais. That truthful Triboullet well discerned my nature and my inward inclinations. For I swear to you that I like better the merry little disheveled shepherdesses, whose tail smells of thyme, than the ladies of the great courts with their rich attire and their perfumes redolent of *maujoint*.[8] I like the sound of the rustic bagpipe better than the quavers of the courtly lutes, rebecs, and violins.

"He gave me a punch on my jolly old lady of a backbone? For the love of God, so be it, and be it that much of a deduction lessening the pains of purgatory! He wasn't doing it to harm. He thought he was striking some page. He's a goodly fool; innocent, I swear to you; and anyone sins who thinks ill of him. I pardon him with all my heart.

"He was flicking my nose: those are little tomfooleries between my wife and me, as happens with all newlyweds."

CHAPTER 47

How Pantagruel and Panurge
decide to visit
the oracle of the Divine Bottle.[1]

"HERE is quite another point, which you're not considering. Never-theless it's the heart of the matter. He gave me back the bottle into my hand. Now what does *that* signify? What is the meaning of that?"

"Peradventure," replied Pantagruel, "it signifies that your wife will be a drunkard."

"On the contrary," said Panurge, "for it was empty. I swear to you by the backbone of Saint Fiacre in Brie that our morosophe [sophomore], the unique but not lunatic [l'unicque, non, lunaticque] Triboullet, is sending me back to the bottle. And once more I refresh my first vow, and swear by Styx and Acheron, in your presence, to wear spectacles on my bonnet and wear no codpiece on my breeches until I have got the Divine Bottle's word about my project. I know a prudent man, a friend of mine, who knows the spot, the region, and the country its temple and oracle is in. He'll take us there safely. Let's go there together. I beseech you not to turn me down. I'll be an Achates to you, a Damis, and a companion on the entire trip. I've long known you to be a lover of foreign travel and wishing always to see and always to learn. We'll see wonderful things, believe me!"

"Gladly," replied Pantagruel, "but before we set out on this long per-egrination, full of risk, full of evident dangers . . . "

"What dangers?" said Panurge, interrupting his remarks. "Dangers flee from me, wherever I may be, for seven leagues around; even as, when the prince comes on the scene, the magistrate ceases to be one;[2] when the sun comes out, the darkness vanishes; and as illnesses used to flee at the coming of Saint Martin's body at Candes."

"By the way," said Pantagruel, "before we set out, we must take care of certain points. First, let's send Triboullet back to Blois (which was done right away, and Pantagruel gave him a robe of braided cloth of gold). Secondly, we must have the advice and leave of my father the king. Besides, we need to find some sibyl as our guide and interpreter."

Panurge replied that his friend Xenomanes would suffice for them, and moreover was planning to pass through the country of Lanternland[3] and there to pick up some learned and useful Lanterness, who would be to them for this trip what the sibyl was to Aeneas when he went down into the Elysian Fields. Carpalim, passing by on his way to take Triboullet back, heard this statement and called out to say:

"Ho there, Panurge, Sir Quit-of-debts, pick up Milord Debt-puty[4] in Calais, for he's a *goud fallot*[5] and don't forget [to forgive] our debtors:[6] those are lanterns. Thus you will have both a torch [fallot] and lanterns."

"My prognosis," said Pantagruel," is that along the way we won't breed melancholy. Already I perceive this clearly. My one regret is that I don't speak good Lanternese."

"I," responded Panurge, "will speak it for you all; I understand it like my mother tongue; I'm as versed in it as in the vernacular:[7]

> Briszmarg d'algotbric nubstzne zos
> Isquebfz prusq; alborz crinqs zacbac.
> Misbe dilbarlkz morp nipp stancz bos.
> Strombtz, Panrge walmap quost grufz bac.[8]

"Now, Epistémon, guess what that is?"

"Those," replied Epistémon, "are names of devils errant, devils passant, devils rampant."

"Your words are bery[9] true, my fine friend," said Panurge. "That's Lanternese courtier language. Along the way, I'll make you up a nice little dictionary of it, which will last hardly any longer than a new pair of shoes: you'll have learned it by heart before you see daybreak. What I said, translated from Lanternese into the vernacular, sings like this:

> When I was under Cupid's yoke,
> Mishaps on me, but no good fell.
> Happier are the married folk
> Panurge is one, and knows it well.

"So what remains," said Pantagruel, "is to hear my father the king's will, and obtain leave from him."

CHAPTER 48

*How Gargantua points out
that it is not lawful for children
to marry without the knowledge
and consent of their fathers and mothers.*[1]

Wʜᴇɴ Pantagruel entered the great hall of the château, he found the good Gargantua[2] coming out of his council, gave him a summary of their adventures, explained their project, and besought him that by his leave and agreement they might put it into execution. That good chap Gargantua, holding in his hands two fat bundles of petitions answered and memoranda for answers, gave them to Ulrich Gallet, his long-time Master of Petitions and Requests, drew Pantagruel aside, and, with an expression even more joyous than usual, said to him:

"I praise God, my very dear son, for keeping you in virtuous desires, and I'm very pleased to have you complete this journey. But I'd like to see you too come to the will and desire to marry. It seems to me that from now on you are coming into the age suitable for it. Panurge has striven enough to break down the difficulties that could have been an obstacle to him. Speak for yourself."

"My very kind father," replied Pantagruel. "I hadn't yet given it a thought. I was referring all that business to your goodwill and paternal command. I pray to God rather to be seen stone dead for having displeased you than without your pleasure to be seen alive and married.[3] I have never heard that by any law whatever,[4] whether sacred or profane and barbarous, it has been up to the fancy of children to marry when their fathers, mothers, and close relatives did not consent, will it, and promote it. All lawgivers have withheld this freedom from children and reserved it for the parents."

"My very dear son," said Gargantua, "I take you at your word, and praise God that into your knowledge come only good and laudable things, and that in through the windows of your senses nothing has entered the domicile of your mind but liberal knowledge: for in my time there was a country[5] on the continent in which I know not what mole-catching image-bearers [pastophores taulpetiers][6] just like the pontiffs of Cybele in Phrygia (if those had been capons, not cocks full of salaciousness and lasciviousness) who have pronounced laws to married people in the matter of marriage. And I don't know which I should abominate more: the tyrannical presumption of these dreaded mole-catchers who do not confine themselves within the gates of their mysterious temples but thrust themselves into dealings diametrically opposite to their estate, or superstitious stupidity of the married people who have ratified and given obedience to such malign and barbaric laws, and do not see (what is clearer than the morning star) how such connubial ratifications all work to the advantage of their priests, none to the welfare and profit of the married people, which is reason enough to make them suspect as unfair and fraudulent.

"By reciprocal temerity they might establish laws for their priests on the matter of their ceremonies and sacrifices, considering that these (men) cut tenths and gnaw from the gain coming forth from their labors and the sweat of their hands in order to feed and keep them up in plenty. And such laws would not (in my judgment) be as perverse and impertinent as theirs are, which they have received from them. For (as you have very well said) there was no law in the world that gave children freedom to marry without the avowal and consent of their fathers.

"By means of the laws I'm telling you about, there is no scoundrel, rogue, criminal, gallows-bird, stinking, putrid, leper, robber, villain in their countries, who may not violently snatch away whatever girl he may want to choose, however noble, beautiful, rich, modest, decent you could possibly say, from her father's house, her mother's arms, in spite of all her relatives, if the scoundrel has once taken on with him some priest who will some day participate in the booty.[7]

"Would the Goths, the Scythians, the Massagetae do worse, and any more cruel act in an enemy site long besieged by them and assaulted at great costs?

"And do the grieving fathers and mothers see dragged out of their houses by a stranger, barbaric, mongrel, all totted, cankered, cadaverous, poor, wretched, their ever so lovely, delicate, rich, and healthy daughters, whom they had brought up so fondly in all virtuous practices, hoping at an opportune time to unite them in marriage with the sons of their old friends and neighbors, (also) born and brought up with the same care to arrive at that felicity of marriage, that they should see born lineage related and inheriting no less the ways of their fathers and mothers than their goods, furniture, and inheritances. What sort of spectacle do you think this is for them?

"Do not think that any more enormous was the desolation of the

Roman people and their confederates, on hearing of the death of Germanicus Drusus [see *Tacitus Annals* 2.72.82].

"Do not think that any more pitiable was the comfortlessness of the Lacedaemonians when they saw Grecian Helen furtively abducted from their country by the Trojan adulterer.

"Do not think that their grief and lamentations are lesser than those of Ceres when her daughter Proserpina was ravished from her; than those of Isis at the loss of Osiris; of Venus at the death of Adonis; of Hercules at the loss of Hylas [Theocritus *Idylls* 13.55 ff.]; of Hecuba at the removal of Polyxena [see especially Euripides' *Hecuba* vs. 391 ff.].

"They, however, are so possessed by fear of the devil and by superstition that they dare not speak against it, since the mole-catcher was present and making the contract. And they remain in their houses, deprived of their dearly-loved daughters, the father cursing the day and hour of his wedding, the mother sorry that she had not aborted in such a sad and unhappy child-bearing; and in tears and lamentations they finish their lives, which by rights they were to finish in joy and good treatment from them.

"Others have been so beside themselves and virtually crazy with grief that they have drowned, hanged, killed themselves, unable to bear such indignity.

"Others have had a more heroic spirit, and, on the example of Jacob's sons avenging the rape of their sister Dina [Genesis 34], have found the libertine, in company with his mole-catcher, clandestinely soliciting and suborning their daughters; they have cut them to pieces and furiously killed them on the spot, later throwing their bodies to the wolves and crows amid the fields. At which most manly and knightly act the mole-catching confriars trembled and lamented miserably, fashioned horrible complaints, and with all importunity begged and implored the secular arm and civil justice, insisting fiercely and demanding that for such cases exemplary punishment be exacted.

"But, neither in natural equity, nor in the rights of man, nor in any imperial law whatever, has there ever been found a clause, paragraph, point, or title, by which any penalty or torture was prescribed for such an act, for reason would oppose this, nature find it repugnant. For there is not a virtuous man in the world who would not naturally and by reason be more perturbed in mind, hearing the news of his daughter's rape, defamation, and dishonor, than by that of her death. Now it is a fact that each and every man, finding the murderer wickedly and treacherously in the act of homicide upon the person of his daughter, by reason may, by nature should, slay him on the spot, and will not be apprehended by the law for it. So it is no wonder then if on finding the libertine trying, on the urging of the mole-catcher to suborn his daughter and steal her out of his house, he should, even if she were consenting, put them ignominiously to death, and throw their bodies to be torn by the wild beasts, as being unworthy to receive the sweet, longed-for, final embrace of that great foster mother Earth, which we call burial.

"My very dear son, after my death, take care that such laws are not received in this kingdom; so long as I shall be living and breathing in this body, I'll see to it in good order, with the help of my God. So since you're referring your marriage to me, I'm for it, I'll see to it. Make ready for Panurge's trip. Take with you Epistémon, Frère Jean, and any others you choose. Do as you will with my treasury. Whatever you do cannot fail to please me. From my arsenal at Thalasse take whatever ships and equipment[8] you want, such pilots, sailors, and interpreters as you want, and, when the wind is favorable, set sail, in the name and under the protection of God our Savior.

"During your absence, I'll make the preparations for both a wife for you and a feast that I want to make famous, if ever there was one, at your wedding."

CHAPTER 49

How Pantagruel made his preparations
to put out to sea and
of the herb named Pantagruelion.

A few days later Pantagruel, taking leave of the good Gargantua as he was praying earnestly for his son's trip, arrived at the port of Thalasse, near Saint-Malo, accompanied by Epistémon, Frère Jean des Entommeures, abbot of Thélème, and others of the noble house, notably Xenomanes the great traveler and voyager across perilous ways,[1] who had come at Panurge's command, because he held some manor or others as a mesne fief[2] of the seignory of Salmagundi.

On arriving there, Pantagruel got the ships equipped and ready, in the number of those that Ajax of Salamis long ago had brought the Greeks as a convoy to Troy. Sailors, pilots, rowers, interpreters, artisans, warriors, victuals, artillery, munitions, clothes, cash, and other goods, he took and brought on board, as was necessary for a long and risky trip. Among other things, I saw that he had a great store loaded on of his herb Pantagruelion, both green and raw and prepared and put up.[3]

The herb Pantagruelion has a small root, rather tough and rough, ending in a blunt white point, with a few filaments, and it burrows no deeper than a cubit into the ground. From the root rises a single stem, round, like a cane, green on the outside, paling to white within, concave, like the stem of *smyrnium olusatrum* [hemp], beans, gentian; woody, straight, friable, a bit crenelated in the form of slightly striated columns, full of fibers, in which consists the entire worth of the herb, especially in the part called *mesa,* meaning middle, and that which is called *mylasea.*

The height of it is usually from five to six feet. Sometimes it exceeds the height of a lance:[4] to wit, when it encounters soil that is sweet, damp, light, humid but not cold, as is that of Olonne and that of Rosea, near Praeneste in Sabine territory, and when it has no lack of rain around the times of the fishermen's festivals[5] and in the summer solstice. And then it surpasses the height of trees and is called, as you say, dendromalache [Greek for "tree-mallow"], on the authority of Theophrastus [see his *Inquiry into Plants*], although it is an herb dying each year, not a tree enduring in its root, trunk, stock, and branches. And from the stem come out strong branches.

It has leaves three times longer than wide, always green, rather rough like bugloss, rather tough, indented all around like a sickle and like betony, ending in a point, like a Macedonian pike, and like a lancet that surgeons use. The shape of it is not very different from that of leaves of ash or agrimony; and so much like liverwort that many herbalists have called it cultivated agrimony, and called liverwort Pantagruelion run wild. And they are in rows spread out at equal distances around the stem, in the number of either five or seven in each row. So much has Nature cherished it that she has endowed it in its leaves with these two odd numbers, so divine and mysterious. The odor of these is strong and unpleasant to delicate noses.

The seed appears near the head of the stem and a little below. Individual seeds are as numerous as of any herb there is, spherical, oblong, or rhomboid, jet black or somewhat tawny, rather tough, covered with a frail coating, delicious to all songbirds, such as linnets, goldfinches, larks, green Provence canaries, yellowhammers, and many others; but in man they extinguish the generative seed in anyone who should eat many of them often; and although long ago, among the Greeks, they used to make of them certain kinds of snack, tarts, and fritters, which they ate after supper as sweetmeats and to enjoy the wine more; yet the fact is that they are hard to digest and bad for the stomach; they engender bad blood, and by their excessive heat they hit the brain and fill the head with harmful and painful vapors. And—as in many plants there are two sexes, male and female which we see in laurels, palms, oaks, yews, asphodels, mandragora, ferns, agarics, birthwort, cypress, turpentine, pennyroyal, peonies, and others—so in this herb there is a male, which bears no flower but abounds in seed, and a female, which abounds in little whitish flowers, useless, and bears no seed worth noting, and, as with herbs like it, has a leaf wider and less tough than the male, and does not grow to the same height.

They sow the Pantagruelion at the first coming of the swallows; they take it out of the ground when the cicadas begin to get hoarse.

CHAPTER 50

How the famous Pantagruelion
is to be prepared and put to use.

PANTAGRUELION is prepared under the autumnal equinox[1] in various ways, according to the fancy of the peoples and the diversity of the regions. Pantagruel's first instructions were: strip the stem of its leaves and seed; macerate it in standing, not running water for five days, if the weather is dry and the water warm, for nine to twelve if the weather is cloudy and the water cold; then dry it in the sun; then in the shade strip off the cortex and separate the fibers (in which, as we have said, consists its entire worth and value) from the woody part, which is useless, except to make a bright flame, to light the fire and to fill pig's bladders for the amusement of little children. Gourmands sometimes use it, on the sly, as siphons to suck up and draw in by one's breath the new wine through the bunghole.

Some modern Pantagruelists, to avoid the manual labor it would take to make such a separation, use certain crushing instruments made in the form in which angry Juno held her hands bound together to prevent the child-bearing of Alcmene, mother of Hercules; and, through this, they shatter and pound the woody part and make it useless, to salvage the fibers from it. In this sole preparation agree those who, against everyone's opinion and in a way paradoxical to all philosophers, earn their living by walking backward.[2] Those who want to bring it up to a more evident value do what we are told was the pastime of the three sister Fates, the nocturnal amusement of the noble Circe, and the long-lasting excuse of Penelope to her foppish suitors during the absence of her husband Ulysses. Thus it is put in possession of its inestimable virtues, part of which I will explain to you (for to explain the whole lot is impossible) if first I may interpret for you the denomination thereof.

I find that plants are named in various ways. Some have taken the name of the man who first discovered them, revealed, cultivated, domesticated, and appropriated them; as *mercuriale* [dog's mercury], from Mercury; *panacea,* from Panacea, daughter of Aesculapius; *armoise* [motherwort], from Artemis, who is Diana; *eupatorium,* from King Eupator [of Pontus]; *telephium* [orpine], from Telephus; *euphorbia,* from Euphorbus, King Juba's doctor; *clymenos* [honeysuckle], from Clymenus; *alcibiadion,* from Alcibiades; *gentian* from Gentius, king of Slavonia.

And so highly was esteemed of old this prerogative of giving one's name to herbs discovered that, even a controversy was stirred up between Neptune and Pallas over which one the land newly discovered by them both together should take its name from, land which later was called Athens after Athene, that is to say Minerva; likewise Lyncus, king of Scythia, made a hard try to kill, by treachery, young Triptolemus,[3] sent by Ceres to show men the still unknown *froment* [wheat],[4] so that by his death he might impose his own name, and, to his immortal honor and glory, be called the discoverer of this grain so useful and necessary to human life. For which treachery he was transformed by Ceres into a lynx or bobcat. Likewise, great long wars were stirred up between certain transient kings in Cappadocia over this sole dispute, after which one's name should be named one single herb, which, for such a dispute, was called *polemonia,* like "warlike."

Others have retained the name of the regions from which they were brought, such as Medie apples, those are lemons from Edeia, in which they were first found; Punic apples, those are pomegranates brought from Punicia (that's Carthage); *ligusticum* (that's lovage), brought from Liguria (that's the coast off Genoa); *rhubarbe,* from the barbarian river named

Rha,[5] as Ammianus attests; *santonica*;[6] fenugreek; *castanes* [chestnuts];[7] *persicae* [peaches]; *sabine* [juniper];[8] *stoechas*,[9] from my Iles d'Hyeres, in antiquity called Stoechades; *spica celtica* [a kind of nard]; and others.

Others have their name from antiphrasis and contrariety: such as *absynthe* and its opposite to *pynthe*,[10] for it is disagreeable to drink; *holosteon* (that's *tout de os*) [meaning "all of bone"], on the contrary, for no plant in nature is more frail and tender than it is.

Others are named for their virtues and operations, such as *aristolochia*,[11] which helps women in childbirth; *lichen*, which cures the skin diseases that bear its name; *mallow*,[12] which mollifies; *callithrichum*,[13] which makes hair beautiful; *alyssum, ephemerum, bechium*,[14] *nasturtium*, which is garden cress, *hyoscyame* [pig-bean], *henbane*,[15] and others.

Others, by the admirable qualities that have been observed in them, such as *heliotrope*,[16] that's *soulcil* [marigold], which follows the sun; for when the sun rises it blooms; when it climbs, it rises, when it sinks it droops, when it goes down and hides, it closes; *adiantum*,[17] for it never holds moisture, although it grows near water and may be sunk under water a long time; *hieracium* [hawkweed],[18] *eryngo*, and others.

Others, by metamorphosis of men and women of similar name like *daphné* (that's the laurel), from Daphne; the *myrtle*,[19] from Myrsine; the *pitys*, from Pitys; the *cynara* (that's the artichoke); *narcissus, saffron, smilax*, and others.

Others, by similitude, like *hippuris* (that's prelle), for it looks like a horse's tail; *alopecuros*, like a fox's tail; *psylion*, which looks like a flea; *delphinium*, like a dolphin; *bugloss*, like an ox-tongue; *iris*, like the rainbow in its flowers; *myosotis*, like a mouse's ear; *coronopous*, like a crow's foot, and others.

By reciprocal denomination [Par réciproque dénomination] are named the *Fabii*, from beans [febves]; the *Pisos*, from peas; the *Lentuli*, from lentils; the *Ciceros*, from chickpeas; as also, by loftier resemblance is named the *Venus's navel, Venus's hair, Venus's basin, Jupiter's beard, Jupiter's eye, Mars's blood, Mercury's fingers (hermodactyles)*, and others.

Others, by their forms; like *trevoil*, which has three leaves; *pentaphyllon*, which has five leaves; *serpolet*, because it creeps [serpentlike] along the ground; *helxine* [or pellitory]; *petasites* [or sunshades]; *myrobalans* [plums] which Arabs call *béen*, for they look like acorns and are oleaginous.

CHAPTER 51

Why it is called Pantagruelion,
and of the admirable virtues thereof.

In all these ways (except the fabulous, for God forbid we should use fable in this ever so truthful history), the herb is called Pantagruelion. For Pantagruel was the discoverer of it: I don't mean as regards the plant, but as to a certain use, which is more abhorred and hated by thieves, more contrary and hostile to them, than are dodder and choke-week to flax, cattail to fern, horsetail to reapers,[1] broom rape [orobanche] to chickpeas, darnel [aegilops] to barley, hatchet-vetch [securidaca] to lentils, antranium to beans, tares to wheat, ivy to walls; than the water lily and *nymphoea heraclia*, to bawdy monks; than the rod and birch to schoolboys at Navarre;[2] than is the cabbage to the bile, garlic to the magnet, onion to the sight, fern seed to pregnant women, willow seed to depraved nuns, the shade of the yew tree to any who sleep under it, aconite to leopard and wolves, the smell of the fig tree to angry bulls, hemlock to goslings, purslane to teeth, oil to trees. For many of these [robbers] we have seen, by such a use, their lives ended, strung up high and short, on the example of Phyllis, queen of the Thracians; Bonosus, emperor of Rome; Amata, wife of King Latinus; Iphis, Auctolia, Lycambes, Arachne, Phaedra, Leda, Acheus, king of Lydia, and others; offended at this alone, that without their being otherwise ill, by Pantagruelion people stopped up the passages by which good remarks come out and good morsels come in, more banefully than would a bad choking spell or mortal quinsy.

Others we have heard, at the moment when Atropos was cutting the thread of their life, grievously complaining and lamenting that Pantagruel had them by the throat. But, alackaday! it wasn't Pantagruel at all; he never was an executioner; it was Pantagruelion, performing its function as a halter and serving them as a cravat. And they were speaking inaccurately and in a solecism, unless they could be excused for it as a synecdoche, taking the discovery for the discoverer, as we say Ceres for bread, Bacchus for wine. I swear to you here and now, by the bright remarks that are in that bottle yonder cooling in that tub, that the noble Pantagruel never took anyone by the throat, unless those who are negligent about forestalling imminent thirst.

In another way it is called Pantagruelion by a similarity. For Pantagruel, when he was born into the world, was as tall as the herb I'm telling you about, and this measurement was taken easily, seeing that he was born in a season of drought, when they gather the said herb, and when Icarus's dog,[3] by his barking at the sun, makes everyone a troglodyte, forcing people to live in caves or cellars or other underground places.

In another way it is called Pantagruelion by its virtues and special properties. For, even as Pantagruel has been the ideal and exemplar of all joyous perfection (I think none of you drinkers is in any doubt about that), so in Pantagruelion I recognize so many virtues, so much energy, so many perfections, so many admirable effects, that if it had been known in its qualities when (by the account of the Prophet)[4] the trees held an election of a wooden king to rule and govern them, without a doubt it would have won a plurality of the votes and suffrages.

Shall I say more? If Oxylus, son of Orius, had engendered it by his sister Hamadryas, he would have taken more delight in its worth alone than in all his eight children, so celebrated by the mythologists, who have set their names into eternal remembrance. The eldest, a daughter, was named Vine; the next-born, a son, was named Fig-tree; another, Walnut-tree; another, Oak; another, Sorb-apple tree; another, Nettle-tree; another, Poplar; the last was named Elm and was a great surgeon in his time.

I forbear to tell you how the juice thereof, squeezed out and dropped into the ears, kills every kind of vermin that might have bred there by putrefaction and any other creature that had got in. If you put some of this juice into a pail of water, you immediately see the water congealed, as if it were curds, so great is its power. And water thus curdled is a handy remedy for horses with colic and griping pains.

The root thereof, cooked in water, softens shrunken sinews, contracted joints, sclerotic gouties, and gouty knots.

If you want to heal a burn promptly, whether from water or fire, apply to it some raw Pantagruelion, that is, just as it comes out of the ground, without any other preparation or compounding. And be careful to change it as soon as you see it drying on the burned spot.

Without it, kitchens would be a disgrace, tables loathsome, even were they covered with every exquisite dish; beds without delight [les lictz sans délices], although abounding in gold, silver, gold and silver alloy, ivory, and porphyry. Without it, millers would not carry wheat to the mill, or bring back flour. Without it, how would advocates' pleas be carried to the courtroom? How would plaster, without it, be carried to the workshop? Without it, how would water be drawn from the well?

Without it, what would scribes, copyists, secretaries, and scriveners do?

Wouldn't official documents and rent-rolls perish? Wouldn't the noble art of printing perish? What would they make the frames of? How would they ring the bells? With it are the priests of Isis adorned, the image bearers clothed, all human beings covered in their original positon. Not all the wool-bearing trees of the Seres,[5] the cotton bushes of Tylos and the Persian Gulf, or those of the Arabs or the vines of Malta, clothe as many people as does this herb all alone. It protects armies against cold and rain, surely more adequately than skins used to do. It protects theaters and amphitheaters against the heat, surrounds woods and groves for the pleasure of hunters, goes down into both fresh and sea water to the advantage of fishermen. By it are shaped and prepared for use ordinary boots, high boots, buskins, shoes, pumps, slippers, gym shoes. By it bows are strung, crossbows bent, slingshots made. And, as if it were a sacred plant, like verbena, and revered by the Manes and Lemurs,[6] dead human bodies are not buried without it.

I will say more. By means of this herb, invisible substances are visibly arrested, caught, detained, and as it were imprisoned. By their seizure and arrest great heavy mill wheels are nimbly turned for the notable profit of human life. And I am amazed how the discovery of such a practice was hidden for so many centuries from the ancient philosophers, in view of the priceless utility that comes out of it, in view of the intolerable labor they endured without it in their mills.

Thanks to it by retention of the waves of the air, the stout cargo ships, the ample cabined barges, the mighty galleons, the ships holding a thousand or ten thousand men, are launched out of their stations and driven forward at the will of the commanders.

Thanks to it, the nations that Nature seemed to keep hidden, impenetrable, and unknown, have come to us, and we to them: a thing the birds would not do, whatever their lightness of wing and whatever freedom is given them by Nature for swimming in the air. Taprobrana [Sri Lanka, once Ceylon] has seen Lapland; Java has seen the Riphaean Mountains; Phebol shall see Thélème; the Icelanders and Greenlanders shall see the Euphrates. By it Boreas has seen the manor of Auster; Eurus has visited Zephyros. With the result that the Celestial Intelligences, the gods of both sea and land, have all been frightened by this, seeing, by the use of this blessed Pantagruelion, the Arctic peoples, in full sight of the Antarctics, cross the Atlantic Ocean, pass the two tropics, turn down beneath the torrid zone, measure the entire zodiac, sport beneath the equinoctial line, have both poles in sight level with their horizon.

The Olympian gods in similar fright have said: "Pantagruel has plunged us into a novel and irksome kind of thought, more than the Aloïdae ever did, by the use and virtues of his herb. He will shortly be married, and by his wife will have children. This destiny we cannot contravene, for it has passed through the hands and spindles of the sister Fates, daughters of Necessity. Perhaps by his children may be discovered an herb of similar energy, by means of which humans will be able to visit the sources of hailstorms, the floodgates of rains, and the workshop producing lightnings will be able to invade the regions of the Moon, enter the territory of the celestial signs, and there take lodging, some at the Golden Eagle,[7] others at the Lamb, others at the Crown, others at the Harp, others at the Silver Lion sit down at table with us, and take our goddesses as wives, which are the only ways to be deified."

Finally they set the remedy for obviating this under deliberation and counsel.

CHAPTER 52

*How a certain kind of Pantagruelion
cannot be consumed by fire.*

WHAT I have told you is great and admirable. But if you should be willing to risk believing some other divine property of this sacred Pantagruelion, I would tell it to you. Believe it or not, it's all one to me. Enough for me to have told you the truth. Truth I will tell you. But, in order to get into it, for it's rather rough and hard to get at, I ask you this: if I had put into this bottle two gills[1] of wine and one of water, very well mixed together, how would you get them apart? How would you separate them, so that you would give me back the water without the wine, the wine without the water, in the same measure in which I had put them in?

Put it another way: If your carriers and boatmen, bringing us provision for your households a certain number of casks, pipes, and puncheons of Graves, Orléans, Beaune, and Mirevaux wines had drunk up and adulterated half of them, filling the rest with water, as the Limousins do by the bootful in carting the wines of Argenton and Saint-Gaultier, how would you get the water completely out? How would you purify them? I quite understand you're going to tell me about an ivy funnel. That's down in writing. It's true, and attested by a thousand experiments. You knew it already. But those who didn't know it and never saw it wouldn't think it possible. Let's move on.

If we were in the time of Sulla, Marius, Caesar, and other Roman emperors, or in the time of our ancient druids, who had the dead bodies of their relatives and lords burned, and you wanted to drink the ashes of your wife or father in an infusion of some good white wine, as Artemisia did the ashes of her husband Mausolus, or otherwise preserve them entire in some urn or reliquary, how would you salvage these ashes apart and separate from the ashes of the pyre and funeral fire? Answer me.

By my foot, you'd have plenty of trouble. I'll discharge you of it, and tell you that if you take as much of this heavenly Pantagruelion as you'd need to cover the body of the deceased and completely enclose the said body in it, tie it and sew it up with the same material; then just throw it on the fire, however great and blazing it be; the fire, through the Pantagruelion, will burn and reduce to ashes the body and bones; the Pantagruelion not only will not be consumed or burned, and will not lose a single atom of the ashes enclosed inside, will not take on a single atom of the ashes of the pyre, but will finally be drawn out of the fire more beautiful, white, and clean than when you threw it in. For that reason it is called asbestos.[2] You will find plenty of it in Carpasium, and in the region of Syene, quite cheap.

O what a great thing! O what an admirable thing! Fire, which destroys, wastes, and consumes everything, cleans, purges, and whitens this Carpasian asbestine Pantagruelion alone. If, like Jews and unbelievers, you don't believe this and ask for demonstration and a customary sign, take a fresh egg and wrap it all around with this divine Pantagruelion. So wrapped, put it in a brazier as big and fiery as you like. Leave it in as long as you want. Finally you will take out the egg hard and burned, without alteration, mutation, or heating, of the holy Pantagruelion. For less than fifty thousand Bordeaux crowns, reduced to the twelfth part of a *pithe* [quarter denier], you'll make the experiment.

Don't talk to me about that paragon the salamander:[3] that's a hoax. I do confess that a little straw fire invigorates and gladdens it. But I assure you that in a great furnace, like any other living thing, it is suffocated and consumed. We have seen this by experience. Galen, long ago, had confirmed and demonstrated it, *lib. 3 De temperamentis* [in his third book, *On the humors*], and Dioscorides maintains it, *lib. 2* [Book 2].[4]

Don't talk to me about feather alum,[5] or the wooden tower in Peiraeus that L. Sulla never could burn, because Archelaus, governor of the town for King Mithridates, had completely coated it with alum.

Don't give me here the comparison with that tree that Alexander Cornelius named *eon,* and said it was like the oak that bears the mistletoe and could not be consumed or damaged by either water or fire, any more than the oak's mistletoe, and said that of this wood had been made and built the ever so famous ship Argo. Try and find somebody to believe that; count me out.

Don't tell me about that other paragon, however marvelous it may be, that kind of tree that you see around the mountains of Briançon and Ambrun, which of its roots produces for us that good agaric; of its body gives us that resin so excellent that Galen dares to match it to turpentine; on its delicate leaves catches for us that fine honey from heaven that is manna; and although it is gummy and oily, it cannot be consumed by fire. You name it *larix* in Greek and Latin; the people of the Alps name it *melze;* the Antenorides [Paduans] and Venetians, *larege.* From which was named *Larignum* the castle in Piedmont that foiled Julius Caesar on his way to Gaul.[6]

Julius Caesar had issued a command to all the residents and inhabitants of the Alps and Piedmont to bring victuals and provisions to the stations set up along the military road, for his army as it passed through. All obeyed except those who were in Larignum, who, trusting in the natural strength of the place, refused the contribution. To chastise them for this refusal, the emperor had his army head straight for the place. In front of the castle gate was a tower built of stout beams of larix, stacked and bound crosswise upon one another like a woodpile, rising up to such a height that from the machicolations one could easily repel with stones and bars those who came near. When Caesar heard that those inside had no other defenses than stones and bars, he ordered his soldiers to throw around it fagots aplenty and set fire to them, which was instantly done. When the fagots were set on fire, the flame was so great and high that it covered the whole castle. Whereby they thought that soon afterward the tower would be burned down and consumed. But when the flames died and the fagots were consumed, the tower appeared, whole and not a bit damaged by it. Considering which, Caesar ordered that all around it, outside a stone's throw, they build a network of ditches and trenches.

Thereupon the Larignans surrendered on terms. And from their account Caesar learned of the admirable nature of this wood, which of itself makes neither fire, flame, nor charcoal. And in this respect it would deserve to be set on the same level as real Pantagruelion—and the more so because Pantagruel willed that of this be made all the doors, gates, windows, gutters, coping and wainscoting, of Thélème; likewise he covered with it the sterns, prows, galleys, hatches, gangways, and forecastles of his great carracks, ships, galleys, galleons, brigantines, light galleys, and other vessels of his arsenal at Thalasse—were it not that larix, in a great furnace of fire coming from other kinds of wood, is finally marred and destroyed, as are stones in a lime kiln: asbestine Pantagruelion is renewed and cleaned by this rather than marred or altered. Therefore,

> Sabaeans, Arabs, Indians, refrain
> From praising incense, myrrh, and ebony so.
> Come see the goodly things of this domain,
> And from our herb take seed back when you go;
> Then, if within your lands this gift can grow,
> Give thanks to heaven by the million,
> Rejoicing that this reign in France can show
> The coming of Pantagruelion.[7]

End of the Third Book of the heroic
deeds and sayings of the
good Pantagruel.

BOOK 4

The Fourth Book
of the
HEROIC DEEDS AND
SAYINGS
of the Good

PANTAGRUEL

Composed by
MASTER FRANÇOIS
RABELAIS
Doctor of Medicine

Old Prologue[1] (1548)

To the Fourth Book.

Most illustrious drinkers, and you, most precious poxies, I have received, heard, and understood the Ambassador that the Lordship of your Lordships [la Seigneurie de voz Seigneuries] has transmitted in the direction of my Paternity, and he seemed to me a very good and very eloquent orator. The summary of this message I reduce to three words, which are of such great importance that of old, among the Romans, with these three words the Praetor responded to all petitions set forth for judgment; with these three words he decided all controversies, all complaints, lawsuits, and disputes; and the days were called unfortunate and ill-starred on which the Praetor did not use these three auspicious and fortunate words, fortunate and auspicious those on which he made use of them: "You give, you say, you adjudge [appoint by judgment]."[2]

O my good folk, I can't see you![3] May the power of God be to you, and no less to me, eternally an aid. Now then, in God's name, let's never do anything unless first His holy name be praised! You give me what? A fine ample breviary.[4] Honest to Gosh, I thank you for it: that will be the most I can do, the least I should. What sort of breviary it was, I certainly was not thinking, seeing the *reigletz*,[5] the rosette, the clasps, the binding, and the cover, on which I did not fail to consider the sword hooks and the magpies painted above and sprinkled in a very beautiful arrangement, by which, if they were hieroglyphics, you would readily say there's no workmanship like a tosspot's magpie-nibbler [crocqueurs de pies]. *Crocquer pie* signifies a certain joyousness derived by a metaphor from the prodigy that happened in Brittany a short time before the battle fought near Saint-Aubin-du-Cormier. Our fathers have expounded it to us; it is right that our successors should not be ignorant of it. It was the year of the good grape crop; they were offering a quart of good tasty wine for a lace lacking one of its tags.

From the region of the Orient flew up a great number of jays from one direction, a great number of magpies from the other, all heading toward the Occident. And they skirted each other in such an order that in the evening the jays were pulling back toward the left (here understand the felicity of the augury) and the magpies toward the right, rather near each other. Whatever region they passed through, there remained neither a magpie that did not join the magpies' camp nor a jay that did not join the camp of the jays. So far did they go, so far did they fly, that they passed over Angers, a city in France on the frontier of Brittany,[6] in numbers so multiplied that by their flight they blocked the sunlight from the lands lying underneath.

In Angers at that time was an old uncle, Seigneur de Saint-Georges, named Frapin; he's the one who wrote and composed the merry Noels in the Poitevin tongue. He had a jay he delighted in because of his chatter, in which he used to invite all the passersby to drink; never did he sing except about drinking; and he called him his Bulgey [son Goitrou]. This jay, in martial fury, broke his cage and joined the passing jays. A barber named Behuart had a very gallant female magpie. With her person she increased the number of magpies and followed them into combat.

Now here are great things, paradoxical but true, witnessed and attested. Take good note of everything! What was the outcome? What came of it, good folk? A wondrous thing! Near the Malchara Cross the battle was so furious that it's a horrible thing just to think of it: the outcome was that the magpies lost the battle and were cruelly slain on the spot up to the number of 2,589,362,109, not counting the females and the little magpie chicks, you understand. The jays remained victorious, not however without the loss of many of their good soldiers; so the damage was great throughout the whole region. The Bretons are gents,[7] you know. But if they had understood the prodigy, they would have easily recognized that misfortune would be on their side. For magpies' tails are in the form of ermines; blue jays have in their plumage a few images of the arms of France.[8]

By the way, Bulgey came back from the wars three days later, all crestfallen and with one eye bloodshot. However, a few hours after he had fed in his usual fashion he returned to his good mood. The dandies, the people, and the schoolboys of Angers ran up in droves to see him thus decked out. Bulgey kept inviting them to drink as usual, adding the invitation, "Crocquez pie!" [Nibble magpie]. I suppose that was the watchword on the day of the battle, and all made it their business to use it. Behuart's magpie was not coming back; she had been nibbled. From this it was said as a common proverb that to drink your fill in great drafts was really nibbling magpie. With such pictures, for immemorial memory, Frapin had his servants' mess and lower hall painted. You can see it in Angers on the Tertre Saint-Laurent.

This figure placed in your breviary made me think that in it there was something, I know not what, of a breviary. And indeed to what purpose would you be making me a present of a breviary? I have some, thanks be to God and to you, from old ones right down to new. In this doubt, opening the said breviary, I soon perceived that it was a breviary wrought on a wondrous conceit, and its ribbons all apt and the inscriptions appropriate. So you want me to drink white wine at prime [see "hours" in the Glossary]; at tierce, sext, and nones likewise; at vespers and compline, claret wine; and this you call nibbling magpie [crocquer pie]; truly you were never hatched by a bad magpie. I'll grant this petition.[9]

You say what? That in no way have I angered you by all my books printed up to now. If in this connection I cite you the saying of an old Pantagruelist, still less will I anger you:

> "It is," said he, "no ordinary thing
> To have known how to entertain a king."[10]

You say further that the Third Book was to your taste and that it is good. True it is that there wasn't much of it, and you don't like what they commonly say: "A little and good"; you prefer what the good Evispande Verron used to say: "A lot, and good!" Moreover you invite me to the continuation of the Pantagrueline story, alleging the utilities and fruits received in the reading thereof by all good people, excusing yourselves for not obeying the request I made you, that you abstain from laughing until the seventy-eighth book. I forgive you for it with all my heart. I'm not as implacable as you might think. But what I was saying about it was not to your detriment. And I say to you in reply, as is Hector's saying set forth by Nevius that it is a fine thing to be praised by praiseworthy people. By a reciprocal declaration I say, and maintain up to the stake, exclusive (you understand, and for good reason), that you are all fine good people, all issued from good fathers and good mothers. Promising you, word of a foot soldier, that if I ever meet you in Mesopotamia, I'll do so well with little Count George of Lower Egypt[11] that he will make each one of you a present of a handsome Nile crocodile and a nightmare[12] from the Euphrates.

You adjudge. What? To whom? All the old quarter moons to the

417

hypocrites, dissemblers, impostors, gumshoes [botineurs], phonies, drones, hairypaws, indulgence-peddlers, catamites.[13] These are horrific names, just to hear the sound of them. On hearing them pronounced, I saw the hair of your noble ambassador stand on end. I didn't understand any of them but the High German, and I don't know what sort of barbarous beasts you include in those denominations. Having done diligent research through diverse countries, I've never met a man who acknowledged them or who put up with being so designated. I assume that these were some sort of barbarous beasts from the time of the high bonnets; now it has perished in nature, as all things have their finish and period, and we do not know what the definition of them is, as you know that, the subject perished, easily perishes its denomination.

If by these terms you understand the calumniators of my writings, more aptly may you call them devils. For in Greek, calumny is called *diabole*.[14] See how detestable, in the eyes of God and the angels, is this vice called calumny (that is when a good deed is impugned, when good things are maligned), that by this one, although several would seem more enormous, are the devils in hell named and called. These people are not (strictly speaking) devils from hell. They are their attendants and ministers. I name them black-and-white devils, domestic devils. What they have done to my books they will do (if they are left free to) to all others. But this is not by their own scheming. I say this so that henceforth they may not pride themselves so much on the surname of old Cato the Censor.

Have you ever heard what it means to spit in the basin? In olden times the predecessors of these private devils, overseers of pleasure, destroyers of decency such as a Philoxenus, a Gnatho, and others of the same ilk, when around the taverns where they ordinarily used to hold their schools, seeing the guests being served some good dishes and tasty morsels, they would foully spit in the platters, so that the guests, seeing their infamous spittle and snot, should give up eating the foods set out, and everything be left to these filthy spitters and snivelers.

Almost like it, but not so abominable, is the story they tell us of the freshwater doctor,[15] nephew of the late Amer's lawyer, who used to say that a fat capon's wing was bad, the rump dangerous, the neck pretty good provided the skin was removed, so that patients should not have any and the whole thing be preserved for his mouth. Thus have these befrocked devils done, seeing everyone in fervent appetite to see and read his writings because of the preceding books: they have spitten in the basin; that is to say, they have all by their handling beshitten, decried, and calumniated them, with the intention that no one should read them except their Dastardships [leurs Poiltronitez], which I have seen with my own eyes, not just with my ears; indeed to the point of preserving them religiously in their nightclothes and using them like breviaries for their daily use. They have taken them away from the sick, the gouties, the unfortunate, for whom I had written them to cheer them up in their trouble. If I took on as patients all those who fell into disability or illness, there would be no longer any need to bring such books into light and print.

Hippocrates wrote a book expressly entitled: *Of the condition of the perfect doctor* (Galen illustrated it with learned commentaries), in which he commands that nothing about the doctor—indeed even to the fingernails—must please and delight the patient. To do this in my own case, in my lowly way, I labor and strain, toward those I take on as patients. So do my colleagues for their part; wherefore we may be called charlatans with long arms and big elbows,[16] in the opinion, as crazily interpreted as stupidly invented, of two hunters of tiny turds.

There is more: over a passage in the sixth of the *Epidemics* of the said father Hippocrates we sweat and dispute to determine, not whether a doctor's face that is gloomy, cross, harsh, unpleasant, unhappy, saddens the patient, and a doctor's face that is joyous, serene, pleasant, laughing, open, rejoices the patient (that is all tested and certain), but whether such saddenings and rejoicings come about by the patient's apprehension and in contemplating these qualities, or by the transfusion of the serene or darksome, joyous or sad spirits, from the doctor to the patient, as is the opinion of the Platonists and Averrhoists.

So since it is not possible for me to be called in by all the sick, for me to take on all the sick as patients, why do they want to take away from the languishing and sick the pleasure and joyous pastime, with no offense to God, to the King, or to anyone else that they take in hearing in my absence the reading of these joyous books?

Now, since by your adjudication and decree these backbiters and calumniators are seized and possessed of the old quarters of the moon, I forgive them. It won't be any laughing matter for them all, henceforth, when we see these lunatic fools, some of them lepers, some buggers, some others both lepers and buggers at the same time, running about the fields, breaking the benches [i.e., going bankrupt], gnashing their teeth, splitting cobblestones, pounding the pavements, hanging themselves, drowning themselves, hurling themselves down head first, and running off unbridled to all the devils according to the energy, faculty, and power of the quarters (of the moon) they have in their noggins, crescent, initial, amphicyritic, on the wane, and closing.

Only toward their malignities and impostures I shall make use of the offer that Timon the Misanthrope made to his ungrateful Athenians. Timon, vexed at the ingratitude of the Athenian people in his regard, one day entered the public council of the city, asking to be given a hearing on a matter of business concerning the public welfare. At his request there was silence in expectation of hearing matters of importance, seeing that he, who for so many years had absented himself from all company and who lived in privacy, had come to the council. Thereupon he said to them:

"Outside my private garden, beneath the wall, it is a great handsome notable fig tree, from which, when desperate, you Athenian gentlemen, women, youths, and maidens have the custom of strangling yourselves in privacy. I give you notice that, to make my house more comfortable, I am planning within a week to take down that fig tree; therefore any one of you in the whole city who will have a mind to hang himself should hurry and get on with it promptly; when the aforesaid term has expired they will not have so suitable a place or so convenient a tree."

Following his example, I proclaim to all these diabolical calumniators that they are all to hang themselves I assign between noon and Faverolles.[17] With the new moon, they will not be received there at such a bargain price and will be constrained themselves at their own expense to buy ropes and choose a tree for hanging, as did Signora Leontium,[18] calumniator of the ever so learned and eloquent Theophrastus.

Liminary Epistle (of January 28, 1552)

To the Very Illustrious Prince and Most Reverend
Monseigneur Odet, Cardinal de Chastillon.[1]

You are duly notified, most illustrious Prince, by how many great
personages I have been and am daily asked, requested, and importuned
for the continuation of the Pantagruelic mythologies,[2] on the grounds
that many languishing, ill, or otherwise vexed and heart-sick people
had, in the reading thereof, beguiled their troubles, passed time joyously, and received new blitheness and consolation. To whom it is my
custom to reply that, in composing these for sport, I aspired to no
glory or praise; I had intended and had regard only to give in writing
what little relief I could to the absent sufferers and sick, which gladly,
when there is need, I give to those who take help from my craft and
service.

Sometimes I expound to them by lengthy reasoning how
Hippocrates, in many places, especially in the sixth book of his *Epidemics,* describing the training of his doctor disciple, and how Soranus of
Ephesus, Oribasius, Cl. Galen, Hali Abbas, likewise other subsequent
authors, have composed him in gestures, bearing, glance, touch, look,
grace, decency, neatness of face, clothes, beard, hair, hands, mouth,
even going into detail about the fingernails, as if he were about to play
the part of some lover or suitor in some notable comedy, or go down
into an enclosed tiltyard to fight some powerful enemy. Indeed, the
practice of medicine is quite aptly compared by Hippocrates to a
combat and farce played by three personae: the patient, the doctor, and
the illness.[3]

Once in reading this passage, I was reminded of a remark of Julia to
her father Octavian Augustus. One day she presented herself before
him in sumptuous, dissolute, lascivious garments, and had greatly
displeased him, although he said not a word about it. The next day she
changed her attire and dressed herself modestly, as was then the custom

421

of chaste Roman ladies. So dressed she presented herself before him.
He, who the day before had not declared in words the displeasure he
had in seeing her in shameless clothing, could not conceal the pleasure
he took in seeing her thus changed, and said to her: "O, how much
more fitting and praiseworthy is this clothing for the daughter of
Augustus!" She had her excuse promptly and answered him: "Today I
dressed for the eyes of my father. Yesterday I was dressed for the
pleasure of my husband."

Similarly the doctor, thus disguised in face and clothes, especially if
dressed in a rich and pleasing gown with four sleeves,[4] as once used to
be the regular custom (and it was called Philonium, as Petrus
Alexandrinus says in *Epidemics,* chapter 6), could reply to those who
might find the costume strange: "Thus have I clad myself, not to show
off and strut, but for the taste of the patient I am visiting, whom alone
I want to please entirely, not offend or vex him in any way."

There is more. Over a passage of father Hippocrates in the book
cited above [*Epidemics* 6], we sweat, seeking and arguing, not whether
the doctor's mien that is gloomy, cross, harsh, Catonian, unpleasant,
unhappy, saddens the patient, and the doctor's face that is joyous, open,
pleasant, rejoices the patient; all that is tested and certain; but whether
such saddenings and rejoicings come about by the patient's apprehension in contemplating these qualities in the doctor and by these conjec-
turing the outcome and catastrophe [result] to follow from the malady:
to wit, by the joyous ones, joyous and desired, by the unpleasant ones
unpleasant and abhorrent; or by the transfusions of spirits that are
serene or darksome, airy or earthy, from the doctor into the person of
the patient. As is the opinion of Plato and Averroes.

Above all, the aforesaid authors give special notice to the doctor
about the words, conversations, and confabulations he should have with
the patients on whose behalf he is called in. This must all lead and tend
to one end: that is to gladden him without offense to God and not to
sadden him in any way whatever. As Hierophilus greatly blames a
doctor, Callianax, who, to a patient who questioned him and asked
him: "Will I die?" impudently replied:

> So had Patroclus to bid life adieu,
> Who surely was a better man than you.[5]

To another one, who wanted to know the state of his illness and questioned him in the manner of the noble Pathelin:

" . . . can you deny
My urine shows that I'm about to die?"[6]

He replied witlessly: "Not if Latona, mother of the lovely children
Phoebus and Diana, had given birth to you." Likewise Galen, *Book 4,
Comment. in 6 Epidemi.*, greatly blames Quintus, his tutor in medicine,
who, when a patient in Rome, an honorable man, said to him: "Master,
you've had lunch, your breath smells of wine," arrogantly replied to him:
"Yours smells of fever; which has the more delightful odor, fever or
wine?"

But the calumny of certain cannibals, misanthropes, *agelastes* against
me had been so atrocious and irrational that it had vanquished my
patience, and I was determined not to write one more jot of this. For
one of the slightest contumelies they used was that such books were
full of divers heresies;[7] however, they could not point to a single one
in any place whatever—of joyous fooleries, without offense to God or
to the king, that's true—that's the sole subject and theme of these
books: Of heresies, [there are] none, unless by interpreting perversely
and against all use of reason and ordinary language what I would not
want even to have thought, on pain of dying a thousand deaths, if that
were possible; as if someone interpreted bread as stone, fish as snake,
egg as scorpion.[8]

Complaining of which once, in your presence, I told you freely that
if I did not think myself a better Christian than for their part they show
themselves to be, and if in my life, writings, words, and even thoughts,
I recognized one scintilla of heresy, they would not be falling so
detestably into the snares of the spirit of calumny, that Διάβολος
[*Diabolos*, the Devil], who by their calumny seek to incite me to such a
crime; I myself, after the example of the phoenix, would pile up the
dry wood and light the fire to burn me in it.

Then you told me that the late King Francis, of eternal memory,
had been informed of such calumnies; and having carefully heard and
understood a distinct reading of these books of mine by the most
learned and faithful reader in the kingdom (I say this because some
infamous false ones have been wickedly imputed to me), had found no
suspect passage whatever; and had held in horror some serpent-eater
who was basing a mortal heresy on an *N* put for an *M* by the fault and
negligence of the printers.[9]

So had his son, so good, virtuous, and heaven-blessed, Henry
(whom God will keep a long time for us), so that he had granted you

for me a privilege and particular protection against the calumniators. This evangel you in your benignity have since reiterated to me in Paris, and furthermore when not so long ago you visited My Lord Cardinal du Bellay, who, to recover his health after a long troublesome illness, had retired to Saint-Maur, a place, or (to speak better and more aptly) a paradise of salubrity, serenity, comfort, and all the honorable pleasures of agriculture and rustic life.

This is the reason, My Lord, why now, free from all intimidation, I toss my pen to the wind [je mectz la plume au vent], hoping that by your benign favor you will be to me like a second Gaulish Hercules in knowledge, prudence, and eloquence; Alexicacos[10] in virtue, power, and authority of whom verily I can say what was said of Moses, the great prophet and captain of Israel, by the wise King Solomon [Ecclesiasticus 45.1–5], a man fearing and loving God, beloved of God and men, whose memory is happy. God in praise compared him to the Worthies, made him great in striking terror into his enemies. In his favor He performed prodigies and frightful things; in the presence of kings He honored him; to the people by him He declared His will, and by him He showed His light. In faith and kindness He consecrated and elected him among all humans. By him He willed His voice to be heard, and to those who were in darkness willed the law of life-giving knowledge to be announced.

Promising you moreover that all those I meet rejoicing in these writings I will adjure to be totally grateful for them to you, to pray Our Lord for the preservation and growth of that mighty stature of yours, but that they should give me credit for nothing more than humble subjection and willing obedience to your commands. For by your highly honorable urging you gave me both courage and inventiveness, and without you my heart and animal spirits had remained dried up. May Our Lord keep you in His holy grace. From Paris, this 28th of January, 1552.

Your very humble and obedient servant,

Franç. RABELAIS, physician

Prologue of the Author

M. François Rabelais
For the fourth book of the heroic deeds and sayings
of Pantagruel.

To readers of good will.

Good people, God save and guard you! Wait till I put my glasses on—my feet![1] Sweet and fair Lent goes its way![2] I do see you. And then what? You've had a good vintage, from what they tell me. I wouldn't be one bit sorry about it. You've found an inexhaustible remedy against all thirsts.[3] That's mighty fine work. You, your wives, children, relatives, and families, are in the health you wish? That's nice going. That's good. I like that. God, the good God, be eternally praised for it, and (if such is His holy will) may you be long maintained in it.

As for me, by His holy benignity I'm the same way, and I commend myself to Him.[4] I am, thanks to a little Pantagruelism (you understand that that's a certain gayety of spirit confected in disdain for fortuitous things), healthy and sprightly, ready to drink, if you wish. Do you ask me why, good folk? Irrevocable answer: such is the will of the very good, very great God, in which I acquiesce, which I obey, whose sacrosanct word of good news I revere, that's the Gospel, in which it is said [Luke 4.23], with horrible sarcasm and biting derision, to a doctor negligent of his own health: "Physician, heal thyself!"

Cl. Galen maintained himself in health not for such reverence, although he had some feeling for the Holy Bible and had known and frequented the holy Christians of his time, as appears from Book 2, *De differentiis pulsuum,* chapter 3, and ibid., Book 3, chapter 2; and the book *De rerum affectibus* (if it is by Galen); but for fear of falling prey to this vulgar and satiric mockery:[5]

'Ιητρος ἄλλων, αὐτὸς ἕλχεσι βρύων.

Although he treats others to good effect,
His running sores attest his self-neglect.

So that with great bravado he boasts, and he doesn't want to be es-teemed a doctor unless, from his twenty-eighth year until his ripe old age, he has lived in full health, except for a few fevers lasting only a day or so, although he was not by nature one of the healthiest and had an unruly stomach. "For," he says, Book 5 of *De sanitate tuenda* [*On preserving health*] "a doctor will not easily be thought to take good care of the health of others who is neglectful of his own."

Vaunting himself with even more bravado was Asclepiades, a doctor, for having come to this pact with Fortune, that he should be reputed no doctor if he had ever been sick from the time he began to practice his craft until his final old age, which he reached whole, and vigorous in all his members, and triumphing over Fortune. Finally without any preced-ing illness, he made the exchange of life for death, by inadvertence in falling from atop some ill-mortised and rotted steps.

If by some disaster Health has emancipated herself from your lordships, above, beneath, to the right, to the left, within, without, far from your territories or near them, wherever she may be, may you, with the help of the blessed Savior, promptly come upon her! Fortunately come upon by you, may she be affirmed on the spot, claimed, seized, repossessed, and taken back by you! The laws allow you this, the king intends it, I advise it; no more nor less than the ancient legislators authorized the lord to claim his fugitive serf wherever he was found. 'Odsbodikins![6] Isn't it written and practiced, by the ancient customs of this most noble, most ancient, most beautiful, most flourishing, most rich kingdom of France, that the dead man seizes the quick?[7] See what was recently expounded about it by the good, learned, wise, most humane, most kind and equi-table André Tiraqueau, counselor to the great, victorious, and triumphant King Henry, second of that name, in that most redoubtable Court of the Parlement de Paris. Health is our life, as Ariphron of Sicyon very well declared [comme très bien déclare]. Without health life is not life, life is not livable: ἄβιος βίος, βιος ἀβίωτος [Aristrophanes *Plutus* 969]. Without health life is nothing but languor; life is but the simulacrum of death. So then you, when deprived of health (that is to say dead), seize the quick, seize life, that is, death.

I have this hope in God, that He will hear our prayer, seeing the firm faith in which we offer them, and will fulfill this wish of ours, seeing that it is moderate. Moderation was called golden by the ancient sages, that is to say precious, praised by all, in all places agreable. Run through the Holy Bible, you will find that never have the prayers been denied of those who asked for moderate things. An example of it is little Zacchaeus, whose body and relics the Musafis of Saint-Ayl near Orléans boast of having, and they call him Saint Sylvanus. He wanted, and nothing more, to see our blessed Savior near Jerusalem. That was a moderate thing and available to everyone. But he was too small, and amid the throng he could not. He hops up and down, he trots to and fro, he strains; he goes off; he climbs a sycamore tree. The all-good God recognized his sincere and moderate desire, appeared to his sight, and not only was seen but heard by him, visited his house, and blessed his family.

A son of a prophet in Israel splitting wood near the river Jordan, had the head of his axe slip off (as is written in 4, Reg. 6) [i.e., II Kings 6.1–7], and it fell into this river. He prayed God to be willing to return it to him. This is a moderate thing; and in firm faith and confidence he threw in, not the head after the handle, as the censorious devils say in a scandalous solecism, but the handle after the head, as you properly say. Promptly two miracles appeared. The axe-head rose out of the depths of the water and it fitted itself onto the handle. If he had made a wish to rise up to the heavens in a flaming chariot like Elisha, to multiply in lineage like Abraham, to be as rich as Job, as strong as Samson, as handsome as Absalom, would he have gotten it? This is a question.

Speaking of moderate wishes in the matter of hatches (have an eye to when it's time to drink), I'll tell you what is written in the Fables of Aesop the Frenchman, I mean Phrygian and Trojan, as Max. Planudes affirms, from which people, according to the most faithful chroniclers, are descended the noble French.[8] Aelian writes that he was a Thracian; Agathias, after Herodotus, that he was a Samian; it's all one to me.

In his time there was a poor villager, born in Gravot, named Couillatris,[9] a feller of trees and splitter of wood, and in this low estate, after a fashion, earning his poor living. It came to pass that he lost his hatchet. Who do you suppose was mighty vexed and unhappy? He was, for on his hatchet depended his welfare and his life; by his hatchet he lived in honor and repute among all well-to-do woodchoppers; without a hatchet he would have died of hunger. Six days later, death, finding him without a hatchet, would have reaped and weeded him out of this world.

427

In this plight he began to cry out, implore, invoke Jupiter by very eloquent prayers (as you know, Necessity was the inventor of Eloquence), raising his face toward the heavens, knee on the ground, head bare, hands high in the air, fingers spread, in every refrain of his prayers saying indefatigably in a loud voice:

"My hatchet, Jupiter! My hatchet, my hatchet! nothing more, O Jupiter, than my hachet! or pennies to buy another! Alas, my poor hatchet!"

Jupiter was holding a council on certain urgent matters, and just then old Cybele, or else bright young Phoebus, was giving an opinion. But so loud was Couillatris's outcry that it was heard as a great racket in the full council and consistory of the gods. "What devil," asked Jupiter, "is that down there howling so horrifically? By the powers of the Styx, haven't we been, aren't we still, troubled enough with more important and disputed matters? We've settled the dispute between Prester John, king of the Persians, and Sultan Sulayman, emperor of Constantinople. We've closed the split between the Tartars and the Muscovites. We've responded to the request of the sheriff. So have we to the prayer of Guolgotz Rays. The status of Parma is settled.[10] So is that of Magdeburg, Mirandola, and Africa (so mortals call the place on the Mediterranean that we call Aphrodisium).[11] By careless guarding Tripoli has changed masters; its time had come.[12] Here are the Gascons repenting [or swearing: *renians*] and asking for the restoration of their bells.[13]

In this corner are the Saxons, Easterlings, Ostrogoths, and Germans, peoples once invincible, now *aberkeids* [German, "villified"], and subjugated by a little man all crippled [Charles V].[14] They're asking us for vengeance, help, restitution of their original good sense and liberty. But what shall we do with this Ramus and this Galland, who, swathed in their scullions, hangers-on, and toadies, are stirring up this entire Academy of Paris? I'm in great perplexity about it and still haven't decided which way I should lean. Both seem to me in other respects good fellows and well-hung [bons compaignons et bien couilluz]. One has sun-crowns, I mean fair and weighty [je diz beaulz et tresbuchans]; the other would very much like to have some. One has some learning; the other is not ignorant. One is a shrewd sly fox; the other a slanderer with tongue and pen, yapping against the ancient philosophers, like a dog. How does it seem to you, you great donkey-prick Priapus? I have often found your counsel equitable and pertinent: "et habet tua mentula mentem [And your penis has a mind]."[15]

"King Jupiter," said Priapus, unwrapping his hood, his head raised, flaming and assured, "since the one you compare to a barking dog, the other to a shrewd sly fox, my advice is that without vexing or troubling yourself further you do with them what you once did with a dog and a fox."

"What?" asked Jupiter. "When? Who were they? Where was this?"

"O what a great memory!" replied Priapus. "This venerable father Bacchus that you see there with his crimson face, to revenge himself on the Thebans, had made a fox enchanted [un renard fée] in such a way that whatever harm or damage he did, he would not be caught or hurt by any other animal in the world. That noble Vulcan wrought a dog of Monesian brass, and by dint of hard breathing made him alive and animate. He gave him to you; you gave him to your cutie Europa; she gave him to Minos; Minos, to Procris, finally Procris gave him to Cephalus. He was likewise enchanted: in such a way that, like today's advocate, he would catch every animal he met; nothing would escape him. It came about that they met. What did they do? The dog by his fated destiny was bound to catch the fox; the fox by his destiny was bound not to be caught.

"The case was reported to your council. You protested that you would not contravene the destinies. The destinies were contradictory. The truth, the end, the result of two contradictories was declared by nature impossible. You sweated with strain from it. From your sweat falling on the ground there sprang up round-headed cabbage [les choux cabutz]. All that noble consistory, for lack of a clear-cut resolution, incurred wondrous thirst, and in that council was drunk up more than seventy-eight puncheons of nectar. On my advice you turned them both to stones. Immediately you were out of all perplexity; immediately a truce on thirst was proclaimed atop this great Olympus. This was the year of the soft ballocks,[16] near Teumesse, between Thebes and Chalcis.

"On this model, my advice is that you petrify this dog and fox; the metamorphosis is not unknown. They both bear the name Peter,[17] and because, according to the Limousins' proverb, three stones are needed to make the mouth of an oven,[18] you will associate them with Master Pierre du Coignet,[19] once petrified by you for the same causes. And these three dead stones will be placed, in the form of an equilateral triangle, in the middle of the porch of the great temple of Paris, with the function of putting out with their noses, as in the game of Fouquet,[20] lighted candles, torches, tapers, and flares; they who when alive ballockwise lit the fire of faction, enmity, ballockish sects, and partisanship among the idle schoolboys, in perpetual remembrance that in your eyes these little ballock-shaped egos [philauties couillonniformes] were rather contemned than condemned. I have spoken."

"You're favoring them," said Jupiter, "from what I see, fair Messer Priapus. You are not that favorable to all. For, seeing that they crave to perpetuate their names and memory, for them it would be much better to be thus converted after life into marble stones than into rot and earth. Behind here, toward that Tyrrhenian Sea and the places around the Apennines, you see the tragedies that are being aroused by certain pastophores? This madness will last its time, like Limoges ovens, then will end but not soon. We'll have much sport from it. I see one drawback: that we have a scant supply of lightning bolts since the time when you fellow gods of mine, by my special permission, kept throwing them unstintingly, for your sport, on the new Antioch.[21] Since then, following your example, the foppish champions who undertook to guard the fortress of Dindenarois against all comers used up all their ammunition in shooting at *moineaux*;[22] they did not have the wherewithal in time of need to defend themselves, and valiantly gave up the place and surrendered to the enemy, who were already raising their siege as utterly crazy and hopeless, and had no more urgent thought than their own retreat, with only utter shame for company. See to this matter, son Vulcan! waken your sleeping Cyclope, Asteropes, Brontes, Arges, Polyphemus, Steropes, Pyracmon! Set them to work and have them drink their fill. O workers with fire you must never spare the wine. Now let's take care of that howler down there. Mercury, see who it is and find out what he's asking for."

Mercury looks out the trapdoor of heaven, by which they listen to what people are saying down here on earth; and it really looks like a ship's scuttle (Icaroménippe used to say it looks like the mouth of a well [à la gueule d'un puiz]); and he sees that it's Couillatris asking for his lost hatchet, and reports this to the council. "Really," says Jupiter, "we're in fine shape! At this time we have nothing to do but give back lost hatchets? Yet give it back to him we must: that is written in the book of Destinies, do you understand? Just as well as if it were the Duchy of Milan. Indeed, his hatchet is to him in just such pride and esteem as to a king his kingdom would be. Here now, here now, have this hatchet returned to him! Let's have no more talk about it. Let's resolve the quarrel between the clergy and the mole-catchery of Landerousse. Where were we?"

Priapus remained standing in the chimney corner. On hearing Mercury's report, he said in all courtesy and jovial seemliness:

"King Jupiter, in the time when, by your order and particular benefice, I was guardian of the gardens on earth, I noted that the term *coignée* [modern *cognée*] is ambiguous, meaning several things. It means (or of old it meant) the female fully ripe and frequently copiocopulated [gimbretiletolletée]; and I saw what each good fellow called his merry girlfriend *ma coignée*. For with this naked steel (this he said exhibiting his half-cubit knocker) they knock up their eyeholes [leurs emmanchouoirs] so fiercely that these girls remain exempt from a fear endemic among the female sex, that these [eye-holes], for lack of clamps, may fall out of their belly down into their heels. And I remember (for I have a mentula, or rather I mean a memory) quite fair and big enough to fill a butter-pot), one day long ago, during the Tubilustria, at the festival of that good Vulcan in May, hearing Josquin des Prez, Olkeghem, Obrecht, Agricola, Brumel, Camelin, Vigoris, La Fage, Bruyer, Prioris, Seguin, De la Rue, Midy, Moulu, Mouton, Gascogne, Loyset, Compère, Penet, Fevin, Rouzée, Richardfort, Rousseau, Conseil, Costanzo Festa, Jacques Berchem, singing melodiously:

> When Big Tibault a newlywed,
> Wanting to make love to his bride,
> Brought along with him into bed
> A battle-axe he sought to hide,
> "O my sweet love," his lady cried,
> "What is that axe for that I see?"
> "That is to split you with," said he.
> "An axe?" said she; "there is no need:
> When Big John comes to work on me,
> With just his ass he does the deed."[23]

"Nine Olympiads and one intercalary year (O lovely mentula, or rather memory! I often commit a solecism in the concurrence and connection between these two words), I heard Adrien Willaert, Gombert, Jannequin, Arcadelt, Claudin, Certon, Manchicourt, Auxerre, Villiers, Sandrin, Sohier, Hesdin, Morales, Passereau, Maille, Maillart, Jacotin, Heurteur, Verdelot, Carpentras, Lhéritier, Cadéac, Doublet, Vermont, Bouteiller, Lupi, Pagnier, Millet, du Moulin, Alaire, Marault, Morpain, Gendre, and other joyous musicians in a private garden, under a lovely arbor, surrounding a rampart of flagons, hams, pasties, and divers well-coiffed chicks, charmingly singing:

If it is true an axe-head is no use
Without a haft, a tool unless it's gripped,
So I may fit you well and not come loose,
Let me be the handle, and you shall be clipped.[24]

"Now we still need to know which sort of *coingnée* this howler Couillatris is asking for."

At these words all the venerable gods and goddesses burst out laughing like a microcosm of flies.[25] Vulcan, with his crookshank, for love of his lady-friend, did three or four nice little platform jumps.[26]

"Here now, here now," said Jupiter to Mercury, "go down there right now, and throw at Couillatris's feet three hatchets, massive, all of the same caliber: his own, another of gold, a third of silver. If he takes his own and is content with it, give him the two others. If he takes one other than his own, cut off his head with his own. And from now on do thus with all these hatchet-losers."

These words completed, Jupiter, swiveling his head around like a monkey swallowing pills made such a frightful grimace that all great Olympus trembled.

Mercury, with his pointed cap, his flat round hat, his heel-wings, and his caducée [staff or wand],[27] casts himself out the trapdoor of the heavens, cleaves the empty air, alights gently on earth, throws the three hatchets at Couillatris's feet, then says to him: "You've yelled long enough to have a drink. Your prayers are answered by Jupiter. Take a look, see which of these is your hatchet, and take it away." Couillatris hefts the golden hatchet, looks at it, and finds it very heavy; then says to Mercury: "I swan,[28] this one sure ain't mine. I don't want any part of it." He does as much with the silver hatchet, and says to him: "It's not this one: this is all yours." Then he takes in his hand the wooden one; he looks at the handle, and thereon recognizes his mark; and, all trembling with joy like a fox on encountering some stray chickens, with his face all wreathed in smiles, he says: "Turd of God![29] This one was mine! If you'll let me have it, I'll sacrifice to you a fine big pot of milk all covered with strawberries on the Ides (that's the fifteenth day) of May." "Good man," said Mercury, "I leave it to you, take it. And because you wished for and chose moderation in the matter of hatchets, by the will of Jupiter I give you these two others. You have enough to make you rich from now on; be a good man."

Couillatris courteously thanks Mercury, reveres great Jupiter, fastens his old hatchet onto his leather belt, and girds it over his tail like Martin of Cambria. The two other, heavier ones, he loads over his neck. Thus he goes galumphing[30] around the countryside, beaming at his neighbors and fellow parishioners, and asking Pathelin's little question: "Do I ever have some?"[31] The next day, wearing a clean white jacket, he loads onto his back the two precious hatchets, betakes himself to Chinon, a notable, ancient town, indeed the first in the world, according to the judgment of the most learned Massoretes. In Chinon he exchanges his silver hatchet for fair testoons and other white [silver] coins; his gold hatchet for lovely angel crowns, long-wooled sheep, fair Agnus Dei crowns, fine Dutch ritters, handsome royals, nice sun-crowns. With them he buys many summer houses, barns, meadows, vineyards, woods, arable pastures, ponds, mills, gardens, willow groves; oxen, cows, ewes, sheep, nannygoats, sows, hogs, donkeys, horses, hens, roosters, capons, chickens, geese, ganders, drakes, ducks, and small fowl. In a short time he was the richest man in the region, even more so than lame Maulévrier.

The "francs gontiers et Jacques Bonshoms" [merry lads and yokels] of the neighborhood, seeing this lucky strike [ceste heureuse rencontre] of Couillatris's, were quite flabbergasted; and in their spirits the pity and commiseration in which earlier they had held Couillatris were changed to envy of such great and unexpected riches of his. And they began to run about, inquire, and pry, to find out by what means, in what place, on what day, at what time, apropos of what, this great treasure had come to him. On hearing that it was by having lost his hatchet, "ho ho ho!" said they, "was the loss of a hatchet all it took for us to be rich? That's an easy way and costs little. And so at the present moment is the revolution of the heavens, the constellation of the stars, such that whoever loses a hatchet will thus immediately get rich? Ho, ho, ha! By God, hatchet, you shall be lost, and no offense."

Thereupon they all lost their hatchets. Devil take the one who had a hatchet left! There was no son of a good mother who did not lose his hatchet. No more wood was felled in the region, for lack of hatchets.

The Aesopic fable says that certain little no-account Jumblemen [Janspill'hommes], who had sold Couillatris the little meadow and the little mill so as to show off better at the periodic review, when informed that this treasure had come to him thus and by this means alone, sold their swords in order to buy hatchets, so as to lose them. You would naturally have supposed that they were Romipètes, selling what was theirs, borrowing from others, in order to buy *mandamuse* [indulgences] from a newly chosen pope. And yelling, and praying, and lamenting, and invoking Jupiter: "My hatchet, my hatchet, Jupiter! My hatchet here, my hatchet there, my hatchet, ho, ho, ho, ho! Jupiter, my hatchet!" All around, the air resounded with the cries and howls of these hatchet-losers.

Mercury was quick to bring the hatchets, offering to each one his own lost one, another of gold, and a third of silver. All chose the gold one and picked it up, thanking the great giver Jupiter; but at the moment when they lifted it off the ground, while bowed and bent over, Mercury cut off their head according to the edict of Jupiter. And the number of heads cut off was equal and corresponding to (that of) the hatchets lost.

That's the way it is, that's what happens to those who in simplicity wish for moderate things [choses médiocres]. Take this as an example, you lowland wiseacres [gualliers de plat pays], who say that not for ten thousand francs a year would you give up your wishes; and henceforth don't talk so impudently, as I've sometimes heard you wishing: "Would God I had right now a hundred and seventy-eight millions in gold! O, how I'd triumph!" A bad case of chilblains to you! What more would a king, an emperor, a pope want?

And so you see by experience that when you've made such excessive wishes, you get nothing but the ague and the scab, and not a penny for your purse; any more than those two beggars, Paris-style wishers, one of whom wished to have as much in sun-crowns as has been spent, bought, and sold in Paris from the time they laid the first foundations to build it right down to the present time; the entire amount estimated at the rate, sale, and value of the dearest year that has passed in that space of time. Had this man lost his appetite, do you think? Had he eaten sour plums without peeling them? Were his teeth set on edge?[32] The other one wanted the temple of Notre-Dame to be filled chock-full of steel-tipped needles from the floor to the topmost point of the vaults, and to have as many sun-crowns as could be put in as many sacks as could be sewn with each and every needle, until they were all broken or blunted. That's a wish for you, that is! What do you think of it? What came of it? That evening each one of them had chilblains on his heels,

> A sore where chin and jawbone met,
> A cough that wheezing lungs repeat,
> Catarrh in throat, and, to complete
> The mess, a boil upon the seat.

And the devil with the old hunk of bread to scour your teeth with![33]

So wish for a moderate lot: it will come to you, and all the better, meanwhile toiling and working.[34]

"All right," you say, "but God might just as well have given me seventy-eight thousand as the thirteenth part of a half, for He is almighty: a million in gold is as little to him as an obol." Heydeho! And who taught you to discourse this way and talk about the power and predestination of God, you poor folk? Peace! Sh, sh, sh! humble yourselves before His holy face, and recognize your imperfections."

That, gouties is what I base my hope on, and I firmly believe that, if the good God please, you will obtain health. Wait a little longer, with half an ounce of patience. Thus the Genoese do not do when in the morning, in their offices and counting-houses, having gone over, planned, and decided from whom and what sort of folk they can extract money that day, and who by their wiles shall be fleeced, rooked, tricked, and cheated, they go out in public, and in greeting one another say *Sanita et guadain, messer.*[35] They do not rest content with health; much more, they wish for gain, indeed the gold crowns of Guadaigne.[36] Wherefore it often comes about that they get neither one. Now, in good health cough one good cough, drink three drinks, give your ears a cheery shake, and you shall hear wonders about the good and noble Pantagruel.

CHAPTER 1

*How Pantagruel put out to sea
to visit the oracle of the divine Bacbuc.*

In the month of June, on the day of the Vestalia festival, the very one on which Brutus conquered Spain and subjugated the Spaniards, on which also the miserly Crassus was defeated and crushed by the Parthians, Pantagruel, taking leave of his father the good Gargantua, while he [Gargantua] earnestly prayed (as was the laudable custom among the saintly Christians of the primitive Church), for a prosperous voyage for his son and all his company, put to sea at the port of Thalasse, accompanied by Panurge, Frère Jean des Entommeures, Epistémon, Gymnaste, Eusthenes, Rhizotome, Carpalim, and others of his old servants and domestics; also by Xenomanes, the great traveler across perilous routes, who had arrived some days before at Panurge's command. This man, for good and sure reasons had mapped out and left for Gargantua, in his great universal hydrography, the route they would take in visiting the oracle of the divine bottle Bacbuc.

The number of ships was such as I exposed to you in the Third Book, with a convoy of triremes, long barges, galleons, and Libernian galleys [feluccas], of the same number, well equipped, well calked, well provisioned, with an abundance of Pantagruelion. The assembly of all the officers, interpreters, pilots, captains, seamen, mate-oarsmen, and sailors, was held on the Thalamège. Thus was named Pantagruel's great flagship, which had on its stern as an ensign a great ample bottle, half of smooth polished silver, the other half of gold enameled in flesh color. Whereby it was easy to judge that white and claret were the colors of the noble travelers and that they were going in order to get the word of the Bottle.

On the stern of the second ship was raised aloft an antiquated lantern, meticulously wrought of transparent and reflecting stone, signifying that they would pass Lanternland.

437

The third had as its device a fine deep porcelain tankard.

The fourth, a two-handled gold pot, as if it was an antique urn.

The fifth, a notable flagon made of coarse emerald.

The sixth, a huge monkish horn-shaped drinking mug made of the four metals together.

The seventh, an ebony funnel all embossed and encrusted with gold.

The eighth, a very precious ivy goblet gold-beaten damascene style.

The ninth, a toasting-glass of fine tried gold.

The tenth, a drinking cup of fragrant *Agalloche* (you call it aloe wood), laced with Cypriot gold, azzimino work.

The eleventh, a grape vat of mosaic work.

The twelfth, a firkin of pale gold covered with a little vine of great Indian pearls, topiary work.

So that there was no one, however sad, vexed, sullen, or melancholy he might be, indeed not even weeping Heraclitus were he here, who would not have rejoiced afresh and smiled in good humor, seeing this noble convoy of ships with their devices, and would not have judged as a sure prognostic that the trip, both going and returning, would be completed in blitheness and health.

So in the Thalamège was held the assembly of all. There Pantagruel made them a short holy exhortation, all supported with passages drawn from the Holy Scripture, on the subject of navigation. With that finished, prayers were said loud and clear to God, heard and understood by all the burghers and citizens of Thalasse, who had come flocking up to the pier to watch the embarkation.

After the prayer, there was a melodious singing of the psalm of the holy King David that begins: "When Israel came out of Egypt."[1] When the psalm was finished, tables were set up on the bridge and the food brought out promptly. The Thalassians, who had also sung the aforesaid psalm, had many victuals and winery brought. All drank to them. They drank to all. That was the reason why no one in the assembly threw up when at sea or had any disturbance in stomach or head. Which troubles would not have been obviated so conveniently by drinking sea water for a few days beforehand, either pure or mixed with wine; or by using the flesh of quinces, or lemon peel, or juice of bittersweet pomegranates; or keeping on a long diet; or by covering their stomach with paper; or doing what foolish doctors prescribe for them for going to sea.

When their nips had been repeated, each man went back to his ship; and at a good time they set sail to a Greek easterly wind, according to which their fleet admiral [pilot principal], James Brayer by name, had mapped out the route and set the needles of the compasses. For his advice, and that of Xenomanes as well, seeing that the oracle of the divine Bacbuc was near Cathay, in upper India, was not to take the ordinary route of the Portuguese, who, crossing the Torrid Zone and rounding the Cape of Good Hope on the southern tip of Africa, beyond the Equinoctial [the Equator], and losing the sight and guidance of the Pole Star [North Star], make an enormous trip; but to follow as closely as possible the parallel of the said India, and turn about the said pole to the westward, so that winding under the North [Star], they should have it at the same elevation as at the port of Olonne, without coming any nearer to it for fear of entering and being caught in the Glacial [Arctic] Sea.

And following this canonical way around the same parallel, they would have it on the right, toward the Orient, which at their departure was on their left. This turned out to their inestimable advantage, for without shipwreck, without danger, with no loss of their men, in great serenity (except for one day near the island of the Macraeons), they made the trip to Upper India in less than four months, which the Portuguese would hardly make in three years with myriad troubles and countless dangers. And I am of the opinion, subject to better judgment, that such a route was followed by those Indians who sailed into Germany and were honorably treated by the king of the Swedes, in the time when Q. Metellus Celer was proconsul in Gaul, as is described by Cor. Nepos, Pomp. Mela, and after them Pliny.

CHAPTER 2

*How on the island of Medamothi
Pantagruel bought several beautiful things.*

THAT day and the next two there appeared to them[1] no land or any other thing. For once before they had covered this route. On the fourth, they sighted an island named Medamothi, fair to the eye and attractive because of the large number of lighthouses and high marble towers that adorned its whole circumference, which was no less great than that of Canada.

Pantagruel, inquiring who was its ruler, learned that it was King Philophanes, then absent for the marriage of his brother Philotheamon to the Infanta of the kingdom of Engys. Thereupon he disembarked at the harbor, contemplating, while the ship's crew had a stop for water, divers pictures, divers tapestries, divers animals, fish, birds, and other exotic objects for sale, which were on the road to the pier and in the open markets of the harbor. For it was the third day of the place's great solemn fairs, to which each year came the richest and most famous merchants of Africa and Asia. Among these (objects for sale) Frère Jean bought two precious rare pictures, on one of which was portrayed to the life the face of an appellant; on the other was the portrait of a valet in search of a master, in all the required qualities, gestures, demeanor, expression, ways of moving, physiognomy, and emotions, painted and imagined by Master Charles Charmois, painter to King Mégiste; and he paid for them in monkey coin.

Panurge bought a big picture copied from the needlework done long ago by Philomela, exposing and representing to her sister Procne how her brother-in-law Tereus had deflowered her and cut out her tongue so that she could not reveal such a crime. I swear to you, by the handle of this lantern, that it was a goodly wondrous painting! Don't suppose, I beg you, that it was a picture of a man coupled upon a girl. That would be too stupid and too crude. The picture was quite different and more intelligible. You can see it at Thélème, on the left hand as you enter the high gallery.

Epistémon bought another one, on which were portrayed to the life Plato's Ideas and Epicurus's Atoms. Rhizotome bought another, showing Echo in her natural form.

Pantagruel had Gymnaste buy him the life and deeds of Achilles in seventy-eight pieces of top-quality tapestry, four fathoms long and three wide 24' x 18', all of Phrygian silk, embroidered in gold and silver. And the tapestries started with the wedding of Peleus and Thetis, continuing with the birth of Achilles, his youth as described by Statius Papinius, his deeds and exploits as celebrated by Homer, his death and funeral as described by Ovid and Quintus Calaber; finishing with the apparition of his shade and the sacrifice of Polyxena, as described by Euripides.

He also had him buy three handsome young unicorns: one male, with a coat of burnt sorrel, and two females with dappled gray coats. Also a tarande, sold him by a Scythian from the land of the Geloni.

A tarande is an animal the size of a young bull, with a head like a stag's, a bit bigger, with remarkable horns, broadly branched; its feet forked; its coat as long as a great bear's; its hide a little less hard than the body of a cuirass. And the Gelonia said there were few of them found in Scythia, because it changes color according to the variety of places where it feeds and stays. And it takes on the color of the plants, trees, shrubs, flowers, places, meadows, rocks, and generally everything it comes near. It has this in common with the marine polyp; with the thoës; with the Lycaons of India; with the chameleon, which is a kind of lizard so wonderful that Democritus composed a whole book about its figure, anatomy, powers and properties in magic. The fact is that I have seen it change color, not merely at the approach of colored things, but of itself according to the fear or emotions it felt: as, on a green rug, I have seen it turn green; but also, on remaining there for a certain length of time, turn yellow, blue, tawny, violet, in succession; as you see the crests of turkey cocks change color according to their feelings. What we found especially wonderful in this tarande was that not only his head and his skin but equally his hair changed according to the color of the things around it. Next to Panurge dressed in his dun-color toga his coat turned gray; next to Pantagruel clad in his scarlet cloak, his coat and skin turned red; next to the admiral clad in the fashion of the Isiacs of Anubis in Egypt it appeared all white. These last two colors are denied to the chameleon. When he was in his natural state, free of any fear or emotions, his coat was such as you see on the donkeys of Meung.

CHAPTER 3

How Pantagruel
received a letter from his father Gargantua
and of a strange way of getting news very promptly
from distant foreign countries.

As Pantagruel was busy with the purchase of these exotic animals, there were heard from the pier ten salvos of small culverins and falcons, and with these a joyful acclamation from all the ships. Pantagruel turns toward the harbor and sees that it is one of the *celoces* [BD: vessels light upon the sea] of his father Gargantua, named the Chelidon because on the stern was a sculpture in Corinthian brass of a sea swallow aloft. This is a fish the size of a Loire dace, quite fleshy, without scales, with cartilaginous wings (as on bats), very long and wide, by means of which I've often seen it fly further than a bowshot one fathom above the water. In Marseille they call it a *lendole*.

Likewise this vessel was as light as a swallow, so that it seemed to fly rather than to sail over the sea. Therein was Malicorne,[1] Gargantua's carver squire, sent by him expressly to learn through him of the state and condition of the good Pantagruel and to bring him a letter of credit.

Pantagruel, after a gracious salutation and a little embrace, before opening the letter or having any other talk with Malicorne, asked him:

"Do you have here the gozal [BD: in Hebrew, pigeon, dove], the celestial messenger?"

"Yes," he replied, "it's wrapped up inside this basket."

It was a pigeon from Gargantua's pigeon-house, who had just been hatching her young the moment the aforesaid *celoce* was leaving. If adverse fortune had befallen Pantagruel, she would now have had black jesses placed onto her feet; but because everything had come out well and prosperously, he fastened onto her feet a little ribbon of white taffeta, and, without further delay left her the full freedom of the air. Instantly the pigeon takes flight, cleaving the air with incredible speed; as you know, there is no flight like a pigeon's when it has eggs or young, because of the obstinate concern planted in it by nature to hurry back and succor its pigeon young. So that in less than two hours it crossed by air the long route that the *celoce,* rowing and at full sail, covered in three days and three nights by extreme diligence and with a continuous stern wind. And she was seen entering the pigeon-house and going to the very nest of her offspring. Thereupon, when the valiant Gargantua heard that she was bearing the white ribbon, he was left in joy and security about the well-being of his son.

This was the practice of the noble Gargantua and Pantagruel whenever they wanted to have news promptly of some matter that greatly concerned them and that they eagerly desired, like the outcome of some great battle on sea or land, the capture or defense of some stronghold, the settlement of some important disputes, or the happy or unfortunate delivery of some queen or great lady, the death or convalescence of sick friends and allies of theirs, and other such matters. They would take the gozal by post, have it carried from hand to hand right up to the places of which they wanted to have news. The gozal, wearing a black or white ribbon depending on the happenings and occurrences, would free them from anxious thoughts on her return, covering more distance by air in one hour than thirty posts had done by land in one normal day. That was to recover and gain time. And believe me as something plausible that throughout the dovecotes of their country houses, every month and season of the year, they found pigeons aplenty upon their eggs or young, which is very easy to arrange in husbandry, with the help of rock saltpeter and the sacred verbena plant.

When the gozal was loosed, Pantagruel read the letter from his father Gargantua, the tenor of which follows:

"My very dear son, the affection a father naturally has for his well-beloved son is in my case so greatly accrued by consideration and reverence for the particular graces placed in you by divine choice, that since you left no other thought has at any time displaced it, thus leaving in my heart this sole anxious fear that your sailing may have been attended by some unhappy blow or trouble: as you know, fear is always attached to a good sincere love. And because, as Hesiod says,[2] the beginning of each and every thing is half the whole, and, according to the common proverb, it's the putting in the oven that gives loaves their crusts,[3] to rid my mind of such anxiety, I've sent Malicorne expressly so that I may be assured of how your health is on these the first days of your voyage. For if it is prospering and such as I wish it to be, it will be easy for me to foresee, prognosticate, and judge of the rest.

"I have got a few books which by the present bearer will be given to you. You will read them when you want a refresher on your best studies. The said bearer will tell you more amply all the news of this court. The peace of the Eternal be with you. Greetings to Panurge, Frère Jean, Epistémon, Xenomanes, Gymnaste, and my good friends your other familiars. From your paternal home, this thirteenth of June.[4]

GARGANTUA."

CHAPTER 4

*How Pantagruel writes to his father Gargantua
and sends him several rare and beautiful things.*

Aᴛᴛᴇʀ reading the aforesaid letter, Pantagruel talked with Squire Malicorne about several matters, and was with him so long that Panurge interrupted and said:

"So when are you going to drink? When are we going to drink? When is My Lord the Squire going to drink? Isn't this enough preaching for a drink?"

"Well said," said Pantagruel. "Have a collation made ready at the nearest inn, the one with the hanging sign that shows the picture of a satyr on horseback."

Meanwhile, to dispatch the squire, he wrote to Gargantua as follows:

"Most kindly father, since of all accidents of this transitory life that are not anticipated or suspected, our senses and animal faculties undergo more enormous and helpless disturbances (even to the point of having our soul thereby separated from our body, even though such sudden news should be for our desire and contentment) than if they had been predicted and foreseen in advance, even so I was greatly moved and perturbed by the unexpected arrival of your squire Malicorne. For I had no hope of seeing any of your familiars or hearing any news from you before the end of this voyage of ours. And I was readily contenting myself with the sweet recollection of your august majesty, inscribed, indeed rather sculpted and engraved, on the hindmost lobe of my brain,[1] often representing it to me to the life in its own natural form.

"But since you have got ahead of me by the beneficence of your gracious letter, and by your squire's message, restored my spirits with news of your prosperity and health, also that of your whole royal house, I am forced to do what in the past was voluntary. First to praise the blessed Savior, Who by His divine goodness keeps you in this long stretch of perfect health; secondly, to thank you eternally for that fervent and inveterate affection that you bear me, your very humble son and unprofitable servant.

"In olden times a Roman named Furnius said to Caesar Augustus, on his receiving into grace and favor his [Furnius's father], who had followed Antony's party: 'By granting me this boon today, you have reduced me to such ignominy that all my life I shall be reputed an ingrate for the impotence of my gratitude.'[2] Even so I say to you that the excess of your paternal affection reduces me to the straits and plight of having to live and die an ingrate. Unless I am acquitted of such a crime by the dictum of the Stoics, who used to say that there were three parts in a good turn: one, of the giver; another, of the receiver; the third, of the recompenser; and that the receiver recompenses the giver very well when he willingly accepts the good turn and retains it in his memory forever; even as, on the contrary, the receiver would be the worst ingrate in the world who should despise and forget a good turn.

"So being oppressed by infinite obligations all created by your immense benignity, and incapable of even the tiniest share of recompense, I will at least save myself from calumny, in that the remembrance of them shall never be blotted from my memory; and my tongue will not cease to confess and protest that to render you condign thanks is something transcending my faculty and power.

"Moreover, I have this confidence in the commiseration and help of Our Lord, that the end of this peregrination of ours will correspond to the beginning, and the whole of it will be in perfect cheer and good health. I shall not fail to reduce to commentaries and logbooks the whole story of our navigation, so that on our return you may have a true account of it to read.

"I found here a tarande from Scythia, an animal strange and wonderful because of the variations in color of his skin and coat, according to the distinction between the surrounding things. You'll like him. He's as manageable and easy to train as a lamb. I'm also sending you three young unicorns, more tame and domesticated than three kittens would be. I've conferred with the squire and told him the way to treat them. They do not graze on the ground, the long horn on the forehead being in the way. They are forced to get their fodder on fruit trees or on suitable food racks, or fed by hand when you offer them plants, sheaves, apples, pears, barley, winter wheat, in short all kinds of fruits and vegetables. I'm amazed at how our ancient writers say that they are so wild, fierce, and dangerous, and have never been seen alive. If you see fit, you will make trial of the contrary; and you will find that in them lies the greatest gentleness in the world, provided they are not maliciously injured.

"Likewise I send you the life and deeds of Achilles on a very lovely and well-wrought tapestry. Assuring you that all the novelties in animals, plants, birds, and precious stones that I can find in this whole peregrination of ours I will bring to you, with the help of God our Savior, Whom I pray to keep you in His holy grace.

"From Medamothi, this fifteenth of June. Panurge, Frère Jean, Epistémon, Xenomanes, Gymnaste, Rhizotome, and Carpalim, after devoutly kissing your hand, return your greetings with hundredfold usury.

"Your humble son and servant,

PANTAGRUEL."

While Pantagruel was writing the aforesaid letter, Malicorne was feasted, greeted, and embraced by everyone many times over. Everything went well, Lord knows, and recommendations from all sides and messages were busily trotting about. Pantagruel, having finished his letter, banqueted with the squire. And he gave him a great gold chain weighing eight hundred crowns,[3] in which, by the septenary links, were set great diamonds, rubies, emeralds, turquoises, union pearls, in alternation. To each one of his seamen he had five hundred sun-crowns given; to his father Gargantua he sent the tarande, covered with a satin horse-blanket brocaded in gold, with the tapestry containing the deeds of Achilles, and the three unicorns, caparisoned in embroidered cloth of gold. Thus they left Medamothi: Malicorne to return to Gargantua, Pantagruel to continue on his voyage. On the high seas he had Epistémon read (aloud) the books brought by the squire. Of these, because he found them merry and entertaining, I'll gladly give you a transcription, if you ask me for it earnestly.

446

CHAPTER 5

How Pantagruel encountered a ship
with travelers returning from Lanternland.

On the fifth day, already beginning to circle little by little around the pole, moving away from the equinoctial line, we[1] sighted a merchant ship sailing toward us to port of us. There was no little joy, both on our part and on the merchants': on ours, to get news of the sea; on theirs, to get news of terra firma.

Coming up to them, we learned that they were Frenchmen from Saintonge. In talk and discussion with them, Pantagruel learned that they were coming from Lanternland. This further increased his joy, also that of the whole noble company, as we inquired especially about the state of the country and the ways of the Lanternese people, and learned that for the end of the forthcoming July was set the general chapter meeting of the Lanterns;[2] and they were making great preparations there, as if people were going to Lanternize very thoroughly there. We were told that, when we stopped at the great kingdom of Gebarim, we would be honorifically received and treated by King Ohabé, ruler of that land, who speaks Touraine French, as do all his subjects likewise.

While we were hearing these pieces of news, Panurge got into a dispute with a merchant from Taillebourg named Dindenault. The occasion of the dispute was this. This Dindenault, seeing Panurge without a codpiece with his eyeglasses attached to his bonnet said about him to his companions:

"That's a nice picture of a cuckold." Panurge, because of his eyeglasses, could hear with his ears much better than usual. So, hearing this remark, he said to the merchant: "How the devil would I be a cuckold, when I'm not married, as you are, as far as I can judge from that boorish snout of yours?"

"Yes," replied the merchant, "and I wouldn't *not* be for all the eyeglasses in Europe, not for all the spectacles in Africa. For I have one of the most beautiful, most decent, most modest women as my wife that there is in the whole region of Saintonge, no offense to the others. I'm bringing her back from my voyage as a homecoming present a handsome eleven-inch branch of red coral.[3] What's that to you? What busines is it of yours?

447

Who are you? Where are you from? O you four-eyed son of the Antichrist,[4] if you are on God's side, answer me!"

"I ask you this," said Panurge: "if by the consent and agreement of all the elements, I had sacksackshakeshookbingbangasspassed [sacsacbezevezinemassé] your ever so beautiful, ever so decent, ever so modest wife, to such effect that that stiff god of the gardens Priapus (who dwells here at liberty, subjection to codpieces being excluded) had remained stuck in her body so disastrously that it would never come out unless you pulled it out with your teeth, what would you do? Would you leave it there eternally? Or would you pull it out with both your teeth?[5] Answer me, you ram-monger to Mahomet, since you're on the side of all the devils."

"I'd hit you," replied the merchant, "a blow with the sword on that eyeglass-bearing ear, and kill you like a ram."

So saying, he was unsheathing his sword. But it stuck in the scabbard; for as you know, at sea all pieces of armor readily rust, because of the excessive nitrous humidity.[6] Panurge runs back toward Pantagruel for help. Frère Jean put his hand to his newly whetted cutlass and would have furiously killed the merchant, but that the ship's master and some other passengers besought Pantagruel that there would be no violence aboard his ship. So their dispute was patched up; and Panurge and the merchant shook hands on it and cordially drank each other's health as a sign of perfect reconciliation.

CHAPTER 6

How, with the dispute pacified,
Panurge bargains with Dindenault for one of his sheep.

WITH the dispute completely pacified, Panurge said in secret to Epistémon and Frère Jean:

"Stand back a bit and have a good time with what you're going to see. There will be fine sport if the line doesn't break."[1] Then he addressed the merchant and drank his health with a full drinking cup of good Lanternland wine. The merchant returned his pledge in all courtesy and civility. That done, Panurge begged him earnestly to sell him one of his sheep. The merchant answered him: "O my, O my, my friend, our neighbor, what a sharpie you are at cheating poor folk! You really are a nice customer! O what a valiant sheep buyer! Honest go Gosh [Vraybis]! You have the look not of a buyer of sheep but of a cutter of purses. Golly Nick, fellow [Deu Colas, faillon]! What fun it would be to have a full purse and be next to you in a tripe shop at the time of the thaw![2] Haw, haw, with anybody who didn't know you, you'd really take him to the cleaners. But hey, good folks, just see how he plays the history pundit![3]

"Patience!" said Panurge; "but by the way, as a special favor, sell me one of your sheep. How much?"

"What do you mean by that?" replied the merchant, "my friend, my neighbor? These are sheep with lots of wool.[4] That's where Jason got the Golden Fleece. The Order of the House of Burgundy was derived from them. Levantine sheep, pedigreed sheep, well-fatted sheep."

"So be it," said Panurge; "but please sell me one, and for good reason; I'll be paying you well and promptly in Western money, pedigreed and low in grease. How much?"

"Our neighbor, my friend," replied the dealer, "listen here a bit with the other ear."

PAN. At your command.

MERCH. You're going to Lanternland?

PAN. True.

MERCH. To see the world?

PAN. True.

MERCH. Merrily?

PAN. True.

MERCH. Your name I believe, is Robin Mutton?[5]

PAN. If you like.

MERCH. No hard feelings.

PAN. So I understand.

MERCH. You are, I believe, the King's Merryman.

PAN. All right.

MERCH. Shake on it! Ha ha! You're going to see the world, you're the King's Merryman, your name is Robin Mutton. See that sheep over there, his name is Robin, like you. Robin, Robin. Baa, baa, baa, baa. O what a beautiful voice!

PAN. Most beautiful and harmonious.

MERCH. Here's a pact we'll have between you and me, our neighbor and friend. You, who are Robin Mutton, shall be in this plate of the scale; my sheep Robin shall be in the other; I'll bet a hundred Buch[6] oysters that in weight, worth, and esteem he will send you up high and short, in the same shape in which some day you will be suspended and hanged.

"Patience. Easy," said Panurge. "But you would do a lot for me and for your posterity if you would sell me this one or else one from lower in your choir. I beg you to, Sir Sire."

"Our friend," replied the dealer, "my neighbor, of the fleece of these sheep will be made the fine cloths of Rouen; the skeins from the Leicester bales, compared to it, are nothing but tow. From the hide will be made handsome moroccos[7] that will be sold as moroccos from Turkey, from Montelimart, or at worst from Spain. From the bowels will be made strings for violins and harps,[8] which will be sold as dear as if they were strings from Munich or from Aquila. What do you think of that?"

"If you please," said Panurge, "you'll sell me one, I'll be very much indebted to the bolt of your front door.[9] Here's ready cash. How much?"

This he said displaying his wallet full of new Henricuses.[10]

CHAPTER 7

*Continuation of the bargaining
between Panurge and Dindenault.*

"My friend," replied the dealer, "our neighbor, this is meat only for kings and princes. The flesh is so delicate, so savory, and so tasty, that it is balm [tant friande, que c'est basme]. I bring them in from a country where hogs (God be with us!) eat nothing but myrobalan plums. The sows when they lie in (no dishonor to this entire company!)[1] are fed only on orange blossoms."

"But," said Panurge, "sell me one, and I'll pay for it like a king, word of a footsoldier.[2] How much?"

"Our friend," replied the dealer, "my neighbor, these are sheep drawn from the very line of the one that bore Phryxus and Helle over the sea named Hellespont."

"Plague take it [Cancre]!" said Panurge, "you are *clericus vel adiscens* [a cleric or a student]."

"Ita, that's cabbages," replied the dealer, "Vere, that's leeks. But rr. rrr. rrrr. rrrrr. Ho, Robin, rr. rrrrrr. You don't understand that language.

"By the way! all through all the fields where they piss, wheat springs up as if God had pissed there:[3] you don't need any other marl or manure. There is more. From their urine the Quintessentials derive the best salt-peter in the world. From their turds (begging your pardon) the doctors of our countries cure seventy-eight kinds of illnesses, the least of which is the evil of Saint Eutropius of Saintes, from which God save and preserve us. What do you think of that, our neighbor, my friend? And so they cost me good and plenty."

"Cost what they may," replied Panurge. "Just sell me one; I'll pay well for it."

"Our friend," said the dealer, "my neighbor, just consider for a bit the wonders of nature residing in these animals you see, even in a member that you would consider useless. Take me these horns, crush them quite a little with an iron pestle or an andiron, it's all one to me. Then bury them in sunlight wherever you will, and water them often. In a few months you will see spring up the best asparagus stalks in the world; I wouldn't even deign to except those of Ravenna. Just try telling me that the horns of you gentlemen the cuckolds have such virtue and such a mirific property."

"Patience!" said Panurge.

"I don't know," said the dealer, "if you're a cleric. I've seen lots of clerics, I mean great clerics, cuckolds. By the way, if you *were* a cleric, you'd know that in the lower parts of these divine animals there is a bone, the heel, that's the hucklebone if you like, with which, not with any other animal in the world except the Indian donkey and the Libyan roebuck, they used to play the royal game of *tali,* at which one evening the Emperor Octavian Augustus won more than 50,000 crowns. You cuckolds aren't likely to win that much!"

"Patience!" said Panurge. "But let's get moving."

"And when," said the dealer, "shall I, my friend, my neighbor, have praised condignly to you the inward parts? The shoulder, the haunches, the legs, the upper ribs, the breast, the liver, the spleen, the tripes, the bowels, the bladder, with which people play ball; the cutlets, with which in Pigmyland they make nice little bows for firing cherry pits at the cranes; the head, from which, with a little sulfur, is made a marvelous decoction to unclog dogs constipated in the belly?"

"Shit, shit," said the ship's master to the dealer, "that's too much haffling here. Sell to him if you want; if you don't, don't string him along any more."

"I'm willing to," said the dealer, "for your sake. But he'll pay three Tours livres to take his choice."

"That's a lot," said Panurge. "In our part of the country I'd get easily five or six for such a sum of deniers. Consider whether that may not be too much. You're not the first one I've known who, wanting to get rich and move up too quickly, has fallen over back into poverty, and sometimes has even broken his neck."

"A batch of tough quartan fevers to you!" retorted the dealer, "stupid nincompoop that you are! By the worthy relic at Charroux, the least of these sheep is worth four times more than the best of those that of old the Coraxians of Tuditania, a region in Spain, used to sell for one gold talent apiece. And what, you goldbricking dumb underling, do you suppose one talent was worth?"

"Blessed Sir," said Panurge, "from what I can see and tell, you're getting hot under the collar. All right! There, here's your money."

Panurge, having paid the dealer, out of the whole flock chose one big handsome sheep and carried it off bleating and crying out, while all the others heard and bleated in unison and watched where their companion was being taken to. Meanwhile the dealer was saying to his sheep-handlers:

"O how well he knew how to pick 'em, that customer! He knows his way around with them, the lecher! Really, really and truly, I was saving that one for Lord de Cancale, since I know his taste very well. For by nature he's all overjoyed and beaming when he's holding in hand a well-fitting attractive shoulder of mutton like a left-handed racket,[4] and, with a good sharp carving knife, how he takes his cuts at it!"[5]

CHAPTER 8

How Panurge had the merchant and the sheep
drowned at sea.

S UDDENLY, I know not how—I had no time to consider it—Panurge, without another word, throws his bleating and bawling sheep right into the sea. And the other sheep, bawling and bleating in unison, started jumping and throwing themselves into the sea one after another after him. They were shoving to determine which one would jump in there first after their companion. It was not possible to keep them from it; for as you know, the nature of a sheep is always to follow the leader, wherever he goes. And so Aristotle, in Book 9 of *De histo. animal,* says it is the stupidest, silliest animal in the world.

The merchant, all terrified to see his sheep perish and drown before his eyes, kept trying with all his might to hinder them and hold them back. But it was in vain. One after the other, they all jumped into the sea and perished. Finally he took one big strong one by his fleece on the ship's deck, thinking in that way to hold him back and so then to save the rest. The sheep was so powerful that he dragged the merchant with him into the sea, and he was drowned, in the same way that the sheep of Polyphemus, the one-eyed Cyclops, carried Ulysses and his companions out of the cave [*Odyssey* 9.425 ff]. The other herdsmen and shepherds did the same thing, taking them some by the legs, some by the fleece. And they were all likewise dragged into the sea, and perished miserably.

Panurge, standing beside the galley holding an oar in his hand not to help the shepherds but to keep them from climbing back aboard and avoiding drowning, kept preaching to them eloquently, as if he were a little Friar Oliver Maillard or a second Friar Jean Bourgeois,[1] pointing out to them by rhetorical topoi the miseries of this world, the beatific felicity of the other life, affirming that the deceased were happier than those living in this vale of tears [vallée de misère], and promising each one to erect a fine cenotaph and honorary sepulcher on the very summit of Mont Cenis on his return from Lanternland, nonetheless wishing them, in case they were not fed up with living among humans, good luck and an encounter with some whale that on the third day thereafter would cast them up safe and sound on some Satinland, following Jonah's example [Jonah 2.10].

With the ship cleared of the dealer and his sheep, Panurge said: "Is there any muttonish soul left here? Where are those of Thibault l'Aignelet, and those of Regnauld Belin, which sleep while others graze. I don't know a thing about it. That's an old wartime trick. What do you think of it, Frère Jean?"

"A good job of yours," replied Frère Jean. "I didn't find anything wrong, unless that it seems to me that just as of old in war, on the day of a battle or assault, they would promise the soldiers double pay for that day: if they won the battle, they had plenty to pay with; if they lost, it would have been disgraceful to ask for it, as did the runaway Swiss after the battle of Ceresole;[2] likewise, when all's said and done, you should have reserved payment; the money would have remained in your purse."

"That," said Panurge, "was a good shit for the money! Power of God, I had more than a thousand francs' worth of fun. Never did a man do me pleasure without getting rewarded by me or at least without my being grateful. Never did a man do me a bad turn without being sorry for it either in this world or in the other. I'm not stupid to that point."

"You," said Frère Jean, "are damning yourself like an old devil. It is written: *Mihi vindictam* [Vengeance is mine],[3] etc. Breviary matter."

CHAPTER 9

How Pantagruel reached the island of Ennasin,[1]
and of the strange relationships of the country.

ZEPHYR [the west wind] kept blowing for us with a little help from Garbin [southwest wind], and we spent one day without sighting land. On the third day, at the flies' sunrise,[2] there appeared before us a triangular island, in shape and site much like Sicily. It was named the island of Relationships [L'isle des Alliances].

The men and women looked like red Poitevins [red-painted Picts], except that they all, men, women, and little children, have noses shaped like the ace of clubs. For this reason, the ancient name of the island was

Ennasin. And they were all kinfolk and interrelated so they boasted; and the Potentate [Potestat][3] of the place said to us freely:

"You people from the other world think it is a wonderful thing that out of one Roman family (that was the Fabii), on one day (that was the thirteenth of the month of February), by one gate (that was the Porta Carmentalia, of old situated at the foot of the Capitol, betweeen the Tarpeian Rock and the Tiber, and since surnamed the Scelerata—the crime-stained), against certain enemies of the Romans (these were the Etruscan Veientes), there went forth three hundred and six warriors, all related with five thousand other soldiers, all vassals of theirs who were slain (that was near the river Cremera, which flows out of the Lake of Baccano).[4] From this land, in case of need, will go forth three hundred thousand, all relatives and of one family."

Their kinships and relationships were of a very strange sort; for while all were kith and kin and related to one another, not one of them was father or mother, brother or sister, uncle or aunt, cousin or nephew, son-in-law or daughter-in-law, godfather or godmother, to another. Except for one tall old denosed man, to be sure, who, as I watched called out to a little girl of four: "My father"; the girl called him: "My daughter."

The kinship and relation between them was such that one man called a woman "my flatfish"; she called him "My porpoise [ma maigre . . . mon marsouin]." "Those two," said Frère Jean, "must really smell of low tide when they've rubbed their bacon together."

One of them, smiling, called out to an elegant lass: "Good day, my currycomb [mon estrille]!" She returned the greeting: "Good day to you, my dun horse [mon fauveau]!" "Haw haw haw," exclaimed Panurge, "Come and see a currycomb, a scythe [une fau] and a calf [un veau]. Isn't that currying favor [estrille fauveau]?" The dun horse with the black stripe must quite often get his tool well curried.[5]

Another greeted a cutie of his, saying: "Good-bye, my desk." She answered: "And the same to you, my lawsuit [mon bureau . . . mon procès]." "By Saint Ninian!" said Gymnaste, "that lawsuit must often lie upon that desk."

One of the men called another woman "My worm" [*Mon verd,* modern *ver*]. She called him her "rascal [son coquin]." Said Eusthenes: "There's a rascally staggerworm [du verdcoquin] there."

Another man, greeting a female relative of his, said "Morning, my hatchet [ma coingnée]!" She answered: "And the same to you, my helve [mon manche]!" " 'Odsbelly [Ventre beuf]!" cried Carpalim, "how is this hatchet helved? How is this helve hatcheted [coingnée . . . emman-chée . . . manche . . . encoingné]? But mightn't this be the great helve that the Roman courtesans asked for? Or a cordelier with a big handle [ou un cordelier à la grande manche]?"

Moving on, I saw an oaf [un averlant] greeting a relative and calling her "My mattress"; she called him "my quilt." Indeed, he looked rather like an oafish loafer [un lodier lourdault]. One man called another girl "crumb"[6] [of bread]; she called him "my crust." One called another his "fire-shovel"; she called him her "oven-fork [sa palle . . . son fourgon]." One called another "my gym-shoe"; she named him "slipper." One called another "my buskin"; she called him her "oversock [estivallet]." One called another his "mitten"; she called him her "love." One called another his "rind"; she called him her "bacon"; and their relation was that between rind and bacon.

In a similar relationship, one called his girl "my omelet"; she called him "my egg"; and they were related like omelet to eggs. Likewise another called his girl "my tripe"; she called him her "faggot." I never could find out what kinship, relation, or consanguinity there was between them relating to our common usage, unless they were telling us that she was "trippe de ce faggot" [Cotgrave: "one of the smallest sticks of the fag-got"].

Another man, greeting his lady kin, said "Hello, my shell." She replied: "And hello to you, my oyster." "That," said Carpalim, "is an oyster in the shell [une huytre en escalle]."

Another man likewise greeted a girl relative of his, saying: "A good life to you, my pod." She replied: "A long one to you, my pea." "That," said Gymnaste, "is a pea in a pod."

Another, a big ugly loafer mounted on high wooden mules, meeting a short stout, fat wench, said to her: "God save my humming top, my spinner, my whip top, my casting top!" She answered him proudly: "Save and save alike [Guard pour guard], my whip!" "Blood Saint Gray!"[7] said Xenomanes, "is he whip enough to spin that top?"[8]

A doctor professor, spruce and well combed, after chatting for some time with a highborn lady, on taking leave of her, said: "Many thanks, good face!" "Why," said she, "very many to you, bad matter!" "The relation," said Pantagruel, "of good face to bad matter is in no way impertinent."[9]

A senior graduate, passing by, said to a young chick: "Hey, hey! Long time no see, Muse!" "I'm always glad to see you, Horn," she replied. "Couple them together," said Panurge, "and blow into their asses: that'll be a bagpipe!"[10] Another man called a relative of his: "my sow"; she called him her "hay [ma truie . . . son foin]." There the thought came to me that this sow liked to be turned out to this hay.

I saw a hunchbacked half-pint gallant greet a girl relative of his: "Good-bye, my hole!" She likewise returned the greeting, saying: "God keep you, my peg!" Frère Jean said: "She, I think, is all hole, and likewise he, all peg. Now we need to know whether this hole can be entirely plugged up by this peg."[11]

Another man greeted his girl by saying: "Good-bye, my molt." She answered: "Good day, my gosling." "I think," said Ponocrates, "that the gosling is often in molt."[12]

A lusty boozer, chatting with a young cutie, said to her: "Remember that, fizzle." "So I shall, fart [Aussi fera, ped]!" she replied. "Do you call those two kinfolk?" said Pantagruel to the Potentate. "I think they're natural enemies, not kinfolk, for he called her a fizzle. In our countries you couldn't insult a woman worse than by calling her that." "Good folk from the other world," replied the Potentate, "you have few people so related and so close as are this Fart and this Fizzle. They both came out invisibly together from one hole in a moment."

"So the Galerne wind [northeast]," said Panurge, "had Lanternized their mother?" "What mother do you mean?" said Potentate. "That's a relationship of your world. We have no father or mother. That's for people from overseas, hayseeds."[13]

The good Pantagruel kept listening to it all and watching it all; but at these remarks, he nearly broke up.[14]

After carefully observing the site of the island and the ways of the Ennasian [Denosed] people, we went into a cabaret to have a little re-freshment. They were holding a wedding there in the manner of the country. Moreover, a good time and a half. In our presence was per-formed a merry marriage of a female pear, a very lively woman as it seemed to us (however, those who had tried her said she was rather soft), to a young cheese with a downy chin and a slightly reddish complexion. I had heard in other days reports of such marriages and several had been performed elsewhere. They still say, in this cow country of ours, that there never has been such a marriage as that of a pear and some cheese. In another room, I saw that an old boot was being married to a supple young buskin. Pantagruel was told that the young buskin was taking the old boot as his wife because she was good goods, in good shape, and as plump as a man could want, even for a fisherman.[15] In another lower room I saw a young dress pump marry an old slipper.[16] And we were told that it was not for the beauty and good grace of her, but for greed and covetousness to get the gold pieces with which she was lined and crammed full.

CHAPTER 10

How Pantagruel went ashore on the island of Cheli,
which was ruled by King Saint Panigon.

THE Garbin [southwest wind] kept blowing astern when, leaving the unattractive Kith-and-Kinners [Allianciers], with their ace-of-clubs noses, we put out to the high seas. As the sun was going down, we landed on the island of Cheli,[1] a big, fertile, rich, and populous island ruled by King Saint Panigon.[2] He, accompanied by his children and the princes of the court, had betaken himself near the harbor to receive Pantagruel, and escorted him right up to his château. Above the donjon gate[3] the queen presented herself, attended by her daughters and all the ladies of the court. Panigon wanted her and all her suite to kiss Pantagruel and his men. Such was the courteous custom of the country, which was done, except for Frère Jean, who took off and stayed apart among the king's officers.

Panigon tried most insistently to keep Pantagruel there for that day and the next. Pantagruel based the excuse he made on the serenity and opportuneness of the wind, which is more wished-for than encountered by travelers, and must be put to use when it comes, for it doesn't come each and every time you want it. When he pointed this out, after twenty-five or thirty drinks downed per man, Panigon gave us leave.

Pantagruel, going back to the port and not seeing Frère Jean, was asking where he was and why he wasn't with everyone else. Panurge didn't know how to excuse him and wanted to go back to the château to call him, when Frère Jean came running up all beaming, and in great rejoicing of heart called out: "Long live the noble Panigon! By the death of a wooden ox,[4] he's at home around the kitchen. I've just come from there, and they serve everything by the ladlefuls. I was really hoping to get some stuffing there to fill out in monkish profit and style the mold and lining of my frock."

"So, my friend," said Pantagruel, "still at those kitchens!"

"Cocksbody!"[5] replied Frère Jean, "I know their customs and ceremonies better than how to shittershatter so much with all these women, *magny, magna, chiabrena* [manyee, manya, shitteryshattery], bow, repeat, once again, the hug, the embrace, kiss your majesty's hand, be most welcome, pish tush. That's crap, known as shit in Rouen! I'm not saying that I might not take a crack at it while it's there, in my clumsy way, if anyone would let me insinuate my nomination. But this turdocrapery of scrapes and bows makes me madder than a young devil, I meant to say a double fast.[6] Saint Benedict never lied about it. You never talk about kissing young ladies. By the worthy and holy gown I wear, I steer clear of that, for fear there might happen to me what happened to the lord of Guyercharois."[7]

"What was that?" asked Pantagruel. "I know him; he's one of my best friends."

"He was invited," said Frère Jean, "to a sumptuous, magnificent banquet given by a relative and neighbor of his, to which were also invited all the gentlemen, the married and unmarried ladies, of the neighborhood. These, while waiting for him to arrive, disguised the pages of the gathering and dressed them as very sprightly, well-dressed ladies. To him as he came in near the drawbridge the ladified pages appeared. He kissed them all in great courtesy and magnificent bows. At the end, the ladies, who were waiting for him in the gallery, burst into peals of laughter, and signaled to the pages to take off their finery. At the sight of which the worthy lord, embarrassed and annoyed, did not deign to kiss the natural-born ladies claiming that, since they had disguised the pages on him so, by the death of the wooden ox! These must be the servants, even more cleverly disguised.

"Power of God! *da jurandi* [forgive my swearing], why don't we instead take all our humanities [ourselves] into one of God's lovely kitchens? And why not consider the rotation of the spits, the harmony of the jacks, the position of the bacon strips, the temperature of the soups, the preparations for the dessert, the order of the wine service? *Beati immaculati in via* [Blessed are those unspotted along the way].[8] That's breviary matter."

CHAPTER 11

Why monks like to be in the kitchen.

"T HAT," said Epistémon, "is spoken like a natural-born monk. I mean a monking monk, not a monked monk.[1] You put me in mind of what I saw and heard in Florence about twenty years ago. We were in good company of studious folk, loving travel and eager to visit the learned men, antiquities, and special sights of Italy. And at that point we were observing carefully the site and beauty of Florence, the structure of the cathedral, the sumptuosity of the magnificent temples[2] and public buildings, and were trying to see who would extol them most aptly by worthy praises, when a monk from Amiens named Bernard Lardon,[3] as if all vexed and baffled, said:

"'I don't know what you find here to praise so. I've observed it just as well as you have, and I'm no more blind than you are. What is it? These are handsome houses. That's all. But, God and our good patron Saint Bernard be with us! In this whole city I haven't yet seen one roast-shop, and I've looked around it carefully and observed. Indeed, I tell you this as one who spies them out and is ready to count and number, both to the right and to the left, how many, and in which direction, we would come upon more roasting roast-shops. Now at Amiens, in four, rather five times less ground than we have crossed in our minds, I could have shown you more than fourteen streets of roasting shops, most ancient and aromatic. I don't know what pleasure you took in seeing the lions and African big cats (so I believe you were naming what they call tigers) near the belfry; likewise seeing the porcupines and ostriches at the palace of Lord Filippo Strozzi. My faith, laddies, I'd rather see a good fat gosling on a spit. These porphyries, these marbles are beautiful; I say nothing against them. But the Amiens *darioles* [custard tarts][4] are better, to my taste. These ancient statues are well made, I'm willing to believe it; but by Saint Ferréol of Abbeville,[5] the young chicks in our country are a thousand times more attractive.'"

"What do they mean," said Frère Jean, "and why do they say that you always find monks in kitchens, and never find there kings, popes, or emperors?"

"Is there," suggested Rhizotome, "some latent virtue and hidden specific property in the pots and racks that attract monks to them, as the magnet attracts iron, and does not attract emperors, popes, or kings? Or is it some natural attraction and inclination, inherent in monks' gowns and cowls, which of itself leads and impels the good monks into the kitchen, even if they had no plan or will to go there?"

"He means," said Epistémon, "forms following matter. That's what Averroes calls them." [6]

"True, right you are," said Frère Jean.

"I'll tell you," replied Pantagruel, "though without speaking to the problem, for it's a bit ticklish, and you would hardly touch it without being pricked. I remember reading that Antigonus, king of Macedonia, going into his camp kitchen one day and there coming upon the poet Antagoras, who was preparing an eel fricassee and holding the pan himself, asked him in great glee: 'Was Homer fricasseeing eels when he described the exploits of Agamemnon?' 'But ha! Sire,' replied Antagoras, 'do you think that Agamemnon, when he was performing such exploits, was curious to know whether anyone in his camp was fricasseeing eels?' To the king it seemed unbefitting for the poet to be making such a fricassee in his kitchen. The poet was pointing out that it was too preposterous a thing to meet the king in the kitchen."

"I'll cap that one [Je dameray ceste-cy]," said Panurge, "by telling you what Breton Villandry [7] replied one day to his Lordship the Duc de Guise. They were talking about some battle of King Francis [I] against Emperor Charles the Fifth, in which Breton was elegantly armed, indeed with steel-trimmed greaves and steel shoes, also advantageously mounted, yet had not been seen in combat.

" 'My faith,' replied Breton, 'I was there, it will be easy for me to prove it, indeed in a place where you would never have dared to be!' When My Lord the Duke took this statement in bad part, as being too insolently and rashly proffered, and as his remarks grew stiffer, Breton easily appeased him into hearty laughter, saying: 'I was with the baggage, in which place your honor would never have led you to hide, as I did.' "

In such talk they reached their ships. And they made no longer stay in this island of Cheli.

CHAPTER 12

*How Pantagruel passed Procuration,[1]
and of the strange way of life among the Shysteroos.[2]*

CONTINUING on our way, on the next day we passed Procuration, a country that is all jumbled and begrimed. I couldn't make out a thing in it. There we saw the Pettifoggers [Procultous] and Shysteroos, monstrous hairywild men.[3] Only, after a long sequence of many learned salutations, they told us that they were all at our service—for pay. One of our interpreters was telling Pantagruel how this people earned their living in a very strange fashion, diametrically opposite to the Romans. In Rome, an infinite number of people earn their living by poisoning, beating, and killing; the Shysteroos earn theirs by being beaten. So that, if they remained a long time without being beaten, they would die of starvation, they, their wives, and their children.

"It's like those," said Panurge, "who, from Cl. Galen's report, cannot raise their cavernous nerve to the equatorial circle unless they are good and soundly whipped. By Saint Thibault, if anyone whipped me that way, he would, on the contrary, wholly unsaddle me, by all the devils!"

"The way they work," said the interpreter, "is this. When a monk, a priest, a usurer, or an advocate is down on some gentleman of his region, he sends after him one of these Shysteroos. Shysteroo will cite him, serve a warrant on him, set him a date to appear, offend him, insult him, independently outrage him, following his orders and instructions, to the point where the gentleman, if he is not paralyzed in sense or stupider than a tadpole, will be forced to give him beatings with swordstrokes on his head, or a nice slash of his hamstrings, or, better yet, throw him off the battlements or out the windows of his château. That done, you have Shysteroo rich for four months, as if beatings were his natural harvests. For from the monk, the usurer, or the advocate, he will receive very good pay, and damages from the gentleman that are sometimes so great and excessive that the gentleman will lose all his means, with the danger of rotting miserably in prison, as if he had struck the king."

"Against such a disaster," said Panurge, "I know a very good remedy that the lord of Basché used to use."

"What was that?" asked Pantagruel.

"The lord of Basché," said Panurge, "was a courageous, valorous, magnanimous, chivalrous man. On his return from a certain long war in which the duke of Ferrara, through the help of the French, defended himself valiantly against the fury of Pope Julius the Second, he was every day cited, summoned, wrangled with, to the taste and for the sport of the fat prior of Saint-Louant.

"One day, lunching with his people (since he was friendly and humane), he sent for his baker, named Loyre, and his wife, also the curate of his parish, named Oudart, who served him as wine steward, as was then the custom in France, and said to them in the presence of his gentlemen and others of his house: 'My children, you see what vexation these scoundrelly Shysteroos cause me every day; I've come to the point of resolving that unless you help me in this I'll plan to leave the region and take the side of the sultan to all the devils. From now on, when they come in here, be ready, you, Loyre, and your wife, to appear in my great hall in your fine wedding clothes, as if you were just getting married, just as you were married in the first place.

" 'Look, here are a hundred gold crowns which I give you so you may get and keep your finery in good shape. You, Sir Oudart, do not fail to appear in your fine surplice and stole, with the holy water, as if to marry them. You too, Trudon (that was the name of his drummer), be there with your flute and drum. When the words are pronounced and the bride kissed to the sound of the drum, you will each give one another mementos of the wedding: those are little punches with your fist [a custom, see below]. So doing, you will sup only the better for it. But when it comes to the Shysteroo, lay it on him as on green rye, don't spare him, whack him, bank hit, I beseech you. Look, right now I give you these young jousting gauntlets covered with kid leather.[4] Keep on striking countless times at random. The one who hits hardest I'll recognize as my best friend. Don't be afraid of being taken to court for it; I'll stand warrant for you all. Such blows must be given with a laugh, according to the custom observed at all weddings.'

" 'Right,' said Oudart, 'but how shall we recognize the Shysteroo? For every day people come into this house of yours from every direction.'

" 'I've planned for that,' replied Basché. 'When up to our gate comes some man, either on foot or pretty badly mounted with a great wide silver ring on his thumb, that will be Shysteroo. The porter, after courteously letting him in, will ring the bell. Then, be ready and come into the hall to play the tragic comedy that I've laid out for you.'

"That very day, as God willed, there arrived a fat ruddy old Shysteroo. When he rang at the gate, he was recognized by the porter for his greasy leggings, his wretched mare, a cloth bag full of writs fastened to his belt, and especially for the big silver ring he had on his left thumb. The porter was courteous to him, brings him in honorably, joyfully rings the bell. At the sound thereof, Loyre and his wife dressed in their finery appeared in the hall putting a good face on it [faisans bonne morgue]; Oudart put on his surplice and stole. Coming out of his sacristy, he comes upon Shysteroo, takes him to drink a long time in his sacristy, while on all sides they were putting on gauntlets, and says to him: 'You couldn't have come at a better time. Our master is in the best of moods. We'll soon have a great time, everything will go by the ladlefuls; we're having a wedding in here. Here, drink up, cheers!'

"While Shysteroo was drinking, Basché, seeing all the people in the hall in the necessary equipment, sends for Oudart to come. Oudart comes, bearing the holy water. Shysteroo follows him. When he came into the hall he did not forget to make numerous humble bows, and served the summons on Basché. Basché gave him the warmest possible welcome, gave him a gold angel, asking him to be present at the contract and the wedding. Which was done. In the end, fists came out and began their thumps and whacks. But when Shysteroo's turn came, they feted him with great blows with the gauntlets, so roundly that it left him all punchy and bruised, with one eye poached in butter sauce, eight broken ribs, his breast bone knocked in, his shoulder blades each in four quarters, his lower jaw in three pieces, and all this done laughing. God knows how well Oudart operated, covering with the sleeve of his surplice the great steel-trimmed gauntlet with the ermine fur, for he was a powerful rascal.

"So Shysteroo goes back to L'Isle Bouchart, cruelly battered, but quite satisfied and content with the lord of Basché; and with help from the good surgeons of the region he lived as long as you like. There was no talk of him from then on. The memory of him expired with the sound of the bells that pealed out at his burial."[5]

CHAPTER 13

*How, after the example of Master François Villon,
the lord of Basché praises his people.*

"WHEN Shysteroo had left the château and climbed back onto his
scrawny blind nag [esgue orbe] (that's what he called his one-eyed mare),
Basché, under the arbor in his private garden, sent for his wife, his ladies,
all his people; had wine brought for a collation, in company with a
number of pastries, hams, fruits, and cheeses, drank with them in great
glee, then said to them:

" 'Master François Villon, in his old age, retired to Saint-Maixent in
Poitou, under the aegis of a worthy man, the abbot of the said place.
There, to offer an entertainment for the people, he undertook to put on
the Passion in Poitevin ways and language. When the roles were
distributed, the players rehearsed, and the theater prepared, he told the
mayor and aldermen that the mystery play could be ready by the end
of the Niort Fair;[1] all that remained was to find costumes suitable for
the characters.

" 'The mayor and aldermen set the date. He [Villon], to dress up an old
peasant playing God the Father, requested Friar Estienne Tappecoue,[2]
sacristan of the cordeliers of the said place, to lend him a cope and stole.[3]
Tappecoue refused him, alleging that, by their provincial statutes, it
was strictly forbidden to give or lend anything to players. Villon replied
that the statute concerned only farces, mummeries, and dissolute plays,
and that he had seen it applied that way in Brussels[4] and elsewhere.
Tappecoue, this notwithstanding, told him peremptorily to get his furnishings elsewhere if he wanted, to hope for nothing from his sacristy, for
he would get nothing there and no mistake. Villon reported this to the
players in great indignation, adding that God would soon mete out vengeance and exemplary punishment on Tappecoue.

" 'On the following Saturday, Villon got word that Tappecoue,
mounted on the monastery's filly (so they called a mare that had not yet
been covered), had gone to beg alms at Saint-Ligaire, and that he would
be back at about two in the afternoon. Thereupon he led the parade of
the crew of devils through the town and marketplace. His devils were all
caparisoned in wolf-skins, calfskins, and ram-skins, spiced with sheep's
heads, ox-horns, and great kitchen hooks; girt with great leather belts

from which hung big cowbells and mule-jangles that made a horrific racket. They held in their hands black sticks full of firecrackers; others carried long lighted firebrands, on which at every crossroads they tossed fistfuls of powdered resin, which emitted terrible fire and smoke. After leading them around to the great satisfaction of the people and great terror of the little children, finally he took them to banquet in a little country inn outside the door of which is the road to Saint-Ligaire. On reaching the inn, he espied from afar Tappecoue returning from seeking alms, and said to them in macaronic verse:[5]

> Hic est de patria, natus de gente belistra,
> Qui solet antiquo bribas portare bisacco.'

> [From an ignoble line this fellow comes,
> Who fills his pouch with moldy crusts and crumbs.]

" ' " " 'Sdeath," said the devils then, "he wouldn't lend a lousy cope to God the Father; let's give him a scare."

" ' ' "Well said," replies Villon, "but let's hide until he passes, and load up your firecracker and brands."

" 'When Tappecou reached the place, they all came out on the road in front of him, with a frightful racket, throwing fire from all sides onto him and his filly, banging their cymbals, and howling like devils: hoo, hoo, hoo, growrowrow, roo, roo, roo, roor! Hoo, hoo, hoo. Ho, ho, ho! Brother Estienne, don't we make good devils?

" 'The filly, badly scared, took off at a trot, with farts, and jumps, and at a gallop, kicking up her heels, stepping high, bucking, and farting: so wildly that she threw Tappecoue to the ground, although he clung with all his might to the pommel of the packsaddle. His stirrups were of rope. On the side opposite the mountingblock [i.e., on the right side], his sandal of leather thongs was so entangled that he never could get his leg free. So he was dragged flayass by the filly, who kicked out againt him harder than ever, always multiplying the kicks against him, and was straying off the road in her fright through the bushes, hedges, and ditches. With the result that she quite bashed in his skull, so that his brains fell out near the Hosanna Cross;[6] then came the arms, in pieces, one here, one there, likewise the legs; then she made one long carnage of the bowels; so that when the filly reached the monastery, all she bore of him was his right foot and the entangled shoe.

" 'Villon, seeing that it had come out as he had planned, said to his devils: "You'll play well, Sir Devils, you'll play well, I promise you. O how well you'll play! I defy the devil-crew of Saumur, Doué, Montmorillon, Langeais, Saint Epain, Angers, or indeed, by God, of Poitiers with their great hall, in case they can even be compared to you. O how well you'll play!"

" 'So,' said Basché, 'I foresee, my good friends, that from now on you will play this tragic farce well, seeing that at the rehearsal and trial you drubbed, whacked and tickled Shysteroo so eloquently. Right now I'm doubling your wages for you all.

" 'You, my dear,' he said to his wife, 'do your set of honors as you like. You have all my wealth in your hands and keeping. As for me, first I drink to you all, my good friends. Come on now, it's nice and cool. Second, you, my steward, take these two gilt silver goblets. Your pages are not to be whipped for three months. My dear, give them my fine white plumes with the gold spangles. Sir Oudart, I give you this silver flagon. This other I give to the cooks. To the valets I give this silver hammer; to the grooms I give this silver gilt vase; to the porters I give these two plates; to the muleteers, these ten soupspoons and this comfit box. You lackeys, take this big saltcellar. Serve me well, friends, I'll remember you; and believe me, I'd rather, by the power of God, endure a hundred blows on my helmet in war in the service of our best of kings than be summoned once by these Shysteroo curs, for the sport of a fat prior like that one!' "

CHAPTER 14

*Continuation of the Shysteroos
drubbed in the house of Basché.*

"Four days later another Shysteroo, young, tall and thin, went to serve a summons on Basché at the fat prior's request. On his arrival he was immediately recognized by the porter, and the bell tolled. At the sound of it all the community of the château understood what was afoot. Loyre was kneading his dough. His wife was sifting the flour. Oudart was minding his office. The gentlemen were playing tennis. Lord Basché was playing three hundred and three[1] with his wife. The younger ladies were playing spillikins.[2] The officers were playing *impériale*.[3] The pages were playing morra[4] with vigorous finger-snaps. Everyone understood immediately that Shysteroo was around. Then Oudart started to get dressed up again, Loyre and his wife to put on their finery, Trudon to play his flute and beat his drum, each one to laugh, everyone to get ready, and forward march, gauntlets.

"Basché goes down to the courtyard. There Shysteroo, on meeting him, fell on his knees before him, asked him not to take it amiss if he cited him on behalf of the fat prior, pointed out to him in an eloquent speech how he was a public personage, a servant of the monkery, summoner for the mitred abbot, ready to do as much for him, indeed for the least in his house, whenever he would like to use and command him. 'Really,' said his lordship, 'you're not going to serve a summons on me without having a drink of my good Quinquenais wine and attending the wedding I'm having shortly. Sire Oudart, see that he has a drink and a chance to freshen up, then bring him into the hall. And do you be welcome!'

"Shysteroo, well supplied with food and drink, comes into the hall with Oudart, in which were all the characters in the farce, in place and ready to go. At his entrance everybody began to smile. Shysteroo was laughing sociably when the mysterious words were spoken over the betrothed, hands clasped, the bride kissed, everyone sprinkled with holy water. While they were bringing on the wine and spices, fisticuffs began to fly. Shysteroo hit Oudart several times. Oudart had his gauntlet hidden under his surplice; he puts it on like a mitten. Then to drubbing Shysteroo, and blows from all sides with young gauntlets raining on Shysteroo.

" 'A wedding,' they kept saying, 'a wedding, a wedding! Remember it!'

"He was so well attended that blood was coming out of his mouth, his nose, his ears, his eyes. Moreover, all battered down, crushed, and bruised, head, neck, back, chest, arms, everywhere. Believe me, even in Avignon at Carnival time, the young men never slapped anyone around more melodiously than was done on Shysteroo. Finally he falls to the ground. They threw wine aplenty on his face, fastened to the sleeve of his doublet a fine green and yellow costume,[5] and put him on his sniffling horse. Back in L'Isle Bouchard, I don't know whether he was well tended and treated by his wife and the local doctors. There has been nothing heard of him since.

"On the next day a similar case occurred, because in the bag and game-pouch of the thin Shysteroo his summons had been found. On behalf of the fat prior a fresh Shysteroo was sent to serve a summons on the Lord of Basché, with two witnesses for his security. The porter, ringing the bell, gladdened the whole family when they understood that Shysteroo was there. Basché was at table, dining with his wife and gentlemen. He sends for Shysteroo, seats him next to him, the witnesses next to the ladies, and they all dined very well and joyously. At dessert Shysteroo gets up from the table, and in the presence and earshot of the witnesses serves his summons on Basché.

"Basché graciously asks him for a copy of his warrant. It was already prepared. He takes written proof of his summons. Four sun-crowns were given to Shysteroo and his witnesses. Everyone had left the room to prepare for the farce. Trudon begins to beat his drum. Basché asks Shysteroo to attend the wedding of an officer of his and to approve the contract,[6] on payment of a good healthy fee. Shysteroo was polite, pulled out his *escriptoire*,[7] promptly got paper, his witnesses next to him. Loyre enters the hall by one door, his wife with the ladies by another, dressed for a wedding. Oudart, in his priestly garb, takes them by the hands, questions them about their intentions, gives them his benediction without sparing the holy water. The contract is signed and recorded. From one direction wines and spices are brought in; from another heaps of livery, white and tanned; from another, gauntlets are secretly brought out."

CHAPTER 15

*How by Shysteroos are renewed
the ancient wedding customs.*

"Shysteroo, after guzzling a big glass of Breton wine, said to the lord: 'Sir, how do you mean that? Don't you give wedding-taps here? Holy Goose's blood,[1] all good customs are getting lost: and so you don't find hares in their lairs any more.[2] There are no more friends. See how in many churches they've abandoned the old tippling to the blessed saints O O[3] at Christmas! The world is in its dotage; it's coming near its end. Now just look: a wedding, a wedding!'

"So saying, he was banging on Basché and his wife, and after them on the ladies and on Oudart.

"Thereupon gauntlets did their work, so that Shysteroo had his skull cracked in nine places; one of the witnesses had his right arm banged out of joint, the other had his upper jaw dislocated, so that it half covered his chin, baring the uvula and knocking out a lot of teeth: molars, masticators, and canines [des dens molares, masticatoires et canines].

"At the sound of the drum changing its beat, the gauntlets were hidden without anyone's noticing, and sweetmeats passed around again, with fresh rejoicing. As the jolly companions drank to each other, and everyone to Shysteroo and his witnesses, Oudart was swearing off and speaking spitefully of weddings, alleging that one of the witnesses had disincornifistibulated his whole other shoulder;[4] this notwithstanding, he kept drinking to him merrily. The demandibulated [Le records démandibulé] witness was clasping his hands and tacitly asking his pardon, for speak he could not. Loyre kept complaining that the de-armed witness had hit him so hard on the other elbow with his fist that he'd got him all shrdlucripplogrillachortlificated[5] way down in his heel.

" 'But,' Trudon kept saying, hiding his left eye with his handkerchief and displaying his drum knocked in on one side, 'what harm had I done them? It wasn't enough for them thus to have roughly nuzzlefizzled-tizzledackbacksocked[6] my poor eye; besides that they've knocked in my drum on me. Wedding drums are ordinarily beaten; but drummers well feted, beaten never. Let the Devil try that one on for a nightcap!'

" 'Brother,' said one-armed Shysteroo, 'I'll give you a nice big old Royal Letter-Patent, which I have here in my baldrick, to patch up your drum; and in the name of God, forgive us. By Our Lady of Rivière, the fair lady, I meant no harm!'

"One of the grooms, as he nipped and swigged, was limping in a good impersonation of the noble Lord de la Rocheposay. He addressed the witness that was driveling from his drooping jaw that hung down like a helmet beaver, and said to him: 'Are you one of the frapins, the heavy hitters, or the belly-bumpers?[7] Wasn't it enough for you to have so roughly snoutcrapgutanbuttmorgatysackbackpopsmashed[8] all my upper members with great kicks from your clodhoppers, without giving us such snatchcatchadoodahodgepodgehumdrummings[9] on our shins with the sharp points of your boots? Do you call that "Youth must have its day?" By God, youth it may be, but it's not play!'[10]

"The witness, clasping his hands, seemed to be begging his pardon for it, murmuring like a baby: 'My, my, fly, fie, bye, bye.'[11]

"The new bride was crying as she laughed, laughing as she cried, because Shysteroo had not been content to baste her with no choice or selection among her members, but, after churlishly disheveling her hair, besides had treacherously swattwotchinkkinkbruiseabused[12] her private parts.

" 'Devil take his share in it!' said Basché. 'It was very necessary that Mr. King here [Monsieur Le Roy] (that was Shysteroo's name) sure had to go give me a bang like that on my little old lady of a backbone! I bear him no grudge, however. Those are little nuptial caresses. But I clearly perceive that he summoned me like an angel and basted me like a devil. He has something of the Banging Friar [Frère Frappart] about him. I drink to him with all my heart, and to you too, Sir Witnesses!'

" 'But,' said his wife, 'to what purpose and on what provocation did he treat and fete me so generously with his best Sunday punches?[13] Devil take him if I want that. However I don't want it, so help me God! But I'll say this for him: he has the hardest knuckles I ever felt on my shoulders.'

"The steward was keeping his left arm in a sling as being all bingbangbroken.[14] 'It's the Devil,' said he, 'who had me attend this wedding. By the Power of God, all I've got out of it is both arms pulpedgulpedpulverized[15] and battered. Do you call that a wedding? I call it a shitty turding.[16] This, by God, is the true-to-life feast of the Lapiths, described by the philosopher from Samosata [Lucian ca. A.D. 115–200].'

"Shysteroo was out of words. The witnesses made the excuse that in thumping so hard they had borne no ill will, and begged forgiveness for the love of God.

"So they leave. A half league from there, Shysteroo felt a little bad. The witnesses arrived in L'Isle Bouchard, stating publicly that they had never seen a finer man than the lord of Basché, or a more honorable house than his. Also, that they had never been to such a wedding. But the fault was all theirs, for they had begun the banging. And they were still alive I don't know how many days afterward.

"From there on out it was maintained as a certainty that Basché's money was more pestilential, deadly, and pernicious to Shysteroos and witnesses than ever was the gold of Toulouse[17] and Sejus's horse to those who possessed it. Since then the said lord has been at peace and quiet, and Basché weddings a common proverb."[18]

471

CHAPTER 16

*How Frère Jean makes trial
of the nature of the Shysteroos.*

"This story," said Pantagruel, "would seem merry, were it not that we must continually have the fear of God before our eyes."

"Better, it would have been," said Epistémon, "if the downpour of those young gauntlets had fallen on the fat prior. He was spending money for his sport, partly to annoy Basché, partly to see his Shysteroos drubbed. A tattoo of fists would have aptly adorned his shaven pate, considering the enormous extortion that we see today among these auxiliary judges under the village elm.[1] What offense had these poor devil Shysteroos committed?"[2]

"I am reminded," said Pantagruel, "in this connection, of an ancient Roman Gentleman named Lucius Neratius. He was of a noble family and rich in his time. But there was in him a tyrannical spirit such that when he came out of his palace, he had his servants' game-pouches filled with gold and silver coins, and when in the street he met some well-dressed, fashionable fops, without any provocation from them he would deliberately give them a few punches in the face. Then right away, to appease them and keep them from filing a complaint at law, he would pass out money to them, so well that he would leave them content and satisfied, by the ordinance of the Law of the Twelve Tables.[3] Thus he spent his income, beating people for the price of his money."

"By the holy tun of Saint Benedict!"[4] said Frère Jean, "I'll know the truth of it shortly." Thereupon he goes ashore, put his hand to his wallet, and pulled out of it twenty sun-crowns. Then he said in a low voice in the presence and hearing of a great mob of the Shysteroovian people: "Who wants to earn twenty crowns for getting a devil of a beating?" "Yo, yo, yo,"[5] they all answered. "You'll beat us senseles, Sir, that's for sure. But that's good money."

And they all came running up in droves, to see who would have first crack at getting such a precious beating. Out of the whole rabble, Frère Jean chose one red-snouted Shysteroo, who wore on the thumb of his right hand a great broad silver ring, in the bezel of which was set quite a big toadstone.[6]

When he had chosen him, I saw all this populace murmuring, and heard a tall thin young Shysteroo, able and well educated so the report ran, a decent man in the ecclesiastical court, complaining and murmuring that the Red-Snout was taking all their practice from them, and that if, in the entire territory, there were only thirty blows of a stick to earn, he would always pocket twenty-eight and a half of them. But all these complaints and murmurs emanated only from envy.

Frère Jean drubbed Red-Snout so much, so very much, back and belly, arms and legs, head and all, with great blows of his stick, that I thought he was beaten to death; then he gave him twenty crowns; and here's my lout on his feet, cheery as a lark or a king or two.[7] The others kept saying to Frère Jean:

"Sir Fra Diavolo,[8] if you'd like to beat anyone else for less money, we're all yours, Sir Devil. We're each and every one yours, sacks, papers, pens, and all."

Red-Snout cried out against them, saying loudly: "FeataGod! you good-for-nothing bums, are you poaching on my territory? Are you trying to steal and seduce my customers? I summon you before the ecclesiastical judge for a week from today, calloo, callay! I'll shyster you like a Vauvert devil!" Then, turning a smiling joyous face toward Frère Jean, he said: "Reverend Father in the Devil, Sir, if you've found me good goods and would like to have some more sport beating me, I'll be content with half the money, as a fair price. Don't spare me, please. I'm all, indeed all, yours, Sir Devil, head, lungs, bowels and all. I tell you this as a friend!"

Frère Jean interrupted his talk and turned off in another direction. The other Shysteroos kept heading toward Panurge, Epistémon, Gymnaste, and others, piously entreating them to beat them at a low price; otherwise they were in danger of some long fasting. But no one would hear of it.

Later, while looking for fresh water for the ship's crew, we came across two local Shysterettes [Chiquanourres], who were wretchedly weeping and lamenting together.

Pantagruel had stayed aboard the ship and was already having them sound recall. We, suspecting that they were related to the Shysteroo who had had the beatings, asked about the causes of such a lament. They replied that they had very good reason to weep, seeing that at the present moment two of the finest worthy people in Shystroovia had been given the monk by the neck at the gallows.[9]

"My page," said Gymnaste, "give the monk[10] by the feet to their comrades when they're sleepy-heads. To give the monk by the neck would be to hand and strangle the person."

"True," said Frère Jean; "you're talking about it like Saint Jean de la Palisse."[11]

Questioned about the reasons for this hanging, they answered that the two had stolen the instruments for Mass [les ferremens de la messe] and hidden them beneath the bell-tower [soubs le manche de la paroece].

"That," said Epistémon, "is spoken in a terrible allegory."

CHAPTER 17

How Pantagruel passed the islands of Tohu and Bohu,
and of the strange death of Bringuenarilles,
the windmill-swallower.

THAT same day Pantagruel passed the two islands of Tohu and Bohu,[1] where we found nothing cooking.[2] Bringuenarilles,[3] the great giant, had swallowed all the pots, pans, caldrons, kettles, dripping-pans, and boilers, for lack of windmills, on which he ordinarily fed. Whence it came about that a little before daybreak, at his time for digesting, he had fallen seriously ill from a certain unreadiness of the stomach brought on (so the doctors say) because the concoctive power of his stomach, naturally apt for digesting windmills in full whirl, had not been able to digest completely the pots and kettles; the caldrons and boilers it had digested pretty well as they (the doctors) said they could tell from the precipitates and sediment in four puncheons of urine that he had voided in two trips that morning.

To make him better they used various remedies in the manner of the art. But the illness was stronger than the remedies. And that morning the noble Bringuenarilles had passed away in a fashion so strange that we should no longer be amazed at the death of Aeschylus.[4] He, since it had been predicted to him as fated by the soothsayers, that on a certain day he would die from the fall of something that would drop on him, on that destined day had moved away from the city, from all houses, rocks, and other things that could fall and harm someone by their fall. And he stayed in the middle of a great open field, entrusting himself to the faith of a clear open sky, in the surest safety, so it seemed to him, unless the sky really fell, which he thought was impossible.

However, they say larks have a great dread of the skies' falling, for if the skies fell, they would all be caught. So was this dreaded in other days by the Celts living near the Rhine: those are the noble, valiant, knightly, warlike, and triumphant French, who questioned by Alexander the Great asking what thing they feared most in the world (in good hope that they would make an exception of him alone in consideration of his great exploits, victories, conquests, and triumphs), replied that they were afraid of nothing except that the sky would fall; that nevertheless they would not refuse to enter into alliance, confederation, and friendship with such a valiant magnanimous king. If you believe Strabo,[5] Book 7, and Arrian Book 1, Plutarch too, in the book he wrote *On the face in the moon,* alleges a man named Phenaces, who was much afraid that the moon would fall upon the earth, and felt commiseration and pity for those who dwell under it, as do the Ethiopians and Taprobanians,[6] if such a great mass fell upon them. He had a similar fear about the earth and sky, if they were not duly sustained and supported on the pillars of Atlas,[7] as the opinion of the ancients held, according to Aristotle, Book 5, *Meta ta phys* [*Metaphysics*].

Aeschylus, this notwithstanding was killed by the drop and fall of a tortoise's carapace, which, falling on his head from the talons of an eagle high in the air, split open his skull.

Besides Anacreon, a poet, who died choking on a grapeseed. Besides Fabius, a Roman praetor, who died suffocating on a goat's hair, as he drank a bowlful of milk. Also {Plus de] that bashful one who, for holding his wind and failing to fart one lousy time, suddenly died in the presence of Claudius, the Roman emperor [Suetonius *Life of Caludius* 12]. Also the one who is buried on the Via Flaminia in Rome, who in his epitaph complains of dying from being bitten by a tabbycat on his little finger.[8] Also Quintus Lecanius Bassus, who suddenly died of a needle-prick on the thumb of his left hand so small you could hardly see it. Also Quenelault, a Norman doctor, who passed away suddenly at Montpellier, as a result of taking a hand-worm out of his hand slantwise with a penknife.

Also Philemon, for whom his valet had prepared as an appetizer some fresh-plucked figs. In the time he spent first at his wine, a ballocky stray donkey had come into the house, and was devoutly eating the figs that were set out. When Philemon came upon him and carefully contemplated the grace of this sycophagous [fig-eating] donkey, he said to his returning valet:

"It's only right that since you've left the figs to this pious donkey, you set out for him some of this good wine you've brought."

Having said these words, he was seized with such excessive merriment of spirit, and burst into such uncontrollable laughter, that such overexertion of the spleen [l'exercice de la ratelle] stopped his breathing entirely, and suddenly he died.

Also Spurius Saufeius, who died gulping down a soft-boiled egg on coming out of the bath. Also the one who Boccaccio says died suddenly from cleaning his teeth with a sprig of sage [*Decameron* 4.7]. Also Philippot Placut, who, when hale and hearty, without any preceding malady, suddenly died paying an old debt. Also Zeuxis the painter, who suddenly died by dint of laughing, as he looked at the sour puss and picture of an old hag whose portrait he had painted [Erasmus *Adages* 3.5.1, after Pliny]. Also a thousand others they tell you about, whether Verrius, or Pliny, or Valerius, or Baptista Fulgosus, or Bacabery the Elder.[9]

The good Bringuenarilles, alas! choked to death eating a pat of fresh butter on his doctors' orders by the mouth of a hot oven.

There, besides, we were told that the king of Cullan on Bohu had defeated the satraps of King Mechloth and sacked the fortresses of Belima.[10] Later, we passed the islands of Pish and Tush [Nargues et Zargues]. Also the islands of Teleniabin and Geneliabin,[11] very beautiful and fruitful in the matter of enemas. Also the islands of Enig and Evig, from which had come earlier the "stab in the back" of the Landgrave of Hesse.

CHAPTER 18

*How Pantagruel came safely
through a mighty tempest at sea.*

THE next day we encountered to starboard nine big transport ships
loaded with monks—Jacobins, Jesuits, Capuchins, Hermits, Augustines,
Bernardins, Celestins, Theatins, Egnatians, Amadeans, Cordeliers,
Carmelites, Minims, and other holy religious—who were going to the
Council of Chesil[1] to scrutinize and garble [grabeler] the articles of faith
against the new heretics. At the sight of them Panurge went wild with
joy, as being assured of having all good fortune for that day and a long
stretch of days thereafter. And after courteously greeting the blessed fathers and commending the salvation of his soul to their pious prayers and
small favors [leurs dévotes prières et menuz suffraiges], he had tossed into
their ships seventy-eight dozen hams, quantities of caviar, tens of black
puddings [cervelatz], hundreds of mullets, and two thousand lovely
angelots for the souls of the deceased.

Pantagruel remained all pensive and melancholy. Frère Jean noticed it
and was asking him the cause of such unaccustomed low spirits, when the
captain, considering the tumblings of the pennant on the stern and foreseeing a cruel squall and then a fresh tempest, ordered a general alert for
sailors, apprentice seamen, and ship-boys, also for us passengers; had sails
lowered, mizzen, after-mizzen [contreméjane], jury sail [triou], mainsail
[maistralle], *épagon,* spritsail [civadière]; had the bowlines loosened, the
main topsail, fore-topsail, mizzenmast taken down, leaving nothing of the
yards but the ratlines and shrouds.

Suddenly the sea began to swell and boil up from the lower depths;
mighty waves to batter our ship's sides; the mistral, together with a furious squall, black thunderstorms, terrible whirlwinds, deadly squalls,
whistling through our yards; from the heavens on high coming thunder
and lightning, rain, hail; the air losing transparency, becoming opaque,
darksome, and obscure, so that no light came to us except thunder and
lightning and breaks in flaming cloud, the gusts, squalls, whirlwinds and
hurricanes flaming all around us from the thunder sheet and forked lightning, and other emissions; we looked all shocked and upset; horrific
typhoons held the mountainous waves up above the surface. Believe me,

it seemed to us to be the ancient Chaos,[2] in which fire, air, sea, land, all the elements were in obstinate confusion.

Panurge, having well fed the scatophagous fishes with the contents of his stomach, remained squarring on deck, all upset, all beat, and half dead; invoked all the blessed saints, men and women to his aid; vowed he would make confession at some time and place, then in great terror cried out and said: "Steward, ho! my friend, my father, my uncle, bring out something salty; we'll soon have only too much to drink, from what I see! Eat light and drink hearty, henceforth that shall be my motto. Would God and the most blessed, most worthy, and holy Virgin, that now, I mean at this very moment, I were on terra firma safe and sound and at ease!

"O how thrice and four times happy are those who plant cabbages! O Fates, why didn't you spin me one to be a planter of cabbages! O how small is the number of those to whom Jupiter confers such favor that he destined them to plant cabbages! For they always have one foot on land, and the other is not far away. Whoever wants to may dispute about happiness and the supreme good; but whoever plants cabbages is now to my decree declared supremely happy, on far better grounds than Pyrrho, who, being in danger like what we're in now and seeing a pig near the shore eating scattered barley, declared him to be most happy in two respects: to wit, that he had plenty of barley, and moreover he was on land.[3]

"Ha! for a divine and lordly abode there is nothing like solid ground [le plancher des vaches]. Savior God, this wave is going to sweep us away! O my friends, a little vinegar! I'm sweating like a horse from the strain.[4] Alas! The halyards have snapped, the bow-rope is in pieces, the eyelets are splitting, the topmast is plunging into the sea, our keel is out sunning itself, our cables are almost all broken. Alas, alack! Where are our topsails? All is *frelore bigoth!*[5] Our main topmast is adrift. Alas! Who will this wreck belong to? Friends, lend me a hand here aft of one of those handrails! Lads, your lantern has fallen. Alas! Don't let go of the rudder nor the bowline, I hear the pintle rattling. Is it broken? For God's sake, let's save the tackle; don't worry about the stays. Bebebe bous bous bous![6] Look and see from your compass needle, Master Stargazer [maistre Astrophile],[7] from where this tempest is coming upon us. My faith, I really am scared. Bou bou, bou bous bous! I'm beshitting myself in a frenzy of panic fear. Bou bou, bou bou! Otto to to to to ti! Otto to to to to ti.[8] Bou bou bou, ou ou ou bou bou bous bous! I'm drowning, I'm drowning, I'm dying. Good people. I'm drowning [Bonnes gens, je naye]."

CHAPTER 19

How Panurge and Frère Jean
behaved during the tempest.

Pantagruel, after first of all imploring the aid of Great God the Savior and offered a public prayer of fervent piety,[1] on the captain's advice held the mast firm and strong. Frère Jean had stripped to his doublet to help out the sailors. The same was true of Epistémon, Ponocrates, and others. Panurge stayed on his ass on deck, crying and wailing. Frère Jean, passing along the quarter-deck, noticed him and said to him:

"By God, Panurge, you calf, you sniveler, Panurge, you howler, you'd do a lot better to be helping us here than crying like a cow over there, sitting on your balls like a monkey!"

"Be be be bous bous bous," replied Panurge, "Frère Jean, my friend, my good father, I'm drowning, my friend, I'm drowning, my friend, I'm drowning! It's all up with me, my spiritual father! It's all over! Your cutlass couldn't save me now! Alas, alas! We're up above Ela![2] beyond the whole gamut! Be be be bous bous! Alas! At this moment we are below *gamma ut!* I'm drowning! Ha my father, my uncle, my all! The water's got into my shoes through the collar. Bou bou bou whoosh hu hu hu ha ha ha ha ha. I'm drowning! Alas, alas, boo hoo hoo boo hoo hoo! Blubblub booblubblub blubblub, oh oh oh oh oh oh! Alas, alack! At this point I'm just like a forked tree, head down, feet in the air.[3] Would God I were right now in the transport we met this morning with the good blessed concilipetic [council-seeking] fathers, so plump, so cheery, so sleek and gracious. Alas, alas! Alack, alackaday! This wave of all the devils (*mea culpa, Deus*), I mean this wave of God will sink our ship. Frère Jean, my father, my friend, confession!"

"Come here, you devil's gallows-bird," said Frère Jean, "and lend us a hand! In the name of thirty legions of devils, come on! . . . Will he ever come?"

"Let's not swear," said Panurge, "my father, my friend, for the time being! Tomorrow, all you like. Alas, alas, alack! Our boat is shipping water. I'm drowning! Alas, alas! Be be be bou bou bou bou. Now we're on the bottom! Alas, alas! I'll give eighteen hundred thousand crowns a year in revenue to anyone who sets me on land, all beshitten and turd-smeared as I am, if ever a man was in my crappy country. *Confiteor!* Just one little word as a will, or at least as a codicil!"

"A thousand devils," said Frère Jean, "jump on the body of this cuckold! Power of God! Are you talking about a will, at this moment when we're in danger and when it's up to us to do our damnedest now or never! Will you come on, you devil? Bosun, my hearty, O lieutenant, good man, back here! Gymnaste, here, on the poop! Power of God, we're really done for this time! There, our lantern's gone out. This is on its way to all the millions of devils."

"Alas, alas!" said Panurge, "alas! Bou, bou, bou, bou! Alas, alack! Was it here that we were predestined to perish? Alas, good folk, I'm drowning. I'm dying! *Consummatum est.*[4] It's all up with me!"

"Magna, gna, gna," said Frère Jean, "Fie! Is he ever ugly, that shitty sniveler! Here, ship's-boy, ho! by all the devils, man the pump! Did you hurt yourself? Power of God hand on to one of these bollards. Here, that way, hey, by the devil! That's it, lad!"

"Ah, Frère Jean," said Panurge, "my spiritual father, my friend, let's not swear! You're sinning. Alas, alas! Blub blubblub, I'm drowning, I'm dying, my friend! I forgive everybody. Farewell! *In manus!*[5] Bou bou bououou! Saint Michel d'Aure, Saint Nicholas, just this time and never again! I hereby make a good vow to you and to Our Lord that if at this time you help me, I mean you set me ashore out of this danger, I'll build you a nice big little chapel or two,

> Between Candes and Montsoreau,
> Where no cow or calf shall go.[6]

"Alas, alas! I've had over eighteen buckets of water come into my mouth. Bous bous bous bous! How bitter and salty it is!"

"By the powers," said Frère Jean, "of the blood, of the flesh, of the belly, of the head![7] If I hear you whimpering any more, you devil's cuckold, I'll keelhaul you like a sea-wolf![8] Power of God! Why don't we dump him down to the bottom of the sea? Oarsman [Hespaillier], good old matey, this way, my friend! Hold tight up there! This is really first-class thunder and lightning. I do believe all the devils are loosed today, or that Proserpina is in labor with child. All the devils are doing a morris dance."

CHAPTER 20

*How quartermasters abandon ship
at the height of the tempest.*[1]

"A HA!" said Panurge, "Frère Jean, my old-time friend, you're sinning! Old-timer, say, for at present I am null, you are null.[2] I'm sorry to tell you so, for I think swearing like that does your spleen a lot of good, even as a wood-chopper gets great relief if at each stroke someone near him shouts 'Hah!' in a loud voice at each stroke, and as a skittles-player is wonderfully relieved, when he hasn't bowled straight, if some smart man near him leans and half twists his body in the direction in which a well-thrown ball would have made contact with the skittles. Nevertheless you're sinning, my sweet friend. But, if right now we eat some sort of goat stews [cabirotades], would we be in safety from this storm? I've read that always safe at sea were the ministers of the Cabiri, gods so celebrated by Orpheus, Apollonius, Pherecydes, Strabo, Pausanias, and Herodotus."

"He's raving," said Frère Jean, "poor devil. A thousand millions and hundreds of millions of devils take the horned devil's cuckold! Help us here, tiger![3] Will he ever come? Here, to starboard! By God's headful of relics! What monkey's paternoster are you muttering there between your teeth? That devil's sea-calf is the cause of the tempest, and he alone won't help the crew! By God, if I get there, I'll punish you as a tempestuous devil would! Come here, apprentice, my cutey, that's a good lad! Would God you were abbot of Talemouze,[4] and the man who now is that was warden of Le Croullay! Ponocrates, brother, you'll hurt yourself there. Epistémon, watch out for that rail! I saw a lightning bolt strike it."

"Hoist!"

"Well said! Hoist, hoist, hoist! Launch the dinghy! Hoist! Power of God, what's that there? The point of the beak-head [le cap] is in pieces. Thunder, you devils, fart, belch, crap! Shit on that wave! Power of God, it just missed sweeping me off under the current! I think all the millions of devils are holding their provincial chapter here, or else plotting for the election of a new rector."

"To port!"

"Well said. 'Ware that pulley! Hey, ship's boy, by the devil, hey! Port, port!"

"Blubblubboo boo," said Panurge, "boo boo blubblub boo boo, I'm drowning. I can't see either heaven or earth. Alas, alas! Out of the four elements all we have left here are fire and water. Boobooboo boo boo! Would to God's worthy Power I were at the present moment inside the close at Seuillé, or at Innocent's pastry shop in front of the Painted Cellar in Chinon, even on pain of having to strip to my doublet to cook the little pasties! Say, matey, do you think you could throw me ashore? You know so many good tricks, I'm told! I'll give you all Salmagundi and my big snailshellery [ma grande cacquerollière], if, by your resourcefulness, I ever get to terra firma. Alas, alas, I'm drowning! Good Lord, my fine friends, since we can't reach a good port, let's ride this out, no matter where. Drop all your anchors. Let's get out of danger, I beg of you. Here honest friend get you into the chains and have the lead, if it please you. Let us know how many fathoms of water we are in. Sound, friend, in Lord Harry's name. Let's find out if you can drink here comfortably standing up, without stopping. I kind of think so."

"Uretacque [To the rigging!],[5] ho!" cried the skipper, "uretacque! Hands to the halyard! Helm a-lee [Amène uretacque]! Halyard! Rigging! Watch out for the sail! Make fast! Make fast below! Hey, to the rigging! Head on to the sea! Unhelm the tiller! Let 'er ride!"

"Have we come to that?" said Pantagruel. "May the good God the Savior come to our aid!"

"Let 'er ride, ho!" cried Jamet Brahier, pilot of the flagship. Let 'er ride! Let everyone think of his soul and fall to prayer, hoping for help only from miracles from the heavens!"

"Let's," said Panurge, "make some nice pretty vow. Alas, alas, alas! Boo hoo blubblubboo boo. Alas, alas! Let's back ourselves a pilgrim [faisons un pèlerin]. Here now, here now, everyone pitch in some nice little liards, here now!"

"On this side, ho," said Frère Jean, "by all the devils! To starboard! Let 'er ride, in the name of God! Unhelm the tiller, ho! Let 'er ride! Let's drink, ho! I mean some of the best and tastiest. Do you understand, up there? Steward, bring it out, put it on! Anyway, all this is on its way to all the millions of devils. Bring me here, my page, my drawer (so he called his breviary).[6] Wait! Draw, my friend, so! Power of God, this really is some hail and lightning! Hold good and fast up there, I beg you. When shall we get to All Saints' Day? I think today is the unfestive festival [l'infeste feste] of all the millions of devils."

"Alas!" said Panurge. "Frère Jean is damning himself well in advance. O what a good friend I'm losing there! Alas, alas, here's worse than ever before! We're going from Scylla to Charybdis, alas, I'm drowning! *Confiteor* [I confess!]! A little word or two about a will, Frère Jean my father; Sir Abstractor,[7] my friend, my Achates; Xenomanes, my everything. Alas, I'm drowning! Two words about a will. Look, here on this ship's ladder."

CHAPTER 21

Continuation of the tempest,
and brief discourse on wills made at sea.

"To make a will at this time," said Epistémon, "when we should be straining to help our crew on pain of being shipwrecked, seems to be as importunate and untimely an action as was that of Caesar's subalterns and favorites when he was entering Gaul, who were squandering their time making wills and codicils, regretting their lot, bewailing the absence of their wives and their Roman friends, when it behooved them to run to their arms and do their utmost against their enemy Arivistus. It's a stupidity like that of the carter who, when his cart was overturned in a field of stubble, was on his knees imploring the aid of Hercules and not spurring his oxen, not reaching out his hand to lift the wheels. What good will it do you to make your will here? For either we will escape this danger or we'll be drowned. If we escape, wills are not valid or authorized except by the death of the testators. If we're drowned, won't it drown with us? Who will take it to the executors?"

"Some kind wave," replied Panurge, "will cast it ashore as one did Ulysses;[1] and some king's daughter, going out to play in the cool of the evening, will come upon it, then will have built for me some magnificent cenotaph,[2] as did Dido[3] for her husband Sichaeus; Aeneas for Deiphobus on the shore of Troy, near Rhoete; Andromache for Hector in the city of Buthrotum; Aristotle for Hermias and Eubulus; the Athenians for the poet Euripides; the Romans for Drusus in Germany and for Alexander Severus, their emperor, in Gaul; Argentarius for Callaeschrus; Xenocrates for Lysidices; Timares for his son Teleutagoras; Eupolis and Aristodice for their son Theotimus; Onestes for Timocles; Callimachus for Sopoles, son of Dioclides; Catullus for his brother; Statius for his father; Germain de Brie for the Breton mariner Hervé."

"Are you out of your mind?" said Frère Jean. "Lend a hand here, in the name of five hundred thousand and millions of cartloads of devils, help us! May the pox get you in your mustaches and three half ells of canker-ous sores, to make you a pair of breeches and a new codpiece! Has our ship run aground? Power of God, how shall we get free? Here's a very devil of a sea running! We'll never escape, or the devils take me."

Then was heard a piteous exclamation from Pantagruel, saying aloud:

"Lord God, save us, we perish![4] Nevertheless not as we wish, but Thy Holy Will be done!"[5]

"God and the blessed Virgin," said Panurge, "be with us! Alas, alas, I'm drowning! Blubblubblubblub, boo boo. *In manus.*[6] Dear God, send me some dolphin to bring me safe to land like a nice little Arion.[7] I'll give out good and loud on the harp, unless it's out of kilter."

"I'll give myself to all the devils," said Frère Jean . . .

"God be with us!" Panurge kept muttering between his teeth.

" . . . If I come down there, I'll show you conclusively that your balls hang down from the ass of a cuckoldy, antlered, broken-horned calf. Nyuh, nyuh, nyuh! Come here and help us, you great blubbering calf, in the name of thirty million devils, and may they jump all over your body! Are you going to come, you sea-calf? What an ugly sight he is, that sniveler!"

"That's all you ever say."

"Come here, my merry drawer, step forward, let me rub your feathers back. 'Beatus vir qui non abiit [Blessed is the man who did not leave].'[8] I know all this by heart. Let's see the legend of Saint Nicholas.

Horrida tempestas montem turbavit acutum.

[A horrible tempest blasted the mountain peak.]

Tempeste was a great whipper of schoolboys at the Collège de Montaigu. If for whipping little boys teachers are damned, he, 'pon my honor, is on Ixion's wheel, whipping the curtal dog that turns it; if for whipping innocent children they are saved, he must be above the . . . "

CHAPTER 22

End of the tempest.

"Land, land!" cried Pantagruel. "I see land! Lads, be brave as lambs![1] We're not far from port. To the north I see sky, and it's starting to clear. Now watch out for the sirocco."[2]

"Courage, lads!" said the skipper," the sea is lighter. Now she will hold up the hullock of a sail. Hands, up to the main top! Hoist away! Haul your aftermizzen bowlines! Tack to port! Helm aweather! Pull on the starboard sheet, you son of a whore!"

"You're feeling mighty good, my fine fellow," said Frère Jean to the sailor, "to be hearing news of your mother."

"Stay close to the wind, but keep her full! Luff the tiller!"

"Luffed it is," answered the sailors.

"Cut along! Head for the harbor! Now to the eyelets! Secure the bonnes [que l'on coue bonnette]. Hoist, hoist!"

"Well said and right on!"[3] said Frère Jean. "Come on, come on, come on, lads, get into it! Good! Hoist, hoist!"

"To starboard!"

"Well said and right on! It seems to me the storm is easing up and ending, and high time. Praise be to God for all that! Our devils are beginning to hit the road [escamper dehinch]."

"The pier!"

"Spoken like a gentleman and a scholar.[4] Pier, pier! Here, in the name of God, Ponocrates, you husky rascal! He'll make nothing but male children, the lecher! Eusthenes, you gallant man, run up the fore topsail!"

"Hoist!"

"Well said, hoist! In the name of God, hoist, hoist!"

"I wouldn't stoop to fearing anything, for today's a holiday, hey, hey, hey!"[5]

"This shout of the seamen," said Epistémon, "is not amiss and pleases me, for it is a holiday."

"Hoist, hoist, good!"

"Oh!" cried Epistémon, "I command you all to have good hope. I see Castor off there to the right."[6]

"Blubblubblub blub boo boo!" said Panurge. "I'm much afraid it may be that slut Helen."

"It really," said Epistémon, "is Mixarchagevas, if you prefer the Argive name for him. Hey, hey! I see land, I see port, I see a large number of people at the harbor. I see a flame atop a lighthouse."

"Hey, hey," said the skipper, "double the point and the rocks."

"Doubled she is," replied the sailors.

"Off she goes," said the skipper, "and so do the rest of the fleet. Help in good weather."

"By Saint John!" said Panurge, "that's the way to talk! O what a nice thing to say!"

"Nyuh, nyuh, nyuh [Mgna, mgna, mgna]," said Frère Jean. "If you get to taste a drop of it, the devil taste me! Do you understand, you devil's ballocksbag [couillu au diable]? Here, matey love, here's a full tankard of the very best. Bring the flagons, hey, Gymnaste, and that great beast of an iambic or ham pasty,[7] it's all one to me. Be sure you bring her in right [Guardez de donner à travers]."

"Courage!" exclaimed Pantagruel, "courage, lads! Let's be polite. See, here, near our ship, two skiffs, three barks, five ships, eight light fliers, four gondolas, and six frigates, sent to our aid by the good people of this next island. But who is that Ucalegon yonder howling and carrying on so? Wasn't I holding the mast securely with both hands, and straighter than two hundred cables would do?"

"It's that poor devil Panurge," replied Frère Jean, "who has calf's ague. He trembles with fear when he's drunk."

"If," said Pantagruel, "he was scared during that horrible perilous tempest, as long as he strove his utmost anyway, I have not a whit less esteem for him. For, even as being afraid at any trouble at all is the mark of a flabby coward's heart, as was Agamemnon, and for that reason Achilles reproached him for the ignominy of having the eyes of a dog and the heart of a stag [Iliad 1.225]; even so, to have no fear when the situation is evidently redoubtable is a sign of some lack of apprehension. Now if there is anything to be feared after offense to God, I do not want to state that it is death. I don't want to get involved in the argument of Socrates and the Academics, that death is not in itself an evil, death in itself is not to be feared. For, as Homer's statement has it [Odyssey 5.312], it is a dismal, abhorrent, and unnatural thing to perish at sea. Indeed Aeneas, in the tempest by which his fleet was caught by surprise near Sicily, lamented not having died by the hand of the mighty Diomedes and said that those were thrice and four times happy who had died in the burning of Troy [Aeneid 1.94]. No one in here is dead: God the Savior be eternally praised for it! But really, our place here is in bad shape; we'll have to repair this wreck. Watch out that we don't run aground!"[8]

CHAPTER 23

How, with the tempest over,
Panurge plays the jolly good fellow.

"Aha!" cried Panurge, "all's well. The storm is past. Please, I beg you, let me get off first. I'd like very much to go about my affairs a bit. Shall I help you there some more? Give me that rope to coil. I have courage, plenty of it, yes indeed. Of fear, very little. Give me that, my friend. No, no, not a trace of fear. True enough, that decuman wave that swept me from prow to stern did alter my pulse a bit."

"Lower sail!"

"Well said. What, you're not doing anything, Frère Jean? Is it really the time for drinking at this point? How do we know but that Saint Martin's lackey may be brewing another fresh storm for us? Shall I give you some more help out of there? Power of a goose [Vertus guoy]! I do indeed repent, but I'm doing so late; I didn't follow the teachings of the good philosophers, who say that walking near the sea and sailing near land are very safe, delightful things, like going on foot when you're holding your horse by the bridle. Ha, ha, ha, by God, all goes well! Shall I help you there some more? Hand me that, I'll certainly do that, or the devil will be in it."

Epistémon had the inside of one hand all skinned and bleeding, from having held one of the cables with might and main, and, hearing Pantagruel's statement, said:

"Believe me, Lord, I felt no less fear and fright than did Panurge. But so what? I didn't spare any efforts to help. I consider that if really it is of necessity fatal and inevitable to die (as it is), at such or such a time, yet to die in such or such a way is in the holy will of God. Therefore we must ceaselessly implore, invoke, pray, ask, supplicate Him. But we must not set our goal and limit there; for our part we should likewise put forth our utmost efforts, and, as the Holy Envoy says, be co-operators with Him. You know what the consul Flaminius said, when by Hannibal's wiles he was hemmed in near the lake of Perugia called Trasimene. 'Lads,' he said to his soldiers, 'you must not hope to get out of here by praying and imploring the gods. We must escape from here by might and valor, and with drawn swords make our way through the enemy.'

"Likewise in Sallust: 'The help of the gods,' says Marcus Portius Cato, 'is not won by idle prayers, by womanish lamentations. By being watchful, working, doing our utmost, all things turn out as we wish—safe and sound. If, in all need and danger, a man is negligent, spineless, and lazy, to no purpose does he implore the gods; they are irritated and indignant.' "

"Devil take me . . . ," said Frère Jean.

"I'll go halves with you," said Panurge.

"If the close at Seuillé wouldn't have been all stripped of grapes and destroyed, if I had just sung *Contra hostium insidias* [against the enemy's wiles] (breviary matter), as all the rest of those poor devils the monks were doing, without rescuing the vineyard by banging the staff of the cross on those Lerné freebooters [contre les pillars de Lerné]."

"Let 'er rip [Vogue la gualère]!" said Panurge, "all goes well. Frère Jean over there is doing nothing. He's known as Frère Jean Donothing, and he's watching me here sweating and straining to help this worthy man. Sailor, first of that name,[1] our dear friend, a word with you, if I'm not bothering you. How thick are the planks of this ship?"

"They," replied the captain, "are a good two inches thick, don't be afraid."

"Power of God!" said Panurge, "so we're continually just two inches from death. Is this one of the nine joys of marriage?"[2]

"Aha! old friend, you do well to measure the peril by the ell of fear!"

"I have none of that, for my part; just call me William the Fearless. As for courage, all that and more! I don't mean courage of a lamb; I mean courage of a wolf, aplomb of a murderer. And there's nothing I fear except dangers."

CHAPTER 24

How by Frère Jean Panurge is declared
to have been scared without reason
during the storm.

"GOOD day, gentlemen!" said Panurge, "good day to one and all! Are you well, each and every one of you? Thank God, yes, and you? Pray do be most welcome and come at a good time. Let's go ashore. Oarsmen, ho, put down the gangplank! Bring that dinghy alongside. Shall I give you a hand again there? I'm hungry as a bear,[1] and with an appetite for doing good and working like four oxen. Really, here's a nice place, and good people. Lads, have you anything more for me to help you with? Don't spare the sweat of my body, for the love of God! Adam, that is man, was born to labor and toil, as a bird is to fly.[2] Our Lord wills (do you understand that?) that we eat our bread by the sweat of our bodies,[3] doing nothing like that drip of a monk you see, Frère Jean, who's drinking and dying of fear. Here's good weather. At this point I know that the answer of Anacharsis, the noble philosopher, was true and well founded in reason, when he, asked what kind of ship he thought was the safest, answered: 'The one that's in port.'"

"Better yet," said Pantagruel, "when he, asked whether the number of the dead or of the living was greater, asked: 'Among which ones do you count people sailing at sea?' Subtly signifying that those who sail on the sea are so close to the continual danger of death that they live dying and die living. Thus Portius Cato used to say that he repented of three things only: to wit, if he had ever revealed a secret of his to a woman; if he had ever spent a day in idleness; and if he had taken a long sea voyage to a place otherwise accessible by land."

"By the worthy rock I wear," said Frère Jean to Panurge. "Old ballock my friend, during the tempest you were scared without cause and without reason. For your fated destinies are not to perish by water. You will certainly be hanged high in the air or burned lusty as a Church Father.[4] My Lord, would you like a good shelter against the rain? Give up those cloaks lined with wolf-skin and badger-skin. Have Panurge flayed and cover yourself with his skin. Don't go near the fire and don't pass in front of a blacksmith's forges, in God's name! In a moment you'd see it in ashes; but expose yourself all you like to rain, snow, and hail.

489

In fact, by God! take a dive in it into the water; never will you get wet from that. Make winter boots from it; never will they let in water. Make of it winter bundles[5] for teaching young people to swim: they'll learn without danger."

"So his skin," said Pantagruel, "would be like the plant called Venus's-hair, which is never wet or dampened; it's always dry, even were it in the deepest water for as long as you wish; therefore, it is called *Adiantos*" [Greek for 'unwetted'].

"Panurge, my friend," said Frère Jean, "never be afraid of water, I beseech you: by the opposite element will your life be ended."

"All right," replied Panurge, "but the devils' cooks sometimes doze off and make mistakes in their work, and often put on to boil what was supposed to be roasted; just as in the galley in there, the master chefs often lard partridges, ringdoves, and pigeons, with the intention (as seems likely) of putting them on to roast; it happens at all events that they put on to boil partridges with cabbage, ringdoves with leeks, and pigeons they put on to boil with turnips. Listen, my friends: I protest in front of the noble company that, as for the chapel [chapelle] I vowed to My Lord Saint Nicholas between Candes and Montsoreau,[6] I mean that it shall be a flask of rosewater [chapelle d'eau rose] in which no cow or calf shall go, for I'll throw it into the bottom of the water."

"That's that sharpie for you," said Eusthenes, "that's that sharpie, sharpie and a half! That shows the truth of the Lombard proverb:

Passato el pericolo, gabato el santo."

[Danger gone and by, saint high and dry.]

CHAPTER 25

*How after the tempest Pantagruel went
ashore on the islands of the Macraeons.*

AT that moment we landed at the port of the island they called the
island of the Macraeons. The good people of the place received us honorably. An old Macrobe[1] (so they called their senior aldermen) wanted to
bring Pantagruel to the town hall to refresh himself at his ease and have a
bit of food. But he wouldn't leave the pier until all his men had landed.
After checking on them, he ordered everyone to change his clothes and
for all the supplies on the ship to be laid out on land, so that all the crews
should have a good feast, which was promptly done.

And Lord only knows what drinking and feasting went on. All the
people of the place brought victuals in abundance. The Pantagruelists
gave them even more. True it is that[2] their provisions were somewhat
damaged by the tempest just before. When the meal was over, Pantagruel
asked each and every one to do his best and his duty to repair the wreck-
age, which they did with a will. The repairing was easy, because all the
people of the island were carpenters and all artisans such as you see in the
Arsenal in Venice; and the big island was inhabited only in three ports and
ten parishes; the rest was overrun with high woods, and as deserted as if
it were the forest of the Ardennes.[3]

On our urging, the old Macrobe showed us what was notable and
worth visiting on the island. And in the dark, uninhabited forest, he
revealed several old ruined temples, several ancient obelisks, pyramids,
monuments, and sepulchers with diverse inscriptions and epitaphs, some
in hieroglyphics, others in the Ionic tongue, others in Arabic, Hagarene,[4]
Slavonic, and other tongues. Of which Epistémon scrupulously made
a copy.

Meanwhile Panurge said to Frère Jean: "This is the island of the
Macraeons here. *Macraeon* in Greek means 'old man, a man who has lived
many years.' "

"What," replied Frère Jean, "do you want me to do about that name?
Do you want me to get rid of it? I wasn't even in the country when it
was baptized."

"By the way," said Panurge, "I think the noun *maquerelle* [bawd] is
derived from it. For running a bawdy-house [maquerellaige] is suited

only for old women. The young ones are suited for tail-pushing. There-fore it would seem likely that here was the Maquerelle island, the original and prototype of the one there is in Paris.[5] Let's go fish for oysters in the shell."

The old Macrobe, in Ionic language, was asking Pantagruel by what labor and assiduity he had reached their port that day, when there had been such a horrific disturbance in the air and tempest on the sea. Pantagruel answered him that the Savior above had had consideration for the simplicity and disinterested motivation of his people, who were not traveling for gain or traffic in merchandise.[6] One sole cause had sent them to sea, to wit, an earnest desire to see, to learn, to inwardly digest, visit the oracle of Bacbuc and get the word of the Bottle about certain prob-lems posed by someone in the company. However, this had not been without great affliction and evident danger of shipwreck. Then he asked what he thought was the cause of this frightful hurricane, and whether the oceans adjacent to this one were ordinarily subject to tempest, as, in the Ocean Sea,[7] are the straits of Saint-Mathieu and Maumusson, and, in the Mediterranean Sea, the Gulf of Adalia, Montargentas [Porto di Telamone, in Tuscany], Piombino, Capo Melio in Laconia, the Strait of Gibraltar, the Strait of Messina, and others.

CHAPTER 26

How the good Macrobe tells Pantagruel about the abode and departure of heroes.[1]

Thereupon the good Macrobe replied: "Peregrine[2] friends, this is one of the Sporades Islands, not one of your Sporades that are in the Carpathian Sea, but one of the Ocean Sporades, once rich, frequented, opulent, mercantile, populous, and subject to the ruler of Britain; now, by the lapse of time and upon the decline of the world, poor and de-serted, as you see.

"In this dark forest you see, more than seventy-eight thousand parasangs long and wide, is the dwelling-place of the Daemons and He-roes who have grown old; and we believe—since the comet no longer shines which appeared to us for three whole preceding days—that one of them died yesterday, upon whose decease was stirred up that horrible tempest you suffered. For, while they live, every good abounds in this place and other nearby islands, and on the sea is perpetual calm and serene weather. At the death of each and every one of these, we ordinarily hear through the forest great piteous lamentations, and see on land plagues, storms, and afflictions, in the air disturbances and darkness, at sea tempest and hurricane."

"There is much likelihood," said Pantagruel, "in what you say. For even as the torch or candle, all the time it is alive and burning, shines on those present, lights up everything around, delights each and every one, and displays its utility and its light, harms and displeases no one at the moment it is extinguished, infects the air by its smoke and vapor, harms those present, and displeases everyone; so it is with these noble and notable souls. All the time they dwell in their bodies; their stay is peaceful, useful, delightful, honorable; upon the moment of their decease, there commonly occur throughout the islands and continent great disturbances in the air, darkness, lightning bolts, hailstorms; on land, tremors, earthquakes, astonishments; at sea, hurricane and tempest, with lamentations of peoples, changes of religions, removals of kingdoms, overthrows of states."

"We," said Epistémon, "have seen this by experience not long ago on the death of the valiant and learned knight Guillaume du Bellay,[3] during whose life France enjoyed such felicity that the whole world was envious of her, all the world wanted to be her ally, all the world dreaded her. Immediately after his death, she came to be held in all the world's scorn for a very long time."

"Thus," said Pantagruel, "after the death of Anchises at Trapani in Sicily [*Aeneid* 3.707–708], the tempest gave Aeneas a terrible time. This may perhaps be the reason why Herod,[4] the tyrant and cruel king of Judaea, seeing himself near a death horrible and frightful in nature (for he died of phthiriasis [pediculosis], devoured by worms and lice [Acts 12.23], as earlier had died Lucius Sulla; Pherecydes the Syrian, tutor of Pythagoras; the Grecian poet Alcman; and others), and foreseeing that at his death the Jews would light bonfires to celebrate, had all the nobles and magistrates from all the cities, towns and castles in Judaea assemble in his seraglio, under the fraudulent color of wanting to communicate to them matters of importance for the governance and protection of the province. When they had come and appeared in person, he had them locked up in the hippodrome of the seraglio. Then he said to his sister Salome and her husband Alexander: 'I'm quite sure the Jews will rejoice at my death; but if you will hear and carry out what I'll tell you, my obsequies will be honorable and marked by public lamentation. The moment I have died, have killed, by the archers of my guard, to whom I have given express commission for this, all these nobles and magistrates who are locked up in here. By your doing this, all Judaea, in spite of itself, will be in mourning and lamentation, and it will seem to foreigners that it is because of my decease, as if some heroic soul had passed away.'

"As much did one desperate tyrant hope for when he said: 'When I die, let the earth be intermingled with fire.'⁵ That is to say: 'Let the whole world perish.' Words which that villain Nero changed, saying: 'While I live,' as Suetonius attests. This detestable statement, mentioned by Cicero, Book 3 *De finibus,* and Seneca, Book 2 *De clementia,* is attributed by Dion Nicaeus and Suidas to the Emperor Tiberius."

CHAPTER 27

How Pantagruel discourses on the departure of
certain heroic souls, and of the horrific prodigies that
*accompanied the demise of the late lord of Langey.*¹

"**I** wouldn't want," continued Pantagruel, "to have been spared the storm at sea, which caused us so much vexation and trouble and so not to have heard what this good Macrobe told us.² Furthermore, I am easily induced to believe what he told us about the comet seen in the air for some days preceding such a decease. For certain such souls are so noble, precious, and heroic, that notice of their departure and death is given us by the heavens for a few days beforehand.

"And as the prudent doctor, seeing by the signs and prognostics his patient entering upon his way down to death, by a few days ahead warns the wife, children, relatives, and friends of the impending decease of the husband, father, or neighbor, so that they may admonish him to put his house in order exhort and bless his children, commend his wife's widow-hood, declare what he knows will be necessary for the upkeep of the underage children, and not be surprised by death without making a will and leaving orders concerning his soul and his household: likewise the benevolent heavens, as if joyful at receiving another of these blessed souls, before their decease seem to light bonfires of joy by such meteoric apparitions, which the heavens wish to be to humans as a certain prognostic and truthful prediction that in a few days such venerable souls will leave their bodies and the earth.

"No more nor less than in Athens of old the Areopagite judges, voting on the judgment of imprisoned criminals, used certain notations according to the variety of the verdicts: by Q [theta] meaning condemnation to death [thanatos]; by T [tau], absolution; by A [alpha] amplification, to wit, when the case was not yet liquidated;[3] these, publicly displayed, freed from worry and anxiety the relatives, friends, and others curious to hear what would be the outcome and the verdict on the malefactors detained in prison. Thus by such comets, as if by ethereal signals, the heavens tacitly say: 'Mortal men, if from these happy souls you want to find out, learn, understand, take in, foresee, anything concerning the public or private utility, make haste to come before them and get their answer from them, for the end and denouement of the comedy is at hand. Once this is past, you will regret them in vain.'

"They do more. This, in order to declare that the earth and earthlings are not worthy of the presence, company, and enjoyment of such remarkable souls, they stun and terrify it [the earth] by prodigies, portents, monsters, and other premonitory signs formed against all order of nature, which we saw several days before the departure of that ever so illustrious, high-minded, and heroic soul of the learned and valorous Lord of Langey, of whom you have spoken."

"I remember it," said Epistémon, "and my heart still shivers at it and trembles within its pericardium, when I think of the extremely varied and horrific prodigies that we clearly saw several days before his departure. So that the lords d'Assier,[4] Chemant, Mailly le borgne, Saint-Ayl, Villeneuve-la-Guyart, Master Gabriel, the doctor from Savigliano, Rabelays,[5] Cohuau, Massuau,[6] Majorici, Bullou, Cercu, called the Burgomaster, François Proust, Ferron, Charles Girard, François Bourré, and many others, friends, domestics, and servants of the deceased, all frightened, kept looking at one another in silence without speaking a word by mouth, all certainly thinking and foreseeing in their understandings that shortly France would be deprived of a knight so perfect and so necessary for her glory and protection, and that the heavens were rehearsing it as being their proper and natural due."

"By the tip of my cowl [Huppe de froc]!" said Frère Jean, "I want to turn scholar before I die! I have a pretty fair sort of mind, I find.[7]

> I ask you, and I ask of you,
> As of his guard a king may do,
> A queen may ask her infant too.

"Can death be the end of these heroes and demigods you've spoken of? By 're Lady [Par Nettre Dene] I was thinking in my thinkeroo [je pensoys en pensaroys] that they were immortal like fair angels, God forgive me. But this venerable Macrobe says that they finally die."

"Not all of them," replied Pantagruel. "The Stoics used to say that they were all mortal except One, Who is immortal, impassible, invisible.

"Pindar clearly says that to the Hamadryad goddesses [ès déesses Hamadryades] no more thread, that is to say no more life, is spun from the distaff and flax of the wicked Destinies and Fates than for trees preserved by them.[8] These are oaks, from which they were sprung, in the opinion of Callimachus, and Pausanias, in Phoci,[9] with whom Martianus Capella concurs. As for the demigods, pans, satyrs, sylvans, will-o'-the wisps, Aegipans, nymphs, heroes, and daemons, many people have, by the sum total resulting from the diverse ages surmised by Hesiod, reckoned their lives to be of nine thousand seven hundred and twenty years, a number composed of unity rising to quadrinity, and the entire quadrinity doubled in itself four times, and then the whole thing multiplied five times by solid triangles.[10] See Plutarch in his book *On the cessation of oracles*" [chaps. 11 and 19].

"That," said Frère Jean, "is not breviary matter. I don't believe a word of it except what you'd like me to."

"I believe," said Pantagruel, "that all intellective souls are exempt from the scissors of Atropos. All are immortal: angels, daemons, and human souls. However, in this connection, I'll tell you a very strange story, but one written and attested by many scholarly learned historians."

CHAPTER 28

How Pantagruel relates a piteous story concerning the decease of heroes.

"A s Epitherses, father of Aemilian the rhetorician, was sailing from Greece to Italy on a ship laden with various goods and many passengers, and the wind died down one evening near the Echinades, islands that lie between the Morea [Peloponnesus] and Tunis, the ship was borne near Paxos [south of Corfu]. When they drew near there, while some of the passengers were asleep, others awake, some eating supper and drinking, there was heard from the island of Paxos a voice of someone loudly calling out *Thamoun*.[1] At which cry they were all terrified. This Thamous was their pilot, a native of Egypt, but not known by name except to a few of the travelers. A second time the voice was heard, which called out *Thamoun* in horrific cries. As no one answered, but all remained in silent trepidation, for the third time this voice was heard, more terrible than before. Wherefore it came about that Thamous replied: 'I am here, what do you ask of me? What do you want me to do?' Then was heard this voice still louder, telling and ordering him, when he was in Palodes, to announce and say that the great God Pan was dead.

"When this word was heard, Epitherses said that all the sailors and travelers were astonished and greatly terrified; and as they were deliberating among themselves which would be better, whether to be silent or to announce what had been commanded, Thamous said his opinion was that in case they had the wind astern, they should go on past without saying a word; but if it happened that it was calm, they should report what he had heard. So when they were near Palodes it came about that they had neither wind nor current. So then Thamous, climbing onto the prow, and casting his eyes to land, said, as he had been ordered to, that Pan the great was dead. He had not yet finished his final word when there were heard great sighs, great lamentations and cries of fright on land not from one person alone but from many together. This news, since many had been present, was soon divulged in Rome. And Tiberius Caesar, then emperor in Rome, sent for this Thamous. And having heard him, he put faith in his words. And on inquiring of the learned men, who were at that time at his court in great numbers, who this Pan was, he learned from their report that he had been the son of Mercury and Penelope.

497

"So Herodotus had written earlier, and Cicero, in the third book of *De natura deorum* [*Of the nature of the gods* 3.22]. Nevertheless, I would interpret it to be about that great Savior of the faithful, Who was ignominiously slain in Judaea by the iniquity of the pontiffs, doctors, priests, and monks of the Mosaic Law.[2] And the interpretation does not seem preposterous to me, for He may rightly in the Grecian tongue be called Pan, seeing that He, is our All. All that we are, all that we live, all that we have, all that we hope for is Him, in Him, from Him, by Him. He is the good Pan, the great Pastor, Who, as the passionate shepherd Corydon[3] attests, holds in His love and devotion not only his sheep but also his shepherds. And at His death there were wails, sighs, cries of terror, and lamentations in the entire machine of the universe, heavens, earth, sea, hell. The time concurs with this interpretation of mine, for this most good, most great Pan, our sole Savior, died outside Jerusalem in the reign in Rome of Tiberius Caesar."

Pantagruel, on finishing this statement, remained in silence and profound contemplation. Shortly after, we saw the tears flow down his cheeks, big as ostrich eggs. God take me if by one single word I'm lying about it.

CHAPTER 29

How Pantagruel passed the island of Coverup,[1]
which was ruled by Fastilent.[2]

WHEN the ships of the joyous convoy were renewed and repaired, the victuals replenished, the Macraeons more than content and satisfied with what Pantagruel had spent there, and our men even more joyous than usual, on the following day we set sail in great cheer to the serene and delightful Aguyon [north wind]. Well on in the day, from afar, was pointed out by Xenomanes the island of Coverup, which was ruled by Fastilent, whom Pantagruel had heard of in other days, and he would have liked to see him in person, were it not that Xenomanes dissuaded him, both because of the long detour out of the way and the meager fun he said there was in the whole island and the Lord's court.

"When all's said and done," said he, "all you'll see there is a great swallower of gray [dried] peas, a great man for shellfish [un grand cacquerotier], a great mole-catcher, a great hay-bundler, a demigiant with a downy beard and double tonsure, sprung from Lanternland, a great Lanterner, standard-bearer of the Ichthyophagi, dictator of Mustardland,[3] whipper of small boys, burner of ashes,[4] father and nursling of the physicians, abounding in pardons, indulgences, and solemn masses, a worthy man, a good Catholic[5] and of great piety. He cries for three quarters of the day. He is never to be found at weddings. True it is that he's the busiest maker of larding sticks and spits there is in forty kingdoms. About six years ago, passing by Coverup, I took away a big one and gave it to the butcher of Candes. They thought highly of them, and not without cause. I'll show you two of them when we get home, fastened over the great portal. The victuals he feeds on are salt hauberks, salt caskets and headpieces, and salt helmets.[6] From which he sometimes suffers a bad hotpiss.[7]

"His garments are merry in both cut and color, for he wears gray and cool, nothing in front and nothing behind, and sleeves to match."

"You'll give me pleasure," said Pantagruel, "if, even as you have described to me his clothes, his food, the way he acts, and his pastimes, you tell me also about his physique and bodily conditions in detail."

"Please do, old ballock," said Frère Jean, "for I've found him in my breviary, and he runs out after the movable feasts."[8]

"I'll be glad to," replied Xenomanes. "We may peradventure hear more about him when we pass the Wild Island, dominated by the stubby Chitterlings, his deadly enemies, against whom he wages eternal war. Were it not for the help of the noble Shrovetide [Mardigras], their protector and neighbor, that great Lanterner Fastilent would already have driven them out of their dwelling-place."

"Are they," said Frère Jean, "male or female? Angels or mortals? Women or maidens?"

"They are," replied Xenomanes, "female in sex, mortal in state, some maidens, others not."

"Devil take me," said Frère Jean, "if I'm not for them! What kind of disorder in nature is that, to make war against women? Let's go back. I'll cut that great villain to pieces [Sacmentons ce grand villain]."

"Fight against Fastilent?" said Panurge. "In the name of all the devils, I'm not that crazy and bold at the same time! *Quid juris* [what legal decision] would there be if we found ourselves caught in a squeeze between Chitterlings and Fastilent, between the anvil and the hammer? A pox on that! Get out of there! Let's sail on past! Farewell, I tell you, Fastilent. I commend the Chitterlings to you, and don't forget the Black Puddings."[9]

CHAPTER 30

How Fastilent is anatomized and described by Xenomanes.

"FASTILENT has (or at least in my time had)," said Xenomanes, "as for his inward parts, a brain comparable in size, color, substance, and vigor, to the left ballock of a male hand-worm.[1]

The lobes thereof, like an auger.

The vermiform excrescence [median lobe], like a croquet mallet.

The membranes, like a monk's cowl.

The optic nerves, like a mason's tray.

The vault [cerebral fornix], like a wimple.

The pineal gland, like a bagpipe.

The *retz admirable* [wondrous network], like a horse's frontstall.

The mamillary tubercles, like mended shoes.

The eardrums, like a whirligig.

The petrous bones [bones of the temple], like a plume.

The nape of the neck, like a cresset light [a kind of lantern].

The nerves, like a spigot.

The uvula, like a sackbut.

The palate, like a mitten.

The saliva, like a weaver's shuttle.

The tonsils, like a magnifying glass.

The bridge of the nose, like a hamper.

The throat, like a vintager's jacket.

The stomach, like a baldrick.

The pylorus, like a pitchfork.

The windpipe, like an oyster knife.

The throat [le guaviet], like a ball of tow.

The lungs, like an amice.

The heart, like a chasuble.

The mediastinum, like an earthenware cup.

The pleura, like a crow's beak.

The arteries, like a watchman's cloak.

The diaphragm, like a cockaded cap.

The liver, like a twibill [two-bladed axe].

The veins, like a windowframe.

The spleen, like a quail call.

The bowels, like a partridge net.

The gall, like a carpenter's axe.

The entrails, like a gauntlet.

The mesentry, like an abbot's miter.

The hungry gut [intestin jeun], like a pincer.

The blind gut [intestin borgne], like a breastplate.

The colon, like a toasting glass.

The bum-gut, like a monk's carousing glass.

The kidneys, like a trowel.

The loins, like a padlock.

The ureters, like a pothook.

The emulgent veins, like two squirts.

The spermatic vessels, like a pastry puff.

The prostate gland, like a feather jar.

The bladder, like a stone bow [crossbow or catapult].

The neck thereof, like a bell clapper.

The abdomen [le mirach], like an Albanian hat.

The peritoneum [le siphach], like an archer's armlet.

The muscles, like a bellows.

The tendons, like a hawking glove.

The ligaments, like a wallet.

The bones, like three-cornered cheesecakes.

The marrow, like a pouch.

The cartilages, like a heath tortoise [mole].

The adenoids, like a pruning knife.

The animal spirits, like heavy punches.

The vital spirits, like long flicks on the nose.[2]

The hot blood, like a flurry of raps on the nose.

The urine, like a popefig.

The sperm, like a hundred lath nails. And his wet nurse was telling us that he, when married to Midlent, begat only a number of locative adverbs and certain double fasts.

He had a memory like a scarf.

Common sense, like a drone.

His imagination, like a carillon of bells.

His thoughts, like a flight of starlings.

His consciousness [or conscience], like an unnesting of young herons.

His deliberations, like a pouchful of barley.

His repentance, like the carriage of a double cannon.

His enterprises, like the ballast of a galleon.

His understanding, like a torn breviary.

His notions, like snails crawling out of strawberries.

His will, like three walnuts in a dish.

His desire, like six trusses of sainfoin.

His judgment, like a shoehorn.

His discretion, like a mitten.

His reason, like a footstool."[3]

CHAPTER 31

*Anatomy of Fastilent
as regards the outward parts.*

"F ASTILENT," said Xenomanes as he continued, "as regards his outward parts, was a little better proportioned except for the seven ribs he had over and above the common form of humans.

Toes he had like a virginal on an organ.[1]

Nails, like a gimlet.

Feet, like a guitar.

Heels, like a mace.

Soles of the feet, like a crucible.

Legs, like a lure.

Knees, like a stool.

Thighs, like a crossbow's gaffle.[2]

Haunches, like a wimble.

Belly big as a tun, buttoned up in the old style and loosely girt.[3]

Navel, like a fiddle [une vielle].

Groin, like a mincemeat pasty.

Member, like a slipper.

Balls, like a little leather vial.

Genitals, like a carpenter's plane.

Cremasters, like a racket.

Perineum, like a flageolet.

Asshole, like a crystal mirror.

Buttocks, like a harrow.

Loins, like a butterpot.

Alkatin [Arabic for sacrum], like a billiard table.

Back, like a large-sized crowbow.

Vertebrae, like a bagpipe.

Ribs, like a spinningwheel.

Brisket, like a canopy.

Shoulder blades, like a mortar.

Chest, like a hand-organ.

Nipples, like the mouth of a hunting horn.

Armpits, like a checkerboard.

Shoulders, like a stretcher.

Arms, like a riding hood.

Fingers, like friary andirons.

Wrist bones, like a pair of stilts.

Forearms [fauciles], like sickles [faucilles].

Elbows, like rat traps.

Hands, like a currycomb.

Neck, like a great drinking cup.

Throat, like a hippocras filter.

Adam's apple, like a barrel from which hung two very fair and harmonious bronze wattles in the shape of a sand hourglass.

Beard, like a lantern.

Chin, like a mushroom.

Ears, like two mittens.

Nose, like a buskin grafted on him like a shield bud.[4]

Nostrils, like a baby's bonnet.

Eyebrows, like a dripping-pan.

Over his left eyebrow he had a mark of the size and shape of a urinal.

Eyelids, like a rebec.

Eyes, like a comb case.

Optic nerves, like a fire-steel.[5]

Forehead, like a false cup.[6]

Temples, like a watering pot.

Cheeks, like two wooden clogs.

Jaws, like a goblet.

Teeth, like a boar-spear. Of his milk teeth such as this you will find one at Colonges-les-Royaux in Poitou, and two at la Brosse [Charente-Maritime] in Saintonge, over the cellar door.[7]

Tongue, like a harp.

Mouth, like a horse blanket.

Face, as misshapen as a mule's packsaddle.

Head, twisted around like an alembic.

Skull, like a game-pouch.

Cranial sutures, like the seal ring of a papal fisherman.

Skin, like a gabardine.

Epidermis, like a bolting cloth.

Hair, like a scrub brush.

Body hair, as has been said."

CHAPTER 32

Continuation of Fastilent's physical features.

"IT'S a natural wonder," said Xenomanes as he went on, "to see and hear of the state of Fastilent.

If he spat, it was basketfuls of wild artichoke.

If he blew his nose, it was little salt eels.

If he cried, it was ducks with onion sauce.

If he trembled, it was big hare pasties.

If he sweated, it was codfish in fresh butter.

If he belched, it was oysters in the shell.

If he sneezed, it was barrels full of mustard.

If he coughed, it was jars of quince marmelade.

If he sobbed, it was pennyworths of watercress.

If he yawned, it was potfuls of split pea soup.

If he sighed, it was smoked ox tongues.

If he whistled, it was scuttlefuls of green monkeys.[1]

If he snored, it was bowls of shelled beans.

If he frowned, it was pigs' feet smoked in lard.

If he spoke, it was coarse Auvergne frieze, a far cry from being crimson silk, of which Parisatis wanted spun the words of those who spoke to her son Cyrus, king of the Persians.

If he blew, it was poor boxes for indulgences.[2]

If he blinked his eyes, it was waffles and wafers.

If he grumbled, it was March-born cats.

If he nodded his head, it was iron-shod wagons.

If he made a face, it was a manual drumbeat.[3]

If he muttered, it was law clerks' revels.

If he hopped up and down, it was delays and five-year respites.

If he drew back, it was sea cockleshells.

If he driveled, it was communal ovens.

If he was hoarse, it was morris dance entrances.

If he farted, it was brown cowhide leggings.

If he fizzled, it was cordovan summer boots.

If he scratched himself, it was new ordinances.

If he sang, it was peas in the pod.

If he crapped, it was toadstools and mushrooms.

If he gorged, it was cabbages cooked in oil, alias *caules amb'olif.*

If he discoursed, it was snows of yesteryear.[4]

If he was concerned, it was about shaven and shorn alike.[5]

If he gave anything, it was at so much for the bearer.[6]

If he daydreamed, it was of pricks flying and rampant against a wall.[7]

If he dreamed, it was of rent rolls.

"A strange case: he worked doing nothing, he did nothing working. He had eyes open sleeping, slept having his eyes open, open like those of hares in Champagne, fearing some sudden raid by the Chitterlings, his ancient enemies. He laughed as he bit, bit as he laughed. He ate nothing fasting, fasted eating nothing. He nibbled out of suspicion, drank in imagination. He bathed on top of high steeples, dried himself in ponds and streams. He fished in the air and there caught decuman crayfish. He went hunting in the depths of the sea and there found ibexes, wild goats, and chamois. He ordinarily poked out the eyes of every crow caught by surprise.[8] He was afraid of nothing but his shadow and the bleating of plump kids. On certain days he pounded the pavements. He played with the ropes of girded friars.[9] Of his fist he made a mallet.[10] On shaggy parchment, with his stout pen-case, he wrote prognostics and almanacs."[11]

"That's the dandy," said Frère Jean, "that's my man. That's the one I'm looking for. I'm going to send him a challenge."

"That," said Pantagruel, "is a strange and monstrous figure of a man, if man I am to call him. You put me in mind of the shape and features of Amodunt and Discord."

"What sort of shape did they have?" asked Frère Jean, "I never heard of them, God forgive me."

"I'll tell you," replied Pantagruel, "what I've read about them in old stories. Physis (that's Nature) in her first brood bore Beauty and Harmony without carnal copulation, since of herself she is richly fecund and fertile. Antiphysis, who from all time has been the party adverse to Nature, was immediately envious over so fair and honorable a delivery, and, contrariwise, gave birth to Amodunt and Discord by copulation with Tellumon.

"They had heads spherical and completely round, like a balloon, not gently compressed on each side, as the human shape is. Their ears were raised up high, big as donkeys' ears; their eyes, sticking out of their heads, on bones like heel bones, without eyebrows, hard, as are crabs' eyes; their feet round as balls; arms and hands turned around backward toward the shoulders; and they traveled on their heads, doing continuous cartwheels, head over heels,[12] with their legs in the air. And (as you know that to female monkeys their little monkeys seem handsomer than anything in the world) Antiphysis praised her children's shape and tried to prove that it was more beautiful and attractive than that of the children of Physis, saying that thus to have your feet in the air, your head down below, was an imitation of the Creator of the Universe, seeing that hair in man is like roots, legs like branches, for trees are more conveniently fixed in the ground on their roots than they would be on their branches; by this demonstration arguing that her children were much better and aptly like an upright tree than those of Physis, which were like a tree upside down. As regards the arms and legs, she proved that they were more reasonably turned toward the shoulders, because that part of the body should not be without defense, considering that the front was adequately protected by the teeth, which a person can use not only in chewing without the help of his hands, but to defend himself against harmful things.

"Thus by the testimony and witness of the brute beasts, she drew all the fools and madmen to her view and was held in admiration by all brainless people unequipped with good judgment and common sense.[13] Since then she engendered the Matagotz,[14] Cagotz, and Papelars, the maniacal Pistols,[15] the demoniacal Calvins,[16] impostors of Geneva, the rabid Putherbeuses,[17] the Gut-guzzlers, Hypocrites, Toadies,[18] Cannibals, and other monsters deformed and misshapen in despite of Nature."[19]

CHAPTER 33

How Pantagruel sighted a monstrous physeter
near the Wild Island.

As we neared the Wild Island [l'isle Farouche] well on in the day,
Pantagruel sighted from afar a great monstrous cachalot coming toward
us, puffing, puffed up, rising higher than the main tops of our ships,
spouting water from its throat into the air ahead of it, as if it were a great
stream tumbling from some mountain. Pantagruel pointed it out to the
captain and to Xenomanes. On the captain's advice the trumpets of the
Thalamège rang out with the message: Watch out! Close up [Guare!
Serre]! At this sound, all the ships, galleons, and brigantines, according to
their orders and to naval practice, drew up in a Y-shaped formation,
Pythagoras's letter,[1] such as you see cranes use in their flight, such as you
find in an acute angle, at the cone and base of which was the said
Thalamège, ready and in position to give valorous combat. Frère Jean,
valiant and ready for action, climbed up on the forecastle with the cannoneers. Panurge began to howl and wail worse than ever.

"Bub-bub-babble-blubblub," he wailed, "this is worse than ever. Let's
run away! This, by gorry [c'est, par la mort boeuf], is Leviathan as described by the noble prophet Moses in the life of that holy man Job [Job
40–41]. He'll swallow us all, men and ships, like so many pills. In his great
infernal gullet we'll take up no more room than would a tidbit of spiced
oats in an ass's throat. Look, here he is! Let's flee, let's go to land! I believe
he's the very sea monster that was destined long ago to devour Andromeda.[2] We're all done for! O, if only there were here now to slay him some
valiant Perseus [Per-se-us]!"

"*Persé jus* [pierced and on his back] by me he shall be!" replied
Pantagruel. "Have no fear."

"Power of God!" said Panurge, "take us out of the causes of fear. When
do you expect me to be afraid, if not when the danger is evident?"

"If such," said Pantagruel, "is your ill-fated destiny, as Frère Jean was
stating a while ago, you should be afraid of Pyroeis, Eous, Aethon, and
Phlegon, the famous flammivomous [flame-vomiting] horses of the Sun,
who breathe out fire through their nostrils; of physeters, which spout
nothing but water from their blowholes and from their throats, you
should have no fear at all. Never from their water will you be in danger

of death. By that element you will rather be made safe and preserved than troubled and harmed."

"Next!" said Panurge ["A l'aultre!" dist Panurge]. "That's hitting the nail right on the thumb! Powers of a little fish [Vertus d'un petit poisson]! Haven't I explained to you enough about the transmutation of the elements and the easy correspondence there is between roast and boiled meat, between boiled and roasted? Alas! Here he is! I'm going and hide below yonder! We're all dead this time! Above the topmast I see cruel Atropos with her scissors newly ground, ready to cut the thread of our lives. Look out! Here he is! O how horrible and abominable you are! You've drowned plenty of others who didn't come back to boast about it. Good Lord! If he spouted good wine, white or red, tasty, delicious, instead of this bitter water, stinking and salty, it would to some extent have been tolerable, and would give us some occasion for patience, after the example of that English milord who, when ordered to take his choice of deaths for the crimes he was convicted of, chose to be drowned in a tun of Malmsey.[3]

"Here he is! Oh, oh! You Devil, Satan, Leviathan! I can't look at you, you're so hideous and detestable! Go off to the hearing, go off to the Shysteroos!"[4]

CHAPTER 34

How Pantagruel slew the monstrous physeter.

THE physeter, coming inside the wedge and angles of the ships and galleons, was spouting water on the former by the barrelfuls, as if it were the cataracts of the Nile in Ethiopia. Darts, arrows, javelins, pikes, spears, halberds flew upon it from all sides. Frère Jean did not spare himself in this. Panurge kept dying of fear. The artillery hurled thunder and lightning like the Devil, and tried its best to prick it and not in jest.[1] But this was doing little good; for the iron and bronze cannonballs, as they sank into its skin, seemed to melt, to see them from a distance, as tiles do in the sun. Then Pantagruel, considering the occasion and the need, unfolds his arms and shows what he could do.

You say, and it is written, that that wretch Commodus, emperor of Rome, could shoot a bow so adroitly that from quite a distance he could send his arrows between the fingers of young children as they held their hand in the air, without touching them at all.

You also tell us about an Indian archer, at the time when Alexander the Great conquered India, who was such an expert shot that from a distance he could send his arrows through a ring, though they were three cubits long and the iron point thereof was so big and heavy that with it he could pierce steel cutlasses, thick bucklers, steel breastplates, generally whatever he could hit, even though it were as firm, resistant, hard, and sturdy, as you could say.[2]

You also tell us wonders about the deftness of the ancient Franks, who were rated above all others in the sagittary art and who, when hunting black or russet animals,[3] rubbed the point of their arrows with hellebore,[4] because the flesh of venison struck with this was more tasty, tender, and delicious, marking off and removing, however, the part all around the spot thus hit.

You also give an account of the Parthians, who fired more cleverly backward than other nations did forward. You also celebrate the Scythians in this dexterity, on whose behalf long ago an envoy sent to Darius, king of the Persians, offered him, without a word, a bird, a frog, a mouse, and five arrows. When asked what such presents meant, and if he had orders to say anything, he answered no. At which Darius was left utterly astonished and dumbfounded, but that Gobryas, one of the seven captains who had killed the Magi, expounded and interpreted it to him, saying: "By these gifts and offerings the Scythians are tacitly saying to you: 'If the Persians do not fly up to the sky like birds, or hide toward the center of the earth like mice, or plunge like frogs to the bottom of the ponds and swamps, they shall be sent to their doom by the power and the arrows of the Scythians.' "[5]

The noble Pantagruel, in the art of shooting and throwing darts, was incomparably more admirable. For with his horrible javelins and darts (which actually looked like the great beams on which rest the bridges of Nantes, Saumur, and Bergerac,[6] and in Paris the pont-au-Change and the Pont-aux-Meusnier, in length, stoutness, weight, and ironwork), from a thousand paces away he would open oysters in the shell without touching the edges; would snuff a candle without putting it out; would hit magpies in the eye; would unsole boots without damaging them; would strip the fur from hoods without harming them; would turn the pages of Frère Jean's breviary, one after the other, without tearing a thing.

With such darts, of which there was a large supply in his ship, on his first shot he pierced the physeter in the forehead so that it went through both jaws and tongue, so that it could no longer open its mouth, or take in or spout water. With the second shot he put out its right eye; with the third, its left eye, and the physeter was seen, to the great jubilation of all, to wear these three horns on its forehead, leaning a bit forward, in the form of an equilateral triangle [en figure triangulaire aequilatérale], turning from one side to the other, wavering and swerving as if stubbed, blind, and near death.

Not content with this, Pantagruel darted him another on the tail likewise leaning a little to the rear; then three others on the spine in a perpendicular line, in equal spaces from tail to prow [head] divided three times precisely.

Finally he shot onto his flanks fifty on one side and fifty on the other. In such a way that the physeter's body looked like the keel of a three-masted galleon mortised by an adequate adjustment of its beams, as if they were the ribs and cablerings of the keel.[7] And it was a very entertaining sight to see.

Thereupon the physeter, dying, rolled over on its back, belly up, as do all dead fish; and overturned thus, with the beams underneath it in the water, it looked like the scolopendria, a serpent with a hundred feet, as described by the ancient sage Nicander [*Theriaca*, note 12].

CHAPTER 35

How Pantagruel goes ashore on the Wild Island,
ancient abode of the Chitterlings.[1]

THE lead oarsmen of the ship with the lantern brought the physeter, tied up, ashore on the next island, called the Wild Island, in order to dissect it and collect the fat of the kidneys, which they said was very useful, and necessary for the cure of a certain malady they called Lack of Money.

Pantagruel took no account of it, for he had seen enough others like it, indeed even more enormous, in the Gallic Ocean.[2] He consented, however, to go ashore on the Wild Island to allow some of his men to dry and refresh themselves, who had been drenched and befouled by the nasty physeter, at a little deserted seaport to the south, located next to a tall, fair, and pleasant wooded grove, out of which flowed a delightful stream of fresh water, clear and silvery. There, under lovely tents, the kitchens were set up without sparing the firewood. When each man had changed his clothes as he saw fit, Frère Jean rang the bell. At the sound of it the tables were set up and the food promptly served. Pantagruel, joyfully dining with his men, noticed certain little tame Chitterlings climbing without a word up a tall tree near the improvised pantry. So he asked Xenomanes: "What kind of animals are those?" thinking they were squirrels, weasels, martens, or ermines.

"They're Chitterlings," replied Xenomanes. "This is the Wild Island, which I was telling you about this morning; between these and Fastilent, their mortal enemy, it has long been war to the death. And I think that from the cannonades fired against the physeter they got some fright and suspicion that their said enemy was there with his forces to take them by surprise or lay waste their island, as he has already tried to do several times in vain and to little advantage, foiled by the care and vigilance of the Chitterlings, whom (as Dido said to the companion of Aeneas, who wanted to make port in Carthage without her knowledge and permission ['sans son sceu et licence': *Aeneid* 1.561–578]) the malignity of their enemy and the nearness of his lands constrained to be on their guard and keep watch continually against him."

"My goodness, dear friend," said Pantagruel, "if you see that by some honorable means we might put an end to this war and reconcile them together, tell me what you think. I'll work on it with all my heart and not spare my pains to moderate and settle the matters in dispute between the two parties."

"That is not possible for the present," replied Xenomanes. "It was about four years ago that, stopping off here and in Coverup Island, I made it my business to discuss peace between them, or at least long truces; and now they would be good friends and neighbors, if either one of the two parties had been willing to put aside their passions about one single matter. Fastilent would not include in a peace treaty the wild Blood Puddings, or the Mountaineer Sausages [les Saulcissons montigènes], their former good friends and allies. The Chitterlings demanded that the fortress of Herringkegs [la forteresse de Cacques] should be ruled and governed at their discretion, as is the castle of Saltingtub [le chasteau de Sallouoir], and that there should be driven out of it I know not what stinking, villainous assassins and brigands who were holding it, which could not be agreed on, and the conditions seemed unfair to both parties.

"So no reconciliation was concluded between them. Nonetheless they remained less harsh and milder enemies than they were in the past. But since then, by the publication of the decisions of the national council of Chesil,[3] by which they [the Chitterlings] were cited, bullied, and denounced, by which also Fastilent was declared to be full of shit, messed up, and dried out as a stockfish [breneux, hallebrené et stocfisé], in case he made any agreement whatever with them, they have become horrifically embittered, envenomed, indignant, and obstinate in their hearts, and it is impossible to remedy this. You'd sooner get the cats and rats, the dogs and hares, reconciled with one another."

CHAPTER 36

How an ambush is laid against Pantagruel by the wild Chitterlings.

As Xenomanes said this, Frère Jean espied twenty-five or thirty young Chitterlings of slender build at the harbor hurrying at top speed back toward their city, citadel, castle, and fortress of Chimneys,[1] and said to Pantagruel:

"There's going to be some monkey business [Il y aura icy de l'asne] going on here, I predict. These venerable Chitterlings might peradventure mistake you for Fastilent, although you don't look a bit like him. Let's leave off our feasting and get ourselves ready to resist them."

"That," said Xenomanes, "would not be too bad a thing to do. Chitterlings are Chitterlings, always duplicitous and treacherous."

Thereupon Pantagruel rises from table to reconnoiter outside the grove; then promptly comes back and assures us that on the left he has discovered an ambush of the stubby Chitterlings, and on the right, half a league away, a great battalion of powerful gigantic Chitterlings in battle array marching furiously toward us along a little hill, to the sound of bagpipes and flageolets, sheeps' paunches and bladders, merry fifes and drums, trumpets and clarions.

By conjecture from seventy-eight ensigns that he counted there, we estimated that their number was no less than forty-two thousand. The order they kept, their proud march and confident faces, led us to believe that these were no Meatballs [ce n'estoient Friquenelles], but veteran warrior Chitterlings. From the front ranks all the way back to the standards, they were all armed cap-à-pie, with pikes that looked small from a distance, but were steel tipped and with very sharp points. On the wings they were flanked by a large number of game Blood Puddings [de Boudins sylvaticques], massive Meat Pasties [de Guodiveaux massifz], and Sausages on horseback, all well set up, wild, insular brigand types.

Pantagruel was quite perturbed and not without reason, although Epistémon pointed out to him that the practice and custom of the Chitterlings might be thus to welcome and receive in arms their friends from abroad, as the noble kings of France are received and saluted in the good cities of their kingdom at their first entries after their coronation [leur sacre] and recent accession to the throne.

"Peradventure," said he, "this is the ordinary guard of the queen of the place, who, notified by the young Chitterlings of the ambush you saw on the tree, and how at this port was appearing the fine pompous fleet of your ships, thought that there must be some rich and powerful prince, and is coming to visit you in person."

Not satisfied with this, Pantagruel called in his council to hear their opinions summarily on what they should do in this doubtful situation where hope was uncertain and danger evident.

So he pointed out to them how such forms of welcome under arms had often, under color of kind usage and friendship, led to deadly harm. "Thus," said he, "on one occasion the Emperor Antoninus Caracalla slew the people of Alexandria; on another he defeated the bodyguards of Artabanus, king of the Persians, under color and pretext of wanting to marry his daughter, which did not go unpunished, for shortly afterward he lost his life. Thus the sons of Jacob, to avenge the rape of their sister Dinah, destroyed the Shechemites [Genesis 34]. In this deceitful way the Roman Emperor Gallienus slaughtered the warriors inside Constantinople.[2] Thus, under color of friendship, Antonius lured Artavasdes, king of Armenia, then had him bound and fettered with chains; finally he had him slain.[3] We find a thousand other such stories amid the ancient record. And rightly, down to the present, is praised for prudence Charles, king of France, sixth of that name, who, when returning victorious over the Flemings and inhabitants of Ghent, to his good city of Paris and to Le Bourget in France, heard that the Parisians with their mallets[4] (which had won them the surname of Maillotins [Malleteers]), had come out of the city in battle formation to the number of twenty thousand combatants, would not enter (although they remonstrated that they had armed themselves thus to welcome him more honorably, with no ulterior motive or hostility), until they had first disarmed and gone home to their houses."

CHAPTER 37

How Pantagruel sent for
Captains Gobblechitterling and Chopsausage,[1]
with a noteworthy discourse
on the proper names of places and persons.

THE council's resolve was that at all events they should stand on their guard. Then on Pantagruel's command Carpalim and Gymnaste summoned the soldiers who were in the ship Cheers [Brindière], whose colonel was Gobblechitterling, and Vinetub [Portouerière], whose colonel was Chopsausage the Younger.

"I'll relieve Gymnaste of that trouble," said Panurge. "Besides, his presence here is necessary to you."

"By the frock I wear," said Frère Jean, "you want to keep away from the combat, old ballock, and you won't ever go back to it, upon my honor! That's hardly a great loss. Anyway, he wouldn't do anything but weep, moan, wail, and dishearten the good soldiers."

"I certainly will go back to it," said Panurge, "Frère Jean, my spiritual father, soon. Only see that those pesky Chitterlings don't climb up on our ships. While you're fighting, I'll pray to God for your victory, after the example of the valiant captain Moses, leader of the Israelite people."[2]

"The names," said Epistémon to Pantagruel, "of these two colonels of yours, Gobblechitterling and Chopsausage, promise us in this conflict assurance, good luck, and victory, if by chance these Chitterlings were to try to attack us."

"You take it rightly," said Pantagruel, "and I'm pleased that from the names of our colonels you foresee and predict our victory. Such a manner of prognosis is not modern. It was celebrated and religiously used, long ago, by the Pythagoreans.[3] Many great lords and emperors of old used it to their good advantage. Octavian Augustus, the second emperor of Rome, on meeting one day a peasant named Eutyche, that is to say Fortunate, leading a donkey named Nicon, that is to say in Greek Victorian [conqueror], stirred up by the meaning of the names of both the driver and the donkey, felt assured of every prosperity, felicity, and victory.[4] When Vespasian, likewise emperor of Rome, was all alone one day at prayer in the temple of Serapis, at the unexpected sight and coming of a servant of his named Basilides,[5] that is to say Royal, whom he had left sick far behind him, he took hope and assurance of getting the imperium of Rome. Regilian[6] was chosen emperor by the soldiers for no other cause and occasion than the meaning of his own name.[7] See the *Cratylus* of the divine Plato . . . "[8]

"By my thirst!" said Rhizotome, "I want to read it: I often hear you citing it."

" . . . See how the Pythagoreans, by reason of the names and numbers, conclude that Patroclus was bound to be slain by Hector, Hector by Achilles, Achilles by Paris, Paris by Philoctetes.[9] I'm quite confounded in my mind when I think about the wonderful discovery of Pythagoras, who, by the even or odd number of the syllables of each and every proper name, expounded on which side humans were lame, humpbacked, one-eyed, gouty, paralytic, pleuritic, and other such afflictions of nature: to wit, assigning the even number to the left side of the body, the odd to the right."

"That's true," said Epistémon, "I saw that tried out at Saintes,[10] during a general procession, in the presence of that most excellent, learned, and equitable President Briand Vallée, Seigneur du Douhet. When a lame man or woman passed, a one-eyed or humpbacked man or woman, they reported to him his proper name. If the syllables of the name were of an odd number, promptly, without looking at the persons, he immediately said they were afflicted, one-eyed, lame, or humpbacked on the right side. If they were of an even number, on the left side. And so it was in truth; never did we find an exception."

"By this discovery," said Pantagruel, "the scholars have affirmed that Achilles, while on his knees, was wounded by Paris's arrow in the right heel; for his name is of uneven syllables (here it is to be noted that the ancients knelt on their right foot); Venus by Diomedes before Troy wounded in the left hand, for her name in Greek was four syllables [A-phro-di-te]; Vulcan lame in his left foot, for the same reason; Philip, king of Macedon, and Hannibal, blind in the right eye. We could also be specific about sciatica, herpias, migraines, by this same Pythagorean reason.

"But to return to names, consider how Alexander the Great, son of King Philip, of whom we have spoken, by the interpretation of one single name succeeded in an undertaking of his.

"He was besieging the strong city of Tyre and had been fighting there with all his might for several weeks; but it was in vain; his machines and endeavors were to no avail; everything was promptly undone and repaired by the Tyrians. So in great melancholy he took a notion to raise the siege, seeing in this breaking off a notable loss to his reputation. In such a plight and vexation he fell asleep. In his sleep he dreamed that a satyr was in his tent, capering and skipping on his goatish legs. Alexander tried to catch him; the satyr kept escaping him. Finally the king, pursuing him into a corner, nabbed him. At that point he woke up, and, on telling his dream to the philosophers and learned men of his court, he came to understand that the gods were promising him victory and that Tyre would soon be taken, for his word *Satyros* [Greek for 'satyr'], divided in two, is *Sa Tyros*, meaning 'Tyre is yours.' Indeed, at the first assault he made, he won the city by force, and in a great victory subjugated this rebellious people.[11]

"On the other hand, consider how from the meaning of a name Pompey fell into despair. Being conquered by Caesar in the battle of Pharsalia, he had no other way of escape than by flight. Fleeing by sea, he came to the island of Cyprus. Near the town of Paphos he espied on the shore a beautiful sumptuous palace. On asking the pilot the name of this palace, he learned that it was called Καχοδασιλέα, that is to say "Bad King." He took such fright and abomination at this name that he fell into despair, as being sure not to escape but to lose his life. So that those present heard his sighs and moans. And indeed, a short time later, a man named Achillas, an unknown peasant, cut off his head.

"We could cite further in this connection what happened to Lucius Aemilius Paulus, when he was elected emperor by the Roman senate, that is to say leader of the army they were sending against Perses, king of Macedonia. That same day, toward evening, on his way back to his house to get ready to move out, on kissing a little daughter of his named Tratia, he noticed that she was a little sad. 'What is it, my Tratia?' he said. 'Why are you so sad and forlorn?' 'Father,' she replied, 'Persa is dead.' That is what she called a little puppy bitch she was very fond of. At that statement Paulus gained confidence in his victory over Perses.[12]

"If time allowed us to scrutinize the Holy Bible of the Hebrews, we would find a hundred notable passages showing us clearly in what consideration and reverence they held proper names and their meanings."

At the end of these remarks the two colonels arrived, accompanied by their soldiers, all well armed and determined. Pantagruel made them a short speech exhorting them to show themselves valiant in combat if by chance they were forced to (for he still couldn't believe the Chitterlings were so treacherous), and forbade them to begin the hostilities; and he gave them Shrovetide [Mardigras] as the watchword.

CHAPTER 38

How Chitterlings are not to be despised among humans.[1]

Now you're laughing at me, topers, and not believing that this is all truly so just as I'm telling it to you. I don't know what I can do for you about that. Believe it if you want; if you don't want to, go there and see. But I know very well what I saw. This was on the Wild Island. I'm giving you its name. And call back to mind the giants of old, who undertook to pile lofty Mount Pelion upon Ossa, and envelop shady Olympus with Ossa, to combat the gods and dislodge them from their nest. That was no commonplace or moderate might. Those, however, were Chitterlings for only half their body, or serpents, lest I tell a lie.

The serpent who tempted Eve was Chitterline; this notwithstanding, it is written of him that he was subtle and wily beyond all other beasts of the field.[2] So are Chitterlings.

They still maintain in certain academies that this tempter was the Chitterling named Ithyphallus, into whom was transformed long ago good old Messer Priapus, the great tempter of women among the paradises in Greek, which are gardens in French. The Swiss [Souisses], peoples now bold and warlike, how do we know but that they were once sausages [saulcisses]? I wouldn't put my finger in the fire to contest it. The Himantopodes, a very noteworthy people in Ethiopia, are Chitterlings, according to Pliny's description,[3] and nothing else.

If these arguments do not satisfy the incredulity of your lordships,[4] shortly (I mean after drinking) go and visit Lusignan, Parthenay, Vouvant, Mervent, and Pouzanges, in Poitou. There you will find witnesses of long renown and honest repute who will swear to you on the arm of Saint Rigomer that Mélusine, their first founder, had a female body down to the prick-purse,[5] and the rest of it below was a serpentine Chitterling or else a Chitterling serpent.

She, however, had fair and lively ways, which are still represented today by Bretons doing their lusty song-and-dances.[6]

What was the reason why Erichthonius was the first to invent coaches, litters, and chariots? It was because Vulcan had begotten him with Chitterling's feet, to hide which he chose to travel by litter rather than on horseback. For in his time Chitterlings were not yet renowned.

The Scythian nymph Ora likewise had a body divided in half between woman and Chitterling. However, she seemed so beautiful to Jupiter that he lay with her and by her had a fine son named Colaxes.[7]

So now stop laughing any more, and believe there is nothing so true as the Gospel.

CHAPTER 39

How Frère Jean joins forces with the cooks
to combat the Chitterlings.

WHEN Frère Jean saw those frenzied Chitterlings thus marching joyously, he said to Pantagruel:

"This here is going to be a fine straw battle,[1] from what I see. Oh! what great honor and magnificent praises there will be for our victory! I'd like you to be just a spectator of this conflict in your ship, and for the rest let me handle it with my men."

"What men?" asked Pantagruel.

"That's breviary matter," replied Frère Jean. "Why was Potophar, master chef of Pharaoh's kitchens—the one who brought Joseph and whom Joseph could have made a cuckold if he had wanted—master of all the cavalry of the whole kingdom of Egypt? Why was Nebuzaradan, master chef of King Nebuchadnezzar, chosen among all other captains to besiege and destroy Jerusalem?"[2]

"I'm listening," replied Pantagruel.

"By the Trou Madame!"[3] said Frère Jean, "I'd dare swear that in other days they had fought Chitterlings, or people as little esteemed as Chitterlings, for whom cooks are incomparably more suitable and adequate to beat them down, combat them, conquer them, and chop them to bits, than all the men-at-arms, Albanian horsemen, soldiers, and infantrymen in the world."

"You bring back to my mind," said Pantagruel, "what is written among Cicero's facetious and joyous responses.[4] At the time of the civil wars in Rome between Caesar and Pompey, he naturally leaned more to Pompey's side, although he was solicited and greatly favored by Caesar. Hearing one day that the Pompeians in a certain encounter had suffered a considerable loss of their men, he succeeded in visiting their camp. In their camp he observed little strength, little courage, great disorder. Then, foreseeing that all would go to ruin and perdition, he began to ridicule now some of them, now others, with bitter stinging jibes, as he knew very well how to do. Some of the captains, playing at being the good fellows like very confident and determined men, said to him: 'Do you see how many eagles [ensigns] we still have?' These were then the ensigns of the Romans in time of war. 'That' said Cicero, 'would be fine and to the point if you were at war against magpies.'

"So, seeing that we must fight Chitterlings, you are inferring that it's a culinary battle and you want to join forces with the cooks. Do as you intend. I'll stay here and await the outcome of these fanfares."

Frère Jean then goes straight to the kitchen tents and in all gayety and courtesy says to the cooks:

"Lads, I mean to see you all today in honor and triumph. By you shall be performed exploits in arms not yet seen in our memory. Belly to belly! Don't they take any other account of these valiant cooks? Let's go fight these whoremonger Chitterlings. I'll be your captain. Let's drink, friends. Come on now, courage!"

"Captain," replied the cooks, "that's well said. We're at your merry command. Under your leadership we mean to live and die!"

"To live," said Frère Jean, "fine! To die, not a bit of it. That's something for the Chitterlings. So now let's set ourselves in order for battle. Nebuzaradan shall be the watchword for you."

CHAPTER 40

*How Frère Jean is set up in the sow
and the valiant cooks are enclosed in it.*[1]

Then on Frère Jean's command was set up by the master engineers the great sow, which was in the ship Drinkingmug.[2] It was a marvelous machine, made in such wise that from the big cannon that ringed it round in rows it fired great stones and steel-feathered bolts, and in its hold two hundred men could easily fight and stay under cover; and it was made on the model of the Sow of La Réole,[3] by means of which, under the reign of the young King Charles the Sixth, Bergerac was taken from the English.

Here follow the number and names of the stalwart valiant cooks who, as into the Trojan Horse, entered into the sow:[4]

Tartsauce [Saulpicquet],
Slickster [Ambrelin],
Panicky [Guavache],
Weak-knees [Lascheron],
Porkfry [Porcausou],
Dirtyrat [Salezart],
Mandragora [Maindeguourre],
Breadpudding [Paimperdu],
Trudgealong [Lasdaller],
Shoveler [Pochecuillière]
Moldymust [Moustamoulue],
Frizzlecrisp [Crespelet],
Master Slipslop [Maistre Hordoux],[5]
Greasygut [Grasboyau],
Poundpestle [Pillemortier],
Sheriff or Lickwine ["L'eschevin" or "Leschevin"][6]
Pea-and-bean stew [Saulgrenée],
Goat stew [Cabirotade],
Carbonado [Carbonnade],

Mixed-grill [Fressurade],
Hodgepodge [Hoschepot],
Pig's liver [Hasteret],
Snoutslash [Balafré]
Gallimaufry [Gualimafré],

All these noble Cooks bore on their coats of arms, on a field gules, a larding-pin vert, scutched with a chevron argent, inclined to the left.[7]

Baconrasher [Lardonnet],
Baconstrip [Lardon],
Roundbacon [Rondlardon],
Nibblebacon [Croquelardon],
Baconsnatch [Tirelardon],
Fatbacon [Graslardon],
Savebacon [Saulvelardon],
Archebacon [Archilardon],
Antibacon [Antilardon],
Frizzlebacon [Frizelardon],
Lacebacon [Lacelardon],
Scratchbacon [Grattelardon],
Baconmarch [Marchelardon],
Lustybacon [Guaillardon], by syncope, born; the name of the culinary doctor was Guaillartlardon; thus you say *idolâtre* for *idololâtre*.
Stiffbacon [Roiddeiardon],
Autobacon [Aftolardon],[8]
Sweetbacon [Doulxlardon],
Munchbacon [Maschelardon],
Chunkybacon [Trappelardon],
Baconnuff [Bastelardon],
Baconspit [Guyllelardon],
Flybacon [Mouschelardon],
Fairbacon [Bellardon],
Newbacon [Neuflardon],
Bitterbacon [Aigrelardon],
Ballbacon [Billelardon],

Spybacon [Guignelardon],
Weighbacon [Poyselardon],
Bagpipe-bacon [Vezelardon],
Lookbacon [Myrelardon],

Names unknown among the maranos and the Jews,[9]

Bigballs [Couillu],
Salad-chef [Salladier],
Cress-fixer [Cressonnadière],
Turnipscraper [Raclenaveau],
Swineherd [Cochonnier],
Rabbitskin [Peaudeconnin],
Gravyman [Apigratis],
Pastrycook [Pastissandière],
Shavebacon [Raslard],
Freefritter [Francbeuignet],
Mustardpot [Moustardiot],
Vintner [Vinetteux],
Porringer [Potageouart],
Madwag [Frelaut],
Ninnyhammer [Benest],
Greensauce [Jusverd],
Potscraper [Marmitige],
Trivet [Accodepot],
Hodgepodge [Hoschepot],
Potbreaker [Brizepot],
Potscourer [Guallepot],
Shivery [Frillis],
Saltythroat [Guorgesalée],
Snaildresser [Escarguotandière],
Drybouillon [Bouillonsec],
Marchsops [Souppimars],
Chinechopper [Eschinade],
Rennet-curdler [Prézurier],

Macaroon [Macaron],

Skewerman [Escarsaufle],

Crumb [Briguaille]: this one was drawn from the kitchen for room-
duty, for the service of the noble Cardinal [Hunter] Le Veneur;

Spoilroast [Guasteroust],

Dishclout [Escouvillon],

Babybonnet [Béguinet],

Firefanner [Escharbottier],

Longtool [Vitet],

Hugetool [Vitault],

Proudprick [Vitvain],

Cutiepie [Jolivet],

Newprick [Vitneuf],

Foxtailduster [Vistempenard],

Victorian [Victorien],

Oldcock [Vitvieulx],

Hairycock [Vitvelu],

Hastycalf [Hastiveau],

Shortriblady [Alloyaudière],

Lego'lamber [Esclanchier],

Milkspoiler [Guastelet],

Mountainscaler [Rapimontes],

Blowinbowl [Soudflemboyau],

Skatefish [Pelouze],

Gibeonite [Gabaonite],

Lubber [Bubarin],

Crocodilekin [Crocodillet],

Dandy [Prelinguant; cf., 1.35 above],

Scarface [Balafré; cf., "Snoutslash" above],

Smudgeface [Maschouré],

Mondam, inventor of Sauce Madam,[10] and for this invention he was
named thus in Scotch-French,

Clatterteeth [Clacquedens],

Dewlapper [Badiguoincier],

Polyglotter [Myrelanguoy],

Woodcockbeak [Becdassée],

Rinsepot [Rincepot],

Drinkspiller [Urelipipingues],

Sloven [Maunet],

Stuffguts [Guodepie],

Waffler [Guauffreux],

Saffroneer [Saffranier],

Unkempt [Malparouart],

Windbag [Antitus],

Turnipgrower [Navelier],[11]

Turnipseed [Rabiolas],

Bloodpuddinger [Boudinandière],

Piglet [Cochonnet],

Robert, inventor of Sauce Robert,[12] so salubrious and necessary for roast conies, ducks, fresh port, poached eggs, salt cod, and myriad other such foods,

Coldeel [Froiddanguille],

Thornback [Rougenraye],

Gurnard [Guourneau],

Rumblegut [Griboullis],

Almscrip [Sacabribes],

Roister [Olymbrius],

Squirrel [Foucquet. cf., 3. Prol.],

Tittletattle [Dalyqualquain],

Salmagundi [Salmiguondin],

Merrywing [Gringualet],

Redherring [Aransor: Harengsaur],

Slaplip [Talemouse],

Grosbeak[13] [Grosbec],

Swipesnack [Frippelippes],[14]

Finickygoat [Friantaures],

Thistlechomper [Guaffelaze],

Well-salted [Saulpouddré],

Panfried [Paellefrite],
Oaf [Landore],
Calabrian [Calabre],
Turnipper [Navelet],
Crapcart [Foyrart],
Bigpighoof [Grosguallon],
Turdiman [Brenous],
Sticky [Mucydan],
Sowslayer [Matatruys],
Mixed-grill [Cartevirade],
Cocklicrane [Cocquecygrue],
Knothead [Visedecache],
Besotted [Badelory],
Bullcalf [Vedel],
Coxcomb [Braguibus].[15]

Inside the sow went these noble cooks, lusty, lively, rough-and-ready, and quick to fight.[16] Frère Jean, with his great cutlass goes in last and locks the doors with a spring lock from the inside.

CHAPTER 41

How Pantagruel snapped
the Chitterlings over his knee.[1]

So close did these Chitterlings come that Pantagruel could see how they were flexing their arms and already starting to lower their lances [to the ready]. Thereupon he sends Gymnaste to find out what their intentions were and for what complaint, without provocation, they were minded to make war against their old friends, who had given them no offense in word or deed.

Gymnaste, before their front ranks, made a great deep bow and called out as loud as he could: "yours, yours, yours are we each and every one and at your command. We are all in dependency upon Shrovetide [Mardigras], your old ally."

Some peole have told me since that he said "Tideshrove" [Gradimars], not "Shrovetide." However that may be, at these words, a great wild stubby Blood Pudding, stepping out in front of their battalion, tried to seize him by the throat.

"By God," said Gymnaste, "You'll get in there only in slices; you never could get in that way whole."

So saying, he pulls out his two-handed sword Kiss-my-ass (that's what he called it) and cut the Blood Pudding in two.

Honest to God, how fat he was! I was reminded of the Fat Bull of Berne,[2] killed at Marignano at the defeat of the Swiss. Believe me, he had no less than four inches of lard on his belly.

With that Blood Pudding bloodied [Ce cervelat écervelé], the Chitterlings attacked Gymnaste, and were foully dragging him down, when Pantagruel rushed up with his men to his aid. Then the martial combat began pell-mell. Gobblechitterling [Riflandouille] kept gobbling Chitterlings, Chopsausage [Tailleboudin] kept chopping sausages, Pantagruel kept snapping Chitterlings over his knee. Frère Jean was keeping quiet inside his Sow, watching and considering everything, when the Veal Patties [les Guodiveaulx], who were lying in ambush, with a great racket, came rushing out upon Pantagruel.

Thereupon, when Frère Jean saw the disarray and tumult, he opens the door of his Sow and comes out with his good soldiers, some carrying iron spits, some andirons, racks, pans, fire shovels, kettles, grills, oven forks, pincers, dripping-pans, chimney brooms, great pots, mortars, pistons, all as orderly as house-burners,[3] and all frightfully together: "Nebuzaradan! Nebuzaradan! Nebuzaradan!" With shouts and commotion they fell upon the Veal Patties and broke through Sausages. The Chitterlings suddenly noticed this new drive and took to their heels at a gallop, as though they had seen all the devils. Frère Jean kept knocking them into little pieces with great blows of a crowbar; his soldiers went at it unsparingly. It was pitiful. The camp was all covered with dead or dying Chitterlings. And the story goes that if God had not taken care of it, the entire Chitterline race would have been exterminated by these culinary soldiers. But a wondrous thing happened. You will believe whatever you want of it.

From the direction of the Transmontane [north wind: across the mountains] up flew a great fat greasy gray hog, with wings as long and as wide as a windmill's sails. And his plumage was crimson red, like that of a Phoenicopter, which in Languegoth is called flamingo. It had flaming red eyes, like red carbuncles; ears green, like an emerald; teeth yellow, like a topaz; tail long, black as Lucullan marble;[4] feet white, diaphanous, transparent like a diamond and were largely webbed, like those of geese and those worn long ago in Toulouse by the Goosefoot Queen [La Royne Pédaucque]. And it had a golden collar on its neck, around which ran some Ionic letters, of which I could read only two words: ΥΣ ΑΘΗΝΑΝ, "swine teaching Athena."[5]

The weather was fine and clear. But upon the arrival of this monster, it thundered on the left side, so loud that we all remained astounded. The Chitterlings, as soon as they espied it, cast down their arms and sticks and all fell on their knees, hands clasped without a word, as if in adoration

Frère Jean, with his men, still kept on striking and impaling Chitterlings. But by Pantagruel's command retreat was sounded, and all fighting ceased. The monster, after flying back and forth several times between the two armies, cast onto the ground over twenty-seven pippes [hogsheads] of mustard, then disappeared, flying through the air and crying out without stopping: "Shrovetide! Shrovetide! Shrovetide! [Mardigras! Mardigras! Mardigras!]."

CHAPTER 42

How Pantagruel parleys with Niphleseth,[1]
queen of the Chitterlings.

As the aforesaid monster made no further appearance, and the two armies remained in silence, Pantagruel asked to parley with the lady Niphleseth (as the queen of the Chitterlings was named), who was in her coach near the two banners, which was easily granted.

The queen alighted from her coach and greeted Pantagruel graciously, and was glad to see him. Pantagruel was complaining of this war. She made her excuses honorably, stating that the mistake had been made because of a false report, and that her spies had announced to her that Fastilent, their old enemy, had come on land and was spending his time seeing the physeters' urine.[2] Then she besought him out of his kindness to pardon this offense, alleging that in Chitterlings was found rather shit than gall; on this condition, that she and her successor Niphleseths[3] would forever hold from him and his successors all the island in faith and homage; would obey his commands in all things and everywhere; would be friends of his friends and enemies of his enemies; each year, in token of this fealty, would send him seventy-eight thousand Chitterlings to serve as his first course at table for six months of the year.

This was done by her, and the next day she sent in six great brigantines the aforesaid number of royal Chitterlings to the good Gargantua, under charge of the young Niphleseth, Infanta of the island. The noble Gargantua made present of them to the great king of Paris. But from the change of air, also for lack of mustard (the natural balm and restorative of Chitterlings), they almost all died. By the permission and will of the great king they were buried in heaps in a spot in Paris that has since been called the Chitterling-paved street [la rue Pavée d'Andouilles].[4]

At the request of the ladies of the royal court Niphleseth the Younger was saved and honorably treated. She has since been married to a good rich man and has several fine children, for which God be praised. Pantagruel graciously thanked the Queen, pardoned the entire offense, refused the offer she had made, and gave her a pretty little penknife from Perche.[5] Then he questioned her carefully about the apparition of the aforesaid monster. She replied that it was the Idea of Shrovetide [Mardigras], their tutelary god in time of war, first founder and original of the whole Chitterline race. Therefore it looked like a hog, for Chitterlings were extracted from hog. Pantagruel asked for what purpose and curative indication it had cast forth so much mustard on the ground. The queen replied that mustard was their Holy Grail [Sangréal][6] and celestial balm, and by putting a little bit of it in the wounds of the felled Chitterlings, in a very short time the wounded were healed, the dead resuscitated.

Pantagruel had no further conversation with the queen, and withdrew into his ship. So did all the good companions with their weapons and their sow.

CHAPTER 43

*How Pantagruel went ashore
on the island of Ruach.*

Two days later we reached the island of Ruach,[1] and I swear to you by the celestial Chicken-brood[2] I found the state and the life of the people stranger than I can say. They live on nothing but wind. They drink nothing, eat nothing, except wind. They have no houses but weather-vanes. In their gardens they sow only the three species of anemones;[3] all rue and other carminatives they carefully weed out of them. The common people use for food fans made of feathers, paper, or cloth, according to their means and capacity. The rich live on windmills. There they feast, happy as at a wedding, and during their meal they argue over the goodness, excellence, and salubriousness of the winds, even as you drinkers do on the matter of wines at your banquets. One praises the Sirocco;[4] another, the Besch;[5] another, the Garbino;[6] another, the Bise; another the Zephyr; another the Galerne;[7] and so forth. Another favors the smockwind [le vent de la chemise], for flirts and lovers. For the sick they invoke a draft [vent couliz], as they feed the sick in our country on meat broth [couliz].

"O!" a little inflated one was saying to me, "if only one could have a bladderful of that good Languegoth wind they call the Circius![8] That noble doctor Schyron,[9] passing through this region one day, was telling me that it's so strong it tips over loaded carts. O what good that would do for that Oedipodic leg of mine![10] The stoutest are not the best."

"But," said Panurge, "what about a stout butt of that good Languegoth wine that grows at Mirevaux, Canteperdris, and Frontignan!"[11]

I saw there a man of good appearance, looking very ventose,[12] bitterly wrathful against a big fat servant of his and a little page, and he was beating them like the devil, with heavy blows of a buskin. Not knowing the cause of his anger, I thought it was on the advice of the doctors, as a healthy thing for the master to get mad and beat someone, and for the servants to be beaten. But I heard that he was reproaching the servants for his having been robbed of half a goatskinful of Garbino wind, which he was keeping dearly, as a rare dish, for the late season.

They neither crap, piss, nor spit on this island. To compensate, they fizzle, they fart, they belch copiously. They suffer every sort and species of malady. Also every malady arises and proceeds from ventosity, as Hippocrates deduces, in his book *On body winds* [*De flatibus*]. But the most epidemic is the windy colic. To remedy it, they use ample cupping glasses [ventoses], and in them void great ventosities. They all die of dropsy or tympanites, and the men die farting, the women fizzling. Thus their soul goes out through their ass.

Later, strolling about the island, we came upon three fat wind-blown specimens, who were going for sport to watch the plovers that abound there and live on the same diet [vivent de mesmes diète]. I noticed that just as you drinkers, going about the region, bear flagons, leather flasks, and bottles, likewise each of them bore at his belt a nice little bellows. If by chance wind failed them, with these pretty bellows they made some of it fresh, by blowing it in and out, as you know that wind, by its essential definition, is nothing else but flowing and undulating air.

At that point, on behalf of their king, we were ordered not to receive on board our ships any man or woman of the country. For he had been robbed of a bladder full of the very wind that that good snorer Aeolus gave Ulysses long ago to guide his ship in calm weather,[13] which he was keeping religiously, like another Holy Grail, and with it was curing many enormous maladies, just by releasing and turning loose to the patients as much as would be needed to make up a virgin's fart:[14] that's what the Sanctimonials[15] call sonnet.[16]

CHAPTER 44

How little rains beat down great winds.

PANTAGRUEL was praising their polity and way of life and said to their Hypenemean Potentate:

"If you accept Epicurus's view saying that the sovereign good consists in sensual pleasure[1] (pleasure, I mean, that is easy and not painful), I consider you most happy. For your victuals, which are wind, cost you nothing or very little; you need only blow."

"True," replied the potentate, "but in this mortal life nothing is in all respects blessed.[2] Often, when we are at table feeding on some good

Godsent wind as on heavenly manna, feeling as good as Fathers [aises comme Pères], some little rain comes up that takes it away and brings it down. Thus many meals are lost for lack of victuals."

"That," said Panurge, "is like Johnny from Quinquenais [Jenin de Quinquenays], who, by pissing on his wife Quelot's fanny, beat down the stinking wind that was coming out of it as out of a masterly Aeolipyle.[3] A while ago I made a pretty little dizain about it:

> When one day Johnny tasted his new wine,
> Cloudy, fermenting, muddied with its lees,
> He asked Quelot to cook up nice and fine
> Turnips for supper, if my lady please.
> This soon was done. Then, merry and at ease,
> They both lie down, sport awhile, snooze away.
> But Johnny, vainly trying, sleepless lay,
> So loudly Quelot farted, and so fast;
> Therefore he pissed on her, and then could say:
> "Small rains indeed beat down great rains at last."[4]

"Besides," said the potentate, "we have an annual calamity, very great and harmful. This is that a giant named Bringuenarilles, who lives on the island of Tohu,[5] every year, on the advice of his doctors, he brings himself here in the springtime to get a purgation and devours a great number of windmills on us as pills, and also bellows, of which he is very fond, which comes as a great misery to us, and because of it we fast three or four Lents each year, except for certain rogations and prayers."

"And don't you know," asked Pantagruel, "any way to prevent this?"

"On the advice," replied the potentate, "of our masters and Mezarim, we have placed inside the windmills, in the time of year he usually comes here, many cocks and many hens. The first time he swallowed them, he wasn't far from dying of it. For they kept singing to him inside his body and flying back and forth around his stomach, from which he would fall into a deathlike swoon, angina pectoris, and a horrific and dangerous convulsion, as if some serpent had got into his stomach through his mouth."

"That," said Frère Jean, "is a very untimely and preposterous as if. For some time ago, I heard that a serpent that has got into the stomach causes no pain, and promptly comes out again if they hang the patient up by his feet and offer him, near his mouth, a pan full of hot milk."

"You," said Pantagruel, "have that on hearsay; so had those who told it to you. But such a remedy was never seen or read of. Hippocrates, in book 5 of *Epidemics* [*lib. 5. Epid.*], writes that the case happened in his time and the patient suddenly died in a spasm and convulsion."

"Furthermore," said the potentate, "all the foxes in the region went into his gullet, chasing the hens, and he would have passed away at any moment, were it not that, on the advice of a playful magician, at the time of the paroxysm he flayed a fox[6] as an antidote and counterpoison. Later he got better advice, and his remedy is to have a suppository given him made up of a concoction of grains of wheat and millet, for which the same hens came running up, also of gosling livers, and for all these the foxes came running up. Also some pills that he takes by mouth, composed of greyhounds and terriers. There you see our misfortune."

"Have no fear, good folk," said Pantagruel, "from now on. That great giant Bringuenarilles, swallower of windmills, is dead. And he died of choking and suffocation, eating a pat of fresh butter by the door of a hot oven, on the doctors' orders."[7]

CHAPTER 45

How Pantagruel went ashore
on the island of the Popefigs.

The next morning we came upon the island of the Popefigs, who were once rich and free, and were known as Swingers[1] [Guaillardetz], but at this time were poor, unhappy, and subject to the Papimaniacs. The occasion of it had been this.

On one annual processional feast day [feste annuelle à bastons], the burgomaster, syndics, and grand rabbis of the Swingers had gone for a pastime to watch the festival in Papimania, the next island. One of them, seeing the papal portrait (since it was the laudable custom to display it publicly on processional feast days), made it the sign of the fig,[2] which in that country is a sign of manifest contempt and derision. To avenge this, the Papimaniacs, a few days later, without a word of warning, all took up arms, surprised, sacked, and ruined the whole island of the Swingers, putting to the sword every man who wore a beard. The women and young males were pardoned, on a condition like the one the Emperor Frederick Barbarossa once used against the Milanese.

The Milanese had rebelled against him and driven his wife the empress out of the city, ignominiously mounted on an old mule named Thacor[3] wrong way round, that is to say with her ass turned toward the head of the mule and her face toward the crupper.

Frederick, on his return, after subjugating and taking back the city, made such a thorough search that he recovered the famous mule Thacor. Thereupon, in the middle of the great Brouet [the marketplace of Milan], on his orders the hangman placed a fig in the pudenda of Thacor, in the presence and sight of the captive townsmen, then proclaimed on behalf of the emperor, to the sound of the trumpets, that any one of them who wanted to escape death must publicly take the fig out with his teeth, then put it back in the right place without using his hands. Anyone who refused would be hanged and strangled on the spot. Some of them felt shame and horror at such an abominable penalty, put it beyond the fear of death, and were hanged. In others the fear of death won out over such sense of shame. These, after pulling out the fig with their teeth, displayed it clearly to the hangman, saying: *Ecco lo fico* [Behold the fig].

In the same ignominy the rest of these poor and desolate Swingers were protected and saved from death. They were made slaves and tributaries, and had the name Popefigs imposed on them, because they had made the sign of the fig to the papal portrait. Since that time the poor folk had not prospered. Every year they had hail, storms, plague, famine, and every kind of misfortune, as an eternal punishment for the sin of their ancestors and forefathers.

Seeing the misery and state of the people, we had no wish to go in any further. Just to take some holy water and commend ourselves to God, we went into a little chapel near the harbor, ruined, desolate, and roofless, as is the temple of Saint Peter in Rome.[4] When we had come into the chapel and were taking some holy water, we noticed in the holy-water basin a man dressed in stoles and wholly hidden in the water, like a duck in his dive, except for a bit of his nose to breathe with. Around him were three priests, well shaven and tonsured, reading from the book of exorcisms and conjuring the devils.

Pantagruel found the case strange, and, on asking what were the games they were playing there, was informed that for the past three years there had reigned on the island a pestilence so horrible that more than half of the country had remained deserted and the lands without owners. When the pestilence had passed, this man hidden in the holy-water basin was plowing a big annual field and sowing it with fine winter wheat [touzelle] on a day and at a time when a little devil (who didn't yet know how to thunder and hail, except on parsley and cabbage), also didn't know how to read or write, had got Lucifer's permission to come play and sport on the island of the Popefigs, on which the devils were very familiar with the men and women, and often went there to pass the time.

This devil, arriving at the spot, addressed the farmer and asked what he was doing. The poor man replied to him that he was sowing this field with winter wheat to help himself to live on through the next year. "All right," said the devil, "but this field isn't yours, it's mine, and belongs to me. For since the time and the moment when you people made the sign of the fig to the pope, all this region has been adjudged, consigned, and given over to us. Sowing wheat, however, isn't my profession. Therefore I leave you the field; but that's on condition that we'll share the profit."

"I'm willing," replied the farmer.

"I mean," said the devil, "that of the yield that comes we'll make two shares. One will be what grows above the ground, the other what will be covered in the ground. The choice belongs to me, for I'm a devil sprung from an ancient and noble race, you're only a peasant. I choose what will be in the ground; you'll have what's above it. At what time of year will the harvesting be?"

"In mid-July," replied the farmer.

"All right then," said the devil, "I won't fail to be there. For the rest do as is your duty: work, peasant, work! I'm going to tempt with the lusty sin of concupiscence the noble nuns of Dryfart [Pettesec], also the hypocritical and gluttonous monks. I am more than sure of their wills. When the two sides meet, the battle will be on."

CHAPTER 46

*How the little devil was fooled
by a farmer from Popefigland.*

WHEN mid-July had come, the devil again appeared on the spot, accompanied by a squadron of little choirboy devils. Meeting the farmer there, he said to him:

"Now then, peasant, how have you been since I left? This is the time and place to divide up into our shares."

"That's right," said the farmer.

Then the farmer and his men began to cut the wheat. The little devils likewise pulled the stubble out of the ground. The farmer threshed his wheat in his barn, winnowed it, put it into sacks, and took it to the market to sell. The little devils did likewise, and at the market sat down near the farmer to sell their stubble. The farmer sold his wheat just fine, and with the money filled an old half-buskin, which he carried at his belt. The devils didn't sell a thing; but on the contrary, the peasants made fun of them right out in the middle of the market.

When the market was closed, the devil said to the farmer: "Peasant, you fooled me this time, next time you won't fool me."

"Sir devil," replied the farmer, "how could I have fooled you, when you chose first? True it is that by this choice you thought you'd fool me, hoping that nothing would come out of the ground for my share, and that under the ground you'd find entire the grain I'd sowed there, so you might tempt therewith the needy, hypocrites, or misers and by temptation make them stumble into your snares. But you're very young in your trade. The grain you see in the ground is dead and rotten, and the corruption thereof was the generation of the other that you saw me sell. Thus you were choosing the worse. That's why you are accursed in the Gospel."[1]

"Let's drop the subject," said the devil. "What will you be able to sow our field with this coming year?"

"For a good husbandman's profit," said the farmer, "it ought to be sown with radishes."

"Well then," said the devil, "you're a good peasant! Sow radishes aplenty, I'll protect them from the tempest and I won't hail on them. But get this: I'm keeping for my share what will be above ground, you'll have what's underneath. Work, peasant, work! I'm going to tempt the heretics: those are the souls fond of carbonadoes; Sir Lucifer is having his colic; it'll be a nice hot snack for him."

When the time came for reaping, the devil showed up at the place, with a squadron of little room-service devilkins. There, meeting the farmer and his men, he began to cut and gather the radish-leaves. After him went the farmer digging and pulling out the hefty radishes and putting them in sacks. So they both go off together to the market. The farmer went selling his radishes very well. The devil didn't sell a thing. What's worse, people kept making fun of him publicly.

"I see very well," said the devil then, "that I'm tricked by you. I want to be done with sharing this field between us. That will be on these terms: that we'll have a scratching-match, and whichever of the two gives up first shall give up his share in the field. It will remain entire to the victor. The date shall be a week from now. Go on with you, peasant, I'll scratch you like the devil. I was going to tempt the thieving Shysteroos, disguisers of lawsuits, forger notaries, prevaricating advocates; but they've sent word to me by an interpreter that they were already mine. As a matter of fact, Sir Lucifer is getting tired of their souls and usually sends them down to the scullery-knave devils, except when they're well seasoned. You folks say there's nothing like schoolboys for breakfast, nothing like advocates for dinner, like vintners for snacks, merchants for supper, chambermaids for late snacks, and hobgoblins for all meals?"[2]

"That's true: in fact, Sir Lucifer takes a bite of hobgoblins as a first course at all his meals. And he used to breakfast on schoolboys. But alas! I know not by what misfortune, for a number of years these have added to their studies the holy Bible:[3] for this reason we can't draw a single one of them to the devil any more. And I believe that unless the hypocrites help us, and take their Saint Paul out of their hands by threats, insults, force, violence, and burnings, we won't have any more of them to nibble on down here.

"On advocates who pervert the law and rob the poor he has dinner ordinarily, and he has no lack of them. But one does tire of always eating just one and the same dish. Not long ago he said right in full chapter meeting that he really would like to eat the soul of a hypocrite who had forgotten to commend himself in his sermon, and he promised double pay and a notable position to anyone who would bring him one hot off the spit [de broc en bouc]. Each one of us went out hunting, but it has done us no good. They all admonish the noble ladies to give to their monastery.

"Snacks he has laid off of since he had his bad colic, which came on because in the northerly countries his nurslings, sutlers, colliers, and pork-butchers had been villainously maltreated. He sups very nicely on usurer merchants, apothecaries, counterfeiters, forgers, coiners, adulterators of merchandise. And sometimes when he's on top of the wave, he has midnight suppers of chambermaids who, having drunk up the good wine of their masters, refill the bottle with stinking water.

"Work, peasant, work! I'm going off to tempt the scholboys of Trebizond[4] to leave their fathers and mothers, renounce the common way of life, emancipate themselves from their king's edicts, live in underground liberty, despise each and every one, make fun of everyone, and, putting on the jolly little baby's bonnet of poetic innocence, make themselves into nice little hobgoblins."

CHAPTER 47

How the devil was fooled
by an old woman of Popefigland.

As the farmer returned to his house, he was sad and pensive. His wife, seeing him so, supposed he had been robbed at the market. But on understanding the cause of his melancholy, also seeing his purse full of money, she gently comforted him and assured him that of this scratchery no harm would come to him, only he had to depend and rely on her: she had already thought of a good way out.

"At worst," said the farmer, "I'll get off with a scratching. I'll give up at the first scratch and leave the field to him."

"No way, no way!" said the old woman; "depend and rely on me and leave it to me to handle it. You've told me he's a little devil: I'll make him give up for you right away, and the field will remain ours. If it had been a big devil, there'd be something to think about."

The day set for the encounter was the day we arrived on the island. Early in the morning, the farmer had made a thorough confession, taken communion as a good Catholic, and dived into hiding inside the holy-water basin, in the state we had found him in.

At the moment when we were being told this story, we got word that the old woman had fooled the devil and won the field. The way of it was this. The devil came to the farmer's door and shouted as he rang:

"Ho there, peasant, peasant! Here, here, with your best claws on!"[1]

Then, entering the house, chipper and fully determined, and not finding the farmer there, he espied his wife on the floor weeping and lamenting.

"What's this?" asked the devil. "Where is he? What's he doing?"

"Ha!" said the old woman, "where he is, the villain, the murderer, the scoundrel? He's wrecked me, I'm done for, I'm dying from the harm he's done me."

"How's that?" said the devil. "What's the trouble? I'll make him do a nice dance for you in a little while."

"Ha!" said the old woman, "he told me, the murderer, the tyrant, the devil-scratcher, that he had an appointment today to scratch it out with you: to try out his fingernails, he just gave me a scratch with his little finger here between my legs, and he's completely wrecked me. I'm ruined! I'll never recover from it. Look! Besides, he's gone off to the blacksmith's to point up and sharpen his claws. You're done for, Sir Devil, my friend! Get out of here! There'll be no stopping him. Go away, I beg you."

Then she uncovered herself up to the chin in the way the Persian women long ago showed themselves to their sons fleeing from battle,[2] and showed him her whatsitsname [comment a nom].

The devil, seeing the enormous solution of continuity in every dimension,[3] cried out:

"Mahound! Demiourgon, Megaera, Allecto, Persephone! He's not catching me! I'm on my way out of here in a hurry! Sure [Cela]. I'll leave him the field."

On hearing the denouement and end of the story, we went back into our ship. And there we made no further stay. Pantagruel gave eighteen thousand gold royals to the collection box for building the church, in consideration of the poverty of the people and utter misery of the place.

CHAPTER 48

How Pantagruel went ashore on the island of the Papimaniacs.[1]

LEAVING the desolate island of the Popefigs, we sailed for a day in serenity and all pleasure, when to our sight appeared the blessed island of the Papimaniacs. As soon as our anchors were weighed in the harbor, before we had tied up with our cables, there came toward us in a skiff four persons variously dressed: one as a monk, befrocked, bedunged, booted [enfrocqué, crotté, botté]; another as a falconer, with a lure and hawking-glove [un leurre et guand de oizeau]; another as a solicitor of lawsuits, holding in his hand a great sack full of accusations, summonses, chicaneries, and postponements; the fourth as a vine dresser from Orléans, with fine cloth leggings, a bread basket, and a vine knife at his belt. The moment they had reached our ship, they all cried out loudly together, asking:

"Have you seen him, you travelers? have you seen him?"

"Whom?" asked Pantagruel.

"The One," they replied.

"Who's he?" asked Frère Jean, "Ox death, I'll clobber him!"[2] thinking they were inquiring about someone guilty of robbery, murder, or sacrilege.

"How's that?" said they. "Don't you know the One and Only?"

"My Lord," said Epistémon. "We don't understand such terms. But explain to us, please, whom you mean, and we'll tell you the truth about it without dissimulation."

"He," said they, "is the One Who Is. Have you ever seen him?"

"The One Who Is," replied Pantagruel, "by our theological doctrine, is God. And in these words He declared Himself to Moses.[3] Certainly we have never seen Him, and He is not visible to bodily eyes."

"We're not talking at all," said they, "about that high God Who reigns in the heavens. We're talking about the God on earth. Have you ever seen him?"

"They mean," said Carpalim, "the pope, on my honor!"

"Yes, yes," replied Panurge, "Lord, yes, gentlemen. I've seen three of them, and the sight of them hasn't done me much good."[4]

"How's that?" said they, "our holy Decretals chant that there's never any but one alive."

"I mean," said Panurge, "three in succession, one after another. Otherwise I've never seen but one at a time."

"O thrice and four times happy people,"[5] said they, "pray be welcome and many times over, welcome."

Then they knelt down before us and wanted to kiss our feet, which we would not allow them to do, pointing out to them that even to the pope, if by chance he came there in person, they could do no more.

"Yes we would, yes indeed," they replied, "that's already decided among us. We'd kiss his ass with no figleaf, and likewise his balls. For he has balls, the Holy Father, we find that in our beautiful Decretals;[6] otherwise he wouldn't be pope. So that in subtle Decretaline philosophy this consequence is necessary: he is pope, so he has balls. And if the world ran out of balls, the world would have no more pope."

Pantagruel meanwhile was asking a ship's boy from their skiff who were these personages. He answered him that these were the four estates of the island, added furthermore that we would be warmly welcomed and well treated, since we had seen the pope, which he pointed out to Panurge, who said to him secretly:

"I swear to God, that's it! All comes in time to him who can wait. The sight of the pope has never done us any good; this time, by all the devils! it will do us good, so I see."

Then we went ashore, and up to us as in a procession kept coming all the people of the country, men, women, little children. Our four estates called out to them loudly:

"They've seen him! They've seen him! They've seen him!"

At this proclamation all the people knelt before us, raising their clasped hands to heaven and crying out:

"O happy people! O most happy people!"

And this cry lasted more than a quarter hour. Then up ran the schoolmaster with all his pedagogues, grammar school boys, and schoolboys, and fell to whipping them magisterially, as they used to whip the little children in our countries when some malefactor was being hanged, so that they should remember it. Pantagruel grew angry at this and said to them:

"Gentlemen, if you don't stop whipping these boys, I'm going back!"

The people were astonished at hearing his stentorian voice, and I saw a little hunchback with long fingers asking the schoolmaster:

"Power of the Extravagantes! Does everyone who sees the pope grow as big as this one who's threatening us? How incredibly I can't wait to see him, so as to grow as big as this one!"

So loud were their exclamations that Grosbeak (Homenaz:[7] that was the name of their bishop) rushed up on an unbridled mule with green trappings, accompanied by his apordinates (as they called them), his subordinates also, bearing crosses, banners, gonfalcons, baldachins, torches, holy-water basins. And he likewise tried with all his might to kiss our feet (as did the good Christian Valfinier with Pope Clement [VII]), saying that one of their hypophetes,[8] a degreaser and glossator of their holy Decretals, had left it in writing that even as the Messiah, so much and so long awaited by the Jews, had come to them at last, just so to this island some day the pope would come; that while they were awaiting that happy day, if anyone arrived who had seen him in Rome or anywhere else, they were to feast him well and treat him with reverence. However, we politely excused ourselves from this.

CHAPTER 49

How Grosbeak, bishop of the Papimaniacs, showed us the uranopète[1] Decretals.

THEN Grosbeak said to us: "By our holy Decretals we are enjoined and ordered to visit the churches first, before the cabarets. Therefore, not falling away from that fine regulation, let's go to church; afterward we'll go and banquet."

"You worthy man," said Frère Jean, "lead on, we'll follow you. You spoke of this in good terms and as a good Christian. We hadn't seen any of them for a long time now. I find myself much rejoiced in my mind from this, and I think I'll feed the better for it. It's a nice thing to meet good people."

As we approached the door of the temple, we espied a great gilded book, all covered with fine precious stones, balas rubies,[2] emeralds, diamonds, and union pearls, more excellent than those that Octavian consecrated to Jupiter Capitolinus [Suetonius *Life of Divus Augustus* 30.4], or at least as excellent. And it hung in the air, fastened by great gold chains to the zoophores[3] of the portal. We kept looking at it in wonder. Pantagruel kept handling it and turning it about at will,[4] for he could easily touch it. And he asserted that at the touch thereof he felt a gentle itching in his fingernails and new life in his arms, together with an urgent temptation in his spirit to beat a sergeant or two, provided they were not tonsured.

Thereupon Grosbeak said to us: "Long ago the law was given to the Jews by Moses, written by the very fingers of God. At Delphi, over the gate before the temple of Apollo, were found these words, divinely written: ΓΝΩΘΙ ΣΕΑΥΤΟΝ [Know thyself]. And after a certain interval of time later was seen ΕΙ [Thou art], also divinely inscribed and transmitted from the Heavens. So was the image of Cybele transmitted from the Heavens to Phrygia in the field called Pessinonte.[5] So was the image of Diana into Tauris, if you believe Euripides [*Iphigenia in Tauris* 85-88]. The oriflame[6] was transmitted from the heavens to the noble and most Christian kings of France to combat the infidels. In the reign of Numa Pompilius, second king of the Romans in Rome, was seen to descend from heaven the potent buckler called *Ancile* [Latin "crooked, curved"]. Onto the Acropolis of Athens once fell from the empyrean the statue of Minerva.[7] Here likewise you see the holy Decretals, written by the hand of an angelic cherub. You Transpontine people won't believe it . . . "

"Not very well," replied Panurge.

" . . . and miraculously transmitted to us here from the heaven of heavens, in the same way as Homer, father of all philosophy (always excepting the divine Decretals), the Nile is called Diipetes.[8] And because you have seen the pope, evangelist and eternal protector to these, by our leave you will be permitted to see and kiss them inside, if you'd like to. But you will have to fast for three days in advance and make confession regularly, carefully culling out and cataloguing your sins so scrupulously that not a single circumstance of them may fall to the ground, as is divinely sung to us by the celestial Decretals that you see here. That takes time."

"Worthy man," replied Panurge, "Decrapppers,[9] or rather I mean Decretals, we have seen many on lanterned parchment,[10] on vellum, both handwritten and in print. By now there's no need for you to take the trouble to show us this copy; we're content with your good intentions and thank you just the same."

"Honest to Gosh!" said Grosbeak, "you just haven't seen these evangelically written ones. Those of your country are mere transcriptions of ours, as we find written in one of our ancient Decretaline scholiasts. Anyway, I beg you not to try to spare me trouble. Just consider whether you're willing to make confession and fast for those three fine little days of God's."

"To cuntsfess [De cons fesser],"[11] replied Panurge, "we consent very readily; only the fast is very untimely for us, for we've fasted so much, so very much, at sea, that the spiders have spun their webs over our teeth. Just look at this good Brother Jean des Entommeures . . . "

At this title Grosbeak courteously gave him a little accolade.[12]

" . . . that moss has grown in his throat for want of moving and exercising his chaps and his jawbones."

"He's telling you the truth!" put in Frère Jean. "I've fasted so much, so very much, that it's left me all hunchbacked."

"Then," said Grosbeak, "let's go inside the church; and pardon us if right now we don't sing you God's lovely Mass. The hour is past midday, after which our holy Decretals forbid us to sing Mass, I mean legitimate High Mass. I'll say a low dry one for you."

"I'd prefer," said Panurge, "one wet with some good Anjou wine. So go ahead and knock it off low and stiff."[13]

"Mother of pearl!"[14] said Frère Jean, "I don't like one bit having my stomach still fasting. For once I'd had a good breakfast and fed well monkish style, if by chance he sings us some Requiem, I'd have brought some bread and wine gone down the hatch.[15] Patience! Sack, clash, push, but truss it up short, for fear it may get filthy,[16] and for another reason too, I beg you!"

CHAPTER 50

How by Grosbeak we were shown
the archetype of a pope.

WHEN the mass was over, Grosbeak drew out of a coffer near the high altar, after great jumble of keys, with which he opened, past thirty-two locks and fourteen padlocks, a window over the said altar, tightly barred with iron bars; then, with great mystery, he covered himself with a wet sack and, pulling back a curtain of crimson satin, showed us a picture, rather badly painted in my opinion, touched it with a longish stick, and had us all kiss the end that had touched it. Then he asked us:

"What do you think of that picture?"

"It," said Pantagruel, "is a likeness of a pope. I can tell him by the tiara, the amice, the surplice, and the slipper."

"Well said," said Grosbeak, "This is the Idea of that good God on earth, whose coming we await devoutly and whom some time we hope to see in this land. O what a happy and long-desired and keenly awaited day!"

"And you, happy and most happy, who have had the stars so favorable that you have seen alive, face to face and in reality, this good God on earth, by seeing merely whose portrait we gain full remission of all our sins that we can remember, also, of our forgotten sins, one-third of them plus thirteen quarantines![1] And so we see it only at the great annual festivals."

At that point Pantagruel said it was such a work as Daedalus used to make. Even though it was an imitation and badly drawn, still there was latent in it some divine energy in the matter of pardons.

"Just as at Seuilly," said Frère Jean, "on one good feast-day when the beggars were boasting, one of getting six half-sous [blancs] that day, another two sous, another seven carolus, one fat bum was boasting of getting three good testoons."

"And so," retorted his companions, "you have a God's game leg [une jambe de Dieu]," as if some touch of divinity were hidden in a leg all infected and rotted."

"When you tell us such stories," said Pantagruel, "remember to bring a basin: I'm almost ready to throw up. To use the holy name of God in such filthy and abominable things! Fie! I say Fie![2] If such an abuse of words is customary in your monkery, leave it there, don't bring it outside the cloisters."

"So," said Epistémon, "the doctors say that in some maladies there is some participation of divinity. Similarly Nero used to praise mushrooms and in a Greek proverb called them 'food of the gods,' because inside them he had poisoned his predecessor Claudius, emperor of Rome."

"It seems to me," said Panurge, "that this portrait is faulty for our latest popes; for I've seen them wearing, not an amice, but a helmet on their head crested with a Persian tiara, and, when all Christendom was in peace and quiet, I've seen them alone waging outrageous cruel war."

"Then that," said Grosbeak, "was against the rebels, heretics, desperate

Protestants, not obedient to the sanctity of this good God on earth. That's not only allowed him and legal but commanded by the holy Decretals, and he must immediately put to fire and the sword emperors, kings, dukes, princes, republics, once they transgress one iota of his commands; despoil them of their goods, dispossess them of their kingdom, proscribe them, anathematize them, and not only slay their bodies and those of their children and other relatives but also damn their souls in the depths of the most burning caldron there is in hell."

"Here, by all the devils," said Panurge, "these are not heretics, as was Raminagrobis and as they are amid the Germanies[3] and in England. You are Christians sifted out on the sieve."

"Yes, honest to Gosh [Ouy, vraybis]," said Grosbeak; "and so we'll all be saved. Let's go take some holy water, then we'll have dinner."

CHAPTER 51

Small talk during dinner
in praise of the Decretals.

Now note, topers, that during Grosbeak's dry mass, three church bell-ringers, each bearing a great basin in his hand, were walking through the people, crying aloud:

"Don't forget the happy people who have seen him face to face!"

While leaving the temple, these men brought Grosbeak their basins all full of Papimanic coins. Grosbeak told us that that was to feast with and that one half of this contribution and tax would be employed to drink well, the other to eat well, pursuant to a mirific gloss hidden in a certain little corner of the holy Decretals.

This was done, and in a handsome tavern rather like Guillot's[1] in Amiens. Believe me, the feeding was copious and the drinking bouts numerous. In this dinner I noticed two memorable things; one, that no meat was brought on, whatever it was, whether roebucks, capons, hogs (of which there is an abundance in Papimania), or pigeons, rabbits, leverets, turkeys, or others, in which there was not a plethora of magisterial stuffing;[2] the other, that all the main courses and desserts were brought on by marriageable young maidens of that place, beautiful, I swear to you, palpitating, blond, sweet and gracious,[3] who, dressed in long, white, loose robes with double girdles, heads bare, hair entwined with little fillets and ribbons of violet silk adorned with roses, carnations, marjoram, dill, southernwood, and other fragrant flowers, at each beat kept inviting us to drink, with charming expert curtseys. And all those present enjoyed watching them. Frère Jean kept looking at them out of the corner of his eye, like a dog carrying off a chicken.

As they cleared off the first course they melodiously sang an epode in praise of the sacrosanct Decretals. As they brought on the second course [the dessert], Grosbeak, all beaming with joy, addressed himself to one of the master butlers and said:

"Cleric, bring a light."[4]

At these words, one of the girls promptly offered him a great beaker of *Extravagant*[5] wine. He took it in his hand and said to Pantagruel with a deep sigh:

"My Lord, and you, my fine friends, I drink to you all right from the heart. Do be ever so welcome!"

Once he had drunk and returned the beaker to the charming maiden, he exclaimed heavily: "O divine Decretals! So good is wine made to taste by you!"

"That," said Panurge, "is not the worst of the lot!"

"It would be better," said Pantagruel, "if they could make bad wine good."

"O seraphic Sixth!"[6] Grosbeak went on, "how necessary you are to the salvation of poor humans! O cherubic *Clementines!* how aptly is contained and described in you the perfect training of a true Christian! O angelic *Extravagantes!* without you how poor souls would perish which wander about in human bodies here below in this vale of tears! Alas! when will come that gift of special grace granted to humans, to desist from all other studies and business to read you, understand you, know you, use, practice, incorporate you, change you into blood and center you in the deepest lobes of their brains, the innermost marrow of their bones, the complex labyrinths of their arteries? O then, and no sooner or otherwise, how happy the world!"

At these words, Epistémon got up and said quite candidly to Panurge: "The lack of a close-stool forces me to get out of here. This stuffing[7] has unstopped my bumgut. I can hardly wait."

"O then," said Grosbeak as he went on, "no trace of hail, frost, fogs, climatic disaster! O then, abundance of all good things on earth! O then, obstinate peace, unshatterable, in all the universe, cessation of wars, pillages, forced drudgery, brigandage, assassinations, except against the accursed heretics and rebels! O then, joyousness, bliss, solace, pastimes, pleasures, delights, in all human nature. But O great teaching, inestimable erudition, deific precepts, mortised by the divine chapters of these eternal Decretals! O how, on reading just one half-canon, one little paragraph, just one sentence of these sacrosanct Decretals, you feel inflamed in your hearts the furnace of divine love, of charity toward your neighbor, provided he is not a heretic, assured disdain of fortuitous and earthly things, ecstatic elevation of your spirits, even up to the third heaven, certain contentment in all that you care about!"[8]

CHAPTER 52

Continuation of the miracles occasioned by the Decretals.

"THIS talk sounds good,"[1] said Panurge, "but I believe as little of it as I can. For I happened one day in Poitiers, at the Scotchman's, the Decretaline Doctor,[2] to read a chapter of it; devil take me if, on the reading thereof, I was not so constipated in my belly that for over four, even five, days, I crapped only one tiny turd. Do you know what kind? Such, I swear to you, as Catullus says are those of his neighbor Furius:

> In one whole year not ten turds do you shit;
> And if by hand you break them up a bit,
> No dirt upon your finger will be shown,
> For each is harder than a bean or stone.[3]

"Aha!" said Grosbeak, "Snyan,[4] my friend, you may just by chance have been in a state of mortal sin."

"That bit," said Panurge, "is wine from another barrel."

"One day," said Frère Jean, "at Seuilly, I'd wiped my ass on a sheet of some wretched *Clémentine,* which Jean Guymard, our bursar, had tossed onto the meadow of the cloister; may all the devils take me if the skin chaps near the anus and the hemorrhoids didn't come upon me so very horrible that my poor little brown asshole was all shot."[5]

"Snyan," said Grosbeak, "that was evident punishment by God, avenging the sin you had committed by beshitting these holy books, which you should have been kissing and adoring, I mean with the adoration of *latria*,[6] or *hyperdulia*[7] at the least. Panormitanus never lied about it."

"Johnny Jumpup[8] in Montpellier," said Ponocrates, "had bought from the monks of Saint-Olary[9] a fine set of Decretals written on great handsome Lamballe parchment, to make into vellum for gold-beating.[10] The trouble with that was so strange that never was a piece struck with it that was any good to him. All were tattered and gutted."

"Divine punishment," said Grosbeak, "and vengeance!"

"At Le Mans," said Eudémon, "François Cornu [Horned Frances], the apothecary, had used for making paper cornets a dog-eared copy of the Extravagantes: I renounce the devil if all that was packed in it was not instantly poisoned, rotted, and spoiled: incense, pepper, cloves, cinnamon, saffron, wax, spices, cassia, rhubarb, tamarind, in fact everything, drugs, purges, and medications."[11]

"Vengeance," said Grosbeak, "and divine punishment. To misuse in profane matters such holy scriptures as these!"

"In Paris," said Carpalim, "Groignet, a tailor, had used some old *Clémentines* for patterns and measures. O what a strange case! All clothes cut on such patterns and measures were spoiled and ruined: robes, hoods, cloaks, gowns, jackets, neckpieces, doublets, smocks, riding coats, and farthingales. Groignet, thinking to cut a hood, would cut the form of a codpiece. Instead of a smock he would cut a hat fit to hold plum pits. On the pattern of a long coat he would cut an amice. On the pattern of a doublet he would cut out the shape of a *paele*.[12] His helpers, after sewing it, would cut holes in it on the bottom, and it seemed like a pan for roasting chestnuts. For a collar he would make a buskin. On the pattern of a farthingale he would cut out a riding hood.[13] Thinking to make a cloak, he would make a Swiss soldier's drum. To such a point that the poor man was condemned in law to pay for all his customer's goods, and at present he's broke [au saphran]."

"Divine punishment," said Grosbeak, "and vengeance!"

"At Cahusac," said Gymnaste, "an archery match was set up between Lord d'Estissac and Viscount de Lausun. Pérotou had chopped up half a Decretals of the good Canon La Carte, and out of the leaves had cut out the white of the target. I'll give myself, sell myself, hurl myself through all the devils, if ever a crossbowman of the region (and these were superlative in all Guyenne) shot one arrow into it. All were to one side. None of the sacrosanct chalkened white was deflowered or touched. Moreover, Sansornin the Elder, who was holding the stakes, kept swearing to us *Figues Dioures,*[14] his great oath, that he had seen clearly, visibly, manifestly, Carquelin's bolt, heading straight into the bull's eye in the middle of the white, on the point of contact and going in, to be deflected a fathom away, to one side, toward the bakehouse."

"A miracle," cried Grosbeak, "a miracle, a miracle! Cleric, bring a light! I drink to you all! You seem to me like real Christians."

At these words the girls began to snicker among themselves. Frère Jean was whinnying from the tip of his nose as if ready to play stallion or at least donkey,[15] and leap them like Herbault[16] onto poor folk.

"It seems to me," said Pantagruel, "that with such whites a man would have been safer from the danger of an arrow than ever was Diogenes long ago."

"What?" asked Grosbeak, "was he a Decretalist?"

"That," said Epistémon, returning from his business,[17] "is hitting the nail right on the thumb!"

"Diogenes," replied Pantagruel, "looking for sport one day, went to watch the archers shooting at the target. Among them was one so wild, inept, and clumsy, that when he lined up to shoot, all the spectators moved away for fear of being hit by him. Diogenes, after watching him shoot so perversely that his arrow fell more than a perche [about five feet] away from the butt, at his next shot, as the crowd moved far away on one side or the other, took his stand right next to the white, affirming that this spot was the safest and that the white alone was in safety from the arrow."[18]

"A page," said Gymnaste, "of Lord d'Estissac, named Chamouillac, spotted the charm. On his advice Pérotou changed the white and used the papers of the Pouillac lawsuit.[19] Thereupon they all shot very well."

"At Landerousse,"[20] said Rhizotome, "at the marriage of Jean Delif, the feast was notable and sumptuous, as was the custom of the region. After supper several farces, comedies, amusing conceits were performed; there were several morris dances with jangles and drums; various masques and mummeries were introduced. My schoolmates and I, to honor the feast as best we could (for we had all in the morning gotten beautiful white and violet liveries), toward the end got up a merry mascarade with many shells from Saint-Michel and pretty snailshells. For lack of arum, burdock, or brown mullein leaves and of paper, out of some leaves of an old *Sextum* that had been left there we made our face masks, cutting them out a bit in the places for the eyes, the nose, and the mouth. A marvelous thing! When our little carols and childish entertainments were done, on removing our false faces we appeared, more hideous and ugly than the devilkins of the Doué Passion,[21] so badly were our faces messed up in the places touched by the said leaves. One of them had the smallpox, another the plague-spot [le tac], another the great pox, another the measles, another great furuncles. In short, each one considered himself unharmed whose teeth had fallen out."

"A miracle!" cried Grosbeak, "a miracle!"

"It's not yet time," said Rhizotome, "to laugh. My two sisters Catherine and Renée had put inside this fine Sextum as in a press (for it was covered with big boards and studded with heavy nails) their wimples, sleeves, and collars freshly soaped, quite white and starched. By the power of God . . . "

"Wait," said Grosbeak. "Which God do you mean?"

"There's only one," replied Rhizotome.

"Yes indeed," said Grosbeak, "in heaven. Don't we have another one on earth?"

"Giddap [Arry avant]!" said Rhizotome. "I wasn't thinking about that one any more, 'pon my soul! By the power, then, of the pope God on earth, their wimples, neckpieces, bibs, headscarves, all other linen turned blacker than a charcoal-burner's sack."

"A miracle!" exclaimed Grosbeak. "Cleric, bring a light here [Clerice, esclaire icy],[22] and note down these fine stories."

"Then how is it," said Frère Jean, "that people say:

> Since first Decrees had wings,
> And soldiers boxed their things,
> Monks had their horse to ride,
> And ills spread far and wide."[23]

"I know what you mean," said Grosbeak. "Those are little japes of the new heretics."

CHAPTER 53

How by virtue of the Decretals
gold is subtly drawn from France into Rome.[1]

"I would like," said Epistémon, "to have paid for a half pint of tripes ready to eat, and for us to have collated from the original those terrifying chapters, *Execrabilis, De multa, Si plures, De annatis per totum, Nisi essent, Cum ad monasterium, Quod dilectio, Mandatum,*[2] and certain others, which in every year draw from France to Rome four hundred thousand ducats and more."

"That, is that nothing?" said Grosbeak. "However, it seems to me rather little, seeing that the most Christian France is the sole nursing mother of the Roman court. But can you find me books in the world, whether on philosophy, medicine, law, mathematics, humane letters, even (by that God of mine) of the holy Scripture, which can extract as much from there? Nix! Pish, tush! You won't find any with this aurifluous energy [ceste auriflue énergie], I assure you. Besides, these heretic devils will not learn and know them. Burn them, tear them with pincers, cut with shears, drown, hang, impale, break their shoulders, dis-embowel, chop to bits, fricassee, grill, slice up, crucify, boil, crush, quar-ter, smash to bits, unhinge, charcoal-broil these wicked heretics, decretalifuges, decretalicides, worse than homicides, worse than parri-cides, decretalictones[3] of the devil.

"Now you worthy people, if you want to be called and reputed true Christians, I beseech you with clasped hands not to believe anything else, not to think anything else, not to say, undertake, or do anything, except what is contained in our holy Decretals and their commentaries: that lovely *Sextum,* those beautiful *Clémentines,* those handsome *Extravagantes.* O what deific books! Thus you will be revered by everyone in this world in glory, honor, exaltation, riches, dignities, preferments, dreaded by each and every one, preferred to all, elected and chosen over all. For there is no estate under the cope of heaven in which you will find people more fit to do and handle no matter what than those who, by divine foreknowl-edge and eternal predestination, have devoted themselves to the study of the holy Decretals.

"Do you want to choose a doughty emperor, a good captain, a worthy chief and leader of an army in wartime, knowing well how to foresee all problems, avoid all dangers, lead his men into the assault and combat in high spirits, risk nothing, always win without loss of his soldiers, and make good use of his victory? Take me a Decretist.[4] No, no! I mean a Decretalist."

"O what a juicy slip!"[5] said Epistémon.

"Do you want to find in peacetime a man apt and adequate to govern well the state of a republic, of a kingdom, of an empire, of a monarchy, maintain the Church, the nobility, the Senate, and the people in riches, sanity, concord, obedience, virtue, honor? Take me a Decretalist.

"Do you want to find a man who by an exemplary life, fine talk, holy admonitions, in a short time and without shedding human blood, will conquer the Holy Land and convert to the holy faith the miscreant Turks, Jews, Tartars, Muscovites, Mamelukes, and Sarabaites?[6] Take me a Decretalist.

"What makes the people in many countries rebellious and unruly, the pages greedy and bad, the schoolboys rubbernecks and lazy asses? Their preceptors, their squires, their tutors were not Decretalists.

"But who (in all conscience) was it that estabished, confirmed, authorized these lovely religious orders, with which in every place you see Christianity adorned, decorated illustrated, as the firmament is with its bright stars? Divine Decretals.

"What has founded, supported, based, what maintains, sustains, nourishes the pious religious throughout the convents, monasteries, abbeys, without whose continual prayers by day, by night, the world would be in evident danger of returning to its ancient chaos? Holy Decretals.

"What makes, and day by day augments in its abundance of all temporal, corporeal, and spiritual goods the famous, celebrated patrimony of Saint Peter? Holy Decretals.

"What makes the Apostolic See in Rome, from all time and today, so redoubtable in the universe that willy-nilly, all kings, emperors, potentates, and lords must depend on it, be indebted to it, be crowned, confirmed, authorized to submit and fall prostrate before the mirific slipper, the picture of which you have seen? God's lovely Decretals.

"I want to divulge to you a great secret. The universities of your world ordinarily bear in their coats of arms a book, some open, some closed. What book do you think that is?"

"I certainly don't know," replied Pantagruel. "I've never read in it."

"It," said Grosbeak, "is the Decretals, without which would perish the privilege of all the universities. I got you on that one! Ha, ha, ha, ha!"

Here Grosbeak began to burp, fart, laugh, drool, and sweat, and handed his great greasy four-codpiece bonnet to one of the girls, who, after kissing it amorously, set it on her lovely head in great delight, as pledge and assurance that she would be the first one married.

"Vivat!" cried Epistémon, "vivat! fifat! pipat! bibat![7] O what an apocalyptic secret!"

"Cleric," said Grosbeak, "bring a light here, a pair of lanterns. On with the fruit, lassies! So I was saying that, by devoting ourselves to the sole study of the holy Decretals, you will be rich and honored in this world. I say consequently that in the other you will infallibly be saved in the blessed Kingdom of Heaven, the keys to which are given to our good Decretaliarch God. O my good God, Whom I adore and have never seen, by Thy special grace open unto us at the point of death, at least, that very sacred treasure of our mother holy church, of which Thou art the Protector, Preserver, Distributor, Administrator, Dispenser! And see to it that the jaws of hell may not engulf us! If pass through purgatory we must, patience! In Thy power and will it lies to deliver us from it, if Thou wilt."

Here Grosbeak began to shed great hot tears, beat his chest, and cross his thumbs and kiss them.

CHAPTER 54

How Grosbeak gave Pantagruel some good-Christian[1] pears.

Epistémon, Frère Jean, and Panurge, seeing this doleful conclusion, under cover of their napkins began to call out: "Meow, meow, meow [Myault, myault, myault]!" meanwhile pretending to wipe their eyes as if they had been crying. The girls were well trained, and offered everyone full beakers of Clémentine wine with plenty of sweetmeats. Thus was the banquet once again rejoiced.

At the end of the meal Grosbeak gave us a large number of big handsome pears, saying: "Here, my friends, are singular pears, which you won't find anywhere else. Not every land bears everything. India alone bears black ebony. In Sheba the good incense grows. On the island of

Lemnos the clay for vermilion.[2] In this island alone grow these lovely pears. Make seedbeds of them, if you see fit, in your countries."

"What do you call them?" asked Pantagruel. "They seem to me very good and with very nice juice. If you cooked them in casseroles with a little wine and sugar, I think it would be a very salubrious dish for both the sick and the healthy."

"We call them no other way," replied grosbeak. "We're simple folk, since God so pleases. And we call figs figs, plums plums, and pears pears."

"Truly," said Pantagruel, "when I'm back home (that, God willing, will be soon), I'll plant and graft some in my garden in Touraine on the bank of the Loire, and they shall be called good-Christian pears.[3] For I've never seen better Christians than these Papimaniacs are."

"I'd just as soon," said Frère Jean, "he gave us two or three cartloads of his girls."

"What for?" asked Grosbeak.

"To bleed them," replied Frère Jean, "between the two big toes with certain highly sensitive pointed probes. In so doing, we would engraft upon them some good Christian children, and the race of them would multiply in our countries, in which they are none too good."

"Lan's sakes!" replied Grosbeak, "we will not, for you'd play your idiot bachelor's tricks[4] on them! I can tell it by your nose, and yet I'd never seen you.[5] Alas! You're a fine one! Would you really want to damn your soul? Our Decretals forbid that. I wish you knew them well."

"Hold on [Patience]!" said Frère Jean. "But, *si tu non vis dare, praesta, quesumus.*[6] That's breviary matter. In that domain I fear no man wearing a beard, even were he a doctor of crystalline (I mean Decretaline) with a triple hood."

When dinner was over we took leave of Grosbeak and of all that good people, thanking them humbly, and in return for so many kindnesses promising them that when we came to Rome we would work on the pope so well that he would shortly go to see them in person. Then we went back to our ship. Pantagruel, out of liberality and gratitude about the holy portrait, gave Grosbeak nine pieces of cloth of gold embroidered upon embroidery, to be placed in front of the iron-barred windows, had their box for repair and construction filled full of double clog-crowns,[7] and had delivered to each one of the girls who had served at table during dinner nine hundred and fourteen gold saluts to get them married at an appropriate time.

CHAPTER 55

How on the high seas
Pantagruel heard some unfrozen words.

O~N~ the open sea, as we were banqueting, nibbling, conversing and making fine short discourses, Pantagruel got to his feet to scan around him. Then he said to us: "Mates, do you hear anything? It seems to me I hear people talking up in the air, but all the same I don't see anyone. Listen!"

We were attentive to his command, and sniffed the air in great earfuls like fine oysters on the shell[1] to hear whether there could be any sound around, and, in order not to miss any, after the example of the Emperor Antoninus,[2] some of us cupped our hands behind our ears. Nevertheless we protested that we heard no voices whatever. Pantagruel kept on affirming that he heard various voices in the air, of both men and women, and then it struck us that we were either hearing them too or hearing things. The more we persevered in listening, the more we made out the voices, until we could understand entire words, which frightened us greatly, since we saw no one, and heard voices and sounds so diverse, of men, women, children, and horses; to the point where Panurge cried out:

"Gorbelly![3] Is this some trick? We're done for. Let's get out of here! There's an ambush all around. Frère Jean, are you there, my friend? Stay close to me, I beseech you. Do you have your cutlass? Be sure it doesn't stick in the scabbard. You don't clean the rust off it at all in our ship. We're done for! Listen: these, by God, are cannon shots. Let's flee! I don't mean with feet and hands, as Brutus said at the battle of Pharsalia, I mean with sails and oars.[4] Let's get out of here! Let's escape! I don't mean for any fear I have, for I fear nothing except dangers; that's what I always say. So did the Free Archer of Baignolet. Therefore let's not press our luck, so we don't get struck.[5] Let's get out! About face! Turn the helm, you whoreson! Would God I were right now in Quinquenais, on pain of never marrying! Let's get out of here! Let's make all the sail we can, for they may be too hard for us; we might not be able to cope with them. After all, they are ten to our one. They are also on their own dunghill, while we do not know the country. They'll be the death of us. That'll be no dishonor to us.

"Demosthenes says that the man who flees will fight again. Let's at least pull back. Port! Starboard! Man the topsail! Man the bowlines [au boulingues]! We're goners! Let's get out of here! In the name of all the devils, let's get out!"

Pantagruel, hearing the uproar Panurge was making, said: "Who's that runaway over there? Let's first see what sort of people they are. They may peradventure be our own. I still don't see anyone, and I can see for a hundred miles around. But let's listen. I've read that a philosopher named Petron[6] was of the opinion that there were several worlds touching one another in the form of an equilateral triangle, at the base and center of which he says were the abode of Truth and the habitat of Words, Ideas,[7] the exemplars and images of all things past and future, and all around these was the Age.[8] And in certain years, at long intervals, part of these fell upon humans like catarrhs, and as the dew fell upon Gideon's fleece;[9] part of them remain reserved for the future, until the consummation of the Age.

"I also remember that Aristotle says that Homer's words are prancing, flying, moving, and consequently animate.[10] Moreover, Antiphanes used to say that Plato's doctrine was like certain words, which in some region or other, in the depths of a hard winter, freeze and turn to ice in the cold of the air, and are not heard. Likewise that what Plato taught young children was scarcely understood by them when they had grown old.[11]

"Now it would be something to think about and look into whether by any chance this might be the place where such words unfreeze [thaw out]. We would certainly be most amazed if these were the head and lyre of Orpheus. For after the Thracian women had torn Orpheus to pieces, they threw his head and his lyre into the river Hebrus; these floated down by this river into the Black Sea and on through all the way to the island of Lesbos, all the time swimming together over the sea. And from the head continually came forth a lugubrious song, as if lamenting the death of Orpheus; the lyre, played on by the moving winds, kept tune harmoniously with the song. Let's look and see whether you can see them around here."[12]

CHAPTER 56

How among the frozen words
Pantagruel found some lusty jests.[1]

THE skipper made answer: "Lord, don't be afraid of anything! Here is the edge of the glacial [Arctic] Sea, on which, at the beginning of last winter, there was a great fierce battle between the Arimaspians[2] and the Nephelibates. Then in the air froze the words and cries of the men and women, the clashing of maces, the banging of armor for men and horses, the neighing of the horses, and every other tumult of combat. Right now, with the rigor of the winter past, and the serenity of the good weather coming on, they are melting and are heard."

"By God," said Panurge, "I do believe he's right! But might we see one of them? I remember reading that by the edge of the mountain on which Moses received the law of the Jews, the people could literally see the voices."

"Look, look!" said Pantagruel, "here are some that are not yet unfrozen."

Then he cast down on the deck for us handfuls of frozen words, and they seemed like candies, variegated in divers colors. There we saw some lusty jests, jests of azure, sable, gold,[3] which all, on being warmed up a little between our hands, melted like so much snow, and we could really hear them, but not understand them, for it was a barbarous language. Except for one rather plump one, which, when warmed by Frère Jean between his hands, made a sound such as chestnuts do when tossed on the coals without being split, and then burst, and made us all start with fright.

"That," said Frère Jean, "was a falconet shot in its day."

Panurge asked Pantagruel to give him some more. Pantagruel replied that giving words was a thing that lovers do.[4]

"Sell me some then," Panurge kept saying.

"That's a thing that lawyers do," replied Pantagruel, "sell words.[5] I would rather sell you silence, and more dear, even as Demosthenes sold it, by means of his argentangine."[6]

This notwithstanding, he tossed three or four handfuls onto the deck. And among them I saw some words that stung, some that drew blood (which the captain said sometimes returned to the spot they were sent from, but it was with their throats cut),[7] some horrific words, and others rather unpleasing to see. When these were melted together we heard: "Hin, hin, hin, hisse,[8] tick, tock, tack, brededin, brededac, frr, frrr, frr, bou, bou, bou, bou, bou, bou, bou, bou, traccc, trr, trrr, trrrrr, on, on, on, ououououououououon, goth, magoth,[9] and I know not what other barbarous words; he said that these were vocables from the crashing and from the neighing of the horses at the time of the clash. Then we heard some other, coarse ones,[10] and in unfreezing they made a noise, some as of drums and fifes, some as of bugles and trumpets.

Believe me, we had lots of good fun. I wanted to put a few lusty jests in reserve in oil, as you keep snow and ice. But Pantagruel wouldn't have it, saying that it was folly to keep a reserve of what you never lack and always have in hand, as are lusty jests among all good joyous Pantagruelists.

Here Panurge angered Frère Jean quite a bit, until he was beside himself, for he took him at his word at the moment when he least expected it,[11] and Frère Jean threatened to make him sorry for it the way G. Jousseaulme was sorry he sold the cloth on his word to the noble Pathelin,[12] and, if it had turned out that Panurge got married, to take him by the horns like a calf, since Panurge had taken him at his word like a man. Panurge flipped his lower lip at him as a sign of derision.[13] Then he cried out and said:

"Would to God that here and now, without going any further, I might have the word of the Divine Bottle!"

CHAPTER 57

How Pantagruel went ashore
at the abode of Messere Gaster,[1]
first master of arts in the world.

On that day Pantagruel went ashore on an island wonderful among all others, both because of its site and of the governor thereof. At the outset on all sides it was rugged, stony, mountainous, infertile, unpleasing to the eye, very hard on the feet, and hardly less inaccessible than the mount in Dauphiné called as it is because it is shaped like a toadstool, and in the memory of man no one has been able to climb it, except Doyac,[2] master of the artillery for King Charles the Eighth, who with wondrous machines got up it and on top found an old ram. It was anyone's guess who had transported him there. Some said that as a young lamb, snatched up there by some eagle or tawny owl, he had escaped among the bushes.

Overcoming the difficulty of the entry, with very great effort and not without sweat, we found the mountaintop so pleasing, so fertile, so healthy and delightful, that I thought it was the real earthly Garden of Paradise, about whose location the good theologians argue and toil so.[3] But Pantagruel asserted that there was the abode of *Arété* (that is virtue) described by Hesiod [*Works and Days* 289], this however without prejudice to sounder opinion.

The governor of the island was Messere Gaster, first master of arts in the world. If you think that fire is the great master of arts, as Cicero writes, you are mistaken and are going wrong, for Cicero never did believe it. If you think that Mercury was the first inventor of the arts, as our ancient druids believed long ago, you are far off the track. The statement of the Satirist[4] is true, who says that Messere Gaster is master of all the arts. With him dwelt peaceably the good lady Penia,[5] otherwise called Want, mother of the nine Muses, to whom long ago in conjunction with Porus, lord of Abundance, was born to us Love, the noble child, mediator between Heaven and Earth, as Plato attests in his *Symposium* [203b].

To this lordly king we had perforce to pay reverence, swear obedience, and bear honor. For he is imperious, rigorous, round, tough, hard, and inflexible. One cannot convince him of anything, point out to him anything, persuade him of anything. He just doesn't hear. And as the Egyptians used to say that Harpocras, god of silence—in Greek called Sigalion—was *astomé* that is to say mouthless,[6] so Gaster was created without ears, as in Candia the statue of Jupiter was without ears. He speaks only by signs. But his signs everyone obeys more promptly than the edicts of praetors and commands of kings. When he gives orders he admits of no delay or deferment. You can say that at the lion's roar all animals far around tremble, as far (that is to say) as his voice can be heard. This is written. It is true. I have seen it. I certify to you that at Messere Gaster's command all heaven trembles and all the earth quakes. The name of his command is: hop to it without delay, or die.

The captain was telling us how one day, on the model of the members conspiring against the belly as Aesop describes it,[7] the whole kingdom of the Somates conspired against him to pull out of their obedience to him. But soon they felt the consequences of it, repented of it, and returned in all humility to his service. Otherwise they would all have perished of dire famine.

Whatever companies he is in, one must not debate over superiority or precedence; always he goes ahead of all, were they kings, emperors, or even the pope. And at the Council of Basil[8] he went first, although they tell you that the said Council was seditious because of the contentions and ambitions over precedence. To serve him everyone is busy, everyone toils. And so in recompense he does the world this good: that he invents for it all arts, all machines, all trades, all devices and subtle contrivances. Even the brute beasts he teaches skills denied them by nature. Crows, jays, parrots, starlings he makes into poets; magpies he makes into poetesses and teaches them to utter, speak, sing the human language. And all for the gut [pour la trippe]!

Eagles, gerfalcons, sakers, lanners, goshawks, sparrowhawks, merlins, hagards, peregrines, wild and rapacious birds,[9] he domesticates and tames so utterly that, leaving them in full freedom of the sky when he sees fit, as high as he wants, as long as he likes, he keeps them suspended, roaming, flying, hovering, playing up to him, paying court to him above the clouds; then suddenly he makes them plunge from heaven to earth. And all for the gut!

Elephants, lions, rhinoceroses, bears, horses, dogs, he causes to dance, fling, prance, fight, swim, hide, bring him what he wants, take what he wants. And all for the gut!

Fish (both ocean and freshwater), whales and sea monsters, he forces out of the lowest depths; wolves he drives out of the woods; bears out of their rocky caves; foxes out of their lairs; snakes he casts out of the ground. And all for the gut!

In short, he is so uncontrollable in his rage that he devours them all, beasts and people, as was seen among the Vascons, when Quintus Metellus was besieging them during the Sertorian Wars,[10] among the Saguntines when besieged by Hannibal, among the Jews besieged by the Romans,[11] six hundred others. And all for the gut!

When Penia his regent starts on her rounds, in all the places she goes, all Parlements are closed, all edicts are mute, all ordinances vain. She knows, obeys, and has no law. All shun her, in every place, choosing rather to expose themselves to shipwrecks at sea and venture through fire, rocks, caves, and precipices than be seized by that most dreadful tormenter.

CHAPTER 58

How in the court of the ingenious
master, Pantagruel detested
the Engastrimyths and the Gastrolaters.[1]

IN the court of this great ingenious master, Pantagruel noticed two sorts of people, importunate yesmen[2] and far too officious menials, whom he held in great abomination. One group was named Engastrimyths, the others Gastrolaters.

On the one hand, the Engastrimyths said they were descended from the ancient race of Eurycles, and on this point they cited the testimony of Aristophanes, in the comedy entitled *The Wasps* [vss. 1017–1020]. Wherefore they were originally called Eurycleans, as Plato writes, and Plutarch, in his book *On the cessation of oracles.*[3] In the holy *Decrees,*[4] 26 question 3, they are called ventriloquists, and thus Hippocrates names them in the Ionic language, Book 5, *On epidemics,* as speaking from the belly. Sophocles calls them *Sternomantes.*[5] They were diviners, magicians, and deceivers of the simple people, seeming to speak and reply not from the mouth but from the belly to those who questioned them.

Such was, around the year of our blessed Savior 1513, Jacoba Rohodigina,[6] an Italian woman of low degree. From whose belly we have often heard, as have an infinite number of others, in Ferrara and elsewhere, the voice of the unclean Spirit, certainly low, weak, and small, nevertheless well articulated, distinct, and intelligible, when, by the curiosity of the rich lords and princes of Cisalpine Gaul, she was called for and summoned. And they, to remove all suspicion of fiction or hidden fraud, had her stripped stark naked and her mouth and nose stopped up. This malign spirit answered to the name Crespelu [Curly], or Cincinnatulus, and seemed to take pleasure in being so called. When he was called so, he promptly answered what was said. If he was asked about present or past matters, he replied pertinently even to the wonderment of his hearers. If about future things, he always lied, never told the truth about them. And often he seemed to confess his ignorance, instead of answering letting a great fart, or muttering a few unintelligible words with barbarous endings.

The Gastrolaters, on the other hand, stayed huddled together in troops and bands, some cheery, lusty, soft, others sad, grave, severe, gloomy, all of them idle, doing nothing, never working, a useless weight and burden to the earth, as Hesiod says,[7] fearing (as far as one can judge) to offend the belly and make it thin. For the rest, masked, disguised, and clad so strangely that it was a lovely sight.

You say, and it is written by many wise old-time philosophers,[8] that Nature's ingenuity is shown forth wondrously in the sport she seems to have had in fashioning seashells: such variety we see in them, so many figures, so many colors, so many traits and forms inimitable by art. I assure you that in the garb of these shell-clad[9] Gastrolaters we saw no less variety and disguise. They all held Gaster as their great god, worshiped him as a god, sacrificed to him as to their omnipotent god, recognized no other god than him, served him, loved him above all things, honored him as their god. You would have said it was precisely about them that the Holy Apostle [Saint Paul] writes in Philippians 3: "There are many of whom I have often spoken to you (I say it to you even now with tears in my eyes) who are enemies of the cross of Christ, of whom Death will be the consummation, of whom Belly is the god [18–19]."

Pantagruel was wont to compare them to the Cyclops Polyphemus, of whom Euripides has spoken as follows:

"I sacrifice only to myself (not at all to the gods), and to this belly of mine, the greatest of all the gods."[10]

CHAPTER 59

Of the ridiculous statue called Manduce,[1]
and how and what the Gastrolaters
sacrificed to their ventripotent[2] *god.*

As, all in utter amazement, we considered the faces and actions of these sluggard magnigulous[3] Gastrolaters, we heard a noteworthy bell-ringing, at which they all lined up as in battle array, each according to his office, rank, and seniority.

Thus they came before Messere Gaster, following a powerful fat young pot-belly, who bore on a long well-gilded pole a wooden statue, ill carved and crudely painted, such as is described by Plautus,[4] Juvenal,[5] and Pompeius Festus. In Lyon, at their carnival, they call it Crunchcrust [Maschecroutte]. Here they called it Manduce. It was a monstrous effigy, ridiculous, hideous, and terrifying to little children, having eyes bigger than its belly and a head bigger than all the rest of its body, with ample, wide horrific jaws with plenty of teeth, both upper and lower which, by the device of a little cord hidden in the gilded pole, were made to clatter frighteningly together, as they do at Metz with Saint Clement's dragon.[6]

As the Gastrolaters approached, I saw that they were followed by a great number of stout valets laden with baskets, hampers, bundles, pots, sacks, and kettles. Thereupon, following Manduce's lead, chanting I know not what dithyrambs, croepalocomes,[7] epaenons, they offered to their god, opening their baskets and kettles:

White hippocras, with a piece of soft dry toast,
White bread,
Soft bread,[8]
Choice white bread,
Bourgeois bread,
Carbonados of six kinds,
Stews,
Shanks of roast veal, cold, spiced with powdered ginger,
Couscous,[9]
Haslets,

Fricassees, nine kinds,
Small pies,
Fat prime dips,
Greyhound dips,
Lyonnaise dips,
Round cabbages with beef marrow,
Hodgepodges,
Salmagundis,[10]

Eternal drink intermixed, first a good tasty white wine, then a cool claret and vermilion wine,[11] I tell you cold as ice, served and offered in great silver cups.

Then they offered:

Chitterlings garnished with fine mustard,
Sausages,
Smoked ox tongues,
Pig's feet and lard,
Pork chines with peas,
Larded veal stewed,
Blood puddings,
Sausages,
Hams,
Boar's heads,
Salt venison with turnips,
Sliced grilled pork livers,
Marinated olives.

All this accompanied by eternal drink. Then they would shovel into his gullet:

Legs of mutton in garlic sauce,
Pasties in hot sauce,
Pork cutlets in onion sauce,
Roast capons with their own gravy,
Cockerels,
Goosanders,

Kids,
Fawns, fallow deer,
Hares, leverets,
Partridges, grown and young,
Pheasants, grown and young,
Peacocks, grown and young,
Storks, grown and young,
Woodcork, snipe,
Ortolans,
Turkey cocks, hens, and chicks,
Ringdoves, small stockdoves,
Hogs in must,
Ducks in onion sauce,
Blackbirds, rail,
Coots,
Sheldrakes,
Egrets,
Teal,
Divers,
Bitterns,
Spoonbills,
Curlews,
Grouse,
Moorhens with leeks,
Fat kids, young goats,
Shoulder of mutton with capers,
Cuts of beef *royale*,
Breasts of veal,
Boiled hens and fat capons in clear jelly,
Pied pheasants,
Chickens,
Rabbits, grown and young,
Quail, grown and young,
Pigeons, grown and young,

Herons, grown and young,
Bustards, grown and young,
Sparrows,
Young guinea hens,
Plovers,
Geese, goslings,
Small stockdoves,
Pigeons,
Thrushes,
Flamingos, swans,
Spoonbills,
Wild ducks, cranes,
Sea-ducks,
Cormorants,
Curlews, great curlews,
Turtledoves,
Coneys,
Porcupines,
Water rail,

Reinforcements of wine amid these, and then great
Pasties of venison,
Of larks,
Of wild goats,
Of roebucks,
Of pigeons,
Of chamois,
Of capons,
Pasties of bacon strips,
Pig's feet with lard,
Fricasseed pie crusts,
Capon drumsticks,
Cheeses,
Corbeil peaches,

Artichokes,
Pastrypuff cakes,
Chards,
Shortbreads,
Fritters,
Tarts of sixteen kinds,
Waffles, crepes,
Quince pastries,
Curds,
Floating islands,
Candied Myrobalan plums,
Jelly,
Hippocras, red and vermilion,
Poupelins,[12]
Macaroons,
Tarts, twenty sorts,
Cream,
Dry and liquid preserves, seventy-eight species,
Sweetmeats, a hundred colors,
Fresh cheese in green rushes,
Wafer with fine sugar.

Wine brought up the rear, for fear of the quinsies.
Item, toasts.

CHAPTER 60

How, on the interlarded fast-days,[1]
the Gastrolaters sacrifice to their god.

WHEN Pantagruel saw this scurvy rabble of sacrificers and the multiplicity of their sacrifices, he grew angry, and would have gone back to the ship, if Epistémon had not asked to see the outcome of this farce.

"And what," said he, "do these knaves sacrifice to their ventripotent god on the interlarded fast-days?"

"I'll tell you," said the captain. "As appetizers, they offer him:

Caviar,
Dried mullet,
Sweet butter,
Pea soup,
Spinach,
Bloaters,
Kippered herring,
Sardines,
Anchovies,
Salt tuna,
Cabbage in oil,
Bean and onion porridge.

"A hundred varieties of salads: cress, hops, wild cress, rampion, Jess's ears (that's a kind of fungus that grows out of old elder trees), asparagus, chervil, so many others yet,

Salt salmon,
Salt eels,
Oysters in the shell.

"At that point it's time for a drink, or the devil would make off with him. They see to this, and no mistake; then they offer him:

Lampreys in hippocras sauce,

Barbels,
Barbel fry,
Mullets, grown,
Mullet fry,
Rays,
Cuttlefish,
Sturgeons,
Whales,
Mackerel,
Shad fry,
Plaice,
Fried oysters,
Scallop-shells,
Crayfish [Languoustes],
Smelts,
Gurnards,
Trout,
Lavarets,
Cod,
Octopus,
Bret-fish,
Flatfish,
Plaice [Maigres],
Sea Bream,
Gudgeon,
Turbot [Barbues],
Sprats,
Carp,
Pike,
Bonito,
Dogfish,
Sea-urchins,
Vielles,[2]
Sea nettles,

Crespions,[3]
Moray,
Swordfish,
Skate-fish,
Small lampreys,
Small pickerel [Lancerons],
Small pike or pickerel [Brochetons],
Carpions [a kind of trout],
Small carp [Carpeaux],
Salmon,
Salmon fry,
Dolphins,
Sea-hogs,
Turbots,
White skatefish,
Soles,
Dover soles,
Mussels,
Lobsters,
Shrimp,
Dace,
Small bleak,
Tench,
Grayling,
Fresh cod,
Cuttlefish [Seiches],
Stickleback,
Tuna,
Gudgeon [Guoyons],
Miller's thumbs,
Crayfish [Escrevisses],
Cockles,
Sea crevices,
Suckers,

Conger eels,
Porpoises,
Dolphins,
Bass,
Morays,
Little graylings,
Small dace,
Eels,
Little eels,
Tortoises,
Snakes, *id est* wood eels,
Giltheads,
Sea-hens,
Perch,
Réalz [Bordelais name for sturgeons],
Loach,
Crabs,
Snails,
Frogs.

"Once these foods had been devoured, Death was waiting two paces away, unless he had a drink. They took the steps to arrange matters [L'on y pourvoyoit très bien].

"Then were sacrificed to him:

Salt cod,
Stockfish.[4]

"Eggs fried, lost,[5] stifled, steamed, dragged through the ashes, thrown down the chimney, jumbled, calked, et cet.

Mussels,
Rock rays,
Haddock,
Marinated young pike.

"To get these properly concocted and digested many drafts of wine were downed. To finish up they offered:

Rice,
Millet,
Oatmeal,
Almond butter,
Butter snow,[6]
Pistachios,
Salt pistachios,
Figs,
Grapes,
Parsnips [Escherviz],
Corn meal,
Wheat broth,
Prunes,
Dates,
Walnuts,
Nuts,
Parsnips [Pasquenades],
Artichokes,

with a continuous flow of drink.

"Believe me, it was no fault of theirs if Gaster, their god, was not suitably, richly, and abundantly served by these sacrifices, indeed more than the idol of Heliogabalus, more than the idol Baal in Babylon, under the reign of Belshazzar. Nonetheless, Gaster confessed that he was no god, but a poor, vile, puny creature. Even as King Antigonus, first of that name, replied to a certain Hermodotus (who in his poetry called him God and son of the Sun) by saying: "My Lasanophore[7] denies it" (a lasanon was a pot and vessel made to receive the excretions of the belly), thus Gaster sent his hypocrite flatterers to his close-stool to see, consider, philosophize, and contemplate what divinity they found in his fecal matter."

CHAPTER 61

How Gaster invented the methods
of getting and preserving grain.

WHEN these devilish Gastrolaters had retired, Pantagruel turned his attention to a study of Gaster, the noble master of arts. You know that, by arrangement of Nature, bread and its appurtenances have been adjudicated to him for food and maintenance, besides this added blessing from heaven that he should lack nothing to find and keep bread.

From the beginning he invented the fabrile art[1] and agriculture to cultivate the land, so that the soil should produce grain for him. He invented the military art and weapons to defend the grain; medicine and astrology, with the necessary mathematics, to keep grain in safety for several centuries and place it out of reach of the calamities of the weather, the ravages of brute beasts, theft by brigands. He invented water mills, windmills, mills run by a thousand other devices, to grind grain and reduce it to flour; leaven to ferment the dough; salt to give it savor (for he knew this, that nothing in the world made humans more subject to maladies than using unfermented, unsalted bread); fire to cook it, clocks and sundials to understand the time needed for making bread, product of grain.

It happened that grain failed in one country: he invented an art and means of bringing it from one country to another. He, by great inventiveness, mingled two species of animals, ass and mare, to produce a third, which we call mules, beasts more powerful, less delicate, more enduring of toil than the others. He invented small wagons and carts to haul it more conveniently. If the sea or streams impeded the transport, he invented boats, galleys, and ships (a thing that astonished the elements) to navigate over the sea, over rivers and streams, and to carry and transport grain from barbarous nations, unknown and distant.

It has happened over a few years that in cultivating the land he has not had rain when needed and in season, without which the grain in the ground is dead and lost. In other years the rain was excessive and spoiled the grain. In some other years the hail spoiled it, the winds crushed it, the tempest beat it down. Already before we arrived, he had invented an art and method of calling down rain from the heavens, just by cutting up a plant common in the fields but known to few people, which he showed us. And I gathered that it was the one of which a single branch, if Jove's priest placed it in the Agrian spring[2] on Mount Lycaeus in Arcadia, in time of drought raised vapors, of the vapors were formed great clouds, and when these were turned into rain, the whole region was watered to suit anyone. He invented the art and means of suspending rain in the air, and making it fall on the sea. He invented the art and method of annihilating the hail, suppressing the winds, turning aside the tempest, in the manner employed among the Methanensians of Troezenia.[3]

Another misfortune occurred. Thieves and brigands kept stealing grain and bread around the fields. He invented the art of building towns, fortresses, and castles to lock it up in and keep it safe. It happened that sometimes not finding grain for bread in the fields, he understood that it was locked up in towns and castles, and defended and guarded by the inhabitants more assiduously than were the golden apples of the Hesperides by the dragons.[4]

He invented an art and method of beating down and destroying fortresses and castles by machines and weapons of war, battering rams, stone throwers, and catapults, of which he showed us the plan, rather ill understood by the ingenious architects, disciples of Vitruvius,[5] as Messer Philibert Delorme, grand architect to the Megistos[6] of kings, has confessed to us. When these ceased to be advantageous, foiled by the malign subtlety and subtle malignity of the fortifiers, he had recently invented cannons, serpentines,[7] culverins, bombards, basilisks, shooting iron, lead, or bronze cannonballs, weighing more than great anvils, by means of a horrific concoction of powder at which Nature herself stood appalled and confessed she was vanquished by art, holding in disdain the practice of the Oxydracians,[8] who by dint of thunderbolts, hailstorms, lightning strokes, and tempests, conquered and promptly put to death their enemies right on the battlefield. For it is more horrible, more frightful, more diabolical, than a hundred lightning strokes; wounds, shatters, breaks, and kills more humans; stuns their senses more; and demolishes more fortress or city walls.

CHAPTER 62

*How Gaster invented an art and means
not to be wounded or touched by cannon shots.*

It happened that when Gaster, taking back grain to store in his fortresses, found himself attacked by his enemies, his fortresses demolished
by this thrice wicked [triscaciste] and infernal machine, his grain and
bread snatched away and pillaged by a titanic force,[1] he then invented an
art and method not only[2] of protecting his ramparts, bastions, walls, and
defenses from such cannon fire, and so that bullets should either not
touch them and should remain short and still in the air, or if they touched
them they should do no harm either to the defenses or to the citizen defenders.

This danger he had already found a very good device to counter, and
he gave us a demonstration of it, which Frontinus[3] used later, and it is at
present in common use among the pastimes and honorable games of the
Thélémites. The demonstration was this (and from now on be readier to
believe what Plutarch assures us he has tried out): if a flock of nannygoats
was running at top speed in flight, put a sprig of eryngo in the throat of
one of the hindmost runners, and immediately they will all stop.

Inside a bronze falcon[4] he would place, upon the carefully compounded
cannon powder, purged of its greasy sulfur and combined with fine cam-
phor in sufficient quantity, a hollow iron ball of the right caliber holding
twenty-four iron-powder pellets, some round and spherical, others in the
shape of the teardrop. Then, after taking aim at a young page as if he
meant to hit him in the stomach, halfway in a direct line between the
page and the falcon, at a distance of sixty paces, he hung in the air on a
rope from a wooden gibbet a great big siderite, that is to say an iron
lodestone, otherwise called Herculean, found in olden times on Ida, in
the land of Phrygia, by a man named Magnes, as Nicander attests;[5] and
we commonly call it a magnet.[6] Then he would put the flame to the
falcon through the touch-hole. When the powder was consumed, what
happened was that to avoid a vacuum[7] (which is not tolerated in Nature;
rather would the machine of the Universe, Heaven, Air, Earth, Sea, be
reduced to the ancient Chaos, than that there should be a void in any
place in the world), the ball and pellets were violently propelled through
the throat of the falcon, so that air might penetrate into the chamber
thereof, which otherwise would have remained in vacuity, so swiftly was

the powder consumed by the fire. The ball and pellets, thus violently shot out, seemed surely bound to hit the page; but at the point when they came near the aforesaid stone, their impetus was lost, and they all remained in the air, floating and turning around the stone, and not one of them, however violent, got as far as the page.

But also[8] he invented an art and method of making bullets turn back upon the enemy, with the same fury and danger as they had been fired with, and the same trajectory. He did not find the matter difficult, considering that the herb named dittany [Aethiopis] opens all the locks presented to it,[9] and that remora [Echineis], such a feeble fish, in the teeth of the tempest, stops the mightiest ships there are at sea, and that the flesh of this fish, preserved in slat, draws gold out of wells, even any as deep as could be sounded.

Considering that Democritus writes, Theophrastus believed and proved, that there was an herb by whose mere touch a wedge of iron deeply and most violently buried in some thick hard piece of wood promptly comes out, which is used by hickwalls [les picz-mars], which you call woodpeckers [pivars], when by some poweful iron wedge is stopped up the hole for their nests, which they have been wont to build and dig out diligently inside the trunk of mighty trees.[10]

Considering that stags and does deeply wounded by shots from darts, arrows, or bolts, if they come upon the herb called dittany, common in Candia, and eat a little of it, immediately the arrows come out and they are left quite unharmed;[11] with which Venus cured her well-beloved son Aeneas, wounded in the right thigh by an arrow shot by Turnus's sister Juturna.

Considering that by the mere scent emanating from laurels, fig trees, and seals, lightning is turned aside and never strikes them.[12]

Considering that at the mere sight of a ram, mad elephants come back to their senses; raging frenzied bulls, when they come near wild fig trees,[13] known as caprifices, become tame and remain motionless as if cramped;[14] the fury of vipers dies out at the touch of a beech branch.[15]

Considering also that on the island of Samos, before Juno's temple was built there, Euphorion writes that they had seen creatures called water-nymphs [Néades], at whose mere voice the earth would break up and crumble into chasms and the abyss.[16]

Considering likewise that the elder grows more melodious and suitable to use for flute playing in lands where cock crowing would not be heard, as the ancient sages have written, according to Theophrastus's report, as if cock crowing numbed, softened, and stunned the matter and wood of the elder; at which crowing similarly heard, the lion, an animal of such great strength and stamina, becomes completely astounded and dismayed.

I know that others have understood this saying to be about the wild elder bush, coming from places so remote from towns and villages that cock crowing could not be heard there. This no doubt is to be chosen and preferred for flutes and other musical instruments over the domesticated kind, which grows around dilapidated houses and ruined walls. Others have chosen a loftier interpretation of this, not according to the letter, but allegorical, after the habit of the Pythagoreans. As, when it was said that the statue of Mercury is not to be made indiscriminately of just any kind of wood, they expound it to mean that God is not to be worshiped in a common way, but in a special, religous way.[17]

Likewise in this saying they teach us that wise and studious people should not devote themselves to trivial and vulgar music but to the celestial, divine, angelic kind, more abstruse and coming to us from a greater distance: to wit, from a region where cock crowing is not heard. For when we want to define some out-of-the-way place where few people go, we say that in it cock crowing has never been heard.

CHAPTER 63

How Pantagruel took a nap near the island of Chaneph,
and of the problems proposed when he waked.[1]

ON the following day, busy in small talk as we pursued our route, we arrived near the island of Chaneph, on which Pantagruel's ship could not land, because the wind failed and there was a calm at sea. We were sailing only by fits and starts, changing form starboard to larboard and larboard to starboard, although they had added the drabblers[2] for the sail. And we were staying there, all pensive, matagrabolized, distempered, and in the dumps, not saying a word to one another.[3]

Pantagruel, holding in his hand a Greek Heliodorus,[4] on a galley's hammock at the end of the trapdoors to the hold, was taking a nap. Such was his custom, that he slept much better by the book than by heart.[5]

Epistémon was looking to see by his astrolabe the elevation of the pole to us.

Frère Jean had betaken himself to the kitchen, and in the ascendant of the spits and horoscope of the fricassees was considering what time it might be then.

Panurge, through a tube of Pantagruelion, was blowing bubbles with his tongue.

Gymnaste was sharpening toothpicks of mastic.

Ponocrates, dreaming, was dreaming,[6] tickling himself to make himself laugh, and scratching his head with one finger.

Carpalim, out of a shell from a crow-ridden walnut tree, was making a pretty, merry little windmill out of four little strips of board of alder.

Eusthenes was playing on a long culverin with his fingers as if it had been a kind of fiddle.

Rhizotome was making a velvet purse out of the shell of a heath tortoise [a mole].

Xenomanes was repairing an old lantern with merlin jesses.

Our captain was pulling worms out of his sailors' noses,[7] when Frère Jean, coming back from the galley, noticed that Pantagruel had awakened. And so, breaking that obstinate silence, in the highest good spirits he asked in a loud voice:

"What's a way to raise a breeze during a calm?"[8]

Panurge promptly followed suit, likewise asking: "A remedy for feeling low?"

Epistémon chimed in third, asking cheerily: "A way to urinate when a person doesn't feel the urge to?"

Gymnaste asked, rising to his feet: "A remedy against dazzling of the eyes?"

Ponocrates, after rubbing his forehead a bit and shaking his ears, asked: "A way not to sleep like a dog?"

"Wait!" said Pantagruel. "By decree of the subtle Peripatetic philosophers we are taught that all problems, all questions, all doubts proposed, must be certain, clear, and intelligible. How do you mean: to sleep like a dog?"

"That means," replied Ponocrates, "to sleep on an empty stomach right in the bright sunlight, as dogs do."

Rhizotome was squatting on the coursey. Then, raising his head and yawning deeply, so much so that by natural sympathy he started all his companions yawning likewise, he asked: "A remedy against oscutation and yawning?"[9]

Xenomanes, as if all screwed up in fixing his lantern,[10] asked: "A way to equilibrate and balance the bulge of your stomach so that it doesn't lean to one side any more than to the other?"

Carpalim, playing with his little mill, asked: "How many operations are there in nature that come up before a person is said to be hungry?"

Eusthenes, hearing the sound of voices, came running on deck and called out from the capstan to ask: "Why is a fasting man bitten by a fasting snake in greater danger than after either man or snake has eaten or both have eaten?"[11] Why is the saliva of a fasting man venomous to all snakes and venomous animals?"[12]

"Friends," said Pantagruel, "for all the doubts and questions you propose one single solution is fitting, and one single medicine for all such symptoms and accidents. The answer shall be promptly exposed to you, not by long circumlocutions and wordy speeches. A famished stomach has no ears. It doesn't hear a thing. By signs, deeds, and results, you shall be satisfied and have a solution to content you. As, long ago in Rome, Tarquin the haughty, last king of the Romans (so saying, Pantagruel pulled the cord of the dinner-bell, Frère Jean immediately went running to the kitchen), replied with a sign to his son Sextus Tarquinius, then in the city of the Gabini,[13] who had sent him a man expressly to find out how he could completely subjugate the Gabini and reduce them to perfect obedience; the aforesaid king, mistrustful of the messenger's fidelity, took him into his private garden, and in his sight and presence, with his cutlass, cut off the highest heads of the poppies that were there. When the messenger went back with no answer and told the son what he had seen his father do, it was easy to understand that by such signs he was advising him to cut off the heads of the foremost men in the city, the better to hold down the rest of the common people in their duty and total obedience."

CHAPTER 64

*How no answer was given by Pantagruel
to the problems proposed.*

THEN Pantagruel asked: "what people live in this lovely dog of an island?"[1]

"All," replied Xenomanes, "are hypocrites, dropsicals, paternosterers,[2] catamites, sanctorum-mumblers [santorons], bigots, hermits. All poor people, living (like the hermit of Lormont, between Blaye and Bordeaux) off the alms that travelers give them."

"I'm not going there," said Panurge, "I swear to you; if I go there, may the devil blow in my ass!" Hermit, sanctorum-mumblers, catamites, bigots, hypocrites, by all the devils, get out of here! I still remember our fat concilipete from Chesil:[3] would that Beelzebub and Astaroth[4] had reconciled them with Proserpina, such terrible tempests and deviltries we suffered from seeing them! Listen, my little potbelly, my squad leader Xenomanes, please: are these hypocrites, hermits, impostors, virgins or married? Are there any of the feminine sex? Might one hypocritically get a little hypocritical sport with one of them?"

"Really," said Pantagruel, "that's a fine joyous question for you!"

"Yes indeed," replied Xenomanes. "There are lovely merry hypocritesses, catamitesses, hermitesses, women of great piety, and there is a profusion of little hypocritkins, catamitekins, hermitkins . . ."

"Take it away [Oustez cela]!" Frère Jean interrupted. "From a young hermit, an old devil. Note this authentic proverb:[5] otherwise, without a multiplication of the line, the island of Chaneph would long ago have been abandoned and desolate."

Pantagruel sent him his alms via Gymnaste in the skiff: seventy-eight thousand nice little lantern half-crowns; then he asked: "What time is it?"

"Nine o'clock and after," replied Epistémon.

"That," said Pantagruel, "is the right time for dinner. For the sacred line is approaching so celebrated by Aristophanes, in his comedy entitled *The Ecclesiazousae,*[6] which falls when the shadow is on the tenth point of the dial. In olden times among the Persians the time for having something to eat was prescribed for kings alone; all the others had their appetite and their belly for their clock. Indeed in Plautus a certain parasite complains, and furiously detests the inventors of clocks and sundials, it being a well-known fact that there is no clock more accurate than the belly.[7] Diogenes, asked at what time a man should eat, answered: 'The rich man, when he's hungry; the poor man, when he has the wherewithal.' The doctors say more aptly that the canonical hours are:

> Five to rise, nine to dine.
> Five to sup, bed at nine.[8]

"The magic of the celebrated King Petosiris was different."

This statement was not completed when the officers of the gullet [officiers de gueule] set up the tables and sideboards; covered them with fragrant tablecloths, plates, napkins, salt cellars; brought tankards, earthenware jugs, flagons, cups, goblets, basins, water jugs. Frère Jean, accompanied by the stewards, butlers, loaf-bearers, cupbearers, food-tasters, brought on four horrific ham pies, so big they reminded me of the bastions of Turin. My Lord, how they drank and had a ball! They didn't yet have their dessert when the west-norhwest wind began to fill their sails, mainsail, mizzen foresail, top-gallants. Wherefore they all sang various canticles of praise of the most high God in the heavens.

At the fruit course, Pantagruel asked: "Consider, friends, whether your doubts are fully resolved."

"I'm not yawning any more, thank god," said Rhizotome.

"I'm not sleeping like a dog any more," said Ponocrates.

"I'm not dazzled any more," replied Gymnaste.

"I'm not fasting any more," said Eusthenes. "For this whole day shall be safe from my saliva:

Asps,[9]

Amphisbenas,

Anerudutes,

Abedissimons,

Alhartafz [sea dragons],

Ammobates [snakes walking on sand],

Apimaos,

Alhatrabans [Arabian dragons],

Aractes [Arabian serpents with black and white spots],

Asterions [a kind of arachnids],

Alcharates [vipers: Avicenna],

Arges [white snakes: Hippocrates],

Spiders,

Ascalabes [lizards: Nicander],

Attelabes [crickets or weevils: Aristotle],

Ascalabotes [or ascalabes, lizards: Aristotle],

Aemorrhoïdes [perhaps horned vipers],

Basilisks [legendary serpents whose glance was fatal],

Ferrets,

Boas,

Buprestids,

Cantharides,

Caterpillars,

Crocodiles,

Toads,

Catoblepes [gnus, whose glance was also considered fatal],

Cérastes [horned vipers],

Cauquemares,

Mad-dogs,

Colotes [lizards: Aristotle],

Cychriodes,

Cafezates [Arabian serpents],

Cauhares [sand-colored snakes],

Vipers,

Cuharsces [or caunares, sand colored snakes],

Chelydri [amphibious snakes: Nicander et al],

Chroniocalaptes [tarantulas?],

Chersydri [Pliny, Lucan et al],

Cenchryni [a kind of spotted snake],

Cockatrices [black vipers],

Dipsades [black vipers: Nicander, Lucan],

Domeses [unknown snakes],

Dryinades [tree-dwelling snakes: Nicander],

Dragons,

Elopes [mutes, of fish: Nicander],

Enhydrides [water moccasins],
Fanuises [Arabic fanjunuis, an unidentified snake],
Galéotes [a kind of lizard],
Harmenes [dragons?: Arabic],
Handons [sea dragons],
Icles [iaculi, nonvenimous snakes: Pliny],
Jarraries [Brazilian snakes],
Ilicines [snakes that sleep under yews: Avicenna],
Ichneumons
Kesudures [Chersydri, as above, sea-hares],
Chalcidic lizards,
Myopes [short-sighted snakes: Nicander],
Manticores,
Molures [molouroi: snakes: Nicander],
Myagres [rat-chasers: Nicander, shrew-mice],
Miliares [Cenchryni, as above: Avicenna],
Mégalaunes [probably melanouroi, black-tails, a fish: Aelian],
Ptyades [spitting asps],
Porphyres [deadly purple Indian snakes],
Paréades [harmless asps: Aesculapius],
Phalanges [a kind of arachnid: Nicander],
Penphredones [a kind of wasp: Nicander],
Pityocampes [a kind of caterpillar],
Rutulas [venomous spiders],
Rimoires [snakes: Albertus Magnus],
Rhagions [arachnids?: Pliny],
Rhaganes [rhagins, above],
Salamanders,
Scytalae [cylindrical snakes: Lucan],
Stellions [lizards with spots like stars],
Scorpenes [dogfish],
Scorpions,
Selsirs [stripped multicolored snakes: Avicenna],
Scalavotins [see ascalabes, above],

Solofuidars [salfuges, snakes poisoned by salt],

Sourds [salamanders, bloodsuckers],

Salfuges [see solofuidars, above],

Solifuges [see solofuidars, salfuges, above],

Sepes [chalcidic lizards: Aelian, Lucan, Pliny],

Stinces [Pliny's scincus, a small Egyptian Saurian: Delaunay],

Stuphes [an unknown snake: Delaunay],

Sabtins [Haemorrhoïs, a snake: Delaunay],

Sepedons [serpents whose bite causes putrefaction: Nicander],

Scolopendres [sea-monsters: Rondelet],

Tarantulas,

Typholopes [blind snakes: Aelian, Nicander],

Tetragnaties [venomous spiders],

Teristales [cerastes, horned vipers],

Vipers."

CHAPTER 65

How Pantagruel enjoys his time
with his household.[1]

"IN which category of such venomous beasts," asked Frère Jean, "would you place Panurge's future wife?"

"Are you speaking ill of women?" retorted Panurge, "you skirt-chaser, you bald-assed monk?"[2]

"By the cenomanic stuffing [la guogue Cénomanique]," said Epistémon, "Euripides writes, and Andromache is his mouthpiece,[3] that a helpful remedy has been found against all venomous beasts by human ingenuity and teaching of the gods. Up to now no remedy has been found against a mean woman."[4]

"That show-off Euripides," said Panurge, "always spoke ill of women. And so by divine vengeance he was eaten by dogs, as Aristophanes taunts him with being.[5] Let's move on. Let him speak that has it."[6]

"I'll urinate shortly," said Epistémon, "all anyone could want."

"Now," said Xenomanes, "my stomach is ballasted to a T. It will never lean to one side more than to the other."

"I don't need," said Carpalim, "either wine or bread. A truce on thirst. A truce on hunger."

"I'm not feeling low any more," said Panurge, "thanks to God and you. I'm cheery as a parrot,[7] joyous as a merlin, lighthearted as a butterfly. Truly it is written by your fine Euripides, and that memorable toper Silenus says it:

> Out of his senses is that man, and mad,
> Who even when he drinks is not made glad.[8]

"Without fail we must highly praise the good God, our Creator, Savior, Preserver, Who by this good bread, this good cool wine, by these good foods, cures us of such perturbations, both of body and of soul, besides the voluptuous pleasure we have in eating and drinking. But you're not answering the question of this blessed venerable Frère Jean, when he asked for a way to raise a breeze?"

"Since," said Pantagruel, "you are content with this easy solution of the doubts proposed, so am I. Elsewhere and at another time we'll have more to say about them, if you see fit. So it remains to clear up what Frère Jean has proposed: a way to raise a breeze.[9] Haven't we raised it all one could wish? Look at the weathervane on the scuttle. See the whistling of the sails. See how taut are the stays, the ties, and the sheets. While we were raising and emptying our cups, the weather likewise rose[10] by occult sympathy of nature. Thus Atlas and Hercules raised it,[11] if you believe the wise mythologizers. But they raised it half a degree too high: Atlas, to feast his guest Hercules the more cheerily; Hercules, because of the thirsts brought on by going through the deserts of Libya . . . "

"Gosh!" said Frère Jean, interrupting his statement, "I've heard from several venerable scholars that Tirelupin [Rascal], your good father's cellarman, each year saves more than eighteen hundred pipes of wine by having the domestics and unexpected visitors drink before they're thirsty."

" . . . For," Pantagruel went on, "as the camels and dromedaries of the caravan drink for the thirst past, for the thirst present and for the thirst to come, so did Hercules. So that by this excessive raising of the weather there came about in heaven a new movement of staggering and shuddering, so controversial and debated among the crazy astrologers."

"That," said Panurge, "is what they say in the common proverb:

> Bad weather leaves, replaced by fine,
> While 'round fat ham we drink our wine."[12]

"And not only," said Pantagruel, "by eating and drinking have we raised the weather, but also greatly unburdened the ship, not only in the way Aesop's basket was unloaded—to wit, by emptying the victuals—but also by freeing ourselves from our fast.[13] For as the body is heavier dead than alive, so is a fasting man more earthbound and heavy than when he has eaten and drunk. And those people do not speak improperly who on a long trip drink and breakfast in the morning, and say: "Our horses will go only the better for it." Don't you know that in olden times the noble Amycleans worshiped noble father Bacchus above all gods and called him *Psila* in an apt and appropriate denomination? *Psila,* in the Doric language, means "wings." For as birds with the help of their wings fly lightly high in the air, by the aid of Bacchus (that's the good tasty delicious wine) are the spirits of humans raised high, their bodies evidently lightened, and what was terrestrial in them is made supple."[14]

CHAPTER 66

How, near the island of Ganabin,
at Pantagruel's commandment
the muses were saluted.[1]

As the good wind and these cheery remarks continued, Pantagruel scanned afar and sighted a certain mountainous land, which he pointed out to Xenomanes and asked him:

"Do you see up ahead there to port a high crag with two humps that looks a lot like Mount Parnassus in Phocis?"

"Very clearly," said Xenomanes. "That's the island of Ganabin. Do you want to go ashore there?"

"No," said Pantagruel.

"You're quite right," said Xenomanes: "there's nothing there worth seeing: the people are all thieves and robbers. There, however, toward that righthand hump, is the loveliest fountain in the world, and around it a very large forest. Your crews can take on water and wood there."

"Spoken," said Panurge, "like a gentleman and a scholar! Heydoho! Let's never go ashore in a land of thieves and robbers. I assure you that this land here is such as in other times I've seen the islands of Sark and Herm to be, between Brittany and England, such as was the Poneropolis of Philip in Thrace, lands of rogues, robbers, brigands, murderers, and assassins, all scraped up out of the deepest dungeons of the Conciergerie. Let's not go there by any means, I beg you! Believe, if not me, then at least the advice of this good wise Xenomanes. By the death of wood [mort boeuf de boys], they're worse than the Cannibals. They'd eat us all alive. Don't go ashore there, for mercy's sake. You'd do better to go down into Avernus.[2] Listen! There I hear, by God, the horrific tocsin, such as some time ago the Gascons in the Bordelais[3] used to ring it against the salt-tax collectors and the king's commissioners. Or else I'm hearing things. Let's get out of here, hey! Let's pass on!"[4]

"Go ashore there," said Frère Jean, "go ashore there. Let's go, let's go, come on, let's go! This way we'll never have to pay for our lodging. Let's go! We'll sack them one and all. Let's go ashore!"

"Let the devil take his share in it!" said Panurge. "This devil of a monk here, this monk of a crazy devil has no fear of anything. He's venturesome as all the devils, and doesn't care a rap about other people. He thinks everybody is a monk like him."

"Go away," replied Frère Jean,"you green leper, to all the millions of devils, and may they dissect your brain and make mincemeat of it. This devil of a lunatic is such a lousy coward that he shits in his pants again and again in a sheer frenzy of panic fear. If you're so paralyzed with vain fear, don't go ashore, stay right here with the baggage. Or else go hide under Proserpina's petticoat, right through all the millions of devils."

At these words Panurge vanished from the company and went and hid down below, amid the crusts, crumbs, and odd bits of bread. "I feel in my soul," said Pantagruel, "an urgent pull backward, as if it were a voice heard from afar, which tells me that we should not go ashore. Each and every time I have felt such an impulsion in my mind, I have found myself well off in refusing and leaving the curse from which it was pulling me back; conversely, I have found myself equally well off on following the course to which it was impelling me; and never have I repented of it."

"That," said Epistémon, "is just like the daemon of Socrates, so celebrated among the Academics."

"Then listen," said Frère Jean; "while the crews are taking on water, Panurge is down there making like a wolf in the straw. Do you want to have a good laugh? Have the fire set to this basilisk you see near the forecastle. That will be to salute the Muses of this Mount Antiparnassus.[5] Anyway, the powder in it is getting spoiled."

"That's well said," replied Pantagruel. "Have the master gunner come here to me."

The gunner promptly appeared. Pantagruel ordered him to put the fire to the basilisk, and in any case reload it with fresh powder, which was done instantly. The gunners of the other ships, frigates, galleons, and galleasses of the convoy, at the first discharge of the basilisk in Pantagruel's ship, likewise each put the fire to one of their loaded big pieces. Believe me, it was a lovely racket.

CHAPTER 67

How Panurge beshat himself in panic fear
and thought the great cat Rodilardus[1]
was a devilkin.[2]

Panurge, like a dumbstruck goat [comme un boucq estourdy], burst out of the storeroom in just his shirt, with just one stocking on one leg, his beard all specked with breadcrumbs, holding in his hand a big cat, which was holding on to the other stocking. And, wagging his jowls like a monkey hunting for fleas on his head, trembling, his teeth chattering, he rushed toward Frère Jean, who was sitting on the starboard chain-wale, and devoutly begged him to have compassion on him, and keep him in safeguard with his cutlass, affirming and swearing by his share of Papimania that he had seen all the devils freed of their chains.

"Looky here, me fren [Agua, men emy]," said he, "me brother, me spiritual father, today all the devils are out to a wedding! You've never seen such preparations for an infernal banquet! Do you see the smoke from the kitchens of hell? (This he said pointing to the gunpowder smoke over all the ships.) You've never seen so many damned souls. And do you know what? Looky here, me fren! They're so blond, so delicate that you'd say they were Stygian ambrosia![3] I supposed (God forgive me!) that they were English souls and thought that this morning the Isle of Horses,[4] near Scotland, must have been sacked and put to the sword by the Lords of Thermes and Hesse with the English who had seized it by surprise."

Frère Jean on approaching him smelled I know not what odor other than that of cannon powder. He pulled Panurge out into the open and perceived that his smock was all crapped on and newly beshitten. The retentive power of the nerve that controls the muscle called sphincter (that's the asshole) was dissolved by the violence of the fear he had had in his fantasy visions, besides the thunder of the cannonades, which is more horrific in the lower quarters than it is on deck. For one of the symptoms and accidents of fear is that by it is ordinarily opened the wicket of the seraglion in which for a time the fecal matter is contained.

An example is that of Messere Pandolfo de la Cassina of Siena, who, passing through Cambéry and stopping at the inn of that good husbandman Vinet,[5] took a pitchfork from the stable, then said to him: "Da Roma in qua io non son andato del corpo. Di gratia, piglia in mano questa forcha, et fa mi paura."[6] Vinet got busy making passes with the fork, always making as if he really meant to hit him. The Sienese said to him: "Se tu non fai altramente, tu non fai nulla. Pero sforzati di adoperarli più guagliardamente."[7] Thereupon Vinet gave him such a great clout with the fork between his neck and his collar that he threw him on the ground head over heels. Then, frothing at the mouth and laughing his head off, he said to him: "Feast o'God Bayard!"[8] That's what you call "Given at Chambéry [Datum Camberiaci]." Just in time the Siennese had taken down his breeches, for suddenly he dunged more copiously than nine buffaloes would have done and fourteen archpriests of the Host. Finally the Sienese graciously thanked Vinet and said to him: "Io ti ringratio, bel messere. Cosi facendo tu m'hai esparmiata la speza d'un servitiale."[9]

Another example is that of King Edward the Fifth of England. Master François Villon, banished from France, had been received at his court. He had taken him into such great intimacy that he concealed from him nothing of even the petty affairs of his house. One day the said king, going to do his business,[10] pointed out to Villon a painting of the coat of arms of France and said to him: "Do you see what reverence I bear your

French kings? I have their coat of arms nowhere but in this privy, near my close-stool."

"Holy God!" retorted Villon, "how wise, prudent, informed and careful about your health you are, and how well you are served by your learned doctor, Thomas Linacer! He, seeing that naturally, in your later years, you were constipated in the belly and obliged to stick an apothecary at your tail, I mean an enema, otherwise you wouldn't have crapped, got you to have painted appropriately here, not elsewhere, the arms of France, by a singular and potent foresight. For just at the sight of them you have such a horrific fizzling fear that you promptly crap like eighteen Paeonian aurochs. If they were painted anywhere else in your house, in your main hall, in your galleries, or elsewhere, Holy God! You'd shit all over the place the moment you'd seen them. And I believe that if you also had there a picture of the great oriflamme of France, at the sight thereof you'd void the bowels of your belly right through your fundament.[11] But harrumph *atque iterum* [and once again] hrrmph!

> A Paris rubberneck am I,
> Paris close by Pontoise, I say.
> A rope shall teach my neck some day
> Exactly what my ass shall weigh.[12]

"A rubberneck, I say, ill-advised, inexpert, ununderstanding, when, coming from here with you, I wondered that you had your breeches taken down in your bedroom. Verily I thought that herein, behind the tapestry or in the alcove beside your bed, was your close-stool. Otherwise the case seemed to me most incongruous, thus to get undressed in your bedroom in order to go to the family seat [au retraict lignagier]. Isn't that a real rubberneck's idea? The case is caused by quite another mystery, in God's name! In so doing you do well, so well, I say, that you could do no bettter. Have your breeches taken down all the way, far off, in plenty of time. For if you came here with breeches not taken down, on seeing all those scutcheons, Good Lord! All, I mean all [notez bien tout, sacre Dieu]! the bottom of your breeches would fulfill the function of a *lazanon*, commode, chamber pot, or close-stool."

Frère Jean, holding his nose tight shut with his left hand, with the index finger of his right pointed out to Pantagruel Panurge's smock. Pantagruel, seeing him thus upset, numbed speechless, beshitten, and scratched by the claws of the famous cat Rodilardus, could not keep from laughing, and said to him:

"What do you mean to do with the cat?"

"With this *cat?*" replied Panurge. "Devil take me if I didn't think it was a devilkin with fur, which I nabbed a while ago on the sly, using my hose for good mittens, inside the great hutch of hell. Devil take the devil! He's shredded my skin here like a crayfish's beard."

So saying, he threw down his cat.

"Go along," said Pantagruel, "go along, in God's name, and take a bath, clean up, get hold of yourself, put on a clean white shirt and get dressed again!"

"Are you saying," said Panurge, "that I'm afraid? Not a bit of it, by the power of God! I'm more courageous than if I'd swallowed as many flies as are put into pies from Midsummer Day [de Sainct Jean] to All Saints' Day.[13] Ha ha ha! Whay! What the devil *is* this stuff? Do you call this turds, crap, droppings, shit, stool, elimination, fecal matter, excrement, fumets, leavings, scybale or spyrathe?[14] It is, I do believe, Hibernian saffron.[15] Ho, ho, hee! It's Hibernian saffron! Sela![16] Let's drink up!"

End of the Fourth Book of the Heroic Deeds

And Sayings of the Noble Pantagruel

BRIEF DECLARATION[1]

*Of Some of the More Obscure Terms
Contained in the Fourth Book
Of the Heroic Deeds and Sayings of Pantagruel.*

[IN THE LIMINARY EPISTLE].[2]

MITOLOGIES: fabulous narratives. It's a Greek term.

PROSOPOPÉE: disguise, impersonation.

TÉTRICQUE: peevish, rough, surly, bitter.

CATONIAN: severe, as was Cato the Censor.

CATASTROPHE: end, outcome.

CANIBALES: a monstrous people in Africa who have faces like dogs and who bark instead of laughing.

MISANTROPES: hating men, fleeing the company of men. That was the surname of Timon of Athens, Cicero 4, *Tusculans*.

AGELASTES: never laughing, sad, cross. This was the surname of Crassus, uncle of that Crassus who was slain by the Parthians, who in all his life was seen to laugh only once, as attested by Lucilius, Cicero 5, *De finibus*; Pliny, Book 7.

IOTA: a point, jot. It's the smallest letter of the Greeks. Cic. 3 *De Orat.*; Martial Book 2.92; in the Gospel, Matthew 5.18.

THÈME: position, subject. What someone proposes to discuss, prove, and deduce.

ANAGNOSTE: reader.

EVANGILE: good news.

HERCULES GAULLOYS [GAULISH]: who by his eloquence drew to himself the noble French, as Lucian describes. *Alexicacos*,[3] defender, helping in adversity, warding off evil. It's one of the surnames of Hercules, Pausanias in *Attica*. To the same effect are used *Apopompaeus* and *Apotropaeus*.

[IN THE PROLOGUE][4]

SARCASME: stinging, bitter mockery.

SATYRICQUE MOCQUERIE: as is that of the ancient satirists Lucilius, Horace, Persius, Juvenal. It's a way to speak ill of each and every one at will, and to blazon [expose] vices, as is done at the revels of the Basoche, by characters disguised as Satyrs.

EPHÉMÈRES FIEBVRES: fevers lasting only a day or so, or which last no more than one natural day, to wit, one of 24 hours.

DYSCRASIÉ: ill-tempered, ill-disposed. People commonly say *biscarié* in corrupted language.

Ἄβις βίς: Life is not life, life is not livable.

MUSAPHIZ [MUSAFIS]: in Turkish and Slavonic language, doctors and prophets.

CAHU, CAHA: a popular expression in Touraine; so-so; after a fashion.

VERTUS DE STYX [BY THE POWERS OF THE STYX]: that is a marsh in hell, according to the poets, by which the gods swear, as Virgil writes *Aeneid* 6.187, and do not perjure themselves. The reason is that Victoria, daughter of Styx, favored Jupiter in the battle with the giants, and in recompense to her Jupiter decreed that the gods swearing by her mother would never fail in their word, etc. Read what Servius writes about it in the place cited above.

CATÉGORICQUE: full, open, and resolved.

SOLOECISME: a faulty way of speaking.

PÉRIODE [TIME]: revolution, conclusion, end of a sentence.

ABER KEIDS: in German, vilified. Bisso.[5]

NECTAR: wine of the gods, famous among the poets.

MÉTAMORPHOSE: transformation.

FIGURE TRIGONE AEQUILATERALE: having three angles equidistant from one another.

CYCLOPES: blacksmiths of Vulcan.

TUBILUSTRE: on which day were blessed in Rome the trumpets dedicated to the sacrifices, in the courtyard of the tailors.

OLYMPIADES: a way of counting the years among the Greeks, which was every five years.[6]

AN INTERCALAIRE: on which falls the leap year, as it does in the present year 1552. Pliny Book 2, chapter 47.

PHILAUTIE [EGO]: self-love.

OLYMPE: the sky [or heaven]. Thus it is called among the poets.

MER TYRHENE: near Rome.

APPENNIN: the Bolognese Alps.

TRAGOEDIES: tumults and disturbances excited for something of little value.

PASTOPHORES: pontiffs among the Egyptians.

DODRENTAL:[7] a half cubit long, or nine Roman inches.

MICROCOSME: little world.

MARMES, MERDIGUES [TURD OF GOD]: oaths of village folk in Touraine.

IDES DE MAY: on which Mercury was born.

MASSORETHZ: interpreters and glosssators among the Hebrews.

ST, ST, ST: sound and whistling by which one imposes silence. Terence uses it in *Phormio* and Cicero *De oratore*.

[FIRST SHEET OF THE BOOK (CHAPTER 1)]

BACBUC: bottle, in Hebrew, from the sound it makes when it is emptied.

VESTALES: feasts in honor of the goddess Vesta in Rome. They're on the seventh day of June.

THALASSE: sea.

HYDROGRAPHIE: book of ocean charts.

PIERRE SPHENGITIDE: transparent as glass.

CEINCTURE ARDENTE: torrid zone.

L'AISSEUIL SEPTENTRIONAL: Arctic Pole.

PARALLÈLE: imaginary straight line in the sky equidistant from its neighbors.

[CHAPTER 2]

MÉDAMOTHI: no place, in Greek.

PHARES: high towers on the seashore in whch they light a lantern in time of tempest at sea to direct the sailors, as you can see at La Rochelle and Aigues-Mortes.

PHILOPHANES: desirous to see and to be seen.

PHILOTHÉAMON: desirous to see.

ENGYS: near by.

MÉGISTE: very great.

IDÉES: invisible forms and species imagined by Plato.

ATOMES: small indivisible bodies, by whose conjunction Epicurus used to say all things were made and formed.

UNICORNES: you call them *Licornes* [Unicorns or their horns].

[CHAPTER 3]

CÉLOCES: vessels light upon the sea.

GOZAL: in Hebrew, pigeon, dove.

[CHAPTER 4]

POSTÉRIEUR VENTRICULE DU CERVEAU [HINDMOST LOBE OF THE BRAIN]: that's memory.

[CHAPTER 6]

DEU COLAS, FAILLON: are Lorrain words; in the name of Saint Nicolas, fellow!

[CHAPTER 7]

SI DIEU Y EUST PISSÉ [IF GOD HAD PISSED THERE]: that's a vulgar way of speaking, in Paris and all over France, among the simple folk, who suppose that all places have had special benediction in which Our Lord had voided urine or any other natural excrement, as is written of saliva in John 9 [vs 6–7]: *Lutum fecit ex sputo.*

LE MAL SAINCT EUTROPE: a colloquial way of speaking, like "le mal sainct Jehan, le mal de sainct Main [Saint Meen, Main, or Mevenius, was thought to cure ailing hands], le mal Sainct Fiacre." Not that these blessed saints had such maladies, but so that they [the sick] might be cured of them.

[CHAPTER 8]

CÉNOTAPHE: an empty tomb, not holding the body of the person in whose honor and memory it is erected. Elsewhere it is called "honorary sepulcher," and thus Suetonius names it.

AME MOUTONNIÈRE [MUTTONISH SOUL]: live and animate sheep.

[CHAPTER 9]

PANTOPHLE [SLIPPER]:[8] this word is derived from the Greek παντόφελλος "all of cork."

[CHAPTER 12]

RANE GYRINE: a shapeless frog. Frogs when first born are nothing but a bit of flesh, black, with two eyes and a tail. Wherefore fools are called tadpoles [gyrins]. Plato, in *Theaetetus;* Aristophanes; Pliny, Book 9, chapter 51; Aratus.

TRAGICQUE COMOEDIE: a farce amusing at the beginning, sad at the end.

[CHAPTER 13]

CROIX OSANIÈRE [HOSANNA CROSS]: in Poitevin, it's the cross elsewhere called *Boysselière,*[9] near which on Palm Sundays they sing "Osanna filio David," etc.

[CHAPTER 15]

MA DIA [SO HELP ME GOD!]: is a colloquial way of speaking in Touraine; at the same time it is Greek Mὰ δία. No, by Jupiter, like *Ne dea,* Nὴ Δία, yes, by Jupiter.

L'OR DE THOLOSE: which Cicero speaks of, Book 3, *De Natura deorum;* Aulus Gellius Book 3; Justinian Book 22; Strabo, Book 4; bore misfortune to all who carried it off, to wit, Q. Cepio, a Roman consul, and his whole army, who all, as sacrilegious, perished miserably.

Le Cheval Séjan: that of Cn. Seius, which brought bad luck to all who possessed it. Read Aulus Gellius, Book 3, chapter 9.

[Chapter 16]

Comme Sainct Jan de la Palisse: a colloquial way of speaking, by syncope, instead of L'Apocalypse; like Idolâtre for Idololâtre [Idolatrous].

Les Ferremens de la Messe [implements for mass]: so the Poitevin villagers call what we call ornaments; and "le manche de la paroece" [the parish handle] what we call "le clochier" [the bell tower], this by a rather clumsy metaphor.

[Chapter 17]

Tohu et Bohu: Hebrew for deserted and uncultivated.

Sycophage: fig-eating.

Nargues et Zargues [Pish and Tush]: names made up at will.

Teleniabin et Geleniabin: Arabic terms, manna and rose honey.

Enig et Evig: German words, "without, with." In the settlement and pact between the Landgraf of Hesse and the Emperor Charles the Fifth, instead of *Enig* (without detention of the person), it was written *Evig* (with detention).

[Chapter 18]

Scatophages: crapcrunchers living on excrements. Thus is Aesculapius called by Aristophanes in his *Plutus*, in general mockery of all physicians.

[Chapter 19]

Concilipetes: like Romipetes, going to the council.

[Chapter 20]

Teste Dieu Plaine de Reliques [By God's headful of relics]: that's one of the oaths of Lord de la Roche du Maine.

[CHAPTER 21]

TROIS RASES D'ANGONNAGES: Tuscan, three half ells of cankerous sores.

[CHAPTER 22]

CELEUSME: song to exhort the sailors and give them courage.
UCALEGON:[10] not helping. It's the name of an old Trojan, celebrated by
Homer 3 *Iliad*.

[CHAPTER 23]

VAGUE DÉCUMANE: great, strong, violent. For the tenth wave is ordinarily
bigger than the others in the Ocean Sea [Atlantic Ocean]. Thus hereafter are big crayfish called decuman, great; as Columella speaks of
decuman pears, and Festus Pompeius of decuman eggs. For the tenth is
always the greatest. And in a camp, decuman gate.

[CHAPTER 24]

PASSATO, ETC.: the danger past, the saint is mocked.

[CHAPTER 25]

MACRÉONS: people who live long.
MACROBE: a long-lived man.
HIÉROGLYPHICQUES: sacred carvings. Thus were called the letters of the
ancient Egyptian sages, and they were made out of the various pictures
of trees, plants, animals, fish, birds, instruments, by whose nature and
function was represented what they wanted to designate. Of these you
have seen the device of My Lord the Admiral [Gaspard de Coligny,
1518–1572] in an anchor, a very heavy intsrument, and a dolphin, a fish
lighter than any animal in the world, which Octavian Augustus had also
borne, meaning: "make haste slowly; use a lazy diligence," that is to say
expedite, but leave nothing necessary undone. Orus Apollo [Horapollo]

599

has written of these among the Greeks. Peter Colonna has explained several of them in his Tuscan book entitled *Hypnerotomachia Polyphili*.

OBELISCES: great tall stone needles, broad at the bottom and tapering to a point at the top. You have one whole one in Rome near the temple of Saint Peter, and several others elsewhere. On these, near the seashore, a fire used to be lit to shine out to the sailors in time of tempest, and they were called Obeliscolychnies, as here above [4.22].

PYRAMIDES: great structures of squared stone and brick, wide at the bottom and pointed at the top, as is the form of fire, πῦρ. You can see several of these on the Nile, near Cairo.

PROTOTYPE: first form, pattern, model.

[CHAPTER 26]

PARASANGES: among the Persians was a measure of the roads, containing thirty stadia (each about two hundred yards). Herodotus, Book 2.

[CHAPTER 29]

AGUYON: among Breton and Norman sailors, a gentle, serene, pleasant wind, as the Zephyr is on land.

CONFALLONNIER: standard-bearer, Tuscan.

ICHTHYOPHAGES: people living on fish in the interior of Ethiopia near the Western Ocean. Ptolemy, Book 4, chapter 9; Strabo, Book 15.

[CHAPTER 32]

CORYBANTIER: to sleep with open eyes.

ESCREVISSES DÉCUMANES [DECUMAN CRAYFISH]: big ones. Explained above.

[CHAPTER 33]

ATROPOS: death.

SYMBOLE: correspondence, relation.

[CHAPTER 34]

CATADUPES DU NIL [CATARACTS OF THE NILE]: place in Ethiopia where the Nile falls from high mountains with such a horrible noise that nearly all those near by are deaf, as Cl. Galen writes. The bishop of Caramith [in Armenia], the man who in Rome was my tutor in Arabic, told me that you hear this noise more than three days' journey away, which is as far as from Paris to Tours. See Ptolemy; Cicero in *Somnium Scipionis*; Pliny Book 6, chapter 9; and Strabo.

LINE PERPENDICULAIRE: the architects say falling in a plumb line, hanging straight.[11]

[CHAPTER 35]

MONTIGENES: engendered in the mountains.

[CHAPTER 36]

HYPOCRITIQUE: feigned, disguised.

[CHAPTER 37]

VENUS: in Greek has four syllables Ἀφροδίτη; Vulcan has three: Hy-phai-stos.

ISCHIES: you call them sciatica, hernias, ruptures of the bowel falling down into the scrotum, either through aquosity, or fleshiness, or varices, etc.

HEMICRAINES: you call them migraines; it's a pain affecting half the head.

[CHAPTER 42]

NIPHLESETH: male member, Hebrew.

[CHAPTER 43]

RUACH: wind or spirit, Hebrew.

Herbes carminatives: which either consume or void the windinesses of the human body.

Jambe Oedipodicque [oedipodic leg]: swollen, fat, as were those of Oedipus the diviner,[13] which in Greek means swollen foot.

Aeolus: God of the winds, according to the poets.

Sanctimoniales: at present they're called nuns.

[Chapter 44]

Hypenemien:[14] windy. Thus are called the eggs of hens and other animals made without copulation with the male, from which are never hatched chickens, etc. Aristotle, Pliny, Columella.

Aeolipyle: gate of Aeolus. It's a closed bronze instrument with a little opening in it, from which, if you put water in it and bring it near fire, you will see wind come continuously. Thus are engendered the winds in the air and windinesses in human bodies, by heatings or by concoction begun but not yet completed, as Cl. Galen explains. See what our great friend and Lord Monsieur Philander has written about it in the first book of Vitruvius.

Bringuenarilles: a name made up at will like a large number of those in this book.

Lipothymie [a deathlike swoon]: a weakening of the heart.

Paroxysme: access, fit.

[Chapter 45]

Tachor: a fig in the fundament, Heb.

Brouet: that's the great hall of Milan.

Ecco lo fico: behold the fig.

Camp Restile: bearing fruit every year.

[Chapter 48]

Voix stentorée: loud and strong, like that of Stentor, of whom Homer writes, 5 Iliad [785]; Juvenal, Book 13.

Hypophètes: who speak of things past as prophets speak of future things.

[CHAPTER 49]

URANOPÈTES: descended from heaven.

ZOOPHORE: bearing animals. It's on one portal and in other places that architects call a frieze, on which place they used to put the manikins, sculptures, writings, and other devices, at will.

ΓΝΩΘΙ ΣΕΑΥΤΟΝ: Know thyself.

EI: thou art. Plutarch wrote an unusual book on the explanation of these two letters.[15]

DIIPETES: descended from Jupiter.

SCHOLIASTES: expositors.

[CHAPTER 50}

ARCHÉTYPE: original, portrait.

SPHACELÉE: corrupted, rotten worm-eaten. A term frequent in Hippocrates.

[CHAPTER 51]

EPODE: a kind of verse such as Horace wrote.

PARAGRAPHE: you say *parafe,* corrupting the diction, which means a sign or note set next to the writing.

ECSTASE: ravishment of spirit.

[CHAPTER 53]

AURIFLUE ENERGIE: power of making gold flow.

DÉCRÉTALICTONEZ: murderers of the Decretals. It's a monstrous word, composed of one Latin word and one Greek word.

COROLAIRES: additions, the surplus. What is adjoined.

PROMECONDE: dispenser, quickly, the guardian who will take good care for the master.

[CHAPTER 54]

TERRE SPHRAGITIDE TERRA SIGILLATA [CLAY FOR VERMILION]: is called terra sigillata "adorned earth," by the apothecaries.

[CHAPTER 56]

ARGENTANGINE: quinsy of money. Thus Demosthenes was said to have it when, so as not to refuse the request of the Milesian ambassadors, from whom he had received a large sum of money, he wrapped his neck in heavy cloths and wool, as if he had the quinsy, to excuse himself from giving an opinion. Plutarch and Aulus Gellius.

[CHAPTER 57]

GASTER: belly.
DRUYDES: were the pontiffs and learned men of the ancient French, of whom Caesar writes, *De bello Gallico,* Book 6; Cicero Book 1, *De divinatione;* Pliny, Book 16, etc.
SOMATES:[16] bodies, members.

[CHAPTER 58]

ENGASTRIMYTHES: speaking from the belly.
GASTROLATRES: worshipers of the belly.
STERNOMANTES: divining through the chest.
GAULE CISALPINE: the old part of Gaul between the Mont Cenis and the river Rubicon, near Rimano,[17] including Piedmont, Monferrato, Astigiano, Vercelli, Milan, Mantua, Ferrara, etc.

[CHAPTER 59]

DITHYRAMBES, CROEPALOCOMES, EPAENONS: drunkards' songs in honor of Bacchus.
OLIVES COLYMBADES [MARINATED OLIVES]: confected.

[Chapter 60]

Lasanon: this term is explained there.

[Chapter 62]

Triscaciste: thrice very wicked.
Force Titanicque: of giants.

[Chapter 63]

Chaneph: hypocrisy, Hebrew.
Sympathie: compassion, consensus, fellow feeling.
Symptomates: accidents occurring in illness, such as pain in the side, cough, hard breathing, pleurisy.

[Chapter 64]

Umbre Decempédale: falling on the tenth point of a dial.
Parasite: buffoon, prattler, looking for his free meals.

[Chapter 66]

Ganabin: thief, Hebrew.
PoneROPLE: city of the wicked.

[Chapter 67]

Ambrosie: food of the gods.
Stygiale: of hell, said of the river Styx among the poets.
Da Roma, etc.: "From Rome here I haven't had a bowel movement. Please take this pitchfork in hand and give me a scare."

SI TU NON FAY, ETC.: "If you don't do it any other way (i.e., any better than that), you're not doing a thing. So please try to go at it a bit more lustily."

DATUM CAMBERIACI: given at Chambéry.

IO TI RINGRATIO, ETC.: "I thank you, fair Sir. By doing this you've saved me the cost of a suppository."

BONASES [AUROCHS]: an animal of Paeonia, of the size of a bull, but stockier, which, when hunted and hard pressed, spurts crap up to four paces away and more. By such means he escapes, burning with his crap the hair of the dogs pursuing him.

LAZANON: this term is explained [chap. 60].

PITAL [COMMODE]: earthenware pot for a close-stool. Tuscan. Wherefore are called *Pitalieri* certain officers in Rome who clean out the close-stools of the most reverend cardinals when they are sequestered in conclave for the election of a new pope.

PAR LA VERTUS DIEU: That's not an oath; it's an assertion, thanks to the power of God. So it is in many places in this book. As Friar Quambouis used to preach in Toulouse: "By God's blood we were redeemed. By God's power we shall be saved!"

SCYBALE: hardened turd.

SPYRATHE: turd of a nannygoat or sheep or ewe.

SELA: certainly, Hebrew.

BOOK 5

The Fifth and Last Book
of the
HEROIC DEEDS AND
SAYINGS
of the Good

PANTAGRUEL

Composed by
M. FRANÇOIS RABELAIS
Doctor of Medicine

in which is contained
the visit to the oracle of the divine Bacbuc,
and the word of the Bottle: to get which
this whole voyage is undertaken
newly brought to light

MDLXIV

Prologue[1] by M. François Rabelais

For the Fifth Book of the Heroic Deeds and Sayings
Of Pantagruel.
To Readers of Good Will.

Indefatigable topers, and you, most precious poxies, while you are at
leisure and I have no business more urgent at hand, I ask you and I ask of
you:[2] why is it that they say nowadays as a common proverb: People
aren't stupid any more.[3] *Fat* is a Languedoc term that means unsalted,
insipid, tasteless; as a metaphor it means foolish, stupid, senseless, with a
hole in the head. Would you mean to say, as might logically be inferred
from the converse, that heretofore people had been stupid, and had
grown wise nowadays? By what and how many conditions were they
foolish? What conditions were required to make them wise, and how
many of them were there? Why were they foolish? Why are they now
supposed to be wise? Whereby do you recognize the present wisdom?
Who or what made them foolish? Who or what has made them wise?
Which is the greater number, of those who like them foolish, or of those
who like them wise? For how long a time were they foolish? For how
long a time have they been wise? What was the source of their previous
folly? What can be the source of the ensuing wisdom? Why, at this time,
not later, did the former folly come to an end? Why, at this time, no
sooner, did the present wisdom begin? What harm did the preceding folly
do us? What good does the present wisdom do us? How may the former
folly have been abolished? How may the present wisdom have been
established?

 Answer, if you see fit, for I shall use no other prayer to your Reverences, fearing to make your Paternities thirsty. Don't be bashful, make
your confession to Her der Tyflet,[4] enemy of Paradise, enemy of Truth.
Courage, lads! If you're on my side, drink three or five times for the first
part of my sermon, then answer my question. If you're on the side of the
Other, *avalisque Sathanas!*[5] For I swear to you by my great hurlyburly that

if you don't help me in some other way to the solution of the aforesaid problem, I repent of having proposed it to you. That even though this is not as bad a plight as if I were holding a wolf by the ears, without hope of help.

How's that [Plaist]? I quite understand: you're not minded to answer. Me neither, by my beard; only I'll cite you what had been prophetically predicted about it by a venerable scholar, author of the book aptly entitled *The Bagpipe of the Prelates!*[6]

> What does he say, the lecher? Listen, you donkeypricks, listen.
> Jubilee Year, when silly tonsuring was done,
> Was supernumerary, number thirty-one.
> What lack of due respect! Foolish it seemed to be;
> But multitudes of lengthy spiels will show it free
> Of any folly, and of gluttony to boot;
> For from that selfsame plant it will take in the fruit
> Whose flower so frightened it once springtime had begun.[7]

You've heard it; did you understand it? The scholar is ancient, the words laconic, the statements Scotine[8] and obscure. Notwithstanding the fact that he was treating a matter deep and difficult in itself, this good father's best interpreters give this explanation: the Jubilee Year exceeding the thirtieth is the year fifteen hundred and fifty, the current year.[9] Never will its flower have anything to fear. Men will no longer be fools. When harvest time comes, the fools, whose number is infinite, as Solomon attests,[10] will perish in their madness, and every kind of madness will cease which is likewise infinite, as Avicenna says, *maniae infinitae sunt species* [infinite are the kinds of madness]. This madness, which during the winter was driven back toward the center, is appearing on the circumference, and has the sap rising in it like the trees. Experience demonstrates this to us, you know it, you see it. And the matter was once explored by that great good fellow Hippocrates, *Aphorisms, Verae etenim maniae* [*Aphorisms* 3.20]. So, as people grow wise, no longer will they fear the flower of beans in the springtime; that is to say (as you may pitiably believe, glass in hand and tears in your eyes), in Lent, a bunch of books that seemed in flower, blooming, flourishing like lovely butterflies, but in truth were boring, tedious, dangerous, thorny, and darksome, like those of Heraclitus, obscure as the numbers of Pythagoras (who was king of the bean, witness Horace).[11] These will perish, no one will have them in hand, no more will they be read or seen. Such was their destiny, and there was their predestined end.

In their place have followed the beans in the pod. These are the joyous fruitful books of Pantagruelism, which for this present day are in renown for their good sale, awaiting the next Jubilee, to the study of which everyone has devoted himself; and so they are called wise. There is your problem solved and resolved; make yourselves good people on the strength of it. Cough a good cough or two and drink nine drinks down the hatch, since the vines are beautiful and the userers are hanging themselves. They'll cost me a lot for rope if the good weather lasts, for I pledge myself to punish them liberally with it without payment every time they want to hang themselves without paying an executioner's fee.[12]

So in order that you may participate in this wisdom to come, emancipated from the former folly, strike me off from your scrolls now the symbol of the old philosopher with the golden thigh,[13] by which he forbade you to eat or use beans, when you consider as a true established fact among all good fellows that he denied you them with the same intent as the late freshwater doctor Amer,[14] nephew of the advocate, Lord of Camelotiere, forbade patients partridge wings, hens' rumps, and pigeon's neck: "ala mala, croppium dubium, colum bonum pelle remota [the wing is bad, the rump doubtful, the neck good with the skin removed]," saving them for his own mouth, and leaving the patients only little bones to gnaw on. He has been succeeded by certain Capuchinaries forbidding us beans, that is to say the books of Pantagruelism, and in imitation of the Sicilians Philoxenus and Gnatho, architects of their monkish cram-gut pleasure, who in the middle of banquets, when the tidbits were served, would spit on the food so that in horror everyone else would leave them uneaten. Thus these hideous, snot-nosed, catarrhal, worm-eaten scums of the earth, in public and private, detest these tasty books and foully spit on them. And although nowadays in our Gallic language we read many excellent works in both verse and prose, and few relics are left of pietistic dissembling and Gothic times; nevertheless, as the proverb goes, I have chosen to warble and whistle like a goose among the swans,[15] rather than be consigned to the ranks of those who serve only as shadows and number, just gaping at the flies, pricking up their ears like an Arcadian donkey at the musicians' song, and by a sign, in silence, signifying that they consent to the performance.

Having taken this choice and option, it seemed to me that I would do nothing unworthy if I bestirred my Diogenic barrel, that you may not say that I live this way without example.

I contemplate a great flock of Collinets,[16] Marots, Drouets, Saint-Gelais, Salels, Massuaus and a long line of other Gallic poets and prose writers. And I see that, for all that they have long frequented Apollo's school and drunk deep drafts from the Caballine spring among the joyous Muses, to the eternal fabrication of our vernacular they bring only Parian marble, alabaster, porphyry, and very good royal cement: they treat only heroic exploits, great things, matters arduous, serious, and difficult; all this is silken, crimson rhetoric; by their writings they produce only divine nectar, precious, tasty, sparkling wine, muscatel, delicate, delicious.

And this glory is achieved not by men alone; the ladies have had a share in it. Among them one sprung from the royal blood of France,[17] not to be cited without further notable mention of her honors, has astonished this whole age both by her writings and transcendent imagination and by ornamental language and wondrous style. Imitate them if you can; as for me, I cannot possibly; not to everyone is it granted to frequent and inhabit Corinth;[18] for the erection of Solomon's temple not everyone might offer a gold shekel [Exodus 30.13]. Since it is not in our faculty to advance as far as they in the art of architecture, I am determined to do what Regnault de Montauban did, to serve the masons, put on to boil for the masons;[19] and since companion I may not be, they shall have me as listener, I mean a tireless one, to their most celestial writings.

You are dying of fear, you Zoiluses, envious emulators; go hang yourselves, and yourselves choose a tree for the hangings; you shall not lack for a halter. Pledging here before my Helicon, in the hearing of the divine Muses, that if I still live a dog's lifetime plus that of three crows, hale and hearty as the sainted Jewish captain [Moses] lived, Xenophilus the musician, Demonax the philosopher, I will prove by not unpertinent arguments and irrefutable reasons, in the teeth of I know not what compilers, bundlers of materials hundreds and hundreds of times hashed over, patchers of old scrap iron, hucksters of old Latin words, all moldy and uncertain, that our vernacular is not so vile, so inept and scorn-worthy, as they think.[20]

And so, beseeching them by special favor—even as of old, although Phoebus divided all great treasures among the great poets, still Aesop found a place and function as a fabulist—likewise, seeing that I aspire to no higher rank, they will not disdain to receive me into the estate of little turnip-painter[21] of the same sect as Pyreicus; they will do so, rest assured of it, for they are so good, humane, gracious, and kindly that nothing can be more so. Wherefore, topers, wherefore, gouties, these men [the Zoiluses] want to have all to themselves the entire enjoyment of these works, for, reciting them in their little monasteries, making a cult of the high mysteries comprised therein, they come into sole possession and singular reputation, as did Alexander the Great in a similar case with the books of prime philosophy composed by Aristotle.

Belly to belly, what boozers! What scalawags!

That is why, topers, I give you timely notice, lay in a good provision of them [R's books] as soon as you find them in bookstores, and you will have not only to shell them but also to devour them like an opiate for the heart and incorporate them into yourselves; it is then that you will discover the good they reserve for all nice bean-shellers. At present I offer you a nice handsome basketfull plucked in the same garden as the ones before, most respectfully beseeching you to content yourselves with the present, while awaiting better the next time the swallows come.

End of the Prologue

CHAPTER 1

How Pantagruel arrived on the Ringing Island,[1]
and of the noise we heard.

Continuing on our way, we sailed for three days without discovering anything; on the fourth we sighted land, and were told by our captain that it was the Ringing Island; and we heard a noise coming from afar, frequent and tumultuous. It seemed to us on hearing it that it was big, medium, little bells ringing together as is done in Paris, Tours, Jargeau, Nantes, and elsewhere, on the days of great festivals, and the closer we approached, the more we heard this reinforced ringing.

We feared that it was Dodona with its caldrons, or the portico called Heptaphone in Olympia, or the eternal sound from the Colossus erected over the tomb of Memnon in Egyptian Thebes, or the jinglings that of old were heard around a sepulcher on the island of Lipara, one of the Aeolian Islands; but the geography was against it.

"I wonder," said Pantagruel, "whether some swarm of bees has not taken flight yonder, and it's not to drive them back that the neighborhood is making this hurlyburly of pans, caldrons, basins, corybantic cymbals of Cybele, great mother of the gods. Let's listen." Coming closer, we heard, amid the perpetual ringing of the bells, what we thought was the tireless chanting of its inhabitants. Since that was what we thought, that was the reason why Pantagruel had the idea that before landing on the Ringing Island we should go ashore with our dinghy on a little rock next to which we could make out a hermitage.

There we found a nice little hermit fellow named Braguibus, a native of Glenay, who gave us full information about the ringing and feasted us in a strange way. He had us fast four days in a row, stating that otherwise we would not be received on the Ringing Island, because there it was then the Feast of the Four times.[2]

"I don't understand this enigma," said Panurge; "it should rather be the Time of the Four Winds, for when fasting we are full of nothing but wind. What then, have you no other pastimes than fasting? It seems to me that that is very meager. We'd do all right without so many palace feasts."[3]

"In my Donatus," said Frère Jean, "I find only three times [tenses] preterite, present, and future; the fourth must be a tip for the server."[4]

"There is," said Épistémon, "an aorist in the pluperfect preterite of the Greeks and Latins, accepted in time of war and of motley.[5] 'Patience!' say the lepers."

"It is fated," said the hermit, "as I've told you; anyone who speaks against it is a heretic fit for nothing but the stake."

"Without fail, father," said Panurge, "when I'm at sea I'm much more afraid of being wet than heated, and being drowned than burned. Oh well, let's fast, in God's name; but I've already fasted so long that the bastions of my body are falling into decrepitude. Another fear I have even more, of angering you as I fast, for I don't know a thing about it, and I do it with very bad grace, as many have assured me, and for my part I believe them, I say; I have very little interest in fasting. There's nothing so easy and ready to hand; I care much more about not fasting in future, for then you need to have the cloth it takes to drape with and the grain it takes to put it in the mill. In God's name, since we've come into the festivals of the goddess Hunger [ès féries ésuriales]; it's been a long time since I renewed my acquaintance with them."

"And if fast we must," said Pantagruel, "there's no other expedient but to go through with it as over a bad road. So I want to have a look among my papers to see whether study at sea is as good as on land. Because Plato,[6] to describe a stupid, inexperienced, ignorant man, compares him to people brought up on ships, as we would speak of people brought up in a barrel who never looked out except through a hole."[7]

Our fasts were terrible and frightening. On the first day we fasted by fits and starts [à battons rompus]; on the second, with foils [à espées]; on the third, in dead earnest [à fer esmoulu]; on the fourth, with fire and the sword [à feu et à sang]; such was the plan of the Fairies.

CHAPTER 2

How the Ringing Island was inhabited
by Siticines, who had turned into birds.

Oun fastings completed, the hermit gives us a letter addressed to
someone he called Albian Camat,[1] the Master Aeditus of the Ringing
Island; but Panurge in greeting him called him Master Antitus. He was a
little old fellow, bald, with a well-lighted muzzle [à muzeau bien en-
luminé] and a crimson face. He gave us a very good welcome on the
hermit's recommendation, on learning that we had fasted as had been
stated above. After we had fed very well, he expounded to us the singularities of the island, stating that it had been first inhabited by the
Siticines; but by order of Nature (since all things change), they had turned
into birds.

There I gained a full understanding of what Atteius Capito, Pollux,
Marcellus, Aulus Gellius, Athenaeus, Suidas, Ammonius, and others had
written about the Siticines and Sicinnists, and it did not seem to us hard
to believe in the transformations of Nyctimène, Procne, Itys, Alcmene,
Antigone, Tereus, and others into birds. We also retained little doubt
about Matabrune's children, transformed into swans, and the men of
Pallene in Thrace, who, as soon as they bathe nine times in shallow Lake
Triton, are transformed into birds.

Later he talked to us about nothing but cages and birds. The cages were
big, rich, sumptuous, and of wondrous construction. The birds were big,
moreover handsome and slick, looking much like the men of my country; they ate and drank like men, farted and slept and hopped their
women like men; in short, to see them, at first glance you would have
said they were men; however, they were not that at all, from what Master
Aeditus told us, protesting that they were neither secular nor lay. Also
their plumage set us musing: on some it was all white, others all black,
others all gray, others half white half black, others all red, others half
white half blue; it was a beautiful sight to see them. The males he called
Clerkhawks,[2] Monkhawks, Priesthawks, Abbothawks, Bishawks, Cardinhawks, and Popehawk, who was one of a kind. The females he called
Clerkkites, Nunkites, Priestkites, Abbesskites, Bishkites, Cardinkites, and
Papesskite. Even, however, said he, as among the bees dwell the drones,
who do nothing but eat everything and mess up everything, so for the last

three hundred years, I know not how, every fifth of the month there have flown in a great number of Cheathawks[3] among these joyous birds, which had befouled and beshitten the whole Island,[4] so hideous and monstrous that they were shunned by everyone. For they had twisted necks [le col tors] and hairy paws [les pattes pelues], the talons and bellies of Harpies, and asses like the Stymphalids,[5] and it was impossible to exterminate them; for one that died, twenty-four more flew in. I was wishing they had some second Hercules there, because Frère Jean went out of touch in vehement contemplation, and there happened to Pantagruel what had happened to Messer Priapus, when he watched the sacrifices to Ceres, for lack of skin.[6]

CHAPTER 3

How on the Ringing Island there is only one Popehawk.

THEN we asked Master Aeditus, seeing the multiplicity of these venerable birds in all their species, why there was only one Popehawk. He answered that that was the original establishment and the destiny fated by the stars. That from Clerkhawks are born Priesthawks and Monkhawks without carnal conjunction, as happens among bees from a young bull bedecked according to the art and practice of Aristaeus. Of Priesthawks are born the bishawks, and of these the fine Cardinhawks; and the Cardinhawks, if not forestalled by death, would end up as a Popehawk; and of these there is ordinarily only one, as in beehives there is only one king, and in the world there is only one sun. When this one dies, another is born in his place out of the entire race of Cardinhawks, you understand still without carnal copulation. So that in this species there is individual unity with perpetuity of succession, no more nor less than with the Phoenix of Arabia.

"True it is that about two thousand seven hundred and sixty moons ago [230 years][1] two Popehawks were born into this world; but this was the greatest calamity ever seen on this island. For," said Aeditus, "these birds pillaged and beat up one another so badly during that time that the Island was in danger of being stripped of its inhabitants, part of them rallying to one of these and supporting him, part to the other and defending him; part of them remained as mute as fish and never sang again; and part of these bells, as if dazed and forbidden, never rang again. During this time of sedition they called to their aid emperors, kings, dukes, marquises, counts, barons, and communities of the inhabited world living on the continent and terra firma; and there was no end to this schism and sedition until one of them was taken from this life and the plurality reduced to unity."

Then we asked what impelled these birds to sing that way without stopping. Aeditus answered us that it was the bells hanging over their cage. Then he said to us: "Now do you want me to have those Monkhawks you see over there hooded like a Hippocras strainer sing like woodlarks?"

"Yes, please," we replied. Then he rang a bell for just six rings, and up came Monkhawks on the run, Monkhawks singing.

"And," said Panurge, "if I rang that bell, will I likewise make those sing whose plumage is the color of a red herring?"

"Likewise," said Aeditus. Panurge rang, and right away up came those smoky birds, and they sang together; but they had unpleasant raucous voices, and Aeditus pointed out to us that they lived only on fish, like the herons and cormorants of the world, and that this was a fifth species of Cheathawks [Cagaux] newly minted. He added further that he had had notice from Robert Valbringue,[2] who had passed that way not long before on his way back from Africa, that there was to fly in here a sixth species which he called Capuchinhawks, [Capucingaux], sadder, crazier, and more troublesome than any species there was on the whole island.

"Africa," said Pantagruel, "is always producing new monstrosities."

CHAPTER 4

How the birds of the Ringing Island
are all birds of passage.

"**B**UT," said Pantagruel, "seeing that you have expounded to us that of the Cardinhawks is born Popehawk, and the Cardinhawks of the Bishawks, the Bishawks of the Priesthawks, and the Priesthawks of the Clerkhawks, I would like to know whence these Clerkhawks are born to you."

"They," said Aeditus, "are all birds of passage, and come to us from the other world: part of them from a wonderfully great country that is named Breadlessdays [Joursanspain]; part from another toward the west that is named Toomanyofem [Tropditieux or Tropdiceux]. From these two countries every year these Clerkhawks fly to us in flocks, leaving fathers and mothers, all friends, and all relatives. The way it happens is this: when in some noble house in this last region there are too many of these children, whether male or female, so that anyone gave part of the heritage to all, as reason wills, nature ordains, and God commands, the house would be disintegrated. That is why the parents unload them onto this Hunchback Island [Isle Bossard]."

"That's the Isle-Bouchard," said Panurge, "adjoining Chinon."

"I mean Bossard," replied Aeditus. "For ordinarily they are hunch-backed, lame, one-armed, gouty, disfigured, deformed, a useless burden upon the earth" [*Iliad* 18.1-4].

"That is a custom," said Pantagruel, "completely contrary to the regu-lations observed of old in the admission of the Vestal Virgins: and Labeo Antistius attests, it was forbidden to select for that dignity any girl who had any vice in her soul, or diminution in her senses, or any spot on her body, however hidden and tiny."

"I am astounded," said Aeditus, going on, "that the mothers out there beyond bear them nine months in their loins, seeing that in their houses they cannot bear them or put up with them for nine years, most often not even for seven; and by merely putting a smock over their robe, cutting I know not how much hair off the top of their head, with certain propitiatory and expiatory words, as among the Egyptians by certain placings-on of linen and shavings, were created the Isiacs, visibly, openly, manifestly, and by Pythagorean metempsychosis, with no lesion or wound whatever, they make them become birds such as you now see them. All the same, my fine friends, I know not how it can be, or should be, that the females (whether Clerkkites, Monkkites, or Abbesskite) do not sing pleasing motets or hymns of thanksgiving, as people used to do to Oromasis [Ormuz], by the teaching of Zoroaster, but *catarates* [the accursed] and *skythropes* [the sullen or the gloomy] such as used to be offered to the demon Ahriman, both young and old, and continually pray for ill to their relatives and friends who transformed them into birds.

"The greatest number of them come to us from Breadlessdays, which are excessively long. For the Assaphis of this region, when they are in danger of suffering Bad Counsel, from not having enough to feed themselves and not knowing how, or not being willing, to work at some decent craft or trade, or else hire themselves out for service, also those who have not been able to enjoy their ladyloves [leurs amours], who did not succeed in their undertakings and are in despair; also those who have wickedly committed some criminal act and are being sought out to put them ignominiously to death, these all fly here: here they have their lives assigned, here they promptly get as fat as dormice, they who before were as lean as magpies: here they have perfect security, impunity, and freedom."

"But," said Pantagruel, "when these fine birds have flown in, do they ever go back to the world where they were hatched?" "A few," said Aeditus, "once very few, very late, and with regret. For the last few eclipses a whole great flock has flown back by virtue of the celestial constellations. This gives us no melancholy; the rest of us have only the greater pittance. And all, before flying back, have left their plumage amid the nettles and thorns." We actually found some of this, and on searching further found a pot of roses uncovered.[1]

CHAPTER 5

How the Gourmander birds are mute
on the Ringing Island.

HE had not finished these words when near us flew up twenty-five or thirty birds of a color and plumage that we had not yet seen on the island. Their plumage was changing from hour to hour like a chameleon's skin or the flower of a tripolion or teucrion. Under their left wing they had a mark that recalls two diameters bisecting a circle, or a perpendicular a straight horizontal. They all had about the same form but not the same color: some were white, some green, some red, some violet, others blue. "Who are these?" asked Panurge, "and what do you call them?"

"They," replied Aeditus, "are half-breeds, we call them Gourmanders,[1] and they have a great number of rich gourmanderies in your world."

"I beg you," said I, "have them sing a little so that we may hear their voices."

"They," he said, "never sing; but to compensate they eat for two."

"Where," I asked, "are the females?"

"They have none," he replied. "Then how," reasoned Panurge, "are they all covered with scabs and eaten up by the pox?"

"That, they say, is a mark of this species of birds, because of the sea, which they often frequent."

Then he told us the motive for their coming. "Here near you is this one to see if he will recognize among you a magnificent species of Goths,[2] terrible birds of prey, at all events not coming to the lure or acknowledging the gauntlet, who they say exist in your world. And of these some wear on their legs very precious jesses, with an inscription on the vervel saying that 'whoever thinks ill of it[3] is condemned to be immediately beshat all over.' Others on the front of their plumage bear the trophy of a calumniator,[4] and others bear a ram's pelt."

"Master Aeditus," said Panurge, "that's true enough, but we don't recognize them."

"Now," said Aeditus, "that's enough conferring, let's go drink."

"And eat," said Panurge.

"Eat," said Aeditus, "and drink well, half on credit and half cash down; nothing is so dear and precious as time; let's use it in good works."[5]

First he wanted to take us to the baths, in the Cardinals' baths, supremely beautiful and delightful, and on coming out of the baths to have us anointed with precious balm by the Alyptes. But Pantagruel told him that he would drink only too much without that. Then he took us into a delightful big refectory and said to us:

"Braguibus the hermit had you fast for four days; here to make up for it you shall spend four days eating and drinking without stopping."

"Shan't we sleep at all in the meantime?" said Panurge.

"You're free to," replied Aeditus "for he who sleeps drinks."

Honest to God, what a feast we had! O what a great good man!

CHAPTER 6

How the birds of the Ringing Island are fed.

Pantagruel wore a gloomy look and seemed unhappy about the four-day stay that Aeditus was laying down for us, which Aeditus noticed and said: "Lord, you know that for seven days before and seven days after the winter solstice [breume], there is never a tempest at sea. This is because of the favor that the elements grant the halcyons, birds sacred to Thetis, which for that time lay their eggs and hatch their young by the seashore. Now here the sea takes revenge for this long calm, and for four days an enormous tempest never stops when a few travelers arrive. The cause, we think, is so that during this, necessity may force them to stay in order to be well feasted on the income from the ringing. Therefore do not consider the time here idly wasted. Forcible force will detain you here. Unless you want to fight against Juno, Neptune, Doris, Aeolus, and all the *véjoves,* just make up your mind to have a good time here."

After the first ravenous mouthfuls gulped, Frère Jean asked Aeditus: "On this island you have nothing but cages and birds; they neither plow nor cultivate the land. Their entire occupation is having fun, chirping, and singing. From what land does this cornucopia come to you, and this abundance of good things and tasty morsels?"

"From the whole world," said Aeditus, "leaving out certain northerly countries, which for a number of years have been stirring up the Camarina.[1] Cheers!

623

They'll rue the day, you'll see, dong ding!
They'll live to rue the day, ding dong!

"Let's drink, friends! But what part of the country are you from?"

"From Touraine," replied Panurge.

"Really," said Aeditus, "you were never hatched by a bad magpie,[2] since you come from that blessed Touraine. From Touraine came to us every year so many good things that one day we were told by people from that area passing this way that the Duke of Touraine, out of all his revenue, hasn't enough to eat his fill of bacon, through the excessive largesse that his predecessors have given to these sacred birds, so as to glut us here with pheasants, partridges, wood hens, young turkeys, fat Loudun capons, venison of all sorts, and all kinds of game. Let's drink, friends. See this perchful of birds, how dainty and plump they are from the income that comes to us from there [Touraine]; and so they sing well for them. You never saw nightingales warbling better in the flat than they do when they see these two batons and when I ring for them these great bells that you see hanging around their cages.

"This is a feast of batons," said Frère Jean.

"Let's drink, friends, it's certainly a lovely day to drink, and so it is every day. Let's drink. I drink to you with all my heart, and do be most welcome. Have no fear that our wine and victuals will fail us, for even were Heaven made of brass and earth of iron, still we would not be lacking victuals, not for seven or eight years—longer than the famine in Egypt lasted.[3]

"Devils," cried Panurge, "what a rare time of it you have in this world."

"This is nothing," said Aeditus, "to what we'll have in the other. Let's drink together in full loving accord."

At least the Elysian Fields will not fail us. Let's drink, friends. I drink to you. It was, I say, the most divine and perfect spirit of your first Siticines to have invented the way by which you have everything that all humans desire and that to few, or properly speaking to none, is granted. It's having paradise in this life and likewise in the other.

O happy demigods are you!
Would God that happened to me too![4]

CHAPTER 7

How Panurge tells Aeditus
the fable of the charger and the donkey.

W<small>HEN</small> we had eaten and drunk well, Aeditus took us into a nicely furnished room well draped with tapestries, all gilded. There he had us brought myrobalan plums, a little preserved green ginger, plenty of hippocras and delicious wine; and by these antidotes, as by drinking of the river Lethe, to cast into heedless oblivion the travails we had endured on the sea; also had victuals in abundance brought onto our ships, which were lying in port. Thus we rested that night, but I couldn't get to sleep because of the eternal tintinnabulation of the bells.

At midnight, Aeditus waked us to drink; he himself drank first, saying: "You people from the other world say that ignorance is mother of all ills; but all the same you by no means banish it from your understanding, and you live in it, with it, by it. That is why so many troubles afflict you from day to day: always you complain, always lament; never are you satisfied: this I now see for a fact. For ignorance holds you here bound in bed, as was the god of battles by the art of Vulcan; and you do not understand that your duty was to be sparing of your sleep, not to be sparing of the good things of this famous island. You should already have had three meals, and take it from me, to eat the victuals of the Ringing Island you've got to get up really early in the morning; when you eat them, they multiply, when you save them up they go a-dwindling. Reap the field in its season, the grass will grow back there all the thicker and the more useful. Don't reap it, and in a few years it will be carpeted with moss. Let's drink, friends, let's drink one and all. The leanest of our birds are all now singing to us: we'll drink to them if you like. Let us drink once, twice, thrice, nine times *non zelus, sed charitas* [not out of zeal but out of love]."

At daybreak likewise he waked us to eat prime dips. Later we had only one meal, which lasted all day, and I didn't know whether it was dinner, or supper, or an early or late snack. Only, for sport's sake we strolled around on the island a few times, to see and to hear the joyous song of these blessed birds.

In the evening Panurge said to Aeditus: "Lord, if you don't mind I'll tell you a merry story which happened in the Châtellerault region twenty-three moons ago. One morning in the month of April a gentle-man's groom was walking his steeds around some fallow fields; then he came upon a jolly shepherdess, who was tending her little lambs in the shade of a little bush, also a donkey and a nannygoat or so. Chatting with her, he persuaded her to climb onto the crupper behind him and go visit his stable, there to have a nice little bite of something, country style. While they stayed there talking, the horse addressed the donkey and whispered in his ear (for in many places animals could talk all that year):

" 'Poor puny little donkey, I feel pity and compassion for you. You work hard all day, I can tell that by the wear and tear on your crupper. That's a good thing, since God made you for the service of humans: you're a good donkey. But not to be sponged off, curried, caparisoned, and fed any better than I see you are, that seems to me a bit tyrannical and outside the bounds of reason. Your coat looks like a hedgehog's, you're all messed up and screwed up, and here you eat nothing but reeds, thorns, and thistles. That's why I summon you, asslet, to toddle along with me and see how we whom nature has produced for war are treated and fed. It will not be without sampling my ordinary fare.'

" 'Really,' replied the donkey, 'I'll be very glad to go, Sir Horse.'[1]

" 'That'll be Sir Steed[2] to you, asslet,' said the charger.

" 'Pardon me, Sir Steed,' replied the donkey, 'that's the way our talk is, incorrect and uncouth, we village yokels. By the way, I'll be happy to obey you, and will follow you from a distance for fear of blows—my hide is all crisscrossed with welts—since you are to do me such a favor and honor.'

"When the shepherdess had mounted, the donkey was following the horse with the firm idea of having a good feed when they reached the house. The groom noticed this and ordered the stable boys to give it the pitchfork and clobber it with sticks. When the donkey heard these words, he commended himself to the god Neptune[3] and began to get out of that place on the double, musing to himself and drawing conclusions:

" 'He also says rightly that my estate is not to follow the courts of the great lords: nature created me only to help poor folk. Aesop had certainly warned me about that by his fable;[4] it was presumption on my part; the only remedy is to get out of here quick, I mean before the asparagus is cooked.' And the donkey trots off, jumping, kicking up his heels galloping, with volleys of farts.

"The shepherdess, seeing the donkey go off, told the groom he was hers and asked that he be well treated, otherwise she meant to leave without going in any further. Then the groom ordered that rather should the horses have no oats for a week than that the donkey should not have his bellyful of them. The worst part was calling him back; it was no use for the stable boys to call and coax him:

" 'Here, boy, come here.'

" 'I'm not going,' the donkey kept saying, 'I'm bashful.'

"The more nicely they called him, the more roughly he flailed about him: and more jumps and fart-volleys. They would still be there but for the shepherdess, who advised them to toss the oats high in the air in a sieve as they called him, which was done; immediately the donkey turned his head, saying:

" 'I dote on oats when that comes, not the pitchfork, I don't say: "I'll pass this up." ' "[5]

"So he went up to them singing harmoniously, as you know it is good to hear the voice and music of these Arcadian animals. When he got there they took him to the stable near the charger, where he was sponged off, curried, fresh litter up to his belly, a rack full of hay, a manger full of oats; when the stable boys were sifting this he flipped down his ears, conveying to them that he would eat it only too well without sifting it, that so much honor was not fitting for him.

"When they had been well fed, the horse questioned the donkey and said:

" 'Now then, poor asslet, and how's it with you? What do you think of this treatment? And yet you didn't want to come.'

" 'By the fig,' replied the donkey, 'from one of my ancestors' eating which Philemon died by dint of laughing, this is balm Sir Steed. But so what? It's only half a feast. Don't you donkey it at all in here, you gentlemen chargers?'

" 'What donkeying are you talking about, asslet?' asked the horse. 'Bad cess to you, asslet! Do you take me for a donkey?'

" 'Ho ho,' replied the donkey, 'I'm a bit slow to learn the courtier language of horses. I ask you: "Don't you stallion it at all in here, you gentlemen Stallions?" '

" 'Keep your voice down, asslet,' said the horse, 'for if the stable boys hear you, they'll belabor you so badly with great pitchfork blows that you won't have any more itch to donkey [baudouyner] it. We don't dare even let the tip get stiff, not even to urinate, for fear of the beatings; otherwise as happy as kings.'

" 'By the pommel of the pack-saddle I bear,' said the donkey, 'It's all yours. I say fie on your litter, fie on your hay, fie on your oats; horray for the thistles in the fields, since there you can play stallion all you like. Eat less and always have your leap [roussiner], that's my motto; out of that we make our hay and pittance. Oh, Sir Steed my friend, if you had seen us at fairs, when we have our provincial chapter meeting how we donkey it up to beat the band, while our mistresses are selling their chicks and goslings!'

"Such was their parting. I have spoken."

With that Panurge was silent and did not say another word. Pantagruel kept urging him to conclude his remarks. But Aeditus responded: "A word to the wise is enough. I quite understand what you mean to say and infer by this fable of the donkey and the horse, but you're bashful. Know that here there's none of that for you, don't speak of it again."

"Yet," said Panurge, "a while ago I saw here a white-plumed Abbess-kite whom it would be more fun to ride than to lead by the hand. And if the others are stag birds,[6] she would seem to me a doe bird.[7] I mean neat and pretty, well worth a sin or two. God forgive me, I meant no harm; may any harm I mean strike me right now."

CHAPTER 8

How Popehawk was shown us
with great difficulty.

THE third day continued in the same feasts and banquets as the first two. On this day Pantagruel urgently requested to see Popehawk; but Aeditus replied that he did not let himself be seen that easily.

"How's that?" said Pantagruel; "does he have Pluto's helmet[1] on his head, or the ring of Gyges on his claws, or a chameleon on his breast to make himself invisible to everyone?"

"No," replied Aeditus, "but still he is by nature very difficult to see. However, I'll arrange for you to see him, if that can be done."

That word uttered, he left us in place still nibbling for a quarter of an hour. Returning, he told us that for this hour Popehawk could be seen; and he took us furtively and silently right to the cage where he was squatting, in the company of two little Cardinhawks and six big fat Bishawks.

Panurge curious, considered his form, his gestures, and his bearing. Then he cried out loudly: "Plague take the beast! He looks like a hoopoe!"[2]

"Keep your voice down," said Aeditus, "in God's name! He has ears, as Michael de Matiscones[3] astutely noted!"

"But he still has a crest," said Panurge.

"If he once hears you blaspheming this way, you're ruined, good folk: do you see a basin here in this cage? Out of this will come thunder, lightning bolts, devils, and a tempest, by which in a moment you will be plunged a hundred feet underground."

"Better it would be," said Frère Jean "to drink and banquet." Panurge remained in intense contemplation of Popehawk and his company, when under his cage he noticed a madge-owl [chevêche]; at that he cried out and said: "Power of God, we're really cheated good and proper, slick-tricked. In this building, by God, there is a pip-off, frip-off, rip-off that and more.[4] Take a look at that madge-owl there: this, by God, is murder!"

"Keep your voice down," said Aeditus; "by God, this is no madge-owl, this is a male, a noble guard bird [chevecier]."

"But," said Pantagruel, "now have Popehawk sing to us a little bit so we can hear his harmony."

"He doesn't sing," replied Aeditus, "except at his hours, nor eat except at his hours."[5]

"Nor do I," said Panurge; "but all hours are mine. And so to prove it let's go drink our fill."

"Now *you*," said Aeditus, "are talking correctly; if you talk that way, you'll never be a heretic. Let's go. I have the same idea."

Returning from there to our drinking we perceived an old green headed Bishawk, who was squatting in the company of three pelicans, merry birds; and he was snoring away beneath an arbor. Near him was a pretty Abbesskite, singing joyously; and we were taking such pleasure in it that we wanted all our members changed into ears so as not to lose any of her song, and to pay complete attention without being at all distracted anywhere else.

Panurge said: "This lovely Abbesskite is bursting her head singing, while this fat ugly Bishawk is snoring. I'll soon get him singing, in the devil's name!"

Then he rang a bell hanging above his cage; but however loud he rang, Bishawk snored louder, not a bit did he sing. "By God, you old buzzard," said Panurge, "in another way I'll really make you sing!"

Then he picked up a big stone, meaning to hit him in the miter.[6] But Aeditus cried out and said: "Worthy man, strike, slash, kill, and murder all kings and princes in the world, by treason, by poison, or otherwise, whenever you want; dislodge the angels from their heavenly nest; for everything you will get pardon from Popehawk; these sacred birds do not touch, insofar as you love life, profit and means, both yours and those of your relatives and friends, alive and deceased; even those who would be born of them later would be harmed by it. Take a good look at this basin."

"Then it's better," said Panurge, "to drink our fill and feast."

"He's talking sense, Master Antitus," said Frère Jean: "here, seeing your devilish birds, we do nothing but blaspheme; as we empty your bottles and pots we do nothing but praise God. So let's go drink our fill. O what a nice term!"

On the third day[7] (after drinking, you understand), Aeditus gave us leave to go. We made him a present of a nice little knife from Perche, for which he was even more grateful than was Artaxerxes for the glass of cold water presented to him by a peasant.[8] And he thanked us courteously; sent into our ships fresh stores of all supplies; wished us bon voyage, and to come through in safety to our persons to the goal of our enterprises made us swear by Jupiter-stone[9] that we would return by way of his territory. Finally he said to us: "Friends, you will note that in the world over there are many more ballocks than men, and remember that."

CHAPTER 9

How we went ashore
on the island of Ironware.[1]

Having well ballasted our stomachs, we had the wind astern, and we raised our mizzen mainsail, whence it came about that in less than two days we arrived on the island of Ironware, deserted and uninhabited. And there we saw a large number of trees bearing pickaxes, mattocks, weeding-hooks, scythes, sickles, spades, shovels, trowels, axes, clippers, saws, planing hatchets [doloueres], shears, scissors, pincers, bolts, toy windmills, wimbles. Others bore pocket daggers, wee penknives, bodkins, swords, tucks, jangers, scimitars, short swords, three-edged daggers, and knives.

Anyone who wanted to had only to shake the tree: immediately they fell like plums; furthermore, in falling to the ground, they encountered a kind of plant that was called scabbards, and promptly sheathed themselves in them.[2] In their fall, you had to be careful not to have them fall on your head, on your feet, or on other parts of the body. For they fell point first (that was so as to sheathe straight) and would have ruined a person.

Underneath some kind of other trees I saw certain kinds of plants that were growing there, like pikes, lances, javelins, halberds, bill-hooks, partisans, prongs, pitchforks, and boar-spears; growing high so as to touch the tree and meet their heads and blade, each one matching one of its kind. The trees already held these higher, ready for their growing and coming, even as you prepare gowns for little children when you want to unswaddle them. More than that, so that from now on you may not abhor the opinion of Plato,[3] Anaxagoras, and Democritus (were they puny philosophers?),[4] those trees seemed to be earthly animals, not differing from the beasts in not having skin, fat, flesh, veins, arteries, ligaments, nerves, cartilages, adenoids, bones, marrow, humors, wombs, brain, and fitting joints, all congruent; for they do have them, as Theophrastus deduced very well; but (differing from animals) in that they have their head (that's the roots) in the ground; and their feet (that's the boughs) up on top, as if a man were playing the forked oak. And just as you, poxies, feel from afar in your sciatic legs, your shoulder blades, the coming of the rains, the winds, the good weather, every change in that: so in their roots, stems, sap, and marrow, they foretell what sort of staves are growing under them, and prepare for them suitable heads and blade.

True it is that since in all things (except God) there sometimes comes error, Nature herself is not exempt from this when she produces monstrosities and deformed animals. Likewise in these trees I noticed an occasional mistake: for one half-pike, growing up in the air beneath these ironware-bearing trees and touching their branches, encountered, instead of a head a broom; well, that's to sweep out the chimneys. A partisan encountered some scissors: all's well, that will be to clean out the caterpillars from the gardens. A halberd shaft met a scythe blade, and looked like a hermaphrodite: no matter, that will be for some reaper. It's a fine thing to put your trust in God!

As we went back to our ships, I saw behind some sort of bush or other, some sort of people doing something or other, and in some way sharpening some piece of ironware or other, which they kept in some place or other, in some fashion or other.[5]

CHAPTER 10

How Pantagruel arrived on Sharpers' Island.[1]

Leaving the island of Ironware, we continued on our way. The following day we came onto the Sharpers' Island, the real Idea of Fontainebleau,[2] for the soil there is so meager that the bones of it (that's rocks) pierce its skin, sandy, sterile, unhealthy, and unpleasant. Our captain pointed out to us two little cubic rocks with eight equal points, which from their white appearance seemed of alabaster, or else covered with snow; but he assured us that they were made of bones. In these, he said, in six stories,[3] was the black abode of twenty devils of chance, so dreaded in our countries, of which the greatest twins and pairs he called *Senes* [double six], the smallest *amb's-ace* [double ones],[4] the others in between *Quine* [double five], *Quaderne* [double four], *Terne* [double three], Double two; the others, not pairs, he called Six and Five, Five and Four, Five and Three, and so on in succession.

Then I noted that all over the world there are few players who do not invoke the devils. For in casting two dice on the table, when they devoutly cry: "Senes, my friend!" that's the big devil; "Am's-ace, my cutey," that's the little devil; "Four and two, my lads," and so on, they are invoking the devils by their names and surnames. And not only do they invoke them, they say they are their familiars. True it is that these devils do not always come instantly on request; for that they are excusable; they are somewhere else, according to the date and priority of the invokers. Therefore one must not say that they have neither senses nor ears. They have them, I tell you, fine ones.

Then he told us that around these square rocks and on their edges there had been more break-ups, shipwrecks, losses of life and property than around all the Syrtes,[5] Charybdise, Sirens, Scyllas, Strophades, and abysses of the whole Ocean. I readily believed him, recalling that of old, among the Egyptian sages, Neptune was designated in hieroglyphic letters by the first cube, as was Apollo by the ace, Diana by the deuce, Minerva by the seven, etc.

There he also said was a flask of *sang-vreal,*[6] a divine thing, known to few people. Panurge had such success with fair entreaties to the Syndics of the place that they showed it to us; but it was with three times more solemnity and ceremony than they show in Florence Justinian's *Pandects,* or the Veronica[7] in Rome. I never saw so many veils, so many flares, torches, lighted reeds, and mumbo-jumbo. Finally what was shown us was the face of a roast coney.[8]

There we saw nothing else memorable except Good Face, wife of Bad Game,[9] and the shells of the two eggs hatched long ago by Leda, from which were born Castor and Pollux, brothers of Helen the Fair. The Syndics gave us a piece of them for some bread. On leaving, we bought a bundle of sharpers' hats and caps, from the sale of which I have no doubt we shall make little profit. I think that those who buy them from us will make less in using them.

CHAPTER 11

*How we passed the Wicket, abode of Clutchpuss,
archduke of the Furred Cats.*

From there we passed Condemnation, which is another wholly deserted island; we also passed the Wicket, where Pantagruel would not disembark, and did very well not to, for there we were taken into custody and in fact arrested by order of Clutchpuss, Archduke of the Furred Cats, because one of our company tried to sell a *serrargent*[1] some hats from Sharpers' Island.

The Furred Cats are mighty horrible, frightful beasts: they devour little children, and feed on marble stones.[2] Consider, topers, whether they shouldn't have very flat noses. Their body hair does not grow outward, but is hidden inside; and each and every one of them wears an open game-pouch as their symbol and device; but not all in the same fashion. Some wear it fastened around the neck like a scarf, others on the tail, some on the belly, others at their side, and all for mysterious reasons. They also have claws so strong, long, and steely, that nothing escapes them once they've got it in their clutches. And they cover their heads sometimes with caps with four gutters or codpieces; others with wrong-way-round caps; some with mortarboards; some with mortified caparisons. As we went into their hideout, a poorhouse beggar, to whom we had given a half testoon, said to us:

"Good folk, God grant you to get out of there soon in good health! Take a good look at the mugs of these valiant pillars,[3] flying buttresses of Clutchpussian justice. And note that if you live six more Olympiads plus the age of two dogs, you will see these Furred Cats lords of all Europe and peaceful possessors of all the property there is in it, unless in their heirs, by divine punishment, should suddenly perish the property and income unjustly acquired by them; take it from a beggar and straight. Among them reign the Sixth Essence,[4] by means of which they clutch everything, devour everything, and beshit everything: they burn, explode, decapitate, maim, imprison, ruin and undermine everything with no distinction between good and evil. For among them vice is called virtue; treachery bears the name of loyalty; theft is called liberality; pillage is their motto; and that performed by them is found good by all humans, excepting only the heretics; and the whole thing they do with sovereign and unbreakable authority.

"As a token of my prognosis you will note that inside here the mangers are above the hayracks.[5] Remember this some day. And if in the world there ever come plagues, famine, or wars, storms, cataclysms, conflagrations, do not attribute them to the conjunctions of maleficent planets, the abuses of the Roman Curia, or the tyranny of the kings and princes of the earth, to the imposture of hypocrites, heretics, false prophets, to the malignity of userers, counterfeiters, testoon-clippers, or to the ignorance of doctors, surgeons, apothecaries, nor to the perversity of adulterous, venal, infanticide wives. Attribute it all to their unspeakable ruining, the incredible, inestimable wickedness that is constantly being fabricated and practiced in the workshop of the Furred Cats. It is no more known to the world than is the cabala of the Jews; therefore, it is not detested, corrected, and punished, as by rights it should be. But if some day it is brought into evidence and manifested to the people, there is not and never was an orator so eloquent that by his art he could hold them [the people] back; nor law so rigorous and draconic that it could ward them off by fear of punishment; nor magistrate so powerful that he could prevent them by force from getting them [the Furred Cats] cruelly burned to death in their rabbit hole. Their very own children, Furred Kittens, and other relatives held them in horror and abomination.

"That also is why, even as Hannibal received from his father, under a solemn religious oath, the command to persecute the Romans as long as he lived, so did I receive from my late father an injunction to remain here outside, while waiting for Heaven's lightning to strike in there and reduce them to ashes like other Titans, profane fighters against God; since humans have their bodies so toughened that they neither notice, feel, nor foresee the evil that has been done them, is being done, or is to come; or, if they feel it, they dare not, will not, exterminate them."

"What's that?" said Panurge, "O no, I'm not going there, by God! Let's go back! Let's go back, I say, in the name of God!

> This noble beggar stunned me even more
> Than would in autumn hearing thunder roar."

On our return, we found the gate closed; and we were told that one went in there easily, as down to Avernus; the hard thing was to get out; and that we couldn't do in any way without getting an authorization and discharge from those present, for this sole reason, that you don't leave a fair the way you do a market, and that our feet were dusty.[6]

The worst was when we passed the Wicket. For to get our discharge we were brought before the most hideous monster ever described. They called him Clutchpuss. I couldn't compare him better than to the Chimaera, or to the Sphinx and Cerberus, or else to the image of Osiris as the Egyptians pictured him, with three heads all joined together: to wit, those of a lion roaring, a dog fawning, and a wolf yawning, entwined by a dragon biting his own tail and with scintillating rays all around. His hands were full of blood, his claws like a harpy's, his muzzle like a crow's beak, the teeth of a four-year-old wild boar, eyes flaming like the mouth of hell, all covered with mortars interlaced with pestles;[7] only the claws showed. His seat and that of all his collaterals the warren cats was on a long brand-new rack above which, in reverse order, were fixed very fine ample mangers, as the beggar had advised us. In place of the principal seat was the picture of a very old woman holding in her right hand the sheath of a sickle, in her left a scale, and wearing spectacles on her nose. The dishes of her scales were made up of two old velvet-covered game-pouches: one was full of bullion and hanging down, the other empty and long, raised above the beam. And it is my opinion that this was the image of Clutchpussian justice,[8] very dissimilar to the institution of the ancient Thebans, who erected the statues of their dicasts and judges after their death in silver or gold or marble, according to their merit, all without hands. When we were brought before him, I know not what sort of people, all wearing game-pouches and sacks, with great strips of writings, made us sit on a little footstool. Panurge kept saying: "My frowsy friends, I'm only too comfortable standing; moreover, this is too low for a man who has new breeches and a short doublet."[9]

"Sit down," they retorted, "and don't make us tell you again. The earth will shortly open wide to swallow you up alive if you don't succeed in getting the answer right."

CHAPTER 12

How a riddle is propounded by Clutchpuss.

WHEN we were seated, Clutchpuss, in the midst of his Furred Cats, said to us in a furious raucous voice: "Here now, here now, here now [Gold here, gold here, gold here]!"[1]

"A drink, a drink, a drink!" Panurge kept muttering between his teeth.

> "A rather tender, very blond young maid
> Conceived a sireless Ethiopian son,
> Then brought him forth, unhurt and unafraid,
> Though his delivery was no easy one;
> Gnawing her side, he left her quite undone,
> In his frantic impatience not to stay.
> Then over hill and dale he went his way—
> Walking on land, but through the air he flew,
> Leaving poor Wisdom's friend in stunned dismay,
> Who thought he was a human creature too.[2]

"Here now [Gold here], give me the answer to that riddle," said Clutchpuss, "and solve that enigma on the spot, here now [gold here]!"

"Now, by God," I replied, "if I had the Sphinx in my house, now by God, as did Verres, one of your predecessors, now by God, I could solve that riddle, now by God; but sure enough I wasn't there, and I am, now by God, innocent of the deed."

"Here now [Gold here]," said Clutchpuss, "by the Styx, since you won't say anything else, I'll show you here now, that better for you it would be to have fallen between Lucifer's paws, here now, and those of all the devils, here now [gold here], than into our claws, here now; do you see that clear, here now, you wretch, are you claiming innocence to us, gold here, as something that deserves to escape our tortures? Here now, our laws are like spiderwebs; here now, the mere gnats and little butterflies get caught, here now, but the big harmful gadflies break out of them, here now, and pass through, here now. Likewise we don't go looking for the big thieves and tyrants, here now; they're too hard on our digestion, and would ruin us! Here now, you nice little innocent, you'll be well innocented here now; the great Devil, here now you will sing a mass here, here now."

Frère Jean, impatient with what Clutchpuss had implied, said to him: "O Sir Furry devil, how do you[3] expect him to respond about a case he doesn't know? Aren't you satisfied with the truth?"

"Here now," said Clutchpuss, "it had never happened during my reign, here now, that anyone spoke without being questioned first. Who turned loose this crazy madman here on us?"

"You're a liar [Tu as menty]," said Frère Jean without moving his lips.

"Here now, when it's your turn to answer, here now, you'll have your hands full."

"You're a liar, you wretch," Frère Jean kept saying silently.

"Do you think you're in the groves of the Academy,[4] here now, with the idle huntsmen and inquisitors of *truth*?[5] Here now, we're after something quite different here; here now, people respond, I say, here now categorically, about what they do not know. Here now, they confess having done, here now, what they never did. Here now, they protest they know what no one ever learned. Here now you take patience as you go mad. Here now they pluck the goose without making it scream.[6] Here now, you're speaking without procuration [power of attorney], here now, I can see that easily, here now. A bad case of quartan fever strike you and wed you, here now!"[7]

"You devils," cried Frère Jean, "archdevils, protodevils, panto-devils, so you want to have monks marry! Hou, ho, hoo, I take you for a heretic."[8]

CHAPTER 13

How Panurge explains Clutchpuss's riddle.

CLUTCHPUSS, pretending not to hear this remark, addresses Panurge and says: "Here now, here now, you wretch, have you nothing to say about it?"

Panurge replied: "Now by the devil there, I clearly see that the plague is upon us, now by the devil there, seeing that innocence is not safe here and that the devil sings mass here, by the devil now I ask you to let me pay for it all, now by the devil there, and let us go. There's nothing more I can do, there by the devil now."

"Go?" said Clutchpuss, "Gold here, it has not yet happened here in three hundred years, gold here, that anyone escaped our clutches without leaving some of his hair, gold here, or more often of his skin, gold here. For what if they did? Here now [Gold here], that would amount to saying they had been unjustly summoned before us, gold here, and by us unjustly treated. Here now, you're quite unhappy, here now; but you'll be even more so, gold here, if you don't answer the enigma propounded; gold here, what does it mean, gold here?"

"It's a black weevil born of a white bean, here by the devil now, by the hole he made in nibbling on it, here by the devil now; now it [the weevil] flies, now it makes its way on land, here by the devil now; that is why it was thought by Pythagoras, first lover of Wisdom (that is to say in Greek 'philosopher'), there by the devil now, to have received from somewhere else a human soul, here by the devil now. If you people were men, here by the devil now, after death your souls, in his opinion, would enter the bodies of weevils there by the devil now. For in this life you gnaw and eat everything; in the other:

> Like vipers you would gnaw and eat away
> Your mothers' flanks some day,
> Here by the devil now."[1]

" 'Odsbody," said Frère Jean, "I could readily wish with all my heart that my asshole would become a bean and all the part around it be eaten by weevils."

Panurge, after these remarks, tossed onto the middle of the floor a big leather purse full of sun-crowns. At the sound of his purse all the Furred Cats began to warm up their claws like fiddlers tuning up. And they all cried out loudly and said: "It's the spices! The lawsuit was very good, very tasty, and well spiced.[2] They're good folk."

"That's gold," said Panurge, "I mean sun-crowns."

"The Court," said Clutchpuss, "understands it, well and good, well and good. Go ahead, lads, well and good, well and good, and Pass Beyond;[3] we're not such devils, well and good, as we are black, well and good."

On coming out of the Wicket, we were conducted to the port by certain griffins; before boarding our ships we were advised by them that we were not to proceed on our way without giving lordly presents to both the Clutchpussic lady and the Furred Tabbycats; otherwise they were under orders to bring us back to the Wicket.

"Crap!" said Frère Jean. "We'll step aside here and turn out the bottom of our purses, and give to everyone's content."

"But," said the clerks and chore-boys "Don't forget the poor devils' wine [their tip]."

"For the poor devils," replied Frère Jean, "never is the wine forgotten; it is memorable in all countries and all seasons."[4]

CHAPTER 14

How the Furred Cats live on corruption.

F RÈRE Jean had not finished these words when he sighted sixty-eight galleys and frigates arriving in port; then he immediately ran over to ask for news, also what merchandise the vessels were loaded with; saw that they were all laden with game: hares, capons, pigeons, kids, lapwings, chickens, ducks, young wild ducks, goslings, and other kinds of game. Amid it he noticed a few pieces of velvet, satin, and damask. So then he asked the travelers whither to whom they were taking these goodies. They answered that it was to Clutchpuss, the Furred Tomcats, and the Furred Tabbycats.

"What," asked Frère Jean, "do you call these tidbits?"

"Corruption," replied the travelers.

"So they live on corruption!" said Frère Jean, "they will die in generation. By the power of God, that's it: their fathers devoured the good gentlemen who by reason of their rank spent their time in hawking and hunting in order in time of war to be abler and already inured to hardship. For hunting game is a kind of simulacrum of battle, and Xenophon was no liar when he wrote that out of the hunt, as out of the Trojan horse, had sprung all the good leaders in war. I'm no cleric, but I've been told that, and I believe it.

"The souls of these men [these gentlemen], in Clutchpuss's opinion, after their death enter wild boars, stags, roebucks, herons, partridges, and other animals which they had always liked and sought out during their first life. Now these Furred Cats, having destroyed and devoured their châteaux, lands, domains, possessions, income, and revenues, are seeking their blood and soul in the other life. What a worthy beggar that was that warned us about them, by the sign of the manger instabled above the rack!"[1]

"Yes," said Panurge to the travelers, "but it has been proclaimed in the name of the Great King that on pain of the halter no one must catch stags or does, wild boars, or kids."

"That's true," replied one of them for all, "but the Great King is so kind and benign, these Furred Cats so wild and thirsting for Christian blood, that we're less afraid if we offend the Great King than hopeful if we support these Furred Cats with such Corruptions: especially because tomorrow the Clutchpuss is marrying off a Furred Tabbycat of his to a fat well-furred Tomcat. In times past they used to be called hay-chompers; but alas! they don't eat that any more. At present we call them hare-chompers, partridge-chompers, woodcock-chompers, pheasant-chompers, chicken-chompers, kid-chompers, coney-chompers, hog-chompers; on no other foods are they fed."[2]

"Crap, crap!" said Frère Jean, "next year they shall be called turd-chompers, dung-chompers, shit-chompers.[3] Will you be guided by me?"

"Lord, yes!" answered the brigade. "Let's do two things: first, let's seize all this game you see here; anyway, I'm very tired of salt meats, they heat up my belly and bowels; I mean, paying well for it. Secondly, let's go back and sack all these Furred Cat devils!"

"No mistake," said Panurge, "I'm not going; I'm a bit of a coward by nature."

CHAPTER 15

How Frère Jean des Entommeures
determines to sack the Furred Cats.

"POWER of the gown!" said Frère Jean, "what sort of a voyage are we taking here? This is a voyage for crappers: we do nothing but fart, fizzle, crap, and daydream, and do nothing. God's head! that's not my nature: if I don't always do some heroic deed, at night I can't sleep well. So you've taken me along as a traveling companion on this trip to sing mass and give confession? Lordamercy [Pasques de soles]! The first one that comes to me for that shall get as a penance to cast himself as a wretched coward to the bottom of the sea, as a deduction from the pains of Purgatory; and I mean head first!

"What brought Hercules into eternal fame and renown, but that, wandering about in the world he set peoples free from tyranny, from error, dangers, and drudgery? He put to death all the brigands, all the monsters, all the venomous serpents and harmful animals. Why don't we follow his example and do as he did in all the regions we pass through? He slew the Stymphalids, the Hydra of Lerne, Cacus, Antaeus, and the Centaurs. I'm no cleric, but the clerics say so.[1] In imitation of him let's slay and sack these Furred Cats: they're of the devil's brood: and let's deliver this country from their tyranny. I renounce Mahomet [Je renie Mahon]; if I were as strong and powerful as he was, I wouldn't be asking for any help or counsel. Now then, shall we go [Cà, irons-nous]? I assure you, we'll slay them easily; and they'll put up with it patiently, I have no doubt, seeing that they patiently put up with more insults from us than ten sows would drink of hogwash. Let's go!"

"About insults," said I, "and dishonor they don't care, provided they have crownpieces in the game-pouch, even if they got all beshitten: and perhaps we *would* slay them, like Hercules; but we're lacking the command of Eurystheus;[2] and nothing more at this point except that I wish Jupiter would take a stroll among them just for two little hours in the form he put on to visit his lady friend Semele, first mother of good old Bacchus."[3]

"God has granted me a fine favor," said Panurge, "by having us escape from their claws; as for me, I'm not going back there. And I still feel bothered and upset from the strain I suffered there. And I was very put out for three reasons: the first because I was put out; the second because I was put out; the third because I was put out. Listen to this with your right ear, Frère Jean, my left ballock; each and every time you want to go to all the devils, before the tribunal of Minos, Aeacus, Rhadamanthus, and Dites,[4] I'm ready to keep you inseparable company; to pass with you across Acheron, Styx, Cocytus, drink a full jug from the river Lethe,[5] pay Charon the toll for his bark for the two of us; as for going back to the Wicket, if by any chance you want to go back there, get yourself some other company than mine, I won't go back there.

"Let those words be a wall of brass to you. Unless I'm dragged there by force and violence, I won't go any nearer to there, as long as I'm alive in this life, than Calpe is to Abila. Did Ulysses go back to get his sword in the cave of the Cyclops? By Zeus, no. At the Wicket I didn't forget anything, I won't go back there."

"Oh," said Frère Jean, "a good heart and a stout companion, with paralyzed hands! Let's talk a bit *par escot,* the subtle doctor:[6] why did you, and what led you to, toss them the purse full of crownpieces? Did we have too many of them? Wouldn't it have been enough to toss them a few clipped testoons?"

"Because," replied Panurge, "at every pause in his talk, Clutchpuss would open his game-pouch and exclaim: 'Gold here, gold here [Here now, here now]!' From that I conjectured how we might escape free and clear by tossing some gold here, gold there, in the name of God, gold there by all the devils.[7] For a velvet game-pouch is not a reliquary for testoons or small change, it's a receptacle for sun-crowns; do you understand, Frère Jean, my little ballock? When you've roasted as much as I have, and have been, you'll talk another kind of Latin.[8] But, by their injunction, it's up to us to pass on."[9]

The lazy ship riggers were still waiting at the harbor in expectation of some handout of *deniers.* And seeing that he meant to set sail, they addressed Frère Jean, letting him know that he wasn't to pass without paying the tip [le vin] for the helpers in keeping with the scale of the spices paid.

"So, by Saint Hurlyburly [Et, sainct Hurluburlu]," said Frère Jean, "you're still here, you griffins of all the devils? Haven't I been hassled enough without your pestering me any more? Gorbelly [Le cordieu]! you'll get your tips right now, I promise you that assuredly." Then, unsheathing his cutlass, he got down off the ship, determined to slaughter them fiercely; but they tore off at a great gallop, and we didn't see them again.

For all that, we were not through with vexations; for some of our sailors, with Pantagruel's permission, had pulled into a hostelry near the harbor, during the time we were with Clutchpuss, to have a banquet and refresh themselves awhile; I don't know whether they had actually paid their bill; but the fact remains that an old hostess, seeing Frère Jean on land, kept insistently letting him know her grievances, in the presence of a moneysqueezer,[10] son-in-law of one of the Furred Cats, and one or two observers as witnesses.

Frère Jean, impatient of their talk and charges, asked: "My frowsy friends [Gallefretiers, mes amis], do you mean in short that our sailors are not good folk? I maintain the contrary, and will prove it to you by justice, that is to say by this master cutlass here."

So saying, he laid about him with his cutlass. The peasants took to their heels at a trot; there remained only the old woman, who affirmed to Frère Jean that his sailors were good folk; her only complaint was that they had not paid anything for the bed they had rested on after dinner, and for that she was asking five Tournois sous.[11]

"Really," said Frère Jean, "that's cheap, they're ingrates, they won't always get one at such a price. I'll be glad to pay for it, but I *would* like to see it."

The old woman took him to the house and showed him the bed, and after praising all its qualities told him she would make no more fuss, but she asked five sous for it. Frère Jean passed her five sous; then with his cutlass he cut in two the feather bed and the pillow and fell to throwing the feathers out the window to the wind. Thereupon the old woman came down, screaming: "Help, murder!" and keeping busy picking up her feathers. Frère Jean, unconcerned about that, took away the cover, the mattress, and the two sheets into the ship without being seen by anyone, for the air was obscured by the feathers as if by snow; and he gave them to the sailors. Then he said to Pantagruel that beds were much cheaper here than around Chinon, although we had the famous geese of Pautilé.[12] For the old woman had asked only five douzains for the bed, which around Chinon would be worth no less than twelve francs.

CHAPTER 16

How we passed Beyond,
and how Panurge nearly got killed there.

IMMEDIATELY we set our course for Beyond,[1] and told Pantagruel our adventures; he was very sympathetic about them, and as a pastime made up several elegies about them. Once we had arrived there, we refreshed ourselves a bit and drew more fresh water and took on wood for provisions. And from their faces we judged the natives to be good fellows and fond of good cheer. They were all bloated and farting [splitting] with grease; and we noted (what I had not seen in any other country) that they slashed their skin to make the fat push out, much as the bedunged dandies in my country slash their breeches to make the taffeta puff out. And they said they didn't do it for show or ostentation, but inside their skins they couldn't do anything else. Also, by doing this they grew taller quicker, as gardeners slit the skin of trees to make them grow sooner.

Near the harbor was a big tavern that from the outside looked fine and magnificent; and seeing a large number of Beyond [Outré] people hurrying in there, of both sexes, all ages and estates, we thought there must be some notable feast or banquet there. But we were told that they were invited to the bursting [crevailles] of our host, and close friends and relatives were going there in a hurry. Not understanding this lingo, and thinking that in this country they called the feast a bursting, as over here we speak of betrothings, weddings, and harvest-time shearings,[2] we were informed that in his time mine host had been a great kidder, a great downer of onion soups,[3] a great clock watcher [for mealtime], eternally dining, like mine host at Rouillac,[4] and having for ten days been farting grease in abundance, had come to his bursting time, and was ending his days by bursting, since his peritoneum and skin, slashed for so many years could no longer close up and hold in the tripes from bursting out, like a pierced barrel.

"How is it, good folk," said Panurge, "that you couldn't fix him up with some good stout girths or good stout rings of sorb-apple wood, or even iron if necessary, to bind his belly? Bound so, he would not spurt out his insides so easily, or bust so soon."

These words were not done when we heard in the air a loud strident sound, as if some great oak were splitting in two; but then the neighbors said that his bursting was over and that that bang was his death fart.

That put in mind of the venerable abbot of Chastelliers,[5] the one who didn't deign to tumble his chambermaids *nisi in Pontificalibus* [except in full pontifical regalia]. He, pestered by his relatives and friends in his last days in his abbey to resign, protested that he would never strip until before going to bed, and that his Paternity's last fart would be an abbot's fart.[6]

CHAPTER 17[1]

How we ran aground, and how we were helped by some travelers from dependencies of the Quint.[2]

HAVING raised anchor and cables, we set sail before the gentle Zephyr. At about two hundred and twenty-two miles there arose a furious whirlwind of various winds, around which we temporized for a little while with the rudder and bowlines, so as not to be called disobedient to the captain, who had assured us, seeing the gentleness of these winds, also seeing their mild confrontation, as well as the serenity of the air and tranquility of the current, that there was no reason to have either any hope of great good or fear of great harm from them; and moreover that the philosopher's saying was appropriate to our situation which recommended that we endure and abstain,[3] that is to say temporize.

However, this whirlwind lasted so long that at our importunate request the captain tried to break free of it and resume our original route. Indeed, raising the great mizzen and setting the rudder right on the compass point, he broke free, thanks to a stiff gust of wind that came up from the aforesaid whirlwind. But it was into like trouble as if, avoiding Charybdis, we had fallen into Scylla; for two miles from that spot our ships were stranded amid shoals much like those of the Saint-Mathieu Roads.[4]

Our whole company was most distressed, and much wind blew through our mizzensails; but Frère Jean gave no ground to melancholy, but with gentle words consoled now one man, now another, pointing out to them that soon we would have help from Heaven and that he had seen Castor over the top of the Mainmast.

"Would God," said Panurge, "that I were right now on land, and nothing more; and that each one of you, who so love the sea, had two hundred thousand crowns; I'd fatten a calf for you and fix up a hundred faggots for your return. All right! I consent never to marry; just arrange for me to be set down on land, and have a horse to get home on; as for a valet, I'll do without very well. I'm never treated so well as when I'm without a valet. On that point Plautus never lied when he said[5] that the number of our crosses, that is to say afflictions, troubles, vexations, varies with the number of our valets, even if they had no tongue, which is the most dangerous and wicked part there is in a valet,[6] and for which alone were invented tortures, questionings, and rackings for the valets; elsewhere no, although the legal beagles [les cotteurs de Droict] outside this kingdom have nowadays drawn from this an illogical, that is to say unreasonable, conclusion."

At this point there came right up to us a ship laden with drums, on which I recognized a few travelers of good family, among others Henry Cotiral, an old comrade, who wore at his belt a great donkeyprick, as women wear beads [patenostres], and held in his left hand a greasy old scald-pate's cap; in his right he held a big stump of cabbage. From the moment he recognized me he shouted for joy and said to me: "Have I ever got some?[7] Look (holding up the donkeyprick), here's the real Algamana;[8] this doctor's cap is our sole Elixo; and this (holding up the cabbage stump) is *Lunaria Major*. We'll make it on your return."

"But," said I, "where are you coming from? Where are you going? What are you carrying? Have you had a sniff of the sea [avez senty la marine]?" He answered me: "From the Quint; to Touraine; Alchemy, up to our ass [Alchimie, jusques au cul]."

"And what sort of people," I asked, "have you with you there on deck?"

"Singers," he replied, "musicians, poets, astrologers, rhymers, geomancers, alchemists, clockmakers; all are from dependencies of the Quint; from there they have fine letters patent."

Before he had finished these words, Panurge, vexed and indignant, said: "So you, since you can do or make anything [Vous donques qui faictes tout], even to children and fair weather, why don't you, without delay, take our bow onto your stern and pull us right back into the current?"

"I was about to," said Henry Cotiral; "this hour, this very moment; you shall shortly be off the bottom."

Then he had 7,532,810 stout drums knocked in on one side, and set that side toward the bow, and lashed the cables fast at every point, to our prow onto his poop and fastened it firmly to the bitts. Then in the first heave he towed us out of the sands with great ease, and not without our delight. For the sound of the drums, combined with the sweet murmur of the gravel and the crew's shanty, gave us a harmony little inferior to that of the rotating stars, which Plato says he heard some nights in his sleep.[9]

We, loath to be ungrateful for this good deed, kept tossing over to them some of our chitterlings, filling their drums with sausage, and were hauling onto their deck sixty-two hogsheads of wine, when two huge physeters bore down impetuously on their ship and spouted into it more water than the Vienne holds between Chinon and Saumur,[10] and filled all their drums with it, drenched all their yardarms, and bathed their breeches through their collars. Seeing this, Panurge burst into such an excess of glee, and exerted his spleen so, that it gave him a bellyache for over two hours.

"I wanted," said he, "to give them their wine [their tip], but they got only water, right on the dot. Fresh water they care nothing about, and use it only to wash their hands. This fine salt water will serve them for borax, niter, and sal ammoniac, in Geber's kitchen."[11]

No other converse was it possible to hold with them; for at first the whirlwind left us no freedom to stay. And then the Captain asked us to let the sea guide us from then on without worrying about anything but enjoying good cheer and said that for the time it befitted us to skirt this whirlwind and give way to the current if we wanted to reach the kingdom of the Quint without danger.

CHAPTER 18

How we reached the kingdom of Quint Essence,
named Entelechy.

A<small>FTER</small> prudently skirting the whirlwind for a half a day's time, on the third day afterward the air seemed to us more serene than usual, and we disembarked safe and sound at the port of Mateotechny, not far from the palace of Quintessence. Disembarking at the harbor, we found ourselves face to face with a large number of archers and warriors [archiers et gens de guerre] who were guarding the arsenal. At first arrival, they almost frightened us, for they made us lay down our arms and questioned us roughly, saying: "Mates, what country are you coming from?"

"Cousins," replied Panurge, "we're from Touraine. We're coming from France, desiring to pay our respects to the Lady Quintessence and to visit this most famous kingdom of Entelechy."

"Which do you say?" they questioned, "Entelechy, or Endelechy?"[1]

"Fair cousins," replied Panurge, "we are simple untutored folks; excuse our countrified talk, since, for the rest, our hearts are frank and honest."

"Not without cause," said they, "have we questioned you about this distinction; for a large number of others from your region of Touraine have passed this way who seemed good yokels and spoke correctly; but from another region have come some arrogant others, haughty as Scotchmen,[2] who right from their entry obstinately insisted on disputing with us; they got a good drubbing, for all their rhubarbative faces.[3] Do you in your world have so much time to waste that you don't know what to spend it on besides thus talking, disputing, and impudently writing about our Lady Queen? It was certainly necessary for Cicero to give up his *Republic* to meddle in it, and Diogenes Laertius, and Theodorus Gaza, Argyropylos and Bessarion, and Politian, and Budé, and Lascaris, and all those wise fool devils, whose number would not have been big enough if it had not been recently augmented by Scaliger, Bigot, Chambrier, François Fleury,[4] and I don't know what other fly-blown young jerks. A bad attack of angina to them; may it choke up their throat and their epiglottis. We'll . . . "

"But what the deuce, they're flattering the devils!" Panurge kept muttering between his teeth.

"You haven't come here to support them in their madness, and you haven't power of attorney for that; so we won't talk about them any more. Aristotle, number one man and paragon of all philosophy, was godfather to our Lady Queen; quite rightly and properly he called her Entelechy. Entelechy is her real name. Anyone who calls her anything else can go take a shit! Whoever calls her anything else is as far off the mark as Heaven is wide. Do be most welcome."

They gave us a friendly embrace; we were delighted. Panurge whispered in my ear: "Comrade, weren't you just a bit frightened at that first encounter?"

"Somewhat," I replied.

"I was," said he, "more than Ephraim's soldiers when they were killed, drowned by the Gileadites, for saying Sibboleth instead of Shibboleth [Judges 12.5–6]. And to put it bluntly, there's not a man in Beauce who wouldn't have been welcome to stop up my asshole with a bundle of hay."

Then the captain took us in silence with great ceremony to the queen's palace. Pantagruel tried to have a few words with him; but he [the captain], unable to climb up as high as he was, wanted a ladder or high stilts. Then he said: "So what? If our Queen had wanted, we'd be as big as you. That will be when she wishes."

In the first galleries we met a great throng of sick people, who were diversely installed according to the diversity of their sicknesses: the leper apart, the victims of poisoning in one place, of the plague in another, the poxies in the front row; and so for all the others.

CHAPTER 19

How the Quint Essence cured the sick by songs.

In the second gallery we were shown by the captain the Lady, young (and yet she was at least eighteen), beautiful, delicate, gorgeously clad in the midst of her ladies and gentlemen. The captain said to us: "It is not the time to speak to her; we must be attentive spectators of what she does. You, in your kingdom, have a few kings who psychologically cure certain maladies, such as scrofula, erysipelas, quartan fever, by mere laying-on of hands. This queen of ours cures all maladies without touch, by just playing them a song appropriate to their trouble."

Then he showed us the organs by playing on which she performed wonderful cures. They were very strangely made, for the pipes were of sticks of cassia, the sounding board of guiacum, the stops of rhubarb, the pedals of turbith, the keyboard of scammony.

While we were considering this wondrous novel way of building an organ, by her Abstractors, Spodizators, Massiteres, Pregusts, Tabachins, Chachanins, Neemanins, Rabrebans, Nereins, Rozuins, Nedibins, Nearins, Segamions, Perazons, Chesinins, Sarins, Sotrins, Aboth, Enilins, Archasdarpenins, Mebins, Giborins and others of her officers, the lepers were brought in. She played them a tune, but what one I don't know. Instantly they were perfectly cured. Then the poisoned were brought in; she played them another tune, and they were on their feet. Then the blind, the deaf, the mute, treating them similarly, which terrified us, not wrongly, and we fell to the ground, prostrating ourselves as people in ecstasy and rapt in contemplation of the powers we saw emanating from the Lady; and it was not in our power to say a single word. So we remained when she, touching Pantagruel with a bouquet of natural-grown roses, restored us to our senses and had us rise. Then she said to us in silken-smooth words such as Parisatis used in addressing her son Cyrus or words at least of crimson taffeta:

"The decency I see scintillating in your circumference[1] makes my judgment certain of the virtue latent in the center of your spirits; and, seeing the mellifluous suavity of your expert salutations, readily persuades me that your heart suffers no vice, no sterility in any lofty liberal branch of learning, but abounds in many rare exotic kinds of lore, which nowadays, due to the ordinary practice of the untutored herd, is easier wished for than found. That is the reason why I, though in the past dominating any private feeling, cannot keep from saying to you the most trivial thing in the world: that is: pray be welcome, very welcome, most welcome."

"I'm no cleric," Panurge kept telling me secretly; "answer if you wish." However, I did not reply, nor did Pantagruel, and we remained in silence.

Then the queen said to us: "From this taciturnity of yours I can tell that not only have you come out of the Pythagorean school in which in successive propagation took root the antiquity of my progenitors, but also that in Egypt, famous factory of lofty philosophy, going back many a moon, have bitten your nails and scratched your head with a finger.[2] In the school of Pythagoras taciturnity was a symbol of knowledge, and silence was recognized by the Egyptians with deific praise; and the pontiffs in Hieropolis sacrificed to the great God in silence without making a sound or uttering a word. My intent toward you is not to be lacking in gratitude, but by a lively formality, even if matter absented itself from me, to excentricate to you my thoughts."

These remarks completed, she directed her words to her officers and said to them only: "Tabachins, to Panacea." At these words, the Tabachins told us that we were to consider the Lady excused if we did not dine with her; for at her dinner she ate nothing except a few Categories, Jecabots, Eminins, Dimions, Abstractions, Harborins, Chelimins, Second Intentions, Caradoth, Antitheses, Metempsychoses, and Transcendent Prolepsies.[3]

Then they took us into a little closet all covered with alarm signals, where we were treated Lord knows how. They say Jupiter, on the diphtera, the skin of the nannygoat that suckled him in Candia, which he used as a shield when he fought the Titans, wherefore it is called Eginchus,[4] writes down everything that is done in the world. Upon my word, my toper friends, even on eighteen goatskins could not be described the good foods that were served us, the tidbits and good cheer offered us, not even were it in letters as small as Cicero says he saw on a copy of Homer's *Iliad*, so small they covered it with a nutshell.[5] For my part, even had I a hundred tongues, a hundred mouths and an iron voice, and Plato's mellifluous abundance,[6] I couldn't expound to you even in four books one-third of a second of it.

And Pantagruel was saying to me that in his opinion the Lady, in saying to her Tabachins "To Panacea," was giving the word, symbolic among them, of sovereign cheer, as Lucullus used to say "In Apollo" when he wanted to offer his friends a special treat, even if he was caught unprepared, as did sometimes Cicero and Hortensius.[7]

CHAPTER 20

How the queen spent her time after dinner.

Dinner over, we were taken by a Chachanin into the Lady's hall, and saw how customarily, after dinner, in company with the ladies and the princes of the court, she would strain, sift, bolt, range, and pass the time through a nice big sieve of blue and white silk. Then I noticed that they brought back antiquity into use as they played and danced:

The Cordax,	The Calabrian,
The Emmelia,	The Molossic,
The Sicinnis,	The Cernophore,
The Iambic,	The Mongas,
The Persian,	The Thermanstria,
The Phrygian,	The Floral,
The Nicatiam [a victory dance],	The Pyrrhic,
The Thracian,	And myriad other dances.

Then by her command we toured the palace, and there saw things so novel, wondrous, and strange, that thinking about it I am still rapt in spirit. Nothing, however, stunned us more than the practice of the gentlemen of her house, Abstractors, Perazons, Nedibins, Spodizators, and others, who told us frankly, without dissimulation, that the Lady queen did all the impossibles; they, her officers, did and cured all the rest. There I saw a young Perazon curing the poxies, I mean those with the finest pocks, what you might call Rouen type, just by touching their dentiform vertebra three times with a piece of clog.

Another I saw perfectly cure a man with the dropsy, some with typanites, ascites, and hyposarcides,[1] by hitting them nine times on the belly with one of Tenes's axes, without solution of continuity.

One cured all fevers on the spot, just by hanging a fox tail on the patient's left side from the belt.

One cured the toothache by three times washing the root of the painful tooth with elderberry vinegar and letting it dry out half an hour in the sun.

Another, every kind of gout, whether hot or cold, natural or accidental, just by having the gouties close their mouth and open their eyes.

Another I saw cure nine gentlemen of Saint Francis's evil [poverty] in a short time by getting them out of all debts and hanging from each one's neck, on a rope, a casket holding ten sun-crowns.

Another, by marvelous device, threw houses out the windows;[2] thus they were left cleansed of any pestilent air.

Another cured all three kinds of hectic fevers—atrophy, wasting, emaciation—without baths, without Tabian [country] milk, without drops, pication or other medication, by making the patients into monks for three weeks.[3] And he maintained that if they didn't fatten up in the monastic state, never, by art or by nature, would they fill out.

Another I saw accompanied by women in large numbers in two groups: one was of appetizing tender young blond girls, and of good will, it seemed to me; the other, of toothless old hags, blear-eyed, wrinkled, swarthy, cadaverous. There Pantagruel was told that he remodeled old women, thus rejuvenating them, and by his craft making them become such as the young girls presented there, whom that day he had remodeled and completely restored to the same beauty, form, elegance, size, and composition of the members, as they were at the age of fifteen or sixteen, except only for the heels, which remained much shorter than they had been in their first youth. That was the reason why, from now on, whenever they meet a man, they will be very easy marks and subject to falling over backward.

The group of old women was waiting most devoutly for the next batch in the oven[4] and impatiently clamoring for it, claiming that it's something intolerable in nature when a willing ass wants beauty.[5]

And in his craft he [the remodeler] had a continuous practice and a better than modest income. Pantagruel inquired whether he likewise rejuvenated old men; the answer was no, but that the way for them to grow young again was by living with a remodeled woman, for thereby one caught that fifth kind of pox named soughing [pellade], in Greek *Ophiasis,* by means of which you change your hair and skin, as snakes do annually and youth is renewed in them, as in the Phoenix of Arabia. That's the real Fountain of Youth. There, suddenly, the man who was old and decrepit becomes young, blithe, and ready for action, as Euripides says happened to Iolaos;[6] as happened to the fair Phaon, beloved of Sappho, by the benefit of Venus;[7] to Tithonus, by means of Aurora [Dawn]; to Aeson by Medea's craft, and likewise to Jason, who, according to the testimony of Pherecydes and Simonides, was held and rejuvenated by her; as Aeschylus says happened to the wet nurses of Bacchus and also to their husbands.[8]

CHAPTER 21

*How the officers of the Quint operate diversely,
and how the queen kept us on
in the estate of Abstractors.*[1]

LATER I saw a large number of her aforesaid officers who were bleaching the Ethiopians in jig time just by rubbing their bellies with the bottoms of baskets.

Others with three pairs of foxes under yoke were plowing the sandy seashore, and were not wasting their seed.

Others were washing tiles and making them lose their color.[2]

Others were squeezing water out of pumices, which you call pumice stones, by pounding them a long time in a marble mortar and making them change substance.[3]

Others were shearing donkeys and finding on them a very good woollen fleece.

Others gathered barberries and figs off of thistles.

Others were drawing milk from billygoats and catching the milk in a sieve, a big help to the household [à grand profit de mesnage].

Others were washing the heads of donkeys and not wasting any soap.

Others were hunting in the winds with nets, and there catching decuman crayfish.

I saw one young Spodizator carefully drawing farts out of a dead donkey, and selling them for five sous an ell.

Another was putrefying some Sechaboth. O what lovely food!

But Panurge foully threw up his guts on seeing an Archasdarpenim putrefying a great potful of human urine with horse dung, with plenty of Christian shit. Fie upon the slob! However, in reply he told us that with this sacred distillation he gave drinks to kings and princes, and thereby lengthened their lives by a good fathom or two.

Others were snapping chitterlings over their knees.

Others were flaying eels by the tail, and the said eels were screaming before being flayed, as the Melun eels do.

Others were making great things out of nothing, and making great things return into nothing.

Others were cutting fire with a knife and drawing water with a net.

Others were making lanterns out of bladders, and, out of clouds, brass stoves.

We saw twelve others of them banqueting under an arbor, and drinking free and hearty, out of nine ample false cups, four kinds of wine, cool and delicious; and we were told that they were enjoying the time[4] in the manner of the place and that once in this manner Hercules enjoyed the time with Atlas.

Others were making a virtue of necessity, and the work seemed to me very fine and to the point.

Others were doing alchemy with their teeth; and in so doing they weren't getting the close-stools full.

Others in a grassy plot were measuring exactly how far the fleas could go at a hop, a skip, and a jump, and they told us that this was exceedingly useful for the ruling of kingdoms, the conduct of armies, and the administration of commonwealths. And Socrates, who first removed philosophy from the realms of heaven and brought it down to earth, as well as from the idle and simply curious, made it profitable and useful; he used half of his study time to measure the leaps of fleas, as Aristophanes, the Quintessential, affirms.[5]

I saw two Giborins [giants] by themselves keeping watch on the top of a tower, and we were told that they guarded the moon from wolves.

I met four others in a corner of the garden disputing bitterly and ready to take each other by the hair; on asking the origin of their disagreement, I learned that four days had passed since they had begun disputing about three lofty metaphysical [plus que phisicales] propositions, for resolving which they were promising themselves mountains of gold. The first was about the shadow of a ballocky donkey, another about the smoke from a lantern; the third about nannygoat hair, to find out whether it was wool. Then we were told that they found nothing strange about two contradictories true in form, in figure, and in time.[6] A thing the sophists of Paris would rather have themselves unbaptized than confess.

As we carefully considered the wondrous operations of these people, up came the Lady with her noble company, as bright Hesperus already shone. On her arrival, we were once again stunned in our senses and dazzled in our vision. Immediately she noticed our affright and said to us:

"What gets human minds lost is not the perfection of the effects, of which they clearly perceive to arise from natural causes by virtue of the ingenuity of the astute artisans; it's the novelty of the experience entering the senses, which does not foresee the ease of the task when serene judgment is paired with diligent study. So keep a clear head, and rid yourselves of all fear, if you are seized by any in considering what is being done by our officers. See, understand, and contemplate to your hearts' content all that my house contains, emancipating yourselves bit by bit from the enslavement of ignorance. The matter is quite to my taste. To give you unfeigned teaching in this, in contemplation of the studious desires of which you seem to me to have made in your hearts a notable pile and sufficient proof, I now retain you in the estate and function of my Abstractors. By Geber, my first Tabachin, you shall be inscribed on my rolls when you leave this place."

We thanked her humbly, without saying a word, and accepted the handsome estate she was giving us.

CHAPTER 22

How the queen was served at supper,
and how she ate.

A<small>FTER</small> saying this, the queen turned her back on her other gentlemen and said to them: "The orifice of the stomach, common ambassador for revictualing all the members, upper and lower, is importuning us to restore to them, by apposition of idoneous aliments, what has been lost to them by continuous action of the natural heat in the radical humidity.[1] Spodizators, Cesinins, Nemains, and Perazons, let there be no delay on your part in having the tables set, abounding in every legitimate species of restoratives. You too, noble Pregusts, accompanied by my gentle Masticators: my experience of your expertise spiced with care and diligence makes me unable to give you any order to be about your business and stay always on your guard. Let me just remind you to go on doing what you're doing."

Having said this, she withdrew with some of her ladies for some little time, and we were told that this was to take a bath, a custom as much preserved among the ancients as among us is that of washing our hands. The tables were promptly set, then covered with precious tablecloths. The serving was this: the Lady ate nothing but celestial ambrosia, drank nothing but divine nectar; but the lords and ladies of the house were served, and we with them, with foods rare, tasty, and precious, if ever Apicius ever thought of any such.

At the end of the meal a potpourri was brought on, in case by chance famishing hunger had granted us no truce; and it was of such amplitude and great size that the golden plane tree that Pythius Bithynius gave King Darius would scarcely have covered it.[2] The potpourri was full of various kinds of pottages, salads, fricassees, bean and pea stews, cabirotades [goat stews], roast meat, boiled meat, carbonados, great hunks of salt beef, vintage hams, deific saltmeats, pastries, tarts, lots of couscous, cheeses, curds, jellies, fruits of all kinds. The whole thing seemed to me good and tasty; however, I didn't touch it, since I was quite full and stuffed. Only I must tell you that there I saw pasties in crust, a rather rare thing; and the pasties in crust were pasties in pot.[3] At the bottom of this [potpourri], I noticed plenty of dice, cards, tarot packs, luettes, chessmen, and checkers, with a cup full of sun-crowns for people who would like to play.

Finally, underneath I saw a number of mules in handsome trappings, with velvet blankets, and a troop of ambling nags, some for men and some for women; I don't know how many litters all lined with velvet and a few coaches Ferrarese style for those who had a mind to take the air.

That did not seem strange to me, but I did find very novel the way the Lady ate. She chewed nothing; not that her foods did not need mastication, but such was her habit and custom. The foods, which her Pregusts had tried, her Masticators took and chewed nobly for her, having their gullets lined with crimson satin with little welts and gold braiding, and teeth of fine ivory; thanks to which, when they had chewed them enough, they poured them down into her throat through a funnel of fine white gold all the way into her stomach. For the same reason we were told that she never defecated except by proxy [par procuration].

CHAPTER 23

How, in the presence of the Quint,
was performed a joyous ball
in the form of a tourney.[1]

THE supper over, in the Lady's presence was performed a ball in the form of a tourney, worth not only looking at but also remembering eternally. To begin it the floor of the hall was covered with an ample piece of velveted tapestry made in the form of a chessboard, to fit, in squares half of which were yellow, half white, three palms wide [twenty-seven inches], and all perfectly square. Then into the room came eight young nymphs,[2] just as the ancients portrayed them in Diana's company; one king, one queen, two guardians of the castle, two knights, and two archers; in like order were sixteen others clad in cloth of silver. Their placing on the tapestry was this: the kings stood in the last row, the golden king on a white square, the silvered on a yellow square; the queens beside their kings, the golden on a golden square, the silvered on a white square; two archers next to them as guards of their kings and queens; next to the archers, two knights; next to the knights, two guardians. In the next row in front of them were eight nymphs. Between the two bands of nymphs four rows of squares remained empty.

Each team had on its side its musicians in matching livery, some in orange damask, some in white; and there were eight on each side all with different instruments joyously inventive, blending well together, and wondrously melodious, changing tone, tempo, and measure as the course of the ball required, which I found admirable, considering the great variety of moves, jumps, vaults, flights, ambushes, retreats, and surprises.

Still more did it transcend human imagination, meseemed, that no sooner had the music given the signal than they moved onto the designated place the diversity of their moves notwithstanding. For the nymphs, which are in the front row, as being ready to start up the combat, march straight ahead against their enemies one square at a time, except for the first move, when they are free to move two squares; they alone may never move backward. If one of them reaches the row of her enemy king, she is crowned queen of her king, and from then on takes and moves with the same privilege as the queen; otherwise, they never strike [take] their enemies except obliquely and on a diagonal, and only from in front. However, neither they nor the others are allowed to take any of their enemies if by taking him they were leaving their king unprotected and in check.

The kings move and take their enemies in all directions in a straight line, passing only from a white square to an adjoining yellow, and vice versa;[3] except that on the first move, if their row should be empty of other officers besides the guardian, they can put him in their place and draw back beside him.

The queens move and take in greater freedom than any others: to wit, on any place and in any manner, on a direct line, as far as they please, provided it is in the same color as their starting place [for that move].[4]

The archers move both forward and backward, both far and near. Also they never change the color of their original position.[5]

The knights move and take in a crotched or gallows [lignéare] fashion, stepping over one free space even if it is occupied by one of his own men or the enemy; at the second square moving one square to the right or left, with a change of color, a jump that is very harmful to the opposite side and hard to watch for; for they never take it head on.

The guardians take on a straight line both to the right and the left, both forward and backward, like the kings, and they can move as far as they like in an empty space, which the kings cannot.

The common rule for both sides was, as the final goal of the combat, to besiege and hem in the king of the opposing team so that he cannot escape in any direction. When he was thus hemmed in, unable to escape or to be rescued by his team, the combat ended and the hemmed-in king lost. So to protect him from this calamity, there is no one on his team who does not offer his own life; and they take one another everywhere once the sound of the music comes. When anyone took a prisoner from the other side, he would bow to him, tap him gently on the right hand, and move him off the field, and move into his place. If it came about that one of the kings was in check [en prise], the adversary was not to take him; but the one who had uncovered him or who held him in check was rigorously commanded to make him a deep bow and warn him by saying: "God keep you!" so that one of his officers should rescue and protect him, or else he should change his position, if by misfortune he could not be rescued. At all events, if he still was not taken by the opposing team, but saluted on bended knee by saying to him: "Good day." That was the end of the tourney.

CHAPTER 24

How the thirty-two persons in the ball fight.

WITH both sides settled in their places, the musicians all together start to play in a martial tone, rather frighteningly, as if at the assault. Then we see both sides quiver and stiffen themselves to fight when the time comes for the attack, and they must be called out of their camp. Then suddenly the musicians of the silver team stopped; only the musicians of the gold team played on, by which we were signaled that the gold team was on the attack, which soon happened; for at a new tone we saw that the gold nymph stationed in front of the queen made a full turn to the left toward her king, as if asking leave to go into combat; at the same time also saluting her whole team. Then in nice modesty she moved two squares forward and curtseyed to the opposing team, which she was attacking. Then the gold musicians stopped, and the silver began. Here it must not be omitted that the nymph had in turn saluted her king and her team so that they should not remain idle; likewise they returned her salute, turning to the left; except the queen, who turned to the right toward her king; and this form of salutation was followed by everyone who moved in the entire course of the ball, and also the return salutation, on both one side and the other.

At the sound of the silver musicians out moved the silver nymph who was stationed in front of her queen, graciously saluting her king, and her whole company, and with them likewise saluting her back, as was said of the golds, except that they turned to the right and their queen to the left; placed herself on the second square ahead, and, bowing to her adversary, stood opposite the first gold nymph with no distance between, as if they were ready to fight, but that they strike only to the sides. Their companions follow them, both gold and silver, in an intercalary figure, and appear to skirmish there, so that the gold nymph who had first entered the field, tapping a silver nymph in the hand, put her off the field and occupied her place; but soon, at a new sound from the musicians, she was tapped in the same way by the silver archer. A gold nymph made him move and close up; the silver knight came out on the field; the gold queen placed herself in front of her king. Thereupon the silver king changes places, fearing the fury of the gold queen, and drew back onto the place of his guardian on the right, which seemed very well supplied and a good one to defend.

The two knights standing on the left, both gold and silver, move out and capture many opposing nymphs (which could not draw back to the rear), especially the gold knight, who gives all his attention to taking nymphs. But the silver knight has more important things in mind, and, concealing his plan, sometimes when he could have taken a gold nymph he leaves her alone and passes on, to such effect that he took his place near his adversaries, where he saluted the opposing king and said: "God keep you!"

The gold team, having this warning to rescue their king, shuddered; not that they could not easily give the king immediate help, but that in saving their king they were losing their right guardian, and no help for it. Thereupon the gold king drew back to the left, and the silver knight took the gold guardian, which was a great loss to them. However, the gold team plans revenge for this, and surrounds him on all sides until he cannot flee back or escape from their hands; he makes myriad efforts to get out; his mates use myriad ruses to protect him, but in the end the gold queen took him.

The gold team, deprived of one of its mainstays, lashes out with might and main, tries rather at random to take revenge, somewhat thoughtlessly, and does much harm amid the enemy hosts. The silver team lies low and awaits the moment to strike back and offers one of its nymphs to the gold queen, having set up an ambush for her, to such effect that when she took the nymph the gold archer just missed taking the silver queen[1] by surprise. The gold knight attempts the capture of the silver king and queen, and says: "Good day."

The silver archer salutes them; he was taken by a gold nymph, she was taken by a silver nymph. The battle is fierce. The guardians come out of their stations to the rescue. Everything is in a dangerous melee. Enyo still does not declare herself. Once all the silvers break through all the way to the gold king's tent, and are immediately repulsed. Among others, the gold queen performs great exploits, on one foray taking the silver archer, then, swerving, the silver guardian. Seeing this, the silver queen charges to the fore and wreaks havoc with the same hardihood, and takes the last gold guardian and also an odd nymph.

The two queens fought a long time, now trying to take one another by surprise, now each one trying to save herself and guard her king. Finally the gold queen took the silver queen, but immediately afterward she was taken by the silver archer. Then all the gold king had left was three nymphs, one archer, and one guardian. The silver still had three nymphs and the righthand knight, which was the reason why from then on they fought more slowly and deliberately.

The two kings seemed mournful over losing their dearly beloved lady queens, and all their planning and effort goes into receiving others, if they can, out of the whole number of their nymphs, into this dignity and new marriage, and loving them joyously, with certain promises of being received into this if they can win through all the way onto the enemy's last row. The golds get ahead, and one of them is made a new queen; she has a crown put on her head and is given new accouterments.

The silver nymphs made haste that they too could be made new queens; one moved forward, but a golden knight lay ready to intercept her, so that she could go no farther.

The new gold queen, on arriving, tried to show herself strong, valiant, and warlike. She performed great feats of arms around the field. But at this point the silver knight took the gold guardian who was guarding the edge of the field, and by this means was made a new silver queen, who also tried to show her prowess on her new arrival. The combat was renewed, more ardent than before. Myriad ruses, myriad assaults, myriad moves were made by one side and the other, to the point where the silver queen clandestinely entered the gold king's tent and said "God keep you!" and he could be saved only by his new queen.

She had no hesitation in standing in the way and saving him. So then the silver knight, curveting around in every direction, took his place beside his queen, and they put the gold king in such disarray that to save himself he had to lose his queen. But the gold king took the silver knight. This notwithstanding, the gold archer and two remaining nymphs defended their king with might and main, but finally they were all taken and put off the field, and the gold king remained alone. Then he was greeted by the whole silver team, and in deep reverence they said to him: "Good day," since the silver king remained the victor. At these words the two bands of musicians began to play together, for a victory. And this first ball came to an end with such great delights, such charming gesture, such honorable bearing, such rare graces, that we were all exhilarated in spirit like people in ecstasy, and not wrongly did it seem to us that we were transported to the sovereign delights and utmost felicity of the Olympian heaven.

The first tourney over, the two teams went back to their original positions; and as they had fought before, so they began to fight for the second time, except that the music was speeded up in its measure half a beat faster [serrée d'un demy temps plus] than it was before; also the course of the ball was totally different from the first. This time I saw that the gold queen, as if vexed at the rout of her army, was drawn out by the tone of the music, and took the field among the first with an archer and a knight, and she barely missed taking the silver king by surprise in his tent amid his offices. After that, seeing her plan discovered she skirmished around amid the troop and slew so many silver nymphs and other officers that it was a pitiable thing to see. You'd have thought it was another Amazon Penthesilea hurling thunderbolts around the camp of the Greeks.

But little did this havoc last; for the silvers, shuddering at the loss of their men but biding their grief, set up an ambush with an archer far off at an angle and a knight roving, and by these she was taken and put off the field. The rest were soon undone. She will be shrewder another time and will stay close to her king, not move so far away, and go off, when go she must, far better accompanied. In that one the silvers remained the victors, as before.

For the third and last ball, both teams took their stations as before, and seemed to wear a gayer and more determined face than in the two before. And the music was more than half again faster, and the mode Phrygian and warlike, like the one that Marsyas once invented.[2] Then they began to ride around and go into the fray with such agility that in one beat [temps] of the music they made four moves, with the corresponding respectful turns, as we have said above; so that it was a rapid-fire sequence of hops, gambols, and curvets, as of rope dancers, interwoven with one another. And seeing them pirouette on one foot after taking the bow, we were comparing these to the motion of a top in a little children's game, spinning under the strokes of the whip, when its turn is so swift that its motion is rest, and it seems still, not moving but sleeping, as they call it. And when it has a colored dot showing on it, it seems to our eye to be not a dot but a continuous line, as Cusa astutely noted in a truly divine work.[3]

This time we hear nothing but handclapping and acclamations repeated at every turn, by both sides. There never was a Cato so severe, or a Crassus the Elder so unsmiling, or a Timon of Athens so misanthropic, or a Heraclitus so set against man's special distinction, which is laughter, that he would not have broken into it on seeing these young men with the queens and nymphs, to the sound of such sprightly music, suddenly move about in such diverse ways, take steps, jump, curvet, gambol, twirl, with such dexterity that never did one get in the way of the other. The fewer were those that remained in the field, the greater the pleasure in seeing the ruses and tricks they used to take one another by surprise, in keeping with what was signaled to them by the music. I will say more; if this superhuman spectacle left us confounded in our senses, stunned in our spirits, and uplifted us, we felt even more our hearts stirred and amazed at the sound of the music; I could readily believe that it was by such strains that Ismenias roused Alexander the Great,[4] when he was at table and dining quietly, to rise and take up arms. In the third tourney the gold was the victor.

During these dances the Lady unobtrusively disappeared, and we did not see her again. We were indeed taken by Geber's sailors and then and there were inscribed into the estate ordered by her. Then, going down to Mateotechny harbor, we boarded our ships, hearing that we had a wind astern, which, if we did not seize it, could hardly be got back in three quarters of a moon.

CHAPTER 25

How we went ashore on the island of Odes,[1]
where the roads go places.[2]

AFTER two days of sailing, there came into view the island of Odes, on which we saw a memorable thing. The roads are animate—if Aristotle's statement is true which says that the invincible proof of an animate being is that it moves of itself.[3] For the roads go places, like animals, and some are wandering roads, in the manner of the planets; others are passing roads, crossing roads, traversing roads. And I saw that the travelers, servants, and inhabitants of the country would ask: "Where does this road go? and this one?" Their answer was: "Between Noontide and Faverolles,[4] to the parish, to town, to the river."

Then, setting forth on the right road, with no more trouble or fatigue, they would find themselves at their destination; as you see happen to those who embark by boat on the Rhone from Lyon to Avignon or Arles.[5] And as you know that in everything there is something wrong and nothing comes out right in every respect; we were told that there were a kind of people they called waylayers [guetteurs de chemins] and pavement-pounders [batteurs de pavez]; and the poor roads feared them and kept away from them as from brigands. These lay in wait for them as they passed by, as we do for wolves in trapping them, or for woodcocks with a net. I saw one of these who was apprehended by the law for unjustly, in despite of Pallas [Malgré Pallas], taking the road for school, that was the longest one; another was boasting of taking, as fair in war, the shortest one, saying that in this encounter it was such an advantage to him that he was the first to get his business done successfully.

And so Carpalim said to Epistémon, one day when he came upon him pisser in hand pissing against the wall, that he was no longer amazed if he always was the first to Pantagruel's levee, for he had the shortest and least ridden.[6]

There I recognized the high road to Bourges [le grand chemin de Bourges], and saw it trudge along at an abbot's amble [à pas d'Abbé], and also saw it flee when some carters threatened to trample it with their horses' hoofs and run their carts over its belly, even as Tullia ran her chariot over the belly of her father Servius Tullius, sixth king of the Romans. Likewise I recognized the old byway [le vieux quemin] from Péronne to Saint-Quentin, and it seemed to me a nice well-groomed way. There I spotted among the rocks the old Ferrate road over the top of a great bear.[7] Seeing it from a distance reminded me of Saint Jerome in the painting[8]—if his lion had been a bear; for it was all mortified; had a long ill-combed white beard. You'd have thought it was icicles; it had on it plenty of ill-planed pine rosaries; and it was as though on its knees, not standing nor completely lying down, and kept beating its chest with great rough stones. It moved us to both pity and fear at the same time.[9]

As we were looking at it, a young local teacher drew us aside, and, pointing to a well-smoothed road, all white and just a bit felted with straw, said to us: "From now on do not disdain the opinion of Thales of Miletus when he said that water was the beginning of all things, or Homer's assertion [Iliad 14.246] that everything had its birth in the ocean. This road you see was born in water and will return to it: two months ago boats were passing along where, now, carts are passing."

"Really," said Pantagruel, "you're making that sound very pitiable! In our world we see five hundred similar transformations, and more, every year."

Then, considering the gaits of these moving roads, he said to us that in his judgment Philolaus and Aristarchus had philosophized on this island; Seleucus here got the notion of affirming that the earth, not heaven, really moved about the poles, even though the contrary seems to be the truth. Just as when we are on the river Loire the nearby trees seem to move, but they do not move; we do, by the progression of the boat. Returning to our ships, we saw that near the shore three waylayers were being racked who had been caught in an ambush and being burned over a slow fire was a big lecher who had beaten a road and cracked one of its ribs; and we were told that it was the road to the dikes and levees of the Nile in Egypt.

CHAPTER 26

How we stopped on the island of Clogs,
and of the order of the Semiquaver [Minimal] Friars.[1]

NEXT we came to the island of Clogs, where they live on nothing but haddock chowder; however, we were well received by the king of the island—named Benius, third of that name, who, after drinks, took us to see a new monastery created, erected, and built, on his plan, for the Semiquaver Friars; so he called his religious, saying that on the mainland lived the Brothers who were Little Servants and Friends of the Gentle Lady,[2] also, the grand and glorious Friars Minor,[3] who were semibreves of bulls; the Friars Minim, akin to smoked herring; also the Crotchet Friars Minim; and the smallest he could make of the name was Semiquavers [Fredons].

By the statutes of the bull obtained from the Quint, which is all in perfect chords, they were all dressed like house burners, except that, even as roof tilers in Anjou wear kneepads, even so they had padded bellies, and belly padders were in great repute among them. They had their breeches' codpiece in the form of a slipper, and each one wore two of them, one sewn in front and the other in back, maintaining that by this codpiecical duplicity were duly represented certain horrific mysteries. They wore shoes round as basins, in imitation of the people who live by the Sea of Sand; for the rest they were clean shaven and iron shod. And to show that they have no care about Fortune, he [Benius] had them shaved and plucked like pigs on the hind part of the skull, from the top down to the shoulder blades. Their frontal hair grew down freely all the way from the parietal bones.[4] Thus they counterfortuned [Ainsi contre-fortunoient] like people caring not a whit about the good things there are in this world. In further defiance of fickle fortune, they each bore, not in hand like her but at the belt, by way of a rosary, a sharp razor, which they ground twice a day and sharpened three times a night.

On his feet each one wore a round ball, because it is said that Fortune has one under her feet. The rear flap of their cowl was attached in front, not in back; that way their faces were hidden, and they could freely make fun of both Fortune and the fortunate, the way our young ladies do when they have on their *cache-laids* [face-savers: masks or mufflers], which you call nose turrets;[5] the ancients called them *charities,* because one of them covers a multitude of their sins. Also they always had the back of their head uncovered, as we have the face; that was how they could go around belly or ass first, as they saw fit. If they went ass first, you would have thought that was their natural walk, because of the round shoes and the preceding codpiece, also a face behind shaven and crudely painted, with two eyes and a mouth, as you see on coconuts. If they went belly first, you'd have thought they were playing blind man's bluff; it was a lovely thing to see them.

Their way of life was this: when bright Lucifer [the morning star] began to appear over the earth, they booted and spurred one another, out of charity. Thus booted and spurred, they slept on, or at least snored; and in sleeping they had spectacles on their nose, or eyeglasses at worst.

We found that way of living very strange; but they satisfied us in reply, pointing out that when the Last Judgment came, humans would be getting their rest and sleep. So to make it more obviously clear that they were not refusing to show up there, they kept themselves booted, spurred, ready to take horse when the trumpet sounded.

At the stroke of noon (note that their bells both church and refectory, were made according to Pontanus's plan, to wit, lined with fine down, with the clapper of a fox's tail), at the stroke of noon they woke up and took off their boots; anyone who wanted to pissed, anyone who wanted to crapped, and anyone who wanted to sneezed.

But all, on compulsion, by a rigorous statute, amply and copiously yawned, and breakfasted on yawns. This seemed to me an amusing sight: for, leaving their boots and spurs on a rack, they went down to the cloisters; there they carefully washed their hands and mouth, then sat down on a long bench and picked their teeth, until the provost gave the signal by whistling in his palm; then everyone opened his throat as wide as he could, and they yawned sometimes for half an hour, sometimes

more, sometimes less, according as the prior thought the breakfast proportioned to the day's festival. After that they formed a fine procession,
carrying two banners, on one of which appeared the prettily painted
portrait of Virtue, on the other that of Fortune. One Semiquaver in front
bore the banner of Fortune; after him marched another bearing that of
Virtue, holding in his [other] hand a sprinkler dipped in Mercurial water,
which Ovid describes in his *Fasti*,[6] with which he kept incessantly whipping the friar who was bearing Fortune.

"This order," said Panurge, "is contrary to the view of Cicero and the
Academics who would have Virtue precede, Fortune follow." All the
same, it was pointed out to us that it was right for them to do thus, since
their intention was to give a whipping to Fortune.

During the procession, they quavered and warbled [fredonnoient] melodiously between their teeth some anthems or other, I know not which,
for I don't understand their gibberish; and on listening attentively, I noted
that they sang only with their ears.[7] O what a lovely harmony, attuned
to the sound of their bells! Never would you find them discordant.
Pantagruel made me one noteworthy observation about their procession,
saying:

"Did you see the cunning of these Semiquavers? To complete their
procession, having come out one door of the church, they went back in
by the other. They were mighty careful not to go back in the way they
went out. 'Pon my honor, these are sharp people, I mean sharp enough
to gild, sharp as a lead dagger,[8] not sharpened sharp but sharpening sharp,
passed through a fine sieve."[9]

"That sharpness," said Frère Jean, "is derived from occult philosophy,
and I don't understand one devilish word of it."

"All the more is it redoubtable," said Pantagruel, "because it is not
understood. For sharpness understood, discovered, loses the essence and
the name of sharpness; we call it dullness [lourderie]. 'Pon my honor,
they know lots of other sharp tricks!"

The procession completed, a healthy walk and exercise, they retired to
the refectory and knelt down, knees beneath the table, each one leaning
his chest and stomach upon a lantern. With them in this posture, in came
a great Clog with a pitchfork in hand, and then and there he belabored
them with the fork; so that they began their meal with cheese and finished it with mustard and lettuce, as Martial testifies was the custom of the
ancients.[10] At the end they offered each one a dishful of mustard, so that
they had mustard after dinner.

This was their diet: on Sunday they ate blood puddings, chitterlings, sausages, meat and vegetable puddings, liver slices, haslets, little quails, always excepting the cheese to start with and the mustard before they left. On Monday, sauce peas and bacon, with ample commentary and interlinear gloss.[11] On Tuesday, holy bread aplenty, *fouaces,*[12] cakes, scones, and biscuits. On Wednesday, country fare: fine sheep's heads, calf's head, badger's head, which abound in the region. On Thursday, seven kinds of pottages and eternal mustard amid them. On Friday, nothing but sorb apples, and at that they were none too ripe, as far as I could judge by their color. On Saturday, they gnawed the bones. Not, however, that they were emaciated for each and every one of them had the benefit of a mighty fine belly. Their drink was an antifortunal;[13] so they called some sort of local beverage. When they wanted to eat or drink, they pulled the flaps of their cowl around them and down in front, and these served as bibs.

When dinner was over, they made a very fine prayer to God, and all in warbles and Semiquavers; the rest of the day, tweaking one another's noses; on Tuesday, scratching one another; on Wednesday, blowing one another's noses; on Thursday, pulling worms out of one another's noses; on Friday, tickling one another; on Saturday, whipping one another.

Such was their regimen when they were in the monastery. If on the cloistral prior's orders they went outside, they were strictly forbidden, under horrific penalty, to touch or eat any fish when at sea or on a river; nor flesh, of any kind, when on terra firma: so that it should be evident they they were not enjoying power of concupiscence, and were no more moved by it than Marpesian rock [Parian marble]; doing all this with fitting antiphones and suitably, still singing with their ears, as we have said.

When the sun set in the ocean, they booted and spurred one another as before, and, spectacles on nose, settled down to sleep. At midnight the Clog came in, and on their feet! Then they ground and sharpened their razors, and, when the procession was over, put the tables over them, and fed as before.

Frère Jean, seeing these joyous Semiquaver Friars and learning their statutes, lost all composure, and shouted out loudly to say: "O what a big rat on the table![14] I'll smash him to bits and go off, by God, out of here![15] O why isn't Priapus here just as he was at the nocturnal rites of Canidia, just to see him fart his guts out, and warble a semiquaver as a counterfart [contrepédant fredonner]! At this point I realize in truth that we are in an Antichthonian and Antipodean land. In Germany they demolish monasteries and defrock monks; here we erect them askew and inside out."[16]

CHAPTER 27

How Panurge, questioning a Semiquaver Friar,
got no answer from him except in monosyllables.[1]

P<small>ANURGE</small>, ever since we arrived, had done nothing but deeply contemplate the pusses of these kingly Semiquavers; at this point he tugged at the sleeve of one of them, lean as a kippered devil, and asked him: "Friar, Semiquaver, Minimal, Warbler, Quaverburbler, where is the wench?"[2]
The Semiquaver answered him: "Down."

> P<small>AN</small>. Do you have many of them in here?—F<small>R</small>. Few.
>
> P<small>AN</small>. How many actually are there?—F<small>R</small>. Score.[3]
>
> P<small>AN</small>. How many would you like?—F<small>R</small>. Five.
>
> P<small>AN</small>. Where do you keep them hidden?—F<small>R</small>. There.
>
> P<small>AN</small>. I suppose they're not all the same age; but what sort of figure do they have?—F<small>R</small>. Straight.
>
> P<small>AN</small>. Complexion like what?—F<small>R</small>. Lilies.
>
> P<small>AN</small>. Their hair?—F<small>R</small>. Blond.
>
> P<small>AN</small>. What color eyes?—F<small>R</small>. Dark.
>
> P<small>AN</small>. Their tits?—F<small>R</small>. Round.
>
> P<small>AN</small>. Their puss?—Dainty.
>
> P<small>AN</small>. Their eyebrows?—F<small>R</small>. Soft.
>
> P<small>AN</small>. Their charms?—F<small>R</small>. Ripe.
>
> P<small>AN</small>. Their glance?—F<small>R</small>. Free.
>
> P<small>AN</small>. What about their feet?—F<small>R</small>. Flat.
>
> P<small>AN</small>. Their heels?—F<small>R</small>. Short.
>
> P<small>AN</small>. What about their lower parts?—F<small>R</small>. Nice.
>
> P<small>AN</small>. And their arms?—F<small>R</small>. Long.
>
> P<small>AN</small>. What do they wear on their hands?—F<small>R</small>. Gloves.
>
> P<small>AN</small>. What kind of rings on their fingers?—F<small>R</small>. Gold.
>
> P<small>AN</small>. What do you use to dress them?—F<small>R</small>. Cloth.
>
> P<small>AN</small>. What kind of cloth do you dress them in?—F<small>R</small>. New.

PAN. What color is it?—FR. *Pers* [bluish].[4]

PAN. How about their headgear?—FR. Blue.

PAN. What sort of shoes?—FR. Brown.

PAN. All the aforesaid cloth is of what sort?—FR. Fine.

PAN. What about their shoes?—FR. Leather.

PAN. But how are they apt to be?—FR. Filthy.

PAN. Do they walk out in public in them that way?—FR. Fast.

PAN. Let's move on to the kitchen, I mean the wenches; and in no hurry let's run down the list in detail. What is there in the kitchen?—FR. Fire.

PAN. What keeps the fire going?—FR. Wood.

PAN. And how is that wood?—FR. Dry.

PAN. What trees do you take it from?—FR. Yew.

PAN. The kindling and the faggots?—FR. Alder.

PAN. What wood do you burn in the bedroom?—FR. Pine.

PAN. And what trees besides?—FR. Linden.

PAN. On the aforesaid girls, I'll go halves with you; how do you feed them?—FR. Well.

PAN. What do they eat?—FR. Bread.

PAN. What sort?—FR. Coarse.[5]

PAN. And what else?—FR. Meat.

PAN. But prepared how?—FR. Roast.

PAN. Don't they eat any sops?—FR. None.

PAN. And pastry?—FR. Lots.

PAN. I'm with them; don't they eat any fish?—FR. Yes.

PAN. How's that? And what else?—FR. Eggs.

PAN. And they like them how?—FR. Cooked.

PAN. I'm asking, cooked how?—FR. Hard.

PAN. Is that all their meal?—FR. No.

PAN. Why then, what else do they have?—FR. Beef.

PAN. And what else?—FR. Pork.

PAN. And what else?—FR. Goose.

PAN. What besides?—FR. Gander.

Pan. Also [item]?—Fr. Cock.

Pan. What do they have by way of seasoning?—Fr. Salt.

Pan. And for the choosy ones?—Fr. Must [New wine].

Pan. For the meal's last course?—Fr. Rice.

Pan. And what besides?—Fr. Milk.

Pan. And besides that?—Fr. Peas.

Pan. But what kind of peas do you mean?—Fr. Green.

Pan. What do you put with them?—Fr. Bacon.

Pan. And for fruits?—Fr. Good.

Pan. Served how?—Fr. Raw.

Pan. What more?—Fr. Nuts.

Pan. But how do they take their drink?—Fr. Neat.

Pan. What drink?—Fr. Wine.

Pan. Which kind?—Fr. White.

Pan. In winter?—Fr. Stiff.

Pan. In spring?—Fr. Straight.

Pan. In summer?—Fr. Cool.

Pan. In autumn and at harvest time?—Fr. Sweet.

"By my slut of a gown!"[6] exclaimed Frère Jean, "how big-bellied these Semiquavering bitches must get, and how they must get the trots,[7] seeing that they feed so well and copiously!"

"Wait till I finish," said Panurge.

Pan. What time is it when they go to bed?—Fr. Night.

Pan. And when do they get up?—Fr. Day.

"Here," said Panurge, "is the nicest little Semiquaver I've ridden[8] this year! Would to God and the blessed worthy virgin Saint Semiquaveress that he were First President[9] of the Paris Parlement! Goshamighty [Vertu goy], my friend, what an expediter of cases [quel expéditeur de causes], what an abridger of lawsuits, what a scanner of sacks, what a leafer through papers, what a summarizer of documents, he would be! Now then, let's get into the other components of living, and let's speak deliberately and dispassionately about our aforesaid sisters of charity."

Pan. What is their receptacle like?—Fr. Stout.

PAN. At the entrance?—FR. Cool.

PAN. In the depths?—FR. Hollow.

PAN. I mean what is it like inside?—FR. Warm.

PAN. What is there around the edges?—FR. Hair.

PAN. What sort?—FR. Russet.

PAN. And on the older ones?—FR. Gray.

PAN. The screwing of them, what is it like?—FR. Prompt.

PAN. The movement of their buttocks?—FR. Brisk.

PAN. Are they all wrigglers?—FR. Too much.

PAN. Your tools, how are they?—FR. Big.

PAN. On the outside, how shaped?—FR. Round.

PAN. The tip, of what color?—FR. Red [Bail].[10]

PAN. When they're done, how do they get?—FR. Still.

PAN. The genitals, how are they?—FR. Heavy.

PAN. And worn trussed up how?—FR. Close.

PAN. When it's all done, how do they get?—FR. Limp.

PAN. Now, by the oath you've taken, when you want to cohabit, how do you toss them?—FR. Down.

PAN. What do they say while tail-pushing?—FR. Nil.

PAN. Only they give you a real good time; meanwhile do they attend to the sweet play?—FR. True.

PAN. Do they get you children?—FR. None.

PAN. How do you lie together?—FR. Nude.

PAN. By the said oath you've taken, on a true count, how many times each day do you ordinarily do it?—FR. Six.

PAN. And at night?—FR. Ten.

"A plague on it!" said Frère Jean, "the lecher's too proud to go beyond sixteen; he's bashful."

PAN. Really, would you do all that many, Frère Jean? By God, he's a green leper. The others do the same?—FR. All.

PAN. Which of you all is the greatest gallant?—FR. Me.

PAN. Don't you ever fail to cope?—FR. Nope.

PAN. This is getting beyond me.[11] When you've emptied and exhausted your spermatic vessels the day before, can there be much left the next day?—Fr. More.

Pan. Unless I'm dreaming, they must have that Indian herb celebrated by Theophrastus.[12] But if by some legitimate blockage or otherwise, in this pleasure comes some dwindling of the member, how does that leave you feeling?—Fr. Bad.

Pan. Then what do the wenches do [or make]?—Fr. Noise.

Pan. And what if you stopped some day?—Fr. Worse.

Pan. Then what do you give them?—Fr. Junk [Trunc].

Pan. And then what do they give you?—Fr. Crap [Bren].

Pan. And what is your response?—Fr. Farts.

Pan. Sounding how?—Fr. Cracked.

Pan. How do you punish them?—Fr. Hard.

Pan. And draw what out of them?—Fr. Blood.

Pan. What does that make their color?—Fr. High.

Pan. Wouldn't anything make it better for you?—Fr. Paint.

Pan. And so you always remain how?—Fr. Feared.

Pan. Then what do they think you are?—Fr. Saints.

Pan. By the said swear-to-wood oath you took,[13] what's the time of year when you're most lax about doing it?—Fr. August.

Pan. In which are you spryest?—Fr. March.

Pan. And the rest of the year how are you doing it?—Fr. Blithe.

Then said Panurge, smiling: "So this is the world's poor Semiquaver?[14] Did you hear how firm, summary, and succinct he is in his answers? He replies only in monosyllables. I think he'd take three bites for one cherry."

" 'Odsbody," said Frère Jean, "he doesn't talk that way with his wenches; he's certainly polysyllabic in that. You talk about three bites for one cherry: By Saint Gray,[15] I'd swear that he would make only two bites of a shoulder of mutton, and one draft of one quart of wine. Just look and see how pooped out he is!"

"That's just the way it is with that lousy junkheap the monks!"[16] said Epistémon: "All the world over they're intractable on the subject of victuals, and then they go telling us they have nothing in this world but their life. What the devil do kings and princes have?"[17]

CHAPTER 28

How Epistémon dislikes the institution of Lent.

"**D**ID you notice," said Epistémon, "how that lousy wretch of a Semiquaver cited March to us as the month for lechery?"

"Yes," said Pantagruel, "and yet it falls in Lent, which was instituted to tame the flesh, mortify the sensual appetites, and restrain the Venerian furies."

"By this," said Epistémon, "you can judge the sense of that pope who first established it, and when that mangy drip of a Semiquaver professes to be never more befouled in lechery than in the season of Lent; also by the evident reasons set forth by all good learned doctors, affirming that in the entire course of the year no foods are eaten that excite a person more to lust than in that period: beans, peas, kidney beans, chickpeas, onions, walnuts, oysters, herrings, salt fish, garo, salads all made up of aphrodisiac herbs, such as rocket, garden cress, tarragon, watercress, water parsley, rampion, river cress, hops, figs, rice, grapes."

"You would be quite amazed," said Pantagruel, "if that good pope who instituted holy Lent, seeing that then was the season when the natural warmth comes out of the center of the body, where it had confined itself during the chills of winter, and spreads over the circumference of the members, as the sap does in trees, should have ordained these foods you have mentioned to assist in the multiplication of the human race. What has led me to think so is that in the baptismal record of Thouars[1] the number of children born in the months of October and November is greater than in any of the other ten months of the year, and all these, by counting back, were made, conceived, and engendered in Lent."

"I'm listening to what you're saying," said Frère Jean, "and taking no little pleasure in it; but the curate of Jambet[2] attributed this copious impregnation of women to the little booted preachers, the stooped shoul-dered little beggars, the little booted preachers, the little bedunged con-fessors, who, all through this time when they have the power, damn the lusty married men three fathoms beneath Lucifer's claws. In their terror the husbands stop bestriding their chambermaids and fall back on their wives. I have spoken."

"Interpret," said Epistémon, "the institution of Lent as your fancy bids; let each man enjoy his own view;[3] but its suppression, which seems to be

676

impending, will be opposed by all the doctors, I know. I've heard them say so. For without Lent their craft would be held in disdain, and they wouldn't earn anything, and no one would be sick. In Lent all illnesses are sown; that's the real nursery, the native seed-bed and dispenser of all ills. Still you are not considering that if Lent rots bodies it also drives souls insane. Then devils make their great efforts; hypocrites then come out of the woodwork;[4] bigots hold their great assizes, many sessions, stations, pardon-handouts, confessionals, flagellations, anathematizations. I don't mean for all that to infer that the Arimaspians[5] are in that respect any better than we are, but I speak to the purpose."

"Here now," said Panurge, "tailpushing and Semiquavering ballock what do you think of this? Isn't he a heretic?"—Fr. Quite.

Pan. Shouldn't he be burned?—Fr. Should.

Pan. And as soon a possible?—Fr. Right.

Pan. Without parboiling him?—Fr. Yes.

Pan. In what way then?—Fr. Live.

Pan. So that what follows in the end?—Fr. Death.

Pan. For he vexed you too much?—Fr. *Las!*

Pan. What did you take him to be?—Fr. Worse.

Pan. What would you want him to be?—Fr. Roast.

Pan. Others have been burned?—Fr. Lots.

Pan. Who were heretics?—Fr. Less.

Pan. Will you let any be redeemed?—Fr. Nix [Grain].

Pan. Must they all be burned?—Fr. Must.

"I don't know what pleasure," said Epistémon, "you have in reasoning with this measly ragbag of a monk; but if you were not known to me otherwise, you'd give me a none too honorable opinion of you in my understanding."

"Let's go, in God's name," said Panurge; "I'd be tempted to take him along to Gargantua, I like him so; when I'm married, he'd serve my wife as a fool."[6]

"Or maybe rather as a tool," said Epistémon, "by a change of just one letter."

"Now," said Frère Jean, "you've got your tip, poor Panurge; you'll never get out of this without being a cuckold up to your ass."[7]

CHAPTER 29

How we visited the land of Satin.

JOYFUL for having seen the religious order of the Semiquaver Friars, we
sailed for two days; on the third our captain sighted a beautiful island
delightful above all others, which was called the island of Frieze, for the
roads were made of frieze. On it was the land of Satin,[1] so renowned
among the court pages, whose trees and plants never lost a flower or
leaves and were of damask and figured velvet. The animals and birds were
of tapestry.

There we saw many animals, birds, and trees, just like what we have
over here, in size, amplitude, and color, except that they ate nothing and
did not sing at all, nor did they ever bite, as ours do. Many also we saw
there that we had not seen; among others we saw various elephants in
various postures; above all I noticed the six males and six females shown
by their trainer in the theater on Rome in the time of Germanicus,
nephew of Emperor Tiberius;[2] elephants that were learned, musicians,
philosophers, dancers, pavane dancers, galliard dancers; and they would sit
at table in fine order and composure eating and drinking in silence like
fine fathers [friars] at the refectory.

They have a muzzle two cubits long, and we call it a proboscis, with
which they draw water to drink, pick up palms, plums, all kinds of eats,
defend themselves and attack, as with a hand; and in combat they toss
men high in the air and make them split and die laughing as they fall.
They have joints and articulations in their legs; those who have written to
the contrary have never seen any except in paintings. Between their teeth
they have two great horns; so Juva called them,[3] and Pausanias says they
were horns, not teeth;[4] Philostratus maintains that they were teeth, not
horns;[5] it's all one to me, as long as you understand that they were real
ivory, and three or four cubits long, and they were on the upper, not the
lower jaw. If you believe those who say the contrary, you'll be wrong,
especially if it should be Aelian,[6] a tiercel [expert] in lying. There and not
elsewhere Pliny had seen some walking and dancing with jingles on tight-
ropes, also passing over the tables in the midst of a banquet without
bothering the drinkers as they drank.[7]

There I saw a rhinoceros just like the one Hans Clerberg had once
shown me and not very different from a wild boar I had once seen in

Limoges;[8] except that he had a horn on his muzzle a cubit long and pointed, with which he dared to take on the elephant in combat, and, sticking him in the underbelly (which is the softest and most vulnerable part of the elephant), would lay him low upon the ground.

There I saw thirty-two unicorns; that is a marvelously fierce beast,[9] entirely like a handsome horse, except that it had a head like a stag, feet like an elephant, a tail like a wild boar, and on its forehead a sharp black horn six or seven feet long, which ordinarily hangs down like the crest of a turkey cock; this, when it [the unicorn] wants to fight or otherwise help himself with it, it raises up straight and stiff. One of them I saw, accompanied by divers wild animals, clean out a spring with its horn. At that point Panurge said to me that his curtal was like this unicorn, not at all in length, but in ability and cleanliness; for just as she [the unicorn] would purify the water of ponds and springs of any filth or venom that was in them, and these divers animals would come and drink after her in perfect safety, so after him [the curtal], one could paddle safely with no danger of cankers, pox, hotpiss, or bubonic pimples, or other such petty favors; for if there were any harm in that stinking hole, he would clean the whole thing out with his sinewy horn [his phallus].

"When you're married," said Frère Jean, "we'll try this out on your wife. For the love of God, so be it, since you're giving us most salubrious instruction about it."

"Yes indeed," said Panurge, "and then suddenly comes that nice little pull in the stomach that brings you close to God, made up of twenty-two dagger stabs Caesarine style."[10]

"Better," said Frère Jean, "would be a mug of some good cool wine."

There I saw the golden fleece conquered by Jason. Those who have said it was not fleece but a golden apple, because *mela* means both "apple" and "sheep" had not inspected the Land of Satin at all well.

There I saw a chameleon such as Aristotle describes it and as I had once been shown one by Charles Marais,[11] eminent physician in the city of Lyon on the Rhône; and it lived on nothing but air, just as the other one did.

There I saw three Hydras, like those I had seen elsewhere. They are serpents that each have seven different heads.

There I saw fourteen Phoenixes. I had read in various authors that there was only one in the whole world for one age; but in my puny judgment, those who have written about them have never seen any unless in Tapestryland,[12] even Lactantius Firmianus.[13]

There I saw the hide of Apuleius's golden ass.[14]

There I saw three hundred and nine pelicans and six thousand and sixteen Seleucid birds,[15] marching in formation and devouring the grass-hoppers amid the wheat; some Cynamolges, Agathiles, Caprimulges, Thynnuncules, Crotonotaries (of course I mean Onocrotaries, or rather I should say Onocrotals [pelicans] with their great gullet), some Stym-phalids, Harpies, Panthers, Dorades, Cemades, Cynocephali [baboons], Satyrs, Cartasonnes [unicorns], Tarands, Ure [aurochs], Monopes [buffa-loes], Pephages, Cepes, Neades, Steres, Cercopitheci, Bisons, Musimones [Sardinian sheep], Byturi, Ophyri, Stryges, Griffons.

There I saw Mid-Lent on horseback (Mid-August and Mid-March were holding his stirrups for him), Werewolves, Centaurs, Tigers, Leo-pards, Hyenas, Cameleopardals [giraffes], Oryxes [unicorns].

There I saw a Remora, a tiny fish, called Echineis by the Greeks, next to a great ship, which did not move although it was at full sail in the open sea; I think it was that of the tyrant Periander, which such a little fish was stopping against the wind. And in this Satinland, not elsewhere, Mutianus had seen it.[16] Frère Jean told us that amid the Courts of Parlement two kinds of fish used to reign, which made the bodies rot and the souls go mad in all plaintiffs, nobles, commoners, poor, rich, great, little. The first kind were April fish [*poissons d'avril,* "April fools"], that's mackerel;[17] the second are venomous remoras; that's an eternity of litigation with no end in judgment.

There I saw Sphinxes, Raphes [jackals], Lynxes Cephes, which have forefeet like hands and [hind] feet like a man's; Crocute, Eales, which are as big as hippopotami, have tails like elephants, jaws like wild boars, horns mobile as are asses ears. Cucrocutes, very light beasts the size of Mirebalais donkeys, have their neck, tail, and crest like a lion, legs like a stag, jaws split wide to the ears; and they have no teeth but one upper and one lower; they speak with a human voice, but they never said a word then.

You say no one has ever seen a saker's nest;[18] truly, I saw eleven of them, and do you take good note of it.

There I saw some left-handed halberds;[19] never had I seen any any-where else.

There I saw some Manticores, very strange beasts; they have a body like a lion, red fur, face and ears like a man; three rows of teeth, fitting in with each other as if you interlaced the fingers of both hands with each other; in their tail they have a spur with which they sting as scorpions do; and they have a very melodious voice.

There I saw Catoblepes, wild beasts with very small bodies; but their heads are disproportionately large; they can hardly lift them off the ground; they have eyes so venomous that anyone who sees them dies instantly like someone who should see a basilisk.

There I saw two-backed beasts,[20] which seemed to me wonderfully joyous and copious in tail-pushing, even more than the wagtail [mocitelle], with eternal movement of the rumps.

There I saw crayfish that gave milk—never had I seen any anywhere else—that were marching in very good order, and it was very good to see them.

CHAPTER 30

How in the land of Satin we saw Hearsay
running a school for witnesses.[1]

Pushing on a little farther into the land of tapestry, we saw the Mediterranean Sea opened up and uncovered down to its deepest abysses, even as in the Persian Gulf the Red Sea opened up to make a roadway for the Jews coming out of Egypt. There I recognized Triton sounding his great shell horn, Glaucus, Proteus, Nereus, and myriad other gods and monsters of the sea. We also saw an infinite number of fish of various kinds, dancing, flying, curveting, eating, breathing, screwing, hunting, skirmishing, laying ambushes, arranging truces, bargaining, swearing, disporting.

In a nook nearby I saw Aristotle holding a lantern in a posture like that in which they paint the hermit next to Saint Christopher,[2] closely watching, considering, putting it all down in writing. Behind him, like sergeants' witnesses, were many other philosophers: Appian, Heliodorus, Athenaeus, Porphyrius, Pancrates the Arcadian, Numenius Posidonius, Ovid, Oppian, Olympius, Seleucus, Leonides, Agathocles, Theophrastus, Damostratus, Mutianus, Nymphodorus, Aelian, also five hundred idle folk, as was Chrysippus, or Aristarchus of Sola, who stayed fifty-eight years contemplating the state of the bees, without doing anything else. Among these I noticed Pierre Gilles,[3] who, holding a urinal in his hand, was deeply contemplating the urine of these fine fish.

After considering this land of Satin at length, Pantagruel said: "I've feasted my eyes for a long time, but I can't get filled up on anything; my stomach is growling mad with terrible hunger!"

"Let's eat," said I, "let's eat, and have a taste of these anacampserotes[4] that are hanging up above there. Fie, that's nothing worth eating."

So I took a few myrobolans that were hanging from a bit of tapestry; but I couldn't chew them or swallow them, and to taste them you would rightly have said they were just twisted silk and had no savor at all. You'd think Heliogabalus had taken there, like a transcript of a bull, his way of feasting those he had forced to fast long, promising them at the end of it a sumptuous, abundant imperial banquet; then he would feed them foods of wax, marble, and pottery, in figured paintings and tablecloths.[5]

So, looking over the said country to see if we could find any victuals, we heard a varied strident noise, as if it were women washing laundry, or mill clappers on the Bazacle near Toulouse. With no further delay we made our way to the place it came from, and there saw a little old man, hunchbacked, misshapen, and monstrous; his name was Hearsay. His throat was split to the ears, and he had in his throat seven tongues, and the tongue each split into seven parts; whatever the subject was, all seven at the same time spoke many different things in diverse languages; he also had, around his head and the rest of his body, as many ears as Argus once had eyes; for the rest he was blind, and paralyzed in his legs.

Around him I spotted some putting on a good face, among whom one was for the time holding a world map, and expounding it to them summarily in little aphorisms, and in short order they were becoming learned clerics and talking elegantly from a good memory about prodigious things, to know the hundredth part of which one man's lifetime would not suffice: the Pyramids, the Nile, Babylon, the Troglodytes, the Hymantopodes, the Blemmies, the Pygmies, the Cannibals, the Hyperborean Mountains, the Aegipans, all the devils, and all by Hearsay [Ouy-dire].

There I saw, I believe, Herodotus, Pliny, Solinus,[6] Berosus, Philostratus, Mela, Strabo and many other ancients, plus Albert the Great Jacobin,[7] Peter Martyr, Pope Pius the Second, Volterrano, Paolo Giovio, that valiant man, Jacques Cartier, Hayton the Armenian, Marco Polo the Venetian, Lodovico the Roman, Pedro Alvarez Cabal, and I know not how many other modern historians, hiding behind a piece of tapestry and covertly writing fine works, and all by Hearsay.

Behind a piece of velvet embroidered with mint-leaves, near Hearsay, I saw a large number of people from Perche and around Le Mans, good students, rather young; and on asking in what Faculty they were studying, we learned that from their youth up they were learning to be witnesses, and in this craft profiting so well that on leaving this place and going back to their province, they made a decent living by the trade of witness-bearing, bearing their witness about all things for those who would give them the most per day, and all by Hearsay. Say what you will about them, they gave us some of their slices of bread, and we enjoyed a full and pleasant drink at their barrels. Then they cordially advised us that we should be sparing of the truth, as far as we should find this possible, if we wanted to get on in the court of the great lords.

CHAPTER 31

How we came in sight of Lanternland.[1]

Poorly treated and poorly fed in the land of Satin, we sailed on for three days; on the fourth, by good fortune, we drew near Lanternland. As we approach, we see upon the sea certain little hovering flames; for my part I thought they were not lanterns but fish, which with their flaming tongues struck fire out of the sea, or else Lampyrides (you call them glow-worms), shining as they do in my country in the evening, when barley comes to its ripeness. But the captain informed us that they were lanterns of the watch, who were reconnoitering around the suburbs and providing an escort for some foreign lanterns who, as good Cordeliers or Jacobins, were going there to attend the provincial chapter.[2] Although we feared that this might herald a tempest,[3] he assured us that they were indeed here for that purpose.

CHAPTER 32

How we disembarked at the port of the Lichnobians and entered Lanternland.

At that moment we entered the port of Lanternland. On a high tower Pantagruel recognized the lantern of La Rochelle, which gave us good light. We also saw the lantern of Pharos, of Nauplion, and of the acropolis of Athens, sacred to Pallas. Near the port is a little village inhabited by the Lichnobians,[1] who are people living on lanterns (as in our countries the lay brothers live off nuns), decent studious folk. Demosthenes had once lanterned[2] there. From this place to the palace we were guided by three lighthouses [Obéliscolychnies], military guards of the harbor, with high bonnets like Albanians, to whom we expounded the causes of our trip, and our intention, which was to obtain there from the queen of Lanternland a lantern to light us and guide us through the trip we were taking toward the oracle of the Bottle. This they promised to do, and gladly, adding that we had arrived there at a good moment, and that we would have a good choice of lanterns then, since they were holding their provincial chapter meeting.

Arriving at the royal palace, we were presented by two lanterns, to wit, the lantern of Aristophanes and the lantern of Cleanthes, to the queen, to whom Panurge expounded briefly in the Lanternese language the causes of our trip. And we had a good welcome from her and a command to attend her supper so as to choose more easily the one we would like for a guide. This pleased us very much, and we were not negligent to note and consider everything both in their gestures, dress, and bearing, and also in the ordering of the service.

The queen was dressed in virgin crystal, with damascene work spangled with great diamonds. The lanterns of the blood were dressed, some with paste jewelry, some with rock crystal; the rest were dressed in horn, in paper, and in oilcloth.[3] The cressets likewise according to the states of antiquity of their houses. Only I noticed one of earthenware, like a pot, among the most gorgeous; amazed at this, I came to understand that it was the lantern of Epictetus, for which they had turned down three thousand drachmas.

I diligently considered the style and arrangement of Martial's polymix lantern,[4] and even more the Eicosimix,[5] long ago consecrated by Canopa,

684

daughter of Tisias. I took very good note of the pensile lantern, taken from the temple of Apollo Palatine in Thebes and later transported to Cyme in Aeolia by Alexander the Conqueror. I noted one other one, remarkable because of a handsome tuft of crimson silk it had on its head. And I was told it was Bartolus, lantern of the law. I likewise noted two other goodly ones because of the two enema bulbs they wore at the belt, and I was told that one was the great, the other the little, luminary of the apothecaries.[6]

When suppertime came, the queen took her seat in the head place, and subsequently the others in order of their rank and dignity. For the first course everyone was served great molded candles except the queen, who was served a great torch of white wax, still flaming, a bit red at the tip; the lanterns of the blood were also treated differently from the others, as was the provincial lantern of Mirebalais,[7] which was served with a walnut oil candle adorned with coats of arms; and Lord knows what light they gave out after that with their wicks. Here make an exception of a number of young lanterns belonging to the retinue of a great lantern. These did not shine like the others, but seemed to me to show lustful colors.

After supper we retired to rest. The next morning the queen had us choose a lantern, one of the most notable, to guide us. And thus we took our leave.

CHAPTER 33

How we reached the oracle of the Bottle.

Wｉｔｈ our noble lantern guiding us, lighting and directing us to our heart's content, we at last found the oracle of the Bottle. As soon as Panurge landed, he danced with delight and said to Pantagruel:

"Today we are where we have wished ourselves for so long. This is the place we have been seeking with such toil and labor."

Then he made a compliment to our lantern who desired us to be of good cheer and not to be daunted or dismayed by what even we might chance to see.

We had to pass through a great vineyard formed of all kinds of wines, such as Falernian, Malmsey, Muscadine, Tabbia, Beaune, Mirevaux, Orléans, Picardent, Arbois, Coussy, Anjou, Graves, Corsica, Verron, Nérac, and others. The vineyard was planted long ago by Bacchus,[1] with such a benediction that in every season it bore leaves, flowers, and fruits, like the orange trees of San Remo. Our magnificent lantern ordered us to eat three grapes per man, put some vine leaves in our shoes, and take a green branch in our left hand. At the end of the vineyard we passed under an ancient arch on which was very neatly insculpted the memento of a drinker, to wit, in one place, a long line of flagons, leather gourds, bottles, phials, barrels, firkins, pots, quart jugs, ancient amphoras, all hanging from a shady trellis; in another, a great quantity of garlic cloves, onions, shallots, hams, caviar, cheese crackers, smoked ox tongues, old cheeses, and that kind of snacks; and at the same time all was very artfully interwoven and packed together with vines. In another a hundred kinds of glasses, such as glasses on foot and glasses on horseback, cups, false cups, ewers, tumblers, goblets, and such Bacchic artillery as that. On the face of the arch, under the zoophore,[2] were inscribed these two verses:

> When you pass this postern, pray
> Let a lantern guide your way.[3]

"For that," said Pantagruel, "we have provided. For in the whole region of Lanternland there is not one lantern better and more divine than ours."

This archway led into a nice spacious alley all made up of vine stocks adorned with grapes of five hundred different colors, and five hundred different forms not natural but fashioned thus by agricultural artifice, yellow, blue, swarthy, azured, white, black, green, violet, striped, speckled, varicolored, long, round, triangular, ballock-shaped, bearded, round-headed, grassy. The end thereof was closed by three ancient ivies, most versant, and all laden with bayberries. There our illustrious lantern ordered each of us to make himself an Albanian hat[4] out of this ivy and cover our head with it. This was done without delay. "Under this trellis," said Pantagruel then, "Jupiter's pontiff would not have passed."

"The reason," said our most brilliant lantern, "was a mystical one. For in passing there he would have had the wine, that's the grapes, over his head, and he would seem as if mastered and dominated by wine; this is to signify that pontiffs, and all persons who devote and dedicate themselves to contemplation of divine things, must keep their spirits in tranquility outside of any perturbation of sense, which is manifested more clearly in drunkenness than in any other passion, whatever it be.

"Likewise you, after going under this arch, would not be received into the Temple unless Bacbuc, the noble Pontiff saw your shoes full of vine leaves, which shows an action wholly and diametrically opposite to the first, clear evidence that by you wine is held in disdain, and by you trodden down and subjugated."

"I'm no cleric," said Frère Jean, "for which I'm sorry; but I find in my breviary that in Revelation [12.1] was seen, as a wonder, a woman who had the moon beneath her feet; that, as Bigot has expounded it to me, was to signify that she was not of the same race or nature as the others who had the moon in their head, and consequently always a lunatic brain; that leads me to believe what you're saying, Madam Lantern my dear [Madame, Lanterne ma mie]."

CHAPTER 34

How we went underground
to enter the temple of the Bottle,
and how Chinon is the first city in the world.[1]

Thus we went down underground through a little archway encrusted with plaster, which on the outside showed in a crude painting a dance of women and satyrs in company with old Silenus, laughing, on his donkey.[2] At that point I said to Pantagruel: "This entry recalls to my mind the Painted Cellar in the first city in the world: for there are similar paintings, and of the same freshness as these."

"Where," said Pantagruel, "is this first city you're speaking of?"

"Chinon," said I, "or Caynon, in Touraine."

"I know," said Pantagruel, "where Chinon is, and your Painted Cellar too; I've drunk many a glass of cool wine there, and I have no doubt that Chinon is an ancient city; its blazon attests it, in which it is said:

Chinon, twice, nay thrice my town,
Numbers small, but great renown,

687

Set on rock since long ago,
Woods above, Vienne below.[3]

"But how would it be the first city in the world? Where do you find
that written? What grounds do you have for that conjecture?"

"I find," said I, "in the Holy Scripture that Cain was the first man to
build cities. So it is likely that he named the first one Caynon, with his
name, as since, in imitation of him, have all the other founders and
establishers of cities imposed their names on them: Athene (that's
Minerva in Greek) on Athens, Alexander on Alexandria; Constantine, on
Constantinople; Pompey, on Pompeyopolis in Cilicia; Hadrian, on
Adrianople; Canaan, on the Canaanites; Sheba, on the Shebans; Assur, on
the Assyrians; Ptolemais, Caesare, Tiberium, Herodium in Judaea."

We were engaged in this small talk when there came out of the great
Flask (our lantern called him a *phlosque*), preceptor of the divine Bottle,
accompanied by the templeguard; and they were all French Bottle-eers.
This man, seeing that we were all Thyrsigers [thyrsis-bearers], as I have
said, and crowned with ivy, also recognizing our lantern, had us enter in
security, and ordered that we be taken straight to Princess Bacbuc, lady of
honor of the Bottle and pontiff of all its mysteries. This was done.

CHAPTER 35

How we went down the tetradic[1] *steps,*
and of Panurge's fear.

Then we went down a marble staircase underground; a landing was
there; turning to the left, we went down two others, and there was a
similar landing; then three to one side, and four more likewise. There
Panurge asked: "Is it here?" "How many steps," said our magnificent
lantern, "have you counted?"

"One," replied Pantagruel, "two, three, four."

"How many is that?" she asked.

"Ten," answered Pantagruel.

"By that same Pythagorean tetrad," said she, "multiply our resultant."

"That," said Pantagruel, "is ten, twenty, thirty, forty,"

"What total does that make?" said she.

"One hundred," replied Pantagruel.

"Add the first cube," said she, "that's eight; at the end of that fated number we'll find the temple door. And here take prudent note that this is the true psychogony [generation of the soul] of Plato, so celebrated by the Academics and so little understood: half of it is composed of the first two plain numbers, two squares, and two cubes."[2]

Going down those numerous flights underground, we needed first of all our legs, for without them we could have got down only by rolling, like barrels into a low cellar; secondly, our excellent lantern; for in this descent no other light appeared to us, any more than if we had been in Saint Patrick's Hole[3] in Hibernia or the cave of Trophonius on Boeotia.[4]

After going down about seventy-eight flights, Panurge, addressing our shining lantern, exclaimed: "Wondrous lady, with a contrite heart I beg of you, let's turn back! 'Sdeath, I'm dying of sheer fright. I consent never to marry; you've gone to much trouble and fatigue for me; God will recompense you in His great recompensery;[5] I'll be grateful to you for it when I get out of this Troglodyte's cave. For mercy's sake let's go back. I'm much afraid that this is Taenarus,[6] which is on the way down into Hell, and it seems to me I hear Cerberus barking. Listen: that's him, or I'm hearing things.[7] I'm in no way a devotee of his, for there's no toothache so bad as when the dogs have us by the legs. If this is the cave of Trophonius here, the lemurs and goblins will eat us alive, as long ago they ate one of Demetrius's halberdiers, for lack of sops. Are you there, Frère Jean? I beg you, my little pot belly, stay close to me, I'm dying of fear. Do you have your cutlass? I still have no weapons at all, offensive or defensive. Let's go back."

"I'm here," said Frère Jean, "have no fear, I have you by the collar, eighteen devils won't take you out of my hands, even though you're without weapons. Arms never failed a man who joined a stout heart to a strong arm; rather will arms rain down from Heaven, as when in the fields of Crau near the Marian Canal in Provence stones once rained down (they are still there) to help Hercules when he had nothing else to fight with in combat against the sons of Neptune.[8] But what of that? Are we going down into the Limbo for tiny infants (by God, they'll shit over us all!), or else into Hell with all the devils? 'Odsbody, I'll really lead them a merry dance now that I have vine leaves in my shoes! O how fierce I'll fight! Where is it? Where are they? All I'm afraid of is their horns. But the two horns that Panurge will wear when married will protect me from them completely. In a prophetic spirit. I can see him now, another Acteon, hornified, horny, horned, horninass [cornan, cornu, cornancul]."

"Take care, frater," said Panurge, "till the time when they let monks marry, that you don't wed a quartan fever. But if you do, may I never return safe and sound from this hypogee if I don't ram her for you, even if only to make you a cornipotent corniger [cornigère, cornipétant]; apart from that I think the quartan fever is a pretty nasty bitch. I remember that Clutchpuss wanted to give her to you to be your wife, but you called him a heretic."

Here our talk was interrupted by our splendid lantern, pointing out to us that there was the place where we should keep a reverent silence, by both suppression of words and taciturnity of tongues; for the rest, she answered us categorically that we should have no concern whatever about possibly going back without having the word of the Bottle, once we had our shoes lined with vine leaves.

"Then let's pass on," said Panurge, "and hurl ourselves head down right through all the devils. You can't die more than once. I *was* saving up my life for some battle! I have that much courage and then some; true, my heart's atremble, but that's from the cold and the odors in this cavern. It's not from fear, no, nor fever. Up an' at 'em, up an' at 'em. Let's pass on, push on, piss on. Just call me William the Fearless."[9]

CHAPTER 36

*How the doors of the temple
opened of themselves.*[1]

At the bottom of the stairs we came to a portal of fine jasper, all built and wrought in Doric fashion and form, on the face of which was written in Ionic letters of very pure gold this saying: ἐν οἴνῳ ἀλήθεια that is to say *en vin vérité* [in wine (is) truth].[2] The two doors were of a brass like the Corinthian, massive, charmingly wrought with raised enamel vine scrolls, as the sculpture required, and they were joined together and closed evenly in their mortise, without a lock or padlock, with no linkage whatever; only there hung there an Indian lodestone [un diamant Indique] the size of an Egyptian bead set at two points in refined gold, hexagonal in shape, and in straight lines; on each side toward our wall hung a clove of garlic.

At that point our noble lantern told us that we were to consider her excuse legitimate if she did not attempt to guide us any further: we had only to obey the instructions of the noble Pontiff Bacbuc, for she herself was not allowed to go in, for certain reasons that it is better not to expose, but to keep from persons living a mortal life. But she ordered us in any event, to keep our minds alert in all circumstances, to have no fear or fright, and to put our trust in her for our return. Then she pulled the lodestone that hung where the two doors joined, threw it to the right into a silver box expressly arranged for this; she also pulled from the hinge of each door a crimson silk cord a fathom and a half long, on which the garlic hung, attached it to the gold buckles hanging on the sides expressly for this purpose, and withdrew.

Immediately both doors, without anyone's touching them, opened of themselves, and as they opened made not a strident noise, not a horrible shudder, as rough heavy brass doors usually do, but a sweet gracious murmur, resounding through the temple vault, the cause of which Pantagruel promptly grasped, as he saw beneath the outer end of each door a little cylindrical roller that met the door above the hinge end, and, when the door swung back against the wall, pivoted on a hard piece of stone, porphyry, very smooth, and also polished by its rubbing, and made that sweet harmonious murmur.

I was marveling how the two doors, each by itself, with no pressure from anyone, were thus opened. To understand this wonder, after we had all come inside, I cast my eyes between the doors and the wall, suspecting that our amiable lantern had placed between their edges the herb Aethiopis,[3] by means of which all closed doors can be opened; but I perceived that the part by which both doors closed into the inside mortise was a plate of fine steel, set into the Corinthian brass.

I saw besides two plates of Indian lodestone half a palm wide and thick, sky blue in color, well smoothed and polished; the whole thickness thereof was set into the wall at the place where the doors, wide open, had only the wall to stop their opening.

So by the violent tug of the lodestone, the steel plates, by an admirable occult plan of nature, were subjugated to this movement; consequently, the doors were gradually pulled out and drawn there, however, not always, but only when the aforesaid lodestone was removed; for by its placement near by, the steel was released from its natural submission to it.

The two cloves of garlic too were removed and discarded, which our joyous lantern had drawn out and hung by the crimson cord, because it deadens the magnet and strips it of its power to attract.

On one of the aforesaid squares, to the right, was exquisitely carved in antique Latin letters this Senecan iambic verse:

Ducunt volentem fata, nolentem trahunt.[4]

[Fate leads the willing, drags those who resist.]

On the other I see on the left in capital letters this saying, elegantly engraved:

ALL THINGS MOVE TO THEIR END.[5]

[TOUTES CHOSES SE MEUVENT A LEUR FIN.]

CHAPTER 37

How the temple was paved
with an admirable mosaic.[1]

After reading these inscriptions, I cast my eyes about to contemplate the magnificent temple and was considering the incredible conjunction of the pavement, to which no other work can in reason be compared that is or has been under the firmament, not even that of the temple of Fortune in Praeneste in Sulla's time, or the pavement the Greeks called Asserotum, which Sosistratus made in Pergamum. For it was in marquetry in the form of little squares, all of fine polished stones, each in its natural color; one of red jasper, pleasingly colored with diverse spots; another, with ophite, a mottled rock, [usually a green marble]; another with porphyry; another with lycophthalamy [or licoptalmy, a dotted red, white, speckled precious stone mentioned by Pliny, then Colonna]; another with agate, with confused wavy streaks without order, milky in color; another with very precious chalcedony; another, with green jasper, with certain red and yellow veins; and they were split up into their situations by a diagonal line.

Over the portico,[2] the structure of the pavement was a marquetry of little stones brought together, each in its native color, forming the design of the figures, over the aforesaid pavement someone had strewn about, serving to make up the drawing of the figures; and it was as if someone had strewn about a bunch of vine leaves without any too careful planning. For in one place it seemed to be strewn lavishly; in another, less so.

And this foliage was striking in every place, but there stood out especially, in a dim light, some snails crawling over the grapes; in another, little lizards running through the vine leaves; in another appeared grapes half ripe and grapes fully ripe, composed and fashioned by the builder with such art and ingenuity that they could have deceived the starlings and other little birds as easily as did the painting by Zeuxis of Heraclea;[3] however that may be, they certainly fooled us; for in the place where the builder had strewn the vine leaves very thick, we, fearing to hurt our feet, went stepping high with long high strides, as one does in passing over some uneven stony place. Later I turned my gaze to contemplate the temple vault and walls, which, with incredible elegance, were all encrusted with mosaic work in marble and porphyry from one end to the other, on which, beginning on the left of the entry, was represented, with incredible elegance, the battle that good old Bacchus won against the Indians, in the manner that follows.

CHAPTER 38

*How in the temple's mosaic work
was represented the battle that Bacchus won
against the Indians.*[1]

At the start there figured various towns, villages, castles, fortresses, fields, and forests, all in flames and fire. Figured also were some frenzied dissolute women, madly tearing to pieces calves, sheep, and lambs, and feeding on their flesh. There it conveyed to us how Bacchus in coming into India put everything to fire and the sword.

This notwithstanding, he was so scorned by the Indians that they did not deign to come out to encounter him, since they had sure information from their spies that in his host there were no warriors, but a little old fellow, effeminate and always drunk, accompanied by some young rustics in the buff, always dancing and leaping, with tails and horns like those of young goats, and a large number of drunken women. That is why they resolved to let them pass on through without offering armed resistance; as if it would be to their shame, dishonor, and ignominy, not to their glory, honor, and prowess, to win a victory over such people.

Thanks to this disdain, Bacchus kept gaining territory and setting on fire, because fire and lightning are Bacchus's paternal weapons, and before he was born he was saluted with lightning by Jupiter (his mother Semele and his maternal house were burned and destroyed by fire), and likewise by blood, for by his nature he makes some in peacetime and draws some in time of war. Evidence of this is the fields of the island of Samos called Panaima, that is to say all bloody, on which Bacchus caught the Amazons fleeing from the land of the Ephesians and put them all to death by phlebotomy,[2] so that the said field was all steeped and covered with blood. From which henceforth you will be able to understand, better than Aristotle explained it in his *Problems* [36.2], why they used to say of old as a common proverb: "In time of war do not eat or plant mint." The reason is this: that in wartime blows are ordinarily dealt out without consideration; so when a man is wounded, if that day he has handled or eaten mint, it is impossible, or at least difficult, to stanch the blood.

Next was figured in the aforesaid marquetry how Bacchus marched into battle, on a magnificent chariot drawn by three pairs of young leo-pards harnessed together; his face was that of a young child, as a teaching that all good drinkers never grow old, pink as a cherub's without a single hair of a beard on his chin; and on his head he wore pointed horns, and above them a beautiful crown made up of grapes and vine leaves, with a miter of crimson red; and he was shod with gilded buskins.

In his company there was not one single man; all his guards and his forces were made up of Bassarids, Evantes, Euhyades, Edonides, Trietherides, Ogaygias, Mimallones, Maenads, Thyades, and Bacchides,[3] wild women, frenzied, mad, girt with dragons and live snakes instead of girdles, their hair flying in the air, with headbands of vine leaves, dressed in skins of stags and goats, bearing in their hands little axes, thyrses, tridents, and halberds with ends like pinecones, and certain little light bucklers that rang noisily when touched however lightly, which they used when necessary as tambourines and drums. The number of these was seventy-nine thousand two hundred and twenty-seven.

The vanguard was led by Dilenus, a man in whom his confidence was total, whose prowess and great-hearted courage he had come to know in the past in many places. He was a tremulous little old man, bowed, fat, gorbellied; and he had long straight ears, a pointed aquiline nose, and big unkempt eyebrows. He was mounted on a ballocky donkey; he held in his fist a staff to lean on, also to fight with gallantly, if by chance he had to get off on foot, and he was dressed in a woman's yellow robe. His company was of young field hands, horned as goats and cruel as lions, all naked, always singing and dancing the cordax.[4] They were called Tityri[5] and Satyrs. Their number was eighty-five thousand a hundred and thirty-three.[6]

Pan led the vanguard, a horrific monstrous man. For in the lower parts of the body he was like a billygoat, his thighs were hairy; he wore horns on his head pointing straight up against Heaven. His face was red and inflamed, and his beard very long, a daring man, courageous, adventurous, easily roused to anger. In his left hand he carried a flute, in his right a crooked stick; his troops likewise consisted of Satyrs, Hemipans, Aegipans, Sylvans, Fauns, Lemurs, Sprites, Goblins, and Hobgoblins, in the number of seventy-eight thousand a hundred and fourteen. The common battle cry for all was the word: *Evohé.*

CHAPTER 39

*How in the mosaic was pictured the clash and assault
of good old Bacchus against the Indians.*[1]

THE next scene portrayed the clash and assault made by good old
Bacchus against the Indians. In that one I observed that Silenus, leader of
the vanguard, was sweating profusely[2] and spurring on his donkey; the
donkey likewise had his jaws open horribly wide, snorted, laid about him
with his heels, bounced around, in a frightful fashion, as if he had a gadfly
in his ass.

The satyrs, captains, drill sergeants, squadron leaders, corporals with
cornets sounding the war chants, made frantic rounds about the army
with goats' capers, jumps, farts, heel kicking, giving the comrades courage
to fight with valor. Everyone in the picture kept crying *Evohé*. The
Maenads charged first on the Indians with horrible cries and frightful
sounds from their drums and bucklers; the entire heaven resounded
with them, as the mosaic showed—this so that you may no longer so
admire the art of Apelles, Aristides of Thebes,[3] and others, who have
painted thunderbolts, lightning strokes, lightning, winds, words, customs,
and minds.

Next was the host of the Indians when warned that Bacchus was laying
waste their country. On the front line were the elephants, laden with
towers, with warriors in infinite number; but the whole army was routed
and fleeing back against them, and upon them the elephants turned and
walked to escape the horrible tumult of the Bacchants and the panic
terror that had robbed them of their sense. There you would have seen
Silenus furiously spurring his donkey and laying about him with his stick
in the old-style sword-play [right and left], his donkey prancing after the
elephants with jaws agape, as if he was braying, and giving a martial bray
with the same vigor as when of old he waked the Nymph Lotis[4] right in
the Bacchanals when Priapus, full of Priapism, tried to Priapize her in her
sleep without asking her, sounded the assault.

There you would have seen Pan hopping about the Maenads on his
crooked legs, and with his rustic flute exciting them to fight valiantly.
There you would have seen a young satyr, afterward, bringing in as
prisoners seventeen kings; a Bacchant, with her snakes, pulling in forty-

two captains; a little faun bearing twelve ensigns taken from the enemy; and that good fellow Bacchus going about on his chariot in safety around the field, laughing, chortling, and drinking to everyone's health. Finally in mosaic was portrayed the trophy of the victory and triumph of good old Bacchus. His triumphal chariot was all covered with ivy taken up and gathered on Mount Meros,[5] and this for the rarity (which raises the price of all things), expressly in India, of those plants.

In this later on Alexander the Great imitated him in his Indian triumph. And the chariot was drawn by elephants harnessed together. In this later Pompey the Great imitated him in Rome in his African triumph. Upon it was the noble Bacchus drinking out of a tankard. In this he was imitated by Gaius Marius, after the victory over the Cymbri that he won near Aix-en-Provence.[6] His whole army was covered with ivy; their thyrses, their bucklers and drums were covered with it. There was only Silenus's donkey that was not caparisoned with it.

At the sides of the chariots were the Indian kings, held and bound with great gold chains; the whole brigade marched in divine pomp, in inexpressible joy and gladness, bearing an infinity of trophies, litters, and enemy spoils, resounding with joyous *epinicia* [victory songs] and little village songs and dithyrambs.

At the far end was pictured the land of Egypt, with the Nile and its crocodiles, cercopithedidae [monkeys], ibises, apes, trochiles [wrens that picked the teeth of crocodiles and kept watch for them], ichneumons, hippopotami, and other animals native to it. And Bacchus marched into that region led by two oxen, on one of which was written in letters of gold: *Apis*; on the other: *Osyris*; because in Egypt, before the coming of Bacchus, there had never been seen an ox or a cow.[7]

CHAPTER 40

How the temple was lighted by a marvelous lamp.[1]

Before I go into an account of the Bottle, I will describe to you the marvelous configuration of a lamp that shed light all through the temple, so plentiful that even though it was underground, you could see there as at high noon we see the sun shining bright and clear upon the earth.

In the middle of the vault was fixed a ring of massy gold the size of a clenched fist, from which hung three chains a little less thick, most artfully wrought, which from two and one-half feet in the air enclosed, in a triangular figure, a round plate of fine gold, of such a size that the diameter was greater than one cubit and a half a span [total about 3,375 feet]. In this were four buckles or openings, in each of which was firmly set a round globe,[2] hollow on the inside and open from the top, like a little lamp with a circumference of about two span [eighteen inches]; and they [the buckles] were all of very precious stones: one of amethyst, another of Libyan carbuncle, the third of opal, the fourth of bloodstone [d'Anthracite]. Each one was filled with colorless spirits [d'eau ardente], five times distilled through a serpentine alembic, inconsumable, like the oil that Callimachus[3] once put into the golden lamp of Pallas on the Acropolis in Athens, with a flaming wick, half of asbestine flax (as there was of old in the temple of Jupiter Ammon, and that most studious philosopher Cleombrotus saw it),[4] half of Carpasian flax;[5] both of which are rather renewed than consumed by fire.

About two and one-half feet below this gold plate, the three chains, in their original arrangements, were buckled onto three handles protruding from a great round lamp of the purest crystal a cubit and a half [twenty-seven inches] in diameter, which at the top was open about two spans [eighteen inches]; in the middle of this opening was set a vessel of the same crystal in the shape of a gourd or urinal, and it went down to the bottom of the great lamp with a quantity of the same spirits such that the flame of the asbestine flax was at the center of the great lamp. So by this means the whole spherical body of this [great lamp] seemed burning and in flames, because the flame was at the center and midpoint of it, and it was hard to hold your gaze on it firmly and constantly, just as you cannot on the body of the sun, since the shine of the material was so marvelous, and the work so subtly transparent, by the reflection of the various colors (which are natural to precious stones) of the four little lamps above the big lower one; and the brilliance of these four was at all points inconstant and vacillating around the temple. Furthermore, when this flickering light came to touch the polish of the marble with which the whole interior of the temple was inlaid, such colors appeared as we see in the rainbow when the bright sunlight touches the rain clouds.

The design was wonderful, but even more wonderful, it seemed to me, was that the sculptor had engraved, around the body of the crystal lamp, a carving of a brisk lusty battle between little naked boys, riding little hobbyhorses, with little whirligig lances and shields subtly contrived of grape clusters interlaced with vine leaves, this with childlike moves and efforts so ingeniously represented by art that nature could do no better. And they seemed to me not chiseled into the material, but in bas-relief, or at least in grotesque work, standing out fully, thanks to the pleasant varied light contained inside, which came out through the carvings.[6]

CHAPTER 41

How the pontiff Bacbuc showed us
a fantastic fountain inside the temple.

As in ecstasy we considered this wondrous temple and memorable lamp, there appeared to us the venerable pontiff Bacbuc with her company, her face joyous and smiling; and seeing us accoutered as has been said she took us without difficulty into the middle of the temple, in which, under the aforesaid lamp, was located the lovely fantastic fountain.

CHAPTER 42

How the water of the fountain gave a taste of wines
to suit the imagination of those who drank it.[1]

Tʜᴇɴ she ordered that we be offered mugs, cups, and goblets of gold, silver, crystal, porcelain, and we were graciously invited to drink the liquid flowing from the fountain, which we did most gladly; for however plaintive, it was a fountain more precious, rare, and wondrous, than Pluto in Limbo ever thought of.[2] Its substructure [soubastement] was of very pure, very limpid alabaster, about three spans in height, a little more; in shape a regular heptagon on the outside, divided equally, with its columns, little arulets, carvings of waves, and Doric undulations around it. On the inside it was exactly round. And the midpoint between[3] each angle of the lip was a rounded column in the shape of an ivory or alabaster circle (modern architects call it *portri*),[4] and they were seven in number, corresponding to the seven angles. The length [height] of these, from the bases to the architraves, was seven span [sixty-three inches], a dimension corresponding precisely and exquisitely to a diameter passing through the center of the inner circumference and roundness.

And such was the arrangement [of these columns] that when we sighted from behind one of them (on alternate sides of it), whichever one it might be around the basin, to look at the others that were opposite, we found that the pyramidal cone of our line of vision ended in the aforesaid center, and from there received, from two opposites, the meeting point of an equilateral triangle [from beyond], two sides of which (if extended forward toward us) divided the column into two equal halves, and, passing, on one side or the other, two parallel columns at the first third of an interval, met their own original baseline, which, extended all the way to the center of it, by a line drawn expressly for that purpose, and divided into two equal parts, by exact division gave the distance between the seven columns opposite in a direct line starting from the obtuse angle of the lip; as you know that in any figure with an odd number of angles, one angle is always intercalated halfway between its neighbors.[5] Whereby it was wordlessly expounded to us that in geometric proportion, amplitude, and distance, seven half diameters make a little less than the circumference of the circular figure on the outside of which they were drawn, to wit, three whole units plus one and one-half eighths, little more, or one and one-half sevenths, little less, according to the ancient teaching of Euclid, Aristotle, Archimedes, and others.

The first column, to wit, the one that on our entry first offered itself to our sight, was of a celestial azured sapphire.

The second, of Hyacinth, naturally representing (with the letters A and I in various places), the color of the flower into which was changed the blood of Ajax [Greek: Aias] in his anger.[6]

The third, of anachite diamond, shining and gleaming like lightning.

The fourth, of male balas ruby shading off to amethyst, so that its flaming gleams verged on the purple and violet of the amethyst.

The fifth, or emerald, five hundred times more magnificent than ever was that of Serapis in the labyrinth of the Egyptians, more brilliant and shining than were those set for eyes in the marble lion lying beside the tomb of King Hermias.

The sixth, of agate more cheerful and varied in the different spots and colors than was that which was held so dear by Pyrrhus, king of Epirus.

The seventh, of transparent selenite, white as beryl, resplendent as Hymettian honey; and on the inside of it appeared the moon, in shape and movement such as it is in the sky full, silent [unseen], waxing, or waning.

These are the stones that the ancient Chaldeans and the Magi attributed to the seven planets of the sky. To make this understood by a cruder Minerva [a less acute mind], above the sapphire first one, raised in a perpendicular line above the capital, was an image of Saturn in very precious Elutian lead,[7] at his feet a crane of gold, artfully enameled in the colors naturally befitting the Saturnian bird.

On the Hyacinth second, turning to the left, was Jupiter in Jovetan tin, on his chest a gold eagle enameled in its natural colors.

On the third, Phoebus in refined gold, a white rooster in his right hand.

On the fourth, in Corinthian brass, Mars, a lion at his feet.

On the fifth, Venus in copper, a material like that of which Aristonides made the statue of Athamas, in reddening whiteness expressing the shame he felt in contemplating his son Learchus dead of a fall at his feet.[8]

On the sixth, Mercury in quicksilver, fixed, malleable, and immobile, at his feet a stork.[9]

On the seventh, Luna in the silver, at her feet a greyhound.

And the statues were of a height one-third of the supporting columns, little more; so ingeniously represented, according to the mathematicians' formula, that in comparison the canon of Polycletus, by making which art was said to have learned from art, would have been barely accepted there.

The bases of the columns, the capitals, architraves, zoophores, and cornices were of Phrygian work, massive, of gold purer and finer than the Lez bears near Montpellier, the Ganges in India, the Po in Italy, the Hebrus in Thrace, the Tagus in Spain, the Pactolus in Lydia. The little arches rising between the columns were of the same stone as these up to the next one in order: to wit, of sapphire toward the hyacinth one, of hyacinth toward the diamond one, and so on in succession. Over the inner face of the arches and capitals of columns was a cupola erected as a cover for the fountain, which began behind the placings of the planets and changed progressively to end up as a sphere; and it was of a crystal so pure, so diaphanous, so perfectly and uniformly polished in all its parts, without veins, clouds, streaks, or stripes, that Xenocrates never saw one that could be compared with it. On the inner side of its circumference were artfully engraved, in order, in requisite form and characters, the twelve signs of the zodiac, the twelve months of the year with their properties, the two solstices, the ecliptic line, with certain of the most notable fixed stars, around the Antarctic Pole and elsewhere, with such artistry and expressiveness that I thought it was the work of King Necepsus or of the ancient mathematician Petosiris.

At the summit of this cupola, corresponding to the center of the fountain, were three pear-shaped union pearls, fashioned into a wholly perfect teardrop shape, all three joined together in the form of a fleur-de-lis, so big that the flower was larger than nine inches square. From the calyx of it issued a carbuncle as big as an ostrich egg, cut in heptagonal form (that is a number well loved by Nature), so prodigious and wonderful that when we raised our eyes to gaze at it we nearly lost the power of sight. For no more flaming or sparkling is the light of the sun, or the lightning, than it then appeared to us; so much so that among fair-minded assessors there would be judged to be, in this fountain and the lamps described above, more riches and singularities than are contained by Asia, Africa, and Europe together. And this would have put in the shade the pantharbas of Iarchas, the Indian magician, as easily as is done to the stars by the sun in bright noonday.

Now let Cleopatra, queen of Egypt, vaunt herself, with her two union pearls hanging from her ears, one of which, a present from the triumvir Antony, she dissolved in water with lots of vinegar, it being assessed at ten million *sexterces*.

Let Pompeia Plautina [Aille Pompéie Plautine] go her way and strut about with her robe all covered with emeralds and pearls sewn in alternation, which drew the whole Roman people in admiration. Rome, they used to say, was the cache and storehouse for all the conquering robbers in the world.

The outflow and draining of the fountain was through three little pipes and channels made of fine pearls in the form of three marginal angles as exposed above; and the channels were led out in the form of double spiral. We had considered these and were turning our gaze elsewhere when Bacbuc ordered us to listen to the water flowing out; then we heard a marvelously harmonious sound, but muted and interrupted, as if coming from afar and underground. In which it seemed more delightful than if it had been heard from near and in the open. So that even as by the windows of our eyes, our spirits were enchanted by the contemplation of the aforesaid things, so much did there remain for the ears, on hearing this celestial harmony.

Thereupon Bacbuc said to us: "Your Philosophers deny that motion is created by the power of figures; listen here, and see the contrary. Merely by the spiral figure that you see to be double here, together with a quintuple mobile infoliature at each inner meeting place (such as is the vena cava at the place where it enters the right ventricle of the heart), this holy fountain is drained and cleaned out; and by this process there flows out a harmony such that it rises all the way out to the sea of your world." Then she ordered them to serve us drink.

For to give you clear notice of it, we are not of the caliber of a bunch of silly geese who,[10] like sparrows, eat only if you tap them on the tail, and who likewise won't eat or drink unless you beat them with a crowbar. Never do we turn down anyone who courteously invites us to drink. Then Bacbuc questioned us and asked what we thought of it. We answered that it seemed to us to be good cold spring water, limpid and silvery, even more so than the Argirondes in Aetolia, the Peneus in Thessaly, the Axius in Mygdonia, or the Cidnus in Cilicia, which Alexander of Macedon saw to be so lovely, so clear, and so cold in the height of summer, that he compared the pleasure of bathing in it to the harm he foresaw would come to him from this transitory pleasure.

"Ha!" said Bacbuc, "that's what it is not to consider in themselves, not to understand the movements made by the muscular tongue when drink flows over it on its way to the stomach. You travelers, are your gullets lined, paved, and enameled, as once had Pythillus, called Teuthes,[11] that you never recognized the taste and savor of this deific liquor? Bring here," she said, "those scourers of wine that you know of, to rake, clean out, and clear out their palate."

So there were brought on plump, handsome, joyous hams, plump joyous smoked ox tongues, nice fair salt meats, black puddings, botargos, fine handsome venison sausages and other gullet-sweeps. By her command we ate to the point where we confessed that our stomachs, thoroughly cleansed of thirst, were pestering us rather annoyingly; so she said to us:

"In olden times a Jewish captain, knightly and learned [Moses], leading his people through the deserts in an extreme famine, obtained from heavens manna,[12] which had for them such a taste, by imagination, as real foods had had for them before; here likewise, drinking this wondrous liquor, you will savor the taste of such wine as you will have imagined. Now, imagine."

Which we did. Then Panurge exclaimed and said: "By God, this is Beaune wine, better than I ever drank, or ninety and sixteen devils take me. Oh oh, to taste it longer, if only anyone had a neck three cubits long, like a crane, as Melanthius wished!"

"Faith of a Lanterner," cried Frère Jean, "it's Greek wine, lively and curveting. Oh, for the love of God, my dear, teach me the way to make it!"

"To me," said Pantagruel, "it seems that these are Mirevaux wines, for so I was imagining before drinking. The only thing wrong with it is that it's cool, I mean cooler than ice, than the water of Nonacris and Derce, cooler than the spring of Conthoperia in Corinth, which used to freeze the stomach and nutritive parts of those who drank of it."

"Drink," said Bacbuc, "one, two, three times. From now on, change your imagining, and such you will find it for taste, savor or texture, as you will have imagined it. And henceforth say that to God nothing is impossible."

"Never," I replied, did we ever say otherwise; we maintain that He is Almighty."

CHAPTER 43

How Bacbuc accoutered Panurge
to get the word of the Bottle.[1]

THESE words and drinkings over, Bacbuc asked: "Which of you is the
one who wants to get the word of the divine Bottle?"

"I," said Panurge, "your humble little funnel."

"My friend," said she, "I have only one instruction to give you; it's this:
when you come to the oracle, take care not to listen to the word except
with one ear."

"That," said Frère Jean, "is wine for one ear."[2]

Then she dressed him in gabardine, covered his head with a nice white
hood, muffled him in a hippocras strainer, at the end of which, instead of
a tuft, she put three points,[3] bathed his face three times in the aforesaid
fountain, finally threw a handful of flout in his face, put three cock
feathers on the righthand side of the hippocras strainer, had him go nine
times around the fountain, do three pretty little jumps, touch his ass to
the ground seven times, while all the time she was muttering some conjuring spells in the Etruscan tongue and sometimes reading in a book of
ritual, which one of her mystagogues carried beside her.

In short, I think that Numa Pompilius, second king of the Romans, the
Caerites of Tuscia [Etruria], and the holy Jewish captain, never instituted
as many ceremonies as I saw then, nor the soothsayers of Memphis to
Apis in Egypt,[4] nor the Euboeans to Rhamnasia in the city of Rhamnes,[5]
nor did the ancients use to Jupiter Ammon, or to Feronia,[6] observances as
religious as those I was considering.

She took him thus accoutered away from our company and led him
by the right hand through a golden door outside the temple, and into a
round chapel made of transparent and reflecting stones, through whose
solid transparency, with no window or other opening, was admitted the
sunlight shining through a cleft in the rock, covering the greater temple
so easily and in such abundance that the light seemed to emanate from
within, not come in from outside. The workmanship was no less admirable than was of old the holy temple in Ravenna,[7] or in Egypt that of the
island of Chemnis.[8]

And it is not to be omitted that the workmanship of this round chapel was put together in such symmetry that the diameter of its projection was the height of the vault.[9]

In the middle of it was the fountain of fine alabaster of heptagonal shape, with unusual workmanship and infoliation, full of water as clear as an element in all its simplicity could be, into which was placed the holy Bottle, all encased in pure crystal of an oval shape, except that the rim was opened up a little more than that form would allow.

CHAPTER 44

How the pontiff Bacbuc presented Panurge
before the said Bottle.[1]

THERE the noble pontiff Bacbuc had Panurge bow down and kiss the lip of the fountain, then get back up and dance around it three *ithymboi* [Bacchic dances]. That done, she ordered him to sit down between two stools prepared there, ass to the ground. Then she opened up her book of ritual, and, blowing into his left ear, had him sing a Bacchic ode, as follows:

Bottle dear
Whence proceed
Things unknown
With one ear
You I heed;
Don't pospone,
But intone
My heart-awaited word.
In the drink let it be heard,
Where Bacchus, who crushed the Indian herd,
Holds all truth concealed inside.
Wine divine, by you denied
Are all things false and all deceit.
Let joy through Noah's era[2] still abide,
Who taught us how to make it, dry or sweet.
Pray speak that lovely word, I do repeat,
And end the woes from which I groan.
No drop be wasted in my need,
Whether of white or claret clear.
Bottle dear,
Whence proceed
Things unknown,
With one ear
you I heed;
Don't postpone.

[O Bouteille,
Pleine toute
De mistères,
D'une aureille
Je t'escoute:
Ne differes,
Et le mot proferes
Auquel pend mon coeur.
En la tant divine liqueur,
Baccus, qui fut d'Inde vainqueur
Tient toute vérité enclose.
Vin tant divin, loin de toy est forclose
Toute mensonge et toute tromperie.
En joye soit l'aire de Noach close,
Lequel de toy nous fist la tempérie.
Sonne le beau mot, je t'en prie,
Qui me doibt oster de misères.
Ainsi ne se perde une goutte.
De toy, soit blanche, ou soit vermeille.
O Bouteille
Pleine toute
De mystères,
D'une aureille
Je t'escoute:
Ne differes.]

This song done, Bacbuc cast I know not what into the fountain, and suddenly the water started boiling hard, as does the great cauldron at Bourgueil when it's a high festival. Panurge was listening with one ear in silence; Bacbuc was kneeling beside him, when from the sacred Bottle there came a noise such as bees make when born of the flesh of a young bull slain and accoutered according to the art and plan of Aristaeus, or such as a bolt makes loosed from the crossbow, or in summer a heavy shower falling suddenly. Then was heard this word: *Trinch.*[3] "By the power of God," said Panurge, "it's broken, or cracked, and that's no lie; that's how crystal bottles speak in our countries when they burst near the fire."

Then Bacbuc rose and took Panurge gently under the arm and said to him: "Friend, give thanks to the heavens, reason demands it of you: you have promptly got the word of the Bottle. I mean the most joyous, most divine, most certain word I've yet heard from her in all the time I've been ministering here to her most sacred oracle. Rise, let's go to the chapter in the gloss of which is interpreted the beautiful word."

"Let's go," said Panurge, "in God's name, I'm just as wise as I was before. Light up: where is this book? Turn pages: where is this chapter? Let's see this joyous gloss."[4]

CHAPTER 45

How Bacbuc interprets the word of the Bottle.[1]

THROWING something back into the fountain that immediately stopped the water from boiling, Bacbuc took Panurge into the greater temple, in the central part of which was the life-giving fountain. There, pulling out a stout silver book in the form of a hogshead or a fourth book of *Sentences,*[2] she filled it from the fountain and said to him:

"The philosophers, preachers, and scholars of your world feed you an earful of fine words. Here we literally incorporate our precepts through the mouth. Therefore I do not say to you: 'Read this chapter, see this gloss.' I say to you: 'Taste this chapter, swallow this fine gloss.' Long ago an ancient prophet of the Jewish nation ate a book,[3] and was a cleric to the teeth; now you shall drink one and so be a cleric down to your liver. Here, open your mandibles."

As Panurge held his gullet open Bacbuc took the silver book—and we were thinking it really was a book, because of its shape, which was that of a breviary—but it was a real natural breviary and a natural flask, full of Falernian wine, all of which she had us swallow.

"This," said Panurge, "is a notable chapter and a most authentic gloss. Is this all that was meant to be conveyed by the word of the greatest of great bottles? It suits me fine, really."

"Nothing more," replied Bacbuc, "for *Trinch* is a panomphaean word,[4] celebrated and understood by all nations, and it means 'Drink' [Beuvez]. You say in your world that *sac* is a vocable common to every language, and rightly so, and accepted correctly by all nations. For, as Aesop's fable has it, all humans are born with a wallet around their neck, needy by nature and begging from one another. There is no king so powerful that he can get along without others; there is no poor man so independent— not even the philosopher Hippias, who did everything—who can do without the rich man. Even less can you do without drinking than you can [do] without a sack [or wallet].

"Therefore we maintain that not by laughing but by drinking does man distinguish himself. I don't say drinking simply and absolutely in the strictest sense, for beasts drink as well as man, but I mean drinking cool, delicious wine. Take note friends, that from wine we incline to the divine [de vin divin on devient]; and there is no argument so sure, nor act of divination less fallacious. Your academics affirm it, in giving the ety- mology of wine, when they say that *oinos* in Greek is like *vis*, strength, power. For power it has to fill the soul with all truth, all knowledge and philosophy. If you have noted what is written in Ionic letters over the door into the temple, you have been able to understand that in wine truth is hidden. The divine Bottle sends you to it; you yourselves be the inter- preters of your own undertaking."

"It is not possible," said Pantagruel, "to say it better than does this venerable pontiff. I said as much to you the first time you spoke to me about it. So *Trinch*; what does your heart tell you when roused by Bacchic enthusiasm?"

"Let's *trinch*," said Panurge, "in the name of good old Bacchus:

> Ho, ho, drink up before wine comes to lack us;
> Meanwhile we'll soon see weighted down with ballast
> Some pretty asses, soon to be well ball-assed

By my modest but strong humanity.
But what of that? for the Paternity
Within my eager heart still makes me sure
That all my marriage plans are quite secure,
And that my wife, as soon as we are wed,
Will be my willing playmate in the bed,
Where we may both enjoy, as man and wife,
Venus's brand of intermarital strife.
Unceasingly; her marital fields I'll till,
And of my plunger let her have her fill;
And since her meals tickle my appetite,
I'll be her valiant husband every night,
Best of the very best. Then Paean ho!
Ho Paean! Once more, Paean ho!
Ho marriage too, three times and more!
An oath, Frère Jean, that must prevail;
Its truth is guaranteed by Fate:
The divine Bottle shall not fail."

CHAPTER 46

How Panurge and the others
rhyme in poetic frenzy.[1]

"HAVE you gone crazy," said Frère Jean, "or are you bewitched? Look how he's frothing! Listen to his rhythmatics [rithmaille]! What the devil's got into him, something he ate? He's rolling his eyes about like a dying nannygoat! Isn't he going to go off out of the way? Won't he take a crap farther on [fiantera il plus loin]? Isn't he going to eat some dog's grass to unburden his tumtum?[2] Or in the monkish practice won't he put his fist down his throat up to the elbow to clean out his belly and bowels? Will he take some more of the hair of the dog that bit him?"[3]

Pantagruel in rebuke says to Frère Jean:

711

"That's true poetic frenzy, believe me,
From Bacchus; this ecliptic wine you see
Seizes his sense and makes him versify.
Don't underrate
His mental state,
Subordinate
Now to his brew;
Laughs spring from cries,
Worst soars to prize,
In this disguise
His gentle heart and true
Spurs him to rhyme anew,
Monarch and victor too
Over our smiles.
And since hysteria has seized his soul,
It would bespeak a madman and a clown
To think to put so fine a toper down.
Over our smiles.
And since his mind by Bacchus is possessed,
A scurvy trick it would be, and ill-born,
To sting so fine a *trincher* with our scorn."[4]

"What's this?" said Frère Jean, "you're rhyming too? Power of God, we've all of us caught it! Would God that Gargantua could see us in this state! 'Gad, I don't know which to do, go ahead and rhyme like you, or not. Anyway, I don't know a thing about it, but we're in rhymatic spirits. By Saint John,[5] I'm going to rhyme like the rest of you; I can feel it coming on. Just wait a bit, and please excuse it if I don't rhyme satin smooth.[6]

God the Father, God paternal,
Who turned water into wine,
Make my ass, pray, more lanternal,
For my neighbor let it shine."

Panurge goes on with his discourse and says:

"Never more responsive word
From the Delphic god was heard,

Clear and sure; this fountain too
From that shrine its power drew;
First at Delphi, then brought here,
To give out its answers clear.
If Plutarch here had had a drink,
He'd have known better what to think,
When he came to wonder why
Oracles had seemed to die.
Like a cloister, not a sound
From an oracle was found.
Muted back in Delphi then,
Here that tripod speaks again,
Telling us what lies ahead:
For Athenaeus truly said
This tripod was a bottle first,
Filled with vintage wine to burst.
The wine I mean is verity.
There is no such sincerity
Hidden in the diviner's art
As now is able to impart
This holy Bottle when it will.
So, Frère Jean, I advise you still;
While we are here, consult the Flask
About the questions you should ask.
Get the word that's right for you
From this magic Bottle too.
Is there something in the way
Of your being wed some day?
Start to learn what she may find.
Meanwhile, lest you change your mind,
Play that comic Moor in heat;[7]
Flour will bleach him like a sheet."

Frère Jean, still in a frenzy, replied and said:

"By Saint Benoit's holy boot
And his legging! Marry? Me?
All my friends could always see,
Sooner I'd give up my beard,
Be tonsured, put to shame, cashiered,

713

Than be so far gone and fond
As to tie a nuptial bond;
Lose my freedom? Take a bride?
From then on to her be tied?
Far from me be such a fate!
Alexander, called the Great,
Caesar, nor his son-in-law,
Nor the best knight you ever saw."

Panurge, doffing his gabardine and mystical accounterment, replied:

"So, a beast unclean and raw,
You'll be damned like any snake,
While my harp I gently rake,
Up in Paradise, I betcha,
Looking down on you, poor lecher,
Now and then to take a pee.[8]
But when the moment comes to be
When Satan takes you down to stay,
If you ever find a way
To prick Proserpina's insides
With the thorn your codpiece hides,
Leaving her infatuate
With that virile piece of bait
And with your Paternity,
Till an opportunity
Comes to closer harmonize,
When you mount her where she lies;
Then, to serve you when you dine,
Lucifer you'd send for wine
From the finest inn in Hell.
Let him bring your food as well.
She would never bring despair
To a monk, though she was fair."

"Go on, you old madman," said Frère Jean. "I don't rhyme any more; rhyme brings rheum to my throat. Let's look to giving a satisfaction here for what we owe [parlons de satisfaire icy]."

CHAPTER 47

*How, after taking leave of Bacbuc,
they leave the oracle of the Bottle.*[1]

"About giving satisfaction here," said Bacbuc in response, "don't
worry! All will be satisfied if you are content with us. Down here, in
these circumcentral regions, we establish the sovereign good not in taking
and receiving, but in handing out and giving, and we consider ourselves
happy not if we take and get much from others, as peradventure the sects
of your world decree, but if we always distribute and give much to
others. All I ask of you is to leave here your names and native countries
in this ritual."

Then she opened a big handsome book, in which, with one of her
mystagogues writing at our dictation,[2] a few strokes were put down with
a golden stylus, as if someone had been writing, but not a trace of writing
was apparent to us.

That done, she filled three leather skins with the magic water, and,
passing them from her hands into ours, said: "Go friends, under the
protection of that intellectual sphere whose center is everywhere and its
circumference nowhere,[3] which [sphere] we call God; and when you're
back in your world, bear witness to the fact that the great treasures and
wonderful things are underground. And it was not wrongly that Ceres—
already revered throughout the universe for having demonstrated and
taught the art of agriculture, and by the discovery of wheat having abolished among humans the brutish eating of acorns—lamented very greatly
the abduction of her daughter into our subterranean regions, foreseeing
with certainty that she [Proserpina] would find more good things and
marvels underground than she herself, her mother, had found above it.

"What has become of the art, invented long ago by Prometheus, of
calling down from the heavens celestial fire and lightning? You have
assuredly lost it. It has departed from your hemisphere; it is in use here
beneath the ground. And wrongly are you sometimes astounded, when
you see cities in flames and burning with ethereal fire and lightning, and
do not know from whom, and by whom, and from where came this
disaster, in your eyes horrible, but to us familir and useful. Your philosophers who complain that everything has been written by the ancients,
nothing new has been left for them to invent, are only too evidently

wrong. What appears to you of heaven and that you call phenomena, what the earth offers to your sight, what the sea and other waters contain, is not to be compared with what is hidden inside the earth.

"Therefore the Sovereign Dominator is in almost all languages equitably named by the epithet for riches.[4] When will they [the philosophers] devote their fervor and toil to good research, by imploring the Sovereign God, whom long ago in their language the Egyptians named the Recondite, the Concealed, the Hidden,[5] and, invoking him by this name besought him to manifest and reveal himself to them, opening up to them the knowledge of him and of his creatures, thus by the guidance of a good lantern. For all ancient philosophers and sages, for the sure and pleasant completion of the road to divine knowledge and the pursuit of wisdom, have considered two things necessary: guidance of God and company of man.

"Thus among the philosophers, Zoroaster took Arimaspes as companion on his peregrinations; Aesculapius, Mercury; Orpheus, Musaeus;[6] Pythagoras, Aglaopheme. Among princes and men of war, Hercules in his most difficult undertakings had as his particular friend Theseus; Ulysses, Diomedes; Aeneas, Achates. You folks have done as much by taking as your guide your illustrious lady lantern. Now go, in the name of God Who guides you."[7]

CHAPTER A16[1]

How Pantagruel arrives on the island of the Apedeftes,
with their long fingers and crooked hands,
and of the terrible adventures
and monsters he found there.

As soon as the anchors were weighed and the vessel secured, they lowered the dinghy. After good old Pantagruel had said his prayers and thanked the Lord for saving him from so great a danger, he got into the dinghy with all his company to go ashore, which was easy for them, since the sea was calm and the winds had subsided; in a short time they reached the rocks. When they had landed, Epistémon, who was admiring the site of the place and the strangeness of the rocks, sighted a few inhabitants of the country. The first one he addressed was clad in a short gown of kingly purple, a doublet half of serge worsted, with satin cuffs, upper sleeves of chamois, and a cockaded cap [le bonnet à la coquarde]; a man of pretty good appearance, and his name, we later learned, was Gainalot [Gangnebeaucoup].

Epistémon asked him the name of those very strange rocks and valleys. Gainalot told him that the land of the rocks was a colony from the land of Proxy [Procuration]; they called it the Charges [les Cahiers], and that beyond the rocks, on crossing a little ford, they would find the island of the Apedeftes.[2]

"Power of the *Extravagantes!*" said Frère Jean. "And you good folk, what do you live on here? Could we have a drink out of your glass? For I don't see any utensils on you but parchments, inkhorns, and pens."

"And that's all we live on; for all who have business on the island have to pass through our hands."

"Why?" said Panurge, "are you barbers, and do they have to get shaved?"

"Yes," said Gainalot, "we shave their purses [quant aux testons de leur bourse]."

"Power of God," said Pantagruel, "you won't get a nickel or a penny [denier ny maille] out of my purse; but I beg you, fair sir, take us to these Apedeftes, for we're just leaving the land of the learned, where I didn't exactly learn much."

As they talked, they arrived on the island of the Apedeftes; for the water was soon crossed. Pantagruel looked with great wonder at the construction of the abode and habitation of the people of the country; for they live in a great winepress, to enter which you climb almost fifty steps; and before you enter the master press (for there are all kinds of them there, large, hidden, medium, and of all sorts), you pass through a great colonnade, where as landscape you see the ruin of almost everybody, so many gallows, great robbers, gibbets, torture racks, that it frightens you. When Gainalot saw that Pantagruel was entertained by this, he said: "Sir, let's go on further; this is nothing."

"How's that?" said Frère Jean, "this is nothing? By the soul of my overheated codpiece,[3] Panurge and I are trembling from sheer hunger. I'd rather drink than look at these ruins."

"Come on," said Gainalot.

Then he took us to a little winepress that was hidden away to the rear, and that in the island's language was called Pithies [Greek *pithoi* "wine jars"]. There, don't ask whether Master Jean and Panurge had themselves a treat, for Milan sausages, turkeycocks, capons, bustards, malmsey, and all sorts of good foods were ready and nicely prepared. A little butler, seeing that Frère Jean had cast an amorous glance at a bottle that was near a sideboard, separated from the bottellic troop, said to Pantagruel: "Sir, I see that one of your men is making eyes at that bottle; I beseech you that it not be touched, for it's for the Gentlemen [pour Messieurs]."

"How's that?" said Panurge, "then there are overseers [Messiers] here? They're harvesting the vineyard, from what I see. Then Gainalot had us go by a little hidden staircase into a room from which he showed us the Gentlemen who were in the big winepress, a place he told us no one was allowed to enter without their leave, but that we could see them well enough through this little peephole of a window, without their seeing us.

When we reached it, in a great winepress we saw twenty or twenty-five stout gallows-birds around a big table[4] garbed in green, looking at each other, their hands the length of a crane's leg and fingernails at least two feet long; for they are forbidden ever to clip them; so they grow crooked like redfing-bills or boathooks; and at that moment they brought in a great cluster of grapes from the vineyards in that country where they cut and gather from the growth of the *Extraordinary*,[5] which often hangs in the *Eschalats*.[6] As soon as the cluster was there, they put it in the press; and there was not even a seed from which they did not squeeze out some golden oil; to such a point that the poor cluster was taken away so drained and dry that there was not one drop of juice or liquid in it. Now Gainalot told us that they do not often get clusters that big, but they always have others in the winepress.

"But comrade," said Panurge, "do they have lots of growths?"

"Yes," said Gainalot. "Do you have a good view of that little one over there on its way back into the press? It's from the growth called the Royal Tithes [les Décimes];[7] they got some out of it the other day right down to the squeezing; but the oil smelled of a priest's hutch, and the Gentlemen didn't find it very tasty."

"Then why," said Pantagruel, "do they put it back into the press?"

"To see," said Gainalot "if there is any juice or remainder left in the skins or in the mother of the grapes."

"Power of God!" said Frère Jean, "and you call these people ignorant? What the devil! Why they'd get oil out of a wall."

"And so they do," said Gainalot; "for often from manors, parks, forests, they draw potable gold."

"You mean portable," said Epistémon.

"I mean potable," said Gainalot: "for in here they drink many a bottle of it that others would not drink. There is some from so many growths that they don't know the number. Pass on up to here and look in this courtyard: there you see over a thousand just waiting for the moment to be pressed. Here are some of the public stock; here, some of the private fortifications, loans, gifts, incidentals, domains, privy purses, positions, offerings, of the Royal Household."

"And which is that big one over there, with all those little ones around it?"

"That," said Gainalot, "is the Treasury, which is the best growth of this whole country. When they squeeze some of that growth, six months later there's not one of the Gentlemen but smells of it."

When these Gentlemen had risen, Pantagruel asked Gainalot to take us inside that big press, which he gladly did. As soon as we had gone in, Epistémon, who understood all languages, started showing Pantagruel the inscriptions in the press, which was big and handsome, made, from what Gainalot told us, from the wood of the Cross: for over each working part was written each thing's name in the country's language. The spindle of the press was named Receipts; the trough, Expenditures; the vice pin, the State; the sideboards, Monies Charged and Not Received; the big beams, Respite from Homage; the branches, *Radiatur*;[8] the side beams, *Recuperetur*; the vats, Surplus age; the two-handled baskets, the Rolls; the treading-vats, Acquittance; the dossers, Validation; the panniers, Authentic Decrees; the pails, Power; the funnel, the Quittance or Quietus.

"By the Queen of the Chitterlings!" said Panurge, "all the hieroglyphics of Egypt never came close to this jargon. What the devil! those terms hit the nail on the thumb like goat turds. But why, old boy, are these people called ignorant?"

"Because," said Gainalot, "they are not and flatly must not be clerics, and because here, by their ordaining, everything must be handled only by ignorance, and there must be no reason offered except that 'The Gentlemen have said it, the Gentlemen will have it so, the Gentlemen have so ordered it.' "

"By the One True God," said Pantagruel, "since they gain so much from the clusters, the branch may be worth a lot to them."

"Have you any doubt of it?" said Gainalot. "There's not a single month when they don't have them. It's not like in your countries, where an oath [serment][9] is worth nothing to you except once a year."

On our way out of there to be taken through myriad little presses, we sighted another little executioner [petit bourreau], around whom were four or five of these ignoramuses, filthy, mad as a donkey that's had a rocket attached to its tail, who, on a little winepress they had there, were putting through the press once more the skins and lees of the clusters after the others; they were called, in the country's language, Auditors.[10]

"They're the most repulsive villains to look at," said Frère Jean, "I've ever seen."

From this great press we went on through an infinity of little presses, all full of harvesters scraping the grapes dry with utensils they call bills of charge [articles de compte]; and finally we arrived in a low hall where we saw a great mastiff with two dogs' heads, the belly of a wolf, and claws like a Lamballe devil,[11] who was fed there on milk of almonds,[12] and so delicately, by order of the Gentlemen, because there wasn't one of them to whom he wasn't easily worth the rent of a good farm; in ignoramus language they called him Dupple [Double fine]. His mother was beside him, who had a similar coat and form, except that she had four heads, two male and two female, and her name was *Quadruple*;[13] and who was the most furious and dangerous beast in there after her grandmother, whom we saw locked up in a dungeon and whom they called Refusal of Fees [Omission de recepte].

Frère Jean, who had twenty ells of bowels empty to swallow an advocate stew, beginning to grow angry, asked Pantagruel to be thinking about dinner and to bring Gainalot with him; so that we left there by the back door, and there came upon an old man in chains, half ignorant, half learned, like some devilish hybrid, caparisoned in eyeglasses like a tortoise in scales, and he lived on only one food, which in their patois they call Review of Accounts [Appellations].[14] On seeing him, Pantagruel asked Gainalot what race this portenotary[15] belonged to and what his name was. Gainalot told us how from all antiquity he was chained in there to the great regret of the Gentlemen, who kept him almost dying of hunger, and that his name was Review [Revisit].[16]

"By the holy ballocks of the pope," said Frère Jean, "there's a pretty dancer for you, and I'm not surprised that the Gentlemen ignoramuses here make much of this phony popelet. By God, it seems to me, friend Panurge, if you look closely, that he looks a lot like Clutchpuss. These people here, ignorant as they are, know what they're doing just as well as anybody else. I'd send him back where he came from with a good eelskin whipping."

"By my oriental spectacles," said Panurge, "Frère Jean my friend, you're right; for if you look at the mug on this false villain Review, he's even more ignorant and wicked than these poor ignoramuses here, who glean the least badly they can, without long lawsuits, and who, to put it in few words, harvest the close without so many interlocutories and decrapperies [décrotoyres], which makes the Furred Cats very angry."

CHAPTER A32

How the lady lanterns were served at supper.[1]

THE bagpipes, other pipes, and rustic horns rang out harmoniously, and the foods were brought on. At the start of the first course, the queen took, by way of before-meal pills,[2] to clean out any grease from her stomach, a spoonful of petasinne.[3]

Then were served [note in the 1564 text: "There follows what was in the margin and not included in the present book"]:

Servato in-4 libr. Panorgum ad nuptias [Preserved in Book 4 for Panurge's wedding].[4]

Three quarters of the sheep that bore Helle and Phryxus on the Propontis.[5]

The two kids of the famous nannygoat Amalthea, wet nurse to Jupiter.

The fawns of the doe Egeria, adviser to Numa Pompilius.

Six goslings hatched by the worthy Ilmatic [bleu-blood] goose who by her song saved the Tarpeian Rock in Rome.

The piglets of the sow . . .

The calf of the cow Ino, once ill-guarded by Argus.

The lungs of the fox that Neptune and . . . Julius Pollux *in canibus.*[6]

The swan into which Jupiter changed himself for love of Leda.

The ox Apis, of Memphis in Egypt, who refused his pittance from the hand of Germanicus Caesar,[7] and six oxen stolen by Cacus, recovered by Hercules.

The two young wild goats that Corydon recovered for Alexis.[8]

The Erimanthian wild boar,[9] the Olympian, and the Caledonian.

The cremasters of the bull so beloved of Pasiphae.[10]

721

The stag into which Actaeon was transformed.

The liver of the she-bear Callisto.[11]

Des corquignolles savoreuses.

Des happelourdes.

Des badigonyeuses.

Des cocquemares à la vinaigrette.[12]

Des cocquecigrues.

Des étangourres.

De ballivarnes en paste.

Des estroncs fins à la nasardine.

Des aucbares de mer.

Des godiveaulx de lévrier bien bons.

Du promerdis grand viande.

Des bourbelettes.

Primeronges.

Des bregizollons.

Des lansbregotz.

Des freleginingues.

De la bistroye.

Des brigailles mortiffiées.

Des genabins de haulte fustaye.

Des starabillatz.

Des cornicabotz.

Des cornameuz revestuz de bize.

De la gendarmeroyre.

Des jerangoys.

De la trismarmaille.

Des ordisopiratz.

De la mopsopige.

Des brebasenas.

Des fundrilles.

Des chinfreneaulx.

Des bubagotz.

Des volepupinges.

Des gafelages.

Des brenouzetz.

De la mirelaridaine.

De la croquepye.

For the second course were served:

Des ondrespondredetz.

Des entreduchz.

De la friande vestanpenarderye.

Des baguenauldes.

Des dorelotz de liepvre.

Des bandyelivagues, viande rare.

Des manigoulles de levant.

Des brinborions de ponnent.

De la pétaradine.

Des notrodilles.

De la vesse coulière.

De la foyre en braye.

Du suif d'asnon.

De la crotte en poil.

Du moinascon.

Des fanfreluches.

Des spopondrilloches.

Du laisse-moy en paix.

Du tire-toy là.

Du boute-luy toy-mesmes.

De la clacquemain.

Du sainct balleran.

Des épiboches.

Des ivrichaulx.

Des giboullées de mars.

Des tricquebilles.

De la bandaille.

Des smubrelotz.

Des je reny ma vie.

Des hurtalis.

De la patissandrye.

Des aucrastabotz.

Des babillebabous.

De la marabire.

Des sinsanbregoys.

Des quaisse quesse.

Des cocquelicous.

Des maralipes.

Du brochaucultis.

Des hoppelatz.

De la marmitaudaille avec beau pissefort.

Du merdiguon.

Des croquinpedaigues.

Des tintaloyes.

Des piedz à boulle.

Des chinfreneaulx.

Des nez d'as de treffles en paste.

De pasque de solles.

Des estaffillades.

Du guyacoux.

For the last course were offered:

Des drogues sernogues.

Des tricquedandaines.

Des gringuenauldes à la joncade.

Des brededins brededas.

De la galimaffrée à l'escafignade.

Des barabin barabas.

Des mocquecroquettes.

De la hucquemasche.

De la tirelytantaine.

Des neiges d'antan, desquelles ilz ont en abondance en Lanternois.

Des gringaletz.

Du sallehort.

Des mirelaridaines.

Des mizenas.

Des gresamines, fruict délicieulx.

Des marioletz.

Des fricquenelles.

De la piedebillorie.

De la mouchenculade.

Du souffle au cul myen.

De la menigance.

Des tritrepoluz.

Des besaibenus.

Des aliborrins.

Des tirepétadans.

Du coquerin.

Des coquilles betissons.

Du croquignologe.

Des tinctamarrois.

For dessert they brought on a full platter of shit covered with turds in bloom: it was a platter full of white honey, covered with a wimple of crimson silk.

Their drinking was in lusty bouts [en tirelarigotz], handsome old vessels, and they drank nothing but Elaiodes [Greek: oily liquids], a rather unpleasant beverage to my taste, but in Lanternland it's a deific drink; and they got drunk just like people, so much so that I saw one toothless old female lantern clad in parchment, as corporal to other, young lanterns, who, as she was calling out to the sleepers: *Lampades nostrae extinguntur* [Our lights are going out: Matthew 25.8], was so drunk from the drink that at that very moment she lost her life and her light; and Pantagruel was told that in Lanternland often lanterned lanterns perished thus, especially in the times when they were holding their chapter.

Supper over, the tables were cleared. Then, as the fiddlers sounded, ever more melodiously, the queen led off a double brawl [bransle double], in which they all, both cresset lights and lanterns, danced together. Then the queen retired to her seat; the others, to the divine tones of the rustic trumpets, danced a variety of dances, such as these that you might name:

Serre, Martin.
C'est la belle franciscane.
Dessus les marches d'Arras.
Bastienne.
Le trihorry de Bretaigne.
Hély, pourtant si estes belle.
Les sept visaiges.
La gaillarde.
La revergasse.
Les crappaulx et les grues.
La marquise.
Si j'ay mon joly temps perdu.
L'espine.
C'est à grand tort.
La frisque.
Par trop je suys brunette.
De mon dueil triste.
Quand m'y souvient.
La galliotte.
La goutte.
Marry de par sa femme.
La gaye.
Malemaridade.
La pamine.
Catherine.
Saint Roc.
Sanxerre
Nevers.
Picardie la jolye.
La doulourouze.
Sans elle ne puys.
Curé, venez donc.

Je demeure seulle.
La mousque de Biscaye.
L'entrée du fol.
A la venue de Noël.
La péronnelle.
Le gouvernal.
A la bannye.
Foix.
Verdure.
Princesse d'amours.
Le cueur est myen.
Le cueur est bon.
Jouyssance.
Chasteaubriant.
Beure fraiz.
Elle s'en va.
La ducate.
Hors de soulcy.
Jacqueline.
Le grand hélas.
Tant ay d'ennuy.
Mon cueur sera.
La seignore.
Beauregard.
Perrichon.
Maulgré danger.
Les grandz regretz.
A l'ombre d'un buissonnet.
La douleur qui au cueur me blesse.
La fleurye.
Frère Pierre.
Va-t'en, regretz.
Toute noble cité.
N'y boutes pas tout.

Les regretz de l'aignau.

Le bail d'Espaigne.

C'est simplement donné congé.

Mon con est devenu sergent.

Expect ung poc ou pauc [wait awhile for me].

Le renom d'un esgaré.

Qu'est devenu, ma mignonne.

En attendant la grâce.

En elle n'ay plus de fiance.

En plainctz et pleurs je prens congé.

Tire-toy là, Guillot.

Amours m'on faict desplaisir.

La patiance du Maure.

Les souspirs du polin.

Je ne sçay pas pourquoy.

Faisons-là, faisons.

Noire et tannée.

La belle Françoise.

C'est ma pensée.

O loyal espoir.

C'est mon plaisir.

Fortune.

L'alemande.

Les pensées de ma dame.

Pensés tous la peur.

Belle, à grand tort.

Je ne sçay pas pourquoy.

Hélas, que vous a faict mon cueur?

Hé Dieu! quelle femme j'avoye!

L'heure est venue de me plaindre.

Mon cueur sera d'aymer.

Qui est bon à ma semblance.

Il est en bonne heure né.

De doleur de l'escuyer.

La douleur de la charte.

Le grand Alemant.

Pour avoir faict au gré de mon amy.

Les manteaulx jaulnes.

Le moût de la vigne.

Toute semblable.

Crémonne.

La mercière.

La trippière.

Mes enffans.

Par faulx semblant.

La valantinoise.

Fortune a tort.

Testimonium.

Calabre.

L'estrac.

Amours.

Espérance.

Robinet.

Triste plaisir.

Rigoron Pirouy.

L'oyselet.

Biscaye.

La doulourouse.

Ce que sçavez.

Qu'il est bon.

Le petit hélas.

A mon retour.

Je ne fay plus.

Paouvres gensdarmes.

Le faulcheron.

Ce n'est pas jeu.

Breaulté.

Te grati, roine.

Patience.

Navarre.

Jac Bourdaing.

Rouhault le fort.

Noblesse.

Tout au rebours.

Cauldas.

C'est mon mal.

Dulcis amica.

Le chault.

Les chasteaulx.

La girofflée.

Vaz en moy.

Jurez le prix.

La nuyt.

A Dieu, m'en voys.

Bon gouvernement.

Mi sonnet.

Pampelune.

Ilz ont menti.

Ma jove.

Ma cousine.

Elle revient.

A la moictié.

Tous les biens.

Ce qu'il vous plairra.

Puysqu'en amour suys malheureux.

A la verdure.

Sus toutes les couleurs.

En la bonne heure.

Or faict-il bon aymer.

Mes plaisantz champtz.

Mon joly cueur.

Bon pied bon oeil.

Hau, bergère, mamye.

La tisserande.

La pavane.

Hély, pourtant si estes belle.

La marguerite.

Or faict-il bon.

La laine.

Le temps passé.

Le joly boys.

L'heure vient.

Le plus dolent.

Touche-loy l'anticaille.

Les hayes.

I also saw them dance to the old songs of Poitou sung by a cresset light from Saint-Maixent, now a great yawner from Parthenay-le-Vieil.[13]

Note, topers, that everything went with spirit; and showing off very nicely were the little cresset lights with their wooden legs. In the end they brought on a wine nightcap with a fine *mouscheenculade*,[14] and a treat was announced on behalf of the queen thanks to a box of pétassine.[15] The queen granted us the choice of one of her lanterns to guide us, whichever one we wanted. Selected and chosen by us was the lady-friend of Mr. Pierre Lamy, a lady I had known favorably and pretty well. She too recognized me, and seemed to us more divine, more *hilique* [celestial], more learned, wiser, more expert, more humane, more kindly, and more suitable to guide us, than anyone else in the company. Very humbly thanking the lady queen, we were accompanied all the way to our ship by seven young cresset-light dancers, as already bright Diana [the moon] was shining.

When we left the place, I heard the voice of a big crookshanked cresset light saying that one good evening is worth more than all the good mornings in the world, even were there as many as there have been chestnuts in stuffing since Gyges's deluge, meaning to convey that there's no time like night for a good time, when lanterns, accompanied by their nice cresset lights, are in place. Such good times the sun cannot look on favorably, witness Jupiter when he lay with Alcmene, mother of Hercules, he had the sun hidden for two days, for shortly before it had revealed the stolen amours of Mars and Venus.[16]

EPIGRAM[17]

Is Rabelais dead? No, one book's still in store.
His better part has brought us back his brain,
To give us something new of him again
That keeps him still alive for evermore.

[Rabelais est-il mort? Voicy encore un livre.
Non, sa meilleure part a repris ses esprits
Pour nous faire présent de l'un de ses escrits
Qui le rend entre tous immortel et fait vivre.]

NATURE QUITE

6

Miscellaneous Writings

(nos. 1–22, 1521–1549)

6.1:

To Guillaume Budé. March 4, 1521. Letter in Latin, with much Greek (translated, in italics in the text).[1]

François Rabelais, a Franciscan, sends respectful salutations to Master Guillaume Budé.

Our dear Pierre Lamy, *I swear by the Graces, a lovable man if ever there was one,*[2] had urged me to write you, and I, led on by his many repeated arguments, consented to accept his invitation; but I insisted on praying and beseeching all the gods to grant me success in this hazardous undertaking. In spite of my keen desire (for why not admit it?) to make my way fully into your friendship, *and that happiness, in my eyes, would be more precious than all the kingdoms of Asia,*[3] I was nevertheles a bit afraid that such a homage, by which I hoped to obtain your good will, might result, not without reason, in the ruin of my hopes. For what indeed can an obscure unknown expect from an inexpert, barbaric letter? What hope can a young man entertain who is *uncultivated and undistinguished, deficient in both ability and any knowledge of fine languages, addressing a man made famous by his eloquence and surpassing all others by his merit and his natural talent?*[4] And so I had thought I should put off any such attempt until such time as I should have refined my written style a bit. But since Lamy kept urging me ever more strongly, I determined, at the risk of losing my reputation, to be one of those who, to judge themselves, would rather trust to others than to themselves. So I did write to you, about five months ago, but so *clumsily* [ἀπειροχάλως] that my having sent it very nearly overwhelms me with simultaneous shame and regrets, since I have not been able to learn the result of that first step; I had not exactly expected a happy outcome from it.

But to think that Budé had taken no account of the feelings shown by a nobody lost in the mass, and that after reading this letter hardly even once, or still worse, while still perusing it, he had thrown it away, that idea, lame as it was, was ruled out for me by the unanimous testimony of all those who even for one day had had the good fortune to be in communication with Budé: they offered assurance that among all his virtues Budé showed admirable spontaneous good will, at least to those who possessed or loved belles lettres, and this despite a certain severity *and rigor* [χαὶ τῆς σπάνης] in regard to those whom with a masterly hand he exposed to the eyes of the learned in their true colors in his book *De asse*,[5] when he goes after the people at court. Amy's assertions urged me in the same direction, whenever he heard me incessantly lamenting my not knowing the result of my overture and reproaching him for inciting me to this boldness, or rather this over-weening presumption. That is why *I was coming to the point of thinking, by Zeus of leveling a terrible accusation against him from which he could not easily get free without paying the penalty I would impose, which in these conditions might well be at the very least the deprivation of all his possessions. And that would not make up even the tiniest part of the punishment we see inflicted on anyone who, as far as he could, has deceived the simple and innocent and made fun of them.*[6]

And what if I declare and prove that it was arranged between us? The written proof is in my hands, and you have read it yourself, for I don't believe you have forgotten what I was saying to you. Anyway if I choose to exercise my full rights in regard to this man, I see no hiding places, no retreats, to which he can go for refuge. And I shall not say how many witnesses I can cite, and those *trustworthy* [ἀξιοπίστους], of course, and impregnable: they will all attest to hearing me stipulate that in case the affair turned out badly, I might prosecute him for fraud. But I'm insisting really too much, whereas truth reveals itself freely and makes itself evident and palpable. And moreover, since learning that my letter *had* reached you, I can't tell you all the pangs of anxiety brought on our friend by the certainty of a rigorous punishment. For I had asserted that in writing you for the second time I was bringing a suit against him.

So here now accept this second letter from me, by which I want to beg your indulgence for coming to knock unscrupulously on your door, for shamelessly pestering you with my silly problems at a time when you are swamped on all sides, I know, with the ruckus of the court, where you work so hard to civilize old Plutus.[7] For he is ashamed (à propos, let me congratulate you on that), ashamed I say, to be the only one to display his ugly ridiculous deformity at a time when all humanity, or nearly all, is regaining its ancient splendor. In that I greatly rejoice, and take pride among my friends, since Heaven has seen fit to grant all my wishes. You remember, at the end of my last letter, the prayer I expressed in Greek verse. That prayer I repeat today; often I even apostrophize Plutus, as if (as sometimes happens) I chance to come upon those whom he ordinarily returns to us after a year and a half and has shaped so well in his own fashion: ignorant wimps,[8] uncouth, a mass of vices; as Homer puts it, *useless burdens upon earth* [τὸ τοῦ Ὁμήρου ἐτώσιον ἄχθος ἀρούρης, *Iliad* 18.104].

And these are the ones that Plutus reveres, in whom he trusts, to whom he entrusts his power, the more to the misfortune of the state. That is why, being reduced to having my eyes swallow such turpitudes, I ordinarily blame Plutus for them with the sharpest of insults and abuse. I load him with vengeful words, since he, knowing that he is blind, as sick in mind as in eyesight, his wits almost gone, incapable of wise administration, lets himself be given tutors who ought to be brought up before a council of kinfolk. How, indeed, could anyone look to the exact conservation of a pupil's property, or property entrusted to him, when he himself, if he does not dissipate it completely, makes inroads into the patrimony that has come down to him by right of inheritance?

If Plutus takes hold of himself, if he shows that he has come back to a better frame of mind, if I see him regret his errors and ask for the assistance of light, and I shall even murmur in his ear a few Greek verses that I might add to my letter, but they are unworthy to come before Budé's eyes; but I will add them just the same; thus you will not go thinking that they are in the same vein as those that the famous impostor used to cure his gout:

> What say you, Plutus, of gods the most impure?
> So now is beauty pleasing to your sight?
> Go find Budé; your prompt return is sure,
> *Proudly rejoicing in a dazzling light.*[9]

But enough of this. Good-bye, and love me. From Fontenay, March 4 [1521].

Yours if truly mine,

FRANÇOIS RABELAIS.

6.2:

To André Tiraqueau. 1524. Epistle in Greek verse (six lines, translated, in italics).
Liminary to the third edition of Tiraqueau's *De legibus connubialibus*.[10]

> *When the gods in Elysium came to read*
> *This book of laws devised by wise André,*
> *They saw to what good marriages these lead;*
> *And to his fellow Frenchmen show the way.*
> *If Plato first to us these laws had shown,*
> *What man's wiser than he, or better known?*

6.3:

To Jean Bouchet. September 6, 1524, from Ligugé. Epistle in French verse,
"Concerning the things one can imagine while awaiting a thing desired."[11]

> The perfect hope of that for which we yearn,
> And full assurance of your glad return,
> Which you vouchsafed us when you went from here
> Have helped to moderate our anxious fear;
> 5   But still, like fretful columbine, we feel
> Over our senses melancholy steal,
> Which vehement desire and long delay
> Have so dislodged and proudly torn away
> From the abode where they are wont to dwell,
> 10   That we believe, and think that we can tell
> That hours are days, and every day a year;
> These nine or ten a century appear:
> Not that we think the stars have gone astray
> From their appointed, regulated way,
> 15   Or really given up their normal round,
> And that such days will once again be found
> As when Gideon fell to Joshua's men,
> For such a day was never seen again,
> Or that we think the nights can really last
> 20   As long as that which went so slowly past
> When Jove, in fable, by Alcmena's side,

738

Gat Hercules, who traveled far and wide.
This seems to us not credible at all;
But all the same, whenever we recall
Your promise to be back within a week,   25
Lost peace of mind and rest in vain we seek,
Since the appointed time has come and gone,
Since when we've counted minutes on and on,
And watched the hour hands in their crawling round,
Expecting you at every slightest sound.   30
Soon after, weary tedium ensued,
And brought on such an apathetic mood
That things seem true to us that we should know
Are not: our very senses tell us so;
Just as it seems to those who are afloat,   35
From place to place proceeding in a boat,
That they can see upon the shore the trees
Are passing, dancing, waving in the breeze,
And moving to the rear in back of you,
Although we think—and know—this is not true.   40
Of all this I have wanted to apprise
Your Lordship, thus to make you realize
How much we want you back among us here;
So when you see your way with honor clear
To leave the study that you love so well,   45
And check your eagerness, just for a spell,
For eloquent and learned litigation,
Brook no delay, pray, or procrastination,
But quick, make ready, and, with heel-wings shod,
Borrowed from Mercury, your patron god,   50
Take blithely to the winds that you select;
For Aeolus will surely not neglect
To send you Zephyr's kindly gentle breeze
To waft you where your coming will most please
Which, I can proudly boast, is right back here.   55
You have no need to learn, it would appear,
About the loving friendship and good will
You'll find; for over half are with us still
Of those you knew as friends when last you came,
From whom the rest may be inferred the same,   60
Or almost; still, if I may speak my mind,

739

When you arrive, the nobles, you may find,
Or show their love for you, and due respect,
May leave their lands and honors in neglect;
65   For they proclaim and swear, at every chance
That no one lives, in Poitou or all France,
With whom they crave more intimate connection,
Or would enjoy more mutual affection.
For all you write, so honey-sweet and fair,
70   Flows smooth for those with leisure time to spare,
A joyous pastime, fit to banish woes,
And troubles, as it brings their hearts repose,
Which then may learn, from worthy, honest ways,
How best to merit honor all their days.
75   For when I read your works, I seem to find
Two qualities inseparably entwined,
To which in learning always goes the prize:
Sweetness and knowledge, treasures of the wise.
Therefore I beg and summon you anew
80   Never to cause them grief by what you do;
So if you honorably can break free,
Don't write; just bring, in answer to our plea,
That eloquence and readiness of speech
Which leads Pallas at last her spring to breach,
85   And let her clear Castalian liquor flow.
Or, if you would jot down a word or so,
Or send me soon a letter you would write,
This, as you know, would give me great delight.
But nonetheless make it your first concern
90   To tame yourself, and be less wild and stern,
But come and see the company back here,
Who from the heart urge you to lend an ear.
From Ligugé, this morning, six September,
Where from my bed within my little chamber,
95   I've roused myself to pen this note and say,
Your friend and humble servant,

Rabellays.

6.4:

Tiraqueau/Manardi. July 9, 1532, from Lyon. Dedicatory Epistle in Latin, with Greek in italics, for Volume II of the Medical Letters of Manardi.[12]

François Rabelais, Doctor, to André Tiraqueau

A Most Equitable Judge in Poitou[13]

S.P.D.[14]

What is the cause, most learned Tiraqueau, that in our time, so full of light, in which we see all branches of learning restored to their former estate by some singular favor of the gods, we find men so constituted that they either will not or cannot break out of the thick, almost Cimmerian fog of Gothic times, or raise their eyes toward the dazzling torch of the sun? Is it because, as Plato says in his *Euthydemus* [307a] *in every profession there are many who are worthless and incapable, but few who are worthy and active?* Or because the power of the darkness is so great that eyes once possessed by it, afflicted with a regular cataract, inevitably suffer from uninterrupted hallucinations and blurrings of vision unresponsive to either spectacles or medication? As Aristotle writes in his *Categories* [10.13a.30], *there may be a passing from possession to privation, but not from privation to possession.*

If we consider things well and weigh them, as the saying goes, on the scales of Critolaus, it seems to me that any such *Odyssey* of errors has no other origin than that infamous self-love [philautia][15] so condemned by the philosophers, which, once it has attacked men who have not reflected well on what they should seek and what avoid, does not fail to blunt their wits and intelligence, fascinate them, and keep them from seeing what they see, from understanding what they understand. Thus there are people who counted for something, in the eyes of the ignorant populace, for something important, because they plumed themselves on having some expertise in some important and exotic field; but if you strip off the mask and the lion's skin,[16] if you make the herd understand that the art that won them such a brilliant success is pure hocus-pocus and the height of stupidity, you will surely pass as having put out the eyes of crows.[17] For those who until then had installed themselves in the orchestra seats will have trouble finding one even in the "peanut gallery,"[18] and will provide a laugh for the populace and for the children, who nowadays have a sharp nose for the ridiculous;[19] but they will outrage and irritate people who are indignant at having let themselves be duped for so long by their ruses and cheats.

People about to die in a shipwreck often grasp, we are told, at the moment when their ship is breaking up and sinking, a beam, a piece of cloth, a fistful of straw; they keep their hands clenched on this; they do not think of swimming, and they are reassured provided that they do not let go of what they are holding, right up to the moment when they are swallowed up in the vast deep. That is almost exactly what happens to our dear little ignoramuses: no matter that they see their ship of pseudoscience breaking up and shipping water on every side, by every possible means they cling to the books they had got used to since their childhood, and, if these were taken from them, they would imagine their souls were being taken from their body.

Thus that legal knowledge of yours has reached such a peak of perfection that its restoration lacks nothing, and yet there are people from whose hands no one can tear these superannuated glosses of barbarism. And in this laboratory of ours that is medicine and whose beauty is growing from day to day, what is the proportion of those who are devoting their efforts to improving the results?

Here, all the same, is one good thing: in almost all classes of society people have begun to realize that if you examine closely those who are physicians or pass as such, you will find them void of knowledge, honesty, and good counsel, but full of arrogance, envy, and squalor. They perform their experiments (as Pliny kept complaining long ago)[20] by killing people, and are a good deal more dangerous than the maladies themselves. Now at last those in high places are beginning to give much heed to those practitioners who follow the purified ancient ways of medicine. If this view of things prevails these charlatans and quacks who had been bent on impoverishing the human body from tip to toe will soon be reduced to beggary.

Moreover, when I was living in your neighborhood, you were wont to applaud, among our contemporaries who have devoted every effort of their minds to restoring the authentic ancient medicine, the name of the illustrious Manardi of Ferrara, a physician full of ability and knowledge, and to take as much stock in his letters as if they were from Paieon[21] or Aesculapius in person. And so, out of extreme deference in your regard, I set my heart on having printed and published, under the aegis of your name, the latest letters of this same Manardi, which I have just received from Italy. For I know and remember all that is owed you by the art of medicine, to the advancement of which I devote myself, and the occasion of your *Commentaries on the municipal laws of Poitou*.[22] Do not inflict on studious minds the torment of waiting for them any longer, I beg you most earnestly and repeatedly. Give my salutations, when you visit him, to the most illustrious Bishop of Maillezais, that Maecenas so abundantly kind to me, as well as to Hilaire Goguet, if by chance he is in the area.

Lyon, June 3, 1532.

6.5:

To Geoffroy d'Estissac. July 15, 1532, from Lyon. Dedicatory Epistle in Latin prose for R's edition, from a Greek MS of his own, of the *Aphorisms* of Hippocrates and some added writings by Galen (Greek translated in italics). Lyon: Gryphius, 1532.

To the Most Illustrious and Learned Lord

Geoffroy d'Estissac, Bishop of Maillezais

François Rabelais, Physician, Greetings[23]

Most Illustrious Prelate, in my course of public lectures given last year at Montpellier before a good-sized audience, I studied the *Aphorisms* of Hippocrates, then the *Medical Art* of Galen.[24] After pointing out several passages whose interpretations did not seem to me satisfactory, I confronted the texts of these with the translations, using a Greek manuscript I possessed besides the current editions, a very ancient manuscript set down with great care and elegance in Ionian characters, and I realized that these editions offered numerous omissions, sometimes additions, certain passages badly rendered, and, quite often, spots that have been not so much converted as inverted.[25]

If in all other areas these are seen as mistakes, in a book of medicine they are crimes or sacrileges, for in this case the addition or suppression of a single tone or syllable, or its displacement, have more than once consigned thousands of men to death. Please do not think that I write this to strike a blow at those who have deserved well of letters: so silence. Indeed, I fully agree that we owe much to their works, and I acknowledge that I have profited much from them. But in every place where they have been mistaken, the fault, to my mind, lies entirely in the manuscripts they were following, which were marred by the same errors.

Hence these little annotations, Sebastian Gryphius, a printer of consummate expertise and great culture, saw them recently among my papers; already for a long time he had been planning to print the works of the ancient physicians with the same care, the likes of which would be hard to find, that he brings to all other works. For a long time he asked me to authorize publication of these notes, which would be a service to all who study; nor did he have any difficulty in obtaining what I myself wanted to entrust to him. The only delicate point was that my personal notes, which I had taken without any thought of publication, he wanted to have arranged so as to be added to the book, which then would take the form of a manual. Indeed, that would have been less work, and it might have been no more trouble to translate the whole thing entirely into Latin.

Since my notes would in themselves have constituted a second volume larger than the other (the text), it was decided, so as not to inflate the book itself to the point of deformity, to confine ourselves to a very summary indication of the passages where one must refer back to the Greek manuscripts.

I shall not state here what reason impels me to dedicate this present work to you. It is to you that by right belongs whatever my efforts accomplish, you whose kindness has always given me such good support that wherever I cast my eyes, there appear to my senses *nothing but the heaven and the sea* [οὐδέν ἤ οὐρανός ἠδὲ θάλασσα, *Odyssey* 12.404 and 14.303] of your munificence. For your part, the Senate and the People[26] of Poitou have called you to the supreme pastoral responsibility; you acquit yourself so well in it that the same is true of you as of the famous Canon of Polycletus:[27] you are an exemplar to our bishops, the most perfect in rectitude, modesty, humanity; they see in you the true idea of virtue,[28] by gazing on which, or setting it up as a mirror to guide them, they either regulate their conduct [by it], or, as Persius says [*Satires* 3.38], eat their hearts out with regret for failing to follow it. So pray give all this a good welcome and love me, as you do: *Good-bye, most estimable of men and continue happy.*

Lyon, Ides of July [July 15], 1532.

6.6:

To Amaury Bouchard. September 4, 1532, from Lyon. Dedicatory Epistle in Latin prose (Greek translated, in italics), addressed to Amaury Bouchard[29] for Rabelais's edition of the Latin *Will of Cuspidius*. Lyon: Gryphius, 1532.

François Rabelais

to Lord Amaury Bouchard

Counselor to the King and

Master of Requests at the Royal Palace

Greetings

Here you have a present from me, most illustrious Amaury, no doubt very slim if you consider its bulk, which indeed is barely a handful; but (to my mind at least) it is not unworthy to hold your attention and that of learned men who see things as you do. It is the will of the famous Lucius Cuspidius which a happy destiny saved from a fire, from the waters, and from ruin by the wear and tear of time. When you left here you set such great store by it that in order to get it one might accept condemnation by default even before the tribunal of such a tough judge as Cassius.[30] I did not think myself obliged to give you, for your private use, a manuscript copy (as you seemed to wish I would), but, at the first chance I got, I had it printed in two thousand copies; thus, even while satisfying your request, under your auspices I shall allow all men of letters to be no longer unaware in what form the ancient Romans, when belles lettres were in honor, drew up their wills. *This document, both original and truly worthy of Daedalus* [δαιδάλεον], it is a pleasure to use Plato's term,[31] *which you spoke to me about as you were leaving,* I have found people who said they had it at home, but I've never seen anyone who showed it to me. *Apropos of matters concerning the illustrious printer Gryphius,* do not fail to remember him. I'm looking forward some happy day to your new little book *On the architecture of the world,*[32] which you must have drawn up and out of the very deepest of the treasures of philosophy. Up to now you have not written or published anything that did not display deep and recondite learning and did not seem to come out of that dark cavern where Heraclitus said truth was hidden.[33] *Good-bye, most worthy and illustrious of friends, and may you long enjoy your honors.*

Lyon, September 4, 1532

6.7:

To Bernard Salignac. November 30, 1532, from Lyon. Missive letter in Latin prose, with much Greek (translated, in italics) to Erasmus (bearing the outside address: To Bernard Salignac).[34]

To Bernard Salignac

Respectful greetings

in the name of Jesus Christ the Savior.

Georges d'Armagnac,[35] the very illustrious bishop of Rodez, sent me recently *The History of the Jewish Wars* (*The Capture of Jerusalem*) by Flavius Josephus.[36] He asked me, because of our old friendsip, to send it on to you at the first chance that came, if I could find a man *trustworthy* [ἀξιόπιστον] who was going your way. That is why I have gladly taken this occasion that has come to let you know, by a service that is a pleasure for me, my most humane Father, what respectful affection I feel toward you. I have called you "father," I would also call you "mother," if by your indulgence that were permitted me. Indeed, pregnant women, we learn from daily experience, nourish a fetus they have never seen, and protect it from the harmful effects of the surrounding air. *You have taken precisely that trouble:* you had never seen my face, even my name was unknown to you, and [yet] you have given me my education, you have never ceased to feed me with the purest milk of your divine learning; whatever I am, whatever I am good for, it is to you alone that I owe it: if I did not make this known, I would be the most ungrateful of men at present and to come.

That is why I salute you, and salute you yet again, most loving father, father and glory of your country, savior of letters [*litterarum adsertor* and in Greek ἀλεξίχαχος],[37] warding off evil, most invincible champion fighting for the truth. I recently learned from Hilaire Bertulfe,[38] with whom I am on very friendly terms, that you were planning some action or other against the calumnies of Jerome Aleander,[39] whom you suspected of having written a pamphlet against you hidden under the pseudonym of a certain Scaliger. I'd like to put an end to your doubts and undeceive you: your suspicion is unfounded. In fact, Scaliger himself was originally from Verona; he belongs to the exiled family of Scaliger, and he too is an exile. But for the time, he is practicing medicine around Agen. I know him well, *and by Zeus, that calumniator does not have a good reputation; to put it briefly, he has some knowledge of medicine but in other respects he's a complete atheist*[40] *without his like anywhere.* As for his pamphlet, I haven't yet been able to see it; not a single copy has arrived here, and I suspect that it has been suppressed by your well-wishers in Paris.

Good-bye, *and may your happiness continue.*

From Lyon, November 30, 1532

FRANÇOIS RABELAIS, doctor

6.8:

Late 1532.[41]

PANTAGRUELINE PROGNOSTICATION.

Certain, Veritable, and Infallible

For the Perpetual Year

Newly Composed for the Profit and Edification

Of Natural-born Dimwits and Daydreamers

By Master Alcofribas

Chief Steward[42] of the said Pantagruel.

Of a Golden Number[43] nothing is said;

I do not find any this year whatever calculation about it

I have performed. Let's pass Beyond.[44]

If anyone has any, let him get rid of his in me;

Anyone who does not, let him look for some.[45]

Turn the page [Verte folium].

To the Reader of Good Will, Greetings

And Peace in Jesus Christ.

Considering the fact that infinite abuses have been perpetrated because of a bunch of prognostications from Louvain,[46] made in the shade of a glass of wine, I have now worked one out for you, the surest and truest that was ever seen, as experience will demonstrate to you. For no doubt, as the Royal Prophet [David] says to God in Psalm 5 [v. 6]: "Thou shalt destroy all who speak lies," it is no slight sin to lie consciously, and mislead the poor public, anxious to learn new things. As the French have been for all time, as Caesar writes in his *Commentaries*,[47] and Jean de

Gravot in his *Gallic Mythologies*. Which we still see from day to day throughout France, where the first thing said to new arrivals is: "What's the news? Do you know anything new? Who's talking? Who's making a name in society?" And they are so attentive that sometimes they grow furious at people who come from foreign countries and don't bring coffers full of news, calling them donkeys [veaulx] and idiots.

So if, even as they are quick to ask the news, so much or more are they easy marks to believe what is announced to them, shouldn't trustworthy people on salary be stationed at each point of entry into the kingdom, with no other function than to examine the news brought there and find out if each item is true? Yes indeed. And that is what my good master Pantagruel did all over the country of Utopia and Dipsody. And so this came out so well for him, and his territory grew so prosperous, that now they can't keep up in their drinking, and they'll have to spread the wine around on the ground if they don't get from abroad a reinforcement of drinkers and good jokers.

So, wanting to satisfy the curiosity of all good fellows, I unrolled all the records and rolls of the heavens, calculated the quarters of the moon, pried open all the thoughts, past and present, of all the Astrophiles, Hypernephelists, Anemophylakoi, Uranopetes, and Ombrophores, and conferred about everything with Empedocles, who commends himself to your good graces. And all the *Thou likewise* [Tu autem][48] about it except what I think, and think nothing about it except what is so, and there's nothing else to say about it for the whole truth except what you will read about it right now. Whatever will be said besides this will have been passed any which way through the large strainer, and peradventure will happen, peradventure never will happen.

Of one possibility I warn you: that if you don't believe the whole thing, you're doing me a bad turn, for which here or elsewhere you will be severely punished. Your shoulders will not be spared little lashes with the eelskin in a sauce of bull's pizzles;[49] and sniff the air like oysters all you want, for to put it bluntly, things are going to get hot around here unless the baker goes to sleep.[50]

Now then, blow your noses, little tots, and you old dotards too, fix your spectacles straight, and weigh these words by the weight in the Sanctuary.[51]

CHAPTER 1

Concerning the Government and Lord for this Year.

Whatever you may be told by those crazy astrologers from Louvain, Nuremberg, Tübingen, and Lyon, who believe that this year there will be any other governor of the universe than God the Creator, Who by His divine Word rules and moderates all things in their own nature, property, and condition, and without Whose maintenance and government all things would in a moment be reduced to nothingness, just as from nothingness they were by Him brought forth into their being. For from Him comes, in Him is, and by Him is perfected all being and all good, all life and movement, as the Evangelical Trumpet, My Lord Saint Paul, says in Romans 11 [v. 36]. So the governor for this year and all others, according to our truthful resolution, will be Almighty God, and not Saturn, nor Mars, nor Jupiter, nor any other planet, certainly not the angels, or saints, or men, or devils, will have any virtue, efficacy, or influence, unless God, in His good pleasure, gives it to them. As Avicenna says, secondary causes have no influence or action, if the primary cause does not influence. Isn't that good little fellow telling the truth?

CHAPTER 2

Of this Year's Eclipses.

This year there will be so many eclipses of the sun and moon that I fear, not wrongly, that therefore our purses will suffer inanition[52] and our senses perturbation. Saturn will be retrograde, Venus direct, Mercury inconstant.[53] And a lot of other planets will not go as you command.

Wherefore this year crabs will go sidewise, rope makers backward, footstools will climb up on benches,[54] spits upon andirons, and caps upon hats; many men's ballocks will hang down for want of game-pouches; fleas will for the most part be black; bacon will shun peas in Lent; the belly will lead the way; the ass will sit down first; people will not be able to find the bean in the cake of the Magi [on Epiphany];[55] they won't find any ace in the flush;[56] the die won't say what you want no matter how you coax it, and often the luck you want won't come; in many places the animals will talk. Fastilent[57] will win his suit; one half of the people will wear a disguise to fool the other; and people will run through the streets like witless madmen; never was such disorder seen in Nature. And this year will be made more than twenty-seven irregular verbs, if Priscian does not keep a tight rein on them.[58] If God does not help us we shall be in plenty of trouble; but on the other hand, if He is for us, nothing can harm us, as the celestial astrologer[59] says who was snatched up to heaven, in Romans VII c [8.31]: "If God is for us, who can be against us?" [Si Deus pro nobis, quis contra nos?]. My word, no one, Lord; for He is too good and too powerful. Here bless His holy name, hoping for the same from Him.[60]

CHAPTER 3

Of this Year's Maladies.

This year the blind will not see much, the deaf will hear rather poorly, mutes will not talk much, the rich will be a little better off than the poor, and the healthy will stay better than the sick. Many sheep, oxen, hogs, goslings, chickens, and ducks will die, and the mortality will not be so cruel among the monkeys and dromedaries. Old age will be incurable this year because of the past years. People who have pleurisy will have much pain in the side. Those who have diarrhea will often go to the close-stool; catarrh will come down this year from the brain to the lower members; eye trouble will be inimical to sight; ears will be short and rare more than usual in Gascony.[61] And there will reign over almost all the universe a most horrible and dreadful malady, malign, perverse, frightening, and unpleasant, which will leave everyone stunned, and many at their wits' end,[62] and quite often as in a dream composing syllogisms about the philosoher's stone and Midas's ears. I tremble with fear when I think about it; for I tell you, it will be epidemic, and Verroës calls it that, VII, Colliget:[63] lack of money. And considering last year's comet and Saturn's retrogradation,[64] in the hospital will die a big scoundrel all rheumy and scabbed with pocks, at whose death there will be a horrible strife between cats and rats, between dogs and hares, between falcons and ducks, between monks and eggs.

CHAPTER 4

Of the Fruits and Good Things
Growing Out of the Earth.

I find by the calculations of Albumazar, in the book of the Great Conjunction[65] and elsewhere, that this year will be very fertile, with plenty of all good things for those who have the wherewithal. But hops in Picardy will have some fear of the cold; oats will do horses much good; there will be little more bacon than hogs. Because of Pisces being in the ascendant, it will be a great year for snailshells. Mercury is something of a threat to the parsley, but nevertheless for a price he will be reasonable. Marigold and columbine ["le soucil et l'ancholye," meaning "care" and suggesting "melancholy"] will grow thicker than usual, with an abundance of anguish pears [play on *angoisse* and *Anjou*]. Of wheats, wines, fruits, and vegetables never have this many been seen—if the wishes of poor folk are heard.

CHAPTER 5

Of the State of Some People.

The greatest madness in the world is to think that there are stars for kings, popes, great lords, rather than for the poor and needy, as if new stars had been created since the time of the Flood, or of Romulus, or Pharamond, at the new creation of kings.[66] Which neither Triboulet nor Caillette would say, who all the same were people of lofty learning and great renown. And peradventure on Noah's Ark the said Triboulet was of the lineage of the kings of Castille, and Caillette of the race of Priam; but this entire error comes only for lack of true Catholic faith. So, considering it certain that the stars care as little about kings as about beggars, I shall leave it to other crazy Prognosticators to talk about the kings and rich folk, and I shall talk about the folk of low estate.

And first of all the folk subject to Saturn, such as the penniless, the dotards, the evil-thinkers, the suspicious, the mole-catchers, the userers, the profiteers in redeeming farm revenues, the riveters, the tanners of leather, the tilers, the bell-casters, the reconcilers of loans, the cobblers who patch up old shoes, melancholy folk this year will not have everything they would like; they will apply themselves to the Invention of the Holy Cross,[67] and they will not toss their bacon to the dogs, and will often scratch themseves where they do not itch.

[Those subject] to Jupiter,[68] such as whited sepulchers, dissemblers, buskineers (i.e., monks), rogation-peddlers, makers of briefs or writs, chancery scribes, bullists, dater-dispatchers, pettifoggers, capuchins [caputons], monks, hermits, hypocrites, catamites, sanctorum-mumblers, hairypaws, wrynecks, paper-splotchers, showy coxcombs, wigmakers (or curlylocks), registry clerks [clercz de greffe], image-peddlers, paternosterers, parchment-smearers, notaries, raminagrobises, missal-peddlers, promotion agents [promoteurs], will get along according to their money. And so many churchmen will die that they'll run out of candidates for benefices, so that many people will hold two, three, four, or more of

751

them. Hypocrisy will bring its former renown into great decay, since people have gone mad and are no longer fools, even as Abenragel says.

[Those subject to] Mars such as hangmen, murderers, adventurers, sergeants, bailiffs, officers of the watch, fortress guards [mortepayes], toothpullers, ballock-cutters, barbers, butchers, counterfeiters, quack doctors, almanac-makers, and maranos, renegades, match-sellers, firebugs, chimneysweeps, free militiamen [franctaupins], colliers, alchemists, egg-sellers [coquassiers], roasters, pork-butchers, trinket-peddlers [bimbelo-tiers], church wardens [manilliers], lanterners, tinkers, will strike some fine blows [de beaulx coups],[69] but some of them will be very subject to receiving something of a beating on the quiet. One of the above mentioned this year will be made bishop of the fields, giving his benediction with his feet to all the passers-by.[70]

[Those subject to] Sol [the sun], such as drinkers, muzzle-illuminators [enlumineurs de museaulx], pot-bellies, beer-brewers, hay-balers, porters, reapers, house-thatchers [recouvreurs], stevedores, packers, shepherds, ox-herds, cowherds, swineherds, bird-sellers, gardeners, barn-keepers, farmers [cloisiers], hospital beggars, journeymen, degreasers of caps, pack-saddle-stuffers, tatterdemalions, chatterteeth, bacon-nibblers, generally all those who wear their shirt knotted over their back, will be healthy and blithe, and will have no gout in their teeth at a wedding feast.

[Those subject] to Venus,[71] such as whores, bawds, wenchers, buggers, showboats, syphilitica, cankered, swaggerers, pandars, lazy bums, hostel chambermaids, names of women ending in *ière*, such as *lingière* [seam-stress], *advocatière* [woman advocate], *tavernière* [barmaid], *buandière* [laun-dress], *frippière* [old clothes woman], will this year be well reputed, but when the sun enters Cancer and other signs, must keep from getting the pox, canker, hotpisses, inguinal pimples, etc. Nuns will hardly conceive without male operation. Very few maidens will have milk in their breasts.

[Those subject] to Mercury,[72] such as sharpers, cheats, adulterators [of metals], panacea-sellers, thieves, millers, pavement-pounders, Master of Arts, Decretists, porters, miners, rhymers, jugglers, sleight-of-hand artists, enchanters, fiddlers, poets, Latin-manglers, rebus-composers, paper-makers, carters, no-goods, sea-scourges will pretend to be merrier than they often will be, will often laugh when they have no urge to, and will be very subject to going bankrupt, if they find they have more money in their purse than they need.

[Those subject] to the Moon,[73] such as meddlers, huntsmen, hunters, austringers, falconers, post-carriers, salt merchants, lunatics, madmen, brainless, harebrained, batty, hawkers, couriers, lackeys, tennis-scorers, glassmakers, stradiots, ferrymen [riverans], sailors, grooms [chevaucheurs d'escurye], gleaners, will hardly ever be stopped this year. All the same, not so many fossilophers [lifrelofres], for philosophers will go to Santiago [de Compostela] as went in the year 1524. From the mountains of Savoy and Auvergne will come down a great abundance of pilgrims bound for Mont-Saint-Michel [Micquelotz],[74] but Saggitarius threatens them with kibes on their heels.

CHAPTER 6

Of the State of Certain Countries.

The noble kingdom of France will prosper and triumph this year in all pleasures and delights, so much so that foreign nations will be glad to retire there. Little banquets, little frolics, myriad joyous things will be done there, in which each and every one will take pleasure; never have so many wines been seen, or tastier; lots of turnips in Limousin, lots of chestnuts in Périgord and Dauphiné, lots of olives in Languegoth [Languedoc], lots of sands in Olonne, lots of fish in the sea, lots of stars in the sky, lots of salt in Brouage; plenty of wheat, vegetables, fruits, garden produce, butters, silk products. No plague, no war, no trouble, shit on poverty, shit on melancholy; and those old double ducats, rose nobles, angels, *aigrefins*, royals, gold Agnus Dei coins, will come back into use, with plenty of seraphs and sun-crowns. However toward midsummer is to be feared some coming of black fleas and mosquitoes from La Devinière. For the fact is that nothing is in every way blessed [Adeo nihil est ex omni parte beatum].[75] But they will have to be checked by dint of vespertime collations.

Italy, Romany, Naples, Sicily, will remain next year where they were last year. They will dream very deep toward the end of Lent, and at times will daydream toward the height of the day.

Germany, the Swiss, Saxony, Strasbourg, Antwerp, etc., will profit if they do not fail; the relic-peddlers must fear them, and not many anniversaries will be founded there.[76]

Spain, Castile, Portugal, Aragon will be subject to sudden alterations and very much afraid of dying, the young as well as the old; and will therefore keep good and warm, and will often count their golden crowns, if they have any.

England, Scotland, the Easterlings will be rather bad Pantagruelists. For them wine would be as healthy as beer, provided it was good and tasty. At all meals their hope will be in the game to follow.[77] Saint Ninian of

Scotland will perform as many miracles and more. But for all the candles they bring to him he will not see a speck more clearly, unless Aries [the Ram] stumbles in rising from its billet and is shorn of its horn.[78]

Muscovites, Indians, Persians, and Troglodytes [cave-dwellers] will often have a bloody stool [cacquesangue] because they won't want to be screwed by the Romanists, considering the dance of Sagittarius as it rises.

Bohemians, Jews, Egyptians will this year not be reduced in the foundation of their expectations. Venus threatens them direly with the king's evil [scrofula] in the throat; but they will consent to do the will of the king of the Butterflies.[79]

Snails, sarabaites, nightmares, cannibals, will be badly molested by gadflies, and few of them will play bottoms up with the girls,[80] unless the guiacum[81] is available on request.

Austria, Hungary, Turkey, 'pon my word, my good hearties, I don't know how they'll make out, and precious little do I care, in view of the valiant entry of the sun into Capricornus; and if you know anything more about it, don't say a word about it, but wait until the lame man arrives.[82]

CHAPTER 7

Of the Four Seasons of the Year,
and First of All of Spring.

In this whole year there will be only one moon; moreover it will not be new; you're very sorry for that, you people who don't believe in God at all, who persecute His holy divine Word and likewise those who maintain it. But go hang yourselves, never will there be any other moon than the one that God created at the beginning of the world, and which by the effect of His aforesaid holy Word was established in the firmament to light and guide humans by night. Good Lord, I don't mean by that it will not show the earth and earthlings dwindling or growth in its brilliance, according as it draws closer to the sun or farther from it. Why so? On account of, etc. And don't pray any more on her behalf that God may protect her from the wolves;[83] for they won't touch her this year, I swear to you.

By the way, you will see in this season half again as many flowers as in every three others. And that man will not be reputed crazy who in this time takes in his stock of money this year better than his stock of spiders. The mountain griffins and *marroni* [mountain litter-carriers] of Savoy, Dauphiné, and the Hyperboreans, which have eternal snows, will be frustrated this year and have no snow, in Avicenna's opinion, who says

754

that spring is the time when snows fall down from the mountains. Take the word of this bearer [porteur]. In my time they used to reckon *Ver* [Latin: spring] when the sun entered the first degree of Aries. If they count differently now, I pass condemnation.[84] *Et iou mot* [and not another word].

CHAPTER 8

Of Summer.

I don't know what wind will be blowing, but I know well that it will be hot and a sea breeze will prevail. However, if it turns out otherwise, that's no reason to deny God. For He is wiser than we, and knows much too much better what we need than do we ourselves, I assure you on my honor, whatever Ali and his henchmen may say. It will be well to keep cheerful and drink cool, although some have said there is nothing more hostile to thirst. I believe it. And then *contraria contrariis curantur* [opposites are cured by opposites].

CHAPTER 9

Of Autumn.

In autumn they will harvest the grapes, or before or after; it's all one to me, provided we have plenty of *piot*. The vintage tricked will be in season; for so-and-so will think he's farting who will blithely shit.[85] Those lads and lasses who have vowed to fast on fast days until the stars are out in the sky can at this time have a good meal, on my authorization and at my expense. And at that they [those people] have been very slow; for they [the stars] have been there before them for sixteen thousand and I don't know how many days; I mean to tell you well fixed there. And from now on don't hope to catch larks when the sky falls down, for upon my honor, they won't fall in your time. Hypocrites, impostors, and ped-dlers of relics and other such knickknacks will come out of their lairs. Let everyone who wants to be on his guard. Beware of bones when you eat fish, and from poison may God guard you!

CHAPTER 10

Of Winter.

In winter, according to my puny understanding, the only wise ones will be those who sell their skins and furs to buy firewood. And thus did the ancients not do, and witness Avenzoar. If it rains, don't let it get you down [s'il pleut, ne vous en mélencholiez]; you'll have that much less dust on the road. Keep warm. Beware of head colds and catarrhs. Drink of the best while you wait for the other stuff to get better, and henceforth don't shit in your bed. O, O, fowls, must you make your nests so high up?[86]

Finis

6.9:

Almanac for 1533. Late 1532.[87]

Almanac for the year 1533 calculated on the meridian of the noble city of Lyon, and on the climate of the kingdom of France.

Composed by me, François Rabelais, doctor of medicine, and professor of astrology, etc.[88]

Of the disposition of the present year 1533.

Because I see blamed among all learned folk the prognostic and judiciary part of astrology for the vanity of those who have treated it and for the annual frustration of their promises, I shall abstain for the moment from telling you what I was finding out about it from the calculations of Claudius Ptolemy and others, etc. I do say, however, considering the frequent conjunctions of the moon with Mars and Saturn, etc., that in the said year, in the month of May, there cannot but be notable mutations not only in kingdoms but also in religions, which is contrived by the agreement of Mercury and Saturn, etc.

But these are secrets of the privy council of the Eternal King, Who governs everything that is and that happens by His free will and good pleasure, which it is better to leave unsaid and to worship them in silence, as is said in Tobit 12 [v. 7], it is good to keep the secret of the King; and David the prophet, Psalm 64 [v. 2], in the Chaldean text:[89] "Lord God, silence befits you in Sion," and he states the reason in Psalm 17 [in NEB, 18.11]: "For He has placed His retreat in darkness," or "He made darkness around him His hiding place."

Wherefore in any case it behooves us to humble ourselves and pray to Him, as our Lord Jesus Christ has taught us to do, that not that be done which we wish and ask, but that which pleases Him and He has established before the heavens were formed, only that in everything and everywhere His glorious name be sanctified. Entrusting the rest to what is written about it in the eternal daybooks, which no mortal man is allowed to treat or know, as is stated in Acts, 1.7 [NEB: "It is not for you to know the dates or moments, which the Father has set within His own power"]. And the penalty for this temerity is established by the wise Solomon, Proverbs, 25. "Whoever scrutinizes the acts of His Majesty shall be put down for that very thing," etc.[90]

6.10:

To Jean du Bellay. August 31, 1534. Dedicatory Epistle for the topography of ancient Rome by Marliani.

François Rabelais, Doctor,

To the very Famous and very Learned

Lord Jean du Bellay

Bishop of Paris, Counselor to the King

In his Privy Council

Greetings

The immense amount of the benefits, most illustrious prelate, with which you have rejoiced and honored me recently is engraved so deeply in the heart of my memory that nothing, I am sure, could dislodge it or reduce me to the forgetfulness that the years bring on. And would God I might also be as able to publish your praises eternally as I am certain always to acquit myself of my debt of gratitude, not by rendering you comparable services (indeed, how could I), but by at least expressing to you my just homage and faithful recollection.

The essential wish I expressed, from the moment I first had any understanding of belles-lettres, was to travel around Italy and visit Rome, capital of the world. Your marvelous kindness has realized this wish, by allowing me not only to see Italy (which was already enviable in itself), but to see it with you, you the most cultivated man there is in the world —and that is a favor whose value I have not been able to assess.

Seeing you in Rome was more precious for me than seeing Rome itself. To have been in Rome is a destiny accessible to all, provided one is not crippled or paralyzed; but it is a pleasure to have seen you in Rome enjoying extraordinary favor; it's a title of glory to have taken part in affairs at the moment when you were charged with that prestigious mission for which our invincible King Francis had delegated you to Rome; it is a happiness for me to have been at your side when you took the floor, in the most venerable and august council in the world, on the affairs of the king of England.

What satisfaction filled us, what joy uplifted us, what cheer transported us when we saw you speaking! Pope Clement himself remained astounded, the sitting cardinals seized with admiration, and they all were applauding! What points you left in the minds of your spellbound auditors! What acuity you showed in your concepts, what finesse in your reasonings, what authority in your responses, what energy in your refutations, what independence in your language!

As for your style, it was of such purity that you seemed, so to speak, to be the only one to speak Latin in Latium, and of a power able to temper its unusual splendor by delicacy and good humor. I often noticed that people of enlightened taste who were there, picking up the expression of Ennius, would call you "the fine flower of the Gauls,"[91] and declare aloud that in the memory of man there was only the bishop of Paris to speak frankly,[92] and that in truth the king of France had mighty good luck to possess some Du Bellays on his council, for most assuredly France has rarely known men whose glory was more brilliant, of more secure prestige, of more refined culture.

Well before your stay in Rome, I had formed in the depths of my mind a notion, an idea of the things for which desire drew me there. First of all, I had decided to call on the famous learned men living in the places where we were to pass, and have informal discussions with them about certain difficulties that had long been bothering me. Next (and this was related to my specialty), I had to see some plants, animals, and remedies that I was told were still unknown in France and were found in abundance in Italy. Finally, using my pen, as I would a brush, I had to depict the appearance of Rome in such wise that on my return home there should be nothing I could not get out of my books for the purposes of my fellow citizens. On this subject, I had brought with me a pile of notes gathered in various Greek and Latin authors.

On the first point, even if my wishes were not exactly granted in full, I did not make out badly. As for the plants and animals there are none in Italy that I did not see and know beforehand. I saw just one plane tree in Diana's grotto in Aricia. As for the last point, I went to so much trouble on it that no one, I think, knows his own house any better than I know Rome and its districts. And you too, all the free time left you by that prestigious and arduous mission of yours, you willingly employed in visiting the monuments of Rome. And you were not content with seeing only those that were on view; you insisted on bringing some up out of the ground, and for that purpose you acquired a pretty good-sized vineyard.

And so, since we were to stay on there longer than you had expected, and I wanted to get some tangible result from my studies, I had started to draw up the topography of Rome, getting from you as associates two men of your house, Nicolas le Roy and Claude Chappuis, honorable men and deeply versed in antiquity. And suddenly Marliani's book starts to come out from the printer; and its having been composed brought me the same relief that Juno Lucina brings to women in labor pains with child. For I had conceived the same child, but the idea of bringing him into the world was causing me anxiety to the point of anguish to the depth of my soul. If the subject in itself was not hard to conceive, nonetheless it seemed no easy task to arrange neatly, with harmonious elegance, a mass of materials piled up without art.

For myself, thanks to the invention of Thales of Miletus [the sundial, which R had set up vertically], by drawing transverse lines from east to west, then from south to north, I was dividing the city into quarters and was drawing them in. Marliani, for his part, preferred to start his drawing from the hills; but far from blaming him for his way of tracing, I congratulate him for bringing about ahead of me what I was trying to do. All by himself he accomplished more work than could have been expected on this by all the learned men of our generation. And he completed his task so well and in a way so in keeping with my own personal ideas that I admit I owe him personally as much as do all other men of learning in love with letters.

The one unfortunate thing was that you, recalled by the clear voice of the prince and the country, left Rome before this volume was completed. But I saw to it that as soon as it was published it should be sent to Lyon, scene of my studies. That was made possible thanks to the obliging help of Jean Savin, truly a most resourceful man; but—I know not how—the book was sent without a dedicatory epistle; so thus, to avoid its appearing as it was, shapeless, so to speak without a head, I decided to edit it under the auspices of your illustrious name. As for you then, with your unique kindness, do approve of all this and love me (as you do). Good-bye.

Lyon, August 31, 1534

6.11:

Almanac for 1535. Late 1534.[93]

Almanac for the year 1535, calculated on the noble city of Lyon, at an elevation from the pole of XLV degrees, XV minutes in latitude and XXVI in longitude.

By Master François Rabelais, doctor of medicine and physician of the great hospital of the said Lyon.

Of the disposition of this year 1535.

The ancient philosophers who concluded for the immortality of our souls had no more valuable argument to persuade us than the reminder of a feeling that is in us, which Aristotle describes in Book 1 of his *Metaphysics*, saying that humans naturally desire to know and to learn, not only things of the present, but especially things to come, because the knowledge thereof is more lofty and admirable. Therefore because in this transitory life they cannot attain to the perfection of this knowlege (for the understanding is never sated with understanding, as the eye is never without covetousness to see, nor the ear to hear, Ecclesiastes 1 [v. 8], and nature has made nothing without a cause, or given appetite or desire for anything that cannot some time be obtained, otherwise that appetite would be either vain or depraved), it follows that there is another life after this one, in which this desire will be satisfied.

I make this statement inasmuch as I see you in suspense attentive, and coveting to hear from me at present the state and disposition of the year 1535. And you would consider it a wondrous gain if someone with certainty predicted the truth to you. But if you want to satisfy this fervent desire completely, it behooves you to wish (as Saint Paul said in Philippians 1 [v. 23] "to be dissolved and be with Christ" [*Cupio dissolvi et esse cum Christo*; NEB: "to depart and be with Christ"], that your souls should be taken out of this dark prison of the earthly body, and be joined to Jesus the Christ. Then will cease all human passions, affections, and imperfections; for in the enjoyment of Him we shall have plenitude of all good, all knowledge and perfection; as long ago sang King David, Psalm 16 [v. 15]: "Then shall I be satisfied, when Thy glory shall appear" [tunc satiabor, cum apparuerit gloria tua].

To predict otherwise about it would be frivolity for me, as it would be simplemindedness for you to put faith in that. And never yet, since the creation of Adam, has a man been born who wrote on the subject or left anything in which one could acquiesce and settle on it with assurance.

True, some studious characters have put in writing a few observations they have taken from hand to hand. And that is what I have always protested, not wanting by my prognostics to be thought conclusive about the future, but to understand that those who have artfully set down long experiences with the stars have decreed in the way I describe it. And what can that be? Assuredly less than nothing, for Hippocrates says, in *Aphorism* 1: "Life is short, art is long" [Vita brevis, ars longa]. The life of man is too short, the sense too frail, the understanding too distracted, to understand things so remote from us.

It is what Socrates used to say in his ordinary remarks: "Things above us are nothing to us" [Quae supra nos, nihil ad nos].[94] It remains that following Plato's advice in the *Gorgias* [484 c], or better, the Gospel teaching, Matthew 6 [vv. 31 and 34]: "For this care-laden concern let us put our trust in the government and changeless decree of God Almighty, Who has created and dispensed everything according to His holy will; let us supplicate and request that His holy will be done, so on earth as it is in Heaven."

Summarily exposing to you about this year what I've been able to extract from the authors in the field, Arab and Latin, we shall begin this year to feel part of the infelicity of the conjunction of Saturn and Mars, which was last year, and will be next year on the 25th of May. So that in this year will come only machinations, carryings-on, bases, and seeds of the unhappiness to follow. If we have good weather, that will be beyond the promise of the stars; if peace, that will be not for lack of inclination and enterprise for war, but for lack of opportunity.

That's what they say. For my part, I say that if the Christian kings, princes, and communities hold in reverence the divine Word of God and according to that govern themselves and their subjects, then never in our time did we see a year more salubrious for bodies, more peaceful for souls, than this one will be: and we shall see the face of heaven, the covering of the earth, and the bearing of the people more joyous, merry, pleasant, and benign, than it has been for fifty years back.

The dominical letter will be C. Golden number 16. Indication for the Romanists 8, cycle of the sun, 4.[95]

6.12:

Letter from Rome to Geoffroy d'Estissac, bishop of Maillezais. December 30, 1535. Missive letter in French prose.

My Lord, I wrote you very fully on the 29th day of November and sent you some seeds from Naples for your salads of all the kinds they eat down here, except the pimpernel of which then I could not get any. I send you some now, not in great quantity, for I cannot load the courier any more for one trip; but if you want a bigger supply of it either for your gardens or for gifts to others, if you write me then I'll send it to you. I had written you earlier and sent you the four signatures concerning the late Dom Philippe's benefices, obtained in the name of those you cited in your memorandum. Since then I have received no letter of yours that mentions receiving the said signatures. I did indeed receive the one dated from l'Ermenaud, when Madame d'Estissac passed that way, in which you wrote me of the receipt of the two packets I had sent you, one from Ferrara,[96] the other from this city[97] with the cipher that I was writing to you. But from what I understand, you had not yet received the packet in which were the said signatures.

For the present, I can inform you that my affair[98] was granted and expedited much better and more surely than I would even have hoped, and for it I had help and counsel from good people, especially from Cardinal de Genutiis, who is a judge of the Palace, and Cardinal Simoneta, who was an auditor and very expert and knowledgeable in such matters. The pope was of the opinion that I should pass my said affair *per Cameram* [through the Apostolic Chamber]. The aforementioned thought it should be the Court of Counterstatements, because *in foro contentioso* [in the settlement of any dispute], it [my affair] is unbreakable in France, and those which pass through the Court of Counterstatements are held to have been judged, whereas those which pass through the Chamber may be both impugned and come into adjudication. In any case, all I have left to do is to raise the lead-sealed bulls [lever les bulles *sub plumbo*].

My Lord Cardinal du Bellay, and with him Monsieur de Mascon, have assured me that the matter will be settled for me gratis, even though the pope in ordinary practice does nothing gratis except what is dispatched *per Cameram*. There will remain to be paid only the *référendaire* [supervisor of signatures], the proctors [procureurs], and other parchment-smearers. If I run short of money, I will commend myself to your alms, for I believe I will not be leaving here until the emperor goes.

At the moment he is in Naples, and will leave there, from what he has written to the pope, on the sixth of January. Already this entire city is full of Spaniards, and he has sent the pope a special ambassador besides his ordinary one to inform him about his coming. The pope cedes him half the palace [the Vatican] and the entire city of Saint Peter's [Borgo San Pietro] for his men, and is having three thousand beds prepared Roman style, to wit, mattresses, for the city is stripped of them since the sack of the Landesknechts [May 6, 1527], and he has laid in a supply of straw, hay, oats, and spelt, and barley, all he could lay his hands on, and for wine, all that has arrived in Ripa. I think it will cost him plenty, which is hardly what he needs in the poverty he is in, which is great, and more apparent than in any pope there has been for three hundred years back. The Romans have not yet decided how they should behave, and often assemblies have been called by the senator, conservators, and governor,[99] but they can't get their opinions together. The emperor has announced to them by his said ambassador that he does not intend for his men to live at their own discretion, that is to say without paying, but at the discretion [i.e., expense] of the pope, which is what most irks the pope, for he understands that by that order the emperor wants to see how, and how fondly, he [the pope] will treat him and his men.

The Holy Father, by the decision of the consistory, has sent to meet him two legates, the cardinal of Siena and Cardinal Cesarini. Since then in addition have gone Cardinals Salviati and Ridulfi, and My Lord de Saintes with them. I understand that this is about the question of Florence and the dispute between Duke Alessandro de Medici and Filippo Strozzi, whose possessions, which are not small, the duke wanted to confiscate; for after the Fuggers of Augsburg in Germany he [Strozzi] was rated the richest merchant in Christendom and had brought men into the city [Rome] to take him [Medici] prisoner or kill him;[100] however that might be, he, warned of this enterprise, obtained permission from the pope to bear arms, and ordinarily went about with a bodyguard of thirty soldiers armed to the teeth. The duke of Florence {Medici], so I believe, informed that the said Strozzi had gone with the aforesaid cardinals to meet the emperor and was offering four hundred thousand ducats just to have people charged to get information about the tyranny and wickedness of the said duke, made Cardinal Cibo his

govenor, and arrived in this city the day after Christmas at twenty-
three o'clock, as figured by Roman time,[101] entered by Saint Peter's
Gate, accompanied by fifty light-horse cuirassiers lance in hand, and
about a hundred harquebusiers. The rest of his retinue was small and
in bad order, and no [ceremonial] entry at all was held for him, except
that the emperor's ambasssador went as far as the said gate to meet him.
When he had entered, he betook himself to the palace and had an
audience with the pope, which did not last long, and he was lodged
in the Palazzo San Giorgio. The next morning he left, accompanied
as before.

For the past week news had come to the city, and the Holy Father
has received letters about it from various places, about how the Sophy,
king of the Persians, has defeated the army of the Turk. Yesterday
evening there arrived there the nephew of Monsieur de Vély, the
king's ambassador to the emperor, who told My Lord Cardinal du
Bellay that that is the truth and that it had been the greatest slaughter
perpetrated for four hundred years back. For on the side of the Turk
were slain more than forty thousand horses. Consider what number of
foot soldiers as fell on the side of the said Sophy. For among people
who are not prone to flee, *non solet esse incruenta victoria* [victory is not
apt to be bloodless].

The principal defeat was near the little town of Cony [Khoï], a
short distance from the big city of Tauris [Tabriz], over which the
Sophy and the Turk are in dispute. The rest of it took place near a
spot named Betelis [Bitliz]. The way of it was that the said Turk had
split up his army and sent part of it to take Cony. The Sophy, warned
of this, with all his army fell upon this part and caught them off guard.
So we see that it's a bad idea to divide up your army before you win
the victory.

The French could tell you a thing or two about it from the time
when before Pavia the duke of Albany went off with the flower and
strength of their camp. When this rout and slaughter was known,
Barbarossa went back to Constantinople to give his country security
and maintained by his good gods that this was nothing in consideration
for the great power of the Turk. But the emperor is rid of that fear he
had that the Turk might attack Sicily as he had planned to do in the
spring. For a long time Christendom can rest easy and well, and those
who were levying tithes on the Church *eo praetextu* [on that pretext],
that they want to fortify themselves against the Turk, will have a weak
supply of convincing arguments.

My Lord, I received a letter from My Lord of San Cerdos, dated from Dijon, in which he tells me of the lawsuit he has pending in this Roman curia. I wouldn't dare give him an answer without running a risk of getting him into big trouble, but I understand he has the best case in the world and is being manifestly wronged and ought to come here in person. For there is no lawsuit so equitable that may not be lost when it is not solicited, especially when there are powerful parties involved, with the authority to threaten those who solicit if they talk about it. The lack of a cipher keeps me from writing you further about it, but I don't like to see what I'm seeing, especially considering the warm affection you bear him, and also that he has always favored me and in my opinion liked me. Monsieur de Basilac, a counselor from Toulouse, certainly came here for much less of a case this winter, and is older and more decrepit than he is, and had it dispatched soon in his favor.

My Lord, this morning the duke of Ferrara returned here, who had gone to meet the emperor in Naples. I have not yet learned what agreement he reached concerning investiture and recognition of his lands, but I understand that he did not come back very content with the emperor. I suspect that he will be constrained to cast to the winds the gold crowns his late father left him, and that the pope and emperor will pluck him at will, especially since he turned down the king's side, after putting off entering the emperor's league for over six months, no matter what remonstrances or threats were made him on the emperor's behalf. In fact, Monsieur de Limoges, who was the king's ambassador to Ferrara, seeing that the said duke, without notifying him of this step, had gone to meet the emperor, went back to France. There is a danger that Madame Renée may have trouble on this account. The said duke has already taken from her her governess Madame de Soubise and had her served by Italian women, which is not a good sign.

My Lord, a few days ago one of Monsieur Crissé's men arrived here by post bearing the news that Lord Rance's band, which had gone to help relieve Geneva, was defeated by the duke of Savoy's men. With him came a courier from Savoy bearing the news to the emperor. This might well be *seminarium futuri belli* [the seedbed of a future war]. For these little squabbles are very apt to bring after them great battle, as it is easy to see from ancient history, not only Greek and Roman but also French, as is apparent in the battle fought at Vireton.

My Lord, two weeks ago Andrea Doria, who had gone to bring victuals to the men holding, under the emperor's orders, Goleta near

Tunis, and especially water—for the Arabs of the region continually make war on them and they dare not come out of their fort—arrived in Naples and stayed only three days with the emperor, then left with twenty-nine galleys. They say this is to meet Il Giudeo and Cacciadiavolo, who burned much territory in Sardinia and Minorca. The Grand Master of Rhodes, a Piedmontese, died lately; elected in his place was the commander of Forton, between Montauban and Toulouse.

My Lord, I'm sending you a book of prognostics that has this whole city buzzing, entitled *De eversione Europae* [*On the overthrow of Europe*].[102] For my part, I put no faith in it at all, but you never saw Rome so addicted to these vanities and divinations as it is right now. I think the cause is since *mobile mutatur semper cum principe vulgus* [ever does the fickle herd shift with the prince]. I'm also sending you the copy of a brief that the Holy Father decreed some time ago for the coming of the emperor. I'm sending you also the entry of the emperor at Messina and at Naples and the funeral oration delivered at the burial of the late duke of Milan.

My Lord, as humbly as I can I commend myself to your good grace, praying Our Lord to give you, in good health, a good long life.

In Rome, this 30th day of December.

Your very humble servant,

FRANÇOIS RABELAIS.

6.13:

Letter from Rome to Geoffroy d'Estissac. January 28, 1536. Missive letter in French prose.

My Lord,

I received the letter you were pleased to send me dated on the second day of December, by which I learned that you had received my two packets, one of the 18th, the other of the 22nd, of October, with the four signatures that I was sending you.

Since then I wrote you very amply on the 29th of November and the 30th of December. I think that now you've received the said packets, for Sire Michel Parmentier, a bookseller living at the Escu de Basle [The Basel Arms], wrote me on the 5th of this present month that he has received them and sent them on to Poitiers. You may rest assured that the packets I shall send you will be kept faithfully from here to Lyon, for I placed them in a great wax-sealed packet that is for the king's affairs, and when the mail arrives in Lyon, it is opened by My Lord the Governor. Then his secretary, who is a good friend of mine, takes the packet that I address on the outer cover to Michel Parmentier. Therefore there is no problem unless from Lyon to Poitiers. That's the reason why it occurred to me to assess it[103] so it would get to Poitiers more safely by the messengers in their hope of earning a bit of change that way.

For my part, I keep the said Parmentier contented by little gifts I send him or his wife of novelties from down here, to keep him more on his toes in seeking out merchants or messengers to deliver these packets to you. And I fully agree with the plan you write me of, that is, not to put them in the hands of the bankers, for fear they may pick them. I would suggest that the first time you write me, especially if it's a matter of importance, you write a note to the said Parmentier, and enclose in your letter a crownpiece for him in consideration of the trouble he takes in sending me your packets and sending you mine. Sometimes worthy people are greatly obliged by a little thing, and it makes them more eager to help in future, when urgent dispatch might be important.

My Lord, I have not yet given your letter to Monsieur de Saintes, for he has not returned from Naples, where he went with Cardinals Salviati and Ridulfi. In two days he is due to arrive here: I'll give him your said letter and request an answer, then I'll send it to you by the first courier that will be dispatched. I understand that their business was not handled by the emperor in such a way as they hoped, and that the emperor told them peremptorily that in response to their request and with it the urging of Pope Clement, their ally and near relative, he had established Alessandro de Medici as duke over the territories of Florence and Pisa, which he had never thought to do and would [otherwise] not have done. To depose him now would be a mountebank's trick, playing "Now you see it, now you don't."[104] Therefore they should make up their minds to recognize him as their duke and obey him as vassals and subjects, and make no mistake about it [et qu'ilz ne y feissent faulte]. As regards the complaints they were making against the said duke, he would take cognizance of them on the spot, for he intends, after staying some time in Rome, to go by way of Siena and from there to Florence, to Bologna, to Milan and Genoa. Going back that way are the said cardinals, also Monsieur de Saintes, Strozzi, and a few others, *re infecta* [mission not accomplished].

On the 12th of this month the cardinals of Siena and Cesarini were back, who had been selected by the pope and the whole college as legates to the emperor. They managed to get the emperor to put off his coming to Rome until the end of February. If I had as many crownpieces as the pope would like to give pardon days, *proprio motu, de plenitudine potestatis* [on his own initiative, by the plenitude of his power], the consecrated official formula and other such favorable circumstances, to anyone who would put it off to five or six years from now, I would be richer than Jacques Coeur ever was.

In this city they have begun great preparations to receive him. And on the pope's command they have made a new road by which he is to enter, to wit, from the San Sebastiano Gate heading toward the capitol [Camp Doly], Temple of Peace, and the Colosseum, and they're having him pass beneath the ancient triumphal arches of Constantine, Vespasian, Titus, Numetianus, and others, then alongside the Palazzo San Marco, and from there to the Campo di Fiore, and in front of the Farnese Palace, where the pope used to stay, then by the banks and under the Castello San Angelo; and to build and level this road they knocked down and demolished over two hundred houses and three or four churches and razed them to the ground, which many interpret as a bad omen [en maulvays présage]. On the Day of Saint Paul's conversion [January 25] our Holy Father went to hear mass at Saint Paul and gave a banquet for all the cardinals; after dinner he went back by the aforesaid road and lodged at the Palazzo San Giorgio. But it's pitiful to see the ruin of the houses that were demolished, and no payment or compensation at all is being made to the lords thereof. Today there arrived here the ambassadors from Venice, four good old graybeards on their way to see the emperor in Naples. The pope went with all his household [sa famille] to meet them, Cubicularii, Camerarii, Genissarii, Landsknechts, etc., and the cardinals sent their mules in pontifical state.

On the seventh of this month were received the ambassadors from Siena in good order, and after making their speech in open consistory, and having the pope respond in good Latin and briefly, they left to go to Naples. I do believe that from all parts of Italy [les Itales] will go ambassadors to meet the emperor; and he knows very well how to play his part to draw *deniers* out of them, as has been revealed for the past ten days, but I'm not yet fully informed about the ploy he used in Naples. I'll write you about it before long.

The Prince of Piedmont, son of the duke of Savoy, died in Naples two weeks ago; the emperor had a very honorable funeral held for him, and attended it in person. The king of Portugal six days ago sent word to his ambassador that he had in Rome that on receipt of his letter he was immediately to come back to him in Portugal, which he did right away, and, all booted and spurred, came to say good-bye to My Lord the most Reverend Cardinal du Bellay. Two days later was killed in broad daylight near the San Angelo Bridge a Portuguese gentleman who was soliciting in this city on behalf of the community of Jews who were baptized under King Emanuel and later was given a bad time by the contemporary king of Portugal so as to inherit their property when they died, and some other exactions he imposed on them beyond the edict and ordinance of the said late king of Portugal. I suspect that there is some sedition in Portugal.

My Lord, by the last packet I had sent you I notified you how some part of the Turk's army was destroyed by the Sophy near Bitliz. The said Turk did not take long to get his revenge, for two months later he fell upon the said Sophy with the most extreme fury ever seen, and after putting a great region of Mesopotamia to fire and the sword, he chased the said Sophy back past the Taurus Mountains. Now he is having a lot of galleys built on the River Tanais,[105] by which they will be able to descend on Constantinople. Barbarossa has not yet left the said Constantinople to keep the country secure, and has left a few garrisons in Bone [Abbaba] and Algiers, on the chance that the emperor should want to attack him. I'm sending you his portrait drawn from life, also [a plan of] the site of Tunis and of the maritime cities around there.

The Landsknechts that the emperor was sending to the duchy of Milan to keep the strongholds have all drowned and perished at sea to the number of 1,200 in one of the biggest and finest ships of the Genoese. And it was near a port of the Luccans named Lerici.[106] The occasion arose because they were getting bored at sea, and, wanting to land but unable to because of tempests and weather problems, came to think that the ship's pilot intended to keep delaying them without landing. For this reason they killed him and a few of the other officers of the said ship, and, with them slain, the ship was left with no one in control, and instead of pulling down the sails the Landsknechts raised them, like people unpracticed on the sea, in such disarray that they perished a stone's throw away from the said port.

My Lord I have heard that Monsieur de Lavaur, who was the king's ambassador to Venice, has been relieved and is going back to France. Going in his place is Monsieur de Rodez, and already has his retinue ready in Lyon for when the king will have sent him instructions.

My Lord to the best of my ability [tant je puys] I commend myself humbly to your good grace, praying Our Lord to give you in health a good life and a long one.

In Rome, this 28th of January, 1536.

Your very humble servant,

FRANÇOIS RABELAIS.

6.14:

Letter from Rome to Geoffroy d'Estissac in French prose. February 15, 1536.

My Lord,

I wrote to you on the 28th day of the month of January just past very fully about all the news I had had, by a gentleman named Tremelière,[107] serving Monsieur de Montreuil, who was returning from Naples, where he had bought a few of the horses of the kingdom for his said master and was going back posthaste to him in Lyon. On the said day, I received the packet you were pleased to send me from Ligugé, dated on the tenth of the said month, by which you know the order I've given in Lyon concerning the delivery of your letters, how they are brought to me swiftly and surely. Your said letter and packet were delivered at the Basel Arms [Escu de Basle] on the 21st of the said month, and on the 28th were brought to me here. And to keep up the speed displayed by the bookseller of the said Basel Arms in Lyon in this matter, for that is the main point, I think that the next time you write me you should write him some sort of note, and in it put some crownpiece or other old gold coin, such as a royal, angel, salut, etc., in consideration of the trouble he takes and the speed he makes. This little gesture will increase his eagerness to serve you better and better.

To answer your letter point by point, I had a diligent search made in the palace registers from the time you asked me about, to wit, the years 1529, 1530, and 1531, to see if they could find the act of the resignation made by the late Dom Philippe in favor of his nephew, and I gave the registry clerks two sun-crowns, which is very little, consider-

ing the great arduous task they performed. In short, they found nothing, and I've never been able to find out anything new about his
transactions. Therefore I suspect fraudulence in his case, or else the
memoranda you wrote me were not sufficient to find them with. And
to get some assurance about this you will have to send me word *cujus
diocesis* [of what diocese] was the late Dom Philippe and whether you
have learned anything to clear up the fact of the matter, such as
whether it was *pure et simpliciter* or *causa permutationis* ["purely and
simply" or "in view of a change," etc.].

My Lord concerning the piece of which I was writing you the
response made by My Lord Cardinal du Bellay when I presented your
letter to him, there is no reason for you to be distressed about it.
Monsieur de Mascon has written you what the story is, and we're not
about to have a legate to France.[108] Quite true it is that the king
presented the cardinal de Lorraine to the pope, but I think that Cardinal du Bellay will try by every means to have the post for himself.
It's an old proverb that says *nemo sibi secundus* [to himself, no one is
number two]. And I see certain moves in progress, by which the said
Cardinal du Bellay will employ the pope in his own favor and lead him
to win over the king. Therefore do not be distressed if his response
seemed just a bit ambiguous in regard to you

My Lord, regarding the seeds [les graines] I sent you I can give you
full assurance that they are some of the very best there are in Naples,
and the same kind that the Holy Father has sown in his private garden
of Belvedere. No other kinds of salads do they have over here, except
garden cress [nasturtium] and orach [fors de Nasidord et d'Arrousse].
But those of Ligugé seem to me quite as good and a fair bit milder and
pleasanter for the stomach, especially for your own person, for those of
Naples seem to me hotter and tougher. As regards the season for
sowing, you will have to tell your gardeners that they don't sow them
anywhere nearly as early as we do on our side [of the Alps], for the
climate there has not turned nearly as warm as here.

They must not fail to sow your salads twice a year, namely in Lent
and in November, and the chards they can sow in August and September; the melons, pumpkins, and such like in March, and protect them
for certain days with rushes and with light manure not wholly rotted,
when they suspect frost. To be sure, they do sell here still other seeds
such as Alexandria marigolds, violes matronales, a plant they use to
keep their bedrooms cool in summer, which they call Belvedere, and

other, medicinal ones; but that would be rather for Madame d'Estissac.[109] If you would like, I'll send you some of everything, and without fail.

But I am constrained once more to have recourse to your alms, for the thirty crowns you were pleased to have delivered to me have almost run out, and yet I have not spent any of it for mischief or for my own mouth, for I ordinarily eat and drink at my Lord Cardinal du Bellay's or at Monsieur de Mascon's. But for petty paperwork and red tape concerning dispatches and renting bedroom furniture and keeping clothes in shape a lot of money goes, though I run my affairs as thriftily as I find possible. If it is your pleasure to send me some sort of bill of exchange [lettre de change], I hope to make use of it in your service and not be ungrateful for it. Moreover, in this city I see myriad little marvels at a low price, imported from Cyprus, Crete, and Constantinople. If you see fit, I'll send you whatever I find most suitable, both for you and for the said Madame d'Estissac. Having it brought from here to Lyon will cost nothing.

Thanks be to God, I have dispatched my whole business[110] and it cost me nothing but the dispatch of the bulls.[111] The Holy Father of his own free will granted me the dispensation, and I think you will consider the means pretty good and I requested nothing in these that is not civil and juridical. But I really had great need of good advice for the formalities. And I do indeed make bold to tell you that I employed in almost nothing My Lord Cardinal du Bellay, nor my lord the ambassador, although they had graciously offered to bring to bear on it not only their own words and favors, but also in full the name of the king.

My Lord, I have not yet passed your first letter over to Monsieur de Saintes, for he has not yet returned from Naples where he had gone, as I wrote you. He is due here in three days. Then I'll give him your first letter, and a few days later your second, and I'll ask for a response. I understand that neither he nor cardinals Salviati and Ridulfi, nor Philippo Strozzi and his crownpieces, were able to get anywhere with the emperor on their mission, even though they were willing to hand over to him, on behalf of all the expatriates and exiles from Florence a million cash in gold, to complete the Rocca, which is begun in Florence, and maintain it in perpetuity with adequate garrisons in the name of the said Emperor, and each and every year pay him a hundred thousand ducats, provided, and on condition, that he restore them in their original lands, possessions, and liberties.

On the contrary, the duke of Florence was received very honorably by him, and when he first arrived the emperor came out to meet him, and *post manus oscula* [after the hand-kissing]—a sign of allegiance—had him taken to the Castello Capuano in the said city, where is lodged his own bastard daughter, fiancée of the said duke of Florence, by the prince of Salerno, viceroy of Naples, the marquis del Vasto, the duke of Alba, and other leading men of his court; and there he [the duke of Florence] talked with her all he wanted, kissed her, and had supper with her. From then on the aforesaid cardinals, bishop of Saintes, and Strozzi never stopped pleading with him. The emperor put them off until he arrived in this city for a final resolution. In the Rocca, which is a wondrously strong place built by the said duke of Florence in Florence, he had painted in front of the portal an eagle with wings as big as the sails of Mirebeau windmills, by way of protesting and making it understood that he depends only on the emperor. And he went about his tyranny so shrewdly that the Florentines attested *in nomine communitatis* [in the name of the community] before the emperor that they want no other lord than him. True it is that he thoroughly punished the expatriates and exiles.

Pasquin some time ago made up a little song in which he says to Strozzi: *Pugna pro patria* [Fight for your country]; to Allessandro, duke of Florence: *datum serva* [preserve what has been given you]; to the emperor: *quae nocitura tenes, quamvis sint chara, relinque* [give up things that harm you to keep, although they are dear to you]; to the king: *quod potes, id tenta* [what you can do, try]; to the two cardinals, Salviati and Ridulfi: *hos brevitas sensus fecit conjungere binos* [these two have joined their meager wits together].

My Lord, in regard to the duke of Ferrara, I have written you how he had come back from Naples and gone home to Ferrara. Madame Renée was delivered of a girl. She already had another lovely daughter six or seven years old and a little son aged three. He could not come to an agreement with the pope, because he [the pope] was asking him for an excessive sum of money for the investiture of his lands, notwithstanding the fact that he had come down fifty thousand crowns for the sake of the said lady, and this on the urging of My Lords Cardinals du Bellay and de Mascon, to keep ever increasing toward her the conjugal affection of the said duke of Ferrara. And that was why Lyon Jamet[112] had come to this city, and no more than a hundred and fifty thousand crowns remained. But they could not reach an agreement with the pope, because the pope wanted him to acknowledge that he held and possessed all his lands in fief from the Apostolic See. This the other would not do, and would acknowledge none but those his late father had acknowledged and which the emperor had adjudicated at Bologna by decree, in the time of the late Pope Clement. So he left *re infecta* [with mission not accomplished] and went off to see the emperor, who promised him that when he came he would certainly make the pope consent to come to the point contained in his said decree and that he [Ferrara] should go back home leaving an embassy to pursue the matter when he should be on this side [of the Alps] and that he was not to pay the sum already agreed on without full notification to him [the emperor].

The sharp thing is that the emperor is short of money and is looking for more everywhere and is taxing everyone he can and borrowing it everywhere. When he has arrived here, he will ask the pope for some, that's quite evident, for he will point out to him that he waged all those wars on the Turk and Barbarossa for the security of Italy and the pope, and he must perforce contribute. The said pope will reply that he has no money and will offer evident proof of his poverty. Then the emperor will ask him, without disbursing anything, for the money for the duke of Ferrara, which depends only on an OK [un fiat]. And that's how they play their games in these mysteries. At all events the matter is not assured.

My Lord, you ask me whether Lord Pierluigi Farnese is a legitimate or a bastard son of the pope [Alessandro Farnese, 1468–1549, Pope Paul III from 1534]. Know that the pope was never married, that is to say that the aforementioned is truly a bastard. And the pope had a wondrously beautiful sister. They still show in the palace, in that central section where the *sommistes* are, built by Pope Alexander [Rodrigo Borgia, 1434–1503, pope from 1492], a picture of Our Lady, which they say was painted from her portrait and likeness.

She was married to a gentleman, a cousin of Lord Renzo, and when he was away at war in the expedition to Naples, the said Pope Alexander used to visit her. The said Lord Renzo, apprised of the fact, notified his said cousin of it, remonstrating to him that he should not allow such an insult to be made to their family by a Spanish pope, and that in case *he* tolerated it he himself would not tolerate it. To sum it all up, he killed her. For which crime his grievance and his mourning, made him a cardinal, although he was still very young, and did many other good things for him.[113]

At this time the pope [still Alexander VI] kept a Roman lady of the house of Roffini, by whom he had a daughter who was married to Signor Bosio [Sforza], count of Santa Fiore, who died in this city since I have been here, and by her he had one of the two little cardinals, the one who is called Cardinal de Santa Fiore.

Also he had a son, who is the said Pierluigi whom you were asking about, who married the Count de Servelle's daughter, by whom he has a whole houseful of children, and among others the little cardinalcule Alessandro Farnese, who was made vice chancellor by the late Cardinal de Medici. By the above statements you can understand why the pope [still Alexander VI?] was not very fond of Signor Renzo, and for his part Signor Renzo did not trust him, also why there is a great feud between Lord Gianpaolo Ceri, son of the said Signor Renzo, and the aforesaid Pierluigi [Farnese]; for he [Pierluigi] wants to avenge the death of his aunt. But as for the role of the said Signor Renzo, he is quits, for he died on the eleventh day of this month, having gone hunting, a sport he was fond of, old as he was.

The occasion was that he had brought back from the fairs at Racanati a few Turkish horses, of which he took one on the hunt that had a soft mouth, so that he fell back on him and choked him with the saddlebow, and thus from that point on he lived no more than a half hour. That was a great loss for the French, and in him the king lost a good servant for Italy. To be sure, they say that his son Gianpaolo will be no less a one in the future, but for a long time he will have no such experience in armed warfare, or such a reputation among the captains and common soldiers as that late good man had. I wish with all my heart that out of his spoils Lord d'Estissac would get the county of Pontoise, for they say it brings in good revenue.

To attend the funeral and console his wife the Marquise, My Lord the Cardinal, sent all the way to Ceri, which is about twenty miles from this city, Monsieur de Rambouillet and the Abbé de Saint-Nicaise, who was a near relative of the deceased (I think you've seen him at court, he's a very alert little man who used to be called Arch-deacon des Ursins), and a few others, of his protonotaries. Monsieur de Mascon did likewise.

My Lord, I'll put off until the next time I write you to inform you at greater length of the news of the emperor, for what he has in mind has not yet been clearly revealed. He is still in Naples; they are expect-ing him [here] for the end of the month and making great preparations for his coming and many a triumphal arch. His four marshals for lodging [mareschaux des logis][114] have already been in this city for some time: two Spaniards, one Burgundian, and one Fleming. It is pitiful to see the ruins of the churches, palaces, and houses, that the pope had knocked down and demolished in order to build him a road and level it. And moreover, for the costs he taxed and levied money on the college of my lords the cardinals on the officers of the curia, the artisans of the city, even to the water-sellers. Already this whole city is full of foreigners.

On the fifth of this month there arrived here, by the emperor's command, the cardinal of Trent [Tridentinus, in Germany] with a great retinue more sumptuous than is the pope's. In his company were over a hundred Germans dressed in a livery, to wit, in red robes with a yellow stripe, and embroidered on the right sleeve the figure of a sheaf of wheat, around which was written *Unitas* [unity]. I understand that he is very desirous of peace and conciliation for all Christendom, and of the council in any case. I was present when he said to My Lord Cardinal du Bellay: "The Holy Father, the cardinals, bishops, and prelates of the Church shrink from a council and do not want to hear about it, although they are summoned to it by the secular arm; but I can see the time coming when the Church prelates will be constrained to ask for one and the seculars will not hear of it. That will be when they have stripped the Church of all the property and patrimony that they had given in the time when by frequent councils the ecclesiastics maintained peace and order among the seculars."

Andrea Doria arrived in this city on the third of the said month in rather poor shape. No honor at all was paid him on his arrival, except that Signor Pierluigi takes him to the palace of the Cardinal Chamberlain, who is a Genoese of the family and house of Spinola. The next day he made his bow to the pope and left the day after on his way to Genoa on behalf of the emperor to get a sense of the general feeling in France now about the war. Here they have had certain news of the death of the old queen of England [Catharine of Aragon], and they say besides that her daughter is badly ill. However that may be, the bull they were working up against the king of England to excommunicate and interdict him and proscribe [outlaw] his country, as I was writing you, was not passed by the consistory, because of the articles *de commeatibus externorum et commerciis mutuis* [concerning foreign travel and international trade], which were opposed by My Lord Cardinal du Bellay and My Lord de Mascon on behalf of the king because of the damage he claimed they would do.[115] They have put off the bull until the emperor has come.

My Lord, I commend myself very heartily to your good grace, praying Our Lord to give you, in health, a good life and a long one. Rome, this 15th day of February, 1536.

Your very humble servant,

François Rabelais.

6.15:

To Estienne Dolet. Undated (1538 or before). Latin dizain about garum.[116]

F. Rabelais to Dolet
Once More about Garum
A Poem

Although by ancient doctors highly prized,
The garum, sent herewith, is now despised.
To oil or vinegar it adds its savors,
To butter too, if you prefer that flavor.
The appetite that scholars often lack,
Garum, better than drugs, will soon bring back.
No drug gives better gastric stimulation,
Or more benign relief from constipation.
So try it, please; you'll be surprised to know
No other spice will satisfy you so.

[Quod medici quondam tanti fecere priores
Ignotum nostris, en tibi mitto Garum.
Vini addes acidi, quantumvis, quantum olei vis;
Sunt, quibus est oleo plus sapidum butyrum.
Dejectam, assiduus Libris dum incumbis, orexim
Nulla tibi melius pharmaca restituent.
Nulla et Aqualiculi mage detergent pituitam;
Nulla alvum poterunt solvere commodius.
Mirere id potius, quantumvis dulcia sumpto
Salsamenta Garo nulla placere tibi.]

6.16:

To Briand Vallée. Undated. Jest by François Rabelais in twelve Latin verses, to and for his friend Briand Vallée, seigneur du Douhet.

JEST BY FRANÇOIS RABELAIS

When fury makes a father's anger clear,
Children flee to their mother's side in fear,
Knowing that there their safety is entire
Against his indignation and his ire.
When wrathful Jove in thunder gives a sign,
The cellar is your refuge, with the wine,
Where Earth's maternal bosom will provide,
For frightened humans, ample room to hide.
Pharos, oaks, towers, Acroceraunia know
The threefold potency of Jupiter's blow;
But casks lie safely underground in caves;
From Jove's thunder and lightning Bacchus saves.

[Patrum indignantum pueri ut sensere furorem
Accurrunt matrum protinus in gremium,
Nimirum experti matrum dulcoris inesse
Plus gremiis possit quam furor esse patrum.
Irato Jove, sic, coelum ut mugire videbis,
Antiquae matris subfugis in gremium:
Antiquae gremium matris vinaria cella est,
Hac nihil attonitis tutius esse potest.
Nempe Pharos sciunt atque Acroceraunia, turres
Aeriae, quercus, tela trisulca Jovis;
Dolia non feriunt hypogeis condita cellis
Et procul a Bromio fulmen abesse solet.]

6.17:

Almanac for the Year 1541.[117] Late 1540. From the few brief fragments still legible, M. A. Screech, in his meticulous critical edition of Rabelais's Almanacs and Prognostications (Droz, 1974, pp. 49–53), has determined their order; the text of title and heading; the few fragments presented here; the type of almanac it was (primarily liturgical, astronomical, and medical), that it was published in Lyon, probably by François Juste; and that it closely followed one for 1534 (author unknown to us) published by Clauda Carcan, widow of Rabelais's first publisher Claude Nourry.

ALMANAC FOR THE YEAR MDXLI,

Calculated on the Meridian of the Noble City of Lyon,

At the Elevation which . . . by . . . degrees . . . minutes

In Latitude . . . in Longitude

By Master Françoys Rabelais

Doctor of Medicine

The year after the nativity of our Savior . . . one thousand five hundred; we shall have:

Dominical letter B.

Golden number iii

Cycle of the Sun x

Indiction xiv

Between Christmas and Shrove Sunday there are iv weeks

Septuagésima the xiiith of . . Feb

Easter the xviith of April.

Rogation Day the xxii of May.

Ascension the xxvi of May.

Pentecost the v of June.

Advent the xxvii of November.

Conjunction of Moon with Mars (Opposition with Saturn)

In the tail of the Dragon

The characters of the 12

Aries Taurus Gemi

Cancer Leo Virgo

Libra Scorp Sagi

Capri Aquar Pis

For the Moon sign of

half a minute

The Sundays since . . .

[two fuzzy lines]

6.18:

To Antoine Hullot. March 1, 1542, from the Château de Saint-Ayl[118] [pron. Saint-Y; near Orléans]. Missive letter in French prose.

"He Pater Reverendissime quomodo bruslis? Quae nova? Parisiis non sunt ova?" These prefatory words addressing your Reverences, translated from Patelinese into our Orleanese vernacular, amount to my saying something like this:

"Sir, a warm welcome home to you from the wedding, the feast, and Paris. If the power of God should inspire you to betake your Paternity into this hermitage, you should have some good ones to tell us; also the lord of the said place would give you certain kinds of carp-like fish that you pull out by the hair. Now, you will do that, not whenever you please, but when you are brought to it by the will of that great, good, pitying god, Who never did create Lent, but certainly did [create] salads, herrings, young cod, carp, pike, dace, umbrines, blays [or bleaks], sticklebacks, etc. Also (Item), the good wines especially the one *de veteri jure enucleando*,[119] which is being saved here for your coming, like the Holy Grail and a second, true quintessence. *Ergo veni, Domine, et noli tardare*, I mean *salvis salvandis, id est, hoc est*,[120] without letting yourself be troubled or distracted from your more urgent affairs.

"Sir, after commending myself with all my heart to your good grace, I shall pray Our Lord to keep you in perfect health.

"From Saint-Ayl, this first day of March, 1542.

"Your humble *architriclin*, servant, and friend,

FRANÇOIS RABELAIS, physician."

The newly-elected Monsieur Pailleron will find here my humble commendations to his good grace, as will Madame, the newly-elected's wife, and Monsieur Daniel the bailiff, and all your other good friends and yourself. I shall ask the [bishop's] keeper of the seal [Monsieur Le Scelleur] to send me the Plato he had loaned me; I'll send it back to him soon.

To My Lord the Bailiff of the Bailiff of Bailiffs.[121]

Honored Master Antoine Hullot, lord of the Court Compin, in Christendom, at Orléans.

6.19:

The Great New True Prognostication. Late 1543. French prose, possibly by R.[122]

THE GREAT NEW TRUE PROGNOSTICATION FOR THE YEAR 1544
Composed for the utility of all true Christians
Studious in honorable fields of knowledge
By Master Seraphino Calbarsy,[123]
Doctor of the very honorable science of astrology, of medicine,
And of the whole encyclopedia. With the fairs of France
And also the dog days.
This year we have three eclipses of the moon,
And one of the sun.
To Readers of Goodwill
Greetings and Peace in Jesus Christ.

On this bit of paper that was still blank I'd like to reply to the calumny of certain idlers. For they commonly say: *quod opportet mendacem esse memorem* [a liar had better have a good memory]. And then you know that "Every man is a liar"; wherefore a man who intends to lie must think well on what he has said so as not to be found out saying two [different] things. So, abandoning such reveries, I turn to exposing to you briefly what I find about this present year. When Hippocrates described the *Epidemics* and other maladies that happened in his time, he always referred the causes thereof not to the present state but to those of the preceding years. So did Thucydides, as was very well noted by the learned Claudius Galen.

I likewise consider not so much the state of this present year as that of those preceding and of the one following 1544, in which Saturn, from the first of March until the 20th of July, will complete its retrogradation,[124] Jupiter from the 7th of March to the 6th of July will be baneful in its retrogradation; Mars, from the 22nd of May until the 26th of July, will retrograde. Venus from the beginning of the year will be retrograde; Mercury, from the 26th of March until the 17th of April and from the 20th of July until the 12th of August. And besides that, from the 14th of November until the 4th of December it will retrocede. And, basing my argument on that, I greatly fear this year an assault of pestilences and dire maladies from this climate, and the start of some great trouble between

781

kings and great princes. There appear also some new upward pressures among the common people.

At all events, about nothing do I offer assurance. But in any event blessed be the holy name of God.

Of the Disposition of
the Goods and Fruits of the Earth.

According to the influences of the celestial bodies, I find that we have a good year for all goods and fruits issuing from the ground, especially for hayseed, vegetables, and cultivated produce, which will be in great danger of being spoiled because of the aforesaid planets, which will reign this year.

Of the Eclipses of This Present Year.

Eclipse of the moon will be on the 10th day of January at 7 hours and 14 minutes of the forenoon[125] at the sign of Cancer at the 24th degree, and it will be completely dark and will last one hour and forty-four minutes.

Eclipse of the sun will be on the 24th of January at 9 hours and 17 minutes before noon at the sign of Aquarius at the 14th degree, and it will not be completely dark and will last one hour.

Eclipse of the moon will be on the 4th day of July at 8 hours and 32 minutes after noon, at the sign of Capricorn; and it will be completely dark and will last 1 hour and 51 minutes.

Eclipse of the moon will be on the 24th day of December at 6 hours and 28 minutes before noon at the sign of Cancer at the 18th degree; and it will be completely dark and will last 1 hour and 48 minutes.

Of the New, Full, and Quarter Moons
throughout the Twelve Months of the Year.

And firstly

On the second day of January will be the first quarter of the December moon at two o'clock in the forenoon, and it will be fine weather. The full moon will be on the 10th day at 6 hours and 12 minutes of the forenoon, and there will be a change in the weather. The last quarter will be on the 17th day of the said month at 6 hours after noon, and the weather will be fine.

The January moon will be new on the 24th of the said month at 9 hours and 32 minutes of the forenoon, and there will be wind, cold, snow. The first quarter will be on the last day of the said month at ten o'clock P.M. and the weather will be fine.

The February moon will be new on the 22nd day of the said month at exactly noon, and there will be rain, wind, snow, and hail. The first quarter will be on the last day of the said month at one o'clock A.M., and the weather will be fine. The full moon will be on the 7th day of April at ten thirty-nine o'clock P.M., and the weather will be fine. The last quarter will be on the 14th day of the said month at one o'clock P.M., and the weather will be fine. The last quarter will be on the fourteenth day of the said month at 1 hour after noon, and the weather will be fine.

The March moon will be new on the twenty-third day of the said month at exactly noon, and there will be rain, wind, snow, and hail. The first quarter will be on the last day of the said month at one o'clock A.M., and the weather will be fine. The full moon will be on the seventh day of April at ten thirty-nine o'clock P.M., and the weather will be fine. The last quarter will be on the fourteenth day of the said month at one o'clock P.M., and the weather will be fine.

The April moon will be new on the twenty-second day of the said month at 2 hours and 28 minutes of the forenoon, and there will be a rainy wind. The first quarter will be on the last day of the said month at five o'clock of the forenoon. The full moon will be on the 7th day of the month of May at 6 hours and 56 minutes,[126] and there will be rainy wind. The last quarter will be the 13th day of the said month at 9 hours after noon, and there will be a gentle rain.

The May new moon will be on the 21st of the said month at 5 hours and 15 minutes after noon, and the weather will be fine. The first quarter will be the 29th day of the said month at seven o'clock after noon, and the weather will be fine. The full moon will be on the 5th day of the month of June at 1 hour and 53 minutes after noon, and there will be a gentle rain. The last quarter will be on the twelfth day of the said month at seven o'clock of the forenoon, and there will be some thunderstorm activity in the weather.

The June moon will be new on the 20th day of the said month at 8 hours and 6 minutes of the forenoon, and there will be a big wind. The first quarter will be on the 28th day of the said month at six o'clock in the forenoon, and the weather will be fine. The full moon will be on the 4th day of July at 8 hours and 30 minutes after noon, and there will be a change in the weather, thunder, rain, wind. The last quarter will be the eleventh day of the said month at eight o'clock after noon, and the weather will be fine.

The July moon will be new on the 19th day of the said month at 10 hours and 43 minutes after noon, and the weather will be fine. The first quarter will be on the 27th day of the said month at two o'clock; after noon there will be a change in the weather to windy. The full moon will be on the 3rd day of August at 4 hours and 8 minutes of the forenoon, and there will be a disturbance with heavy wind and dark. The last quarter will be on the 10th day of the said month at eleven o'clock of the forenoon, and there will be rather a bit of wind.

The August moon will be new on the 18th day of the said month at 1 hour and 5 minutes after noon, and there will be a rainy wind. The first quarter will be on the 25th day of the said month at eight o'clock after noon, and there will be cloudy weather and rain. The full moon will be on the 25th of the said month at eight o'clock after noon, and the weather will be cloudy with rain. The full moon will be on the first day of September at 1 hour and 46 minutes after noon, and the weather will be fine. The last quarter will be the 9th day of the said month at 5 o'clock of the forenoon, and the weather will be dangerous.

The September moon will be new on the 17th day of the said month at 2 hours 50 minutes of the forenoon, and there will be thunder, rain, hail, wind, and storm. The first quarter will be on the 24th day of the said month at two o'clock of the forenoon, and the weather will be cloudy, cold. The full moon will be on the 1st day of October at 2 hours before noon, and the weather will be fine. The last quarter will be on the 9th day of the said month at 1 hour of the forenoon, and the weather will be fine.

The October moon will be new on the 16th day of the said month at 3 hours and 39 minutes after noon, and the weather will be fine. The first quarter will be on the 23rd day of the said month at 9 hours of the forenoon, and there will be rain and wind. The full moon will be on the 30th day of the said month at 5 hours and 20 minutes after noon, and the weather will be fine. The last quarter will be the 7th day of the month of November at 8 hours after noon, and there will be rather a bit of wind.

The November moon will be new on the 15th day of the said month at 3 hours 23 minutes of the forenoon, and there will be a rainy wind. The first quarter will be on the 21st day of the said month at 6 hours after noon, and there will be rain, wind, snow. The full moon will be on the 29th day of the said month at 11 hours and 12 minutes after noon, and the weather will be fine. The last quarter will be on the 7th day of December at 3 hours after noon, and there will be a cold wind.

The December moon will be on the 14th day of the said month at 2 hours and 10 minutes after noon, and the weather will be fine. The first quarter will be on the 21st of the said month at 6 hours of the forenoon, and there will be rather a bit of wind. The full moon will be on the 29th day of the said month at 6 hours and 27 minutes of the forenoon, and there will be wind, rain, and snow.

Of the Four Parts of This Present Year.

In spring the sun will be entering Aries on the 10th of March at 9 hours and about 36 minutes, in the ascendant of the second triplicity of Gemini,[127] of which, in our hemisphere, by multiple dignities [effects], the dominator is Saturn. So after February has passed, which will be of very bad weather, windy, rainy, and in the mountains bringing heavy snows, there will follow the said spring, more gracious, although very inconstant; as is usual, it is (mainly in the month of May) very windy and rather cold, more so than anyone would need. There will reign very long and often mortal maladies. The gains will be small, except in what concerns the act of war, ruining many places and strongholds, and the weather will be very favorable for women to conceive and deliver children.

On the 11th of June around eight o'clock at night the Sun will enter Cancer, as the 3rd of Capricorn is rising in our hemisphere which will be the beginning of the summer quarter, less hot than usual and very windy. The populace and common run of people will suffer much because of men-at-arms. Some great prince or princes, through illness, will be in fear of death, and spring will be fatal to them. Wives [or, women] will be fine and apt for generation and will undertake great enterprises, in sea voyages, but at great peril.

Autumn, which is the sun entering Libra, will begin on September 12th at about 10 hours of the forenoon and about 22 minutes, while rising in our hemisphere is the 23rd degree of the Scorpion, in the beginning very humid, then cold and dry and very windy around Saint Clement's Day [November 23] or a little before the quarter, for the rest rather well inclined.

On the 11th of December at 3 hours and about 29 minutes will begin the winter quarter, as the 24th of Gemini rises in our east with cold but no excess of it. Many illnesses will reign, in both the common people and persons of state, besides the ordinary disposition of winter, and many of them mortal. Women will not be well and will be very subject to miscarriages and especially in danger of their life. May God by His benign grace change [their] trouble into good.

The Fairs of Lyon and France:[128]

The fairs of the kings begin on the 11th of January.

The same end on the 30th of the said month.

Those of Easter open on Low Monday.[129]

Those of August open on the 4th of the said month.

And end on the 23rd of the said month.

Those of All Saints [All Hallows] Day open on the 3rd of November.

The same close on the 20th of the said month.

The Lyon fair always opens on the Monday after New Year's Day.

The fair at Saint-Germain-des-Prez on the 3rd day of February.

The Rouen fair on that said day; the second on Saint Roumain's Day.[130]

The Gien Race[131] on the second Monday in Lent.

The fair at Crépy-en-Valois[132] on that said day; and the second one on the second day in November.

The fair at Sens on the 18th day of March; and the second one on the 18th of October.

The fair at Compiègne begins on the Monday in mid-Lent, and lasts two weeks.

The Reims fair named La Cousture begins on the Thursday after Easter; the second one on Saint Rémy's Day [October 1].

The fairs at Troyes on the 8th of May; the second one on All Saints' Day [November 1].

The fair at Meaux in mid-May; the second one in the winter Saint Martin's Day [November 12].

The Château-Thierry fair on Ascension Day [40 days after Easter].

The Antwerp fair on the Wednesday after Pentecost [7th Sunday after Easter].

The Lendit[133] begins on the Wednesday after Saint Barnabas Day [June 11].

The Guibray, on the second Wednesday in August.

The Saint-Denis, on the 9th of October.

The Dog Days [Les jours caniculaires].

Note on the dog days, which begin on the 10th of July and end on the 20th of August, one should not be bled or take a laxative. However there are days noted, so that in case of necessity, the least harmful may be chosen.

Almanac for the Year 1544.

Dominical letter F. E	Easter the 13th of April.
Golden Number 6.	Rogation Day will be the 18th of May.
Cycle of the Sun 12th.	Ascension on the 22nd of May.
Indiction 2nd.	Pentecost on the 1st of June.
Septuagésima, the 10th of Feb.	Advent on the 30th of November.

Between Christmas and Shrove Sunday there are 8 weeks, 4 days.

Finis.

6.20:

To Cardinal du Bellay. February 6, 1547. From Rabelais in Metz. Missive letter in French prose.

My Lord, if Monsieur de Saint-Ayl[134] had had any convenient chance to pay you his respects when he left, I would not right now be in such need and anxiety, as he will be able to explain to you more fully, for he was assuring me that you were kindly disposed to grant me some alms, if there happened to be some reliable man available coming from your side [of the Alps]. Certainly, My Lord, if you do not take pity on me, I don't know what I have to do, unless, as a last desperate resort, I take service with someone around here, with evident harm and loss to my studies. It is not possible to live more frugally than I do, and you could not give me so little of the property that God has put in your hands that I would not get through by just keeping body and soul together and getting along decently, as I have done until now, for the honor of the house I had come out of when I left France.

My Lord, I commend myself very humbly to your good grace, and I pray Our Lord to give you, in perfect health, a very good life and a long one.

From Metz, this sixth of February (1547?).

Your very humble servant,

FRANÇOIS RABELAIS, physician.

6.21:

The Shadow Battle [La Sciomachie]. Between March 4 and December, 1549. In French prose.[135] Lyon: Gryphius, 1549.

THE SHADOW BATTLE AND FEASTS

Given in Rome

At the palace of My Lord The Most Reverend Cardinal du Bellay

For the Happy Birthday

Of My Lord of Orléans

The whole piece extracted

From a copy of the letter written to My Lord

The Most Reverend Cardinal de Guise

By M. François Rabelais

Doctor of Medicine.

On the third day of February, 1549, between three and four o'clock in the morning, was born in the château of Saint-Germain-en-Laye ... Duke of Orléans,[136] younger son of the most Christian king of France, Henry of Valois, second of that name, and of his good wife the very illustrious Madame Catherine de Medici. That very day, through the banks, there was a very widespread rumor, of uncertain authorship, of this happy birth, not only of the aforesaid place and date but also of the time, to wit, around nine o'clock according to the way Romans reckon time. That was a prodigious and wondrous thing, although not so to my mind, for I could cite, from Greek and Roman history, remarkable receptions of news, such as of battles lost or won more than five hundred leagues away, or other matters of great importance, having been disseminated the very same day, and even before, without any known author.

Moreover, we saw some like these in Lyon on the day of Pavia, in the person of the late lord of Rochefort, and recently in Paris on the day of the duel between the lords de Jarnac and Chastaigneraye;[137] and myriad others. And it is a point on which the Platonists based their belief in the participation of divinity in tutelary gods, which our theologians call guardian angels. But this subject would reach beyond the proper length of a letter. What it amounts to is that all through the banks this news was believed so stubbornly that many people on the French side,[138] toward evening, lit bonfires in celebration and marked with white chalk on their calendars[139] this heaven-sent happy day. Seven days later this good news

788

was more fully substantiated by certain bank couriers, some coming from Lyon, others from Ferrara.

My lords the Most Reverend French cardinals who are at this Roman court [the curia], together with Lord d'Urfé, ambassador of His Majesty, not having any other private information, were still holding back from declaring their joy and gladness at this eagerly awaited birth, until Signor Alessandro Schivanoia, a Mantuan gentleman, arrived on the first day of this month of March, sent expressly by His Majesty to inform the Holy Father, the French cardinals, and the ambassador, or the above. Thereupon on all sides were held feasts and celebratory bonfires for the next three evenings.

My lord the Most Reverend Cardinal du Bellay, not content with these commonplace and trivial manifestations of gladness for the birth of so great a prince, destined for such great things in knighthood and heroic deeds, as appears from his horoscope, if he doesn't come to grief in marriage, wanted (in a manner of speaking) to do what Signor Gianguirdano Orsini did when King Francis (of happy memory) won the victory at Marignano. This man, seeing that on the enemy's side, from a false report celebratory bonfires were being lit in Rome, as if the said king had lost the battle, some days later, informed of the outcome of his [King Francis's] victory, bought up a row of continuous houses, in the form of an island, near Monte Giordano, had them filled with kindling, firewood, and casks, with plenty of cannon powder, then set fire to it all. It was a new *Alosis*,[140] and a new celebratory bonfire.

That is what the most reverend lord [Du Bellay] wanted to do, to display his extreme gladness over this good news: to put on some sort of spectacle, whatever the cost, never yet seen in Rome within our memory. However, unable to carry this out to his taste and satisfaction (then) because of an illness that at that time had struck the said lord ambassador, who because of his position was also concerned and involved in this, he was relieved of his perplexity by the intermediary of Signor Orazio Farnese, duke of Castres, and Lords Roberto Strozzi and de Maligny, whose ardor matched his own. These four put their heads together. In the end, after considering several schemes, they decided to put on a shadow battle [une Sciomachie], that is to say a simulation and representation of a battle on both water and land.

The Naumachie, that is to say the battle on water, was set up upstream from the Ponte Aeliano, right in front of the private garden of the Castrello San Angelo. The late Guillaume du Bellay, Lord of Langey, with his troops had fortified, guarded, and defended for quite a long time against the Landsknechts, who later sacked Rome. The order of this combat was this: fifty small vessels, such as little galleys, galliots, gondolas, and armed frigates, attacked a great monstrous galleon put together from the two biggest vessels there were in this navy, which they had towed up from Ostia and Porto by the power of wild oxen.

And after many feints, assaults, repulses, and other customary features of a naval battle, in the evening they set a fire inside the said galleon. There was a terrible bonfire of celebration, in view of the great number and quantity of fireworks they had placed inside. Already that galleon was set for a fight, the little vessels ready to attack, and painted to match the liveries of the attacking captains, with a very gallant-looking target-fence [la pavesade] and crew. But this combat was canceled because of a horrible rise of the Tiber and much too dangerous whirlwinds (or waterspouts); as you know, it's one of the most dangerous rivers in the world, and rises unexpectedly, not only by flooding from the waters pouring down from the mountains, from the melting snows or other rains, or by overflows from the lakes that drain into it, but also in a stranger way by the southerly winds which, blowing straight into its mouth near Ostia, suspend its flow, and, keeping it from running out into the Etruscan [Tyrrhenian] Sea, force it to swell and turn back on itself, with miserable calamity and devastation of the adjacent land.[141] Besides the fact that two days earlier one of his gondolas had been shipwrecked, which had on board some mountebanks unfamiliar with the sea, who thought they could show off and fool around on the water just as they do very well on land. Such a Naumachia was scheduled for Sunday the tenth of this month.

The Sciomachie on land was held on the following Thursday. To understand this better it should be noted that in order to put this on perfectly was chosen the Liazza Sant' Apostolo, because next to that of Agona [now Navone], it is the longest and most beautiful in Rome; also, and chiefly, because the palace of the most reverend lord[142] is along the length of this square. So in this [square], in front of the great gate of this palace, by the plan of Captain Gianfrancesco de Monte Melino,[143] was erected a castle in the form of a quadrangle, each face [side], of which was about a hundred and twenty-five paces wide, and half as much high, including the parapet, like that of the said wall. And this wall, on the main face [side], which looked out on the length of the square and the contour of its two turrets, up to the curtain was formed of strong planks and boards; the upper part was of brick, for the reason that you shall hear presently. The other two faces [sides] with their turrets were all made up of planks and boards. The wall of the palace gate served as a fourth face [side].

At the corner of this, on the inside of the castle, was erected a square tower of similar material three time as high as the other, small towers. On the outside everything was suitably joined, glued, and painted, as if they were walls of great stones cut rustic fashion, in the way you see the great tower at Bourges. The entire circuit was girded with a moat four paces wide and over half a fathom deep. The gate was modeled on the approach to the great gate of the palace, raised by the machicolation about three feet higher than the wall, from which a drawbridge came down all the way to the counterscarp of the moat.

On the aforesaid day, the fourteenth of this month of March the sky and the air seemed to favor the festivities. For not for a long time had there been seen a day as clear, serene, and cheery as this one was for its whole duration. The influx of the people was incredible. For not only the Most Reverend lord cardinals, almost all the bishops, prelates, officers, lords and ladies and common people of the said city had flocked there, but also from the lands up to fifty leagues around there had assembled a marvelous number of lords, dukes, counts, barons, gentlemen, with their wives and families, at the report that had been bruited abroad of this new tourney—besides the fact that on the preceding days had been seen all the fringers, tailors, embroiderers, plume-makers, and other workmen in similar trades busily occupied in completing the accouterments required for the festivity. With the result that not only the palaces, houses, lodges, galleries, and stands, were filled with a great crush of people, although the square is one of the biggest and most spacious to be seen, but also the roofs and tops of the neighboring houses and churches. In the middle of the square hung the coat of arms of my said lord of Orléans, with a very big margin appearing on both sides, surrounded by a festoon of myrtles, ivy, laurels, and orange boughs, charmingly edged in gold lace, with this inscription: "Cresce, infans, fatis nec te ipse vocantibus aufer" [Grow, child, and do not shun the destiny that calls you].

Around eighteen o'clock, by Roman timekeeping, which is between one and two in the afternoon, while the combatants were putting on their armor, the two Colonna leaders[144] came into the square with their swordsmen, looking in rather poor shape. Then came the Swiss of the pope's guard with their captain, all with metal cuirasses, pike in hand, toward the square. Then, to fill time and entertain the magnificent assembly, were turned loose four terrible fierce bulls. The first and second of them were turned over to the gladiators and bestiaries with sword and cape. The third was fought by three big Corsican dogs, a combat that provided a great pastime. The fourth was turned over to the long wooden weapons, to wit, pikes, partisans, halberds, long javelins, Bolognese boar-spears, because it seemed too frenzied, and might have done great harm among the common people.

When the bulls had been killed and the square emptied of people as far as the barriers, there came on Moreto [le Moret], Italy's archclown, mounted on a very powerful curtal horse and holding in his hand four lances bound and grafted into one, boasting that in one ride he would break them all on the ground. This he tried to do, spurring his horse fiercely; but all he broke was the handle, and decked out his arm like a clown jouster [en coureur buffonique].

That done, there entered the square, to the sound of fifes and drums, a company of footsoldiers, all elegantly accoutered, armed in harnesses nearly all gilded, both pikesmen and pistoleers, in the number of three hundred and more. These were followed by four trumpeters, a squadron of horsemen, all servants of his majesty on the French side, the most elegant you could ask for, in the number of fifty horses and more. These, with visors raised, took two turns around the square in sprightly fashion, making their horses prance, jump, and stamp their feet, moving in and out among one another, to the great satisfaction of all the spectators. Then they withdrew to the left side of the square toward the San Marcello Monastery. Captain of this band for the footsoldiers, was Lord Astorre Baglione. His ensign and his men's scarves were in the colors white and blue. Lord Duke Orazio [Farnese] was the leader of the men-at-arms, whose names I have gladly listed below, to honor them.

His Excellency the said Lord Duke.[145]

Paolo Battisto Fregosi.

Flaminio di Languillare.

Alessandro Cinquino.

Luca d'Onane.

Theobaldo de la Molare.

Filippo di Serlupis.

Dominico de Massimi.

Padre Luis Capisucco.

Padre Paolo de la Cecca.

Bernardino Piovene.

Lodovico Cosciari.

Gianpaolo squire to His Excellency.

All in guilt armor, mounted on stout chargers their pages mounted on jennets and Turkish horses for the sword-fighting.

His Excellency's livery was carnation and white, which could be seen in the dress, horse armor, caparisons, plumes, lances, sword scabbards, both of the aforesaid knights and of the page and lackeys who followed them in good numbers. His four trumpeters, clad in blouses of carnation velvet, scalloped and lined with cloth of silver. His Excellency was richly clad over the armor with an accouterment made up in the ancient style of carnation satin stitched with gold, covered with crescents fashioned of rich embroidery of silver cloth and purl. Likewise clad and covered with similar costume were all the aforesaid men-at-arms, and likewise their horses. And it should be noted that among the aforesaid embossed silver crescents, in certain squares were placed four embroidered sheaves of wheat in rich green needlework, around which was written the word flavescent [they will turn golden], meaning to signify, in my opinion, that some great hope was nearing maturity and fruition.

When the two bands had gone away and left the square empty, immediately there entered, by the right side of the lower end of the square, a company of beautiful young ladies, richly decked out, and clad in nymphal style, just as we see the nymphs on the ancient monuments. Of whom the leader, taller than the others and standing out among them, representing Diana,[146] wore on top of her forehead a silver crescent, her blond hair strewn over her shoulders, plaited over her head with a garland of laurel, all intertwined with roses, violets, and other lovely flowers, dressed, under the cassock and farthingale, in red crimson damask with rich embroideries, a fine Cyprus cloth all trimmed with gold [toute battue d'or], intricately plaited as if it were a cardinal's rochet, coming halfway down her legs, and over it all a very precious leopardskin, attached over her left shoulder with great gold buttons. Her buskins gilt, carved, tied in nymphal style, with laces of cloth of silver; her ivory horn hanging under her left arm; her quiver, preciously embroidered and wrought with pearls hung from her right shoulder on stout cords and tassels of white and carnation silk. She held in her right hand a little silvered dart.

The other nymphs differed little in accouterments, except that they did not have the silver crescent on their forehead. Each one held in her hand a very handsome Turkish bow, and a quiver like their leader's. Over their rochets some wore skins of tigers, others of lynxes, others of Calabrian martens. Some led greyhounds on a leash; others sounded on their hunting horns. It was a beautiful sight to see them. As they strolled thus around the square, with pleasing gestures as if they were going to the hunt, it happened that one of the troop, busy apart from the company tying a cord of her buskin, was seized by certain soldiers who came unexpectedly out of the castle. At this capture a horrible dread came over the company. Diana kept crying loudly for her to be given back, likewise the other nymphs with piteous and lamentable cries. No reply was made them from those who were inside the castle. Thereupon, firing a certain number of arrows over the parapet and fiercely threatening those inside, they went back with faces and gestures as sad and piteous as they had been joyous and merry when they came in.

When at the end of the square they met his excellency and his company they joined together in uttering frightful cries. Diana, after explaining the mishap to him as to her darling and favorite, witness the silver crescents strewn all over her accouterments, demanded help and vengeance, which was promised and assured her. Then the nymphs left the square. Thereupon His Excellency sends a herald out to those who were inside the castle, demanding the instant return to her of the abducted nymph, and threatening him stoutly and firmly, in case of refusal or delay, with putting them and the fortress to fire and the sword. The people inside the castle made reply that they wanted the nymph for themselves, and that, if they wanted to get her back, they would need knife play and not to forget anything in the store.[147] And then they not only did not give her back on that summons but they took her up to the very top of the square tower in view of the party outside. When the herald had returned and the refusal had been heard, His Excellency summarily held council with his captains. There it was resolved to destroy the castle and all those who should be inside.

At that moment there entered by the right side of the lower end of the square, to the sound of four trumpets a troop [un estanterol] of horsemen and a company of footsoldiers marching furiously, as if meaning to force their way inside the castle to the rescue of those who were holding it. Of the footsoldiers the captain was Signor Ciappino Orsini [Chappin Ursin], all gallant men, and superbly armed, both pikesmen and harquebusiers in the number of three hundred and more. The colors of his ensign and scarfs were white and a sort of orange. The horsemen, numbering fifty horses and more, all in gilded armor, richly clad and armed, were led by Lords Roberto Strozzi and Maligny. Lord Roberto's livery, his accouterment over his armor, his horses' trappings, caparisons, plumes, pennons, pages, and lackeys, were in the colors white, blue, and a sort of orange. That of Lord Maligny and of the men led by him was in the colors red, white, and black. And if those [horsemen] of His Excellency were well and advantageously mounted and richly accoutered, these men were in no respect worse off. The names of the men-at-arms I have set down here in their honor and praise.

Lord Roberto Strozzi.

Lord de Maligny.

Lord Averso di Languillare.

Lord de Malicorne the Younger.[148]

Sir Giambattisto de Vittorio.

Lord de Piébon.

Sir Scipio de Piovene.

Lord de Villepernay.

Spagnino.

Battisto, Pikesman of the lord ambassador.

The Cavalcador [Squire] of Lord Roberto.

Giambattisto Altoviti.

Lord de la Garde.

These last two were not in the combat, because, a few days before the festival, testing themselves inside the Baths of Diocletian with the company, the first got a broken leg, the second a cut the length of his thumb. So when these bands came proudly into the square, they were met by His Excellency and his companies. Then the skirmish was engaged, among those of both sides, with honorable courage, but without shattering lances or swords, however, as those last to enter kept pulling back toward the fort, the first entrants still pursuing them, until they were close to the moat. Thereupon from the castle came considerable heavy and medium artillery fire, and His Excellency and his troops pulled back inside his camp; the last two bands to arrive entered the castle.

When the skirmish was over, out came a trumpeter from the castle, sent to His Excellency, to find out whether his knights wanted to test their prowess in single combat [Monomachie], that is to say man-to-man [one-to-one] against the occupants. To which the reply was that they would do so right gladly. When the trumpeter had gone back, out of the castle came two men-at-arms, each one lance in hand and visor down, and took up a position on the ravelin of the moat, facing the assailants, from whose ranks likewise two men took up their shields, lance in fist, visor down. Then as the trumpets sounded on one side and the other, the men-at-arms came together, furiously spurring their warhorses. Then, with lances broken on one side and the other, they took sword in hand and fought one another so hard that their swords flew into pieces. When these four withdrew, out came four others and fought two against two, like the first ones, and thus subsequently fought all the horsemen of the two opposing bands.

When these individual combats were finished, while the footsoldiers were beating a retreat, His Excellency and his company, changing horses, took up new lances, and presented themselves in a troop in front of the castle. The footsoldiers, on their right flank, covered by some shield-bearers, brought up ladders, as if to take the castle unawares, and had already set up two ladders beside the gate, when from the castle came such heavy artillery fire, and were hurled so many petards, grenades, fire-pots, and flame-throwers, that the entire neighborhood resounded,[149] and all you could see around you was fire, flames, and smoke, with horrible thunderings from such a cannonade. Wherefore those outside had to pull back and abandon the ladders. A few soldiers came out of the fort beneath the smoke and charged the footsoldiers outside, in such a way that they took two prisoners. Then, following up their good fortune, they were surrounded by a certain squadron of the outsiders hidden in ambush.

At that point, fearing that a battle would ensue, they pulled back on the double, and lost two of their men, who were similarly taken prisoner. Upon their retreat, out of the castle came the horsemen, in rows of five, lance in fist. The assailants likewise came forward and broke lances in a throng, in many charges, which is a very perilous thing. At all events, Lord de Maligny, having made a pass without a hit against His Excellency's groom, on the return charge hit him so violently that he knocked man and horse to the ground. And on the spot the horse died, which was a very fine powerful charger. Lord Maligny's was left with a broken shoulder.

During the time when they were dragging off the dead horse, in another more joyous harmony rang out the bands of musicians, which had been set up on various stands over the square, such as oboes, cornets, sackbuts, German flutes, trombones, little bagpipes, and the like, for the enjoyment of the spectators at each stage of the entertaining tourney. When the square was emptied, the men-at-arms on both sides, Lord de

Maligny mounted on a fresh jennet and the groom on another (for their wounds were slight), putting aside the lances fought with swords in a crowd mingled in on one another, rather fiercely; for at least one man broke three or four swords; and although they were adequately protected, several were disarmed.[150]

The end came when a band of attacking harquebusiers, firing long pistols, charged the occupants, whereby they were forced to pull back to the fort, and they got down on foot. When that happened, to the sound of the castle bell, a great salvo of artillery was fired, and the assailants withdrew, likewise got down on foot, and planned to give battle, seeing all the occupants come out of the fort in combat order. Therefore each man took his blunted pike in hand, and, their ensigns unfurled, at a slow deliberate pace came forth in view of the occupants, for a time of silence long enough for the saying of the Lord's Prayer.[151]

Throughout the entire course of the preceding tourney great was the noise and applause of the spectators on every side. At this prayer there was silence everywhere, not without dread, especially on the part of those who had not been in battle at another time. The combatants, having kissed the ground,[152] at the sound of the drums got up instantly, and, pikes in hand, with a frightful howling came to grips; likewise the harquebusiers on the flanks fired tirelessly. There were so many pikes broken that the square was all covered with them. With their pikes broken, they set hands to their swords, and there was so much flailing about in every direction that in one round the occupants drove back the attackers more than two pikes' lengths; in the other the occupants were driven back all the way to the ravelin of the turrets. Then they were saved by the artillery, firing from every vantagepoint in the castle, whereat the attackers withdrew. This combat lasted rather long. And a few scratches were dealt by the pikes and swords, however not in anger or ill feeling. Retreat having been beaten on both sides, there remained on the field, amid the broken pikes and shattered armor, two dead men; but they were straw men, one of which had its left arm cut off and its face all bloody; another had a pike splinter through his body at the chink in his armor.

Around these sprang up fresh entertainment while the music played. For Frérot,[153] with his accouterment of carnation velvet laminated with cloth of silver, in the form of bats' wings, and Fabrizio with his laurel wreath, joined them. One of the two admonished them as men who died for the faith; the other searched them in the gussets and the codpiece to find their purses. Finally, uncovering and stripping them, they showed the public that they were only straw men. Whereat a great laugh arose from the spectators, amazed at how they had been placed and tossed there during this furious combat.

At this retreat, with the air cleared of the smoke and odors of the cannon fire, there appeared in the middle of the square eight or ten gabions in a row, and five pieces of artillery on wheels, which had been placed there during the battle by His Excellency's cannoneer. When this had been perceived by a sentinel posted on the high tower of the castle, to the sound of the bell was expressed and heard great fright and howling by those inside. And then there was so much artillery fire, from all parts of the fort, and so many shots, rockets, cannonballs, flame-throwers,[154] toward the emplaced gabions, that you would not have heard thunder from the sky. This notwithstanding, the artillery emplaced behind the gabions fired two furious salvos against the castle, to the great terror of the attending public. From which the wall fell down right from the outside to the curtain wall, which, as I have said, was brick. From this it came about that the moat was filled up. At this fall, the artillery inside was left uncovered. A bombardier fell dead from the top of the great tower, but it was a dressed-up straw bombardier. Then those inside began to raise ramparts behind this breach, with great effort and diligence. Meanwhile those outside made a mine by means of which they set fire to one of the castle's turrets, which, falling halfway to the ground, made a horrible noise. One of them kept continuously burning; the other made such a hideous thick smoke that you couldn't see the castle any more.

From then on came a new exchange of fire, and the five great artillery pieces fired two salvos against the castle. Thereby down fell the whole scarp of the wall, which, I have said, was made of planks and stout boards. Whereby, since it fell outward, it formed a sort of bridge entirely spanning the moat right up to the ravelin. There remained only the barrier and rampart that the occupants had erected. Then, to prevent an attack by those outside, who were all in battle array at the end of the square, there were fired ten fireballs, cannonballs, fire-bricks, and fire-pots, and from the rampart a great big balloon was hurled onto the square, from which all at once came out thirty spitfires, more than a thousand rockets all together, and thirty rocket-bombs [razes]. And the said balloon went racing around the square spurting fire from every side, which was a terrifying thing, fashioned by Messer Vincenzo, a Roman, and Francesco, a Florentine, cannoneers to the Holy Father. Frérot, playing the good fellow, ran after the balloon, calling it "Jaws of Hell" and "Lucifer's head," but, when he hit it once with a length of pike, he found himself all covered with fire, and was screaming like a madman, fleeing this way and that, and burning those he touched. Then he turned as black as an Ethiopian, and so strongly marked on the face it will still show three months from now.[155]

Upon the consummation of this balloon the assault was sounded on behalf of His Excellency,[156] who, with his men-at-arms, on foot, covered with great bronze shields, gilded in the old style, and followed by the rest of his bands, entered upon the aforesaid bridge. Those inside confronted him on the rampart and barrier. At this last the fighting was fiercer than it had been yet. Finally perforce they got over the barrier and onto the rampart. At which moment was seen on the high tower the coat of arms of His Majesty,[157] embossed with cheery festoons. To the right of which, a little lower, were those of My Lord of Orléans; to the left, His Excellency's which was about two o'clock at night. The abducted nymph was presented to His Excellency, and returned on the spot to Diana, who was in her place as if returning from the hunt.

The attending public great and small, nobles and commoners, religious and secular, men and women, fully and utterly delighted, content, and satisfied, applauded for joy and gladness on all sides, loudly shouting and singing: "Hooray for France! France, France! Long live Orléans! Long live Orazio Farnese!" Some added: "Long live Paris! Long live Bellay! Long live the Langey side!" We may say what they used to sing at the declaration of the games held once in a century: "We have seen what no one alive in Rome has ever seen, in short what no one living will ever see!"[158]

It was already getting late and a good time for supper, which, while His Excellency took off his armor and changed his clothes, as did all the valiant champions and noble combatants, was set in such great sumptuosity and magnificence that it could efface the celebrated banquets of many ancient Roman and barbarian emperors, indeed, even Vitellius's table and cuisine, so celebrated that it came to be a proverb, at whose banquet were served a thousand cuts of fish. I shall not speak of the number and the rare species of the fish served here; it is much too excessive. To be sure, I *will* tell you that at this banquet were served more than one thousand five hundred pieces of pastry, I mean meat pies, tarts, and *darioles* [little vegetable pies]. If the foods were copious, so were the drinks numerous. For thirty puncheons of wine and a hundred and fifty dozen servings of light white bread lasted hardly any time, not to mention the other common white bread. And so my said Most Reverend Lord's house was open to all comers, whoever they might be, all that day.[159]

At the first table of the middle room were counted twelve cardinals, to wit:

The Most Reverend Cardinal Farnèse.

The Most Reverend Cardinal di Santangelo.

The Most Reverend Cardinal Santa Fiore.

The Most Reverend Cardinal Sermonetti.

The Most Reverend Cardinal Ridulfi.

The Most Reverend Cardinal du Bellay.

The Most Reverend Cardinal de Lenoncourt.

The Most Reverend Cardinal de Meudon.

The Most Reverend Cardinal d'Armagnac.

The Most Reverend Cardinal Pisano.

The Most Reverend Cardinal Cornare.

The Most Reverend Cardinal Gaddi.

His Excellency Signor Strozzi, Ambassador from Venice. Ever so many other bishops and prelates.

The other halls, chambers, galleries of this palace were all full of tables served likewise with bread, wine, and victuals. When the tablecloths were taken up, for washing hands were offered on the table two artificial fountains all interwoven with fragrant flowers, with compartments in the old style. The top of these flamed with pleasing redolent fire, composed of musk-scented brandy. Below, by various channels out came Angel Water [myrtle-flavored], naphtha water. When Grace had been said to honorable music, by Labbat[160] with his great lyre was recited the Ode[161] that you will find here at the end, composed by my said Most Reverend Lord.

Then, when the tables were cleared and put away, all the lords came into the main hall, which was all decked and adorned with fine tapestries. There it was thought that a comedy would be performed; but it was not, because it was already after midnight. And at the banquet given earlier by My Lord the Most Reverend Cardinal d'Armignac, one had been put on which angered the spectators more than it pleased them, both by its length and rather insipid Bergamask gags, and by its frigid ingenuity and hackneyed plot.[162] In place of the comedy, to the sound of cornets, oboes, sackbuts, etc., in came a company of new *mattacini* [jesters, strolling players], who greatly delighted the entire audience. After which were brought on several troupes of masked guests, both gentlemen and ladies of honor, with rich devices and sumptuous attire. Then began the ball, which lasted until daybreak, during which my said Most Reverend lords, ambassadors, and other prelates, retired in great jubilation and contentment.

In this tourney and festival I noted two remarkable things; one, that there was no trouble, dissension, dispute, or tumult whatever; the other that, of all the silverware with which so many people of diverse estates were served, not a thing was lost or mislaid.[163]

On the next two days bonfires of celebration were lit in the public square, in front of the palace of my said Most Reverend Lord, with much artillery fire, and such a variety of fireworks that it was a wondrous thing, such as great balls, great mortars that each time fired over five hundred shots and rockets, spinningwheel and windmill firecrackers, fire clouds full of sparkling stars, cannon shots, some consecutive, some reciprocating, and a hundred other kinds. The whole thing was fashioned by the ingenuity of the said Vincenzo and of Le Bois le Court, the great saltpeter expert of Le Maine.[164]

6.22:

Sapphic Ode.[165] Latin, 84 verses, to the infant son of King Henry II, Louis d'Orléans (1549–1551), by the Most Reverend Cardinal Jean du Bellay, by common agreement published in the same volume with Rabelais's *Shadow Battle* (no. 21 above).

SAPPHIC ODE

Wing-footed deity, by Zeus assigned
To bring the gods' commands to humankind,
Speeding communication, day and night,
    By rapid flight.

Come tell the blessed sires,[166] the aged pastor,
In whom the gods in council look as master,
To whom Quirites[167] find reflected still
    The divine will,

That far from Arno's and from Tiber's shore,
Which once had been her homes, the goddess bore
To France and Rome a star, hard by the Seine,
    Under his father's reign.

Long since she'd sailed inside the Phocian port,[168]
As thronging Tritons banded to escort,
Under the shelter of its ramparts steep,
   Fearless of raging deep.

Happy the day to Frank and Tuscan hearts
That brought her to her prince and to these parts,
Her lovely form, good mind, and radiant face,
   And every grace.

Auspicious wedding-knot, by Venus tied,
That brought nuptial delights to groom and bride!
Great Juno also on this union smiled,
   And soon she brought a child.

What happy nights for Catherine, wedded queen![169]
What days for Henry, happy and serene!
What bliss for both, for your descendants too!
   Answers to prayers, fond wish come true.

What help from Juno with that first-born son!
Nor did she let you down after that one:
Two girls, the fourth child next, another boy,
   His smile a mother's joy.

This fourth the gods gave not to France alone;
Italian youth proclaim a share their own,
And hail the birth, as do the youth of France,
   With song and dance.

If French youth claimed to him exclusive right,
While his sire held the kingdom for him tight,
And Jove has vowed his empire to extend
   To the earth's end,

It would tempt the Fates, make jealous gods and men.
Better allow the Latin bees again
From all these buds their honeyed share to glean,
   Than pick the flowers clean.

The Graces, Henry's comrades, will not yield
Their title to the first blooms of the field,
Or to another mortal let them go;
   And neither would the Nymph of Fontainebleau.[170]

Nor would you Muses, dwelling still in Rome,
Whom Gauls would lure to a transalpine home,
And who by now, accustomed to that clime,
    Adopt Gaul's song and rhyme.

And that lone pearl of women, like the rest,
Margaret,[171] Minerva's rival, would protest,
As would her likeness, young Jeanne of Navarre,
    Follow her mother's star.

So would the nymph from down beside the Po
Deal all such arrogance a mighty blow,
Whose royal spouse joins Hector's valiant arm
    To Paris's charm.

And you, Horace,[172] oft subject to desire;
The one for whom your heart is now on fire,
With the assent of those who hold you dear,
    Would make refusal clear.

Catherine, for all the good here heaped on you,
You'd owe all; full return would never do:
Our geniuses in chorus, I expect,
    Would both object.

Our greatest hope being thus denied by Fate,
Let's be content our aims to moderate:
Let him take back this budding flower to Rome[173]
    To her new Latian home.

If she's too young, you fear, unweaned, you say,
Let her be suckled in the Roman way.
Romulus did not long lack milk: to save
    Him, of her own the she-wolf gave.

And if no Christian name is yet assigned
The child, do not let that disturb your mind:
Romulus also lacked his own cognomen
    Till the priest took the omen.

And if this better set your heart at ease,
Here on this child's birth everyone agrees,
The gods, the goddesses and Rome entire:
    Well born of Roman sire.[174]

[Mercuri, interpres superum, venusto
Ore qui mandata refers vicissim,
Gratus hos circum volitans, et illos,
   Praepete cursu,

Adveni sanctis Patribus, senique,
Praesidet qui concilio deorum,
Quem sui spectat soboles Quiritum
   Numinis instar.

Dic iubar, quod Sequanidas ad undas
Edidit Gallis Italisque mixtim
Diva, quam primum Tyberi tenellam
   Credidit Arnus,

Tritonum post hanc comitante turba
Phocidum celsas subiisse turres,
Nec procellosum timuisse vidit
   Nereis aequor.

O diem Hetruscis populis colendum,
Et simul Francis, juveni puellam
Qui dedit, forma, Genio, decore,
   Ore coruscam!

Fauste tunc in quos Hymenaee, quos tu
In iocos, Cypri, es resoluta! vel quas
Iuno succendit veniente primum
   Virgine taedas!

Ut tibi noctes, Catharina, laetas,
Ut dies, Errice, tibi serenos,
Demum ut ambobus, sobolique fausta es
   Cuncta precata!

Ut deam primo dea magna partu
Juvit! ut nec defuerit subinde,
Quartus ut matri quoque nunc per illam
   Rideat infans.

Quartus is, quem non superi dedere
Galliae tantum: sibi namque partem
Vendicat, festisque vocat iuventus
   Nostra choreis.

Laeta si Franciscum etenim iuventus
Hunc petat, cui res pater ipse servat
Gallicas, et cui imperium spopondit
    Iuppiter orbis:

Provocet divos hominesque, tentet
Pensa fatorum: fuerit Latinis
Et satis Tuscis apibus secundos
    Carpere flores.

Nam sibi primos adimi nec ipsae
Gratiae Errici comites perennes,
Nec sinat raucis habitans Bleausi
    Nympha sub antris.

Nec magis vos, O Latio petitae
Celticis, sed iam Laribus suetae, et
Vocibus Musae, ac patriis canentes
    Nunc quoque plectris.

Et puellarum decus illud, una
Margaris tantum inferior Minerva,
Ac Navarraeae specimen parentis
    Iana reclamet.

Ne quidem Nympha id probet illa, ab imis
Quae Padi ripis juvenem secuta est,
Si Parim forma, tamen et pudicum
    Hectora dextra.

Nec tuos haec quae patefecit ignes,
Ignibus praeclare aliis Horati,
Cuncta dum clamant tibi iure partam
    Esse theatra.

Tu licet nostro a Genio tributam ob
Gratiam nil non, Catharina, nobis
Debeas, nostro at Genio tuoque heic
    Ipsa repugnes,

Spe parum nixis igitur suprema
Sorte contentis media, faveto,
Et recens per te in Latios feratur
    Flosculus hortos.

At nihil matrem moveat, quod ipsis
Vix adhuc ex uberibus sit infans
Pendulus: nullae heic aderant daturae
    Vbera matres?

Nec tamen lac Romulidum parenti
Defuit, neve heic quiriteris, esse
Lustricas nondum puero rogatum
    Nomen ad undas.

Nominis si te metus iste tangit,
Sistere infantem huc modo ne gravere,
Diique divaeque hunc facient, et omnis
    Roma Quirinum.]

ΤΕΛΟΣ [175]

Notes

1. Donald M. Frame, review article,"*Rabelais. By John Cowper Powys*," *RR* 42 (1951) 287.
2. See Defaux, "Rabelais et son masque comique," *ER* 11 (1974) 89-136.
3. When uprooting a tree to use as a lance in 1.36, Gargantua is presumably at most 100 feet tall; when a pilgrim's staff hits a nerve in a tooth in 1.38, he must be nearer 1,000 feet. When Pantagruel's mouth holds a whole world for AN to explore (2.32), the giant must be 1,000 miles or more tall; a chapter later, when the miners clean out his bowels, his height might be one or two thousand feet—a fraction of a mile.
4. For more on Pierre Amy and his friendship with R, see Henri Busson, "Les Dioscures de Fontenay-le-Comte: Pierre Amy-François Rabelais," *ER* 6 (1965) 1-50.
5. Hippocrates' *Aphorisms* and Galen's *Ars parva;* April 17-June 24, 1531. R's text was a Greek MS of his own, later published with his notes.
6. We do not know Du Bellay's illness; but R served him many years and on three such trips, his only ones to Rome, January-March, 1534, July-February, 1535-1536, and summer, 1547 to some time in 1549.
7. His first work, in the Italian macaronics (verses mingling Latin with Italian) favored for such burlesque romances, rated perhaps the best of all these.
8. Mellin de Saint-Gelais (1491-1558), vastly popular court poet (mainly improviser), whose publication of his works in 1547 did not enhance his reputation as poet. The moot question of authorship of this enigma is well treated by R. L. Frautschi in *French Studies* 17 (1963) 331-340. The last ten verses are by R, and Frautschi shows that the entire poem may well be his as well. See also Screech, p. 195.
9. Defaux (n. 2 above and n. 39 below) and Duval (n. 41 below), and especially La Charité (n. 15 and n. 41 below); also, I think, Bowen (n. 37 below), Cave (n. 40 below) and Rigolot (n. 14 below) may be so described.
10. Lucian: "To one who said to him, 'You are a Prometheus in words,'" in *Works*, Loeb Classics ed., 6.424.
11. In 3.FM, R enlarges at great length on this and on his fear of the implications.

12. A kind of hash. Here R nods—unless it is Pantagruel—who had given that castleship to AN after his visit inside his mouth (2.32).
13. A practice described in the text, like the consultation of the Bible at random for advice, once practiced in certain Christian homes.
14. *ER* 10 (1972) 186 pp.
15. See Raymond C. La Charité: "An Aspect of Obscenity in Rabelais," in *Renaissance and Other Studies in Honor of W. L. Wiley,* ed. George B. Daniel, Jr. (Chapel Hill: University of North Carolina Press, 1968) 166–189.
16. The original is this: "je vous supplie on nom et révérence des quatre fesses qui vous engendrèrent et de la vivificque cheville qui pour lors les coupploit."
17. Blaise Pascal (1623–1662), whose *Pensées* are models of concision, and one of whose *Provincial Letters* (1656–1657) ends in his memorable apology for not having had the time to make it shorter.
18. A note often sounded in Strunk and White's admirable—and concise— *Elements of Style,* 3d ed. (New York: Macmillan, 1979).
19. Jacques Boulenger, *Rabelais à travers les âges* (Paris: Le Divan, 1925).
20. In the chapter on "Of the Works of the Mind," in his *Caractères,* ed. Robert Garapon (Paris: Garnier, 1962).
21. In his *Philosophical Letters,* in *Oeuvres complètes,* ed. Louis Moland (Paris: Garnier frères, 1877–1885), vol. 22, p. 174. For all this section, fuller treatment may be found in my *FRS,* pp. 169–191, 212–216.
22. In a letter dated 1767; see *Correspondence,* ed. Theodore Baterman (Geneva: Institut et Musée Voltaire, 1953–1977).
23. In *Les Contemplations* written in 1856.
24. Jacques Boulenger, *Rabelais à travers les âges,* pp. 134–138.
25. Quoted from his *Correspondence,* p. 159; cf., pp. 156–158.
26. See Boulenger, pp. 127–131.
27. Goldsmith was an admirer; Fielding and Dr. Johnson regretted his obscenity but admired his genius; Smollett drew on his in his political *Adventures of an Atom.*
28. Walter Besant mixes the highest of praises with a damning conclusion that I think was not atypical in *The French Humorists* (London: R. Bentley, 1873). Although he considers him "a glorious wit and satirist" and "a great moral teacher," he finds his obscenity extreme and his drollery a pernicious enemy of seriousness"; see pp. 122–128, especially 128; see also pp. 89–131.
29. In *Do What You Will* (London: Chatto & Windus, 1929), pp. 307–328.
30. See *Collected Essays, Journalism, and Letters of George Orwell,* eds. Sonia Orwell and Ian Angus (New York: Harcourt, Brace, and World, 1968), 2:45–46; 3:285.
31. The book he had read is Lazare Sainéan, *La Langue de Rabelais,* 2 vols (Paris: E. Boccard, 1923). See Alfred G. Engstrom, "A Few Comparisons and Contrasts in the Word-Craft of Rabelais and James Joyce," pp. 65–82 of the festschrift for W. Leon Wiley (see n. 15 above).

32. *Die Wortbildung als stilistisches mittel exemplifiziert a Rabelais* by Leo Spitzer (Halle a. S., M. Niemeyer, 1910).

33. Horace, *Ars poetica* and *Epistle to the Pisos* (London: Cadell, 1783). Flaubert in coaching the young Maupassant is said to have stressed the quest for such nuggets as invaluable treasures. The sense of Horace's remark was this: "You can recognize a lion (*leonem*) by its claw (*ex ungue*)."

34. In German, 1946; English trans. by Willard Trask (Princeton: Princeton University Press, 1953).

35. "Rabelais et les rabelaisants," *Studi Francesi*, 12 (1960) 401–423.

36. Trans. Hélène Iswolsky (Bloomington: Indiana University Press, 1984).

37. *The Age of Bluff: Paradox and Ambiguity in Rabelais & Montaigne* (Urbana: University of Illinois Press, 1972). See also Manuel de Diéguez, *Rabelais par lui-même* (Paris: Seuil, 1960) and Alfred Glauser, *Rabelais créateur* (Paris: Nizet, 1966).

38. *Pantagruel et les sophistes* (The Hague: Nijhoff, 1973).

39. See n. 2 above, and *Le Curieux, le glorieux et la sagesse du monde dans la première moitié du xvi siècle* [*LCLGLSM*], *FFM* 34 (1982).

40. *The Cornucopian Text* (Oxford: Clarendon Press, 1979).

41. Raymond C. La Charité, "An Aspect of Obscenity in Rabelais" (see n. 15 above); "The Unity of Rabelais's *Pantagruel*," *French Studies*, 26 (1971) 257–265; "Interpenetration in Rabelais's *Pantagruel*: A Study of the Lion-Fox Episode," in *French Renaissance Studies in Honor of Isidore Silver*, ed. Frieda S. Brown, *Kentucky Romance Quarterly* 21, Supplement No. 2 (1975) 239–264; "*Mundus Inversus*: The Fictional World of *Pantagruel*," *Stanford French Review*, 1 (1977) 1–12; "Réflection-divertissement et intertextualité: Rabelais et l'Ecolier Limousin," in *Mélanges Alfred Glauser*, eds. Floyd Gray and Marcel Tetel (Paris: Nizet, 1979) 95–105; *Recreation, Reflection and Re-Creation: Perspectives on Rabelais's* Pantagruel, *FFM* 19 (1980); "Gargantua's Letter and *Pantagruel* as Novel," in *A Rabelais Symposium*, ed. Jerry C. Nash, *L'Esprit Créateur*, 21 (1981) 26–39; "Lecteurs et lectures dans le prologue de *Gargantua*," *French Forum*, 10 (1985) 261–270; ed., *Rabelais's Incomparable Book, Essays on His Art*, *FFM* 62 (1986); and "Par où commencer? Histoire et narration dans le *Pantagruel*," in *Le Signe et le Texte. Etudes sur l'écriture au XVIe siècle en France*, ed. Lawrence D. Kritzman, *FFM* 72 (1990). Edwin M. Duval, "Panurge, Perplexity, and the Ironic Design of Rabelais's *Tiers Livre*," *Renaissance Quarterly*, 35 (1982) 381–400; "Pantagruel's Genealogy and the Redemptive Design of Rabelais's *Pantagruel*," *PMLA*, 99 (1984) 162–178; "Interpretation and the 'Doctrine absconce' of Rabelais's Prologue to *Gargantua*," *ER*, 18 (1985) 1–17; and "The Medieval Curriculum, the Scholastic University, and Gargantua's Program of Studies (*Pantagruel*, 8)," in *Rabelais's Incomparable Book*, pp. 30–44.

To the Reader: Not all chapters have notes.

BOOK 1

1: AUTHOR'S PROLOGUE

1. World: in the passage R has in mind, Plato has Socrates say that auxiliaries (who assist the rational rulers in his ideal commonwealth) need the qualities of a good watchdog: gentle obedience to the good (their masters), and courageous anger toward strangers.

1.1: OF THE GENEALOGY AND ANTIQUITY OF GARGANTUA.

1. French jurists in R's day claimed this descent for their monarchy, which was widely accepted, although many, like Lemaire de Belges and Ronsard, preferred Aeneas and the Trojans (idealized by Virgil) to his perfidious Greeks as ancestors.
2. The phrase "return to our sheep" is still valid today and was already proverbial in R's day, from a great favorite of R's, the late fifteenth-century *Farce de Maistre Pathelin*. When the shrewd lawyer Pathelin has procured some cloth from draper and sheep farmer Guillaume but claimed not to have gotten it, and then takes on the defense of a shepherd of Guillaume's charged with killing and eating one of his sheep, he gets the draper confused between the crimes he charges to the point where the judge must remind him that the present case concerns his sheep.
3. An imaginary allusion: Aristotle nowhere speaks of such an art, although in his *Problems* he touches on maladies of vision.

1.2: THE ANTIDOTED FRIGGLEFRAGGLES.

1. French: "les Fanfreluches antidotées, trouvées en un monument antique." In this long piece of nonsense verse, the omission of the initial characters of many verses is deliberate, aiming to support the narrator's claim that the manuscript has been nibbled and gnawed by rats and moths or other harmful creatures.

1.4: HOW GARGAMELLE, WHILE PREGNANT WITH GARGANTUA, ATE A GREAT ABUNDANCE OF TRIPES.

1. *Diableries* (deviltries) were regular features of mystery plays but never had as many as four devils; so this term suggests a baffling confusion.
2. The *quille* "skittle or nine-pin" is a handy symbol for the phallus.

1.5: THE PALAVER OF THE POTTED.

1. Or "at my canonical hours" (times for daily prayers), in French "à mes heures."
2. "... comme un beau père guardian."
3. By forcing horses to bend down too far to reach water.
4. "... bouteille est fermée à bouchon, et flaccon à viz." The pun hinges on *con* "cunt."
5. "C'est bien chié chanté": meaning crudely "well said."
6. A sponge epitomizes thirst, and *esponge* sounds like *sponsus* "bridegroom," the second claim later.
7. The speaker says *duos* (acc.) where *duobus* (abl.) is correct here.
8. Here end two rhymed couplets:
   > Ainsi se feist Jacque Cuer riche.
   > Ainsi profitent boys en friche.
   > Ainsi conquesta Bacchus l'Inde.
   > Ainsi philosophie Melinde.

   I.e., says the speaker, love of the wisdom of Bacchus (wine) allowed Vasco da Gama to take Melinda, a fabled city on the east coast of Africa.
9. "Longues beuvettes rompent le tonnoire." Allowed as a variant spelling of *tonnerre*, "thunder," *tonnoire* suggests, and makes better sense as *entonnoir*, "funnel."
10. "... estrillons-le (ce fauveau) à profict de mesnaige." Our version here gives the parts of the phrase; but "estriller fauveau" means to curry favor by flattery.
11. A Basque saying meaning: "Drink up, mate!" Many lackeys were Basques.
12. "I thirst": John (19.28) makes this the next-to-last words of Jesus on the Cross.
13. The speaker might be a boastful Cordelier or other monk, but Panurge will use it of himself simply or as boast of his sexual urge and prowess.
14. "Tear of Christ": name of a renowned Italian muscat wine.
15. Presumably a smooth but undistinguished wine.
16. "One-eared" means pleasing even connoisseurs. The wool suggests better than taffeta and seems a sequel to it.
17. A gag from gambling; this raise is no doubt of his elbow, for good reason.

1.7: HOW THE NAME WAS GIVEN TO GARGANTUA.

1. "... mammallement scandaleuse, des pitoyables aureilles offensive, et sentent de loing hérésie."

1.8: How they dressed Gargantua.

1. "*Les Exponibles* de M. Haultechaussade." Probably a dig at both Ockham and Duns Scotus.
2. A comical imaginary book title.

1.9: Of the colors and livery of Gargantua.

1. First mention of the object of the later quest by Pantagruel and party in books 4–5.
2. The word is *trepelu*, "paltry," which also sounds much like *très peu lu*, "very little read."
3. "... entre les pudicques matrones." The sense seems as much "against" as "among."
4. The vaunted mini-Renaissance in France under King Francis I (1515–1547).
5. Admiral: then title of a very high military commander, at this time Philippe de Chabot, seigneur de Brion, Count of Buzançais, Admiral of France and Burgundy, conqueror of Piedmont in 1535. The admiral referred to here, with the anchor and dolphin in his device, was the good friend and commander of Francis I, Guillaume Gouffier, Lord of Bonnivet (1488?–1525), killed in the disastrous French defeat at Pavia.
6. If R (or Alcofribas Nasier) ever meant to do so, no trace of it remains today.

1.10: Of what is signified by the colors white and blue.

1. In legend, Aeneas's son Ascanius discovers a white sow at the site of the then future Alba Longa (Long White).
2. Ovation was a great victor's honor in Rome but much less so than a triumph.
3. Plutarch, in his *Life of Pericles* (27), tells of his doing this at the siege of Samos to give more troops a chance in battle.
4. For Aristotle and noted commentators of R's day like Jacques Lefèvre d'Etaples in his *Commentaries*, two main groups of *spirits*, prominent in psychic theory, were the vital (looking after life and the functioning of the organism; seated in the heart but able to tend toward the brain or spread through the body; subject to dilation and dispersal from the sudden onset of great heat, which for some helped explain sudden deaths from excessive joy or laughter); and secondly our noblest spirits, the animal (of the soul, *anima* or *psyche*) and much discussed in R's day. Notable among these were the *visive*, which emanate from the eyes (thus reducing their substance) to form a radiation that makes sight possible for the visual spirits, despite this loss.
5. A legal formula.

1.11: Of the childhood of Gargantua.

1. This and the ensuing actions by the child Gargantua are a mixture of the childish silly, the proverbial (usually figurative and metaphoric), and the idiomatic, some of them a combination of these types.
2. Scolded a subordinate in the hope of giving a lesson to a superior.

1.13: How Grandgousier recognized the marvelous mind of Gargantua by the invention of an ass-wipe.

1. *Malzoin* (maljoint or maujoin), here used to contrast with *benjoin* (benzoin), but also designating a woman's genitals.
2. Opening words of a verse marking the end of each Bible reading during the mass.
3. French: "as-tu prins au pot?" Urquhart translates this: "hast thou been at the pot?" W. F. Smith makes it: "hast thou burnt to?" (this last, a phrase used of milk which is boiling sticks to the pot, seems to fit best here).

1.14: How Gargantua was instructed by a sophist in Latin letters.

1. Gothic was the heavy black-letter print and script that in R's time was being steadily and rather swiftly replaced by the italic favored by humanists, which then prevailed for a century or so. Most unlearned books for popular consumption, however, were still printed in Gothic, among them both R's *Gargantua* and his *Pantagruel*.
2. The cupola of Saint-Martin d'Ainay in Lyon was supported by four stout columns.
3. A dull scholastic treatise on the ways or modes of signification.
4. The term *brelingant* signified a woman's genitals.
5. R closes on Thubal with a couplet borrowed in adapted form from his friend the poet Clément Marot and written as prose: "et fut l'an mil quatre cens et vingt—de la vérolle que luy vint."
6. Here R puns in conclusion on *enfournames* "baked in an oven" and the likelier *en fourneasmes-nous* "as we ever furnished, or came up with."

1.15: How Gargantua was put under other teachers.

1. Both names (of man and country) honor Erasmus, whose epistle to his friend Johannes Paladanus (des Marais) introduces a panegyric to Don Felipe, viceroy of Castile. *Papeligosse* may be a rough mix of *Pampeluna* and *Saragossa*; but it also approximates another Méridional, name for an imaginary kingdom—*Pamperigouste*.
2. " . . . voz resveurs matéologiens" (cf., Greek *mataio* "vain, empty, idle").

1.16: How Gargantua was sent to Paris.

1. One François de Fayolles, a relative of Geoffroy d'Estissac, R's protector and Maecenas, may be the fictive ruler R has in mind here.
2. An ancient massive quadrangular ruin near Chinon. I cannot identify any saint bearing that name.
3. Inversion of a familiar claim by and about the clergy.
4. A joke on their proverbial poverty.

1.17: How Gargantua paid his welcome to the Parisians.

1. The *proficiat*, at first a wish for success, was for R a welcoming gift.
2. "Saincte Mamye": the divers oaths in many tongues in this passage parody the many languages heard in Paris, the university especially.
3. The Hôtel de Nesle (Left Bank): R had first written here "Sorbonne," which explains the remark about a neglected oracle; prudence led to the change.

1.18: How Janotus de Bragmardo was sent to recover the great bells from Gargantua.

1. Short and fuzzy.
2. No longer needing to be changed to wine.
3. A play on *in artibus* and *inertes*; "a" and "e" were sounded much alike.

1.19: The harangue of Master Janotus de Bragmardo.

1. A corruption and contraction of *Bona dies*, "Good day!"
2. Although there is such a locality outside Paris, Bordeaux is in Gironde, Guyenne.
3. The famous *Sermones aurei de Sanctis* (pub. 1473) of Friar Leonardi de Utino (Udine). *Sermones* is of course a plural, used for a singular by Janotus. The *Utino* presumably leads to the *utinam* (so that) that follows.
4. A concluding scholastic formula with the meaning of QED.
5. Third of nine modes of the first figure of the syllogism.
6. By mixing up the order, Janotus here attributes God's powers to the Virgin.
7. Gibberish deformation of an old adverb signifying affirmation.
8. An obvious boner when he means "the colic."
9. Formula for ending the work of a scribe or a buffoon.

1.20: How the sophist took home his cloth.

1. The first chapter of the *Parvalogicalia*, introduction to scholastic logic. Already here, as later, R makes Janotus speak against his own side and its abuses.

1.21: Gargantua's mode of study according to the teaching of his sophist tutors.

1. Heavy irony: to rise so late was scandalous when daylight was essential.

1.22: Gargantua's games.

1. "A la cheveche" was perhaps a form of backgammon. As we have noted elsewhere, the edition of *Gargantua* by W. F. Smith is a valuable guide here.

1.23: How Gargantua was taught by Ponocrates.

1. Hot baths being hard to come by in R's France, oil rubdowns were often substituted.
2. The twelve sections of the zodiac, from Aries to Pisces, in the sky, traversed by the planets in their daily apparent circling around the earth.
3. Here apparently, as in Plato's *Republic* (530–531), harmonics, considered the most exacting (or one of these) of the mathematical sciences.
4. The newer, clearer Roman script, not the crude old Gothic; and note the importance of a clear correct handwriting when printing was still new, and until recently all copying and copies of a text had to be made by hand.
5. The sporting event that gave rise to the modern shot put.

1.24: How Gargantua used his time.

1. Chauny (Aisne) is a small town on the Oise in NE France fabled for skillful jugglers.
2. I.e., slick at passing off phonies as extraordinary, rare animals.

1.25: How there was aroused between the *fouaciers* of Lerné and the men of Gargantua's country a great dispute.

1. " ... trop diteulx, breschedens, plaisans rousseaulx, galliers, chienlictz, averlans, limes sourdes, faictnéans, friandeaulx, bustarins, talvassiers, riennevaulx, rustres, challans, hapelopins, trainne-guainnes, gentilz flocquetz, copieux, landores, malotruz, dendins, baugears, tézez, gaubregeux, gogueluz, claquedans, boyers d'étrons, bergiers de merde. ... " My debt to Urquhart is considerable for help with such litanies as this.
2. As noted above, this is a medieval form, then still in popular use, of "Par la mère de Dieu" (By the Mother of God), but also a near homonym of "Par la merde" (By shit).
3. An omission thought by some to bring bad luck.
4. A large red grape, which Cotgrave finds better suited to medicine than to eating or wine-making.

1.26: How the inhabitants of Lerné . . . made an unexpected attack.

1. This list is of artillery pieces smaller than cannons, larger than most guns.
2. Lengthened cannons, like culverins.

1.27: How a monk of Seuillé saved the abbey close.

1. A *lance* is not only a knight with a lance but the group attending him.
2. *Entommeures,* a variant of *Entamures,* "hashes," befits a scrapper with a prodigious appetite for good food and drink.
3. Stunned, when on breaking the mold the bell turns out flawed or even cracked.
4. This is a syllabic breakdown of the monks' chant: *impetum inimicorum ne timueritis:* "You shall not fear the enemy's attack," (from a response in the Breviary); missing some syllables.
5. "C'est bien chien chanté"; expressing scorn for the pointless crappery of merely chanting.
6. Ironic proverbial saying meaning crooked, thus like English "straight as a corkscrew."

1.29: The tenor of the letter that Grandgousier wrote to Gargantua.

1. The apparent pessimism this shows about man's nature seems to clash with R's optimism in 1.50 (growth of gratitude in the "man of reason") and in the only rule of Thélème (Do what you will) but probably merely qualifies it, implying this: The Thélémites and the man of reason, knowingly or not, are obeying God and doing His will; but when a man (here, Picrochole) abandons God by disobeying Him, God in turn abandons him, with the results that R notes in Picrochole.
2. This date places the action during vintage time.

1.32: How Grandgousier, to buy peace, had the *FOUACES* returned.

1. The words *couille et molle* suggest scant virility, hence scant courage, a sissy. However, *couille* may also mean "mortar," and *molle* may mean "mill," though why here I do not see.
2. In R's time all surgical cutting and such was done by the barbers on the direction of the surgeon, for whom such manual work on a patient was considered infra dig.
3. " . . . oignez villain, il vous poindra; poignez villain, il vous oindra."
4. " . . . de la pance vient la dance." To express the same idea, we say that an army marches on its stomach.

1.33: How certain counselors of Picrochole, by rash advice, placed him in the utmost peril.

1. In R's day men, like women, often wore hats indoors as well as out but doffed them before a superior. It was a marked courtesy for a king or prince to invite a noble to remain covered, as does Picrochole here, and Pantagruel to Kissass and Sniffshit (2.11).
2. "... pour veoir de leur urine," means "to check their urine."
3. Arabia was counted as triple in R's day: *felix*, *petraea*, and *deserta*.
4. A deformation of *Marcoul* to make *Malcon*, "Bad-cunt."
5. This comic inversion of victim and prize aims to express murderous frenzy.

1.34: How Gargantua left the city of Paris to succor his country.

1. "... le mestayer de Gouguet": this translation assumes Gouguet is a person; if it should be a placename, the French would mean "the farmer from Gouguet."

1.35: How Gymnaste killed Captain Tripet.

1. This unidentified gymnastic stunt is presumably like a series of cartwheels.

1.37: How Gargantua, in combing his hair, made artillery shells fall out of it.

1. Such disdain seems to fit Master Alcofribas and need not be R's but might be. Chroniclers, obsessed with exploits, sometimes wrote like today's "male chauvinist pigs."
2. This is not the familiar west English Cornwall but one in Quimper in Brittany.
3. This Benedictine abbey in Chinon was governed by Philippe Hurault de Cheverny, Abbé de Turpenay.
4. One of the noble Essards family of Langeais, near Chinon.

1.38: How Gargantua in a salad ate six pilgrims.

1. At the famous abbey of Cîteaux (Côte-d'Or) in Burgundy.
2. The elaborate Latin account is from Psalm 124 (123 of the Vulgate). These and others like them were continually being applied to contemporary events, specially by preachers, which is what R is ridiculing here.

1.39: How the monk was feasted by Gargantua.

1. A Eurasian freshwater fish related to the dace, ill regarded in R's day.
2. This, often followed by "Dieu te gard de mal, masson," was a standard way of completely changing the subject.

3. This old prophecy of the coming of Christ involves multiple puns: it implies fertility; and the preceding *moust* "must" suggests its homophone *mou* "soft"; and a lack of softness (in the male member) suggests fertility. Then the sounds of Jesse were those of "j'ay sé" (modern "J'ay soif"), for some, the last words of Jesus on the Cross.

4. This is my guess for "Les perdrys nous mangerons les aureilles mesouan."

5. An actual neighbor of R's, referred to in the Prologue to Book 4 as "le boiteux," the lame or the limper. The name itself means "bad greyhound" (lévrier); one or more of these reasons may explain why Frère Jean is not sure whether he did wrong.

1.40: WHY MONKS ARE SHUNNED BY EVERYONE.

1. According to Aulus Gellius *Attic Nights* 2.22.
2. This is the only time in R that Gargantua contradicts his father.
3. These quarrels were square-headed bolts or arrows to fire from a crossbow.
4. These proctors (ecclesiastical judges) were reputed to take gifts (*épices* or spices, as they were called) from both sides in a single case.
5. *Ad te levavi* or "I raised to Thee," begins Psalm 123; but the Latin sounds like French *leva vit* "prick rose," which is more in keeping with Frère Jean's themes.

1.41: HOW THE MONK PUT GARGANTUA TO SLEEP.

1. The chill of the wee hours brought out the colds afflicting many monks.
2. In falconry, purges for the bird. The other term used here, *tyrouer*, is explained in the text; but since it also is related to *tiroir*, one of Gargantua's terms for his flask-breviary, off we go again.
3. Here "use" means the particular form of the ritual used.
4. "Come, let's drink": a clear parody of the beloved old hymn *Venite adoremus* "O come, let us adore Him."

1.42: HOW THE MONK ENCOURAGES HIS COMPANIONS.

1. A topos that R uses often with jocular irony (4.8 etc.).

1.43: HOW PICROCHOLE'S SCOUTING PARTY WAS MET BY GARGANTUA.

1. *Gregorian* water was water blessed according to Saint Gregory's formula; but R has named this water *Gringorian*, after the dramatic poet Pierre Gringore, 1475–ca. 1538 (whose popular *sotie, Le Jeu du Prince des Sots,* aimed mainly at Pope Julius II, portrays the Church as the Frère Sotte), and who Victor Hugo popularized (as Gringoire) in his novel *Notre-Dame de Paris* (1831).

1.50: The speech that Gargantua made to the vanquished.

1. " . . . au vent vesten Nordest," meaning "west northeast." R's likely intent here and the wind the context calls for, would be either NE or ENE.

1.51: How the Gargantuist victors were rewarded after the battle.

1. The town of Logrono, in Spanish Navarre.
2. These places, all presumably near Chinon and La Devinière, are rewards Gargantua gives his warriors, leaders, and friendly helpers for help in winning the war.

1.52: How Gargantua built for the monk the abbey of Thélème.

1. This tidy truism recalls and may derive from Socrates, Erasmus, or both.
2. R writes *quoy vault toille?* "What is the value of cloth?" but means: "What is she good for?" (*Que vault-elle?* a homophone). The *toille* suggests the shirts.
3. " . . . bien formées et bien naturées"; the "well natured" makes this the likely meaning of R's critical "well born" (1.57) rather than the other possible sense "nobly born."

1.53: How the abbey of the Thélémites was built and endowed.

1. " . . . estoille poussinière," suggested also by the astronomical sun-crowns.
2. Châteaux famed for their splendor, of which all but Bonnivet still exist.
3. In an exhaustive lexical study in *ER* 5 (1964) 71–78, Robert Marichal shows that either of these meanings is quite possible; and Cotgrave also lists "elembic." Marichal notes in passing that Thélème lacks not only any common chapel but also both a kitchen and a refectory.

1.54: Inscription placed over the great gate of Thélème.

1. "Vieulx matagotz, marmiteux, borsouflez." These seven stanzas (though not the seven shorter refrains) abound in intricate internal rhymes as well as the standard ones ending each verse: e.g., " . . . bigotz, / Vieulx matagotz" and later: "Entrez, qu'on fonde icy la foy profonde, / Puis qu'on confonde," etc. Like all earlier translators, I have found these quite beyond my powers to reproduce or emulate and have settled for doing my lame best with the end rhymes and the meter.
2. "Ny Ostrogotz, précurseurs des magotz."
3. " . . . de Dangier palatins.": palace guards of *Dangier*, the jealous husband, hating any lover, of the *Romance of the Rose* and its many epigones.

1.55: How the manor of the Thélémites ran.

1. " . . . bains mirificques à triple solier," i.e., marvelous baths at three stories or levels.

1.57: How the Thélémites were regulated in their way of life.

1. The master of contemporary Rabelais studies, especially in matters theological, M. A. Screech, illuminates much of the Thélème episode and thus of these final chapters of Gargantua in "Some Reflexions on the Abbey of Thelema" in *ER* 8 (1969) 107–114. The reader must please allow me to quote him at length:

   The principal aim of the episode, summed up in the rule *Fay ce que vouldras,* is to show how subservient obedience must be dispensed with. If Socrates cannot govern himself and so declines to govern others, who—on earth—could lay claim to the ability to do so? . . . That is why the abbey is the Abbey of Will (*thelema*); that is why the one and only rule insists on doing what one will, building discipline and right uniformity of conduct on the right thinking resulting from a proper exercise of the trained power of synderesis (here called *honneur*). (p.111)

   Webster's International Dictionary, unabridged (sec.ed., 1936), s.v., syntheresis (or synderesis), defines this as "habitual knowledge of the primary principles of moral action."

1.58: A prophetic riddle.

1. " . . . la machine ronde," a common term for the earth in R's day.
2. "Quand sur un filz de Titan fut jectée."
3. Inarime: Virgil's name and story (*Aeneid* 9.857) of the volcanic island of Ischia in the Tyrrhenian Sea not far from Naples.
4. Curiously, in R's day tennis (our court tennis) was played with just a cord separating the sides instead of a net; so a ball passing close to it (just over or under) might be called either way; one more reason why scorers were so widely used, besides the main reason, the extreme complexity of the game and the scoring.

BOOK 2

2: PROLOGUE

1. Hugues Salel (ca. 1504–1553) of Cohors, a minor poet in the "school" of his fellow townsman Clément Marot (1496–1544) and like him for a time a "valet de chambre" (a sort of secretary) to King Francis I, came later to be known for his own poems (1540) and especially for his translation of Books 1–10 of Homer's *Iliad* (1545). Beyond this dizain nothing is known of his relations (presumably friendly) with R. The dizain first appeared only in the third edition (Lyon: François Juste) in 1534, the probable year of the *Gargantua*. In the Lyon: Juste editions of 1534 and 1537 the dizain was followed by the cry: Long live all good Pantagruelists!

2. The reference is not (as some once thought) to R's own *Gargantua*, not published until after *Pantagruel*, but to one of several popular little storybooks about the legendary giant Gargantua, presumably the one that gave R the excellent idea of writing a "sequel," his own *Pantagruel*.

3. This comparison with the oral religous tradition of the Jews is R's earliest comic suggestion that his book contains profound and abstruse doctrines.

4. The *Institutes* are Justinian's, in R's day still renowned and important in the law. Raclet is presumably Raimbert Raclet, a teacher of law at Dôle whom R clearly did not admire.

5. Unbaptized children and other blameless nonbelievers were thought to be held after death in limbo, a dismal region in the confines of hell. R applies the term to the sweat baths where poxies (syphilitics) were put to sweat out the infection. Saints' lives were one of the few available diversions and highly prized.

6. Latin: *exclusively*. R's favorite bit of gallows humor, meaning of course: up to the stake but not into the fire. However, as Louis de Berquin (1529) and Estienne Dolet (1545) could testify, burning at the stake for heresy was no joke at the time.

7. *Prestinators*, short for *predestinators* "believers in predestination" and "impostors" are both added to R's text in the 1542 edition, which was the first shot in a limited but fierce verbal battle between R and Calvin, whom in 4.32 R would brand a demoniacal impostor and son of Antiphysis (Anti-Nature). Calvin in *De scandalis* (1550) was no kinder to R.

8. The titles in this paragraph are a grab bag of names of medieval romances, real and imaginary, by authors known and unknown. No *Fessepinte* "Tosspint" is known to exist; *Orlando Furioso* is Ariosto's popular verse romance (1532) about the madness of the French hero Roland; *Robert the Devil, Fierabras, William the Fearless,* and *Huon of Bordeaux* are the Englished titles of popular French medieval stories of derring-do. *Montevieille* probably refers to the popular fourteenth-century French *Travels of Sir John Mandeville. Matabrune* was the title of one reworking of *The Knight of the Swan.*

9. Onocrotary, crotonotary, and crock-notary, are parodic deformations of French *protonotaire* "protonotary." The apostolic protonotaries (notaries in the Roman chancellery) were reputed to be lusty blades.

2.1: OF THE ORIGIN AND ANTIQUITY OF THE GREAT PANTAGRUEL.

1. The ancient Greeks had a reputation as topers but had no calends. The Druids reckoned time not by days (as suggested here) but by months. I do not think they counted forty days in a month.

2. Dative plural of word for *debtors,* as in the Lord's prayer: " . . . as we forgive our debtors."

3. In the story of the Flood and the ensuing years (Genesis 6–9), God chose Noah to build the ark and thus allow human and animal life on earth to survive; so Noah reintroduced crops of all kinds. His special association with wine and the vine comes from the sequel when his unmarried daughters, desperate to have children and lacking access to other men, got him drunk one night and conceived children by him in his sleep. Nearly a century before, François Villon had addressed one of his ballades to "Father Noah, who planted the vine."

4. A phrase of harsh condemnation in Saint Paul, here used as a parody of a bit in the Creed regularly sung in Mass and a clear allusion to pot-bellied arch-conservative Noël Béda of the Sorbonne, chief persecutor of any who favored Church Reform.

5. French *Mardi gras* "fat Tuesday," the day before the start of Lent, hence marked by feasting and merrymaking.

6. *Iambus* is both an *iam* and the etymon of French *jambe,* "leg." This form could be either nominative singular or nominative plural, meaning "legs." In prosody, an *iambus* is a foot made up of one short syllable, then one long: a short head then a long leg.

7. The heraldic term for *red.*

8. "Naso and Ovid" is an inside joke, since Ovid is Publius Naso.

9. The text, in this case Latin, is *Ne reminiscaris* "Do not be mindful" to which must be added "of our sins," an old chant sung at mass before and after the seven Psalms of Penitence. This jape was already old in R's time, since Latin *ne* and French *nez* "nose" are homonyms, lists of "noses" (phrases beginning in *Ne*) soon flourished; R's is in this tradition. English *knows,* also very common homonym of nose, is our best approximation.

10. The long genealogy that follows (fifty-odd names) is a parody of the Bible account (Matthew 1.1–17) of the descent of Jesus from Abraham through David. R draws on almost all conceivable sources (legend, mythology, literature, mainly Biblical, Greco-Roman, and medieval) and on his own fertile imagination. It was presented in his time as one of his lists, that is, with a new line of type for each new name. It has seemed preferable here not to follow that practice but to run them on as in ordinary discourse; and, to avoid a plaguy swarm of notes, many of which would be mere pleas

of ignorance, these names, however strange, have been here annotated only in clusters. Thus here: Chalbroth, Sarabroth, and Faribroth are purely imaginary.

11. Fracassus is a character in the comic macaronic poem *Merlini Coccaii macaronicon* or *Baldus* (1521) by the Italian monk Teofilo Folengo ("Merlin Coccai" 1496–1544).

12. Of these thirteen giants (Ferragus-Roboaster) the first and last named are drawn from popular medieval tales; Morgante (above) is the hero of Luigi Pulci's *Morgante maggiore* (1483); Galahad is the successful seeker of the Holy Grail in late Arthurian romances; the others appear to be creatures of R's imagination, as do most of the ones that then follow; but Bruslant de Monmiré, Bréhier (Bruyer), and Maubrun (Mabrun) are characters from medieval tales.

13. R's account of Hurtaly, especially later when he returns to him a few lines below, recalls a Hebrew tradition of a giant named Ha-Palit (the escapee) who escaped the Flood by taking refuge on the roof of the ark, where Noah fed him.

14. French name for the scene, in northern Italy near Milan, of an important French victory over the Swiss (1515).

15. Source unknown but possibly the tag line of a song or proverb popular in R's day.

2.2: OF THE NATIVITY OF THE HIGHLY REDOUBTABLE PANTAGRUEL.

1. The verses 1 Kings 17–18 tell how, at the request of the prophet Elijah, God punished the idolatry of the wicked king Ahab by denying the land rain or even dew for three years. In the summer of 1532, just before *Pantagruel* appeared, France had suffered a terrible drought.

2. This term for "dead, dry, or parched," is found not in Homer himself but in Plutarch, commenting on the *Odyssey*, in his *Table Talk* (*Symposiaca* or *Quaestiones conviviales*).

3. "Meagerly not eagerly" emulates the wordplay of R's "lâchement, non en lancement." *Lâchement* means "laxly," while *en lancement* plays on the sound of German *Landsmann* "compatriot" used of one another by Swiss soldiers, who, like the Germans, were noted drinkers..

4. " . . . à tout le poil": suggesting strength, comparable to English "with hair on his chest."

2.3: HOW GARGANTUA MOURNED FOR THE DEATH OF HIS WIFE BADEBEC.

1. From scholastic logic: acccording to the modes and figures of the syllogism, here ridiculed for their futility.

2. "Mouse in pitch" is a proverbial provincial French term descended from Greek via Latin *mus in pice* "the more he struggles, the tighter he sticks."

3. *Mementos:* priests' prayers for the dead, beginning: *Memento mori* "Remember to die," meaning "Remember that you must die."
4. "Foy de gentilhomme!": the favorite oath of King Francis I.
5. Latin: "Allow my swearing," a way of apologizing for it.
6. Meaning: "I don't believe you are there."

2.4: OF PANTAGRUEL'S CHILDHOOD.

1. The "Giant's Bowl," a stone trough in front of the palace of the Dukes de Berry, in olden times filled once a year with wine for the poor.
2. La Grande Françoise (2,000 tons), then the biggest ship yet built in France, completed in 1527, but never got out of port. The name Françoyse today means Frances; it then might also be the feminine adjective meaning "French" (now *Française*).
3. The passage here from "What did he do?" through "my hearties? Listen" began in the first edition (1532) as simply "Here is what he did." In the 1534 edition R changed this to "What did he do?" Finally in the 1542 definitive edition he kept the question to the reader but enlarged it further, as we see in our version. These changes in the French are from initial "Voicy qu'il fist" to "Que fist-il? Il essaya" to the final "Qu'il fist, mes bonnes gens? Escoutez." Even as it offers a glimpse of R's way of composition, it illustrates nicely his love, and increasing use, of dialogue and an oral style.

2.5: OF THE DEEDS OF THE NOBLE PANTAGRUEL IN HIS YOUTH.

1. Now forgotten, this great long rack-bent crossbow was of the type used in defense from the ramparts against enemy besiegers. Chantelle (Allier) is a village that had a castle of the Dukes of Bourbon.
2. "Pass-lumpkin": a grotto in a cliff not far from Poitiers.
3. A phrase from Horace's *Art of Poetry* (vs. 9–10) on the right of poets and painters to the free exercise of their imagination.
4. The medical school of the University of Montpellier, then rivaled in France only by that of Paris, was where R took his own medical degrees (bachelor, 1530, licentiate and doctor, 1537), and then taught in 1530 or 1531 or both, in 1537, and perhaps at other times as well.
5. The University of Valence in Dauphiné, founded in 1452 and now no longer in existence, was notorious for bad town-and-gown relations.
6. In R's time there was still an underground passage beneath the Eglise Saint-Pierre just outside the town that was said to run underneath the Rhône.
7. A more literal version would go like this:
   A tennis ball in your codpiece,
   In your hand a racket,
   A law in your *cornette* [an item rather like a doctor's hood],
   A slow-paced dance in your heel,
   Now you've passed your doctor's hood.

This quatrain seeks to render five verses of R:

> Un esteuf en la braguette
> En la main une raquette,
> Une loy en la cornette,
> Une basse dance au talon,
> Vous voylà passé coquillon.

2.6: How Pantagruel met a Limousin.

1. Person coming from Limoges or the surrounding region (le Limousin) in central France.

2. The opening part of this speech is borrowed from Geoffroy Tory's book *Le Champfleury* (1529), a treatise mainly on elegant printing. (A nineteenth-century American analogue is the poem "Aestivation, by my late Latin tutor," in Oliver Wendell Holmes's *Autocrat of the Breakfast Table*.)

   The sense of it up to this point is roughly this: "We cross the Seine at dawn and dusk; we stroll through the squares and streets of the city; we 'skim off' Latin, and, as if really in love, we gain the good graces of the all-joining, all-formed, and all-bearing feminine sex. On some days we visit the brothels and, in sexual transport, plunge our penises into the depths of the pudenda of these most pleasant little whores."

3. Translation: "then we feast in the fine inns of the Pomme de Pin, the Château, the Madeleine, and the Mule, on lovely shoulders of lamb larded with parsley; and if by bad luck we are broke (we have no money or coins in our purses), we leave our books and clothes as pledges, counting on the arrival of messengers to come from home."

   Laires and penates are Roman gods of house and cupboard of each family's home.

4. Translation from "No, signor": "No, My Lord," said the student; "for most freely, as soon as the slightest glimmer of day breaks, I go into one of these well-built churches, and there, sprinkling myself with fair holy water, I mumble a snatch of some prayer from the mass in our rituals. And, muttering my prayers from the hours, I wash and clean my soul of its night's stains. I revere the Gods of Olympus, I worshipfully venerate the Almighty on high who rules the stars. I obey the Ten Commandments, and, according to my feeble powers, do not stray one nail's breadth from them. It's true that since I have no money coming in, I rarely give alms to the poor who seek their bread from door to door."

   This student goes through the motions of a truly pious believer but makes no offering or alms, saving up for uses closer to his heart, while scrupulous in ritual. His smug hypocrisy doubtless helps explain Pantagruel's harshness with him.

5. Translation from "Signor Missayre": "My Lord and master, my nature is not suited to what this insulting knave says, to flay our French vernacular, but I labor diligently in the opposite cause, and strive with sails and oars to fill it out from the abundance of Latin."

6. Translation of the student's speech: "My ancestors came originally from the region of Limoges, where lies the body of the most holy Saint Martial."

7. Ironic antiphrasis for "what a foul odor!" much as Panurge's will be at the end of Book 4. Saint Alipentin is a comic name perhaps drawn from the medieval mystery plays.

2.7: How Pantagruel came to Paris.

1. Although this is probably not historical fact, in R's time this cemetery was grievously overcrowded, so that skeletons were constantly being dug up and piled in charnel houses nearby, where some people set up shops and others used to come by for a stroll.

2. This is the library of the Abbey of Saint-Victor, noted for its richness in theological works. The list of some sevenscore titles that follows and fills the chapter is a mixed bag that includes even a few actual titles, but most are imaginary: about one-third Latin; two-thirds French; perhaps one-quarter mainly comic with no clear satiric intent; the majority are satiric. Principal butts of the satire and sources of the comic are the standard monastic shortcomings of the flesh and the unending contrast between the portentous-sounding Latin of the titles or of the author's name and credentials, or both, and the unwavering triviality, more often than not obscene, of the subjects of the books.

   In attempting to render these as well as I could, I have always given an English version, trying in it to convey usually the sense, and when possible also the sound and the imagery—not to mention something of the comic effect. Beyond this I have not seen as desirable any consistency but that of intent, and so have simply used my judgment to decide when, and when not, to offer the original text as well as the translation.

   The first item in the "catalogue" illustrates the usual styling when both translation and original are given.

3. The French for saltpeter is *hanebane*, then considered an aphrodisiac.

4. The name was Mamotret, a Biblical commentator. R added the "r" to create an analogy with *marmot,* a monkey, about which the treatise was written.

5. Comical parody of the scholastic habit of giving leading theologians honor-ific epithets to modify "Doctor" such as "Angelic, Subtle, Cherubic," etc. For example, Aquinas was called "angelic"; Bonaventure, "seraphic"; Duns Scotus, "subtle"; Occam, "invincible"; see below note 26. Pasquin's here is well deserved, since he (and Marforio below) are facing marble statues in Rome where lampoons and the like were posted.

6. Apparently a mystery play on the manufacture of crown coins stamped with the cross, hence counterfeit, by unscrupulous clerics.

7. Noël Béda, professor of theology at the Collège de Montaigu and syndic of the arch-conservative Sorbonne (Faculty of Theology of the University of Paris), was the enthusiastic persecutor of heresy (which he found all around) and consequently bête noire of the Erasmians and other humanist

Evangéliques. Besides his humped back, Béda was deformed by a famous, enormous paunch, which explains this title and most other allusions to him by R.

8. These *dragées,* like the judges' *épices* were bribes, a notorious abuse.

9. A traditional comic figure of the cowardly soldier given literary form by the fifteenth-century poet François Villon.

10. "Mustard after dinner" was a proverbial saying, later used by Montaigne; see *Essais* 3.10, Pléiade ed. p. 987 (Montaigne, *Oeuvres complètes,* ed. by Albert Thibaudet and Maurice Rat [Paris: Gallimard, 1962]) for the futility caused by bad timing; cf., our "lock the barn after the horse is stolen."

11. Apparently an allusion (not in the first edition) to the invasion of Provence and burning of it to a crisp (the red of Brésil) in 1542 by the Imperial army under Leiva.

12. Marforio was the name of an ancient statue facing that of Pasquin. See above note 5.

13. "Coqueluche" also means "whooping cough," but I doubt that that matters here.

14. Brother (Frai) Inigo has not been identified with anyone.

15. Estienne Brûlefer (Ironburner) was a Scotist professor at the Sorbonne.

16. "Callibistratorium Caffardie, actore M. Jacobo Hoctratem hereticometra." *Callibistratorum* means "a woman's genitals"; *caffardie,* "of hypocrisy." Jacob Hochstraten, a Cologne Dominican, was Grand Inquisitor for Germany.

17. Johann Maier von Eck (Eccium, 1486–1543) strongly opposed Luther, obtained a papal bull condemning him and continued opposition to Reform. R's ascription on sweeping out flues may well aim at an erotic connotation.

18. A medley of Greek prepositions serving as a nonsense book title.

19. Bishops *in partibus* were also known as *portatifs;* hence the irresistible pun *potatifs* "hard-drinking," here, *potative.*

20. A cause célèbre in the early sixteenth century was the fierce opposition of conservative obscurantists to Professor Johann Reuchlin, led by Johann Pfefferkorn and centered in Cologne for a time, because Reuchlin, a Greek and Hebrew scholar, wanted to spread the knowledge of Hebrew in Germany. Humanists, led by Erasmus, backed Reuchlin.

21. "To play the cymbals" here could also mean to have sexual intercourse.

22. *Martingale* here means "long underpants that open at the bottom."

23. The actual title of a book (1414) by the eminent theologian Jean Gerson, onetime chancellor of the University of Paris, a leader in restoring the unity of the Church after the Western Great Schism (1378–1417).

24. In the full title a little later of the book by Dytebrodius, the *libellus acephalos* may go back to Plato's phrase *mythos akephalos* in *Phaedrus* 264.

25. Master Guingolfus is unknown to all scholarly editors and to this translator. He may well be a creature of R's fertile imagination.

26. See above, note 5 on this chapter. "Moillegroin, Doctoris cherubici, De origine patepelutarum." The name "Cherubic Doctor" was one of those

given to Aquinas. "Hairypaws," rather like our "gumshoes," meant spies, observers, or especially snoopers.

27. *Godemarre* is also a partial homophone of *Gaude Maria* "Hail Mary."

28. Aquinas is "the Angelic Doctor" and the *Summa* his master work.

29. This is the actual title of a book by Dr. Symphorien Champier (1528) of Lyon against Arab medicine and Arab doctors.

30. Tübingen was indeed a center for printing; otherwise this statement is fantasy and fun.

2.8: HOW PANTAGRUEL, WHILE IN PARIS, RECEIVED A LETTER FROM HIS FATHER GARGANTUA.

1. Much of this idea is from Aquinas. For this sense of "period" as "revolution, conclusion, end of a sentence," see for example 4.BD.

2. The contemptuous French Renaissance humanists referred to everything medieval, including their own ancestors, as Goths and Gothic.

3. Dissections of the human body were still rare in R's day and anathema to the Sorbonne conservatives. R performed some publicly, both at Montpellier and at Lyon, and was praised in verse for it by Estienne Dolet (*Carmina,* Book 4).

4. A commonplace of the time was the contrasting but complementary pairing of the macrocosm (the universe) and microcosm (man); the fine Lyon poet Maurice Scève (1500–1564) used the title *The Microcosm* for his longest poem, an encyclopedic history of man since the Fall.

5. The phrase "against all comers" is a curious, disputatious, seemingly late scholastic touch, but typical of the time, and preparing for what follows in 2.10 and 2.18–20. In R's day this was how you made a name and proved yourself in higher knowledge.

6. Science without conscience was a formula coming from Saint Bernard of Clairvaux (1090–1153) and current in scholastic theology. Faith formed of charity was a phrase recalling one of St. Bonaventure's and dear to the Erasmian humanist évangéliques of the French sixteenth century.

7. To Evangelicalists such as R, lovers of Paul and of 1 Corinthians 13, this was a key phrase and concept at the heart of true Christianity.

2.9: HOW PANTAGRUEL FOUND PANURGE.

1. The comic device basic to this whole chapter is that the new character Panurge, though nearly starving and quite broke, persists in answering all Pantagruel's normal well-meant questions (who he is, from where, doing and seeking what?) in thirteen languages (four of these imaginary) unintelligible to most of his listeners, as well as to most of R's readers then and now. A few inconsistencies need bother us no more than they did R: the listeners' apparent ignorance of Latin, and that neither Pantagruel nor Epistémon (elsewhere said to know all languages) seem to make any sense

of any but French. This first piece, rather pompous and antiquated, in a German with a touch or two of Latin, means approximately this:

"My Lord, God give you happiness and good fortune. First, my dear Lord, you must know that what you are asking me about is a sad and unfortunate thing, which it would be unpleasant for you to hear and for me to tell, even though poets and orators in other times have said that the recollection of poverty and misery in the past is a great pleasure."

2. If not a fictive Antipodean (East Indian) piece at times it recalls Arabic and near the end in the name of R's hometown Chinon. Jourda (in G) calls it untranslatable; Demerson (LI), with thanks to Emile Pons, summarizes the gist of it thus: "In a language colored with Oriental images, Panurge demands cakes and stew; or else he will sodomize Pantagruel in Scottish style."

3. Italian: "Sir, you see by example that a bagpipe will not play unless its belly is full. So I likewise cannot possibly tell you about my adventures unless first my ill-treated belly has its wonted food, for which it thinks my hands and teeth have lost their natural function and are totally annihilated."

4. The weatherbeaten Scottish conveys approximately this meaning: Panurge hopes that the giant's spirit is as lofty as his build but fears that the equality of the giant's and his own nature may not be recognized, since virtue is often misprized. In editions after 1542 an English text replaced the Scottish.

5. In a very vulgar Basque, presumably picked up from a lackey: "Sir, for all troubles a remedy is needed. To do exactly as we should is hard. I have implored you so! Arrange it so that we can have an orderly talk; that will be, with no hard feeling, if you have me brought enough to eat. After that, ask me whatever you wish. You could even ask a double share of questions, if God please."

6. As LI suggests a Lanternese might have gathered from this gibberish that Panurge asks the Lord of La Devinière to give him a drink; God will pay him back doubly in wine from the Cordeliers's stock.

7. Now, in a kind of Dutch, Panurge protests that he is speaking Christian talk; but why must he? His rags eloquently bespeak what he wants.

8. In Spanish: "Lord, I am tired from talking so much. So I beseech Your Reverence to consider the evangelical precepts so that You may be moved to what conscience requires; if these do not suffice to move Your Reverence, I beseech you to consider natural pity, which, I believe, will touch you as it is only right. And I say no more."

9. In Danish: "Sir, even in case I, like infants and animals, were not to speak any language, my clothes and the emaciation of my body would clearly show what I need: to eat and drink. Have pity on me and have someone give me enough to calm my baying stomach, as they place a sop before Cerberus. Thus you will live a long happy life."

10. As Epistémon recognizes, this is Hebrew: "Lord, peace be with you. If you wish your servant well, give me a scrap of bread right away, as it is written: 'He lends to the Lord who has pity on the poor man.'"

11. In ancient Greek: "Excellent master, why don't you give me some bread? You see me miserably pale with hunger, and yet you have no pity and keep asking me things beside the point. Nevertheless, all who love letters agree that words and speeches are superfluous when the facts are evident. Speeches are necessary only where the facts under discussion do not appear clearly."

12. This is one more of R's imaginary languages.

13. Latin at last: "Several times already I have implored you by all that is holy, all the gods and all the goddesses, if you have any pity, to relieve my poverty; but my cries and lamentations have had no effect. Permit me, permit me, impious men, to go off to where the Fates call me, and weary me no longer with your vain interrogations, remembering the old proverb that says that an empty belly has no ears." Although "whither the Fates call me" (*quo me fata vocant*) strongly recalls phrases in both Lucan and Ovid, I think it likeliest to be a conflation of two pieces from Virgil, the *fata vocant* of *Georgics* 4.49 and the more evident *quo fata trahunt /sequamur* of *Aeneid* 5.709.

14. In 1502 the French, at the pope's request, tried to besiege Mytilene, chief city of Lesbos, in the Aegean near Asia Minor; but they were beaten off and lost some men as prisoners to the Turks.

2.10: How Pantagruel equitably judged a marvelously difficult and obscure controversy.

1. In a standard university practice, one might present, by posting them in advance, conclusions (theses or propositions) that one was prepared to discuss and defend in debate against all comers. Near the end of chapter 8 above, Gargantua had instructed his son to do this soon to demonstrate his knowledge.

2. The French *ergotz* "spurs of a cock" implies cockiness (*monter* or *estre sur ses ergots* means "to get up," or "be on one's high horse"), and is also the homophone of Latin *ergo* "therefore," a favorite word of disputants.

2.11: How Lords Kissass and Sniffshit pleaded.

1. An invitation showing great politeness on Pantagruel's part. Many men wore hats then indoors as well as out, but never a social inferior in the presence of a superior, unless with such permission as this. In the three chapters that follow (11–13) relating the pleas and Pantagruel's decision in this lawsuit, any cogency or coherence is of course strictly coincidental.

2. "A kind of British daunce" (Cotgrave).

3. Scene of a severe defeat (April 29, 1522) of Lautrec and his French army by the Imperials. A *bicoque* is "a small insignificant stronghold."

4. The French original of this quatrain was this:

> La Penthecoste
> Ne vient foys qu'elle ne me couste;

> May, hay avant,
> Peu de pluye abat grand vent.

5. "Sa, Dieu gard de mal Thibault Mitaine!" He is an unidentified man in a song.

6. Opening words of two anthems, here presumably automatically muttered: Hail Mary's and Hear us's.

7. Presumably terms from an unidentified game perhaps (Cotgrave) like "Whirlebone."

8. R has of course inverted a verse proverb that said: "He who walks wisely does not fall from the bridge."

9. A didactic allegory in verse (1493) by the *Rhétoriqueur* Jean Meschinot. These spectacles should have Prudence and Justice as lenses, Force as mounting, Temperance as joining-pin.

10. Inversion of *in verbo sacerdotis* "on the word of a priest" (presumably Gospel).

2.12: How Lord Sniffshit pleaded before Pantagruel.

1. Proverbial (Villon and before) for an easy distinction to make.

2. A euphemism aiming to avoid but skirt swearing, much like *corbleu*, for *boeufs*, like *bleu*, rhymes with *Dieu*. *Quatre boeufs* means "four oxen"; these oxen will return later in the chapter.

3. The French original goes as follows:

> Qui boit en mangeant sa souppe
> Quand il est mort, il n'y voit goutte?

4. A term designating one figure of the syllogism.

5. The French *ambesace* means "two aces" (cards) or "two ones" (dice).

6. Charles VIII, who died in 1498.

7. The French original is this:

> Incontinent les lettres veues,
> Les vaches luy furent rendues.

8. Probably a fantasy name of R's invention.

2.13: How Pantagruel gave his decision.

1. A paragraph from the *Digest* (q.v.) dealing with indivisibility.

2. " ... et autant pour le brodeur"; this seems to mean "as much again for good measure."

3. The Flood. This prediction was proverbial in R's day.

2.14: How Panurge relates the way in which he escaped.

1. Lords and scholars.

2. Of these names, Astaroth and Rappallus appear in medieval mystery plays; Grilgoth and Gribouillis are inventions of R.

3. This Christian invocation in Greek, surprising among Turks, is less so assuming this takes place still near Mytilene in Greek-speaking Lesbos.

4. François Villon (1431–?) used this line as the refrain of his "Ballade of the Ladies of Yesteryear" (*Ballade des dames du temps jadis*), probably his best-known poem.

5. Proverbial for smelling strong (from underarm sweat?) for fear; the leg of mutton is clearly overripe, gamy, or higher yet.

6. Corinthian women included many prostitutes and were considered notoriously free.

7. A very popular expression at this time.

2.16: OF THE WAYS AND DISPOSITIONS OF PANURGE.

1. Lead being ill-suited for daggers, the effect of this phrase is much like English "like a lead balloon," i.e., futile, pointless.

2. " . . . au demourant, le meilleur filz du monde": probably the most famous line by R's friend the poet Marot, ending the introductory stanza of his "Epistle to the King, for having been robbed."

3. Formula for saying Grace after a meal.

4. Pierre d'Ailly (1350–1420), Chancellor of the University of Paris and later Bishop of Cambrai and cardinal, was indeed the author of a book entitled *Suppositions,* which formed a section of the logic of the scholastics. Beyond that we have R.

5. " . . . courir les rues": the French equivalent of English "street walking."

2.17: HOW PANURGE GOT PARDONS.

1. The authorized open selling of pardons and indulgences by the Church was a main trigger of revolutionary reform in the early sixteenth century by Luther and others.

2. Formed from the formula for "thanks," *grates vobis do* "I give you thanks," to give you a comically incorrect form of *dominus*, "Lord or Master." "Thank you, my lords" would be *grates vobis, domini.*

3. Urquhart's term for French *le reniguebieu* (euphemism for *renie-Dieu*). OED and Cotgrave offer no help. Lefranc suggests: "Sans doute jeu de Cassette [puzzle game] qui fait jurer."

4. An unknown saint, possibly of R's invention. Sainéan has suggested as a source Latin *ad auras* "in the air."

2.18: HOW A GREAT SCHOLAR FROM ENGLAND WANTED TO DEBATE AGAINST PANTAGRUEL.

1. Onetime residence of abbots of Saint-Denis, in R's day a college for Benedictines, where R, as a Benedictine monk, may have stayed.

2. The verse 2 Chronicles 9.1–12; see also Matthew 12.42.

3. Meaning "of Memphis" in Egypt but resembling and suggesting *mephitic,* "stinking and possibly poisonous."

4. A saying of Democritus, not of Heraclitus.

5. Editions from 1534 through 1537 added here the following fearsome and impresssive list; to express R's loathing for the monsters infesting the Sorbonne: Sorbillans, Sorbonagres, Sorbonigènes, Sorbonicoles, Sorboniformes, Sorbonisecques, Niborcisans, Borsonisans, Saniborsans.

2.19: How Panurge made a monkey of the Englishman.

1. "Vous avez parlé, masque!": i.e., you broke your own rules for this debate. Panurge's signs range from merely making faces to elaborate nose-thumbing and on to the sign of the fig and the other without a name I know of but expressing English "Screw you!" or words to that effect, these last two of course expressing obscene, insolent contempt.

2.21: How Panurge was smitten by a great lady of Paris.

1. Apparently a common errand for children, freeing parents for other jobs.

2. " . . . venir au dessus de": means "get the better of, dominate," but literally "come over" or "come on top of," as is clearly meant here.

3. Here used by R in the sense of what in animals we call "cover" (sexually).

4. This and the "antic dance" a bit later refer of course to sexual intercourse.

5. " . . . bouttepoussenjambions": the bit on Panurge's predestination for this is from the 1542 edition and may be an early swipe at Calvin. In the first (1532) edition, the sentence had read: "By God, that will be me, I see it clearly: for already you are madly in love with me, I know it. So, to save time, let's do it."

6. Our imitation of the *équivoque* making "A Beaumont le Vicomte" into "A beau con le vit monte" or "a creek rises for a handsome punt" into "the prick rises at a lovely cunt."

7. By this pun ("on my youth" for "on my oath"), I have tried perhaps vainly to approximate the French: "par mon sergent" for "par mon serment."

2.22: How Panurge played a trick on the Parisian lady.

1. R uses a French learned creation, *lycisque orgoose,* which I see no way to approximate in English. Ordinary French, Latin, and Greek seem to offer no help; Cotgrave gives, for *licisque* alone, "A dog engendered between a wolf and a dog" (cf., Greek *lukos* "wolf," Latin *lycus*), nothing for *orgoose* alone; and for *licisque orgoose* "a sault bitch" or "a bitch in heat."

2. Here is the French original of this rondeau:

> Pour ceste foys que à vous, dame très belle,
> Mon cas disoys, par trop feustes rebelle
> De me chasser sans espoir de retour,
> Veu que à vous oncq ne feis austère tour

En dict ny faict, en soubson ny libelle.
Si tant à vous déplaisoit ma querelle,
Vous pouviez par vous, sans maquerelle,
Me dire: "Amy, partez d'icy entour
   Pour ceste foys."

Tort ne vous fays, si mon cueur vous décelle,
En remonstrant comment l'ard l'estincelle
De la beaulté que couvre vostre tour;
Car rien n'y quiers, sinon qu'en vostre tour
Me faciez de hait la combrecelle
   Pour ceste foys.

2.24: A LETTER THAT A MESSENGER BROUGHT TO PANTAGRUEL.

1. "... du sel ammoniac destrempé en eau." This is diluted ammonium chloride. The list, which begins here, of devices for secret writing, mainly in invisible ink, comes to R from many sources, this one from the *Polygraphia* (1518) of Trithemius; the next from Pliny, *Natural History* 25.8. The works and many of the authors cited further on are apocryphal, and "Francesco di Nianto" is literally "Francis of Nothing."

2. Christ's last words on the cross (Matthew 27.46 and Mark 15.34, but not in Luke or John; cf., Psalms 22.1) usually rendered "Eli, Eli, lema sabachthani?" and translated "Lord, Lord, why has thou forsaken me?"

3. "Dy, amant faulx": for its homonym "diamant faulx" (fake diamond).

4. All these places up to and including Melinda are in or off Africa on the route Spanish and Portuguese explorers took around Africa at the Cape of Good Hope from western Europe to the Indies: down south along the African west coast, around the Cape, and back up north along its eastern coast. Melinda is a special case: there was a real one in modern Zanzibar, won over with wine by the Portuguese, but how closely identifiable with the town and kingdom of fantasy, home of Hans Carvel, is not fully clear. For it and the following fantasy ports on this trip, see the Glossary.

5. In Herodotus's *History of the Persian Wars* (Book 3), a Persian noble under Darius who cut off his own nose and ears to persuade the besieged Babylonians that he was a deserter to their side and ultimately to give him full authority over their army; whereupon he opened the gates of the city to be taken and sacked by the Persians. Erasmus tells the story in his *Adages* 2.10; but R had long been a devotee of Herodotus and already in 1524 had been busy translating Book 2 of the *History* into Latin.

6. In Aeneas's account of the fall of Troy (*Aeneid* 2.56 ff.), the treacherous Greek who, by a similar though less drastic ruse, persuaded the Trojans to drag the great Trojan horse into the city, where later the Greeks, hidden inside the horse, came out and opened the gates to their army.

2.26: HOW PANTAGRUEL AND HIS COMPANIONS WERE FED UP WITH EATING SALT MEAT.

1. Suppposed to confer invulnerability on the wearer; cf., *Gargantua,* chap. 8.

2.29: HOW PANTAGRUEL DEFEATED THE THREE HUNDRED GIANTS.

1. These are all three popular tales in medieval France: a long poem attributed to Bishop Turpin the fighting churchman of the *Song of Roland;* the beloved story of Saint Nicholas, subject of Jean Bodel's early miracle play (thirteenth century) *Le Jeu de Saint Nicolas;* and the ancestors of the Mother Goose Tales, in France called *contes de la cigogne* (Stork's Tales) or *contes au vieux loup.*

2. A combination or conflation of Constantine's motto, *Hoc signo vinces* "with this sign thou shalt conquer," which he is said to have seen in the sky over Christ's monogram (ICHTHUS) after his great victory of Saxa Rubra (312) over Maxentius, and Jesus' command to the lawyer (Luke 10.28) who, to test him, asked him what he must do to inherit eternal life: *Hoc fac et vives* "This do, and thou shalt live."

3. When he breaks the mold and finds the bell defective: a proverbial mishap.

4. *Riflandouille*: a name that appears in medieval drama, the *mystères;* R will use this name for a captain sent to fight the Andouilles (4.37).

2.30: HOW EPISTÉMON HAD HIS CHOP HEADED OFF, AND WAS CLEVERLY CURED BY PANURGE.

1. "La couppe testée" instead of "la teste coupée": one of R's favorite forms of his beloved inversions.

2. The French word, *lanternier,* like the verb *lanterner,* suggests sexual intercourse.

3. Like Artaxerxes two spaces below, Achilles is here given a second posthumous vocation.

4. The original French, "de pain et de souppe," parodies the pardoner's formula, "de peine et de coulpe," or "of penalty and guilt or sin."

5. Prototype of the cowardly medieval free-lance bowman, of whom François Villon wrote, and whose *Stratagems* we encountered in the Library of St. Victor (above, chap. 7).

6. Ergotism, a common disease of the time, was marked by cramps and spasms, one of those invoked as threats to unbelieving readers in the Prologue (see above). It was represented in painting on hospitals where patients ill with it were treated. Present opinion is that the disease was contracted by eating spoiled rye flour.

2.31: HOW PANTAGRUEL ENTERED THE CITY OF THE AMAUROTS.

1. *Pervers,* homophone of *pers* "blue" plus *vert* "green."

2. "Monsieur du roy de troys cuittes": sugar was then sold as once, twice, and thrice cooked; and the thrice cooked "de troys cuittes" was considered much the best.

2.32: How Pantagruel with his tongue covered a whole army.

1. Gorgias was a noted fifth-century B.C. Greek sophist, who figures in Plato's dialogue of that name, where Socrates' doctrine of rhetoric is contrasted with that of the sophists. *Les Gorgias,* in French, then meant the "sumptuous, the wealthy and swanky."

2.33: How Pantagruel was sick.

1. Here follows a list of leading hot mineral baths of France and Italy, their origin at last correctly explained by R or Alcofribas Nasier.
2. Roman goddess who personified the sulphur dioxide fumes that came out of the ground in some spots, and whose name is preserved in *mephitic,* "stinking" and sometimes also "poisonous." The marsh of Camarina was in Sicily near the city of that name. Strabo (*Geography* Book 16) writes of a stinking lake Serbonis whose name gave comfort to R's fellow humanists.

2.34: The conclusion of the present book.

1. Wine, generally harvested in September.
2. This, the book's original conclusion, seems a sort of apology to his potential literate and discriminating readers for writing a book aimed lower, and seems to me a prediction or preparation for the more outspoken *Gargantua* and more discursive and learned later books.
3. Such as the space between robe and the hood in a monk's cowl. For R such people are the wrynecks or hypocrites, whom above all others he detests.

BOOK 3

1. R's Book 3 is the first of his narratives in which he put aside his "comic mask" (Defaux), his anagrammatic pseudonym of the fictive ancient Arab sage Master Alcofribas Nasier and signed it with his own name and real title as Doctor of Medicine, to be sure, adding, in the first few editions only, the fictive title "Priest of the Isles of Hyères" (Calloïer des Iles Hières) facetious because these islands (just off the French Riviera coast near Toulon), were a popular hideout for pirates and brigands.

Since his debut in printed narrative some fourteen years before (*Pantagruel* 1532) as a learned humanist physician of modest repute, R had come far, mainly in the company of such greats as the brothers Du Bellay; Guillaume, lord of Langey (1491–1543), able commander, governor, statesman; Bishop Jean (1492–1560), soon to be archbishop and cardinal, skilled diplomat and prelate, later Cardinal Odet de Chastillon; much earlier a lesser but protective helper, Geoffroy d'Estissac, bishop of Maillezais; and although Books 1 and 2 sought, at least ostensibly, a more plebeian, less erudite public than such as these, their enthusiastic readers included both R's kings (Francis I, then Henry II) and Francis's sister, the learned and high-minded Margaret of Navarre (see n. 2 below).

Here and now, with apparent unease or even trepidation (shown in the story of Ptolemy, son of Lagus, that he borrowed from Lucan to use as that master had done) R undertakes a bold new venture, new in several ways: he abandons the story of the giants, and with it that ready-made plot pattern and indeed any clear-cut story line whatever; completes the change, begun earlier in the parts of 1–2 on education and crowned there in the victorious wars, from the crude, rather oafish young giant cubs he began with into the Pantagruel of the last few books, the Evangelicalist Christian philosopher-king (or prince), rivaling Plato's in all but the rigors of his preparatory curriculum, and far merrier, sunnier, and more merciful. R addresses his new nobler public explicitly from the first, and throughout the book by his erudition and concern with serious moral problems—and unconcern for physical action and prowess; also by his change from a plebeian publisher such as Claude Nourry or François Juste of Lyon to one who issued more serious fare, Christian Wechel of Paris; and finally in his election of Roman print (such as we still use), then favored by humanists, over the lowly Gothic used for chapbooks and old romances—and for R's own first two books. For R the seas he now set sail onto were uncharted.

3: "To the Spirit of the Queen of Navarre"

1. Margaret of Navarre (1492–1549), born d'Angoulême, then by her first marriage d'Alençon, before becoming queen of Navarre by her second (1527), to Henri d'Albret; older sister of King Francis I of France; called by some Margaret d'Angoulême to distinguish her from another Margaret of Navarre, both her grandniece and her granddaughter-in-law (1553–1610), best known as Margaret of Valois, sister of French King Henry III and (for a time) ill-matched wife of French Protestant leader King Henry of Navarre, from 1589 to 1610 King Henry IV of France.

   Margaret (Marguerite) of Navarre, learned and mystically religious, strongly favored Church Reform (to which for a time in the 1520s she nearly won over King Francis) and protected as patron innovative writers and all victims of persecution—this even in her desolate late years. Herself a versatile and prolific writer, she left many deeply-felt religious poems; several fine plays (*théâtre profane* "secular drama") dealing squarely but tactfully with religious and moral issues; and her best-known (and arguably best) work, the seventy-odd tales and discussions of these by ten stranded noble friends, modeled on Boccaccio's *Decameron* but incomplete and posthumously published, that we know as her *Heptameron*. The mystical streak so marked in her later years helps explain R's invitation in his dedicatory dizain to her to return down to earth a bit for a fresh taste of *Pantagruel*.

3: ROYAL PRIVILEGE (OF 1545)

1. Here we depart from our usual guides, our edition of reference (LI) and the other two French scholarly reader's editions (PL and G) that we generally also follow, for not one of these gives the original Royal Privilege (by Francis I, for 6 years, dated Sept. 19, 1545; they give only the later, longer, ten-year one issued by Henry II (with R's benign supporter Chastillon present), on August 6, 1550. Only M. A. Screech in TL offers both documents; but with the original one as a variant in a note, the other alone as the text. None of the English translations give either one. Although the two are much alike, both are short, and seem to us important enough to be presented here, and as text, in order of their appearance: first that of 1545 (Francis I), then that of 1550 (Henry II).

2. Francis I of the house of Angoulême (1494–1547), king of France from 1515, enjoyed war as a noble sport and won at it in invading Italy until taken captive at Pavia in 1515 by Emperor Charles V's army, then imprisoned by Charles for a year and sick much of it. Also fond of arts and letters, he fostered their blooming in France, paying well to bring in Italian artists and building many handsome châteaux and palaces. Detesting the Sorbonne, which had bitterly opposed his 1515 Concordat with the pope giving the king much control over French high clerical appointments (a source of funds and power), and influenced by his peacefully Reformist sister Margaret of Navarre (see note 2 just above), for many years he tolerated and protected peaceful Reform such as Evangelicalism; but provocations in October 1534 and January 1535 alienated him and left him alternating between toleration and harsh repression as determined advisers on either side drew him now one way now the other.

3. The justices and officers listed included many of the main supporters of the crown in the struggle with the nobility to try to unify and strengthen the nation.

4. A favorite charge of R's but ill-supported by such evidence as we have.

5. R's dedicatory epistle to Book 4, addressed to his greatest protector and supporter in his late years, Cardinal Odet de Chastillon, and dated January 28, 1552, states that R had indeed at some point resolved to stop writing and publishing his story, so weary and heartsick was he at the venom and malice of his calumniators and other critics; but that Chastillon's encouragement, moral support, and promise of protection gave him fresh heart and stomach to resume and continue. Some such thing may well have happened, and the likeliest time was probably around 1543–1545.

3: ROYAL PRIVILEGE (OF 1550)

1. Note that R asked for a ten-year privilege but got one for six; his luck was to be better with Henry II and with Chastillon. The repetition of the threat of penalties for disobedience is probably a mistake, but it is not ours; so reads the text as reproduced in TL (p. 4, variant).

2. Henry II of France (1519–1559), son of Francis I, and his successor; like him, physically robust and vigorous but also weak willed, easily swayed (Diane de Poitiers, mistress); long harshly intolerant in his Catholicism, influenced by François de Guise and others but also at times by advisers favoring tolerance (Anne de Montmorency, Jean du Bellay, et al); opposed Emperor Charles V, with modest success for European hegemony; married Catherine de Medici, died suddenly (1559) in a jousting accident; like his father, greatly enjoyed R's stories.

3: PROLOGUE OF THE AUTHOR

1. R regularly calls his giant hero "le bon Pantagruel," which sounds better to me in French than the literal English, which we have used here, but which, regrettably, has somehow acquired an aroma of priggish self-righteousness that ill befits R. We have therefore rendered it at times by the inexact but homier "good old Pantagruel." We have used similar freedom in rendering "le bon Gargantua."

2. Meaning metaphysically. Since Aristotle's *Metaphysics* directly follows his *Physics* and since Greek *Meta* with the accusative means "after," this work was named his *Metaphysics* (ta meta ta physika), and the name stuck.

3. Nothing besides this text is known of this artillery piece, whose name suggests that its power and efficiency made it popular with the soldiers who used it.

4. The long list that now follows (sixty-odd verbs in the imperfect active) conveys a sense of rolling, bustling, knocking, and driving to and fro, up and down, in a frenzy of activity for activity's sake. Since their sequences and groupings seem determined more by sound than by sense, we follow suit with little regard for the sense of each verb but close heed to the clusters of similar sounds.

5. "Je pareillement, quoy que soys hors d'effroy, ne suis toutesfoys hors d'esmoy."

6. " . . . repetasseurs de vieilles ferrailles latines": a puzzling phrase, since it might be applied to R's great hero Erasmus, who, however, was a confirmed pacifist, as shown by his *Complaint of Peace* (*Querela pacis*).

7. " . . . feust-ce portant hotte, cachant crotte, ployant rotte ou cassant motte": all among the humblest of activities, which shows his goodwill to help if he can.

8. " . . . ceste insigne fable et tragicque comédie": the later defined as a drama that begins sadly or tragically but ends happily, as a comedy.

9. Allusion to Saint Mary the Egyptian, a popular subject for medieval and Renaissance artists. Reputedly rather wanton until her conversion to Christianity, once later on, under high obligation to cross a stream but no swimmer and not having money for the fare she allowed a boatman to have sex with her to pay him for taking her across.

10. Another puzzle, for we know of no epilogue by R to any book.

11. Normal body temperature was the first degree; the second degree was a very low fever.

12. A word-play suggesting idle time-wasting (by others, of course). Recalling Horace, *Epistles* 1.17.36, renewed by Erasmus in his *Adages* 1.4.1.

13. These *sentences pantagruélicques* are of course R's Books 3 and 4, which were both (4 to be sure, in a short incomplete version of 1548) soon to appear, and in rather swift succession.

14. "... me auront ... pour Architriclin loyal," as in the wedding feast at Cana (John 2.1–11).

15. Pronounced "la passion acuton": this suggests first the agony of Jesus Christ, then (from the *cu*, which sounds like *cul* or "ass"), a pain in the ass.

16. *Mars* in French means both "Mars" and "March": so this might mean the plausible "unless in Lent" (as it often does).

17. "... pour Vénus advieigne Barbet le chien": in knucklebones the best shot is called "Venus," the worst one "the dogs."

18. "... la couppe guorgée": one of R's favorite équivoques (word-plays) rather like spoonerisms in English. See Epistémon's *couppe testée* "chop headed off" in 2.30.

19. "... lifrelofres": a deformation (comic) of "philosopher, philosophers"; but also a name suggesting "boozer" applied to German and Swiss mercenaries; thus R will force no one to drink willynilly, as do the German Lutherans and the Swiss Calvinists.

20. Some legends assigned Pandora a box, others a bottle.

21. Danaids (daughters of King Danaus) were punished in death by having to keep refilling with water a vessel full of holes.

22. These giants, who were symbols of impiety, were the judges, devouring gold (money), the more obvious bribes that they demanded (see 5.11–15).

23. Here spelled "au cul passions" so as to mean "passions" in the ass or the tail; but the sound is that of French *occupations,* which the context leads us to expect—one more reminder of the oral style R loves and employs and how new in his day silent reading, usually alone, still was.

24. "Je renonce ma part de Papimanie": R heralds here an episode of Book 4 (4.48) but already scoffs at that mania.

3.1: HOW PANTAGRUEL TRANSPORTED A COLONY OF UTOPIANS INTO DIPSODY.

1. An allusion to Machiavelli and his many admirers and emulators. R disagrees.

2. The remark by Hesiod comes not from his *Theogony* but from his *Works and Days,* chapter 5, and is found also in Plutarch, *Of Isis and Osiris* 12.

3. Aurelian (Lucius Domitius Aurelianus, A.D. 212–275, emperor from 270), a great Roman emperor, consolidated the then shaky Roman Empire and regained Britain, Gaul, Spain, Egypt, and much of the Near East.

4. R quotes Virgil only in a French translation (presumably his own) as the following couplet:

> Il, qui estoit victeur, par le vouloir
> Des gens vaincuz faisoit ses loix valoir.

5. "... Flamens habitans en Saxe, embeurent les meurs et contradictions des Saxons."

3.2: HOW PANURGE WAS MADE LORD OF SALMAGUNDI IN DIPSODY.

1. The *royal* was a medieval gold coin. Cotgrave sets its value at "about 68 solz" (sous). E. C. rates it at this time at about 13–14 gold francs.

2. A *seraph* was a Turkish gold coin worth about a French crown (Cotgrave).

3. The French *dilapida* means "squandered," but literally "tore it down stone by stone," which explains R's play on Panurge's not spending the money on building for hospitals, schools, or the like.

4. "... et mangeant son bled en herbe": proverbial for counterproductive wild spending.

5. "... par li bon Dieu et li bons homs!" This is an old mild oath in Old French forms and an archaism dear to R.

6. The following couplet translates a statement in Latin from a tragedy of Seneca (*Thyestes* v. 619).

> Oncq' homme n'eut les Dieux tant bien à main,
> Qu'asceuré feust de vivre au lendemain.

7. Commutative justice sets limits on unearned profits or increments.

8. Distributive justice, as the name suggests, is recompensing each man according to his merits, his deserts.

9. The French original, "jouant des haulx boys," was a popular gag in a period when many nobles, lacking ways to earn a living, were forced by relentless inflation to sell off some of their lands or timber.

10. Thestylis, in Virgil's *Eclogue* 2.10, is a peasant girl who prepares the meal for the harvesters.

11. "It is consumed" or "It is accomplished," in John 19.30: for John these are Christ's last words as he was dying on the cross. Reportedly Thomas Aquinas spoke the words once when, dining with Saint Louis (Louis IX of France), his mind on a sermon, he absentmindedly ate a lamprey meant for the king, then found the phrase apt and spoke it.

3.3: HOW PANURGE PRAISES DEBTORS AND CREDITORS.

1. Caesar (*Gallic Wars* 6.13) is the authority here on the Gauls. Dis or Pluto, god of the underworld, was held to be extremely rich with treasures underground. But possibly also either Caesar or R here confuses Plutus with Pluto.

2. Another pun: *la manche,* "the sleeve," is also *la mancia,* Italian for "tip"; but to call it a sleeve and pair it with arm makes a neater claim.

3. "... en ronfle veue": showing my hand, from a different game, amounts to being "behind the eight-ball" from a wild form of pool. Cotgrave calls this game "hand-ruffe."

4. "... je le maintiens jusques au feu exclusivement": the heroic claim bursts in the final word, a favorite formula for R.

5. In *Works and Days* 5.289: a popular allegory in the Renaissance.

6. *Licence, Licentiate:* French academic higher degree qualifying the holder to teach.

7. This figure, of man as a microcosm (of the cosmos), is a Renaissance topos.

8. On the revolt of the members against the stomach.

9. Implying that by paying his debts he would be tossing his money to all the devils.

3.4: CONTINUATION OF PANURGE'S SPEECH IN PRAISE OF CREDITORS AND DEBTORS.

1. Brittany was noted for its extreme piety and its many bishoprics and saints. A great favorite was Saint Ives or Yves (1253–1303), Breton born, patron of lawyers; festival May 1.

2. From the *Farce of Master Pathelin* vs. 172–173:

> Et si prestoit
> Ses denrées à qui en vouloit.

3. "Sang est le siège de l'âme": so said Empedocles, Lucretius, and Virgil, among others.

4. "La bouteille du fiel en soubstraict la cholère superflue." The bile was then considered the cause of irascibility. Nothing is drawn off by the bile duct.

5. The verb *devoir* means "to owe," the noun "duty." R links his brilliant paradox in Panurge's praise of debt to the main theme of Book 3—marriage.

3.5: HOW PANTAGRUEL DETESTS DEBTORS AND CREDITORS.

1. Apollonius, according to his *Life* by Philostratus 4.4–10. Philostratus reports that when the plague threatened Ephesus, and the Ephesians asked for help, Apollonius had them stone a ragged old beggar to death. When they then removed the stones, they found underneath not the dead beggar, but a huge mad dog the size of a lion that had disguised itself beneath the rags. This story suggests that this dog was the plague.

2. So says Plutarch, according to Erasmus *Adages* 2.7.98: "Felix qui nihil debet."

3. *Laws,* as quoted by Plutarch *De vitanda usura (On avoiding usury)* 1.827d.

4. This request was reported by Bonaventure Des Périers (ca. 1500–1544) in story 34 of his *Nouvelles récréations et joyeux devis.* It was almost proverbial by 1546.

5. This is the closest Pantagruel seems to come to losing patience with Panurge.

3.6: Why newlyweds were exempt from going to war.

1. This is the French original of this quatrain:

> Patenostres et oraisons
> Sont pour ceulx-là qui les retiennent.
> Un fiffre allans en fenaisons
> Est plus fort que deux qui en viennent.

2. Panurge's respect for Galen's great learning springs from his own lack of it.

3.7: How Panurge had a flea in his ear.

1. Presumably to keep this mark of serious purpose always ready at hand.

2. "Chascun abonde en son sens" (Romans 14.5). The *abonde* is a subjunctive that needed no *que* in R's day. NEB: "On such a point everyone should have reached a conviction in his own mind." Reformists often cited this verse to distinguish dissent from heresy; and R plays safe by his Erasmian stress on its soundness in extraneous, irrelevant matters.

3. Apparently another pun on *bureau*, though why apropos here is not clear to me. See the Glossary.

4. "O le grand mesnaiger que je seray": as the text shows, in one respect at least.

5. Lengthening certain *esses* would change "ss" (sous) into "ff" (francs), so that he would be wrongly charged many times too much.

3.8: How the codpiece is the first piece of harness among warriors.

1. "Par la dive Oye guenet": euphemistic oath, recalling "Ventre Sainct Quenet" (1.5) but also suggesting "Holy Mother of God!" or the like.

2. In Nancy, on the first Sunday in Lent, persons were chosen out of a merry society of pranksters to be named *Valentins* and *Valentines* and to serve as kings and queens for a day or two. The identity of Viardière is unknown.

3. " . . . le genre humain aboly par le déluge poëtique." Not the (true) flood in the Bible, from which God saved Noah (Genesis 6). R's is Ovid's story in his *Metamorphoses* 1.348 ff., when human wickedness led Zeus to plan to kill them all by a flood. Prometheus warned Deucalion and his wife Pyrrha, who built a boat and escaped onto Mount Parnassus. Obeying an oracle, they threw stones on the ground, which grew into men and women.

4. A title already listed in the Library of Saint-Victor (above, 2.7).

5. Lord de Merville is unknown.

6. I.e., the male genitals; cf., the book title *The Marriage Packet,* also in the Library of Saint-Victor (above, 2.7).

843

7. Yet another book title from the same library (above, 2.7).

8. Here is the French original of this octave, which appeared in an anthology
   in 1534:

> Celle qui veid son mary tout armé,
> Fors la braguette, aller à l'escarmouche,
> Luy dist: "Amy, de paour qu'on ne vous touche,
> Armez cela, qui est le plus aymé."
> Quoy? tel conseil doibt-il estre blasmé?
> Je diz que non; car sa paour la plus grande
> De perdre estoit, le voyant animé,
> Le bon morceau dont elle estoit friande.

3.9: HOW PANURGE TAKES COUNSEL OF PANTAGRUEL.

1. To Panurge's concluding "ne me marier poinct," Pantagruel replies:
   "Poinct doncques ne vous mariez," setting the pattern for this whole chapter, where the comedy of Panurge's dithering with changes back and forth
   is enhanced by Pantagruel's plan of beginning each of his responses with the
   last words or sounds (or nearly those) of Panurge's preceding voiced anxiety
   or refusal: what Panurge thereupon (3.10) will call "the Ricochet song,"
   and reproach him for. R manages this neatly; we have done our best to
   emulate him.

2. The tercel is a kind of male falcon, so called because he is one-third smaller
   than the female. Job's tercel presumably suffers a full two-thirds of Job's
   miseries.

3. A popular saying compared women of sweet appearance with sweet wine,
   as being more likely than most to turn sour or bitter (from *vin doux* to *vin
   aigre*, vinegar).

4. Here, to Panurge's preceding "de mon mal riez" he replies "Mariez-vous
   doncq, de par Dieu!"

3.10: HOW PANTAGRUEL POINTS OUT TO PANURGE THAT ADVICE ABOUT MARRIAGE IS A DIFFICULT THING.

1. Cotgrave says this of "C'est la chanson du Ricochet": "tis an idle, or
   endlesse tale, or song; a subject whereof one part contradicts, marres, or
   overthrowes, another."

2. The Thebaid (Egypt) and Montserrat (Catalonia) were arid desert retreats
   for hermits.

3. A translation following the ancient verse indicates a translation of R's
   French rendering of the ancient verses. A translation in brackets indicates a
   direct translation of the ancients.

4. Pierre Amy or Lamy, friend of R's at Fontenay-le-Comte (1521–1523)
   and his initiator there into Greek studies, fled from there when their books
   were confiscated by order of the Sorbonne (1523) and spent his few
   remaining years, like his master Jacques Lefèvre d'Etaples, at refuge with

Margaret of Navarre, and in Basel near his admired friend Erasmus. A devout Evangelical humanist, he probably did not go all the way to Protestantism.

3.11: How Pantagruel points out that fortune-telling by throwing dice is unlawful.

1. The *Libro delle sorti,* by Lorenzo Spirito of Perugia (Bologna, 1476), was translated in 1528 and often reprinted and widely read in R's day.
2. In a game in May played by many, players had to wear a green leaf all month or pay a fine if caught without it, whence the expression "prendre sans vert." Panurge is saying that his dice are his green leaf and help him foil the devil. The Coccai book is imaginary.
3. Or more properly, unprotected.
4. In modern tennis as in its royal ancestor so popular in R's day, which we call court tennis, the first two points in each game each count for fifteen, those later for ten. Pantagruel's idiosyncratic scoring counts Panurge's initial failure (on his first try) as fifteen, then adds one to that for his ensuing success, to make sixteen. The term fault in modern tennis is used only of the service, in which two faults (misses in serving) make up a loss of a point for the server, or, better, an added point for the receiver of service.
5. Besides the literal *mitten, mitaine* has metaphoric uses, one of which seems not unlikely here–gloved hand-taps between friends at wedding feasts (a bit like modern American "high fives" in congratulation).
6. The goddesses of lots.

3.12: How Pantagruel explores by Virgilian lots.

1. An etymological pun: the father from whose head she was born.
2. It is really not Virgil but his commentator Servius who mentions Vulcan's name at this point and in this connection.
3. A *cordelier* is a Franciscan, Gray Friar (Franciscan girt with a cord; R was one); a *bordelier,* a wencher, or more specifically, a man who frequents bordellos; R's play makes them seem interchangeable.

3.13: How Pantagruel advises Panurge to foresee by dreams.

1. A theory, Platonic in origin and very popular in the sixteenth century.
2. Both these terms mean interpreter of dreams. Throughout this chapter R draws heavily on two works especially, J. C. Scaliger's commentary (1539) on Hippocrates' *Peri hupnion* (*On dreams*) and *De occulta philosophia* by Henry Cornelius Agrippa (1533).
3. R, by calling this man "the Frenchman Villenovanus," makes it clear that he means not Miguel Servetus (1511-1553), whose railing against the Trinity, then against Calvin and seeking to oust him, led to his death at the

stake, but Simon de Neufville, d. 1530, a Walloon, who was a teacher of Estienne Dolet at Padua and probably died there.

4. Homer (*Odyssey* 19.562) and Virgil (*Aeneid* 6.894) tell how dreams come through one of two gates: the true and to-be-accomplished through the gate of horn (which R, in explanation, calls diaphanous) and the false and deceptive through the gate of ivory (which R pronounces opaque). This poetic notion, on which both poets (or Odysseus and Virgil, at least) agree, has captivated many western imaginations ever since.

5. The visive spirits, as noted earlier and as explained by Macrobius in his commentary on Cicero's *Somnium Scipionis* (*Scipio's Dream*) 1.3, are a kind of animal spirits that the eye emits and that create an illuminated field that makes vision possible.

6. "Vous voulez inférer," dist Frère Jean, "que les songes des coquz cornuz, comme sera Panurge, Dieu aydant et sa femme, sont tousjours vrays et infallibles."

3.14: PANURGE'S DREAM AND THE INTERPRETATION THEREOF.

1. The remark of Joseph's brothers to one another (Genesis 37.19), jealous of the prestige he had got from his interpretations of dreams. As we noted just above, R, having just reintroduced Frère Jean into his tale, now joins him and the others with three more regulars (Ponocrates, Eudémon, Carpalim) "and others" to enrich his plot from this point on.

2. "J'en suys bien chés Guillot le songeur," a proverbial type whose company brought on mental drowsiness or stupor.

3. " . . . comme il feist en la position des cornes bovines." This tale goes back to Lucian; Erasmus alludes to it in *Adages* 5.74: "Momo satisfacere"; and see also Conti *Mythology* 5.6.

4. In *The Interpretation of Dreams* 2.12.

5. Drum and drummer were indispensable parts of wedding parties.

6. Curiously, one Sorbonne theologian in 1533, Pierre Cornu, bore that name in the Latinized form of his own.

7. Panurge follows the correct *fiat* (Latin passive: "Let it be done!") with the barbaric, overkill passive *fiatur,* then notes his difference in this from the pope.

8. " . . . proculteurs," which of course grafts *cul* "ass" onto the word *procureurs.*

9. Ovid (*Metamorphoses* 3.138 ff.) tells how hapless Actaeon, for having accidentally come upon Diana bathing nude, was changed by her into a stag and caught and torn to bits by his hounds.

10. In rhetoric, taking the antecedent for the consequent, or vice versa.

11. Calling them "foundling" or "bastard," or both.

12. The French original of this couplet reads thus:

> D'enfer aille au gibbet,
> Noel nouvelet.

13. " . . . le premier sensitif": the heart. Brain and spinal marrow were considered insensible still.

14. Sophocles, quoted in Erasmus's *Adages*.

3.15: PANURGE'S EXCUSE.

1. "Dieu," dist Panurge, "guard de mal qui void bien et n'oyt goutte!" Proverb quoted by Cotgrave and rendered thus: "For my part, I am loath to conceive it, though I see it, well enough." Urquhart's reading has much the same sense.

2. Maistre Mousche, a popular type of "magician" or sleight-of-hand artist.

3. In theory, 9 hours after dawn, but actually around noon; see Glossary s.v., hours.

4. " . . . souppes de lévrier": a very hearty (greasy) snack, usually involving the hare's saddle.

5. " . . . aux abboys du parchemin": at the raucous chanting of liturgical texts written on parchement.

6. "Le sort, l'usure, et les intérestz je pardonne. Je me contente des despens."

7. Friend as close to my heart as is my baldrick (a belt that would carry a sword, a bugle, or the like worn next to the chest). Cf., Hamlet to Horatio (III.ii) "I will wear him in my heart's core."

8. A favorite in R's time, this fable of Aesop's is found in the *Adages* (1.7.90) of Erasmus, who lists it in his index under the rubric *philautia* "self-love." Already Epistémon's learning makes him often a ponderous bore.

3.16: HOW PANTAGRUEL ADVISES PANURGE TO CONSULT WITH A SIBYL OF PANZOUST.

1. " . . . feust-ce d'un sot, d'un pot, d'une gedoufle, d'une moufle, d'une pantoufle?" I have tried to do justice to the sound as well as the sense of this comic list.

2. I.e., virtually infallible for the essentials.

3. The French *maunettes* or *mal nettes* means "unclean," like the sibyl of Panzoust and no doubt many others. *Monettes* (from Latin *moneo,* "to warn or remind") means "women who notify, remind, or warn."

4. Latinized name of Master Hardouin de Graes of Cologne, fierce foe of Reuchlin and Erasmus, ridiculed as such by humanists, listed by R (above, 2.7) as author of an imaginary book in the Library of Saint-Victor. He had caused a scandal by fathering a bastard child by a maid-servant; so R creates a comic shock by using him to cap this list of eminent and self-respecting philosophers.

5. French *zibeline* "sable," hence, smooth as sable, with an obvious pun on *sibylline*.

3.17: HOW PANURGE SPEAKS TO THE SIBYL OF PANZOUST.

1. This is a learned pun of R's, since Heraclitus was known as *skoteinos* "darksome, shadowy, obscure," hence *scotiste*. Since his *floruit* was about 500 B.C., he obviously could not have had a disciple or follower of Duns Scotus (1266–1308).

2. "... officialement": in a pisspot, *official*, also of course "officially." The homely tale of the genesis of Orion is in Ovid *Fasti* 5.499–536 and Servius's commentary on the *Aeneid* 6.136. It is this. Jupiter, Neptune, and Mercury, inspecting men and the earth incognito to know their true nature, were most handsomely lodged, fed, and entertained by the poor but hospitable peasant Hireus (aka Oenopion). Having nothing else of theirs to leave, as asked, as a parting gift, they urinated and filled a chamber pot (*ourein*, Greek "to urinate"); and from this sprang Orion.

3. "Verd et bleu!": green and blue, clear euphemism for "Mère de Dieu!" or "Mother of God!"

4. Plucked by Aeneas at the Cumaean sibyl's bidding as his passport through the underworld (*Aeneid* 6.136); title of James Fraser's fine 1922 book.

5. A precious tone common in Beuxes, near Loudun, which some said was drawn from the head of a toad.

6. "Par le sambre guoy de bois, voylà le trou de la Sibylle." Allusion to the sibyl's grotto described in *Aeneid* 6.11–12.

7. Here is the French original of these verses:

> T'esgoussera
> De renom.
>
> Engroissera
> De toy non.
>
> Te sugsera
> Le bon bout.
>
> T'escorchera,
> Mais non tout.

The play in the fourth line rests on the ambivalence of the preposition *de,* whose object may be either the future father or the future child. The likelier meaning seems to be English "by," i.e., that Panurge will not be the father; but he of course takes it, rightly, to mean that he will not be the child his wife will bear. English *with* or *from* seem both possible; we have chosen *with*.

3.18: HOW PANTAGRUEL AND PANURGE DIVERSELY INTERPRET THE VERSES.

1. Here continues (from the end of preceding chap. 17) the ambiguity of French *de* in this context, whose object may be either the prospective father or the prospective child (English *by* or *with*). See note 7 above (3.17).

2. "... et en suys là, sans praejudice de meilleur advis."

3. A red die is made from dried bodies of some insects sucked up off oaks.

4. "C'est bien à propous truelle, Dieu te guard de mal, masson!" This is a standard formula in R's day for changing the subject.

5. "Frère Artus Culletant." *Artus* is an old form of "Arthur." *Culletant* is from *culeter*, which Cotgrave defines as "to move the taile in a wanton time."

6. " . . . par le sainct sang breguoy": formed to sound a bit like "Saint sang de Dieu."

7. " . . . vous me alléguez de gentilz veaulx! Ilz feurent folz comme poëtes et resveurs comme philosophes, autant pleins de fine follie comme estoit leur philosophie."

3.19: HOW PANTAGRUEL PRAISES THE COUNSEL OF MUTES.

1. On this live question of language "arbitrary or natural in its meanings," Pantagruel, and presumably R, follow Aquinas, Dante, Sperone Speroni, and soon followed also by Joachim Du Bellay in his *Deffence et Illustration.*

2. Probably Lucian *Dialogue on the dance* 60, though he does not mention Tiridates by name.

3. " . . . dam Royddimet": a name that also offers a pun on *redimet* in *ipse redimet Israel*, "He alone will set Israel free," Psalms 130.8.

4. Punished thus for their revolt against Moses (Numbers 16.30–33). Dathan and Abiram rebel against God and Moses, and upon Moses' prayer were swallowed up in the earth and went down alive into Sheol.

3.20: HOW GOATSNOSE REPLIES TO PANURGE IN SIGNS.

1. " . . . son pistolandier": meaning of course his member.

2. Five, or, consisting of five, or, made up of fives.

3. As though the odd numbers were left over and unnecessary for counting.

4. Literally, "Power of a wooden ox," a very different sense but comparable euphemistic oath.

5. "Cicéron en dist je ne sçay quoy . . . ": the only such vague claim in R's book.

6. Imitating the sound of a fart with lips and tongue.

3.21: HOW PANURGE TAKES COUNSEL OF AN OLD FRENCH POET NAMED RAMINAGROBIS.

1. Much speculation, especially early in this century by Abel Lefranc and his biohistorically minded colleagues, has centered about the identity of the historical model, if any, for Raminagrobis; and names suggested include those of the aged poet Guillaume Crétin (d. 1525), whose work R admired, and which included the poem on which is modeled the one that ends this chapter; of Jean Lemaire de Belges (b. 1473), a far abler poet and prose-writer who died about the same time as Crétin; and of the peaceful Evangelical Reformist Jacques Lefèvre d'Etaples (d. 1536). Although a case has been made for each of these, none has convinced most students of R. The

name derives probably from *rominer* or *ruminer* "to ruminate," and *grobis* "tomcat"; but this is no more enlightening than the relationships here alleged by R with "La Grande Guorre" (syphilis) and "la belle Bazoche" (see note 4 below). The source of his account of the vermin he had to drive out to die in peace is a *Colloquy* of Erasmus; the *Funus,* "the vermin," seem clearly to be monks.

2. See especially Plato's *Phaedo* and Plutarch, *On the daemon of Socrates* 593.

3. Normally reckoned as the dangerous sixty third year, but for Du Bellay, his fifty second.

4. For "La Grande Guorre" as syphilis, see note 1 above. The Basoche was a notable society of Paris law-clerks, who elected their own king (a Lord of Misrule) for their annual revels, and performed plays, principally farces and *soties* that included the *Farce de Maistre Pathelin* (later fifteenth century), a favorite of R's often quoted or cited by him in these pages.

5. The last words of Socrates, as reported by Plato (*Phaedo* 118a) were that they owed a cock to Aesculapius.

6. This is the French original of Raminagrobis's verses:

> Prenez-la, ne la prenez pas.
> Si vous la prenez, c'est bien faict;
> Si ne la prenez en effect,
> Ce sera oeuvré par compas.
> Gualloppez, mais allez le pas;
> Recullez, entrez y de faict;
>   Prenez-la, ne . . .
>
> Jeusnez, prenez double repas,
> Défaictez ce qu'estoit refaict.
> Refaictez ce qu'estoit défaict,
> Soubhaytez-luy vie et trespas,
>   Prenez la, ne . . .

This rondeau is by rhétoriqueur poet Guillaume Crétin (d. 1525), in this popular tradition in which his friend Marot began, and in which R wrote the verses of his we have quoted on 3.21: R's conclusion to this chapter closely follows Erasmus's *Colloquy* "Funus" in speaking of monastic death-bed pests as if they were insect pests.

3.22: HOW PANURGE CHAMPIONS THE ORDER OF THE MENDICANT FRIARS.

1. Meaning "beating about the bush," but meanwhile suggesting the naval (umbilicus) and the vagina.

2. Approximately: counterweights in the dynamics of matters heavenly.

3. Periphrastic weak-mindedness.

4. "Je suys aussi saige que oncques puys ne fourneasmes-nous": a common play on the similarity of *fournir* "furnish" and *enfourner* "put in the oven." The sense is much like English "as smart as ever came down the pike."

5. In dialectic, expressing mutually exclusive alternatives.

6. A comic imaginary substitute for the pilgrimage spot Santiago de Compostela.

7. "Ce que je diray adviendra ou ne adviendra poinct." Recalls Horace *Satires* 5.59; quoted by Erasmus *Adages* 3.3.35.

8. The problem was whether men or women enjoyed sexual consummation more; Tiresias, who had once been a woman, answered "women, nine times more" so angry Juno put out both his eyes.

9. " . . . congnoistre mousches en laict": a time-honored phrase (as in Villon's *Débat*) for being capable of, and practicing, elementary observation and discrimination.

10. According to a much later commentator, in the early days of Reform in La Rochelle, a magistrate had a clock burned at the stake with its Huguenot maker.

11. A Greek god living in the center of the earth, identified by many in the Middle Ages with the Devil, and mentioned in Arnoul Gréban's *Mystère de la Passion,* ca. v. 1500.

3.23: HOW PANURGE MAKES A SPEECH FOR RETURNING TO RAMINAGROBIS.

1. Two terms for ceremonies celebrating the anniversaries of deaths, lucrative for the clerics.

2. The cross here is the one stamped on many coins.

3. A ford over the stream of Vède or Négron not far from La Devinière on the road from Seuilly to Chinon in the heart of the R country; the scene, or near the scene, of Gargantua's birth (1.4–7 above) and of much of his war with Picrochole (1.28, 34–38, 48, and passim), including a piss-flood, two major victories, the rout of Picrochole's army and capture of his stronghold, and finally his flight and disappearance.

4. The name of course suggests *couille* and *couillon* "testicle, ball, ballock."

5. First and last words of this penitential Psalm (no. 51). The *vitulos* were sacrificial oxen. This was a popular pairing in monastic circles.

6. EC calls this a fur-trimmed capuchin or hood.

7. " . . . pinthe et fagot": a common pairing suggestive of hospitality.

8. " . . . docteur subtil en lard": *lard* for *l'art*, of course.

9. Milan-born Trivulzio (1448–1518) was Grand Marshal of France under Charles VII, but died in disfavor, probably at Châtre (Arpajon), not Chartres.

10. One of R's favorite terms, most often used of "woman's wound," as in 2.15 above (lion-fox-old woman) and 4.47 below (old Papefigue's wife and naive little devil).

11. Maistre Hordoux, who also appears (called Master Slipslop) as one of Frère Jean's fighting cooks in 4.40 below.

3.24: How Panurge takes counsel of Epistémon.

1. The Friars Minim (the Good Men), founded by Saint François de Paule (1416–1507) but the good men the ladies liked were *les Hommes bons,* the deft and durable lovers.
2. In the Argolid, Herodotus *Histories* 1.82, tells of this fight and what then followed.
3. Parts of the traditional cap of the fool.
4. Enguerrand de Monstrelet (ca. 1390–1453), continuator of Jean Froissart's *Chronicles* for 1400–1444.
5. One of Horace's most-used images (*Art of Poetry* v. 139), treated and cited by Erasmus *Adages* 1.9.14. The mountain gave birth to a mouse.
6. *Aphorisms* 1.1 concludes: "jugement difficile."
7. His daemon or guardian spirit that watches over a man and looks out for him. A Platonic or primarily neo-Platonic notion.
8. " . . . depuis à mort ignominieusement mise." See Tacitus *Annals* 12.22.
9. Saint Paul the Anachorète (d. A.D. 342) hermit, lived and died in the deserts of the Egyptian Thebaid; he was reportedly the founder of monasticism in the East.

3.25: How Panurge takes counsel of Her Trippa.

1. From the client's horoscope the astrologer identified his house of heaven ("sa maison du ciel") from the planetary positions, zodiac signs, and other such variables.
2. Here and for much of their interview, Her Trippa addresses Panurge using the familiar pronoun *tu,* clearly in its belittling and demeaning sense; Panurge of course answers in kind. When later on (see note 8 below) he changes to *vous,* it is clearly not as the polite singular but the general plural; for from this point on he alternates, addressing Panurge alone as *tu* at times, and at other times both men as *vous.*
3. In the circle of generation, this is the place, or house, of marriage.
4. A character described in Martial's *Epigram* 7.10, "Ad Olum."
5. " . . . tenoit le brelant": once a card game, in R's time meant a bawdy house.
6. Homer's Iros (Irus), the fawning but bullying beggar in Ithaca (*Odyssey* 18. 1–116), who taunts the ragged, returning, unrecognized Odysseus until that hero easily thrashes him soundly.
7. Lamia is a character from Plutarch's treatise *On curiosity* (*Peri polypragmosunes*) in *Moralia.* R has added a detail or two: the clog to hide her eyeglasses.
8. Pyromancy is divination by fire. Most of the "mancies" (arts of divination) that Her Trippa practices and recommends, filling the chapter, are explained by him in the text. Here for the first time Her Trippa uses *vous,* not *tu.*

9. Divination by air. The reference to *The Clouds* seems to be a general one.

10. Divination by a mirror or mirrors.

11. Jacoba Rhodigina, a ventriloquist named for her natal town of Rovigo, Italy, was possessed of a devil named Cincinnatulus in her body (see 4.58).

12. Divination by fish. R's source for this item is Pictorius Vigillanus.

13. Choeromancy is divination by hogs, from their bladders.

14. Divination by a cock.

15. These are the first letters in Greek of Theodosius, who succeeded Valens as emperor in A.D. 379.

16. Here Her Trippa, as noted above, starts using *vous* for "you," presumably because from here on he addresses both his visitors, not Panurge alone.

17. I find the ill will of this wish clearer than whatever harm it may do.

18. Scene of Pompey's decisive defeat by Caesar, in Thessaly, in 48 B.C.

19. Many Albanians, who favored pointed hats, served as mercenaries, usually horsemen used as scouts or Estradiots in the armies of the pope and the king of France. Like the Bulgarians later (*bougres,* "buggers"), they had an unsavory reputation for sodomy.

20. A semiprecious stone once thought to be made from a hyena's eye.

21. According to Philostratus *Life of Apollonius* 1.20.

22. Imaginary money coined by R to pair up with the (real) nobles (nobles à la rose), gold coins current not long before R's time.

3.26: How Panurge takes counsel of Frère Jean des Entommeures.

1. A community between La Villaumère and Chinon and near both.

2. Befuddled.

3. Like amalgam, a mixture of mercury with another metal.

4. "... bardable": a puzzler. Two possibilities are "fit to trim (barder) with lard"; and "fit to wear a donkey's saddle" (barde). Both seem only faintly possible. A third possibility is the most likely: "bardable" in the sense of being fit to bear barbed armor.

5. *Couillon pimpant,* brought on by its predecessor *timpant* "clashing."

6. Arab *alidada:* a diopter, an optical instrument for leveling, measuring heights, etc.

7. The poet Eustache Deschamps (1346–1406), in his "Ballade d'Antichrist," wrote that the Antichrist, on coming, will enjoy Solomon's treasures.

8. The Latin is of course utterly garbled; for the verb forms mean: "you" increase, "we" who are alive, "you" multiply.

9. The French of this couplet, Marot's paraphrase of one of Martial's (*Spectacula* 25), is this:

> Si, en allant, je suys de vous choyé,
> Peu au retour me chault d'estre noyé.

Martial's reads as follows:

Parcite dum propero,
Mergite dum redeo.

10. Since the pelican (onocrotale) was said to bray like a donkey, R seems here to endow it with that animal's sexual drive and to suggest: "as lustily as a donkey turned loose."

11. The capital Y, like its ancestor the Greek capital upsilon, may be seen as a schematic outline of a man's genitals.

3.27: How Frère Jean joyously advises Panurge.

1. By implication, their chastity (which he will guard against all others, but not himself); cf., "My Paternity" as myself or my virility.

2. Who probably never existed but had a name for lechery—perhaps because London whores were called "Winchester geese," since bishops of Winchester licensed their houses.

3. Hercules and Caesar are well known for their sexual appetites and prowess. Proculus Caesar, self-proclaimed emperor of Rome in A.D. 280, reportedly raped ten Sarmatian virgins in one night and a hundred in two weeks; see Cornelius Agrippa *De vanitate scientiarum* 60.

4. Like Priapus, the god of the erect phallus, noted above, chap. 19.

5. The phrase *prime del monde* means "first in the world" (compare contemporary American "We're number one").

6. There is such a town, near Niort in west central France, but the anecdote seems fictional, even to there having then been a passion play there.

7. "Caton le Censorin, lequel, voyant par sa praesence les festes Floralies en désordre, désista estre spectateur."

3.28: How Frère Jean comforts Panurge about his fear of cuckoldry.

1. Mountains in the African interior are always covered with snow.

2. The Hyperborean Mountains were far to the north, "above Boreas."

3. The part of rhetoric that deals with *topoi,* commonplaces.

4. Having malanders, cracks at the bend of a horse's knee.

5. I.e., in upsetting the divinely ordained government of things.

6. An East African city discovered by Vasco de Gama and conquered by the Portuguese, which typified remoteness in R's day much as does Timbuctoo today; noted twice in *Gargantua* (above, 1.5 and 1.8) the second time with mention of Hans Carvel as grand lapidary of the king of Melinda.

7. A type of joke common in R, when a noted book, act, or event is taken for a person. Compare the references later by Perrin Dendin to "Concile de Latran" and to "Pragmaticque Sanction" and by Bridoye to *Brocadium juris* (below, chap. 41). A concordat is a formal pact between a pope (as leader of the Church) and a king; the one designated here is that of 1516 between

Pope Leo X and Francis I of France, abolishing the Pragmatic Sanction of Bourges (1438) and requiring papal confirmation of the king's appointments of French archbishops, bishops, abbots, and priors.

8. "La légende des preudes femmes": an edifying medieval work aimed at wives, but as always, *femmes* could mean not only "wives" but "women."

3.29: HOW PANTAGRUEL CALLS A MEETING OF A THEOLOGIAN, A DOCTOR, A JURIST, AND A PHILOSOPHER.

1. Love (Greek *phil-*) of self (Greek *autos*, etc.), here personified, a favorite target of Renaissance moralists and other writers.

2. Probably not the Nicaean martyr celebrated March 13. The name is common in Poitou, and the saint often invoked before R's day.

3. The name of this theologian still eludes explanation. It can hardly stand for Hippotades, another name for Aeolus, god of the winds. R probably formed it from Greek *Hippo* "horse," hence knightly or superior + *Thadée* (Thaddaeus or Judas or Jude), a saint and apostle, one of the twelve disciples but probably not the author of the Epistle of Jude; mentioned by each of the four Evangelists and in Acts 1.13 (as Judas, son of James); probably martyred in Persia with Saint Simon, with whom he shares the feast day October 28; but if so, why Thaddaeus? We can only guess.

4. The name is much like that of R's friend, colleague, and one-time teacher at Montpellier, Guillaume Rondelet (1507–1566), who apparently also played in the farce of the man who married a dumb wife (chap. 34). The ending, however, is just a little like that of R's own name. Rondibilis may represent simply a typical physician.

5. Bridlegoose. R and his contemporaries never tired of the comedy of bridling a goose or gosling, as one does a horse, presumably also to carry a rider or haul a load (see *Gargantua,* Prologue); and although the term could mean a goose with a feather stuck through its nose to keep it from flying off through thorns or hedges, it still suggested idiotic stupidity. Bridoye, though an exemplar of modesty, earns his name by his ingenious folly and occasional lunatic logic in his interpretation of legal classic texts and maxims. R's extremely gentle treatment of him may reflect his hopes to be so treated by readers of this book.

   Well over two centuries later, in *The Marriage of Figaro* (1784), Beaumarchais revives this ancient gag, while taking revenge on counselor Goezman, by putting on stage a stammering idiot and naming him Don Guzman Brid'oison (Bridlegosling).

6. As Sainéan pointed out long ago, this name suggests the Poitevin word *trouil* "reel" or "winder"; therefore, two recent translators have rendered it by a meaningful English word, Jacques Leclercq as *Skeinwinder,* J. M. Cohen as *Wordspinner.* However, Cotgrave and others show no reason to suspect that the name would have meant or suggested any such thing to a contemporary of R's; so we follow Urquhart in leaving the name as R had it in French.

7. Jean de Boyssonné (ca. 1505–1508 to 1558 or 1559) was a friend and admirer of R's, an outspoken opponent of the old scholastic methods of teaching law, and until 1539 a professor of law at the University of Toulouse.

3.30: HOW HIPPOTHADÉE, THE THEOLOGIAN, GIVES ADVICE TO PANURGE.

1. Theories abound about R's choice of this name for this theologian. See above note 3 (3.29). Possible contemporary models have been seen in Melanchthon and in Lefèvre d'Etaples, both peaceful Reformists.

2. Saint Paul, forced to choose between chastity and marriage, praised chastity most highly for those fit for it, but summed up his advice for Christians on the choice (1 Corinthians 7.9) in the Vulgate's famous "melius est nubere quam uri" which translates "It is better to marry than to burn." But to "burn" could bear more than one interpretation: was it "burn in the fires of Sheol?" or was the burning the figurative combustion of lust, of simple sexual desire? Evangelicalists and most Reformists opted for that reading; and R makes his Hippothadée one by adding "on feu de concupiscence"; even as NEB translates the whole precept "Better be married than burn with vain desire."

3. A favorite coinage of R's, combining *circum* "around" with *umbilicus* "naval" and *vagina,* partly just for comic effect, partly to suggest a prurient beating about the bush.

4. *Corpe de galline!* "Body of a hen," from Italian *corpo di gallina,* a euphemism for the popular *Cordieu!* "Body of God!, 'Odsbody!"

5. A term in dialectic fitting the examples Panurge gives.

6. "Vous romperoient tout le testament," with stress on *testa* "head."

7. Wine mulled with cinnamon and named for its early sponsor Hippocrates.

3.31: HOW RONDIBILIS, THE DOCTOR, ADVISES PANURGE.

1. Possibly Saussenac, in the diocese of Albi (Tarn), but more probably an imaginary name. Of such monks or such a remark nothing is known.

2. French *Cauldaureil,* presumably from hearing too many steamy confessions.

3. For Aristotle, food was made usable by the body by three digestive processes: the first in the stomach, the second in the liver, the third in the interior of the tissues. And sperm is a superfluity left over after and from the assimilation of foods.

4. A play on the likeness between *casta* "chaste" and *castra* "camp" in Latin.

5. The "common sense" was the part of the brain that received the impressions from all the other, outgoing, senses.

6. To involve them not simply with living in general but with the good of the soul.

7. Plato *Phaedo* 64a.

8. "... l'esguarement des oeilz": a story told by Cicero (*Tusculans*), then by Plutarch (*On curiosity*), then most recently by Tiraqueau in *De legibus connubialibus*.

9. Apparently on this reasoning: since in a studious man sperm may be produced in the brain, cutting off his carotid arteries would cut off access of such sperm to his testicles.

10. From beyond the Hellespont, hence from the fabled and spice-rich East.

3.32: HOW RONDIBILIS DECLARES THAT CUCKOLDRY IS NATURALLY ONE OF THE ATTRIBUTES OF MARRIAGE.

1. This deflationary parody (meaning "as little as nothing," about like English "practically nothing" or "nothing of consequence") is of course a take-off of the world-famous acronym attesting the might and unity of Rome, S. P. Q. R. (Senatus Populus Que Romani) and as such a popular jest in R's time.

2. "... s'estre esguarée de ce bon sens ... quand elle a basty la femme." Much of this material comes from Tiraqueau's *De legibus connubialibus*.

3. "... ou des animaux raisonnables, ou des bestes brutes": see *Timaeus* 90–91.

4. First in a series of types of Bacchants; the others follow.

5. "Vertus d'aultre que d'un petit poisson": conceivably a veiled slap at swearing by the powers of Christ, symbolized by the outline of a fish, Greek *ichthus* (I. CH. Th. U. S.) were the initials of the words: Jesus Christ, Son of God, Savior.

6. "... en autheur célèbre, passé a dix-huyct cens ans": Aesop, according to Plutarch in his *Letter of consolation to his wife* (6.609a), soon to be translated by Montaigne's friend La Boétie (1530–1563), and the translation published by Montaigne in 1570 in memory of his dead friend.

7. "... cestuy hanat nestorien": gigantic, like the one Homer assigns to Nestor in the *Iliad* 2.631 ff. One that is worthy of the thirst of a Homeric hero.

3.33: HOW RONDIBILIS, THE DOCTOR, GIVES A REMEDY FOR CUCKOLDRY.

1. The Bishop of Auxerre who tried so ineptly to reform the calendar was not Françis de Dinteville but a predecessor of his.

2. One of two saints Vitalis, probably the martyr, husband of Saint Valeria and father of saints Gervasius and Protasius; he was racked and then buried alive, in Ravenna, about A.D. 171, where a fine Byzantine church is named for him. His festival day is April 28.

3. Proverbial to expresss absolute impossibility.

4. His or her (Jealousy's); the French *ses* could mean either.

3.34: How women ordinarily covet forbidden things.

1. "... la morale comoedie de celluy qui avoit espousé une femme mute": performed as part of their merry annual Twelfth Night festivities, probably on January 6, 1531, by a group of friends, students, and faculty members. The play, which Epistémon sketches in the text, was a rather well-known medieval farce now lost to us; but in the 1920s Anatole France, a devotee of R, composed a reconstruction of it to be found in his *Oeuvres complètes illustrées* (Paris: Calman-Lévy, 1925–1935, 25 vols., 18:423–481). Although the identity of the speaker here is less clear than usual, it seems to be Ponocrates, continuing after his story of the pope and the nuns. (It is clearly neither Panurge nor Epistémon, nor presumably Carpalim or Frère Jean. The regal, hostly manner suggests Pantagruel himself; but his remarks rule that out.)

2. "... ce patelinage": the husband's feigned deafness recalls the shepherd's trick on the sharpster Pathelin in the fifteenth-century *Farce de Maistre Pathelin,* a great favorite of R's often used by him and cited in these pages.

3. On checking pregnancy in a widow to determine whether a child is legitimate.

3.35: How Trouillogan, the philosopher, treats the difficulty of marriage.

1. Tobias's dog: although no dog is named in the Book of Tobit (Apocrypha), in 6.1 a dog appears in the text out of nowhere during Tobias's trip with the angel (in the NEB, which there reads: "and the dog came out with him and accompanied them"). Leaving aside questions of authenticity and canonicity of texts, we note that EC traces the dog to *Liber Tobiae* 11.9 in the Vulgate, which gives homey details such as the dog's wagging his tail. Many in R's day were dog lovers, it appears; and even earlier, Filippino Lippi (1460–1515) put what looks to be a small spaniel into his picture of "Tobias and the Angel." Before long others followed suit, and the scene was a popular subject. R's naming this dog (also Gargantua's) Kyne seems a sort of "inside joke." Tobias's dog is given no name in any Biblical text; the Vulgate speaks of him simply by the Latin generic name, *canis* "dog, a dog, the dog." Likewise *Kune* is the generic Greek name for a dog. R's may have been a mild joke like our naming a dog "Dog."

2. " 'Je l'ay,' dist-il, 'amie; mais elle ne me a mie. Je la possède, d'elle ne suis possédé.' "

3. "On luy demanda si jamais elle avoit eu affaire à un homme. Respondit que non jamais, bien que les hommes quelquesfoys avoient eu affaire à elle." Both this and the preceding deft response are related by Plutarch in his *Moralia:* in *Conjugal precepts* and Laconian *Apophthegms* respectively, then quoted and commented on by Erasmus in his *Apophthegms* 2. *Apophtegmata Lacaenarum* 30.

4. Saint Paul (here, The Holy Apostle), 1 Corinthians 7.29. This passage of course figured prominently in Christian discussions of marriage in R's time.

3.36: CONTINUATION OF THE REPLIES OF TROUILLOGAN.

1. Ephectic (from Greek *epecho* "I abstain") is used of a philosopher who, as a true skeptic, withholds judgment or abstains from judging.
2. "Vous dictez d'orgues": roughly, you talk like organ music.
3. Dialectical term: distinctions among things, persons, or times, leaving uncertainty.
4. Or a wife: "Je ne peuz me passer de femme": *femme* has both meanings.
5. "Houstez ces villaines bestes": Trouillogan alludes to the devils Panurge has just sworn by.
6. Dido's lament just before her suicide: *Aeneid* 4.550–551 (*The Aeneid of Virgil* [Berkeley, Los Angeles, London: University of California Press, 1981]).
7. "Pé le quau Dé": this is medieval Poitevin for "Par le corps Dieu!" "By God's body!"
8. Precisely the rule of the Abbey of Thélème (1.57), though phrased here in the plural or more polite singular *vous* form of "Ce que vouldrez" instead of the more familiar *tu* form of "Fay ce que vouldras."
9. "Tarabin tarabas": this may have been originally a magical invocation.
10. "Par le ventre beuf de boys": either *beuf* or *boys* may be a euphemism for *Dieu*.
11. The first chastity belts were made in Bergamo (Lombardy).
12. "C'est bien chien chié chanté pour les discours."
13. These are all regions around the thorax and solar plexus.
14. A coinage of R's, meaning literally "to pass through a narrow passage such as that of a cornet": hence (Cotgrave) "to beat the brains about."
15. "Trut avant!" words normally used by donkey drivers to stir up their donkeys.
16. Meaning of course the flesh, blood, and body of Christ.
17. Followers of Pyrrho of Elis (ca. 360–270 B.C.), fountainhead of systematic skepticism. These are all terms for skeptics, who find knowledge so unlikely for man that wisdom is withholding judgment.
18. " . . . on pourra dorénavant prendre les lions par les jubes, les chevaulx par les crains, les boeufz par les cornes, les bufles par le museau, les loups par la queue, les chèvres par la barbe, les oiseaux par les piedz; mais jà ne seront telz philosophes par leurs parolles pris." His praise of God here is presumably rueful, not enthusiastic; and he leaves as inexplicably and mysteriously as he had come: just for these remarks?
19. In R's time and long after, dining tables, like chairs, might be moved often, indeed sometimes after each use.

3.37: HOW PANTAGRUEL PERSUADES PANURGE TO TAKE COUNSEL OF SOME FOOL.

1. French *fol* (modern *fou*), like English *fool*, may of course also mean "jester"; and Triboulet was the official court jester of Francis I.

2. The simile of the mouse stuck in pitch, getting more stuck the more it struggles, is very old, going back to proverbial Greek *mus en pitte,* but best known in its Latin form *Mus in pice,* in which Erasmus treats it in *Adages* 2.3.68, *Mus picem gustans,* which R surely knew and presumably has in mind here.

3. More precisely, *fatuus,* which meant both "fool" and "diviner" or "prophet."

4. " . . . un mesme généthliaque": thus, some would say, "destined for much the same fate."

5. The *Responsa* or *Consilia* of Giasone de Maino (d. 1519), the noted jurist's masterwork.

6. "Ouy, par le sambreguoy": or "par le sang de l'oye," a euphemism for "par le sang de Dieu" or "By the blood of God" or " 'sblood."

7. An old silver coin, minted at Tours and worth 12 Tournois deniers, bearing the stamped effigy of King Philip V.

8. " . . . martres cingesses": fake, perhaps monkey, marten skins.

9. " . . . que chascun se retire en sa chascunière": a popular expression ever since R, probably his own expression.

3.38: How Triboullet is blazoned by Pantagruel and Panurge.

1. Blasonner "to blazon" is to offer a thorough list of attributes of a person or thing, either in praise or in denigration. Thus it is a device allowing R to give two extremely long lists, in alternation between Pantagruel and Panurge, of things it is possible to say about the famous court fool Triboullet.

2. Arrant fool: "Fol de haulte game."

3. "Fol cotal": phallic (Italian, referring to the phallus).

4. "Fol primipile": standard-bearing (as for a Roman legion).

5. "Fol a latere": from the side or flank or on it; suggests the French *altéré* "thirsty" or "altered," which follows it.

6. "Fol branchier," used of a fledgling bird hopping the branches after its mother.

7. "Fol supercoquelicantieux": cockier than a rooster.

8. From the Latin word for "tenth," a term of the highest praise because of the great reputation of Caesar's tenth legion.

9. Arabic: of amalgam "a mixture of gold and mercury."

10. A Summist is a student or commentator of Aquinas's *Summa.*

11. Interpreting the meaning of a text by its tropes or turns of speech.

12. " . . . epaticque": modern French *hépatique,* hepatic, "pertaining to the liver."

13. Arabic word for a circle of the celestial sphere parallel to the horizon.

14. A sort of damascene, a form of Persian metal-work.

15. I.e., the hearing where his method of decision-making will be judged by his colleagues of the Myrelingues Parlement.

16. Presumably the king and court were then staying at the château de Blois.

3.39: HOW PANTAGRUEL ATTENDS THE TRIAL OF JUDGE BRIDOYE.

1. This makes a highly honorific comparison of these counselors to the senators of ancient Rome, considered to share power and responsibility with the people.

2. A fictive name, in Poitou meaning "Round copse."

3. Composed of a hundred men.

4. The place appointed for the hearing.

5. Judge Bridoye (Bridlegoose) will talk this way in the chapter of his self-defense that here begins, supporting each statement with abbreviations of legal passages that are meant to support his claims. As M. A. Screech has shown, their comedy lies not in what to us is their pedantic erudition (less disconcerting then than now), but in their irrelevance to his points. See TL, notes on chaps. 39–40, and especially M. A. Screech, "The Legal Comedy of Rabelais in the Trial of Bridoye in the *Tiers Livre de Pantagruel*," in *ER* 5 (1964) 175–195. This first such passage means this: "are noted by the Archdeacon in Distinction 86 of the Canon." Except for this initial sample, we have left all the rest of these untranslated in their original Latin as in R's text. For however familiar most of them may have been to most of R's first (French) readers, we think that today they are almost as puzzling and intimidating to the modern Francophone reader as to his modern Anglophone counterpart. We have added our translations only when that seemed worth doing.

6. Genesis 27. Bridoye is of course pleased to cite honorable precedent for his own poor vision.

7. As a sample of Bridoye's lack of pertinence and the resulting comedy, the first law cited here states the right of men with only one testicle to serve in the army.

8. These are the "dice of judgments," i.e., in common legal parlance, the inevitable hazards pertaining to any litigation. Bridoye is unique, however, in taking the term quite literally. All this helps explain his constant refrain: "comme vous autres, Messieurs," which means "like you gentlemen," or "as you gentlemen do" and his sincere conviction that he is at all times following regulations and normal procedures.

9. "And there (on that point), Bartholo." The reference is to Bartolus (1314–1357), widely renowned Italian jurist of the dialectical school, and long the star of the law school of the University of Perugia. His *Commentary* on Justinian's *Code,* cited here, rivaled the *Code* itself in authority.

10. Henri Ferrandat of Nevers, a jurist, commentator of the Decretals.

11. Like most people who claim they will be brief, Bridoye goes on forever.

12. The title, here ironic, is *Moderns love brevity.*

13. *Spec* is Guillaume Durand, expert in canon law, author of *Speculum judiciale* (*Judicial Mirror*), Lyon, 1531. For Bridoye all legal red tape and the law's delays are just that many goodies and spices.

14. "Comme vous aultres, Messieurs": the first of many examples of his pet refrain.

15. "Always in stipulations," abbreviated legal heading for the subject now given in verse.

16. Functioning now as might Roman judges, tribunes, and praetors.

17. The gist of this is roughly "First come best served." Put more legalistically, "Whoever is prior in time is more potent in law."

3.40: HOW BRIDOYE EXPLAINS THE REASONS WHY HE EXAMINED THE LAWSUITS.

1. A saying of Dionysius Cato much quoted in legal circles in R's day.

2. As the text shows, a game in which at some point one player is buffeted by the others.

3. One of a family that goes back to one Honoré Picquet, Régent (a high administrator or moderator) of the Faculty of Medicine of Montpellier in the late fifteenth century.

4. The world of the law courts, which are located in the Palais de Justice.

5. Joannes de Prato, a noted jurist from Prato in Tuscany. Here as often elsewhere, the comedy lies mainly in the pile of irrelevant citations.

6. *Autent.* (Justinian's *Novellae constitutiones*) on restitutions and on a woman who bears a child, and *Speculator* under the heading *Of requests of counsel*.

7. A verse modeled on the one in *Aeneid* 7.53.

3.41: HOW BRIDOYE TELLS THE STORY OF THE SETTLER OF LAWSUITS.

1. The French is *Brocadium juris,* the English *Axioms of the law*. The sense is very different, but the effect comparable: taking a famous basic text for a person.

2. A tiny hamlet near Poitiers in Vienne (Poitou, near Ligugé).

3. Bridoye seems to ignore or not to see the tactless implications of his remark.

4. French *relevailles*. Webster's defines churching as "a ceremony by which, after childbirth, women are received in church with prayers, blessings, and thanksgiving."

5. Diminutive of *Etienne,* thus roughly equivalent to English "Steve." A name with about the force of English Petey Booby. C.f., Molière's Georges Dandin.

6. Found in the legal anthology *Flores legum* and familiar to many laymen as a proverb.

7. For "Qui non laborat non manducet." A parodic deformation of Saint

Paul's often-quoted saying given just after it from 2 Thessalonians 3.10: "He who will not work, let him not eat." Bridoye is probably led astray by French *manger* "to eat," which suggests the *manige*.

8. A breaking up of the common saying: "Deficiente pecunia, deficit omne," which translates "If money is lacking, all is lacking."

9. Ovid *Amores* 3.11.35.

3.42: How lawsuits are born.

1. Here Bridoye takes Arg. (Argument, subject) for a commentator, then as usual piles one irrelevant authority on another, ending with a chapter title and gloss on solemn occasions.

2. This theory that a bear had to be licked into shape was prevalent in R's time.

3. Acts 20.35 NEB: "Happiness lies more in giving than in receiving."

4. A distich of Cato's, quoted by P. Bellon in his *Communes juris sententiae,* Lyon, 1559.

5. Ovid *Remedia amoris* (*Remedies for love*), a long elegiac poem, v. 426.

6. Horace *Ars poetica* 359.

7. When the Danes besieged it in 1518; this anecdote is inspired by one in Aretino's *Dialogo del Giuoco* (1545), perhaps also by Horace's *Luculli miles, Epistles* 2.2.26 ff.

8. Antonio da Budrio of Bologna, a fifteenth-century jurist.

9. " . . . les mies bingt et quouatte baguettes." To the French ear at least, the Gascons confused their Bs and Vs. Among many meanings of *baguette,* Cotgrave lists this: a small brass Gascon coin. EC translates it (into modern French) as *vachette;* but neither Cotgrave nor any good modern French dictionary I know of offers any appropriate sense for that word.

10. " . . . qui boille (for *veuille*) truquar ambe iou à belz embiz?"

11. "Hundred-pounders." Curiously, these "English" speak nothing but bad German.

12. Of a family from Anjou related to the Du Bellays.

13. "Cap de Sainct Arnault . . . " Perhaps Arnault of Bresica, a disciple of Abelard, delivered to his enemies by Frederick Barbarossa (q.v.), martyred by them in 1155.

14. Giovanni Andrea, a fifteenth-century Italian humanist jurist, who relates this anecdote.

3.43: How Pantagruel excuses Bridoye about the verdicts rendered by the chance of dice.

1. Antoine Ardillon of Poitiers, a friend of R's from his years at Fontenay-le-Comte.

2. A small town in Essonne, in the environs of Paris. Nothing is known of this provost.

3.44: How Epistémon tells a strange story.

1. Here we leave our usual guides for the French text (Pl, G, and mainly LI, also TL and EC), because they follow a text that I (DMF, the translator) consider clearly defective in not making good sense, that of the 1552 edition of Book 3 rather than the 1546 text, which makes good sense. Walter Kaiser pointed this out already in 1963 in his fine book *Praisers of Folly* (Harvard University Press) and made the case thoroughly (p. 170 note). Briefly, it is this.

The two chapters (43–44) of the 1552 ed. and since were originally one (41) bearing the title "How Pantagruel excuses Bridoye about the judgments rendered by the chance of dice." Both versions of the story begin as Pantagruel comes before the Parlement of Myrelingues hoping to help his old friend Bridoye, summoned there to explain one verdict of his found not equitable by the Court (1552 chaps. 38–39), the summons that had kept Bridoye from joining Pantagruel's panel of experts convoked to help and advise Panurge. Pantagruel then listens with the others as Bridoye confesses to failing eyesight (which may have made him misread the dice) and then in his main defense tries to prove, by numberless legal references (mostly misinterpreted or misapplied) that his methods are just like everyone else's, including of course those of his listeners ("comme vous aultres, Messieurs"), as he chimes in interminably at every opportunity.

He is then questioned by the presiding judge in detail about his method (why then did he examine his case at all? Since he did so, why not right away or very soon? Why all the delay?). On these matters, too, he is ready with answers that to him at least are plausible. With Bridoye's defense over, the 1552 chapter 43 tells that he is sent from the courtroom while the court discusses his case. Pantagruel is asked, as prince but also and mainly as wise arbiter, to settle it himself; but he rightly declines and elects the role of suppliant, pleading strongly for Bridoye's pardon on a few reasonable conditions (urging on his behalf his age and weakened sight, and most of all his almost flawless record of over forty-odd years, in which he finds a touch of God's hand; and asking further that if they find they must depose Bridoye as judge, they bestow him on him, Pantagruel, who will gladly place him suitably and well in his own kingdom, and who will meanwhile pray to God for this boon to keep them in His grace. With this he takes his leave, joins his friends, and together they leave on their return journey to Gargantua's palace, presumably located in the Loire valley near or at Thélème. On the way Pantagruel relates in detail the story of Bridoye and his judgment; others comment. Panurge finds such continuous successes hard to believe, then Epistémon mentions the parallel story of a provost of Montlhéry, and adds that a few such happy coincidences, especially in matters complex, ambiguous, and obscure, would not surprise him.

Here R, in his 1552 edition, breaks this long chapter in two (43–44), ending 43 and starting a new one (44) on the perplexities of human judgment. Since this does no harm to the sense or anything, we follow in this; but not in the detail of it, for this reason. In the 1546 edition he had had

Epistémon (still in the then chap. 41) go on directly with the story of Dolabella and the woman of Smyrna, introducing it simply with the words: "As was the controversy argued before Cneius Dolabella," telling it succinctly in less than two pages, and ending with the confession: "But in Bridoye, the continuation over so many years astonishes me."

Thereupon Pantagruel (still in the 1546 text), "conjecturally (he says)," as befits such matters, but with some apparent confidence, fills most of the rest of the chapter with the richer explanation and apparent solution to the problem, that Bridoye's simple trust in God, by itself, led God to intervene to help him, having the Moving Intelligences cause the dice to fall so as to lead Bridoye to a just decision, since chance in itself is not evil, and when man is perplexed the divine will often uses it to manifest itself.

Thus R fills out another triad (besides the three expert consultants—theologian, doctor, jurist) by adding, to his professional fool Triboullet and his human fool Panurge, the Christian fool Bridoye, whose folly in the eyes of man may be wisdom in the eyes of God.

Once Bridoye has been heard, Pantagruel offers a tentative and still vague, but wholly sound explanation of the near-miracle, which at least provisionally satisfied all; and for about two pages, or one chapter, there follow relevant comments and stories by the friends, ending as Epistémon confesses his puzzlement, thus prompting Pantagruel to his fuller, final explanation.

In the 1552 edition, however, Pantagruel once again, at about the midpoint of the two-page chapter 43, offers the tentative explanation that he senses the hand of God in this mystery which had left Epistémon and the others wholly baffled; then two pages later, halfway through chapter 44, he confesses his puzzlement and must have Epistémon explain the mystery. Not only is this internally inconsistent—ludicrously so—but it clashes with R's entire tale by taking away Pantagruel's wisdom and bestowing it on Epistémon.

In short, it appears that at some time between 1546 and 1552, R (or a printer or editor acting for him) made two important changes, one harmless, one disastrous. He did no harm by his long chapter 41 (now as 43-44); but he also broke up Epistémon's long speech after the shorter first part to give Pantagruel the longer second part, the story of Dolabella and the woman of Smyrna. But this change, by the logic of dialogue, leaves it to Pantagruel on ending that story to confess his puzzlement and thus allows Epistémon to give the fuller explanation that will be the last word on the subject, a change that here and in the whole work defies consistency and sense, indeed stands them on their head.

Lacking any evidence how and why R came to make this change (which so clearly seems a blunder), we can only conjecture. He does nod at times, we know: having Pantagruel give Salmagundi to Alcofribas in 2.32, then without explanation give it to Panurge in 3.2; abruptly bringing back into the group and the story Frère Jean in 3.13 (last previously seen in 1.58) and the next moment, in 3.14, with the other companions; and then having Frère

Jean (one of the older generation, that of Gargantua) twit Panurge (3.28 and passim) about his graying hair and advancing years; later starting Book 4 with Alcofribas seemingly not among the travelers (4.1–4), then from 4.5 on, among them; and then leaving out the name Alcofribas anywhere in Book 4, whereas Panurge twice clearly addresses him by a title of sorts, once as Master Stargazer (4.18), once (4.20) as "Sir Abstractor."

There was much to distract him from his story between 1546 and 1552: the burning at the stake in 1546 (August 3, 1546); much work of the Council of Trent (in R's eyes, the Council of Chesil: Fools); the long stay in Rome attending Cardinal Jean du Bellay and writing up the *Shadow Battle* (*La Sciomachie,* our item 6.22); the fierce attacks of Dupuyherbault and Calvin, as well as the addlepated Jean Postel (1549–1550); the precarious living he had in Metz, which forced him to send a piteous appeal for help to Du Bellay; and the soliciting that his generous Royal Privilege of 1550 must have required. Like most of his years, these were hardly idle or peaceful; and they held distractions enough to explain a lapse in memory such as we find in 3.43–44.

2. The French text reads "Comme feut, dist Pantagruel." In English "As was, said Pantagruel."

3. Here the speech that follows was attributed to Epistémon, not to Pantagruel, with the words: "respondit Epistémon . . . "

4. The two main texts on which Roman law was based.

5. Strong spikes so firmly set in the ground as to threaten attacking vehicles or men.

3.45: How Panurge takes counsel of Triboullet.

1. A cultivated apple that many enjoyed.

2. " . . . est-il fol comme un chou à pommes": perhaps suggested by a proverbial popular couplet:

> Grosse teste et petit cou
> C'est le commencement d'un fou.
>
> [Little neck, big head, they say:
> One more fool is on the way.]

3. "Par Dieu, Dieu, fol enraigé, guare moine! cornemuse de Buzançay!" The French word for bagpipe, *cornemuse,* explains the puns on *cornes* "horns."

4. Cybele, a potent Asiatic goddess of Phrygian origin, represented all the powers of nature. Her cult, in some ways like the Bacchic, took hold in fifth-century B.C. Athens, then much later flourished in Rome in early third century (A.D.) under Heliogabalus, a former priest of Cybele.

5. *Asinaria* 2.3.405. A farcical comedy derived from a Greek model, the *Onagos* of Demophilus.

3.46: HOW PANTAGRUEL AND PANURGE DIVERSELY INTERPRET THE WORDS OF TRIBOULLET.

1. See note 1 for 3.37.
2. From the Greek, meaning "fool-wise": compare the English converse, *sophomore*.
3. "Dict oultre que serez la cornemuse de Buzançay." See above, chapter 45, note 3.
4. The presumably joking charge is that Panurge robbed little children of their pig's bladders (used as balls?) to make the bagpipe that he is.
5. Ecclesiastes 1.15: repeated in Erasmus *Adages* and *Praise of Folly*.
6. See Erasmus *Adages* 4.7.4: "Nihil potest nec addi nec adimi." For all this part on the ubiquity of folly, compare of course Erasmus's *Praise of Folly*.
7. The French for monk, *moine,* suggests *moineau* "sparrow," and this in turn the beloved (and hated) Lesbia of Catullus (ca. 84–ca. 54 B.C.), the elegiac poet of love and passion, and her cherished sparrow, who inspired a few of the poet's tenderly playful lines.
8. *Maujoint* is a term for vagina. R and others like to play with its obvious contrast with *benjoin,* "benzoin," a hard aromatic resin used in perfumes.

3.47: HOW PANTAGRUEL AND PANURGE DECIDE TO VISIT THE ORACLE OF THE DIVINE BOTTLE.

1. R's first mention of the Divine Bottle as what it will now become, the goal of the questing voyage that will be the theme of all Book 4 and also of the dubious (probably inauthentic) Book 5.
2. "... advenent le prince, cesse le magistrat": an old saying in law that the magistrate's powers and functions cease in the presence of the king, to whom they then revert.
3. The *pays de Lanternoys*, which means "the land of crazy ideas," is found first in R's source for it, the anonymous, derivative *Disciple de Pantagruel* or *Navigation du compagnon à la Bouteille* (1537), which was often printed with R's own stories. This meaning is related to the phrase for the ultimate in gullibility, "prendre des vessies pour des lanternes" which means "to take bladders for lanterns." *Lanterne* is also used to mean the male genitals; cf., Cotgrave on *lanterner:* "to buggar or be buggared"; and of course R does not forget that sense. Book 5.33 will bring the travelers to Lanternois, and in it, later and at last, to their goal, the long-sought oracle of the Divine Bottle.
4. "Millort Debitis": Latin for "debts," a near-homophone of *Deputy*.
5. The French *fallot* means "cresset light," but *goud fallot* sounds like "good fellow."
6. The Latin *debitoribus* (dative plural after *dimittimus*) from the Paternoster.
7. By speaking thus as though French were a second language to him, Panurge

is presumably pretending that his wide learning makes Latin more natural for him.

8. Pieces of similar gibberish appear in several mystery plays, which may have given R the idea; but he had used "Lanternese" before; see 2.9.

9. Gascon pronunciation of very.

3.48: HOW GARGANTUA POINTS OUT THAT IT IS NOT LAWFUL FOR CHILDREN TO MARRY.

1. This entire chapter, centered on Gargantua's indignant diatribe against clandestine marriages (those authorized by a priest but not by the parents of one of the new couple), is a very bold attack by R (bolder than those of either Erasmus or Vives) on a practice authorized by the Roman Catholic Church but regarded by many Reformists (Protestant or Evangelical) as viciously subversive of family and social values; and in this his position is close to Luther's and places Imperial law above canon law.

2. We noted earlier the unfortunate aroma of smug sanctimonious piety that mars our English "the good Pantagruel" as it does not mar its French equivalent; and we offer instead, though it may be too familiar and even slipshod, "good old Pantagruel." But whereas Pantagruel in this book (3) allows a good deal of familiarity, and (to Panurge at least) occasional impudence (as on 3.18), in this book the born-again Gargantua is so fierce as not to permit any such liberty; so we leave this bit as "the good Gargantua."

3. The French is this: "Plustost prie Dieu estre à vos piedz veu roydde mort en vostre desplaisir que, sans vostre plaisir, estre veu vif marié," which seems to come down to this: "If I had displeased you, I'd rather be dead than alive and married." I have rendered it rather freely in this sense.

4. In spite of this statement, control over marriage was a bone of fierce contention in these years. The old way, handed down from ancient Greece and Rome, had left this control entirely in the hands of the parents; and to this extent and in this sense Pantagruel's claim here is justified. But the Roman Catholic Church, to control this critical act that it considers a sacrament, had granted this power to priests to permit and perform marriages between consenting parties even without parental consent. Most Frenchmen, notably the Gallican clergy, saw this move, understandably, as a basically Italian and clerical power grab. King Francis sent the cardinal of Lorraine to the recently opened Council of Trent to protest and urge repudiation of these "clandestine" marriages (as they were called, often rightly); but the appeal was rejected by the rigidly pro-papal, pro-Italian Council. These facts help explain Gargantua's fierceness and the length and fervor of this unique chapter.

5. This hapless country seems to be France, but Italy need not be ruled out.

6. " . . . ne sçay quelz pastophores taulpetiers." Voltaire will borrow *pastophores*, also his *apedeftes* (for which see 5.16), in chapter 11 of his fiercely anticlerical tale *L'Ingénu,* published in the same year (1767) in

which he first recognized in writing that R was not just a foul-mouthed drunken monk but a valuable ally in his struggle against *l'infame*.

7. This vengeful ferocity, unmatched anywhere else in R, springs from the conviction that by overriding the need for parental consent for marriage the Church is threatening the corruption and dissolution of the family and thus of all society.

8. The word *équippage* "equipment," now "crew," seems here to mean both the ships and the furnishings needed, but not the crew, listed separately.

3.49: How Pantagruel made his preparations to put out to sea.

1. "... grand voyagier et traverseur des voyes périlleuses": see 6.3, text and note. This was the chosen sobriquet of R's poet, friend, Jean Bouchet.

2. Intervening: used of a lord holding land as a tenant for a king or prince but having a tenant or tenants of his own on that land. French: "arrière-fief."

3. R devotes the last four chapters of this book (49–52) to the properties of his wondrous herb, which partake of those of hemp, flax, and asbestos. Although Screech dismisses it as simply a learned joke based upon Pliny's *Natural History*, other good readers have sensed a serious meaning in it. In the best such interpretation we have, Thomas Greene simply equates it with Pantagruelism (*Rabelais*, pp. 78–80). For other views see my *François Rabelais: A Study*, pp. 61–62.

4. Of course a variable measure, usually about 10–12 feet.

5. In ancient times the fishermen's festivals on the Tiber were held on or about June 7.

3.50: How the famous Pantagruelion is to be prepared and put to use.

1. About September 23, when the sun crosses the equator, and day and night are of equal length all over the world.

2. Like rope-makers who move backward as they complete more and more rope.

3. As related by Ovid *Metamorphoses* 5.642–661.

4. The approximate sense of the term in Greek.

5. Rha is the modern Volga.

6. Wormseed (in Latin: in or from Saintonge).

7. *Fenugreek* means "Greek hay." *Castanes* comes from Latin *castaniae*, "chestnuts."

8. Juniper was said to be of Sabine origin.

9. *Stoechas* is the old name for lavender.

10. Or *pinte* "pint," the familiar half-quart liquid measure.

11. *Aristolochia* (from Greek), a plant promoting childbirth.

12. From Latin *malva*.
13. Greek *callithricum* "having beautiful hair."
14. Greek *bechion*, Latin *bechium*, a plant considered good for a cough.
15. Or *Jusquiame*, hogsbane, a form of henbane.
16. Heliotrope: from Greek *helios*, "sun" + *tropeim* "to turn," hence turning toward the sun.
17. *Adiantum*: Greek for waterproof or non-absorbent.
18. Hawkweed: from Greek *hierax* "sparrowhawk," a plant thought good for vision.
19. Myrtle from Greek *myrtine* or *myrsine*, named for an Athenian girl, Myrtine or Myrsine, famed both for her beauty and her strength.

3.51: WHY IT IS CALLED PANTAGRUELION.

1. Because it tends to dull their blade.
2. At the noted Paris Collège de Navarre, whips and canes were still highly rated incentives to learning.
3. The constellation Icarius Canis or Canis Major.
4. According to Jotham in Judges 9.8.
5. In his *Natural History* 6.20, Pliny tells of the Seres, who live in Serica, a land north of India that he says has trees that bear wool.
6. Manes are the souls of the good dead; Lemurs souls of the evil dead.
7. The first of five fictive taverns on Olympus whose names recall those of French and English hostels of the time and may defy chronology by being borrowed from them.

3.52: HOW A CERTAIN KIND OF PANTAGRUELION CANNOT BE CONSUMED BY FIRE.

1. " . . . deux cotyles": Cotgrave defines *cotyle* as an ancient measure containing about 24 spoonfuls.
2. The French *asbeston* is from Greek *asbestos*, which means both "inextinguishable" and, like our English, "a material to make fabric fireproof."
3. A mythical animal immune to fire. R calls it a hoax from his sense of betrayal that King Francis (whose emblem was the salamander), after long defending peaceful Reformists in 1534–1535 turned against them and led their persecution.
4. Galen *De temperamentis* 3.4; Dioscorides *Materia medica* 2.54; Pliny *Natural History* 10.86.
5. French *alum de plume* (natural aluminum sulfate) in filaments is gathered into bundles.
6. According to Coelius Rhodiginus *Antiquae lectines* who here is following Plutarch *Life of Caesar* and Vitruvius.
7. Here is the original French verse:

Indes, cessez, Arabes, Sabiens,
Tant collauder vos myrrhe, encent, ébène.
Venez icy recongnoistre nos biens,
Et emportez de nostre herbe la grène;
Puys, si chez vous peut croistre en bonne estrène,
Grâces rendez ès cieulx un million,
Et affermez de France heureux le règne
Onquel provient Pantagruelion.

BOOK 4

Book 4 is unique in the baggage it adds to the definitive 1552 text: two texts in all, each with prologue, a dedicatory epistle to the final text, and a curious, dubious piece claiming to explain some obscure locutions, known as the Brief Declaration (BD). Briefly, what happened was this: R, after a long delay since Books 1 and 2, brought out Book 3 in 1546; then he promptly started to tell the story of the voyage to which he had just committed Pantagruel and his company of domestic friends: to help Panurge decide about marriage by getting the word of the Divine Bottle from its priestess Bacbuc.

R worked in haste to get something ready to give a printer before leaving for Rome, perhaps for years, a physician to Cardinal Jean du Bellay (q.v.). When he set out from France in summer 1547, he left a Lyon printer the MS of a sketchy version of about one-third of the final completed book. Published in 1548, known now as the Partial Edition, it has ten complete chapters (and ends in midchapter, almost midsentence, in chapter 11); but that chapter 11 corresponds to the 1552 chapter 25, and brings the travelers, after the terrible tempest, safe into haven amid the venerable Macraeons (4.25). Between 1548 and 1552 R had split many chapters into multiple shorter ones, and inserted several others, besides making notable additions in many places. But despite differences, the parts common to both versions are much alike, enough so to justify omitting the 1548 text from modern scholarly readers' editions: EC. PL, G, LI, even QL; the 1548 edition is available only in Marichal's facsimile edition: *ER* 9 (1971) 151–174; and we follow their sound example.

No English translation available includes any of all this but the 1552 text and prologue. Inclusion of the BD invites criticism for its doubtful authenticity; but we think its brevity, interest, and relevance, and possible genuineness, earn it its place. While following our French guides in choices for inclusion, we prefer our own order: (1) Old Prologue (OP) to the partial, 1548 edition; (2) Dedicatory Epistle to Odet, Cardinal de Chastillon (OC); (3) definitive (1552) Prologue (P); (4) the definitive completed text of 1552, marked by its chapter numbers; (5 and last), the Brief Declaration (BD).

4. OLD PROLOGUE

1. So titled here for the obvious reason. The title was "Prologue."
2. Latin terms, as the text explains, for routing cases.

3. Implying "Perhaps you are not there"; i.e., perhaps I have no readers.

4. Two points: flasks were sometimes made in R's day to look like breviaries. More to the point, however (as Demerson notes in LI) is R's equation of their effect with the casting [la cure] given a falcon, an emetic to empty his belly and prepare him to hunt again. Frère Jean of course just wants to be ready to drink again. This also explains why he calls it his *tiroir* "drawer," since it draws food up out of his belly.

5. The ribbons marking the pages.

6. This occurs before France annexed Brittany.

7. I.e., nobles. Most Frenchmen regarded Bretons as rather dull folk with nobiliary pretentions.

8. The fleurs-de-lis.

9. Proverbial praise: "Vous ne fustes oncques de mauvaise pie couvez."

10. Here is the French:

> "Ce n'est," dict-il, "louange populaire,
> Aux princes avoir peu complaire."

11. Either fictive or possibly a leader of a gipsy band or troupe.

12. The French *cauquemarre,* modern *cauchemar,* but here suggesting a monster.

13. Here not pedophiles but fantastic monsters.

14. Even as *diabolos* means "slanderer."

15. Presumably not ready to sail the rough seas of medicine.

16. Implying rententiousness and greed.

17. A common gag, dear to R, mixing a time with a place.

18. She had written against him but repented of it and sought a tree.

4: LUMINARY EPISTLE TO CARDINAL ODET DE CHASTILLON

1. Odet de Coligny, Cardinal de Chastillon (1517–1571), older brother of the famous Admiral Gaspard, chief target and victim of the Massacre of Saint Bartholomew's Day (1519–1572), was Cardinal from 1533 at age sixteen, a humanist and sympathizer with religious Reform who late in R's life became his principal supporter and protector, meeting at least three times with him, and by R's account persuading him to resume writing his tale at a point when R, weary of the constant attacks of his enemies, was ready to give it up as a game not worth the candle. Late in life Chastillon followed his brother's example in being converted to Protestantism and emigrated to England for his last years.

2. These are, of course, the books of R's tale *Gargantua and Pantagruel.*

3. This is not a comparison made by Hippocrates but made by R on the basis of Galen's commentary on him, specifically on his *Epidemics.*

4. The flowing sleeves of the formal doctor's gown looked to be double; each one looked like two, so that two made four.

5. From the *Iliad* 21.107, adapted into a French couplet.

6. *Farce de Maistre Pathelin* 656–657.
7. A common charge from extremists of both sides, Sorbonists and Calvinists.
8. A probable reminiscence of Luke 11.11.
9. A frequent complaint of R's, sometimes justified.
10. Protector against evil. The only other man of and to whom R uses this praise is Erasmus; see below.

4: PROLOGUE OF THE AUTHOR

1. "Attendez que je chausse mes lunettes." This French, less cumbrous than the English, is also less forced; for *chausser* may at times be used other than of footwear.
2. "Bien et beau s'en va Quaresme!": a mainly Lenten salutation.
3. Or, altérations: "contre toutes altérations."
4. " . . . et me recommande": usually said by someone leaving a conversation.
5. An inexact quotation from Galen *De sanitate tuenda,* 5.1, who himself quotes it approximately from Euripides, frag. 171. Both Erasmus (*Adages*) and Tiraqueau (*De nobilitate*) compare it with the proverb that Luke (4.23) reports Jesus as quoting, the famous "Physician, heal thyself."
6. "Ly bon Dieu et ly bons homs!": one of R's deliberate archaisms.
7. " . . . le mort saisit le vif": epitomizing that inheriting is instantaneous; the *saisit* in this sense means "gives possession of," not "takes possession of."
8. This legend of Trojan descent convinced many French in R's century, including belletrist Jean Lemaire de Belges and the poet Pierre de Ronsard.
9. An obvious derivative of *couille, couillon,* the male testicle, ball, or ballock. Urquhart translates the name as "Tom Wellhung"; Putnam, as "Ballocks"; Leclercq, as "Puddingballocks"; Cohen, as "Ballocker." This is one of the many of R's proper names that we have preferred to annotate but then to leave in R's original French.
10. Between Henry II of France and Emperor Charles V, R speaks of a settlement a bit early, but it came soon after this appeared.
11. Modern El Mehedia or El Mahedia, Tunisia.
12. R blames destiny for this; some blamed Henry II for lack of help. Tripoli's resistance (by the Knights of Malta) was weak.
13. A revolt by Bordeaux citizens against the salt tax (1548) was crushed and harshly punished by Montmorency, and the city's warning bells confiscated.
14. Emperor Charles, lamed by gout and ailing in other serious ways.
15. *Mentula* "penis" is also a diminutive of *mens* "mind."
16. A phrase used earlier by Picrochole (1.32) to belittle Grandgousier (that nonmacho appeaser) as being short of virility. It also puns on *coues moles* "mortar mills," which could also be written, like this phrase, "couilles molles."
17. Latin Petra or French Pierre, both of which mean "rock" or "stone."

18. " . . . à faire la gueule d'un four sont trois pierres nécessaires."
19. Pierre de Cognières, king's advocate-general to Philip VI (1293–1350), who successfully defended the royal authority against Decretalist canonists. In reprisal his name was given to a stone marmoset in Notre-Dame de Paris used to snuff out candles, tapers, etc., and called Pierre du Coignet, meaning "petit coin, toilet."
20. Literally squirrel; here a game in which players tried to blow out a candle by puffing only through the nose.
21. Perhaps an old "new" one in Asia Minor, more probably a new settlement in South America at or near Antiochia.
22. Normally sparrows, but also meaning sentry boxes; here probably the latter.
23. Here is the French original of this doleful dizain:

> Grand Tibault, se voulent coucher
> Avecques sa femme nouvelle,
> S'en vint tout bellement cacher
> Un gros maillet en la ruelle.
> "O! Mon doux amy," ce dict-elle,
> "Quel maillet vous voy-je empoingner?"
> "C'est," dist-il, "pour mieux vous coingner."
> "Maillet?" dist-elle, "il n'y fault nul:
> Quand gros Jan me vient besoingner,
> Il ne me coingne que du cul."

24. The French original quatrain is this:

> S'il est ainsi que coingnée sans manche
> Ne sert de rien, ne houstil sans poingnée,
> Affin que l'un dedans l'aultre s'emmanche,
> Prends que soys manche, et tu seras coingnée.

25. " . . . comme un microcosme de mouches": the sense of this simile escapes me.
26. Probably a small gymnastic stunt, just what kind, we do not know.
27. Mercury's standard equipment is given in Virgil *Aeneid* 4.238–258; others, like R, since that time have followed it as the locus classicus.
28. A rustic colloquialism for "I swear."
29. "Merdigues," euphemism for "Mère de Dieu," but with the sound that we show in our translation.
30. We take this to mean, as Carroll once said, a triumphant gallop.
31. "En ay-je?" From *La Farce de Maistre Pathelin* 352, 356.
32. "Avoit-il les dens esguassées?" Possible reminiscence of Jeremiah 31.29: "The fathers have eaten sour grapes, and the children's teeth are set on edge."
33. The French for this jolly quatrain (monorhyme) is this:

> Le petit cancre au menton,
> La male toux au poulmon,
> Le catarrhe au gavion,

Le gros froncle au cropion,
Et au diable le gros boussin de pain pour s'escurer les dens.

34. " . . . et encores mieulx deuement, ce pendent labourans et travaillans."
35. "Health and profit (gain) to you, Sir."
36. Thoma Guadagni, a very rich Italian banker established in Lyon.

4.1: How Pantagruel put out to sea.

1. Psalm 114 (first verse), adopted by all Reformists as symbolic of their subjection to, and persecution by, conservatives. Also, R quotes the words in French, not Latin, i.e., in a way favored by Reformists.

4.2: How on the island of Medamothi Pantagruel bought several beautiful things.

1. This unobtrusive *them* [leur] alerts us to the apparent absence of the narrator from the traveling company at this point, and the concomitant question: Who is the presumed narrator here? It was apparently Alcofribas Nasier (as the titles announced) in Books 1–2, but clearly R in Book 3, where there is no mention or appearance of AN. Here in Book 4 his name is never spoken and is listed as author on the title page; but AN is twice addressed by Panurge (using his title or function) in the tempest (below 4.18 as "Maistre Astrophile": Master Stargazer) and again on 4.20 as "monsieur l'abstracteur" (Sir Abstractor). To complicate matters further, the narrator (whoever he is) seems not to be on the voyage in the first few chapters (1–4) but on it from chap. 5 on in the 1548 edition, from early in chap. 2, where he refers to the party as a whole as they or them, but on it from then on (for more on this see my "Notes on R by a Recent Translator," *ER* 22 (1989).

4.3: How Pantagruel received a letter from his father Gargantua.

1. Malicorne: it is not clear how this fictive Malicorne is related to two real-life Malicornes we know of. The first is mentioned by R in his *Shadow Battle* (*Sciomachie*) as "Malicorne the Younger" (le Jeune), a participant in the pageant (6.21). Another Malicorne figures in Montaigne's life: Jean de Chourses, governor of Poitou. Early in 1587, Catherine de'Medici writes to her son Henry III, telling him that she has commanded Malicorne to look after Montaigne as the king had wanted, presumably having him escorted home from the Colloquies of Saint-Brice with Henry of Navarre, to which she had summoned him. See my *Montaigne: A Biography* (1965; rpt. New York: Harcourt, Brace & World, 1984), p. 267.
2. Perhaps because of a similar statement (*Works and Days* 40), Erasmus mistakenly attributes this to Hesiod (*Adages* 1.2.39) and R follows him.
3. A Greek maxim said: The beginning is half the whole (Our "Well begun is

half done"). The French is: "à l'enfourner on faict les pains cornuz," a proverb of the thirteenth century or earlier.

4. This date, taken with data in chaps. 1–2, yields a strange chronology. The party sailed June 9; reached Medamothi "on the fourth day," i.e., June 12. Malicorne arrives that day (apparently) after a 3–4 day trip, bearing a letter dated the next day, June 13. Is this "Back to the Future," or simply, in Alice's words (*Wonderland,* chap. 2) "curiouser and curiouser?"

4.4: How Pantagruel writes to his father Gargantua.

1. Reputedly the seat of memory.
2. From Seneca *De beneficiis* 2.25, via Erasmus *Apophthegms* 8.42.
3. Presumably the weight of gold in that many gold crown pieces.

4.5: How Pantagruel encountered a ship.

1. Here for the first time the narrator's use of the pronoun *we* shows that now at last (cf., note 4.2 above) the narrator is a member of the party, as on the same evidence he will be from now on until the title of 5.47.
2. In the Middle Ages, *lanterne* could mean a woman's genitals. For R's day Cotgrave lists many senses for *lanterner:* "To cog, foist, fib; dally, or play the foole with; also, to trouble, or be tedious unto; also, to loiter; also, to buggar, or be buggared; also, to quaffe, revel, feast all night long, or many nights together."
3. An obvious boast about the size and readiness of his member after months of forced inactivity at sea.
4. The Antichrist was expected by many to bring evil before Christ's Second Coming; and these could come almost any time.
5. The "both" is not in R but seems in the spirit of the chat.
6. The nitrous element was thought to foster rusting.

4.6: How, with the dispute pacified, Panurge bargains.

1. "Il y aura bien beau jeu, si la chorde ne rompt": a metaphor presumably from fishing, since Panurge is planning to play Dindenault as a fisherman plays a hooked fish.
2. Presumably because at that time the tripe shops were packed with bargain-hunters, hence a happy hunting ground for pickpockets.
3. ". . . comment il taille de l'historiographe!" These positions were coveted and well rewarded (like a PR man's today) for their power over the place the patron might find in history.
4. ". . . moutons à la grande laine": meaning gold pieces bearing the Agnus Dei stamp.
5. Robin Mouton, one of the commonest names for a sheep.
6. The oysters of Tête-de-Buch in the Arcachon basin (Gironde) were justly renowned.

7. True Moroccos are made of goatskins not sheepskins: one of many proofs that Dindenault is a fraud.

8. The two favorite sources of strings for violins and such stringed instruments.

9. A feudal sign of homage: "j'en seray fort bien tenu au courrail de vostre huys."

10. Brand new gold coins struck, by an ordinance of 1549, for the accession of King Henry II.

4.7: CONTINUATION OF THE BARGAINING BETWEEN PANURGE AND DINDENAULT.

1. A prudishness or decorum surprising in R; hogs must be edible but unmentionable.

2. "... foy de piéton": a parody of Francis I's favorite oath, "Foy de gentilhomme!"

3. "... comme si Dieu y eust pissé": see below, 4.BD chap. 7 for note and comment.

4. Seemingly a popular gag then like our "left-handed monkeywrench."

5. "Dieu sçait comment il s'en escrime!"

4.8: HOW PANURGE HAD THE MERCHANT AND THE SHEEP DROWNED AT SEA.

1. Two popular fifteenth-century preachers, one a Minor, the other a Franciscan.

2. The Duc d'Enghien needed a similar ruse to win at Ceresole (April 1544), where he needed loot to pay his troops; the enemy Swiss ran away and were not paid.

3. Deuteronomy 32.34–35; sharpened as quoted by Saint Paul in Romans 12.19. NEB: "Justice is mine," says the Lord, "I will repay."

4.9: HOW PANTAGRUEL REACHED THE ISLAND OF ENNASIN.

1. Suggestive of *Enasé* "noseless, denosed," which was a special brand of infamy inflicted on certain criminals. The *-in* ending resembles the Hebrew plural form in *-im* found further in this book in such ugly terms for ugly types as *gebarim, ganabin,* etc.

2. "... aube des mousches": when flies, wide awake, get really busy.

3. "Le Potestat," modeled on Italian *potesta* and southern French *poestat* "chief magistrate."

4. This story is told by both Livy (*History* 2.49–50) and Ovid (*Fasti* 2.195–342), then again by Aulus Gellius (*Attic Nights* 17.21).

5. "Ce fauveau à la raye noire doibt bien souvent estre estrillé." Here are the elements in this chain of gags: *estrille . . . fauveau* "treat a horse kindly,"

fauveau "dun horse," then *fau* "beech tree" and *veau* "calf." The climax is Panurge's triumphant cry: "Venez veoir une estrille, une fau et un veau. N'est-ce Estrille fauveau?" Then yet another pun that would require tedious explanation. Since these abound in this chapter that we do not consider one of R's best, from here on in we have tried to explain them briefly or else not at all.

6. "Ma mie": evident play on "m'amie" (modern *amie* "my dear").
7. "Sang sainct Gris!": perhaps a euphemism for "Blood of Christ."
8. ". . . est-il fouet compétent pour mener ceste touppie?"
9. "De bonne mine," dist Pantagruel, "à mauvais jeu n'est alliance impertinente."
10. "Accouplez-les," dist Panurge, "et leur soufflez au cul: ce sera une cornemuse."
11. ". . . si ce trou par ceste cheville peult entièrement estre estouppé."
12. ". . . que cestuy oizon est souvent en mue."
13. "C'est à faire à gens de delà l'eau, à gens bottez de foin."
14. ". . . à ces propous, il cuyda perdre contenence."
15. ". . . elle estoit bonne robbe, en bon poinct et grasse à profict de mesnaige, voyre feust-ce pour un pescheur." This because a fisherman needs good boots.
16. ". . . un jeune escafignon espouser une vieille pantophle."

4.10: HOW PANTAGRUEL WENT ASHORE ON THE ISLAND OF CHELI.

1. From Hebrew *scheli* "peace."
2. Literally "little bread," in the south of France an old term for an easy going "nice guy."
3. ". . . l'entrée du dongeon": the gate beneath the main tower of a castle, usually its main gate above the dungeon.
4. "Par la mort beuf de boys": one of R's euphemisms for oaths.
5. "Corpe de galline": another similar euphemism.
6. ". . . me fasche plus qu'un jeune diable; je voulois dire un jeusne double."
7. Lord of La Guerche, whose château still stands, about thirty miles south of Tours.
8. Psalms 119.1 NEB: "Happy are they whose life is blameless."

4.11: WHY MONKS LIKE TO BE IN THE KITCHEN.

1. "Je diz moine moinant, je ne diz pas moine moiné."
2. R regularly uses the term for both churches and temples.
3. The name means roughly Bernard Baconslice, and thus suggests a monk who likes his food and drink.
4. An Amiens specialty: a small spicy meat-and-vegetable pie.

5. Whom Henri Estienne, no friendly critic, reports to have been a noted tender of geese: *Apologie pour Hérodote* 1566.
6. "... formes suyvantes la matière. Ainsi les nomme Averroïs."
7. Jean Breton, sieur de Villandry, comptroller General for War, friend of Jean du Bellay, may have met Duke Claude de Guise in the campaign against the Imperials in Picardy in 1536–1537.

4.12: HOW PANTAGRUEL PASSED PROCURATION.

1. To "pass procuration" is to give power of attorney. R enjoys treating procuration as a place.
2. "Les chicquanous": name formed from *chicane* "chicanery, etc.," but the actual Chicanous are the process-servers, often beaten in the line of duty, often collecting good damages for beatings received.
3. "... gens à tout le poil": this idiom defies translation.
4. "... jeunes guanteletz de jouste, couvers de chevrotin."
5. "La mémoire en expira avecques le son des cloches, lesquelles quarillonnèrent à son enterrement."

4.13: HOW, AFTER THE EXAMPLE OF MASTER FRANÇOIS VILLON, THE LORD OF BASCHÉ PRAISES HIS PEOPLE.

1. Saint Maixent in the canton of Niort (Deux-Sèvres), site of an abbey, but no trace of a passion play. Fairs were held in Niort three times a year and widely attended, especially the one in May. As was noted earlier, legends about Villon's last years abounded in R's France and of course in R.
2. Friar Taptail (*coue*, is modern *queue*).
3. In the mystery plays, God the Father was dressed in these vestments.
4. Where in 1540–1560 every year were performed the *Sept Joies de la Vierge,* preceded by a large procession called the *omnegange.*
5. Verse in mixed Latin and a vernacular (here, Italian).
6. BD: "In Poitevin, it's the cross elsewhere called Boysselière, near which on Palm Sundays they sing 'Osanna filio David'," etc.

4.14: CONTINUATION OF THE SHYSTEROOS DRUBBED IN THE HOUSE OF BASCHÉ.

1. Apparently a card game won by whichever player first scored 303 points.
2. Or jackstraws dropped in a pile; player tries to remove one at a time without disturbing the others.
3. Italian card game named after the strongest, highest card used. The main card was called the *impériale.*
4. Italian morra (cf., 1.22) in which the players in turn guess at the number of their adversary's fingers extended out of their sight.

5. The traditional motley of the professional fool or jester, of course to ensure that no one took his drubbing seriously.

6. Necessary to make the marriage legal.

7. Here this polyvalent word presumably means his writing-case.

4.15: HOW BY SHYSTEROOS ARE RENEWED THE ANCIENT WEDDING CUSTOMS.

1. "Sainsambreguoy!": deformation of "Saint sang de Dieu."

2. "... aussi ne trouve-l'on plus de lièvres au giste."

3. In the week before Christmas a new anthem was sung each day starting "O sapientia," "O Adoinai," "O Radix," "O Clavis," etc., and accompanied at times by other pleasant customs like passing out wine, etc.

4. "... luy avoit desincornifistibulé toute l'aultre espaule."

5. "... esperruquancluzelubelouzerirelu."

6. "... morrambouzevezengouzequoquemorguatasacbacguevezinemaffressé."

7. "Estez-vous des Frappins, des Frappeurs ou des Frappars?"

8. "... morcrocassebezassevezassegrigueliguoscopapopondrillé."

9. "... morderegrippipiotabirofreluchamburelurecoquelurintimpanemens."

10. "Appelez-vous cela jeu de jeunesse? Par Dieu, jeu n'est-ce."

11. "Mon, mon, mon, vrelon, von, von!"

12. "... trepignemampenillorifrizonoufressuré."

13. "... m'a-il tant et très tant festoyée à grands coups de poing?"

14. "... tout morquaquoquasse."

15. "... tous les braz enguoulevezinemassez."

16. "Appelez-vous cecy fiansailles? Je les appele fiantailles de merde." Note that *fiente* is another word for excrement.

17. The text explains the dire effect of this gold and that horse on their possessor.

18. It seems likely that this proverb, unknown to us, prompted R to write this episode.

4.16: HOW FRÈRE JEAN MAKES TRIAL OF THE NATURE OF THE SHYSTEROOS.

1. Judges called *pédanes* "mobile, ambulatory," attached to no seat or bench, dispensed justice *soubs l'orme* "under the elm" and none too well says R.

2. "En quoy offensoient ces paouvres diables Chiquanous?" Perhaps implying: "What offense against God?"

3. A very ancient Roman law cited in Aulus Gellius's text.

4. "Par la sacre botte de sainct Benoist!" The great tun was in his monastery in Bologna. Frère Jean seems to have been a Benedictine.

5. "... io, io, io!": Italian for "Me, me, me!"

6. "... une bien grande crapauldine": considered a remedy for headaches.

7. "... ayse comme un Roy ou deux."

8. "Monsieur frère Diable": a notorious Italian bandit named Michele Pezza (1771–1806), was known as Fra Diavolo; although our "Fra Diavolo" is a bad anachronism, the sense is much the same.

9. "... l'on avoit au gibbet baillé le moine par le coul aux deux plus gens de bien qui feussent en tout Chiquanourroys."

10. Give trouble; rather like our "give a headache to," but often much stronger.

11. BD: For "Saint Jean de l'Apocalypse," meaning that what is being said is too obvious to deserve mention.

4.17: HOW PANTAGRUEL PASSED THE ISLANDS OF TOHU AND BOHU.

1. BD: "Hebrew: deserted and uncultivated." From Genesis 1.1.

2. "... èsquelles ne trouvasmes que frire": i.e., we found nothing to do. Our version tries to suggest both this and the real meaning.

3. The name means nothing but suggests wide or slit nostrils. Urquhart and Leclercq call him Widenostrils; Putnam, Nosesplitter; Cohen, Slitnose. Since none of these (or any other we can dream up) seems right, we have stayed with R's French original.

4. This story of Aeschylus's death, already cited in 3.23 above, comes down from Pliny's *Natural History* 10.3 via Valerius Maximus 9.12, and of course Erasmus *Adages* 2.9.77.

5. Strabo 7; Arrian 1.4. Plutarch calls the man Pharnaces; but R follows Erasmus (*Adages* 5.64) in making his name Phenaces.

6. Sri Lankans, whom until recently we were calling Ceylonese.

7. In Greek mythology, the pillars on which Atlas supported heaven and held it apart from earth were thought to rest in the sea beyond the western horizon.

8. So says an unknown in a fairly well-known epitaph (for himself) in an Augustinian church near Rome, which R himself may have seen in one of his stays there.

9. A fictive name: EC suggests it is an anagram for *Rabelais cy en bas* "Rabelais here listed last," which we find more ingenious than convincing.

10. *Mechloth* in Hebrew means "illnesses"; *Belima*, "nothing."

11. BD: Arabic words meaning "manna" and "rose honey."

4.18: HOW PANTAGRUEL CAME SAFELY THROUGH A MIGHTY TEMPEST AT SEA.

1. Hebrew *Kessil*, "crazy." R clearly refers thus to the Council of Trent (1540–1563).

2. Chaos, in Greek, was the first state of the universe before spirit gave things form. See also Genesis 1.1–2.

3. See Plutarch *Apothegms* 7.18 and Diogenes Laertius *Lives of the Philosophers,* but R changed these sources somewhat.
4. "Je tressue de grand ahan": compare English "sweating gumdrops."
5. "Tout est frelore bigoth": garbled German and English for "verloren, By God."
6. "Bebebe bous bous bous!": blubbering, teeth-chattering noises.
7. Stargazer is French *Astrophile.*
8. More blubbering in tearful fright.

4.19: HOW PANURGE AND FRÈRE JEAN BEHAVED DURING THE TEMPEST.

1. This vital prepositional phrase, from "after first" through "fervent piety" is one of many 1552 additions to the story as it appeared in the partial edition of 1548.
2. "... nous sommes au-dessus de Ela, hors toute la gamme!" Musicians in R's day recognized one uniform gamut or range of musical sounds, in which the highest note was *Ela,* the lowest *gamma ut,* which also meant the entire range and gave rise to the term *gamut* to designate that particular range.
3. "A ceste heure foys bien à poinct l'arbre forchu, les pieds à mont, la teste en bas."
4. NEB: "It is accomplished!" Saint John (19.30) offers these as Jesus' last words on the Cross. See 3.2, note 11.
5. According to Saint Luke, the last words of Jesus (23.46) NEB: "Father, into Thy hands (*in manus tuos*) I commend my spirit."
6. Here is the French:

> Entre Quande et Monssorreau,
> Et n'y paistra vache ne veau.

This is an old proverb meaning "nowhere," since Candes and Montsoreau are villages adjoining each other.
7. In all these oaths, "of God" is implicit.
8. "... je te gualleray en loup marin!"

4.20: HOW QUARTERMASTERS ABANDON SHIP AT THE HEIGHT OF THE TEMPEST.

1. "Comment les nauchiers abandonnent les navires au fort de la tempeste." A puzzling title partly because it has nothing to do with its chapter, but especially because the sense of *nauchiers* is not clear. Cotgrave, Littré, and Marichal do not list it in this the old spelling, but only under *nocher.* Cotgrave calls that "Pillot, or Steeres-man"; Urquhart makes it in the title "Pilots"; Cohen makes them "Captains." None of these seem to make much sense, but Littré offers another possibility that seems likelier: *Contre-maître* "Quartermaster," concerned mainly with the ship's cosmetics, not its overall safety and welfare.

2. "Ancien, dis-je, car de praesent je suys nul, vous estes nul." Worth noting here is Panurge's use of the *vous* (presumably deferential) to his comrade, whose fury at Panurge's base cowardice has led him to lapse into the *tu* form for a time just before now even as Panurge had stuck to the *vous* (4.19). They have usually both used the *tu* to each other, as in the consultation over Panurge's marriage (3.26–28), but at the end of 4.8, in a to-and-fro movement that puzzles me, Panurge asks what Frère Jean thought of it all with a *tu,* Frère Jean responds with a *vous*, then after another *tu* from Panurge, replies with a *tu* to end the chapter. Since this question of the *tu* and *vous* does not affect the translation, I have not studied it throughout, and have for now only these random observations to offer.

3. Here used much like our English metaphor, and here clearly ironic.

4. A cake, out of place here; in 1548 R had written Talmont.

5. One of R's puzzling nautical terms *uretacque* may mean a single line to the mizzenmast or more probably the rigging in general.

6. As explained above in 1.41, a *tiring* is a purge for a falcon making him ready to hunt, as a wee time with his breviary leaves Frère Jean ready to drink.

7. "Maistre Alcofribas" makes another appearance in his own narrative.

4.21: CONTINUATION OF THE TEMPEST AND BRIEF DISCOURSE ON WILLS MADE AT SEA.

1. When it cast him ashore (*Odyssey* 5.443 ff.) in Phaeacia, there to enjoy the delightful rescue by the king's daughter Nausicaa (6.17 ff.).

2. The first three of these cenotaphs are mentioned by Virgil, the others by many others.

3. Widowed by her brother's (Pygmalion's) murder of her husband: *Aeneid* 1.334–361, although with no mention of a cenotaph R probably compiled this list from Virgil, Diogenes Laertius, Pausanias, Suetonius, Catullus and others.

4. The frightened disciples in Matthew 8.25.

5. The pious corrective is in Luke 22.42: Christ in Gethsemane to God.

6. In Luke 23.46 the last words of Jesus; cf., above, 4.19, note 5.

7. Who in Greek legend got a ride for a song from a dolphin.

8. Leave, that is, in the context of Psalm 1.1, to follow and join the wicked sinners.

4.22: END OF THE TEMPEST.

1. "Enfans, couraige de brebis!": a rather mocking reminder that the worst was over, so that from then on a little more courage would be needed.

2. In the Mediterranean, a southeast wind.

3. "C'est bien dict et advisé": our colloquialism was very tempting.

4. "Cest bien et doctement parlé."

5. "... car le jour est fériau, Nau, Nau, Nau!": this last is the refrain of an old Poitevin Noel.

6. The Dioscuri (Castor and Pollux) were considered lucky stars by sailors, except when close to a third, their sister Helen, an omen of shipwreck and possible death.

7. "... ce grand mastin de pasté Jambique ou Jambonique, ce m'est tout un."

8. "Guardez que ne donnons par terre!"

4.23: How, with the tempest over, Panurge plays the jolly good fellow.

1. Jesting use of a formula normally reserved for princes, dukes, or other high nobles.

2. Allusion to *Les Neuf Joies de Mariage,* a popular sardonic tract of the late fifteenth century.

4.24: How by Frère Jean Panurge is declared to have been scared without reason.

1. "Je suis allouy": i.e., hungry as a wolf.

2. Paraphrase of Job 5.7 with a start from Genesis 3.19.

3. As in Genesis 3.19.

4. "... ou bruslé guaillard comme un Père": meaning like a good Cordelier. See 3.11 above, and below, 4.44. A possible allusion to the many Reformist martyrs.

5. Like our water wings, bundles of reeds provided buoyancy for a beginning swimmer.

6. A proverbial phrase meaning nowhere, since these two towns were adjacent, with no room between.

4.25: How after the tempest Pantagruel went ashore.

1. Greek *makrobios, -on* for "long-lived" (people).

2. Here the 1548 edition abruptly ended, with this phrase lamely filled out as follows to form a complete sentence: "True it is that he/she says no more about it" (Vray est que qui a plus n'en dict). See Marichal's facsimile ed. in *ER* 10 (1971). For more on the relation of the 1548 partial edition to the final definitive one of 1552, see our introductory note to this book.

3. The Ardennes (Shakespeare's Arden in *As You Like It*) is a large region, wooded and mountainous, covering parts of Belgium, Luxembourg, and the northeast corner of France, and to this day rather sparsely populated.

4. Moorish (as distinct from other Arabs): formed from Hagar, in Genesis 16.3 ff. and originally thought to be descended from her.

5. L'Ile aux Cygnes, between the Passy and Grenelle bridges. In R's day was notorious for its prostitutes.

6. Financial disinterestedness was then thought a worthy Christian motive or assurance of some purity of motive.

7. The Atlantic Ocean. The following places were well-known danger-spots for sailors.

4.26: How the good Macrobe tells Pantagruel about the abode and departure of heroes.

1. In Greek religion and thought, heroes were famous men (normally heroic) who after death were worshiped as quasi-divine. In this they bore some resemblance to daemons, spirits intermediary between gods and men, some of whom like guardian angels, looked out for men they felt responsible for, such as Socrates. See the note on them in the Glossary. Also see Augustine's definition of them in *City of God* 10.21.

2. Traveler or traveling.

3. Lord of Langey (1491–1543) and older brother of Cardinal Jean; R's most beloved and admired patron; excellent governor first of Turin, then of all Piedmont. The next chapter (4.27) gives R's moving account of his death.

4. King of Judaea under the Romans 37–34 B.C. See note in the Glossary. What follows is mainly a compilation from Pliny 7.52 and 11.39; for Herod see Acts 12.23.

5. For all this see Erasmus *Adages* 1.3.80: "Me mortuo terra misceatur incendio."

4.27: How Pantagruel discourses on the departure of certain heroic souls.

1. For Langey see chapter 26, note 3 above.

2. "Je ne vouldroys," dist Pantagruel continuant, "n'avoir pâti la tormente marine . . . pour non entendre ce que nous dict ce bon Macrobe." To make it less convoluted in translation by changing one negative ("n'avoir pâti") to an affirmative ("to have been spared"); but the sense, if clearer, is the same.

3. This excursus is derived from Erasmus *Adages* "praefigere" in either 4.56 or 5.56 (so at least say PL, G, and QL; but I find nothing so clear in either place. *TH* (theta) obviously stands for *thanatos* "death," A (alpha) presumably for *anabole* in its sense of "deferral, delay"; but like other inquirers, I am baffled by the *tau*.

4. François de Genouillac, sieur d'Assier, was killed in 1544 in the battle of Ceresole.

5. Our author, who seems to have been present and deeply moved.

6. Claude Massuau, seigneur de Belle-Croix (parish of Saint-Ayl) who translated into French R's lost work on the *Stratagemata* of Langey. Of those listed here by R, Chemant (François Errault) was President at the Parlement (q.v.) of Turin; Mailly was an officer under Langey; Villeneuve-la-Guyart was a nephew of Langey; Gabriel, the doctor from Savigliano, was Langey's doctor; Lord of Saint-Ayl (pron. Saint-Y), Etienne Lorens,

a friend of R's, was captain of the Turin castle. Except for these and those noted individually, all were unidentifiable members of Langey's large household.

7. Here is the French original of these three lines of verse:

> Je vous demande en demandant,
> Comme le roy à son sergent
> Et la Royne à son enfant.

8. Sylvan nymphs who each resided in her tree, in which she was born and died.

9. In the chapter on Phocis of his *Description of Greece* 10.32.9.

10. R gives us a clear total figure, but his account of how it is reached is less clear and has been variously read. For the best reading we know of and have used our great debt is to K. H. Francis, "R and Mathematics," *BHR* 21 (1959), 85–97; he notes other theories, but here is his: "Unity rising to quadrinity": 1+2+3+4: 10. "The entire quadrinity doubled in itself four times: 4 × 10: 40. The whole thing multiplied five times by solid triangles. These amount to 84 + 84 + 35 + 20 + 20, which comes to 243. 243 × 40: 9,720."

4.28: How Pantagruel relates a piteous story.

1. *Thamoun* is the accusative form of *Thamous,* Syrian name for Adonis, whose worshipers mourned him every year, chanting: "The Very Great One is dead"; so says Marichal; see above 4.25, note 2. This of course fits Plutarch's account in *The Cessation of Oracles,* here reported by R.

2. R of course updates the story to put blame on priests and monks of his day.

3. Corydon was a shepherd in Virgil; see the *Eclogues* 7 and 2.33 and *Bucolics* 2. Saint John the Evangelist, perhaps because of his terms for Jesus in John 10–11, is here called by that name as a "passionate shepherd."

4.29: How Pantagruel passed the island of Coverup.

1. "...l'isle de Tapinois," from *tapir* "hide"; Urquhart: "the Sneaking Island"; Cohen: "Sneaks' Island"; any of these will do.

2. "Quaresmeprenant," ruler of Tapinois; means "Lent-observer"; Urquhart: "Shrovetide"; Cohen: "Lent." Here I have used "Fastilent."

3. "...dictateur de Moustardois": mustard was important in Lenten diets.

4. A jibe at the ritual of Ash Wednesday, the start of Lent.

5. Apparently ironic toward the conservative claim to be the only true Catholics.

6. All these are of course promoters of thirst.

7. "...pissechaulde": gonorrhea.

8. "...les festes mobiles": those whose dates depend on Easter and thus change from year to year.

9. "...et n'oubliez pas les Boudins."

4.30: How Fastilent is anatomized.

1. " ... la cervelle en grandeur, couleur, substance et vigueur semblable au couillon guausche d'un ciron masle."
2. "Les espritz vitaulx, comme longues chiquenauldes."
3. "La raison, comme un tabouret." The French *tambourin* now means "drum, tambourine"; but Urquhart gives "cricket stool," and LI, Demerson's modern French version is *tabouret* for "stool."

4.31: Anatomy of Fastilent as regards the outward parts.

1. "Les orteilz avoit comme une espinette orguanisée."
2. "Les cuisses, comme un crenequin."
3. "Le ventre à poulaines, boutonné scelon la mode antique et ceinct à l'antibust."
4. "Le nez, comme un brodequin anté en escusson."
5. Or, like a gun *un fuzil*.
6. "Le front, comme une retombe."
7. " ... sus la porte de la cave."

4.32: Continuation of Fastilent's physical features.

1. "S'il subloit, c'estoient hottées de cinges verds." A popular example of imaginary creatures.
2. "S'il souffloit, c'estoient troncs pour les Indulgences." Indulgences were of course an especial bête noire to all Reformists.
3. "S'il faisoit la moue, c'estoient battons rompuz."
4. "S'il discouroit, c'estoient neiges d'antan": another nod to the great fifteenth-century poet François Villon, who wrote a fine ballade, best loved, with the refrain "Mais où sont les neiges d'antan?" (But where are the snows of yesteryear?).
5. "S'il se soucioit, c'estoient des rez et des tonduz."
6. "Si rien donnoit, autant en avoit le brodeur."
7. "S'il songeoit, c'estoient vitz volans et rampans contre une muraille."
8. "De toutes corneilles prinses en tapinois ordinairement poschoit les oeilz."
9. "Se jouoit ès cordes des ceincts." *Ceincts* and *saints* are homophones.
10. "De son poing faisoit un maillet."
11. "Escrivoit ... prognostications et almanachs."
12. " ... cul sus teste": unlike the English, the French phrase makes sense.
13. " ... toutes gens écervelez et desguarniz de bon jugement et sens commun."
14. Literally, apes of a certain kind; here, and elsewhere in R, "hypocrites," with a suggestion of Goths from the homonymous final syllable -*gotz*.
15. Pistoletz: allusions to Guillaume Postel (1510–1581), Middle East expert and Royal Lecturer, polygraph, proud, with wild ideas, tried to reconcile

the Koran with the Bible. Postel had bitterly attacked R as a heretic not long before R's Book 4.

16. Calvin was one of R's fiercest and most detested enemies. R had made a thinly veiled crack at him in his 1542 ed. of Book 2; Calvin attacked him as a monstrous heretic in *De scandalis* (1550); this is R's response.

17. Another fierce censor of R: see GL for note.

18. *Chattemites,* which usually means "catamite," but probably not here.

19. "... et aultres monstres difformes et contrefaicts en despit de Nature."

4.33: How Pantagruel sighted a monstrous physeter.

1. The capital upsilon looks much like our capital Y, which through Latin is derived from it. As a numeral it meant 400,000. For Pythagoras it had a symbolic meaning.

2. Until Perseus saved her, as related in Ovid *Metamorphoses* 4.673–739.

3. George, duke of Clarence, brother of King Edward IV of England, of whose choice R may have read in Philippe de Commynes (1447–1511), *Mémoires* 1.13.

4. "Vestz à l'audience, vestz aux Chiquanous!"

4.34: How Pantagruel slew the monstrous physeter.

1. "... et faisoit son debvoir de le pinser sans rire." In modern French, "pince-sans-rire" denotes sarcasm in its user: i.e., petty malice in intent.

2. "... tant ferme, résistant, dur et valide feust, que sçauriez dire."

3. "... en chasse de bestes noires et rousses."

4. Hellebore, valued against insanity, was credited with other uses as well.

5. "... tous seront à perdition mis par la puissance et sagettes des Scythes."

6. In R's day, these were some of the biggest bridges in France outside Paris.

7. "... comme si feussent cosses et portehausbancs de la carine."

4.35: How Pantagruel goes ashore on the Wild Island.

1. "... manoir antique des Andouilles."

2. The Atlantic Ocean between France and Newfoundland, where the French fished mainly for cod on the Newfoundland banks, and sometimes found whales.

3. "... du concile national de Chesil": R calls it "national," because for all its claim to be a general council, it was so wholly dominated by Italians.

4.36: How an ambush is laid against Pantagruel.

1. "... leur ville, citadelle, chasteau et rocquette de Cheminées." Another meaning for chimney was the council room of sheriffs or magistrates in certain villages.

2. See Trebellius Polli *Historia Augusta* 7.
3. " . . . finablement le feist occire": see Tacitus *Annals* 2.3.
4. " . . . avecques leurs mailletz": war hammers. The word may also mean "battle-axe," but here it seems clearly to be the hammer that gave its name to the 1382 uprising of the Maillotins.

4.37: How Pantagruel sent for captains Gobblechitterling and Chopsausage.

1. Riflandouille and Tailleboudin.
2. " . . . du chevalereux capitaine Moses, conducteur du peuple Israëlicque": while Joshua was fighting the Amalekite champion Amalek; Exodus 17.8–11.
3. According to Henry Cornelius Agrippa *De vanitate scientiarum* 15, *De sorte Pythagorica*.
4. Suetonius cites this story in his *Life of the Divine Augustus* 96.5.
5. A name clearly suggesting "king's son." Suetonius again, *Life of Vespasian* 7.2.
6. In Latin, *rex, regis* is the word for "king"; this name clearly suggests it.
7. Trebellius *Thirty tyrants* 10.
8. Plato's dialogue on the origin of language and on onomastics, the study of words and proper names, their origins, meanings, and connotations.
9. Cornelius Agrippa *De vanitate* 3.15.
10. The capital of the old county of Saintonge, on the Charente, now chief town of Charente-Maritime, not far north of Bordeaux. For R's friend Briand Vallée see the Glossary.
11. Plutarch tells this story in his *Life of Alexander*; Celio Calcagnini repeats it.
12. "A ce mot print Paulus asceurance de la victoire contre Persés."

4.38: How Chitterlings are not to be despised among humans.

1. "Comment Andouilles ne sont à mespriser entre les humains."
2. Genesis 3.1. The French is: "il estoit fin et cauteleux sus tous aultres animans."
3. Pliny *Natural History* 5.8.
4. " . . . ne satisfont à l'incrédulité de vos seigneuries."
5. " . . . jusques aux boursavitz": the term *bourses-à-vits* refers to the female genitalia.
6. " . . . par les Bretons balladins dansans leurs trioriz fredonnize": lively, lusty, Breton dances.
7. Valérius Flaccus *Argonautica* 6.48.58.

4.39: How Frère Jean joins forces with the cooks.

1. "Ce sera icy une belle bataille de foin."
2. See Genesis 29 and Kings 25.8–11. Nebuzaradan was already changed into a cook in medieval popular literature.
3. Cotgrave defines *Trou Madame* as "The Game called Trunkes, or the Hole." Here it seems to be used as a mild oath.
4. Plutarch *Apophthegmata Ciceronis* 19, translated from Greek into Latin by Erasmus.

4.40: How Frère Jean is set up in the sow.

1. "Comment par Frère Jean est dressée la Truye et les preux cuisiniers dedans enclous."
2. ". . . la grande Truye, laquelle estoit dedans la nauf Bourrabaquinière."
3. Jean Froissart relates in his *Chronicles* how in 1378 under Charles V (not VI), the French hauled the huge siege engine called The Sow (La Truye) all the way over land and water from La Réole (Gironde) to Bergerac, which with its help they recaptured from the English.
4. R's long list of warrior cooks is a mock-epic parody of Homer's famous catalogue of the Greek ships and warrior leaders that fills Book 2 of the *Iliad*. Imitations of this had become, long before R's time, standard features of long heroic poems. Homer tells us little about the Trojan horse (*Odyssey* 4.272; 8.494–504 ff.) and gives no list of the warriors it held; most of our details come from two poems of the "Trojan Cycle," the *Sack of Troy* by Aektinos of Ephesus and the *Little Iliad*.

   Since many of the names that follow either have or suggest clear meanings but most fare poorly in translation, we offer here R's French original as well as our version of each. Several of the cooks' names are borrowed from earlier chapters and episodes in R's book, and we indicate most of these in individual notes.
5. Another "Maistre Hordoux" (there called by us Master Slipslop) on 3.23 is a typical cook deserving that typical name.
6. QL gives *L'eschevin* "the sheriff"; LI gives *Leschevin* "Lickwine"; for a cook in this list the latter seems far likelier, but the pun intentional.
7. ". . . en leurs armoiries en champ de gueulle, lardouoire de sinople, fessée d'un chevron argenté, penchant à guausche."
8. *Aftolardon* would be modern Greek pronunciation of the word *autolardon*.
9. Neither of which ethnic groups eats any bacon.
10. A popular sauce dating from the Middle Ages. The Scotchmen of the Guard were said to pronounce it Sauce Mondam.
11. One of several names here formed from *navelet* "turnip," then in wide use in France.
12. A popular tangy sauce (browned onions, mustard or vinegar in white wine) to liven up overly bland meat or fish.

13. The same name, inevitable here, we used for Homenaz: 4.48. Grosbeak in the Glossary.
14. R owes the name Frippelippes to Marot, whose Epistle in verse against his vindictive enemy François Sagon he entitled as being by his valet Frippelippes.
15. This will also be the name of the hospitable hermit in 5.1–2.
16. " . . . cuisiniers guaillars, guallans, brusquetz et prompts au combat."

4.41: HOW PANTAGRUEL SNAPPED THE CHITTERLINGS OVER HIS KNEE.

1. "Comment Pantagruel rompit les Andouille aux genoulx." A proverbial expression for doing something ludicrously impossible.
2. At the battle of Marignano (1515) a stout bullhorn-blower for the Swiss was called "the Bull of Berne" for leading a few comrades in a raid that ruined several pieces of French artillery; he was killed in the process. Cf., 2.2. At this battle of Marignano, near Milan (September 13–14, 1515), the French, helped by their Venetian allies, won one of the bloodiest battles of the Franco-Italian Wars, and thus for a time gained control over the opulent duchy of Milan.
3. Ironic, of course. "House-burners" were normally undisciplined looting soldiers.
4. A treasured Egyptian marble introduced into Rome by Lucullus.
5. A proverb popularized (after Cicero *Posterior academics* 5, and Plutarch *Demosthenes* 11) by Erasmus in his adage *Sus Minervam* intended to humble pretentious idiots: "dici solitum cum quis id dovet alterum cujus ipse est inscius."

4.42: HOW PANTAGRUEL PARLEYS WITH NIPHLESETH.

1. Hebrew: the male member.
2. To see someone's urine (veoir son urine) meant to test his mettle (which is the sense here), but also, more literally, to check or test the urine.
3. This seems to be as much a title as a proper name.
4. On the Montagne Sainte-Geneviève; perhaps the present Rue Séguier. In R's time many streets were named "Rue pavée."
5. Perche: a former county in the Parisian basin noted for manufacture of small knives, penknives, etc., often used for small gifts.
6. This, the old form of the term, helps explain the derivation favored by some from royal blood, i.e., the blood of Christ.

4.43: HOW PANTAGRUEL WENT ASHORE ON THE ISLAND OF RUACH.

1. BD: "Hebrew: wind or spirit." We might render it "afflatus."
2. "Poussinière" is an ancient name for the Pleiades.
3. *Anemone* is related to Greek *anemos,* "air, wind."

4. Southeast wind.

5. Languedoc word for a southwest wind.

6. In Italian *garbino,* also meant southwest wind but milder than the preceding ones.

7. Northeast wind.

8. Northwest wind.

9. Born at Anduse, died in 1556, physician to Queen Margaret of Navarre, a good friend of R's who had been his sponsor (patron) at the Medical Faculty of Montpellier.

10. "... à ma jambe oedipodicque." BD: "swollen, fat, as were those of Oedipus the diviner," which in Greek means "swollen foot." Cf., Shelly's title "Swellfoot the Tyrant."

11. Some of the best muscat and summer pear wines came from Frontignan and Mirevaux.

12. "... bien ressemblant à la ventrose": big-bellied (from *ventre* "belly"), but looking and sounding like words from *vent* "wind."

13. "... pour guider sa nauf en temps calme."

14. Presumably the most modest, decorous wind-breaking imaginable.

15. See BD: "at present are called nuns."

16. Already this new Italian import had taken the world of verse by storm, to the point of inspiring such jokes as this one.

4.44: HOW LITTLE RAINS BEAT DOWN GREAT WINDS.

1. "... le bien souverain consister en volupté."

2. "... béat de toutes pars." The phrase "most happy" above is *bienheureux.*

3. BD: "gate of Aeous. It's a closed bronze instrument, with a little opening in it, from which, if you put water in it and bring it near fire, you will see wind come continuously. Thus are engendered the winds in the air and windiness in human bodies, by heatings or by concoction begun but not yet completed, as Cl. Galen explains. See what our great friend and lord Monsieur Philander has written about it on the first book of Vitruvius."

4. The original French of this edifying dizain is this:

> Jenin, tastant un soir ses vins nouveaulx,
> Troubles encor et bouillans en leur lie,
> Pria Quelot apprester des naveaulx
> A leur soupper, pour faire chère lie.
> Cela feut faict. Puys, sans mélancholie,
> Se vont coucher, belutent, prenent somme.
> Mais ne pouvant Jenin dormir en somme,
> Tant fort vesnoit Quelot, et tant souvent,
> La compissa. Puys: "Voylà," dist-il, "comme
> Petite pluie abat bien un grant vent."

5. This name for an island, like the preceding Bringuenarilles, comes, by a

kind of reverse borrowing, from the highly derivative *Panurge disciple de Pantagruel* (1538), better known as the *Navigation de Panurge*. BD defines "Tohu et Bohu" as "Hebrew: deserted and uncultivated."

6. " . . . il escorchoit un renard": he threw up.

7. "Et mourust suffocqué et estranglé, mangeant un coin de beurre frays à la gueule d'un four chault, par l'ordonnance des médicins."

4.45: How Pantagruel went ashore on the island of the Popefigs.

1. We are using "Swingers" loosely to mean simply living free and easy.

2. An international sign of obscene and insolent defiance, made by projecting a thumb out from between two knuckles of a closed fist.

3. BD: "a fig in the fundament, Heb."

4. When R was in Rome, Saint Peter's still had no roof. The building was completed only in 1626.

4.46: How the little devil was fooled by a farmer.

1. "C'est pourquoy estez mauldict en l'Evangile." R's allusion is not to a Gospel text but to the pun (on homonyms *mauldit* and *mot dit*) in an old pseudo couplet noted in print much later in *Synonyma et aequivoca gallica* (Lyon, 1619, p. 138): "il est mot dict en l'Evangile / Tel choisit qui prend le pire" (One man chooses and takes the worse is a piece said in the Scripture).

2. "Vous dictez qu'il n'est desjeuner que de escholiers, dipner que d'advocatz, ressiner que de vinerons, soupper que de marchans, reguoubilloner que de chambrières, et tous repas que de farfadetz?"

3. "Mais (las!) ne sçay par quel malheur, depuys certaines années ilz ont avecques leurs estudes adjoinct les saincts Bibles."

4. Once an important Black Sea port and offshoot of the great Byzantine empire, it is modern Turkish Trabzon. Just why R chooses to use it here is not clear. From its context, Demerson (LI) thinks it is an allegory of fractious students who abuse their clerical immunity by practicing anarchy in the name of freedom. One may recall, however, how Voltaire often uses Babylon to represent Paris, especially in showing its luxury and vice.

4.47: How the devil was fooled by an old woman.

1. "O villain, villain! çza, çà à belles gryphes!"

2. " . . . les femmes Persides se praesentèrent à leurs enfans fuyans de la bataille." This is an anecdote repeated by Erasmus *Apophthegms* 6 "Varie mixta," 90, from Plutarch *Moralia,* "De virtutibus mulierum" (On the virtues of women).

3. " . . . voyant l'énorme solution de continuité en toutes dimensions."

4.48: HOW PANTAGRUEL WENT ASHORE ON THE ISLAND OF THE PAPIMANIACS.

1. "Comment Pantagruel descendit en l'isle des Papimanes."
2. "Par la mort beuf, je l'assommeray de coups!"
3. "Et en tel mot se déclaira à Moses." See Exodus 3.14: NEB: "I am; that is who I am."
4. "... ouy dea, messieurs, j'en ay veu troys, à la veue desquelz je n'ay guères profité."
5. "O gens," dirent-ilz, "troys et quatre foys heureux."
6. Papal decrees in the form of epistles, which formed a large part of canon law. Of the nine books of these, two, the *Extravagantes* of Pope John XXII (1244–1334), pope from 1316–1334, and the *Extravagantes communes,* were so called because they were outside (extra) the main collection, which included Books 1–5 (of 1234) and 6 (of 1298), and the *Clementines* (1313) of Pope Clement V.
7. The name Homenaz has been variously translated: as Dumbell (Putnam), Stoutmoron after one introductory "Homenais (sic) or Stoutmoron" (Leclercq), and Greatclod (Cohen), while Urquhart had left it as Homenaz. We have chosen Grosbeak for this reason: we consider conclusive Robert Marichal's demonstration that the name stands for *Homme-Nez* (English "Nose-Man"); (compare Nazdecabre-Goatsnose, the mute in 3.20 who could answer Panurge's questions only by signs) and designates a caricature of the bellicose Pope Julius III, at that time a bitter foe of R's King Henry II and the French, and noted for his great beak; see his "Quart Livre: Commentaires," p. 131, and the portrait of Julius III facing p. 65, in *ER* 5 (1956). Thus the name we are using, Grosbeak, seems to fit both Homenaz and Julius III quite well, better than any used earlier and than any available alternative. To be sure, it is even better suited, as the name of a bird, to one of the cleric birds of the Ringing Island (5.1–8), but we found no occasion for it there.
8. Hypophetes: BD "Who speak of things past as prophets speak of future things"; i.e., who have, as we say, 20–20 hindsight.

4.49: HOW GROSBEAK, BISHOP OF THE PAPIMANIACS, SHOWED US THE URANOPÈTE DECRETALS.

1. BD: "fallen from heaven."
2. A variety of the gem ruby spinel or spinel ruby.
3. BD: "bearing animals. It's on one portal and in other places that architects call a frieze, on which place they used to put the manikins, sculptures, writings, and other devices at will."
4. "Pantagruel le manyoit et tournoyt à plaisir."
5. A city in Galatia famous for its temple of Cybele. For this story see Livy *History* 29.10.

6. Lit., "golden flame": the banner of Saint Denis symbolic of devotion and courage, borne into battle by most of the early kings of France and by some later ones also.

7. See Pausanias *Attica* 26.6.

8. BD: "descended from Jupiter." Diipetes is from the Greek.

9. Decrappers: *Décrotouères.*

10. " . . . parchemin lanterné": perhaps, seriously, diaphanous parchment then used in lanterns because less fragile than glass; or one more gag on lantern; q.v., Glossary.

11. "To whip cunts," homonym for *confesser,* "to confess."

12. The embrace given to a *brother,* a fellow churchman.

13. "Boutez doncq, boutez bas et roidde!": a phrase suggested by Homenaz's talk of a low mass, but now with sexual implications from the *roidde* "sexual thrusting by the male phallus."

14. "Verd et bleu!" Although these words mean "green and blue," this is a euphemism for "Mère de Dieu!"

15. " . . . je y eusse porté pain et vin par les traictz passez": note the pun between the homophones *traictz passez* "down the hatch" and *trespassez* "dead."

16. " . . . troussez-la court, de paour que ne se crotte": tuck up your pants before your bowels move, for fear they may get filthy. The sense here seems to be what we mean by "make it short and sweet."

4.50: HOW BY GROSBEAK WE WERE SHOWN THE ARCHETYPE OF A POPE.

1. This is a puzzler, and our version is less clear than it might be. R wrote that seeing the portrait gave full remission of all remembered sins, "ensemble la tierce partie avecques dix-huict quarantaines des péchez oubliez!" A *quarantaine* is a 40-day period. I assume (much as Urquhart seems to have done) that R's intended meaning is "one-third of the forgotten sins, plus eighteen 40-day periods" (720 days, very nearly two years) of complete remission for these as well as all other sins; the puzzlement comes from the place where R inserted the "quarantaines." Cohen, however, takes the eighteen quarantaines to mean 18/40, and translates it as "the third part and eighteen fortieths"; this seems just possible but much less likely. The sum of the two would be about 78 percent. Leclercq does better than that, I think, writing: "one third of all the sins we have overlooked, plus eighteen times forty for good measure." This keeps what *quarantaine* means.

2. "Fy! j'en diz fy!": This is as close as Pantagruel ever comes to profanity.

3. Germany, ever divided, was therefore often referred to in the plural, as here.

4.51: SMALL TALK DURING DINNER.

1. Guillot's was a first-class inn and restaurant run by Guillaume Artus

(Guillot), at the Sign of the Silver Dolphin on what was then the Rue du Beffroi (Belfry St.). Thirty years later Montaigne is reminded of it by another great one in Levanella, near Florence, considered the best in Tuscany, and where "they say the nobility of the region often gather there, as at Le More's in Paris or Guillot's in Amiens" (see the North Point ed. of the *Travel Journal*, p. 116 and Levanella, May 1, 1581; and my translation, Stanford University Press's *The Complete Works* [1957], p. 980.) But he made no such comment about any inn in Florence on either of two brief visits there on the same trip.

2. " . . . abondance de farce magistrale": farce may of course also mean "farce."

3. " . . . saffrettes, blondelettes, doulcettes et de bonne grâce."

4. "Clerice, esclaire icy." This jest, involving two homonyms in the usual pronunciation of Latin in R's time, is a favorite of R's, as we shall shortly see.

5. The term means extravagant and of course alludes to the Extravagantes.

6. "O séraphicque Sixiesme!" and a few lines below "O chérubicques Clémentines!" Books 6–7 of the Decretals; see above 4.48, note 6.

7. "Ceste farce me a desbondé le boyau cullier." This farce is probably "stuffing," not "farce"; cf., note 2 above.

8. " . . . contentement certain en toutes vos affections!"

4.52: CONTINUATION OF THE MIRACLES.

1. "Voicy," dist Panurge, "qui dict d'orgues."

2. Presumably Robert Irland, professor of law at Poitiers from 1502 to 1561. The title R gives him parodies those given to Thomas Aquinas, Duns Scotus, and other notable clerics.

3. The French quatrain, an excremental adaptation of Catullus, *Carmina* 23 *Ad Furium* vss. 20–23. The French is this:

> En tout un an tu ne chie dix crottes,
> Et, si des mains tu les brises et frottes,
> Jà n'en pourras ton doigt souiller de erres [with traces]
> Car dures sont plus que febves et pierres.

4. "Inian," a popular, corrupt shortening of French Saint Jean.

5. " . . . le paouvre trou de mon clous bruneau en feut tout déhinguandé."

6. The cult of *latria:* veneration in worship reserved for God.

7. The cult of *hyperdulia:* veneration owed to the Virgin Mary. The following, Panormitanus, is a reference to Nicola Tedesco (b. 1386), Sicilian prelate and revered authority as professor of canon law, whose service as bishop of Palermo (once known as Panormus) led to his surname Panormitanus.

8. Jean Chouart, a popular nickname suggestive of both cupidity and lechery. Chouart is the name of the male owl.

9. Saint-Olary is the name of an abbey in Montpellier noted for its parchments.

10. "... pour en faire des vélins pour batre l'or." Gold-beaters used to place sheets of parchment between their sheets of gold.

11. "... drogues, guoges et senogues": laxatives.

12. A liturgical veil, shroud, or hood. What follows depends on a pun with *poêle,* a pan such as is used for roasting chestnuts.

13. "Sur le patron d'une verdugualle tailloit une barbutte."

14. Gascon for *Foi d'or* "Faith of Gold!" thus possibly a sort of euphemism in French.

15. "... comme prest à roussiner ou baudouiner pour le moins."

16. The name of a medieval figure representing Need, and thus ever ready to jump on any but the rich; also of course the Latin name of the "rabid Putherbeus," R's bitter enemy and censor Gabriel Dupuyherbault; see above, 4.32 and our Introduction to this volume.

17. "... dist Epistémon retournant de ses affaires": i.e., having paid a successful visit to the close-stool.

18. "... le blanc seul estre en sceureté du traict."

19. "... les papiers du procès de Pouillac." This village is near Jonzac in Charente-Maritime; the case is unknown to us.

20. An undetermined placename, probably fantasy, seen above as an abode of usurpers (3.3) and of clerics and mole-catchers (4.P).

21. Doué-la-Fontaine, about 30 miles from Chinon. In 3.3 R alludes to a *diablerie* (deviltry or devil-play) there; but we know nothing about it or any passion play there.

22. As in chap. 51, note 4 above: "Clerice, esclaire icy ... "

23. Depuis que Décretz eurent ales [Ailes, Latin alae],

> Et gens d'armes portèrent males,
> Moines allèrent à cheval,
> En ce monde abonda tout mal.

This quatrain first appeared in Pierre Grosnet Proverbs (1536), then in R's probable source, Bonaventure Des Périers *Nouvelles Récréations* (*Novel Pastimes*), no. 67 (published later but presumably known to R before DP died in 1544); then Henri Estienne, *Apologie ... pour Hérodotus,* chap. 39, in 1566.

4.53: HOW BY VIRTUE OF THE DECRETALS GOLD IS SUBTLY DRAWN FROM FRANCE INTO ROME.

1. "Comment par la vertus des Décrétales, est l'or subtilement tiré de France en Rome."

2. These works are taken from the *Extravagantes, Decretals,* and *the Clementines*; they forbade the piling up of benefices, discussed such subjects as dispenses, mandates, the eating habits of religous etc., all of which brought much money into Rome.

3. The term *decretalictones* is defined in BD 248: "murderers of the Decretals. It's a monstrous word, composed of one Latin word and one Greek word."

4. "Prenez-moi un Décrétiste": an expert on Gratien's honorable *Decretum*. A Decretalist is of course an authority on, or strong admirer of, the Decretals.

5. This, "O le gros rat!" has several possible meanings, any or all of which R may well have had in mind here: the literal "a fat rat" (as Frère Jean reads it); or as we render it; or finally a pun on the homonym *raz* "tonsured," hence, a monk.

6. "... les mescréans Turcs, Juifz": in the literal sense of unbelievers. Conversion was at least an avowed intention of the Crusades.

7. *Vivat!* is of course "Long live!" The others are similar alien deformations: *fifat* Germanic, Landsknecht style; *bibat* Gascon, confusing V's and B's; and *pipat* (from French piper, "to cheat" in the sense of "Let him cheat!" Their torrential outpouring marks Homenaz's frenzied enthusiasm for his Decretals, all they bring him, and all their sectarians.

4.54: HOW GROSBEAK GAVE PANTAGRUEL SOME GOOD-CHRISTIAN PEARS.

1. "Comment Homenaz donna à Pantagruel des poires de bon Christian." The repeated suggestion in this chapter that Homenaz and his Papimaniac flock are all the best of Christians is puzzling, for here as elsewhere he is clearly an object of ridicule and perhaps contempt. Yet here they are explicitly proclaimed to be good Christians; even Pantagruel calls them the best he has ever seen. I think it must be basically ironic, perhaps in U.S. terms a bit like calling Roy Cohn a 100 percent American in Joseph McCarthy's heyday, or Agnew and the Watergate "Plumbers" under Nixon. In R's day "good Catholic" was defined by a Church led by a bellicose pope and counseled in matters of dogma by the Sorbonne, legislated largely by the anti-Reformist Council of Chesil (Fools) that we know as Trent. I think much of this is the full context of these surprising pieces of the highest praise. I am convinced there is much more to this than this sketch can even suggest; but I think that is about it in outline.

2. "... la terre Sphragitide": i.e., with a seal, the stamp showing it comes from Lemnos (q.v.). It is a clay used for plasters in medicine and for paints.

3. "... poires de bon Christian" again: and this time it is Pantagruel who christens them thus.

4. "... car vous leurs feriez la follie aux guarsons."

5. "... je vous congnoys à vostre nez et si ne vous avoys oncques veu."

6. "If you won't give, lend, we beg you." Of all this, *Quaesumus* alone is in the breviary.

7. "... tout de doubles escuz au sabot": fictive fantasy coins based on the many divers distinguishing marks of crown coins (sun, rose, cross, etc.); the clog is of course one mark of the monk; cf., 5.26–27, 74–84, passim.

4.55: HOW ON THE HIGH SEAS PANTAGRUEL HEARD SOME UNFROZEN WORDS.

1. "... et à pleines aureilles humions l'air comme belles huytres en escalle." The comparison seems visual, not auditory.

2. According to Dion Cassius A.D. 150–235, *Roman History* 77.17, the Emperor Antoninus Caracalla had a huge police force including secret police and spies.

3. *Ventre bieu!*: euphemism for *Ventre de Dieu!* "God's belly!"

4. "... je diz à voiles et à rames." Erasmus *Apophthegmata* 5.2, following Plutarch. The Roman proverb "with sails and oars" is quoted by Erasmus in *Adages* 1.4.19.

5. "Pour tant n'hazardons rien à ce que ne soyons nazardez": literally, "let's not risk anything so we don't get a flick on the nose!"

6. Plutarch, in *Of the cessation of oracles,* says that Petron believed in a triangular universe containing 186 worlds; see above 3.3.

7. As usual in R, in the Platonic sense of archetypes, the true eternal realities.

8. "... les Exemplaires et protraictz de toutes choses passées et futures; autour d'icelles estre le Siècle."

9. "... comme tomba la rousée sus la toizon de Gédéon": Judges 6.37–40.

10. "... et par conséquent animées": Fragment 151a.

11. "... à peine estre d'iceulx entendu lorsque estoient vieulx devenuz": according to Plutarch *De profectibus in virtute* 15.

12. "Reguardons si les voirons cy autour": for this, the standard myth of the murder of Orpheus, see Virgil *Georgics* 4.523 ff.; and especially Ovid *Metamorphoses* 11.50 ff.

4.56: HOW AMONG THE FROZEN WORDS PANTAGRUEL FOUND SOME LUSTY JESTS.

1. "Comment entre les parolles gelées Pantagruel trouva des motz de gueule." Much of the wordplay in this chapter hinges on the polysemism of the French word *mot*. Normally meaning simply "word," it can also mean a jest or a joke, as in the expression *bon mot*. The word *paroles* in the title also means "word," but usually the spoken word, whereas a *mot* may be either spoken or written. Since *gueule* may mean either "throat" or "mug" or the heraldic color red (gules), that will lead, a little later, into the listing of colors of words. Late in the chapter we shall learn of *paroles gelées* that thaw out into sounds other than words: clarion notes, neighing of horses, clash of arms, other battle sounds, etc.

2. A Scythian people mentioned by Pliny (*Natural History* 7.2) and Herodotus (*History* 5.27), who says that their name meant "one-eyed." "Nephelibates" (Greek) means those who travel on clouds. Saulnier has suggested that the -Arimaspians may represent for R the Lutherans and Papists in "Le silence de Rabelais et le mythe des paroles gelées," in *François Rabelais,* 1553–1953

(Geneva: Travaux d'Humanisme et Renaissance, 1953), p. 239; this is so for complicated reasons that include the unending recurrence of their wars.

3. "Nous y veismes des motz de gueule, des motz de sinople, des motz de azur, des motz de sable, des motz dorez."

4. "Pantagruel luy respondit que donner parolles estoit acte des amoureux."

5. "C'est acte de advocatz," respondit Pantagruel, "vendre parolles."

6. " . . . argentangine": R likes this story told by Plutarch, then Aulus Gellius, then Erasmus *Adages* 1.7.19; summed up in BD as follows: "quinsy of money." Thus Demosthenes was said to have this "money quinsy" because of his strategy in avoiding having to refuse a request of the Milesian ambassadors, from whom he had received much money: he wrapped his neck in heavy cloths and wool to simulate the quinsy (sore throat).

7. These were "paroles sanglantes," which came back to the sender "la guorge couppée."

8. The reader must of course imagine these sounds with a French pronunciation.

9. Peoples R regularly uses to epitomize barbarism.

10. "Puys en ouysmes d'aultres grosses": *parolles* again.

11. " . . . car il le vous print au mot sus l'instant qu'il ne s'en doubtoit mie." I still find it unclear what remark by Panurge had given offense to Frère Jean.

12. In the *Farce de Maistre Pathelin,* the draper sells the lawyer the cloth on Pathelin's word, i.e., promise to pay for it.

13. "Panurge luy feist la babou, en signe de dérision": this is placing a finger in one's cheek and making a popping noise.

4.57: How Pantagruel went ashore at the abode of Messere Gaster.

1. "Sir Belly": Italian plus Latin. R may have found the most gluttons in Italy.

2. Doyac, a great engineer who enabled the French artillery to cross the Alps, was wrongly credited with the supposedly impossible ascent, of the Aiguille (Needle) in the Vercors in the northern French Alps. The captain who did found chamois on top.

3. " . . . le vray Jardin et Paradis terrestre, de la situation duquel tant disputent et labourent les bons théologiens."

4. Persius (Aulus Persius Flaccus A.D. 34–62), Stoic satirist, in *Choliambi* 8 ff.

5. It is R (perhaps remembering Horace *Epistles* 2.2.51) who makes Lady Penia the mother of the Muses. She appears as goddess of poverty in Aristophanes, *Plutus.*

6. See Plutarch *Of Isis and Osiris* 68; Erasmus *Adages* 4.1.52. For more about the statue of Jupiter, see Plutarch, loc cit.

7. Fable of the stomach and the members of the body; cf., 3.3 above.

8. Held between 1431–1449, declared a heretical anticouncil; treated tough problems: Hussite movement; popes vs. councils; unifying East and West Church.

9. "... émerillons, oizeaux aguars, pérégrins, essors, rapineux, saulvaiges."

10. Wars of the Vascones (first century B.C.) against Sertorius: see Valerius Maximus 7.6.

11. All these tales of cannibalism come from Erasmus *Adages* 1.9.67, whose sources include Livy 21.2, for the Saguntines and Josephus *De bello judaico,* for the siege of Jerusalem by the Romans in A.D. 69.

4.58: HOW IN THE COURT OF THE INGENIOUS MASTER, PANTAGRUEL DETESTED THE ENGASTRIMYTHS AND THE GASTROLATERS.

1. "Comment en la court du maistre ingénieux Pantagruel détesta les Engastrimythes et les Gastrolâtres." BD defines the former as "ventriloquists" and the latter as "worshipers of the stomach."

2. For the expression "appariteurs," see "apparatchik" today.

3. R draws most of his material on diviners from Coelius Rhodiginus *Antiquae lectiones* (1517) 5.10 (see also 8.10); some also from Plato *Sophist* 252c, and Plutarch *On the cessation of oracles* 9.

4. By Gratian (fl. ca. 1140). Italian scholar monk, founder of science of canon law, as respected by humanists as Decretalists were despised. The *Decretum* was his summa.

5. BD calls them "divining through the chest." The Sophocles comment is from a fragment cited by Plato *Sophist* 252c.

6. Unrelated to Coelius Rhodiginus except that also native of Rovigo; already cited (3.25) by Her Trippa as an Engastrimyth practicing gastromancy, as is related here in the text at length.

7. Homer, not Hesiod (*Iliad* 18.104, Achilles in self-reproach for the death of his dear friend Patroclus) is a favorite of R's, especially for monks.

8. From Erasmus *Adages* 5.2.20, "Conchas legere," citing Pliny 9.52.

9. So called here for their varicolored habits, seen as resembling seashells.

10. "... cestuy mon ventre, le plus grand de tous les Dieux": Euripides *Cyclops* 335.

4.59: OF THE RIDICULOUS STATUE CALLED MANDUCE.

1. Approximate imperative of Latin *manduco,* "eat, gorge."

2. Belly-potent.

3. Having big gullets.

4. *Rudens* 2.6.67. Here again R's source is Coelius Rhodiginus.

5. *Satires* 3.174.

6. The dragon Saint Clement had drowned in the river Seille, an event celebrated yearly in Metz. Saint Clement (Pope Clement I) was pope from A.D. 88 to 97. Now known as the *Graulli* or *Graouilli,* it was led in Metz in the processions for Saint Mark (April 25) or on Rogation Days.

7. Drunkards singing Bacchic drinking songs called *croepalocomes* and *epaenons.*

8. "Pain mollet."

9. A polysemous term: a stew of divers kinds, a flavored rice dish, etc.

10. A kind of hash; also the name of Panurge's seigniory (chastellenie) given him in 3.2.

11. "Breuvaige éternel parmy, précédent le bon et friant vin blanc, suyvant vin clairet et vermeil frays." The French might mean that either wine came first. Note that in R's day claret (clairet) was, according to Cotgrave: "commonly made of white and red grapes mingled or growing together."

12. An Angevin and Provençal pastry named for a term for a woman's breast.

4.60: How on the interlarded fast-days, the Gastrolaters sacrifice to their god.

1. Half fast-days and half free. These fast-days allowed certain specified exemptions from dietary rules.

2. *Vielles*: QL and LI combine to make this a Breton name for a large marine tench; Cotgrave calls these "Poules de mer," and calls this "a small-mouthed sharp-toothed, broad-scaled, little-eyed rock-fish," which he says is transparent and covered with varicolored beautiful spots.

3. A Mediterranean molusc called the crepidulam.

4. Stockfish: haddock, or most often cod, dried hard in the open air to preserve it without salting. For all the centuries before refrigeration much used because the only fish available, and eternal salt meats wearying at last.

5. An unexplained (in the context, probably rough) way of cooking eggs, but not one of the others listed. Urquhart offers both "bedaten" and "buttered"; Cohen opts for "buttered."

6. "Neige de beurre"; Urquhart does not give it; Cohen "whipped cream"; I find no clue to what R meant in dictionaries, recent cookbooks, or anywhere I have looked.

7. *Lasanophore*: bearer (hence emptier) of the chamber pot, *lasanon* in BD: Lazanon.

4.61: How Gaster invented the methods of getting and preserving grain.

1. ". . . l'art fabrile" (Latin *fabrilis*): that of the worker with metal, wood, or stone, the artificer, whose work is manufacture.

2. Spring or fountain, "la fontaine Agrie." Pausanias, who relates this (8.38), calls the spring Agno.

3. Troezen was in the Argolid, Peloponnesus, Greece. The inhabitants used to bury a white rooster in a procession after carrying it around their territory, which they held protected them from excessive winds. See Pausanias again, then Nicolas Leonicenus *Varia historia* 1.67.

4. This was proverbial. See Conti *Mythology* 7.7.

5. Vitruvius Pollio, eminent and influential Roman architect, saw military service (ca. 50–26 B.C.) under Julius Caesar and Augustus, and wrote his

ten-book treatise *De architectura,* dealing not only with that but all aspects of building, extending this to water-supply, water-clocks, and sundials, and from construction to decoration. His work was in the Renaissance the main, almost unquestioned, authority in all such matters.

6. The Greatest (Greek *Megistos*), here Francis I. R calls him "grand architecte du roy Mégiste."

7. A kind of small cannon.

8. An Indian people living near the Ganges whom the gods protected in war by thunder and lightning. See Philostratus A.D. third century *Life of Apollonius* of Tyana 2.33.

4.62: HOW GASTER INVENTED AN ART AND MEANS NOT TO BE WOUNDED OR TOUCHED BY CANNON SHOTS.

1. BD defines Titanic force as that "of giants."

2. Here we render French *non* "no" by "not only" for two main reasons. First, the "no" makes no sense, indeed contradicts the sense expected by the context; and some editors ignore it (G, QL), or write it off as a typo. However, Demerson in LI explains that it must mean "non seulement"; and I agree, the more so because of my second reason. The incomplete statement left here by this reading should be completed, by reading the *Mais* "But" near the end of that chapter (4.62) as meaning "But also," which is suggested by the LI reading but by no other I know of. It is a long wait for a completion, but worth it, since it restores badly needed sense to the account, at these two critical points. For Plutarch's report, see *De sera vindicata* 14 and *Quaestiones conviviales* "Table Talk" 2.1.

3. A puzzler: the French *Fronton* suggests the third century rhetor Fronton of Emesa, who seems no fit or a bad one; a likelier candidate is Sextus Julius Frontinus (A.D. 40–103), author of a book on *Stratagems,* but he does not speak of this remarkable stunt.

4. A small piece of artillery, as has been noted before.

5. Like much of this chapter, borrowed from Pliny *Natural History;* here 36.25.

6. Note that the French word here for magnet, *aymant,* bears no resemblance to the proper name Magnes or the region Magnesia.

7. "Pour éviter vacuité." I cannot trace or explain R's theories here about explosives and gunnnery.

8. *Mais:* see above, this chapter, note 2.

9. Most of R's stories here about magical powers (remore, dittany, etc.) come from Pliny *Natural History,* esp. 2.46; 8.51; 9.41; 10.20; 13.64; 15.40; 16.79; 26.9; 36.25.

10. "... lesquelz ilz ont accoustumé industrieusement faire et caver dedans le tronc des fortes arbres."

11. "... soubdain les flèches sortent hors et ne leurs en reste mal aulcun."

12. "... est la fouldre détournée, et jamais ne les férit."

13. "... les taureaux furieux et forcenez approchans des figuiers saulvaiges."

14. " . . . se apprivoisent et restent comme grampes et immobiles."
15. " . . . la furie des vipères expire par l'attouchement d'un rameau de fouteau."
16. " . . . à la seule voix desquelles la terre fondoit en chasmates et en abysme."
17. "Comme, quand il a esté dict que la statue de Mercure ne doibt estre faicte de tous boys indifféremment, ilz l'exposent que Dieu ne se doibt estre adoré en façon vulgaire, mais en façon esleue et religieuse."

4.63: How Pantagruel took a nap.

1. "Comment, près de l'isle de Chaneph, Pantagruel sommeilloit et les problèmes propousez à son réveil." *Chaneph*, a Hebrew word, means "hypocrisy."
2. " . . . quoyqu'on eust ès voiles adjoinct les bonnettes trainneresses."
3. "Et restions tous pensifz, matagrabolisez, sesolfiez et faschez, sans mot dire les uns aux aultres."
4. No doubt the Greek original of his popular romance, whose French version by Jacque Amyot *L'histoire Aethiopique de Heliodorus* (1548; we call it *Theagenes and Chariclea* as a rule in English), was a bestseller.
5. " . . . que trop mieulx par livre dormoit que par coeur": a play on "knowing by the book" and "knowing by heart."
6. "Ponocrates resvant, resvoit": the point of this Lapalissade escapes me, and I find no help in earlier editors or commentators.
7. Or, worming out their secrets: "Nostre pilot tiroit les vers du nez à ses matelotz."
8. "Manière de haulser le temps en calme?"
9. "Remède contre les oscitations et baislements?"
10. "Xenomanes, comme tout lanterné à l'accoustrement de sa lanterne."
11. " . . . que après avoir repeu, tant l'homme que le serpent?" This theory is of course from Pliny 7.2 and 28.4, as are most of the tall stories in this chapter. Aristotle had treated such matters in his *History of Animals* 8.29.
12. " . . . de l'homme jeun vénéneuse à tous serpens et animaulx vénéneux?": Pliny 28.7.
13. The inhabitants of Gabies, in Latium. Livy tells the story in his *History* 1.54.

4.64: How no answer was given by Pantagruel.

1. "Quelz gens habitent en ceste belle isle de chien?"
2. Compulsive mumblers of rote prayers such as the paternoster (the Lord's prayer).
3. The Council of Fools: R's term for the Council of Trent; see above, this book, chap. 18.
4. Beelzebub (Hebrew Ba'al zebub, Lord of Flies), is the Devil, or, as in *Paradise Lost,* a leading devil, Satan's chief assistant devil. Astaroth or

Astarte, the Phoenician goddess of fertility (R's Astarotz), had often appeared as a lesser devil in medieval mystery plays.

5. "De jeune hermite, vieil Diable. Notez ce proverbe autenticque."

6. R calls it Les *Prédicantes* (*Women at the Assembly*), vs. 652, quoted by Erasmus *Adages* 3.4.70.

7. ". . . il n'est horloge plus juste que le ventre." Again see Erasmus, loc. cit.

8. Lever à cinq, dipner à neuf,
   Soupper à cinq, coucher à neuf.

The well-known traditional sequel to the couplet was "Font vivre d'ans nonante neuf" (Make a man live ninety-nine years); *nonante* is an old term, now dialectal, for "ninety" and still is found in some regional French usages.

9. "Aspicz," one of many words for asps in the lengthy list that follows, which seems one of R's many encyclopedic digressions amusing to his readers in the 1550s but which have not worn well for most readers today. The list is copied from the Latin *Canon of Avicenna,* of which a new edition had appeared in 1527.

4.65: How Pantagruel enjoys his time.

1. "Comment Pantagruel haulse le temps avecques ses domesticques." Throughout this chapter, much wordplay depends on the diverse meanings of "hausser le temps": enjoy the time, liven up the time, raise a breeze (the weather), etc. Our renderings have been guided by the contexts.

2. "Dis-tu mal des femmes," respondit Panurge, "ho guodelureau, moine culpelé?"

3. "Euripides escript, et le prononce Andromache": in *Andromache* vss. 269–273.

4. "Remède . . . n'a esté trouvé contre la male femme."

5. ". . . comme luy reproche Aristophanes." Byzantine scholar, author of a *Life of Euripides,* this detail comes from the *Adages* of Erasmus 1.7.74.

6. "Qui ha, si parle": this is the name of a card game, one of Gargantua's: see above, 1.22.

7. "Je suys guay comme un papeguay."

8. Furieux est, de bon sens ne jouist,
   Quiconques boyt et ne s'en resjouist.

The French couplet is a version of Euripides *Cyclops* vs. 168.

9. Another meaning, frequent in this chapter, of "haulser le temps."

10. Yet again: "s'est pareillement le temps haulsé."

11. "Ainsi le haulsèrent Athlas et Hercules": Lucian *Caron* 4.

12. Le mal temps passe et retourne le bon,
    Pendent qu'on trinque autour de gras jambon.

13. ". . . sçavoir est vuidants les victuailles." Aesop is said to have chosen a load of provisions as his share for a trip, knowing that each meal would leave it lighter, as indeed happened, until at last he had no burden left.

14. From Pausanias *Laconca* 19.6. Amycleans was a village located next to Sparta.

4.66: How, near the island of Ganabin, at Pantagruel's commandment the Muses were saluted.

1. "Comment près l'isle de Ganabin, au commandement de Pantagruel, feurent les Muses saluées." BD: "Ganabin: thieves, Hebrew."

2. The lake near Cumae in Campania, not far from Naples and by extension the cave near it through which Aeneas went down into the world below (*Aeneid* 6.272 ff.). The name is usually traced to Greek *Aornos,* supposedly meaning "birdless, without birds," because of the foul fumes emanating from it, a feature noted by Virgil.

3. In 1548 the Bordelais revolted against the salt tax; but the revolt was crushed and harshly punished by Montmorency for the king, and the bells confiscated.

4. "Tirons vie de long. Hau! Plus oultre!"

5. "...pour saluer les Muses de cestuy mons Antiparnasse." Much like Parnassus in appearance, as noted earlier, but its opposite or much worse in its nefarious influence.

4.67: How Panurge beshat himself in panic fear.

1. Rodilardus seems a misnomer for a cat, since it suggests "bacon-nibbler," which better fits a mouse, which a cat would rather nibble; but it names a rat in R's apparent source, a neo-Latin mock epic imitation by Calenzio of the famous *Batrachomuomachia* (*Battle of the Frogs and the Mice*) often attributed to Homer.

2. "Comment Panurge par male paour se conchia et du grand chat Rodilardus pensoit que feust un Diableteau."

3. BD: "ambrosia: food for the gods," and "Stygian: of or relative to the Styx."

4. Inchkeith, in the Gulf of Forth opposite Edinburgh, also known as the Isle of Horses, taken earlier by the English, was recaptured on July 5, 1548 by the French troops led by the Landgraf of Hesse, who was succeeded soon after by Paule, seigneur de Thermes.

5. This Vinet, otherwise unknown to us, was probably an innkeeper whose hospitality R thought well of and may at times have enjoyed on his trips to and from Italy.

6. "Since I left Rome I haven't had a bowel movement. Please take this pitchfork in hand and give me a scare."

7. "If you don't do it some other way, you're doing nothing. So please try to go about it more lustily."

8. "Feste Dieu Bayart!": favorite oath of the great French paladin and leader Pierre Terrail, seigneur de Bayard (1476–1524).

9. "I thank you, fair Sir. By doing this you've spared me the cost of a suppository."

10. "Estant à ses affaires." This story, one of myriad about Villon's last years, had been told two centuries earlier about a juggler named "Hugues le Noir" (Black Hugh or Hugh Black). François Villon (b. 1431) was banished from Paris in 1463 and thenceforth is lost to our sight. Edward V of England (1470–1483) reigned only a few months before his uncle the duke of Gloucester had him assassinated.

11. *Fundament* for once here means just "bottom, rump."

12. Sometimes called Villon's Epitaph for Villon, this quatrain runs thus:

>Ne suys-je badault de Paris,
>De Paris, diz-je, auprès Pontoise?
>Et d'une chorde d'une toise
>Sçaura mon coul que mon cul poise.

13. From June 24 (Midsummer Day or Saint John's Day) to November 1.

14. *Scybale* in BD: "hardened turd." *Spyrathe*; BD: "turd of a sheep or ewe or nannygoat."

15. Saffron: a flower and the powder from it, prized as a dye (yellow) and as a perfume base and as a medicament, widely grown and used. Why Hibernian here is not clear.

16. *Sela* in BD: "certainly, Hebrew."

4.BD: BRIEF DECLARATION OF SOME OF THE MORE OBSCURE TERMS CONTAINED IN THE FOURTH BOOK OF THE HEROIC DEEDS AND SAYINGS OF PANTAGRUEL.

1. The word declaration here, like its Latin etymon, means "clarification" as well as the usual "announcement." This curious document, which appeared only in a few later copies of the completed 1552 Book 4, has long been suspect for many reasons—curious publication record, definitions, and spellings, and other apparent incompatibilities and inconsistencies with the 1552 Book 4 and other texts by R; but French editors even the most scholarly ones today (PL, G, QL, and LI) all include it, often with little or no comment on its uncertain authenticity. Most recent intensive study has found it suspect or even spurious as a work of R's: from R. Arveillier's "La *Brief Declaration* est-elle de Rabelais?" (*ER* 5 [1964] 9–10) to André Tournon's "La Brief Declaration n'est pas de Rabelais" (*ER* 13 [1976] 133–138); and M. A. Screech in 1979, in his magisterial *Rabelais* (p. 369) clearly implied that someone else compiled it. However, in 1981 Mireille Huchon showed serious flaws in Arveillier's and Tournon's negative arguments and concluded, from her exhaustive grammatical study, that it was a vade mecum that R offered to help the reader follow his linguistic experiments, composed between his completing the 1552 Book 4 and his thorough revision of Book 3 "on the basis of the ancient censure," as its title page proclaims (Huchon "Rabelais grammarien," *ER* 16 [1981] 406–411, 491–

495); and as I write this in 1990 her grounds and arguments are still standing strong.

Seeking maximum fullness in minimal space, we present these definitions in this way: Since the French form often differs between text and BD, wherever the differences seem significant we offer both forms; and we offer the English version as well wherever it differs from the French.

2. This is of course the "Liminary Epistle" to Odet, Cardinal de Chastillon.

3. R had used this term to praise his hero Erasmus in his 1532 letter to him, 6.7.

4. The definitive complete Prologue of 1552. The reader will do well to be wary of these (often incorrect) notations purporting to locate terms: absent from the earliest editions, these were added by later editors.

5. This notation, misread by some editors as a puzzling "Biffo," is identified by Demerson in LI as "Bisso," meaning Nicolas Bischof of Basel (d. 1563), a humanist printer and friend of Erasmus.

6. A puzzling boner (five years instead of four) for either R or another apparent Hellenist.

7. From Latin *dodrans, dodrantis* "nine-twelfths of anything," hence nine inches (nine-twelfths of a foot).

8. Even in R's age of zealous Hellenists and subjective etymologies, this one seems surprising, since Pantoufle (pantophle), now traced to Italian *pantofola* "slipper," is found in French from 1465 on; but as Mireille Huchon notes ("R grammairien"), in this R is following the illustrious Hellenist Guillaume Budé.

9. From *boisseau* "bushel or one-bushel container," by way of *boisselier* "bushel-maker" or "cooper," a maker of wooden bushel kegs or tubs.

10. As Oukalegon, a Trojan elder and adviser to King Priam (*Iliad* 3.148). The Greek name does indeed mean "uncaring, heedless." Virgil (*Aeneid* 2.425) notes the burning of Ucalegon's palace as the Greeks are burning down Troy.

11. The Latin etymon suggests this definition, very common in R's day, but limiting the meaning of the term far more than those in modern French or English.

12. Another baffling boner (upsilon for eta) in an author who seems to know some Greek.

13. A curious definition for Oedipus, fitting him only in *Oedipus at Colonus,* and that rather loosely.

14. From Greek *hupo (hypo),* "under or beneath," and *anemos,* "wind."

15. *On the meaning of EI.*

16. From Greek *somata,* "bodies, members."

17. I find no mention of Rimano in any atlas or commentator of the many I have consulted.

BOOK 5

Introductory Note on Book 5: Authentic or Inauthentic?

As noted already above, several items included in our volume may well be spurious: the *Brief Declaration* Book 4 and two of R's spoofs of the best-selling books of divination, his *Almanac for 1541,* and his *Great new true prognostication for 1544* (our items 6.17 and 6.19). But these are minor: the one major doubtful item is Book 5 of his tale *Gargantua and Pantagruel.* It has been suspect from the first, but most editors, by their almost tacit acceptance of it in including it as part of his tale, have lent it more authority and respectability than it may deserve; and like the camel in the proverb, it has wriggled its way into the text. Few critics today accept it unreservedly, but few flatly and utterly reject it as bearing no trace of R's own hand and work.

A dozen years ago I wrote of it that I found most judgments ultimately subjective, and I leaned to the view that parts at least are mainly if not wholly by R; but I was sorry to learn that the two men I think the best authorities, Michael Screech and Gérard Defaux, agreed with Alfred Glauser in finding it spurious. A rereading of Glauser after translating much of the book and finding many parts dull has brought me to the negative view but not to the polar negative that I find in him and implicitly in Screech's total ignoring of it as even a problem.

Book 4 so obviously leaves R's story dangling that I am convinced he must have left, when he died in 1553, some notes or other such indications of his further intent; and I am taken with Mireille Huchon's richly supported theories about this, especially that of his leaving rough drafts or *brouillons* of such episodes. Such, I think, may include the Ringing Island (chaps. 1–8), the Furred Cats (11–15), and the Semiquaver Friars (27–28). And now that Richard Berrong has shown that what may seem excessive angelism in the dominance of Bacbuc in the final chapters is nicely undercut by the crude eroticism of the Bacchic rhyming in chapter 46, so that even though Bacbuc has the last word in 47, Dionysius is not forgotten at the end; this sharpened awareness of the variety found in the conclusion leaves me satisfied with that too, as an ending I think R might have considered—at least after many more books of the tale than his life span was to allow him—and us his readers.

The main arguments against acceptance en bloc as authentic are in my judgment three: (1) the nine years between R's death and the appearance of any part of Book 5; (2) the clear differences between the three texts we have for chaps. 1–16, and between the two texts we have for the remainder; and (3) the large amounts of flatly borrowed material (descriptions of the temple from Colonna's "Dream Battle of Polyphile") and dull material (passim). Those arguments against total rejection as spurious are again three: (1) the lack of any other conclusion to R's tale, and the fact that this one meets the reader's expectations and seems to fit the story well; (2) the considerable resemblance of many episodes to others in Book 4; and most of all (3) the brilliance of many parts that raise the question whether anyone else in the 1550s seems capable of having totally conceived and executed them.

The more I ponder this vexed question, the closer I find myself, as before, to the view expressed by Thomas M. Greene in 1970 in his brilliant short introduction to R entitled *Rabelais: A Study in Comic Courage* (Englewood Cliffs, N.J.: Prentice-Hall, 1970, p. 102) that when he died R probably left some materials on where to go on from Book 4; that some time later some editor-compiler, after some adding and padding, "tried to shape them, clumsily and hurriedly, into a book." This view, as Greene noted, is hinted in the enigmatic couplet at the end. In short, I think we may see R's hand in the broad outline and, at least in rough draft, in several episodes; but I do not find it either clearly or largely authentic, and therefore do not consider it fully and truly R's book.

5: Prologue by M. François Rabelais

1. This prologue is an almost certainly spurious part of its dubious book. Only one of our three texts (see Demerson, p. 783) has it complete. The *Isle Sonnante* has no prologue; the manuscript has only a fragmentary version of it; and it is wholly unworthy of R, who, in the parts we know are his or his tale and elsewhere does not copy himself. This piece copies chunks of 3 Prologue, pieces of 4 Prologue, and odd other bits from R; also (adapted) parts from Joachim du Bellay's 1549 *Defense and Illustration of the French Language,* with the author pleading for a modest place, much like Aesop's earlier, for R in French letters.

2. " . . . je vous demande en demandant": copied from 4.27 and one of many.

3. " . . . le monde n'est plus fat." *Fat* means "foolish" or "stupid."

4. *Her der Tyflet*: a sort of German for *Herr der Teufel,* "Lord of the Devil."

5. An exorcism in Languedoc: "Behind me, Satan!" See Matthew 4.10.

6. Borrowed from the Library of Saint-Victor; see above, 2.7.

7. The French original of this seven-verse piece is the following:

   > L'an Jubilé, que tout le monde raire
   > Fadas se feist, est supernuméraire
   > Au dessus trente. O peu de révérence!
   > Fat il sembloit; mais en persévérance
   > De longs brevets, fat plus, ne gloux sera:
   > Car le doux fruict de l'herbe esgoussera,
   > Dont tant craignoit la fleur en prime vère.

8. *Scotine* is both a play on Greek *skoteinos* "shadowy, obscure," the standard epithet for the philosopher Heraclitus, and an adjective formed from (Duns) Scotus, and thus suggesting the obscurity of the "Subtle Doctor."

9. Thus dating this piece at 1550, presumably a ploy to argue authenticity.

10. This is the version of Ecclesiastes 1.15 given by Erasmus in T*he Praise of Folly* chap. 63; see Radice trans. in Penguin ed. (1871), pp. 187–188, text and notes.

11. Se Horace's *Satires* 2.6.63.

12. Borrowed also from Old Prologue to 4, last paragraph.

13. Pythagoras, according to a story in Lucian.

14. Renowned for his obscurity; cf., note 8 above.

15. Goose among swans: one of Erasmus's *Adages* 1.7.22.

16. Possibly Jacques Colin of Auxerre, reader to Francis I and translator of Castiglione's *Il Corteggiano* into French. Of the names that follow, Drouet is unknown; Masuel is probably Claude Massuau (q.v. Glossary); Saint-Gelais a popular court poet under Francis I; and R's friend Marot, the best poet of his time.

17. This is Queen Margaret of Navarre (q.v., Glossary), sister of Francis I, poet, dramatist, best remembered as a storyteller; R's dedicatee of Book 3.

18. Another copying from 3 Prologue; a Greek proverb shaped by Horace in *Epistles* 1.17.36, then repeated by Erasmus in *Adages* 1.4.1.

19. Another borrowing from 3 Prologue.

20. Taken verbatim from Joachim du Bellay's *Defense and Illustration*.

21. Belittled as a *riparographe* "painter of mean or squalid" subjects because he chose not to idealize all he treated. The author claims the same distinction.

5.1: How Pantagruel arrived on the Ringing Island.

1. "L'Isle Son(n)ante": subject of chaps. 1–8, subject and title of the first part of Book 5 to appear, chaps. 1–16, in 1562. Bells seem to have symbolized and epitomized for R the futile regimentation he found in monastic life. Note that Book 5 is begun and presented in no way as a continuation of 4.

2. "Jeusne des quatre temps." The church then prescribed not only the Lenten fast but also one of a few days to start each of the four seasons.

3. Palace or palate: the French word *palais* has both meanings.

4. " . . . icy le quatriesme doit estre pour le vin du valet."

5. " . . . en temps guerre et bizart": making this a dubious rule of the Church.

6. Plato *Phaedrus* 243c; then Erasmus *Adages* 4.7.92.

7. See Erasmus *Adages* 1.8.61.

5.2: How the Ringing Island was inhabited by Siticines.

1. Name not in *Isle Sonnante*. MS reads: *Abihen Camar,* roughly Hebrew for "Pagan Priest."

2. "Clergaux, Monagaux," etc., through "Papegaut." *Papegaut,* like *Papegai,* means "parrot" or "popinjay"; the *-gaux* endings are homophones of *Gots* "Goths"; also the singular forms, in *-al,* are thus much like many minor ecclesiastical titles.

3. *Cagots* means "hypocrites."

4. " . . . lesquels avoient honny et conchié toute l'Isle."

5. Or Stymphalian Birds, man-eating monsters living around Lake Stymphalus in Arcadia, which it was one labor of Hercules to destroy. They were sometimes confused in references with the Harpies, who were more repulsive but less dangerous.

6. Not in *Isle Sonnante*; a reminiscence of Erasmus *Praise of Folly* par. 54 (in Penguin Classics 1871 ed., p. 170), telling how Folly, at the exquisite idiocy

of the views expounded by one old dotard, says: "I nearly split my sides like the figwood Priapus who had the misfortune to witness the nocturnal rite of Canidia and Sagana."

5.3: HOW ON THE RINGING ISLAND THERE IS ONLY ONE POPEHAWK.

1. The so-called "Babylonian captivity" of the Papal See at Avignon (Vaucluse, France, 1309–1378), then the Great Schism (1378–1408) that saw antipopes there as well as the regular popes in Rome. If we count back from R's death in 1553, this date (for no reason known to us) would be 1323, during the papacy (1316–1334) of John XXII in Avignon.
2. The name may possibly be meant to suggest that of the explorer Canada Roberval.

5.4: HOW THE BIRDS OF THE RINGING ISLAND ARE ALL BIRDS OF PASSAGE.

1. Or, rose-pot (pot for roses: a French proverb for unearthing a secret).

5.5: HOW THE GOURMANDER BIRDS ARE MUTE.

1. Literally *gormandizers* a play on *commandeurs* and thus a crack at the myriad military religious orders—Malta, Rhodes, Templars, and Saints Anthony, Lazarus, James-of-the-sword, etc.
2. *Gotz*, another homonym of *-gaux* thus adds a type of Goths to the ugly list of repulsive birds.
3. A reference to "Honni soit qui mal y pense," motto of the Order of the Garter.
4. The collar of the French Order of Saint-Michel showed the saint slaying the dragon, who represented the Devil; hence here the Calumniator (*Diabolus* in Greek).
5. " . . . rien si cher ne précieux est que le temps; employons-le en bonnes oeuvres."

5.6: HOW THE BIRDS OF THE RINGING ISLAND ARE FED.

1. A lake so foul-smelling that it was a Roman proverb not to stir it up.
2. " . . . vous ne fustes onques de mauvaise pie couvez": proverb for good parents.
3. Seven years: Genesis 41.30–57.
4. Recalling Victor Brodeau's epigram "A deux frères Mineurs" ("To two Friars Minor") which R's friend Clément Marot published with his own works:

> Mes beaux pères religieux,
> Vous disnez pour un gramercy.
> O gens heureux, O demi dieux,
> Pleust à Dieu que je feusse ainsi.

[Fair brothers in religious ranks,
Of demigod felicity,
You get your dinner for your thanks.
Would that the same were true of me.]

5.7: How Panurge tells Aeditus the fable of the charger and the donkey.

1. *Roussin:* a strong horse often used for war, rarely for menial drudgery, here rendered sometimes as "Charger," sometimes as "Steed": a proud, nobile equine type.
2. "Monsieur le Roussin": note that the horse calls the donkey simply *baudet* and uses the *tu*; the donkey learns the respectful address, but uses the *vous* from the first.
3. This donkey sees Neptune, mythic creator of horses, as being also protector of donkeys.
4. " . . . un sien apoloigue": either "The Donkey and the Little Dog," or, more probably, "The Dog and his Master."
5. " . . . non la forche; je ne dis: 'qui me dit, passe sans flux.' " Our version aims to approximate the sense of this saying from a card game.
6. " . . . dains oiseaux": *daims* means "stags."
7. " . . . daine oiselle": close to *damoiselle* or "lady."

5.8: How Popehawk was shown us with great difficulty.

1. *Iliad* 5.845 (Lattimore: helmet of death); Erasmus *Adages* 2.10.74; it made the wearer invisible.
2. " . . . il semble une huppe": whose crest recalls a tiara in a way.
3. An unidentified Michel de Macon, possibly a bishop.
4. "Il y a, par Dieu, de la pipperie, fripperie, et ripperie tant et plus en ce manoir."
5. Here, as elsewhere, *heures* may mean canonical hours, or, times of his choosing.
6. This MS reading *mitre* seems likelier than the 1564 edition's *moitié*, "midriff."
7. " . . . troisième jour": *Isle Sonnante* gives the likelier reading *quatriesme* "fourth."
8. So Plutarch reports in his *Life of Artaxerxes.*
9. " . . . par Jupiter-pierre": Aulus Gellius says this was an ancient oath often used. Our author may be hinting at paganism in linking so closely Jupiter and Peter, the first bishop of Rome.

5.9: How we went ashore on the island of Ironware.

1. "Comment nous descendismes en L'Isle des Ferrements." The translation

of *ferrements* as "tools" (Urquhart and Cohen) is defective, since many items here are weapons, and some are kitchen utensils.

2. " . . . et s'engainoient là-dedans."
3. Plato *Philebus* and *Sophist* and Plutarch *Questiones naturales* 1.1.
4. "Furent-ils petis philosophes?"
5. " . . . je vis derrière je ne sçay quel buysson je ne sçay quelles gens, faisans je ne sçay quoy, et je ne sçay comment, aguisans je ne sçay quels ferremens, qu'ils avoient je ne sçay où, et ne sçay en quelle manière."

5.10: How Pantagruel arrived on Sharpers' Island

1. "Comment Pantagruel arriva en l'Isle de Cassade." Cassade means a "trick" or "act of cheating."
2. " . . . vraye Idée de Fontainebleau": notable for rough terrain.
3. The six stories represent the six dots or spots on a die, the top number.
4. Sometimes in some circles known as "snake-eyes."
5. The notoriously dangerous Gulf of Sidra (Surt) in the Mediterranean off Libya.
6. This old spelling *sang-vreal* (of modern Saint Graal) suggests a derivation favored by some, from royal blood (i.e., Christ's).
7. The tightly-guarded veil with which reportedly Saint Veronica wiped off the sweat from the brow of Christ on the Cross.
8. Here R mocks phony miracles, but why a coney (rabbit) here is beyond me.
9. This play on putting a good face on a bad hand (Bonne Mine femme de Mauvais Jeu) is proverbial and here taken from 4.5.

5.11: How we passed the Wicket, abode of Clutchpuss.

1. Play on *sergent* "sergeant": *serrargent* means "moneysqueezer."
2. The Paris Hall of Justice had a famous marble table.
3. By its sound, *pillers* meaning "pillars" suggests *pilleurs* "pillagers" and not by accident.
4. See Glossary under Quintessence; a Sixth Essence is still more fanciful, but here it explains the magic or sorcery by which the Furred Cats get away with all the wicked crimes they perpetrate.
5. In the upside-down world of the Furred Cats, the judges' fodder does not come down to them from above but rises to them from the pile of sacks on the registrar's table.
6. Suggesting low estate: they had come on foot, not by horse or carriage.
7. A play on *mortiers* "mortars": first as the mortarboard cap of the presiding judge, then, literally, as a hard bowl in which to grind plaster or the like with a pestle.
8. " . . . le pourtraict de justice Grippe-minaudière.
9. " . . . qui a chausses neuves [which can split], et court pourpoint."

5.12: How a riddle is propounded by Clutchpuss.

1. Clutchpuss's incessant refrain is "Or ça": either legal "Here now" or the greedy "Gold here." The ideal reader will try to keep both meanings in mind each time this comes.

2. Clutchpuss's riddle is in the form of this dizain:

> Une bien jeune et toute blondelette
> Conceut un fils Etyopien, sans père.
> Puis l'enfanta sans douleur, la tendrette,
> Quoyqu'il sortist comme faict la vipère:
> L'ayant rongé en mout grand vitupère
> Tout l'un des flancs, pour son impatience.
> Depuis passa mons et vaux en fiance,
> Par l'air volant, en terre cheminant:
> Tant qu'estonna l'amy de sapience,
> Qui l'estimoit estre humain animant.

3. " . . . comment veux-tu qu'il responde": note the contemptuous *tu* here.

4. "Pense-tu estre en la forest de l'Académie (Plato's school)?"

5. " . . . avec les ocieux veneurs et inquisiteurs de vérité?"

6. "Orça, on plume l'oye sans la faire crier."

7. " . . . orça tes fortes fièbvres quartaines, orça, qui te puissent espouser, orça."

8. " . . . ho, hu, ho, hou, je te prens pour hérétique."

5.13: How Panurge explains Clutchpuss's riddle.

1. Here is the French original of this bit of verse and appendage:

> Vous rongerez et mangerez, comme vipères,
> Les costez propres de vos mères,
> Or de par le diable-là.

2. The *espices* (lit. "spices"), expected gifts from litigants to judges, an old and dishonorable custom already then in France, and with a long life ahead of it.

3. " . . . et passez outre." In 5.16 *outre* will become a land they sail past, while still meaning basically to pass on or beyond (Latin *ultra*).

4. " . . . jamais n'est en oubly le vin, mais est mémorial en tout païs, et toutes saisons."

5.14: How the Furred Cats live on corruption.

1. " . . . à l'enseigne de la mangoire instablée au-dessus du ratelier!"

2. "Nous de présent les nommons mâche-levraux, mâche-perdrix, mâche-beccasses, mâche-faisans, mâche-poullets, mâche-chevreaux, mâche-connils, mâche-cochons; d'autres viandes ne sont alimentez."

3. " . . . l'année prochaine on les nommera mâche-estrons, mâche-foires, mâche-merdes."

5.15: HOW FRÈRE JEAN DES ENTOMMEURES DETERMINES TO SACK THE FURRED CATS.

1. "Je ne suis pas clerc, les clercs le disent."
2. Hercules performed his labors on orders from King Eurystheus of Argos; and the narrator says he would be readier to emulate Hercules in this if he too were under orders to.
3. In his full splendor as a god, in which his lightning consumed Semele, Bacchus's "first mother." Zeus rescued their unborn child from the ashes and hid him in his own thigh, from which later he was "born again," a second time.
4. In Hades, the judges of the souls of the dead.
5. Greek for oblivion: the river in Hades whose waters souls drank when about to be reincarnated, leaving them no memory of their previous life. In *Aeneid* 6.703 ff., Virgil presents Aeneas as watching this happen.
6. Meaning: "Let's talk this over and decide together," but suggestive of cryptic speech like that of Duns Scotus, the "Subtle Doctor": cf., above, Prologue, note 8.
7. ". . . or là, de par tous les diables-là."
8. ". . . tu parleras autre latin" i.e., you'll see the matter in a different light.
9. "Mais par leur injonction il nous convient outre passer."
10. ". . . présent un serrargent": a moneysqueezer; the word of course puns on *sergent* "sergeant."
11. I.e., 5 sous, since a franc was worth 20 sous, 12 francs would make 240 sous.
12. The geese of Pautilé (or Ponthille), a village not far from Chinon, were renowned for the quality and the quantity of their down.

5.16: HOW WE PASSED BEYOND.

1. Already noted is the play on using *Outre* "Beyond" as an island they pass.
2. ". . . enfiansailles, espousailles, velenailles, tondailles, mestivales."
3. ". . . beau mangeur de souppes Lionnoises."
4. A small town near Angoulême. The host was clearly no friend of fasting.
5. Undeservedly forgotten, but presumably attached to the Abbey in Castilliers, not far from Sanxay (Deux-Sèvres).
6. ". . . et que le dernier ped que feroit Sa paternité seroit un ped d'Abbé."

5.17: HOW WE RAN AGROUND.

1. This is chapter 5.17 in the 1564 edition, hence also in G and LI, our guiding edition of reference.
2. "Comment nostre nauf fut encarrée, et feusmes aidez d'aucuns voyagiers qui tenoient de la Quinte." La Quinte is, of course, Quintessence, the kingdom of Entelechy, visited in chapter 18.

3. "... du philosophe, qui commendoit soustenir et abstenir," which epitomizes the position of Epictetus and the Stoics.

4. In Brittany, Le Raz Saint-Mathieu, near the end of Finistère; see 4.25. Here we follow the MS; the 1564 ed. reads "Sainct-Maixant," which makes no sense.

5. "Plaute jamais n'en mentit disant le nombre de nos croix, c'est à dire afflictions, ennuits, fascheries, estre selon le nombre de nos valets." This citation, taken from Erasmus *Adages* 2.3.31, was attributed to Cato and is found in Seneca *Ep* 47.5 and not in Plautus.

6. "... qui est la partie plus dangereuse et mâle qui soit à un valet."

7. "En ay-je?" Taken from *Pathelin* and used in 4 Prologue.

8. *Algamana* means "amalgam," a mixture of mercury with another metal. *Elixo* (in the manuscript *elixir*) is another name for mercury.

9. "... laquelle dit Platon avoir par quelques nuicts ouye dormant." See 3.4 above.

10. Saumur, not in the Vienne like Chinon, is probably here because the word for salt water, *saumure,* a homophone, suggests it.

11. A comical term for alchemy. Geber was a famous eighth-century Sevillian alchemist.

5.18: How we reached the kingdom of Quint Essence.

1. *Entelechy* means "efficacious activity"; *endelechy,* "continuous duration."

2. Scots were reputed intellectually arrogant and fierce debaters.

3. A wordplay on *rebarbative* "repellent, surly," especially on French *rubarbatif.*

4. J. C. Scaliger (1484–1558), Italian philologist, physician, and Latinist, learned but arrogant; G. Bigot, humanist professor (Tübingen, Nîmes), author of a *Prelude to Christian Philosophy* dedicated to Langey; Fleury, a defender of Latin.

5.19: How the Quint Essence cured the sick by songs.

1. I.e., in the queen's fluent Quintessential, shining on your surfaces.

2. See Erasmus *Adages* 3.16.96.

3. Two Hebrew abstract terms precede and two follow: abstractions—truths, images, and then concepts, dreams; and after scholastic second intentions, Hebrew frightening visions, before returning (for dessert?) to familiar French expressions, antitheses, metempsychoses, transcendent prolepses (anticipations, prefigurations).

4. From Greek *Aigiochos* "Aegis-bearer"; see Conti 6.2; and for the skin that Zeus writes everything on, see Erasmus *Adages* 1.5.24, "Of facts older than the diphtera skin."

5. "... tellement qu'on la couvroit d'une coquille de noix." After Pliny, *Natural History* 7.21.

6. A topos in R's day traceable through Quintilian (*De institutione oratoriae* 10.1) to Cicero.
7. So Plutarch reports in his *Life of Lucullus* 41.

5.20: HOW THE QUEEN SPENT HER TIME AFTER DINNER.

1. Three forms of dropsy. Erasmus reports (*Adages* 1.9.29) that Tenes, ruler of Tenedos, posted a guard with an axe behind each sitting judge.
2. One of several ingenious but impossible activities of these officers. These and others more insane clearly prompted Swift's Academy of Projectors in Lagado (*Gulliver's Travels* 3.5).
3. "... seulement les rendant moyennes par trois mois."
4. "La bande des vieilles attendoit l'autre fournée": obviously in an erotic sense.
5. "... quant beauté faut à cul de bonne volonté." This is a reminiscence of Marot *Deuxième Epistre du Coq à l'Asne* 30.
6. In *The Heracleidae* 849–863.
7. Lucian *Dialogues of the Dead* 9.2.
8. From *Medea* of Euripides. See Conti *Mythology* 5.13.

5.21: HOW THE OFFICERS OF THE QUINT OPERATE DIVERSELY.

1. Here begins the first explanation of how narrator M. Alcofribas Nasier got his title "Abstractor of Quintessence," used by R in presenting him in Books 1–2, then later elsewhere. Evidently his entire party share that title with him.
2. As these occupations get wackier, Swift derives more and more for his works. One or two are from the description of Fastilent in 4.32 and passim. Many may be inspired by the *Adages* of Erasmus, which includes many as examples of well-meaning idiocy.
3. "... et luy changeoient substance." One of many of these activities recalled later by Jonathan Swift in those of the projectors in his Grand Academy of Lagado (*Gulliver's Travels* 3.4), where Gulliver also confesses that "I had myself been a sort of projector in my younger days." See note 2 above, chapter 20.
4. "... haulsoient le temps": another borrowing from R. See 4.63 and 4.65.
5. This point, used by Aristophanes to ridicule Socrates (*Clouds* 144 ff.) is used later by Cicero to praise him; see *Tusculans* 5.4. R often cites Aristophanes, but as "Quintessential" only in this chapter, where of course this epithet befits him best.
6. "... chose estrange ne leur sembloit estre deux contradictoires vrayes en mode, en forme, en figure, et en temps."

5.22: HOW THE QUEEN WAS SERVED AT SUPPER.

1. A polite way of speaking of loss of perspiration.
2. Pliny tells this story in his *Natural History* 33.47.
3. " . . . et les pastez en paste estoient pastez en pot": a feeble gag or perhaps a big puzzle.

5.23: HOW, IN THE PRESENCE OF THE QUINT, WAS PERFORMED A JOYOUS BALL.

1. "Comment fut, en présence de la Quinte, faict un bal joyeux en forme de tournay." A chess game pageant follows.
2. We have chosen to follow the French nomenclature (giving the normal English equivalents of their terms) rather than converting all this to the English terms. Of the pieces (chessmen), kings, queens, and knights are labeled alike in both languages. Their nymphs are our pawns; their archers our bishops; and their guardians of the castle, our castles or rooks. Their polite forms for "check" and "checkmate" are noted as they appear. Also noted below are some errors by the author (or his likely source Colonna) in descriptions of the pieces' moves. Such ballets, mostly inspired by Colonna's *Hypnerotomachia Poliphili,* translated into French by Jean Martin under the title *Songe de Poliphile,* were very popular at the court of King Henry II (1547-1559).
3. Incorrect. I believe the rules of chess have not changed: the king may move one space in any direction and take any piece that close to him.
4. Again, there is no such limitation on the queen's free movement: it is any open distance in any direction.
5. Clearer would be this: the archers move as far as they like, forward or backward, but only on a diagonal line. Thus they never change the color of their original position.

5.24: HOW THE THIRTY-TWO PERSONS IN THE BALL FIGHT.

1. Almost surely a mistake; read: "the silver archer nearly took the gold queen."
2. A Greek myth (Conti 4.15) tells how one day Athene wearied of her invention the flute and threw hers away but put a curse on anyone who should pick it up and use it. The satyr Marsyas did so, then went on to invent both Doric music and the two-tubed flute; but later rashly challenged Apollo to a musical duel, winner to do as he would with the loser. The Muses found Apollo to be the winner; and he had Marsyas flayed (in most accounts; cut to bits in one) to death.
3. Nicolas of Cusa or Cusanus (1401?-1464), German philosopher, statesman, and mystical philosopher, best known for *De docta ignorantia,* perhaps the work intended here.
4. Suidas tells this story, but about Timotheus (fifth and fourth century B.C.), able Athenian general and diplomat, not about Alexander.

5.25: How we went ashore on the island of Odes.

1. *Odes* means a kind of poem but comes from Greek *odos* "road," hence the name of the island (then spelt *hodos* but pronounced *odos*, and now spelt so).
2. Language generally speaks of roads going here or there, thus implying that they move; R in effect says "Why not." Compare moving belts in air terminals, museums, etc.
3. " . . . argument invincible d'un animant, si se meut de soymesme": *Physics* 8.1–6, already quoted in 3.32.
4. A popular gag mixing a time and a place; already seen in 4. Old Prologue.
5. Both these cities are of course on the Rhône downstream from Lyon.
6. " . . . car il tenoit le plus court et le moins chevauchant." A short road impeded by few horses would of course be a quick one, but since Epistémon is holding his penis to urinate, Carpalim's point is to twit him by saying that it is both short and little used for (sexual) riding.
7. " . . . le bon vieux chemin de la Ferrate sus le mont d'un grand ours": this road from Limoges to Tours crossed the Mont du Grand Ours (Great Bear Montain).
8. Saint Jerome was popularly portrayed translating the Bible in his hermit's cell with a tame lion by his side.
9. Aristotle (*Poetics*) says that tragedy should arouse both of these.

5.26: How we stopped on the island of Clogs.

1. "Comment passasmes l'Isle des Esclots, et de l'ordre des Frères Fredons." The *Esclots* "clogs" must symbolize the contempt for luxury shown by their crude dress. The name *Fredons* means "Semiquavers," minuscule musical notes, and is also a reduction ad absurdum of the modest names of religious orders, descending from Minors to Minims, then Crotchet Friars Minim, finally the tiniest of all, our *Semiquavers,* to whose name we have therefore added the parenthetical "Minimal" to suggest the meaning.
2. " . . . les Frères petits Serviteurs et Amis de la douce Dame" (the Virgin Mary).
3. " . . . les glorieux et beaux Frères Mineurs": the humble title was chosen for his order by Saint Francis of Assisi (ca. 1182–1226); Calabrian Saint Francis de Paule (ca. 1416–1507) went one better with the name Friars Minim (least) for his order; and from that the semimusical competition proceeds to Crotchet Friars Minim, who amount to Semiquavers and are barely a note, more of a hum (Fredon); so that these are the humblest, tiniest, saddest of all.
4. "Les cheveux en devant depuis les os bregmatiques, croissoient en liberté."
5. " . . . touret de nez": lit. nose turret, a partial mask worn normally to cover a disfigurement.
6. *Fasti,* originally important dates (festivals, etc.) came to mean a history.
7. " . . . apperçeu qu'ils ne chantoient que des aureilles": i.e., inaudibly.

8. Made for display only, not for use; cf., our "like a lead balloon."

9. "... fins non affinez mais affinans, passez par estamine fine."

10. "... et l'achevoient par moustarde et laictue, comme tesmoigne Martial avoir esté l'usage des Anciens." Martial (*Epigrams* 13.14) writes thus only about lettuce; but our author adds the French proverb about a good thing come too late: "moustarde après disner." Montaigne will use the phrase in this sense in 3.10 (Stanford University Press ed., p. 772).

11. This combination, of a simple humble dish with a learned Latin title and commentary, was irresistibly popular, and R had used it in his Library of Saint-Victor 2.7, above.

12. The popular rustic food (bread, roll, or cake) that led to war in 1.25.

13. A counter to Fortune (as here) or to a tempest (fortunal).

14. "O le gros rat à la table": literally, as translated, but *rat* could mean a "gaffe, verbal slip, or boner"; finally, its homophone *ras* "shaven or shorn," i.e., "tonsured" could designate a monk. His ensuing statement suggests meaning 1 or 3.

15. "Je romps cestuy là, et m'en vois par Dieu de pair." I find this also unclear.

16. "... icy on les érige à rebours [de bides] et à contrepoil."

5.27: HOW PANURGE, QUESTIONING A SEMIQUAVER FRIAR, GOT NO ANSWER.

1. We have not always managed to translate the friar's answers in this way.

2. "Frater, fredon, fredon, fredondille, où est la garse?"

3. I.e., twenty.

4. Mansion's unabridged: "sea-green, grey, or purplish-blue according to contexts: "Minerve aux yeux pers," nor "grey-eyed Minerva."

5. *Pain bis* in R's time was a coarse grayish-brown wholemeal bread.

6. "Pote de froc." Jourda, in G, traces *pote* to Italian *potta*.

7. "... comment elles devroient aller au trot." This French does not mean diarrhea.

8. "Voicy ... le plus gentil Fredon que je chevauchay de cest an." This verb is common in R for a man "mounting" a woman for copulation; this seems unlikely here, and the context suggests something closer to our *ride* in the sense of "tease, rib, deride."

9. French Parlements in R's day had several numbered presidents, all presiding judges or their potential successors. The first president indeed presides.

10. *Bail* seems between *bay* "chestnut" and *maroon* "brownish-red or reddish-brown."

11. "Je perds mon sens en ce poinct."

12. In his *Historia plantarum* 9.20.

13. "Par ledit serment de bois qu'avez fait."

14. "Voice le pauvre Fredon du monde."

15. " . . . par sainct Gris": an unidentified saint, possibly Saint Francis of Assisi, from the color of the order's habit, as Cohen takes it.
16. "Ceste . . . meschante ferraille de moines."
17. "Que diable ont les Roys et grans Princes dadvantaige?"

5.28: How Epistémon dislikes the institution of Lent.

1. A town in Deux-Sèvres near Bressuire, but why chosen here is not clear to me.
2. Near Le Mans, Saint-Christophe-du-Jambet was one of R's curacies in his last years.
3. " . . . chascun abonde en son sens": Romans 14.5 NEB: "Everyone should have reached conviction in his own mind."
4. "Caffards alors sortent en place": "the woodwork" is ours, not R's.
5. Here clearly Reformist types not observing Lent; cited in 4.56.
6. Here we depart far from the French, where the wordplay is on *fou* "fool, jester" and *fouteur* "copulator"; but this is the best approximation we could find.
7. " . . . tu n'eschappe jamais que tu ne sois cocu jusques au cul."

5.29: How we visited the land of Satin.

1. Proverbially a kind of neverneverland of infinite ease and abundance.
2. Pliny in his *Natural History* (8.2–4) states that Germanicus was not the nephew of Tiberius but his adopted son.
3. Again, see Pliny 8.3.
4. " . . . et dit Pausanias estre cornes, non dents": Pausanias *Description of Helles* 5.12.
5. "Philostrate tient que soient dents, non cornes": Philostatus *Life of Apollonius* 2.13.
6. Claudius Aelianus (fl. ca. A.D. 200), learned but uncritical author of *Characteristics of Animals*.
7. " . . . sans offenser les beuveurs beuvans."
8. Here the MS reads "Ligugé," where R stayed with his patron d'Estissac for much of the year 1524. Either reading is of course possible.
9. This author says just the opposite of Pantagruel's assurance to his father in sending him three from Medamothi; see above 4.4.
10. Reportedly the number of blows (23) dealt Caesar by his murderers.
11. The doctor friend who replaced R at the Hôtel-Dieu in Lyon when R suddenly left his position there in February 1535.
12. " . . . au pays de tapisserie": of course a wholly imaginary country.
13. The Christian apologist and rhetor Lactantius of Firmium A.D. fourth century, who may be the author of a poem, *The Phoenix*, on the resurrection of Jesus Christ.

14. "J'y vy la peau de l'asne d'or d'Apulée": title of Apuleius's ever popular tale, whose hero is first transformed by magic into an ass, then later changed back by the favor of the goddess Isis, whose worshiper he has become.

15. Birds dear to the dwellers on Mount Cassius for eating the grasshoppers that kept destroying their crops, so that they prayed to Jupiter to send them again, Pliny *Natural History* 10.27. Pliny is the source for many of the exotic, imaginary birds listed below.

16. Mutianus was a minor source for Pliny, who reported that Periander's ship had indeed been stopped, but by *murex* "molluscs."

17. "Ce sont maquereaux." These abounded in April, and the noun was already coming to be used also in the modern connotation of "pimp."

18. "Vous dites qu'on ne vit onques aire de sacre." The saker is an old world falcon.

19. Presumably an ingenious impossibility like the left-handed racket already noted (4.7 above) or our own left-handed monkeywrench.

20. Two-backed beasts: couples engaged in a popular and populating activity often noted by R in these pages from 1.3 (the birth of Gargantua) on; Shakespeare uses the phrase in Othello (1.i) when Iago tells Brabantio that Desdemona and Othello are indulging in it.

5.30: How in the land of Satin we saw Hearsay running a school for witnesses.

1. "Comment au pays de Satin nous veismes Ouy-dire, tenant escole de tesmoignerie."

2. "... en semblable contenance que l'on peint l'hermite près sainct Christophle." Popular pictures of Saint Christopher showed the hermit (who in the legend had lit a lantern and used it to guide the giant saint as he bore the infant Jesus across the raging river through the storm) staying near him, watching and recording everything.

3. Not Erasmus's friend Peter Giles, but Pierre Gilles of Albi, who in 1533 brought out in Lyon a *Natural history* based on Aelian, Porphyry, Oppian, and other shaky ancient authors, with a treatise on the names of fishes in Latin and Greek. This last of course explains how R says he found him occupied.

4. A plant which, Pliny reports (Book 24), by its touch reconciled quarreling lovers.

5. Source: the *Life of Heliogabalus* by Aelius Lampridius in the collection of biographies of Roman emperors from A.D. 284–117, known as the *Historia Augusta*.

6. Julius Solinus A.D. third century, who wrote an epitome of Pliny's *Natural History*.

7. Albert the Great (1194–1280), noted Aristotelian philosopher, was a Jacobin.

5.31: HOW WE CAME IN SIGHT OF LANTERNLAND.

1. "Comment nous fut descouvert le païs de Lanternois."
2. Meeting of canons or chapter.
3. "Doutans toutesfois que fust quelque prognostic de tempeste.": the fear of this as a bad prognostic is traceable to the tempest in Book 4.18 above.

5.32: HOW WE DISEMBARKED AT THE PORT OF LICHNOBIANS.

1. *Lichnobians* is from Greek *Luchnobios* "living in lamplight."
2. For the sexual connotations of *lanterne, lanterner,* see 4.9 above.
3. " . . . estoit vestu de corne, de papier, de toille cirée."
4. "The lamp with many wicks" is the title of Martial's *Epigram* 14.41.
5. The 20-wick lamp or lantern. Canopa's father was not Tisias, but Critias, leader of the Thirty that ruled Athens for a time (404–403 B.C.).
6. Titles of two large pharmacopeias of the late fifteenth century.
7. Mirebeau had a Cordelier monastery served by a candle that burned walnut oil.

5.33: HOW WE REACHED THE ORACLE OF THE BOTTLE.

1. If all vineyards' claims were true, Bacchus must have done little but plant them.
2. The frieze in a church that represents symbolic animals.
3. The French original couplet is this:

> Passant icy ceste poterne
> Garny-toy de bonne lanterne.

4. A pointed cockaded hat like that worn by the stradiots, the widely-used mercenary light cavalry from Albania first organized by Louis XII.

5.34: HOW WE WENT UNDERGROUND TO ENTER THE TEMPLE OF THE BOTTLE.

1. "Comment nous descendismes soubs terre pour entrer au Temple de la Bouteille, et comment Chinon est la première ville du monde."
2. This Silenus was always portrayed.
3. The French original of this quatrain—also the device written with the city's coat of arms and beneath it—was the following:

> Deux ou trois fois Chinon,
> Petite ville, grand renom,
> Assise sus pierre ancienne,
> Au haut le bois, au pied Vienne.

5.35: How we went down the tetradic steps.

1. Tetradic: relative to the number four or to groupings thereof. The author, using the term *degrez* for steps in a staircase, suggests a relation of this descent to initiation rites leading to the arcana contained in the holy Tetragrammaton (the Hebrew letters JHVH, forming Jahveh, one of their names for God) and handed down from Moses on down to R's time; a subject discussed at length by Marsilio Ficino.

2. "... de laquelle la moictié est composée d'unité, des deux premiers nombres plains, de deux quadrangulaires et de deux cubiques."

3. "... au trou de sainct Patrice": a famous Irish cave inevitably associated with the saint.

4. Trophonius, a son of Apollo, prophesied at the mouth of this cave in Lebadia, Boeotia, as noted by R in 2.24. Erasmus (*Adages* 1.7.77) had associated these two caves.

5. "Dieu vous le rendra en son grand rendouer."

6. On cape Matapan, site of the ave through which Hercules went down into Hades.

7. "Escoutez, c'est luy, ou les aureilles me cornent."

8. Pomponius Mela (*Chorographia* 2.5) reports that Hercules, weaponless and hard pressed by the sons of Neptune, ran out of arrows; so then Jupiter, to help him, sent down a rain of stones, which still clutter the Marian Canal near Crau in Provence.

9. "Boutons, boutons, passons, poussons, pissons: je m'appelle Guillaume sans peur."

5.36: How the doors of the temple opened of themselves.

1. "Comment les portes du Temple par soy-mesme admirablement s'entr'ouvrirent."

2. Surely a common maxim in languages wherever the grape is grown or known.

3. So says Pliny *Natural History* 26.4; cf., above, 4.62.

4. From the Greek Stoic, Cleanthes, put in Latin by Seneca *Epistles* 107; Seneca quoted by Epictetus *Enchiridion* (*Manual*) 51; and finally see Erasmus *Adages* 3.3.41 and 5.1.90.

5. A Greek maxim: "Pros telos auton panta kineitai."

5.37: How the temple was paved with an admirable mosaic.

1. "Comment le pavé du Temple estoit faict par emblémature admirable."

2. The text reads *dessus* "over," but the context suggests *dessous* or *dessoubs* "under."

3. Pliny *Natural History* 35.36.

5.38: How in the temple's mosaic work was represented the battle that Bacchus won against the Indians.

1. "Comment en l'ouvrage mosaïque du Temple estoit représentée la bataille que Bacchus gagna contre les Indians."
2. Blood-letting, long practiced as a near panacea, but not in this case.
3. A variety of Bacchants, as are many that follow. Lucian mentions many of these groups in his Bacchus, but as subjects of unlikely reports, not as facts. See also Pliny *Natural History* 35.10 and 36.
4. The cordax is a lascivious Bacchic dance.
5. Dorian name for satyrs.
6. In old-style numbers: "octante cinq mille six vingts et treize."

5.39: How in the mosaic was pictured the clash and assault.

1. "Comment en l'emblémature estoit figuré le hourt et l'assaut que donnoit le bon Bacchus contre les Indians."
2. " . . . suoit à grosses gouttes": cf., English "was sweating gumdrops."
3. Two painters living and working in the fourth century B.C.
4. Ovid tells the story in his *Fasti* 1.415–440; cf., above, 5.2.
5. Both Theophrastus (4.4) and Pliny (16.34) tell us that in India ivy grew only on Mount Meros.
6. After his first great victory over the Cimbrians at Aqua Sextiae in 102 B.C.
7. Plutarch *Of Isis and Osiris* 354 ff., notes the identification of Osiris with Bacchus, and LI gives that as reference here; but I do not find this point in it.

5.40: How the temple was lighted by a marvelous lamp.

1. "Comment le Temple estoit esclairé par une lampe admirable." This puzzling chapter and the following three (40–44) show the same relish we noted in R for lavish details of sumptuous feasts, of mind and eye as well as palate, and for mathematical problems and oddities, both arithmetical and geometrical. This creates myriad enigmas, which are augmented and reinforced by the galimatias taken over from the Colonna original. This combination leaves the translator baffled and groping his way through the maze as best he can. Besides the obvious guideposts, the texts of 5.40–44 and of the Colonna fantasy romance, I have found help (for which I am grateful) in Marcel Françon's two articles "Rabelais and Numbers" in *Isis* 41 (1950) 398–399, and Francesco Colonna's *Polyphili Hypnerotomachia* and *Pantagruel*, in *Italica* 31 (1954) 135–137; more from the excellent article by K. H. Francis, "Rabelais and Mathematics," in BHR 21 (1959) 85–97, already cited here for its invaluable help with the calculations in 4.27; and most of all from the notes and the modern French version by the Demerson team in LI. Despite this valued help and my own best efforts, many passages in these five chapters still puzzle me and may have escaped me; so I wish the reader much patience and much luck.

2. "... en chascune desquelles estoit fixement retenue une boule vuyde."
3. So says Pausanias *Atticus* 1.26.7.
4. According to Plutarch *Of the cessation of oracles* 2.
5. From around Carpasia in Cyprus. This flax was highly esteemed.
6. "... moyennant la diverse et plaisante lumière, laquelle dedans contenue ressortissoit par la sculpture."

5.42: HOW THE WATER OF THE FOUNTAIN GAVE A TASTE OF WINES.

1. "Comment l'eau de la fontaine rendoit goust de vin selon, l'imagination des beuvans."
2. "... plus rare et mirifique, qu'onques n'en songea dedans les limbes Pluto." Here the MS gives the likelier name of Daedalus, legendary craftsman-inventor (Joyce's "old artificer"), instead of that of Plutus, god of riches but without known qualifications as a craftsman.
3. Here the puzzling French text is "Sus le poinct moyen de chascun angle, et marge, estoit assise une coulomne ventricule, en forme d'un cycle d'yvoire ou alabastre."
4. Here the French MS reads *potrye*, which also seems to make little or no sense.
5. "... comme vous sçavez qu'en toute figure angulaire impare, un angle tousjours est au milieu des deux autres trouvé intercalant."
6. Sophocles, in his *Ajax,* dramatizes this tragic piece of the Trojan story. When the armor of the dead Achilles was awarded to Odysseus not to himself, Ajax, insane with anger, slaughtered a flock of sheep that he mistook for the Greek army, then, in shame and frustration, killed himself with his own sword. Poets later declared that his blood was the source of the flower hyacinth; see Ovid *Metamorphoses* 13.371–398.
7. "... en plomb élician bien précieux." The gods were often portrayed with their special birds and metals; in this list of the planetary gods with theirs, only Venus and her doves are missing.
8. "... avoit contemplant Léarche son fils mort d'une cheute, à ses pieds." For the sculptor Aristonides and the murderous father Athamas, see Pliny *Natural History* 34.14.
9. "Sus la sixiesme, Mercure en hydrargyre, fixe, maléable, et immobile, à ses pieds une cigogne."
10. "... nous ne sommes du calibre d'un tas de veaux." We mix the fauna but keep the sense.
11. Athenaeus, in his *Connoisseurs in Dining* 1.6 tells how this expert taster used to coat his tongue with an oil that retained flavors for leisurely savoring, then wiped it clean off in between tastings.
12. "... impétra des cieux la manne": Moses, to whom God gave manna for his famished people (Exodus 16.31 ff.).

5.43: How Bacbuc accoutered Panurge to get the word of the Bottle.

1. "Comment Bacbuc accoustra Panurge pour avoir le mot de la Bouteille."
2. "C'est," dist Frère Jean, "du vin à une aureille": for rather mystifying reasons, this means a first-class wine; poorer wines were called "for two ears" (à deux oreilles).
3. Points in the old sense of laces for tying two garments together (Old French *obélisques* here: modern *aiguillettes*).
4. "... n'aussi les vaticinateurs Memphitiques à Apis en Egipte": see Conti *Mythologie* 6.13.
5. "... ny les Euboyens en la cité de Rhamnes à Rhamnasie": Rhamnasia was a goddess of forests and orchards.
6. Feronia, a goddess of childbirth, is mentioned by Virgil *Aeneid* 8.563.
7. A temple to either Apollo or Hercules, on the site of the present cathedral.
8. A temple on a floating island on the Nile near Thebes; Herodotus 2.91.
9. "... l'ouvrage d'icelle chapelle ronde estoit en telle symmétrie compassé que le diamètre du project estoit la hauteur de la voûte."

5.44: How the pontiff Bacbuc presented Panurge before the said Bottle.

1. "Comment la Pontife Bacbuc présenta Panurge devant ladicte Bouteille."
2. "... l'aire (l'ère) de Noach close": when Noah's vineyard (or era) is closed.
3. The Germanic word for imbibing: English *Drink*, German *Trink*.
4. "Esclairez: où est ce livre? Tournez: où est ce chapitre? Voyons ceste joyeuse glose."

5.45: How Bacbuc interprets the word of the Bottle.

1. "Comment Bacbuc interprète le mot de la Bouteille."
2. Here the French makes a pun we see no way to match: "un gros livre d'argent en forme d'un demy muy ou d'un quart de sentences": *muy* and *quart* (etymon of English *quart*) are measures of volume; but "quart de sentences" points to the famous central fourth book of Peter Lombard's *Sentences,* one of the most influential guidebooks of the Middle Ages.
3. "... mangea un livre": Ezekiel 3.2–3, NEB, "Then he said to me, 'Man, eat what is in front of you, eat this scroll; then go speak to the Israelites.' ... So I ate it and it tasted as sweet as honey."
4. "... panomphée": from Greek *panomphaios* "giving oracles in all languages," used of Zeus in *Iliad* 8.250: Lattimore, "Zeus of the Voices." Ovid repeats it later in *Metamorphoses* 11.198.

5.46: HOW PANURGE AND THE OTHERS RHYME IN POETIC FRENZY.

1. "Comment Panurge et les autres rithment par fureur poëtique."
2. "... mangera il de l'herbe aux chiens pour descharger son thomas?" This herb seems to be an emetic or purgative, and *thomas* a sort of pet name for *estomac.*
3. "... reprendra il du poil de ce chien qui le mordit?" This exactly matches our current English expression.
4. Here is the Old French original of the last two lines.

> Ce me seroit acte de trop piqueur,
> Penser moquer un si noble trinqueur.

5. "Par sainct Jean": he means the visionary author of the Apocalypse.
6. "... et m'ayez pour excusé si je ne rithme en cramoisi."
7. "Et jouë la marabaquine": a stock comic figure in the farces.
8. Here is the French:

> Lors bien sus toy, pauvre paillard,
> Pisseray-je, je t'en asseure.

5.47: HOW, AFTER TAKING LEAVE OF BACBUC, THEY LEAVE THE ORACLE OF THE BOTTLE.

1. "Comment, avoir prins congé de Bacbuc, délaissent l'oracle de la Bouteille." Note again here the reference to the travelers in the third person plural, not the first: the first such reference since early in Book 4 (4.5); it had been to "them" earlier, on 4.2. From the present point on, for the rest of chapter 47, the first person plural will be used by the narrator in speaking of Pantagruel and the party with him.
2. "... nous dictans, une de ses mystagogues excepvant."
3. "... en protection de ceste sphère intellectuale de laquelle en tous lieux est le centre et n'a en lieu aucun circonférance, que nous appellons Dieu." This is a favorite and overworked definition in Renaissance France, traceable to Empedocles, but usually attributed to the so-called Hermes Trismegistus, author of the second century neoplatonic *Pimander,* already quoted by R (3.13), probable source of the paraphrase here. Its vogue was durable: Pascal (1623–1662) used the same definition for Nature (*Pensées,* Krailsheimer trans. [Harmondsworth, England: Penguin ed. 1966], p. 89); "Nature is an infinite sphere whose centre is everywhere and circumference nowhere."
4. "Pour tant est équitablement le Soubterrain Dominateur presques en toutes langues nommé par épithète de richesses": presumably the Pluto-Plutus thing.
5. "... lequel jadis les Egyptiens nommoient en leur langue l'Abscond, le Mussé, le Caché."
6. "Zoroaster print Arimaspes pour compagnon de ses pérégrinations, Esculapius, Mercure; Orpheus, Musée; Pythagoras, Agléophème."

7. "Or, allez, de par Dieu qui vous conduit." The MS has a longer and richer conclusion in place of this last three-sentence paragraph. From "guidance of God and company of man," it continues:

> "Thus, among the Persians, Zoroaster took Arimaspes as companion in all his mysterious philosophy; Hermes Trismegistus, among the Egyptians, had —; Esculapius had Mercury; Orpheus in Thrace had Musaeus; there too Aglaophemus had Pythagoras; among the Athenians, Plato had, first, Dion of Syracuse in Sicily, on whose death he took, secondly, Xenocrates; Apollonius had Damis.

> "So when your philosophers, guided by God, and accompanying some bright lantern, devote themselves to diligent research, investigating (as is the nature of humans, and of that quality Herodotus and Homer are called *alphestai* [Greek: "enterprising"] that is to say researchers and inventors), they will find true the reply made by the sage Thales to Amasis, king of the Egyptians, when, asked by him in what thing there was the most wisdom, replied: 'In Time: for by Time have been, and by Time shall be, all hidden things invented'; and that is the reason why the ancients called Saturn 'Time,' father of Truth, and Time for a daughter had Truth. Infallibly, knowledge of themselves and their predecessors, is scarcely the tiniest part of what is and they do not know [See Erasmus *Adages* 2.4.17].

> "From these three wineskins that I now give you, you will take judgment knowledge, as the proverb says, *Ex ungue leonem* ["You can tell the lion by its claws," from *Adages* 1.9.84]. By the rarefaction our water herein enclosed, the intervention of warmth from bodies above it, and the fervor of the salt water, in the normal transmutation of elements, will very salubrious air be engendered that will serve you as a clear, serene, delightful wind; for wind is nothing but floating, undulating air. Thanks to this wind, you will follow a straight route, without touching land if you want, right to the port of Olonne in Talmondois, by loosing through your sails out of this little gold mouthpiece you see attached as to a flute, as much [wind] as you think is enough to have you sail slowly ever safely and pleasantly, with no danger of any tempest.

> "Have no doubt of this; do not suppose a tempest will issue forth and come out of this wind; for wind comes from the tempest that burst out of the abyss. Don't suppose rain comes from impotence of the heavens' retentive powers and weight of the hanging clouds. It comes by evocation from the regions underground, as by the evocation of higher bodies it is imperceptibly drawn up from below; and the Prophet King attests you this, saying in song that deep calls to deep [David in Psalms 42.8].

> "Of the three wineskins, two are full of the aforesaid water; the third is drawn from the Indian sages' well called 'the Brahmins' cask' [see 3.FM. above].

> "Moreover, you will find your ships well provided with all that you

might find useful and necessary for the rest of your company's supplies, for I had given very good orders about that.

"Go, friends, in blithe spirits, and take your King Gargantua this letter; bring our greetings to him and all the princes and officers of his noble court."

These words completed, she gave us a letter sealed closed, and, after offering prayers of undying thanksgiving, had us leave by a door next to the chapel, where Bacbuc invited them [again!] to ask [a list of] questions twice as high as Mount Olympus.

Through a countryside full of all delights, pleasant, more temperate than Tempe in Thessaly, more salubrious than that part of Egypt that looks toward Libya, more irrigated and verdant than Thermischria, more fertile than the part of Mount Taurus toward Aquilon [north], more fragrant than the Hyperborean Island in the Judaic Sea or Caliges on the Caspian Mountain, gracious and as serene as is the region of Touraine, at last we found our ships in port.

5. A16: How Pantagruel arrives on the island of the Apedeftes.

1. "Comment Pantagruel arriva en l'Isle des Apedeftes à longs doigs ès mains crochues, et des terribles aventures et monstres qu'il y trouva." This is the final chapter (no. 16) of *L'Isle Sonnante* "The Ringing Island," hence also no. 16 in PL and G, Urquhart, and Cohen. Here as always we follow LI and the 1564 edition.

2. From the Greek *Apaideutoi,* then pronounced *apedeftoi,* meaning "uneducated, ignorant, stupid."

3. "Par l'âme de ma braguette eschauffée."

4. " . . . à l'entour d'un grand bourreau": here the context suggests *bureau* "table or desk," but the word *bourreau* means "executioner."

5. A special, very heavy war tax.

6. A probable allusion to the fate of Jean Poncher, treasurer of the Extraordinaire, who was hanged (and his property confiscated) for misappropriation of funds.

7. *Décimes:* a ten percent tax levied upon the clergy.

8. I have failed to find the precise meaning of these two legal terms, as have earlier commentators; presumably *radiatur* means "funds to be disseminated" and *recuperetur* "funds to be recovered."

9. Punning on what then were virtual homonyms, *serment* and *sarment.*

10. The term *courracteurs* is a pun on *correcteurs,* which probably also meant to suggest *courroyer* "to curry or comb clean (a horse's coat)" hence "to pluck or fleece."

11. Presumably a performer in a devil-play (diablerie) in Labaille, a town near Saint Brieuc (Côtes-du-Nord).

12. " . . . nourry de laict d'amendes": puns on the homonyms *amendes* "fines" and *amandes* "almonds."

13. As the name indicates, a fourfold fine.

14. G and LI: "a technical term for reviews of accounts": see note 8 above.

15. One of the myriad plays on the term *protonotaire* "protonotary."

16. Cotgrave, s.v. *Revisit:* "A Review taken by the King of his officers' accounts."

5. A32: HOW THE LADY LANTERNS WERE SERVED AT SUPPER.

1. "Comment furent les dames Lanternes servies à soupper." This chapter, listed as 32 *bis* in G, is there placed between nos. 32 and 33; in PL, listed as *bis,* between nos. 33 and 34. Both Urquhart and Cohen simply leave it out.

2. A play on two near homonyms about pills, *qui sentent si bon* "which smell so good" and *ante cibum* "before a meal."

3. Here *ptisane* "herb tea, infusion" is changed to suggest a donkey's fart *pétasine.*

4. These comic indications in bad Latin are a jest of the author's not ours.

5. In Greek myth, King Athamas of Thebes, son of Aeolus, by his first wife Nephele had two children, Phryxus and Helle, whom his second wife Ino tried to kill. They fled on a winged ram with golden fleece that started to carry them across the sea, but Helle fell off and was drowned in the body of water since named for her, the Hellespont.

6. Presumably recalling the dog and fox turned to stone in 3.P.

7. Pliny, *Natural History* 8.46.

8. For Cacus (Greek *Kakos* "the Bad One"), see Virgil *Aeneid* 8.194–290; for Corydon and Alexis, *Eclogues* 2.40–42.

9. A boar born in Mount Erimanthus in Arcadia, which in vengeance Artemis (Diana) loosed on Arcadia and all Phocis. One of the labors of Hercules was to tie it up and bring it back thus "gift wrapped" to King Eurystheus (Conti *Mythologje* 8.1). The somewhat similar story of the Calydonian boar hunt (in Aetolia) is told by Ovid *Metamorphoses* 8.270–430. I can find nothing about the Olympian boar listed here.

10. Which by her, in Greek legend, begat the Minotaur.

11. Raped by Jupiter, then turned into a she-bear by angry Juno, she was then again transformed, this time by Jupiter, into the constellation The Great Bear; Ovid 2.408–520; Conti 9.9.

12. Lazare Sainéan has convincingly shown, in "Le Chapitre XXXIII du Ve livre," in *Revue des Etudes Rabelaisiennes* 8 (1910) 191–199, that the salty foods and the dances so lavishly listed in this chapter are a farrago of borrowed materials, mainly from R's own earlier books of the story, especially the list of battling cooks in 4.40 some unchanged, such as "Cocquecigrues"; some slightly altered, such as "Badigonyeuses" from "Badiguoincier." They are also from works inspired by R but not by him, e.g., *Les Navigations de Pantagruel.* This being a highly derivative chapter in a highly suspect book, we have seen little point in offering translations or even full annotations of all these, and have chosen instead to leave the

author's Jabberwocks and Jubjub Birds in the brightness of their original French.

13. "... or ung grand baislant de Partenay le Vieil," located just outside the town itself (Deux-Sèvres), on the Thouet, about 30 miles west of Poitiers.

14. Untranslatable, but clearly suggesting a fly in the ass "mousche en cul."

15. The same gag as in note 3 above: *pétassine* to suggest a donkey's fart.

16. For the amours of Mars and Venus (Ares and Aphrodite), see *Odyssey* 8.267–319; Conti *Mythologie* 2.6.

17. This epigram appears only in the 1564 edition (not in the other two basic texts), and there on the last page of the Table of Contents. The signature, "Nature Quite," although apparently an anagram, has resisted even the best efforts of the best scholars over four centuries to decipher it.

6. MISCELLANEOUS WRITINGS

The 22 items that follow and complete our text are all R's other known extant writings besides the tales, prologues, and other liminary and appended material. They vary vastly in interest and claims for inclusion. For example, item 22 (Du Bellay's *Sapphic Ode*) is not even by R; but both men wanted it published in R's *Shadow Battle* (no. 21), and so it was. Two others (items 17 and 19, an almanac and a prognostication) may well not be by R; several are trivial (the six Greek verses of no. 2; the verbose French of 3; the two short pieces of Latin verse, nos. 15–16, but their great brevity suffices for our putting them in. My favorites are the seven missive letters (nos. 1, 7, 12–14, 18, 20) for the glimpses we get of R and the insights and information they provide, and the spoofing items offered as divination: the tiny almanacs for 1533, 1535, and 1541, and the copious *Pantagrueline Prognostication* for 1533 (no. 8).

Among the missives, I like especially the three from Rome to Geoffroy d'Estissac in winter 1535–1536 (nos. 12–14), always informative, often amused and often amusing, including many details of daily life, its routines and problems and ranging from complicated arrangements for communicating from afar and across frontiers by mail before regular postal systems came to be to an account in outline of how R went about seeking absolution from the pope for his apostasy from monastic residence, how the reigning pope, Paul III, himself offered welcome advice on procedure, and how R's quest succeeded completely, at little cost and with little other help. Besides such matters, these letters show us R as reporter, alert, well informed, and incisively informative, his accounts cutting through the hugger-mugger of the politics of the time, both local and international—papal, Imperial, Italian, Mediterranean, even Eurasian at times—as diplomats and minor potentates scurry about seeking, and paying dearly for, the favor of the stronger in a kaleidoscopic pace, while money talks the loudest, for it pays the troops, and the strongest troops give authority. True as the French maxim is: "Plus ça change, plus c'est la même chose" (The more it changes, the more the same it is), the spectacle, and, however superficial, the differences, are both entertaining and instructive.

Besides these missives, illuminating are two others (nos. 1, 7) to two humanist giants of R's day, Guillaume Budé (q.v., the Glossary for information about the people discussed here) and Desiderius Erasmus. He writes to Budé in 1521, as a mere unknown cloistered monk and priest and novice in Greek studies, presuming to address the leading French Hellenist, intellectual adviser to the king and eminent public servant. R at this point is understandably diffident overly apologetic, and almost obsequious in praise; but he ventures to show off his novice Greek, and his Latin is fluent if florid. When he writes Erasmus eleven years later (November 30, 1532), although addressing a longtime hero, he has become a personage himself: an established physician with his doctorate (not like many), and just lately, with the wild success of his first giant story, *Pantagruel,* a celebrity in his own right, courted by sales-hungry publishers; and better yet, he has in hand a book ready to send that he knows Erasmus wants: the volume of Josephus's *Jewish Wars* on the fall of Jerusalem. His praise, effusive as it is, can come man to man, and it does; and it illuminates much of the earnest side of R that is humanistic and Evangelicalist.

Besides these various groups—missive letters, prophetic spoofs and parodies, and odd bits of verse (one French and long, one tiny Greek, two short Latin)—the main remaining group is the dedicatory letters, in Latin to Latin works not written by R but either published or republished by him: four in all, two on medicine (nos. 4 and 5 in 1532), to d'Estissac and to Tiraqueau; one, a Roman will (1532), to Amaury Bouchard; the fourth (no. 10, in 1534), to Jean du Bellay, on Marliani's *Topography of Ancient Rome.* Considering the constraints of the genre, these tell us quite a lot about some of R's preoccupations and activities in the years he wrote them.

Lastly there is the longest item in this lot, the *Shadow Battle* (*Sciomachie*). R's account of the great lavish pageant offered by Jean du Bellay to celebrate the recent birth of Henry II's second son, seems to promise light on his skills in direct reportage and perhaps the passion R's time had for pageantry, however insubstantial (entertainment was so scarce!), a passion exceeding that of our own time. But R's piece, almost copied (with minimal adaptation for the gratification of his patron) from the account composed in March 1549 in Italian by Antonio Buonacorsi for Cardinal Ippolito d'Este.

Moreover, and ironically in view of the Du Bellay-Guise rivalry, R's account, when published, announced it as an extract from a letter to the Cardinal de Guise, though of course it might have been just that, sent him to spite him. At the actual event, on March 14, 1549, R was present; but he must have preferred to leave the dull chore of chronicler of details to someone else, then borrow the result. Although all these items are presented in all the complete French scholarly readers' editions (PL, G, LI), but in none of the English translations do any of them appear. In French again, the EC, far from finished with Book 4 of R's tale, of course does not give any of these items; and there is no critical edition of them all. For all the works of divination, however, we have had since 1974 M. A. Screech's edition of all five of these works, notably the starter and best, the *Pantagrueline Prognostication* for the year 1533. For the rest there is nothing of the sort. So for the items in it we have generally followed Screech's edition; for all the rest, our guide has been our usual excellent lantern, Demerson's LI.

Our 22 items are a mixed bag resistant to neat categorization; genre and date have seemed their main determinants. So despite the vagueness and inadequacy of most dates (including some of these) involving R, we came to adopt, as the best available, a chronological order of presentation, and have begun each with date and place of origin and brief sketch of type of document. With 22 items and some 175 notes, we thought it would be too choppy to number them item by item; and so we have numbered them all together, from 1 to 175.

1. We have of course translated passages originally in Greek into English; we have pointed some of them out by a note indicator at the end of the passage and others by italics.

2. For Pierre Amy or Lamy (as here), see Amy, Pierre in the Glossary.

3. For the Greek, see Demerson, p. 936, column one.

4. Ibid., column two.

5. Budé's first magnum opus, building a rich picture of Roman life from a close study of its coinage and measures, and these of the base of their smallest unit of weight and money value, the *As: De asse et partibus ejus libri quinque* (Paris: Josse Bade, 1515, new style).

6. This long Greek passage occurs in Demerson on column two page 936 and column one page 937.

7. Here and later in this letter, R uses the name of this god of riches to embody and personify the greed and lazy frivolity he finds rampant in his society and seeks earnestly to educate and cure.

8. Here we render Latin: "Ignavos quidem illos, rerum imperitos."

9. The Greek verse appears to be R's own composition.

10. Tiraqueau's *De legibus connubialibus* first appeared in 1513, presented as a guidebook to its subject, but in the spirit of the time and in anticipation of the similar rules of Arnolphe in Molière's *School for Wives* (1662), a clear statement of the right of the husband to absolute rule in his house; then many times expanded in its third edition (1524), to which R contributed the six Greek verses honoring his friend.

11. "Epistre . . . traictant des ymaginations qu'on peut avoir attendant la chose désirée."

12. Dr. Giovanni Manardi (1462–1536) of Ferrara had published there in 1525 the first volume of his *Medical Letters* (*Epistolarum medicinalium*), mainly studying and discussing manuscripts of Greek and Latin medical texts. When R wrote this dedicatory epistle, the second volume, dealing with Dioscorides and other ancient Greek and Roman doctors and natural historians, had just been published in Ferrara; R knew it would interest Tiraqueau and deserved to be better known and more accessible to all.

13. The full title is "Franciscus Rabelaesus Medicus Andreae Tiraquello ludici Aequissimo apud Pictones."

14. I fail to find a certain explanation of "S. P. D." but assume it stands for "Salve Paxque Domino," meaning "Health and Peace in the Lord," which clearly is about the sense.

15. Cf., 3.29 above, where Pantagruel tells the puzzled Panurge: "I recognize that *philautia* or self love is deceiving you."

16. Latin and Greek: "si personam hanc, χαὶ λεοντῆν." This is the traditional garb of Hercules; and in Aristophanes's *Frogs* Dionysus puts it on to go down into Hades to bring back a real tragedian, preferably Aeschylus (v. 46 ff.).

17. A proverbial Roman phrase for doing something ultra difficult, coming from Cicero, *Pro Murena* 25, used later in Erasmus *Adages* 1.3.75: "Cornicum oculos confixisse."

18. Or more properly (*in subselliis*), to the ill-placed unreserved folding seats.

19. " . . . qui nunc passim nasum rhinocerotis habent."

20. " . . . ut est Plinii querela vetus": Pliny *Natural History* 29.18.

21. Paieon was the healing god, whom Zeus (*Iliad* 5.401, 899) sends to heal Ares when he is wounded by Diomedes with decisive help from Pallas Athene.

22. The Greek ὑπομνήμασι is equivalent to the Latin Commentary. Tiraqueau's *De legibus connubialibus* was presented as part of his *Latin Commentaries on the municipal laws of Poitou.*

23. "Clarissimo Doctissimoque Viro D. Gotofredo ab Estissaco Malleacensi Episcopo Franciscus Rabelaesus Medicus. S. P. D."

24. The Latin headnote says: "Hippocratis et Galeni libri aliquot, ex recognitione Francisci Rabelaesi medici omnibus numeris absolutissimi, Lyon: Gryphius, 1532."

25. " . . . non pauca invertisse verius quam vertisse."

26. " . . . quam omnibus Senatus Populique Pictonici": imitation of the famous S P Q R (Senatus Populusque Romanus), symbol of Roman unity and power.

27. Polycletus or Polyclitus (Polukleitos, fl. 450–420 B.C.), Athenian sculptor rated just after Phidias in ancient sculpture, whose aim was to show postures of calm and repose and the precise proportions of the parts of the body. His observations were influential in medieval and Renaissance theories of principles of sculpture.

28. In the Platonic sense of forms or archetypes.

29. Lieutenant General of the Seneschal of Saintonge, a mutual friend of both R and Tiraqueau, author in 1522 of a defense of womankind against Tiraqueau, which in turn prompted Tiraqueau's third edition of his *Laws of marriage*, noted above. When R wrote him this dedication, he was a counselor to the king and his Master of Requests.

30. Cassius Longinus Ravilla, who was consul in 127 B.C., was proverbially notorious for the severity of his tribunal.

31. Plato once uses the term (*Epigram* 22) to describe the skilled hand of a sculptor.

32. This document, prized and coveted by scholars at the time as shedding light

on an ill-known aspect of Roman law, has been since shown to be spurious. Clearly R did not know, or apparently suspect, this.

33. This is by Democritus: ἐν βυθῷ γὰρ ἡ ἀλήθεια It seems that R confuses Heraclitus's formula: φύσις δὲ χρύπτεσθαι φιλεῖ.

34. So often were letters opened in transit that they often bore an address on the outside not to the intended recipient but to a third party who would redirect them right.

35. Georges d'Armagnac (ca. 1500–1585), a humanist patron and protector of letters, friend of Margaret of Navarre and trusted by Francis I, was bishop of Rodez from 1529, ambassador to Venice 1536–1539, then transferred to Rome, a cardinal from 1544, later archbishop of Toulouse from 1562, then of Avignon from 1577. R, a friend of his, saw him in Rome on his third trip there.

36. An account in Greek of the Roman wars on the Jews from 170 B.C. to their recapture of Jerusalem in A.D. 70, by the Jewish soldier and statesman Flavius Josephus, much esteemed by Vespasian and Titus and honored with Roman citizenship.

37. BD: "defender, helping in adversity, warding off evil. It is one of the surnames of Hercules." R also uses it of and to Cardinal Odet de Chastillon in his liminary epistle to Book 4.

38. Or Bertoul, a Hollander, once a teacher of grammar in Toulouse, later for a time a secretary to Erasmus. He lived in Lyon for some time from 1532 on.

39. Aleander (1480–1542), an Italian humanist and theologian, who led the opposition to Luther at the Diet of Worms and drew up the edict against him, and much later led the persecution in the Netherlands and brought about many burnings for heresy. Several times a papal nuncio, he was made a cardinal in 1536. Erasmus was convinced that he authored or sponsored an attack on him dated 1531 for his *Ciceronianus* of 1528; but R was probably right in ascribing it, as he says here, to Julius Caesar Scaliger.

40. Possibly true, but as Febvre has shown, then a common charge, often groundless.

41. This *Prognostication* is R's first, and successful, attempt to cash in on the smashing success of his *Pantagruel* in fall 1532; and it is closely tied to that first book of the giant story that R wrote, and primarily a comico-satiric parody of the vastly popular almanacs and prognostications that enchanted readers in R's day. Although in his *Pantagruel* he has Gargantua speak harshly of divining astrology, it was less sharply distinguished from astronomy than it is today, and Ficino had helped to foster a widespread wishful belief in the quasi-magical powers exerted by the stars over human lives and events; the target of R's spoof is no straw man.

42. *Architriclin*: wine steward, or steward of the feast, as in John 2.8–9. R uses it of himself as narrator in 3 Prologue, seeming to relish the notion of himself as pouring out the wine of his tales as from a bottomless cask.

43. The golden number is the place of the year in the lunar cycle (of 19 years); it is found by adding one to the current year, dividing that sum by 19; the final undivided part, the remainder, is the golden number. Thus for 1533 the dividend would be 1534; divide that by 19, and the result is 80 with a remainder of 14 (1534−1520).

44. "Passons oultre": compare the use of this as a gag in 5.17.

45. The preceding sentence, from "If anyone" on, is found only in the 1533 ed., not in any of the later ones.

46. Louvain, in Belgium, a commercial and cultural center with a fine university, was an early center of printing and spawned many almanacs and such.

47. Caesar, *De bello Gallico* 4.5.

48. The first words of a verse repeated in Catholic services at the end of each scripture reading, meaning "all this, to the very end," and here, "you shall know all this."

49. I.e., a generous assortment of lashes with whips.

50. " . . . si le fournier ne s'endort": a common old saying, probably suggesting a most unlikely mishap. The whole sentence is an addition to R's original text made in later editions of it.

51. A Biblical expression: the Jews kept their standards for weights and measures in the temple. This too is part of an addition to the original text.

52. R's joke here is that for alchemists the sun stood for gold, the moon for silver.

53. These gaits or courses may seem strange but are normal for these planets.

54. This series of actions includes some absurd, some odd but normal (crabs, ropemakers), some almost proverbial.

55. In the age-old game of trying to find the bean hidden in this special cake.

56. The flush, a sequence of four cards of the same suit, is of course far easier to get if aces are wild and with an ace or two to help. See Book 1.22.

57. Quaresmeprenant, for whom see Book 4.29−32.

58. Priscian, a fifth-century Latin grammarian, was still respected in R's time.

59. Yet another term for Saint Paul, for whose ravishment to heaven see 2 Corinthians 12.2.

60. Another addition to the 1533 ed.: "Icy bénissez son sainct nom, pour la parreille."

61. Pillaging soldiers had their ears cut off; this often happened to Gascons.

62. " . . . et dont plusieurs ne sçauront de quel boys faire flèches."

63. A medical treatise by Averroes, but of course with nothing about this malady.

64. Turning backward from its normal course, reversing it.

65. The apparent meeting, passing, or coming close of two or more celestial bodies in the same degree of the Zodiac. The ninth-century Arab astronomer Albumazar had a book on the great conjunctions still widely cited in R's day; these were considered as having great influence on human affairs.

66. An ancient theory of history dear to Pico della Mirandola and other Neoplatonists divided it into eras determined by the stars; one of these was to bring a new creation of kings, as noted here.

67. A mystery play about a clerical trick for counterfeiting crown coins; cf., 2.7.

68. Turning from the saturnine (under Saturn) to the jovial (under Jupiter). Thus subject to Mars will be men at home with violence and killing; to Venus, the wenchers and other lustful lechers; to Sol, drinkers and generally men living much out of doors in the sun.

69. Presumably for often selling defective matches that could start unwanted fires.

70. This is literally gallows humor from an age when hanging was common. The "bishop of the fields" is a hanged man, high up hanging from his gallows; the kicking of his feet in his death-throes is sardonically called "giving the benediction."

71. Here and in this group things will be found in their usual place or places.

72. On the influence of Mercury, see 3.48 above.

73. This category held mostly loonies and other types who worked by night.

74. These were apparently an annual midsummer pestilence in R's neighborhood.

75. A reminiscence of Horace *Odes* 2.16, vv. 27–28; cf., Book 4.44.

76. I.e., Catholic practices will not thrive in Protestant countries or regions.

77. "A toutes tables" may mean not meals but the kind of backgammon noted in 1.22 as one of the child Gargantua's games.

78. " . . . si Aries ascendent de sa busche ne trébusche et n'est de sa corne escorné."

79. " . . . du Roy des Parpaillons": in Book 1.3, father of Grandgousier's wife Gargamelle.

80. " . . . peu joueront des cymbales et manequins."

81. Then considered a remedy for venereal disease, the latest scourge of the lusty.

82. " . . . et si plus en sçavez, n'en dictes mot, mais attendez la venue du boyteux": the *boyteux* here is Father Time.

83. A cherished sign of lunacy was trying to protect the moon from the wolves.

84. I.e., I condemn the change.

85. " . . . car tel cuidera vessir qui baudement fiantera." See Book 1.25, "cuideurs de vendanges," who suffer the same misadventure as is noted again here in the text.

86. "O, o! poullailles, faictes-vous vos nidz tant hault?": these were low.

87. This fragment, like item 6.8 above, and others is preserved in the seventeenth-c. MS lat. 8704 of the Paris Bibliothèque Nationale. R of course usurps the title Professor of Astrology. At a time of French anxiety over Imperial power, Screech finds this almanac discrediting astrology to strengthen French resolve to resist.

88. This is the first book that R signed with his own name, adding (as he was
to do with Books 3–4 and as was done with Book 5) his profession; and
here for good measure if not for truth or accuracy, he adds: "professor of
astrology." He seems to have enjoyed not only spoofing prognostications
and almanacs but also composing them, since he wrote not only these three
(our items 6.8, 6.9, and 6.11) but quite possibly two or three others (6.17
and 6.19, perhaps yet one more); and in our item 6.12, his letter of December 30 to d'Estissac, he says he is sending him "a book of prognostics that
has this whole city buzzing, entitled *De eversione Europa* (*On the overthrow* or
destruction of Europe), adding that he himself puts no faith in it but that
Rome seems more addicted than ever to "these vanities and divination."

89. Screech identifies it as a Biblical Syriac known as Aramaic, one of the
earliest texts of the Bible. Chaldea is Southern Mesopotamia.

90. This is about the gist of Proverbs 25.3 and 25.5–8, though not an exact
quotation.

91. ". . . vocare te Galliarum florem delibatum," from Ennius *Annals* 309:
"Flos delibatus populi suadaeque medulla."

92. ". . . post hominum memoriam antistitem Parisiensem uere παρρησιάζειν":
this last word is in Greek and makes a clear play with the Latin *Parisiensem*
(Parisian, of Paris); R had already used the same pun in *Gargantua* 1.17.

93. Whereas the almanac for 1533 was close to R's *Pantagruel*, this one, for
1535, is close to its contemporary, *Gargantua,* in scope and concerns. It
starts with the strongest rational argument for immortality of the soul, sup-
ports that with Christian and secular examples and kindred ideas, urges
goodness and self-reliance for all, and finally peace and harmony for rulers,
who above all others should set good Christian examples, but by all their
war and troubles too often do the opposite.

94. Adapted from Xenophon *Memorabilia* 4.7.6.

95. Taking these four final cryptic items together: dominical letter "C": means
the letter marking all the Sundays, as days 3, 10, 17, 24, 31, 38, etc. of the
year. The golden number: see above, note 43. By the same calculation, the
golden number for 1535 will be 1535 + 1 ÷ 19 = 80 with a remainder of 16,
as stated in the text. The Romanist cycle of indiction is a period of 15
(Julian) years; the cycle of the sun is the 28-year period at the end of which
the same weekdays return on the same days of the month; R locates 1535
in the fourth such year (of the 28).

96. R and Cardinal du Bellay had stopped in Ferrara in late July, 1535 at the
court of Reformist sympathizer Renée de France, duchess of Este, and
evidently R had carried out a commission or two for d'Estissac, as he would
continue to do in Rome.

97. In and around Rome. In all matters of herbs, planting, etc., R is mindful of
the big differences in climate, seasons, and consequent requirements between Rome and Maillezais, over 700 miles further north.

98. "My affair" is R's request, ultimately granted, for papal absolution for his
apostasy in quitting monastic residence, and for full authorization to continue, as a lay cleric, his practice of medicine. This and the next two letters

(items 13–14) give further details about a matter much on R's mind and in his heart.

99. The governor was named by the pope; the conservators were elected by the people; the senator was the theoretical head of the city administration, but in the sixteenth century was under the thumb of the pope.

100. Just one more reminder that these people played rough, and of how precarious was the pope's police power even in Rome.

101. At that time the Romans counted the time of day from one sunset to the next, and in winter reckoned sunset at about 5 P.M.

102. Thought to be just possibly by R himself.

103. The term *le taxer* apparently meant a sort of registering.

104. "Maintenant le déposer ce seroyt acte de batelleurs qui font le faict et le deffaict."

105. Tanais is the ancient name of the river Don; but that cannot be the one described here that must be the Aassi, which runs past Antioch (Antakya).

106. Lerici: presumably a tiny port serving Lucca, about 15–20 miles inland.

107. La Tremelière is probably Joachim du Bellay's brother René, sieur de La Turmelière.

108. "Et ne sommes pas prests d'avoir légat en France." R's text explains the circumstances and the reason for his gloomy prediction.

109. Madame d'Estissac, a niece of the bishop's, was living in his house.

110. "My whole business" is the absolution, etc., noted above.

111. " . . . et ne m'a cousté que l'expédition des bulles." Clearly no great sum.

112. Jamet was the well-placed friend to whom the poet Marot addressed, from one of his prison stays, one of his most delightful epistles, his fable of the lion and the rat, the "Epistre à son ami Lion." Jamet was a clerk of finances in the service of the duke of Ferrara.

113. As, from R's account, well he might.

114. These are a sort of squadron sergeant-majors performing a very demanding though unglamorous task.

115. " . . . pour les intérêts qu'il y prétendoit."

116. For this prized condiment of marinated fish intestines see the Glossary.

117. Taken from M. A. Screech's critical edition (Droz, 1974) of the *Pantagrueline Prognostication pour l'an 1533 avec les Almanachs pour les ans 1533, 1535 et 1541. La grande et vraye Pronostication nouvelle de 1544.* The version in Demerson is more complete.

118. Antoine Hullot was Bailiff of Saint-Laurent-des-Orgerils-lez-Orléans; Hullot had once been a schoolmate of Calvin.

119. "How to clear up the ancient jurisdiction," but with a pun on *ju* and *jus* "juice (of the vine)."

120. "While preserving what is to be preserved, that is to say, that's it." Apparent parody of legalese, as in his address of the letter.

121. The address seems boyishly playful in its deliberately silly order.

122. A luscious title but probably not R's, and just a wee fragment.

123. Seraphino Calbarsy is one more near-anagram of François Rabelais.

124. Retrogradation: reversal of normal course (of a celestial body).

125. The French phrase used throughout this piece for A.M. is "avant midi," which of course could mean, as it does literally, that many hours before noon (i.e., eleven hours would mean 1 A.M., six hours 6 A.M., one hour 11 A.M., and so on.) Although I can find no clearcut answer to the question how morning times were counted in R's day, both the contexts here and the inherent probabilities seem to point out the interpretation used in our translation.

126. Whether this is A.M. or P.M. is not stated here or a few lines earlier.

127. The time when the two twin Gemini appear to us on earth to be three.

128. In R's time many from southern France thought of France as the northern part only, and spoke of going there as "going to France." We find little information about these fairs available or relevant.

129. "... le lundy de Quasimodo": Low Monday, thus the eighth day after Easter.

130. I am not sure of this date, but it seems to be October 6.

131. "Le cours de Gien": a town on the Loire about 40 miles southeast of Orléans. I can find nothing about this race, if such it was.

132. A town on the Oise about 40 miles northeast of Paris. About this fair, like most of those listed, I find details hard to come by, and perhaps not worth the attention of the reader. Almost all those listed were in the northern and northeastern part of central France and even then within reasonable range of Paris.

133. The Lendit fair, notable and mentioned in R's story, was held in the plain between La Chapelle and Saint-Denis.

134. Saint-Ayl is the home and château of R's good friend Estienne Lorens, seigneur de Saint-Ayl, a squire and man-at-arms in the company of Guillaume du Bellay, seigneur de Langey, with whom R was staying. Epistémon (4.27) lists him as present at Langey's death. R's waggish greeting is borrowed straight out of his old favorite the *Farce de Maistre Pathelin*, vv. 957–961.

135. Two facts deserve mention in this long laudatory account of the elaborate pageant and festival put on in Rome to celebrate the birth of a second son to King Henry II: R's heavy debt, demonstrated thirty-odd years ago by Richard Cooper, to a much earlier account in Italian, composed in March 1549 for Ippoito d'Este by Antonio Buonacorsi, which R followed in the main pretty closely even while enlarging and embellishing the parts and aspects most favorable to his cardinal patron and patient; the other, that R presents such an account as being part of a letter he wrote to Cardinal Louis de Guise (1527–1578), one of the leaders of this powerful and ambitious family, conservative in religion then as later, then as always competing strenuously with the liberal Du Bellay faction for influence with the king. The fact, Screech notes (*Rabelais*, p. 318) "is not without a certain irony."

136. The occasion, as the text explains, was the birth at Saint-Germain-en-Laye, between 3 and 4 A.M. on February 3, 1549, of a second son, Louis, duke of Orléans (between the future Kings Francis II and Charles IX), to King Henry II and Queen Catherine de Medici of France. The unfortunate infant was to die in 1550 after only twenty-one months of life. In those days bank couriers were often the earliest bearers of news—true and false—and of rumors, especially across national frontiers.

137. The famous duel (July 10, 1547) between these two favorites of Henry II ended in the death of La Chastaigneraye and led the king to ban all such duels.

138. In Rome in a time like this there were naturally groups of partisans favoring each of the competing sides, the French and the Imperials.

139. Erasmus notes in *Adages* 1.5.54 the ancient Roman custom of marking with white chalk the outstandingly blessed days, like our "red-letter" days, but stronger.

140. In Greek "burning": this is the title of the poem on the burning of Troy that Nero was singing while Rome burned.

141. As the text explains, the Tiber is treacherous and very dangerous at times, subject in spring especially to violent heavy sudden flooding with only short warning.

142. This of course is Cardinal Jean du Bellay.

143. A gifted military architect and engineer.

144. Two great, old, and powerful Roman houses were hereditary enemies: the Colonna and Orsini families. In R's time the Colonnas were pro-Empire and anti-France; the Orsini, for France against the Empire.

145. His Excellency is of course Cardinal Jean du Bellay.

146. Diana figured in all pageants under Henry II as a tribute to his mistress and favorite, Diane de Poitiers (1499–1566). In myth, literature, and portrayals, Diana was always represented as standing about a head taller than her attendant nymphs.

147. " . . . il failloit jouer des cousteaux et n'oublier rien en la boutique."

148. Malicorne the Younger: this is the same Jean de Chourses, seigneur de Malicorne, who was to become governor of Poitou in 1585, and as such be ordered by Queen Mother Catherine de Medici to see to Michel de Montaigne (presumably make sure he enjoyed a safe return home) after she had summoned Montaigne to the Colloquies (Conférences) at Saint-Brice near Cognac (Charente) in midwinter 1586–1587; see EC Vol. 6 (Book 4, chaps. 1–17), p. 93, where we also learn that in 1549 he was an "écuyer d'écurie" (a groom in the royal stables, I believe); see also my *Montaigne: A Biography* (New York; Harcourt, Brace and World, 1965), p. 267. The connection between him and R's fictive Malicorne (in 4.3), however, is not clear.

149. " . . . tant jetté de mattons, micraines, potz et lances à feu, que tout le voisinage en retondissoit."

150. "... et, quoy qu'ilz fussent couvers à l'advantage, plusieurs y furent désarmez."

151. This and the prayer before it were common practice before battle in R's day.

152. "... ayant baisé la terre": a standard custom then of Christian armies before going into battle.

153. Frérot and Fabrizio were apparently a team of two performing apart from the "archclown" Moreto [le Moret], but in a supporting role.

154. "... et tant de sciopes, fusées en canon, palles et lances à feu."

155. "... qu'il y paroistra encores d'icy trois mois."

156. Jean du Bellay, once more.

157. King Henry II of France.

158. "Nous avons veu ce que personne en Romme vivant ne veit, personne en Romme vivant ne verra."

159. "Aussi fut la maison de mon dit Seigneur Révérendissime ouverte à tous venans, quelz qu'ilz fussent, tout iceluy jour."

160. Labbat, unknown to us, was clearly an eminent singer-reciter then in Rome, presumably in Du Bellay's employ.

161. Cardinal du Bellay's Latin Sapphic Ode, here our next item as no. 22.

162. "... en avoit esté jouée une, laquelle, pus fâcha que ne pleut aux assistans, tant à cause de sa longueur et mines Bergamasques assez fades, que pour l'invention bien froide et argument trivial."

163. "Il n'y eut rien perdu n'esgaré."

164. "Le tout fait par l'invention dudit Vincentio, et du Bois le Court, grand salpêtrier du Maine." Vincenzo (Vincentio), a Roman was one of the pope's bombardiers.

165. A more lyrical, less complex strophic verse form than the Pindaric ode, the Sapphic ode is yet a highly complex and demanding form, which Cardinal Jean du Bellay must have known well and probably attempted in Latin in practice for him to undertake—and bring off successfully—in so conspicuous a place and on such a gala occasion. It testifies to the rich learning and culture of him and the likes of him.

166. The blessed sires are the cardinals, in the College of Cardinals; the aged pastor, the pope (Paul III, then past 80), who was to die later that year.

167. The "race of the Quirites" were the people of Rome.

168. Marseille, founded by a colony from Phocis in northern Greece west of Boeotia. When King Francis of France sent for Catherine de Medici as his future daughter-in-law she came by sea, landing in triumph at Marseille.

169. Surely no irony intended. The union was fruitful, but if Catherine had had any hopes for loving fidelity, Henry's undying devotion to Diane de Poitiers must soon have crushed it.

170. Unlike others in the poem, this nymph is a purely allegorical figure.

171. This cannot be Margaret of Valois (see Demerson and LI, p. 987), for she

was born in 1553. But this hardly narrows down much the question who this is; and I have no answer or clear clue to offer. The Jeanne cited soon after is Jeanne d'Albret (1528–1572), mother-to-be of Henry IV.

172. Orazio Farnese, son of the grand Pierluigi Farnese and grandson of Pope Paul III, at this time engaged to Diane de France, legitimized daughter of Henry II and Diane de Poitiers.

173. Young Diane, the bride-to-be.

174. This legerdemain of Du Bellay's is complicated and depends on a theory he liked, as did many, of the Trojan descent of the French kings.

175. This Greek term for end, in Greek capital letters, is a final flourish.

Glossary

Few authors need annotation as much as Rabelais (R) for even an intelligible translation; and in this Glossary (GL) our aim is to provide the necessary minimum as briefly as possible while also avoiding note duplication. We offer the first or most typical use of each glossed term. The Glossary includes most proper names and many other words or phrases calling for elucidation that recur several times, but few trivial place-names such as many in R's neighborhood around Chinon and La Devinière. This Glossary may not be complete, but we think it is nearly enough to be useful to supply new information or a brief review, sometimes even background information. A complete set of notes would swamp the text, and a complete index or glossary would, we think, risk outweighing it. What follows is a compromise; we ask the reader to accept it as that and not expect more of it than it is designed to offer. It is long and complements a long set of notes; but any acceptable alternative would, we believe, have to be unacceptably longer.

NOTES ON OUR ALPHABETIC ORDERING

References to saints are listed under the given name (Anthony, Saint; John, Saint, etc.); but when they refer to something named for the saint (and whenever hyphenated) we alphabetize under Saint. And we usually list hyphenated words as though without hyphens (Saint-Brigitte and Sainte-Barbe before Saint-Innocent and Saint-Mesme). We have used few cross-references for saints' names, but many elsewhere. We have generally assumed the q.v., and not expressed it. Each item ends with a reference to book and chapter in Rabelais; this reference is either the first occurrence or a typical entry.

947

ABEL: Genesis 4.4–9; son of Adam and Eve; slain by brother Cain; the first man to die: 2.1.

ABSALOM: son of David, revolted and tried to kill him, but riding into battle, caught his head between two branches of a tree and hanged himself (2 Samuel 18.9): 1.42.

ABSTRACTOR (OF QUINTESSENCE): the original title assumed by the purported author-narrator, Master Alcofribas Nasier, later extended (5.21) to the whole traveling party as honorary officers of hers, joining regular titleholders: 1.opening page.

ABYDOS: a Phrygian city on the Hellespont, across which young Leander often swam to visit his ladylove Hero, a priestess of Aphrodite. When he was drowned in a storm, she soon after drowned herself for love and grief: 3.26.

ACADEMY, ACADEMIC(s): Plato's school (the Academy) in Athens and its philosophers: 3.3.

ACCURSIUS, ACCURSIAN, ACCURSIANTIST(s): Francesco Accorso (1180–1260) of Bologna, influential law professor whom R despised for his orderly glosses in barbaric Latin: 2.5.

ACHATES: Aeneas's faithful companion in Virgil's Aeneid: 2.9.

ACHERON: one of the four rivers of Hades; Milton's "Acheron of sorrow, black and deep" (Paradise Lost 2.578): 2.30.

ACHILLAS: unknown peasant who cut off the head of fleeing Pompey the Great after defeat at Pharsalia (in Thessaly, 48 B.C.): 4.37.

ACHILLES: Homer's noble Greek warrior-hero in the Iliad, whose anger at King Agamemnon is the subject of the book: 2.30.

ACHORIA, ACHORIAN(s): from Greek achoros "without the dance"; Thomas More's Utopians; the epithet is used of Ares as sign of the grimness of war; here apparently a fictive African kingdom near Gargantua's fictive kingdom of Utopia: 2.24.

ACRISIUS: a mythic king of Argos whose daughter Danae Jupiter seduced: 3.12.

ACROPOLIS: in Greek "upper city"; used especially of that of Athens, a massive citadel with grand temples, notably that of Athena: 4.49.

ACTEON, ACTAEON: in Greek myth, then Ovid's Metamorphoses (3.140 ff.), a princely Greek huntsman who by ill chance came upon Artemis bathing nude; she, furious, changed him into a stag, and, as such, he was torn to pieces by his own hounds: 3.14.

ACTS OF THE APOSTLES: in New Testament, spreading the Gospel of Christ: 2.8.

ADALIA (OR ANTALYA OR SATALIA): see Satalia.

ADAM: in Genesis 1, the first man: 4.24.

ADAM COUSCOIL: see Couscoil, Adam.

ADMIRAL (AMIRAL): in R's time a chief military (not merely naval) commander; here means Philippe de Chabot (1480–1543), Lord of Brion, Count of Buzançais, Amiral of France, Brittany, Guyenne; once governor of Burgundy; conqueror of Piedmont (1535): 1.9.

ADONIS: perhaps drawn from a Semitic vegetation myth; in Greek myth a beautiful youth loved passionately but vainly by Aphrodite; killed hunting a boar; Ovid's *Metamorphoses* 10 traces origins of some flowers to his blood and her resulting tears: 1.6.

ADRASTEA, ADRASTEIA: one of the Cretan nymphs to whom Rhea entrusted the infant Zeus: 1.8.

AEDILE: a Roman official in charge of public works and games, police, and the grain supply.

AEDITUS: from Latin *aedituus* "guide"; the title, here used as a proper name, of Albian Camat, sacristan of the Ringing Island: 5.2.

AEGISTHUS (AIGISTHOS): in Greek legend and drama, the son by incest of Thyestes and his daughter Pelopia; lover of Clytemnestra of Mycenae and her accomplice in killing her husband King Agamemnon, thus causing the tragedy presented in Aeschylus's *Oresteia*, a trilogy: 3.31.

AELIAN (CLAUDIUS AELIANUS, FL. CA. A.D. 200): uncritical author of historical miscellanies in Greek: 1.23.

AEMILIUS PAULUS, LUCIUS: see Paulus, Lucius Aemilius.

AENEAS (AINAIAS): Greco-Roman legend, epic; son of Aphrodite and mortal Anchises; in I*liad* a brave but not topnotch Trojan warrior and leader; but as hero of *Aeneid*, the godly slave of duty and conquering hero; founder of a future Rome and progenitor-to-be by his marriage (to come) with Latian princess Lavinia, still ahead at end of book: 2.9.

AENEID: Virgil's twelve-book Latin epic poem about the perilous voyages of Aeneas from fallen, burned Troy to Italy (his *Odyssey*, Books 1–5); his visit (6) to Hades and dead Trojan heroes, where Anchises continues Sibyl's prophecy by foretelling much of Rome's future; and finally (his *Iliad*, Books 10–12) the taxing war for the future Roman territory with the indigenous Latians spurred on by vengeful Juno and led by Latian hero-prince Turnus, whom Aeneas finally kills in single combat. Virgil greatly condenses Homer's starker material, glamorizes and stylizes it, making it more worthy of the Augustan majesty of imperial Rome, but gives clear hints of the dangers of absolute power. Read parts of it to his backer Emperor Augustus, and spent his last eleven years (30–19 B.C.) writing and revising it; but died dissatisfied, urging it be burned: 3.10.

AESCHINEAS: this one not Demosthenes's famous rival orator but a lesser rhetor, philosopher, and disciple of Socrates, but for whom Plato had little respect: 3.10.

AESCHYLUS (AISCHULOS, 525–456 B.C.): first in time of the three great Greek tragedians, all from Athens; a nobleman, proud of fighting at Marathon; left some nondramatic poems and about 90 tragedies, of which 7 survive, including the plays of his Oresteia trilogy: *Agamemnon, The Libation Bearers,* and *The Eumenides*; the four others are *Prometheus Bound, The Suppliants, The Persians,* and *The Seven against Thebes.* He is noted for treating great issues, characters larger than life, lofty, heroic speeches, and faith in the ultimate though slowly emerging justice of the gods. R loves the story of his death that has a myopic high-flying eagle mistake his bald head for a rock and drop a tortoise it was carrying on his head, breaking the shell but also his skull: 3.P.

AESCULAPIUS (ASKLAPIOS): in Greek myth the son of Apollo and Cofinis; because of her infidelity, entrusted to tutelage of the centaur Chiron, who taught him medicine. At the prayer of Artemis he restored to life her favorite Hippolytus, victim of Aphrodite; but Zeus, angry at his interference with actions of a goddess, slew him with a thunderbolt. God of medicine, he fathered physicians Machaon and Podaleirios (*Iliad*); his worship centered in Epidaurus (in Argolis, Peloponnesus): 3.3.

AESOP (AISOPOS): lived mid-sixth c. B.C.; slave of a Thracian, says Herodotus; the traditional composer of fables, usually moral, about animals that represent men: 2.1.

AFRICA: medieval name of Tunisia, N of the town of Meheddia: 4.P.

AFRICA, AFRICAN(S): the great continent: 1.16.

AGAMEMNON: in Greek legend, the king of Mycenae, son of Atreus, brother of Menelaus king of Sparta; leader of the great Greek expedition that after ten years took and burned Troy, killed their men, and enslaved their women, then had troubles getting back home and once back there: 3.21.

AGELASTES: Greek *agelastoi,* "the unlaughing": 4.OP.

AGENOR: in Greek myth the king of Tyre and of Europa, by whom Zeus, in the form of a bull, sired Minos, Rhadamanthus, and perhaps Sarpedon: 3.12.

AGESILAUS (CA. 444–361 B.C.): lame but able generally; led Spartans to defeat Persians (396–395) then both Athenians and Thebans at Coronea (395); but less fortunate later; killed in a campaign undertaken to raise money for needy Sparta: 2.15.

AGNUS DEI: one-crown gold coins stamped with Paschal lamb, a symbol of Jesus, and a banner with a cross and a halo; R often calls them "long-woolled sheep" ("moutons à la grand laine"): 4.P.

AGRICOLA: presumably Alexander Agricola (d. 1506), musician active in Italy from 1472 on: 4.P.

AGRIPINA (OR AGRIPPINA): third of that name; mother of Nero; married again, to Claudius (Roman emperor A.D. 41–64); her son Nero had her killed A.D. 59: 3.24.

AHASUERUS: Biblical form of Greek Xerxes, Persian Ksharshaya; king of Persia 486–465 B.C.: 1.51.

AJAX: in Greek Aias, plural Aiantes; in legend and *Iliad*, the greater, of Salamis, son of Telamon; and, as here, the lesser, of Locris, son of Oileus: 3.12.

ALANUS IN *PARABOLIS*: Alanus de Insulis (Alain de Lille, bishop of Auxerre [thirteenth c.]); wrote a standard class text, the *Liber parabolarum*: 1.14.

ALBA: or Alba Longa: "the White," whose founding prefigured Rome's; long Rome's rival: 1.10.

ALBANIA, ALBANIAN(S): here used mainly of their light cavalrymen or stradiots, hired as guards by French kings; noted for their tall pointed caps: 2.31.

ALBERICUM DE ROSATA: Aubry (Albericus) de Rosata, of Bergamo, a fourteenth-c. expert on canon law, whom some called the Doctor Practicus: 2.7.

ALBERTUS (LEONE BATTISTA ALBERTI, LATE FIFTEENTH C.): Florentine architect; author of the influential *De re aedificatoria*: 2.7.

ALBUNEA: a site of an ancient oracle near Rome: 3.24.

ALCIBIADES (CA. 450–404 B.C.): brilliant, daring Athenian leader, but unscrupulous and unreliable; admirer and one-time pupil of Socrates; changed sides repeatedly in the Peloponnesian Wars, ending on the Persian side when they moved in: 1.P.

ALCMAN (SEVENTH C. B.C.): Spartan poet born in Sardis: 4.26.

ALCMENE: in Greek myth, the wife of Theban general Amphitryon, whose likeness Zeus, desiring her, put on to lie with her while Amphitryon was away at war; she bore Iphicles, held to be son of Amphitryon; and Hercules (Herakles q.v.) held to be the son of Zeus, the great and mighty slayer of monsters, bandits, all enemies to man: 1.3.

ALCOFRIBAS NASIER (AN), MASTER: R's favorite pseudonym (and anagram); narrator and purported author of Books 1–2; also a character in these (not in 3); and seemingly in 4. See Abstractor, Stargazer.

ALCORAN (CORAN, KORAN): the holy book of Islam; words of Mohammed: 2.14.

ALECTO: see Allecto.

ALEXANDER: Alessandro Tartagno, a fourteenth-c. Italian jurist: 2.10.

ALEXANDER: a squire of Gargantua:1.51 and Salome's husband: 4.26.

ALEXANDER, POPE: Alexander VI (Borgia, 1431–1503); pope from 1492: 1.21.

ALEXANDER CORNELIUS: a natural historian quoted by Pliny: 3.52.

ALEXANDER MYNDIUS: a third-c. philosopher from Myndus in Caria, Asia Minor: 3.21.

ALEXANDER OF APHRODISIAS (FL. CA. A.D. 200): author of *Problemata*; a very important early commentator in Greek of Aristotle; often quoted later: 1.10.

ALEXANDER SEVERUS: succeeded Heliogabalus in A.D. 222 as emperor of Rome: 3.10.

ALEXANDER THE GREAT: Alexander III of Macedon (356–323 B.C.); the greatest of ancient western conquerors; trained by father Philip II; tutored by Aristotle; devotee of *Iliad* and of Achilles; succeeded on father Philip's death (336); after a tough struggle, capped father's conquest of Greece by leading Greeks in war of conquest, invaded Asia, defeated Persians (the Granicus, 334) to win Asia Minor; on plain of Issus in Cilicia (333) beat them again, captured King Darius and his queen; in 332–331 conquered Syria and Egypt after tough siege of Tyre; then on to conquer most of India; but there his battered and exhausted troops made him turn back; made his great empire a fusion of Europe and Asia; died of a fever in Babylon in summer 323, aged 32: 1.14.

ALEXANDRIA: great Egyptian port city named for Alexander, with grand library: 2.18.

ALI: Ali Abenragel; eleventh-c. Arabian astronomer, often spoofed in almanacs: 6.8.

ALIBANTES: Greek "parched or withered"; but despite R, not in Homer as a proper name: 2.2.

ALKATIN, AL KATIM: Arabic terms for the sacrum: 3.20.

ALLECTO (OR ALECTO): in Greek myth, one of the Furies (Erinyes), avengers of dead kin: 4.47.

ALLIACO, DE: PIERRE D'AILLY, 1350–1420: theologian, author of a *Perpetual Almanac* and of *Suppositions* and *Insolubilia*: 2.16.

ALLOBROGIANS: warlike Gauls from Gallia Narbonensis (roughly Languedoc): 1.33.

ALMAIN, JACOB: a sixteenth-c. Ockhamist theologian and author: 1.21.

ALOÏDAE: rebel giants who once tried to scale Mount Olympus: 3.51.

ALPHARBAL: fictive king of fictive Canarre; showed his boundless gratitude for Grandgousier's benign clemency: 1.50.

ALPS, ALPINE: the great mountain chain separating France and Switzerland from Italy: 3.52.

AMALTHEA: either the nannygoat who gave milk or the nymph who gave nannygoat's milk to the infant Zeus when his mother Rhea hid him on Crete from jealous Cronos: 5.A32.

AMATA: Latin for "beloved"; wife of King Latinus, mother of Lavinia and fiancée of Aeneas in Virgil's *Aeneid*; her grief for her city's fate and her role in it leads her to hang herself (*Aeneid* 12.604): 3.51.

AMAUROT(S): Greek for "indistinct"; named for the capital of More's *Utopia*; similarly here their city is the capital of Pantagruel's country and its citizen subjects, which he comes and saves from the attack by the Dipsodes: 2.2.

AMMON: chief god of the ancient Ammonians (Egypt-Libya); identified with Jupiter as Jupiter Ammon: 3.12.

AMPHIARAUS: in Greek myth, an Argive seer and hero; an Argonaut and a member of the Caledonian boar hunt. His wife Eriphyle, bribed with a fatal necklace, got him to join the expedition of the Seven against Thebes, though he knew all who did would die; in retreat swallowed up in the earth; avenged in good time by his son Alcmaeon: 3.13.

AMPHION: in Greek myth, the son of Zeus and Theban Antiope; a harper so gifted that he could move stones by playing; and thus built the walls of Thebes: 3.P.

AMPHITRYON: in Greek myth, Theban general, husband of Alcmene (q.v.): 3.12.

AMY (OR LAMY), PIERRE: R's friend and Greek tutor in monastery at Fontenay; led him to write to Budé; fellow member of Tiraqueau's Hellenist circle in that town; when his and R's books taken from them there, fled monastery and order for good; lived in Basel among peaceful Reformists; died young in 1525; see Henri Busson (*ER* 6 [1965]:1–50): 3.10.

ANACHARSIS: a sixth-c. B.C. Scythian sage who traveled to study many countries and, says Herodotus, tried to bring their ways into Scythia, but was killed by their king: 2.18.

ANACREON: a noted playful early Greek poet (sixth c. B.C.) cited by R for his strange death: 4.17.

ANARCHE: Greek for "unruler": aggressor king of Dipsodes in Pantagruel, comically punished: 2.28.

ANAXAGORAS: early fifth-c. B.C. Greek philosopher of nature; saw matter as infinitely varied, the mind as organizing and directing it: 2.18.

ANCENIS (LOIRE-ATLANTIQUE): a small town on the Loire near Nantes: 1.38.

ANCHISES: in Greco-Roman myth and story, one of Trojan royal houses; loved by Aphrodite, who bore him Aeneas; boasted of this, maimed by Zeus's thunderbolt; carried by Aeneas from burning Troy, taken on wanderings; died in Sicily and buried there on Mount Eryx: 2.29.

ANDRÉ, JO: Giovanni Andrea, fifteenth-c. Italian humanist; tells story of Seigny Joan: 3.37.

ANDROMEDA: girl saved from sea monster by Perseus (q.v.): 4.33.

ANGEL CROWNS, ANGELOTS, ANGELS: once gold one-crown coins showing St. Michael; slowly devalued to ca. 50–80 percent of that: 3.25.

ANGERS, ANGEVIN(S): Maine-et-Loire, on the Maine, former capital of Anjou, ca. 180 miles SW of Paris; cathedral, big strong old castle: 2.4.

ANGOULÊME (CHARENTE): capital of old Angoumois; small city ca. 270 miles SW of Paris, on the Charente: 1.33.

ANIMAL SPIRITS: see spirits.

ANTHONY, SAINT (SAINT ANTOINE, CA. A.D. 251–350): hermit, founder of hermit colony near Egyptian Thebes and, in effect, of European monasticism; cited here for his order but mainly for his fire, a kind of ergotism, then widespread and potentially dangerous: 1.17.

ANTICHRIST, THE: the great antagonist destined to bring much evil to the world but will finally be beaten not long before the world ends: 3.25.

ANTICYRA: Greek city on Phocis, noted for its hellebore, then rated the best cure for insanity: 1.23.

ANTIDOTED FRIGGLEFRAGGLES (FANFRELUCHES ANTIDOTÉES): a nonsense title for some nonsense verse; a reportedly ancient document introducing Gargantua: 1.2.

ANTIOCH: modern Antakya, Turkey; ancient capital of Syria, on the Orontes near the Mediterranean; a great trade center and pleasure city; founded ca. 400 B.C. by Seleucus I and named for his father, as were other cities founded later by other Seleucid kings: 3.24.

ANTIOCHUS: name of Seleucus; here probably Antiochus I Soter, son of Alexander's officer Seleucus (ruled 323–281 B.C.) who succeeded to rule in Asia; Antiochus Soter (324–261 B.C.), king of Syria, was noted as a founder of cities: 2.30.

ANTIPODES: lands on the opposite side of the earth from Eurasia and Africa (ca. modern Australia); their existence, denied by Augustine, still therefore doubted by many, generally questioned: 2.2.

ANTITUS: a traditional name for a witless pedant: 5.2.

ANTONINUS (MARCUS AURELIUS ANTONINUS, A.D. 188–217): best known, by nickname Caracalla, for his infamy and cruelty and the baths he built: 2.30.

ANTWERP: French Anvers; a big busy N Belgian North Sea port on the Scheldt: 2.11.

ANUBIS: Egyptian god of the dead and of embalming; has dog or jackal head: 4.2.

APEDEFTE(S): Greek *apaideutai* or "ignoramuses; judges and minions," possibly of the Chambre des Comptes, concerned with taxes, audits, accounts; perhaps less menacing than the Furred Cats of the Wicket (Book 5, chapters 11–15), but quite as greedy and financially devastating: 5.A16.

APHRODISIUM: the gods' name for the Mediterranean Tunisian port men call Africa, near Mehedia; captured in August 1551 by pro-papal Spaniards, which led the Turks to enter the war on the side of the French: 4.P.

APHRODITE: Greek love goddess; Roman Venus; wife of Hephaistos, mistress of Ares, mother of Eros (Cupid) and by Anchises of Aeneas: 4.37.

APICIUS, QUINTUS GAVIUS: a Roman gourmet under Tiberius: (q.v.): 5.22.

APIS: Egyptian bull worshiped as a god in the form of a bull: 3.24.

APOLLO, APOLLONIAN (PHOEBUS): Greco-Roman god of sunlight, music and poetry: 1.45.

APOLLO CLARIUS: of Clarus, Asia Minor, near Colophon; site of a famous oracle: 3.24.

APOLLO CYNTHIUS: born of Cynthus: 3.45.

APOLLONIUS OF RHODES OR RHODIUS (CA. 295–215 B.C.): unrelated to the above; author of a still extant Greek epic poem in four books, *Argonautica*: 4.20.

APOLLONIUS OF TYANA (BORN CA. 4 B.C. IN CAPPADOCIA): Pythagorean philosopher, mystic, thaumaturge whose powers some considered divine: 3.18.

APOSTLE, THE HOLY: one of several such names for Saint Paul: 3.5.

APOSTLE(S) OF JESUS: scorned by Frère Jean for cowardice at Gethsemane: 1.39.

APULEIUS, LUCIUS (FL. CA. A.D. 155): Roman philosopher and storyteller; left a defense of magic, a study of Plato, some verses, and above all his tale of desire and of magic *The Golden Ass* or *Metamorphoses*, a Latin prose romance still fully alive today: 5.29.

AQUINAS, SAINT THOMAS (1225–1274): the "Angelic Doctor"; main source of scholasticism; in 1879 pronounced official Catholic doctrine by Pope Leo XIII: 3.2.

ARAB(S), ARABIAN, ARABIC: a major source of lore and culture, including the Greco-Roman, in the European late Middle Ages and Renaissance: 1.23.

ARACHNE: in Greek myth, a brash Lydian woman who challenged Athena to a weaving contest, then in her web showed the gods' amours; Athena beat her, tore up her web; she hanged herself; Athena relented and changed her into a spider to weave at will (Ovid *Metamorphoses* 6.1–150): 2.16.

ARCADIA (N): a mountainous region in the central Peloponnese: 3.P.

ARCHIMEDES (CA. 287–212 B.C.): great Syracusan inventor, astronomer, mathematician, and physicist: 2.7.

ARCHYTAS OF TARENTUM (FL. CA. 400 B.C.): a Pythagorean philosopher and mathematician; also a military leader: 2.18.

ARDILLON, ABBÉ ANTOINE: humanist friend of André Tiraqueau: 2.5.

AREOPAGUS, AREOPAGITE(S): in Greek myth, hill of Ares; a hill on the side of the Acropolis in Athens; the court of justice sat there, and its judges reputed most just; in myth, Ares was tried there for killing his daughter, a son of Poseidon. More famous, in legend, was the trial of Orestes for killing his mother Clytemnestra to avenge her murder of his father, her husband, Agamemnon, he being bound to avenge his father the king. Pursued and persecuted by the Furies (Eumenides) for this murder of his, he was saved by Athena, who gave him asylum at her temple, submitted his case to the Areopagites and when their all-human jury split their votes, herself cast the deciding vote for acquittal; a court fabled for wisdom and justice: 3.34.

ARGO, ARGONAUT(S): in Greek myth, Jason's ship and shipmates on voyage north to remote Colchis to recover the Golden Fleece of the winged ram who bore Phrixus and Helle over the Hellespont until she fell in and drowned: 3.52.

ARGOS, ARGIVE(S), ARGOLIS: important city and state and inhabitants in E Peloponnesus; also Homer's term for all Hellenes who sailed against Troy: 1.10.

ARGUS: in Greek myth, the hundred-eyed herdsman sent by Hera to watch Io but killed by Hermes; name also of the Argo's builder and (as Argos) of Odysseus's dog in the *Odyssey* (17.292): 1.5.

ARIMASPIAN(S): Herodotus (3.113–114; 4.13, 27) says this is a remote tribe of one-eyed Scythians who rob griffins of the gold they guard; here they may represent the N European peoples who reject observance of Lent: 5.28.

ARISTAEUS: a Greek god of bee-keeping and hunting; lusting for Orpheus's wife Eurydice, pursued her; in her flight, she trod on a snake and was bitten and died; the Dryads killed his beloved bees, but when his fit sacrifice of bulls and heifers appeased her spirit, they produced a new swarm to replenish his hives (Virgil *Georgics* 4.315 ff.): 5.3.

ARISTOPHANES (448-CA.-380 B.C.): the great Athenian dramatist of the Old Comedy from the 420s to the 380s B.C., including *Acharnians, Knights, Clouds, Wasps, Peace, Birds, Lysistrata,* combining satires of politicos and novelties and constant earnest appeals for peace from the insane, continuing Peloponnesian Wars: 3.21.

ARISTOTLE (OF STAGIRA, IN THE CHALCIDICE, 384–322 B.C.): great Athenian philosopher and organizer of human knowledge; student, then critic, of Plato; trusting reason less, experience more; in Middle Ages and for many later, the philosopher; but challenged more and more by Plato in the Renaissance; in R's day noted especially for his *Organon* (logic), *Categories* (terms and predicates), *Metaphysics* (or First Philosophy), *Ethics, Politics, Rhetoric, Poetics*, only after 1536, then influential: 1.1.

ARMENIA, ARMENIAN(S): ancient SW Asian kingdom in mountains SE of Black Sea, SW of Caspian Sea; now part of the USSR: 1.33.

ARMORICA, ARMORICAN ISLANDS: old name for Brittany and islands off its coast in NE Atlantic: 1.50.

ARTAXERXES I (ARDASHIR, 464–425 B.C.): king of Persia, during whose reign the kingdom lost much of its power to rebels: 2.30.

ARTEMIDORUS DALDIANUS: A.D. second-c. Roman soothsayer, whose books on dreams were among those Pantagruel studied in preparing to debate Thaumaste: 2.18.

ARTEMIS: in Greek myth, daughter of Zeus and Leto, thus Apollo's sister; virgin goddess of hunt, like Roman Diana, of childbirth, and the very young; finally of the moon; Ephesus the center of her worship: 3.50.

ARTHUR: legendary Briton king, head of Round Table of chivalrous knights; his legend based on exploits of a sixth-c. military leader: 2.30.

ARTOIS: old county in NW France next to Flanders; capital, Arras: 1.33.

ASCLEPIADES: not the noted epigrammatist but a cocky doctor whose lasting health won him a bet with Fortune: 4.P.

ASIA: the largest continent; home of China, India, Siberia, Japan, etc.: 3.26.

ASIA MINOR: the large, mainly Turkish, far western promontory of Asia: 1.26.

ASSYRIA, ASSYRIAN(S): a mighty ancient Mesopotamian culture and empire: 1.1.

ATE: early Greek myth; blind folly personified, downward step on path from hubris (arrogant pride) to nemesis (righteous indignation of the gods) and that to man's complete downfall: 1.2.

ATHENA OR ATHENE (PALLAS): Greek goddess of wisdom like Roman Minerva and of Athens; daughter of Zeus and his wife Metis (Counsel); swallowed by Zeus lest she bear him a son stronger than he; Athena sprang full-grown from Zeus's head, split open with an axe by Hephaestus; Athena joins wisdom with power: 3.50.

ATHENAEUS (ATHENAIOS, FL. CA. A.D. 200): of Naucratis, best known for his Greek *Deipnosophistai* (*Connoisseurs in dining*), 15 books of talk among 23 learned Romans who converse anecdotally about food and countless other matters: 1.23.

ATHENS, ATHENIAN(S): in fifth c. B.C. especially, by far the leading Greek city-state, in power, trade, politics, government, all branches of culture, including drama, letters, philosophy; a democracy of its citizens: 1.10.

ATLANTIC (SEA OR OCEAN): between Europe and the Americas; then thought to be the edge of the world, west of the known world: 1.31.

ATLAS: in Greek myth, a Titan's son, once comrade to Hercules; for his part in Titans' revolt, condemned to hold up the heavens with his head and hands, somewhere far in the unknown west: 2.1.

ATOMS (OF EPICURUS, Q.V.): in his system the indivisible (atomoi) units by whose junction (as they swerve slightly in their fall) all matter as we know it is formed; on this, Lucretius is our best source: 4.2.

ATROPOS: in Greek myth, of the three Fates (moirae), the one whose scissors cut the thread of life: 3.51.

AUGSBURG: a large city in Bavaria (SW Germany) on the Lech River; in R's day a great trade and banking center; home of the proverbially rich Fugger family of bankers: 1.8.

AUGUSTUS (JULIUS CAESAR OCTAVIANUS, 63 B.C.–A.D. 14): first emperor of Rome, assuming the new name Augustus with the imperium: 2.6. See also Octavian(us).

AULULARIA (*THE POT OF GOLD*): a comedy by Plautus (q.v.); 254–184 B.C.: 3.P.

AULUS GELLIUS (A.D. SECOND C.): compiled *Latin Noctes Atticae* (*Attic Nights*) in 20 books; mainly anecdotes and minor points about minor writers: 1.3.

AUNIS (MODERN DEUX-SÈVRES AND CHARENTE-MARITIME): a French Atlantic region, former province N of Saintonge and S of Vendée: 1.33.

AURELIANUS (LUCIUS DOMITIUS; AURELIAN, CA. A.D. 213–275): emperor of Rome 270–275; fortified Rome and the Empire; made conquests in Near East: 3.1.

AVE MARIA(S): a Roman Catholic prayer to the Virgin (Hail, Mary); salutation leading to a plea for her intercession: 1.40.

AVENZOAR (ABD EL-MALIK IBN ZUHR, ABU MARWAN, ELEVENTH-TWELFTH C.): noted Arab physician; teacher of Averroes (q.v.); author of the *Liber Teisir, sive rectificatio medicationis et regiminis*: 6.8.

AVERNUS: from Greek *aornos* "birdless"; a lake near Naples with nearby cave, on Aeneas's route to visit his father and other Trojan dead in Hades (*Aeneid* 6.293 ff.): 4.66.

959

AVERROES, AVERROIST: Muhammad Ibn Rochd, twelfth-c. Arab physician, philosopher, and commentator on Aristotle; had great influence in Europe from Middle Ages on: 4.OC.

AVICENNA (IBN SINA, 979–1037): Arab doctor and philosopher; long widely read in France; Islamic, Persian-born, best known for his *Canon of medicine*: 1.10.

AVIGNON (VAUCLUSE): a city on the Rhône, upstream from Arles but still near its mouth; archbishopric, papal palace; site of "Babylonian captivity" of Papacy, 1309–1378; in R's day merry, free-living, notorious for its fleshpots: 2.5.

AVOISTRE: already in R's day an old term for a bastard: 3.14.

AYMON, THE FOUR SONS OF: a popular medieval tale of derring-do: 1.27.

BABIN: a Chinon cobbler: 1.16.

BABOLIN ("SAINCT BABOLIN LE BON SAINCT"): R's tribute to Abbé Babolin of Sain-Maur: 3.3.

BABYLON, BABYLONIA, BABYLONIAN(S): a great ancient capital city, on the Euphrates, and its Mesopotamian empire; from after the downfall of Assyria and the time of its own great founder and lawgiver Hammurabi (fl. 1792–1750 B.C.); a scene of Jewish slavery and captivity so often lamented in the Old Testament, but crucial to maturing of Jewish religious thought: 1.33.

BACBUC: in BD, "bottle, in Hebrew, from the sound it makes when it is emptied"; compare English "chugalug," etc.; also the Bottle's pontiff or high-priestess: 4.1.

BACCHUS (BAKCHOS), BACCHANT(S), BACCHIC, ETC.: a Greco-Roman god (probably originally Thracian) of wine, intoxication, frenzy, ecstasy; Nietzsche's Dionysiac side of man; also of poetry, music, comedy, and tragedy; subject of myriad myths and legends, such as this one of conquest of India; a latecomer among Olympians, not in Homer; son of Zeus and queen Semel of Thebes; she was consumed by fire in their intercourse; Jupiter hid unborn babe in thigh, later "bore" him; Bacchus later ruined Thebans for not honoring him enough. See Euripides's tragedy *The Baccants*, produced posthumously in 405 B.C.: 1.P.

BACTRIA, BACTRIAN(S): ancient S Asian region (now Balkh, N Afghanistan): 3.P.

BADEBEC: wife of Gargantua, mother of Pantagruel; dies in childbirth; praised in death by Gargantua in verse: 2.2.

BAGNOLET, BAIGNOLET: now a suburb E of Paris (Seine-Saint-Denis); then a sizeable town best known for the proverbial cowardice of its Francs-Archers (Free Archers), a militia started ca. 1450 by Louis XI but soon dropped; subject of a clever monologue in 1468 ascribed by some to François Villon: 2.7.

BALDUS (PETRUS BALDUS DE UBALDIS, FOURTEENTH C.): legal authority; rated after Bartolus (q.v.) at the top of the field: 2.10.

BALEARIC, ISLANDS OR SEA: a cluster of islands in Mediterranean E of Spain; Majorca, Minorca, Obiza, etc., and the sea around them: 1.33.

BANDOUILLE, JOUSSE: see Jousse Bandouille.

BARALIPTON: a synthetic mnemonic device to recall the fifth (of nine) modes of the syllogism in scholastic disputation; 1–4 are Barbara, celarent, darii, ferio: 1.17.

BARBARIANS: originally a term used by Greeks of all non-Greeks: 1.35.

BARBAROSSA (1): Redbeard; surname of Frederick of Hohenstaufen (ca. 1125–1190), duke of Swabia, Holy Roman Emperor from 1155; conciliated Pope Eugene III in 1153 to gain and consolidate the Empire; fitly punished rebellious Milanese for shameful insult to his empress in his absence: 4.45.

BARBAROSSA (2): the Turkish corsair Khaï-ad-Din (1483–1546); long a pirate scourge of the Mediterranean; later the commander of Charles V's imperial fleet: 1.33.

BARBARY: coastal W. Africa: 1.33.

BARBE (BARBARA), SAINT (D. A.D. 235): a virgin martyr tortured and killed by her pagan father when she professed her faith; festival December 4; since lightning killed him, she is the patron saint of storms, miners, artillerymen et al.: 1.27.

BARTACHIN (OR BERTACHIN) DE FERNO: fifteenth-c. Italian jurist: 2.1.

BARTHOLUS (OR BARTOLUS) OF SASSOFERRATO (1314–1357): a potent Italian jurist: 1.10.

BASCHÉ: René Du Puy, lord of Basché, not far from Chinon; expert, R shows us, in handling summons-serving Shysteroos—roughly; part of trying to preserve rights of nobles against judicial encroachments by the Crown, which made litigation a popular sport: 1.23.

BASEL: a city and canton in German-speaking N Switzerland; held by Empire in R's day: 4.57.

BASEL, COUNCIL OF: 1431–1449; declared councils had power over popes; so Pope Eugene IV pronounced it no council but an anticouncil, hence null and void; this was one battle in a long war of attrition, basically between papacy and secular powers: 4.57.

BASOCHE (OR BAZOCHE): dramatic society of Paris law-clerks; held annual revels ruled by a Prince of Fools (Prince des Sots), there performing satiric farces called *soties*: 3.21.

BASSUS, CALPURNIUS: wrote a book on illegible (invisible) letters: 2.24.

BASSUS, QUINTUS LECANIUS: suddenly died from barely visible needle-prick: 4.17.

BASTE THE BEAR: a game in which a player, losing in turn, then briefly becomes "the Bear" and is playfuly buffeted by the other players; the French is "à la mousche": 1.22.

BAUDICHON: hero of an old popular song: 2.11.

BAUMETTE, LA: see La Baumette.

BAVARIA (BAYERN, SW GERMANY): a former duchy, now a large state; capital Munich: 1.33.

BAYARD: "Feast of God Bayard" (Feste Dieu Bayart): favorite oath of the great French paladin and leader Pierre Terrail, seigneur de Bayard, 1476–1524: 4.67.

BAYARD, PIERRE TERRAIL, SEIGNEUR DE BAYARD (1476–1524): a noble French captain deservedly called "without fear and without reproach": 1.39.

BAYONNE (PYRÉNÉES-ATLANTIQUES): resort and seaport on Atlantic N of Spain on French Atlantic coast; also known for good hams: 1.3.

BEAST, TWO-BACKED: see two-backed beast.

BEAUCE, LA: a large wheat-growing plain in S Parisian Basin; Gargantua's mare leveled trees to drive off insects; R offers new etymology: 1.16.

BEAUNE (CÔTE-D'OR): eponymous center of a region noted for a fine Burgundy wine: 3.52.

BÉDA, NOEL: paunchy Sorbonne leader in fierce fight against all Reform: 2.7.

BELLAY, GUILLAUME DU, SEIGNEUR DE LANGEY: see Langey.

BELLAY, JEAN DU: see Du Bellay.

BENEDICT, SAINT, OF NURSIA (CA. A.D. 480–CA. 544): the patriarch of western monks; Saint Gregory our only informant; good Umbrian family; sent to study in Rome; shocked by its licentiousness, he fled into Abruzzi mountains, clothed in monastic habit by a monk friend, Romanus, who kept him fed while Benedict spent three years of early manhood alone in a cave in prayer and contemplation. The word, and soon fame, spread, and disciples flocked; was asked to head a monastery, but again found immorality there; founded his own monastery on top of Monte Cassino, overlooking that town, about midway between Rome and Naples, which became a center of Christianity in W Europe; he virtually Christianized rustic Italy, trained numberless young Romans as monks, and set down in his Rule (in a prologue and 73 chapters) a sane monastic way of life, which Gregory calls one of discretion, in rather normal dress, involving much reading and much field work; replaced the usual extreme asceticism by moderation; monks lived all in common in their abbey. His order grew under his rule; and although later orders often differed sharply in ways, most were in part at least modeled on this one. His "boot" or tun is a great cask: 1.39.

BERCHEM, JACQUES: a noted Flemish musician; at court of Mantua in 1555, he and the other musicians and composers listed here include, among others, most of the best in western Europe in R's day; and many of them enjoyed such obscene songs as these just as R did. For R's fondness of music and expert knowledge of it, see Nan Cooke Carpenter, *Rabelais and Music*, ed. Berchem et al. (Chapel Hill: University of North Carolina Press, 1954): 4.P.

BERGAMASK, BERGAMOT: of the town of Bergamo, in Lombardy (N Italy); used here of rustic dance and barely intelligible speech; known also for chastity belts and for fine pears: 3.13.

BERN OR BERNE: city and canton W central Switzerland; now national capital; since fourteenth and fifteenth centuries a leader of the Swiss Confederacy; see also Bull of Bern: 2.1.

BERRY (OR BERRI): a region, former county, south of the Parisian basin; main occupation was farming; the old capital was Bourges (Cher): 1.45.

BESANT(S): a Byzantine coin (here, gold), same as the *solidus* (later *sol* or *sou*) widely current in western Europe in fifteenth and sixteenth centuries: 1.31.

BEUSSE AND BIBAROIS: R's invented names, suggesting Gascon pronunciations of Beuxes (Vienne) and Vivarais (modern Ardèche in Languedoc) that sound like forms of *boire* "to drink"; to use in bibulous context; both names together: 1.6; Beusse alone 3:17.

BIBLE, THE HOLY, BIBLICAL: a bestseller in R's day: 2.P. See also Holy Scripture, Holy Word, Holy Writ, Gospel.

BICOQUE, LA: scene of a disastrous defeat of the French by Imperials in 1522: 2.11.

BIGASS, SISTER (SOEUR FESSUE): a naïve, well-meaning nun impregnated by a friar: 3.19.

BITHYNIA: country in Asia Minor bordering on both Black Sea and Sea of Marmora: 1.33.

BLANC(S): coin; a small silver coin worth about one half a *sou* (*sol*): 2.16.

BLOIS (LOIRE-ET-CHER): a large town with château on the Loire ca. 110 miles S of Paris: 3.47.

BLOWHARD (TOUCQUEDILLON): one of Picrochole's military chiefs: 1.26.

BOHEMIA: W Czechoslovakia; a plain ringed with mountains, well suited for sausages: 1.33.

BONA: a Mediterranean cape on NE tip of Tunisia and Atlas mountain chain: 1.33.

BONNETS, HIGH: see high bonnets. A bonnet is an added piece of canvas at the foot of a jib or foresail: 4.22.

BONNIVET, GUILLAUME GOUFFIER DE (1488–1525): a favorite of Francis I; Amiral (top military commander); grand château; killed at Pavia defeat (1525): 1.53.

BOOBY, FRIAR: one translation of the common name Frère Lubin (q.v.): 1.P.

BORDEAUX (GIRONDE): important Atlantic port city on the river Garonne; former capital of Guyenne; cathedral, archbishopric, university (not a strong one then); R rates it low: 2.5.

BOTTLE, THE DIVINE: Bacbuc or the shrine she tends; object of Pantagruel's long voyage with Panurge and the company to get its word on Panurge's marriage plans: 3.47.

BOUCHET, JEAN: a rhétoriqueur poet and friend of R; R wrote him a French verse epistle in 1524 (our item 6.3), which Bouchet published in his *Epistres morales et familières* (1545): 6.3.

BOUGUIER, GUY: Montpellier friend of R and fellow player with him in the farce of the mute wife with Rondibilis, Epistémon, and others: 3.34.

BOURBONNAIS: Pas-de-Calais area of N coastal France; said to breed very long ears: 2.1.

BOURGES (CHER): a city ca. 140 miles S of Paris; once capital of Berry; cathedral, citadel built under Philip Augustus (twelfth c.); palace of wealthy Jacques Coeur; and the famous Butter Tower ("Tour de Beurre"); replacement for one destroyed, paid for by dispensations allowing buyers some butter in Lent; in R's day Bourges boasted a great law facility starring Alciati, Jacques Cujas, and others: 2.4.

BOURGUEIL (INDRE-ET-LOIRE): a town near Chinon; soon after famous for Ronsard's Marie, his second "poetic mistress": 1.47.

BOYSSONÉ OR BOISSONNÉ (JEAN DE, 1505–1558): humanist poet in French and Latin, foe of scholasticism; law professor at Toulouse and at Chambéry; highly esteemed friend of R: 3.29.

BRABANT: province in central Belgium; once a duchy in Germany: 1.23.

BRAGMARDO, JANOTUS DE: see Janotus de Bragmardo.

BRAGUIBUS: neat, dandy, but suggesting *braguette* "codpiece"; the little hermit living on a rock offshore who prepares the travelers (fasting, a few good tips for a good reception on the Ringing Island): 5.1.

BRAHIER (OR BRAYER), JAMET: chief steersman of Pantagruel's fleet; also the name of a relative of R's (d. 1533), a merchant on the Loire: 4.1.

BRAHMINS (OR BRAHMAN): an upper-class Hindu assigned to the priesthood: 2.18.

BRAYER, JAMET: see Brahier.

BRAZIL, BRAZILIAN(S): the great S American country, then recently invaded by the Spaniards: 3.26.

BRÉHÉMONT: a village near Chinon rich in pastures, dairy farms: 1.7.

BRENNE, LA: a swampy region between Indre and Creuse rivers with many hog farms: 1.3.

BRETON: see Brittany.

BRETON VILLANDRY, BRETON: see Villandry, Claude Breton.

BRIAREUS (BRIAREOS): in Greek myth, a friendly hundred-handed giant when giants as a group revolted, attacked Olympian gods, but were defeated and confined under the earth: 1.5.

BRIDÉ, JOBELIN: see Jobelin Bridé.

BRIDGET (OR BRIDE), SAINT (453–523): Irish virgin who founded a great monastery at Kildare: 2.17.

BRIDOYE: then a common name for an idiot, Bridlegoose; the judge in Myrelingues who settled cases by rolling dice, then defended his practice by citing countless legal Latin abbreviations of irrelevant alleged precedents: 3.39.

BRITTANY, BRETON(S): the NW region of France, on the Atlantic; long an independent duchy, until joined to France by a royal marriage (1492) and later a vote by the independent estates of Brittany (1532); Breton wine is not grown in Brittany but in the Verron region near Chinon, from Breton stock: 3.4.

BRUTUS, MARCUS JUNIUS (78–42 B.C.): a protégé of Julius Caesar but a passionate republican against empire; joined in assassination of Caesar, with Cassius; then killed himself when their army was beaten at Philippi (42 B.C.) by that of Antony and Octavian: 2.30.

BUDÉ, GUILLAUME (1457/8–1540): the great exemplar and champion of French Hellenism; also a top authority on Roman society; public servant, king's adviser, persuaded Francis I to found free trilingual College of Royal Lecturers (now Collège de France), first French institute of higher learning free of Church domination; in 1520s, answered letters from R (our item 6.2): 6.1.

BUGSCRATCHER (GRATELLES), PRINCE: apparently an ally of Picrochole: 1.31.

BULGARIA: a Balkan country N of Greece, S of Romania, W of Black Sea: 1.33.

BULL OF BERN: name given a Bernese bullhorn-blower killed at battle of Marignano (q.v.) but only after spiking several French big guns: 2.1.

BUREAU: used by R in several senses (the usual table, desk, or office); also as *bure* a course dark brown cloth (as in a monk's robe) used by Panurge as dress: 3.7.

BURGUNDY (BOURGOGNE): large territory in eastern France; once a kingdom, once part county, part duchy; at times linked to Germany; as such, in fifteenth c., a strong bitter rival to France until beaten by Louis XI; annexed by him upon the death of Charles the Bold, Duke of Burgundy 1467–1477: 4.6.

BUTTER SAUCE, EYE POACHED IN ("OEIL POCHÉ AU BEURRE NOIR"): a luminous black eye: 4.12.

BUZANÇAIS (INDRE): a small town near Châteauroux, famous for making bagpipes: 3.45.

CABALA, CABALIST(S): an ancient mystical Jewish system of theosophy and thaumaturgy believing in creation through emanation and in a ciphered interpretation of Scripture: 2.8; monastic cabala: 3.15.

CABALLINE: equine, horse-related; used of the Hippocrene Spring on Mount Helicon (sacred to the Muses), a spring in myth created by a hard hoof-beat from the winged horse Pegasus; used also by analogy of the spring at Croustelles outside of Poitiers: 2.5.

CACUS: from Greek *kakos* "evil"; a fire-breathing monster who stole the Latins' cattle and hid them underground until routed out and killed by Hercules (*Aeneid* 8.258 ff.): 2.1.

CAESAR, GAIUS JULIUS (102–44 B.C.): a Roman noble, great general, very good writer; brilliant conquests in Gaul (58–49); led to fear and censure of him in Rome; returned, defeated, and drove out Pompey and other foes; showed them clemency; planned reorganization of Rome and the Empire; but assassinated (Brutus, Cassius, et al.) by foes of any empire; left 3 books on civil war, his great *Commentaries* on the Gallic War(s), some minor works now lost: 1.16.

CAHUSAC (LOT-ET-GARONNE): a seigniory of a nephew of Geoffroy d'Estissac remote from the scene of our action, which appears to be near Thélème and the Loire valley: 1.12.

CAILLETTE: a famous French jester (fool), second only to Triboullet: 2.30.

CAIN: brother and murderer of Abel (Genesis 4.1–9): 2.1.

CAJETAN (OR GAIETAN, GAETANUS): from birthplace Gaeta, Italy; Giacomo de Vio (1469–1534); General of Dominican Order; Cardinal, worked for reform in Lateran Council (1518–1519); tried to reconcile Luther with Church; failing, helped in his excommunication: 2.7.

CALABRIA: the peninsular toe of the Italian "boot," opposite Sicily, between Tyrrhenian Sea and Ionian; mainly mountainous; fishing, some farming on coastal strips: 1.33.

CALENDS: Greek; proverbial for a nonexistent time or date, hence "never": 1.20.

CALIGULA: nickname of Gaius Caesar, son of Germanicus and Agrippina, emperor of Rome A.D. 37–41; arrogant, bloodthirsty, perhaps insane; finally murdered: 3.2.

CALLIOPE: the Muse of epic poetry, once invoked by R before the fight with the giants: 2.28.

CAMARINA: a marsh in southern Sicily so foul smelling that a Roman proverb warned against stirring it up: 2.33.

CAMBRAI (NORD): a small city in the N of France near Belgium; "Martin of Cambrai" was the name given to a stone marmoset used to strike the cathedral bell: 4.P.

CAMILLA: a swift-footed maiden warrior allied to Turnus; kills many Trojans in battle, then is killed by one; no Amazon (despite Carpalim), but much like one (*Aeneid* 8.809 ff., 12.1085): 2.24.

CAMILLUS, MARCUS FURIUS (FOURTH C. B.C.): a great Roman general; saved Rome from the Gauls; often chosen dictator: 1.39.

CANA: a Galilean town; scene of wedding feast where Jesus changed water to wine (John 2.1–11): 3.P.

CANADA: then meant the known part near the St. Lawrence going from its mouth west to its juncture with the Saint-Maurice: 4.2.

CANARRE, CANARRIAN(S): a fantasy land whose name may be suggested by that of the Canary Islands and apparently confused with them once: 1.27.

CANARY ISLANDS: seven real islands in the NE Atlantic near the Spanish Sahara (Africa); the "Fortunate Isles" of the ancients, ruled by Spain since 1496: 2.24.

CANDES (OR CANDE): a hamlet next to Montsoreau near Chinon holding many relics of Saint Martin: 1.27.

CANDIA, CANDIOT(S): Greek Herakleion, largest city of Crete: 1.33.

CANE: measure of length; about 5 feet 10 inches: 1.8.

CANIDIA: a witch or prophetess mentioned by Horace: 3.16.

CANNAE: in Apulia, S Italy, heel of the Italian "boot"; scene of the crushing Roman defeat (216 B.C.) by Hannibal and his cavalry with enormous losses: 1.10.

CANNIBAL(S): man-eating New World tribes strangely defined in BD; mainly from Lesser Antilles and Brazil; in R's day recently discovered: 1.56.

CAPE BLANCO: in Senegal near the westernmost tip of Africa: 2.24.

CAPE OF GOOD HOPE: cape near the S tip of Africa; now also a South African province: 2.24.

CAPE VERDE (ISLANDS): a Portuguese archipelago in Atlantic W of Senegal: 2.24.

CAPUCHIN(S): a member of the austere Franciscan Order of Friars Capuchin Minor; but it may also mean a monkey capped with what looks like a monk's cowl: 3.22.

CARIA, CARIAN(S): an ancient region in SW Asia Minor (now Turkey): 1.33.

CARMANIA, CARMANIAN(S): old name for the main Asian part of Turkey: 1.33.

CAROLUS: silver coins each worth ten *deniers*: 3.17.

CARPALIM: Greek "the Swift"; one of Pantagruel's domestic companions: 2.9.

CARRASIA: capital of ancient Lydia in Asia Minor: 1.33.

CARTHAGE, CARTHAGINIAN(S): the Tunisian capital and heart of the great

Phoenician empire; trade and military rival to Rome from the sixth c. B.C. to the third; who in the third fought three successive bitter wars with Rome, invaded Italy, and threatened Rome at times, before their final defeat by Scipio Africanus at Zamia (203 B.C.) and final demolition (146 B.C.) by Scipio Aemilianus after long vehement urging by Cato the Censor: 1.2.

CARVEL, HANS: fictive; Grand Lapidary of the king of Melinda; protagonist of R's comically obscene fable about what is called his ring: 1.8.

CASPIAN SEA: the greatest inland body of water in the world; salt; between European USSR and Asian Iran. The Caspian mountains lie mainly south of it and form that frontier of the kingdom of fabled Prester John (q.v.): 1.33.

CASSIA: a spice and medicament (laxative, etc.) popular in R's day: 2.33.

CASSIUS, GAIUS: an able soldier; once pardoned by Caesar, but led conspiracy that assassinated him (44 B.C.); later he and Brutus routed, he killed, at Philippi (42 B.C.): 2.30.

CASTALIAN SPRING: at Delphi on Mount Parnassus; sacred to Apollo and the Muses: 3.24.

CASTAMENA (MODERN KASTAMOUNI): once Castra Comneni, a fortified town in Asia Minor, now Turkey: 1.33.

CASTOR: in Greek myth, he and Pollux (q.v.) are the two Dioscuri (sons of Zeus and Leda, brothers of Helen of Troy); as deities, protectors of seamen; in the sky they form the constellation Gemini (Twins): 1.6.

CATEGORIES: by Aristotle; a theory and book of terms and predicates: 6.4.

CATO THE ELDER, THE CENSOR: Marcus Portius Cato, 234–149 B.C.; a farmer's son; became military tribune, then consul, from 184 censor; opposed Greek influence and all luxury, license; long demanded total destruction of Carthage; made it happen soon after his death; left works on great cities, husbandry (*De agricultura* or *Rustica*): 1.24.

CATO THE YOUNGER: of Utica, great-grandson of the Censor, 95–46 B.C.; rigidly Stoical, noble, strongly opposed Caesar and his party; when defeated and all hope lost, killed himself in protest; never mentioned by R unless he is the Cato meant on 3.P.

CATULLUS, GAIUS VALERIUS (84–CA. 54 B.C.): gifted Roman poet of the sweets and the bitters of love: 3.45.

CAUCASUS, MOUNT: mountain chain between Black Sea and Caspian SE USSR; at the point dividing Europe from Asia: 2.18.

CELESTINE(S): an austere branch of the Benedictine Order founded in the thirteenth c. by the future Pope Celestine V, and later named for him: 2.7.

CELLAR, PAINTED: see Painted Cellar.

CENOTAPH: Greek *kenotaphon* "empty tomb": 4.8.

CENSOR: one of two magistrates in early Rome acting as census-takers, assessors, and inspectors of morals and conduct.

CEPOLA: a Veronese jurist; wrote book of tricks to evade the law, his *Cautelae*: 2.10.

CERBERUS: in Greek myth, the ravenous, many-headed watchdog of Hades: 3.15.

CERES: Greek Demeter; Roman goddess of cereal foods; festival the great mid-April Cerealia: 3.4.

CHALDEA, CHALDEAN(S): Southern Mesopotamia and its ancient people, whose language is needed for thorough Old Testament study: 2.8.

CHALYBEA, CHALYBEAN(S): a land and people in Pontus (now Turkey) on the Black Sea, noted for good steel: 2.29.

CHAMBÉRY (SAVOIE): a sizeable town, once capital of duchy of Savoy; Alpine, next to Switzerland on the road between France and Italy: 1.25.

CHAMBORD: a large elaborate château near the Loire built for Francis I; reportedly outdone in splendor by Thélème: 1.53.

CHAMPAGNE: the region and its great wine in the eastern Parisian basin; once a duchy; annexed to France in 1203: 1.33.

CHANEPH: flatterers; in BD Hebrew for "hypocrisy"; a fictive island passed near at hand by the travelers on their way to the Bottle: 4.66.

CHANTILLY: town and famous château (Seine-et-Oise) ca. 30 miles N of Paris built in the Middle Ages, embellished by Montmorency 1527–1532; home of Musée Condé; another château reportedly outshone by Thélème: 1.53.

CHAOS: the primordial state before matter received form; formless matter: 4.18.

CHAPPUYS: possibly the poet Claude but presumably the naval commander Michel: 1.8.

CHARANTON BRIDGE: just outside Paris on the road from Paris to Charanton-le-Pont (Val-de-Marne): 1.24.

CHARLEMAGNE: King Charles I of the Franks or of France, 742–814; king from 768; the great legendary Christian ruler and leader of continental western Europe: 3.1.

CHARLES V, KING OF SPAIN (1500–1558): from 1518 emperor of the Holy Roman Empire; from then on the great power rivaling kings of France for W European hegemony; in his later years badly crippled by gout, arthritis, etc.; R calls him lame and crippled; in 1555–1556 abdicated both rules (king, emperor) in favor of son Philip II; spent his last few years retired to a monastery: 4.P (unnamed), 4.11.

CHARLES VI OF FRANCE (1368–1422): king from 1380; fought well for France until he went mad in 1392; wrongly listed by R (instead of Charles VII) for capture of Bergerac: 4.40.

CHARLES VIII OF FRANCE (1470–1498): king from 1483; whose second marriage, to Duchess Anne of Brittany, led movement later to joining Brittany to France; his unsuccessful invasion of Italy (1497) led France into its Italian Wars, which lasted for decades: 2.12.

CHARMOIS, CHARLES: a French painter working for Francis I at Fontainebleau, 1554–1557: 4.2.

CHASTILLON, CARDINAL ODET DE (ODET DE COLIGNY, 1517–1571): older brother of the famous Amiral Gaspard de Coligny (1519–1572), army chief and potent adviser to young King Charles IX (1550–1574), whose pro-Protestant power with the king made him (Gaspard) chief target and victim of the Catholic Massacre of Saint Bartholomew's Day (August 23, 1572). Odet de Chastillon, a cardinal since 1533 at age 16, already sympathetic to peaceful Reform, became R's last great patron and protector from the 1540s on, whose reassuring support, says R, led him to resume writing his story after being ready to give it up, so that he finished books 3–4. Chastillon turned Protestant and married (in 1564), moving to England, where he died: 3.Royal Privilege (1550) and 4.OC.

CHAUNY (IN PICARDY): a town noted for producing expert jugglers and mountebanks: 1.24.

CHESIL, COUNCIL OF: in BD Hebrew for fool; R's clear damning reference to the Council of Trent (q.v.), which he also calls "national" for its Italian dominance: 4.18.

CHIABRENA (SHITTERSHATTER): synthetic word from two terms for feces: 2.7.

CHILON: a Spartan ephor (one of five ruling magistrates) in 556 B.C., rated as one of the Seven Sages of Greece: 1.10.

CHINON (INDRE-ET-LOIRE): an old city on the Vienne near the Loire, rising up a steep hill to the castle on top; in effect R's home town; R ingeniously traces the name back to Biblical Cain, proclaims it the first city in the world, quoting its official description in verse: 1.27.

CHITTERLING(S), CHITTERLINE: in Webster "the intestines of hogs especially when prepared as food; fashioned like sausages"; here an imprudent warrior race so fearful of Fastilent that they mistake Pantagruel for him and attack him—to their own heavy cost, in spite of his generous pardon: 4.35.

CHOPSAUSAGE (TAILLEBOUDIN): an aptly-named Pantagrueline captain in the Chitterline War: 4.37.

CHRIST, JESUS, CHRISTIANS: named mainly by attributes like Savior, Redeemer, etc.; by this name: 1.29.

CHRISTOPHER: Greek "Christ-bearer"; Saint, third c.; a martyr from Asia Minor. In his legend he carries a child over a rushing river; when weight becomes unbearable, he learns it was the infant Jesus with the world in his hands; long the patron saint of travelers, especially motorists nowadays. His "burden" here is of course the Christ-child bearing the world in His hands: 3.23.

CIBO (OR CYBO), INNOCENZO, CARDINAL: cousin of Alessandro de Medici; later when Alessandro was assassinated, Cibo took charge of determining his successor: 6.12.

CICERO, CICERONIAN(S): Marcus Tullius, 106–43 B.C.; an able Roman statesman and potent orator; son of a well-to-do Roman knight; served in Social War; studied philosophy, rhetoric, law; his legal pleading showed both skill and courage (81–80); married (79); a liberal, supported Pompey (70); consul (64–63); foiled Catiline's attempted coup, got him convicted and executed—no mean feat. His boasting of his good works led to disfavor. Caesar, once back in Rome and consul (60–59), courted his support; but Cicero held off, fearing Caesar's excessive power, later fled from Rome; his later return humiliating; twice divorced; grief over daughter's death (45) led to much writing on oratory, philosophy, theology, duty, old age, friendship, consolation in grief, Fate, nature of the gods; many orations; Tusculan disputations on happiness. Generally skeptic, Stoic, eclectic; a great authority in R's day, attacked by some but honored by most as master of rhetoric, Latin prose, style, etc.: 1.15; see also Marcus Tullius.

CILICIA: ancient region in SE Asia Minor (S Turkey) between Taurus Mountains and the Mediterranean Sea: 1.33.

CIMBRI, CIMBRIAN(S): an ancient German tribe who fought the Romans in Gaul in the second c. B.C.: 1.2.

CISALPINE GAUL: see Gaul, Cisalpine.

CLARET WINE: in R's day (says Cotgrave), formed of red and white grapes growing together; but Robert Marichal (in QL) calls it wine mixed with honey or spices; and Demerson (LI, p. 583) calls it a red; Littré (1863 ed.) defines the adjective *clairet* as "D'un rouge clair"; but in speaking of wine, he agrees with Marichal. One of his two definitions of the noun is "Infusion de plantes odorantes dans du vin miellé et sucré." The modern meaning (1969 Petit Robert) is "vin rouge léger, peu coloré," is more like the present sense of English claret (Webster's Collegiate, 9th ed.), which calls it simply either "A red Bordeaux wine" or "a similar wine produced elsewhere"; the Compact OED (1971) notes the change in meaning but does little to help date it; it seems to have come mainly in about the eighteenth c.: 4.1.

CLAUDIUS I: Tiberius Drusus Nero Germanicus, emperor of Rome, A.D. 41–54; stammering historian, antiquarian: 3.24.

CLAUDIUS II: Divinus Claudius, emperor of Rome, A.D. 268–279; called Gothicus for conquering the Goths when they threatened Rome: 3.42.

CLEMENT VII, POPE: Giulio de Medici, 1478–1534; pope from 1523: 4.48.

CLERBERG, HANS: a German-born Lyon merchant ennobled and re-named by Francis I: 5.29.

CLERIC: see "clerice."

"CLERICE, ESCLAIRE ICY": two near homophones to say "bring a light": 4.52.

CLOUAUD, SAINT: of Sinays, near La Devinière; a grandson of Frankish King Clovis: 1.27.

CLUNY, HÔTEL DE: in Paris: 2.18.

CLUTCHPUSS, CLUTCHPUSSIAN, CLUTCHPUSSIC (GRIPPEMINAUD, ETC.): archduke of the Furred Cats: 5.11.

COCAI, MERLIN: pseudonym of Italian monk Teofilo Folengo, 1491–1544; author of *Baldus* or *Opus macaronicum*, a long verse tale, half in Latin, half in Italian; one of R's major sources for characters and incidents: 2.1.

COCKLICRANES (COCQUECIGRUES): imaginary creatures, probably half bird, half seashell, whose coming, like that of the Greek Calends, was proverbial for never: 1.49.

COCKSBODY (CORPE DE GALLINE): euphemism for 'Odsbody, Corbleu or Cordieu: 3.30.

COCYTUS: one of the four rivers of Hades; Milton's "Cocytus, named of lamentation loud" (*Paradise Lost* 2.578): 2.30.

COEUR, JACQUES: a fabulously rich Bourges businessman: 1.5.

COL D'AGNELLO: Italian pass to which some Picrocholeans fled in defeat: 1.51.

COLLÈGE DE MONTAIGU: a notoriously harsh, austere Paris school; Erasmus among many others loathed it; Gargantua mentions its vermin, later the cruelty of one master, Tempeste: 1.37.

COLLÈGE DE NAVARRE: a solid school in the Paris University quarter, whose students did not love the rod of iron discipline: 2.16.

COLONNA, FRANCESCO: whose Latin romantic fantasy *Polyphili Hypnerotomachia* (*The Strife of Love in a Dream*), Florence, 1499, is a source of much of R's Book 4 and even more of Book 5; curiously, BD refers to him as "Peter Colonna": 4.BD.

COLOPON: an ancient city in Lydia (Asia Minor, Turkey), one of Homer's many reputed birthplaces: 2.33.

COMMODUS, LUCIUS MARCUS AURELIUS (A.D. 160-192): emperor of Rome from 180; son and successor to Marcus Aurelius; reversed his policies and ways; claimed wrestling prowess; reveled in luxury and license; showed signs of insane pride: 2.30.

COMMUTATIVE JUSTICE: that which governs commerce and trade: 3.2.

COMPOSTUM: either the *compotus* (much studied old calendar) or more probably Johannes Sinthen's old *Composita verborum*, a textbook derided by many humanists: 1.14.

CONCIERGIE: R's term for the Conciergerie, a medieval dungeon, widely dreaded, in the Paris Hall of Justice; in Revolution, last stop on way to guillotine: 4.66.

CONCILIPETIC: seeking the Council (Concilium); here, heading for the Council of Trent: 4.19.

CONDEMNATION, TO PASS: to make that the verdict; R treats this act as a place: 5.11.

CONSTANTINOPLE (MODERN ISTANBUL): chief city of Turkey; long the capital of the Eastern Roman Empire as well as of the Eastern Orthodox Christian Church; in R's day capital of the great Ottoman Empire (q.v.): 1.33.

CONSUL: either of two annually elected chief magistrates of the Roman republic.

"CONTINUITY, SOLUTION OF": see "solution of continuity."

CORAN: see Koran, Alcoran.

CORBLEU, CORDIEU: see Cocksbody.

CORDAX: a licentious dance linked to drunken Bacchic rites, common in Attic comedy before Aristophanes but not in him or later: 5.20.

CORDELIER: a Franciscan Gray Friar—a Franciscan girt with a cord; R was one: 3.12.

CORNELIUS NEPOS: see Nepos, Cornelius.

CORPUS CHRISTI, FESTIVAL OF (FESTE-DIEU OR CORPS-DIEU): the Thursday after Trinity Sunday, thus 57 days after Easter: 2.22.

CORSICA: big Mediterranean island W of Italy and just N of Sardinia: 1.33.

COS (KOS): a Greek island in the Dodecanese (SE Aegean): 3.24.

COURT: usually means the Court of the Parlement (q.v.); often used alone in that sense; once seems to stand for the assembled Sorbonne faculty: 1.20.

CRANION: a hill and promontory near Corinth; a favored abode for Diogenes: 3.P.

CRAPHAM (MERDAILLE): one of Picrochole's officers: 1.33.

CREATOR: as attribute of God: 1.23.

CRETE, CRETAN(S): the great long island in the Mediterranean well S of Greece; long the seat of the great Minoan power and civilization: 1.10; see also Candia, Candiots.

CRITOLAUS: an Athenian popular in Rome in second c. B.C.; imagined a scale (later proverbial) precisely balanced for weighing spiritual as against material goods: 3.32.

CROUSTELLES: site of a noted spring near Poitiers (Vienne): 2.5.

CROWN(S), SUN-CROWN(S) (ESCUS AU SOLEIL): gold coins stamped with French arms and a crown; in R's time worth 36 *sous*, 3 *deniers*: 1.51.

CRUSTUMENIA(N): a town in Italy noted of old for fine pears: 3.13.

CRYERE: Greek *krueros*, French *icy;* name of the NE tower of Thélème: 1.55.

CUBIT(S): Latin *cubitum* "elbow"; ancient measure of length (fingertip to elbow); slightly variable, but normally ca. 1.5 feet (18 inches): 4.34.

CUCKOLD(S): victim of a sexually unfaithful wife; Panurge's greatest terror about marriage: 3.9 to end of 5; see particularly 3.30.

CUMAE, CUMAEAN(S): a Greek colony in Campania S of Naples and nearby cave abode of Sibyl, priestess of Apollo, and entrance to underworld (*Aeneid* 3.576 ff.): 3.23.

CUNAULT (ANJOU), OUR LADY OF: a famous priory: 1.27.

CUPID: Greek Eros; Roman boy god of Love, son of Venus; arousing or inflaming love by shooting his arrows; ubiquitous in Renaissance poetry and arts: 3.31.

CURTAL (OR CURTAIL): a horse or dog with a docked tail: 2.12.

CURULE: used of a seat in ancient Rome reserved for the use of the highest dignitaries.

CUSANUS (OR DE CUSA OR DE CUES), NICOLAS, 140–1454: German humanist, natural philosopher, statesman; from 1448 a cardinal; renowned for his D*e docta ignorantia* (*On learned ignorance*), 1440: 2.14.

CUSPIDIUS, WILL OF: see *Will of Cuspidius*.

CYBELE: an Asian nature goddess (see Greco-Roman Rhea, q.v.); worshipped by many Romans during the stressful Punic Wars; her priests notoriously lewd and cruel: 3.45.

CYCLADES: a circle of S Aegean islands including Andros, Kos, Melos, Syros, Delos, Naxos, Paros, Tenos, but not (pace R) Thasos: 1.33.

CYCLOPS, CYCLOPAS: round-eye(s); monstrous giants with just one round eye; Vulcan's helpers; arrogant, unafraid of gods; one, a man-eater, is Polyphemus (*Odyssey* 1.70 ff.; 9.423 ff., whom Odysseus tricks, later blinds, and escapes): 1.2.

CYNIC(S): a Greco-Roman school of philosophy founded by Antisthenes in 440 B.C.; made famous (infamous to some) in fourth c. B.C. by Diogenes of Sinope: see Diogenes of Sinope.

CYNTHUS, CYNTHIUS: see Apollo Cynthius.

CYPRIAN: goddess Aphrodite; her worship strong in Cyprus; one story has her come to land there: 3.18.

CYPRUS, CYPRIOT(S): the large triangular island in NE corner of the Mediterranean, now a republic of the British Commonwealth: 1.33.

CYRENE: a former Greek colony near coast of Libya; prosperous from herbs and trade: 1.33.

CYRUS (KUROS), THE GREAT (FL. CA. 550 B.C.): first of that name, founder of the Persian Empire and the line of Achaemenid dynasty; conquered Lydia and King Croesus, then Greek Asia Minor: 2.30.

DACIA: modern Denmark: 1.33.

DAEDALUS: in Greek myth, prototypical craftsman-inventor (Joyce's "Old Artificer" in his *Portrait of the Artist*); built the labyrinth for Minos, who then confined him in it; built wings, flew out with son Icarus in the first human flight: 4.50.

DAEMON(S): mediating spirits between men and gods (Plato's *Symposium*) or spirits within men that guard them and watch over them (like that of Socrates) or yet some such beings: 3.20.

DANAIDS: in Greek myth, daughters of King Danaos of Argus, forced by the sons of Aegyptus to be their brides; so Danaos had the Danaids kill their new husbands, and all but one did; these were sent to Hades and forced to keep filling a water jar full of holes: 3.P.

DANGIER (DANGER): since the *Romance of the Rose*, the jealous husband's threatening guard: 1.54.

DARII: third of the nine modes of the first syllogism (a memory aid): 1.19.

DARIUS I (DARIAVUSH): king of Persia, 521–486 B.C.: greatly increased royal power at home and abroad; E to NW India, W into Greece, until beaten at Marathon (490): 4.34.

DARIUS III (CODOMANUS): king of Persia, 336–330 B.C.; defeated by Alexander the Great at the Issus, then at Gaugamela (333, 331); murdered by his satrap Bessus (330): 2.30.

DAUPHINÉ: modern Isère, Drôme, Hautes-Alpes: 2.5.

DAVID: the Israelite shepherd lad who killed Goliath; succeeded Saul as king; became Israel's greatest; left the hymns of praise, prayer, and thanks, that we call his Psalms: 1.21.

DE CASTRO: a famous fifteenth c. Neapolitan professor of canon law: 2.10.

DE CUSA (OR DE CUES), NICHOLAS: see Cusanus, Nicolas.

DE LYRA, NICOLAS: see Lyra, Nicolas de.

DECIUS, PHILIPPUS (D. 1535): law professor at Pavia, then counselor at Parlement (q.v.) of Bourges: 2.10.

DECRETALS, DECRETALINE: a body of conciliar and papal decisions compiled ca. 1250–1350 as basis for canon law; challenged in R's day as mainly the chief source of the Church's power and revenue: 4.48.

DECRITISTS: believers in Gratian's *Decretum* (A.D. 1140), a handbook of all church law: 4.53.

DECUMAN: from Latin for tenth, strong, great: 1.51.

DEMIURGON: since Boccaccio (fourteenth c.), a prime god of ancient mythology; "adopted" as a Christian demon by Arnoul Gréban in his *Mystère de la Passion* (1457): 3.22.

DEMOCRITUS, DEMOCRITIZE: of Abdera in Thrace, b. ca. 460 B.C.; atomistic philosopher who wrote also on mathematics, music, and morals; from a note by Juvenal (*Satires* 10.33), got name of "the laughing philosopher"; contrasted in a Renaissance topos with "weeping Heraclitus": 1.20.

DEMOGORGON: see Demiurgon.

DEMOSTHENES (384–322 B.C.): Athenian orator and statesman who tried hard but vainly to persuade Athens to try to check Philip of Macedon's aggressions before he grew too strong for that to be possible. He was greedy, as an episode in R shows: 1.P.

DENDIN, PERRIN AND TENOT: this surname, as with Georges Dandin a century later, is used to denote a simpleton, a booby. Here, however, while the son is that, the father is not: 3.41.

DENIER: Roman *denarius*, worth 10 *asses* in R's day, the smallest French monetary unit; 12 to one *sou*, 240 to one *livre* (pound), which then was a gold coin worth one *franc*: 2.17. See *denare* (here translated in context as penny) and *denrées* then plural of "one denier's worth": 4.2.

DENIS (DIONYSIUS), SAINT (A.D. THIRD C): first bishop of Paris, patron saint of France; martyred on the Paris Mount of Martyrs, now known as Montmartre: 1.38.

DES MARAIS, PHILIPPE: see Marais, Philippe des.

DES PRÉS (OR DES PREZ), JOSQUIN (CA. 1440–1521/1527): the leading composer of his time and great creator of polyphonic music; after many years in Italy, returned to France as a musician to Louis XII; left many masses, motets, etc. Of the 50–60 musicians listed here in two groups, only the most notable are here annotated individually. They all come from or live and perform in France, England, Germany, Italy, and the Low Countries, and make up nearly all the musical leaders of the time: 4.P. For further evidence of R's keenness and expertise in this field, see Nan Cooke Carpenter, *Rabelais and Music* (Chapel Hill: University of North Carolina Press, 1954).

DEUCALION: in Greek myth, the one good man spared, with his wife Pyrrha, spared as God-fearing when Zeus flooded the earth to destroy the wicked human race (Ovid *Metamorphoses* 1.314 ff.); the couple then began a novel way of repopulating the earth: 2.28.

DEVIL: in Christianity, the archfiend, adversary, tempter, aka Beelzebub, Lucifer, Satan, enemy of God and man; for R, the great Calumniator (Greek *Diabolos*, q.v.): 1.2.

DEVIL(S) VAUVERT: see Vauvert devils.

DEVILKIN: the naive neophyte demon tricked and intimidated by the Popefigger's wife and her enormous "wound": 4.45⁻47.

DEVINIÈRE, LA: see La Devinière.

DIABOLOS: a favorite term in Rabelais: 4.OP; see Devil.

DIAGORAS OF RHODES: first of several so named; Olympian victor in boxing in 464 B.C.; honored by Theban poet Pindar and statue at Olympia of him and his champions—two sons and three grandsons: 1.10.

DIANA: like Greek Artemis; Roman maiden goddess of the hunt; also like Hecate, a moon goddess: 4.OC.

DICTATOR: a person granted absolute emergency power; esp. one appointed by the Senate of Rome.

DICTE, MOUNT: one of two mountains in Crete (Ida is the other), which in a cave Rhea (q.v.) hid the infant Zeus to save him from his father Cronus: 3.12.

DIDO: *Aeneid,* 1 and especially 4; the widowed founding queen of Carthage; Venus made her fall in love with Aeneas; he loved her in return, but on Jupiter's orders, he left her to seek a Roman bride; she had a bitter suicide: 2.24.

DIGEST (OR PANDECTS): the main part of Justinian's *Corpus juris civilis*; see Justinian.

DIGNITY OF CODPIECES, ON THE: one of R's mock-learned book titles: 1.P.

DINA: Genesis 34; Jacob's daughter, raped by Shechemites, bloodily avenged by her brothers who killed all their men: 3.48.

DINA'S POND: in Lycia, named for an unknown Dina; this Dina is noted by Henry Cornelius Agrippa *On occult philosophy*: 3.25.

DINDENAULT: cf., modern dinde, dindon, turkey, turkeycock; a suggestive fictive name for the boorish, sleazy sheep dealer who starts a lively war of words with Panurge and ends up silenced by drowning: 4.5⁻8.

DIODORUS SICULUS (OF SICILY, FL. CA. 40 B.C.): a contemporary of Julius Caesar; wrote in Greek a 40-book Rome-centered world history, uncritical but useful: 3.31.

DIOGENES (DIOGENIC) OF SINOPE (ON THE EUXINE OR BLACK SEA, FOURTH C. B.C.): the best-known Cynic philosopher; chose to live mainly in sophisticated Athens and Corinth, feeding countless legends and anecdotes by frugal life and defiance of rules of decorum and propriety; hero and model of the Prologue to Book 3: 2.30.

DIOGENES LAERTIUS (OR OF LAERTE IN CILICIA, ASIA MINOR, CA. A.D. 200–250): left ten books on lives and opinions of ancient philosophers, 82 of them in all, not fully reliable but useful; best for anecdote and Greek folklore: 3.10.

DIOMEDES: a king of Thrace, son of Ares and Cyrene; fed his horses human flesh; killed by Hercules (eighth labor) protecting those horses: 1.36.

DIOMEDES (OR DIOMED): *Iliad*; led forces of both Argos and Tiryns against Troy; in Book 5, with Athena guiding, dominated fighting, wounding even Aphrodite when she intervened to protect her son Aeneas and Ares in 10; with Odysseus on a night foray killed Dolon and many sleeping Trojans. After Troy fell, vengeful Aphrodite led his wife Aihaleia into adultery; he left her, wandered around Italy, founded a few cities, died and was buried there. In *Aeneid* (11.225 ff.), mindful of Aeneas's toughness, refuses to join Latian fight against him: 3.23.

DIONYSIUS (1): see Bacchus.

DIONYSIUS (2), UNRELATED TO (1) OR I: a friend of Democritus: 3.32.

DIONYSIUS I, TYRANT OF SYRACUSE (405–367 B.C.): a low-born demagogue and mediocre general; but walled his city and the heights (Epipolai) above it; conquered all Sicily and part of Italian mainland; died celebrating his one victory in a contest in tragic poetry; succeeded by son Dionysius II, who ruled badly and died 354 B.C.: 1.10.

DIOSCORIDES (OR DIOSCURIDES): a Greek physician; served in Roman army under Nero (A.D. 54–68); his book on plants, herbs, and medicine was basic for Renaissance pharmacology: 1.23.

DIPSODY, DIPSODE(S): Greek Thirsties; fictive neighbors of Pantagruel's Amaurots and their Utopia; follow their aggressor King Anarche (Unrule) into unprovoked invasion of Utopia, but are routed by Pantagruel and his army and made his subjects (as the title page had announced): 2.P.

DISCORD (PERSONIFIED AS DISCORDANCE): daughter of Antiphysie (Antinature) thus sister or half-sister of R's foes Calvin, Postel, Putherbeus (q.v.): 4.32.

DIVE, LA: a tiny nonnavigable stream near La Devinière comically incapable of producing such revenue as R facetiously suggests: 1.53.

DIVINE BOTTLE: see Bottle, Divine.

DOCTRINALE PUERORUM: by Alexandre de Villedieu (13th c.); a Latin grammar in barbaric verse, popular in R's day but not with him: 1.14.

DODONA: in Epirus, site of a great oracle of Zeus; noted for ringing caldrons: 3.27.

DODRENTAL: Latin 3/4, hence 9/12, thus nine inches or one half-cubit: 4.P.

DOLABELLA, CN: at one time proconsul in Asia: 3.44.

DOM PEDRO OF CASTILE: see Pedro of Castile.

DOMINE, DOMINUS: Latin "Lord": 1.10.

DOMINIC, SAINT (DOMINGO GUZMAN OF CASTILE, 1170?–1221): preached and practiced poverty, abstinence; founded the Dominican Order; sent to S France to oppose Albigensians; festival August 4: 3.33.

DOMITIAN (TITUS FLAVIUS DOMITIANUS): emperor of Rome A.D. 81–96; loved ease, games: 3.46.

DONATUS, DONAT: here as a simple version of Aelius Donatus's good Latin grammar: 1.14.

DORIA, ANDREA (1466–1560): great Genoese commander, admiral, statesman; served France, Empire, lastly Genoa; brought it law and order but under Empire's aegis: 6.12.

DOUZAIN: worth twelve *deniers* or one *sou,* thus one twentieth of a franc.

DRACHMA: now the smallest Greek coin and weight; then worth 3 obols (q.v.): 5.32.

"DRAW WORMS FROM NOSE, TO": see "worms, from nose, to draw."

DREAME OF LOVE: near the title in English translation of Francesco Colonna's fantasy romance (q.v.) *Polyphili Hypnerotomachia:* see Colonna.

DROOPYTAIL (BASDEFESSES): one of Picrochole's captains: 1.31.

DRUIDS: Celtic priestly rulers; reputedly magicians: 2.1.

DRUSUS: name of a high noble Roman family; here probably Germanicus (15 B.C.–A.D. 19); a great Roman hero, nephew and adopted son of Tiberius, but poisoned probably with his approval or connivance or both: 2.30.

DU BELLAY, GUILLAUME, SEIGNEUR DE LANGEY: see Langey.

DU BELLAY, JEAN (1492–1560): notable French prelate, diplomat, statesman; bishop of Paris from 1532, cardinal from 1535, ambassador to England, then to Rome, dean of the Sacred College; serious contender for pope in 1555, when Paul IV won; influential adviser to Francis I; urged tolerance and peaceful Reform, as did brother Langey: 4.OC.

DU DOUHET, BRIAND VALLÉE SEIGNEUR: see Vallée.

DUCAT: a small gold coin, originally Venetian (from *doge*); later in wide use; worth about 1.2 gold francs: 2.21.

DUNS SCOTUS (JOHN OF SCOTLAND): see Scotus, Duns.

"EAR, FLEA IN THE": see "flea in the ear."

EASTERLING(S), ESTRELINS: Baltic or Hanseatic north coastal Germans: 1.33.

ECCIUS, ECCIUM (JOHANN MAIER VON ECK, 1486–1543): persuaded Rome to condemn Luther: 2.7.

ECHEPHRON: Greek for "having sense"; one sane man in Picrochole's council of war: 1.33.

ECLIPTIC WINE: eclipsing the senses on the way to Bacchic revelation: 5.46.

EELS: of Melun, that scream; strange result of the cry of the Melun eel-hawkers; Melun eels before they are skinned: 1.47.

EGESTA: while standing near a stream, raped by a man in the form of a bear or dog; bore a monster: 3.34.

ELIJAH: 1 Kings 17–18; Hebrew prophet for whom God withheld rain for three days: 2.2.

ELL(S) (AULNES): an old measure of length, usually 45 inches: 1.8.

ELYSIUM, ELYSIAN FIELDS: or Islands of the Blessed; in Greek myth the lovely place (locus amoenus) reserved after death for the gods favorites, heroes, patriots: 1.13.

EMBER DAYS: in Roman Catholicism, for fasting and prayer on Wednesday, Friday, or Saturday in any of three special weeks: 2.7.

EMBLIC PLUMS: from around Alexandria, supposedly an aphrodisiac: 2.14.

EMILIUS, PAULUS (OR AEMILIUS PAULLUS), LUCIUS (D. 160 B.C.): in his consulship, found Rome weak against attacking Macedonians under Perses; restored army discipline and order, turned the tide of war; in 168 routed Perses at Pydna; he bore the same name as his father, killed at the terrible Roman defeat by Hannibal at Cannae (216 B.C.) in Apulia (S. Italy). Plutarch wrote a *Life* of the son as a Roman hero: 1.15.

EMPEDOCLES (FIFTH C. B.C.): of Acragas, Sicily; scientist, natural philosopher; recognized air as a substance; saw matter as a varied product of the four elements (fire, air, earth, water) that combine and split apart to create our changing universe: 2.14.

EMPEROR: here of the Holy Roman Empire; mattered most to France; in R's day Charles V of Spain (1517–1556), in later years suffered from arthritis, gout, etc.; R refers to him as lame, crippled, etc.: 4.16.

EMPIRE: of antiquity, means that of Rome; elsewhere, the Holy Roman Empire, meaning mainly Austria and Spain, but also much of Germany and Italy; has great strength from component parts but weakened by the distance between them and by much revolt or at least disaffection in several parts, religious and secular (Germany, Low Countries, etc.); see also Imperial(s).

EMULGENCES: kin to indulgences; also a growth industry in R's day: 2.35.

ENDELECHY: Greek for "continuation, perpetuity"; sometimes misused instead of *entelechy*: 5.18.

ENGASTRIMYTHS: Greek for "belly-speakers"; one group of Gaster-worshipers whom Pantagruel detests as much as the other group, the Gastrolaters: 4.58.

ENNIUS, QUINTUS (239–169 B.C.): one of the best early Roman poets, born in Calabria; spoke and wrote in Latin 18 books of verse *Annals*, a history of Rome from its early years, with brief lives of many heroes and other greats: 1.P.

ENTELECHY: Greek *entelecheia*; Aristotle; the actualization of form-giving cause (as contrasted with potential existence); here, kingdom of Queen Quintessence, visited by Pantagruel's party: 5.18.

ENTOMMEURES (ENTOMMERIC), FRÈRE JEAN DES: fantasy name suggesting both funnels (for drinking) and slashes or hash (making mincemeat of enemies); the hyperactive, cheery, courageous, lusty, breviary-quoting, resolutely uneducated monk or antimonk who shares center stage with Panurge for the liveliest parts of Books 3–5 after sharing it with Gargantua in Book 1; rewarded for extraordinary heroic exploits in Picrocholean War with ideal antimonastery of Thélème made to his order: 1.27.

ENYO: Greek myth; cf., Roman Bellona; a minor war goddess, below Ares: 3.6.

EPHOR: one of five ancient Spartan magistrates having power over the king.

EPICTETUS (A.D. 60–140): Phrygian, a freed slave; Stoic; left *Manual* and lectures: 2.30.

EPICURUS (EPIKOUROS, 341–270 B.C.): born in Samos; founded school (gardens) in Athens; atomist in physics, hedonist in ethics and pleasure, or lack of pain, the supreme good, harmony and plain living the way to it; few writings remain; best known from Lucretius (99–55 B.C.): *On the nature of things*, a Latin heroic, didactic poem in six books: 4.2; see Atoms.

EPIPHANY: normally an astonishing apparition; the Christian one, the coming of the Magi, on Twelfth Night (January 6): 3.4.

EPISTÉMON: Greek for "knowing, understanding"; first of Pantagruel's tutor-companions, then simply one of his domestic companions; relentlessly learned; despises Lent, heresy-hunters; refuses to give Panurge advice on his marriage although asked to; a voice for R's erudition: 2.5.

EPODE(S): (1) a long lyric poem alternating long and short verses; or (2) the third part of an ode, following the strophe and antistrophe: 4.51.

ERASMUS, DESIDERIUS (CA. 1466–1536): great Dutch humanist and peaceful Reformist; leader of "Evangelicalists"; scholar; great satirist, as in *Praise of Folly*; edited Greek New Testament, Saint Jerome, Church Fathers; *Adages,* a great sourcebook; R's great hero in faith and writings, as his letter to him shows: 6.7.

ERGO, ERGOS, ERGOING, ETC.: from Latin, meaning "therefore"; here used as a mark of dispute for dispute's sake, as scholastics were (mostly rightly) charged with doing: 1.17.

ERICHTHO: a Thessalian witch from Lucan's *Pharsalia*, magical prediction: 3.25.

ERICHTHONIUS: in Greek myth, a son of Dardanus (son of Zeus), whose grandsons Tros and Ilus gave names to Troy; father of legendary King Erechtheus; cited by Euripides and Virgil: 4.38.

ESAU: Genesis 27–30 ff.; Bridoye's weak eyesight reminds him of Isaac's, which allowed Jacob to cheat Esau of his birthright: 3.39.

ESTE, CARDINAL IPPOLITO (1509–1572): is not mentioned by R, but for him was composed the Italian model for R's *Shadow Battle*.

ESTE, DUKE ERCOLE (1508–1559): of Ferrara (first name not given in R); of highest nobility; art patron; anti-Reformist; married Renée de France (q.v.); pro-Reform; much friction ensued; late in life, she retired to France and died there: 6.12.

ESTISSAC, GEOFFROY D' (D. 1543): nobleman, bishop of Maillezais, R's first and long-lasting protector-patron; probably managed his transfer from Observantine confinement to the freer, more literate Benedictine house of his at Maillezais, and probably sponsored and paid for his Paris medical studies, perhaps also those at Montpellier; later employed him as reporter in Rome on his trip there with ailing Jean du Bellay in winter 1535–1536; helped with loans when R's expenses topped his income. His death (May 30, 1543) surely a heavy blow to R: 6.5. Also mentioned by R are a niece, "Madame d'Estissac" (6.12), Anne de Daillon, and a nephew Louis: 4.52.

ESTRADIOTS (OR STRADIOTS): Albanian light horsemen; served in France as guards; conspicuous for tall pointed caps or bonnets: 6.8.

ETHIOPIA, ETHIOPIAN(S): a large NE African country and people esteemed by Herodotus (2.13); founded tenth c. B.C. by Menelik I, son of Solomon and Queen of Sheba; long ruled as part of vast empire of fabled Prester John (q.v.): 2.18.

ETRURIA, ETRUSCAN(S): ancient land and people that is modern Tuscany and part of Umbria, in Italy NW of Tiber; until sixth c. B.C. Italy's highest civilization; widespread until conquered by Rome after long struggle; Greek-influenced script still puzzled all: 1.1.

EUCLID (EUKLEIDES, FL. CA. 300 B.C.): a great mathematician; left *Elements* (*Stoicheia*) on geometry and number theory; until ca. 1900 still *the* great authority in plane geometry: 2.7.

EUCLION: in Plautus's *Pot* or *Aurlularia* (Pot of Gold), owner of an ill-fated rooster whose lot R once says he fears he may share: 3.P.

EUDÉMON: Greek *eudaimon* for "fortunate"; a page first to Philippe des Marais (q.v.), then to Gargantua, finally (Books 3–5) one of Pantagruel's companions: 1.15 to end of 5.

EUPATOR: Mithridates Eupator, king of Pontus; much admired in later years: 3.50.

EUPHORBIUM: a bitter drug often used as an emetic: 2.16.

EUPHRATES: the great SW Asian river joining the Tigris in defining and embracing Mesopotamia on their way through Iraq and Syria into the Persian Gulf: 1.33.

EURIPIDES (480–406 B.C.): latest of the three great Greek tragedians; most controversial; most concerned to show pathos, passion, gods as malignant to men, heroes as mere mortals; 17 tragedies remain, including *Trojan Women, Hecuba, Helen, Orestes, Medea, Hippolytus, Alcestis, Bacchae*; his dialogue not highflown but plain; badly missed after death: 4.2.

EUROPA: the continent: 4.P.

EURUS: the SE wind: 3.51.

EURYCLES, EURYCLEAN(S): an Athenian who divined by ventriloquy; hence here called an ancestor of the Engastrimyths (q.v.): 4.58.

EURYDICE: a dryad (wood nymph); loving wife of loving Orpheus; when pursued by lustful Aristaeus, bitten by a snake, died; Orpheus came down with his music into Hades to bring her back, under pact with Hades, but on her way back up, leading her, forgot pact, looked back in love; she vanished forever: 3.14.

EUSTATHIUS: twelfth-c. bishop from Thessaloniki; commentator on Homer: 1.P.

EUSTHENES: Greek, "The Strong"; a domestic companion to Pantagruel: 2.10.

EUTROPIUS, SAINT: a Saint Eutropius founded the church at Saintes (Charente-Maritime); pilgrims went there hoping inanely for a cure for dropsy, but only connection was a pun (Eutrope-hydrope): 1.27.

EVANGEL: Greek for "good news"; Gospel; here used in literal Greek sense: 4.OC.

EVANGELICAL, EVANGELICALISM: an irenic Christian Reformist position (and its adherents) seeking reform with the Church; stressed authority of Bible over Church or other interpreters; of faith over works; rejected separate (celibate) priesthood and all Catholic sacraments as such except baptism and communion; urged wide dissemination of Bible and its free translation into vernaculars; return past Jerome's Latin Vulgate to original Greek and Hebrew Bible texts; a view largely mystical and spiritual with Margaret of Navarre (q.v.); more intellectual and satirical with Erasmus (q.v.); Rabelais warmly revered both, adhered to this position: 1.17.

EVE: Genesis 1–3; first woman, Adam's wife, mother of us all; ate forbidden fruit: 3.33.

EVERGETES (BENEFACTOR): a surname given to Osiris and some others: 3.1.

"EVERYONE TO HIS EVERYHOME": "chascun s'en va à sa chascunière"; original with R: 2.14.

EVISPANDE VERRON: a puzzler; Verron a region but Evispande unknown: 4.OP.

EXTRAVAGANTES: large group of Decretals (q.v.) collected under Pope Gregory IX (pope from 1227–1241), hence outside (Extra) Gratian's original basic Decretum (q.v.); plus those compiled under John XXII (pope from 1316–1334); these all combined in 1500 with Gratian et al.,

into vast *Corpus juris canonici,* also including *Sextum* and *Clementines:*
4.51.

FABIUS, FABII: a great Roman noble family; cited here is Fabius Maximus
Verrucasus (d. 203 B.C.), called Cunctator "Delayer"; who after bad
Roman defeat at Trasimene (217 B.C.) managed to hold up and harass
mighty army of Hannibal, ever avoiding pitched battles; finally won out:
2.27.

FACETUS: a childish old guide to good child behavior: 1.14.

FACULTY, WHERE UNSPECIFIED, READ "FACULTY OF THEOLOGY": University
of Paris (q.v.): 1.18.

FAIRIES, LAND OF THE: fictive happy, aging Gargantua "translated" there:
2.23.

FALCON(S): a kind of small cannon: 1.36.

FASTILENT (QUARESMEPRENANT "LENT OBSERVER"): embodiment of
Sorbonic fasting and such conservative ritual: 4.29.

FATES (GREEK *MOIRAI, PARCAE*): three sisters, Clotho, Lachesis, Atropos,
who spin and cut threads of human lives; Atropos, the cutter, was the
most feared: 3.51.

FATHOM(S): an old measure of length, esp. depth; ca. 6 feet: 2.5.

FAUNUS: a grandson of Saturn; a nature god often identified with Pan:
3.24.

FAVEROLLES: a common place-name used in old place-time gag "between
noon and Faverolles": 4.OP.

FAYE MONJAU, LA (OR LA FOYE MONJAULT): fine wines; crooked approach road: 1.34.

FAYOLLES: fictive fourth king of Numidia; sent Gargantua his gigantic
mare: 1.16.

FEAST OF GOD BAYARD (FESTE DIEU BAYART): see Bayard, Feast of God.

FÉCAMP (SEINE-MARITIME): near Le Havre; site of a Benedictine abbey; its
"use" means its ritual practice: 1.41.

FEE FIE FO FUM (MOUFLIN, MOUFLART): a mild nonsense oath but less
bloodthirsty in French: 2.12.

FERRARA, FERRARESE: large city, then a cultural center, in Emilia, N
Italy; see also Este (Duke of) and Renée de France, Duchess of: 2.15.

FESSEPINTE (TOSSPINT OR TOSSPOT): an unknown tale casually claimed
once by R: 2.P.

FEURRE (FOURRE), RUE DU: on Paris Left Bank, near university; site of the Faculty of Arts: 2.10.

FIACRE (FIACHRA), SAINT: seventh-c. Irishman, founded monastery in Brie; his remains preserved in Meaux: 3.47.

FIERABRAS: a Saracen giant featured in an old tale: 2.1.

FIFY, MASTER: name given the man who empties, scours privies: 2.17.

FLACCUS, QUINTUS HORATIUS: see Horace.

FLANDERS, FLEMISH, FLEMING(S): a region and its people in coastal Belgium and NE France on the North Sea; some inland farming: 1.33.

"FLAY THE FOX" (ESCORCHER LE RENARD): to vomit (usually from too much drink): 1.11.

"FLEA IN THE EAR, TO HAVE" (AVOIR LA PUCE À L'OREILLE): to have an overpowering urge, often sexual: 3.7.

FLEECE, GOLDEN: see Golden Fleece.

"FLIES, LAUGH LIKE A PILE OF": burst with laughter: 1.12.

"FLIES IN THE MILK TO RECOGNIZE": cf., Villon, *Débat*; a proof of minimal wit or sense: 1.12.

FLOOD: Biblical, Genesis 10.6–9; sparing only Noah, his wife, animal couples: 2.1.

FLORA: Roman goddess of fertility and flowers: 3.4.

FLORENCE: a great city in Tuscany (N Italy); a center of trade, banking, culture: 1.33.

FLORIN(S): an old Florentine gold coin stamped with a fleur-de-lis: 2.17.

FLUSH: in cards, a four-card sequence in the same suit; also name of a game: 1.22.

FLYCATCHER (GOBEMOUSCHE): once, a fictive ancestor of our giant heroes: 2.1; another time, another, unidentified fictive character: 1.24.

FONSBETON: spring and hamlet near Poitiers where Bridoye long judged well: 3.30.

FONTAINEBLEAU (SEINE-ET-MARNE): a great forest ca. 40 miles SSE of Paris, and the château, then brand new, built there for Francis I: 6.22.

FONTARABIE: an obscene deformation Foutarabie, a town in Guipuzocoa, NW Spain not far S of France; not noted for embroidery: 1.33.

FONTENAY-LE-COMTE (VENDÉE, THEN POITOU): a sizeable town not far from both La Rochelle and Poitiers; R spent 2–3 years there as monk and priest in an Observantine Franciscan monastery, Le Puy Saint-

Martin (1520–1523); learned Greek from Pierre Amy, a fellow member of Tiraqueau's Hellenist circle; letters to Budé: 2.5.

"FOOTSOLDIER, WORD OF A" (FOY DE PIÉTON): parody of Francis I's "Word of a Gentleman": 4.OP.

FORD OF VÈDE: see Vède.

FOU: locality, which Panurge places near Toul in NE France: 3.46.

FOU, LORD DU: Jacques du Fou, Lord of Lusignan, Maître d'Hotel to King Louis XII in 1514; here cited once as domestic to giant cub Gargantua: 1.22.

FOUACE, FOUACIER(S): a thick cake (or rich bread or roll) baked fast on a hot hearth under hot embers; covered with burning coals; a regional delicacy; here the cause or pretext of the Picrocholine War in *Gargantua*: 1.25.

FOUR METALS: gold, silver, copper, steel: 1.8.

FOUR SONS OF AYMON: see *Aymon, the Four Sons of*.

FOURNILLIER: the most resourceful of the pilgrims Gargantua ate in a salad: 1.38.

FOUTARABIE, FOUTIGNAN: see Fontarabie, Frontignan (both obscene comic deformations): 2.16.

FOYE MONJAULT: see Faye Monjau, La.

FRACASSUS: hero of a tale by Merlin Coccai (Teofilo Folengo, q.v.): 2.1.

FRANC-ARCHER DE BAGNOLET (OR BAIGNOLET): Bagnolet Free archer; a proverbially timid rural constable from a town near Paris; subject of a clever verse monologue with that title (1468) ascribed by some to no less a writer than François Villon: 2.30.

FRANCISCAN(S): the religious order of R for many years; founded in 1209 by Saint Francis of Assisi: 3.22.

FRANCS-TAUPINS (FRANCTOPINUS): rural militia also renowned for poltroonery; then used at times for just N France or even the Ile-de-France: 1.35.

FRANKFURT: a busy city in Hesse, W Germany; renowned for its many fairs: 1.12.

FRAPIN: "an old uncle"; R had an uncle of that name, his mother's maiden name: 4.OP.

FRATER LUBINUS, FRATRIS LUBINI, FRÈRE LUBIN: see Lubin, Frère.

FRIAR BOOBY, FRIAR GULLIGUT SMELLSMOCK: see Lubin, Frère.

FRIESLAND (OR FRISIA), FRIESLANDER(S): a province of the N Netherlands: 1.12.

FRIGGLEFRAGGLES, ANTIDOTED (FANFRELUCHES ANTIDOTÉES): nonsense title of a long nonsense poem: 1.2.

FROGIER: innocent shepherd of Gargantua, whiplashed by unprovoked Marquet, hits back hard: 1.32.

FRONTIGNAN: usually deformed into Foutignan, small town near Montpellier, good wine region: 2.16.

FUGGER(S): of Augsburg; fabulously rich merchant prince family: 1.8.

FUNDAMENT: derrière, both basis and bottom; old joke: 1.2.

FURRED CATS (CHATS FOURRÉS): of the wicket and of the law courts; note that homophone *chaffourés* suggests the blurred, smeared confusion of the legal system: 5.11.

GABINI: citizens of an old town near and E of Rome: 4.63.

GAETAN, GAETANUS, GAIETAN: see Cajetan.

GALEN (GALENOS OF PERGAMUM, ASIA MINOR, A.D. 129–209): of Greek parents; after only Hippocrates as the outstanding medical authority, esp. in anatomy and biology; lived long in Rome; friend of Marcus Aurelius (q.v.): 1.P.

GALEN RESTORED (NO RELATION TO THE ABOVE): a medieval lord fighting in Spain to renew knighthood: 2.30.

GALICIA: the one in Spain, not in Poland, Ukraine: 1.33.

GALILEE: region in Palestine N of Judea; saw much of Jesus' teaching: 3.P.

GALLAND, PIERRE (1510–1559): defender of Aristotle against colleague Ramus in a dispute that stirred all Paris (the academia) around 1550: 4.P.

GALLET, ULRICH: Gargantua's envoy, spokesman, Master of Requests: 1.30.

GALLI: gelded priests of Isis, notoriously cruel and lecherous: 3.45.

GALLIA NARBONENSIS: a Roman province including most of Languedoc, S France: 1.33.

GALLUS, GAIUS CORNELIUS (69–26 B.C.): Gaul-born Roman soldier-poet; restored elegiac form to repute; esteemed by Virgil: 1.3.

GAMBIA, GAMBIAN(S): W African country, a bit N of midpoint: 2.24.

GAMES (GARGANTUA'S): R spends one chapter on Gargantua's games to display a waste of time: 1.22.

GANABIN: in BD "Island of Thieves"; island so wicked that Pantagruel will not land: 4.66.

GARGAMELLE: daughter of the king of the Parpaillons, wife of Grandgousier, mother of Gargantua: 1.4.

GARGANTUA: eponymous hero of Book I; father of Pantagruel; aging, translated to fairyland, but returns at a good time in 3, but not to stay: 1. passim.

GARGANTUIST(S): Gargantua's supporters in Picrocholine War: 1.48.

GARUM: a condiment dear to ancients; praised by Pliny; fish guts marinated in brine: 6.15.

GASCONY, GASCON(S): an old French duchy joined to Aquitaine in 1052, extending from Spain and the Pyrenees to the Garonne on NE, with Atlantic Ocean on W; Gascons were often bellicose and quick to claim nobility and to mix up "b" and "v" in speech: 1.1.

GAUDE MARIA(S): Rejoice, Mary; announcement of coming birth of Christ: 2.11.

GAUL, CISALPINE: "on this side" of the Alps, the Roman side, i.e., N Italy: 4.58. Beyond the Alps lies transalpine Gaul.

GAUL, GAULISH: the Roman name for much of W. Europe (N Italy, France, Germany, Low Countries, Spain, and Portugal); conquered for Rome by Julius Caesar (ending 27 B.C.); split into four huge provinces in A.D. third c.; invaded by Germanic tribes, then in fifth c. by Visigoths, Burgundians, and Franks: 3.3. See also Gallia.

GELLIUS, AULUS (A.D. CA. 130–180): studied in Athens and Rome, wrote (in Latin) 20 books of *Attic Nights* (*Noctes Atticae*), mainly anecdotes and odds and ends: 1.3.

GENOA, GENOESE: a big Italian port on Gulf of Genoa on the Mediterranean Sea; R finds men greedy and money-mad: 1.33.

GENOU, SAINT: supposedly able to cure gout; abbey named for him near Nantes: 1.45.

GENTLEMEN, THE (MESSIEURS): the greedy paper-pulling Apedeftes of Book 5: 5.A16.

"GENTLEMAN, WORD OF A" (FOY DE GENTILHOMME): Francis I's favorite oath: 2.3.

GENTLEMEN OF THE TREASURY: i.e., members of that body: 2.11.

GEOFFREY SABERTOOTH (GEOFFROY DE LUSIGNAN): a brigand but related by marriage to Pantagruel: 2.5.

GEORGICS: Virgil's four-book poem on husbandry (completed 30 B.C.); for some, his best work: 1.24.

GERMANICUS (GERMANICUS DRUSUS OR GERMANICUS CAESAR, 15 B.C.–
A.D. 19): nephew and adopted son of Tiberius (q.v.); heroic conqueror
of Germanic tribes; popular, promising but poisoned very young;
Tiberius probably involved: 3.48.

GERMANY, GERMANIES, GERMAN(S), GERMANIC: the large strong European country and people (see also High Germany); then under Empire
but very fragmented: 1.23.

GERTRUDE, SAINT (B. 1302): a German nun famous for her *Revelations*:
2.7.

GERVASIUS (OR GERVASE), SAINT: martyred with his brother Saint
Protasius in Milan under Nero; R mentions not him but the church
named after him on the Paris Right Bank near the Hôtel de Ville: 2.17.
See Saint-Gervais.

GERYON: his oracle noted by Suetonius B.C.–A.D. 69 in *Life of Tiberius*:
3.11.

GETHSEMANE (OR OLIVET), GARDEN OF: scene of transfiguration of Jesus
(Luke 22.39 ff.): 1.39.

GIANTS (1): their revolt against Jupiter threatened Olympus; punished:
3.28.

GIANTS (2): See Werewolf.

GIBRALTAR: the N of the two "Pillars of Hercules," on the Spanish side
of the strait separating the Mediterranean Sea from the Atlantic Ocean.
The "hole" may be a cave on its side: 1.2.

GILDAS, SAINT (SEVENTH C.): British missionary; founded monastery in
Brittany; patron of madmen; festival January 29: 1.45.

GLACIAL (OR ARCTIC) SEA: the big ocean mass around the North Pole:
1.33.

GOATSNOSE (NAZDECABRE, I.E., NEZ-DE-CHÈVRE): the rude mute consulted by Panurge: 3.19–20.

GOBBLECHITTERLING (RIFLANDOUILLE): one of two aptly-named Pantagrueline commanders in the war against the Chitterlings, but also earlier
name used, curiously, for one of Werewolf's giants destroyed by
Pantagruel's ingenuity: 4.37.

GOBELINS: the great Parisian firm of dyers, weavers, tapestry makers, who
indeed used some water (from underground Bièvre stream) containing
untreated sewage; their country seat, a fancy pleasure house in the Saint-
Jacques (not the Saint-Marceau) suburb, was called their folly: 2.15.

"GOD KEEP YOU": a chess term in those days meaning "Check!": 5.23.

GODERAN, SAINT (1063 OR 1070–1158): bishop of Saintes and abbot of Maillezais; buried there: 1.58.

GOGUET, HILAIRE: a Fontenay lawyer friend of R's: 6.4.

GOLDEN FLEECE: Greek myth; that of the winged ram that carried Phrixus all the way to Helle until she fell off, across the Hellespont (named for her fall); much later recovered by Jason and his Argonauts, helping restore his father to throne of Iolchos: 4.6.

GOLFARIN: sworn by one of Werewolf's giants as nephew of Mahomet: 2.29.

GOLIATH (OF GATH): 1 Samuel 2.9; gigantic Philistine champion; taunted, terrified Israelites until shepherd boy David fought him, killed him with a stone shot from his sling: 2.1.

GOMORRAH: Genesis 14; twin wicked city of the Jordan plain (with Sodom); both destroyed for their evil ways by Jehovah: 2.P.

"GOOD DAY!": then a chess term meaning "Checkmate!": 5.24.

GOOD JOHN: name for typical nice peasant; here a Franc-Taupin captain: 1.35.

GOOD NEWS OR GOOD TIDINGS, OUR LADY OF (NOSTRE DAME DE BONNES NOUVELLES): a pilgrimage spot at Loreto (in Ancona, E Italy) on a hill overlooking the Adriatic Sea: 1.27.

GORGIAS (CA. 485–380 B.C.) OF LEONTINI: in Sicily, potent Sophist rhetorician, whom Plato presents in the dialogue named for him, on truth and persuasion. Here R uses this familiar name for a pun on French *gorge* or "throat" when the narrator is inside Pantagruel's mouth: 2.32.

GOSLING, BRIDLED (OYSON BRIDÉ): like a bridled goose, a figure of fancy in R's day and often since. Note such names as Judge Bridoye (Bridlegoose), Beaumarchais's Bridlegosling (Bridoison), etc.: 1.P.

GOSPEL: Evangel or Good Tidings; here rarely means the four Gospels or the Evangelists; normally means simply the Bible (q.v.): 1.12. See also Holy Word, Holy Scripture, Holy Writ.

GOTH(S), GOTHIC: R regularly uses this term for barbarian hordes to damn the many people and institutions that opposed all the "new learning" and rediscovered the riches of ancient Israel, Greece, and Rome; this term often used to describe the "Dark Ages" and esp. of scholasticism; R clearly enjoys the fact that this word (pronounced "go") is thus a homophone of the common ending "gaux" that he uses for all the names of his hominoid clerically-named birds who represent steps on the ecclesiastical ladder (from *Clergaux* up to *Papegaux*) in the episode of the Ringing Island: 1.14.

GOTHIA: southern Sweden: 1.33.

GOZAL: carrier pigeon or dove: 4.3.

GRACCHUS, GRACCHI: a noble Roman family justly renowned for fairness in arbitrating property disputes between rich and poor: 1.15.

GRACES: in Greek myth, three lesser goddesses personifying loveliness, grace, etc.: 1.55.

GRAIL, HOLY (SANGREAL): reportedly the cup, bowl, chalice, or platter used by Christ at the Last Supper and since His death holding His blood; object of numerous knightly vain quests in Arthur's time and later: 4.43.

GRAMMONT: lord of one or two fiefs in Chinon parish: 1.37.

GRANDGOUSIER: from *Grand Gosier* or "Big-throat"; husband of Gargamelle and father of Gargantua; under threat of war seems a gentle but tired, feeble old man but later gives wise, kindly advice to pilgrims that leaves them ecstatic (1.45) and treats captured prisoner Blowhard most generously (1.46), as we learn in 1.50 to King Alpharbal and his defeated Cararrians long before; serves as a model and guide to his son Gargantua vis-à-vis the Picrocholeans, but with those exceptions he vanishes after 1.37 to reappear never and be remembered seldom: 1.3–5; the only exceptions are 1.45–46; 1.50; and 2.1; even in 3.48 there the revivified Gargantua inveighs so fiercely against marriages lacking parental consent, no mention is made of Grandgousier, by name or without it.

GRAVES: wine; esteemed Bordeaux wines from the left bank of the Garonne: 3.5.

GRAVOT: hamlet or hamlets near Bourgueil (Indre-et-Loire), hence also near Chinon; given to Sebaste after the victory; probably the R family had land there: 1.9. The woodchopper Couillatris of 4.P was born there.

GRECISMUS: by Eberhard de Béthune (twelfth c.); a grammar in barbaric Latin verse claiming to offer etymologies of Greek-derived Latin words: 1.14.

GREECE, GRECIAN, GREEK(S): the great ancient language and culture that are a major source of modern W European tradition and others derived from them; in R's day highly prized (but hard to learn) as key to the New Testament and the best in secular literature, philosophy, science, medicine; opposed by most conservatives as a threat to their (real or fancied) authority; cherished by humanists, Evangelicalists; R learned it well from 1520–1523 from Pierre Amy, his friend and fellow monk and priest at Fontenay-le-Comte: 1.1.

GREEK CALENDS: see Calends, Greek.

GREENLAND, GREENLANDER(S): the huge Arctic island in the far N Atlantic: 1.33.

GRIBOUILLIS, GRILGROTH: plus Astaroth and Rapallus, burlesque demons' names, here invoked by a Turk whose house and goods have just burned down, at least as reported by Panurge: 2.14.

GRIPPEMINAUD OR GRIPPEMINAULT: see Clutchpuss.

GROSBEAK: used once to translate Grosbec, one of Frère Jean's fighting cooks (4.40), but far more often and importantly the name of Homenaz who stands for Pope Julius III; Homenaz-Grosbeak is the ebullient bishop of Papimania, who drools in adoration of popes and decretals and would like to torture and slaughter anyone so heretical as not to share these feelings: 4.48.

GROVE, WILLOW: see Willow-Grove.

GRYPHIUS, SEBASTIAN (GREIFF): a fine scholarly Lyon publisher who issued a few of R's books: 6.5.

GULES (GUEULE): in heraldry, red; "mots de gueule"; starts gags on words' colors, since it may also mean "gules jests": 4.56.

GUORRE (OR GORRE): puzzling here; usual meanings "sow" or "syphilis"; may also mean foppish showiness; here it may even be a fantasy term: 3.21.

GUZZLER (MORPIAILLE): an ally or commander of Picrochole in his war with Gargantua: 1.31.

GYMNASTE: nimble domestic companion of both giants; a minor character: 1–5, passim.

HADES (HAIDES, AIDES): "the Unseen"; or Pluto "the Rich," god of the underworld, the mineral-rich domain; abode of body-less shades flitting after death; not in R, but Epistémon's visit, despite the label, takes him there, not to any Christian Hell: 1.2.

HADRIAN (AELIANUS HADRIANUS, EMPEROR OF ROME A.D. 117–138): an able organizer and builder, he strengthened the empire: 3.10.

HAGARENE: Moorish; the Moors were reputedly descendants of Hagar via Ishmael (Genesis 16.15–16): 2.2.

HAINAULT, HAINAULTER(S): a region, once German, in NE France near Belgium: 1.33.

HAIRYPAWS: pussyfooters and sneaks; a favorite pet name here for monks: 2.7.

HALF SPAN: 2.15; see span.

HALI ABBAS (OR ALI BEN-AL ABAS): tenth-c. Arab physician: 4.OC.

HAMILCAR BARCA: able Carthaginian general, fierce foe of Rome, not cited by R.

HANNIBAL (247–182 B.C.): greatest Carthaginian general, routed Romans at Cannae (216 B.C.); threatened Rome: 1.46.

HARDUIN (OR ORTUINUS) DE GRAES: fierce foe of Erasmus and all Reformists: 2.7.

HASDRUBAL: another able son of Hamilcar Barca, brother of Hannibal, who worked well with him: 2.30.

HASTYCALF (HASTIVEAU): rash commander and bad adviser to Picrochole; unprovoked, mortally insults fellow commander Blowhard who rightly kills him; cruelly avenged by Picrochole (1.47); the name is also used for one of Frère Jean's fighting cooks: 4.40.

HAVRE DE GRÂCE: Normandy, now Le Havre; then a big French Atlantic port; now the biggest: 2.4.

HEBREW(S), HEBRAIC: Old Testament chosen race; language of the Old Testament: 1.7.

HECALE: a needy old woman who entertained young Theseus most hospitably: 3.17.

HECTOR: the great Trojan hero; keeps them in the fight; kills Patroclus and is killed by Achilles: 2.30.

HECUBA (GREEK HEKABE): queen, then widow of King Priam of Troy; cruelly treated by Greek victors; see Euripides tragedy named for her: 3.14.

HELEN (OF TROY): daughter of Zeus (as swan) and Leda; wife of Menelaus; pretext or cause of Trojan War: 3.48.

HELICON: mountain in Boeotia sacred to the Muses, site of their worship: 3.P.

HELLEBORE: an herb then favored for dementia and other ills: 3.24.

HELLESPONT (OR DARDANELLES): a large, wide strait between European and Asiatic Turkey and connecting Sea of Marmora and Aegean Sea: 4.7.

HER TRIPPA: see Trippa, Her.

HERA: Greek myth; like Latin Juno; see Juno.

HERACLITUS (FL. CA. 500 B.C.), HERACLITIZE: of Ephesus, now Turkish Asia Minor; philosopher believing in unity of all substance and universal constant flux; considered melancholy, so ever contrasted with supposedly laughing Democritus: 1.20.

HERBAULT: medieval embodiment of Want, Misery; above all, main part of name (Dupuyherbault, Putherbeus); a fierce foe of R: 4.52; see Putherbeus.

HERCULES, GAULISH: Gaulish Hercules; a legendary leader so eloquent that he draws peoples after him as he likes by a golden chain that connects their ears to his tongue; this figure is drawn from Lucian: 4.OC.

HERCULES (GREEK HERAKLES): Greco-Roman myth; son of Zeus and Alcmene; mighty destroyer of myriad scourges of man; some of these among the Ten Labors assigned him by King Eurystheus of Tiryns (ten or twelve); but also reputedly given to lust and gluttony; persecuted by Hera, jealous of Zeus's infidelity; rescued Alcestis from Hades when she gave her life for her husband; driven mad by Hera: 1.2.

HERCULES, PILLARS OF: the ancient name for the two rocky promontories flanking the eastern end of the Strait of Gibraltar (q.v.): 1.33.

HERM: like nearby Sark, a little island in the English Channel infamous for robbers who plundered foundered ships and often murdered survivors: 4.23.

HERMES: in Greek myth, messenger god, much like Roman Mercury; see Mercury but see also Hermes Trismegistus.

HERMES TRISMEGISTUS (THRICE GREATEST): a name first used of the Egyptian god Thoth; then since A.D. third c. applied to the author of the Neoplatonic *Pimander*, stressing the common nature of all things: 3.13.

HERMOLAUS BARBARUS (ERMOLAO BARBARO, 1454–1493): Italian humanist: 3.25.

HERO, HEROES: a more distinctive term in Greek, though imprecise; one almost superhuman mighty warrior or great patriot; like daemons in that their death was often marked by portents such as terrible storms: 4.6.

HERO (IN GREEK ROMANCE *HERO AND LEANDER*): a young priestess of Aphrodite in (European) Sestos, loved by Leander of (Asian) Abydos, who many times swam Hellespont to court her; when he drowned in a blinding storm, in her grief and bereft love she drowned herself in turn: 3.26.

HERO (OR HERON; DATES UNKNOWN) OF ALEXANDRIA: noted inventor and mathematician; but not known as author of any book *De ingeniis*: 2.7.

HEROD "THE GREAT": Antipater; virtual king of Judaea under the Romans 37–34 B.C.; bloodthirsty, perhaps mad: 4.26, n. 4.

HERODOTUS (CA. 480–425 B.C.) OF HALICARNASSIS IN COASTAL ASIA MINOR, NOW TURKEY: the Greek "Father of History"; struggles to extricate history from myth, legend, epic; wide travels and studies aspects of the entire then known world including cultures, religions, main events and persons, esp. the "Persian War" (512–479 B.C.); Greek repulse of invasion by mighty Persia; great storyteller; R translated some of his Book 2 (on Egypt, etc.) by 1524: 2.26.

HEROPHILUS (OR HIEROPHILUS) FOURTH–THIRD C. B.C. OF ALEXANDRIA: noted anatomist, who discovered the nervous system; founded a medical school: 4.OC.

HERVÉ (DE PRIMAUGUET): naval commander; fought heroically against the English (1512): 4.21.

HESIOD (FL. CA. 800 B.C.): early Greek poet; highly renowned for his *Works and Days:* 1.24.

HESPERIA (GREEK FOR WESTERN): W tower of Thélème; used of Italy: 1.53.

HIARCHAS: an eastern sage, apparently an Indian brahmin; visited by Apollonius of Tyana: 2.18.

HIBERNAIAN (LATIN FOR IRISH): but why Hibernaian saffron?: 4.67.

HIEROPHILUS: see Herophilus.

"HIGH BONNETS" (TIME OF THE): fast faded fifteenth-c. custom used by R to deride any outdated, old-fashioned idea or thing that he dislikes: 1.9.

HIGH GERMAN (OLD): an old Alpine dialect proverbially unintelligible: 1.23.

HIPPO: Saint Augustine's bishopric, near Bona in NW Algeria: 1.33.

HIPPOCRAS: a mulled wine supposedly invented by Hippocrates (q.v.): 3.30, n. 7.

HIPPOCRATES (B. CA. 460 B.C.) OF COS: Greek father of western medicine; still the great authority in R's day; famed today for "Hippocratic Oath": 1.3.

HIPPOLYTUS: Greek myth and tragedy by Euripides (q.v.); son of Theseus and Amazon Antiope; an ultra-chaste huntsman; adored Artemis but scorned and flouted Aphrodite; she, vengeful, made his stepmother Phaedra love him madly, try to lure him, then, when roughly rebuffed hanged herself and left note accusing him of trying to rape her. Theseus cursed him, got him killed in horrible fashion when horses bolted in fear; restored to life for a time by Aesculapius, to his cost: 3.18.

HIPPONAX (FL. CA. 540 B.C.): a coarse, sometimes amusing satirist: 2.18.

HIPPOTHADÉE: subject of various interpretations and various suggested models; the benign Evangelicalist theologian (note his stress on continence as a "gift and special grace" and his interpretation of Saint Paul's dictum in 1 Corinthians 7.9. Vulgate is "melius nubere quam uri," the NEB more explicitly "Better be married than burn with vain desire"; at Pantagruel's urging, Panurge consults him about his dilemma over marriage, only to ignore his wise advice: 3.30.

HISPANIOLA: an Antilles island holding modern Haiti and the Dominican Republic; R's time known (by choice of Columbus) as Isabella (the queen): 1.50.

HOBGOBLINS (FARFADETS): here means monks (once, those at Fontenay): 3.10.

HOGSHEAD(S) (MUIDZ): huge but imprecise measures of liquid volume; seems to mean something between 63 to 140 gallons; P. calls it 270 liters; and (or) casks to hold these: 2.14.

HOLE, SAINT PATRICK'S: a cave in Ireland that was inevitably linked to the saint: 1.2.

HOLE OF GIBRALTAR (SO-CALLED): see Gibraltar.

HOLLAND: a major province of the Netherlands; name often used for the entire country: 1.33.

HOLOFERNES, THUBAL: see Thubal Holofernes.

HOLY APOSTLE: one of the many names used for Saint Paul: 3.5.

HOLY SCRIPTURE(S), HOLY WORD, HOLY WRIT: the Bible: 2.8; see also Gospel.

HOMENAZ: R's name for the prelate we translate as Grosbeak; see Grosbeak.

HOMER, HOMERIC: the great ancient Greek epic poet; wrote *Iliad* and *Odyssey*; life unknown but conjectures abound; blind; from coastal Asia Minor; clearly the fountainhead of all Greek, all western literatures; vast influence: 1.P.

HONDRESPONDRE(S): a corruption of both English "hundred-pounder" and German "hunder-punder"; a derisive term for the ubiquitous predatory mercenaries, mainly German and Imperial, then infesting France and most of W Europe: 3.42.

HONFLEUR (CALVADOS AT SEINE MOUTH): in R's day a busy Atlantic port: 2.23.

HORACE (QUINTUS HORATIUS FLACCUS, 65–8 B.C.): excellent Roman poet; left *Art of Poetry, Epistles, Epodes, Satires*: 1.P; see also Flaccus.

HORAPPOLLO: see Orus Apollo.

HORTENSIA: daughter of orator Hortensius (114–50 B.C.): made speech in forum 42 B.C.: 2.30.

HOSANNA CROSS: in BD "near which on Palm Sunday they sing 'Osanna filio David',": 4.13.

HOSPITALERS: a religious military order founded twelfth c. in Jerusalem: 1.39.

HÔTEL-DIEU: a Paris public hospital near Notre-Dame on Ile de la Cité; another of the same name in Lyon; R was a doctor there (1532–1535).

HOT-PISS (GONORRHEA): Fastilent got it from his strange diet: 4.29.

HOURS: the seven daily canonical times for monastic prayers and devotions; about every three hours, from matins 3 A.M. and lauds, tierce, sext, nones (about noon), vespers, complines: 1.41.

HUNGARY, HUNGARIAN: a country in E central Europe then ruled by Turks; noted for fine embroidery: 1.33.

HUON DE BORDEAUX: hero of a medieval tale of exploits, chivalry, etc.: 2.P.

HURLYBURLY (CONFUSION): Frère Jean swears by his and by Saint Hurlyburly, not on most calendars: 5.P.

HURTALY: giant steersman of Noah's Ark, ancestor of Gargantua: 2.1.

HYÈRES, ILES D' (STOECHADES): tiny French Mediterranean islands near Toulon; pirate hideout: 3.50.

HYPOGEE: an underground trip: 5.35.

HYRCANIA, HYRCANIAN SEA: the Caspian Sea and region E of it (now in N Iran): 1.8.

IAMBLICHUS (D. CA. A.D 330): a Syrian neoplatonic mystic who wrote on Epicureanism: 3.13.

IAMBUS, IAMB: prosody; one short syllable followed by two longs (here one short body, two long legs); cf., French *jambe*, "leg": 2.1.

IBERIA, IBERIAN PENINSULA: Latin names for Spain and Portugal: 3.P.

ICAROMENIPPUS: Daedalus's son playing Menippus in the tall tale named for him: 3.P.

ICARUS: Greek myth; son of Daedalus; escaping with father from Crete by flight but flew too high; sun melted wax in wings; he fell, drowned in part of Aegean named Icarian for him; his "dog" in the sky is the Dog Star, Canis Major: 3.51.

ICHTHYOPHAGIA, ICHTHYOPHAGI: Land of the Fish-eaters; an Egyptian tribe and land in Herodotus: 3.22. Also the subject of Erasmus *Colloquy* deriding Catholic stress on dietary ritual.

IDA: name either of a wet nurse of Zeus in Crete or mountain Rhea hid him on: 1.8. Could also be a mountain range in Troad (S. Phrygia) from which Zeus watched Trojan War: 1.8.

IDEA(S) (PLATONIC): Plato saw reality only in eternal, unchanging forms or archetypes (ideas) of which our "realities" of sense-objects and such are to him mere imitations or representations: 4.2; see Plato.

IDES: old Roman calendar; 15th day of March, May, July, or October; 13th of all other months; thus Ides of May are May 15: 1.31.

ILIAD: Homer's great epic about the wrath of Achilles and the Trojan War (successful attack on Troy by Greek armies): 1.P.

ILLIERS, MILES D': a happy debtor: 3.5.

INNOCENT, SAINT: cemetery of; see Saint-Innocent.

INSINUATE ONE'S NOMINATION: to slip in one's candidacy (often erotic): 1.5.

Insolubilia of Alliaco by Pierre d'Ailly, 1350–1420; for humanists, an out-dated text: 3.30.

INTELLIGENCES, MOVING: angels charged with moving the celestial spheres: 3.28.

INTERCALARY: intercalated, interpolated: 4.P.

IOLAUS (IOLAOS): Greek myth; helped Hercules face two monsters at once, the many-headed Hydra and a giant crab Hera sent to support it as Hercules cut off Hydra's heads; he seared the stumps so that heads could not grow right back again: 5.20.

IONIA, IONIC: W coastal Asia Minor; important source of Greek thought, language (its oldest form), and letters: 1.8.

ISAAC: Genesis 21–27; son of Abraham, father of Jacob and Esau: 3.21.

ISABELLA: modern Hispaniola, Antilles; Haiti and Dominican Republic; see Hispaniola.

ISHMAEL: Genesis 16.1; son of Abraham and Hagar; sent away but to found a great nation, many cities: 3.3.

ISIS, ISIAC(S): Egyptian goddess of female fertility; sister-wife of Osiris and with him ruler of the lower world; her priests very cruel and licentious: 3.48.

ISLE-BOUCHARD: small islet and town in the Vienne near Chinon: 1.47.

ISRAEL, ISRAELITE(S): the ancient Hebrews from Jacob's time on: 1.50.

ITALY, ITALIAN(S): the great S European peninsula; home of Rome, Naples, Florence, Genoa, Milan, Venice; cultural leader in R's day, but then also a mixed bag of often warring principalities: 1.33.

ITHYPHALLUS: Greek for "the male member at the ready": 3.19.

IVES (OR YVES), SAINT (1253–1303): a Breton saint widely worshiped by his countrymen; patron of all who are involved with the law: 3.4.

IXION: Greek myth, when pardoned by Zeus for murder of father-in-law, tried to seduce Hera; so bound on a racking wheel turning for eternity: 4.21.

JACOB: Genesis 25–50; son of Isaac, father of Joseph and his brothers: 3.14.

JACOBIN(S): a religious order; Dominicans, so named because their first monastery was on the Rue Saint-Jacques (Saint James), Paris: 3.22.

JAFFA (OR JOPPA), ISRAEL: once a large port city, now the S part of Tel Aviv: 1.33.

JAMES, SAINTS: two, both of the twelve disciples; (1) "The Greater," killed by Herod in 43 B.C.; (2) "The Lesser, the Evangelist," author of the Epistle; this mention could mean either one: 1.32.

JANEQUIN (OR JANNEQUIN), CLÉMENT (1480–1558): eminent French composer-musician; inventor of polyphony: 4.P.

JANOTUS, JANOT (APPROXIMATELY JOHNNY-O) DE BRAGMARDO (CF., BRAGUEMARD, BRAGMARD "CUTLASS"): the comical wheezing Latin orator delegated by Sorbonne to beg Gargantua to return the bells of Notre-Dame de Paris: 1.18–20.

JASON: mythical Greek hero; sailed ship Argo to remote Colchis; won back the Golden Fleece, thanks to sorceress Medea; married her; then when they took refuge in Corinth, he planned to marry the king's daughter; Medea killed her and the king by witchcraft and killed both of her and Jason's own two children, leaving him childless; then fled to Athens for asylum with King Aegeus and married him; see the *Medea* of Euripides (431 B.C.), a powerful tragedy: 2.30.

JASON (ANOTHER, UNRELATED): Giasone del Maino d. 1519; noted Paduan jurist: 2.10.

JAVA: rich populous Indonesian island, long renowned for coffee, spices: 3.51.

JAVERZAY (POITOU): a hamlet not far from Chinon; pilgrimage spot because of relics from Rome deposited in church there by Cardinal Perrault, born there: 1.27.

JEALOUSY: personified and deified; indispensable to produce cuckoldry: 3.33.

JEAN DE PARIS: hero of an old romance named for him: 2.30.

JEAN DES ENTOMMEURES, FRÈRE: see Entommeures, Frère Jean des.

JENON (JOHNNY) DE QUINQUENAIS (Q.V.): his "little rain" beat down great winds: 4.44.

JERUSALEM (ISRAEL): holy city of Jews, Christians, and Muslims: 1.33.

JESSE: 1 Samuel 17; father of King David of Israel: 1.39.

JESUIT(S): military teaching order founded by Loyola in 1534: 4.18.

JESUS: see many references to Him by role or attribute (Lord, Savior, Redeemer): 1.39.

JEW(S): Jewish, Jewry; chosen people of the Bible; 1.29; see also Judaea, Judaic: 1.8.

JOB: a model of piety and eponymous hero of a book of the Old Testament; proverbially patient; endured and passed God's terrible testing on Satan's prompting; duly rewarded; a model for Jews during Babylonian Captivity: 3.2; see 4.33 for Job's name used instead of Jonah.

JOBELIN BRIDÉ: the second "old wheezer" to mishandle Gargantua's education: 1.14.

JOHN, SAINTS (2): both sons of Zebedee; (1) one of the twelve apostles, probably "the disciple whom Jesus loved," and to whom, dying, he put in charge of his mother Mary; traditionally the author of the fourth Gospel, the three Epistles of John and the book of Revelation; (2) brother of "James the Greater," mentioned also in other Gospels and Epistles and the Book of Acts; made one visit to Rome; long exiled to Patmos in Aegean near Asia Minor; probably died of old age in Ephesus about A.D. 28–30; June 24, our "Midsummer Day," French "la Saint-Jean," is celebrated as his birthday: 1.10 refers clearly to the author of Revelation; 2.P to the Evangelist; 2.6 and 2.14 refer to either John 1 or 2 or one to each; 3.33 to John the Baptist; the two references in 4 BD could be to either John (1) or (2) or one to each.

JOHN OF SCOTLAND: see Scotus, Duns.

JOHN THE BAPTIST (OR HERE THE BEHEADED, DIED CA. A.D. 28–30): Jewish prophet who chose to live in the desert; preached the coming of Jesus as Messiah and meanwhile repentance of sins; when Jesus came, hailed Him as Son of God and baptized Him; condemned and opposed King Herod, who on a whim of Herod's wife and daughter was beheaded (3.33); "La Saint-Jean" (June 24) is celebrated as his birthday: 3.33. Saint Jean de La Palisse in 4.16 relates to the author of the Apocalypse (Revelation); 4.22 could refer to any Saint John.

JOHN XXII, POPE FROM 1245–1334: pope in Avignon from 1316; tried to centralize pontifical administration; in R, easily proved to nuns that they, being women, could not be trusted to keep secrets: 3.34.

JOHN-CALF (JEAN LE VEAU): a traditional name for a dolt; here a pedant: 1.14.

JOHNNY (JENON DE) OF QUINQUENAIS: see Jenon de Quinquenais.

JOHNNY JUMPUP (JEAN JEUDI): the penis: 2.21.

JONAH: hero of a popular Old Testament book; he was a pious servant of God whom He sent to denounce and warn Nineveh; when, on the way, swallowed by a whale; lived three days in his belly; then God heeded his prayers and saved him. At first he had sought to escape from God; hence thrown into the sea. This was a favorite story ever since: 4.8. In 4.33 cited under name of Job.

JOUSSE BANDOUILLE: a colleague and helper of Janotus de Bragmardo (q.v.): 1.20.

JOUSSEAULME: the sheep-farming draper victimized by lawyer Pathelin (q.v.) in the fifteenth-c. farce named for him that R loved and often used: 3.4.

JOVE, JOVIAN: another name for Jupiter; see Jupiter.

JUBILEE (YEAR): in most Christian creeds every 50 years; in Roman Catholicism every 25; in R's time, 1500, 1524, and 1550; Catholics could get plenary indulgences for certain specified acts of piety, penance, or both: 2.13.

JUDAEA, JUDEA, JUDAIC: Palestine between the Dead Sea and the Mediterranean; the heart of Judaism: 4.26.

JUDGMENT (DAY, NIGHT, LAST): the world's last day, when Christ returns to judge mankind: 2.14.

JULIA: daughter of Emperor Augustus (q.v.) who failed to correct her; finally banished her for profligacy: 1.3.

JULIAN: a notable jurist; Salvius Julianus Severus (A.D. second c.): 3.45.

JULIAN "THE APOSTATE": Flavius Claudius Julianus, "Divus Julianus"; emperor A.D. 361–363; anti-Christian; may never have been Christian: 3.25.

JULIUS CAESAR: see Caesar, Julius.

JULIUS POLLUX (FL. A.D. 180): a Greek grammarian; wrote a lexicon of hunting terms: 1.23.

JULIUS II, POPE (GIULIANO DELLA ROVERE, 1443–1513): pope from 1503; first pope to wear a beard; militant; fiercely anti-French: 2.30.

JULIUS III: pope never named by R but clearly his model for Bishop Homenaz (Grosbeak) of the Papimaniacs; see Grosbeak.

JUNEBUGGERY (HANNETONNIÈRE): a major source of revenues for Panurge: 3.5.

JUNO, JUNONIC: the greatest Roman goddess (cf., Hera), sister and wife of Zeus; often furious at his countless infidelities; takes it out on his victims (Alcmene, Io et al.): 1.2.

JUNONIC GADFLY: like the one Juno inflicted on Io because Jupiter lusted for her: 1.44.

JUPITER: chief Roman Olympian god (cf., Greek Zeus); wields thunder and lightning; incurable womanizer, even rapist; Panurge fears this for his own wife: 1.2.

JUPITER AMMON: see Ammon.

JUPITER PHILIOS: Jupiter as special patron god of friends and friendship: 3.24.

JUS GENTIUM: law accepted by all nations and peoples (or nearly all): cf., the notion of "natural law," a notion pervasive in 3.48 but not so named there; named as such: 1.10.

JUSTINIAN (JUSTINIANUS, A.D. 527–565): Roman emperor at Constantinople; helped into power by his uncle Justin; his great general Belisarius won him back Africa from the Vandals; Rome and all Italy from the Goths; by the work of Tribonianus and his staff he organized Roman law better than ever, into a four-part *Corpus juris* rising from the *Novels* (*Novellae*) to the *Digest* (or *Pandects*); to the *Institutes*, and on up to the famous *Code* (*Codex*); built the great Church of Saint Sophia in Constantinople; in 529 closed Athenian schools of philosophy: 2.7.

JUTURNA: in *Aeneid* (12.140 ff.) a nymph of streams and pools; trying to save her brother Turnus, she broke truce, wounded Aeneas with an arrow: 4.62.

JUVENAL (DECIMUS JUNIUS JUVENALIS, BORN CA. A.D. 65–70): an able Roman poet; wrote 16 verse Satires in 5 books (prob. ca. A.D. 98–128); fierce attacks on Roman vices and follies, then and before; emulated since in all W literatures, in English notably from Chaucer through Dryden and on down to our time: 4.59.

JUVENTIUS (MARCUS JUVENTIUS TALVA): died of joy: 1.10.

KATIM, AL: see Alkatin.

KING, THE GREAT: for R, a Frenchman, Francis I of France (q.v.): 3.41.

KINGS (SPARTA): Sparta long had two kings, one each from two royal families; strong from time of legendary Lycurgus through the seventh c. B.C.; progressively weaker in and from the sixth c.

KISSASS (BAISECUL): one of two nonsense litigants reconciled by Pantagruel: 2.10–12.

KNUCKLEBONES: *osselets* or *tales*, from Latin *talos;* either a game of chance like dice; or a form of backgammon (tables); or yet the skill game of jacks, jackstones, dibs: 1.22.

KORAN (CORAN, ALCORAN): the holy book of Islam; words of Mohammed: 2.14.

KYNE: Greek term for "bitch"; R's "inside joke" is to use it as a proper name: 3.35.

LA BAUMETTE: a Franciscan monastery near Angers, perhaps where R entered religious orders, surely where he studied for a time: 1.12.

LA BRENNE: see Brenne, La.

LA DEVINIÈRE: farmhouse or country house of R's family in the fields S of the Vienne, near Chinon; our author's probable birthplace; home also of a good wine: 1.5.

LA FOYE MONJAULT (OR LA FAYE MONJAU): a popular wine from near Niort (Deux-Sèvres), about 35–40 miles E of La Rochelle and SW of Poitiers: 1.34.

LA LENOU: possibly meant for Limoux (Aude), another pilgrimage spot: 1.27.

LA PALISSE, SAINT JEAN DE: BD says "a colloquial way of speaking, by syncope, instead of L'Apocalypse": 4.16.

LA ROCHE-CLERMAUD (LA ROCHE-CLERMAULT): a château site near La Devinière where R's family had property: 1.4.

LA ROCHELLE (CHARENTE-MARITIME): an old walled city and Atlantic port: 2.4.

LACEDAEMON (SPARTA), LACEDAEMONIAN(S): capital of state of Laconia in SE Peloponnesus; the strong Dorian-sprung warrior city-state that led the allied Greek aristocracies against the expanding democratic empire of Athens and its allies in the Peloponnesian War (431–404 B.C.) or wars (starting earlier) until new-learned Spartan naval skill and Athenian discord and overreaching brought Athens to its knees in 404: 1.20.

LACHRYMA CHRISTI ("TEARS OF CHRIST"): a noted Italian muscatel: 1.5.

LACONIA, LACONIAN(S): SE Peloponnesian state with capital Sparta: 3.13.

LACTANTIUS, CAECILIUS OR CAELIUS (BORN CA. A.D. 250): African rhetor; Christian apologist: 3.12.

LANDES, LES: a large département on the Atlantic in SW France; sandy ponds, scrubby pines: 2.21.

LANDSKNECHT(S): German mercenaries, footsoldiers in Imperial armies; hated and feared for wanton, greedy cruelty in their terrible sack of Rome in 1527; also Landsmann: 1.4.

LANGEAIS: near Chinon; site of an ancient ruin: 1.16.

LANGEY: Guillaume du Bellay, seigneur de Langey (1490–1543); one of R's great heroes; superb commander, governor, diplomat; R worked for him closely 1539–1543 as doctor and secretary in Piedmont and on trips with him back to France; mourned him deeply; helped escort his body to Le Mans for funeral and went back there for that: 4.26.

LANGUEDOC (LANGUE D'OC, HERE ALSO AS LANGUEGOTH): the tongue and area where Middle Ages (until about the eleventh or twelfth c.) used *oc* for "yes," whereas in N France it was *oïl,* which soon became *oui;* roughly the area of the Roman Gallia Narbonensis (q.v.); good wine region; home of troubadours, courtly love, much high medieval culture: 1.16; see also Languegoth.

LANGUEGOTH: in R's day considered by some the true etymon and spelling of Languedoc; used as a gag by R who loves to bring in the Goths wherever he can: 4.41.

LANS, LANS TRINGUE: invites a comrade to drink: 1.4.

LANS, LANSQUENETS: see Landsknechts.

LANTERN: in all forms, uses, and compounds still retains its slang connotation of copulation, since medieval French *lanterne* could also mean a woman's genitalia: 2.9.

LAOMEDON: Greek myth; king of Troy, father of Priam; cheated Apollo and Poseidon on their building walls of Troy, then, later, Hercules when he killed a sea monster for him; so Hercules took the city and gave Laomedon's daughter Hesione to Telamon (*Iliad* 24.443): 3.P.

LAPITHS (LAPITHAI): a Thracian people living near the Centaurs; when at a wedding feast some drunken Centaur guests tried to carry off the bride and other Lapith women, the Lapiths killed many in the ensuing battle, as Nestor relates in 11.209 ff. of Ovid's *Metamorphoses*. Strangely, R has Basché's steward, who mentions this battle, ascribe the story to Lucian, not Ovid: 4.15.

LARIGNAN: a strong castle in Piedmont that held off Caesar once; named for its use of the wood larix as a defense, almost unburnable: 3.52.

LASCARIS, JANUS (1445–1536): an Italian humanist; taught Greek; librarian for Francis I; R claims him as a friend, as is very likely: 1.24.

LASDALLER: pilgrim leader Trudgealong; see Trudgealong.

LAST JUDGMENT: see Judgment Day.

LATERAN COUNCIL: here probably the fifth of these (1512–1517); taken for a person: 3.41.

LATIN(S): still the European language of the educated and of serious books; but from long universal use, long butchered by many, even educated, like Janotus; butts of humanist mockery; also the people of Latium and their King Latinus: 1.15.

LATONA (GREEK LETO): a Titan's daughter but loved by Zeus; bore him twin gods, Apollo and Artemis: 3.10.

"LAURENCE, MY GREAT-AUNT": a fictive character from the *Farce de Maistre Pierre Pathelin*, ca. 1464: 3.7.

LAVAUGAUDRY (OR LA VAUGAUDRY): see Vaugaudry and Vauguyon.

LAWRENCE, SAINT (D. A.D. 258): a Roman deacon martyred for his Christianity; said to have been roasted to death on a grid: 3.33.

LAWS: by Plato; criminal and general, for a new colony; his last dialogue: 3.5.

LE GENDRE (LEGENDRE OR GENDRE), JEAN: a Parisian chapel cantor for Francis I, then for Henry II: 4.P.

LEAGUE(S): a variable measure of distance; between 2.4 to 4.6 miles, but usually about 3 miles: 2.23.

LEANDER: lover of priestess Hero: see Hero (and Leander).

LEDA: Greek myth; princess of Aetolia; Zeus took the form of a swan to lie with her; she bore him mortal Helen of Troy, also two demigods Dioscuri (Castor and Pollux); despite R, she probably did not hang herself: 1.6.

LEMURS AND LAMIAS: Roman malevolent spirits of dead ancestors: 3.24.

LENT: Christian, esp. Catholic; 40 days of fast and penitence before Easter: 2.11.

LEONICUS (NICOLAUS LEONICUS THOMAEUS): Italian humanist in R's time a recent author of a Latin treatise on the game of *tali, De ludo talaris*: 1.24.

LERNÉ: a village near Chinon famed for fine *fouaces* (q.v.); home of their *fouaciers;* Picrochole's capital and headquarters so important in the Picrocholine War: 1.25.

LESBIA: mistress of the poet Catullus who praised her sparrow in two of his poems: 3.46.

LESBOS: a large island off W Asia Minor, home of the able poet Alcaeus and the powerful poet Sappho (q.v.): 3.24.

LETHE (GREEK FOR "FORGETFULNESS"): the river in Hades that gives oblivion: 2.30.

LETO: see Latona.

LEUCADIA (IONIAN ISLAND): oracle of Apollo; mainland town near Mount Helicon; site of oracle of Trophonius: 3.24.

LEUCECIA: pun on Greek leukos "white" plus old Latin name for Paris, Lutetia Parisiorum; R ascribes his new name to Strabo: 1.17.

LEVANT, LEVANTINE: of or from the Levant, the Orient in general, the Mediterranean Middle East in particular: 3.38.

LEX: Latin word for "law"; often found in Bridoye's source references: 3.39-41.

LIARD(S): a small French brass coin worth 3 *deniers* or 1/3 *sol* or *sou*: 2.17.

LIBYA, LIBYAN(S): the big coastal N African country between Algeria and Egypt: 1.2.

LICENCE, LICENTIATE: the French higher degree qualifying the holder to teach: 1.9.

LIGUGÉ: a priory in Maillezais where R (presumably with Geoffroy d'Estissac) spent most of his years 1523-1530 between monastery in Fontenay and Paris medical school: 2.5.

LIGURIA, LIGURIAN SEA: Gulf of Genoa and region around Genoa: 1.33.

LIMOGES, LIMOUSIN(S), LEMOVIC: a city and surrounding province (now

Haute-Vienne); origin of the Latin-mangling Limousin schoolboy of 2.6.

LINACER (OR LINACRE), THOMAS (1460-1524): humanist, physician to Henry VIII; founder of the London School of Medicine: 4.67.

LISBON: a large Atlantic port city, capital of Portugal: 1.33.

LITHUANIA: a large former grand-duchy on the Baltic Sea, now part of the USSR: 1.33.

LIVIA (LATER JULIA AUGUSTA, 58 B.C.-A.D. 29): mother of Tiberius; grand-mother of Claudius; later wife then widow of Emperor Octavian Augustus: 2.30.

LIVY (TITUS LIVIUS, 59 B.C.-A.D.17): Roman historian of Rome in 142 books; a friend of Augustus but loved the republic; book shows high early standards, deep decline leading to Civil Wars: 1.10.

LOIRE: France's longest river (ca. 630 miles); flows first mainly N, then mainly W, into the Atlantic at Saint-Nazaire, past Blois, Orléans, Tours, Nantes, mainly navigable; great châteaux, good wines: 1.52.

LOLLIA PAULINA: mistress of Emperor Claudius: 3.24.

LOMBARD, PETER (PETRUS LOMBARDUS, CA. 1100-1160): potent Italian theologian; for a time, bishop of Paris; often called Magister Sententiarum, for his most notable work; not named in R, but see *Sententiae.*

LOMBARDY, LOMBARD(S): the large region (capital Milan) in N Italy bordering on Switzerland; in R's day a very rich major banking center: 1.3.

LONDON (LONDRES): England's capital and chief city, to the S, on the Thames: 2.20.

LONG-WOOLLED SHEEP (MOUTONS À LA GRAND LAINE): usually French Agnus Dei gold crown coins, first issued by Duke Jean de Berry; from 1380 one of the regents for nephew child-king Charles VI of France (1368-1422): 1.53.

LORETO: Italian town on Adriatic lodging the alleged home of the Virgin Mary miraculously flown there; then a great pilgrimage site: 1.27.

LORRAINE (OLD LOTHARINGIA FOR NAME, BUT SMALLER): from region assigned to Lothaire I, a grandson of Charlemagne and Emperor of the West (A.D. 794-855) by his father Louis I ("the Pious") of France, also emperor; in modern times ruled now by Germany, now by France; in sixteenth c. won by the Guise branch of the House of Lorraine; said by Pathelin, Panurge, and long tradition, to breed men with huge ballocks: 1.33.

LOT: Genesis 12–19; nephew of Abram-Abraham; warned by God to leave wicked Sodom and Gomorrah; did so safely but wife disobeyed, looked back, turned into a pillar of salt: 2.14.

LOUDUN (VIENNE): town and region SW of Chinon; famous for capons: 1.37.

LOUIS XI OF FRANCE (1423–1483, KING FROM 1461): rebellious youth; twice exiled for it; but as king, struggled long and hard to consolidate all France and all authority in the crown; weakened clergy and great nobles after grave threats to himself and crown; on the death of great rival Charles the Bold of Burgundy, seized that, also Artois, Boulogne, Franche-Comté, and Picardy; and later Anjou, Bar, Maine, and Provence: 3.5.

LOUIS XII OF FRANCE (1462–1515): king of France from 1498; discarded first wife to marry Anne of Brittany, widow of Charles VII of France, his predecessor; invaded Italy, took Milan; but beaten at Novara (1513); had to accept forced peace: 3.46.

LOUZEFOUGEROUSE: a fantasy name perhaps suggested by a real place-name: 2.12.

LOYRE: fictive baker of Lord Basché; helps in seriocomic drubbing of Shysteroos: 4.12.

LÜBECK: a large Baltic port in NE Germany: 1.33.

LUBIN, FRÈRE (FRATER LUBINUS, FRATRIS LUBINI): here usually rendered as Friar Booby, but once as "Friar Gulligut Smellsmock"; time-honored name for a stupid, gluttonous, lecherous monk (there were some): 1.P.

LUCCA: a city in Tuscany (central Italy): in R's day an independent republic: 1.33.

LUCIAN (LOUKIANOS, CA. A.D. 115–200): of Samosata on the Euphrates; rhetor, parodist, debunker; teller of tall tales (*True History, Icaromenippus*); best known for satirical *Dialogues of the Dead*; R translated some of his work, borrowed much with scant acknowledgment: 2.1. See also for two mentions of "the philosopher from Samosata": 3.24.

LUCIFER: Latin for Light-bearer; fallen archangel; Satan or the Devil; name also used for the Morning Star: 2.4.

LUCILIUS GAIUS (CA. 180–102 B.C.): creator of Roman satire; left 30 books of verse *Sermones* on familiar, often personal incidents; also fierce attacks, satiric on politicians, writers, general mores, etc.: 3.P.

LUGA: an unidentified place seemingly in Asia Minor: 1.33.

LULL (OR LULLY, LULLIUS), RAYMOND (OR RAMON, 1232–1316): a Catalan religious philosopher, opposed Averroes; tried to reconcile reason and faith, philosophy and religion; also to Christianize Moslems: 2.7.

LUNETTES DES PRINCES (*PRINCES' SPECTACLES*): any one book of edification for princes by way of allegory, a popular genre in R's day: 2.11.

LUSIGNAN (VIENNE): village and old château near Poitiers, home of seemingly human-sized ancestors of Pantagruel including furious Geoffrey Sabertooth: 3.41.

LUTETIA, LUTECE: old names for Paris; see Leucecia.

LUXEMBURG: small independent grand-duchy (then) and its capital city, among France, wedged in with the three: 1.33.

LYCIA, LYCIAN(S): an ancient mountainous coastal country in Asia Minor: 1.33.

LYDIA, LYDIAN(S): an ancient country in W Asia Minor; mighty under Gyges and later strong tyrants, but in 546 B.C. ultra-rich Croeses was crushed by Cyrus and his tough Persians; Lydia absorbed into Persian empire: 1.33.

LYON, LYONNAIS: on Saone and Rhône, large city, trade and cultural center, also printing, rivaling Paris; R's probable home for his last twenty years (1533–1553): 1.12.

LYRA OR LIRA, NICOLAS DE (FOURTEENTH C.): noted Italian Bible commentator: 2.4.

LYRIPIPION: Sorbonne doctoral hood: 1.18.

MACEDONIA (MACEDON), MACEDONIAN(S): ancient country N of Greece in SE part of Balkan Peninsula; now part Greece, part Bulgaria, part Yugoslavia; stood apart in Persian Wars; later with Alexander I (d. 450 B.C.); a Grecophone royal family entered Greek politics; built a strong army under Philip II (359–336 B.C.); extended power into, finally over, Greece; his son Alexander the Great (356–323 B.C.) conquered most of Mediterranean Europe, also Asia eastward to India; he loved the *Iliad*, hero Achilles; on his death his empire broke up into small pieces: 1.1.

MACRAEON(S), MACROBE(S): good, long-lived neighbors of heroes: 4.25.

MACROBIUS (ALSO KNOWN AS THEODOSIUS, FL. CA. A.D. 400): an able Roman observer and philosopher, whose *Saturnalia* shows Romans grouped at that mid-December festival from which our Christmas festivities are probably descended: 1.3.

MADERA (OR MADEIRA): an Atlantic Portuguese archipelago near Morocco; a hilly resort; grows rich, sweet wines, Malmsey, etc.: 2.24.

MADGE-OWL, MADGE-OWLET: female owl; as a game: 1.22.

MAGDALEN, SAINT MARY: once a sinner, then devoted follower of Jesus (all four gospels): 3.33.

MAGNIFICAT AT MATINS: a song of praise due later at the first canonical hour; proverbial for premature and thus inappropriate action: 1.11.

MAGUS, MAGI: Zoroastrian priests, considered magicians; also, for Christians, the three wise men who at Christ's birth followed the star from the East to over Bethlehem (Matthew 1.2–12): 2.18.

MAHOMET: Mohammed, Mahound, Mahometans, Mohammedans, etc. (ca. A.D. 570–632); the prophet and founder of Islam (Mohammedanism); since his time Christendom's great rival in the western, then Mediterranean, world; some Christians thought him a devil or a wencher: 1.33.

MAILLEZAIS (VENDÉE; THEN IN POITOU): the village where Bishop Geoffroy d'Estissac, R's first eminent patron-protector, welcomed R into his Benedictine monastery of Saint-Pierre de Maillezais in 1523 or 1524 and remained his host until R left for Paris medical studies, then later from his return until he left for further study and degrees at Montpellier: 2.5.

MAINZ: a West German city on the Rhine noted for good ham: 1.3.

MAISTRE MOUSCHE (MASTER SLICK): probably a priest of note: 2.16; for *mousche* as a game; see also "Baste the Bear."

MAJORCA: the largest Balearic Island in the Mediterranean E of Spain: 1.33.

MALADERIE, LA: A big leper hospital near Chinon, now Saint-Lazare hamlet: 1.43.

MALCON: obscene corruption of Marcoul; used in a counter by Echéphron: 1.33.

MALENCOUNTER, STRAIT OF: a fictive symbol of a plight of R's unknown to us: 3.P.

MALICIOUS SPIRIT: the Devil: 3.19.

MALICORNE: (1) Gargantua's fictive carver squire and messenger; brought Pantagruel letter and swift carrier pigeon for fast return message, then took back letter: 4.3–4; also (2) a real live Malicorne, mentioned on 6.21; as "Malicorne the Younger," is the same Jean de Chourses, seigneur de Malicorne, whom several decades later, as Governor of Poitou, Queen Mother Catherine de Medici instructed to watch over Michel de Montaigne and see to his safe return home from her unavailing Colloquies of Saint-Brice near Cognac in early 1587; see my *Montaigne: A Biography* (New York: Harcourt, Brace, and World, 1965), p. 267.

MALTA: an independent island state in Mediterranean S of Sicily, noted for cotton: 2.7.

MANES: spirits much like lamias, lemurs; see lemurs.

MANS, LE, MANCEAU(S) (SARTHE): a city and area 140 miles S of Paris; a center of farming and industry: 1.31.

MANUBIAE (LATIN): bolts of thunder or lightning or both: 3.12.

MARAIS, PHILIPPE DES: fictive viceroy of Papeligosse; helped his friend Grandgousier find a better tutor than before for his son Gargantua: 1.15.

MARANO(S), MARRANO(S): Moors or Jews "converted" usually by force or threat to Christianity: 4.40.

MARC: a weight of one-half pound: 1.8.

MARCUS TULLIUS (CICERO): see Cicero.

MARDIGRAS (SHROVETIDE): protector of Chitterlings against Fastilent: 4.29.

MARGARET OF NAVARRE (NÉE OF ANGOULÊME, 1492–1549): older sister of French King Francis I; learned, mystical Reformist; protected many writers; wrote poems, plays, especially *Heptaméron* (72 tales with discussions); dedicatee of R's Book 3: 3. "To the Spirit of the Queen of Navarre."

MARIGNANO: near Milan, N Italy; scene of Francis I's great 1515 victory over Swiss and allies: 2.1.

MARINUS, ANATOMIST: maybe Italian astronomer Marino: 1.23.

MARIUS, GAIUS (157–186 B.C.): led Roman plebeians in bloody civil wars ending 83 B.C against Sulla and aristocrats; ended as consul; cruel; died probably mad: 3.51.

MARO: see Virgil.

MAROT, CLÉMENT (1496–1544): light court poet but pro-Reform; translated Psalms; many troubles for his beliefs; friend of R, who borrowed from him. See Marotus du Lac, a spoof on him and on Lancelot of the Lake, Round Table hero: 2.23.

MARQUET: pugnacious Picrocholine *fouacier* who touched off the war unprovoked: 1.25.

MARRIAGE PACKET: the male member: 2.7.

MARS: Greek Ares; war god; lover of Venus; also the French name for March (month): 1.2.

MARSAULT, SAINT (SAINT MARTIAL): pronounced by terrified Limousin schoolboy: 2.6; see Martial, Saint.

MARSEILLE: France's main Mediterranean port and now second city: 3.31.

MARTIAL, SAINT (A.D. THIRD C.): apostle to the Limousin and first bishop of Limoges, where his relics are preserved: 2.6.

MARTIN, SAINT (A.D. CA. 316–397): born in Pannonia; split his coat with a poor man, the bishop of Tours; won western Gaul for Christianity; festival Nov. 11: 1.36.

MARVELOUS: (Latin *rete mirabilie*) or "wondrous network": a small dense network of blood vessels issuing from one large one and usually rejoining it further on: 3.4.

MASSAGETAE: an equestrian nomadic people from E of Caucasus and Caspian Sea; repulsed Cyrus's Persians (Herodotus 1.205–216); to the Greeks, cruel savages: 2.18.

MASSORETES: Hebrew Old Testament scholars: 1.2.

MASSUAU, CLAUDE: a friend of R and follower of Langey; present at his death; translated into French R's now lost Latin *Stratagemata of Guillaume de Langey*: 4.27.

MASTER SLICK: see Maistre Mousche.

MATABRUNE: a rearrangement of the romance *The Knight of the Swan*: 2.P.

MATAGOT(S OR Z): a trained trick monkey; a hypocrite, often a monk; last syllable of a handy homophone of Goth(s); the third group denied entrance to Thélème: 1.54.

MATAGRABOLIZE, MATAGRABOLISM: *mataios* "vain" plus *grabeler* "imagine vainly": 1.19.

MATEOTECHNY: *mataios* plus *techne* "art, craft"; vain craft; port or kingdom of Quintessence: 5.18.

MATHURINS, MATURINS, CHURCH OF THE: a Trinitarian order founded in 1198, and their church in Paris, site of Sorbonne faculty meetings: 1.20.

MAUGIS (D'AIGREMONT): hero of popular old tales of derring-do: 1.27.

MAULÉVRIER: Michel de Ballan, a neighbor of R's; apparently rich, stingy, lame: 1.39.

MEANDER (MAIANDROS, TURKISH MENDERES): Turkish Asia Minor; a river flowing so slowly in great S-curves, as to form English term for leisurely ambling: 3.20.

MECCA: capital of Hejax, Saudi Arabia; birthplace of Mohammed, holy city of Islam; goal of prayers and pilgrimages: 1.33.

MEDAMOTHI: one of R's many Greek terms for nowhere, like Utopia; first stop of Pantagruel's on the voyage to the Bottle; exchange of letters; sends presents home to Gargantua: 4.2.

MEDIA, MEDIC, MEDE(S): W Asia (modern Azerbaijan); in eighth-sixth c. B.C., a great empire until Cyrus and Persians annexed it to theirs: 1.1.

MEDITERRANEAN SEA: between Europe and Africa; the great cradle of European civilization: 1.33.

MÉDOC: large region, excellent wines, in SW France near Bordeaux: 1.33.

MEGAERA: one of the four Furies or Erinnyes (*Aeneid* 12.846 ff.): 4.47.

MELINDA: African town won by Portuguese with wine; its location in R seems imaginary or else near Zanzibar, off E Africa in Indian Ocean: 1.8.

MELUN (SEINE-ET-MARNE): a city ca. 25–30 miles SE of Paris; famous for its eels: 1.47; see eels of Melun.

MÉLUSINE: a fabled fairy's daughter who could change into a snake; reputed ancestress of the eminent, respected Poitevin family of the Lusignans: 4.37.

MEMPHIS, MEMPHITIC: capital of Egyptian Old Kingdom, near Cairo and Nile delta: 2.18.

MEN-AT-ARMS (HOMMES D'ARMES): horsemen: 1.48.

MEPHITIS, MEPHITIC: a Roman goddess personifying SO_2 (sulfur dioxide) fumes, stinking and poisonous: 2.33.

MERCURY: Greek Hermes; messenger of the gods; also god of the wheat trade and of thieves: 3.3.

MERDAILLE (CRAPHAM): another of Picrochole's captains: 1.33.

MERLIN: legendary magician and seer; teacher and adviser to King Arthur: 1.58.

MERLIN COCAI (TEOFILO FOLENGO): see Cocai, Merlin.

MESOPOTAMIA: Greek for "Mid-rivers"; ancient region (in modern Iraq) between and near the Tigris and Euphrates rivers in SW Asia; cradle of empires and cultures; Assyria, Babylonia, etc.: 1.33.

MESSALINA, VALERIA: grand-niece of Augustus, wife of Claudius; notorious for debauchery; Claudius either killed her or forced her suicide: 3.27.

METALEPSIS: transposition: 3.14.

METAMORPHOSES: work by Ovid; here sometimes abbreviated to *Met.*; the rich collection, in 15 books of Latin verse, of main myths, legends, and tales of ancient Greece and Rome; named for their core, the magical changes made in humans by gods, mainly into plants or the like; an enduring favorite in Europe ever since, and a rich source for R, although rarely cited as such (in one of the few instances, R names Ovid for a popular moralized version by Thomas of Wales, worsened in R's day by Pierre Lavin, who in this context is R's Frère Lubin): 1.P.

METRODORUS OF LAMPSACUS (D. 277 B.C.): an Epicurean who believed, says Plutarch, in an infinite number of worlds: 3.3.

MICHELOTS (OR MICQUELOTS): pilgrims to Mont-Saint-Michel (Manche), that gem of a church on a small rocky island on the English Channel: 1.38.

MIDAS: in Greek legend, king of Phrygia, granted one wish by grateful guest, chose to have all he touched turn to gold; poor diet; rued his wish; released from it; but for another like stupidity, his ears grew long into ass's ears: 3.P.

MILAN, MILANESE: big Lombard city in N Italy, then capital of a rich duchy ruled 1532–1535 by Duke Francesco Sforza: 4.P.

MILETUS, MILESIAN(S): a major Ionian port on W coast of Asia Minor: 4.BD.

MILO OF CROTON (SIXTH C. B.C.): legendary strong man, wrestler; once led city's army into battle; died caught in a tree-trunk he tried to split barehanded: 1.23.

MINERVA: like Greek Pallas Athene; Roman goddess of wisdom; also potent: 1.6.

MINIM(S): humble name of religious order founded 1435 by Saint Francis de Paul: 3.22.

MINORCA: a Balearic Island (q.v.) ENE of the largest, Majorca: 1.33.

MINOS: legendary Cretan king; in death made a judge of the dead in Hades: 1.2.

MIRANDOLA, PICO DELLA (COUNT GIOVANNI PICO DELLA MIRANDOLA, 1463–1494): a great leader in Neoplatonic philosophy; handsome; richly and broadly learned; adept in Hebrew, Greek, and other languages; leader of Lorenzo de Medici's Florentine Academy; tried above all to reconcile Platonism and Christianity: 2.18.

MIREBALAIS, MIREBEAU: Vienne, near Poitiers; locality famous for its windmills: 1.11.

MIREVAL, MIREVAULX (HÉRAULT): a region noted for fine wines such as muscatel: 2.5.

MISERERE: Latin "have mercy"; the first word giving its name to the Penitential Psalm (50); its last word is *vitulos* (sacrificial calves); Couscoil here claims that Dodin would be reduced to crying loud and long for mercy: 3.23.

MISTRAL: the bitter cold N Alpine wind blowing down the Rhône valley into S France: 4.18.

MITHRIDATES (VI, EUPATOR): from 115 B.C. sole king of Pontus; long resisted Rome; in 86 driven out of Europe by Sulla; in 63 chose death rather than captivity: 3.52.

MITYLENE (OR MYTILENE): modern Mitilini; chief port and city of Lesbos (q.v.): in 1502, while held by Turks, besieged by French; Panurge was captured by the Turks: 2.9.

MIXARCHAGÉVAS: Argive name for Castor: 4.22.

MOHAMMED: see Mahomet.

MOLECATCHER, MOLECATCHERY (TAULPETIER, TAULPETERIE): one of R's pejorative terms for two bêtes noires of his, monk and monastery: 3.48.

"MONK, TO HAVE OR GIVE THE": to have trouble, give trouble, and the like: 1.12.

MONKEY'S PATERNOSTER: *patenostre du cinge*; mumbo-jumbo, mumbled perfunctory prayer; epitome of lip-service, for R all too common among monks: 1.11. More generally, got off the subject or answered not to the point.

MONS JOVIS: Mount of Jupiter, palmistry; small rise in palm of hand at base of index: 3.25.

MONT CENIS: mountain mass in French alps above the high (6,831 feet) Mont Cenis Pass, at the border on the road between Lyon (France) and Turin (Italy): 4.9.

MONTAIGU, COLLÈGE DE: see Collège de Montaigu.

MONTLHÉRY: a village about 17 miles from Paris, to the northeast of it: 3.43.

MONTMARTRE (MARTYRS' MOUNT): hill on Right Bank of Paris; site of Sacré-Coeur (Sacred Heart); hot spots; mentioned by R only in a variant to 1.23.

MONTPELLIER (HÉRAULT): a large city in Languedoc near Mediterranean; site of France's top medical faculty then, when R took his degrees; did some teaching: 2.5.

MONTSOREAU (MAINE-ET-LOIRE): a village on the Loire outside Saumur: 1.8.

MOOR(S), MOORISH: nomadic N Africans; Moslems who in early A.D. 700s conquered Spain and southern France until Charles Martel drove them back at Tours in 732; left rich legacy of ideas and arts where they ruled, and their mark elsewhere; English Morris dance was once "Moorish dance"; R's "Morris dance of the Heretics" (2.7) describes the short-lived writhing of hanged men: 1.37.

MORAVIA: a region in Czechoslovakia E of Bohemia: 1.33.

MOREA: an ancient name for the Peloponnesus: 1.33.

MORGAN, MORGAN LE FAY: in old romances, a sister of Arthur with magical powers: 2.23.

MORPHEUS: Greek god of dreams; son of Somnus (Sleep): 3.13.

MORPIAILLE (GUZZLER): Viscount; either an ally or a captain of Picrochole's: 1.31.

MORRIS DANCERS: see Moor.

MOSES (MOÏSE, MOYSE): the great Hebrew prophet who led Israel out of captivity in Egypt (Exodus) and received the Law (Ten Commandments) from God on Mount Sinai; allegedly wrote the Pentateuch (Books 1–5 of the Bible, Genesis through Numbers) at God's dictation; this is the written Torah of the Jews, and with the Talmud, commentaries, their basic Holy Book; Moses was allowed to see but not enter the Promised Land: 1.50.

MOTHER OF GOD! (PAR LA MER DÉ): euphemism for Par la Mère de Dieu! but R does not forget that it includes the sound of the word *merde* "shit": 1.13.

MUSAFIS (OR MUSAPHIS): BD "In Turkish and Slavonic language, doctors and prophets": 2.14.

MUSCOVITE(S): from the Grand Duchy of Muscovy or Moscow; roughly the European part of the modern USSR: 4.P.

MUSES: in Greek myth, daughters of Mnemosyne (Memory) and goddesses of literature and the other arts; abode of Pieria, near Thessalian Mount Olympus, and on Boeotian Mount Helicon; at first nine in number, unspecialized; later each specializing in one art or another: 3.31.

MYRELINGUES, MYRELINGUOIS: means of myriad tongues or languages; all references to it are to a city, whose model might be Lyon: 3.36; related Millelingo, Myrelangault or Myrelingault, which means "giant" (2.1).

MYSIA, MYSIAN(S): a region near Troy in NW Asia Minor, now Turkey: 1.33.

MYTILENE: see Mitylene.

"NAIL ON THE THUMB, THAT'S HITTING THE": that's beside the point; "C'est bien rentré de picques noires" or "de treuffes noires"; the point is unclear to me: 1.45.

NANCY (MEURTHE-ET-MOSELLE): on Marne-Rhine canal; once capital of Lorraine, one of its three large cities and bishoprics: 3.8.

NANTES (LOIRE-ATLANTIQUE): a large Atlantic port city at confluence of Erdre with Loire near its mouth; site of Henry IV's 1598 Edict of Toleration allowing Protestant as well as Catholic worship in France; château of dukes of Brittany: 1.38.

NAPLES (NAPOLI): metropolis in Campania, Italy; on gulf of Naples; in R's day one of the "twin kingdoms" of Naples and Sicily; the French called syphilis "le mal de Naples" the Naples ailment: 6.12.

NARGUES ET ZARGUES (PISH AND TUSH): fictive islands passed by the fictive voyagers: 4.17.

NASIER, ALCOFRIBAS: see Alcofribas.

NASO (PUBLIUS OVIDIUS NASO, 43 B.C.–A.D. 18): the poet known as Ovid; thus R's "Naso and Ovid" (2.1) is a wee "inside joke" of his: see Ovid.

NAUSICLETE: Greek for "famous for ships"; ship's supplier for the Thélémites: 1.56.

NAVARRE, COLLÈGE DE: see Collège de Navarre.

NAVARRE, MARGUERITE DE: see Margaret of Navarre.

NAVELET, NAVELIER (TURNIPPER, TURNIP-GROWER): cooks named for a vegetable then much used: 4.40.

NEBUCHADNEZZAR (NABUCHODONOSOR): king of Babylon, ca. 605–562 B.C.; after soon defeating the Egyptians, a setback led to Jewish revolt under Jehoiakim; crushed this 597; after taking Jerusalem, deported many Jewish nobles, thus starting their "Babylonian captivity" (586–538 B.C.); later (Daniel 4.33) shows him hubristic, mad, eating grass; Jeremiah prophesizes his fall (25.12 ff.); name also written Nebuchadrezzar; cf., 2 Kings, 24–25: 3.3.

NEBUZARADAN (NABUZARADAN): twice listed in 2 Kings 25, as captain of the king's bodyguards; here, as in an allegory in 1180, as his master chef (Maistre queux) of his kitchens: 4.39.

NECEPSOS: a legendary king of Egypt; reputed magician and disciple of both Aesculapius and Anubis: 1.8.

NEOPTOLEMUS: see Pyrrhus.

NEPOS, CORNELIUS (CA. 100–25 B.C.): Roman born in Gaul, friend of Catullus (q.v.) in Rome; wrote on geography, world, and Roman history; biography (Cato, Cicero et al.); 24 biographical sketches remain: 4.1.

NEPTUNE: like Greek Poseidon; god of the sea, also of horses; with Apollo built walls of Troy for Laomedon; with nymph Tyro, fathered Peleus (q.v.) and Neleus (q.v.): 1.3.

NERO (LUCIUS DOMITIUS AHENOBARBUS): later Nero, emperor of Rome A.D. 54–68; gifted but narcissistic and cruel, fond of display, grew unpopular; said to have "fiddled while Rome burned," and, by some, to have caused the fire himself: 2.30.

NESTOR: wise but verbose old counselor to Agamemnon and king of Pylos in *Iliad* (1.247 ff.) and *Odyssey* (3.32 ff.), where he entertains Telemachus in his quest to find his father Odysseus: 2.30.

NETWORK: see marvelous network.

NEW TESTAMENT: referred to as "Holy Scriptures": 2.8.

NICANDER (NIKANDROS, SECOND C. B.C.) OF COLOPHON: a Greek didactic poet; left works on poisonous bites and antidotes for them: 1.23.

NICHOLAS, SAINT: A.D. fourth-c. bishop of Mysia (country in S coastal Asia Minor); patron saint of Russia, also of little children (Saint Nick, Santa Claus): 4.21; cf., "Golly Nick": 4.6.

NICHOLAS III, POPE (1220–1280), POPE FROM 1277: R's tag for him here is a pun on Pape Tiers (third pope) and *papetier* "papermaker": 2.30.

NIGHTMARES (CAUQUEMARRES): same sense as modern French "cauchemars": 6.8.

NILE: world's longest river, 4,160 miles; flowing from Burundi (Central Africa) N through Sudan and Egypt through the delta around Alexandria into the Mediterranean Sea: 1.45.

NÎMES (GARD): old city near Mediterranean with fine Roman ruins: 2.5.

NIMROD: Genesis 10.8; Ham's grandson, son of Cush, "a mighty hunter before God": 2.1.

NINE JOYS OF MARRIAGE (*LES NEUF JOIES DE MARIAGE*): a sardonic late fifteenth-c. tract on the tribulations (and supposed delights) of marriage for the husband: 4.23.

NINIAN (OR RINGAN, SAINCT TREIGNAN): patron saint of Scotland; started first church there: 1.33.

NIORT (DEUX-SÈVRES): a large town 40–50 miles from both Poitiers and La Rochelle; scene of three popular fairs each year: 3.13.

NIPHLESETH: BD, Hebrew for "male member"; name and title of the Queen of the Chitterlings: 4.42.

NOAH: the one good man God saved from the Flood; also the first vintner: 1.1.

NOEL: Latin *natalis* "natal, birthday"; Christmas; also Christmas carol: 3.14.

"NOMINATION, INSINUATE ONE'S": 1.5; see "insinuate one's nomination."

NORMANDY, NORMAN(S): a region (once a province) in NW France on English Channel E of Brittany, now forming five départements; and its inhabitants (Normans), who as Norsemen were dreaded pirates in the early Middle Ages: 1.33.

NORWAY, NORWEGIANS: the large Scandinavian country W of Sweden: 1.33.

NOTRE-DAME (OR NOSTRE-DAME) DE PARIS: the great metropolitan Paris church: 1.17.

NOUS: Greek "mind, reason, purposive intelligence": 3.13.

NOYER, BALTHAZAR: a friend of R who played at Montpellier in the *Farce of the Mute Wife*: 3.34.

NUMA POMPILIUS: legendary successor to Romulus and second king of Rome, whose reign later came to be regarded as a wondrous Golden Age: 2.30.

NUMIDIA, NUMIDIAN(S): ancient N African country and people; part of modern Algeria, chief city Hippo, near modern Bône: 1.15.

OBOL: a tiny old Greek weight and coin, later widely used elsewhere: 4.P.

OBSERVANTINE(S): the strict Franciscan order to which R belonged: 3.23.

OCEAN SEA: see the Atlantic Ocean.

OCKHAM (OR OCCAM, OLCAM), WILLIAM OF (CA. 1285–1349): eminent English Franciscan, nominalist Scholastic philosopher; called "the Invincible Doctor": 1.8.

OCTAVIAN (GAIUS OCTAVIUS, 63 B.C.–A.D. 14): he made himself first emperor of Rome (27 B.C.) with the new name Augustus: 1.3.

ODET, CARDINAL DE CHASTILLON: see Chastillon, Cardinal Odet de.

" 'ODS-BELLY (OR OX-BELLY) OF WOOD" (VENTRE BEUF . . . DE BOYS): a euphemistic oath instead of "God's belly": 3.36.

" 'ODSBODY" OR " 'OD'S-BODY" (CORDIEU OR CORBLEU): euphemistic oath for "God's body": 1.12.

ODYSSEUS: Greek form, Latinized as Ulysses; hero of the *Odyssey* (q.v.); see Ulysses.

ODYSSEY: see Homer.

OEDIPUS, OEDIPODIC, OIDIPOUS: legendary tyrant of Thebes, hero-victim of Sophocles (two plays of a probable trilogy: *Oedipus the King, Oedipus at Colonus*), in this century spotlighted again by Freud; I have no idea why in BD he is identified as "the diviner": 4.43.

OGIER THE DANE: a peer of France and hero of many medieval verse tales: 2.1.

OLIVER: peer of France, wise friend of Roland in the *Song of Roland*: 2.1.

OLIVET OR MOUNT OF OLIVES (GETHSEMANE): scene of Christ's prayer, agony, and arrest (Mark 4.): 1.39.

OLONNE (SABLES-D'OLONNE, VENDÉE): a French Atlantic beach and fishing port; off of it a stretch of sea very dangerous for sailors: 1.16.

ORION: in Greek myth, Boeotian killer of wild beasts; also pursued Pleiades (daughters of Atlas); they and he metamorphosed into constellations (he with belt and sword): 3.17.

ORKNEY ISLANDS (ORCHADES): far N part of Scotland N of the mainland: 1.33.

ORLÉANS (LOIRET): city on Loire, ca. 70 miles S of Paris; once provincial capital; university; in R's day studded with tennis (q.v.) courts: 1.15.

ORPHEUS: a legendary pre-Homeric Thracian poet, son of a Muse, follower of Dionysus; his lyre-playing enchanted even animals; when his wife Eurydice died, he almost brought her back to earth from Hades but forgot pact, looked back in love, lost her; later died torn to pieces by Thracian maenads: 1.8.

ORUS APOLLO: Horapollo; credited with Hieroglyphica, popular in west since fifteenth c.: 1.9.

OSIRIS: a widely-worshiped Egyptian god of male reproductive power incarnated in the bull Apis; myth says he educated and civilized Egypt but was murdered and chopped to pieces by his brother Set; his wife-sister Isis collected and buried his remains and avenged him on Set; since then he has been god of the dead and (thanks to the sun, Horus) of renewed life. The Greeks identified him with Dionysus (q.v.): 3.P.

OSSA, MOUNT: like Mount Pelion, a high mountain in Thessaly; seldom mentioned anywhere (never in R) in any other context than this one: 3.12.

OSTROGOTH(S): the eastern Goths (as against the western Visigoths); Germanic Goths long living in the Ukraine, under Attila the Hun until his death in 453; then more in Hungary; allies of Eastern (Byzantine) Roman Empire (493) and held it until Justinian's general Belisarius (from 535 on) drove them out; they lost national identity; Roman uneasy detestation made them favorite bêtes noires of French humanists such as R as wantonly crude barbarians: 1.20.

OTHOMAN VADARE: possibly represents François Hotman (1534–1590), a doctor in Basel and historian; author of *Franco-Gallia*, showing Germanic origins of Franks: 3.40.

OVID (PUBLIUS OVIDIUS NASO, 43 B.C.–A.D. 18): charming Roman poet of lament for exile (*Tristia*), love (*Amores, Ars Amatoria, Heroides*), and legends (*Metamorphoses*); often used by R but rarely cited (the mention on 1.P is not to him but to a moralised dull version then strangely popular); and R's "Naso and Ovid" (2.1) is an "in joke": 3.31.

"OX-BELLY OF WOOD": see 'Od's belly.

OXYLUS: son of Orius; by his sister Hamadryas had eight tree-nymph daughters, the Hamadryads: 3.51.

PAINTED CELLAR (CAVE PEINTE OR PAINCTE): a noted Chinon tavern that R liked: 4.20.

PALAZZO SAN GEORGIO: in Rome, a palace of the chancellery: 6.12.

PALESTINE: Biblical Holy Land; in SW Asia Minor between Dead Sea and Mediterranean: 1.33.

PALLAS ATHENE: see Athena.

PALM: a unit of measure; variable length of palm of hand; here about 3 inches: 5.36.

PALTRY (TREPELU): one of Picrochole's commanders: 1.26.

PAMPHYLIA: ancient coastal region in SW Asia Minor between Lycia and Cilicia: 1.33.

PAN: Greek "all"; the great Greek nature god, whose death Pantagruel sees as symbolizing or even here meaning the death of Christ: 3.14.

PANDECTS: Justinian's digest of his huge *Corpus Juris,* body of Roman civil law, ably annotated by Guillaume Budé (1508, q.v.) in his first major work: 2.5.

PANDORA: in Greek myth, given to man by Prometheus's brother Epimetheua (Afterthought); she bore a box or bottle (stories differ) containing all human ills, which came out when it was opened; but left in it at the bottom was Hope: 3.P.

PANIGON, KING SAINT: lit. "little bread" meaning "nice little guy"; ruled Cheli (Peace): 4.10.

PANORMITANUS (SICILIAN NICHOLAS TEDESCO, B. 1368): great authority on canon law; so named for his service as bishop of Palermo (once Panormus): 2.10.

PANTAGRUEL, PANTAGRUELINE: giant fictive son of Gargantua and hero of Books 2–5 of R's tale; gives name to "prognostication" and to the other derivatives listed next here: Books 2–5.

PANTAGRUELION: a wondrous plant (with properties of flax, hemp, and asbestos) named for Pantagruel and used in his fleet; treated at some length in Book 3, chapters 42–52.

PANTAGRUELISM, PANTAGRUELISTS, PANTAGRUELIZE: a philosophy that seems to be R's own; grows from a simple love of wine and good tall tales into a merry Stoical unconcern about matters beyond our control: 1.1.

PANURGE: Greek *pan-ourgos* "who will do all things"; meaning he will stop at nothing; hence wicked, devilish; Pantagruel's friend for life once met, also entertainer and problem child: 2.9.

PANZOUST: a village between Chinon and Isle-Bouchard, the unlikely abode of a sibyl: 1.47.

PAPELIGOSSE: a fantasy name; but cf., S French Pamperigouste "fantasy-land" or Papagoce, a land of chimeras in some mystery plays; or even both: 1.14.

PAPIMANIA, PAPIMANIAC(S): mad pope-worshipers and their island domain: 3.P.

PAPINIAN (AEMILIANUS PAPINIANUS, D. A.D. 212): learned, able, upright Roman jurist; killed by Caracalla for refusing his defense in Senate for the murder of his brother: 2.8.

PARASANG: see Herodotus, etc.; ancient Persian distance measure, normally ca. 6,000 years, i.e., 3–4 miles: 4.25.

PARIS: (1) or Alexandros (*Iliad* 3.16 ff.), son of Priam; in myth, as a youth, decided beauty contest between goddesses Hera, Pallas, and Aphrodite, the winner, who promised him earth's loveliest woman (Helen of Troy, wife of Spartan King Menelaus); so he seduced or abducted her; cause or pretext of Trojan War. A bowman, his arrow was to give Achilles his fatal wound; one from Philoctetes was to give him his own death: 2.21.

PARIS: (2) Parisian(s); French capital and chief city (old Lutetia Parisiorum), where R studied medicine some time in 1527–1530; also, with Sorbonne and Parlement (q.v.), center of religious obscurantist conservatism and of persecution of Reform; here, place of Gargantua's good education; Pantagruel's headquarters when war broke out: 1.16.

PARISATIS: Achaemenid mother of Cyrus the Great (q.v.) of Persia, twice mentioned for her insistence that he be addressed always smoothly and respectfully: 4.32.

PARLEMENT(S): not a legislative (Parliament) but a judiciary body; the highest under the Old Regime; king's right arm for judicial means (peaceful) in unending power struggle against the high nobility. The term is used both of the entire corpus (7–8, variable) area courts and of each one, then Paris (oldest, strongest), Toulouse, Aix, Bordeaux, Grenoble, Rouen, etc.; the venality of office made these sources of royal revenue as well as strength: 3.36.

PARMA: N Italy, provincial capital; pro-French but disputed by Emperor Charles V until 1551 settlement with Henry II of France: 4.P.

PARPAILLONS: fantasy name suggesting papillons (butterflies); homeland of Gargamelle, wife of Grandgousier and mother of Gargantua: 1.3.

PARTHENAY AND NEARBY PARTHENAY-LE-VIEUX (DEUX-SÈVRES): on Thouet river; big cattle fairs; walls demolished 1487 by Charles VIII; all well settled since: 3.41.

PARTHIA, PARTHIAN(S): ancient land and people in SW Asia, now NW Iran; expert horsemen and bowmen (Herodotus 3, 7), even in firing backward in flight: 1.23.

PARVA LOGICALIA: by Alexandre de Villedieu, a scholastic text derided by humanists: 1.20.

PASIPHAE: in Crete, legendary queen of Minos; bore him Phaedra; Aphrodite made her lust for a bull, and she bore the Minotaur (half bull, half man): 3.34.

PASQUIN (PASQUILIUS): a statue in Rome used for posting satiric verses: 2.7.

PASSAVANT: probably a fourteenth-c. Italian monk; wrote dully on penitence: 1.14.

PATAC: a Picard coin of very small value: 3.26.

PATERNITY (PANURGE'S TERM): either himself or his sexual urge: 1.5.

PATERNOSTER: either the Lord's Prayer or a rosary to use in saying prayers: 2.21; see also monkey's paternoster.

PATHELIN, PATELIN: late fifteenth-c. farce and hero, *La Farce de Maistre Pierre Pathelin*; a great favorite of R's, often quoted, very often mentioned: 1.20.

PATRAS (PATRAI): capital and big port of Achaea in Peloponnesus: 3.24.

PATRICK, SAINT: Apostle to Ireland; founded its first church; converted the country (ca. A.D. 385–461); brought there at sixteen as captive slave; later a voice called him to Gaul; studied, converted, consecrated as missionary; slowly but surely won the entire island to Christ: 1.2; see also Saint Patrick's Hole.

PATROCLUS: in Greek legend (*Iliad*); Greek warrior friend of Achilles; his killing brings on Achilles's return to war, thus fall of Troy: 3.10.

PAUL, SAINT (D. CA. A.D. 67): originally Saul; "Apostle to the Gentiles"; never knew living Christ; convert; chief missionary and founder of Christian theology; his Epistles fill most of New Testament: 4.46.

PAULUS, AEMILIUS (OR EMILIUS): also called Aemilius Paulus (or Paullus); d. ca. 160 B.C.; consul for second time when Macedonia War going badly; restored order, discipline; in one campaign won the war at Pydna; combined Greek mind with Roman valor; formed first private library in Rome; father of Scipio Aemilianus; Plutarch left a *Life* of him: 1.15.

PAUSANIAS (A.D. SECOND C.): a Lydian geographer whose *Description of Hellas* was an informative tourist guidebook and is still a useful resource: 2.8.

PAVIA: city in Lombardy (N Italy) near scene of disastrous French defeat by Imperials (Feb. 24, 1525); led to Francis I's long imprisonment by Charles V: 1.39.

PECK-POINT (LA VERGETTE): child's game pecking rods or wands (Cotgrave) at a heap of points; not one of child Gargantua's myriad games: 2.18.

PÉDAUQUE, REINE ("GOOSEFOOT QUEEN"): legendary; name of a bridge still in Toulouse; and of Anatole France's fictive roast-shop in a novel of 1893: 4.41.

PEDRO OF CASTILE (PEDRO THE CRUEL, FOURTEENTH C.): fought for dominance over nobles; got some: 2.15.

PEGASUS: in Greek myth, winged horse sprung from Medusa's blood when Perseus killed her; helped Bellerophon kill Chimaera; tried in vain to fly to heaven; with a stamp of one hoof opened Hyppocrene spring on Mount Helicon sacred to Muses, Boeotia: 2.24.

PELEUS: in Greek legend (*Iliad*), father of Thetis and Achilles: 4.2.

PELION: in Greek myth, high mountain in Thessaly piled upon Mount Ossa by rebelling Titans, then both on top of Mount Olympus; since, proverbial for "piling on": 3.12.

PELOPONNESUS, PELOPONNESIAN(S): here once called the Morea (1.33); the large half of Greece S of Isthmus of Corinth and joined by it to the N part; chief cities Argos, Corinth; in fifth c. B.C. dominated by Sparta; not mentioned by name by R.

PENELOPE: Odysseus's patient, resourceful wife in *Odyssey*; model of the "woman back home," as such often contrasted with Clytemnestra: 3.25.

PENIA: in Greek myth, goddess personifying want, poverty: 4.57.

PENTECOST (SHROVETIDE): see Shrovetide.

PENTHESILEA: Amazon queen; fought for Troy; killed by Achilles; not in Homer; idea of her selling cress may come from the epic by Quintus of Smyran (A.D. fourth c.) *Meth' Homeron*, covering the interval between the events of *Iliad* and *Odyssey*: 1.2.

PERCEFOREST: a name given King Bethis of Great Britain; a hero of medieval romance: 2.30.

PERCHE: a region (former county) in Parisian basin; apple country; pickers were often ragged: 2.9.

PERICLES (CA. 500–429 B.C.): a great leader of democratic Athens in building empire and in Peloponnesian War (431–404 B.C.); statesman, leader, orator, ideal leader for Thucydides: 1.10.

PÉRIGORD: onetime country in SW France; now most of Dordogne; capital Périgueux: 1.33.

PERIPATETIC(S): philosophy school in Athens founded by Aristotle; named because he walked around as he taught; he headed it while he lived (others later): 2.18.

PERLAS, ISLANDS OF: SOURCES OF PEARLS IN S ANTILLES: 1.56.

PERRIN DENDIN: about like "Pete Ninny"; "settler of lawsuits"; expert on their ripening; friend of Judge Bridoye: 3.41.

PERSEPHONE: Roman form of Proserpina; daughter of Zeus and Demeter; goddess of Hades; Hades abducted and married her; spends half each year since above ground, half below; here hailed as if a devil: 4.47.

PERSEUS: in Greek myth, son of Zeus and Danaë; cast away as a child with his mother; later, with help of gods, killed Medusa, rescued Andromeda; his son reputed to be the founder of the Persian empire: 2.24.

PETRUS DE PETRONIBUS: Peter of the Lumpkins; a medieval commentator, unknown to us or imaginary: 2.10.

PHANTASUS: god of dreams, son of Somnus (Sleep); name suggests phantasm, fantasy: 3.13.

PHARAMOND: legendary Frankish king who some thought was of Trojan descent: 2.23.

PHARAOH: title of ruler of ancient Egypt; here, the one whose eunuch Potiphar bought young Joseph as a slave (Genesis 39): 4.39.

PHARSALIA (IN THESSALY): scene of Caesar's decisive victory (48 B.C.) over Pompey: 3.25.

PHARYNX: fictive city (paired with Larynx) in Pantagruel's throat: 2.32.

PHEBOL: a little-known island in Persian Gulf of the Arabian Sea: 3.51.

PHERECYDES (OF LEROS, FIFTH C. B.C.): chronicler; lived in Athens; left a genealogy of the gods: 5.20.

PHILAUTIA: Greek and BD "self-love"; a neologism in R, current since; once translated here as "egos" (in plural): 3.29.

PHILEBUS: a dialogue by Plato on relation of pleasure and of wisdom to the good: 1.1.

PHILEMON: several; probably the poet of the New Comedy (361–262 B.C.); after Aulus Gellius, R often cites him as one who died of too much laughter: 1.10.

PHILIP OF MACEDON (CA. 382–336 B.C.): Philip II; younger son of Amyntas; schooled in that of Epaminondas of Thebes; reorganized and enlarged army; gradually gained power in all Greece, at last over it; big victories won him peace at home, gold mines in east, allowing him to pay and bribe as needed; conquered Amphipolis (Thrace), later both Athens and Thecea (338); at war with Persia, planned to invade Asia Minor; but a jilted wife got him murdered, perhaps with his son Alexander's knowledge: 1.14.

PHILIPPIANS: Paul's Epistle to the Church in Philippi, Macedonia: 6.11.

PHILIPPIDES AND PHILISTION: a comic poet and a poet-mime, both listed by Ravisius Textor in his *Officina* (ca. 1503), who has many sources, as dying strange deaths: 1.10.

PHILIPPUS: originally a gold stater (a coin) with a portrait of Philip of Macedon (q.v.); by R's time a term used of almost any gold coin: 1.32.

PHILIPPUS DECIUS, PHILIPPUS (D. 1535): see Decius, Philippus.

PHILISTINE(S): Judges, Samuel, etc.; a people of S Palestine who first oppressed the Israelites, then (after David beat Goliath) were dominated by them: 1.37.

PHILOCTETES: in Greek legend and epic, given bow and arrows by his dying friend Hercules; both these needed for taking Troy; suffered a stinking snakebite, so Greeks abandoned him on deserted island Lemnos; later coaxed him back; Machaon healed him; he rejoined Greeks, used bow to shoot Alexandros (Paris), enabling Greeks to conquer Troy; subject of Sophocles' tragedy *Philoctetes* (409 B.C.): 4.37.

PHILOGROBILIZED: another neologism of R; baffled, bewildered; "in a fog": 2.10.

PHILOMELA: in Greek myth, daughter of king of Athens; raped by brother-in-law King Tereus of Thrace, who then, to silence her, cut out her tongue; she wove story into a fabric, sent this to her sister (and his wife) Procne; she then killed Itys, her son by Tereus, cut him up, served pieces to Tereus to eat; he was then changed into a hoopoe, the sisters into a swallow and a nightingale (Ovid, *Met.* 6.430–672): 4.2.

PHILOPHANES, PHILOTHAEMON: Greek and BD "desirous to see and to be seen": 4.2.

PHILOTOMIE: fond of carving and serving; steward and a companion to Gargantua: 1.18.

PHILOXENUS AND GNATHO: two repulsive "basin-spitters" from Plutarch's *Moralia*: 4.OP; see "spit in the basin."

PHOBETOR: a son of Morpheus and like him a god of dreams: 3.13.

PHOCIS: a region of central Greece N of Bay of Corinth, includes Delphi and Mount Parnassus: 4.65.

PHOENICIA, PHOENICIAN(S): great ancient Near Eastern power, mainly in trade, later, by its one-time colony Carthage in Tunisia, Rome's greatest and most threatening rival ever: 2.18.

PHOENIX: in Greek myth, a wondrous bird that lived 500 years, then burned itself on a pyre and rose from its own ashes to live another 500 years; only one said to live at one time; now a proverbial figure in language and thought: 4.OC.

PHORNUTUS OR CORNUTUS (L. ANNAEUS, A.D. FIRST C.): wrote a *De natura deorum* to follow an edition of Aesop's *Fables*: 1.P.

PHRONTISTE: Greek for "deep thinker," used of Socrates; the name R gives one of Gargantua's captains: 1.48.

PHRYGIA, PHRYGIAN(S): the ancient region around Troy in NW Asia Minor: 1.33.

PHYSETER: Greek *phuseteros* "blower," hence also sperm whale; these were often seen by some French Atlantic fishermen; here (after) Lucian inflated into a real monster: 4.33.

PICARDY, PICARD(S): former province in N Parisian basin in NE France: 1.24.

PICATRIS, PICATRIX: thirteenth-c. author of a compendium of ancient magicians: 3.23.

PICROCHOLE, PICROCHOLINE: from Greek "bitter bile"; a former friend of Grandgousier, but now (says Gallet) abandoned by God to his own free choice, hence arrogant, insanely aggressive; comically punished when beaten: 1.26.

PIEDMONT: Italian *piemonte* "foot of the mountains"; region in NW Italy bordering both France and Switzerland; capital Turin (Torino); in R's time (about 1539–1543), governed superbly and generously by R's great hero, chief, and patient, Guillaume du Bellay, seigneur de Langey: 3.52; see Langey.

PIETRO (OR PEDRO OR PETER) OF CASTILE, DON (1333–1389, KING FROM 1349): escaped from prison in 1356; bloody wars with dragon earned him his cognomen, with many vicious murders; was finally murdered himself: 2.15.

PILLARS OF ATLAS: rebel Titan Atlas, doomed to hold up heaven forever, was placed in or beyond the Atlantic at the far west end of the earth: 4.17.

PILLOT: one of several nicknames for Pierre (Pete): 1.28.

PINDAR, PINDARIZE (CA. 520–440 B.C.): the great Theban poet of the *Odes*; inimitable, as Ronsard found later to his dismay; "Pindarizing" amounts to pretentious Latinizing or other such talk: 2.6.

PINEAU (OR PINOT): a Burgundy grape and wine, normally red; the R's grew a white: 1.5.

Piombino (Italy): a W Tuscan town opposite the island of Elba: 4.25.

PIONEERS, PIONNIER(S): footsoldiers, who are expert sappers and demolition engineers, hence sent ahead of the others to wreck or weaken the enemy's fortifications: 1.47.

PIOT: cf., *pier* "to nip or swig"; a wee drop ; a friendly term for a drink, esp. of wine: 1.5.

PIPE: unit of measure of volume; for dry matter, one-half bushel; for liquid (as here), variable; a hogshead, cask, butt, or large barrel (225 liters): 1.7.

PITHO (OR PEITHO OR PYTHO): Greek goddess of persuasion, smooth talk: 3.20.

PLATO, PLATONIST(S) (CA. 427–348 B.C.): great Greek thinker, founder of western philosophy; pupil of Socrates (hero of his dialogues); teacher of Aristotle (q.v.); wrote little, taught by dialogue; like Socrates; left a few epistles, many dialogues, mainly moral and ontological; nature and interrelationships of goodness, truth, justice, pleasure, and happiness; reality only in "ideas" (*ideai*); forms or archetypes, universal and unchanging, on which our "realities" merely imitate or represent (the cave, in *The Republic*); goodness indispensable for happiness; ideal ruler a philosopher-king; centrality of (Socratic) quest for self-knowledge. Plato overshadowed by Aristotle in Middle Ages, finds great popularity and influence in R's day: 1.P.

PLAUTUS, TITUS MACCUS OR MACCIUS (CA. 254–184 B.C.): the earlier of the two great Roman comic playwrights (see also Terence); 21 of his plays survive; R cites his *Pot* (*Aularia*); others include his *Trinummus* (*Three Coins*): 1.3.

PLEIADES: in Greek myth, daughters of Atlas, turned into a group of stars; the conspicuous cluster in Taurus; six clearly visible; also (not here) used of two groups of poets; the stars: 2.1.

PLESSIS-LEZ-TOURS: the village adjoining Tours where Saint Francis de Paul ("Francis the Younger") died in 1507: 3.24.

PLINY (THE ELDER, GAIUS PLINIUS SECUNDUS, A.D.23/24–79): R never mentions his nephew Pliny (the Younger); author of 37 books of *Natural History*, a credulous but entertaining compilation of tall tales and wonders dear to R: 1.3.

PLOTINUS (B. CA. A.D. 205, IN EGYPT): eminent Neoplatonic philosopher and mystic; author, in Greek, of six books of *Ennead*: 2.18.

PLUTARCH (PLOUTARCHOS, A.D. 46–CA. 120): of Chaeronea in Boeotia; a persuasive biographer, observer, and moral and social commentator; best known today for his *Parallel Lives* (23 pairs, 4 singles) of great Greeks and Romans and the many treatises or pre-essays (mostly posthumous) usually called his *Moralia* or *Moral Essays*; R owned three copies of the *Moralia*; both these big works ably translated into French by Amyot, later into English by North (the *Lives* 1579); he was soon adopted as their own by both literatures, and gratefully used by Montaigne, Shakespeare, and countless other topnotch authors ever since: 1.39.

POITIERS, POITOU, POITEVIN(S): capital of former province in central France; city known for the weight of its bells. The "Red Poitevins" (Poitevins rouges) are the ancient red-painted Picts: 1.31.

POLAND: the large, central European country; in R's day a strong monarchy: 1.33.

POLITIAN (ANGELO POLIZIANO, 1454–1494): Italian humanist poet, whose work on Homer had drawn criticism from Budé: 1.P.

POLLUX: one of the Dioscuri, with Castor; also called Polydeuces: 1.6.

POLLUX, JULIUS (FL. A.D. 170): Egyptian-born Greek grammarian; wrote on hunting: 1.23.

POLYBIUS (POLUBIOS, CA. 202–120 B.C.): an able Arcadian historian who readily accepted Roman domination; so was deported to Rome; made his career there; friend of Scipio Africanus Minor, ca. 185–129 B.C.: 1.23.

POLYPHEMUS: in Greek myth and *Odyssey* 9.187–565; a son of Poseidon and chief of monstrous one-eyed man-eater met by homeward-bound Odysseus and his men; he ate several and confined the rest, but was tricked and blinded by Odysseus; Virgil (*Aeneid* 7.556–590) has him and other Cyclops working for Vulcan (Hephaestus): 2.1.

POLYPHILUS, POLYPHILI: hero of fictive *Hypnerotomachia Polyphili* by Francesco Colonna (q.v.), a source for R: 1.9.

POLYXENA: in Greek legend and drama, sacrificed to the shade of Achilles by his son Neoptolemus (Purrhos); see Euripides *Trojan Women* (415 B.C.): 3.48.

Pomona: Roman goddess of fruits and gardens: 3.4.

POMPEY ("THE GREAT," GHAEUS POMPEIUS, 108–46 B.C.): a powerful Roman military leader; for Sulla against Marius; once consul jointly with Crossus (70 B.C.); then after many vicissitudes, fought Caesar in Civil War (49–48 B.C.); crushed by Caesar at Pharsalia in Thessaly (48 B.C.); murdered soon after in Egypt; Plutarch left a *Life* of Pompey: 1.39.

POMPEY, SEXTUS POMPEIUS: son of Pompey the Great; continued father's fight against Caesar but lost and was killed (35 B.C.): 3.25.

PONEROPOLIS: Greek and BD "City of the Wicked"; founded (say Plutarch and Erasmus) by Philip of Macedon to hold criminals; surprisingly, it formed a sound and stable polity: 4.66.

PONOCRATES: Greek "taskmaster, work director"; originally tutor to Eudémon for Philippe des Marais; then able tutor to Gargantua; tutor-designate to Picrochole's son on Gargantua's direction; meanwhile one of Gargantua's domestic companions; and then (from 3.14) one of Pantagruel's domestic companions both before and on their voyage to the Bottle: 1.16.

PONS ASINORUM (ASS'S BRIDGE): a stumbling-block in logic; or a critical test of acumen like proving equality of base angles of an isosceles triangle: 2.28.

PONT AUX MEUSNIERS (MILLER'S BRIDGE): one of the three Paris Seine bridges in R's day, just downstream from the Pont aux Changes (Exchange Bridge): 2.11.

PONT DU GARD: in Provence, a fine old Roman aqueduct (almost 200 feet high) and bridge across the Gard near both Arles and Nîmes: 2.5.

PONTANUS (GIOVANNI PONTANO, 1426–1503): Italian poet, historian, statesman: 1.19.

PONTOISE (VAL-D'OISE): a town (then village) ca. 20 miles NW of Paris on the Oise; Villon's quip in his supposed epitaph may date back to before his time: 4.67.

PONTUS: ancient country in NE Asia Minor (now Turkey) on Black Sea coast: 3.50.

POPE, MISTER DE: an ironic sneer by an adviser to Picrochole: 1.33.

POPEFIG(S), POPEFIGLAND: land where some people made the "sign of the fig" (one thumb thrust out between two fingers of a closed fist), a widely-used obscene gesture of insolent defiance at or to the pope: 4.46.

POPILIA: character from Macrobius *Saturnalia* (q.v.); practices and preaches copulation during pregnancy: 1.3.

PORPHYRY: a fictive giant, Porfirio, ancestor of Gargantua and Pantagruel: 2.1.

PORPHYRY, PORPHURA: Tyrian purple; a hard purple or dark red stone: 5.37.

PORPHYRY (PORPHURIOS, CA. A.D. 233–301): a Tyrian pupil of Plotinus and a leading Neoplatonist; wrote a history of philosophy, a life of Pythagoras, and an introduction to Aristotle's *Organon*: 3.18.

PORT-HUAULT: a river port and forest near Chinon to the NE on way to Tours: 1.49.

PORTO SANTO OR SANCTO: in Atlantic Madera archipelago N of Canaries: 2.24.

PORTUGAL, PORTUGUESE: Iberian country W of Spain on the Atlantic side of the peninsula; expert mariners; active early in New World discovery and conquest: 1.33.

POSEIDON: Greek god of the sea, like Roman Neptune; see Neptune.

POSIDONIUS (CA. 135–161 B.C.): Syrian philosopher, historian, scientist; head of Stoic school at Rhodes; wrote a continuation of Polybius's history: 3.21.

POTATIVE BISHOPS: parody of "portative"; presumably topers: 2.7.

PRACONTAL, HER: perhaps Humbert de Pracontal, lord of Ancona, Italy: 1.8.

PRAENESTE: an ancient town (modern Palestrina, composer's birthplace) in Latium, central Italy; great temple of Fortune noted for its oracles: 3.24.

PRAETOR, PRAETORIAN: one of two high Roman officials just below consuls and having chiefly judicial functions: 3.44.

PRAGMATIC SANCTION: a sovereign's decree having the force of law; best known is that of Bourges (1438); French King Charles VII freed Gallican church from domination by Rome and found councils dominant over popes; revoked in 1461, replaced by a milder one 1493, then superseded in 1516 by Francis I's Concordat with Pope Leo X; Bridoye here must refer to that of 1493: 3.41.

PRELINGAND: "Sprightly"; name of a scout for Gargantua: 1.34; also as Prelinguand "Dandy" name of one of Frère Jean's fighting cooks: 1.34.

PRÉS (PREZ), JOSQUIN DES: see Des Prés, Josquin.

PRESTER JOHN: since twelfth c. the legendary Christian priestly ruler of a vast ill-defined empire in Africa (Ethiopia) or Asia (Persia) or both: 2.34.

PRIAM: king of Troy (*Iliad*); defeated by Greeks in war and killed: 2.30.

PRIAPUS, PRIAPISM, PRIAPIZE: Asian, the Greco-Roman, god of gardens and fertility; figured with a mighty phallus always at the ready: 3.8.

PRIMUS ET SECUNDUS: a game involving spillikins (jackstraws): 2.18.

PROCLUS (PROKLOS, A.D. FIFTH C.): of Byzantium; a Neoplatonist who wrote on sacrifice and magic; R finds this item in Marsilio Ficino: 1.10.

PROCNE: sister of ravished Philomela; see Philomela.

PROCONSUL: a governor or military commander of a Roman province.

PROCULUS CAESAR (A.D. THIRD C.): self-proclaimed emperor; chief distinction that he reportedly raped 100 captive women in less than two weeks: 3.27.

PROCURATOR: an officer of the Roman empire entrusted with management of the financial affairs of a province and often having administrative powers as agent of the emperor.

PROFICIAT: a libation or collation of welcome: 1.17.

PROPERTIUS, SEXTUS (CA. 50–16 B.C.): able Greek-inspired Roman elegiac poet; knew and admired Virgil; in Maecenas's circle; left four books of elegies: 3.18.

PROSERPINA: Greek goddess of the underworld; Roman Persephone: 5.46.

PROTEUS: in Greek myth, an omniscient sea god, "The Old Man of the Sea"; could assume myriad shapes to elude questions; questioned by becalmed Menelaus (*Odyssey* 4.385–608): 3.13.

PROVENCE (LATIN PROVINCIA): onetime province including most of southern France, east to west: 1.33.

PRUSSIA: a large part of W Germany bordering on the Baltic Sea: 1.33.

PSALM(S): of King David, Old Testament, hymns of prayer and thanksgiving: 1.38.

PSAMMETICHUS (PSAMTIK, D. 609 B.C.): ingenious and inquisitive early king of Egypt (Herodotus 2.2 ff., 2.29); reputed inventor of the labyrinth: 3.19.

PTOLEMY: the great astronomer, geographer, mathematician; Claudius Ptolemaios, A.D. second c.; of Ephesus; his *System of Mathematics* summed up the astronomical knowledge of his time: 4.BD.

PTOLEMY I: Soter, putative son of Lagus, and king of Egypt 323–283 B.C.; first of the Ptolemy dynasty that ruled Egypt from death of Alexander to Roman conquest; his mother was a concubine of Philip of Macedon: 3.P.

PUNIC, PUNICIA, PUNICIAN(S): this term usually applies to Carthage and especially to its wars with Rome known as the Punic Wars (262–204 B.C.); see Punic Wars.

PUNIC WARS (262–204 B.C.): between Rome and Carthage for hegemony in W central Mediterranean; in the first (262–241) the Romans drove the Carthaginians out of Sicily; but in 247 Carthage found a fine general Hamilcar Barca; the Second Punic War (or Hannibalic War, 218–201, after the son of Hamilcar, Carthage's greatest general, Hannibal) saw Rome repeatedly in serious danger as Hannibal, with his superior cavalry, took over most of Italy; but crossing the Alps on land and Roman naval power weakening his supply lines and unending harassment by Fabius "Cunctator" (q.v.) slowed and finally stoped him; in the end, Roman will, organization, and economic power prevailed, thanks to the leadership and generalship of the several Scipios (q.v.) culminating in the great victory at Aama in 203. The so-called Third Punic War (149–146) was really little but the Roman attack that led to the destruction of Carthage so long and fiercely demanded by Cato the Elder.

PURGATORY: Roman Catholic doctrine; area of purification for souls destined for Heaven, where sins are successively purged and the soul unburdened: 3.46.

PUTHERBEUS: Latin form of Dupuyherbault (Gabriel de), ultra-conservative Sorbonne-trained theologian who in 1549 fiercely attacked R in his *Theotimus*; 4.32; cf., Herbault (4.52); see Henri Busson "Les Eglises contre Rabelais," *ER* 7 (1967) 1–70.

PYGMY, PYGMIES, PYGMYLAND: Greek *pugmion* "13 inches"; for most Greek writers, a race of tiny humans in Africa at war with the cranes; here similar result, but engendered by Pantagruel's fart and fizzle: 2.29.

PYRACMON: a Cyclops noted here (after *Aeneid* 8.425) as working for Vulcan: 4.P.

PYRRHA: in Greek myth, Deucalion's wife; the other good human spared from the great flood by Zeus; when flood receded, they found a novel way to renew the human race; see Ovid *Met.* 1.314. ff.: 3.8.

PYRRHO (OR PYRRHON, PYRRONIAN, PYRRHONISM, PYRRHONIST[S]) OF ELIS (CA. 360–275 B.C.): went into India in Alexander's army; founded school of skeptics on his return; from Greek *skeptomai* "look about, consider, look into contradictions between the senses and generally between mind and sense"; Pyrrho concluded, that the only wisdom lay in suspending judgment while going on living normally; he left no writings; his doctrines or views come from a later follower, the doctor Sextus Empiricus (fl. ca. A.D. 190) in his *Outlines of Pyrrhonism*: 3.36.

PYRRHUS (1) (PURRHOS) OR NEOPTOLEMUS: son of Achilles (*Aeneid*, mainly 2), probably the cruelest of the many cruel Greek victors after the fall of Troy; killed Priam; had his daughter Polyxena sacrificed; took Hector's widow Andromache as a prize. R makes no clear reference to him by either name unless he is the Pyrrhus on 2.30.

PYRRHUS (2), KING OF EPIRUS (319 OR 318–272 B.C.): a second cousin of Alexander the Great; led a big army of Italian Greeks in revolt against Rome; one big victory cost him such losses that we still call such "victories" "Pyrrhic"; killed trying to take Argos; probably the Pyrrhus intended on 2.30.

PYTHAGORAS, PYTHAGOREAN(S): of Samos, then Athens (ca. 582–507 B.C.); great mathematician and mystic philosopher; believed in metempsychosis (transmigration of souls) and in the number as the ultimate reality; formed a quasi-religious sect; persecuted and exiled for a time; but soon after Christ, revered, with added Jewish and Hellenistic elements; Ovid's devoted admiration shows in final book (15) of *Met.*: 1.P.

PYTHIA, PYTHIAN: the priestess of Apollo at Delphi: 3.45.

QUAESTOR: one of numerous ancient Roman officials concerned chiefly with financial administration.

QUEBECU, DE: for Quercu (Duchesne); an ally of Béda (q.v.): 2.7.

QUENET, SAINT: obscene fantasy name; a diminutive of *con* "cunt": 1.5.

QUENTIN, JAN: a friend of R who played in the farce at Montpellier: 3.34.

QUID EST: title of a popular school text ridiculed by the humanists: 1.14.

QUINCUNCIAL: a plan for five items, one in the center of a rectangle, others at corners: 1.53.

QUINQUENAIS: a hamlet and good wine near Chinon; R's family may have owned land there: 1.47.

QUINTAIN: a rotating man-sized dummy, target for a lance in jousting practice: 2.1.

QUINTESSENCE: Greek and medieval natural philosophy; the fifth and highest element (above the standard four—fire, air, water, earth), all pervasive, forming the celestial bodies; and more and more often used to mean central essence or nature, thus in some way the highest and most refined part (as generally here): 5.19.

QUINTESSENTIALS: alchemists, here ironic; no alchemy is needed for such extraction: 4.7.

QUINTILIAN (MARCUS FABIUS QUINTILIANUS, A.D. 35–CA. 95): eminent Roman rhetor and authority on oratory; left *Institutio oratoria* (*The Education of an Orator*) in 12 books; notably 10 (authors to study); judgments on individual writers; most of 8–12, on style and delivery; and 12 on moral requirements: 2.8.

QUINTILIUS: brother of Emperor Claudius; agreed to join in rule, but soon killed: 3.10.

QUINTUS CALABER OR GALABER (QUINTUS OF SMYRNA, FL. CA. A.D. 350–400): his poem, discovered in Calabria in 1450, continues Homer's story from the end of the *Iliad* through the fall of Troy and departure of the Greek fleet on to its dispersal in a storm: 3.13.

QUIRINALS (QUIRINALIA): Feast of Fools (Stultitiorum Feria); an annual festival held on our February 17: 3.38.

RABANIST(S): commentators, as contrasted with Rabbinical scholars: 2.10.

RABBI BEN EZRA (OR ABEN EZRA OR IBN EZRA): Abraham ben Meir, 1098–1164; a learned rabbi and Biblical commentator: 2.17.

RABBI KIMY: probably Joseph ben Isaac Kinhi or Kimchi (1105–1170?) or another of that notable family of grammarian scholars in France or Spain: 2.17.

RABELAIS, FRANÇOIS (C. 1490–1553): our author, named in the text just once, as "Rabelays"; among mourning friends and domestics present at the death of Guillaume de Langey (q.v.): 4.27.

RACLET, RAIMBERT: law professor at Dole whom R finds most incompetent: 2.P.

RACQUEDENARE (OR RAQUEDENARE "SCRAPEPENNY"): the duke heading Picrochole's rearguard: 1.26; also author of a book in the Library of Saint-Victor: 2.7.

RAGOT: a famous ne'er-do-well rated king of the beggars in R's day: 2.11.

RAMINAGROBIS, RAMINAGROBIDIC: fantasy name based on grobis "cat"; name of the beatific dying poet of Book 3.21–23; modeled, some think, on Evangelicalist theologian Jacques Lefèvre d'Etaples (d. ca. 1536), whose serene views he recalls; others think, on Gallican poet-pamphleteer Jean Lemaire de Belges, who died some time in the 1520s; others think, on rhétoriqueur poet Guillaume Crétin (d. 1525), some of whose verses he uses: 3.21.

RANCE: see Renzo.

RAPALLUS OR RAPPALUS: a fairly familiar medieval demon: 2.14.

RAPHAEL: one of the four archangels in Hebrew and Old Testament tradition: 1.10.

RAVELIN(S): a small fortified firing-point protruding from a fortress wall: 3.P.

RAVENNA: a city in Emilia-Romagna, N central Italy NE of Florence, on a canal to the Adriatic; long a big port and market center: 5.43.

RECTOR (OF THE UNIVERSITY OF PARIS): apparently little but an honorific post and a chance to make an opening address, but fiercely contested at the periodic elections: 3.3.

REDEEMER: one of the many names used in R's book for Jesus Christ: 1.29.

REGNAULT (OR RENAUD): a folklore shepherd, presumably the "Regnauld Belin" whose sheep are said to sleep while others graze: 1.41.

RENAUD DE MONTAUBAN: a hero of medieval romance who as a penance served the masons: 3.P.

RENÉ: a French proper name that literally means reborn: 3.18.

RENÉE DE FRANCE (1510–CA. 1575): pro-Reformist daughter of King Louis XII of France, wife of anti-Reformist Duke Ercole d'Este (see Este) of Ferrara; protected Reformists as well as she could; troubled marriage; for her last years returned to France, retired to Montargis, worked for Reform: 6.12.

RENZO, SIGNOR (DA CERI, D. 1536): Lorenzo Orsini, aka Renzo da Ceri, of that illustrious Roman family, rivals of the Colonna tribe, long Guelfs; a condottiero on the side and in the service of the French, fiery, proud, vengeful. The cousin and husband, first a cuckold then a widower, was Orsino Orsini. Lorenzo Orsini bravely but vainly defended Rome and the Castel San Angelo against the Imperials of Charles V (1527).

REPUBLIC: work by Plato; his widest-ranging, most inclusive dialogue, arguably his best; his main theme goodness (justice) and its relation to happiness; the ideal state (philosopher rulers); the nature of reality (as forms, archetypes, or "ideas," of which objects as sense are mere imitations or representations (parable of the cave): 1.P.

REUCHLIN, JOHANN (OF COLOGNE, 1455–1522): lawyer, Greek and Hebrew scholar; fiercely attacked by conservative Cologne theologians; strongly defended by many concerned humanists and Reformists: 2.7.

RHADAMANTHUS: in Greek myth, son of Zeus and Europa; for his just life on earth, made ruler of Elysium and a judge of the dead; all of which makes Master Pathelin a comically unlikely candidate for post of his treasurer: 2.30.

RHEA: in Hesiod, a Titan; mother of Zeus by Cronus, who promptly planned to swallow him to avoid a dire prophecy. To save him, Rhea bore the baby in Crete, hid him in a cave on Mount Ida or Mount Dicte, where he was nursed either by the nannygoat Amalthea or by the nymph Amalthea or nanygoat's milk: 1.28.

RHINE: the great river; ca. 600 miles long of Switzerland, the Low Countries, and mainly Germany, flowing N into the North Sea at Rotterdam: 1.33.

RHIZOTOME: in Greek "Rootcutter"; Gargantua's botanist page, then one of Pantagruel's domestics and companions: 1.23.

RHODES (RHODOS): a sizeable island in SE Aegean near coast of Asia Minor: 1.33.

RHÔNE: a long river, ca. 500 miles, flowing S from Switzerland through SE France into the Mediterranean, after passing Lyon, Avignon, Nîmes, Arles, Valence, and through its own delta: 2.5.

ROBINET, FRANÇOIS: a friend of R who played in the farce at Montpellier: 3.34.

ROCQUETAILLADE: Provençal "cut out of rock"; a fairytale giant: 1.6.

ROLAND: Charlemagne's greatest French warrior; hero of twelfth-c. *Song of Roland*; died at Roncesvaux (778) after killing myriad Saracens: 1.10. "Roland's death" (La mort Roland) means dying of thirst: 2.6.

ROMIPETES: Rome-seekers, i.e., pilgrims headed for Rome: 4.BD.

ROMULUS: with Remus, legendary co-founder of Rome; and its first king and ruler: 2.30.

RONDIBILIS: Panurge's medical doctor consultant, perhaps named for R's friend, onetime sponsor, and colleague Rondelet, also of the Faculty of Medicine at Montpellier: 3.29.

ROSATA, ALBERICUM (OR AUBRY) DE: a fourteenth-c. jurist: 2.7.

ROSE NOBLE(S): originally an English coin, named for the roses of York, worth one third of a pound; later used to mean any of many kindred coins: 6.1.

"ROSE POT, UNCOVER THE": to discover or reveal secrets or both: 2.12.

ROSTOCOSTOJAMBEDANESSE: a fantasy name, literally Rostocostosheass's leg; our version follows the rhythm of R's and, we think, its spirit, but not its letter: 2.7.

ROTA: the Vatican's final court of appeal in Rome: 3.37.

ROUEN (SEINE-MARITIME): former capital of Normandy; a sizeable city on the Seine about 75 miles NW of Paris: 2.23.

ROUERGUE, LA (MODERN AVEYRON): an old region of S France, capital Rodez: 1.3.

ROYAL(S): a French or English gold coin; the French one dropped in value from 68 to 55 *sous* after being issued in 1300 at 10.74 gold francs: 3.2.

RUACH (AFFLATUS): BD, "wind or spirit, Hebrew"; the name of one island where wind was the food: 4.43.

RUBICON: the river that once separated Italy from Cisalpine Gaul; crossing it has been proverbial for making a critical decision since in 49 B.C. when Caesar, by crossing it into Italy against the Senate's orders, declared war on the Senate and on Rome: 4.BD.

RUSSIA, RUSSIAN(s): then as now, a great Eurasian land power: 1.33.

RUSTICUS: a poem by Politian (Angelo Poliziano; 1454–1494) in praise of country life, imitating Hesiod's *Works and Days* and Virgil's *Georgics*: 1.24.

SABA (OR SHEBA), SABAEANS OR SHEBANS: a city and region in S Arabia on a trade route to the Far East; known for riches in spice trade, etc.; fabled queen reportedly came to Jerusalem to visit wise King Solomon of Israel (1 Kings 10): 2.18.

SABAOTH: cognomen of Jehovah as Lord of Armies or Hosts (Isaiah 1.9; Romans 9.29; James 5.4): 3.P.

SABINE(S): an ancient Italian people from Sabine Hills NE of and near Rome: from early times, intermarried with Romans whence legend of Roman rape of Sabine women; fought Rome pretty long but finally joined them; were absorbed: 3.49.

SAFFRON, SAFFRON-TINTED: i.e., bankrupt; in banking halls a broken bench (bank) was marked with yellow: 3.23.

SAINT ANTHONY, ORDER OF: See Anthony, Saint.

SAINT ANTHONY'S (OR SAINT ANTON'S) FIRE: nickname for an extremely painful form of ergotism then extremely common and dangerous, restricting circulation, caused by eating ergot; an infection found in some wheat: 1.13.

SAINT-ANTOINE, PARIS: a Cistercian abbey on the site of today's Hôpital Saint-Antoine: 2.9.

SAINT-AUBIN-DU-CORMIER: Ille-et-Villaine near the Norman-Breton border on the English Channel and Mont-Saint-Michel; site of a great battle (1488) in which the French beat the Bretons and captured their duke, which soon led to their duchess having to marry King Charles VIII of France; and this finally, in 1532, along with other factors, to the French annexation of Brittany: 1.50.

SAINT-AYL (PRONOUNCED "SAINT-Y"): Estienne Lorens, sieur de; Captain of the Castle in Turin; a good friend of R's, also present at Langey's death; had a château near Orléans, where he held a modest public office;

from there in 1542, on a trip back to France with Langey, R wrote a friend a merry clowning letter (our item 6.18): 4.P.

SAINT CADOUYN: the name of an abbey of d'Estissac's near Bergerac housing a shroud said to be that of Jesus Christ: 1.27.

SAINT-CLOUD (HAUTS-DE-SEINE): now a town near Paris, then a nearby picnic spot: 1.24.

SAINT-DENIS, HÔTEL: a Benedictine house in Paris (of the Abbots of Saint-Denis on the Rue Saint-André-des-Arcs), where R may have stayed when in Paris; see also Denis, Saint.

SAINT-ESTIENNE: name of the great cathedral of Bourges (Cher), ca. 140 miles S of Paris, whose great tower, crumbled down in 1506, had been replaced by the famous "Butter Tower" (Tour de Beurre), funded by selling indulgences for eating butter in Lent: 2.29.

SAINT-FLORENT, ABBEY OF: with Bourgueil, one of France's richest: 1.50.

SAINT-GENOU (INDRE): a town near Châteauroux hard hit by the plague in 1526: 1.45.

SAINT-GERVAIS: a large church and square on the Paris Right Bank near the Hôtel de Ville: 2.17; see also Gervasius, Saint.

SAINT-INNOCENT: cemetery, so named for Innocent I, pope 401–417, champion of papal power over councils and Church; opposed Visigoth sack of Rome (410); the great Paris public cemetery for the poorer classes overflowing with exhumed bones; hangout of tramps and beggars: 1.37.

SAINT-JACQUES: see James, Saint and Santiago de Compostela.

SAINT-JACQUES, BOURG: then a town near Chinon, now one of its faubourgs: 1.47.

SAINT JAMES'S WAY: Milky Way, which some thought led to Santiago de Compostela (q.v.): 2.2.

SAINT-JEAN (PARIS): one of two; Saint-Jean-en-Grève (Right Bank) or Saint-Jean-le-Rond, near Notre Dame, more probably: 2.17.

SAINT-JEAN-D'ANGÉLY (CHARENTE-MARITIME): on the Boutonne and not far from Niort and La Rochelle: 1.27.

SAINT-JEAN-DE-LUZ (PYRÉNÉES-ATLANTIQUES): in SW France, on the Nivelle near Bayonne and the Atlantic Coast: 1.33.

SAINT-LOUAND, SAINT-LOUANT: a village downstream from Chinon; Benedictine abbey, whose fat prior Jacques le Roy set Shysteroos on Lord Basché, bringing ingenious retaliation: 4.12.

SAINT-MAIXENT (DEUX-SÈVRES): now, site of a military school, Saint-Maixent-l'Ecole, then in Poitou; near Niort, a walled Breton port; in R's time a big Atlantic port; no passion play is known there: 4.13.

SAINT-MAUR-DES FOSSÉS (VAL-DE-MARNE): site of Jean du Bellay's Benedictine (later secularized) abbey and residence; took in R to abbey as a canon (then a secular priest); R's headquarters and quite possibly home in his last seventeen years (1536–1553): 4.OC.

SAINT-MESMES: parish of Chinon (from Saint Maximus, ca. 580–662); a Byzantine Greek mystic and theologian; abbot of Chrysopolis monastery; drew pilgrims who came to pray to him: 1.27.

SAINT PATRICK'S HOLE (LE TROU SAINT PATRICE): a cave in Donegal, Ireland, inevitably traced and related to Saint Patrick (q.v.): 1.2.

SAINT-SÉBASTIEN: Loire-Atlantique, now Saint-Sébastien-sur-Loire; a town and pilgrimage site on L bank of the Loire (1.45); for the saint, see Sebastian, Saint.

SAINT-SEVER (LANDES): on the Adour near Mont-de-Marsan; old Romanesque abbey; in adapting this Aretino story, R made up claim he was Gascon patron saint: 3.42.

SAINT-SOFIA OR SOPHIA (SAINT SOFIA OR GREEK HAGIA SOPHIA OR TURKISH AYA SOFIA): the vast Christian Byzantine masterpiece built A.D. 532–537 for Emperor Justinian (q.v.); later a Moslem mosque, now a museum; in old Constantinople (now Istanbul); the saint was martyred in A.D. 137 in Rome with three daughters; festival September 30: 2.32.

SAINT-VICTOR: abbey, near modern Halle aux Vins, Paris Left Bank; noted library that R stocks with grotesque, often obscene, parody titles of pseudo-scholastic books that fill a whole chapter (2.7); name also for a city gate and of the underground stream better known as La Bièvre (Ruisseau Saint-Victor); the saint was Pope Victor I, bishop of Rome 189–199; festival July 28: 1.23.

SAINTE-CROIX, CHURCH OF THE: the grand old Orléans cathedral; its festival May 3: 2.33.

SAINTE-GENEVIÈVE: the hill, with square and fine library (now also Pantheon) in and overlooking the university quarter (Paris, Left Bank): 2.16.

SAINTE-RADÉGONDE: rocky hillside grotto above Chinon. The saint (ca. 520–587), queen of Frankish King Clotaire, sick of the crimes of her royal house, became a nun, founded the Sainte-Croix monastery in Poitiers: 3.31.

SAINTES (CHARENTE-MARITIME, SAINTONGE): on Charente near mouth; old capital of Saintonge, a region on Atlantic between Vendée and Gironde, homeland of Dindenault and his men: 1.33.

SAINTS (ALPHABETIZATION): see Introductory Note to the Glossary.

SALLUST (GAIUS SALLUSTIUS CRISPUS, 86–35 B.C.): acute but often biased historian; riches from public office gave leisure for writing on struggles with Jugurtha and Catiline; and on Rome in the years just after Sulla (78–67 B.C.): 2.10.

SALMAGUNDI (HASH): name of the fictive castleship Pantagruel gave first to Alcofribas Nasier (2.32), then to Panurge for keeps (3.2), who soon spends its revenues past and future: 2.32.

SAMOS, SAMIAN(S): a large Greek island and people in SE Aegean near Asia Minor: 4.P.

SAMOSATA: old city on Euphrates, birthplace of Lucian (q.v.) one of R's masters, whom he twice calls "the philosopher of Samosata" (see also Lucian): 3.24.

SAMSON: a judge and mighty man of Israel (Judges 13–16): 1.37.

SANDY SEA (OR SEA OF SAND): a term for the shallow Baltic straits between Denmark and Sweden: 1.33.

SANTIAGO DE BRESSUIRE: a small town in Deux-Sèvres; an apparent parody of the revered, vastly popular, pilgrimage goal Santiago de Compostela (q.v.): 3.22.

SANTIAGO DE COMPOSTELA: in Galicia, NW Spain; site of supposed tomb of Saint James the Greater; a shrine built over this in ninth or tenth c.; in R's day one of the three greatest goals of pilgrimages; R makes no mention of it.

SAPORTA, ANTOINE: a friend of R, player in the farce at Montpellier: 3.34.

SAPPHO (SEVENTH C. B.C.): of Lesbos, a priestess of Aphrodite; moved to Sicily and there gathered fellow women worshipers; probably married and had a daughter; beyond these mere probabilities we know of few, but tales abound that she vainly loved a man, Phaon, and killed herself for love; that she and her women followers were homosexuals, whence French Saphisme and English lesbianism to mean female homosexuality. She left nine books of finely wrought Odes mainly telling of passionate love; Plato an admirer; imitated by Catullus in Latin, Tennyson and Swinburne in English: 5.20; and our final item (6.22) is an 84-line Latin Sapphic Ode by Cardinal Jean du Bellay.

SARABAITES: in ancient times, debauched Egyptian monks: 2.34.

SARACENS: a general European term for all Arabs and Moslems, specifically those in Spain, Portugal, etc., known as Moors; who in the eighth c. overran all NW Africa and the Iberian Peninsula and invaded France, but were defeated in battle at Tours and mainly Poitiers (732) by Charles Martel's French. However, their long rule (7–8 centuries) over Iberia, and more briefly in southern France, left fine artifacts of their culture far and wide. Christians reconquered; meanwhile, from Charlemagne (778) to Ferdinand and Isabella (1492) was slow and long: 1.46.

SARAGOSSA(NS): chief city of Aragon in NE Spain, then renowned for fine swords: 1.8.

SARDANAPALUS: an Assyrian king cited by Greek Ctesias (fl. ca. 400 B.C.) as wallowing in luxury; but when besieged by threatening Medes, set fire to his court and burned to death in it: 1.33.

SARDINIA: the large Mediterranean island W of Italy and just S of Corsica; now Italian; in R's day under Spanish rule: 1.33.

SARMATIAN(S): ancient land and people E of the Vistula River and W of the Caspian Sea; modern Poland and USSR; pastoral nomads kin to Scythians, speaking an Indo-Iranian tongue; expert falconers: 1.33.

SATALIA (OR ADALIA, ANTAKYA): Turkish SW Asia Minor; Mediterranean port and province; cited here once, as Adalia: 4.25.

SATAN: Christianity; the Great Tempter, Adversary, etc.; the Devil: 3.14.

SATIN, SATINLAND, LAND OF SATIN: an imagined utopia (lovely fabrics, designs, forms, etc.) but finally disappointing; no life, no food or drink; travelers visited it with great interest but left it with greater relief: 5.29.

SATURN: Saturnus "the sower," Italian god of agriculture; later identified with Cronus (Kronos) whom Hesiod classed as a Titan. Confined from birth to Tartarus by father Ouranos (Uranus, Heaven), Kronos rebelled, castrated Ouranos. One legend makes Saturn's the Golden Age; in another, warned his children will overthrow him, he tries to swallow them all; but Rhea (q.v.) saves Zeus on Crete to become new king of the gods when he overthrows and succeeds Kronos. Such stories concern only Kronos, not Saturn; he survives as god of crops, celebrated in three-day sowing time in mid-December, Saturnalia, a wild happy festival, probably prototype of modern western Christmas: 2.31.

SATURNALIA: by Macrobius, fl. ca. A.D. 400; a collection of dialogues among eminent Romans, mostly pagan, in seven books; much concerned with Virgil: 1.3; see under Saturn.

SAUL: Samuel 1–2; first king of the Hebrews; anointed by Samuel; first defended, later succeeded, by David: 3.25.

SAULIEU (CÔTE-D'OR): a small town near Dijon in E central France; an apparent rival to Buzançais for making good bagpipes: 3.46.

SAUMUR (MAINE-ET-LOIRE): a town where the Thouet meets the Loire; site of a passion play remembered fondly, as a player in it, by Panurge: 2.4.

SAVOY: a region in SE France bordering on Switzerland and Italy; once in turn a county, then a duchy (capital, Chambéry); annexed to France between 1792 and 1813: 1.33.

SAXONY, SAXON(S): a large region in eastern W Germany whose size has varied and its people; now heavily industrialized; chief cities include Dresden, Leipzig, Magdeburg: 3.1.

SCATOPHAGOUS: BD, "excrement-eating": 4.18.

SCIPIO(S): eminent Roman family of leaders: Scipio Africanus Major (236/235–183 B.C.) was consul at the end of the second Punic War; at Ticinus (218 B.C.) saved his father's life but was wounded; in 210 drove the Carthaginians out of Spain; consul again in 215; led army into Africa in 214, then at Zama (202) ended that war and the military power of Carthage; successful campaign in Asia with help of brother Lucius; but had many enemies (Cato the Elder et al.) in Rome; temporarily charged with taking bribes and public money; charges later dropped: 1.46; R's term "the Scipios" presumably incudes the two just mentioned; the eldest son of Scipio Africanus Major, and his adoptee, the general who finally destroyed Carthage, Publius Cornelius Scipio Aemilianus Africanus Numantianus (185–129 B.C.): 2.27.

SCOTIST(S): disciple(s) in theology of Duns Scotus; see Scotus, Duns.

SCOTLAND, SCOTTISH, SCOTS: the large country in the UK N of England, and its inhabitants, reputed haughty; many served as guardsmen; spoke bad French: 1.33.

SCOTUS, DUNS (OR JOHN OF SCOTLAND, 1266?–1308): John Scotus; Latin for Irishman or Scot; Scottish-born scholastic theologian and philosopher, known as the "Subtle Doctor"; a Franciscan; taught at Oxford, Paris, and Cologne; works include *On the First Principle* and *Commentaries* on Peter Lombard's *Sentences* (*Sententiae*); used Aristotle's philosophy to serve Christian theology; founded a Scotist school of scholasticism in contrast with Aquinas's Thomism, stressing "univocity" (much like ubiquity or universality) of being; saw the individuation of things in what he called each one's "thisness" (haecceitas), dependent not on the Divine Intelligence but the Divine Will: 1.13.

SCRAPEPENNY (RACQUEDENARE): a duke, military leader for Picrochole: 1.26.

SCRIPTURE(S): the Bible; see also Bible, Holy Word, Holy Writ.

SCYCOPHAGIUS: in Greek and BD "fig-eating": 4.17.

SCYLLA (SKULLA): *Odyssey* 12.75, 12.245 ff.; a many-headed man-eating monster facing the deadly whirlpool Charybdis across a strait Odysseus had to pass through on his way home; she ate several of his men, but the rest got through; passing between these two has ever since epitomized the hardest kind of dilemma: 5.17.

SCYTHIA, SCYTHIAN(S): a vaguely-defined ancient Eurasian land (and its people) reaching E from the Danube all the way to the Chinese border; a warlike nomadic people of bowmen and horsemen combined; Herodotus, Book 4: 1.16.

'SDEATH: euphemistic oath for God's death, like *morbleu* for *mort Dieu*: 1.12.

SEBASTE: in Greek "venerable"; a troop leader under Gargantua, minor but rewarded: 1.48.

SÉBASTE (OR SEBASTA): in Cappadoica, which is SE central Turkey and Asia Minor on border of Cilicia: 1.33.

SEBASTIAN, SAINT (FL. A.D. THIRD C.): a respected Roman officer martyred by Emperor Diocletian's orders when known to be a Christian; shot full of arrows and left for dead; when later found alive, beaten to death (for keeps); his body covered with arrows was a popular subject for Renaissance painters: 1.45; cf., Saint-Sébastien, a town near Nantes (Loire-Atlantique) or Saint-Sébastien-sur-Loire named for him and a point from which Gargantua's pilgrims are returning home: 1.45.

SEIGNY JOAN (FOR SEIGNEUR JEAN): a famous Paris "fool" or jester; shows Solomonic wisdom: 3.37.

SEINE: Sequana in Latin; a great French river and commercial artery, mostly navigable, flowing gently NNW through Troyes, Champagne, Paris, Rouen, into English Channel at Le Havre; receiving on its way the waters of the Marne, Aube, Oise, and Eure: 1.23; as Sequana: 2.6.

SEJUS (OR SEIUS): reputed original owner of a baneful horse that brought harm to all owners: 4.15.

SELEUCUS: a third C. B.C. natural philosopher (unrelated to Alexander's general bearing that name) who believed the earth revolved around the sun: 5.25.

SEMIRAMIS: a legendary Assyrian queen; reputed founder of Babylon; noted for beauty and wisdom; in one story, vanished in the form of a dove, worshiped since as a goddess; but in another (as implied here) fell prey to lust for a horse: 3.34.

SENTENCES (LIBER SENTENTIARUM): the popular and influential school manual by Peter Lombard, twelfth c.: 2.17.

SEPTEMBER BROTH (OR SAUCE OR POTION): wine from grapes harvested then: 1.7.

SEPTIMUS SEVERUS (OR, SIMPLY, SEVERUS), LUCIUS (A.D. 146–211): emperor of Rome from 193; an able general; enlarged and consolidated the empire: 3.7.

SEQUANA: Latin name for the river Seine: 2.6; see Seine.

SERAPH(S) OR SERAPHIN(S): oriental gold coins: 2.14.

SERAPIS: a synthetic Egyptian god formed from Osiris and the Apis bull who came to be worshiped as the godhead by some Gnostic sects: 3.24.

SERES: an ancient Far Eastern country, probably China: 3.51.

SERVIUS, MARCUS HONORATUS (A.D. FOURTH–FIFTH C.): wrote an influential commentary on Virgil (q.v.): 1.3.

SESTERCES, SEXTERCES: small ancient Roman coins worth one quarter of denarius (denier): 5.42.

SEUILLÉ (OR SEUILLY): a Benedictine abbey near La Devinière and Chinon; attacked by Picrochole's pillaging troops, but heroically defended (and troops routed) by the claustral monk Frère Jean des Entommeures (q.v.): 1.27.

SEVERUS, ALEXANDER: see Alexander Severus.

SEVERUS, SEPTIMIUS: see Septimius Severus.

SHEBA, SHEBAN(S) (OR SABA): see Saba, Sabaean(s).

"SHEEP, TO RETURN TO ONE'S": to come back to the point; recalling the Farce de Maistre Pierre Pathelin and its confused angry draper-sheep farmer: 1.11.

SHEKEL(S): any of various ancient units of weight; esp., a Hebrew unit of ca. 352 grains troy; or a coin, gold or silver, of that weight; or the value of such a coin, usually of silver.

SHROVETIDE: the three-day period just before Ash Wednesday: 1.4.

SHYRON (OR SCURRON), JEAN: R's sponsor at Montpellier and friendly colleague: 4.43.

SHYSTEROO(S), SHYSTERETTE, SHYSTEROOVIA (CHICQUANOUS, ETC.): the process-servers and their homeland who earn ther living by getting beatings for doing their job: 4.12.

SIBYL, STRAIT OF (STRAIT OF SEVILLE, OR, BETTTER, OF GIBRALTAR): 1.33.

SICILY: the great triangular island just off and W of the boot of Italy; in R's day one of the twin kingdoms (of Naples and Sicily), now part of Italy: 1.33.

SIDON: the chief, purely Phoenician port, on the Mediterranean, in modern Lebanon: 3.16.

SIENA: a hill city in Tuscany, central Italy; rich in art and architecture, much fought over; its cardinal then was Archbishop Giovanni Piccolomini: 6.12.

SIGEILMÈS (SEGELMISSA OR SIDJILMASSA): an old city in the Moroccan Sahara: 1.33.

SILENUS: probably once a Phrygian god; in Greek myth, a creature of forests and mountains, part human, part animal; in Bacchus's entourage, fat, bearded, pot-bellied, and drunken; also one of the boxes or caskets described in text: 1.P.

SILOAM (OR SILOAH): the Philistine tower pulled down in ruins by captive Samson on top of the Philistines and himself (Judges 16); and famous pool noted in both Testaments (Isaiah 8.6 and Nehemia; also Luke 13.4 and John 9.7): 1.37.

SIMONIDES (OF CEOS, CA. 556–468 B.C.): an able, versatile Greek lyric poet: 5.20.

SINAI, MOUNT: where Jehovah gave the Law to Moses (Exodus 3.4): 1.33.

SINON: the crafty Greek (*Aeneid* 2.110 ff.) who conned the Trojans into bringing the great wooden horse inside their city, then later opened it and let the Greek warriors out to sack and burn the city: 2.24.

SIREN(S): in Greek myth, fabled females who could draw men to destruction by the charm of their song; Odysseus needed all his craft and Circe's advice to get his men and himself past this peril on their voyage home (*Odyssey* 12.39–55): 1.P.

SISYPHUS: mythical crafty king of Corinth; aptly punished after death by having to roll a heavy stone forever over and over up a hill, then seeing it roll back down: 2.1.

SITICINE(S): reputed ancestors of Ringing Island's humanoid birds: 5.2.

SIXTUS IV, POPE (1414–1484, pope from 1471): who, Panurge claims, paid him well for curing him of an agonizing cankerous tumor; and whom Epistémon later found anointing poxies in hell: 2.17.

SMALLFRY (MENUAIL): one of Picrochole's commanders and advisers: 1.31.

SNIFFSHIT (LORD): a fictive, nonsense litigant in his suit with Lord Kissass, at a trial well judged by Pantagruel: 2.10.

SOCRATES (469–399 B.C.): father of Greek—and western—philosophy; professed ignorance, shook some supposed certainties in his teaching, all by questioning; left nothing in writing; known to us by works of disciples or pupils or both—Xenophon, especially Plato; put to death by fellow Athenians at a time when his political views were in disfavor: 1.P.

SODOM: with Gomorrah, two very sinful Palestinian cities destroyed by Jehovah (Genesis 18–19): 2.P.

SOLOMON (TENTH C. B.C.): son of David and the king of Israel; proverbial for wisdom; therefore visited by queen of Sheba (q.v.; Kings 1.10–13) and many others bearing rich gifts: 1.33; the Solomon quoted by Swashbuckler (Spadassin) on 1.33 is not the real one, but the fictive sage of the medieval *Dyalogus Salomonis et Marcolphi*, which contrasts the lofty wisdom of the sage-king with the crude good sense of the "fool," the jester: 1.33.

SOLON (CA. 640–558 B.C.): great Athenian statesman and lawgiver and part-time poet: 2.18.

"SOLUTION OF CONTINUITY": R's favorite way of expressing and describing "woman's wound": 2.15.

SOMATES: in Greek *somata*; BD "bodies, members": from Aesop's fable of their conspiracy against the belly: 4.57.

SOPHIST(S): Greek teaching rhetors who helped seek persuasion, not truth; condemned by Plato but vastly popular; in R, used from 1534 on, replaces in Books 1–2 mainly his earlier, more dangerous "Sorbonist": 1.18.

SOPHOCLES (496–405 B.C.): one of the three great Athenian tragedians; author of the two Oedipus plays (*Oedipus the King* and *Oedipus at Colonus*, perhaps two parts of a trilogy now lost) and of many others, seven remain, including *Antigone*: 1.10.

SOPHRONE: in Greek "wise, temperate"; a Gargantuist captain rewarded after victory: 1.51.

SOPHY: the title used for the king of Persia in R's day: 3.41.

SORBONIST(S) AND DERISIVE DEFORMATIONS WITH THAT SENSE, SOR-
BONICOLES, SORBONAGRES, SORBONISANS, SANIBORSANS, SIBORCISANS,
ETC.: inhabitants (always meaning teachers and/or doctorate holders) of
the Sorbonne (q.v.), hence potent archconservative theologians (often
obscurantist), fierce enemies and dangerous persecutors of even peaceful
Reformists; their leader, Noel Béda (q.v.); as noted above s.v. Sophist(s),
that term replaces this in all but earliest editions of G and P in hopes of
reducing risk.

SORBONNE: properly, the name of the first college in the University of
Paris, founded in 1253 by Robert de Sorbon for theology students who
were not friars and so lacked lodging; gained great importance in the
ensuing centuries; and in the sixteenth c. came to be the meeting place
for the normally dominant theological faculty; so use of the name was
extended to that faculty and often to the entire University, as is still true.
Thanks to its age-old interpretive rights in the Catholic Church, in R's
day it was the stronghold of entrenched ultra-conservatism and fierce
opposition to all Reformist sects and creeds, however peaceful. The
name no longer appears in R's final editions, but is signified by all its
replacement forms and often hinted at by Parisian place-names. The
only exception is a facile humanist pun where R uses the name for the
notoriously foul-smelling lake Serbo (Serbonis), once mentioned by
Strabo: 2.33.

SORTIBRANT OF COIMBRA: in W central Portugal; a Saracen king of
Coimbra in the medieval tale *Fierabras* here also one of the myriad listed
ancestors of Gargantua and Pantagruel: 2.1.

SOU(S), SOL: a very old French coin; once a gold piece worth 1/20 livre
(or pound or franc); for Cotgrave the *sou* is the French shilling, worth
1/10 of an English shilling: 2.17.

SPADASSIN (SWASHBUCKLER): one of Picrochole's commanders and advisers: 1.33.

SPAIN, SPANIARD(S), SPANISH: the great Iberian country; in R's day a European power, with the Empire in Europe and wealth from New World
colonies: 1.56.

SPAN: a measure of length, normally 9 inches; some variation: 2.15.

SPARTA, SPARTAN(S): the strong Peloponnesian military city-state, which,
with her aristocratic allies, fought against Athens and her allies in the
Peloponnesian Wars (459–446 B.C., and 431–404); and finally thanks to

their blunders, defeated them (see Thucydides for a full account by an astute informed participant); today little remains of their city; in its heydey little more than a huge armed camp: 3.35.

S.P.D.: presumably *Salve Paxque Domino* "Health and Peace in the Lord": 6.4. S.P. alone (Health and Peace): 6.7.

SPIRITS (WITHIN US): gases or fluids acting in the body; the animal (noblest) allow the soul to function, formed in brain and heart and distributed; the vital (maintaining life) located in the heart's left ventricle; among the vital are the visive, which, emitted from the eye, create a lighted field that makes vision possible: 1.10.

"SPIT IN THE BASIN": i.e., pay cash on the line: 1.11. Could also mean throw up, but see 4.OP for still another possibility.

SPORADES: Plutarch mentions these ocean Sporades, but what islands he and R mean is not clear to us: 4.26.

S.P.Q.R.: the famous acronym symbolizing the unity of Rome (Senatus Populsque Romani or "The Senate and People of Rome"); R's French parody of it (Si Peu Que Rien "As Little as Nothing") is not original and is best known as the motto or device of belletrist Jean Lemaire de Belges (q.v.): 3.32.

SPURIUS SAUFEIUS: one of the many whose bizarre deaths Erasmus reports in *Adages* (3.5.1): 4.17.

SPYRATHE (SPURATHOS): a lamb or goat turd; for Panurge, "Hibernian saffron": 4.67.

STADIUM, STADIA: ancient measure of distance, ca. 80 meters, but variable, sometimes as much as 250 yards: 2.23.

STENTOR: in *Iliad* (5.785) loud-voiced Achaean, Greek army public announcer: 1.23.

STOICISM, STOIC(S), STOICAL: a potent school of philosophy founded ca. 315 B.C. in Athens by Zeno of Citium (in Cyprus, fl. ca. 300 B.C.); viewed world as an organic whole ruled by a supreme intelligence and having an active part (God) and a part acted on (matter); saw man's true aim as a life of virtue, i.e., in harmony with nature; a doctrine part resembling, part contrasting with, its great rival Epicureanism, and congenial to Roman character (hence helping mold Roman law) and contributing to Christianity: 3.3.

STRABO (CA. 64 B.C.–A.D. 19): of Amasia in Pontus (NE Asia Minor), on Black Sea; a Stoic author of geographies in Greek and a history; entertaining but uncritical, of the Roman world of his time: 1.17.

STRADIOT(S): see Estradiots.

STROZZI, FILIPPO II: son of Filippo I, 1489–1538; a wealthy, powerful Florentine noble: 6.12.

STYRIA, STYRIAN(S): a province (capital, Graz) in central and SE Austria: 1.33.

STYX, STYGIAN: in Greek myth, the main river of the underworld (Hades), which the shades of all the dead must cross on the way to their final abode there: 2.30.

SUETONIUS (GAIUS SUETONIUS TRANQUILLUS, A.D. 70–160): a nobleman, secretary to Trajan; left *Lives of the Caesars* and other works on grammar, literature, and other famous men: 4.26.

SUEVI (SWABIANS): an ancient Germanic people from Swabia, SW West Germany; clearly the ones meant by the "Swedes" (*Les Suedes* for *Les Sueves*): 4.1.

SULLA, LUCIUS CORNELIUS (138–78 B.C.): showed military prowess and skill early against Jugurtha and then the Cimbri (107 ff.); led aristocratic party against Marius (q.v.) and his plebeians in the brutal civil war of 84–82 B.C. once on top, finally lost: 2.30.

SUMMIST(S): admiring students or followers (or both) of Aquinas; named thus after his *Summa theologica*, his great masterpiece: 3.38.

SUN-CROWNS: see crowns.

SWASHBUCKLER: see Spadassin.

SWEDEN, SWEDE(S): largest and strongest Scandinavian country: 1.33; see also Suevi.

SWITZERLAND, SWISS: then as now, a small mountainous central European confederation of member cantons, speaking mainly German, some French, some Italian, a little Romanish; borders mainly on France, Germany, Austria, Italy; about half Catholic, half Protestant (Calvinist, Zwinglian, etc.); a military force until crushed by French at Marignano (1515); a major source of mercenaries for France: 1.13.

SYMPOSIUM (*LE BANQUET*): Plato's (ca. 384 B.C.) great dramatic dialogue centering on love: 1.P.

SYNESIUS, SUNESIOS (CA. A.D. 370–413): a versatile learned Neoplatonist country gentleman from Cyrene (q.v.), who became the Christian bishop of Ptolemais in Libya; left a discourse (*Dion*) and some hymns and letters: 3.13.

SYRACUSE, SYRACUSAN(S): strong, rich Sicilian port city, founded 734 B.C. by Corinthian colonists, whose defeat of the Athenian invaders was essential in bringing about the downfall of Athens that ended the Peloponnesian Wars. Plato made three vain visits there between 389 and 361 B.C. hoping to install there a true philosopher-king: 1.10.

SYRIA, SYRIAN(S): in R's day a big ill-defined country in SW Asia, including Lebanon, Mesopotamia, and modern Syria; capital, Damascus; official language, Arabic: 1.16.

SYRIAN SEA: that part of the E Mediterranean off and near Lebanon: 1.33.

TABLES: a name used of several games, mainly backgammon: 1.22.

TABRIZ: a big city in mountainous NW Iran, then Persia: 6.12.

TAKMONDOIS: area around Les Sables-d'Olonne (Vendée) on French Atlantic coast: 5.32.

TALENT: value and weight; ancient, both variable but considerable; e.g., 3,000 shekels in Palestine or Syria, 6,000 drachmas in Greece; one gold talent (the claim here) was a fortune: 4.7.

TALES: Latin *talus, tali* "ankle-bones"; our knucklebones (q.v.), an old game of skill or chance.

TALMUD, TALMUDIST(S): the huge authoritative body of Hebrew law and expert commentary: 2.8.

TANAIS: normally and in theory, the E European River Don; but R's account here fits much better the Nahr-al-Assi River in Asia Minor: 6.13.

TAPROBANA, TAPROBANIAN(S): modern Sri Lanka (until recently Ceylon): 3.51.

TAROT: Italian game; any of a set of 22 pictorial playing cards used for fortune-telling and as trumps in the popular central European game of tarok, where regular playing cards make up a total of 40, 52, or 56 cards in all (accounts and definitions vary widely): 1.22.

TARTAR(S) OR TATAR(S): a warlike Turkic people of the Caucasus and parts of W Siberia (now a republic in the USSR): 1.37.

TARTARETUS (PIERRE TARTARET): a Sorbonist commentator on Aristotle; tarter was a slang term for defecate, which explains the book title attributed to him: 2.7.

TAURUS MOUNTAINS: a massive chain in SW Asia Minor (Turkey) near the Mediterranean: 6.13.

TEIRESIAS (OR TIRESIAS): see Tiresias.

TEMPE, VALE OF: Greek Tembi; a Thessalian valley (NW Greece) renowned for balmy climate: 5.32.

TEMPLAR: knight of a military religious order formed in the twelfth c. to protect the Church of the Holy Sepulcher in Jerusalem; notable drinkers: 2.16.

temple: a term often affected by humanists, such as R, to mean a church: 4.P.

TENITES: in Greek myth, the goddesses controlling lots: 3.11.

TENNIS: in R and his time, always means what we call "Court Tennis," ancestor of the modern game; then the sport only of the rich, but played by kings, nobles, and many others; the game and its rules are so complicated that we must direct the reader to a big dictionary, an encyclopedia, or a specialized book on racket sports; but we note first that each court involved enclosing walls and roofs and small openings on each side and end called galleries; also numbered crosswise lines on the court important for scoring: 1.23.

TERCEL: a male hawk or falcon, one-third smaller than the female; hence the name: 1.12.

TESTOON (TESTON): a small French silver coin stamped with a head (teste); in R's day worth ten *deniers* (q.v.): 2.12.

THALASSA, THALASSIAN(s): Greek *thalassa* "sea"; a fictive port (possible model Saint-Malo), from which Pantagruel's party and convoy sail in quest of the Divine Bottle and its word about Panurge's wishes for marriage: 3.49.

THASOS: 3.13; see Cyclades.

THAUMASTE: Greek *thaumastos* "wondrous"; a famous English scholar, come to debate with Pantagruel, is worsted in debate in signs with Panurge; heaped praise on both: 2.18.

THEATINO(s): a religious order founded in 1524 to reform Church, combat Lutheranism: 3.23.

THEBES, THEBAID: (1) ancient city and desert in upper Egypt on the Nile near Kaenak: 3.10.

THEBES, THEBAN(s): (2) an ancient Boeotian city-state NNW of Athens; in myth, home of the royal house of Labdacus (Laius, Oedipus, et al.); much later, in history, of Epaminondas (410–362 B.C.), admirable man, great general, and statesman; made Thebes dominant in Greece, defeating the Spartans decisively at Leuctra (371) and keeping Thebes strong; but killed in big victory at Mantinea (362) after which Theban strength and prestige declined: 3.P.

THÉLÈME, THÉLÉMITE(s): Greek *thelema* "will"; R's utopian antimonastic abbey created by Gargantua to reward Frère Jean for his exploits in the war; its only rule, "Do what you will (Fay ce que voudras)": 1.56.

THEMISTOCLES (D. 459 B.C.): daring Athenian commander who led Greeks in defeating and repulsing the Persians at Salamis (480 B.C.); later ostracized under Cimon; died in Asia Minor: 1.39.

THENAUD, JEAN: a Friar Minor who published two travel books around 1530: 1.16.

THENOT (OR TENOT): nickname for Etienne or Dendin: see Dendin.

THEOCRITUS THEOKRITOS (FL. CA. 270 B.C.): Greek pastoral poet, author of *Idylls*: 3.13.

THEODORE, MASTER: the name that in later editions replaced his second anagrammatic pseudonym, Seraphin Calobarsy: 1.23.

THEON: of many possible Theons, probably the Neoplatonic mathematician and philosopher of Alexandria (A.D. fifth c.), father of Hypatia, but Theon of Smyrna (eleventh c.), a commentator on Plato: 2.7.

THEOPHRASTUS (CA. 371–287 B.C.): pupil and friend of Aristotle and his successor as head of the Peripatetic School (q.v.); prolific and diverse writer, treating plants and their growth, style in writing, human characters, and metaphysics: 1.23.

THESEUS: in Greek myth, Greek hero, son of King Aegeus of Athens; killer of brigands and monsters like another Hercules; rescued Athens from yearly tribute of youths to Crete and killed their Minotaur; later life less happy; on a false accusation from his wife Phaedra, sent accused son Hippolytus to his cruel death: 3.17.

THETIS: in Greek myth, a Nereid, sea goddess, daughter of "Old Man of the Sea" Nereus; loved by Zeus but on his order (to avoid a dire prophecy that her son would be stronger than his father) was married to a mortal, Peleus; bore him Achilles; pleads with Zeus on his behalf (*Iliad* 9.18): 3.18.

THIBAULT OR TIBAULT, BIG: a lusty but uninformed bridegroom: 4.P.

THOMAS AQUINAS, SAINT: see Aquinas, Saint Thomas.

THOMAS THE ENGLISHMAN: Saint Thomas à Becket, 1118–1170, English martyr; once friend and adviser to King Henry II; but once ordained on his urging, he fought ably and hard for rights of the Church against Crown's encroachments; Henry got him killed: 1.27.

THRACE, THRACIAN(S): region N of Greece, S of Macedonia, and its inhabitants, considered barbaric by the Greeks for their savagery in warfare: 1.10.

THRASYBULUS: Athenian naval commander; helped lead overthrow of the 400 oligarchs in 411 B.C., then in 404–403 was leader of the Athenian democratic party: 3.1.

THUBAL HOLOFERNES: composite Biblical name (from the Book of Judith in the Apocrypha and Ezekiel 38.1–4); the name R gave to the first stupid "old wheezer" embodying the worst in the bad old education: 1.14.

TIBER: the great yellow river of Rome and central Italy, mouth at Ostia on the Mediterranean; very dangerous for backups and all kinds of floods: 6.21.

TIBERIUS (TIBERIUS CLAUDIUS NERO CAESAR, 42 B.C.–A.D. 37): Roman emperor from A.D. 14: 3.2.

TIBULLUS, ALBIUS (CA. 60–19 B.C.): a Roman elegiac poet, friend of Horace; left two books of poems, *Delia* and *Nemesis* from the names of the women celebrated in them: 3.18.

TIGRIS: a SW Asian river running parallel with the Euphrates, then joining it, enclosing Mesopotamia (q.v.), on its way S into the Persian Gulf: 1.33.

TIMON OF ATHENS (FIFTH C. B.C.): a citizen whose friends' ingratitude reportedly made him a misanthrope, and so called; subject of a dialogue by Lucian and of part of Plutarch's *Life of Antony*, also of numberless anecdotes like the one here: 3.4.

TIMOTHEUS: of Miletus, a jealous and over-solicitous music teacher: 1.23.

TIRAQUEAU, ANDRÉ (1488–1558): able Hellenist lawyer and jurist; good host to R and Pierre Amy and other friends in Fontenay-le-Comte in early 1520s; later a counselor in the Paris Parlement (q.v.); R broke into print with his six lines of Greek verse to his friend (our item 6.2) helping introduce the vastly enlarged second edition of Tiraqueau's *De legibus connubialibus* (*On the laws of marriage*), 1524; and R dedicates to him (our item 6.4) his 1532 edition of Manardi's *Letters on Medicine*, vol. 2: 2.5.

TIRAVANT (OR TYRAVANT), COUNT: Forwardmarch; one of Picrochole's commanders: 1.43.

TIRESIAS (OR TEIRESIAS): in Greek myth, a Theban changed for a time into a woman; blinded by Hera for maintaining (with Zeus) that woman enjoys the sexual act more than man; but Zeus in compensation gave him long life and power of true prophecy; foretells future in *Odyssey* (11.90–137), even in Hades after death; later in many tragedies (esp. of Sophocles) gives sound but vain warning to hubristic hero: 3.22.

TIRIDATES: a king of Armenia lavishly received in Rome by Nero: 3.19.

TITANS: in Greek myth, children of primeval Heaven (Ouranos or Uranus) and Earth (Ge); led by Cronus (Kronos), they deposed their father, ruled the universe; but were overthrown in turn by Zeus and his Olympians and punished variously, mostly in Tartarus: 2.1.

TITHONUS: in Greek myth, despite claim of author of Book 5, an ancestor of Swift's Struldbrugs (*Gulliver*, 3.10); son of King Laomedon (q.v.) of Troy; loved by Eos (Dawn), who bore him Memnon, and won from Zeus immortality for him but forgot to ask also for eternal youth; later, when he shriveled away with age and became only a voice, he was kindly changed into a grasshopper; this mention betrays the story: 5.20.

TOBIAS: in the Book of Tobit (Apocrypha), son of Tobit; when Tobit sent him on a journey, Tobias's dog came along; Renaissance painters liked this scene: 3.16.

TOBIT (IN TOBIT 5.9): greets Raphael with a lament for his blindness: 1.10.

TOLEDO: a small but potent archepiscopal city in New Castile, Spain; its "school" here means the home of R's fictive "Diabological Faculty": 3.23.

TOLET (OR TOLLEX): a friend of R, played in the farce at Montpellier: 3.34.

TOMÈRE (HARDY, AUDACIOUS): one of Gargantua's commanders, rewarded in victory: 1.49.

TOSSPINT (TOSSPOT): see Fessepinte: 1.7.

TOUCQUEDILLON: see Blowhard.

TOUL (MEURTHE-ET-MOSELLE): town in NE France on the Moselle and the Marne-Rhine Canal; pronounced "tou," so rhyming with "fou": 3.46.

TOULOUSE (HAUTE-GARONNE): a big city in SW France, once capital of Languedoc; Parlement (q.v.), archbishopric, academy, university: 2.5.

TOURS (INDRE-ET-LOIRE), TOURAINE, TOURANGEAU: sizeable city on the Loire, once capital of Touraine; ca. 140 miles SW of Paris; university; today boasting faculties of medicine, pharmacy, and letters/human sciences: 2.9.

TRAJAN (MARCUS ULPIANUS TRAJANUS): Spanish-born emperor of Rome A.D. 98–117; unassuming, with simple tastes and ways; able general, conquered Dacia (Denmark), etc.: 2.30.

TRANCHELION, ABBÉ: apparently an old toper friend of Frère Jean: 1.45.

TRANSPONTINE: from across the Hellespont; here meaning from Asia, source of fabled spices and great riches: 3.31.

TRANSYLVANIA: a fair-sized region on a high plateau forming most of central Romania: 1.33.

TRASIMENO, LAKE: W of Perugia in Umbria, central Italy, where in 217 B.C. Hannibal used his cavalry well to crush a Roman army led by Flaminius: 4.23.

TREBIZOND (MODERN TRABZON, TURKEY): a Black Sea port, once (1204–1461) seat of a modest empire, but this allusion by the little devilkin is puzzling: 4.46.

TRENT (TRIDENTINUM, TRENTO): a city now in far N Italy (in R's day in Empire), on the Adige river and the road to the Brenner Pass; capital of Trent Province and site of Council of Trent (q.v.): 6.14.

TRENT, COUNCIL OF (1545–1547, 1551–1552, 1562–1563): the nineteenth ecumenical council of the Roman Catholic Church, called to meet the crisis caused by Luther's revolt and Lutheranism; assured by the election (1534) of a pro-Reformist pope (Paul III, Alessandro Farnese, 1468–1549), who pressed to have it convoked; but opposition in the Church to Reform, and dispute over site (Italy or Empire) delayed this long; and later interruptions came with a plague outbreak in Trent, instability in much of host Germany, and variously motivated popes. Decisions are embodied in the Catechism of the Council of Trent (1566); they demand many Church reforms, but mostly embody the hostility toward Protestant or other Reform that reflects the domination of the Council by Italians, which explains why R refers to the council once as a "national" council (i.e., not ecumenical, as it purported to be) and repeatedly as "the Council of Chesil" (of Fools); and represents it as consecrating stubborn conservatism against all humanistic Reform; for references to it, see Chesil.

TREPELU (PALTRY): one of Picrochole's commanders: 1.26.

TRIBOULLET OR TRIBOULET: Francis I's official "fool" (court jester); on Pantagruel's advice, consulted by Panurge about his hesitations over marriage: 3.38.

TRIBOULLETINALS: fictive festivals modeled on Roman Quirinals but honoring Triboullet: 3.38.

TRIBUNE: a Roman official under the monarchy and the republic with the function of protecting the plebeian citizen from arbitrary action by the patrician magistrates.

TRINQUAMELLE: name suggestive of Tiraqueau but meaning "honey-drinker"; president of the Parlement (q.v.) of Myrelingues in the hearing for Judge Bridoye: 3.39.

TRIPET: little goblet; diminutive of Tripe; one of Picrochole's commanders: 1.34.

TRIPPA, HER: arrogant mantic consulted by Panurge; possible parody of Henry Cornelius Agrippa: 3.25.

TROGUS POMPEIUS (OR POMPEIUS TROGUS): first c. B.C.; wrote a "universal history" centered on Macedonia, which survives only in Justin's abridgment: 2.26.

TROY, TROJAN(S): the Asian power on NW Asia Minor coast destroyed by Greeks (Achaeans) after a long war (*Iliad*): 2.29.

TRUDGEALONG (LASDALLER): leader of the pilgrims eaten in Gargantua's salad: 1.38; also the name of one of Frère Jean's fighting cooks: 4.40.

TUBILUSTRIA: an annual Roman festival blessing the sacrificial trumpets (May 23): 4.P.

TÜBINGEN: small city in SW Germany on Neckar, then a big printing city: 2.7.

TUMBLETORIUM (CULLEBUTATORIUM): part of a comic fictive title: 2.7.

TUNIS, TUNISIA: large port city and kingdom in NW Africa on the Mediterranean: 1.33.

TURIN (TORINO): a big city; capital of Piedmont (N Italy); R was there most of 1539–1542 in service of the French governor Guillaume de Langey (q.v.), his commander and patient: 4.64.

TURKEY, TURKISH, TURK(S): in R's day the mighty Ottoman Empire, a great power in Asia, western and central Europe, the whole Mediterranean world: 1.33.

"TURN OR RETURN TO SHEEP": see "sheep, to return to."

TURNMILL (TOURNEMOULE): one of Picrochole's commanders: 1.31.

TURNUS: see *Aeneid* 7,11.12; Rutulian king, Aeneas's great rival in love and war, losing to Aeneas the war, his fiancée Lavinis, and finally his life: 3.14.

TUSCANY, TUSCAN(S): a large central Italian region (capital, Florence); potent cultural source; long the center for the purest classical Italian: 1.53.

"TWO-BACKED BEAST, TO PLAY THE": a favorite image of R's for human copulation; cf., *Othello*, Act I, Scene i: 1.3.

TYANA: in Cappadocia, now in E central Turkey; home of the mystic Apollonius (q.v.): 2.18.

TYLOS: an island in the Persian Gulf: 3.51.

TYRE, TYRIAN(S): modern Sur, Lebanon; important Mediterranean seaport, originally Phocian, whose colonists founded Carthage: 4.37.

UCALEGON: Greek and *oukalegon,* "uncaring, heedless"; in *Iliad* 3.42, a Trojan elder and adviser to king Priam; in *Aeneid* 2.425, a neighbor of Deiphobus whose palace also burns down during the sack and burning of Troy: 4.22.

UDEM: Greek *oudem,* "nowhere"; another place-name with this sense like Utopia, Medamothi: 2.24.

ULPIAN (DOMITIUS ULPIANUS): a famous A.D. third-c. Roman jurist whose many long commentaries form the basis for much of Justinian's *Digest*: 2.10.

ULRICH GALLET: see Gallet, Ulrich.

ULYSSES: Roman name for Greek Odysseus, hero of *Odyssey*; patient, resourceful survivor; wins his way through to get back home, win back wife and kingdom: 1.36.

UNICORN: fabled equine curiously related to virginity: 4.2.

UNIVERSITY (OF PARIS): the seat of the Sorbonne (q.v.); stronghold of reaction and of persecution of all Reformists: 1.17.

URANUS (OURANOS): the Greek means "deified, heaven"; with Ge (earth) engendered Cronus and the other Titans, Cyclops, and the hundred-handed giants such as Brareus: 3.12.

URBAN, POPE: probably the one then latest, Urban VI (ca. 1318–1389); pope from 1378: 2.30.

URETACQUE: apparently "rigging," hence "to the rigging"; puzzling cry often heard in the tempest: 4.20.

UTINO, LEONARDO MATTAEO: a fifteenth-c. Dominican author of volumes of sermons cited by Janotus not too perversely but in the best childlike Latin: 1.19.

UTOPIA: Greek "nowhere"; name taken from Thomas More; country of Badebec and of the Amaurots, which Pantagruel rescued from invading Dipsodes whose king Pantagruel becomes by both marriage and military victory: 2.2.

VADARE, OTHOMAN: no such person is known, but both EC and TL propose as a possibility a German doctor named Hotmann Werder.

VALENCE (DRÔME): a city on Rhône in old Dauphiné province; cathedral; bishopric, university: 2.5.

VALENCIA, VALENCIAN(S): in French also Valence; Spain's third-largest city; capital of Valencia province; in R's day noted for swords, metalwork: 1.8.

VALENS (ca. 328–378 A.D.): Roman Emperor of the East 364–378; an Arian Christian hostile to all other sects and religions: 3.25.

VALENTIN: hero of a medieval romance of chivalry: 2.30.

VALLA, LORENZO (ca. 1407–1457): Italian Hellenist scholar; clearly proved the myriad flaws and errors in Jerome's Latin Vulgate text of the Bible, leading Erasmus and others into Biblical textual study and to Erasmus's New Testament (1516): 1.10.

VALLÉE, BRIAND, SEIGNEUR DU DOUHET (D. 1544): good friend of R; counselor in Bordeaux Parlement (q.v.); most entries are references to him as Du Douhet: 2.10.

VARENNES-SUR-LOIRE: near Saumur; R's family owned property there; R notes their bells and their preachers: 1.51.

VARRO, MARCUS TERENTIUS (116–27 B.C.): Roman antiquarian and polygraph: 2.10.

VASCON(S): an ancient people of old Hispania Tarraconensis (Navarre): 4.57.

VAUBRETON: a hamlet near L'Isle-Bouchard and Chinon.

VAUGAUDRY AND VAUGUYON: small hamlet near Chinon: 1.34.

VAUVERT DEVIL (DIABLE VAUVERT): an imaginary wild man named for the Paris Hôtel Vauvert, which, long abandoned, became a notorious hangout for shady types: 2.18.

VÈDE: a hamlet, wood, and ford (over the Dive?) near La Devinière to the east; hence also near Chinon and to the south, across the Vienne; often cited by R: 1.4.

VEDIOVIS, PLURAL VEDIOVES OR VEJOVES (LATIN FOR ANTI-JOVES): Pluto; and in pl. maleficent deities much like Christian demons or devils: 1.45.

VENICE, VENETIAN(S): the canal-lined Adriatic Italian city; in R's day a potent state thanks to their sea power (trade and navy); for many the model of a fair, free republic: 1.55.

VENUS: Greek Aphrodite, goddess of love: 2.21. ·

VERDELOT: cantor at Saint Mark's in Venice and Vermont; musician in Francis I's chapel; two musicians listed by R in his fictive concerts: 4.P.

VERRON: region at confluence of Vienne and Loire; source of Breton wine: 1.13.

VESPASIAN (TITUS FLAVIUS SABINUS VESPASIANUS): emperor of Rome A.D. 70–79; an able administrator.

VESTA: Roman goddess of the hearth; Vestal(s) her virgin acolytes; Vestalia, her annual festival, mainly June 9 but June 7–15 in all: 4.1.

VIA LACTEA: milky way: 2.2.

VIENNE (ISÈRE): (1) a large town on the Rhône downstream from nearby Lyon; fine swords: 1.46; (2) the French river flowing past Chinon and into the Loire: 1.1.

VILLANDRY, CLAUDE BRETON, SEIGNEUR DE: a secretary to Francis I; adroitly answered Guise: 4.11.

VILLANOVANUS (SIMON DE NEUFVILLE, D. 1530): a noted erudite born in Hainaut; here called "the Frenchman" to distinguish him from the Spaniard Miguel Serveto (Servetus), who, from his family home in Villanueva, took the name Michel de Villeneuve (Villanovanus), who later fought Calvin in Geneva, lost, and was burned in 1553 on Calvin's orders: 3.13.

VILLAUMÈRE, LA: a hamlet near Chinon; home of the dying poet Raminagrobis (q.v.): 1.47. Speculation about whom (if anyone) he represents has fueled some also about this place; if he represents belletrist Jean Lemaire de Belges, the place-name might stand for "Ville au Maire (Ville à Lemaire, Lemaire's town) or possibly Ville Homère (Homer town, since Lemaire's grandest work treats material from Homer and led some admirers to compare him with Homer). Other models proposed for the poet (not affecting the sense of the place-name are Evangelicalist theologian Jacques Lefèvre d'Etaples (d. ca. 1536), whose serenity he recalls, and rhétoriqueur poet Guillaume Crétin (d. 1525), whose verses the poet (or R) borrows and uses: 3.21.

VILLEDIEU: now Villedieu-les-Poêles (Manche), near Saint-Lô; copper and aluminum works: 2.4.

VILLEGONGYS: a hamlet near Saint-Genou (Berry); birthplace of Eudémon (q.v.): 1.15.

VILLON, FRANÇOIS (1431–TO AFTER 1463): a great French poet, free spirit, often in trouble with the law; lost from our sight when banished from Paris in 1463; his fierce independence and daring engendered countless legends about his supposed later years, several of which, in these pages, R relates with evident zest: 2.14.

VINET: a Chambéry innkeeper who may be either fictive or real or both: 4.67.

VIRGIL (PUBLIUS VERGILIUS MARO, 70–19 B.C.): see also Maro; arguably the greatest Roman poet; wrote *Eclogues* (42–37 B.C.), *Georgics* (completed 30 B.C.) and his masterwork, the national epic *Aeneid*, which he thought still weak, ordered burned (it was not): 1.3.

VIRGO: Latin for virgin; a zodiacal constellation just south of the handle of the Big Dipper; also, in astrology, the sixth sign of the zodiac: 2.1.

VITAULT, VITET, VITVAIN, VITVIEULX: named among Frère Jean's battling cooks; all formed from *vit*, "prick, cock, penis," or a homophone: 4.40.

VITRUVIUS (VITRUVIUS POLLIO, FIRST C. B.C.–A.D. FIRST C.): served in Caesar's army in the period 50–26 B.C. and wrote treatise *De architectura* covering a vast field, all construction of any sort; the book was gospel in the Renaissance: 2.7.

VITULOS: Latin "sacrificial oxen"; the penitential Psalm (51) begins with *miserere* (have mercy) and ends with *vitulos*, which is the point here: 3.23.

VIVARAIS (IN S CENTRAL FRANCE): ca. modern Ardèche; paired here with Beuxe, a region near La Devinière, pronounced like *beusse,* a form of *boire* "drink"; the same is true of Vivarais, pronounced Gascon fashion with B's for V's; see Beusse and Bibarois.

VULCAN (VOLCANUS): early Roman god of fire; perhaps also of the smithy; c.f., Greek Hephaistos; here and in *Aeneid* 2.224 and *passim*, works with a crew of Cyclops in a cavern under Mount Etna: 3.12.

VULGATE (VULGATA EDITIO): oldest extant version of the entire Bible; put into Latin ca. 383–485 by St. Jerome on pope's urging; the official authorized Bible of Roman Catholicism; not named by R.

WALACHIA (OR WALLACHIA): S Romania between Transylvanian Alps and the Danube; chief city Bucharest: 1.33.

WEAKKNEES (TEVOT): obviously, a reluctant warrior: 2.7.

WEREWOLF (LOUPGAROU): leader of the 300 well-armed giants fighting for Anarche, who together require all Pantagruel's courage and ingenuity to kill them: 2.26.

WHISKERS (BARBET LE CHIEN): clearly an unlucky card (unlike lucky card Venus) in some card games common then but unknown to us: 3.P.

WHITSUNDAY (OR PENTECOST): seventh Sunday after Easter: 3.5.

WILL OF CUSPIDIUS: a Latin will prized and coveted as genuine in R's day, since then found to be spurious; but published by R in 1532 (Lyon: Gryphius) with a dedicatory epistle to Amaury Bouchard: 6.1.

WILLAERT (OR VILLART), ADRIEN: a musician still living in 1562: 4.P.

WILLIAM THE FEARLESS (GUILLAUME SANS PEUR): hero of a medieval tale: 4.23.

WILLOW-GROVE: scene on the lively celebration of Gargantua's birth: 1.4.

WINDSWALLOWER (ENGOULEVENT): (1) one of Picrochole's commanders; and (2) also a giant ancestor of Gargantua and Pantagruel: 2.1.

WONDROUS NETWORK (RETE MIRABILIE): a network of blood vessels near the heart along the course of a vein or artery: 3.31.

"WORMS FROM THE NOSE, TO DRAW": "worm out" secrets: 1.11.

WORTHIES: presumably the traditional nine, Joshua, David, Judas Maccabaeus, Hector, Alexander, Caesar, King Arthur, Charlemagne, Godfrey of Bouillon: 4.OC.

WRYNECKS (TORCOUS, TORTICOLLIS): men (for R all monks) with necks twisted from continual snooping and spying; among his favorite bêtes noires: 1.54.

WÜNDERBERLUCH, LAKE (LAKE WONDERFUL): apparently lovely Lake of Thun, N Switzerland, not far from Bern: 3.28.

WÜRTTEMBERG: SW Germany; once an independent state, now part of the modern state of Baden-Württemberg: 1.33.

XENOCRATES (396–314 B.C.): a disciple of Plato, successor as head of the Academy to Plato's nephew Speusippus (fl. 349–337 B.C.): 3.3.

XENOMANES: "Crazy about foreign things": steersman (or pilot) of Pantagruel's flagship on the long voyage to the Divine Bottle: 4.1.

XERXES I, THE GREAT: Ksharshaya, the Ahasuerus of the Biblical book of Esther; the Xerxes in Tobit is surely a later one of that name; emperor of Persia, Egypt, and W Asia, 485–465 B.C.; led a huge army into Greece, with early success; but badly beaten by Greeks (as earlier, 490 Marathon) at Salamis, Plataea, and Mycale (480) and forced to withdraw: 2.30.

ZACCHAEUS (LUKE 19.1–10): later legends made him a hermit bishop who died in the woods, and this named him for the Roman deity of pasture and woodland Sylvanus and possibly some little-known earlier Sylvanus; thought to have died in the woods of Berry; relics and tomb are in collegiate church of Levroux near Châteauroux (Indre), ca. 140 miles SW of Paris: 4.P.

ZEELAND: a province of the Netherlands N of Belgium and E of the North Sea, bordering on both; mostly below sea level: 1.33.

ZEPHYR (ZEPHUROS): the gentle west wind, and its origin, the west: 3.51.

ZOILUS (OF AMPHIPOLIS, FOURTH C. B.C.): a carping critic of Homer, taken as a prototype: 5.P.

ZOPYRUS: Herodotus 3.153–160; a feigned Persian defector whose self-mutilation let him fool, then betray, the Babylonians, and let the Persians take Babylon; Erasmus notes him as a master spy in *Adages* 2.10.64: 2.24.

ZOROASTER (PERSIAN ZARATHUSTRA, CA. 628–551 B.C.): the great Persian founder of Zoroastrianism, a dualism of good versus evil forces in all things: 5.4; also cited by that name is an unrelated first-c. Roman grammarian who wrote a treatise on undecipherable written characters: 2.24.

Designer: Linda Robertson
Compositor: Modern Design
Text: 10/12 Bembo
Display: Bembo
Printer: Edwards Bros., Inc.
Binder: Edwards Bros., Inc.